THE AMERICAN PEOPLE

THE AMERICAN PEOPLE

CENSUS 2000

REYNOLDS FARLEY AND JOHN HAAGA

EDITORS

RUSSELL SAGE FOUNDATION
NEW YORK

Library of Congress Cataloging-in-Publication Data

Library of Congress Cataloging-in-Publication Data

The American people : Census 2000 / Reynolds Farley and John Haaga, editors.
  p. cm
Includes bibliographical references.
ISBN 0-87154-273-0
  1. United States—Population—Statistics. 2. United States—Census, 22nd, 2000. I. Farley, Reynolds, 1938– II. Haaga, John, 1953–

HA201.122.A45 2005
304.6'0973'021—dc22   2005050433

CONTENTS

PART IV   IMMIGRATION AND AMERICA'S RACIAL GROUPS

Introduction

By Reynolds Farley and John Haaga

The Framers of the Constitution faced challenging problems about how to allocate representation in Congress, how to levy taxes—this was long before the days of an income tax—and how to deal with slaves when counting the population. Recognizing that if census taking were left to the individual states, the results might be uneven, they mandated that Congress take a census within three years and then every ten years thereafter. As a result, this nation's continuous history of census taking, dating from 1790, is the longest worldwide.

The leaders of the fragile new nation believed that the United States was a dynamic, rapidly growing country destined to exploit the riches of North America, while they viewed European nations as stagnant or in decline. Thomas Jefferson, who as Secretary of State oversaw the first census, realized that the census could be an ideal tool not just to count people but also to chart the industriousness and entrepreneurial activities of Americans. He was the first to propose adding questions to the basic count. The findings, he believed, would both measure the nation's progress and convince Europeans of this country's stability, strength, and growth. The first additional questions concerned industrial activity. By 1830, census takers also sought information about the health of the population, deafness and blindness, and, one decade later, insanity. Prior to the Civil War, questions concerning literacy and school enrollment were added, reflecting the growing national dedication to developing a public school system.

For several decades after the Revolution, few migrants arrived from Europe, but this changed in the 1830s. By 1850, the census contained questions about citizenship and country of birth. Concerns about the rapid growth in the number of foreigners and the radical changes immigration might produce prompted the addition of numerous questions in the late nineteenth century, about mother tongue, parents' places of birth, and the frequency of childbearing. A growing awareness of public-health issues after the Civil War led to census questions about mortality within a household in the year before the enumeration. As the nation became predominantly urban, innovative questions sought to measure and describe the nation's housing stock and the occupations or activities of adults.

The Depression of the 1930s generated monumental changes in the nation's statistical system, since more information was needed to assess the relative effectiveness of federal economic policies. The economic crisis of the 1930s led to the inclusion of questions about weeks of employment, hours of work, duration of unemployment, specific occupations and industry of employment, income, educational attainment, and migration within the country. The 1940 census was the first modern enumeration and served as a model for all subsequent counts. It was the first time that statistical sampling was used, with some individuals answering more questions than others. More recent censuses replicate Census 1940, although many questions have been altered, a few have been deleted, and several have been added, including inquiries about transportation to work and, for the first time in 2000, the care of grandchildren, and a new approach to getting a better picture of the country's ethnic and racial mix.

Sampling has been used in the last seven censuses. In 2000, all households filled out a brief census questionnaire providing basic information about age, sex, race, household relationships, and tenure. One household in six answered a longer questionnaire, yielding detailed information about how this nation is changing and why.

Since 1900, the Census Bureau has issued special reports following the enumeration summarizing new findings or synthesizing fresh data with the old. Since 1930 the Russell Sage Foundation has supported the writing and publication of these volumes, a tradition that continued with Census 2000. In cooperation with the Population Reference Bureau, the Russell Sage Foundation sponsored fourteen short chapters designed to lucidly synthesize key findings from Census 2000, thus making them highly accessible to a broad audience of policymakers, journalists, college students, and interested citizens. Authors and topics were selected with the help of a distinguished review panel from among a much larger number of excellent proposals. The authors of the chap-

REYNOLDS FARLEY is professor of sociology at the University of Michigan and research scientist in its Population Studies Center. As author, editor, advisor to the U.S. Census Bureau, and interviewer, he has been an active participant in each of the last four censuses.

JOHN HAAGA was director of Domestic Programs and director of the Center for Public Information on Population Research at the Population Reference Bureau. He is now deputy associate director of the National Institute on Aging.

ters met on several occasions during the work and were urged by the series editors to put census findings into the context of social, economic, and demographic trends. This volume brings the chapters together, providing a variety of perspectives on the state of the nation at the beginning of the new century.

Numerous federal surveys and economic data systems provide useful information on a monthly, quarterly, or annual basis, but they can only tell us what has happened at the regional or state level or, on the national level, provide broad-brushstroke data. Their sample sizes are not sufficient to allow comparisons of particular groups, be they recent immigrants from different countries, occupational groups, or persons with specific skills or physical handicaps. Surveys also have sample sizes too small to allow fine-grained geographic comparisons. To understand what happened in local areas and to groups of special interest, we need to analyze information provided by the 17.6 million householders who answered the long-form census questionnaire in April and May of 2000.

Traditional enumeration methods proved to be highly effective in counting the population in 2000—but this was hardly a foregone conclusion for those who had followed the technical and political debates related to undercounts in previous censuses. Beginning in the 1950s the Census Bureau scientifically measured census undercount using sampling, reinterviews, and demographic methods. Their results showed not only substantial undercount but also a disturbing pattern of racial differences; blacks were twice as likely to be omitted as whites—8 percent were missed in 1950—leading to an inequitable distribution of political representation. Strategies were designed to improve the count, but those used for Census 1990 did not work well. Net undercount in that year, 1.8 percent—was higher than in 1980, 1.2 percent. Demographic changes—more single-person households, more cohabitation, fewer people speaking English, more mother-only families—suggested that Census 2000 might be even less accurate than Census 1990. The Clinton administration sought simultaneously to reduce the cost of the enumeration and improve quality by using sampling, first to follow up for nonresponse and then to adjust for net census undercount.

The results of Census 2000 would be highly charged with implications for the political life of the nation. Republicans won control of Congress in 1994, and they realized that their chances to remain the majority party in the twenty-first century would be strongly influenced by Census 2000. If that enumeration counted many voters who were more likely to vote Democrat than Republican, it could be used to draw districts favorable to the Democratic party, and Republican control would be at risk. Legislators of both parties feared the potential consequences of a flawed count, since it could affect both

reapportionment of congressional seats among states and the redrawing of legislative boundaries by the states using census estimates. Fearing that sampling and statistical adjustments for undercount might be done capriciously to aid Democrats and harm Republicans, Speaker of the House Newt Gingrich sued President Clinton about how the population would be counted. The Supreme Court expedited its hearing of this fundamental constitutional issue, and in January 1999—just fifteen months before the census was to begin—ruled 5 to 4 that sampling could not be used to obtain the count that would determine the allocation of congressional seats. Congress provided the necessary funds to recruit a small army of enumerators to visit the 34 percent of American households that had not responded to the mail inquiry for census information. Demographers feared that these efforts to complete the count might fail, since many householders are hard to locate, and others are reluctant to give out information about themselves to the government, are unfamiliar with the census, or speak no English.

Kenneth Prewitt, appointed by President Clinton as director of the Census Bureau, summarizes in this volume the bitter political controversy that surrounded Census 2000, but goes on to demonstrate that the quality of the count was exceptionally high. Statistical analyses show that Census 2000 was virtually complete in its count of whites, Asians, and Hispanics but missed about 1.8 percent of African Americans. Despite this racial gap in the accuracy of the results, Census 2000 was a great improvement over 1990, when almost 6 percent of blacks were missed. More so than any previous enumeration, Census 2000 fulfilled the hopes for representative government of those who drafted our Constitution.

Federal statistical reports in the 1990s had revealed favorable economic trends, especially following 1993. The census, with its long-form sample of one household in six, allows us to dig deeper and learn about local areas, specific groups, and detailed occupations or educational attainment categories. The economic analyses of Census 2000 data show that the 1990s were years of improvement for most such groups. Controlling for inflation, the typical adult in 2000 earned 15 percent more than the typical adult a decade earlier, meaning that he or she could purchase 15 percent more goods and services. This image of the 1990s as a decade of large SUVs, much larger new homes, spas, health clubs, and vacation centers had a basis in fact.

But as several authors show in this volume, a closer analysis reveals more uneven progress. Sheldon Danziger and Peter Gottschalk focus upon trends in economic inequality among Americans. Census 1990 found that 13 percent of the nation's total population and 18 percent of children under age 18 lived in households with incomes below the poverty line. The booming economy of the 1990s raised incomes and reduced poverty, but the declines in the percentages of those living in poverty were modest. By 2000, this figure fell to 12 percent for the total population and 16 percent for children. Older Americans were a bit better off, as the poverty rate for those aged 65 and over fell from 13 to 10 percent.

William P. O'Hare describes trends in the welfare of children. For the most part, his findings give grounds for optimism: there is evidence of rises in income for families with children, sharp increases in the educational attainment of parents, less poverty, higher rates of school enrollment, and lower mortality rates. Some challenges for policymakers remain, since 37 percent of children living in single-parent families were impoverished. This is a substantial improvement from 1990, when 46 percent of such children were poor, but children living with just one parent remain at high risk of deprivation.

Poverty rates for older people are much lower on average than for children, thanks mainly to a relatively generous Social Security system that currently provides more than half the family income for the majority of households headed by older people. The sustainability of this system of public pensions (and public health insurance for those age 65 and over) is questioned by those who foresee a "generational storm" brought on by the retirement of the outsized baby boom cohorts; the older baby boomers will start retiring before the end of the current decade. Finding efficient and fair ways to head off generational conflict requires understanding the likely economic and family circumstances of the baby boomers. Mary Elizabeth Hughes and Angela M. O'Rand show how diversity of experiences has produced cohorts about which it is dangerous to generalize.

Dowell Myers also uses cohorts as an analytical framework to examine economic progress, for example, to document the rising proportion of American households that own their own homes rather than rent. Despite concerns about the educational and linguistic diversity of newcomers, the immigrant cohorts that Myers defines by decade of arrival do seem to catch up to their native-born counterparts in several indicators of material and social progress. Sustained economic growth has led to reduced unemployment rates for all groups, provided opportunities for a large flow of immigrants (18 million, or 14 percent, of the nation's 130 million jobs in 2000 were filled by immigrants), increased per capita hours of employment, especially for the highly educated, and raised the labor force participation rate of women, although not that of men.

Census 2000 confirmed huge differentials in population growth by race, a topic cogently described in chapters 12, 13, and 14, by Rogelio Saenz (for Hispanic Americans), by Michael A. Stoll (African Americans), and by Yu Xie and Kimberly A. Goyette (Asian Americans). Thanks to substantial immigration, during the 1990s the Hispanic population increased by at least 58

percent and the Asian population by 52 percent. By comparison, the groups whose growth was minimally influenced by migration from overseas grew slowly: the African American population increased by 16 percent, and the low-fertility non-Hispanic white population by just 3 percent. Census 2000 reported the Hispanic and black populations were nearly equal in size: 35.2 million of Spanish origin and 36.2 million African Americans. Subsequent data show that in the early years of the twenty-first century, the Hispanic population surpassed the black in size. A common theme emerging from these three chapters is that within-group differences in social, economic, and demographic conditions are wide and significant for policy. Since most data sources have insufficient samples to allow meaningful study of variation within these large racial and ethnic categories, these chapters nicely illustrate our contention that the census is indispensable.

No other data source can as effectively as the census reveal the composition of the immigration flow, a topic explored extensively by Mary M. Kritz and Douglas T. Gurak. Census data enable us to understand the diversity of immigrants: in their origins, in their educational attainments, and in the different gender composition of immigrant streams—some streams are predominantly male while others are gender-balanced. Many immigrants report great educational attainments while many others report few years of schooling. Among Asian immigrants, the highly educated greatly outnumber those with few years of education, whereas the majority of Mexican and Central American immigrants have little formal schooling.

Furthermore only the census documents the current Hispanification of the entire nation—the rapid spread of the Spanish-origin population from their traditional ports of entry to most all regions of the country. Who would have imagined, in 1960, that the Pennsylvania Dutch cities in the old Pretzel Belt would become centers for a Spanish-speaking population or that many smaller metropolises in the Carolinas and the Midwest would include thousands of Mexicans working at semi-skilled as well as skilled jobs?

Frank D. Bean, Jennifer Lee, Jeanne Batalova, and Mark Leach continue the "who would have imagined?" theme so often provoked by immigration studies. They examine how immigration is affecting not only the racial and ethnic composition of the American population but also in all likelihood the very conception of what long-used categories mean. The 2000 census was the first in which respondents could identify themselves as belonging to more than one race. The published results will likely contribute to the trend they document, since Americans will become increasingly accustomed to fairly complex descriptions of a reality that was long described, literally, in terms of black and white. Sonya M. Tafoya, Hans Johnson, and Laura E. Hill study the multiracial population, supplementing the national-level data with detailed information from California.

California is particularly interesting as a test case, since we knew from Census Bureau surveys in the 1990s that many native-born Americans were leaving California and that their places were being taken by even more immigrants from Mexico, Latin America, and Asia. Those surveys were less successful in telling us about rapid population growth throughout the Rocky Mountain states, attributable in part to that exodus from California. And they provided little information about another crucial demographic phenomenon affecting very different parts of the country—sustained population loss. Continuing a decades-long trend, population was lost in the 1990s in a broad swath of contiguous counties stretching from the Appalachian mountains in the east, through much of the interior South, into the upper Midwest and then across the Great Plains including northern Texas. Census 1890 led the historian Frederick Turner to declare the American frontier closed, since most counties had population densities exceeding one per square mile. Census 2000 reports that quite a few counties now fall below that density. Will these losing counties be able to sustain health services, schools, good policing, fire protection, and civic improvements if fewer and fewer people are spread thinly across vast areas? Many of the older suburbs bordering central cities in the Northeast and Midwest also reported substantial population losses. Will they successfully adjust to the changes forced upon them as their populations—and tax revenues—decline by a quarter, a third, or more in the course of a couple of decades? Whereas there is an extensive planning and policy literature describing how communities might best cope with rapid population growth and the prosperity it often brings, almost nothing has been written about how cities and counties should cope with equally rapid population declines.

The 2000 census also gave us surprising information about population growth in some older central cities—places whose population peaked right after World War II, just before the suburban boom. Thanks to immigration linked to economic growth, New York's population set a record in 2000, and Chicago grew for the first time since the 1940s. Eight of the nation's ten largest cities in 1990 grew in the subsequent decade, Detroit and Philadelphia being the two exceptions.

The racial and ethnic groups studied in this volume participated in these national and metropolitan migration streams in different degrees. Residential segregation of the races declined somewhat overall, but remained high in national averages. Only the detailed decennial census gives the precise information needed to study residential segregation at the level of neighborhoods. The chapters on Latinos, blacks, and Asians each document the levels and trends of residential segregation as it affects each group. The residential segregation of

blacks from whites declined in the 1990s, as it had for several previous decades, though it remained higher than most Americans realize. In southern and western metropolises, where most of the housing stock was built after the Open Housing Law prohibited racial discrimination in the housing market (1968), blacks and whites are only moderately segregated from each other. Segregation persists at much higher levels in the older metropolises of the Northeast and Midwest, but even in these places, black-white segregation decreased, by just a little in some metropolises but rapidly in others. Throughout the nation, the shift of African Americans from central cities to the suburbs that began in the 1980s accelerated in the 1990s.

Hispanic and Asian populations grew rapidly and their segregation from non-Hispanic whites increased modestly, but they remain much less segregated from non-Hispanic whites than are blacks. Meanwhile, Hispanics and Asians are just about as highly segregated from African Americans as whites are. In the melting pot of the nation's twenty-first-century metropolises, Asians and Hispanics are highly segregated from native-born African Americans.

The historic purpose of the census was to produce enumerations for the geographic distribution of political representation, and so the economic, social, and demographic data have always been keyed to location: where people live. The fundamental social group that can be studied with long-form census data is the co-residential family, anchored by the person who answers the questionnaire and other household members related to her or him and sharing household expenses. Of course, families have always been more complicated social realities than this statistically convenient unit would suggest. They form, dissolve, and re-form; familial obligations and caregiving relationships link people who may live in separate households. Still, as several of our chapters demonstrate, the census is an excellent source of data on the results of long-term changes in the family and how they are experienced by adults and children, women and men, newcomers and native-born. The 1990s saw some notable changes in the tempo of change. On all indicators, the rate of change was much slower in the 1990s than in previous decades, a theme developed in several chapters, especially by Daniel L. Lichter and Zhenchao Qian. Increases in the proportion of children living in mother-only families were small, the rate at which unmarried women bore children declined, and the trend toward higher divorce rates either tapered off or was reversed. Linked to this—as described in "Women, Men and Work," by Liana C. Sayer, Philip N. Cohen, and Lynne M. Casper, and "Gender Inequality at Work," by David A. Cotter, Joan M. Hermsen, and Reeve Vanneman—was a slowdown in several long-standing trends affecting work and family and gender roles. The labor-force participation rates of adult women may have reached a peak, and the rate of convergence of men's and women's occupational roles—and pay—appears to have slowed.

Census 2000, documented one unexpected but persistent trend toward family stability: adult children are not leaving their parental home at the rate of their predecessors, or, if they leave, more of them quickly return. Of all persons aged twenty to twenty-four in 2000, one-third lived with one or both of their parents and, among those aged twenty-five to twenty-nine, one in seven lived with their father, their mother, or both. At no point in the previous 150 years documented by the decennial censuses had such a high proportion of those in their twenties and thirties lived with their parents.

The secular trend toward greater investments in education continued in the 1990s. The percentage of the nation's young adults, those aged twenty-five to twenty-nine, with a secondary school diploma or a General Educational Development test degree is very high, though significant racial differences remain: 96 percent of native-born Asians, 91 percent of native-born whites, 81 percent of African Americans, and 77 percent of Latinos born in this country have a high school diploma or equivalent. Census data suggest that between 60 and 66.6 percent of high school graduates are now enrolling in postsecondary education, be it a regular university, a community college, or a specialized training program. The challenge of minimizing dropout rates formerly focused upon high school students. Now it is time to turn attention to those many individuals who begin a postsecondary program but fail to complete it.

Less heralded is the continuing feminization of collegiate and professional education in the United States. Forty-nine percent of Americans aged eighteen to twenty-four were women, but the census reported that 55 percent of those working on bachelor's degrees were women. Of those with a four-year degree and studying for an advanced or professional degree, 54 percent were women. A continuation of current trends implies that within two decades the majority of new doctors, lawyers, and MBAs may be women. Several chapters in this volume provide information about the increasing numerical domination of college enrollment by women and its possible consequences with regard to the occupational achievements of women.

Finally, in a subtle fashion, Census 2000 introduced the American public to a new concept of race, one that differs significantly from past perceptions. Throughout our history, from the Colonial and antebellum eras to the Civil War and Reconstruction, on into the twentieth century and the civil rights struggle, race has been the nation's most divisive domestic issue. In the twentieth century, racial tension underlay both bloody urban riots and pivotal Supreme Court decisions, both those that strongly upheld white dominance and others that were the epitome of equity. Despite this divisive history of

bitter disagreement, there was consensus that everyone in the United States could readily be classified into one of two racial groups because everyone was thought to have one primary racial identity. Since 1790, the federal statistical system gathered information on the basis of that assumption. But this assumption no longer can form a credible basis for American demographic statistics.

Increases in interracial marriages after the civil rights decade of the sixties led to a growing population of people with parents and grandparents from different races. A vibrant social movement sprang up in the 1990s demanding that the census include a new racial category: multiracial. The Census Bureau tested innovative questionnaires and the Office of Management and Budget received input from interested parties. Many traditional civil rights organizations feared that a multiracial category might minimize the size of their group; parents argued their children suffered psychological damage when they had to identify with either the race of their mother or the race of their father but not with both races.

For the first time, Census 2000 used a "check all that apply" question with regard to race. A person could check off just one race or as many as five: white; black or African American; American Indian or Alaska Native; Asian; Native Hawaiian or other Pacific Islander; and "some other race." Sonya Tafoya, Hans Johnson, and Laura Hill provide an authoritative summary of what happened when Americans were given the opportunity to identify with several races simultaneously. About one resident in forty marked two races, and about one-third of those people were multiracial because they marked "some other race" and then wrote a term designating a Spanish origin for their race such as Mexican or Dominican.

The census research reports in this volume will likely be the last in a century-long series. With backing from both political parties, the federal statistical system is being modernized and the system of data collection is being changed. Although there will be a head count in 2010 to determine how many congressional seats go to each state, the detailed decennial questionnaire to be answered by a large fraction of households has been eliminated, and this will obviate the need for the decennial research reports.

The merit of a decennial census with its detailed questions and huge sample size is its ability to tell us about small groups and the residents of local areas. But there is a tremendous offsetting disadvantage in this approach when it comes to the generation of useful data: the census is taken only once a decade, so we have to wait ten years to see what changes have occurred, and why.

Instead, the Census Bureau is now implementing the American Community Survey, a large representative sample to be selected each year for interviews that is comparable to a rolling census. This ongoing survey will provide fresh information about the nation, states, and large cities and metropolises every year. The sample size is so large that we will be able to study small groups such as recent immigrants from Africa or women employed in the skilled crafts trades more frequently than once a decade. For smaller geographic areas or relatively small groups, data can be aggregated on a rolling basis for periods of three years or five years (see appendix to this introduction).

As we noted at the outset, Thomas Jefferson was the cabinet secretary responsible for the daunting task of conducting a census of the scattered inhabitants of a vast, newly independent country. He was also a social and natural scientist of great talent and wide interests, and his *Notes on the State of Virginia* covered everything from human population growth to the health of towns and the size of animal fossils. We like to think that he would have enjoyed the eclectic scientific conversation in the chapters that follow, and shared our admiration for his successors at the Census Bureau who followed through on the daunting task he set in train.

APPENDIX: THE AMERICAN COMMUNITY SURVEY

The chapters in this volume rely heavily on supplementary questions to the decennial census (called the "long form," though it is hardly long for a household survey) sent to one-sixth of households in 2000. This design principle for the census—a few core questions answered by every household and a more extensive list answered by a sample—was introduced in 1940 and was used in all subsequent enumerations up to Census 2000.

After each of these censuses, the Russell Sage Foundation commissioned monographs and the Population Reference Bureau published nontechnical reports for wide audiences, in both cases drawing heavily on analyses of sample data. The present volume might be the last flowering of these parallel traditions, for the Census Bureau plans to discontinue use of the sample questionnaire for the 2010 decennial census. Instead, it will conduct only the basic short-form census in 2010, which will produce counts of the population by age, sex, race, and ethnicity (the latter two characteristics are needed to monitor compliance with voting rights legislation), and housing counts. The more detailed information on demographic, economic, and housing characteristics formerly produced by the Census sample questionnaire will be collected separately on a continuous basis under the American Community Survey (ACS).

The ACS is a continuous survey of approximately 3 million households per year, selected at random in every county, American Indian or Alaskan Native area, and Hawaiian homeland in the United States, and Puerto Rico. It uses an instrument very similar to the sample form used in the 2000 census. A test program for the ACS began in 1996, eventually including thirty-one test sites around the country. In 2000, 2001, and 2002, national-level tests collected data from about 750,000 households each year. Full implementation began in 2003.

The reason for this changeover that data users will most readily understand is the need for continuously updated information about the nation's population. Proponents of the ACS often use a metaphor from photography: the traditional decennial census gives us a snapshot of the nation once every ten years, whereas the ACS will provide a continuous video (or perhaps a webcam) showing us how social, demographic, and economic characteristics change almost in real time. The ACS design calls for a smaller number of households in the sample in any one year than the census questionnaire had, but sample sizes for estimates pertaining to small areas or small subpopulations will be brought up to acceptable levels for statistical purposes by means of pooling data collected over a period of some years.

Estimates based on ACS data for geographic units with populations of 65,000 were released beginning in 2004. Estimates for places with populations of 20,000 to 65,000, based on three years of ACS data from 2003, 2004, and 2005, will be released in 2006. For places with populations smaller than 20,000, estimates based on five years of pooled data will begin to appear in 2008. The pooling of data is required both to produce estimates of acceptable precision and to protect the confidentiality of respondents.

For example, the 2003 ACS data can be used to produce estimates for the population of Macomb County, Michigan (population over 805,000 in 2003). Based on one year of data, the Census Bureau estimates that the number of county residents over age 5 who speak a language other than English at home was 101,645. To show the variability in any estimate based on a sample rather than a complete count, the Bureau also publishes lower- and upper-bound estimates, corresponding to a statistical 90-percent confidence interval: between 89,357 and 113,933 Macomb County residents speak a language other than English at home. For the city of Warren in Macomb County (which had 138,247 residents according to the 2000 census), estimates centered on 2004 will be the first available, based on data collected during the three years from 2003 to 2005. The city of New Baltimore, Michigan, also in Macomb County, which had a population of 7,405 in the 2000 census, will require 5 years of ACS data collection to produce a sample size acceptable for any estimate; under current plans, these will be published in 2008.

The value of continuous measurement is best understood when we consider indicators that have recently passed inflection points, points in time when long-standing trends slow or reverse. A good example is the proportion of children living in single-parent households. As William O'Hare points out (this volume, chap. 7, fig. 2), we know from Current Population Survey (CPS) data that at the national level, the percentage of children living in single-parent homes peaked in the mid-1990s and has declined since then. But this percentage was still higher in the 2000 census than in the 1990 census—the downward trajectory had not taken it back to the 1990 level. The CPS sample sizes are insufficient for small areas and small groups to produce reasonable year-to-year estimates of this important indicator. With ACS continuous measurement, we will not need to wait until 2010 long-form data are published in 2012 or so to find out whether small subpopulations such as that of Tompkins County, New York, or Chinese Americans nationally, are part of this general trend: We will have updated estimates throughout the decade to tell us whether their paths diverge.

Less apparent to users, but vitally important to those responsible for producing accurate data, is the managerial efficiency gained by the switch to continuous operations. To gear up once every ten years to implement a census, then virtually to dismantle the field operation, only to repeat the cycle after a hiatus, is a massive undertaking, as Kenneth Prewitt shows clearly in his chapter. Hiring, training, and supervising hundreds of thousands of temporary interviewers, address finders, and data processing clerks for each operation, only to let them go again after a few months is a needlessly costly way to gather information about the population. The continuous nature of the ACS makes it possible for the Census Bureau to hire people for all these jobs and give them training that will pay off for a longer term. It also allows highly trained workers to treat ACS work as part of a career rather than a temporary job, so that they invest in the development of their skills and perhaps advance to supervisory or managerial positions, having gained a solid grounding in the frontline work of the organization.

The ACS uses both computer-assisted telephone interviewing and computer-assisted personal interviewing to follow up the initial mailing of questionnaires to sample households. The ability of trained interviewers to concentrate on nonresponding households should lower "nonresponse error," such as items or whole questionnaires left blank, or inaccurate answers given because questions were misunderstood. Census Bureau analysts and outside researchers evaluated data quality by comparing data from the Census 2000 sample with data from a version of the ACS administered nationwide, and the ACS-type data generally showed higher quality. For example, the ACS-type data had lower rates of imputed data (for skipped items or skipped persons) than the Census data[1] and much higher rates of intelligible responses to problematic items such as the question on ancestry.[2]

In the past, the Census Bureau always had a fairly short window of time in which to get the questionnaires and methods tested and refined for the decennial census. If an error or anomaly was not detected until after the data had been collected and analyzed, it was too late to make any changes and demographers had to wait for another ten years. Questionnaire items appearing late in the census preparations were particularly subject to this uncertainty. For example, the first question on Hispanic ethnicity was added to the 1970 questionnaire at the last minute, with little time taken for testing whether respondents shared an understanding of what was meant by the term "Hispanic." Similarly, the decision to include the question about grandparents caring for grandchildren, this time motivated by congressional interest, was taken late in the planning for the 2000 census. The ACS can readily be used to pretest innovative questions. The ACS schedule is also more forgiving—an item that seems not to work as intended can be replaced without a decade of delay. The ACS questions on disability, for example, have recently been modified to fit better the needs of analysts and planners.

Nothing is perfect, and there are some drawbacks to the change. One is the loss of simplicity inherent in using rolling averages of different periodicity to produce estimates. The clarity of a statement like "This is the picture as of April 1, 2000, everywhere in the nation" is lost when one compares, for example, a 2004 estimate based on three years of data for the large city of Detroit with an estimate based on three years of data for the small but contiguous city of Hamtramck. The different periodicity matters most when one or both of the geographic regions or small populations is changing rapidly—but that is also exactly the circumstance in which having to rely on a snapshot from some years ago is unsatisfying.

This drawback may cure itself over time. People will get used to moving-average estimates from the census, just as they will get used to multiple-choice racial data. The ACS is not the only rolling survey. Unemployment estimates from the Current Population Survey, for example, can be produced every month for states and large metropolitan areas, but for relatively small occupations or groups of workers they must be aggregated over different time periods. Another example: The National Health and Nutrition Examination Survey used to be fielded every decade or so, but it is now collected continuously. National obesity trends can be tracked on a quarterly basis, but valid estimates for rarer conditions require pooling of data from longer time periods.

Calculating standard errors for estimates based on smoothed time series can be difficult. But those sufficiently numerate to worry about standard errors are also likely to be able to use the approximate standard errors provided on the Census Bureau website.

Another concern, one that time and familiarity may not cure so easily, is with the geographic hierarchy that the ACS design uses. When estimates for places of all sizes were released more or less at once, aggregating up to "user-defined geographies" was relatively straightforward. For example, the Appalachian region as defined by the Appalachian Regional Commission currently includes 410 counties in thirteen states and eight Virginia cities (which are not included in counties in Virginia). Census 2000 estimates based on long-form data for these data all appeared around the same time. Anyone with spreadsheet software could produce a weighted average estimate for the whole region and subregions, precisely centered on April 1, 2000, even though no estimates for Appalachia appeared in Census Bureau publications.

In the new ACS era, though, an analyst wanting an estimate for, say, the proportion of college graduates in the adult population in northern Appalachia, would have to average an estimate based on one year of data for Allegheny County, Pennsylvania (a populous county that includes Pittsburgh); estimates based on three years of data centered on the same date for most Appalachian counties, and estimates based on five years of data centered on that date for the smallest counties. This problem may require long footnotes in future reports—though once again, the problem is most acute in the situation of rapid change and wide variation, precisely the situation in which extrapolating trends from the last decennial census is also least satisfactory. Trading some simplicity for greater frequency is likely to look like a good deal to most data users.

In 1937, Guy Irving Burch, the founding president of the Population Reference Bureau, published a discursive examination of the demographic history and prospects of the United States.[3] Many of his topics were remarkably similar to those discussed in this volume—an aging population, rural outmigration, even the apparent diminution of the native-born population of California to which we alluded earlier. In many ways he was premature—he foresaw neither the baby boom, which was so well chronicled by Mary Elizabeth Hughes and Angela O'Rand in this volume, nor the great postwar wave of immigration, analyzed by several of our authors. He titled his articles "Headed for the Last Census?" a provocative allusion to depopulation and decline that he detected in so many features of American demography. Nearly seventy years later we can amend his rhetorical question. We may have seen the last *bifurcated* census. The new model of a basic decennial census supplemented by rich continuous information from the American Community Survey looks, on balance, like an improvement.

REFERENCES

1. U.S. Census Bureau. May 2002. *Meeting 21st Century Demographic Data Needs—Implementing the American Community Survey.* Report 2, *Demonstrating Survey Quality.* Washington: U.S. Census Bureau.
2. Raglin, David A., Theresa F. Leslie, and Deborah H. Griffin. 2003. "Comparing Social Characteristics Between Census 2000 and the American Community Survey." Washington: U.S. Census Bureau.
3. Burch, Guy Irving. 1937. "Headed for the Last Census?" Part 1, "Overpopulation or Underpopulation: A Review of Conflicting Opinions," and part 2, "The Differential Birthrate." *Journal of Heredity* 28: 203–12, 241–54.

PART I

THE CENSUS

Politics and Science in Census Taking

By Kenneth Prewitt

GOVERNMENT AND DEMOCRACY, POLITICS AND SCIENCE

Mention the word "census," and what comes to mind is a dull counting project that the government carries out from time to time. Ask why a census is taken, and most Americans will vaguely reply that the government seems to need all these numbers. A few might add that it has something to do with who goes to Congress and even with how federal monies are spent.

Not many Americans know that the census is required by the Constitution and that since 1787 it has protected basic democratic principles. Many will be surprised to hear that there is an intense politics of census taking and that in recent times these politics have turned sharply partisan. Americans will be equally surprised to learn that the census is the nation's longest continuous scientific project. Dull and technical though it may sound, the census is a drama at the very center of our political life.

This drama has four subplots: providing the government a read on society, insisting that democratic principles be honored, determining political winners and losers, and applying statistical science on a scale nowhere else matched. In the best of times, these four subplots flow comfortably together. Sometimes, though, they don't, creating tension and confusion. Such was the case in the 2000 Census. Government goals were pulled in different directions. Principles of democratic fairness were in jeopardy. Issues of racial justice were contested. The politics were intense and partisan. Census science was vigorously debated, even attacked as unconstitutional. The Supreme Court had to weigh in, twice in two years. This report is about these conflicts, using them to show how policymaking, democratic principles, partisan politics, and science come together in the census.

We briefly introduce each of the subplots before subsequent sections reveal how, when, and why they link in a single narrative.

Guiding Government

In the fourth book of the Old Testament, aptly titled Numbers, God tells Moses: "Take ye the sum of all the congregation of the children of Israel, after their families, with the number of their names, every male … from twenty years old and upward." Moses is being told to take a census of those "able to go forth to war." There is also a census in the New Testament, central to the nativity story that brought Mary and Joseph to Bethlehem, where they were enumerated in order to be taxed. These biblical stories describe ancient practices in which census taking was used by the state to protect the security of its territory and its citizens and to raise revenue. Military conscription or taxation, and often both, are linked with census taking from the beginning of recorded history.

Think of the census as a map—a map of the society rather than of the territory. Both maps and censuses tell us what is out there. An ambitious 17th century annual census is proposed to France's Louis XIV in these terms:

"Would it not be a great satisfaction to the king to know at a designated moment every year the number of his subjects, in total and by region, with all the resources, wealth and poverty of each place? … [Would it not be] a useful and necessary pleasure for him to be able, in his own office, to review in an hour's time the present and past condition of a great realm of which he is the head, and be able himself to know with certitude in what consists his grandeur, his wealth, and his strengths?"[1]

The French king did not get this ambitious census, but modern governments do. In the United States, the 2000 Census form asked questions ranging from veteran's status to place of birth, from age and race to education and ancestry, from distance traveled to work to the costs paid for home heating fuel.

These are not matters of idle curiosity. Every question asked in the U.S. census connects to a specific government program or purpose: locating medical services for veterans, enforcing the Voting Rights Act, monitor-

KENNETH PREWITT first saw census taking up close when, in the 1960 Census, he was a crew leader for large sections of Boston's Back Bay. Then a student at the Harvard Divinity School, he hired Harvard MBA students as enumerators. They proved reasonably competent, earning him a promotion with citywide responsibilities for the enumeration of the transient hotel population. Nearly four decades later, he again was sworn to census duty—this time as director of the Census Bureau. He filled the slow years in between as a professor (mostly University of Chicago), director of NORC, senior vice president of the Rockefeller Foundation, and president of the Social Science Research Council. He is currently the Carnegie Professor of Public Affairs, School of International and Public Affairs, Columbia University.

ing the changing skill level of the work force, planning transportation networks, designing energy policies.

Imagine that you had the task of targeting educational support to children in poverty or medical services to physically disabled veterans. The size and geographic location of such specific subpopulations are provided by the census and its many derivative surveys. Every year, census numbers help determine where approximately $200 billion in federal funds are spent for welfare, education, health, transportation, and dozens of other programs.[2] To pay for these programs, government turns to the census to assess the size, wealth, age structure, and employment patterns of the tax-paying population and designs a taxation system accordingly.

Think of the census as a huge report to the government, portraying what is out there so that laws and programs can be anchored in information that is systematic, comprehensive, current, and objective.

So far, so good, but there is more. Knowing what is out there can lead to a variety of policies, not all of them benign. Governments around the world, for example, generally want to control who enters or leaves their country. In addition to border controls, visas, and the like, they use immigration statistics to determine how many of what kinds of people from what regions of the world qualify to enter the country. A government may also want to influence the overall size of the population, and will use fertility rates and statistics on the age structure of the population to design family planning policies.

The boundary between routine population policy and abusive exercise of power by a government is easily breached, and census history offers instances of the latter. Fertility regulation and forced sterilization in China and India come to mind. Population relocation is another example, and the United States provides a dismal illustration with the internment of Japanese Americans at the beginning of World War II. In this instance, census data helped the government quickly round up large numbers of citizens of Japanese origin, especially on the West Coast, who were said to pose security risks and thus were isolated in guarded camps.

In its darkest misuse, census information has facilitated genocides. Small-area tabulation of a Dutch census of religions taken in 1930 was later used in dot maps of Amsterdam to indicate density of the Jewish population, making it easier for German occupation forces to deport them. The 1939 German census went further, being used to identify specific Jews and Gypsies targeted for concentration camps.

These perversions are few in comparison with the majority of cases where the public gains from fairness and policy efficiency because a census draws an accurate portrait of the population. But like any powerful instrument of government, a census can be used for ill as well as for good.

Insisting That Democracy Be Fair

America had its first national census in 1790, for a purpose that was new to census taking. America's Constitution took on the historically unprecedented task of establishing a government based on the popular will. Perplexing questions faced the writers of the Constitution. What theory of political representation would work for the new republic? How could this republic avoid the seductive temptation of empire?

Allocating Representatives

The Constitution establishes a government based on democratic representation—a few citizens are elected by popular vote to represent the will of the many. This elementary principle of democracy leads to a practical question: What groupings of the population will elect representatives? One possibility is an at-large election in which a long list of candidates is presented to voters across the country, and candidates with the most votes then represent the entire population. But the nation's founders were seeking a way to bring elected representatives closer to the people being represented—that is, elections in which specified groupings of voters would each select their own representative. What principle might define these groupings? The Constitution writers could have divided the population occupationally—farmers, manufacturers, tradesmen, professionals—with each occupation electing its representatives. Or perhaps religious groupings—Anglicans, Congregationalists, Quakers, Methodists—could have served as the basis for representation. Such alternatives were not seriously considered.

Political representation in America is based on territory. Representatives are elected by voters from a politically defined area. This was the principle most familiar to the Constitution writers when they gathered in Philadelphia. In the decade between independence and the Constitutional Convention, each of the 13 original states had its own political identity, rooted in its economy, its religious tradition, its size, and how it had been governed during the colonial period. Following independence the country was governed under the Articles of Confederation, which gave one vote to each state in determining broad policy for the country while also accepting that most policy—including taxation, education, and criminal justice—would be made at the state level. This allowed the Southern states to continue their plantation economy based on slave labor while the Northern states could turn to small-scale farming and commerce. It allowed for differences in religion and cultural outlook; for instance, Puritanical Calvinists concentrated in Massachusetts, Quakers in Pennsylvania, Catholics in Maryland, and Anglicans in Virginia.

The delegates to the Constitutional Convention in 1787 were sent by their respective state legislatures, mostly composed of leaders fiercely protective of state interests. The delegates to Philadelphia knew that a stronger federal constitution to replace the weak Articles of Confederation would be politically acceptable only if state interests were clearly recognized. The result was political representation based on territory: Voters in each of the 13 founding states would elect their representatives to represent their interests in the new Congress.

Immediately there was an issue. How many representatives should be elected from each state? The smaller states wanted every state to have equal voting power. The more populous states cried "unfair," arguing that power over national policy should be proportionate to the size of the state's population. In perhaps the most important compromise of the Constitutional Convention, this sharp controversy was sidestepped by creating a two-house Congress. In the Senate, each state has equal voting power; in the House of Representatives, voting power is proportionate to the population of the state.

The first Congress would have a total of 105 House members, with large states getting more members than small states. This posed the question of how to be fair in determining the exact number of members each state would get. The first step was to take a census to establish the share of the total population that lived in each of the 13 states. The nation's first census took place in 1790, and with the results in hand, an allocation formula written by Thomas Jefferson fixed the number of seats each state would have in the House of Representatives, ranging from one for Delaware, the least populous state, to 22 for Virginia, the most populous.

These differences in state-by-state power in the House put firmly in place the fundamental principle that representation is based on residency and is proportionate to population size. This principle has guided American democracy for more than 200 years. But if the 1790 Census solved the initial problem of democratic representation, why did the Constitution require that a census be taken every 10 years?

Admitting New States to the Union

The boundaries of the United States were not fixed by the War for Independence, which resolved only that 13 British colonies were free to govern themselves. Nor were the boundaries fixed by the Constitution, which resolved that the 13 original states would come together in a federal government. Not at all clear was the status of Americans who lived outside the boundaries of these 13 states.

This uncertainty had to be addressed. Already restless people were leaving the 13 states, crossing the Appalachian mountain range, spreading into the Ohio Valley and down the Mississippi to the Gulf of Mexico. Among the drafters of the Constitution were visionaries who imagined a nation that might one day reach across the sparsely settled continent even to the Pacific Ocean. Territorial expansion was much on the mind of the new nation.

And what was to be the political status of these Western territories—so rich in land, minerals, furs, and forests? They could be annexed as colonies, and their resources exploited for the benefit of the Eastern Seaboard states. Alternatively, the Western territories could be encouraged to form themselves as independent states that would join the Union on equal footing with the original 13. Principle won out over economic expediency, as a majority of the framers felt that an Eastern Seaboard empire with Western colonies violated the principles for which they had waged the War for Independence. Empire was rejected in favor of allowing the new territories, as quickly as they were settled, to apply for statehood with powers and responsibilities equal to the original states. The key phrase is "as quickly as they were settled"; a decennial census was needed to determine when a territory was sufficiently populated to become a state.

The difficult issues of designing a democracy were hardly all resolved at the Constitutional Convention. American political history is the ongoing story of democratic principles evolving in response to conditions unforeseeable in 1787. Were we to recount that entire history, we would see that the census was often central. Our subject, however, is primarily the recent period, and especially how democratic principles were invoked in arguments about the census in 2000.

Determining Winners and Losers

The size, geographic distribution, and characteristics of the population are linked to power, to money, to civil rights. With such high stakes, there will be sharply competing interests in census results.

In the late 20th century, a vigorous political debate emerged about how census taking should address an old problem, the difficulty of counting everyone in the census. The problem was not new: After the census of 1790, the first presidential veto in American history set aside the census apportionment formula prepared by Alexander Hamilton, which favored commercial and manufacturing interests, opening the way for Thomas Jefferson to propose a formula that benefited agricultural interests. Two hundred years later, census methods were being debated before the Supreme Court in a case brought by congressional Republicans against the Democratic president, Bill Clinton. The issue again was how competing interests could be advanced by population numbers.

A census is unfair when some areas or groups are more fully counted than others, because the less well counted do not get their rightful share of benefits—such as legislative seats or public monies. If racial minorities are among the less-well-counted groups, as they are in the United States, issues of social justice and equality are joined to the census. There can be no account of America's census without looking at the

MAJOR PHASES OF THE CENSUS

The old saw that the devil is in the details is especially true of census taking. This note sets out the major phases of the U.S. census as practiced in 2000. Readers will find it helpful to refer to this outline as different phases of the census are discussed in subsequent sections.

Step 1-Construction of an Address File. The U.S. census is based on residency. It starts with a master address file that is assembled from post office delivery addresses; block-by-block canvassing by census workers; the updating of addresses by local governments, adding new construction; and the filtering out of duplicate addresses. The master address file, of approximately 120 million addresses, is the control against which all subsequent census steps unfold. If it is incomplete, the census is incomplete. If it has unrecognized duplicates, the census will have duplicates.

Step 2-Form Delivery. A census form is delivered either by mail (the vast majority) or by hand (where there is no residential mail delivery) to every address, with instructions to return the form by mail. This is the critical mail-out/mail-back phase of the census. Lack of cooperation—that is, low levels of mailing the census form back—drives the costs of the census up and the quality of census data down. There are two census forms. The seven questions on the short form are asked of every household. An additional 47 questions are asked of a sample of one in six households on what is known as the long form.

Step 3-Appeals for Public Cooperation. Auxiliary operations are closely associated with the mail-out/mail-back phase—an advertising campaign, help from organizations that partner with the Census Bureau, mobilization by local leaders, and heavy media coverage—all designed to increase mail response and cooperation with follow-up operations.

Step 4-Nonresponse Follow-up. Not every form is mailed back, requiring several hundred thousand census takers, often called enumerators, to follow up with nonresponding households. Approximately one-third of the addresses on the master address file had to be contacted in this labor-intensive way in 2000.

Step 5-Quality Control. An independent sample of the population was used to estimate the rate of undercounting or overcounting of specific subpopulations, such as renters, children, or racial minorities. This Accuracy and Coverage Evaluation (A.C.E.) of Census 2000 was by far the most ambitious part of the quality-control operation. Others focused on checking census coverage—who was missed, who was erroneously included—and on data quality.

Step 6-Data Capture. Census answers—mostly tick marks in survey-form boxes—are converted to electronic records for tabulation and reporting. In Census 2000, technically sophisticated optical scanning methods were successfully used in digital data capture.

Step 7-Dissemination of Results. The first instance of announcing and disseminating census results is the all-important announcement of state populations, which determine the allocation of seats in the House of Representatives. By law, this census result is delivered to the president, who then transmits it to the Congress within nine months of census day (April 1 since 1930). The next major census product, due three months later, is the redistricting data file detailing the age, gender, and ethnic-racial breakdown of the population to the block level. This census product is used to redraw the geographic boundaries of congressional districts, state legislative districts, and county and city election areas to reflect population changes since the previous census. Subsequent and much more detailed census products are released as soon as feasible and are posted on the Census Bureau website.

Step 8-Evaluation and Planning. Even as one census is underway, its procedures are being evaluated with an eye to designing the next census. Studies embedded in one census point to improvements for the next. Did the advertising campaign work as intended? Did asking local governments to update the address file solve more address problems than it created? Could absolute confidentiality be protected if people filled out the form online? Could greater use of administrative records, such as school enrollment, improve coverage? These and dozens of other issues were part of Census 2000 evaluation studies. Studying such questions during the census process is far preferable to conducting less realistic studies outside the census environment. In this regard, conducting a census is like sending a spaceship to Mars. All the tests, plans, and experiments cannot substitute for actually doing it.

politics of numbers—how many, how many where, how many of what groups.

Advancing Science

We have not said much about census taking itself—how the census is conducted (see "Major Phases of the Census") and, more important, how accurate it is. It is not easy to enumerate a population that is mobile, busy, and easily distracted; that is often indifferent to its civic duties; that is sometimes resentful toward government and not inclined to be cooperative; that speaks dozens of languages and is spread from the edge of the Bering Sea to the tip of Florida; and that is mostly ignorant of what is at stake in the census numbers.

A few dozen U.S. marshals carried out the first census. The most recent census involved nearly a million employees, making it the largest peacetime mobilization in American history. Census taking could not have kept pace with the enormous changes in the country and the population over the last two centuries without itself changing. As a vast scientific and technical enterprise, each census works to correct the flaws and build on the accomplishments of the one that preceded it, making it the nation's longest continuous scientific project.

The Census Bureau has been home to many scientific and technical accomplishments. Modern computing traces its origins to the late 19th century, when a bureau employee, Herman Hollerith, invented a primitive punch-card device and then created the first automated data tabulation system. (He later helped found IBM.) The Census Bureau was the first government agency to use a mainframe computer. In the 1930s the bureau used modern sampling theory for large-scale surveys, paving the way for today's vast polling industry. The science brought to bear in the 2000 Census involved mathematical statisticians, geographers, demographers, psychometricians, sampling theorists, information specialists, and computer scientists, all joining in the demanding task of accurately counting the population.

Accuracy is a technical and scientific matter, but in the case of the census it is also a term tangled up with the larger issues of governing and democracy. Power is allocated, funds are distributed, and civil rights guaranteed on the basis of census numbers. But what if the numbers are inaccurate? For better or for worse, census accuracy is where the politics and the science collide, and how the resulting conflicts are resolved carries into government policy and democratic practice.

CENSUS ACCURACY PROVES ELUSIVE

On Dec. 28, 2000, I announced the first results from Census 2000 to journalists thronging the National Press Club in Washington. I reported that America's new, official population numbered 281,421,906, commenting that "Never have we been so diverse; never have we been so many; never have we been so carefully measured." Below we will consider what lay behind the first two claims; first let us focus on the phrase "never so carefully measured." The wording was itself carefully chosen. I would have been much happier to say, "Never have we been so accurately counted." But that claim could not then or even now be defended. "Accuracy" is not an adjective easily attached to the census.

To begin with, there are two types of census accuracy: population counts and population characteristics. The latter, which will not get much attention in this report, refers to whether, for example, income, education, or race has been accurately recorded in census statistics. Complete accuracy is unlikely. Questions are not always understood the way the Census Bureau intended them. We ask for your race, meaning African American, Asian, and so forth, and you answer "American." Misunderstanding is one problem. Deliberate misinformation is another, often given in response to the income question. Errors also occur in transferring the answer on the census form to a digitized record or in the process of aggregating answers before they are published. Even the most rigorous quality control procedures—and the bureau applies dozens of them—cannot prevent some errors from slipping into the census record.

Accuracy of population characteristics is of great importance, and the Census Bureau quietly focuses on doing this part of its task well. It is not a task that gets much public notice, certainly not in comparison with the much more hotly debated issue of accuracy of population counts. In this and subsequent sections, the term "census accuracy" is about how closely the census estimates the true size of the population of particular geographic areas and of subpopulations.

Numerical Accuracy

The 2000 Census counted 281,421,906 people resident in the United States on April 1. The 1790 Census also reported an exact population—3,929,214. Thomas Jefferson, who as secretary of state oversaw this first census, delivered the results to President George Washington. The president was not pleased.

Historical Significance

Washington had expected a population about 5 percent higher and blamed the "inaccuracy" on avoidance by some residents as well as on negligence by those responsible for taking the census. Uncooperativeness and flaws in the census administration had produced a population count that underestimated the true size of the nation's population (see Box 1).

This was not an idle irritation on Washington's part. The new nation's first census, he knew, would be of great interest in Europe. The president worried that a small population would tempt America's European enemies to military action. He no doubt recalled that population numbers had given confidence to the country during the War for Independence, or at least had been used as wartime propaganda. Revolutionary leaders routinely cited demographic data—based on a mixture of colonial censuses, guesses, and wishful thinking—to assert that the infant nation was numerically strong and could if necessary "withstand war with England for many years."[3]

The diplomat John Adams later took up this revolutionary theme. In the early years after independence, he warned England that Americans "are not to be trifled with. Their numbers have increased fifty percent since 1774." A people that can multiply at this rate, wrote Adams, "will in twenty years more be too respectable to want friends."[4] Thomas Jefferson, his fellow diplomat in Paris, added an economic argument. The rapid growth of the American people offers an important market for French goods, he claimed. "For every article of the productions and manufacturers of [France] then, which can be introduced into the habit [of the United States], the demand will double every twenty or twenty-five years."[5]

The steady growth of the young nation's population also mattered for those who saw the American experi-

ment in self-government as a test of Enlightenment doctrine. The nation's leaders were influenced by the French political philosopher Rousseau, who wrote that the most certain sign of the prosperity of a government "is the number and increase of population."[6] Political thinking in the young America held that a growing population "was both a product of and a tribute to the blessings which America enjoyed—blessings not only of Nature, but of government, economy, and society."[7] A flourishing population was a comforting sign that the new form of Republican government was working, especially important to the early leaders who had risked much in defending an untried Constitution.

If the nation's leaders were disappointed when the 1790 Census count was lower than expected, it was a disappointment soon set aside. Rapid population growth quickly became America's demographic story (see Figure 1). The 19th-century population story combines fertility, immigration, imperial wars, and territorial purchase, with immigration being the major driver.

Immigration was substantial across the 19th century and into the first decades of the 20th. To farm, mine, and forest the new continental nation pulled in immigrants from every corner of Europe as well as from the Far East. Late 19th-century industrialization required factory workers at a scale greater than natural fertility could provide. Thomas Jefferson's vision of a nation of farmers spreading across the Western territory and Alexander Hamilton's competing vision of a manufacturing nation combined to ensure a permissive immigration policy that explains much of the growth from a nation of 4 million at the first census to one that by the 1920 Census exceeded 100 million.

Population growth surged again in the late 20th century because of new immigration policies adopted in the 1960s; this growth shows every sign of continuing in the 21st. Current estimates indicate that the population will number close to 400 million by midcentury. The old reasons for paying attention to population growth remain relevant. A growing population signals a strong country, one conducive to fertility and attractive to immigrants.

Contemporary Concerns

Because of the importance of population size, the accuracy of the census count has always attracted political attention. It did so in 2000, in terms not so different from the concerns voiced by President Washington two centuries earlier. Communities saw economic gain in a growing population; federal and state funds along with airports, shopping malls, and other enterprises go to growing parts of the country. After the 2000 Census, several hundred jurisdictions around the country filed complaints that their census count was too low. None complained that it was too high. In the little town of Patterson, La., the mayor claimed that the census missed 1,699 people. He worried that his town would lose $1.4 million a year in programs such as the state's tobacco tax rebate, which are distributed based on community size. But, said the mayor, "Money's not the only thing at stake." Echoing President Washington, though probably unwittingly, he continued: "Pride in the community is involved. I want people to really know how big we are. We aren't just a little burgh in south Louisiana."[8]

Because there are significant rewards linked to population size, disappointment is built into census taking. No city or state is satisfied with its count and would rather blame the census than accept that other places hold more attractions to a population always on the move. Complaints are adjudicated through a special program initiated by the Census Bureau, called Count Question Resolution, which after the 2000 Census reviewed 461 complaints (or about 1 percent of the 39,000 civil jurisdictions in the country). Most problems can be traced to faulty addresses. For example, a prison gets all of its mail at a post office box that may be some distance away, and it is a simple matter to reallocate this prison population to its correct location. Sometimes, however, there is no evidence of a mistake, and the community has to accept the Census Bureau's numbers. Among my least pleasant moments as Census director were angry phone calls from mayors about numbers we had released. One mayor, from a large Northeastern city, shouted over the phone that I was "killing" his city with a number he knew to be flawed. He demanded that I fly to his city the next day, issue a corrected number, and publicly apologize. (We checked our numbers; they were sound; they were not changed.)

Numerical accuracy in census taking is a challenge, but not half as difficult as achieving distributional accuracy.

Distributional Accuracy

Whereas numerical accuracy points to the overall census count, distributional accuracy points to the proportional distribution of the population by geography or subpopulation groups. This matters when benefits from a fixed resource are allocated in proportion to population shares.

A census can be numerically inaccurate but still achieve distributional accuracy. If, for example, the cen-

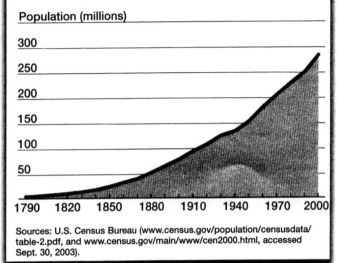

Figure 1

U.S. RESIDENT POPULATION, DECENNIAL CENSUSES, 1790–2000

Sources: U.S. Census Bureau (www.census.gov/population/censusdata/table-2.pdf, and www.census.gov/main/www/cen2000.html, accessed Sept. 30, 2003).

sus misses the same percentage of the population in every state, then each state will still get the number of congressional representatives it would had the census counted 100 percent of the population. It is only when the percentage of errors differs from one state to the next that there is distributional inaccuracy. The simple illustration in Table 1 shows two censuses that miss the same overall percent of the population, but in one census those missed are proportionately higher in State A than State B. This second census then awards to State B a higher share of the final census count, and shares matter when a fixed pie is being sliced.

The journalists who packed the National Press Club in December 2000 came because there were going to be losers and winners in the population-determined allocation of seats in the House of Representatives. When the numbers were announced, 10 states lost congressional seats, with New York and Pennsylvania each losing two. Four fast-growing states—Arizona, Florida, Georgia, and Texas—gained two seats, and four other states each gained one seat. Dramatically and instantly, the census had reduced the political power of the Northern industrial states and increased political power in the South and West. More than legislative power is at stake. In the Electoral College, which technically elects the president of the United States, each state's voting strength is based on the size of its congressional delegation—that is, its two senators plus its seats in the House of Representatives, with the latter determined by census results.

The allocation of seats based on rates of population growth or decline is called reapportionment. This term,

Table 1

DISTRIBUTIONAL ACCURACY ILLUSTRATED

	Census misses 10% of the population but is distributionally accurate	
	State A	State B
True Size	1 million	5 million
Census Count	0.9 million	4.5 million
% Missed	10 percent	10 percent

	Census misses 10% of the population and is distributionally inaccurate	
	State A	State B
True Size	1 million	5 million
Census Count	0.8 million	4.6 million
% Missed	20 percent	8 percent

to which we will refer often, describes the distribution of House seats across the 50 states depending on their proportionate share in the total U.S. population. The term reapportionment is frequently paired with another term, redistricting, which is the redrawing of congressional district boundaries within each state. Under a Supreme Court ruling familiarly known as the one-person, one-vote principle, congressional districts must be drawn to be nearly identical in population size. Because of population shifts that take place from one census to the next, many congressional districts have to change their boundaries, an especially political process in states losing a congressional seat. To achieve the precision required by the Supreme Court ruling, block-by-block census numbers are used. A similar process occurs for other election areas—such as those from which state legislators, county commissioners, and city councilors are selected—though the requirement of nearly identical size is somewhat relaxed.

During the 19th century, as the population grew and territories became states, the size of the House of Representatives was steadily expanded: from 105 members for 13 states in the first Congress to 435 members in 1912, following the admission to the Union of the final two continental states, Arizona and New Mexico. This steady expansion took much of the sting out of reapportionment. The size of the pie changed, and established states did not necessarily lose members even as new states joined the Union. But when in 1912 all of continental America was divided into 48 states, Congress permanently fixed the size of the House of Representatives at 435. Despite a tripling of the nation's population in the 20th century, there it has remained (except briefly, when Alaska and Hawaii gained statehood in the 1950s

and each was assigned one seat in the House until the 1960 Census could again reapportion the 435 seats).

That the size of the House is fixed means that a state can grow in population but still lose a congressional seat. If it grows less rapidly than other states, its share of the total population declines. Both New York and Pennsylvania suffered this fate in 2000. New York, with a population of nearly 18 million in 1990, had 31 members in the House of Representatives as Census 2000 approached. Its leaders were elated to learn that it had grown by almost a million people, but were quickly disappointed because its share of the total U.S. population dropped, from 7.23 percent to 6.74 percent. The combination of population growth but percentage loss also happened in Pennsylvania.

For the all-important reapportionment of congressional power every decade, as mandated in the Constitution, it is distributional accuracy that has political bite. It is difficult to achieve, both because it is hard to enumerate everyone and because it is hard to establish residency.

For its constitutional task of reapportioning Congress, the census must do two things: enumerate and assign every resident to a specific address. The census determines how many Americans there are and where they live.

The Constitution bases political representation squarely on the principle of residents and residency. The census, then, is not limited to citizens or even to legal residents. It includes everyone in the United States on census day (except temporary visitors and tourists). It includes people with citizenship in other countries who have taken up residence here even if they expect someday to return to their home country. It excludes American citizens living abroad, except members of the armed forces, the diplomatic corps, and other federal employees and their dependents. These citizen groups are included on the premise that they have been assigned abroad by the government, and, unlike other overseas Americans, government records make it comparatively easy to count them accurately (see Box 2).

Why is the census based on residency and not citizenship? One reason traces to the Constitution. National citizenship was not yet established in 1787, and in mandating a census, the Constitution took the expedient step of saying that residents should be counted. But there is a more principled reason. American democracy expects elected officials to represent the interests and needs of whoever lives in their state or district—voters and nonvoters, young and old, citizens and noncitizens. The idea is simple. The roads, schools, and public services are there for everyone. Noncitizens go to school, have jobs, pay taxes, and join the army. People in the country illegally still drive on the roads and send their children to school—and are subject to payroll, sales, and property taxes.

A residency-based census implies that there is a workable definition of residency, which is not as self-evident as it sounds. The country's first census law, passed in March 1790, required people to be included where they usually resided, even if they were absent at the time of enumeration. Only if they had no "settled place of residence" were they to be counted where they happened to be on census day.

In 2000 the census used a residency rule not much different from that of 1790. The census assumes that the vast majority of the population has a "usual place of residence." Though someone may not be there on census day, he or she considers it a current residence. This of course need not be a single-family dwelling. For many, it is group quarters—college dormitories, military barracks, jails, nursing homes, shelters for the homeless, training camps, and many other arrangements that house groups of people.

The Census Bureau knows that a "usual place of residence" is difficult to apply in many cases. Migrant workers, traveling salesmen, commuters, students, the briefly jailed, the homeless, children of divorced parents moving back and forth between households, Americans temporarily abroad, retirees who winter in the South and summer in the North (and are en route on April 1) are just a few of the groups that make fixed residency rules difficult to design, to explain, and to implement. (See Box 3, page 12, for an example of residency rule confusions in a noncensus setting.)

Political representation based on the population size of a state or election district requires that everyone in the census be assigned to some piece of geography. No one is in the census without a census-day residence. The "residence" can be a park bench or the back of a truck, but it nevertheless has to be located in one, and only one, of the geographic units into which the census divides the country.

Distributional accuracy is, then, affected by whether everyone in the census is located at his or her true place of residence. In a project as vast as a census, with its 120 million addresses, mistakes will be made. Every day new houses are built; industrial lofts, commercial buildings, even churches are converted to residential spaces; homes are subdivided into multiple units and garages converted to rental units. Reverse processes lead to subtracting housing units: abandoned houses are torn down; homes are destroyed by natural disasters or are converted to

Box 2
COUNTING AMERICANS ABROAD: CHALLENGE TO DISTRIBUTIONAL ACCURACY

In the midst of taking Census 2000, a minor agitation erupted because the census was not including all Americans living overseas. In a congressional hearing on the issue, proponents argued that being left out of the census was "taxation without representation." Why, they asked, were they taxed and allowed to vote but denied census participation. As I testified in response, there are major technical challenges, and if a reliable methodology, which would be costly, were not implemented, the results would be vulnerable to court challenge. The issue is distributional accuracy. Only in a limited number of countries do resident Americans report their whereabouts to the local embassy. In some instances, Canada being a prime example, Americans do not even need a passport. If the census includes all of the Americans working for oil companies in the Middle East, because they are comparatively easy to locate, but only some of the retirees living in Canada, who are more difficult to locate, distributional accuracy would be affected. Oil industry workers often come from Texas, Oklahoma, and Louisiana, and retirees in Canada often come from Washington and Oregon. The latter states would be disadvantaged relative to the former in the apportionment process. The disadvantaged states would sue and probably win.

An example occurred after the 2000 Census. The allocation formula used to distribute congressional seats works its way from the first seat allocated down to the 435th and final seat. By a narrow margin, the final seat went to North Carolina. If Utah had had only 857 more residents in the census, it would have received the 435th congressional seat. The governor of Utah quickly realized that his state had many Mormon missionaries temporarily assigned overseas—11,000, or many more than the 857 Utahans needed to claim the congressional seat that had gone to North Carolina. Utah had excellent records on the temporarily absent missionaries and argued in a lawsuit that it would be easy and accurate to include them in the census. The court threw the case out on the logic that not just the overseas Mormon missionaries of Utah but overseas Americans from every state would have to be included in the apportionment count, and a retrospective census of overseas Americans was impractical.

Congress has now instructed the Census Bureau to investigate whether overseas Americans can be included in future censuses in a manner that will not advantage some states relative to others. The difficulty is that there is nothing similar to a master address file that can be used as a control to determine who has been included and who missed. Any method that works better for the overseas residents of some states compared with others will be distributionally inaccurate and difficult to defend in the inevitable legal challenge by disadvantaged states.

other uses. Some of these processes are illegal, which means they never appear in any property records the Census Bureau uses to build its master address file. People living in neighborhoods restricted to single-family residences don't report student rental rooms above the garage; urban apartments in areas with high immigration may be rented to only one family but be home to temporary boarders. Addresses themselves are changed, as old rural route numbers are converted to a more up-to-date system. Streets change names, and sometimes carry two names for years. Ask a New York taxi driver to take you to an address on Sixth Avenue, and you will wind up, correctly, on the Avenue of the Americas.

It is easy to see why every census locates some people incorrectly. This matters in the allocation of representation and resources. There is, however, another feature of distributional accuracy. It is demographic as well as geographic. And it is this feature that loomed large in recent censuses.

Accuracy and the Differential Undercount

On census day, April 1, 2000, the true population size of the United States was unlikely to be the announced 281,421,906. This is because of the two types of counting errors that plague census taking: missed people and people erroneously included—mostly duplicates, but also people mistakenly thought to meet the residency requirements.

A large-scale census always has some of both errors, and this is why it is correct to describe a national census as a statistical estimate of the population. Except in the highly unlikely event that the two types of errors balance exactly, the census will report either too few or too many people—it has an undercount or an overcount. No large-scale count is immune to these measurement errors. Recall the difficulties of counting Florida votes in the presidential election of 2000, a dispute that finally had to go to the Supreme Court. A year after the terrorist attack on September 11, 2001, there was not yet a definitive report on the number of lives lost in the collapse of the World Trade Center towers. "Thousands of people who had initially been reported as missing turned out to be alive. Others were counted twice or even three times in the original tally. And several dozen people fraudulently tried to add names to the list, hoping to grab a piece of the millions in relief money."[9]

What Causes an Undercount

In census taking, the number of people missed is normally greater than those erroneously included or double-counted. The difference between the two types of error is the net undercount: the number missed minus the number erroneously included. A census that misses 2 million people but erroneously includes 1 million has 3 million errors, but a net undercount of 1 million. As we see when we examine Census 2000 results, there can also be a net overcount. Historically, however, it has been the undercount that has drawn political as well as scientific attention.

There are many reasons for a persistent net undercount in census taking. There are those who won't be counted. George Washington complained of this in 1790, and there is still a small but not insignificant number who avoid the census. These may be people in the country illegally who fear that the census could lead to deportation. This is not true (the census does not even ask legal status), but someone suspicious of government authorities won't take that chance. There are criminals who don't want to be located. There are people with unlisted phones who live in gated communities or behind the protective wall of guards and doormen and don't want to be bothered. And there are those who choose not to cooperate as a matter of principle. It is doubtful that the census managed to include every militia member living in remote cabins in the mountains of Idaho, all the marijuana growers in Northern California, the very wealthy in Park Avenue penthouses, the illegal migrant farm workers, and other uncooperative groups.

There is a larger group who, though not attitudinally uncooperative, are still likely to be missed. They might return the form if they noticed it or might answer the census taker if they were ever home. But their lifestyles make them difficult to reach. Perhaps they travel constantly, use transient hotels, don't have phones, and ignore their mail.

People are missed in a census not only because of the attitudes and lifestyles of our complex population, but as the result of problems inherent in census taking itself. Census 2000 started with 120 million addresses. Eighty percent of the households received the form in the mail. For the other 20 percent of the addresses, mostly in rural areas without mail delivery, the bureau hand-delivered the forms. How likely is it that every household got a mail questionnaire or a visit? Some surely were missed. There are remote and unusual housing arrangements in the United States—house-boats, hunting camps, tree houses—even, I am told, a scattering of people who live as hermits in caves.

Delivering the questionnaire is just the first step. Not all of them are mailed back. In 2000, only about two-thirds of the census forms were returned in the mail (see Box 5, page 31). The Census Bureau sent census takers to the 40 million residences that had failed to mail their form back. This required staffing 520 census offices around the country and hiring more than 900,000 mostly part-time employees. Were all of those people well trained, good at their work, and honest? Most were, but not all. Assignments are misunderstood, forms are mis-filed, oversight procedures break down. Inefficiency and even falsification happen often enough that the census makes a heavy investment in quality control: a 5 percent sample of the work of every enumerator is redone, allowing for quick dismissal of poor performers. In one instance, because of suspected irregularities, the bureau re-enumerated an entire community.

A number of factors, then, produce census errors: public avoidance and indifference, missed addresses, logistic difficulties, and enumerator performance, to name just a few. These factors occur in every census, and not just in the United States. China took a census in 2000, and reported that its undercount of nearly 2 percent was sharply up from the prior census because China now has a large, elusive migrant worker population and because of growing concerns about privacy. The 2001 census in the United Kingdom reported an undercount of approxi-mately 2 percent, which was attributed to a young and mobile population as well as to a large number of asylum seekers and immigrants who avoid the census.

Measuring the Undercount

Although census professionals long presumed that there were errors in the census count and that they most likely netted out in the negative, it was in the latter half of the 20th century that statistical practice was advanced enough to measure the undercount. A moment's reflec-tion will suggest why systematic assessment of census errors is difficult. There is only one census. With what, then, can it be compared to determine how complete it is? To reliably assess census accuracy, you would need two (or more) population counts so the results of one could be used to check the other. Historically this would have been prohibitively expensive.

After decades of anecdotal evidence suggesting an undercount higher in some subpopulations than others, there was an unplanned opportunity to study the undercount. When the shock of Pearl Harbor in 1941 drew America into World War II, the government quickly ordered universal registration of young men eli-gible to be drafted into the armed services. Though obviously not its intent, this universal registration gave statisticians two independent estimates of the number of American males between ages 21 and 35—one reported in the 1940 Census and the other from military records. Comparing these two numbers provided the first reliable measure of how many people, at least among young males, are missed in the census.

This comparison indicated an undercount in the 1940 Census of approximately 3 percent, not surprising to demographers and statisticians. Initially this census fact attracted little interest beyond technical circles. But with civil rights pressures coming to the foreground in the 1950s and then, explosively, in the 1960s, one feature of the undercount gained wide prominence: African Ameri-can males of draft age had been missed in the 1940 Cen-sus at much higher rates than white males. Black men were undercounted by 13 percent, more than four times the rate for whites. Here was the first systematic evidence of an undercount that penalized African Americans.

This definitive demonstration of the differential undercount marked a major turning point in both the politics and the science of census taking. The political con-sequence, discussed in the next section, emerged in the context of the civil rights revolution sweeping the country. Inevitably the politics of racial justice became intertwined with the technical task of trying to reduce the differential undercount. The scientific consequence was a sustained search for statistical methods that could reliably measure the undercount and its distribution across demographic groups and adjust for these systematic errors.

Census taking involves a continuous program of self-evaluation and self-criticism so that steady improve-ments can be introduced. It is the Census Bureau itself that reports how well it did. When it announces that the decennial census missed X percent of young black males

Table 2

NET UNDERCOUNT, 1940–1990

Census Year	Percent Net Undercount
1940	5.4
1950	4.1
1960	3.1
1970	2.7
1980	1.2
1990	1.8

Note: Based on a comparison of census results with a population estimate from demographic analysis. One source of the comparatively low net undercount of 1980 was the large number of suspected duplicates in that census, which had the result of increasing the overcount and thus depressing the net undercount. Census-to-census comparisons are difficult because procedures, including how suspected duplicates are removed, vary from one census to the next.

in central cities or overcounted Y percent of middle-age white women in the suburbs, the natural question is: "How do you know?" If there is only one census, there is only one count. There is no other government agency or private firm counting the entire American population. The bureau evaluates its own work by comparing the census with two other estimates it produces of the country's population size, one using demographic analysis and the other dual-system estimation.

Demographic Analysis. Demographic analysis is, in theory, quite simple. It starts with a basic population number and then, using administrative records such as birth certificates and immigration records, updates it by adding every birth and every arriving immigrant, and subtracting every death and every person who moves out of the country. The starting point is a compilation based on historical estimates of the four basic factors: births, deaths, immigration, emigration, which are then carried forward as age cohorts and corrected on the basis of special studies of the completeness in administrative records and further adjustment as appropriate in light of recent census results.

> **(Base + Births and Immigration)**
> **– (Deaths + Emigration)**
> **= Demographic Estimate of the Population**

The actual calculation is more complicated because it has to estimate the completeness of birth and death records by age, gender, and race. And allowance has to be made for the less-than-precise estimates of immigration, especially the probable number of undocumented residents, and the estimates of out-migration, on which records are incomplete.

Table 2 shows the half-century trend in the net undercount calculated by comparing the census with

estimates from demographic analysis. This table indicates steady improvement in census taking. The slight rise in 1990, after the net undercount had fallen to almost 1 percent, played a significant role in the partisan politics that emerged in preparing for the 2000 Census, discussed below.

Of even more political consequence is what happened to the differential undercount across this half-century. The pattern displayed in Table 3 concerned the Census Bureau. Despite steady decline in the net undercount, the magnitude of the difference for blacks in contrast to other racial groups did not improve; in fact, it was higher at the end of the 50-year period than at the beginning. African American civil rights organizations took notice and were not pleased.

Eventually, concern extended beyond the persistent black undercount. By 1990, statistical work by the Census Bureau produced counts showing how many other minorities were missed. For Hispanics and American Indians, the 1990 rates were even higher than those for African Americans. Asians were missed at about half the rates for blacks but still much more frequently than whites. (The section on "Who Decides Which Count Counts," beginning on page 32, reports these data and updates them for 2000.)

Demographic analysis can indicate the national magnitude of the differential undercount but cannot fix it. The method works at the national level reasonably well, subject to inadequacies in the vital statistics of the nation, but for reapportionment and redistricting purposes, it has glaring weaknesses. For example, it has no measure of internal population movement. It can report where babies are born in one year but not where they were living a year later. For this and other reasons, the method cannot be applied at small geographic levels, and certainly not at the block level required by the Voting Rights Act and by the one-person, one-vote principle of redistricting.

The Census Bureau needed another way to take a second count. It had to work at small areas of geography if the undercount and its differences across groups and areas were to be fixed for purposes of apportioning congressional seats and drawing election boundaries within states.

Dual-System Estimation. In the 1930s statisticians began to work out the theory and practice of statistical sampling, with the first large-scale application being surveys of unemployment during the depression years. By 1940, the Census Bureau was using sampling statistics to reduce the costs of the census and the burden on the public by asking some questions only of a repre-

Table 3
CENSUS UNDERCOUNT, BLACK/NONBLACK, 1940–1990
Percent

	1940	1950	1960	1970	1980	1990
Black	8.4	7.5	6.6	6.5	4.5	5.7
Nonblack	5.0	3.8	2.7	2.2	0.8	1.3
Difference	**3.4**	**3.6**	**3.9**	**4.3**	**3.7**	**4.4**

Note: Based on demographic analysis.

sentative sample of households. This sampling-based innovation in 1940 was carried forward into every subsequent census, eventually leading to a census based on the short form and long form.

By 1950, when the differential undercount became clear for all to see, the question was whether statistical sampling might offer a way to assess the census itself. The idea is simple (though the execution is not!). The Census Bureau would first take the census and then follow it with a large sample survey, known as a post-enumeration survey (PES). The sample survey offers a second population count that is compared with the census. Starting in 1950 the method was steadily improved from one census to the next, though not until 1990 did the bureau believe that dual-system estimation, as this method came to be called, could be applied in a way that would compensate for the undercount. What happened in 1990, and then in 2000, is central to the political story of census taking, taken up in the next section. First we review the scientific rationale for using dual-system estimation to fix the census undercount.

Dual-system estimation rests on the idea that two sources of information, independently produced, offer a better estimate of the population than does one source. The statistical procedure comes from wildlife studies, where it is known as capture/recapture. Fish in a lake are captured, tagged, and returned to the lake. On a successive visit, fish are again taken from the lake. This is the recapture phase. By determining how many of the tagged fish from the first visit are not recaptured, and how many fish in the second visit are untagged, an estimate is made of the fish population that is statistically more reliable than either of the counts taken alone.

Dual-system estimation in the census environment permits case-by-case matching of the results from the census with those in the sample. This means that the household information in the sample survey can be used to determine if a household, or person in the household, was in the census (was "tagged") and whether a person was erroneously included in the census—perhaps died just before April 1, or was born shortly after that date, but nevertheless appears on the census form.

This specific matching cannot itself fix the census because it is limited to those households that fall into the sample. But the results of the matching can be statistically generalized (as with any random sample) to estimate the probability that different demographic subgroups are missed. This makes it a very valuable method for the census. With a large enough "recapture" sample, the method can compare undercount rates for different racial groups or other subpopulations, such as renters and owners or central city and suburban residents.

In principle, dual-system estimation can be used to adjust the differential undercount. Imagine a community that actually has 3,000 young African American males, but only 2,700 are counted in the census. If dual-system estimation has independently estimated that for this population group in these types of communities there is a 10 percent undercount, the census can statistically add 300 census records of young African American males, bringing the total to the true number of 3,000. The census does not, of course, add actual people; it simply adjusts the statistical record upward by this number. If there is a measured overcount of a different population group, perhaps college students who are counted both at home and in their dormitories, the statistical record can be proportionally adjusted downward.

This description of dual-system estimation oversimplifies a complex set of statistical and field procedures, and as in any large-scale effort to count human populations, the practice does not always measure up to the plan. Statisticians skeptical of the Census Bureau's adoption of dual-system estimation voice a number of concerns, especially about the reliability of precision estimates and the attempt to apply the method to small geographic areas such as census blocks.[10] We will consider actual implementation issues in later sections.

Summary

Census accuracy matters to democratic fairness and governmental efficiency. But accuracy is not easily achieved. As it prepared for Census 2000, the Census Bureau believed that dual-system estimation was the statistical method best able to measure and adjust for the persistent differential undercount in census taking. The method was supported by committees of the National Academy of Sciences and the American Statistical Association and by many of the bureau's technical advisers. There were also leading statisticians skeptical about both the practical and technical challenges in dual-system estimation. These legitimate scientific differences were magnified when the census came under intense political fire. As we will see, the effort to do something about the persistent undercount attracted political attention like no other statistical procedure in census history. We turn now to how the Census Bureau struggled with both the scientific and the political dimensions of accuracy, as well as with other challenges unique to the 2000 Census.

UNPRECEDENTED CHALLENGES IN 2000

No census is easy, except perhaps in countries where there is a national population registration system. No such thing exists (at present) in the United States. Nor do we take a census the way it is taken, for instance, in Turkey, where everyone is required to stay home on census day. The American census enumerates a large, diverse, and constantly moving population. All the regular problems besetting census taking confronted the Census Bureau as it prepared for the 2000 Census. But many longtime census observers felt that the familiar challenges were nothing compared with the unprecedented circumstances in 2000.

This section first describes a challenge common to census taking since 1790—population attitudes and characteristics that President Washington complained about—but suggests how these problems have been magnified by recent trends. Beyond the familiar difficulties, however, are three other challenges that made Census 2000 uniquely difficult: the shadow of a so-called failed census in 1990; a government evenly split between political parties with radically divergent views about how the census should be taken; and unprecedented levels of census oversight and scrutiny.

Changing Demographics and Attitudes

In 1790, U.S. marshals were sent to every dwelling place in America and asked a few questions. This basic census strategy was repeated every decade for almost two centuries, though eventually temporary census workers replaced the marshals. In 1970, a radical redesign took place. Instead of sending census takers to every household, the Census Bureau mailed the form and asked that it be completed at home and mailed back. Nearly four of five households did so. The mail-out/mail-back

design was repeated in 1980, when there was a noticeable but not sharp drop-off to 75 percent in the mail-back response. The next decade saw a much sharper decline, down to 65 percent in the 1990 Census (see Box 5, page 31). The bureau feared that this decline would continue, dropping perhaps as low as 55 percent in 2000.

When households fail to return the form, census takers go out to collect the information in person. This also became increasingly difficult over the decades, requiring more effort from one census to the next. Census costs reflected these rising difficulties (Table 4).

Changes in the attitudes and lifestyles of Americans were among the factors that made census taking more difficult and costly between 1970 and 1990. Although this period saw some helpful changes, such as higher levels of education, most of the trends worked against census taking.

What kind of household is most likely to be counted by the census? If you pause to reflect on this question, you are likely to imagine the easy-to-count household as one with a stable family where the family members have only one address and have had it for some time, where mail is delivered and read, where English is spoken, where civic responsibilities are taken for granted, where there is trust in the government.

What kind of household is least likely to be counted accurately? Reflect on this and you will imagine a hard-to-count household as one where unrelated people share living quarters; where household members are seldom at home; where there is a low sense of civic responsibility and perhaps an active distrust of the government; where occupants have lived but a short time and will move again soon; where English is not spoken; where community ties are nonexistent.

Easy-to-count households are much less common now than they were a quarter-century ago, and the portrait of the hard-to-count describes an ever-increasing percentage of our population. Today, for example, married couples living together are about one-half of the nation's households. Single-person households are rapidly increasing, having doubled from 13 percent to 26 percent since 1990. Deferred marriage and high divorce rates are one reason. Another is the increasing life expectancy, which results in one elderly person living alone after the spouse has died. Commuter marriages are increasingly common. There is also an increase in the number of households with unrelated people living together, especially around large universities or in fast-growing areas attractive to young adults.

Americans are on the move. Between 15 percent and 20 percent of us change addresses every year.

Women have joined the work force and are not sitting at home waiting patiently for the census taker to arrive. Increasingly, Americans have two homes and shift often from one to another. Recreational travel is more common. People are busy. They don't want to be bothered by such troublesome tasks as filling out a government form. Although the law says they have to, this is not a law that is enforced (for fear of backlash against the census that would further depress cooperation).

Changes in what we think of as our address and phone number make census taking more difficult. Before e-mail and mobile phones, an address and a phone number belonged to a fixed place. Not now. They exist in electronic space, not on some geographic grid—but the census is inevitably anchored to a geographic grid.

Immigration rates have been extraordinarily high in recent decades, and by 2000 the foreign-born had become 10 percent of America's population. Not all of these 28 million or so recent immigrants speak English; not all of them understand or care about the census. Not all of them welcome contact with government authorities, especially those here illegally. The estimated illegal population doubled between 1990 and 2000, from 3.5 million to 7 million. Many immigrants crowd into city apartments, often without the landlord's knowledge. On the border with Mexico, immigrants often live in large unofficial communities with no basic services and few ties to anything resembling the government. Others live in transitory migrant work camps, staying in one place only as long as there is work.

Civic responsibility and trust in government have steadily declined for several decades. In 1960 about two-thirds of the population said that they trusted the federal government. This percentage fell sharply with the Watergate cover-up and Nixon's resignation. It never recovered, and by the 1990s only about 20 percent of the population trusted the federal government. There are growing concerns about privacy, and public fear that information given to the government will not be kept confidential. The willingness to respond to mail surveys has also fallen sharply. Marketing appeals flood mailboxes, and tossing out the junk mail is a daily chore.

The Census Bureau tracks these demographic and attitudinal changes and knew that taking the 2000 Census was going to present greater challenges than ever before.

The Shadow of the 1990 Census

Every census is conducted against the fresh memories and lessons of the one before, and the 2000 Census had the burden of following one that was widely if incor-

Table 4
COST OF THE CENSUS, 1970–1990

$13 per household in 1970
$24 per household in 1980
$32 per household in 1990

Note: Cost is in constant 2000 dollars.
Source: U.S. General Accounting Office (GAO), *2000 Census: Significant Increase in Cost Per Housing Unit Compared to 1990 Census* GAO-02-31 (Washington, DC: GAO, December 2001): 7.

rectly dubbed a failure. By any reasonable standard, the 1990 Census was not a failure. All of its major functions were performed on schedule. Congress was reapportioned, new election boundaries were drawn, governments used the data for public policymaking, businesses relied on the data for investment decisions, the United Nations incorporated the results in its worldwide statistical reports, and thousands of journalists and scholars turned to the data to provide serious analysis of how the country was changing. Measured by whether its data were accepted, the census succeeded.

However, as Martha Riche, Census Bureau director in the mid-1990s, usefully observed: Though the 1990 Census was a statistical triumph, it was a public relations disaster. To understand how this came about, we refer to Table 2 (page 14), where we saw that the census undercount steadily improved from 1940 to 1980 but then got worse in 1990. It was largely this reversal of an improvement that led the 1990 Census to be labeled a failure. The steady decline in the net undercount had become an easy if imprecise way to say that the census was becoming more accurate. When the net undercount then increased, it was easy to conclude that the census had become less accurate—that is, a "failure."

A cost overrun during the 1990 Census also contributed to its negative image. In the midst of taking the census, the bureau needed a budget supplement. The reason was simple. There was a sharp drop-off in the mail-back response rate compared with the previous census, requiring the bureau to hire more enumerators to find nonresponding households. The need for additional funds, though hardly the fault of the bureau, generated unfavorable publicity. Added to that was continuous media coverage of the many lawsuits brought against the Census Bureau, and the politically charged atmosphere that the lawsuits reflected (discussed below). It was easy, even if misleading, to put the word "failure" on a census that was seen to be inaccurate, over budget, and sufficiently flawed that it had to be taken to court. Congress demanded that the Census Bureau "do better" in 2000, that it come up with a design that would cost less but improve accuracy.

Overcoming the view that the 1990 Census was a failure was important, because lack of confidence in the agency translates into lack of confidence in its statistical products. The stakes are high. A loss of confidence in census data ripples through public policymaking and economic planning. In preparing for 2000, with the shadow of the previous census much in mind, the Census Bureau was more than usually determined to have a successful census.

Then, as planning got underway, Congress began to play a more complicated role. Republicans and Democrats began a prolonged battle over the census design.

Partisan Politics

A census is inevitably a blend of politics and science — politics because power and money are linked to how many people live where, science because the technically complex undertaking draws on many scientific disciplines.

The initial political purpose of the census has been noted — to adjust the regional distribution of power to match changes in the distribution of the population. With one exception, congressional seats have been reapportioned according to census results. Following the 1920 Census, Congress refused to reapportion (suggesting that 1920 rather than 1990 was a "failed census," though it was the Congress not the Census Bureau that failed). What produced that anomaly?

Between 1910 and 1920, there was a massive wartime population movement from the rural, Southern states to industrial Northern cities. In 1920, for the first time in American history, the census included more city dwellers than rural residents. An urban America was something new and disturbing, especially to those who held to the Jeffersonian belief that independent farmers best protected democracy. Among those of this persuasion were rural, conservative congressmen in the South and West. They saw that reapportionment would shift power to factory-based unions and politically radical immigrants concentrated in Northeastern cities. Conservatives in Congress blocked reapportionment, complaining among other things that because January 1 was then census day, transient agricultural workers were "incorrectly" counted in cities rather than on the farms to which they would return in time for spring planting. (Census day was later shifted to April 1, where it has remained.) The

arguments dragged out for a decade, and Congress was not reapportioned until after the next census.

It is instructive to compare 1920 with the even more intense politics later in the century. The 1920 battle aligned the rural Southern and Western regions against the urban Northeast. These regional politics turned on whether to use the census results and were only incidentally about how the census was taken.

Recent controversies have not been regional but partisan, reflecting the sharp divide between Republicans and Democrats that now defines the political culture of America. And now, unlike earlier periods, census politics are focused on the science used to take the census.

These changes mark a significant turning point. For nearly 200 years, under bipartisan congressional oversight, census professionals had designed the methods by which data were collected and the results reported. If politicians sometimes argued about how the results would be applied, that was of no concern to the Census Bureau. Over time the bureau became a professional, scientific agency, careful to maintain distance from the partisan consequences of the statistics it generated. Its thousands of employees take for granted that it is the bureau's reputation for nonpartisan, independent science that earns public cooperation and respect. To tarnish this reputation would put at risk data collection itself and would eventually lessen public confidence in census statistics.

How, then, did it come to pass that a technical and nonpartisan government agency was caught up in a sharply polarized partisan battle late in the 20th century?

Under-Representation

The civil rights laws of the 1960s are an important part of the story. These laws were intended to guarantee equal opportunity to America's racial minorities and to overcome a long history of racial discrimination. But conditions were slow to improve, and civil rights leaders in and out of government began to search for stronger policy instruments. Rather quickly in this effort, statistical proportionality became a favored legal and administrative tool. Statistical proportionality involves comparing how many members of a racial or ethnic minority group occupy particular positions compared with their numbers in the general population. If African Americans are 12 percent of the population, but only 5 percent of college entrants or only 1 percent of the nation's business leaders, African Americans are under-represented. Under-representation is simply the ratio of the proportion of a group in a given position to its proportion in the general population. The denominator for this ratio comes from the basic population numbers of the census.

Under-representation became presumptive evidence of racial discrimination. In dozens of settings—higher education, health access, home mortgages, construction contracts—attention focused sharply on who was under-represented. The nation entered a period in which social justice politics became the calculation of proportionality, and these calculations moved into court cases, college admission practices, hiring and firing decisions, and government contracting. Racial minorities other than African Americans fell under the protection of civil rights laws. And soon women and the disabled made claims similar to those of racial minorities—that they were proportionately under-represented.

The civil rights influence on the politics of census taking was reinforced by a second if less dramatic government initiative of the late 1960s. The Republican administration of Richard Nixon believed that the legacy of New Deal policies and of World War II had shifted too much power to the federal government. It was time to rebalance by returning authority to state and local governments through revenue sharing. Taxes collected at the federal level would be shared with state and local governments, which would know better how to spend them. Health and education programs, public transportation initiatives, and many other state and local government activities began to receive federal funds in significant amounts.

The laws under which federal funds are distributed specify what groups and areas will receive them. Spending formulas routinely incorporate population size as a factor. Cities with more children in poverty receive greater school funds than cities with few such children; communities with large elderly populations receive more health care funds than communities with younger populations; faster-growing cities receive more transportation dollars than cities with declining populations. Although these formulas do not specify minorities, they often use measures—central city residence, crowded housing, low income—that correlate with race.

The political stage was set. The visionary social scientist, Daniel Patrick Moynihan, later to be senator from New York, was the guiding hand behind a "Conference on Social Statistics and the City" that drew out the obvious implication:

"Where a group defined by racial or ethnic terms and concentrated in special political jurisdictions is significantly undercounted in relation to other groups, individual members of that group are thereby deprived of the constitutional right to equal representation in the House of Representatives and, by inference, in other legislative bodies. They are also deprived of their entitlement to partake in federal and other programs designed for areas and populations with their characteristics. In other words, miscounting the population could unconstitutionally deny minorities political representation or protection under the Voting Rights Act. It could also deny local jurisdictions grant funds from federal programs."[11]

These themes gathered political currency in the turbulent 1970s, putting pressure on the Census Bureau as it prepared for the 1980 Census. After all, the census was constitutionally established to ensure that political power and representation would be equitably allocated. Big-city mayors and civil rights leaders were fully aware that to count some groups more completely than others puts equal treatment at risk.

What should or could the bureau do about the increasingly unacceptable differential undercount? There were two possibilities: one, conduct a traditional census more effectively—that is, count better. This led the bureau to introduce a number of coverage improvement methods, including using more advertising to increase cooperation, hiring multilingual census takers who could reach out to hard-to-count population groups, and making multiple callbacks to nonresponding households. The reduction of the undercount from one census to the next gave some hope that the bureau could use traditional methods to count better. But the differential undercount between whites and blacks persisted.

Adjustment

This left the second possibility: dual-system estimation. This statistical procedure held out the hope that the raw census counts could be adjusted to more accurately align them with the true size of different population groups. Specifically, and most important, it could correct differences in how well blacks were counted compared with whites. At least this was the hope.

In the 1980 Census, there was a post-enumeration survey designed to be used for dual-system estimation. The Census Bureau evaluated the results and concluded that there were problems that precluded statistically reliable adjustment. It announced that there would be no adjustment in the 1980 Census, but promised that it would continue its statistical work on dual-system estimation in anticipation of adjusting the next census.

This promise did not satisfy political interests that cared deeply about the rights of minorities, which they saw as denied by the undercount. More than 50 lawsuits were filed seeking to require the adjustment of the 1980 Census to compensate for missed minorities and city dwellers. The most serious legal challenge, brought by Detroit, New York City, and New York state, sought to stop the release of the 1980 Census results until they were adjusted. Under court order, the results were released on schedule, but the case was allowed to proceed to trial. A court ruling eventually upheld the Census Bureau's decision because it had not acted in an "arbitrary and capricious" manner.[12]

During the 1980s, the bureau continued its statistical work, convinced that there was a good chance that adjustment methods could be improved and used in the 1990 Census. It planned accordingly.

By now, however, it was naïve to presume that census planning could be insulated from partisan politics. The Republican and Democratic parties were roughly balanced. Small changes in reapportionment and redistricting could decide which political party controlled the Congress or the White House. The one-person, one-vote ruling of the Supreme Court put pressure on the parties to squeeze every possible advantage in the redrawing of congressional districts after the 1990 Census. Increasingly sophisticated computer-assisted methods allowed the parties to make fine-grained decisions down to the block level.

In this strongly partisan environment, the Census Bureau announced in mid-decade that the 1990 Census would include a post-enumeration survey and that the raw census data would most likely be adjusted to minimize the differential undercount. The Commerce Department, which has formal authority over the Census Bureau, rejected the bureau's plan. The department was quickly taken to court by a coalition of local governments and advocacy groups insisting that the plan be reinstated. There was an out-of-court settlement that allowed the Census Bureau to include a post-enumeration survey in the 1990 Census design, but then gave to the secretary of commerce the authority to set the criteria by which its results would be evaluated and to make the final decision about whether the raw census results would be adjusted.

Why did the Commerce Department try to stop its own bureau from designing the 1990 Census as it saw fit? Census politics had become partisan politics. By the time we got to the 1990 Census, it was obvious that among the population subgroups consistently undercounted were urban minorities, and the subgroups most likely to be overcounted were suburban whites. Leaders in the Democratic Party, understandably, wanted a cen-

sus method that would increase urban populations in order to increase the number of districts likely to elect Democratic candidates. Eliminating the undercount would move in this direction. Republican Party strategists, also understandably, favored a traditional census, especially because it was known to work reasonably well in the white suburbs, where many of the Republican Party's supporters were and are concentrated.

Census method had collided with partisan interests. Both sides dressed their arguments in high-minded language. Democrats spoke of fairness, not partisan advantage. They insisted that the Census Bureau be allowed to apply whatever scientific methods it thought would improve census accuracy. Republicans cited the constitutional provision that an "actual enumeration" be taken as reason to reject any plan using sampling, and they argued that there was no guarantee of a more accurate census using sampling and dual-system estimation. Both sides found support among reputable statisticians, though the weight of professional judgment favored the bureau's design.

Leading up to the 1990 Census, it was a Republican secretary of commerce who tried but had been unable to stop the Census Bureau from including a post-enumeration sample survey. The subsequent out-of-court settlement then produced a curious directive. The bureau would execute the census, evaluate its work, and then decide whether adjustment would improve the raw count. But its decision would take the form of a recommendation to the secretary who had opposed the design in the first place. This set the stage for a confrontation—and that is what happened with the 1990 Census.

The Census Bureau's statisticians concluded that dual-system estimation had worked well enough to warrant statistical adjustment. Barbara Bryant, director of the Census Bureau and a Republican appointee, agreed with this conclusion and presented her recommendation to Commerce Secretary Robert A. Mossbacher. He rejected the recommendation. Overruling a statistical agency in this way was unprecedented, as was one reason the secretary gave for his decision:

"The choice of the adjustment method selected by the Census Bureau officials can make a difference in apportionment, and the political outcome of that choice can be known in advance. I am confident that political considerations played no role in the Census Bureau's choice of an adjustment model for the 1990 Census. I am deeply concerned, however, that adjustment would open the door to political tampering with the census in the future."[13]

This was the first time in American history that a high government official voiced the charge that the nonpartisan, professionally managed Census Bureau might choose a data collection methodology in order to favor one political party over another. The secretary's language was cautious, and he was careful to say that it could happen, not that it had, but in the highly charged political atmosphere cautionary language was soon forgotten. In the close presidential election of 1992, Arkansas Governor Bill Clinton defeated the incumbent Republican, George Bush. Republicans felt that an outsider, and an untrustworthy one at that, had captured the White House. Partisan polarization reached new highs in the 1994 congressional elections, which brought to Congress a number of conservative Republicans deeply mistrustful of Clinton. The Republican Party gained control of the House of Representatives in 1994, and kept control during the entire period in which the 2000 Census was being planned and conducted.

As inevitable as it was unfortunate, census design became a target of partisan animosities. Statistical adjustment, often though inaccurately reduced to the label "sampling," became a political football. The Democratic Party, with its control of the White House, had no doubt that the census could improve its political fortunes. Clinton's first secretary of commerce was the popular African American, Ron Brown, who died in a plane crash, and was replaced by Bill Daley, son of renowned Chicago Mayor Richard Daley, remembered by Republicans as the party boss who had "stolen" the election that barely sent Kennedy to the White House three decades earlier. Republicans were deeply distrustful of what they saw as a very political Commerce Department, and certainly this department did forcefully protect the bureau's right to prepare a 2000 Census that incorporated the adjustment methodology.

Congressional Republicans were now in control of the key subcommittees that reviewed the census plans and appropriated their funds. Their position was clear: In 1997, Jim Nicholson, chairman of the Republican National Committee, sent the following call to arms to local party leaders:

"I am contacting you to recruit your assistance in addressing an issue of unusual importance to the future of the Republican Party. At the heart of the matter is one of the federal government's most fundamental constitutional functions: the United States census. At stake is our GOP majority in the House of Representatives, as well as partisan control of state legislatures nationwide.

"The Clinton administration is implementing a radical new way of taking the next census that effectively will add nearly four and one-half million Democrats to the nation's population. This is the political outcome of a controversial executive decision to use a complex mathematical formula to estimate and 'adjust' the 2000 Census. ...

"... The GOP would suffer a negative effect in the partisan makeup of 24 congressional seats, 113 state senate seats, and 297 state house seats nationwide. ... An adjusted census could provide Democrats the crucial edge needed to prevail in close contests to control several state legislative chambers."[14]

This prediction of how many Republican seats would be "lost" was never documented or subjected to independent analysis. Most students of reapportionment and redistricting believe it is probably impossible a priori to calculate partisan shifts in legislatures resulting from a decennial census, and consider the predictions in this memo highly implausible. As Census Bureau director, I knew that there were far too many factors at work in the census to expect one particular statistical method to have consequences of the scope set forth in Mr. Nicholson's memo.

Plausibility, however, was not the issue. If the Republicans thought sampling would hurt their interests, Democrats were just as certain that it would help theirs. Civil rights organizations argued in favor of the adjustment methodology, claiming that the Republican Party did not care about racial minorities and social justice. The Congressional Black Caucus—all Democrats—took up the census as a leading civil rights issue, and they were often joined by Hispanic and Asian members of Congress. Dozens of congressional votes taken on census issues in the 1990s split on party lines.

One hardly surprising consequence of this partisanship was an unprecedented layer of official oversight and ongoing scrutiny of the Census Bureau. It was in the oversight system that the two political parties, one with control of the Congress and the other with control of the White House, jockeyed for advantage. This back and forth, with the Census Bureau in the middle, is the fourth of the major challenges that faced the bureau as it made final preparations for the 2000 Census.

The Census Under Scrutiny

I became director of the Census Bureau in late 1998, never having been active in party politics or worked in the federal government. After my appointment was announced, but before I got to Washington, the sentence I most frequently heard was: "You're taking on an impossible task." After a few weeks in Washington, it was clear that could not be so, for everyone I met was telling me how to do my job. In fact, the director of the Census Bureau does have many bosses. To give a full account of all of them, and of the oversight to which the 2000 Census was subjected, would turn this into an epic. Here I list the main [organizational] players, all of which had views, often strong views, about how to take the census in 2000.

- As part of a compromise reached during legal and budgetary battles over the census in 1998, the Congress and the White House agreed to jointly appoint a Census Monitoring Board—the first of its kind in census history. This eight-person board, evenly divided between Republicans and Democrats, had its own professional staff and budget ($3 million). Its task, as its name implies, was to monitor the census, hold hearings, inspect census operations, make recommendations, and periodically issue reports on how it thought the census was going. Because the board was evenly divided, few joint reports were issued. The Republican side would issue its report, worrying that the bureau was going to rely on sampling rather than work hard to count everyone. The Democratic side would issue its report, generally defending the census design and the performance of the bureau.

- The Census Bureau's own collection of eight different advisory committees held a total of 25 meetings as the census was underway. Five of these committees, respectively representing African Americans, Asians, Hispanics, American Indians, and Native Hawaiians/Pacific Islanders, focused sharply on the differential undercount issues, defending the sampling design but each also insisting that every effort be made to count fully in their particular community. Other advisory groups, such as one from the National Academy of Sciences, focused on technical issues, particularly on how to improve the statistical adjustment methodology.

- The main congressional investigating agency is the General Accounting Office (GAO). It had a professional staff dedicated to the 2000 Census, which issued a dozen reports (each requiring detailed information supplied by bureau staff) sprinkled with alarming comments such as, "The census faces … several methodological, technological, and quality control challenges. … The country can ill afford an unsatisfactory census at the turn of the century. … Maps still have problems. … With less than four months remaining until census day, significant operational uncertainties continue. … Uncertainties

raise concerns that the 2000 Census may be less accurate than the 1990 Census. … [The] Census Bureau still has not resolved the longstanding challenge of motivating public participation in the census." Each of these reports concluded with specific recommendations of action to be taken by the bureau.

- The parent agency of the Census Bureau, the Commerce Department, had a number of departmental reviews, mainly focused on budgeting, staffing, and related management issues. As director, I reported to an undersecretary in the department, who had a small staff dedicated nearly full-time to the census and was determined that the 2000 Census not be tagged a "failure" as it had been in 1990. This staff was also preoccupied with political strategies that would protect the adjustment methodology. In addition, the Commerce Department, like all federal departments, has its own inspector general's office, whose duty it is to investigate fraud or mismanagement of funds. In a few instances where there were questionable practices by enumerators, this office conducted an investigation and issued its findings and recommendations.

- The White House also took a close interest in the census, though it was careful not to do anything that could be interpreted as trying to politically influence the Census Bureau. The White House mounted a vigorous defense of statistical sampling and worked to reassure its civil rights and urban constituencies that they would be well counted.

- The Office of Management and Budget (OMB) had the responsibility to ensure that budgets submitted by the Census Bureau were consistent with general requirements of the administration, and it had its own budget inspectors who scrutinized dozens of planned census operations. OMB also houses the Office of the Chief Statistician of the United States, responsible, for example, to help coordinate between the Census Bureau and other federal statistical agencies. The judgment of the chief statistician, Katherine Wallman, regarding major census operations helped the White House form its views about the likelihood of a successful census.

- The most sustained oversight was provided by the U.S. Congress, whose responsibility traces to constitutional language—the census is to be carried out "in such Manner as [Congress] shall by law direct." A number of committees and subcommittees with jurisdiction over one aspect or another of the census held hearings. In 1999 and 2000, I appeared in formal hearings before Congress more than 20 times, defending, explaining, and otherwise attempting to convince Congress that it was too late for it to micromanage the taking of the census itself. The House Subcommittee on the Census was the most active (see Box 4). In addition to holding hearings, this subcommittee frequently sent lengthy letters to the Census Bureau requesting that it explain, account for, or otherwise justify particular operations.

In addition to the formal processes of monitoring and oversight listed above, governments and community organizations everywhere in the country were quick to demand of the Census Bureau that it fix any problems they detected—asking if enough staff been hired; complaining that the advertising budget was insufficient; probing into whether enumerators had language skills relevant to local needs; and, above all, monitoring whether their cities were being enumerated as rapidly and completely as others. They often communicated with the bureau through the local newspapers, and much time was spent responding to media stories about problems with the census.

In short, the enterprise that was monitoring the census sometimes seemed to be as vast as the census process itself, and at the Census Bureau we often felt under siege. Mostly, of course, the flow of recommendations—for better or worse—came too late to have much effect. A member of Congress wanted census forms in 33 languages rather than the six languages already printed, a highly impractical suggestion only a few months before census day. Arguments over whether the bureau could hire noncitizens threatened to derail a recruitment effort already underway.

In other instances, the bureau took advantage of advice. Its own advisory committees were especially helpful because these committees were informed and made recommendations consistent with tight schedules and existing budgets. Efforts by local governments to improve the address list materially improved the address file and led to a better census in many cities. The frequent and well-informed warnings by the GAO that the census was at risk seldom said anything the bureau did not already know but reminded political leaders of the importance of the census and helped worry Congress into appropriating the necessary funds.

Box 4

OVERSIGHT OF THE 2000 CENSUS: HEARINGS BY THE HOUSE SUBCOMMITTEE ON THE CENSUS

Community-Based Approaches for a Better Enumeration ....Jan. 29, 1999
Examining the Benefits of Post-Census Local Review ....Feb. 11, 1999
Examining the America Counts Today (ACT) Initiatives
    to Enhance Traditional Enumeration Methods......................March 2, 1999
Examining the Census Bureau's Policy to Count Prisoners,
    Military Personnel, and Americans Residing Overseas..........June 9, 1999
Community-Based Approaches for a Better Enumeration ....June 28, 1999
Examining the Census Bureau's Advertising Campaign ....July 27, 1999
Discussion of the Effects of Including Puerto Rico
    in the 2000 U.S. Population Totals ....Sept. 22, 1999
A Midterm Evaluation of the Local Update
    of Census Addresses Program ....Sept. 29, 1999
Examining the Status of Key Census 2000 Operations..............Feb. 8, 2000
Examining the GAO's Census 2000 Oversight Activities............Feb. 15, 2000
Status of Census Bureau Operations and Activities ....March 8, 2000
Status of Key Operations ....March 14, 2000
Mail-Back Response Rates and Status of Key Operations........April 5, 2000
Status of Nonresponse Follow-up ....May 5, 2000
Nonresponse Follow-up and Other Key Considerations...........May 11, 2000
Accuracy and Coverage Evaluation (ACE)—Still More
    Questions Than Answers ....May 19, 2000
Status of Nonresponse Follow-up and Closeout.......................June 22, 2000
The American Community Survey—A Replacement
    for the Census Long Form? ....July 20, 2000

Although the seemingly endless scrutiny of the census occupied management time that might otherwise have focused on the job at hand, we welcomed its contribution to an open and transparent census. The unprecedented oversight was a consequence of the polarized partisan battles over census design, with its subtext that the Census Bureau could have a partisan agenda. This charge was groundless and even silly. An agency said to have "failed" in 1990 was, a few years later, suspected of being so clever and competent that it could design a census able to shift seats from one party to another a number of years in the future. We could answer this accusation only by complete transparency.

In fact, neither the culture nor the competencies of the Census Bureau are suited to advancing a partisan agenda. The professional statistical community—inside and outside the government—is the bureau's peer community, and the bureau would not jeopardize its high standing among its peers for a short-term political purpose. Of even greater importance, the Census Bureau has the confidence of the American public—a confidence indispensable for public cooperation with its large complement of mainly voluntary statistical surveys and studies (see "The Census Bureau Is More Than the Decennial Census"). To risk public trust and cooperation for a one-time political outcome would be an act of institutional suicide.

Even if its culture were to allow it, the Census Bureau does not have the competence to decide partisan outcomes. There is no expertise in the bureau on trends in voting behavior or in the fine art of drawing election lines. To deliberately influence partisan outcomes, the Census Bureau would need to bring to bear such expertise when making decisions on methodologies—several years in advance of when census results are going to be used for redistricting.

These factors notwithstanding, the concern that the bureau could be subjected to partisan influence was in the air. Active cooperation with the oversight process was the only means available to the bureau to answer this concern. In the end, all the oversight processes, advisory groups, and public watchdogs failed to find partisan intention in the design or conduct of the census. Given the scope of the monitoring effort and the number of groups intent on finding partisan bias, that is powerful evidence that there simply was none to be found.

Summary

In addition to the always tough task of taking a census, the bureau in 2000 faced unprecedented challenges. There was the ever-rising difficulty of getting the American public to cooperate, aggravated by a shadow of the so-called "failed census" in 1990, and the pressure on the Census Bureau to do better. These conditions were in turn greatly complicated by the political environment of mistrust, which led to a level of oversight that itself became a whole side industry in the midst of the census.

THE CENSUS BUREAU IS MORE THAN THE DECENNIAL CENSUS

What does the Census Bureau do in the other nine years when it is not taking the census? It takes other surveys for the federal government. One of the largest of these is the Current Population Survey (CPS), sponsored by the Bureau of Labor Statistics and other agencies. This survey began in 1942 and is fielded every month, year in, year out. It is the basic source of information on employment and labor force participation and is used to set the official poverty line. Also sponsored by the Bureau of Labor Statistics is the Consumer Expenditure Survey, begun in 1979 and conducted quarterly. This survey generates data for the Consumer Price Index, to which are linked the growth of Social Security checks and private pension payments, interest paid on inflation-adjusted bonds, and the positioning of tax brackets. These are just a few of the household surveys conducted by the bureau, often through agreement with other federal agencies.

There is also an extensive Economic Census taken every five years, in years ending in a "2" or a "7" (so it will be off-cycle with the decennial census). This is a census of America's business establishments—from accounting to automobiles, energy to entertainment. It offers a detailed picture of the nation's economy. The underlying classification of business activity by industry group has recently been updated and is now calibrated with Mexico and Canada (the North American Industry Classification System) to better understand economic transactions with our immediate neighbors.

Adding to the nation's economic data are an Agriculture Census and a Census of Governments that reports detailed expenditure information from 39,000 government jurisdictions—states, counties, cities, townships, and tribal councils. Economic statistics are used by the Bureau of Economic Analysis to assess the nation's economic performance, including estimating the Gross National Product (GNP). The quality of the data matters. A mistake in GNP-growth estimates of only one-tenth of one percent (0.1 percent) translates into a $230 billion error in a 10-year federal budget estimate.

The Census Bureau is the nation's largest statistical agency, but in the large task of providing official statistics for the country it is joined by nearly 70 additional federal government statistical programs—listed in *Statistical Programs of the United States Government*, published annually by the Office of Management and Budget, and also available on the Internet: www.whitehouse.gov/omb/inforeg/statpolicy.html#sp. The one-stop shopping site for federal statistical data is www.fedstats.gov.

DESIGN, EXECUTION, ACCOMPLISHMENTS

The 2000 Census, like all censuses, had multiple tasks and purposes. But powerful forces lifted one of these purposes—reduce the undercount and its differential consequences for racial groups—to a privileged position. The forces came from inside and outside the Census Bureau. Within the bureau, there were memories of the charge that 1990 was a failed census, and professional pride had been wounded. More tellingly, for a half-century the bureau had worked to understand the undercount well enough to fix it, thus far without success. It prepared for the 2000 Census confident that sampling methodology could solve the undercount problem.

Politics as well contrived to make the undercount the centerpiece of the census design. An active coalition speaking for historically undercounted groups—Asians, Hispanics, and American Indians as well as African Americans—declared the undercount to be the "civil rights issue of the decade." Leaders of states and cities with high undercount rates in 1990 had, they insisted, lost huge amounts of federal funds as a result, and they did not want a repeat in 2000. Both political parties, each for its own reasons, put the undercount at the center of their divergent strategies for taking the census. Less political interests—a huge and varied group of data users—wanted an accurate census, and this they took to be one without an undercount.

From all sides, the pressure mounted. The bureau had two possibilities: improve traditional census methods or statistically adjust (using dual-system estimation). In the world of census methods, this is not an either-or choice. A full-scale application of traditional methods would not preclude use of adjustment if the effort fell short. The political world did not see it that way. The Republicans said no to adjustment, no matter the results from the traditional census. The Democrats held that the undercount was so resistant to traditional methods that only statistical adjustment could ensure fairness.

These predetermined, strongly held partisan positions ruled out what, in effect, political leadership had said in earlier times: "We expect the most accurate census possible and instruct the Census Bureau to use its experience and scientific judgment to select and administer a census design that has the highest probability of accuracy." That was not the message. There was no single message, but contradictory instructions.

Congressional Republicans ritualistically chanted: "Sampling in census taking is illegal, unworkable, and suspect." The White House and the congressional Democrats, no less ritualistically, responded: "Let the Census Bureau professionals use the most modern scientific methods available to fix the injustice of undercounting the poor and racial minorities."

Caught between the congressional Republican majority and the Democratic administration, the bureau was instructed to plan for two censuses—one using traditional methods only and the other using sampling. In late 1998, only a few weeks into my directorship, I appeared before the Census Monitoring Board, where I was asked what I thought of the "two-track" planning effort. "It feels," I quipped, "as if you are giving me Yogi Berra's famous advice: 'When you come to a fork in the road, take it.'"

The awkward period of two-track planning had been put in place pending the outcome of a lawsuit working its way to the Supreme Court. This case (explained below) would presumably settle the political fight by allowing or forbidding sampling in Census 2000. The case was heard in the late fall of 1998, and announced in January 1999. To follow the story of the census, we need a broad overview of how the Supreme Court ruling influenced the census design (see Table 5).

Note that prior to the Supreme Court ruling, statistical sampling had two purposes, as described below. Second, note that the Supreme Court ruling dealt with

---

Table 5
THE 2000 CENSUS DESIGN

Design Factors	Before the Court Ruling	After the Court Ruling	
		Results Used for Apportionment*	Results Used for Redistricting*
Traditional Methods	Yes	Yes-plus	Yes-plus
Sampling for Nonresponse	Yes	No	No
Sampling for Adjustment	Yes	No	Perhaps

*Apportionment refers to the state-by-state counts that determine how many seats in the House of Representatives each state will get after every decennial census. Redistricting refers to the drawing of election boundaries within the state for congressional elections and, by extension, boundaries for state legislative and other election districts.

census results used in apportionment. This ruling left open the possibility that census results used for apportionment could differ from those used for redistricting. Whether the Supreme Court intended this inconsistency is unclear. Finally, note that traditional census methods will vary in their extensiveness depending on the level of funding provided. The "yes-plus" means that the Congress provided more funds than initially anticipated, allowing for a more thorough traditional census than initially planned.

To understand what the bureau designed following the Supreme Court ruling, we must see why there were two kinds of sampling in the preruling design—sampling those who failed to return a form in the mail and sampling for dual-system estimation.

Sampling in the Census Design Prior to the Supreme Court Ruling

In 1992, Bill Clinton became president. From 1994 forward, Republicans controlled Congress. The Constitution grants Congress authority over how the census will be conducted, but the statutes governing the census vest responsibility in the secretary of commerce, who has customarily delegated authority to the Census Bureau director. Martha Riche, a distinguished demographer, was Clinton's first director.

When census planning first got underway, the government was mired in red ink. The high costs of census taking looked like a good candidate for savings. Under instruction to holds costs down, the Census Bureau turned to what, in its professional view, was obvious—the increased use of sampling. The bureau had had a long and successful experience with sampling in its many surveys (see "The Census Bureau Is More Than the Decennial Census," page 24) and in the census itself, with the administration of the long form and of quality control procedures, but it had never proposed sampling as an aid to the basic count of the population. In the early 1990s, it recommended just that, with support and technical advice from committees of the National Academy of Sciences.

A Sample of Nonrespondents

As usual, in 2000 the census form would be delivered to every household on the address list. When there was no response, a census taker would be sent to get the answers. Every reasonable effort would be made to get information—making up to six return visits or telephone calls, taking proxy answers from neighbors or apartment building managers, and so forth. That is, tra-

ditional enumeration methods would be used for every household in the country.

Knowing how unlikely it was that it would be able to reach every household, however, the bureau would draw a sample of nonresponding households. After all reasonable effort had been made using traditional methods, the focus would shift to this sample. Because resources would be concentrated and only the most skilled enumerators used, there was a much better chance of getting replies from a sample of the very hardest-to-count households than from every household. On the basis of this sample, the census could statistically estimate the household size and characteristics of the other nonresponding households. Great Britain successfully used this method in its census of 2001.

A Post-Enumeration Sample Survey (PES)

The design included a second use of sampling, along the lines reviewed in the section on census accuracy. Census 2000 would conduct a large post-enumeration sample survey that could be matched to census results, and the matching would be used to calculate the rate at which discrete population groups were under- or overcounted. The census would then be adjusted accordingly. The post-enumeration sample survey was itself expected to be a mammoth operation of 750,000 households. This huge sample was needed to provide statistically reliable estimates for each individual state.

This census design was announced in early 1996. The American Statistical Association and other professional organizations endorsed it, but it was not well received by congressional Republicans and other critics of sampling for the basic population count. They noted, correctly, that there were technical problems not yet worked out. In a less politically heated atmosphere, the Census Bureau would have worked on these problems in field tests, with evaluation studies, and by consulting advisory committees, but the congressional Republicans with census oversight responsibilities wanted to drop "sampling methods to complete or adjust the actual enumeration of the 2000 Census," and Jim Nicholson sent his inflammatory memo, quoted earlier.

Political battles simmered throughout 1996 and 1997. In frustration at being unable to derail the census plan, the Republican-led Congress finally attached anti-sampling language to an unrelated bill (on flood relief) that it believed Clinton would be unable to veto. The president did veto the bill, signaling the importance of the census for the Democratic White House.

The partisan struggle continued through congressional hearings; arguments between experts on both sides; the resignation of Census Bureau Director Riche; compromises that left the bureau trying to plan for a rapidly approaching census without yet knowing whether sampling would be allowed; and always the heavy oversight by Congress and its investigating arm, the GAO. Then, in early 1998, a federal lawsuit was brought by Newt Gingrich, the Republican speaker of the House, seeking court action to prevent the Clinton administration from any use of sampling in producing the apportionment numbers.

Following expedited procedures, in January of 1999, the Supreme Court ruled against sampling (in a narrow 5-to-4 decision). The court cited language in the basic census statute that was ambiguous but could reasonably be interpreted as prohibiting the decennial census from using sampling to produce the state-by-state apportionment counts. Contrary to widely circulated reports, the court did not rule that sampling was unconstitutional. It set aside sampling as part of nonresponse follow-up. It prohibited the application of a post-enumeration sample survey to adjust the census results for apportionment. The critics of sampling were initially enthusiastic about the ruling, but their victory was a mixed one—it would be two years before we finally learned the fate of sampling in Census 2000. The court did not rule on whether sampling could be used for other census products, which included redistricting data.

In the paragraphs that follow, we see how the mixed message on sampling moved the partisan politics to a different battlefield. In the remainder of this section, we will review how, following the court ruling, the Census Bureau planned a census using traditional methods that have their origins in the 1790 Census overseen by Thomas Jefferson.

The Budget for the 2000 Census

With the Supreme Court having settled the issue of sampling for nonrespondents, the bureau focused on procedures that would maximize coverage and reduce the net undercount as well as differences in the completeness of the count for different population groups.

This effort was going to be expensive, but in the heady economy of the late 1990s, tax revenues were sharply up. In this fiscally comfortable environment, the Republican-led Congress was willing to pay the bill. Having successfully challenged a less costly plan designed to reduce the undercount, Republicans were accused of not wanting a census fair to racial minorities. Their strongest answer was to fund the census generously, and in particular to provide dollars for efforts tar-

geted to reducing the undercount of racial minorities: more money for community partnerships and promotional campaigns, higher salaries for enumerators working in difficult-to-count areas, and additional support for outreach programs in remote areas and places with high immigrant concentrations.

Ironically, though the initial planning for the census was guided by firm congressional direction to hold costs down, Congress eventually funded the 2000 Census at nearly twice the level of the previous one. To a bureau long accustomed to pleading for every extra dollar, the unexpected boon was a pleasant surprise.

Almost without exception, every census has been more expensive than the one before—having more people to enumerate accounts for some of the cost increase, but even on a per capita basis, the costs increased. In the first census in 1790, it cost an average of 10 cents per person. By 1900 this had multiplied 30-fold (in constant dollars). Costs rose throughout the 20th century, and by 1990 the per capita cost was four times higher than in 1900. Of course the quality and quantity of the data and the speed with which they are released improved substantially. The modern census is probably four times better than the census was at the beginning of the 20th century, and maybe more than 100-fold better than a century before that. Quality improvements explain part of the increased costs. The other cost driver is a population increasingly difficult to enumerate, for reasons noted in the section on "Unprecedented Challenges in 2000" (beginning on page 16).

The 2000 Census was initially budgeted at more than $7 billion; it came in half a billion under budget (approximately $56 per household). For the first time ever, the Census Bureau was treated by the Congress much as the military is in time of war. Military leaders are told to go where necessary and do what is needed to win the war. They don't stop to ask whether there are funds to respond to the unexpected. If the census, the nation's largest peacetime mobilization, is to be successful, it must also rapidly deal with the unexpected. Census taking is a gigantic operation crowded into a short time frame. Not everything can be anticipated. In 2000, for instance, major floods in North Carolina and widespread fires in Arizona required special action by the bureau; the bureau had to hire nearly a million people in a tight employment market.

In addition to allowing intelligent planning and response to the unexpected, the healthy budget for the 2000 Census allowed for expansion of the various efforts urging public cooperation. This expanded effort is indicated by the "yes-plus" in Table 5 (page 25).

Traditional Census Methods in 2000

The term "traditional census" took on two, related meanings. It described the use of procedures—from public announcements urging cooperation to repeated call-backs when no form is returned—that had traditionally been used to maximize coverage and minimize errors in the census. In the political arena, the term was also used to describe a census using only enumeration to arrive at the basic population count. The Supreme Court ruling meant that the basic population count for apportionment would be traditional in both ways the term was being used. The Census Bureau planned accordingly.

A User-Friendly Census

In dozens of ways, the 2000 Census was more user-friendly than ever before. Advanced technology based on intelligent character recognition facilitated improvements in questionnaire design. This technology was used in data capture, or the process of transferring information from a census form to a usable data file. Historically, census forms came into data capture centers where hundreds of people manually transferred the information to whatever the current tabulation medium was—paper, punch cards, or computer tapes. This human transfer is prone to error. These errors can be minimized by designing forms that are easy to code, but there is a catch. A design made easy for data capture has features that make it more difficult for the person filling in the form. Questionnaire design involves trade-offs.

In 2000, for the first time, data capture was based on digital scanning, which permitted forms that are easy to fill out without worrying about how hard they would be to code. This was part of a "keep-it-simple" rule set by the bureau's director, Martha Riche, early in planning for the 2000 Census.

Questionnaires were printed in five commonly used languages in addition to English, and telephone assistance centers were multilingual, as was the enumerator staff that went door-to-door. Every household received three mailings—an advance notice, the census form itself, and then a postcard thanking respondents and reminding others to return the form. (These outreach efforts got results: One person even returned a 1990 form, found in the bottom of a desk drawer, with a note saying she hoped she was not too late.)

Multiple languages and multiple mailings were combined with multiple ways for the public to respond—by mail, by phone, by Internet, or by going to a walk-in assistance center. For those who felt that they had been missed, there were "Be Counted" forms placed in community centers and other convenient locations. Providing multiple ways to respond increased the risk of including some people twice, and in the next section we discuss duplicates in the 2000 Census.

Paid Advertising

We mounted an extensive, targeted paid advertising campaign to increase public awareness and to encourage high rates of cooperation. Previously the Census Bureau had relied on free public service ads that typically ran late at night and could not be pitched to particular groups. Census 2000 had the benefit of paid promotional advertisements carefully designed to reach hard-to-count population groups, and it took advantage of every major outlet—TV, radio, newspapers, magazines, billboards, placement of posters in buses, and dozens of other high-visibility spots. Even the most expensive ads were not out of reach; for example, a well-received census ad ran during the Super Bowl in January of 2000. The advertising budget, $165 million, was second in size only to McDonald's and Wendy's during the early months of 2000.

A leading Madison Avenue advertising agency, Young and Rubicam, designed the campaign, working closely with specialty firms experienced in reaching African Americans, Hispanics, Asians, American Indians, and immigrant groups. The ads appeared in more than 50 languages. Independent evaluations gave high marks to the quality of the advertising copy and to the effectiveness of the campaign.

Every ad included a facsimile of the census form itself, along with the tag line "This is your future, don't leave it blank." Ads emphasized that cooperating with the census would benefit one's own community in tangible ways—less crowded schools, more public transportation, better emergency service. The not-so-subtle message was that an uncooperative community would get less than its share of publicly funded benefits. One proposed ad, not used because we felt it was perhaps too blunt, showed a tax form and a census form side-by-side, with the message: "This form taketh away. This form giveth back."

Partnerships

The Census Bureau established an unprecedented number of partnerships with state and local governments, community groups, and businesses—140,000 in all. Nearly 12,000 were Complete Count Committees that engaged state, county, and city government officials in promoting the census; 60,000 volunteers staffed community sites in churches, schools, clubhouses, and similar meeting places where "Be Counted" forms were available. A school program placed census-related curricular material and lesson plans in thousands of classrooms. Churches promoted the census. The Catholic Church was especially active in reaching out to recent Mexican and Central American immigrants, stressing that census answers were confidential. Census vans, first seen on NBC's Today Show, toured the country, visiting fairs, sporting events, hard-to-count neighborhoods, and other places where they would be covered by the local media.

Special events and promotional efforts numbered in the many hundreds across the nation. In addition to the Census Bureau's own partnership budget of $143 million, promotional dollars were contributed by hundreds of local and state governments and by private businesses and other groups. California alone had a state budget of $35 million to promote Census 2000. A few specifics illustrate the range of promotional efforts and donated contributions through this partnership program:

- McDonald's in Detroit rewarded homeless people who completed a form with a free meal and a yellow button saying, "I'm Important, I've Been Counted."
- Radio Fiesta, a network of 20 South Florida stations, aired a special series of announcements that reached 100,000 migrant and seasonal workers.
- The Carolina Panthers of the National Football League gave free exhibition space at their home games, allowing census workers to reach tens of thousands of football fans throughout North and South Carolina.
- Milwaukee spent $350,000 on its "I Will Count in Census 2000" campaign, one of hundreds of instances where state and local governments spent their own funds on census promotion.
- Univision, the Spanish-language TV channel, carried a national broadcast of a census Mass at the San Antonio Cathedral, where the archbishop, the local congressman, and I spoke.
- The Navajo Nation hosted a Tribal Leadership Conference to promote census cooperation and to help recruit Navajo-speaking enumerators.
- The Goodyear Blimp displayed census messages during its nighttime flights across the Southern California sky.
- New York City funded a special Black Advisory Committee, bringing together African American, Caribbean American, and recently arrived immigrants from dozens of African countries, which organized promotional activities with grassroots groups and churches.
- Unalakleet, a remote Alaskan village on the edge of the Bering Strait, served a huge community meal, including whale blubber and other local foods, to journalists from the *New York Times*, the *Washington Post*, *USA Today*, and dozens of other media that had arrived to cover the first person to be enumerated in Census 2000.

If the scope and magnitude of this partnership effort was unprecedented, so was an invitation to thousands of organizations to help conduct the census. There were risks in blurring the boundary between a tightly controlled, quality-focused statistical operation by trained professionals and an often enthusiastic and spontaneous effort geared to local interests. For example, the Census Bureau had strict criteria for who would be hired to staff its local offices, but in a tight labor market, it asked partners to help recruit workers. People put forward by partner organizations did not always meet the recruitment criteria, and some had to be rejected. To ask for help and then not take it made for some strained relations. In one large Northeastern city, the mayor—a big census booster—wanted to appoint city census watchers on every block who would pressure the nonrespondents to cooperate. He asked the bureau to tell his workers who had not mailed a form in, and it took more than one exchange to convince him that laws guaranteeing the confidentiality of census responses, including no response, absolutely prohibited us from sharing any information with his census watchers. Then there were congressional concerns that a business or, in one instance, a political party, was misappropriating the census logo in a manner suggesting that its product, or candidate, was being endorsed by the Census Bureau. The bureau widely distributed its materials, including a website where they could be downloaded, and could not, in the final analysis, control how they were used in hundreds of promotional events.

On balance, however, the partnership effort was a rousing success. It gave many communities a stake in how well the census was conducted, and it educated the public about the importance of the census and its results. Over time, this will increase the public's use of census information.

Above all, the partnership program served the basic goal—it contributed to a higher percentage of households returning the census form by mail than was expected (see next section). Even the habitually cautious GAO, which audited the census partnership program, concluded that "it appears as though key census-taking activities, such as encouraging people to return their questionnaires, would have been less successful had it not been for the bureau's partnership efforts."[15] Readers knowledgeable about the GAO's obligation to find and report poorly invested tax dollars and mismanagement by executive branch agencies will recognize this as welcome praise.

The user-friendly innovations and the partnership and advertising efforts were elaborations and extensions of traditional census methods focused on improving levels of census cooperation and reducing the differential undercount. Of particular importance was halting the two-decades-long decline in the percentage of households that returned the form by mail. We noted that there had been a 10 percent drop between 1980 and 1990, and the bureau feared that 2000 would continue this sharp decline.

Public Cooperation With the 2000 Census

Whether the public mails back the census form has significant repercussions for data accuracy and census costs. A low mail-back response rate reduces census accuracy because many forms are then completed weeks after census day. Errors increase because memories fade. It is easy for a householder who moved into a vacant house shortly after April 1 to have forgotten his move date and to answer an enumerator in June that yes, he had lived there on April 1. Thus a location vacant on April 1 is incorrectly recorded as an occupied house. Or, in households with a lot of coming and going, perhaps by transient workers or part-time students, it is easy to mis-recall several months later about who was there on April 1.

A low mail-back rate also drives up costs sharply. Census takers make up to six visits to every household that does not return a form. There are high salary, transport, and management costs in this nonresponse follow-up effort. In the initial planning for the 2000 Census, the bureau feared a mail-back response rate as low as 55 percent. In the early 1990s, it conducted studies on how to keep the rate from slipping further. Some studies led to the "keep-it-simple" principles discussed above. Another suggested that the mandatory nature of the census should be emphasized. Though it is the law that everyone has to complete a census form, this had not been stressed in recent censuses—for fear of alienating parts of the population. But with the response rate plummeting, and on the basis of evaluation studies, the bureau decided that the legal obligation should be emphasized in 2000. Based on these and other modifications, the bureau revised its expected mail-back response rate for the 2000 Census to 61 percent.

With this estimate in mind, the bureau presented its budget requests and began the mammoth task of recruiting a census staff that would eventually number a staggering 900,000 office and field workers. If the response rate fell below 61 percent, the bureau would face budget and staffing problems. If it unexpectedly climbed above that rate, even by 1 percent, pressure in the critical follow-up period would lessen. With an address file of 120 million residences, 62 percent rather than 61 percent mail-back is 1.2 million fewer households to visit.

"1990 Plus 5 percent" Campaign

As the census got underway, we launched a special "1990 plus 5 percent" campaign (called the "get it up" campaign by some census staffers). This was the challenge to every city, county, and state in the nation to improve its 1990 Census response rate by 5 percent. This ambitious campaign declared that the nation should not only stop the declining cooperation rate but actually reverse it. No one knowledgeable about the changing attitudes and lifestyles in the population really expected the response rate to reach this target, but it was hoped that the special campaign could at least keep it from falling below the budgeted target of 61 percent. The key strategy was to report day by day to 39,000 jurisdictions in the country—villages, towns, cities, Indian reservations, counties—what its own mail-back "score" was, one of the very few procedures added late in the census process (to satisfy the director). Untested procedures introduced late in a census are high risk and generally avoided. The special "1990 plus 5 percent" campaign required heroic efforts by headquarters staff.

The day-by-day scores were widely cited in the press, with USA Today reporting the national totals as well as the response rate for each of the 50 states. Cities competed with each other, and at least one case of wine passed from a mayor to his colleague in a neighboring town whose rate came in higher. I entered a friendly wager with the bureau's major inspector from the GAO, who doubted that we could exceed the 1990 rate. (When he lost, he graciously agreed to donate my modest winnings to National Public Radio for its excellent coverage of census issues.)

The early days of April were a tense time in the Census Bureau. If the target of 61 percent mail response was not reached, the next phase of the census—the field-based nonresponse follow-up—would be understaffed and more expensive than planned. And even if that target were reached but the nation fell short of the 1990 rate, the huge promotional effort would have failed.

The news trickled in as hundreds of trailer trucks delivered the mail to four data capture centers around the country. Our anxious waiting turned to relief and then to elation. Two-thirds of America's households had mailed in their form by the date when the bureau

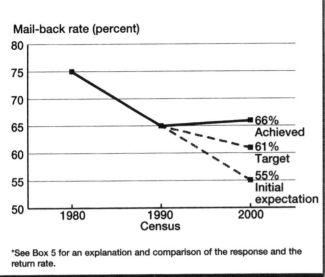

Figure 2

MAIL-BACK RESPONSE RATE: TARGET AND ACHIEVEMENT*

Mail-back rate (percent)

- 66% Achieved
- 61% Target
- 55% Initial expectation

Census: 1980, 1990, 2000

*See Box 5 for an explanation and comparison of the response and the return rate.

had to start its field operation of nonresponse follow-up (see Figure 2).

In fact, the news was much better than we knew at the time. The denominator for the initial response rate is the number of addresses to which a form is delivered. At the time of the census, the master address file includes an unknown number of vacant houses and apartments. When the bureau has completed all its many quality checks, it determines how many addresses on the file represented occupied households. With this as the denominator, it calculates a final return rate (see Box 5). In 2000 the return rate was 78.4 percent, well over three percentage points higher than the comparable number in 1990.

We had not only stopped the three-decade decline in cooperation, we had reversed it. Harvard professor Robert Putnam, author of *Bowling Alone* and the nation's leading commentator on civic disengagement, congratulated the bureau for defying the odds, remarking that we had "managed to run up the down escalator." The combination of the keep-it-simple strategy, partnership program, advertising campaign, and feedback about response rates had been successful far beyond expectations. When we saw the final return rate, we realized that the nation came close to meeting the extraordinary challenge of improving its cooperation by the "1990 plus 5 percent" goal we had set.

Targeted Publicity

Survey evidence confirms that the promotional efforts had increased census awareness, motivated coopera-

Box 5

WHY THE RESPONSE RATE DIFFERS FROM THE RETURN RATE

Response Rate = Percentage of all households on the master address file, whether occupied or not, that mail back the form.

Return Rate = Percentage of households occupied on census day that mail back the form.

In preparing for and then conducting the census, we harped on the response rate, the percentage of households sent a form that they mailed back in. Often we stressed that this rate had fallen in recent decades, most sharply from 1980 to 1990 (by 10 percent). In an effort to motivate cooperation in 2000, I often said that "only 65 percent" had mailed their forms back in 1990, and then pleaded that doing better in 2000 would prove that Americans took civic responsibility seriously. That endlessly repeated fact about the 1990 response rate is true, but it is not the whole story. When the master address file is compiled, the Census Bureau does not know which houses or apartments are occupied. It is not until a form has been delivered, not returned, and there has been a personal follow-up that the bureau learns if a given residency is occupied or vacant. It takes many months to complete all the checks required to determine how many households are vacant on census day, which can be as many as 10 percent of the residences in the United States. After vacancies (and other address errors) are subtracted, the Census Bureau has a list of valid occupied households. Using that as the denominator, it recalculates the mail-back return rate. This corrected calculation is a more meaningful indicator of civic responsibility. In 1990 it was 75 percent, or 10 percent higher than the initially announced "response rate." But of course as Census 2000 got underway, we again were forced to talk about the response rate—it was the only measure available to compare 1990 and 2000 as the census was being conducted. Long after the census had disappeared from public view, the bureau completed all its evaluations and determined that the final return rate in 2000 was 78.4 percent, significantly higher than the comparable measure in 1990.

tion, and reached the targeted hard-to-count population groups. During the phase of maximum publicity, the portion of the population aware of the census climbed to nearly 90 percent (see Figure 3, page 32).

Racial minorities were more strongly influenced by the campaign than were others, confirming that the effort to target publicity had worked. Higher levels of exposure increased levels of census cooperation especially among African Americans and Hispanics (see Figure 4, page 32).

A mail-back response rate that exceeded expectations was welcomed in all quarters, but there were still

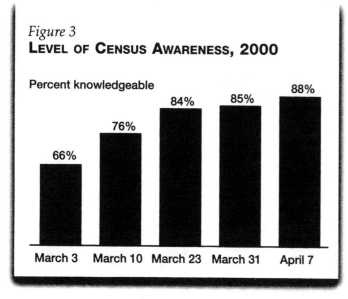

Figure 3

LEVEL OF CENSUS AWARENESS, 2000

Percent knowledgeable

66%	76%	84%	85%	88%
March 3	March 10	March 23	March 31	April 7

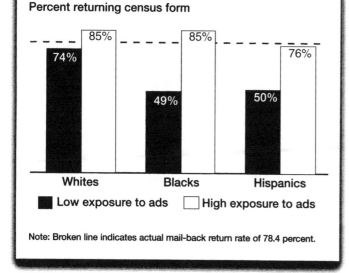

Figure 4

SUCCESS OF TARGETED ADVERTISING: MAIL-BACK RESPONSE RATE, BY RACIAL/ETHNIC GROUP, 2000

Percent returning census form

Whites	Blacks	Hispanics
74% / 85%	49% / 85%	50% / 76%

■ Low exposure to ads □ High exposure to ads

Note: Broken line indicates actual mail-back return rate of 78.4 percent.

40 million households to visit. Moreover, we knew that however important it was to improve cooperation with the mail-back phase of the census, success in eliminating the differential undercount was the outcome that mattered politically.

Summary

When the Supreme Court ruled that statistical adjustment could not be used for the basic apportionment numbers, it put in motion an extraordinary and well-funded effort to conduct the best traditional census in

history, including an unprecedented advertising and promotional campaign. This effort exceeded its first target—to convince a higher proportion of the American population to mail their census form back than had done so in 1990.

But the inescapable fact about census taking is that it can be a huge success for the vast majority of the population yet still have an undercount that differs from one population group to another. This can be illustrated hypothetically:

> **There are 120 million households, of which
> 90 million mail back their forms, leaving
> 30 million to be visited by enumerators, of which
> 28 million cooperate, leaving
> 2 million households not in the census, of which
> 1.5 million are racial minorities.**

In this hypothetical census, a small percentage of the households are missed, but those missed are disproportionately concentrated among minorities. The differential undercount is a stubborn problem, and in the next section we ask whether a census relying only on traditional enumeration methods can eliminate it.

WHO DECIDES WHICH COUNT COUNTS

Table 5 (page 25) showed that the Supreme Court ruling on Census 2000 prohibited sampling for apportionment but not for redistricting, allowing for the possibility of two census counts.

It is understandable if the reader is asking, "How can there be two population figures?" The answer is: In the same way that there can be two, or more, drafts of a text. Any census is a process of successive approximations and refinements, each an improvement over the preceding one. For example, early results from the census are known to have duplicates—the student who is counted both by the parents and by the college dormitory, the child shuttled between separated parents and counted by both. If the Census Bureau can find those duplicates before releasing results, it of course takes them out. This is but one of several such quality checks. Each of them modifies the census, until time runs out and official population numbers are produced.

Time runs out differently for different census purposes. By law, the Census Bureau has to produce the apportionment results within nine months of census day, or by Dec. 31. This is the raw count of how many residents there are in the United States and how they are distributed across the 50 states. These initial numbers tell us nothing about the characteristics of the population—how many men and women, young and old, urban dwellers and suburbanites.

The redistricting data are more complex. To carry out redistricting requires assigning each resident to an address on a specific block. The data also indicate age, race, and gender. This more detailed information takes longer to produce, and the census has an additional three months to produce redistricting data. Even more time is needed to provide data used for federal funding and for general public use because these data products are successively more refined.

In fixing on a design after the 1999 Supreme Court ruling, the bureau built the most robust traditional census possible—which by the end of 2000 would produce population totals for the nation and the 50 states to be used for congressional reapportionment. But the census was not then finished. An evaluation of the results from the post-enumeration survey would determine if dual-system estimation could improve the results to be used for redistricting and/or fund allocation.

It was this possibility that sustained the partisan battle until early 2001, when the decision about adjusting the census for redistricting purposes was scheduled.

The Supreme Court ruling, probably unintentionally, led to a situation unprecedented in U.S. history. Congress appropriated funds to conduct the best full-scale traditional census possible, while at the same time the court ruling left in place a methodology for potential statistical adjustment. The political and practical uncertainty was whether the well-funded traditional census would be so thorough no adjustment would be necessary, or whether there would still be a differential undercount that required adjustment.

Scientific Recommendations

At the center of both the science and the politics of the census remained the differential undercount. The more completely a given group is counted by the census, the greater its voice in presidential elections, Congress, state legislatures, and local governments. The Census Bureau cannot escape the fact that democratic fairness is affected by how well it does its job, which of course is why discovering the differential undercount initiated the long, technically challenging task of trying to fix it. The task did not get easier in a half-century of statistical work, because the groups likely to be missed in the census steadily grew proportionately and because census taking grew more difficult in our mobile, preoccupied, and civically disengaged society.

Risking oversimplification, we label a traditional, enumeration-only census "good" if it reduces the differential undercount; we label a post-enumeration survey "good" if it accurately measures the proportion of various groups who are missed and erroneously included. There were four possible outcomes in Census 2000:

1. **Good Traditional Census* and Flawed PES**
2. **Flawed Traditional Census and Good PES**
3. **Good Traditional Census and Good PES**
4. **Flawed Traditional Census and Flawed PES**

*An undercount is a net number and is zero if the undercount and overcount are equal in size, even if both are very large. Thus a census with a large number of gross errors can be labeled "good" by the criteria used here, but it would not overall be a good census.

Before the census results were known, in a number of political and scientific meetings, I announced that if the outcome were number 1, statistical adjustment would not be used. If the outcome were number 2, adjustment would be used to improve the raw census counts for redistricting data and other census purposes. I said that how to proceed under outcomes 3 and 4 was less clear because there is a difficult statistical judgment about whether adjustment in these cases introduces as much error as it removes.

The outcome of the 2000 Census confounded the expectations of many, including me. The Census Bureau discovered serious technical flaws when it attempted to match the results from the post-enumeration survey to the raw census. It also learned, later in its evaluation, that the well-funded traditional census had erased the net undercount, even producing a small net overcount.

Not all of this was clear to the bureau in the frantic weeks of early 2001, as it faced the looming deadline of March 31 for releasing the redistricting data. During this period, the bureau's statisticians struggled to understand a large discrepancy between the census, if adjusted by PES results, and the independent estimation of the population size from demographic analysis. This discrepancy led the professional staff at the bureau to conclude that, at least within the time available, statistical adjustment would not improve the census results. This was an unexpected turn in the decade-long political controversy, but there is more to the story.

Although the reasons for this intense political focus on sampling and statistical adjustment have been set forth, the reader might still be perplexed by a lingering anomaly. Why is it only adjustment methods and not other statistical procedures that have so exercised the political process? Adjustment is not the only statistical procedure that affects the final census results.

While it decided not to recommend adjustment, the Census Bureau did proceed with two other statistical procedures that affect final census results and consequently influence where boundaries are drawn. One such procedure is imputation, which occurs when an enumerator has strong evidence that a house or apartment is occupied but is unable to retrieve any information—for example, an apartment where a newspaper is delivered and neighbors report that late at night they hear someone enter or leave, but repeated visits by an enumerator never find anyone home (or willing to open the door). The bureau then statistically imputes how many people live here based on characteristics of neighboring households. If every other apartment in this building is occupied by a single resident, it is reasonable to assume the same for this nonresponding apartment. This imputation makes for an overall more accurate census than if the apartment were recorded as vacant.

The Census Bureau has used statistical imputation for a half-century, and it is a practice common to census taking around the world. In the 2000 Census, imputation increased the final population count by 1.1 million, or about a half-percent. Imputation disproportionately increased the numbers of population subgroups, such as urban racial minorities, which were the focus of partisan battles over statistical adjustment.

Another quality control procedure with similar ramifications was the removal of suspected duplicates from the census file. The Census Bureau worried that the many different ways in which a census form could be submitted would lead to duplicate responses. In the summer of 2000, well before the final apportionment count, the bureau identified approximately 6 million forms suspected of being duplicates. It matched these forms as best it could—was Susan Mullin at 112 Price, Apt. 6, the same person as S. Mullin at 112-114 Price Street, 6th floor? If Susan and S. were the same gender and the same age, they were judged to be duplicates. If they were different genders and different ages, they were treated as different people. But what if they were both female, but Susan was 40 and S. was 41? Is that a big enough difference to judge them different people? In the time available, it was not possible to revisit Price Street and the other 6 million suspected duplicates to be sure. A computer-based de-duplication algorithm was used: 3.6 million of the suspected duplicates were deleted from the census; the other 2.4 million were considered legitimate responses and remained in the census.

Imputation and de-duplication are procedures with as much potential as statistical adjustment to impact apportionment, redistricting, federal fund allocation, and other uses of the census. The census unfolds as a series of quality-control efforts which, it is expected,

progressively bring the census closer to the true number and characteristics of America's resident population. Like other quality-control procedures, statistical adjustment is, in the view of the Census Bureau, to be used if it improves the census results, not if it fails to.

In Census 2000, the bureau examined statistical methods designed to improve the census; it applied them if, in its professional judgment, they would increase accuracy. Two of these methods—imputation and de-duplication—combined to account for 3.5 million records in the final census, more than what was at stake in the statistical adjustment battle. Why were two significant statistical procedures left to the discretion of professionals while another was handled politically?

The answer can be traced to lawsuits trying to force the 1980 Census to be adjusted, despite the statistical reservations of the Census Bureau, and from there to the unfortunate language used by the secretary of commerce after the 1990 Census, when he opined that the adjustment method could lend itself to manipulation for partisan advantage. Sampling in the census became political ideology, for both parties—Democrats seeing a census without sampling as undemocratic and Republicans seeing one with sampling as unconstitutional.

Sampling, or more correctly dual-system estimation, is of course not a political ideology. It is a statistical method intended to make the census more accurate, one that the Census Bureau has now evaluated in three censuses. In each, there were technical difficulties, and its future in census taking is much in doubt.

Political Process

The most politically visible census results are the state-by-state numbers that apportion congressional seats. At 10 a.m., on Dec. 28, 2000, I delivered the results to the secretary of commerce—the first time they were seen by anyone outside the bureau. The secretary immediately transmitted them to the president of the United States, and less than an hour later, the secretary and I presented the Census 2000 results to the nation at the packed National Press Club.

No one so much as suggested that the national and state-by-state census results might be reviewed in advance by the secretary, the president, or congressional leaders. There was no opportunity for anyone to instruct the bureau to modify the census by not using imputation or the algorithm that removed suspected duplicates. The apportionment numbers were announced exactly as they emerged from the procedures applied by the bureau.

Two months later, the statistical adjustment decision was handled quite differently. Recall that in 1980 it was the Census Bureau itself that decided against statistical adjustment. In 1990 it was Secretary Mossbacher who made the decision. Assigned that authority in a legal compromise, he overruled his own Census Bureau director.

As the 2000 Census got underway, neither William Daley, then secretary of commerce, nor I, then Census Bureau director, wanted a repeat of 1990. In the summer of 2000, Daley prepared an executive order assigning full and final authority over the release of all census results, including the decision whether to adjust statistically, to the director. This executive order was issued prior to the election of 2000, and no one knew who would be in the White House or who would be the Census Bureau director by March 2001, when the decision about statistical adjustment of the results for redistricting would be made.

When President George W. Bush took office on Jan. 20, 2001, I was immediately replaced by an acting director. Dan Evans, a close associate of the new president, became the secretary of commerce. One of his first acts was to rescind the executive order issued several months earlier. He announced that he would make the final decision about statistical adjustment, calling on advice from statistical consultants of his choice. When the Census Bureau, for technical reasons noted above, recommended against adjustment, Secretary Evans quickly accepted the recommendation. It is unknowable whether he would have overruled the bureau had it recommended adjusting the redistricting data file.

What is certain is that the secretary treated the results differently from every other major statistical product produced by the federal government; he asserted his political right to make the final decision.

The ramifications of this extraordinary assertion are clear if we again consider how the initial census results for apportionment were reported. They were under the sole control of the Census Bureau. If it had been otherwise, if in December of 2000 the Democratic secretary of commerce had asserted his authority to review the state-by-state apportionment counts before they were announced, had brought in his own experts, and had then decided whether to allow the imputation methodology, there would have been a political firestorm. And there should have been. In principle, it was possible in December 2000 for the secretary, or for the president himself, to see that imputation rates shifted the 435th congressional seat from Utah to North Carolina (see Box 6). Had the secretary told the Census Bureau to remove the 1.1 million imputed cases from the census file, Republican leaders and the press would, with rea-

Box 6

IMPUTATION GOES TO THE SUPREME COURT

It emerged after the 2000 Census was completed that the imputation procedure shifted a congressional seat. A higher rate of imputation in North Carolina (0.42 percent) than in Utah (0.25 percent) handed the former the 435th seat in Congress. Utah sued to have all imputed records removed from the census. If it won this case, its congressional delegation would increase from three to four, and North Carolina would lose a seat. The case reached the Supreme Court, where, to the relief of statisticians, the Republican administration successfully defended imputation. It is one of the ironies of Census 2000 that the political party that for decades had fought statistical adjustment as an inappropriate method for improving the census now defended a method that also, statistically, improved the census, and this despite the probability that their court victory cost them an additional Republican seat in the House from Utah.

son, have charged political bias. I would have resigned in protest at the compromising of the bureau's independence. This level of political interference did not, obviously, occur. No one even thought of it.

Nor has interference like this ever been attempted with other key statistics. The Bureau of Labor Statistics does not first show its unemployment rate to the secretary of labor and then defer to his or her political judgment about what method should be used to calculate it. Should that happen, public confidence in this vital number would be shaken. If health and education statistics were routinely subjected to political review before they were announced (as they were in Communist Russia), the nation would never know if it was being given a true reading of social conditions or one that satisfied whatever political party happened to be in power.

The nation's statistical agencies operate under a strong system of safeguards designed to insulate them from political pressure. These safeguards, codified in formal statements of principles and practices, cover such issues as methodological transparency, standardization and predictability in release of data products, open dissemination, protection of respondent confidentiality, forthrightness about error structure, ethical standards to prevent misuse of data, and independence from political influence or manipulation. It is seriously troubling that these principles were not fully adhered to with respect to the census adjustment decision in 2001 (see "Politics and Accuracy—A Personal Comment," page 36).

With the political story behind us, we return to the science of Census 2000 and ask what happened to the undercount.

The census was politically radioactive in 2000, and it may remain so. Is the science of census taking, then, imperiled? Not necessarily. But the science has to be designed and applied in the light of some distasteful political realities. These included, in 2000: the political manipulation of symbols for partisan gain; a frequent disregard of inconvenient facts; an oversight process that occupied time and resources hugely disproportionate to what it achieved; and an atmosphere of suspicion surrounding a scientific agency.

These realities notwithstanding, I left the directorship convinced that census science can be made to work as it is intended. I also left with a clearer sense of the director's responsibility in this regard. Although he or she is appointed by the president, and confirmed by the Senate, the director must be resolutely nonpartisan. In retrospect, I see instances where I fell short—for example, in sometimes describing the adjustment process as "correcting the census," thereby implying that an unadjusted census would be incorrect. Using the phrase suggested that those who opposed adjustment wanted an incorrect census. Perhaps the phrase worked as political spin, but it was scientifically misleading. Such lapses (I hope few in number) made it more difficult to claim what is in fact true, that census methodologies are selected for their scientific and not political properties.

A much-needed reform could help further insulate the director from the political battles of the moment. At present the director has no fixed term, but serves at the pleasure of the president. Representative Carolyn B. Maloney, formerly senior Democrat on the House Census Oversight Subcommittee, has introduced a bill (HR 1571), which would set a five-year fixed term for the director. If a fixed term were to start in a year ending in "7" or "2," no president could dismiss the director in midcensus—as I was when President Bush came to office. This would signal that the Census Bureau directorship is a scientific rather than a political position, as is the case for the head of other statistical agencies such as the Bureau of Labor Statistics, as well as for the director of the National Science Foundation and of the National Institutes of Health. These too are presidential appointments but all with fixed terms. In fact, among all high-level presidential appointees with scientific responsibilities, the Census Bureau director is unique in not having a fixed term.

A more ambitious reform, and one that I urge, would be to make the Census Bureau an independent agency, reporting directly to the president. It should then have a prestigious and bipartisan national board, similar to that of the National Science Foundation. This would insulate it from the sometimes shortsighted partisan fights than can so easily capture congressional debate, and it would bring American practice in line with Great Britain and Canada, countries with high-quality, nonpartisan, and politically independent census taking.

I emphasize the importance of greater institutional independence because I reluctantly have concluded that both of America's major political parties would, up to a point, sacrifice census accuracy for partisan advantage. This is a serious accusation, which I put this way: A political party believing that a slightly less accurate census would guarantee its control of Congress for a decade will want that census—rationalizing that, after all, the census falls short of accuracy anyway, so what's another percent or so? I doubt that I am alone in this suspicion; it seems clear that the leaders of each party believe that the other party would, if it had the chance, cheat with census numbers.

If my suspicion is correct, it is the Census Bureau, certainly including its director, that must finally insist that census accuracy, however elusive, be the only standard against which its scientific methods are evaluated. Of course the Census Bureau does not stand alone; protecting the integrity of the nation's statistical products is a cause joined by all federal statistical agencies and by the Office of the Chief Statistician. There are times when the standards by which the professional staff of these agencies do their work are not welcomed by their political bosses, but the job of the scientist-in-government is to let the facts speak for themselves no matter the political fallout.

The refusal to compromise scientific and professional standards in government work extends well beyond statistics—it matters when testing the feasibility of missile defense systems, when deciding if a new drug should be released, when predicting the consequences of climate change, when evaluating Head Start, when selecting a method to store nuclear waste, when writing an intelligence report on terrorist threats. The tension between politics and science in census taking is but one among many instances where short-term political gains cannot be allowed to overrule the best facts that science can offer.

Sampling, Statistical Adjustment, and the 2010 Census

The end result, after the scientific recommendations were made and the politics played out, was that the undercount had become an overcount. After two years of evaluating its work, the Census Bureau announced in March 2003 that its best estimate for the 2000 Census was an overcount of a half-percent. The ambitious traditional census had counted 5.8 million people twice and had missed 4.5 million people, for a net overcount of 1.3 million.[16]

These final calculations showed something even more remarkable—a significant improvement in reaching members of racial minorities (Table 6).

For a half-century, the census had reduced the net undercount without making headway on the differential rate at which minority groups were left out of the count. The money put into a huge effort in 2000 to reach the hard-to-count paid off. The African American undercount was reduced by more than half, and for Asians, Hispanics, and American Indians, the undercount vanished.

This long-sought outcome came at a price. On the principle that no good deed goes unpunished, the sustained effort to eliminate the undercount had created its opposite: an unacceptably high number of duplicates. From the perspective of democratic fairness, replacing an undercount of minorities with an overcount of the white population is not progress. With whites overcounted at 1.13 percent, and blacks undercounted at 1.84 percent, the white/black differential remained nearly 3 percent.

An ambitious traditional census runs the risk of double-counting too many of the easy-to-reach because, with multiple ways of being included in the census, the population groups most likely to have duplicate responses are also those most likely to be included in the first place.

Looking to the future, the challenge is to correct the overcount problem without allowing minority undercounts to revert to earlier levels. The Census Bureau is now working on ways to avoid duplicates in future censuses. It does not, however, plan to use statistical adjustment in this effort. When the bureau concluded that, because of technical problems the 2000 Census results should not be adjusted, it also decided to leave dual-system estimation out of its plans for the 2010 Census. Director Louis Kincannon, responding to a question by congressional Democrats, wrote in June 2003 that the Census Bureau has concluded that "science is insufficiently advanced to allow making statistical adjustment" in the time frame within which redistricting data have to be released.[17]

This implies another expensive census in 2010. Census taking is not going to get easier—on the contrary, the hard-to-count groups are a growing proportion of the population as a whole, just as the number of two-home families, unconventional household patterns, and other conditions contributing to duplications are growing.

There is a limit to how much the country will (or should) pay for census accuracy. There is a trade-off between costs and quality of census data, just as there is a trade-off between expenditures on highway safety and traffic deaths, or expenditures on education and literacy rates. If it were given the entire federal budget, the Department of Transportation could reduce traffic deaths to near zero. Similarly, the Census Bureau, given the entire federal budget, could reduce census errors to near zero. But trade-offs between traffic safety and census accuracy, to say nothing of defense, public health, and dozens of other needs, have to be made. At a certain point, increases in the quality of census data are not worth the significant marginal costs of trying to achieve that last 1 percent of accuracy.

Table 6

CENSUS UNDERCOUNT OF MINORITIES IN 1990 AND 2000

	1990	2000
African American	4.57 percent	1.84 percent
Asian	2.36 percent	*
Hispanic	4.99 percent	*
American Indian	12.20 percent	*

* Calculated rates were not statistically different from zero. Rates for both 1990 and 2000 are based on post-enumeration surveys.

At a budget level that should reasonably be expected, the census will have errors. The well-funded census in 2000 had errors: it still missed 4.5 million people and double-counted 5.8 million. Those missed were disproportionately racial minorities, the poor, single householders, and immigrants, and those included twice were disproportionately college students, people who own two houses, and others among the well-off.

The partisan political positions that were so aggressively staked out in Census 2000 have been temporarily muted by the decline in the undercount, but not permanently erased. Whether they reappear will depend on the level of confidence in the census methodology planned for 2010 and whether differential undercounts return to earlier levels after that.

AMERICAN DEMOCRACY AND THE CENSUS—LOOKING AHEAD

On July 25, 2000, a Republican congressman from Tennessee, John J. Duncan, addressed his colleagues:

"Madam Speaker, the Census Bureau is proving that it is another arrogant federal agency with a power-mad, public-be-damned attitude. Despite the huge public outcry against the personal, intrusive questions on the census long form, the bureau wants to keep prying with the same or similar personal questions on the form called the American Community Survey to be sent to 250,000 homes each month. The lame defense of questions on the long form was that these questions had been approved by Congress and that they had been asked before. Well, Congress never had a vote on specific questions, and no member saw those questions beforehand except possibly a few on the Subcommittee on the Census. Also, if those nosy personal questions were asked in the past, it was *before the federal government got as big and out of control as it is today and before the age of the Internet. I guess with the computer-controlled society we have today, true privacy is a thing of the past. But the Congress should offer at least a little resistance and not allow the Census Bureau to keep butting its nose into areas that should be none of our federal Big Brother's business."*[18]

Setting aside the congressman's ignorance of how questions appear on the census form (by law, all proposed topics are submitted to the entire Congress three years before census day, and then every specific question is resubmitted, again to the entire Congress, two years before census day), his comments bring to attention both new and old issues central to the role of the census in American democracy.

Privacy, Confidentiality, and Census Taking

For as long as information has been collected, there has been concern about privacy and confidentiality. Privacy is about what can be known—it shrinks when record keeping or surveillance expands against our will, which includes of course the census asking questions considered intrusive. Confidentiality is about what can be shared—it shrinks if information, from medical records to bank transactions, from school grades to census answers, is given to others without our permission. Think of privacy as "don't even ask that question," and confidentiality as "don't tell anyone else what I just told you."

The census occupies a unique place in the public's uneasiness about violations of privacy and confidentiality. The questions the government insists that you answer go far beyond the minimum needed to count the population. In the very earliest censuses, Thomas Jefferson and James Madison wanted to add a question about occupation so that the new government could better know "the conditions of the people" and thereby make more intelligent policy. Census questions on many topics were steadily added across the 19th and 20th centuries, for a simple reason. Once a staff is sent to the field to conduct the basic enumeration, obtaining useful additional information has low marginal cost.

What Jefferson and Madison proposed more than 200 years ago was based on their view of what distinguished a democracy from an autocracy: In an autocracy, the government makes policy through edicts, whereas in a democracy, it must give reasons for its policies. Here we glimpse an important proposition about information in a democracy. The reasons given for one policy over another are founded on inquiry. This premise is evident in the power granted to Congress to hold hearings and to investigate but is also apparent in government data collection and record keeping.

It is a cliché that politicians are fond of anecdotes and rely, perhaps too much, on their personal experiences. But when they turn to the tough task of offering policy solutions to social problems, they seek out information about the shape, scope, durability, and trajectory of the conditions causing the problem. The growing number of elderly without insurance is given as a reason to reform health policy; the educational success of parochial schools leads to arguments on behalf of school vouchers; new patterns of traffic congestion are cited to justify highway construction. A government without information is unable to explain its decisions; it fails a test of democracy.

There is more to the interplay of information and democracy. As American democracy matured, statistical information took on enormous importance not only in making the society legible to the government, but in the reciprocal of this. Information tells the public what its government is doing, or failing to do. The idea of electoral accountability is about candidates competing for votes by offering conflicting views on how well the government in power has performed. This powerful model of democracy presumes that the voters have a basis on which to assess government performance. Statistical trends can be this information. Is the economy growing or stagnating? Are education, health, or housing conditions improving? Is the crime rate up, or down? Are water and air cleaner than they were? Is the war on terrorism being won? Back and forth claims about who can take credit for improvements, or should be blamed for failure, are the currency of competitive elections. The indicators cited, more than is generally understood, come from the large federal statistical system, at the core of which is the census.

In a democracy the people should know as much about their government as it knows about them. For this reason our government (usually) goes to great lengths to make its official statistics easily available. And the Freedom of Information Act is designed to correct any inappropriate withholding of information.

Congressman Duncan, quoted above, wrongly understands government information as something an out-of-control agency collects; it is a resource integral to a functioning democracy and economy. But the congressman is right to draw attention to privacy as highly valued in our democracy. His reference to a "huge public outcry" against the census long form in 2000 is no exaggeration.

Beginning in 1940, the Census Bureau sought a way to collect a large amount of data needed by the government, and increasingly requested by the business community, without burdening the population. This effort matured into the short and long census forms, with the former being asked of the entire population and the latter of only a sample. The long form data range across many topics—education, income, employment, disability, ancestry, and housing characteristics—all of which serve public policy and private sector purposes.

In 2000, the census long form was sent to one in six households. The latent public suspiciousness of an intrusive government was inflamed when talk show hosts, local leaders, a few members of Congress, and even a presidential candidate complained that the long form was intrusive and asked questions the government had no right to ask. Then a candidate, George W. Bush, said he could understand "why people don't want to give over that information to the government. If I had the long form, I'm not so sure I would do it either."[19] Late-night comics took cheap shots (see Box 7). This flared up into a minicrisis in the middle of taking the census, as the mail-back response rate for the long form suddenly dropped well below historical patterns, and many refused outright to answer particular questions, such as income or amount of rent paid. Data quality was affected.

Public concern about privacy makes census taking difficult, putting the nation on a collision course between conflicting but equally important values: privacy and information. There is no escaping that we live in a "knowledge economy," one whose efficiency and productivity depend on massive amounts of information rapidly disseminated. Information flows are to the 21st century economy as the steam engine was to the 19th and the telephone to the 20th. Economic data enhance productivity; other data contribute to well-being in other ways—epidemiological data protect public health; job data reveal patterns of gender or racial discrimination.

Statistical information is assembled from the traits and behaviors of millions of people, and the decennial census is critical. It is, firstly, the only source of information for the entire country that is available in fine geographic detail. Also, it is the benchmark against which all scientifically designed surveys are standardized. For instance, if a population sample survey has 55 percent female and 45 percent male respondents, it would not be truly representative. Not until it is corrected (weighted is the technical term) to match the actual distribution of women and men in the popula-

---

Box 7
EXAMPLES OF WHAT SOME SAW AS INTRUSIVE LONG-FORM QUESTIONS

A question on plumbing facilities—hot water, flush toilet, shower—was widely derided.
Uses—Federal and state agencies use information from this question to determine areas eligible for public assistance and rehabilitation loans. Public health programs use it to locate areas vulnerable to ground water contamination and waterborne diseases.

A question on how people get to work, and how long it takes, was said to be intrusive.
Uses—Transportation planning, the allocation of highway funds, and disaster relief (to pinpoint areas of likely congestion) depend on answers to this question because there is information on where one lives and works.

A question on whether a person has difficulty dressing, bathing, or getting around the home was the target of many talk-show jokes.
Uses—Police and fire departments use the information to identify neighborhoods where vulnerable and helpless older people live. Funds for home nursing programs are allocated to areas with high percentages of people unable to care for themselves.

---

tion, as reported by the census, can it be used for reliable analysis. The fine print accompanying scientific public surveys normally reports: "The results have been weighted to … adjust for variation in the sample relating to geographic region, sex, race, age and education."[20] The census is the uncited benchmark for assigning necessary weights. A poor census reverberates through the entire information system of the nation because it provides incorrect statistical controls for other data collection efforts.

There is no simple trade-off between the need for information and the right to privacy. Public alarm would be lessened if the public better understood how a statistical agency differs from other agencies that collect information. Statistical data are never about individuals; statistics are counts, rates, proportions—the percentage of the population living in poverty, the ratio of the number of minorities in higher education compared with their numbers in the general population, the growing concentrations of households in fire-prone areas.

In contrast, regulatory and enforcement agencies need to know about specific identifiable people. They collect administrative, not statistical data. The Social Security Administration sends payment to an identifiable person, and the Internal Revenue Service collects taxes in the same way. The FBI keeps records on individuals. A statistical agency may report crime rates, but it never tries to find the individual criminal.

The public, unfortunately, has generally failed to understand the character of statistical data, and is skeptical when we say that there are strict laws safeguarding the confidentiality of census and other statistical data. A Census Bureau employee that released an individual's census answers could be imprisoned for up to five years. The bureau invests heavily in secure transmission and in firewalls to deter hackers. It submits all data releases to procedures that ensure against backtracking from aggregate statistics to individual respondents (making it impossible, for example, to find the only dentist in a small town). These safeguards are a matter of law, of professional practice, and above all honor the commitment of confidentiality that statistical agencies make to citizens when asking for their cooperation.

There is no easy way to reconcile the right to privacy and the need for information. Both are basic to our democracy and economy. The census is an unusually visible target for anxieties about the loss of privacy, particularly because it is required by law, and it will no doubt continue to be the focus of public debate about how much the government should know about private citizens and whether the government's pledge of confidentiality can be trusted.

Better Data for Democratic Governance

The information about population and housing characteristics that comes from the decennial census long form suffers from one striking weakness—it grows steadily out of date. With a mobile and changing population and a dynamic economy, collecting basic data on a 10-year cycle does not meet 21st-century needs. In 2008 the Social Security Administration will need to assign a multilingual staff to areas where English is the second language; the city agency responsible for emergency evacuation will want to store its evacuation vehicles near where the elderly live alone; the entrepreneur will want to open a Starbucks in a neighborhood of young adults. Census data will be the best available information—but it will be eight years out-of-date.

The Census Bureau has worked for years on an idea to provide more current information. Instead of collecting long-form information from a huge sample every 10 years, the idea is to collect it from a much smaller sample every month, and then combine the monthly samples to provide annual data of a quality and geographic detail comparable to what the decennial long form now

provides. The design, known as the American Community Survey, has undergone extensive testing and is ready to be fielded in 2004. It has numerous advantages over the current once-in-a-decade long-form data collection. Its biggest hurdle, however, is the need for Congress to appropriate funds on an ongoing basis rather than on a 10-year cycle. The American Community Survey must also overcome opponents in Congress who would get the government out of information gathering altogether (as illustrated in the Duncan quotation at the start of this section).

To accommodate critics like Congressman Duncan, the Census Bureau and the Congress are reviewing the implications of making the American Community Survey nonmandatory. This will lower response rates and lessen data quality but is a trade-off that may have to be made as the government tries to balance the insistence from many quarters for more timely information and the growing public anxieties about the loss of privacy in an information-saturated society.

The Multiple-Race Option in Census 2000

We have focused on how the census determines the size of America's population, ignoring an equally interesting question: What does the census tell us about the characteristics of our population? In only a small way can we get to that question, which in any event is taken up in the several other reports in this series.

In these final pages, however, we emphasize that a census never just counts, it always classifies as well. In the political and economic life of a nation, it is both "how many" and "how many of what" that matter: how many young males, how many taxpayers, how many women of childbearing age, how many noncitizens, how many farmers, how many below the poverty line, and on and on.

In thinking about classification—separating people into groups—probably nothing rivals in importance how America, and many other countries, chooses its ethnic and racial categories. The American ethno-racial classification—including what is racial and what is ethnic about it—is in a period of unprecedented uncertainty.

The politics of statistical proportionality that emerged from the civil rights laws passed in the 1960s and 1970s help us see why. From the very beginning of the nation, discrimination directed at people because of their ethnicity and race was embedded in official policy. Slavery is an obvious example, but even after emancipation a rigid racial segregation had the backing of law, as did forcing American Indians to reservations, denying citizenship to Chinese and Japanese, exploiting Mexican labor, and more in a long, dark chapter of American history.

The civil rights revolution put an end to state-sanctioned discrimination. It gave birth to laws and policies that would right old wrongs and would actively benefit groups historically discriminated against. The idea of statistical proportionality entered our political vocabulary and legal doctrine. The question frequently asked was whether African Americans were under-represented—in universities, in employment, in government contracts, in bank loans, in political office. Under-representation is a statistical concept, and it became a useful tool for detecting racial discrimination and for designing corrective policies. In law, it was joined by the term "disparate impact," where courts were asked to determine if a policy or practice had a disparate impact on racial groups. Concepts such as under-representation and disparate impact require a population denominator, and this is provided by the census.

Groups other than African Americans were quick to bring their cases forward on the basis of statistical proportionality: Hispanics, Asians, American Indians, women, the disabled. In each instance, the census provided the percentage of the group in the population at large—the denominator against which to assess who was being given equal treatment and opportunity, and who was not.

The racial classification system that gave rise to statistical proportionality in the 1960s had a few discrete categories—white, black, and Indian, to which was added Asian and then, in the 1980 Census, Hispanic as an ethnic category. By 1990 every resident of America, in census statistics, belonged to one and only one of four primary racial groups—white, black, American Indian/Native Alaskan, or Asian—or to "some other race." Prior to the 2000 Census, Native Hawaiian/Pacific Islanders became a fifth primary category (they had previously been included with Asians). Being of Hispanic origin is treated in official government statistics as an ethnic, not a racial distinction. A Hispanic can be of any race.

The dramatic change in the 2000 Census was to allow people to choose two or more races, to be multiracial. This upends assumptions that have defined "race" since the beginning of census history. The multiple-race option resulted from a broad review of racial measurement by the Office of the Chief Statistician of the United States, which has oversight responsibilities for the federal statistical system. The office concluded that respondents answering any federal survey or filling out any federal form could declare themselves to be two or more races. The 2000 Census was the first and most visible implementation of this policy, but it is scheduled to become practice for the entire federal statistical system, and it will gradually spread across business, education, medical, and other record keeping. The old idea of a small number of discrete races is on the way out.[21]

Only 6.8 million people used the multiple-race option in 2000.[22] This low percentage allowed government agencies that enforce nondiscriminatory laws to avoid disruptions in current policies and administrative practices. We can expect, however, that the use of the multiple-race option will grow, especially among the younger population. Marrying across racial lines is on the increase, and many Americans are becoming comfortable with the idea that we are a blend of many races.

We have seen that the nation's history of racism and racial politics has been at the center of disputes about how the population is counted. It will increasingly be at the center of what characteristics are counted. Census measurement is a powerful ally of the politics of identity, and of groups claiming rights over public resources.

This is easily seen if we pause and ask: Why do we classify by race and ethnicity?

The simple answer is that the classification is used to facilitate public policy. During the past four decades, the policies that have made fullest use of racial classification have been in the areas of voting rights, affirmative action, and related social justice measures focused on redressing historical discrimination.

But this answer cannot explain why the country suddenly accepted the idea of two or more races as a valid census option. Groups that advocated for this option justified it with the language of social identity more than civil rights.

In congressional hearings about the multiple-race option, the differences between a public policy rationale and a social identity justification were strongly presented.[23]

The NAACP argued that the standard race and ethnic categories were fashioned "to enhance the enforcement of antidiscrimination and civil rights law" and not as "vehicles for self-identification." Its testimony worried that:

"The creation of a multiracial classification might disaggregate the apparent numbers of members of discrete minority groups, diluting benefits to which they are entitled as a protected class under civil rights laws and under the Constitution itself. In our quest for self-identification, we must take care not to re-create, reinforce, or even expand the caste system we are all trying so hard to overcome, the caste system that the NAACP was created to oppose."

The National Council of La Raza agreed:

"The purpose of the census is both to enforce and implement the law and to inform lawmakers about the distinct needs of special historically disadvantaged populations."

But this standard argument was countered in the testimony of the Association of Multiethnic Americans:

"We want choice in the matter. We want choice in the matter of who we are, just like any other community. We are not saying that we are a solution to civil rights laws or civil rights injustices of the past. But I find it ironic that our organization and our people are being asked to correct by virtue of how we define ourselves all of the past injustices of other groups of people."

Project Race, also a multiracial advocacy group, took a similar position:

"The reality is that not all Americans fit neatly into one little box. The reality is that multiracial children who wish to embrace all of their heritage should be allowed to do so. They should not be put in the position of denying one of their parents to satisfy arbitrary government requirements."

The arguments between traditional civil rights organizations and the newer advocates for multiple-race designations make clear that the uses of an ethno-racial classification now go beyond enforcement, which requires a small number of discrete categories. A second purpose is now to be served—choice, expression, identity—and this requires a proliferation of categories. As Harvard professor Jennifer Hochschild put it, "Who would have expected that stodgy data collection agency, the Census Bureau, to be a leading force for deconstruction?"[24]

The introduction of the multirace option in official statistics is not the end of the story. There are growing political efforts to prohibit any ethnic and racial measurement by the government. These efforts, led by groups opposed to affirmative action, believe that the government will not be able to base laws or policies on what it has not recorded.

It seems that the census will continue to be at the center of political debate, though perhaps now more focused on how it classifies the population than how it counts them. The stakes remain high, especially against the backdrop of a demographic diversity unprecedented in history.

The Census and Democracy in the 21st Century

We define democracy as a government that, in principle, allows all voices to be heard and all interests the right to be taken seriously. This means that the government has to mediate the assertion of strongly conflicting economic and ideological views across different groups in American society. This was not easy even in 1787, but the nation's founders had advantages compared with what faces our political leaders today. The 18th-century population was small and contained within a comparatively limited geographic area. Involvement in civic life was strictly limited to white property-owning males, and those heard from politically shared a common English ancestry, language, and the Protestant faith. These commonalities lowered the political temperature when differences erupted between slave-owning and free states, between agricultural and manufacturing interests, between those intent on a strong central government and those protecting states' rights.

The nation did not long remain small and culturally homogeneous. A nation that started with a population mostly English and Protestant became in the course of the 19th century more broadly European, adding Catholics and Jews to the Protestant base. The 20th century continued apace. America now has Hindu, Buddhist, and Muslim populations. Its immigrants arrive from every world region, sending children to public schools where as many as 100 languages are spoken, and settling in the urban neighborhoods of New York, Chicago, Houston, and Los Angeles, where dozens of nationalities share the streets and shops. The political parties are wooing the fast-growing voting population of Hispanics. Universities try to gain competitive advantage by trumpeting the diversity of their student body. Pop culture blends music and fashion from different world cultural traditions. Civil rights have long ceased to be about black-white issues; they have become about the rights of Mexican agricultural workers, Chinese political refugees, and Bosnian immigrants.

However diversity is defined—linguistically, culturally, religiously, ethnically—the United States today is perhaps the most demographically diverse nation in world history.

Democratically governing a multicultural, pan-world nation is a challenge easily equal to those confronting the Constitution writers in 1787. Democratic practice and theory face tough questions. Cultural differences often deepen conflicts as groups compete for jobs, housing, or university places. Some suggest that these conflicts must be managed by recognizing the rights of groups; others believe that democracy must be based solely on the rights of individuals. How can a democratic constitutional state supposedly committed to universalism accommodate identity politics that reject appeals to universalism? Can there be a common "public interest" in a multicultural society? Tolerance is an often-voiced principle of democracy, but are we to be tolerant of religious beliefs that sanction female circumcision, polygamy, or animal sacrifice? Can cultural relativism proceed so far that tolerance becomes a contradiction in terms? Another facet of our democratic history is captured in the metaphor of a "melting pot," which assumes the gradual dissolving of cultural differences into a mainstream culture. But the very idea of a mainstream culture is challenged in a nation that prides itself on being multicultural, which of course presumes the persistence of many cultures among which the "mainstream" becomes simply another option.

Fashioning democratic principles for multicultural societies is the task of the 21st century (and not only in the United States). One thing is certain: The census will be a contested battlefield in this effort. The census counts and the census classifies—both processes are necessarily central to democratic government. The government will be urged to move democratic practice in one direction or another, as is illustrated by the successful advocacy for the multirace option in 2000 or by the more recent advocacy to remove ethnic and racial categories from government record keeping altogether. The contrasting justifications for racial classification voiced by traditional civil rights groups and the newer advocates for categories that express identity mark the beginning of what promises to be a major transition in our democratic practices.

The census makes its most significant contribution to democracy by offering a common map of the society. Democratic debate—especially the difficult debate about justice and equality in multicultural society—is more rational, more fair, and, one hopes, more civil if based on a shared understanding of who we are as a people. The nation cannot reach such an understanding without a census.

REFERENCES

1. James Scott, *Seeing Like a State: How Certain Schemes to Improve the Human Condition Have Failed* (New Haven: Yale University Press 1998): 11.

2. Committee on National Statistics of the National Research Council, *Statistical Issues in Allocating Funds by Formula* (Washington, DC: The National Academies Press, 2003).

3. Margo J. Anderson, *The American Census: A Social History* (New Haven, CT: Yale University Press, 1988): 11.

4. Letter from John Adams to Matthew Robinson, March 2, 1786, in *Works of John Adams, Second President of the United States*, vol. 8 (Boston: Little, Brown and Company, 1851-1865): 385.

5. Letter from Thomas Jefferson to the Count de Montmorin, June 23, 1787, in *Writings of Jefferson*, ed. A.E. Bergh, vol. 6 (Washington, DC: Jefferson Memorial Association, 1904-1905): 186.

6. Cited in Henry Steele Commager, *Jefferson, Nationalism, and the Enlightenment* (New York: George Braziller, 1975): 27.

7. Commager, *Jefferson, Nationalism, and the Enlightenment*: 46.

8. Mayor Jimmy Bernauer, quoted by Cain Burdeau in "With Tax Dollars at Stake, Patterson Fighting Census," *The Advocate* (Baton Rouge, LA), Oct. 14, 2002.

9. Eric Lipton, "Death Toll Is Near 3,000, but Some Uncertainty Over the Count Remains," *New York Times*, Sept. 11, 2002.

10. Lawrence D. Brown et al., "Statistical Controversies in Census 2000," *Jurimetrics* 39 (Summer 1999): 347-75.

11. David M. Heer, ed., *Conference on Social Statistics and the City, Washington, D.C., 1967* (Cambridge, MA: Joint Center for Urban Studies of the Massachusetts Institute of Technology and Harvard University, 1968): 11.

12. Margo J. Anderson and Stephen Feinberg, *Who Counts? The Politics of Census Taking in Contemporary America* (New York: Russell Sage Foundation, 1999).

13. Robert A. Mossbacher, "Decision of the Secretary of Commerce on Whether a Statistical Adjustment of the 1990 Census of Population and Housing Should Be Made for Coverage Deficiencies Resulting in an Overcount or Undercount of the Population," *Federal Register* 56, no. 140 (July 22, 1991): 33583. The passage cited presents only one of the reasons presented by the secretary; other considerations were technical and operational.

14. Jim Nicholson, memo dated May 20, 1997. The Census Bureau itself does not collect information on political party affiliation, does not conduct analysis of possible partisan outcomes, and took no position on the plausibility of Mr. Nicholson's forecast.

15. General Accounting Office (GAO), *2000 Census: Review of Partnership Program Highlights, Best Practice for Future Operations* GAO-01-579 (Washington, DC: GAO, August 2001).

16. The number of duplicates—5.8 million—differs from the earlier number of 3.6 million suspected duplicates that the Census Bureau removed from the census in the summer of 2000. The 5.8 million number was calculated nearly two years later, using dual-system estimation.

17. Terri Ann Lowenthal, *Census News Brief*, Aug. 27, 2003 (available from the author by e-mail at Terriann2K@aol.com).

18. House of Representatives, Representative John J. Duncan of Tennessee, Floor Statement, "American Community Survey," 106th Cong., 2nd sess., *Congressional Record* (25 July 2000): H6783.

19. Michael Kelly, "Census and Nonsense" (editorial), *Washington Post*, April 5, 2000.

20. *New York Times*/CBS News poll, cited in Adam Nagourney and Janet Elder, "Bush's Backing, Still Strong, Shows Steady Decline," *New York Times*, Jan. 24, 2003.

21. The census form allows anyone to "mark one or more" of the five primary races (as well as the "other" line). This allows for 63 separate categories, using the formula of two to the sixth power minus one. Moreover, because each respondent is also Hispanic or non-Hispanic, an ethnic category, to get the full array it is necessary to multiply the 63 by two, producing 126 categories of race/ethnicity.

22. Nicholas A. Jones and Amy Symens Smith, "The Two or More Races Population: 2000," *Census 2000 Brief* C2KBR/01-6 (November 2001).

23. Quotations appear on pages 309, 324, 382, and 286 of "Federal Measures of Race and Ethnicity and the Implications for the 2000 Census," hearings before the Subcommittee on Government Management, Information, and Technology of the Committee on Government Reform and Oversight, House of Representatives, 105th Cong., 1st sess., 23 April, 23 May, and 25 July 1997, 57.

24. Jennifer Hochschild, conversation with the author, May 2002.

FOR FURTHER READING

Alonso, William, and Paul Starr, eds. *The Politics of Numbers.* New York: Russell Sage Foundation, 1987.

Brown, Lawrence D., et al. "Statistical Controversies in Census 2000." *Jurimetrics* 39 (Summer 1999).

Bryant, Barbara, and William Dunn. *Moving Money and Power: The Politics of Census Taking.* New York: New Strategist Publications, Inc., 1995.

Choldin, Harvey. *Looking for the Last Percent.* New Brunswick, NJ: Rutgers University Press, 1994.

National Research Council. *Counting People in the Information Age,* ed. Duane L. Steffey and Norman M. Bradburn. Report by the Panel to Evaluate Alternative Census Methods, Committee on National Statistics of the National Research Council. Washington, DC: National Academy Press, 1994.

Darga, Kenneth. *Sampling and the Census: A Case Against the Proposed Adjustments for Undercount.* Washington, DC: The American Enterprise Institute, 1999.

Kertzer, David I., and Dominique Arel, eds. *Census and Identity: The Politics of Race, Ethnicity, and Language in National Censuses.* Cambridge, England: Cambridge University Press, 2001.

National Research Council. *Measuring a Changing Nation: Modern Methods for the 2000 Census,* ed. Michael L. Cohen, Andrew A. White, and Keith F. Rust. Report by the Panel on Alternative Census Methodologies, Committee on National Statistics of the National Research Council. Washington, DC: National Academy Press, 1999.

National Research Council. *Modernizing the U.S. Census,* ed. Barry Edmonston and Charles Schultze. Report by the Panel on Census Requirements in the Year 2000 and Beyond, Committee on National Statistics of the National Research Council. Washington, DC: National Academy Press, 1995.

Prewitt, Kenneth. "Race in the 2000 Census: A Turning Point." In *Counting Races, Recognizing Multiracials,* Joel Perlmann and Mary Waters, eds. New York: Russell Sage Foundation, 2002.

Skrentny, John David, ed. *Color Lines: Affirmative Action, Immigration, and Civil Rights Options for America.* Chicago: University of Chicago Press, 2001.

Wright, Tommy, and Howard Hogan. "Census 2000: Evolution of the Revised Plan." *CHANCE: A Magazine of the American Statistical Association* 12, no. 4 (Fall 1999).

ACKNOWLEDGMENTS

Although I did not know it at the time, this monograph began to take shape in 1985, when I was a Fellow at the Center for Advanced Studies in the Behavioral Sciences. Then I wrote an essay on "Public Statistics and Democratic Politics" for a volume titled *The Politics of Numbers*, part of a series on the 1980 Census. I had intended to expand the essay but never found the time and am relieved finally to recognize my debt to the special way that the center frees one to take up new ideas. The Social Science Research Council and the Russell Sage Foundation, two extraordinary forces in the American social science world, sponsored the series on the 1980 Census. My indebtedness to both is a pleasure to record, and a visiting scholar appointment at the Russell Sage Foundation in 2002 offered ideal writing conditions for this monograph.

Colleagues who tellingly commented on an early draft include Reynolds Farley and John Haaga, the well-informed editors of this series, and also Norman Bradburn, Tom Hofeller, John Thompson, and Kathleen Wallman, all people with a keen insight into census taking. My best critic—and not only in this effort—has been Susan, my wife, whose contribution includes, but went much beyond, a sharp editorial pencil.

What deepened my thinking about statistics and democracy was an extraordinary (in many senses of that term) two years as director of the U. S. Census Bureau. Here the number of people I should acknowledge by name is, dare I say, uncountable. So I resort to the less satisfactory listing of groups, starting with several dozen census staff, in headquarters and in the regional offices, who gave me a crash course on my job.

They know their stuff. They have to, as they work under difficult conditions, not least of which was having an inexperienced outsider suddenly dropped in as their new director. And I brought in my own outsider, Ellen Lee, who as my chief assistant skillfully navigated me through an endless flow of the unexpected. Washington, D.C., is also home to many—in the Congress, the Department of Commerce, the GAO, and the OMB and in scientific and advocacy organizations—who worked and rooted for a good census. They can rightly lay claim to having helped make it so in 2000. The network of key supporters is larger yet, for it certainly includes advisory groups around the country who gave time, energy, and even devotion to the cause. The list continues to the nearly 1 million temporary census workers and beyond them to thousands upon thousands of unpaid census workers who urged their fellow Americans to be counted. The extended census family, which comes together every decade, was out in force in 2000; it will be back in 2010.

As anyone with a major responsibility in public life knows, there is no effective way to acknowledge all of those without whose support you simply could not do your job. Perhaps my account of Census 2000 will help Americans who hardly noticed that there was one appreciate why so many who worked on its behalf care so much about whether the country has a good one. As a civic event with the ambition to include every person in the nation, the only such civic event in America's democracy, the census counts. This, I suspect, is why members of the family take such pride and pleasure in their work. It is why I did.

PART II

ECONOMIC TRENDS AND EMPLOYMENT

Diverging Fortunes:
Trends in Poverty and Inequality

By Sheldon Danziger and Peter Gottschalk

INTRODUCTION

Following World War II, the American economy experienced a quarter-century of sustained economic growth, rising real wages, and low unemployment rates. The benefits of this prosperity were widely shared among most of the poor, the middle class, and the wealthy. But even though poverty had fallen rapidly from the late 1940s to the early 1960s, popular authors and economic analysts raised concerns in the late 1950s and early 1960s that many families—especially those headed by less-educated workers, minorities, and women—were not benefiting much from the prosperous economy.[1] These observers called for government to target policies and programs at those being left behind.

Responding to these concerns, President Lyndon B. Johnson directed his economic advisers to develop plans for a "War on Poverty." Based on extant research, Johnson's advisers concluded that economic growth alone would not be sufficient to eliminate poverty within a generation and that the government should intervene to raise the employment and earnings prospects of the nation's poorest workers. Johnson announced the War on Poverty on Jan. 8, 1964. In a transmittal letter to Congress accompanying the 1964 *Economic Report of the President*, he declared:

> "We cannot and need not wait for the gradual growth of the economy to lift this forgotten fifth of our nation above the poverty line. We know what must be done, and this nation of abundance can surely afford to do it. Today, as in the past, higher employment and speedier economic growth are the cornerstones of a concerted attack on poverty.... But general prosperity and growth leave untouched many of the roots of human poverty." [2]

This *Economic Report* discussed many strategies for reducing the number of poor people, estimated at the time to represent one of every five Americans. The strategies outlined in the report—some of which were restatements of long-standing policy goals, and some of which were new approaches—included maintaining high employment, accelerating economic growth, fighting discrimination, improving labor markets, expanding educational opportunities, improving health, and assisting the elderly and disabled.

The conventional wisdom among policy analysts when the 1964 *Economic Report* was issued held that, because stable economic growth at the pace of the prior two decades was likely to continue, government could eliminate poverty by keeping the economy moving and by devoting a modest amount of additional resources to antipoverty programs. This line of thinking also held that poverty was high because the poor were not able to find enough work or because their lack of appropriate labor market skills left them with low earnings even if they worked full time all year.

Policy analysts also saw other fundamental problems that contributed to high poverty rates: lagging economic growth in some areas of the country (such as Appalachia); a shortage of training opportunities; lack of access to education for the poor; and labor market discrimination. These analysts argued that government had a role to play in addressing these problems—by focusing government fiscal and monetary policies on improving the performance of the economy, by funding new education and training programs to raise the skills and productivity of the poor, and by enforcing laws to remove discriminatory barriers in labor and housing markets.

However, poverty in America was not eliminated in the generation after Johnson declared the War on Poverty, and the vision of Johnson and his planners still remains unfulfilled. Why? In part, the optimistic economic forecasts of the 1960s that underpinned Johnson's strategy were based on the prosperity of the quarter-century following World War II—an era of rising real wage rates for most workers and steady economic growth that had raised living standards for most families.

But this "golden age" of prosperity ended in the early 1970s, and powerful economic forces in the decades that followed changed the way that labor markets operated and caused rising economic hardships for many workers and their families. These forces include labor-saving technological changes; the globalization of

SHELDON DANZIGER is Henry J. Meyer Collegiate Professor of Public Policy and co-director of the National Poverty Center at the Gerald R. Ford School of Public Policy, University of Michigan.

PETER GOTTSCHALK is professor of economics at Boston College.

markets; and resulting adjustments in labor market institutions (for example, declines in both the inflation-adjusted minimum wage and in the percentage of workers covered by union contracts).

The last quarter of the 20th century proved to be a period of unanticipated changes in labor market performance, as the economy generated diverging fortunes and diminished prospects for many workers. From the early 1970s to the early 1990s, unemployment rates were high; growth in median earnings (adjusted for inflation) was slow; and access to employer-provided health insurance and pensions fell for the average worker. Men without any formal education beyond high school lost ground as employers reduced their demand for less-educated workers. Inflation-adjusted annual earnings of male high-school dropouts were 23 percent lower in 2002 than in 1975, and earnings for male high school graduates were 13 percent lower.

At the same time, employers increased their demand for the most-educated workers and raised their wages relative to those of the average worker. In 2002, men who had college or higher degrees earned 62 percent more than they did in 1975. In addition, the stock market boom that lasted from the mid-1980s until 2000 raised the property incomes (dividends, interest, and rents) of the wealthiest Americans. As a result of these developments in the labor and stock markets, income inequality increased dramatically among families between 1973 and 2001. The inflation-adjusted average income of the poorest one-fifth of families increased by 8 percent (to about $14,000), whereas the average income of the richest 20 percent increased by 65 percent (to about $160,000).[3]

Income Inequality in a Market Economy

Market economies promote the efficient allocation of resources by providing incentives for consumers and firms to make efficient decisions. But as a result, market economies also generate income inequality—individuals with more skills earn more than those with fewer skills, and individuals who work longer and harder earn more than those who work less.

Although much public and policy attention was focused on trends in the poverty rate after the declaration of the War on Poverty, little attention was paid to income inequality until the mid-1980s. Robert Lampman, a Johnson administration antipoverty planner and a proponent of the development of an official U.S. measure of poverty, did not consider reducing income inequality to be an explicit goal of the War on Poverty. Instead, he linked the antipoverty goal with ongoing economic policy goals, and argued that government should focus on raising the incomes of poor people.[4]

Income inequality received little attention until the 1980s because it hardly changed from the late 1940s through the mid-1970s. Economist Henry Aaron wrote in 1978 that analyzing changes in the income distribution "was like watching the grass grow."[5] A quarter-century later, however, sociologist Christopher Jencks wrote that:

> "The economic gap between rich and poor has grown dramatically in the United States over the past generation and is now considerably wider than in any other affluent nation. This increase in economic inequality has no recent precedent, at least in America."[6]

Despite three decades of rising income inequality, there is still little public discussion about the likely causes and consequences of that inequality, and no consensus on how government might make program or policy changes to reduce it. Analysts differ about whether inequality is even a problem. Liberals consider it socially divisive; conservatives believe that it fosters entrepreneurship.

This disagreement presents a difficulty for policymakers: How does a society determine whether inequality has become so high that it exacerbates social problems and diminishes economic opportunities, or so low that it undermines the efficient operation of the economy and causes individuals to work less and to save less? Jencks concludes that there is little evidence that would allow a neutral observer to select the precise level of inequality that would balance competing goals.[7]

It is beyond the scope of this report for us to formulate an inequality-reduction goal comparable to the antipoverty goal adopted four decades ago. Instead, we review long-run trends in poverty, the percentage of people who are rich, median family income, and family-income inequality. We find that, since the mid-1970s, the American people have experienced diverging economic fortunes.

We begin by describing a series of measurement issues that guide our analyses of available historical data. We then place changes in poverty and the level and distribution of income in historical context by providing a brief economic and policy history of the last half of the 20th century in the United States. Next, we review decade-by-decade changes (from 1959 to 1999) in poverty for all people; for people classified by their race or ethnicity; for U.S.-born people and immigrants; and for people of different ages.

We follow that analysis by examining annual changes in labor market outcomes—wage rates and work hours—for male and female workers for the period from 1975 to 2002. Finally, we analyze how changes in the level and distribution of family income as well as changes in the demographic composition of the population have affected the trend in poverty over this period.

Our review suggests that the economic prospects of those at the bottom and at the top of the income distribution have parted ways over the past quarter-century, and that the United States is likely to remain (in the absence of dramatic economic and public policy changes) an economically divided nation. In the 40 years since the War on Poverty, progress against poverty has been very slow. The poverty rate remains high for many segments of the population—in particular, children (especially those who do not live with both parents); racial and ethnic minorities; and workers who have completed no more than a high school education. The main exception to the pattern of slow progress against poverty is for the elderly, whose poverty rates have declined dramatically over the past 40 years because of increases in Social Security benefits and a congressional mandate that those benefits be indexed for inflation.

An increasing economic divide between rich and poor was unforeseen by the planners of the War on Poverty. But an era in which a "rising tide" lifted the incomes of all families gave way to an era of "uneven tides" during which the incomes of those at the bottom stagnated while those at the top increased. And while economic inequalities that had widened from the mid-1970s to the mid-1990s stopped increasing during the economic boom of the 1990s, income inequality at the end of the 20th century was much greater than it had been a quarter-century earlier.

MEASURING TRENDS IN POVERTY AND INCOME INEQUALITY

For this study, we analyze the Public Use Microdata Samples (PUMS) from the decennial censuses for 1960 through 2000; we also analyze the annual March Current Population Surveys (CPS) of 1976 through 2003. We have devoted considerable attention to preparing comparable samples and income concepts for measuring poverty and inequality across these two data sources. The census data cover a longer time period and have large samples that allow us to focus on detailed demographic groups. The CPS data allow us to track yearly changes from 1975 through 2002 and evaluate how poverty and inequality change as the economy grows and contracts over the business cycle.

Although the census defines a *family* as "a group of two or more persons related by birth, marriage or adoption and residing together," we treat unrelated individuals—persons who do not live with their children or with other relatives—as one-person families. Incomes of all family members who reside together are summed when we measure poverty and family income. If unrelated individuals share a housing unit, they are treated as separate units when we measure poverty and family income. Our sample includes all persons except those in the armed forces; those living in group quarters (such as college dor-

mitories and prisons); and children younger than 15 years old who do not live with any relatives.

Individuals are classified as "poor" if the ratio of their family's money income to the poverty line—which varies by family size—is less than or equal to 1.0. This ratio of *family income relative to needs* corrects the trend in family income for changes in mean family size over time. Sample weights are used throughout the analysis so that trends in both poverty and in family income adjusted for family size are measured on a consistent basis for all persons.

Absolute and Relative Poverty

The poverty thresholds used to construct the official U.S. poverty statistics were established by the federal government in the 1960s. The thresholds provide an "absolute" measure of poverty that specifies the income level the government defines as necessary to provide minimally decent levels of consumption. Such measures do not vary with changes in the overall standard of living. In other words, if we lived in a world in which there were no inflation, the poverty line today would be the same as it was in 1959, the first year for which the Census Bureau measured the official poverty rate.

Some researchers prefer to use "relative" poverty lines that rise and fall with societal income.[8] A typical relative poverty measure establishes a constant value for the ratio of the poverty line to median family income. For example, the poverty line might be set at 40 percent or 50 percent of the median. Thus, if inflation-adjusted incomes doubled for all families, the *absolute poverty rate* would fall as the incomes of some poor families rose above the fixed absolute poverty line. However, the *relative poverty rate* would not fall, because the relative poverty line would rise and the position of the poor would not have changed relative to the positions of other families.

Because a relative poverty line would probably be substantially higher than the current official line, a relative poverty rate for a current year would be much higher than the official rate for that year. For example, one recent study uses a relative poverty line of 50 percent of median family income and finds that the relative poverty rate in 1999 was about twice the official poverty rate.[9]

We use an absolute poverty line in our analysis because we conclude that an absolute measure captures the notion of poverty that motivated the War on Poverty. For example, Robert Lampman noted that the poverty line reflects concern about "a national minimum—an income level for each family size below which we do not want any American to live."[10] Lampman went on to argue that, once the elimination of poverty using the official measure had been achieved, it would be appropriate for a new generation to set a new poverty standard. Because poverty in the United States has not been eliminated under the official measure, we consider it appropriate to use such an absolute measure to examine the historical record from 1959 to the present. We do address issues of the relative economic status of people when we analyze trends in income inequality.

Which Price Index to Use?

The Census Bureau adjusts the poverty thresholds each year to reflect changes in the cost of living. If prices rise by 3 percent, for example, and a family's income rises by the same amount, then the family's standard of living remains constant in the bureau's measurement. The bureau uses the Consumer Price Index for Urban Consumers (CPI-U) to make these annual adjustments. For 2002, the official poverty thresholds ranged from $8,628 for a single person over age 65 to $37,062 for a family of nine or more. The average poverty threshold for a family of four in 2002 was $18,392.[11]

We depart from official procedures by using an inflation adjustment that differs from the one used by the Census Bureau. Economists Gary Burtless and Timothy Smeeding point out that "most economists believe that BLS [Bureau of Labor Statistics] estimates of the changes in the CPI-U overstated increases in consumer prices in many of the years after 1959."[12] The most recent price index developed by the BLS—the Consumer Price Index Research Series (CPI-U-RS)—shows that prices grew more slowly in the past 35 years than does the CPI-U. For example, over the 21-year period from December 1977 to December 1998, the CPI-U-RS increased by 141 percent, whereas the CPI-U increased by 164 percent.

We use the CPI-U-RS instead of the CPI-U to adjust the official poverty thresholds for inflation for years after 1969 because it allows us to measure poverty consistently using the best available measure to control for inflation. Because the new price index records less inflation than the official price index, our poverty thresholds increase at a slower pace than do the official thresholds. In 2002, for example, the official poverty threshold for a family of three was $14,348, whereas the CPI-U-RS poverty threshold for a family of three was $12,307. With the CPI-U-RS line, we classify 9.8 percent of people in the United States as poor in 2002, compared with 12.1 percent in the official census series. Because the threshold for each index is the same in 1969, our poverty series also shows a bigger reduction in poverty since 1969 than does the official series.[13]

What is Considered "Income"?

Family income is defined as the sum of *money income* from all sources for a family during the calendar year preceding the March CPS or April Census. The Census Bureau measure of income includes wages and salaries; self-employment income; property income (such as interest, dividends, and net rental income); cash trans-

fers from government income-maintenance programs; and other cash receipts. The bureau's measure of income does not include capital gains; imputed rents; or government or private benefits provided in kind (such as food stamps, Medicare, or employer-provided health insurance), even though all these items affect a family's current standard of living. The measure also does not subtract taxes paid or add tax credits received (such as the Earned Income Tax Credit).

Alternative Poverty Series

The Census Bureau publishes an experimental poverty series for years since 1979 that corrects for many of the deficiencies of the money-income concept. In any year, those poverty measures that subtract taxes paid and add noncash transfers and tax credits to an individual's income all show a lower poverty rate than the official measure. For example, while the official poverty rate rose from 11.7 percent to 12.1 percent of the population between 1979 and 2002, one widely cited experimental measure in this series increased from 8.9 percent to 9.4 percent. Because trends in the experimental series and the official series are similar and because our analysis begins in 1959, we use the official U.S. definition of income (postcash transfer, pretax money income).

Defining Who is "Rich"

The poverty rate measures changes in absolute income at the bottom of the income distribution. In order to generate a corresponding measure for changes in absolute income at the top of the distribution, we calculate the proportion of people in the United States who are "rich," which we define as people living in families with incomes greater than seven times the poverty line for a family of that size. (As mentioned above, we use a poverty line that is adjusted for inflation using the CPI-U-RS.) For a family with two adults and two children, this threshold is equivalent to $118,265 in 1999 dollars.[14]

Because we use a poverty line that does not vary with changes in the average living standard, our threshold for measuring the proportion of people who are rich is also adjusted only for inflation. Seven times the poverty line was about four times the median income adjusted for family size in 1959, but only about twice the median in 1999. In the same period, the official poverty line fell from 56 percent to 27 percent of the adjusted median.

While analysts who prefer relative measures accept that absolute thresholds provide good measures of the number of poor and rich in 1959, they suggest that such absolute measures are outdated today because average living standards have grown over the past 40 years. These analysts argue that, given the income growth noted above, absolute thresholds in 1999 measured not poverty but extreme poverty, and not the rich but the merely prosperous. We consider it appropriate to measure poverty and the percentage rich using fixed thresholds, as that is official practice of the U.S. government. Because we also believe that it is appropriate to consider relative measures of poverty and inequality, we supplement our analyses of these absolute measures with analyses of inequality measures.

Measuring Inequality: The P90/P10 Ratio

Income growth affects absolute measures of who is counted as poor or rich, but it does not necessarily change relative measures of poverty and inequality. For example, if everyone's income increased by the same percentage, there would be no relative improvement for either those at the bottom or those at the top of the distribution, and relative measures of poverty or income inequality would not change. But because fewer individuals would have incomes below a fixed low-income threshold and more individuals would have incomes above a fixed high-income threshold, this proportional increase in income would lower the poverty rate and increase the percentage of people counted as rich.

There are many widely used measures of income inequality. Inequality increases whenever the incomes of people above the mean increase by more than the incomes of those people below the mean. For this report, we measure inequality by using the ratio of income adjusted for family size at the 90th percentile to income adjusted for family size at the 10th percentile. This P90/P10 ratio is a commonly used measure of inequality. (A family at the 10th percentile has an income that is below that of the other 90 percent of the population; conversely, one at the 90th percentile has an income that is below that of only the richest 10 percent of persons.)

Throughout this report, we compute for every person the ratio of family income divided by the poverty line. Recall that the poverty line varies by family size because the amount of income needed to reach any level of economic well-being is greater for larger families than it is for smaller ones. Thus, if a family has two people, we divide its income by the poverty line for a two-person family; if another family has five people, we divide its income by the poverty line for a five-person family. Each person in a family is assigned the resulting ratio.

Dividing the income of each family by the poverty threshold uses the official poverty threshold as an "equivalence scale" that controls for differences in family size. We use the terms *family income adjusted for family size* and *family income-to-needs ratio* interchangeably to denote that we have computed for every person the ratio of family income divided by the poverty line when we are measuring median income, when we are classifying people as rich or poor, or when we are classifying people at the P10 or P90 of family income.

The CPS allows us to estimate trends in hourly wage rates for workers.[15] When we turn to labor market analyses below, we focus on men and women between the ages of 22 and 62 who had positive potential labor market experience, who had worked in the calendar year prior to the March interview, and who reported positive earnings, as wage rates cannot be computed for nonworkers.

ECONOMIC TRENDS AND PUBLIC POLICY CHANGES: A BRIEF HISTORY

The economic history of the United States since the end of World War II can be divided into two broad periods, distinguished by sharply contrasting economic and public policy experiences.[16]

The first period—the quarter-century following the end of World War II—was an era during which a "rising tide lifted all boats," as real earnings (earnings adjusted for inflation) and family income increased rapidly and the official poverty rate declined rapidly. During the 1950s and 1960s, most men were employed at jobs paying wages that tended to increase annually by more than the inflation rate. During these decades, the percentage of employers who provided subsidized health insurance and pensions also increased.

By the end of the 1960s, most family heads (typically the husband) alone earned enough to support a family at an income above the poverty line. The incomes of rich, poor, and middle-class families increased rapidly during this era. In fact, between 1949 and 1969, the earnings of workers and incomes of families at the bottom of the income distribution increased somewhat faster than those in the middle and the top of the distribution, resulting in small declines in earnings and income inequality.

This economic era ended abruptly after the rapid oil price increase and resulting recession of the early 1970s. What followed was a decade—labeled by Frank Levy as "the quiet depression"[17]—with three recessions, rapid inflation, slow economic growth, and rising inequality of earnings and family income. Taken together, the 1970s and 1980s was a period of "uneven tides" characterized by slow economic growth, not much change in poverty, and rising earnings and income inequality. Employers reduced their demand for workers with the least education, so that many jobs offer lower real wages today than they did 25 years ago. Fewer jobs now provide subsidized health insurance and pensions, and wages are such that many families rely on the earnings of two workers. As a result of economic changes, earnings inequality and income inequality were higher at the end of the 20th century than they were at the end of World War II. And the official poverty rate was about the same in 2002 as it was in the early 1970s.

In addition to differences in economic experiences, there were dramatic differences between social policies of the first quarter-century following World War II and the policies of the next 25 years. In the aftermath of the War on Poverty, spending on government social welfare programs (such as Medicare, Medicaid, Head Start, Social Security, and Aid to Families with Dependent Children) increased from 11.0 percent to 18.2 percent of gross domestic product (GDP) between 1965 and 1975. The government introduced new public programs, and benefit levels and the number of recipients of existing programs increased.

Then, after the mid-1970s slowdown in economic growth, the early 1980s saw reductions in government social expenditures on income transfer and employment programs for the nonelderly. The Reagan administration's 1982 *Economic Report of the President* offered a view regarding the relationship between government spending and poverty reduction that differed dramatically from the view of the 1964 *Economic Report*:

"Many of the Administration's policies have reduced government expenditures for various groups or provided less of an increase in such outlays than has been expected. The fundamental premise behind these reductions is that they ultimately will lead to substantial and sustainable economic growth. This has particular relevance for the poor, most of whom probably have historically benefited more from sustained economic growth than from government transfer programs." [18]

As a result of this policy reorientation, the era of social-welfare policy expansions ended. Social-welfare spending as a percentage of GDP fell slightly from 18.2 percent in 1975 to 17.8 percent in 1985; it then increased to 20.9 percent by 1995. But all of the growth in public social-welfare spending as a percentage of GDP after 1975 can be attributed to increases in Medicare, Medicaid, and other health-care spending. Excluding health-related expenses, social welfare as a percentage of GDP increased from 8.8 percent to 15.0 percent between 1965 and 1975, and was at about that same percentage two decades later.

The economic environment also changed in the mid-1970s—from one in which both favorable economic conditions and increased government spending were lifting the incomes of the nonelderly poor to one in which both the wage rates and government benefits of the nonelderly stagnated or declined relative to inflation.[19] The late-1970s oil price increases, increased global competition for manufactured goods production, labor-saving technological changes, and recessions in the early 1980s and the early 1990s meant that an American generation had experienced only a modest increase in its average standard of living at the same time that economic inequality had increased.

Although economic performance in the last quarter of the 20th century was disappointing compared with the performance of the previous quarter-century, the last few years of this period were ones of sustained economic growth. And the employment experience of the 1990s was both different from that of the period from the early 1970s to the early 1990s and was almost as good as it had been in the 1960s. The annual unemployment rate for men over the age of 20 was below 5 percent in 23 of the 25 years between 1950 and 1974, but below 5 percent in only four of the 20 years between 1975 and 1994.[20] The rate again fell below 5 percent in 1995 and stayed below that level for the next seven years before rising during the recession that began in 2001. In 2000, the U.S. male unemployment rate had fallen to 3.3 percent, the lowest rate since 1973.

In contrast to the experiences of the 1970s and 1980s, the recovery of the 1990s was similar to that of the 1960s—one in which real earnings and family incomes increased for those at the bottom of the distribution as well as for the affluent. For example, the real average hourly earnings of private-sector production workers fell by 24 percent between 1973 and 1993, but then increased by 8 percent between 1993 and 1999. The official Census Bureau poverty rate declined from 15.1 percent in 1993 to 11.8 percent in 1999, only slightly higher than the historical low of 11.1 percent in 1973. But the 1999 poverty rate is higher than one would have expected, given that inflation-adjusted per capita income increased substantially between 1973 and 1999. And as the century ended, both the inflation-adjusted value of the minimum wage and the wages of the average production worker were more than 15 percent lower than they had been three decades earlier.

Indeed, poverty in the United States at the end of the 20th century was higher than it was in many industrialized countries, even though U.S. living standards on average are higher than living standards in these countries. In part, this disparity is attributable to the labor market problems mentioned above. In addition, the federal minimum wage (which can be increased only through congressional legislation) has been raised infrequently in recent decades. Poverty is also higher in the United States than in other industrialized countries because the American social safety net provides smaller benefits to fewer low-income families.

Recent research has used the official U.S. poverty threshold to compare the poverty rate in the United States in the mid-1990s with the rate in 10 other advanced economies.[21] The researchers translated each country's currency into U.S. dollars and used a poverty line that is similar to the official census line. According to their calculations, the U.S. per capita GDP in the mid-

1990s was about 20 percent higher than that in the other 10 countries, but the U.S. poverty rate (13.6 percent) was much higher than the other countries' average of 8.6 percent.

The period since 1975 has been an era of rising inequality in the United States. While family income inequality almost always increases during recessions, the increase in inequality during recent economic recoveries is a new phenomenon. Prior to the mid-1970s, economic expansions tended both to increase average family income and to reduce family income inequality, with both changes contributing to poverty reductions. Since the mid-1970s, expansions continued to increase average family income; but inequality increased during expansions as well as during contractions. As a result, people at the bottom of the distribution experienced smaller income increases than average and (at times) even actual income declines.

THE LONG VIEW—TRENDS IN POVERTY AND INCOME INEQUALITY, 1959 TO 1999

In this section, we compare trends in *poverty*; in the percentage of people who are *rich* (those whose family income exceeds seven times their poverty line); and in *inequality* over the past four decades. In Figure 1, the percentage of people classified as poor or rich is shown for each census year. Poverty fell substantially between 1959 and 1979, but only modestly in the next two decades. The decade with the largest poverty decline was the 1960s, when the rate dropped by 9 percentage points, from 23.3 percent to 14.3 percent. Poverty fell 2.9 percentage points in the 1970s to 11.4 percent, did not change in the 1980s, and then declined 1.3 percentage points in the 1990s to 10.1 percent.

As outlined above, we calculate the poverty rates in Figure 1 by adjusting the official poverty line for inflation using the CPI-U-RS from 1969 onward instead of using the CPI-U. Thus the poverty rate we calculate is lower for each year than the official rate. The trends over time, however, are similar regardless of which price index is used to determine the poverty thresholds. Between 1969 and 1999, our calculated poverty rate falls from 14.3 percent to 10.1 percent, whereas it falls from 14.3 percent to 12.3 percent using the official line. In historical context, these differences are small. In the aftermath of the War on Poverty, for example, many analysts expected that poverty according to the official measure would be eliminated by 1980.[22]

One indication of the diverging fortunes of those people at the bottom of the income distribution compared with those at the top of the distribution is appar-

Figure 1

POVERTY RATE AND PERCENTAGE OF PEOPLE WHO ARE RICH, 1959–1999

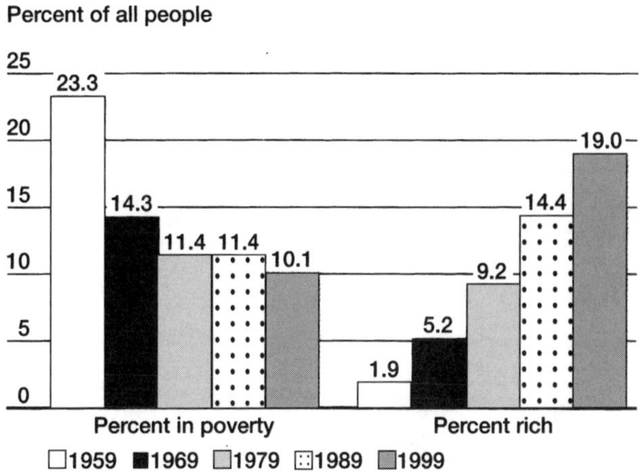

Source: Authors' calculations using the Integrated Public Use Microdata Series (IPUMS), 2003.

ent if one compares the two sides of Figure 1. Our measure of the proportion of Americans who are rich shows that people living in families with incomes above seven times the poverty line (right side of Figure 1) increased from almost 2 percent in 1959 to 19 percent in 1999.[23]

There are substantial differences in the trends in income inequality between the period from 1959 to 1979 and the period from 1979 to 1999. As we discuss in more detail later, labor market changes that began in the late 1970s contributed to declining earnings for male workers with the least education. These changes also increased earnings for the most-educated workers. In addition, married women continued to increase their labor force participation over the latter period—a development that kept some married-couple families whose husbands had declining earnings from falling into poverty, and helped the incomes of other married-couple families move to levels above seven times the poverty line. The 1980s and 1990s differ from the earlier two decades primarily because, while poverty had declined before 1979, those at the bottom gained little after that date. The income gains people at the top of the income distribution made during the 1980s and 1990s were also higher than the gains their counterparts made during the earlier decades.

Figure 2 (page 56) shows the slowdown in economic growth over the period from 1959 to 1999. The left-side bar for each decade shows the percentage change in inflation-adjusted median family income-to-needs (family income divided by the poverty line). The right-side bar shows the percentage change in the real median annual earnings of male workers between the ages of 22 and 62 (a group that has high labor force participation rates).

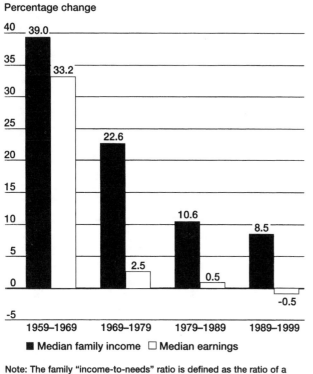

Figure 2

PERCENTAGE CHANGE BY DECADE IN MEDIAN FAMILY INCOME-TO-NEEDS RATIO AND IN MEDIAN ANNUAL EARNINGS OF MALE WORKERS, 1959–1999

Percentage change

■ Median family income □ Median earnings

Note: The family "income-to-needs" ratio is defined as the ratio of a family's income to the poverty line for a family of that size. An income-to-needs ratio of 1.0 indicates that family income is equal to the poverty line.

Source: Authors' calculations using the Integrated Public Use Micro-data Series (IPUMS), 2003.

Between 1959 and 1999, median family income-to-needs doubled to 3.7 times the poverty line. The most rapid rate of growth (39.0 percent) was in the 1960s, with substantially lower growth in subsequent decades. As with the poverty rate, there is a substantial difference between the first two decades of the period and the last two: Median adjusted family income increased by 71 percent between 1959 and 1979, but only by 20 percent over the next 20 years.

Real median annual earnings of male workers grew substantially less than median family income divided by the poverty line over the 40 years. Whereas the family income-to-needs ratio doubled, median male earnings grew by only 36 percent during the period, from $23,544 in 1959 to $32,100 in 1999 (as measured in constant 1999 dollars). And most of the growth in male earnings occurred in the 1960s—these median annual earnings were $31,360 in 1969 and $32,100 in 1999. No economist or policy analyst working in the late 1960s would have

produced such a dismal forecast for the labor market prospects of men: For a full generation, there was no increase in these workers' inflation-adjusted median annual earnings.

If families at the end of the 20th century were as dependent on male earnings as they had been several decades earlier, family incomes would have been much lower and poverty rates higher than they actually were. Growth in income adjusted for family size continued after 1969 in part because of the increased labor market work of women over these years. By 1999, two-earner families were much more common than they had been 40 years earlier: While 41 percent of married women worked at some time during the year in 1959, this figure had increased to 74 percent by 1999. The declining size of families was another source of growth in income adjusted for family size during this period—a smaller proportion of families had children, and families who did have children had fewer of them. While the average household in 1960 contained 3.35 people, by 2000, that average had fallen to 2.62.

Median family income adjusted for family size more than doubled between 1959 and 1999. However, because growth was unevenly distributed across families after 1979, income inequality increased. Figure 3 shows the income-to-needs ratio for persons at the 90th percentile and at the 10th percentile in each decennial year as well as the P90/P10 ratio—our measure of inequality.

In 1959, a person at the 10th percentile of the income distribution lived in a family with an income that was about one-half of the poverty line, while a person at the 90th percentile lived in a family with an income over four times the poverty line. The P90/P10 ratio in 1959 was 8.2, meaning that a person near the top of the distribution had income more than eight times as large as one near the bottom. The P90/P10 measure of inequality declined to 7.3 in 1969 and increased slightly to 7.5 in 1979, reflecting similar rates of income growth at both ends of the distribution.

But in the 1980s, income inequality surged. While people at the 10th percentile experienced a slight income decline, those at the 90th percentile saw their income grow by 20 percent, to 8.1 times the poverty line. As a result, the P90/P10 ratio rose by 21 percent during the decade, to 9.1. And while the rate of increase in inequality declined in the 1990s, inequality still increased because income at the 90th percentile increased more than it did at the 10th percentile. Indeed, income growth at P90 was quite similar in the 1970s, 1980s, and 1990s; but income growth at P10 in the 1990s was only about half the growth at P10 two decades earlier. The 1980s stand out as the beginning of an era of increased inequality in the United States that continues to the present.

The growth rate and distributional performance of the economy since the late 1970s provide little evidence, given recent economic and public policy experiences, to

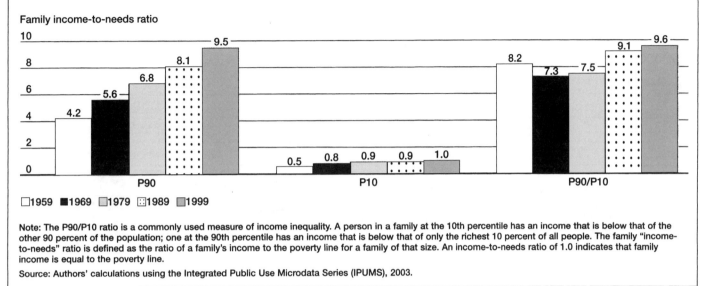

Figure 3

INCOME INEQUALITY, ALL PEOPLE, 1959–1999

Family income-to-needs ratio

□1959 ■1969 ▨1979 ⠿1989 ▨1999

Note: The P90/P10 ratio is a commonly used measure of income inequality. A person in a family at the 10th percentile has an income that is below that of the other 90 percent of the population; one at the 90th percentile has an income that is below that of only the richest 10 percent of all people. The family "income-to-needs" ratio is defined as the ratio of a family's income to the poverty line for a family of that size. An income-to-needs ratio of 1.0 indicates that family income is equal to the poverty line.

Source: Authors' calculations using the Integrated Public Use Microdata Series (IPUMS), 2003.

expect a return in the near future to the lower levels of inequality of the 1960s or 1970s. As we show below in more detail, the earnings differentials between college graduates and high school graduates have widened over the past quarter-century and show no sign of diminishing. For example, a return to the 1979 P90/P10 ratio of 7.5 would require income at the 10th percentile to grow by 25 percent more than income at the 90th percentile. But during the 1990s, when economic growth was stronger overall than it had been in 30 years, the income at P10 grew by only 10 percent, while incomes at the top of the distribution grew by 16 percent.

HOW DIFFERENT DEMOGRAPHIC GROUPS FARED FROM 1959 TO 1999

Racial and Ethnic Differences in Poverty and Family Income

The reduction of racial disparities in economic status was a key goal of the War on Poverty. In addition, concerns regarding racial/ethnic disparities in economic status have a long history in Russell Sage Foundation studies of census data.[24]

About 15 years ago, the Committee on the Status of Black Americans, appointed by the National Research Council (NRC), issued the report *A Common Destiny: Blacks and American Society*. The report presented a com-

prehensive review of changes in the social, economic, and political status of black Americans between 1940 and the mid-1980s.[25]

When the NRC committee was deliberating, data on the relative economic status of African Americans and whites was available for the period of study through the mid-1980s. As noted earlier, the economy performed poorly during the period from the mid-1970s to the mid-1980s. Given this background of slow growth and rising inequality, the report's conclusions were pessimistic.

The availability of data from the 2000 Census allow us to revisit the relative economic status of racial and ethnic minorities after the long economic boom of the 1990s. We document that there was much economic progress in the 1990s for all population subgroups—as poverty fell and wage rates, work hours, and family incomes increased. But our review of the most recent data also demonstrates that economic growth on its own is necessary but not sufficient for reducing persistent between-group economic disparities. The gaps between whites and blacks and between whites and Hispanics remain so large that economic parity between these groups is likely to remain decades away.

The 5% PUMS include samples that are large enough to measure poverty and inequality for a wide range of demographic groups. We classify all persons into one of four mutually exclusive racial/ethnic groups—white persons who are not of Hispanic origin, African Americans who are not of Hispanic origin, other racial groups not of Hispanic origin, and Hispanics. Persons who are classified by the census as neither white nor African American include Asian Americans, American Indians, Native Hawaiians, and Other Pacific

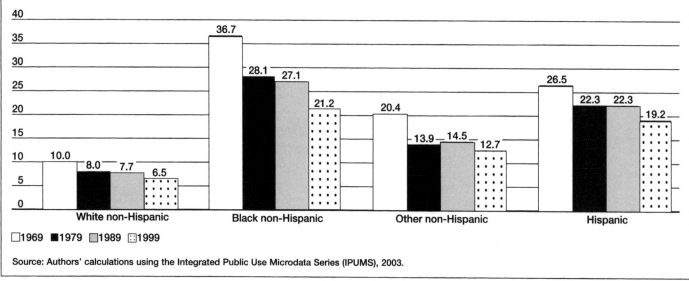

Figure 4

POVERTY RATE FOR ALL PEOPLE, BY RACE/ETHNICITY OF FAMILY HEAD, 1969–1999

Percent of people poor

□1969 ■1979 ▨1989 ⊡1999

Source: Authors' calculations using the Integrated Public Use Microdata Series (IPUMS), 2003.

Islanders: These groups are labeled in Figures 4 and 5 as "Other non-Hispanic." All persons living in a family are classified according to the race/ethnicity of the family head. Because the 1970 Census was the first to ask questions concerning Hispanic origin, we take 1969 as the starting point for our analysis of trends in poverty and inequality across these groups.

Figure 4 shows the trends in poverty for these four groups. In 1969, while 10 percent of whites were living in poverty, the poverty rate for African Americans was 3.6 times higher (at 36.7 percent). For other non-Hispanics, the rate was about twice that of whites (20.4 percent); for Hispanics, the rate was 2.6 times that of whites (26.5 percent). For all four groups, poverty declined substantially during the 1970s, but was virtually the same in 1989 as in 1979.

During the economic boom of the 1990s, poverty once again declined for all four groups. But despite these gains during a period of low unemployment rates, the 1999 poverty rates for African Americans and Latinos were still about three times the rate for non-Hispanic whites, and the rate for other non-Hispanics was about twice that of whites. The 1999 rates for African Americans and Latinos (both about 20 percent) were still higher than the mid-1960s white poverty rate—about 15 percent. In 1999, racial and ethnic minorities made up around 30 percent of all people in the United States and 55 percent of all poor persons.

We also examined trends in the percentage of people who are rich in each of these racial/ethnic groups (data not shown). For each group, the percentage of people whom we classify as rich increased much more rapidly between 1969 and 1999 than the numbers in

poverty fell over the same period, reflecting increased inequality within each racial/ethnic group. In 1969, 6.2 percent of whites had incomes above seven times their poverty line, compared with 3.5 percent of other non-Hispanics, 1 percent of African Americans, and 1.4 percent of Hispanics. By 1999, 23 percent of whites had incomes that we classify as rich, compared with 17.5 percent of other non-Hispanics, 8.9 percent of African Americans, and 6.3 percent of Hispanics.

The ratio of rich people to poor people was greatest for whites. In 1999, there were about 3.5 times as many rich whites as poor whites, while for other non-Hispanics, the rich were 1.5 times as numerous. For African Americans and Hispanics, however, the number of rich people was only a small fraction of the number of poor people. Only 8.9 percent of African Americans were classified as rich, compared with 21.2 percent who were poor. And only 6.3 percent of Hispanics were rich, compared with an Hispanic poverty rate of 19.2 percent.

In addition, inequality of family income adjusted for family size is also higher for racial/ethnic minorities than it is for white non-Hispanics (data not shown). In 1999, the P90/P10 ratio was 7.8 for white non-Hispanics, 15.0 for black non-Hispanics, 11.2 for other non-Hispanics, and 10.0 for Hispanics. Inequality increased for each of these groups between 1969 and 1999.

The declines in poverty and increase in the proportion of people who are rich over these 30 years reflect increased living standards for all ethnic and racial groups. Figure 5 shows trends in median family income adjusted for family size. Between 1969 and 1999, this median grew by 55 percent for whites, by 80 percent for

African Americans, by 62 percent for other non-Hispanics, and by 32 percent for Hispanics.

Even though median family income grew more slowly for whites than for African Americans and other non-Hispanics, the racial/ethnic gaps remain large. In 1999, median family income adjusted for family size for Hispanics was 52 percent of that for white non-Hispanics, while median family income for African Americans was 58 percent of that for white non-Hispanics. Median income-to-needs ratios in 1999 for African Americans (2.5) and Hispanics (2.2) were somewhat below the 2.7 ratio of whites in 1969.

These large racial/ethnic economic disparities are not likely to be eliminated in the near future, given prevailing economic trends and public policies. For example, consider the experience of the last three decades for African Americans. If African Americans' median family income adjusted for family size were to grow by 34 percent over the next 20 years (the same rate as it grew over the last 20 years), then it would increase by 2019 to 3.3 times the poverty line—similar to the 1979 level of white non-Hispanics.

The economic status of the Hispanic population has lagged that of both whites and African Americans in recent years because increasing numbers of Hispanics are recent immigrants. Recent immigrants have incomes that are lower on average than those of the U.S.-born.[26] While 29 percent of Hispanics in the United States in 1970 were foreign-born, that percentage had increased to 43 percent by 1999. Because Hispanic immigrants tend to

have low incomes when they arrive in the United States (in part because they have lower educational attainment than the U.S.-born population), an increase in the immigrant share of the total U.S. Hispanic population contributed to a higher poverty rate and a lower level of family income for Hispanics relative to both white non-Hispanics and African Americans.

Immigrants are included in the data for each of the racial/ethnic groups in Figures 4 and 5. We now examine differences in poverty rates and family incomes between the U.S.-born and foreign-born to see how the trends shown in Figures 1 and 2 differ by immigration status.

Poverty and Family Income by Nativity

The United States has from its beginning been a nation of immigrants. However, immigration slowed after Congress imposed immigration controls in the 1920s. Some researchers have labeled the period between 1915 and 1965 as the "Immigration Pause."[27] Thus, there was relatively little immigration during the quarter-century following World War II, when poverty fell rapidly and real family income doubled. Between 1960 and 1980, between 5 percent and 6 percent of all persons were foreign-born.

But in response to legislative changes, particularly the Immigration Reform and Control Act of 1986, immigration to the United States surged. The number of immigrants increased by 40 percent between 1980 and 1990 and by almost 60 percent between 1990 and 2000.[28] Because immigration has increased rapidly over the last

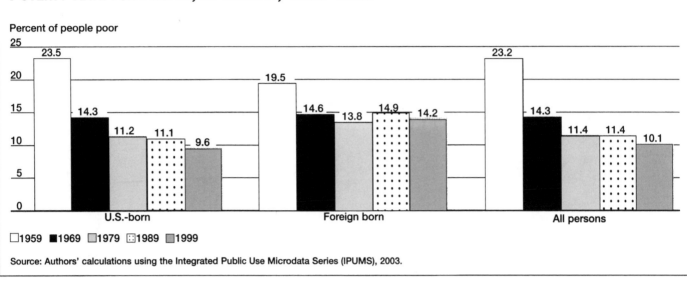

Figure 6
POVERTY RATE FOR PEOPLE, BY NATIVITY, 1959–1999

Percent of people poor

U.S.-born: 23.5, 14.3, 11.2, 11.1, 9.6
Foreign born: 19.5, 14.6, 13.8, 14.9, 14.2
All persons: 23.2, 14.3, 11.4, 11.4, 10.1

☐1959 ■1969 ☐1979 ⊡1989 ▨1999

Source: Authors' calculations using the Integrated Public Use Microdata Series (IPUMS), 2003.

two decades while economic progress has slowed, some observers have suggested that immigration accounts for a large share of the recent slowdown in economic progress and increased inequality.[29]

Immigrants are heterogeneous—not only by country of origin, but also by their citizenship status and by how recently they immigrated. In 2002, 12 percent of all people in the United States were foreign-born, and about 40 percent of the foreign-born had become naturalized citizens. The official poverty rate for naturalized citizens

regardless of country of origin—10.0 percent—was lower than the 11.5 percent poverty rate for U.S.-born citizens. Immigrants who were not naturalized had a poverty rate (20.7 percent) about twice as high as both of these rates. However, immigrant noncitizens represented a small fraction both of the total population and of the poor—7.2 percent and 12.4 percent, respectively.[30]

In Figures 6 and 7, we divide the population into two mutually exclusive groups—those who were born in the United States, and those who were born abroad.

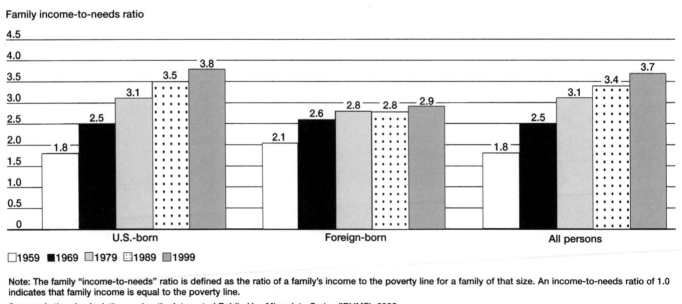

Figure 7
MEDIAN FAMILY INCOME-TO-NEEDS RATIO FOR PEOPLE, BY NATIVITY, 1959–1999

Family income-to-needs ratio

U.S.-born: 1.8, 2.5, 3.1, 3.5, 3.8
Foreign-born: 2.1, 2.6, 2.8, 2.8, 2.9
All persons: 1.8, 2.5, 3.1, 3.4, 3.7

☐1959 ■1969 ☐1979 ⊡1989 ▨1999

Note: The family "income-to-needs" ratio is defined as the ratio of a family's income to the poverty line for a family of that size. An income-to-needs ratio of 1.0 indicates that family income is equal to the poverty line.

Source: Authors' calculations using the Integrated Public Use Microdata Series (IPUMS), 2003.

Figure 6 shows that between 1959 and 1999, the poverty rate for the U.S.-born fell by 13.9 percentage points, from 23.5 percent to 9.6 percent—a decline not much different from the 13.1 percentage-point fall (from 23.2 percent to 10.1 percent) for all people. If we assume that the poverty rate among the U.S.-born in any year is not much affected by immigration, then increased immigration over the period from 1959 to 1999 had little effect on the overall poverty rate.

However, if immigrant workers do compete for jobs with U.S.-born workers and do exert downward pressure on the latter's wage rates, comparing poverty trends for the foreign-born and the U.S.-born provides a lower-bound estimate of the effects of immigration on poverty. Indeed, the existing literature does indicate that immigration affects the labor market status of some U.S.-born workers. Researchers estimate that, while the effect is relatively small for the nation as a whole, it is substantial for specific industries or local labor markets where the immigrant share of workers is relatively high.[31]

Trends in poverty from 1969 to 1999 differ from those between 1959 and 1969. In 1959, when most foreign-born Americans were not recent immigrants, the poverty rate for the foreign-born was lower than that for the U.S.-born. By 1969, the situation had changed: The poverty rate was virtually the same for these two groups. But while poverty among the foreign-born was fairly constant between 1969 and 1999—14.6 percent in 1969, and 14.2 percent in 1999—it declined among the U.S-born from 14.3 percent to 9.6 percent. Thus, the increase in the immigrant share of the population since 1969 has contributed somewhat to an increase in the overall poverty rate. Note, however, that the size of this effect is very small: The poverty rate in 1999 for the U.S.-born was only 0.5 percentage points lower than the rate for all persons in 1999.

The lack of economic progress in recent decades for the foreign-born relative to the U.S.-born is mirrored in the trends for family income divided by the poverty line. Figure 7 shows that, in 1959, the median income adjusted for family size was somewhat higher for foreign-born persons (2.1 times the poverty line) than that for U.S.-born (1.8 times the poverty line).

Yet, as the number of immigrants increased between 1969 and 1999, median income grew at a much faster rate for U.S.-born persons than for the foreign-born (52 percent versus 12 percent). In 1999, the median income-to-needs ratio of the foreign-born (2.9 times the poverty line) was about one-quarter less than that for people born in the United States (3.8 times the poverty line). Again, the overall difference directly attributable to immigration is small: In 1999, the median was about 3 percent higher for the U.S.-born than for all persons.

Between 1959 and 1999, inequality within the foreign-born population increased much more rapidly than it did among the U.S.-born (data not shown). The

P90/P10 ratio of family income divided by the poverty line increased from 6.8 to 11.1 for the foreign-born, while it increased from 8.4 to 9.1 among the U.S.-born.

Trends in Poverty by Age

Over the past 40 years, the economic status of the elderly has increased relative to that of the nation's children and nonelderly adults. Figure 8 (page 62) shows the dramatic reduction in poverty among the elderly. In 1959, the poverty rate of elderly persons was 37.1 percent, more than twice the 17.4 percent rate for adults ages 18 to 64. By 1999, the rate for the elderly had fallen to 7.0 percent—lower than the 9.1 percent rate for adults.

During the 1960s, poverty rates declined significantly for children, nonelderly adults, and the elderly. Yet between 1969 and 1999, there was little progress in reducing poverty rates for children and nonelderly adults because of the slow economic growth and rising inequality discussed earlier. In addition, neither the minimum wage nor cash welfare payments for families with children kept up with inflation during this period, and a smaller percentage of the unemployed received unemployment insurance.

Poverty rates continued to fall for the elderly in each successive decade. This decline is primarily attributable to increased government benefits. Between 1965 and 1973, there were seven across-the-board increases in Social Security benefits. Congress increased these benefits by 13 percent in 1968, by 15 percent in 1969, by 10 percent in 1971, and by 20 percent in 1972.[32] In 1973, Congress mandated automatic inflation-indexation of Social Security benefits beginning in 1975.

From the early 1970s to the early 1990s, the earnings of workers failed to keep up with inflation. As a result, Social Security benefits increased relative to earnings, relative to the poverty line, and relative to the government benefits available to the nonelderly. In 1960, for example, the mean annual Social Security benefit for an elderly married couple was 80 percent of that couple's poverty threshold; that mean benefit rose to match that couple's poverty line in 1970 and then to exceed that line in 1980 by 34 percent.[33] In 1964, the Social Security benefit for a single male retiree was 20 percent of the mean annual earnings of a nonsupervisory production worker. By 1999, this ratio had increased to 45 percent.

In addition, the Supplemental Security Program (SSI), enacted in 1972, provides a minimum monthly cash payment to poor elderly, blind, and disabled persons. SSI is available to those people who did not work long enough to qualify for Social Security benefits; it also provides benefits to those who had very low earnings during their working years and hence receive a low Social Security benefit. As a result, all of the poor elderly—but not all poor children or adults—are eligible for a government monthly cash benefit.

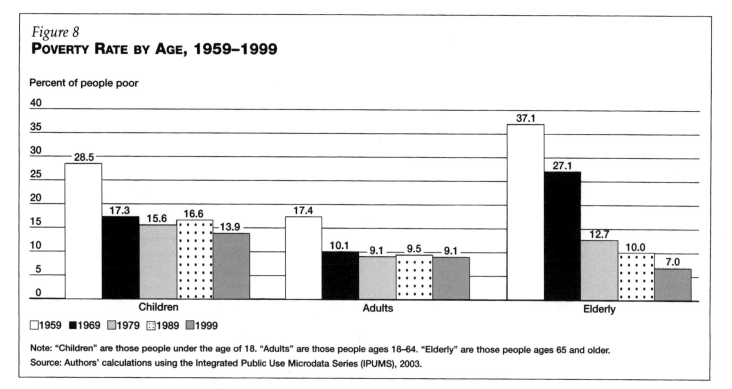

Figure 8
POVERTY RATE BY AGE, 1959–1999

Percent of people poor

Children: 28.5 (1959), 17.3 (1969), 15.6 (1979), 16.6 (1989), 13.9 (1999)
Adults: 17.4 (1959), 10.1 (1969), 9.1 (1979), 9.5 (1989), 9.1 (1999)
Elderly: 37.1 (1959), 27.1 (1969), 12.7 (1979), 10.0 (1989), 7.0 (1999)

☐1959 ■1969 ☐1979 ⊡1989 ▨1999

Note: "Children" are those people under the age of 18. "Adults" are those people ages 18–64. "Elderly" are those people ages 65 and older.
Source: Authors' calculations using the Integrated Public Use Microdata Series (IPUMS), 2003.

Over the past 40 years, the labor force participation rate of the elderly has declined. In 1959, 49 percent of men between the ages of 65 and 74 worked at some time during the year; by 1979, this rate had fallen to 35 percent, and by 1999, it had declined to 31 percent. In contrast, work hours in a typical family have increased over these decades due to the increasing work of married women. The rising economic status of the elderly relative to the nonelderly is even more impressive when viewed in the context of these changing patterns of employment. In 1959, the median family income adjusted for family size of persons between the ages of 65 and 74 was 65 percent of that of persons between the ages of 35 and 54 (the age group most likely to have additional earners). However, by 1999—when the elderly were working less and the nonelderly were working more—this median family income ratio had increased to 82 percent.

Trends in Child Poverty by Living Arrangements

In contrast to the poverty rates for the elderly, poverty rates for children have remained at about the same levels for over three decades. One reason poverty has remained high for children is that a declining number of them live in married-couple families, which have relatively low poverty rates. Between 1959 and 1999, as marital fertility declined and both the divorce rate and the rate of nonmarital childbearing increased, the percentage of children living in married-couple families fell from 91 percent to 71 percent.

Figure 9 shows that the poverty rate for children in married-couple families fell from 24.8 percent to 6.9 percent between 1959 and 1999, and that the rate for children in other living arrangements fell from 66.2 percent

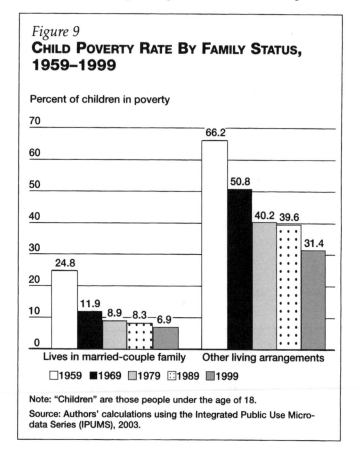

Figure 9
CHILD POVERTY RATE BY FAMILY STATUS, 1959–1999

Percent of children in poverty

Lives in married-couple family: 24.8 (1959), 11.9 (1969), 8.9 (1979), 8.3 (1989), 6.9 (1999)
Other living arrangements: 66.2 (1959), 50.8 (1969), 40.2 (1979), 39.6 (1989), 31.4 (1999)

☐1959 ■1969 ☐1979 ⊡1989 ▨1999

Note: "Children" are those people under the age of 18.
Source: Authors' calculations using the Integrated Public Use Microdata Series (IPUMS), 2003.

to 31.4 percent. While children living in married-couple families have benefited from the trend toward two-earner families, children in other living arrangements primarily live with single mothers who work fewer hours and have lower earnings.

In addition, government benefits for poor children fell in real terms after the mid-1970s, as these benefits were not indexed to inflation and were not legislatively increased. Some research has shown that other industrialized countries provide more government benefits to families with children than does the United States.[34] These benefits are particularly important for children living outside of married-couple families.

RECESSIONS AND RECOVERIES: 1975 TO 2002

The decennial census data do not allow us to distinguish how individuals and families fare in terms of poverty and family income at different points in the business cycle. But the annual March Current Population Survey data allow us to compute time series for the period between 1975 and 2002—the earliest and most recent years that provide estimates of hourly wage rates and a period characterized by several recessions and recoveries.[35]

Business cycles are the "ups and downs" in economic activity, defined by periods of expansion or recession. During expansions, the gross domestic product grows and the unemployment rate tends to fall; during recessions, economic activity contracts and the unemployment rate tends to rise. Business cycles have particularly large effects on the employment and annual earnings of workers. In contrast, Social Security payments to the elderly do not vary with the unemployment rate, so their family incomes and poverty rate are not very sensitive to the business cycle.

The Census Bureau changed its data collection methods between the March 1993 and March 1994 surveys in such a way that economic measures are not comparable for years prior to and after this change. We therefore use a dotted line to connect the data points between calendar years 1992 and 1993 to warn the reader that these changes reflect changes in data collection procedures as well as economic changes.

The Level and Distribution of Hourly Wage Rates

To this point, we have emphasized the distribution of family income adjusted for family size, which is the income concept the government uses to measure poverty. Annual earnings—by definition, the product of the hourly wage rate and annual hours of work—are the income source that accounts for the largest share of total family income for the nonelderly. We now focus extensively on wage rates and annual hours.

Individuals who have higher wage rates are less likely to be poor than those who have lower wage rates, holding hours worked constant. And at any given hourly wage rate, someone who works more hours per year is less likely to be poor than someone who works fewer hours. Wage rates reflect both the willingness of workers to supply their labor and the willingness of employers to put them to work. Wage rates are also assumed by economists to be determined primarily in the market, based on a worker's productivity and skills.

Labor economists focus on differences in wage rates over time as well as across different kinds of workers. Accordingly, we examine how hourly wage rates have changed over time as well as how hourly wages differ for different types of workers. This section is followed by a discussion of changes in annual hours of work.

Figure 10 (page 64) shows mean hourly wages in constant 1999 dollars for male and female workers between the ages of 22 and 62 in each year between 1975 and 2002. For men, the economic recovery of the 1990s represented a break in the disappointing experience of the prior two decades. While mean male wages increased by 3 percent between 1983 and 1989, those gains were lost during the recession of the early 1990s. The mean hourly wage (in constant 1999 dollars) was virtually the same in 1993 ($15.39 per hour) as it had been in 1975 ($15.28). But between 1993 and 2002, the mean male hourly wage grew by 14 percent to $17.51— the first sustained increase in nearly 20 years.

The trend in mean real wages of female workers over the period from 1975 to 2002 is dramatically different. First, the overall growth rate for women was much more rapid. Female wages were 46 percent higher in 2002 than they were in 1975 (an average of $14.14 per hour versus $9.71 per hour), while male wages gained only 15 percent. Second, female wages increased steadily throughout the period—by 15 percent between 1979 and 1989, and by another 15 percent between 1989 and 1999.

The trends in mean wages mask different experiences across the distribution of workers. Figure 11 (page 64) plots the percentage change between 1975 and 2002 in real hourly wages for male and female workers between the ages of 22 and 62 throughout the income distribution. The figure shows increased wage-rate inequality for both men and women between 1975 and 2002—the lines slope upward to the right, indicating that percentage changes in wages were higher for workers at the top of the wage-rate distribution compared with those at the bottom of the distribution.

For men, the relationship between percentile rank and real wage growth is nearly *monotonic*—the lower the rank, the smaller the increase (or the larger the decrease) in wages. Real wages declined at every point on the dis-

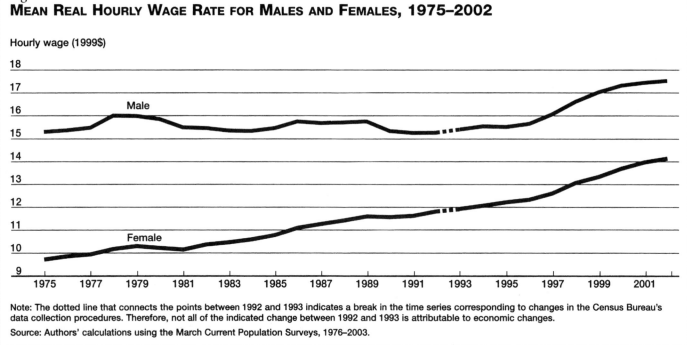

Figure 10

MEAN REAL HOURLY WAGE RATE FOR MALES AND FEMALES, 1975–2002

Hourly wage (1999$)

Note: The dotted line that connects the points between 1992 and 1993 indicates a break in the time series corresponding to changes in the Census Bureau's data collection procedures. Therefore, not all of the indicated change between 1992 and 1993 is attributable to economic changes.

Source: Authors' calculations using the March Current Population Surveys, 1976–2003.

tribution for men up through the 35th percentile. At the top of the distribution, however, males at the 95th percentile in 2002 had wages that, at $48.12 per hour, were 47 percent higher than the wages of their counterparts in 1975 ($32.84). Meanwhile, the increased wage inequality over this period reflected an absolute as well as a relative

decline for men at the lower end of the distribution. For male workers, the P90/P10 ratio of wage rates increased from 3.9 to 5.3 between 1975 and 2002.

By contrast, the line representing female workers in Figure 11 is positive at all percentiles, indicating women across the distribution had higher wage rates in 2002 com-

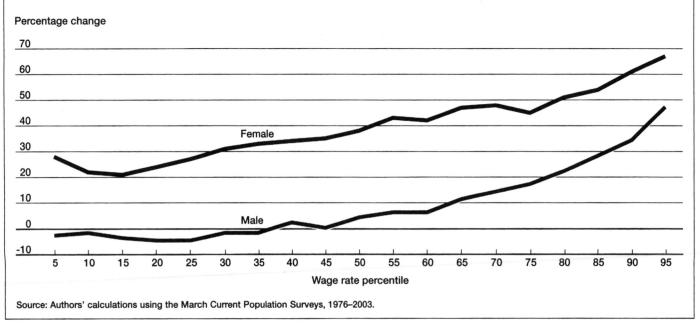

Figure 11

PERCENTAGE CHANGE IN REAL HOURLY WAGE RATE FOR MALES AND FEMALES, BY WAGE-RATE PERCENTILE, 1975–2002

Percentage change

Wage rate percentile

Source: Authors' calculations using the March Current Population Surveys, 1976–2003.

pared with 1975. The line for female workers is also above the line for male workers at every percentile in the distribution, showing that female workers experienced greater growth in wage rates than did male workers. Over the time period, the median wage for males increased by 4 percent, whereas it increased by 38 percent for females. In 2002, females earned 78 cents for every dollar earned by males ($12.16 per hour versus $15.59 per hour).

As with men, however, wage inequality among female workers also increased, as growth in wage rates was highest at the top deciles and lowest at the bottom deciles. As a result, the P90/P10 ratio of wage rates for female workers increased from 3.7 to 4.9 between 1975 and 2002.

Figures 12 and 13 (pages 65, 66) show the same information as Figure 11, but present the data on wage-rate changes for the 1982–1989 and 1993–2000 economic recoveries. Each of these figures depicts wage growth from the trough year (the calendar year in which the recession ended) to the peak year (the calendar year in which the economic recovery ended) of the business cycle.

There has been substantial controversy concerning the extent to which economic growth "trickles down" to workers at the bottom of the wage and income distributions. The Reagan administration, for example, viewed macroeconomic policy as its major antipoverty policy and tailored its policies accordingly. An alternative view contends that, after the early 1970s, economic growth during recoveries has tended to benefit the least-educated and lowest-paid workers relatively little.[36] According to this view, macroeconomic policies that lower the unemployment rate are important in raising average wage rates and annual earnings. But to substantially reduce poverty, such policies must be supplemented by additional policies for low-wage workers.

A comparison of Figures 12 and 13 reveals that most workers, especially those toward the bottom of the wage-rate distribution, fared worse during the economic recovery of the 1980s than they did during the 1990s recovery. These figures allow us to compare patterns of both wage-rate growth and wage-rate inequality.

Wage growth was higher in the recovery of the 1990s than in the recovery of the 1980s. For both male and female workers (Figure 13), wage-rate increases between 1993 and 2000 were above 9 percent at all percentiles. In contrast, for male workers during the 1980s recovery, wage-rate increases (Figure 12) were only 5 percent at the 90th percentile and were negative or close to zero for all workers up to the 80th percentile. For women, wage-rate growth was positive at all points above the 15th percentile during the 1980s recovery. But the rate of increase was higher toward the bottom of the distribution during the 1990s expansion—between 1982 and 1989, wage rates at the 20th percentile grew by 4 percent, compared with 12 percent at the 20th percentile between 1993 and 2000.

The differences in the slopes of the lines in Figures 12 and 13 show that wage inequality for both male and female workers increased more during the recovery of the 1980s than during the 1990s recovery. The lines in Figure 12 are upward sloping, indicating that wage growth was higher during the 1980s for workers toward the top of the wage distribution than for those toward the bottom of the wage distribution. Figure 13 (page 66), however, shows relatively flat lines, indicating that wage growth was spread fairly evenly throughout the distribution during the 1990s.

We now distinguish between *cyclical* changes related to the expansion and contraction of the economy during the business cycle and *secular* changes related to long-run trends in the economy.

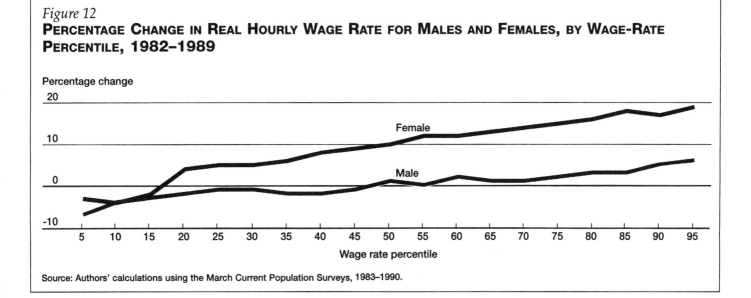

Figure 12

PERCENTAGE CHANGE IN REAL HOURLY WAGE RATE FOR MALES AND FEMALES, BY WAGE-RATE PERCENTILE, 1982–1989

Source: Authors' calculations using the March Current Population Surveys, 1983–1990.

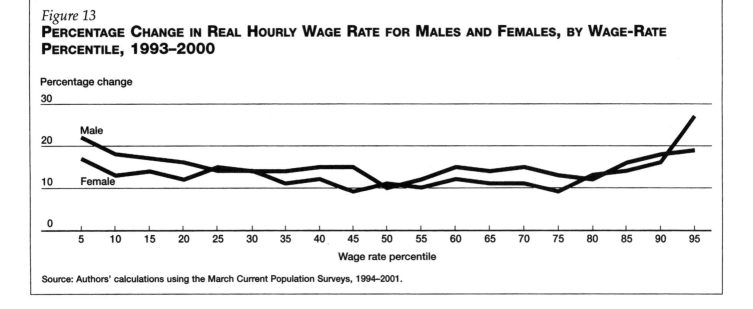

Figure 13

PERCENTAGE CHANGE IN REAL HOURLY WAGE RATE FOR MALES AND FEMALES, BY WAGE-RATE PERCENTILE, 1993–2000

Percentage change

Source: Authors' calculations using the March Current Population Surveys, 1994–2001.

Figure 14 plots the P90/P10 ratio of male wages (on the y-axis) against the employment to population ratio (on the x-axis) for males over age 20. During a recession, the economy contracts and the employment rate falls, so a movement to the left along the x-axis in Figure 14 indicates a recessionary period; a movement to the right indicates an increase in the employment rate associated with an economic expansion. If wage-

rate inequality is affected by the business cycle, then decreases in the employment rate will be accompanied by increased inequality, indicated by an upward-sloping line. This means that the wage rates of workers at P10 fall more than those of workers at P90 during recessions. Long-run increases in wage-rate inequality (secular changes) are reflected by upward shifts in the line, indicating that inequality is higher at a given

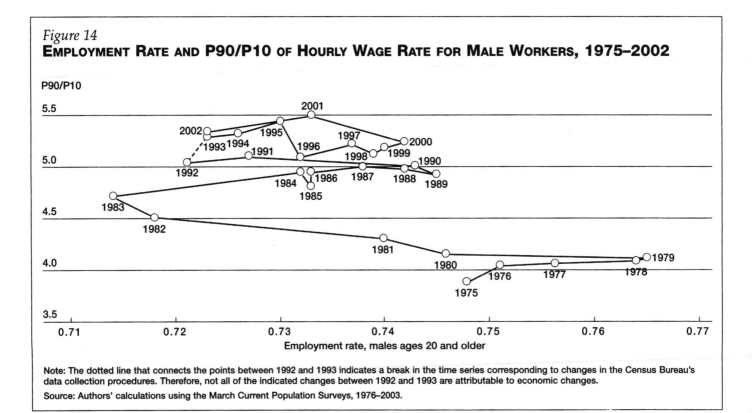

Figure 14

EMPLOYMENT RATE AND P90/P10 OF HOURLY WAGE RATE FOR MALE WORKERS, 1975–2002

P90/P10

Note: The dotted line that connects the points between 1992 and 1993 indicates a break in the time series corresponding to changes in the Census Bureau's data collection procedures. Therefore, not all of the indicated changes between 1992 and 1993 are attributable to economic changes.

Source: Authors' calculations using the March Current Population Surveys, 1976–2003.

employment rate regardless of whether the economy is in a recession or a recovery.

From 1975 to 1979, the employment rate increased from 74.8 to 76.5 percent (the high point during the period) and the P90/P10 ratio increased from 3.9 to 4.1. This increase in inequality does not reflect a cyclical change because it occurred during an expansion. In contrast, the period from 1980 to 1983 was marked by two recessions. The employment rate fell by 5.1 points between 1979 and 1983 to 71.4 percent (the low point during the period), and the P90/P10 increase of 0.6 points to 4.7 represents a cyclical change due to recession. The employment rate increased by 3.1 points during the 1983-1989 expansion, but this increase was accompanied by another secular increase in the P90/P10 ratio, to 4.9.

During the recession of the early 1990s, the employment rate fell again, but the P90/P10 ratio did not increase by much. There was a 0.3 percentage point increase in wage inequality between 1992 and 1993, but this increase also coincides with the change in CPS data-collection methods—so one cannot tell how much of this increase can be attributed to real economic changes and how much to changes in measurement procedures. By the end of the 1990s expansion, however, the employment rate had risen back to around 74 percent (the same level as at the end of the 1980s expansion). The 1990s expansion produced only a slight decline in wage inequality, from 5.3 to 5.2 between 1993 and 2000. As the economy went through another recession, the P90/P10 ratio increased and was higher in 2002 than in 2000. In essence, wage-rate inequality did not decrease during the 1990s recovery.

Roughly half of the increase in wage inequality over the 1975–2002 period occurred between 1979 and 1989. But Figure 14 shows that, at any given employment rate, the P90/P10 ratio was higher in later years than in earlier years. Inequality increased most during the recessions of the early 1980s, but did not decline in subsequent expansions. And even though the economy of the 1990s was as good as it had been since the 1960s, low-wage male workers did not gain enough to significantly close the gap between them and high-wage workers. This analysis suggests that increased wage inequality primarily reflects long-run secular changes in labor markets, not fluctuations attributable to the business cycle.

Most economists agree that a number of factors have contributed to long-run changes in labor market outcomes, although there is disagreement over the importance of various factors that have contributed to increased inequality. Labor-saving technological changes have simultaneously increased the demand for skilled workers who can run sophisticated equipment and reduced the demand for less-skilled workers, many of whom have been displaced by automation. Global competition has increased worldwide demand for the goods and services produced in the United States by skilled workers in high-tech industries and financial services. Lower-skilled workers in U.S. manufacturing industries increasingly compete with and are displaced by lower-paid production workers in developing countries. Immigration has also increased the size of the low-wage workforce and the competition for low-skilled jobs that remain in the United States. And institutional changes—such as the decline in the real value of the minimum wage and shrinking unionization rates—also have moved the economy in the direction of lower real wages for less-skilled workers and higher earnings inequality.[37]

CHANGES IN WAGE-RATE INEQUALITY

The increased wage inequality among all male workers and among all female workers is attributable to changes in inequality both between groups of workers (for example, high school graduates compared with college graduates, or African Americans compared with whites) and within groups (for instance, increased inequality among white male high school graduates). To further explore these changes, we estimated a set of standard log wage-rate equations (results not shown) for workers between the ages of 22 and 62. These equations allow us to examine how different groups of workers have fared over the last quarter-century.[38]

Gender Differentials

As shown earlier, mean wage rates for females grew faster than those for males over the entire period. As a result, the male/female wage-rate gap declined. This decline was partially due to increases in human capital of working women, reflected in their increased education and labor force experience (both in absolute terms and relative to the education and experience of men). But when we hold these factors constant, the decline in the male/female wage-rate gap also reflects an increase in the wage rates of women workers relative to male workers. This gap closed steadily from 47 percent in 1975 to 27 percent in 1993.

However, this decline in the female/male wage-rate differential halted after 1993, as the real wage rates of men began to increase during the economic boom of the 1990s after almost 20 years of decline and/or stagnation. As a result, the gender wage-rate gap was about the same in 2002 (25 percent) as it had been at the start of the 1990s expansion.

The gender gap in annual earnings is affected both by the changes in the wage-rate differential and by changes in the hours women work compared with those men work. The gender gap in annual earnings fell even more than the wage-rate gap over the period in question, because women increased their hours of work relative to the hours worked by men. Between 1975 and 2002, the percentage of women between the ages of 22 and 62 who worked at some time during the year increased from 57 percent to 72 percent. For men, there was no upward trend, as the percentage working in 2002 was the same as in 1975—82 percent. The mean annual hours of working women also increased, while the hours of working men remained constant. Among all women in this age group, average annual hours worked increased from 920 to 1,353 hours per year, while hours for men stayed constant at 1,869.

Racial/Ethnic Differentials

If we hold personal characteristics constant, we find there was little change in the black/white male, the black/white female, the Hispanic/white male, and Hispanic/white female wage-rate differentials from 1975 to 2002. The black/white female wage rate gap had virtually closed by the mid-1970s before increasing to 7 percent in 1993 and then falling back to 4 percent in 2002. The Hispanic/white female wage-rate gap was 4 percent in the mid-1970s and 9 percent in 2002.

In every year studied, the black/white male and Hispanic/white male wage-rate gap is much greater than the black/white female gap, and the Hispanic/white male wage-rate gap is much greater than the gap between Hispanic females and white females. For African Americans, the gap increased from 15 percent in 1975 to about 20 percent during the 1980s recession, before falling in 2002 to 16 percent. For Hispanic men, the size and pattern of their income gap with white males is quite similar to that of African American men to white males. Hispanic men had 16 percent less wages than white males in the mid-1970s, 20 percent less in the mid-1990s, and 17 percent less in 2002.

At the end of the 20th century, an African American or Hispanic man with the same education, experience, and region of residence as a white man earned on average 84 cents for every dollar earned by that white man. Holding education, experience, and region of residence constant, an African American woman earned 96 cents and an Hispanic woman earned 91 cents for every dollar earned by a white woman.[39]

The annual earnings gaps between black and white men and Hispanic and white men are greater than the wage-rate gaps because, on average, black men and Hispanic men work fewer hours per year than white men. In 2002, for example, white men worked an average of 1,941 hours annually, compared with black men at 1,533 hours (20 percent less) and Hispanic men at 1,798 hours (7 percent less).

On the other hand, wage-rate gaps and annual earnings gaps between black and white women are similar because black women and white women work similar hours on average. In 2002, white women worked an

average of 1,392 hours per year, while black women averaged 1,399 hours of work. The Hispanic/white annual earnings gap is higher than the wage-rate gap because Hispanic women worked 1,146 hours—18 percent less than white non-Hispanic women—in 2002.

Differentials Between Education Groups

The increased wage inequality of the 1980s reflected a large increase in the *returns to a college education* (the increase in wages attributable to having a college degree relative to a high school degree) and a lesser increase in the *returns to experience*. Figure 15 shows the returns to a college degree relative to a high school degree for male and female workers between the ages of 22 and 62. The patterns shown are quite similar for male and female workers, with the returns to a college degree for men lower than those for women in every year. One reason for the lower relative return to education for men in any year is the availability of relatively high-paying manufacturing jobs that employ high school graduates, mainly men. These jobs increase the average wage rate of male high school graduates and lower the relative return to college for men more than they do for women.

The benefits of having a college degree relative to having a high school degree fell by a few percentage points between 1975 and 1979 for both men and women. However, between 1979 and 1989, this "college differential" in mean wage rates increased from 21 percent to 35 percent for male workers and from 29 percent to 45 percent for female workers. These differentials also rose in the 1990s, but at a slower rate, reaching 44 percent for males and 49 percent for females in 2002. Thus, one factor that accounted for the rising wage-rate inequality of the 1980s—the college premium—was still trending upward during the 1990s, but exerting less upward pressure on the wage differential than in the 1980s.

From 1975 to 2002, the college/high-school graduate annual earnings differential for men rose even more than the wage-rate differential (data not shown), since the percentage of men who did not work during the year increased somewhat for high school graduates but decreased somewhat for college graduates. For women, there were large increases in labor force participation for workers at all education levels, so the trend in the college/high-school annual earnings differential was similar to that of the wage-rate differential.

Changes in Within-Group Wage-Rate Inequality

Wage-rate inequality increased during the 1980s—not only among those with different observable traits (such as gender, race, ethnicity, experience, and education), but also within groups of workers with the same gender, race, ethnicity, experience, and education.[40]

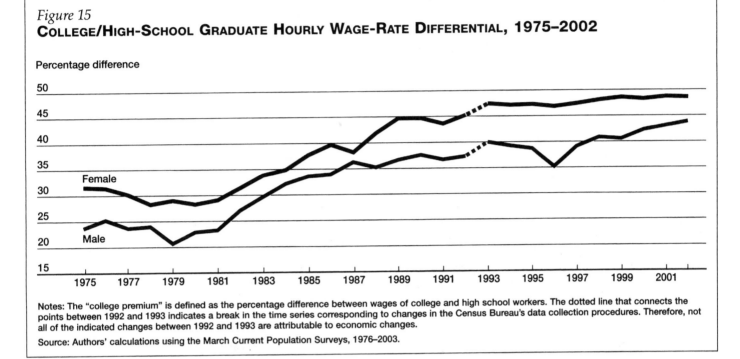

Figure 15
COLLEGE/HIGH-SCHOOL GRADUATE HOURLY WAGE-RATE DIFFERENTIAL, 1975–2002

Percentage difference

Notes: The "college premium" is defined as the percentage difference between wages of college and high school workers. The dotted line that connects the points between 1992 and 1993 indicates a break in the time series corresponding to changes in the Census Bureau's data collection procedures. Therefore, not all of the indicated changes between 1992 and 1993 are attributable to economic changes.

Source: Authors' calculations using the March Current Population Surveys, 1976–2003.

Figure 16 plots the P90 and P10 of the regression residuals for male and female workers. The series for both the P90 and the P10 are benchmarked to equal 1.00 in 1975 in order to express trends relative to this baseline value. For example, the indexed value for the P90 for males goes up by 10.4 percent between 1975 and 1985 (from 1.000 to 1.104). Each point in Figure 16 represents the wage a person at this point in the distribution would receive in each year, compared with the wage a person with the same characteristics would have received in 1975. A male with a wage rate higher than the other 90 percent of males with the same characteristics in 1985 had wages that were 10.4 percent higher than a comparable man at the top of the distribution 10 years earlier.

The patterns are striking. For men and women at the bottom of the income distribution and with the same characteristics, wage rates fell continuously from 1975

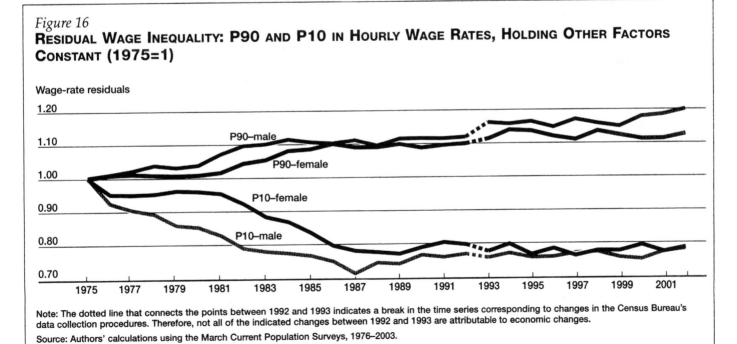

Figure 16
RESIDUAL WAGE INEQUALITY: P90 AND P10 IN HOURLY WAGE RATES, HOLDING OTHER FACTORS CONSTANT (1975=1)

Wage-rate residuals

Note: The dotted line that connects the points between 1992 and 1993 indicates a break in the time series corresponding to changes in the Census Bureau's data collection procedures. Therefore, not all of the indicated changes between 1992 and 1993 are attributable to economic changes.

Source: Authors' calculations using the March Current Population Surveys, 1976–2003.

through the late 1980s, at which point a male at the 10th percentile had a wage rate that was roughly 30 percent lower than a similar male worker at the 10th percentile in 1975. For a woman at the 10th percentile, the decline in wage rate was 25 percent. The P10 of the residuals then stabilized, remaining relatively constant for both men and women throughout the 1990s, with the value in 2002 about 20 percent lower than the 1975 value for both genders.

In contrast, the wage rate at the 90th percentile of the within-group distribution increased from 1975 through the mid-1980s, at which time it was roughly 10 percent higher for both males and females than it had been in 1975. The relative position of the 90th percentile wage rates for both sexes then stabilized, rising only between 1992 and 1993 (a rise that coincides with the change in CPS survey procedures). This pattern indicates that within-group inequality among people with the same characteristics stopped increasing until the end of the 1990s, when the P90 for males increased from 1.15 to 1.20 between 1999 and 2002, compared with the 1975 benchmark of 1.00.

If within-group inequality were to converge back to the level of the mid-1970s, those workers at the bottom of the income distribution would have to experience wage growth that exceeds that of those at the top of the distribution by about 30 percent for both male and female workers. This convergence would require a pattern of wage-rate changes unlike anything that has been experienced in the last several decades.

Changes in Annual Earnings Inequality

As we mentioned earlier, labor economists focus primarily on the distribution of wage rates, as these changes reflect changes in labor demand, labor supply, and/or institutional wage-setting mechanisms. We are also interested in changes in the distribution of annual earnings, as these changes provide the link between labor market outcomes and the distribution of family income. Because annual earnings make up about three-quarters of family income, changes in the distribution of annual earnings have a large effect on the poverty rate.

Annual earnings are by definition equal to hourly wage rates times annual hours worked. Changes in either component will affect annual earnings inequality. If annual hours increase the most for those with the highest wage rates, then changes in hours reinforce the inequality-increasing effects of the wage-rate changes discussed above, and earnings inequality will increase more than wage inequality. If, however, low-wage earners increase their hours of work to offset their real wage-rate losses and maintain their living standards (assuming that employers allow them to work the additional hours), then earnings inequality will not increase as much as wage-rate inequality.

We examined changes in annual hours worked over the 1975-2002 period (data not shown). For men at the 90th wage-rate percentile, annual hours worked increased by 8 percent; but for men at the 10th percentile, annual hours worked increased by less than 1 percent. Thus, changes in hours did not offset the dramatic rise in wage-rate inequality among male workers.

On the other hand, relative changes in annual hours that women worked reduced inequality over the long run. Women at P10 increased their annual hours by 47 percent over the period, while those at P90 increased their hours by 18 percent. Because women at P10 worked less than those at P90 in every year, annual earnings inequality is greater than wage-rate inequality in any year. However, the convergence in annual hours between low-wage and high-wage workers contributed to a decline in annual earnings inequality for women. The P90/P10 ratio of hourly wages increased by 32 percent from 1975 to 2002, whereas the ratio for annual earnings actually declined by 37 percent.

Changes in Family Income Inequality

Changes in the distribution of male and female annual earnings affect the distribution of family income—but these changes can be offset or reinforced by changes in the level and distribution of other income sources. For example, the distribution of family income for married couples is affected by the earnings of both spouses. If increases in wives' earnings are concentrated in families with low-earning husbands, then the trend toward increased male earnings inequality will be reduced. But there were no significant factors that reduced family income inequality from 1975 to 2002. The last quarter of the 20th century was one of significant increases in inequality of wage rates, annual earnings, and family income adjusted for family size.

Figure 17 presents the P90/P10 ratio for the distribution of family income adjusted for family size for all persons from 1975 to 2002. The P90/P10 ratio is benchmarked to 1.00 in 1975. Family income inequality rose throughout the period, reaching 1.46 in 2002—indicating that the gap between the top and the bottom was 46 percent higher that year than in 1975.

As with the labor market outcomes reviewed earlier, most of the increase in inequality occurred during the recession of the early 1980s. The P90/P10 ratio increased from 1.03 to 1.30 between 1979 and 1982, as the unemployment rate rose from 5.8 percent to 9.7 percent—the highest annual unemployment rate since the Great Depression of the 1930s. And the ratio continued to increase during the economic recovery of the 1980s and fell only slightly during the economic recovery of the 1990s. In 2002, a family at P90 had an income that was 9.2 times that of a family at P10. In 1975, this ratio had been 6.3.

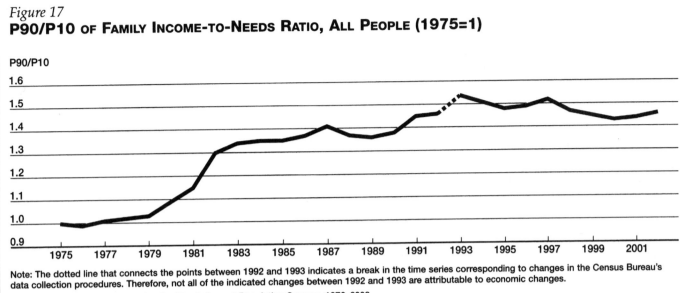

Figure 17

P90/P10 OF FAMILY INCOME-TO-NEEDS RATIO, ALL PEOPLE (1975=1)

Note: The dotted line that connects the points between 1992 and 1993 indicates a break in the time series corresponding to changes in the Census Bureau's data collection procedures. Therefore, not all of the indicated changes between 1992 and 1993 are attributable to economic changes.

Source: Authors' calculations using the March Current Population Surveys, 1976–2003.

FAMILY INCOME, DEMOGRAPHIC CHANGES, AND POVERTY

We have shown that the period between 1975 and 2002 was one of slow economic growth and rising income inequality. We now analyze how changes in the level and distribution of family income adjusted for family size and changes in the demographic composition of the population account for changes in the poverty rate. We follow a procedure described in our earlier research that decomposes changes in poverty into components that reflect changes in mean income, income inequality, and the demographic composition of the population.[41]

To derive these three components of change in the poverty rate, we carry out the following calculations. First, we estimate what the impact of growth in mean family income (adjusted by family size) would have been had there been no changes in either inequality or in the demographic composition of the population. To obtain this counterfactual, we first calculate what the poverty rate for all persons would have been if adjusted family income had grown at the same rate for all families and if the demographic composition had remained constant. The difference between this simulated rate and the actual 1975 rate is the change in poverty that is accounted for by income growth.

We then contrast this simulated poverty rate with a second simulated rate that incorporates actual demographic changes. The difference between these two simulated poverty rates is the change in the poverty rate accounted for by demographic changes. The difference between the second simulated poverty rate and the

Table 1

SOURCES OF CHANGE IN THE POVERTY RATE FOR ALL PEOPLE, 1975–2002

	1975–2002
(1) Observed Percentage Point Change in Poverty Rate	-2.3
% point change owing to:	
(2) Income Changes	-4.3
(a) Growth in mean adjusted income	-6.1
(b) Change in income inequality	1.8
(3) Demographic Changes	2.0
(a) Racial/ethnic composition	1.0
(b) Family structure composition	1.2
(c) Interaction	-0.2

Source: Authors' calculations using the March Current Population Surveys, 1976–2003.

actual 2002 rate is the change in poverty that is accounted for by changes in income inequality.[42]

The first row in Table 1 shows that the poverty rate fell by 2.3 percentage points between 1975 and 2002, from 12.1 percent to 9.8 percent of all people. If economic growth had been equally shared across all families and individuals and if there had been no demographic changes, the poverty rate would have fallen instead by 6.1 percentage points to 6.0 percent. Increases in income inequality added 1.8 points to the poverty rate, offsetting roughly one-third of the poverty-reducing impact of income growth.

Demographic changes also increased poverty. A larger percentage of the population now lives in family units whose heads have a higher-than-average poverty rate (such as Hispanics and female-headed families). In contrast, a smaller percentage of the population lives in units headed by white non-Hispanic married couples, whose poverty rate is lower than that of any of the other 15 demographic groups. Between 1975 and 2002, the percentage living in families headed by nonelderly white males fell from 61 percent to 43 percent. The percentage living in a family whose head was Hispanic increased from 5 percent to 13 percent; the percentage living in families headed by a nonelderly female increased from 10 percent to 13 percent.

Demographic changes added 2.0 points to the poverty rate, making these changes about as important as rising inequality. We can divide the effect of demographic changes into two components. The first—changes in the racial/ethnic composition of the population, or the decline in the percentage of all persons who are white non-Hispanics—is associated with a 1.0 percentage point increase in poverty. The second—changes in family structure, or the decline in the percentage of all persons who live in nonelderly male-headed families—is associated with a 1.2 percentage point increase in poverty.

These results can be placed in historical context. In earlier research, we presented a similar decomposition of the decline in poverty between 1949 and 1969.[43] Over those two decades, the poverty rate fell by more than 25 percentage points, from 39.7 percent to 14.4 percent. Income growth was so rapid that, if it had been equally shared across all families and individuals, poverty would have fallen by 21.4 points. During this period, people at the bottom of the income distribution actually experienced higher income-to-needs increases than people at the top of the scale—and this reduction in inequality contributed an additional 5.5 percentage point drop in poverty. Between 1949 and 1969, demographic changes added 1.2 percentage points to the poverty rate.

Therefore, economic changes, not demographic changes, account for the difference between the rapidly declining poverty rate from 1949 to 1969 and the slowly declining poverty rate of the last quarter of the 20th century. Poverty fell so much more in the first period than in the second period because of rapid economic growth and declining inequality.

We conducted another simulation that included the observed demographic changes between 1975 and 2002 but was based on the assumption that the economic performance of the last 27 years was similar to that of the 1949-1969 period. That is, we assumed that incomes had grown just as rapidly in recent years as it had during the economic "golden age" of the two decades following World War II. This simulation assumes that family income adjusted for family size had doubled between 1975 and 2002, instead of

increasing by 53 percent, and also assumes that income inequality was the same as it was in 1975.

We mentioned earlier that planners of the War on Poverty expected the official poverty rate to fall dramatically in the 1970s and 1980s, based on the assumption that economic growth would continue to be rapid and that inequality would not increase. This simulation suggests that these expectations would have been fulfilled had economic growth not slowed and had inequality not increased. Even with the observed changes in the demographic composition of the population, the poverty rate in 2002 would have been 4.6 percent instead of 9.8 percent.[44] This simulated rate is quite similar to the poverty rate of other industrialized countries.[45]

SUMMARY

Poverty remains high because economic growth in the last quarter of the 20th century was so much slower and inequality so much higher than in the previous quarter-century. While the experience of the 1990s was more favorable than that of the 1980s, there are no prospects—given existing labor market conditions and public policies—for significant declines in poverty or a substantial reduction of inequality in wage rates, annual earnings, or family income.

While most presidents since Lyndon Johnson have given major addresses on welfare reform, we are not aware of any major presidential addresses that focused on antipoverty policies. Since the Nixon administration, poverty has fallen from the top of the public's agenda to its periphery. A recent survey found that only 10 percent of the population considered poverty, welfare, or a similar issue as one of the top two issues government should address. More than 20 percent of the survey's respondents cited health care, education, or tax reform as one of their top two public policy issues.[46]

In contrast to the U.S. approach, British Prime Minister Tony Blair made a Johnsonian "War on Poverty" pledge in 1999. As Blair put it, "Our historic aim will be for ours to be the first generation to end child poverty, and it will take a generation. It is a 20-year mission but I believe it can be done."[47] The antipoverty policies enacted by the Blair government are based to a significant extent on American poverty policy research. For example, the U.S. experience in moving recipients from welfare to work was very influential with Blair's advisers. However, as some analysts have noted, the Blair government used the theme "work for those who can, security for those who cannot" to demonstrate its desire both to reform welfare and to reduce poverty.[48]

The Blair government established new programs and increased funding for existing programs in order to promote work, to increase investments in children, and to expand opportunity and intergenerational mobility. In response to these new initiatives, child poverty in the United Kingdom has fallen dramatically in recent years.

As this recent example demonstrates, if there is a political will to reduce poverty, there are many public policies that could be put in place in the United States to achieve President Johnson's 1964 goal—the elimination of income poverty within a generation.

ACKNOWLEDGMENTS

Yuanyuan Chen, Petia Petrova, and Olga Sorokino provided outstanding research assistance for this article; Joanna Parnes prepared the charts. Reynolds Farley, John Haaga, Deborah Reed, Kristin Seefeldt, and Lesley Turner provided helpful comments on a previous draft. This research was supported by funds provided by the Russell Sage Foundation.

REFERENCES

If provided by the authors, additional text and data associated with this report are available at www.prb.org/AmericanPeople.

1. John Kenneth Galbraith, *The Affluent Society* (New York: New American Library, 1959); Michael Harrington, *The Other America: Poverty in the United States* (New York: Macmillan, 1962); and Robert Lampman, *The Low Income Population and Economic Growth*, U.S. Congress Joint Economic Committee Study Paper no. 12 (Washington, DC: U.S. Government Printing Office (USGPO), 1959).

2. U.S. Council of Economic Advisers, *Economic Report of the President* (Washington, DC: USGPO, 1964): 15.

3. U.S. Census Bureau, accessed online at www.census.gov/hhes/income/histinc/f03.html, on Dec. 1, 2004.

4. Robert Lampman, *Ends and Means of Reducing Income Poverty* (Chicago: Markham, 1971): 49-50.

5. Henry Aaron, *Politics and the Professors* (Washington, DC: Brookings Institution, 1978): 17.

6. Christopher Jencks, "Does Inequality Matter?" *Daedalus* 131, no. 1 (2002): 49.

7. Jencks, "Does Inequality Matter?": 50.

8. Lee Rainwater and Timothy M. Smeeding, *Poor Kids in a Rich Country: America's Children in Comparative Perspective* (New York: Russell Sage Foundation, 2004).

9. John Iceland, "Why Poverty Remains High: The Role of Income Growth, Economic Inequality, and Changes in Family Structure, 1949-1999," *Demography* 40, no. 3: 499-519.

10. Lampman, *Ends and Means of Reducing Income Poverty*: 49.

11. For a history and critique of the official poverty line and a proposal for a new measure of poverty, see Robert Michael and Connie Citro, *Measuring Poverty: A New Approach* (Washington, DC: National Academies Press, 1995).

12. Gary Burtless and Timothy M. Smeeding, "The Level, Trend and Composition of Poverty," in *Understanding Poverty*, ed. Sheldon Danziger and Robert Haveman (Cambridge, MA: Harvard University Press, 2002): 46.

13. Burtless and Smeeding show that annual changes in the official poverty series and a series using the CPI-U-RS are similar from 1969 to 1998. Both series show large increases in poverty during the recessions of the early 1980s and the early 1990s, and declines in the rate during the ensuing economic recoveries. Yet both series show little progress against poverty between the mid-1970s and the late 1990s. See Burtless and Smeeding, "The Level, Trend and Composition of Poverty": 45-46.

14. Any threshold for defining the rich or poor is arbitrary. In previous research, we experimented with setting the threshold for the rich at eight or nine times the poverty line instead of seven times and found little difference in long-run trends in the proportion of people who are rich. Sheldon Danziger and Peter Gottschalk, *America Unequal* (Cambridge, MA: Harvard University Press, 1995); and Sheldon Danziger, Peter Gottschalk, and Eugene Smolensky, "How the Rich Have Fared, 1973-1987," *American Economic Review* 79, no. 2 (1989): 310-14.

15. The term "hourly wage rates" is defined as annual earnings divided by the product of weeks worked last year and usual hours worked per week.

16. This section draws heavily from Danziger and Gottschalk, *America Unequal*.

17. Frank Levy, *Dollars and Dreams: The Changing American Income Distribution* (New York: Russell Sage Foundation, 1987).

18. U.S. Council of Economic Advisers, *Economic Report of the President* (Washington, DC: USGPO, 1982): 44.

19. Real wages and government benefits for the nonelderly have declined in real terms over the past 30 years because they tend not to be indexed for inflation. This real decline is particularly true for the minimum wage and cash welfare benefits, as these payments tend to be fixed in nominal terms and only change as a result of federal and/or state legislation.

20. Employment rates are defined as the total number of persons over the age of 16 who are employed divided by the civilian population over age 16. Thus, the employment rate depends both on the unemployment rate and the labor force participation rate.

21. Timothy M. Smeeding, Lee Rainwater, and Gary Burtless, "United States Poverty in a Cross-National Context," in *Understanding Poverty*, ed. Sheldon Danziger and Robert Haveman (Cambridge, MA: Harvard University Press, 2002). For detailed information on trends in relative poverty for the United States and other industrialized countries as well as information about how government social programs vary across countries, see Lee Rainwater and Timothy M. Smeeding, *Poor Kids in a Rich Country*.

22. Lampman, *Ends and Means of Reducing Income Poverty*; and James Tobin, "It Can Be Done! Conquering Poverty in the U.S. by 1976," *New Republic*, June 3, 1976.

23. If we had used a threshold of eight times the poverty line instead of seven times the line to define the rich, the increase would have been from 1.4 percent to 14.4 percent between 1959 and 1999 rather than from 1.9 percent to 18.9 percent, as shown in Figure 1.

24. Reynolds Farley and Walter Allen, *The Color Line and the Quality of Life in America* (New York: Russell Sage Foundation, 1987); Stanley Lieberson and Mary Waters, *From Many Strands: Ethnic and Racial Groups in Contemporary America* (New York: Russell Sage Foundation, 1988); and Frank Bean and Marta Tienda, *The Hispanic Population of the United States* (New York: Russell Sage Foundation, 1987).

25. Gerald Jaynes and Robin Williams, eds., *A Common Destiny: Blacks and American Society* (Washington, DC: National Academies Press, 1989).

26. James Smith and Barry Edmonston, *The New Americans: Economic, Demographic, and Fiscal Effects of Immigration* (Washington, DC: National Academies Press, 1997).

27. Philip Martin and Elizabeth Midgley, "Immigration: Shaping and Reshaping America," *Population Bulletin* 58, no. 2 (2003).

28. Martin and Midgley, "Immigration: Shaping and Reshaping America."

29. George J. Borjas, *Heaven's Door: Immigration Policy and the American Economy* (Princeton, NJ: Princeton University Press, 1999); and Steven A. Camarota, "Importing Poverty: Immigration's Impact on the Size and Growth of the Poor Population in the United States," *Center Paper* 15 (Washington, DC: Center for Immigration Studies, 1999).

30. The Census Bureau does not obtain a full count of all immigrant noncitizens, since illegal immigrants are likely to avoid contact with government authorities.

31. Martin and Midgley, "Immigration: Shaping and Reshaping America."

32. Martha Derthick, *Policy Making for Social Security* (Washington, DC: Brookings Institution, 1979): 431-32.

33. Eugene Smolensky, Sheldon Danziger, and Peter Gottschalk, "The Declining Significance of Age in the United States: Trends in the Well-Being of Children and the Elderly Since 1939," in *The Vulnerable*, ed. John Palmer, Timothy Smeeding, and Barbara Boyle Torrey (Washington, DC: Urban Institute Press, 1988).

34. Rainwater and Smeeding, *Poor Kids in a Rich Country*.

35. A committee of economists convened by the National Bureau of Economic Research (NBER) sets the official dates for the beginning and end of recessions and economic recoveries. The NBER defines a recession as a significant decline in economic activity spread across the economy and lasting for more than a few months. During the last quarter-century, there have been four recessions: January 1980–July 1980; July 1981–November 1982; July 1990–March 1991; and March 2001–November 2001.

36. Danziger and Gottschalk, *America Unequal*; and Frank Levy and Richard Murnane, *The New Division of Labor: How Computers are Creating the Next Job Market* (Princeton, NJ: Princeton University Press, 2004).

37. Danziger and Gottschalk, *America Unequal*; Eileen Appelbaum, Annette Bernhardt, and Richard Murnane, eds., *Low-Wage America: How Employers Are Reshaping Opportunity in the Workplace* (New York: Russell Sage Foundation, 2003); and Levy and Murnane, *The New Division of Labor*.

38. The framework for these equations is as follows: The dependent variable is the natural logarithm of the hourly wage rate. The independent variables include a set of education dummies ("completed less than a high school degree," "high school degree," "some college," "college," and "more than college"); a quadratic in experience (defined as age minus years of completed schooling minus 6); a gender dummy; dummies for race and ethnicity ("white non-Hispanic," "black non-Hispanic," "Other non-Hispanic," and "Hispanic"); and regional dummies ("Northeast," "Midwest," "South," and "West"). These regressions were estimated separately for each year from 1975 to 2002.

The estimated regression coefficients represent wage-rate differences between groups in any year. For example, the coefficient on the dummy variable indicating that the worker is a woman represents for that year the estimated wage-rate differential between female and male workers (holding race and ethnicity, education and experience, and region constant). Similarly, the estimated coefficients on other variables hold other factors constant while indicating race and ethnicity differentials or returns to education and experience. If the size of a coefficient is rising over time, it means that the wage-rate gap between that group and the reference group is increasing.

Gender, race or ethnicity, and educational differences represent the between-group portion of wage-rate inequality. Within-group inequality is the remaining variation in wage rates (holding all factors constant), and is measured by the standard deviation of the regression residuals.

39. We cannot compute hourly wage rates prior to 1975. Peter Gottschalk reports that the earnings gap between full-time black workers and full-time non-black workers declined by 2.1 percentage points per year from the mid-1960s to the mid-1970s. This gap decline is greater than the 0.4 points per year decline in the black/white wage gap reported here. The difference is attributable, in part, to the greater cyclicality of black work hours relative to white hours. See Peter Gottschalk, "Inequality, Income, Growth, and Mobility: The Basic Facts," *Journal of Economic Perspectives* 11, no. 2 (1997): 21-24

40. The growth in within-group inequality is reflected by a wider dispersion of the residuals in the log wage regressions. If there were no within-group inequality, then every individual in a specific group (such as people of the same gender, race, ethnicity, experience, and education) would have the same wage rate. This is not the case, as there is substantial dispersion in wage rates even among persons with the same characteristics. The dispersion around the mean wage rate for the group is measured by the dispersion of the residuals around the regression line.

41. Danziger and Gottschalk, *America Unequal*.

42. In order to determine the impact of demographic change, we divide all individuals into one of 16 mutually exclusive demographic groups based on the characteristics of their family head. These groups are based on classifying family heads into one of four race/ethnicity categories (white non-Hispanic, black non-Hispanic, other non-Hispanic, and Hispanic) and then further dividing each of the four groups into four categories based on the age/gender of the family's head

(nonelderly male family heads; nonelderly female family heads; nonelderly unrelated individuals; and the elderly, both as heads of families and as unrelated individuals). In all calculations we weight by the number of people in the family so that we can derive the poverty rate for all people.

We begin with the 1975 microdata for each family and calculate a simulated income distribution for 2002 in which every unit's income is increased by the observed growth in adjusted family income over the entire time period—in other words, by 53 percent, as the mean family income-to-needs ratio increased from 3.15 to 4.82 between 1975 and 2002. Because this simulation uses the 1975 data, there is by definition no demographic change. Also, because all families experienced the same percentage increase in income relative to the poverty line, there is no change in inequality. These simulated data have a different poverty rate—one that is lower because of the uniform income growth. The difference between this simulated poverty rate and the actual 1975 rate equals the change in poverty attributable to income growth.

Using these simulated microdata that have the 2002 mean income/poverty line, we then compute the group-specific poverty rates for the 16 demographic groups—in other words, what would have been the 2002 poverty rates for each group if only the mean had changed since 1975. Next, we take these 16 group-specific poverty rates and weight them using the 16 demographic weights that reflect their observed population shares in 2002. This second simulation of the overall poverty rate for 2002 is based on the 1975 inequality level, but with the demographic composition of the population and the mean income held at observed 2002

levels. The difference between the poverty rates from the two simulations equals the percentage point change in poverty accounted for by demographic changes. The difference between this second simulated poverty rate and the actual 2002 poverty rate is equal to the change in poverty accounted for by changes in income inequality.

43. Danziger and Gottschalk, *America Unequal*: 102.
44. Both the simulation's calculated poverty rate of 4.6 percent and the actual 2002 poverty rate of 9.8 percent cited here were calculated using CPI-U-RS adjusted poverty thresholds. Had our simulation used official poverty thresholds, it would have calculated an adjusted poverty rate of 5.5 percent for 2002, versus the official rate of 12.1 percent.
45. Smeeding, Rainwater, and Burtless have estimated absolute poverty rates of between 4 percent and 7 percent in the mid-1990s for Canada, Germany, the Netherlands, Sweden, Finland, and Norway; for the same period, they report, the United States had a poverty rate of 13.6 percent. See Smeeding, Rainwater, and Burtless, "United States Poverty in a Cross-National Context."
46. Henry J. Kaiser Family Foundation, *National Survey on Poverty in America* (2001), accessed online at www.kff.org/kaiserpolls/3118-index.cfm, on Oct. 22, 2004.
47. Tony Blair, "Beveridge Revisited: A Welfare State for the 21st Century," in *Ending Child Poverty: Popular Welfare for the 21st Century?*, ed. Robert Walker (Bristol, England: Policy Press): 17.
48. John Hills and Jane Waldfogel, "A 'Third Way' in Welfare Reform? Evidence from the United Kingdom," *Journal of Policy Analysis and Management* 23, no. 4 (2004): 765-88.

Women, Men, and Work

By Liana C. Sayer, Philip N. Cohen, and Lynne M. Casper

INTRODUCTION

In 1997, Robert Reich made what he described as one of the most painful decisions of his life. He resigned from his job as the U.S. Secretary of Labor. Why? He wanted to spend more time at his other job: being a good dad to his two teenage boys in Boston.

Two years earlier and a quarter of the way around the globe, Penny Hughes, then president of Coca-Cola U.K. and Ireland, resigned from her job to care for her two young sons and pursue other interests.

These two examples represent choices made by two people at the pinnacle of their careers in order to strike a more reasonable balance between work and family. These are of course unusually rich and successful people who can afford to resolve work and family conflict by withdrawing from paid work. But difficult work and family choices are also made by families of more modest means.

In April 2004, Zoila and Manuel Martínez testified in front of the U.S. Senate Health, Education, Labor, and Pensions Subcommittee on Children and Families about the difficulties they face arranging their lives to earn enough to support their family and to provide adequate care for their two school-age children and Zoila's diabetic mother. Zoila and Manuel work the equivalent of three full-time jobs to make ends meet; with the help of their employer, they organize their paid work schedules to maximize the time one of them can care for their children and to minimize child-care costs. While these choices are not necessarily available to all women and men, they illustrate solutions to the dilemma faced by the vast majority of people in this country as they arrange and rearrange their lives to accommodate the demands of work and family.

Work and family are the two most important domains of adulthood, and both involve time and labor. Paid work outside the home is necessary for the income it provides to purchase food, shelter, health care, and other goods and services on which individuals and families rely. Paid work also provides people with a sense of purpose and satisfaction, although it can produce stress. Unpaid work within the home—cooking, cleaning, shopping, home maintenance, and caring for children—is also necessary for the health and well-being of individuals and families. As with paid work, unpaid work provides satisfaction and fulfillment, but much of this work is mundane and tedious.

In the United States, paid and unpaid work have been historically divided along gender lines. For example, in the 1950s, men were typically breadwinners who worked outside the home for pay, and women were homemakers who worked at home to ensure the smooth functioning of everyday life. Even when families differed from this "separate spheres" arrangement, men still had primary responsibility for supporting the family whereas women had primary responsibility for childrearing and housekeeping. This arrangement was well suited to a time in which the vast majority of women and men were married, could maintain a comfortable standard of living on one salary, and could count on their partner to provide that part of work they were not doing themselves. In stark contrast, today many women and men such as Robert Reich, Penny Hughes, and the Martínezes participate in both work spheres. Increases in divorce and single parenthood,

LIANA C. SAYER is an assistant professor of sociology at the Ohio State University. Her research interests include gender inequality, relationship dynamics and outcomes, and time use. Sayer's current research focuses on gender differences in the relationship between spousal resources and marital processes and outcomes, crossnational and historical variation in gendered patterns of time use, and gender and class differences in attitudes about fertility and marriage.

PHILIP N. COHEN is an associate professor of sociology at the University of California, Irvine. He teaches in the areas of social inequality, sociological theory, and demography. His research is concentrated in two areas: families and inequality over time and across various social contexts, and macro and micro linkages in social inequality.

LYNNE M. CASPER is a health scientist administrator and demographer in the Demographic and Behavioral Sciences Branch at the National Institute of Child Health and Human Development (NICHD), where she directs the family and fertility research portfolio and the training program in population studies. She is currently building new research initiatives in the areas of work, family, health and well-being, and family change and variation. Prior to her current position, she was a senior statistician and demographer at the U.S. Census Bureau.

Note: The authors contributed equally to this report and are listed in reverse alphabetical order. The findings and opinions expressed are attributable to the authors and do not necessarily reflect those of the National Institute of Child Health and Human Development.

changes in attitudes about appropriate adult roles for women and men, changes in the economy, and rising demands for consumer goods have impelled more women and men to combine paid work and unpaid work. Although this arrangement yields positives—increased satisfaction for women from paying jobs and for men from participating more in family life—it also yields negatives, including increased time pressures, stress, and poor health outcomes.

The shift in the gender division of labor has created new work and family challenges throughout society. On an individual level, every man and woman is confronted with the challenge of arranging their lives to meet both types of work demands, and the decisions they make affect their co-workers, spouses, children, other family members, and even employers. According to a recent study, eight of 10 American adults say they have problems and stress in their lives and nearly two of three say their stress level is higher than they would like it to be.[1] Women and men who said that they are stressed out reported feeling more stress in their lives than they did even five years ago, and both blame trying to integrate work and family. Women are more likely than men to claim their lives are stressed, and the primary source of stress differs: Women blame family work more and men blame paid work more.[2] Stress weakens the body's ability to fight off sickness and also causes or worsens hypertension, cardiovascular disorders, migraine headaches, cancer, arthritis, respiratory disease, ulcers, colitis, and muscle tension. Stress is a source of anxiety, panic attacks, depression, eating disorders, hypochondria, and alcoholism, and is the second most disabling illness for workers after heart disease.[3]

Employers are aware of work-family conflicts and their effects on worker absenteeism, productivity, and turnover. Some have adopted policies and practices to deal with these issues, such as providing onsite elder care and child care, flextime and flexible work arrangements, and paid leave banks. Policymakers, too, have begun to focus on the problem, and in 2003, they introduced various bills related to work and family issues, including the Fair Minimum Wage Act of 2003, the Family Time and Workplace Flexibility Act, and the Family and Medical Leave Expansion Act. Nonetheless, the United States still lags behind other countries in the support it provides for women and men trying to integrate work and family responsibilities.

For several decades, conflicts between work and family were defined as women's issues because, since 1950, women's work and family roles have changed more dramatically than men's. Women in the 1950s, such as Marian Cunningham on "Happy Days" or June Cleaver on "Leave It to Beaver," got married and had children soon after they graduated from high school and devoted their work time exclusively to unpaid work in the home. By contrast, women in the new millennium, such as Monica, Phoebe, and Rachel on the popular television series "Friends," hold down jobs and live on their own before getting married and most remain in the labor force even after starting a family.

Compared with women, men's work lives have changed relatively little; the vast majority of men in both time periods were employed full time. Recent evidence suggests, however, that men are beginning to change their behavior in unpaid work within the home. The 1990s saw the emergence of a new "fatherhood" movement, questioning assumptions that men's family responsibilities were only financial. Many men have increased their share of family work and some have even given up their jobs entirely to become at-home-dads. Additionally, in a recent study, more than four of five young men declared that having a job schedule that allows for family time is more important to them than money, power, or prestige.[4] Yet important gender differences still exist in the time devoted to work and the type of work done, suggesting that inequalities still remain. Women continue to be less likely to work for pay, and when they do they work fewer hours than men. Women are also more likely to do unpaid family work and devote more hours to this type of work than men do.

Why has this situation changed so dramatically over such a short period of time? Far-reaching shifts in gender relations, family structure, and the economy have altered the context in which work occurs. Changing attitudes about the appropriate roles for men and women have made it more acceptable for women to engage in paid work outside the home and for men to participate in unpaid domestic work within the home. Delays in marriage, declines in fertility, and increases in cohabitation and divorce mean adults, especially women, are spending less time married and raising children and more time working for pay.[5] Increased educational levels of women, shifts in the skills required and valued by firms, and a greater demand for "female" labor have made it easier for women to find and keep good jobs. At the same time, declining wages for men with less than a college education, and the loss of manufacturing jobs (usually held by men), have increased the need for women to work for pay.[6] The demand for consumer goods and services has risen dramatically over the past several decades. For many families, no longer is one car or television enough. Home computers and CD and DVD players are now considered a must. Fifty years ago these things did not even exist.

In past decades, most research on gender and work focused on the causes and consequences of women's dramatic increase in paid work. But now that changing patterns of unpaid work among men are garnering increased attention, scholars have turned toward examining women's and men's paid and unpaid labor. Issues of gender equality, gender differences, and "appropriate" adult roles for women and men are fundamental to questions about the changing nature of work. Whether the issue is the division of labor in and out of the home, the breakdown of the traditional family and its future, the entry of women into previously male-dominated occupations, or welfare reform, the debate inevitably returns to the question of gender equality.

Sociologists and demographers have long recognized the interconnectedness of people's family and work lives. A decade ago, prominent demographer and sociologist Andrew Cherlin noted that the steady movement of married women into the labor force is the "only constant" in the turbulent work and family landscape of the last 50 years.[7] In the past decade, the pace of change in work and family lives has slowed considerably,[8] suggesting that the decisions people make about with whom to live and how, whether to work in the labor market, and how much to work—and the context of opportunities and constraints in which they make these decisions—are related in fundamental ways. But have we reached a plateau in the pervasive increase in women's paid work, and is this connected to a slowdown in the transformation of work and family lives as well? Did the trend toward greater gender similarity in employment and household labor continue through the 1990s? Has the story of gender equality changed over recent cohorts, and does it differ for people in different types of families with different skills? What has had the most impact on changing gender inequality in paid and unpaid work?

In this report, we begin by describing changes in society that set the context for changes in women's and men's paid and unpaid labor. We then assess how women's and men's work lives have changed over the past three decades and whether these lives are becoming more or less equal. We describe some of the leading theories proposed to explain the allocation across gender lines between paid and unpaid work. Because changes in family structure and skill levels have affected men and women differently, we then investigate how they have altered men's and women's paid and unpaid work. Finally, because population change occurs in part because of shifts in the composition of the population, such as in the percent of people in various family statuses, and partly because of changes in people's behaviors, we attempt to sort out which factor is the most important in driving change in women's and men's work and in reducing the gender gap in both work domains.

We concentrate mainly on the 1980 to 2000 time period because this affords the most comparable data on paid and unpaid work and family arrangements and because trends for earlier periods are well documented elsewhere.[9] Unless otherwise noted, we restrict our analysis to adults ages 25 to 54 because this is the age range during which women and men are most likely to be combining work and family responsibilities in their own households.

A CHANGING ECONOMY AND SOCIETY

Young women today begin their lives much differently than women did in the mid-20th century. Consider the life of a young woman reaching adulthood in the 1950s or early 1960s. Such a woman was likely to marry straight out of high school or take a clerical or retail sales job until she married—and was not likely to go to college. She would have moved out of her parents' home only after she married. She was likely to have children soon after she married, and in the unlikely event that she was working when she became pregnant, she would probably have quit her job and stayed home to care for her children while her husband had a steady job that paid enough to support the entire family.

Young women's lives follow a very different course today. A young woman reaching adulthood in the early 2000s is not likely to marry before her 25th birthday. She is likely to strike out on her own before marrying and may live with a partner or live on her own or with roommates before she marries. She is more likely than not to attend college and work at a paid job before and after marrying. She is not likely to drop out of the labor force after she has children, although she may curtail the number of hours she is employed to balance work and family responsibilities. She is also much more likely to divorce compared with a young woman in the 1950s, increasing the chances that she will need to work for pay to support herself and perhaps her children. Even if she remains married and prefers not to have a job, she may find she needs to work outside of the home so that the family can makes ends meet. Similar to her counterpart in the 1950s, this woman is likely to bear the responsibility for unpaid work within the home, although she is likely to devote fewer hours to housework.

Men's lives have not changed nearly as drastically, although they have experienced many of the same changes with regard to family patterns. Compared with the 1950s and 1960s, men are marrying later, having fewer children later in their lives, and are more likely to divorce. However, unlike women, most men were employed full time in the 1950s and 1960s and continue to be employed full time today. The big changes in men's lives have occurred in terms of household labor. More men today do not have spouses to perform unpaid work within the home, so they are doing it themselves. Even among married men, the amount of time spent caring for their children and doing housework has increased, in part because their wives are spending more time in paid work and thus have less time available for household work.

Although these scenarios depicting change in people's lives are truer for white and middle-class men and women than for minorities and the poor, most of these differences are matters of degree; the norms described here have been remarkably widely held. This sketch shows in broad strokes how life has changed for women and men in recent generations.

Many of the changes in when women and men finish their education, marry, have children, and enter the labor force reflect changed economic circumstances since the 1950s. After World War II, the United States enjoyed an economic boom characterized by rapid economic growth, nearly full employment, rising productivity, higher wages, low inflation, and increasing earnings. The economic realities of the 1970s and 1980s were quite different. The two decades following the 1973 oil crisis were decades of economic uncertainty marked by a shift away from manufacturing and toward services, stagnating or declining wages (especially for less-educated workers), high inflation, and a slowdown in productivity. The 1990s were just as remarkable for the turnaround: sustained prosperity and low unemployment, albeit with increased inequality in wages, but with economic growth that seems to have reached many in the poorest segments of society.[10]

Material aspirations were lower during the mid-20th century, following 15 years of reduced consumption during the Great Depression of the 1930s and the war years of the early 1940s, than they are now. Despite the labor force difficulties for unskilled workers in the 1970s and 1980s, rising affluence continued in the United States. Per capita income and family income rose even as men's wages stagnated because women contributed earnings in a growing number of families. Demand for consumer goods also continued to increase. Expectations of "minimal standards of living" continued to rise and were substantially higher than at mid-20th century. These rising expectations created additional pressures for more market work on the part of women to meet families' consumption goals.

CHANGING WORK AND FAMILY NORMS

In 1950, there was one dominant and socially acceptable way for adults to live their lives. Those who deviated could expect to be censured and stigmatized. First and foremost, adults were expected to form a family. The idealized family consisted of a homemaker-wife, a breadwinner-father, and two or more children. Most Americans shared an image of what a family should look like and how everyone should behave. These shared values reinforced the importance of the family, the institution of marriage, and the division of paid and unpaid labor along gender lines.[11] This vision of family

life showed amazing staying power, even as its economic underpinnings were eroding.

For this 1950s-style family to thrive, Americans had to support distinct gender roles and the economy had to be strong enough for a man to financially support a family on his own.[12] Government policies and business practices perpetuated this family type by reserving the best jobs for men and discriminating against working women when they married or had a baby. After 1960, women and minorities gained legal protections in the workplace and discriminatory practices began to recede. A transformation in attitudes toward family behaviors also occurred. People became more accepting of divorce, cohabitation, nonmarital childbearing, voluntary childlessness, and sex outside marriage; less certain about the universality and permanence of marriage; and more tolerant of blurred gender roles.[13] The realization that marriage is no longer the only avenue to certain benefits such as companionship, raising children, and income pooling has made marriage more of an individual choice and less a requirement for adulthood. Among many adults, cohabitation and nonmarital childbearing are now seen as acceptable alternatives.

As women have become more similar to men in the labor market, attitudes about women's labor force participation have become increasingly liberal. Since the 1970s, there has been a relatively steady increase in approval of women's paid work. Nonetheless, disapproval remains of *mothers* working outside the home, more so among men than among women and particularly when young children are involved. That is, popular ideas about women's place in the workforce have become much more supportive of paid work for women, but many people are still concerned about the consequences for children of both parents combining paid work with family responsibilities.

Data from the General Social Survey show that the percent of Americans, men or women, who disapprove of a married women working even if her husband can support her declined from about one-third to under one-fifth between 1977 and 1998 (see Table 1). A dramatic decline also occurred in the percent agreeing it is more important for a wife to help her husband's career than to have one herself. In 1977, more women than men (61 percent and 53 percent, respectively) agreed with the statement, but by 1998 agreement slipped to 19 percent for both men and women.

Men and women disagree to a greater extent as to whether it is better if a man achieves outside the home and a woman cares for home and family. Although both women and men are much less likely to agree with this gendered division of labor in 1998 than they were in 1977, slightly more men (36 percent) than women (34 percent) continue to favor specialization.

Fewer people are concerned about women combining paid work and childrearing than in the past, as

Table 1
CHANGE IN ATTITUDES ABOUT WOMEN'S ROLES AS WIFE, MOTHER, AND WORKER, 1977 AND 1998

Attitudes about gender roles	1977 % women	1977 % men	1998 % women	1998 % men
Disapprove of married woman working if her husband can support her.	35	32	18	17
Agree it is more important for a wife to help her husband's career than to have one herself.	61	53	19	19
Agree it is better for everyone if man achieves outside home and woman takes care of home and family.	63	69	34	36

Attitudes about mother's paid work and childrearing	1977 % women	1977 % men	1998 % women	1998 % men
Say a working mother cannot have as warm and secure relationship with child as nonworking mother.	45	58	25	41
Say a preschool child is likely to suffer if mother works.	63	73	37	49

Source: Authors' tabulations of the General Social Survey (GSS), 1977 and 1998.

smaller percentages of both women and men think children will suffer if a mother is employed outside the home. A large gender difference exists, however, in these responses, and a relatively high proportion of men still question whether children do as well when their mother works for pay. Forty-one percent of men, compared with 25 percent of women, feel a working mother cannot have as warm and secure a relationship with her child as a mother who is not employed. And nearly half of men and more than one-third of women still feel that a preschool child is likely to suffer if a mother works for pay. By 1998, women and men seemed to hold similar attitudes about the desirability of women holding a job, but they differed when it came to believing children would suffer negative effects if their mothers worked, with men expressing greater concern about the costs to children and family life.

While the transformation of many of these attitudes occurred throughout the 20th century, the pace of change accelerated in the 1960s and 1970s. A new ideology was emerging during these years; it stressed personal freedom, self-fulfillment, and individual choice in living arrangements and family commitments.

CHANGES IN PAID AND UNPAID WORK

People seek employment out of economic need—because work provides a sense of purpose and an arena for social contact—and because of cultural beliefs that assign prestige to people who are employed. Employment rates and levels are also influenced by life course stage and, increasingly, education.

Paid Work
Paid work tends to be less common among women and men under age 25, many of whom are still in college, and for those over age 55, many of whom are retired. More highly educated women and men are more likely to work for pay than are less educated women and men. Gender is also related to workforce participation, but it matters less than it used to because sharply demarcated adult roles associated with marriage and parenting have eroded since the 1970s and because women have become more educated and skilled over time. As such "supply" factors and cultural attitudes toward employment shift, so too does the pattern of opportunities and constraints people face when they decide whether to work and then try to get a job. For example, many employers depend on female employees, and workplaces have become more hospitable to women.

Without a doubt, the most remarkable transformation in work in the last century was the increase in women's paid work. Women's employment rates climbed throughout the 20th century, but then skyrocketed between the 1950s and the 1980s with the surge of women with children entering the labor force.[14] Between 1950 and the mid-1960s, older women who had completed childbearing (and in many cases childrearing) accounted for most of the increase, in part because high rates of early marriage and fertility over this period limited the labor supply of young women.[15] Since the late 1960s, however, paid work has increased fastest among younger women, in particular among mothers with young children.[16] Substantial increases continued through the 1980s but have slowed over the past decade to an incremental trickle, as shown in Table 2 (page 81). Thus, after decades of monumental progress toward narrowing the gender gap in paid work, the revolution in women's paid work appears to have stalled.

The proportion of women ages 25 to 54 who were employed increased 16 percent in the 1980s, from 67 percent to 78 percent, but grew only an additional 1 percent in the 1990s. Over the same period, the proportion of men who were employed in the previous year fell slightly, from 93 percent in 1980 to 90 percent in 2000. Consequently, the gap separating women's and men's employment rates narrowed more sharply in the 1980s

Table 2

PAID WORK FOR WOMEN AND MEN AGES 25–54, 1980–2000

Paid work	Women			Men			Ratio women/men (per 100)		
	1980	1990	2000	1980	1990	2000	1980	1990	2000
Percent employed previous year*	67	78	79	93	92	90	72	85	88
Percent employed full-time/year-round**	32	42	46	69	68	68	46	62	68
Average annual hours employed***	1,037	1,305	1,396	1,955	1,951	1,950	53	67	72

* Ratios are the number of women employed in the previous year for every 100 men employed in the previous year.

** Ratios are the number of women employed full-time/year-round for every 100 men employed full-time/year-round.

*** For those employed, ratios are the number of hours women work for pay for every 100 hours men work.

Source: Authors' tabulations using the Integrated Public Use Microdata Series (IPUMS), 2003.

than in the 1990s: 72 women were employed for every 100 men in 1980, increasing to 85 per 100 in 1990, and to 88 per 100 in 2000.

Although examining employment differences in the past year provides us with valuable information about the continued transformation in women's labor force participation, it is perhaps not the most relevant indicator of women's progress in paid work in this day and age. Because women continue to be more responsible for home and family, they have less time to devote to paid work. The inability to work full time can have deleterious consequences for women's careers by reducing the amount of experience they gain over their lifetimes and forcing them into less desirable jobs. Employers may view part-time employees, who are mostly women, as less dedicated, and may therefore be less likely to promote them and bestow other work-related privileges upon them. Thus, a more relevant approach for examining women's recent progress in paid work is to examine the degree of attachment or commitment to paid work by considering the amount of time spent on the job. Time commitment can be measured by the average annual hours of work among those who are employed or the percent of women and men who are employed full-time/year-round. Perhaps the best measure of equality in paid work is that of full-time/year-round employment, since that measure captures those with the greatest investment in paid work.

Not only are women more likely to be employed than they were two decades earlier, but they also spend more time working for pay. Table 2 shows that the percent of women who were employed full-time/year-round rose from 32 percent in 1980 to 46 percent in 2000, with the majority of change occurring in the 1980s. Here we use the official definition of full-time/year-round work: at least 35 hours per week for 50 weeks. The number of average annual hours women worked (among those who worked) also increased the most between 1980 and 1990—from 1,037 hours to 1,305 hours. By 2000, women worked 1,396 hours per year, an average of 27 hours per week. Over the same period, only slightly more than two-thirds of men worked full-time/year-round, and average annual

hours declined slightly between 1980 and 2000, again with the majority of this small change occurring in the 1980s.

As the gender gap in employment declined over this period, so did the gap in time spent working for pay. In 1980, there were only 46 women working full-time/year-round for every 100 men, but by 2000, the gap had narrowed to 68 women for every 100 men. Similarly, in 1980, women worked 53 hours for every 100 hours men did, but by 2000, they were putting in 72 hours for every 100 hours men did. Note again that the majority of change occurred in the 1980s.

Employment rates have risen among women and declined among men of all races and ethnicities. Nonetheless, racial and ethnic differentials in employment levels among adults persist, as shown in Box 1.

Unpaid Work

In the previous section we documented the tremendous increase in women's labor force participation and in the amount of time worked for pay, but the pace of change in the 1990s was much slower than in the 1980s. Has women's and men's unpaid labor in the home also become more similar, and does the pace of change parallel that for paid employment?

While women's entrance into the labor force garnered the attention of researchers for the past 40 years, in the last two decades much attention has also been paid to the trends and gender differentials in unpaid household work. Why? Because time is finite. That is, the amount of time women spend doing household chores takes away from the time they could spend working for pay. In addition, gender specialization in families across the domains of paid and unpaid work is linked to a variety of negative labor market outcomes for women, including lower wages, lower lifetime earnings, diminished career advancement, and occupational segregation. Hence, it is important to know the extent to which women's time continues to be invested more in the family than in the economic sphere and whether the opposite remains true for men.

Decennial census data are well suited to examining gender differences in employment but do not provide information on women's and men's time in unpaid work at home. However, information collected in time diary surveys can fill this gap (see Box 2, page 83).[17] Data on the time adults spend in unpaid work were collected in time diary surveys in 1965, 1975, 1985, and from 1998 to 1999, and we use this data to describe differences in women's and men's time spent on unpaid housework.

Figure 1 (page 83) shows changes in housework and child care in 1965, 1975, 1985, and 1999 for women and men ages 25 to 54. Women's total weekly household work—housework and child care—declined from 37.8 hours in 1965 to 23.8 hours in 1999. The entire decline, however, was concentrated in housework, which dropped 13.6 hours per week over the period (from 30.4 hours to 16.8 hours). Although dipping slightly between 1965, 1975, and 1985, time caring for children was spent nearly the same in 1965 and 1999 (about seven hours per week) despite declines in fertility. Hence, women have balanced increased time in paid work with decreased time in unpaid housework, but have preserved time with children.

Box 1

RACIAL AND ETHNIC DIFFERENCES IN WOMEN'S AND MEN'S EMPLOYMENT

In 2000, 81 percent of white women, 79 percent of black women, 68 percent of Latina women, and 74 percent of Asian women were employed in the previous year (see table). The slightly higher employment rate among white women relative to black women represents a reversal from the historical trend, as throughout the 20th century full-time domesticity was more common among white women than black women.[1] What explains these trends?

Many people assume that women's increased employment results from a drop in men's earnings. That assumption would fit with the historical pattern of black women having higher employment rates than white women. However, we also saw booms in both women's employment and men's earnings simultaneously in the post-World War II period. Moreover, women's employment rates increased faster during the 1980s than they did in the 1990s, even as men's employment rates fell faster during the 1990s.

A closer look at the trends by race and ethnicity shows that white women had the fastest increases in the 1980s. In the 1990s, however, white women's employment increases cooled off, and black women actually had steeper increases, although no group approaches the increases white women had in the 1980s.

One possible reason for white women's higher employment rates could be their more favorable labor "supply" characteristics, particularly higher levels of education. But that condition has long been the case. A more promising explanation is that the demand for jobs in which white women are concentrated increased more quickly than the demand for jobs typically held by black women. In a separate analysis, sociologist Philip Cohen has shown that, in the late 1970s, black women were about twice as likely as white women to work in those occupations that subsequently declined at the fastest rates in the following 20 years—and white women were twice as likely to work in the fastest-growing occupations.[2] Thus, economic development was concentrated in those sectors of the economy in which white women were already employed.

As shown in the table, men's employment levels also vary across racial and ethnic groups. In 2000, 93 percent of white men, 79 percent of black men, 87 percent of Latino men, and 90 percent of Asian men were employed during the previous year. Over recent decades, black men's employment rates

Percent of Women and Men Employed Previous Year by Race and Ethnicity, 1980–2000

	Women			Men		
	1980	1990	2000	1980	1990	2000
White	68	79	81	95	94	93
Black	69	75	79	83	82	79
Latino	59	66	68	90	89	87
Asian/Pacific Islander	69	72	74	91	90	90

Note: Race/ethnic groups are mutually exclusive, with descending selection: Latino, black, Asian/Pacific Islander, white.

Source: Authors' tabulations using the Integrated Public Use Microdata Series (IPUMS), 2003.

have declined more than those of other groups. The employment gap between white men and black men increased from 12 percentage points to 14 percentage points between 1980 and 2000. Racial inequality in employment is linked with changes in the industrial structure of the U.S. economy, which have reduced the supply of blue-collar manufacturing jobs and relocated jobs away from areas of black residential concentration.[3] Industrial restructuring has also increased the premium employers place on higher education, and black men continue to lag behind white men in college attainment.

The end result is that gender differences in employment rates have decreased for all groups, although the changes were more modest in the 1990s for all groups except blacks. The employment gender gap has been eliminated among blacks, not because black women's employment rate outstrips that of other women, but because of black men's relatively low levels of employment. The gap is largest among Latinos, but in contrast to blacks this gap results from Latina women's weak employment picture. Nonetheless, women's and men's economic roles have become much more similar over recent decades for all major racial and ethnic groups.

References

1. Bart Landry, *Black Working Wives: Pioneers of the American Family Revolution* (Berkeley: University of California Press, 2000).

2. Philip N. Cohen, "Demanding Work: Black and White Women's Employment, 1976-2000" (unpublished manuscript).

3. Ted Mouw, "Job Relocation and the Racial Gap in Unemployment in Detroit and Chicago, 1980 to 1990," *American Sociological Review* 65, no. 5 (2000): 730-53.

TIME DIARY DATA

In time diary studies, respondents are asked to provide a chronological accounting of the previous day's activities from midnight to midnight, including what they were doing, what time the activity started and stopped, where they were, whether they were doing anything else, and who else was present. We use these data to calculate weekly hours of housework and child care. Considerable research has established that estimates of unpaid work from time diary studies are more accurate than estimates from stylized survey questions such as "how much time do you typically spend in [activity] over an average day/week?"[1]

Trends over time in market work are more readily measured than trends in unpaid work. Federal data collections (most important, the Current Population Survey) monitor paid work on a monthly basis in order to produce estimates of unemployment for the system of national accounts. Work done in the home for one's family has never been included in measures of national wealth, such as the gross domestic product, and therefore the measurement of household work has been far less systematic and frequent.

The federal government is currently collecting time diary information in one module of the Current Population Survey. This is the first federal time diary study conducted in the United States; earlier studies were conducted at the University of Michigan (1965 and 1975) and the University of Maryland (1985 and from 1998 to 1999). As a result, existing time use studies have relatively small samples that do not allow examination of time in household labor by detailed family status, race and ethnicity, and socioeconomic differences. They do allow researchers, however, to look at gender differences and change over time.

Reference

1. F. Thomas Juster, "The Validity and Quality of Time Use Estimates Obtained From Recall Diaries," in *Time, Goods, and Well-Being*, ed. F. Thomas Juster and Frank P. Stafford (Ann Arbor, MI: The University of Michigan Survey Research Center, 1995); Margaret M. Marini and Beth A. Shelton, "Measuring Household Work: Recent Experience in the United States," *Social Science Research* 22, no. 4 (1993): 361–82; and John P. Robinson, "The Validity and Reliability of Diaries Versus Alternative Time Use Measures," in *Time, Goods, and Well-Being*, ed. F. Thomas Juster and Frank P. Stafford (Ann Arbor, MI: The University of Michigan Survey Research Center, 1995).

CHANGES IN WOMEN'S AND MEN'S WEEKLY HOURS OF UNPAID WORK, AGES 25–54, 1965–1999

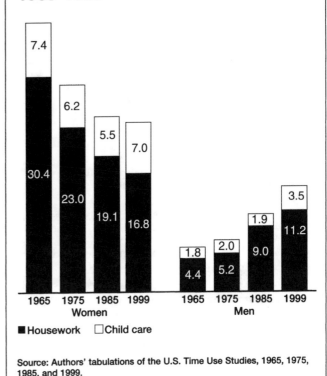

Source: Authors' tabulations of the U.S. Time Use Studies, 1965, 1975, 1985, and 1999.

children. (We will narrow our focus later in this report to examine how gender differences in family status affect unpaid work.)

Table 3 reports the types of housework women and men did in 1965, 1975, 1985, and 1999. Housework is separated into core tasks (cooking meals, meal cleanup, housecleaning, and laundry) and more discretionary and less time-consuming tasks (outdoor chores and repairs, gardening/animal care, and bill-paying).

Most housework time is spent cooking, cleaning, and doing laundry, and women continue to spend more time in these core tasks than do men. Nevertheless, the gap between women's and men's core housework has shrunk substantially. Whereas women put in 12 hours per week for every one hour men spent cooking and cleaning up after meals in 1965, by 1999 women were spending only twice as much time in these activities as men. The ratio of women's to men's time in routine housecleaning and laundry also declined significantly over the period, falling from 18.8 to 1.8 and 29.0 to 4.5, respectively. The dwindling difference between women's and men's cooking and cleaning time is due both to men's increased time in these activities as well as to women's decreased time. Sociologist Liana Sayer finds that two factors contribute to these changes: Fewer women are spending time cooking and cleaning and their average time has declined,

Men's time doing housework and taking care of children more than doubled over the period, rising from 6.2 hours in 1965 to 14.7 hours in 1999. Nonetheless, although the gap is smaller today than in 1965, women continue to do about 40 percent more unpaid work than men. For women, time in unpaid labor declined the most between 1965 and 1975, with slower declines occurring thereafter. For men the story is quite different: Unpaid labor increased the least between 1965 and 1975, while the greatest gains were realized between 1975 and 1985. Increases in men's unpaid labor continued into the 1990s, but at a slower pace. Of course, the number of hours spent caring for children depends in part on family status—whether one is married or has young

Table 3

TRENDS IN AVERAGE WEEKLY HOUSEWORK HOURS FOR WOMEN AND MEN AGES 25–54, 1965–1999

	Women				Men				Ratio women's hours to men's hours			
	1965	1975	1985	1999	1965	1975	1985	1999	1965	1975	1985	1999
Total housework	30.4	23.0	19.1	16.8	4.4	5.2	9.0	11.2	6.9	4.4	2.1	1.5
Core housework (total)	27.4	20.8	15.7	13.2	1.7	1.8	3.8	5.7	16.1	11.6	4.1	2.3
Cooking meals	9.5	8.4	6.6	5.4	0.8	1.0	1.9	2.3	11.9	8.4	3.5	2.3
Meal cleanup	4.6	2.5	1.8	1.0	0.4	0.2	0.3	0.6	11.5	12.5	6.0	1.7
Housecleaning	7.5	6.4	5.0	4.1	0.4	0.4	1.2	2.3	18.8	16.0	4.2	1.8
Laundry, ironing	5.8	3.5	2.3	2.7	0.2	0.1	0.3	0.6	29.0	35.0	7.7	4.5
Other housework (total)	3.0	2.2	3.3	3.6	2.7	3.5	5.2	5.5	1.1	0.6	0.6	0.7
Outdoor chores	0.2	0.6	0.4	1.0	0.5	0.9	1.0	2.2	0.4	0.6	0.6	0.7
Repairs	0.4	0.6	0.6	0.5	1.3	1.6	1.9	1.5	0.4	0.7	0.4	0.5
Gardening, animal care	0.6	0.5	0.8	0.8	0.2	0.3	0.8	0.8	0.3	0.4	0.3	0.3
Bills, other financial	1.7	0.6	1.6	1.3	0.7	0.7	1.6	0.9	2.4	0.9	1.0	1.4

Source: Authors' tabulations of the U.S. Time Use Studies, 1965, 1975, 1985, and 1999.

whereas more men are spending some time cooking and cleaning and their average cooking and cleaning times have increased.[18] Laundry appears to be the household task men resist the most. Declines in the gender "laundry" gap are mostly due to the three-hour drop in women's time, likely because of decreased ironing, rather than larger increases in men's time. The introduction of permanent-press clothing has reduced the need to iron some clothes. Women today may also be more willing to send clothes to the cleaners for pressing, in contrast to the 1950s when housekeeping standards mandated careful ironing of family members' clothes and even bed linens. Despite lingering differences in laundry, the growing similarity in women's and men's core unpaid work parallels growing similarity in paid work.

In terms of other housework, there was a marginal increase in the time women devoted to these tasks, from 3.0 hours in 1965 to 3.6 hours in 1999; and a larger increase among men, from 2.7 to 5.5 hours over the same period. Except in 1965, when women and men were putting in about the same amount of time, women have spent about 60 percent as much time as men in noncore housework. The distribution of time across tasks has changed somewhat. Since 1985, women and men have been more equal with regard to gardening and animal care than other tasks. In 1999, compared with men, women spent less time doing outdoor chores and repairs and more time paying bills and dealing with other financial matters.

Change Across Cohorts

As discussed earlier, women's and men's decisions about whether and how much to work both in and outside the home are influenced by the demographic, economic, legislative, and normative environments they experience as they enter adulthood. The societal context in which

young women and men evaluate alternative work and family paths (and the array of options available) varies tremendously over time. Consequently, a useful way of examining changing patterns of work given these varied environments is to look at the experiences of different cohorts or generations. A *cohort* consists of a group of individuals who share a unique constellation of circumstances, and is often defined by year of birth. Table 4 (page 85) describes the birth cohorts used in this report—adults ages 25 to 54 in 1980, 1990, and 2000—and details the social and economic circumstances occurring at the time they reached adulthood.

The World War II cohort consists of women and men born from 1936 to 1945 who came of age from the mid-1950s to the mid-1960s. The post-World War II period was one of sustained economic growth fueled by an unprecedented expansion of consumption. The G.I. Bill allowed many men to attend college and buy homes in suburban developments that were once farmland. Even among less-educated men, the growth of stable and well-paying blue-collar jobs meant they too could earn a wage sufficient to support a family in middle-class style. Marriage was early and nearly universal. Good economic prospects for the majority of men, in tandem with employment discrimination against married women, also meant this was a period of unusually high fertility and gender specialization, with women tending to the house and children while men provided financially. Despite the economic good times, a family consisting of a breadwinner husband and a caregiving wife was more common among whites than minorities. The growing Civil Rights Movement was demanding that the benefits of economic prosperity be shared more equally among all racial and ethnic groups. Additionally, a revitalized women's movement was gaining strength, calling into question the desirability of the extreme gender speciali-

Table 4
BIRTH COHORTS BY PERIOD OF ADULT TRANSITIONS AND AGE IN 1980, 1990, AND 2000

Birth cohort	Description	Transition to adulthood	Work and family societal context	Age at U.S. census in		
				1980	1990	2000
1926-1935	Parents of Baby Boom	Mid-1940s/mid-1950s	Idealization of separate spheres; sustained economic expansion	45–54	55–64	65–74
1936-1945	World War II	Mid-1950s/mid-1960s	Questioning gender specialization; economic expansion	35–44	45–54	55–64
1946-1955	Early Baby Boom	Mid-1960s/mid-1970s	Civil Rights Act; sexual freedom; economic restructuring begins	25–34	35–44	45–54
1956-1965	Late Baby Boom	Mid-1970s/mid-1980s	Demise of male breadwinner model; economic restructuring and downsizing	15–24	25–34	35–44
1966-1975	Generation X	Mid-1980s/mid-1990s	Shared breadwinning/caregiving; fatherhood rights; economic turbulence; welfare reform	5–14	15–24	25–34

zation characteristic of the 1950s. Both developments set the stage for a different work and family context experienced by subsequent generations.

The early baby-boom cohort consists of the large numbers of people born from 1946 to 1955 who came of age from the mid-1960s to the mid-1970s. This was a period of heady social transformation and continued economic prosperity. The renewed feminist movement was in full swing, supported by passage of landmark legislation such as Title VII of the Civil Rights Act of 1964, which prohibited firms with 15 or more employees from discriminating on the basis of sex, race, national origin, and religion; passage of Title IX in 1973, which prohibited discrimination against women in federally funded educational institutions; and the Pregnancy Discrimination Act of 1967, which prohibited discrimination in hiring and firing pregnant women. Additionally, the introduction of the birth control pill and the legalization of abortion helped liberalize attitudes on premarital sex. Together, these shifts led to major expansions in women's educational and economic opportunities and further questioning of sharply differentiated male and female adult roles.

The late baby-boom cohort consists of individuals born from 1956 to 1965. This generation came of age in the mid-1970s to the mid-1980s during economic conditions quite different from those enjoyed by prior generations. When baby boomers hit working age in the 1970s, the economy was not as hospitable as it had been for their parents. These late baby boomers postponed entry into marriage, delayed having children, and found it difficult to establish themselves in the labor market. They came face to face with industrial restructuring and downsizing. Many of the jobs being created replaced or at least complemented work previously done by women at home—cooking and cleaning, caring for the elderly and the sick—and most of these jobs were filled by

women who were pouring into the paid labor market.[19] The shift from manufacturing to service industries meant men's job opportunities and wages stagnated while demand for women's labor increased. The necessity of women contributing economically to the family increased over the period, in particular among working-class and nonwhite families. Social change also quieted among increasingly strident claims that women's growing employment opportunities were threatening the future of the family. The optimism of the feminist movement that women could "have it all" was being replaced by growing recognition of the "second shift" of household labor many women experienced after putting in a first shift of paid work.

Finally, the Generation X cohort consists of women and men born from 1966 to 1975 who entered adulthood in the mid-1980s to the mid-1990s. These young adults came of age during more favorable economic times than the late baby-boom cohort but also during times of rapid swings in the business cycle. In general, wage growth was slow, job markets tight, job security shaky, and housing costs were soaring ever upward, yet unemployment was also low. Times were also better for some groups than others; economic fortunes were increasingly dependent on educational attainment. College-educated workers experienced rising wages and favorable employment opportunities, whereas industrial shifts eroded less-educated men's economic circumstances and meant they could no longer provide a middle-class standard of living for their families on their wages alone. Poor single mothers, facing the slipping economic prospects of potential spouses—and then punitive welfare reform that required paid work—entered employment in increasing numbers. Finally, this generation grew up in an environment of legal and normative equality in opportunity (if not yet equal outcomes) between women and men, and most

Table 5

PERCENT OF WOMEN AND MEN WHO ARE FULL-TIME/YEAR-ROUND WORKERS, BY AGE AND COHORT

Cohort	Ages 25–34	Ages 35–44	Ages 45–54
Women			
1966-1975 Generation X	44	—	—
1956-1965 Late Baby Boom	42	46	—
1946-1955 Early Baby Boom	32	43	47
1936-1945 World War II	—	32	41
1926-1935 Parents of Baby Boom	—	—	31
Men			
1966-1975 Generation X	64	—	—
1956-1965 Late Baby Boom	65	70	—
1946-1955 Early Baby Boom	66	71	69
1936-1945 World War II	—	73	70
1926-1935 Parents of Baby Boom	—	—	71
Ratio women/men (per 100)			
1966-1975 Generation X	69	—	—
1956-1965 Late Baby Boom	65	66	—
1946-1955 Early Baby Boom	48	61	68
1936-1945 World War II	—	44	59
1926-1935 Parents of Baby Boom	—	—	44

— Not applicable.

Source: Authors' tabulations using the Integrated Public Use Microdata Series (IPUMS), 2003.

people in Generation X have reached adulthood expecting to combine employment, marriage, and parenting. While behavior lags normative changes, work and family have been redefined as men's issues too, in part because of the growing cultural emphasis on fathers' daily involvement with children.

Table 5 shows the percent of women and men who worked full-time/year-round in the cohorts of the parents of the baby boom, World War II, early baby boom, late baby boom, and Generation X. The rows show changes in labor force attachment as each birth cohort ages; the columns show how labor force attachment has changed across birth cohorts.

The table shows that each succeeding cohort of women had higher rates of full-time/year-round employment. The greatest change for women ages 25 to 34 occurred between the early baby-boom and the late baby-boom cohorts, with the latter group having a 10-point higher rate of full-time/year-round employment. Among young women, change between the late baby-boom and Generation X cohorts is relatively small by comparison (only 2 percentage points). Note that large gains were made for women ages 35 to 44 between the World War II and early baby-boom cohorts and for older women between each successive cohort shown in the table. The patterns are the same regardless of whether one examines full-time/year-round employment, labor

force participation in the previous year, or the average annual number of hours worked.

Sociologist Suzanne Bianchi's analysis of cohorts through the late baby boom indicated that the replacement of cohorts was an important aspect of women's growing labor force attachment, as younger cohorts with higher rates of full-time/year-round employment "replaced" older cohorts with lower rates of full-time/year-round employment.[20] However, women in one cohort—early baby boomers who brought the feminist movement into the workplace—dramatically increased their employment rates as they moved from early to mid-adulthood. The late baby boomers, despite starting out at higher rates, have not shown the same pattern of increase. Finally, women in the last cohort, Generation X, have started their young adulthoods with only slightly higher rates of employment than previous generations. The patterns of these last two cohorts account for the slower employment growth among women in the 1990s.

Table 5 confirms that men's labor force attachment has remained quite similar across generations. This pattern also holds regardless of whether one examines full-time/year-round work, labor force participation in the past year, or average annual hours worked. This trend, along with the slowing pace of generational change among women, means that gender differences in employment diminished only slightly between the late baby-boom cohort and the Generation X cohort. Despite economic and cultural changes, women's labor force participation, full-time/year-round employment, and hours in the labor force continue to be less than men's. On the one hand, these data make it clear that in the past decade the revolution in women's paid work has sputtered; consequently gender specialization has weakened only slightly and significant gaps in men's and women's labor force attachment still remain. On the other hand, the data also indicate that Generation X has not "solved" the problem of managing both work and family responsibilities by retreating to the 1950s' pattern of separate spheres, because women continue to make small gains relative to men in the sphere of paid work.

Generational changes also occurred in unpaid labor. Table 6 (page 87) shows changes in the number of hours per week women and men spent doing housework. Because the data for this table are from 1965, 1975, 1985, and 1999, the cohorts are not exactly the same as those presented in Table 4. With the exception of Generation X, each birth cohort range is actually five years later than the range in Table 4. We could have presented numbers for the exact cohorts in the table, but this approach would have changed the age ranges. For example, the same group of people who were ages 25 to 34 in the 1980 Census would have been 20 to 29 in the 1975 time diary data. Because both paid and unpaid labor are sensitive to age categories, we kept the age categories the same and used the same cohort labels.

Table 6

AVERAGE WEEKLY HOURS OF HOUSEWORK BY AGE, SEX, AND COHORT

Cohort*	Ages 25–34	Ages 35–44	Ages 45–54
Women			
Generation X	16.9	—	—
Late Baby Boom	17.3	18.3	—
Early Baby Boom	20.7	20.3	14.9
World War II	30.2	23.2	20.3
Parents of Baby Boom	—	31.2	26.1
Men			
Generation X	8.4	—	—
Late Baby Boom	7.2	13.1	—
Early Baby Boom	4.3	10.3	12.1
World War II	3.7	5.0	10.1
Parents of Baby Boom	—	4.5	7.2
Ratio women's hours/men's hours			
Generation X	2.0	—	—
Late Baby Boom	2.4	1.4	—
Early Baby Boom	4.8	2.0	1.2
World War II	8.2	4.6	2.0
Parents of Baby Boom	—	6.9	3.6

— Not applicable.

* Birth cohort ranges are five years later than ranges shown in Table 4.

Source: Authors' tabulations of the U.S. Time Use Studies, 1965, 1975, 1985, and 1999.

Table 6 shows that, with the exception of Generation X, women are spending appreciably less time doing housework across each successive cohort. Compared with their World War II counterparts, Generation X women are spending about 13 fewer hours per week on housework. Among young women, however, most declines in housework occurred between the World War II and early baby-boom cohorts, concurrent with declines in fertility and the rise of the women's movement. The drop-off in housework seems to have stalled among young women in Generation X; these women are doing nearly the same amount of housework as their late baby-boom counterparts.

In contrast, men in each successive cohort are spending substantially more hours doing housework, with the most substantial gains occurring between the early and late baby-boom cohorts. Generation X men continued the trend toward doing more unpaid labor, but the relative increases were less than they had been in previous generations. Additionally, whereas women reduce housework time as they age, men spend more time in household chores over their life course. For example, whereas the housework gap is 16 hours per week comparing early baby-boom women with men ages 25 to 34, the gap is only three hours per week comparing early baby-boom women and men at ages 45 to 54. Women reduce housework later in their adult lives because the

demand for child-generated housework such as daily laundry and frequent housecleaning drops as children grow older. Men may increase housework over their life course because fewer of them at ages 25 to 34 are married and raising children, and those who are married are becoming established in their careers. Empirical research suggests that some couples integrate work and family responsibilities when their children are young by adopting a traditional division of labor, but that specialization decreases once children enter school.[21] This pattern may be more common among more recent cohorts, however, as women's greater investments in housework vis-à-vis men continue into older ages for earlier cohorts. Nevertheless, because men are doing more housework and women less, women's and men's housework time is becoming more equal across successive cohorts, although the gains registered by Generation X are relatively small in comparison to previous cohorts.

Explaining Allocation of Time Between Paid and Unpaid Work

Researchers have advanced three different theories to explain how women and men divide their time between paid and unpaid work. Economic and bargaining perspectives emphasize rationality and relative resources and why allocations should have changed in response to demographic, economic, and normative shifts. The gender perspective emphasizes the resiliency of the gender system and elements that work against change in the division of labor.

Economic models of time use posit that households rationally and efficiently allocate time, typically through specialization of one partner in paid work and the other in unpaid work. These models also posit that the reason specialization is more efficient and the reason men specialize in paid work while women specialize in unpaid work is because of human capital and biological differences. Since women are the ones who bear and care for infants, they are assumed to be more productive in unpaid work than are men. Since men generally have more education and work experience than women, they are assumed to be more productive in paid work than are women.[22]

The second perspective focuses on bargaining or exchange among partners: The person with more power will do less unpaid work because household labor is less desirable than paid work. People use resources such as education and income to strike the best bargain they can. Husbands' higher resources mean they have more leverage to buy out of tasks they do not wish to perform, such as unpleasant domestic chores, and to engage in things they prefer, such as leisure.[23] Additionally, whereas women's education and employment have increased over the past 30 years, they continue to earn less than men; once married, women are more dependent on the economic resources provided by men. As a result, this perspective posits, women have less bargaining power and less leverage to negotiate higher levels of housework and child care from husbands. Empirical evidence suggests that men do more unpaid work in the home when their wives earn a higher percent of the household income, especially if women are defined as co-providers.[24]

The third perspective posits that the purpose of the gendered division of labor is not simply to produce household goods and services but also to define and express gender relations within families. This perspective was developed to explain why women and men in married or cohabiting relationships appear not to simply trade off time spent in paid and unpaid work.[25] Housework and child care are not neutral chores but instead are "symbolic enactments" of unequal gender relations. Women display femininity and family caring by cooking, cleaning, and raising children; men display masculinity by avoiding these same tasks.[26]

Studies show that women and men in marital households, compared with other household types, have the greatest gap in housework time.[27] When couples marry, women's housework hours go up while men's decline.[28] In other words, wives and husbands are displaying their "proper" gender roles through the amount and type of housework they perform.

What do these theories have in common? All suggest that family status affects how women and men allocate their time between paid and unpaid labor. In the next section, we narrow our focus to how family status affects paid and unpaid work among women and men.

FAMILY STATUS

All women and men need to attend to the basics of life: securing money to buy necessities and maintaining their health and well-being and that of their families. Yet the options for meeting these needs are altered by whether one has a partner who can help to meet these needs and whether one is also responsible for children. Because the number of hours in a day is fixed, the work and family roles associated with meeting these needs compete for men's and women's time and energy. Work affects family formation decisions, and family formation affects work decisions. Recent evidence suggests that work also exerts a strong influence on the scheduling of day-to-day activities and the organization of family life.[29] Marriage can make things easier because theoretically there are two people available to do the two types of work that need to be done. Historically, many married women specialized in the family sphere by taking primary responsibility for housework and child care, whereas many married men specialized in the work sphere by taking primary responsibility for providing financially for the family. Today, marriage still increases

a woman's unpaid labor because she has a new husband to care for, and increases a man's paid labor because he has a new wife to provide for. Children mean more unpaid work because they require regular care and increase the amount of housework a family has to do. Children also increase the paid work needed to cover additional food, clothing, and health care costs. Hence, in married-couple families, children tend to increase women's unpaid work and increase men's paid work. Gender roles have become less rigid, and today more couples expect to share responsibility for both work and family spheres. There are also more single-parent families who must manage work and family roles, more couples without children, and more individuals living by themselves. How have these changes affected women's and men's work, and have they led to more or less gender equality across work spheres?

An adequate answer to these questions hinges on understanding how the family has changed. In recent decades, the family share of U.S. households has been declining. In 1960, 85 percent of households were family households—households having two or more individuals related by marriage, birth, or adoption; by 2000, just 69 percent of households were family households.[30] At the same time, nonfamily households, which consist primarily of people who live alone or who share a residence with roommates or with a partner, have been on the rise. The fastest growth was among those living alone. The proportion of households with just one person doubled from 13 percent to 26 percent between 1960 and 2000. These changes are important to consider in examining trends in women's and men's work overall, because a shift from married-couple households to one-person households affects the choices people have in allocating time between paid and unpaid work and because single childless women and men tend to have more similar paid and unpaid work patterns. Not taking these changes into account could lead one to mistakenly conclude that work allocation has changed, when those changes are really due to these demographic shifts.

Most of the decline in the number of family households reflects the decrease in the share of married-couple households with children. Declines in fertility within marriage between 1960 and 1975, later marriage, and frequent divorce help explain the shrinking proportion of households consisting of married couples with children. The divorce rate rose sharply between 1960 and 1980 and then eased, while the rate of first marriages declined steadily after 1970. Two-parent family households with children dropped from 44 percent to 24 percent of all households between 1960 and 2000, while single-parent family households grew from 4 percent to 9 percent of all households.[31] These shifts have implications for examining changes in women's and men's work overall, because now fewer people have children to care for and women are more likely to be single parents. Again, if we do not take these changes into account, we cannot know whether changes in work are due to changes in work behavior or shifting demographics.

Paralleling changes in work, change in household composition began slowly in the 1960s, as society was facing some of the most radical social changes in U.S. history and the leading edge of the huge baby-boom generation was reaching adulthood. The steepest decline in the share of family households was in the 1970s, when the first baby boomers entered their 20s. By the 1980s, change was still occurring but at a much slower pace. By the mid-1990s, household composition had apparently stabilized.

Television shows reflect the norms and culture of the time periods in which they are set and can help illustrate the changes just described. "Happy Days," a popular sitcom from the mid-1970s to mid-1980s, was set in the 1950s and reflected a time in which young men and women got married relatively young, presumably had children shortly after, and most likely stayed married for life. Although some young women on the show postponed marriage and childbearing, they did not cohabit, live with male roommates, or have children outside of marriage. In stark contrast, the award-winning sitcom "Friends," set in the 1990s and the early years of 2000, depicts young adult lives that involved multiple marriages and divorces, opposite-sex roommates, cohabitation, and children born out of wedlock.

To get a better idea of how these two television shows stack up against reality, we can examine changing family statuses among young adults who are just beginning to adopt family and work roles. Table 7 shows the percent of women and men ages 25 to 34 who have remained single (have never been married) and childless (not living in the same house with an own child under age 18) across cohorts. Both women and men are remaining single longer in recent cohorts. For example, 22 percent of Generation X women ages 30 to 34 have never married, compared with only 10 percent of early baby-boom women. Men experienced a similar increase in singlehood. About 29 percent of Generation X men were not married by ages 30 to 34, almost double the percent of early baby-boom men who never married.

Generation X women and men are also more likely than past generations to remain childless or delay parenthood well into their 30s. Among women ages 30 to 34, less than one-quarter of early baby-boom women were childless (not living with their own biological, step, or adopted children), compared with nearly one-third of Generation X women. Many Generation X women are simply delaying parenthood until their late 30s, but some will never become mothers. About twice as many women ages 40 to 44 in 2000 (the ages at which most childbearing has occurred) were childless in 2000 compared with 1980 (19 percent versus 10 percent). Higher

	% never married*		% childless*	
Cohort	Ages 25–29	Ages 30–34	Ages 25–29	Ages 30–34
Women				
1966-1975 Generation X	38	22	49	32
1956-1965 Late Baby Boom	32	18	47	30
1946-1955 Early Baby Boom	21	10	41	23
Men				
1966-1975 Generation X	49	29	69	51
1956-1965 Late Baby Boom	45	25	67	47
1946-1955 Early Baby Boom	32	15	60	38
Ratio women/men (per 100)				
1966-1975 Generation X	78	76	71	63
1956-1965 Late Baby Boom	71	72	70	64
1946-1955 Early Baby Boom	66	67	68	61

Table 7

WOMEN AND MEN WHO HAVE REMAINED SINGLE AND CHILDLESS, BY AGE AND COHORT

* Percent remaining single are the percent who have never married. Percent childless are the percent not living with any children under age 18.

Source: Authors' tabulations using the Integrated Public Use Microdata Series (IPUMS), 2003.

rates of childlessness as well as delays in becoming a mother appear to be common strategies among women to increase their chance of landing and keeping a good job and establishing their economic independence.[32] Generational increases in childlessness or delayed parenthood are also apparent among men. As with trends in work, the majority of the increases among men and women who remain single and childless occurred between the early and late baby-boom generations. Change continued to occur between the late baby-boom and Generation X cohorts, but at a much slower pace.

How do young women and men compare in adopting family roles? Simply put, at any given age men are less likely to have these responsibilities than women, but the gap is closing. For example, among 25-to-29-year-olds, men are more likely to remain single than women within each generation. But whereas in the early baby-boom generation there were only 66 never-married women for every 100 never-married men, in Generation X the number increased to 78 women for every 100 men. The patterns are similar for childlessness; more men than women are childless.

Comparing gender differences in remaining single and remaining childless highlights an important finding. Although women and men have become more similar in terms of singlehood, more women than men are raising children, and gender differences are quite similar across cohorts. For example, among 30-to-34-year-olds, there were 61 childless women for every 100 men in the early baby boom, compared with 63 per 100 in Generation X. These findings have important implications for women's

Table 8
WOMEN AND MEN AGES 25–34 IN DIFFERENT FAMILY STATUSES, BY COHORT

Cohort	% married with children*	% married without children	% single with children*	% single without children
Women				
1966–1975				
Generation X	43	15	16	26
1956–1965				
Late Baby Boom	47	15	15	23
1946–1955				
Early Baby Boom	55	14	12	18
Men				
1966–1975				
Generation X	34	18	6	42
1956–1965				
Late Baby Boom	39	17	4	41
1946–1955				
Early Baby Boom	49	17	2	32

* Living with at least one child under age 18.

Source: Authors' tabulations using the Integrated Public Use Microdata Series (IPUMS), 2003.

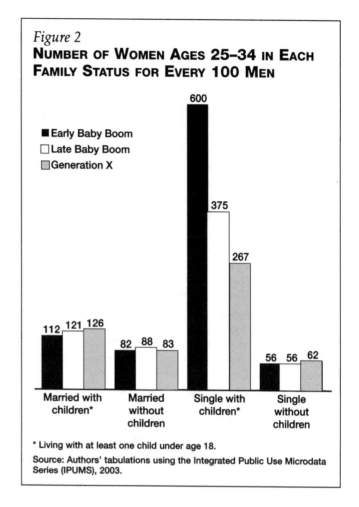

Figure 2
NUMBER OF WOMEN AGES 25–34 IN EACH FAMILY STATUS FOR EVERY 100 MEN

* Living with at least one child under age 18.

Source: Authors' tabulations using the Integrated Public Use Microdata Series (IPUMS), 2003.

and men's paid and unpaid work. The longer people remain single and without children, the fewer family responsibilities they have and the more time they have to get an advanced education and to devote to their careers. The data in Table 7 show that young women continue to be disadvantaged comparatively in terms of parenthood; they are more likely to raise children and are younger when they do so.

Table 7 gives us an idea of how two important domains of family—marriage and parenthood—have changed, but many people get married and don't have children and others have children without getting married. Table 8 shows how the combination of these two statuses has changed over the past three generations among women and men ages 25 to 34, the prime family-building stage. The category "single with children" refers to women and men who are not married (never married, separated, divorced, or married spouse absent) and who are living with a biological, step, or adopted child under age 18. The category includes women and men who are cohabiting with an unmarried partner who may or may not be the child's parent.

Both women and men in Generation X are less likely to be married with children, more likely to be single with children, and more likely to be single without children when compared with previous generations. The greatest changes were in the declines in the proportions married with children: from 55 percent for women and 49 percent for men among the early baby-boom cohort to 43 percent for women and 34 percent for men

among Generation X. The proportions who are single people without children also changed dramatically, increasing from 18 percent for women and 32 percent for men in the early baby boom to 26 percent for women and 42 percent for men in Generation X.

How do women and men compare in these family statuses, and are they becoming more or less similar? Figure 2 shows generational differences in the number of women for every 100 men in a given family status. The closer the bars are to 100, the more similar women and men are in their family statuses. Not unexpectedly, more women than men are in the family statuses with children (bars above 100) and more men than women are in the family statuses without children (bars below 100). The gap in the proportions of women and men who are married with children has grown consistently over the past three generations. In the early baby boom there were 112 married women with children for every 100 men. In the late baby boom this number increased to 121 and in Generation X the number was 126. Women and men are the most dissimilar, however, when it comes to single parenting. Differences are less substantial in later cohorts because there was a dramatic increase in the number of single fathers, although even among Generation X relatively few men are in this family status. Whereas there were 600 single mothers for every 100 single fathers in the early baby-boom cohort, the difference fell to 375 single mothers for every 100 single fathers in the late baby-boom generation and to 267 single mothers for every 100 single fathers in Generation X.

At each time point, men are more likely to be in the status with the fewest family responsibilities—single without children—than are women. In the early and late baby-boom cohorts, there were only 56 women for every 100 men in this category, compared with 62 women per 100 men in the Generation X cohort. Men are also more likely than women to be married with no children in each cohort. Thus, more young women than young men continue to occupy the most time-intensive family roles. While more Generation X than early baby-boom fathers are raising children in single-parent families, women are still more than 2.5 times more likely than men to be in the most time-poor family status.

When one considers all parenting combined—single and married—the gender *gap* in parenting responsibilities actually increased from the early baby-boom to the Generation X cohort. Women were about one-third more likely to be parents (married or single) than were men in the early baby-boom cohort, but this gap increased to 50 percent for the Generation X cohort.

Paid and Unpaid Work

How do gender differences in family statuses affect paid and unpaid work among the working-age population? In 2000, women's and men's paid work were the most similar when they were single with no children (see Table 9). Single women and men without children were equally as likely to be employed in the previous year (84 percent) and to be working full-time/year-round (about 55 percent). They also had similar average annual hours of work (about 1,600). The greatest discrepancy in paid work is found between women and men who are married with children: Seventy-five percent of married mothers were employed last year, compared with 95 percent of married fathers; 38 percent of married mothers worked full-time/year-round, compared with 77 percent of married fathers; and married mothers worked only 57 percent of the average annual hours of married fathers.

Women and men who are married with no children are more equal in terms of work than their married counterparts who have children. But even though they don't have children, these married women are still much less likely to work full-time/year-round and work many fewer hours than married childless men. These findings indicate that marriage and parenthood augment the gender gap in paid work. Economist Claudia Goldin's longitudinal analysis of cohorts of college graduates indicates that, among women from the 1944–1957 birth cohort, fewer than one in five were able to combine full-time/year-round employment with marriage and motherhood con-

Table 9

PAID WORK FOR WOMEN AND MEN AGES 25–54 BY FAMILY STATUS, 2000

Paid work	Married with children*	Married without children	Single with children*	Single without children
Worked for pay (%)				
Women	75	81	83	84
Men	95	90	89	84
Ratio women/men (per 100)	79	90	93	100
Worked full-time/year-round (%)				
Women	38	51	49	55
Men	77	68	62	56
Ratio women/men (per 100)	49	75	79	98
Average annual hours of work				
Women	1,233	1,514	1,473	1,600
Men	2,156	1,941	1,818	1,677
Women's hours as % of men's hours	57	78	81	95

* Living with at least one child under age 18.

Source: Authors' tabulations using the Integrated Public Use Microdata Series (IPUMS), 2003.

tinuously over their adult lives. About one-half of women with successful careers had forgone motherhood.[33] While our data are not longitudinal, they suggest that "having it all" continues to be an unattainable goal for many women. Balancing work and family often means making trade-offs such as withdrawing from paid work, shifting from full-time to part-time work, or scaling back career opportunities by switching to less-demanding jobs.[34]

Single mothers and single fathers are nearly as likely to have worked in the past year (83 percent for women and 89 percent for men). But only 79 single mothers for every 100 single fathers work full-time/year-round, and they work about 20 percent fewer hours than single fathers. Some readers may be surprised that single fathers work so many more hours than single mothers, but about 62 percent of single fathers are cohabiting, living with their parents, or living with other adults, compared with just 46 percent of single mothers.[35] More single fathers than single mothers have household members who provide child care and help with housework.

Gender differences in the trade-offs between time for childrearing and time for paid employment are evident in the reasons adults give for nonemployment. Data from the 1996 Survey of Income and Program Participation show that, among nonemployed women ages 25 to 44, taking care of children or adults was the main reason for not being employed. In contrast, men were more likely to cite long-term health problems and disability as reasons for not being employed. Only 2.6 per-

Table 10

AVERAGE WEEKLY HOURS OF UNPAID WORK FOR WOMEN AND MEN AGES 25–54 BY FAMILY STATUS, 1999

Unpaid work	Married with children	Single without children
All housework		
Women	20.0	11.4
Men	11.2	8.1
Ratio women's hours to men's hours	1.8	1.4
Core housework*		
Women	17.0	6.5
Men	6.5	4.0
Ratio women's hours to men's hours	2.6	1.6
Other housework**		
Women	2.9	4.9
Men	4.7	4.1
Ratio women's hours to men's hours	0.6	1.2

* Core housework includes cooking, meal cleanup, housecleaning, laundry, and ironing.

** Other housework includes repairs, outdoor chores, gardening, animal care, and bill-paying.

Source: Authors' tabulations of the U.S. Time Use Study, 1999.

Table 11

FULL-TIME/YEAR-ROUND PAID WORK FOR WOMEN AND MEN AGES 25–34, BY FAMILY STATUS AND COHORT

Cohort	Married with children*	Married without children	Single with children*	Single without children
Women (%)				
1966–1975				
Generation X	33	56	44	55
1956–1965				
Late Baby Boom	30	59	36	57
1946–1955				
Early Baby Boom	20	51	36	53
Men (%)				
1966–1975				
Generation X	75	64	59	57
1956–1965				
Late Baby Boom	75	69	53	54
1946–1955				
Early Baby Boom	74	68	52	52
Ratio women/men (per 100)				
1966–1975				
Generation X	44	88	75	96
1956–1965				
Late Baby Boom	40	86	68	106
1946–1955				
Early Baby Boom	27	75	69	102

* Living with at least one child under age 18.

Source: Authors' tabulations using the Integrated Public Use Microdata Series (IPUMS), 2003.

cent of men ages 25 to 64 gave taking care of children as the reason for their nonemployment.[36]

Does family status also affect unpaid work? Data limitations preclude us from examining all the groups we were able to examine for variations in paid labor using the census data. However, we can look at differences for married women and men with children (the family status with the most gender inequality in paid labor) and for single women and men without children (the family status with the most gender equality in paid labor), Table 10 shows that, in 1999, married women with children devoted nearly twice as many weekly hours to total housework as did single women without children (20.0 hours versus 11.4 hours). The increased demand for household labor that accompanies marriage and motherhood is evident in differences among women in core household tasks: Married mothers spend nearly triple the time that single women without children do cooking, cleaning, and doing laundry (17.0 hours versus 6.5 hours). However, husbands may relieve wives of some household chores, because single women without children spend more time on other household tasks than married women, including doing repairs, doing outdoor chores, gardening, taking care of pets, and paying the bills. Nonetheless, the time married fathers and single men without children devote to unpaid labor is much more similar than is the case for women. For example, married fathers spend 6.5 hours on core household tasks, compared with 4.0 hours for single men without children.

As was the case with paid work, single women and men without children are more similar in their unpaid work hour totals than are married mothers and fathers. Married mothers devote almost three times more hours to core household tasks than do married fathers. By contrast, single women without children spend only 60 percent more time on these tasks.

Table 11 shows generational changes in full-time/year-round employment for women and men ages 24 to 35, the ages at which most young adults are adopting family roles and establishing their careers. Full-time/year-round employment increased for married women with children in each successive generation, with the most dramatic increase occurring between the early and late baby boom. By contrast, married men with children did not make similar gains across generations. In fact, it is quite surprising that only 75 percent of men with wives and children work full-time/year-round. The gender gap in labor force attachment declined between married mothers and fathers across the generations because of the increase in married mothers' attachment to the labor force. The most progress in closing this gap was achieved between the early and late baby boom.

Box 3

SINGLE MOTHERS, EMPLOYMENT, AND WELFARE REFORM

Historically, single mothers have been much more likely to be employed than married mothers. The gap between married and single mothers' employment rates narrowed during the 1980s; but in the 1990s, single mothers increased their employment faster than did married mothers. All groups of single mothers saw steep increases in employment rates during the 1990s (see figure). Employment shot up especially quickly for black and Latina single mothers, substantially narrowing what had been a persistent racial and ethnic employment gap.

There are two leading explanations for this phenomenon. On the one hand, welfare policy could have successfully driven single mothers into the labor force. On the other hand, it's possible that the booming economy of the late 1990s increased employment opportunities for single mothers. Although it's not yet possible to resolve this debate, we can shed some light on it.

Federal and state programs to aid low-income families were transformed during the 1990s, culminating in the 1996 Personal Responsibility and Work Opportunity Reconciliation Act (PRWORA) at the federal level. This law replaced the Aid to Families with Dependent Children program, which had been a federal entitlement for poor families, with a program of block grants to the states called Temporary Assistance to Needy Families (TANF). The biggest effect of the change— and its principal aim—was to force single mothers into the labor force. Additionally, the expansion of the Earned Income Tax Credit (EITC) during the 1980s and 1990s also spurred poor women to enter paid employment. At the same time as welfare and tax policy was changing in the 1990s, the economy experienced a sustained recovery following the 1991 recession, with rapid job growth, falling unemployment rates, and job opportunities that reached uncommonly far down the socioeconomic ladder.

Employment Among Single Mothers

Among those without college degrees, never-married mothers had steeper employment rate increases in the 1990s than married mothers: 15 percentage points (62 percent to 77 percent), compared with just a 1 percentage point increase for married mothers (72 percent to 73 percent). Employment also increased for single mothers who had finished college, but not nearly as steeply, and the difference in the increase between never-married mothers and married mothers was not as great. Thus, employment growth was the greatest among those who had been the least likely to be employed before: single mothers with less than a college degree.

The greater growth in employment among single mothers with less education could be evidence for either the welfare-reform or the good-economy explanation. But if the good economy were helping poor mothers in general get jobs, it is likely that the increase would have been similar for married and never-married mothers.

Looking at 1990 versus 2000 is slightly limiting, however, if what we are interested in varied across the decade, as was the case with both economic growth and welfare policy. We

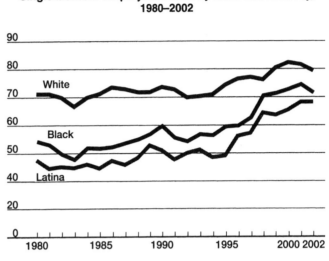

Single Mothers' Employment Rate by Race and Ethnicity, 1980–2002

Note: Black and white categories do not include Latinas.

Source: Authors' tabulations of the March Current Population Surveys (women ages 25–54).

use annual data from the Current Population Survey (CPS), a large, nationally representative employment survey, to get a better idea of the timing of the increase in employment for single mothers.

Major welfare reform was signed into law in 1996, and the time limits for welfare receipt that the new law imposed started to take effect in 1998. The figure above shows that the upward trend predates national welfare reform. In fact, the increase in single-mothers' employment began as soon as the 1990s recession ended, after 1992.

It is important to note, however, that welfare reform started at the state level, and a number of states were taking steps to move single mothers into the labor force even before the national program changed in 1996. So we cannot yet conclude welfare reform was not the driving force for single mothers' employment. We can learn a little more by looking at the effect of the 2001 recession. Both white and black single mothers saw decreases in employment again in 2002, for the first time since the end of the last recession. Clearly, economic conditions are an important factor in these trends.

Additionally, several analyses conducted by the Urban Institute, using their 1999 and 2002 National Survey of America's Families, have concluded that the economic recession hit single mothers hard, undermining the success of welfare reform in moving poor women into employment. The report shows that 50 percent of those leaving welfare from 1997 to 1999 reported working and not receiving TANF anymore in 1999. That number fell to 42 percent in the 2002 report, for those leaving welfare from 2000 to 2002. Hence, opportunity changes from the growth of the economy are probably more important than welfare policy in explaining these trends, although welfare reform and the expanded EITC undoubtedly contributed as well.

Single parents made little progress in improving their labor force attachment between the early and late baby-boom cohorts. Full-time/year-round work stayed steady across these generations for single mothers at 36 percent, while it increased slightly for single fathers from 52 percent to 53 percent. The interesting story for single parents is the large increase in full-time/year-round work that occurred between the late baby boom and Generation X for both women and men. Full-time/year-round employment increased from 36 percent to 44 percent among single mothers and from 53 percent to 59 percent for single fathers. This finding is all the more striking when one considers that this increase is the first change we have seen that was greater between the late baby boom and Generation X than between the early and late baby booms. Substantial gains were also made by Generation X in the percent of single mothers in the labor force and the number of hours they worked (data not shown). Welfare reform and the strong economic recovery of the 1990s had a hand in these increases (see Box 3).

The gender gap in full-time/year-round work among single parents decreased substantially between the late baby-boom and Generation X cohorts. In the late baby-boom cohort, 68 single mothers for every 100 single fathers worked full-time/year-round, whereas in the Generation X cohort, 75 single mothers for every 100 single fathers worked full-time/year-round.

In contrast to increases among women with children, full-time/year-round employment among women without children actually declined between late baby-boom and Generation X women. To our knowledge, this is the first evidence of a reversal in women's steady march toward increased full-time/year-round employment. However, more women in the Generation X cohort were enrolled in college compared with their counterparts in the late baby-boom cohort, and increasing enrollments could have depressed full-time/year-round employment, a topic we turn to in the next section.

Full-time/year-round employment also decreased substantially between the late baby-boom and Generation X cohorts for married men without children (from 69 percent to 64 percent) but not for single men without children. Greater decreases in full-time/year-round employment for men than for women who are married without children resulted in a slight narrowing of the gender gap in employment for this group. In the late baby-boom cohort, single women without children were actually more likely than their male counterparts to work full-time/year-round; but in Generation X, this pattern reversed, so that Generation X women were slightly less likely than men to be employed full-time/year-round. Nonetheless, the gender gap in full-time/year-round employment is still smaller among single women and men with no children than among women and men in other family statuses.

Table 12
AVERAGE WEEKLY HOURS OF CORE HOUSEWORK FOR WOMEN AND MEN AGES 25–54 BY FAMILY STATUS, 1975–1999

Family status	1975	1985	1999
Married with children			
Women	23.6	19.0	17.0
Men	1.1	4.1	6.5
Ratio women's hours to men's hours	21.5	4.6	2.6
Single without children			
Women	10.7	9.8	6.5
Men	3.1	3.8	4.0
Ratio women's hours to men's hours	3.5	2.6	1.6

Note: Core housework includes cooking, meal cleanup, housecleaning, laundry, and ironing.

Source: Authors' tabulations of the U.S. Time Use Studies, 1975, 1985, and 1999.

In sum, with the exception of single women and men with no children, the gender gap in full-time/year-round employment continues to close, albeit at a much reduced pace. But what about unpaid labor? Have married women and men with children made progress in this domain as well? The relatively small sample size of the time diary data does not allow us to investigate change in unpaid labor by family status for those ages 25 to 34, but we are able to investigate these trends for all age groups (ages 25 to 54). The data in Table 12 show that the answer to this question is a resounding yes. Married women with children have decreased the time they devote to cooking, cleaning, and doing laundry, while married men with children have increased the time they spend in these tasks. Thus, whereas in 1975 married mothers were doing more than 21 times as much core housework as married fathers, by 1999 married mothers were doing only 2.6 times as much.

Married mothers continue to do more absolute child care compared with fathers, but gender differences have diminished here too, as shown in Figure 3 (page 95). Married mothers did three times more child care in 1975 compared with married fathers, but by 1999 they were doing only about 1.6 times as much. This is not because mothers decreased the amount of time they were spending in child care but rather because married fathers increased their time with children more than married mothers did. Married mothers' child-care time increased more than one hour between 1975 and 1999, whereas married fathers' child-care time increased almost three hours over the same period. Married dads are also spending more time in routine child-care activities, suggesting that fathers are getting more involved in their children's day-to-day care. Still, mothers continue to do more of the day-to-day care of children.

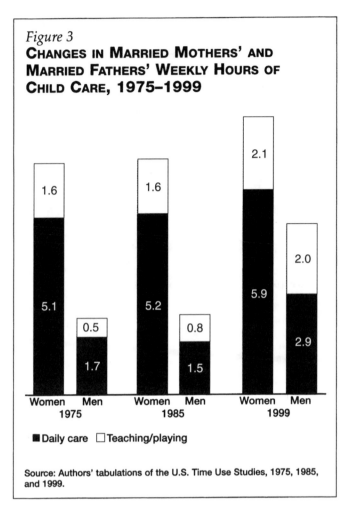

Figure 3

CHANGES IN MARRIED MOTHERS' AND MARRIED FATHERS' WEEKLY HOURS OF CHILD CARE, 1975–1999

■ Daily care □ Teaching/playing

Source: Authors' tabulations of the U.S. Time Use Studies, 1975, 1985, and 1999.

Gender differences in unpaid work have also diminished for single women and men without children (see Table 12, page 94). Single men have increased the time they spend cooking, cleaning, and doing laundry, and single women have decreased their time on these tasks. Most of the decline for single women without children occurred between 1985 and 1999; most of the increases made by men occurred between 1975 and 1985. The combination of these trends resulted in a steady reduction of the gender gap in housework among single women and men.

In sum, women and men's unpaid work is more similar across family statuses today than in the mid-1970s. Nevertheless, single women and men without children are more equal in terms of time in unpaid work than are married women and men with children.

These results parallel those shown for paid work. Single women without children have been able to close the employment gap with men, but married women with children are still employed at lower rates and work fewer hours compared with married men with children. Women's greater responsibility for unpaid work likely underlies continuing gender differences in paid work. And women's and men's time in housework and child care remains far from equal.

EDUCATIONAL ATTAINMENT

Two of the theories introduced earlier to explain women's and men's allocation to paid and unpaid work emphasize differences in human capital. Human capital includes the set of skills and experiences employees bring to the job. One component of human capital is educational attainment. Women and men with diplomas and degrees are more attractive to employers, tend to get the best jobs when they leave school, and are better protected against unemployment during tough economic times than are their less-educated counterparts.

Like changes in the family, the institution of higher education was transformed by changes in society and the economy. Prior to the 1970s, opportunities to attend college were more common for men than for women. The gender gap in educational attainment reached its peak in the parents of the baby-boom generation, when many women married early and stayed home to raise their children while their husbands went to college under the G.I. Bill. Gender differences in educational attainment diminished with passage of Title IX of the Education Amendments of 1972, which opened the doors to institutions of higher learning for women by prohibiting sex discrimination in all public and private schools receiving federal funding. This legislation was passed at about the same time that reproductive rights were being bolstered by increased access to the birth control pill and the legalization of abortion. During this time, shifts in the economy translated into an increased demand for educated workers, giving women an alternative to early marriage and motherhood: the pursuit of higher education and the attendant qualifications to land a good job.

Figure 4 shows that women have benefited from these societal changes, having improved their level of education in each successive cohort. Generation X women are much more likely to have college degrees and much less likely to have only a high school degree or less when compared with their counterparts in the early and late baby-boom cohorts. Late baby-boom women made some inroads into college compared with early baby-boom women, but they did not seem to be able to translate their increased college attendance into a degree. The change in the proportion of women who were college graduates did not actually occur until Generation X, when a record 30 percent were college graduates, compared with only 22 percent of late baby-boom women.

By contrast, men did not vastly improve their educational attainment from generation to generation. The most noteworthy change for men occurred with the increase in the proportion with some college. But most of this change occurred between the early and late baby-boom cohorts. The proportion of men who were college graduates increased slightly between the late baby-boom and Generation X cohorts, but because there was a

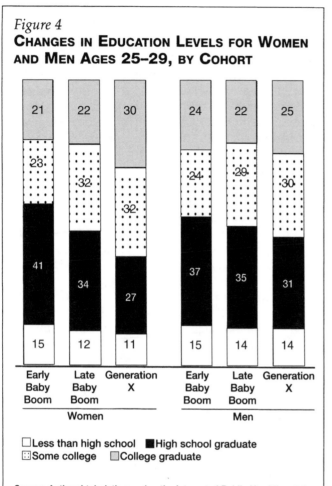

Figure 4

CHANGES IN EDUCATION LEVELS FOR WOMEN AND MEN AGES 25–29, BY COHORT

	Early Baby Boom	Late Baby Boom	Generation X	Early Baby Boom	Late Baby Boom	Generation X
College graduate	21	22	30	24	22	25
Some college	23	32	32	24	29	30
High school graduate	41	34	27	37	35	31
Less than high school	15	12	11	15	14	14
	Women			Men		

☐ Less than high school ■ High school graduate
▨ Some college ☐ College graduate

Source: Authors' tabulations using the Integrated Public Use Microdata Series (IPUMS), 2003.

Table 13

PAID WORK FOR WOMEN AND MEN AGES 25–54 BY EDUCATION LEVEL, 2000

Paid work	Less than high school	High school graduate	Some college	College graduate
Worked for pay (%)				
Women	55	75	84	87
Men	77	88	93	96
Ratio women/men (per 100)	71	85	90	91
Worked full-time/year-round (%)				
Women	24	43	51	50
Men	44	65	73	77
Ratio women/men (per 100)	55	66	70	65
Average annual hours of work				
Women	852	1,294	1,490	1,607
Men	1,473	1,855	2,033	2,191
Women's hours as % of men's hours	58	70	73	73

Source: Authors' tabulations using the Integrated Public Use Microdata Series (IPUMS), 2003.

decline in this proportion between the early and late baby-boom cohorts, the net improvement over three generations was only 1 percentage point. Improvements in the educational attainment of women and the relative stability in men's educational attainment across generations means that Generation X women have achieved something no other generation before them has: A greater proportion of women than men have college degrees (30 percent and 25 percent, respectively).

Even though women have made phenomenal progress with regard to education, men continue to have higher employment rates and spend more time working for pay than women, even within education levels (see Table 13). Women and men with at least some college tend to be more equal in terms of paid work than their less-educated counterparts. For example, in 2000, there were 91 female college graduates in the labor force for every 100 male college graduates, and these women worked 73 hours for every 100 hours worked by men. In stark contrast, among those with less than a high school education in 2000, 71 women worked per 100 men, and these women worked only 58 hours for every 100 hours worked by men. In general, as educa-

tional attainment increases, paid work and the amount of time worked also increases for both women and men. Why might women and men with more education spend more time in paid work compared with those with less education? More highly educated women and men may have more interesting or enjoyable careers than the often tedious work in jobs held by less-educated individuals. In addition, occupations requiring more education, such as scientist, professor, or physician, are more often full-time jobs compared with those requiring little education that are typically part-time, such as salesperson or fast-food cook. It is also possible that changes in the economic environment have intensified the time demands required in white-collar jobs. Downsizing of middle management along with shifts of some tasks formerly handled by administrative staff (such as professionals preparing their own documents on computers) has meant more work spread among fewer people.

Despite gains in higher education among women, men are still more likely to be engaged in paid work and tend to work more hours at all educational levels. Is the same true for unpaid labor? Do women spend more time in unpaid work than men regardless of education level, and are women and men more equal at higher levels of education? When one considers all housework, women do spend more hours engaged in this type of work than men in both education categories (see Table 14, page 97). But men and women with a high school degree or less appear to be more equal than their more

Table 14
AVERAGE WEEKLY HOURS OF UNPAID WORK FOR WOMEN AND MEN AGES 25–54 BY EDUCATION, 1999

Unpaid work	High school or less	More than high school
All housework		
Women	18.5	15.4
Men	13.7	9.4
Ratio women's hours to men's hours	1.4	1.6
Core housework*		
Women	14.4	12.1
Men	6.1	5.5
Ratio women's hours to men's hours	2.4	2.2
Other housework**		
Women	4.0	3.3
Men	7.6	3.9
Ratio women's hours to men's hours	0.5	0.8

* Core housework includes cooking, meal cleanup, housecleaning, laundry, and ironing.

** Other housework includes repairs, outdoor chores, gardening, animal care, and bill-paying.

Source: Authors' tabulations of the U.S. Time Diary Study, 1999.

Table 15
FULL-TIME/YEAR-ROUND WORK FOR WOMEN AND MEN AGES 25–34 BY EDUCATION AND COHORT

Cohort	Less than high school	High school graduate	Some college	College graduate
Women (%)				
1966–1975				
Generation X	21	39	48	53
1956–1965				
Late Baby Boom	20	38	46	51
1946–1955				
Early Baby Boom	19	33	37	36
Men (%)				
1966–1975				
Generation X	43	62	70	73
1956–1965				
Late Baby Boom	42	64	69	74
1946–1955				
Early Baby Boom	49	67	69	71
Ratio women/men (per 100)				
1966–1975				
Generation X	49	63	69	73
1956–1965				
Late Baby Boom	48	59	67	69
1946–1955				
Early Baby Boom	39	49	54	51

Source: Authors' tabulations using the Integrated Public Use Microdata Series (IPUMS), 2003.

highly educated counterparts. A closer examination of the data, however, indicates that most of this difference is because among those with a high school degree or less, men spend much more time than women doing other housework, while women and men with at least a high school degree spend more similar numbers of hours on these tasks. Women and men with a high school degree or less also spend more time on core housework compared with women and men with more education. More highly educated people generally have higher incomes than those of more modest educational attainment and may purchase household services such as prepared food and lawn care. Less-educated women and men spend fewer hours in paid work compared with the more highly educated, so they may have more time to spend in unpaid work and less discretionary income to purchase outside help.

Recall that many social and economic changes over the past several decades altered the context in which women and men obtain their educations and enter the labor force. Many of these changes, such as the postponement of marriage and childbearing and the softening of norms against women in the labor force, have favored women's educational advancement. Changes in the economy have shifted jobs from manufacturing toward service, and these changes have favored women's employment. Table 15 shows that women's full-time/year-round employment increased for each successive cohort, but increases were negligible among

women with less than a high school education compared with women with more education. For men the story is quite different. The proportion of men with full-time/year-round employment remained relatively stable across cohorts for those with at least some college, whereas full-time/year-round employment actually decreased substantially for men with a high school degree or less, most likely due to the decline in manufacturing jobs.

Due mainly to men's stagnating or worsening labor force attachment and to the increasing labor force attachment for those women with at least a high school degree, the gap in full-time/year-round employment within each educational category closed substantially. For example, among those with less than a high school education in the early baby-boom cohort, there were 39 women for every 100 men who worked full-time/year-round, but by Generation X this number had increased to 49 women per 100 men. Among those with a college degree, there were 51 women for every 100 men working full-time/year-round in the early baby-boom generation, compared with 73 women per 100 men among Generation X. The most progress in closing the gender gap occurred between the early and late baby-boom cohorts.

Table 16

AVERAGE WEEKLY HOURS OF CORE HOUSEWORK FOR WOMEN AND MEN AGES 25–54 BY EDUCATION, 1975–1999

Education	1975	1985	1999
High school or less			
Women	22.0	17.2	14.4
Men	2.1	3.4	6.1
Ratio of women's hours to men's hours	10.5	5.1	2.4
More than high school			
Women	17.7	13.9	12.1
Men	1.3	4.1	5.5
Ratio of women's hours to men's hours	13.6	3.4	2.2

Note: Core housework includes cooking, meal cleanup, housecleaning, laundry, and ironing.

Source: Authors' tabulations of the U.S. Time Use Studies, 1975, 1985, and 1999.

Has progress been made in closing the gap in unpaid work as well among women and men with differing amounts of education? The answer seems to be yes. In 1975, among those with a high school education or less, women spent about 10 hours for every hour men spent cooking, doing dishes, cleaning house, and doing the laundry (see Table 16). By 1985, this differential was narrowed to five hours; and by 1999, women spent a little more than two hours doing these tasks for every hour men spent doing them. In 1975, for those with more than a high school degree, the gap in housework between women and men was greater than it was for less-educated women and men. Women with more than a high school education spent almost 14 hours on these tasks for every hour men spent on them. But by 1985, the difference in the time men and women spent in housework was smaller among those with more than a high school education than among those with a high school degree or less.

Educational attainment is tied to family status and norms about the appropriate roles for men and women. We now turn to examining whether compositional shifts or behavioral modifications are accounting for changes in women's and men's work, and the slowing of these changes in the most recent cohort.

ACCOUNTING FOR TRENDS IN PAID AND UNPAID WORK

How women and men divide their time between paid and unpaid work changes over time, both because the demographic characteristics of people change (compositional shifts) and because people modify their behavior.

As we have described, women and men in more recent generations are better educated and are delaying entry into marriage and parenthood well into their 30s. Generation X women and men are both more likely to be single without children and single with children compared with earlier generations. But how do all these changes affect the paid and unpaid work of women and men?

In this section we first discuss how population changes in family status and education should affect paid and unpaid work. We then explore how shifting behaviors shape changes in paid and unpaid work. Finally, we examine the roles that changing behavior and changes in the composition of family status and education play in explaining shifts in paid and unpaid work.

Higher levels of educational attainment likely account for some of the increase in women's paid work hours as well as changes in time allocated by women to child care and housework. Shifts in the economy from manufacturing toward services translate into increased demand for workers with higher levels of education. More highly educated people are more likely to be employed and to work more hours than those with less education. Women's increasing education levels have no doubt played a role in boosting their employment and labor force attachment. Better-educated parents spend more time with children than less-educated parents spend. Thus, increases in women's education have helped them preserve time with children. Some research suggests that college-educated men do more housework compared with men without college degrees, whereas college-educated women do less housework compared with women with less education. Thus, women's gains in education have likely reduced the time women spend doing housework.

Also, college-educated women and men generally have more egalitarian attitudes about gender roles. For example, they believe that paid and unpaid work should be shared equally. The increase in women's education over time has likely augmented the number of women who favor more egalitarian gender roles and thus has acted to further spur the growth in women's employment. Because men's education has not changed appreciably since the early baby boom, it should not affect men's paid and unpaid work.

If education were all that mattered for explaining change in paid and unpaid work, women's continued improvement in education and men's lack of improvement should have substantially decreased the gender gap from the early baby boom through Generation X. But progress toward closing the gender gap in both paid and unpaid labor has slowed to a crawl since the late baby boom, and yet family status has changed over this period as well. Can changes in the composition of family status help explain this apparent anomaly?

For women, marriage and parenthood increase unpaid work and decrease paid work. More men and women are single without children and single with children than in the past. The increase in singles without children should boost employment and labor force attachment and dampen time spent in unpaid work for women and men because the people in this status do not have the family responsibilities that require more unpaid work. By contrast, the increase in single parents should dampen labor force attachment and unpaid work for both women and men because people in this family status have to do both types of work themselves. This dampening should be stronger for women than for men, who are more likely to have live-in help from a cohabiting partner or other relatives. Thus we have two trends in family status that have counterbalancing effects on paid and unpaid work. If one examines the statuses of marriage and parenthood, however, the gap between men and women has actually increased from the early baby boom to Generation X, so that over time women are increasing their family responsibilities vis-à-vis men. If family status were all that mattered, women should be losing ground to men in both work spheres.

Because young women and men are delaying parenting until older ages, family size has decreased and parents are older. Having fewer children in the home decreases housework and child-care time.[37] However, older parents are more likely to have chosen to become parents rather than to have become parents through an unintended pregnancy, and they might want to spend more time in child care and the household labor that goes along with children. Older parents will typically also have more competing demands on their time, especially from paid work. As a result, population changes in family size should act to decrease unpaid work and increase paid work among both women and men, whereas changes in the age of parents should work to increase both.

The increase in women's employment should also account for some of the change in housework and child care, because the more hours women spend doing paid work, the fewer they have to devote to unpaid work in the home. In fact, studies show that employed women do less housework and child care compared with women who do not work for pay.[38] In contrast, men's employment has little or no association with time in housework and child care.

Changes in women's and men's allocation of time to paid and unpaid work also reflect behavioral shifts associated with the cultural and social transformations discussed in previous sections. For example, attitudes about women's involvement in paid work have become increasingly liberal, and norms about the appropriateness of women attending college have changed. Changes in the social acceptance of women working and going to college have allowed more women to change their behaviors, increasing employment and college attendance. Housekeeping standards are also more relaxed than in the past, and convenience products such as take-out meals are more common. These changes have allowed

women to decrease the amount of time they spend on housework. It has also become more socially acceptable for men to cook, clean, and take care of their children. By contrast, however, parenting practices have become more time-intensive as mothers and fathers are expected to devote most nonemployment hours to their children. Changes in parenting norms mean that parents have increased the time they spend with children.

Up until this point, we have addressed how women's and men's paid and unpaid work time have changed in relation to changes in a single demographic characteristic. Yet these characteristics tend to be grouped. For example, single mothers tend to be younger and have less education compared with married mothers. What our earlier discussion could not tell us is how changes in family status and human capital *combined* have affected changes in women's and men's paid and unpaid work, and to what extent these changes are due to the changing family status and human capital characteristics of the population versus shifts in men's and women's behaviors. For this information, we adjust paid and unpaid work hours to account for the combined effect of changes in women's and men's human capital characteristics (employment, education, and age), family status characteristics (marital and parental status), and alterations in their behavior. We then separate the change in these paid and unpaid work hours into that part due to shifts over time in the characteristics of people and that part due to changes over time in how people behave.[39]

Table 17 shows adjusted annual hours of paid work for women and men in 1980 and 2000, and the difference in adjusted annual hours between 1980 and 2000. We calculated the adjusted annual hours under the assumption that all women (men) have the family status and human capital characteristics of the average woman (man) in 1980 and in 2000. We can then partition the difference in the adjusted annual hours between 1980 and 2000 into two components: the portion that is the result of shifts in women's and men's characteristics and the portion due to shifts in behavior. This partitioning allows us to determine whether the inclination of women and men to spend time in paid work changed between 1980 and 2000, or whether the observed difference in annual hours of paid work reflects merely a change in the structure of the population, such as how many women and men are married, have children, and have a college education.

The results indicate that, between 1980 and 2000, behavioral modifications and shifting demographic characteristics worked to increase women's annual employment hours. Nonetheless, the effect of behavior was a bit stronger. Changes in characteristics account for 47 percent (241 hours) and changes in behavior account for 53 percent (268 hours) of the 509-hour increase in annual paid work time. Women spent more time in paid work in 2000 than in 1980 because fewer of them are married, are par-

Table 17

PORTION OF CHANGE IN ADJUSTED ANNUAL HOURS OF PAID WORK ATTRIBUTABLE TO BEHAVIORAL AND COMPOSITIONAL FACTORS, 1980 AND 2000

Adjusted annual hours of paid work	Women	Men
2000	1,282	1,959
1980	773	1,954
Difference 2000-1980 adjusted annual hours	509	5
Change due to shifts in characteristics	241	44
Change due to shifts in behavior	268	-39

Source: Authors' tabulations using the Integrated Public Use Microdata Series (IPUMS), 2003.

Table 18

PORTION OF CHANGE IN ADJUSTED WEEKLY HOURS OF HOUSEWORK AND CHILD CARE ATTRIBUTABLE TO BEHAVIORAL AND COMPOSITIONAL FACTORS, 1975 AND 1999

Panel A:

Adjusted weekly hours of housework	Women	Men
1999	21.2	17.0
1975	25.2	12.2
Difference 1999-1975 adjusted weekly hours	-3.9	4.8
Change due to shifts in characteristics	-1.9	-0.3
Change due to shifts in behavior	-2.0	5.1

Panel B:

Adjusted weekly hours of child care	Mothers	Fathers
1999	16.0	14.2
1975	11.7	7.8
Difference 1999-1975 adjusted weekly hours	4.4	6.4
Change due to shifts in characteristics	-0.9	0.5
Change due to shifts in behavior	5.3	5.9

Source: Authors' tabulations of the U.S. Time Use Studies, 1975 and 1999.

ents, and have less than a college education, and because they are more likely to want to spend time in paid work.

For men, changes in demographic characteristics and shifts in behavior contributed about equally to the small change in annual employment hours. However, changes in characteristics and behavior worked in opposite directions: If men in 2000 had similar levels of education, marriage, and parenthood as did men in 1980, annual employment would have increased by 44 hours. But shifts in men's behavior also occurred, pulling annual employment down by 39 hours and resulting in only a five-hour increase over the period. Hence, changes in women's behavior and characteristics both worked to increase their annual employment hours, whereas men's behavior has counteracted compositional shifts that alone would have increased paid work time. Overwhelming majorities of young men today state that they desire jobs that will allow them to spend time with their families. The results of the decomposition suggest that men have changed their behavior to ratchet down paid work time, possibly because they are spending more time in unpaid work and possibly because of the scarcity of good jobs. But do we find similar patterns for unpaid work time? Are changes in unpaid work due to shifts in the propensity of women and men to spend time in housework and child care, or are the observed changes merely the result of shifts in women's and men's characteristics?

Table 18 shows change in adjusted weekly hours of housework between 1975 and 1999 (Panel A) and child care between 1975 and 1999 (Panel B). The results in Panel A indicate that, for men, almost all of the five-hour-per-week increase in housework time between 1975 and 1999 is related to behavioral change rather than changes in characteristics. Men's inclinations to cook, clean, and do laundry have increased since 1975. In contrast, if behavior had not changed, and men in 1999 were just like men in 1975, housework time would have declined by about 18 minutes.

For women, behavioral change and compositional shifts both contributed to the almost four-hour decline in housework between 1975 and 1999. About 49 percent of the decline is due to the larger proportion of women who are employed and college-educated and the smaller proportion who are married with children. For example, if women in 1999 were just like women in 1975—with the same lower rates of labor force participation and higher rates of marriage—the decline would have been 1.9 hours per week, not 3.9 hours. Because women's behavior also changed over the period, however, housework declined an additional two hours. Women have simply become less likely to want to spend time doing housework.

Some sociologists argue that women's housework can decline only to a certain point, because doing unpaid work is still considered part and parcel of being a good wife and mother.[40] Our results indicate that the activities in which women's housework have declined are the easiest to outsource entirely or piecemeal, suggesting that we may have reached the limits of behavioral change. For example, many services such as banking or ordering groceries can now be done online. Modern appliances, plus the inclination to "eat out," do appear to play a part in the reduction of women's housework time in the United States.[41] Consequently, women's housework time may have declined in some activities while their production of household goods has remained at "acceptable" levels.

It is also likely that what constitutes an "acceptable" level of housework has changed, as some research indicates that standards of housekeeping have fallen since the mid-1970s.[42] The use of cleaning products for more discretionary tasks such as cleaning the oven and shampooing carpets dropped sharply between 1986 and 1996.[43] Given the increased hours women spend working for pay, it is entirely possible that women are simply doing the bare minimum amount of housework. If this were the case, a further reduction in women's hours spent in housework would not be possible even with these technological advancements and the ability to purchase substitute goods and services.

What about mothers' and fathers' child-care time? Conventional wisdom has held that changes in the family have necessarily reduced parents' time with children. Results in Panel B of Table 18 indicate, however, that mothers and fathers have changed their behavior more than enough to make up for changes in the family that alone would have decreased time with children.

Between 1975 and 1999, predicted weekly hours of child care increased 4.4 hours for mothers and 6.4 hours for fathers. If mothers in 1999 had the same demographic characteristics as mothers in 1975, compositional differences alone would have *decreased* child-care time by almost one hour, with most of the decline due to increases in maternal employment (results not shown). However, negative compositional changes were more than outweighed by behavioral shifts that worked to increase mothers' time in child care by 5.3 hours per week. For fathers, compositional and behavioral shifts both contribute to the 6.4-hour increase in child-care time between 1975 and 1999, but the relative contribution of behavior is much greater. Increases in married fathers' propensity to spend time caring for children explain 92 percent (or 5.9 hours) of the change. In contrast, shifts in demographic characteristics account for only 8 percent of the increase in fathers' child-care time (or about 30 minutes per week), with most of this attributable to increased levels of paternal education (results not shown).

Behavioral changes among mothers and fathers likely stem from the increasingly voluntary nature of parenthood, burgeoning parental concern over the safety of children, and pervasive changes in the cultural context of parenthood.[44] The widespread availability of contraceptives and lessened normative pressure to become a parent suggest that women and men who decide to become parents may increasingly be selected from those who have greater motivation and desire to invest heavily in children. The erosion of community bonds within neighborhoods and heightened parental fears about children's safety appear to have increased the level of parental supervision of children's activities. Changes in the cultural context of parenting and childhood have also driven up the amount of parental time necessary to produce a "good" childhood.[45]

The results in Tables 17 and 18 suggest that, although shifts in characteristics and behavior both play

a part in explaining changes in paid and unpaid work, behavioral alterations account for a larger share of change. But what about change over the past decade? Results from the same type of analysis (not shown) indicate that behavioral change in the realms of paid work and housework has slowed to a crawl. Only about one-quarter of the changes in women's paid work and housework hours over the 1990s is attributable to behavioral shifts. Additionally, the small uptick in men's housework over the past decade occurred because men's characteristics changed, not because of further behavioral modification. In contrast, though, behavioral shifts of mothers and fathers continued to drive child-care hours up in the 1990s, similar to the story of change in the 1980s. The declining importance of behavioral modifications in explaining change in paid work and housework hours suggests that women and men have reached a limit in the extent to which they can rearrange their lives to accommodate both paid and unpaid work.

PROGRESS MADE, GAPS REMAIN

At the beginning of this report, we wondered whether the slowing pace of family change portended a plateau in the steady movement toward greater gender similarity in employment and household work that occurred between 1960 and 1990. Our findings suggest that sweeping changes in women's paid and unpaid work have slowed to a crawl. And while the transformation of men's household work was not as dramatic as women's paid-work transformations, here too change has slowed.

We find that gender differences in all measures of paid work—employment in the previous year, full-time/year-round employment, and annual employment hours—narrowed more sharply in the 1980s than in the 1990s. Additionally, Generation X women do not appear to have increased their labor force attachment appreciably over that of late baby-boom women, in sharp contrast to the substantial increases evident between early baby-boom women and late baby-boom women.

The plateau in paid work appears to be interrelated with a slowdown in gender equality in unpaid work as well. The steady decline in housework has stalled among young women: Generation X women are doing about the same amount of housework as their late baby-boom counterparts. Among all women, declines in housework are smaller after 1975 than they were from 1965 to 1975. In each successive cohort, men are doing more housework, but the relative increase was less for the Generation X cohort compared with previous cohorts. Fathers increased child-care time substantially between 1985 and 1999; however, mothers also increased their child-care time, so a large gender gap in parental child-care time remains.

Although to a lesser degree than in 1970, marriage and parenthood continue to differentiate women's and men's paid and unpaid work time. Paid and unpaid work time allocations are most similar among single women and men without children and most dissimilar among married mothers and fathers. Among young adults, more women and men in Generation X are single with no children than in the early and late baby-boom cohorts. However, the gender gap in marriage and parenthood has increased over time, so that Generation X women have even more family responsibilities than their male counterparts when compared with early baby-boom women and men.

Finally, education levels for women skyrocketed between the early baby-boom and Generation X cohorts. Women in Generation X did something no other cohort before them has: More women than men in this cohort have college degrees.

All of these population changes have affected the shifts we documented in women's and men's paid and unpaid work. But work and family change between the late baby-boom and Generation X cohorts was incremental, in sharp contrast to the more sweeping change that took place between the early baby-boom and late baby-boom cohorts. Women have altered their behavior so they spend more time in paid work and child care and less time in housework. Men have changed too, making behavioral modifications to decrease time in paid work and increase time in housework and child care. Nonetheless, our analysis indicates that, with the exception of child care, behavior appears to have changed little between 1990 and 2000—most change occurred between 1980 and 1990. In fact, the relatively small population shifts away from being married with children toward being single with no children and increased education explain the vast majority of the small gain in women's labor force attachment in the past decade. And increased labor force participation in conjunction with these trends explains about three-quarters of the small decline in housework for women over the same period. For men, shifts away from being married with children toward being single explain the vast majority of the small increase in their housework over the past decade.

The timing of change for men in the domestic sphere is more recent than that for women. Change in men's involvement in the home may be slowing but does not show quite the "stall" that characterizes women's market work trends. The data presented in this report suggest that women changed first. They increased their paid work and decreased their housework as much as they could. But women may have reached a limit on the amount of domestic work that they can shed and still maintain a comfortable life at home. Similarly, mothers made adjustments to include more market work in their lives, but also may have reached a limit on how much paid work they can add and still care for their children—unless they want to dramatically sacrifice time with children either by not having children in the first place or spending little time with them; or, for single mothers, by granting physical custody to the nonresidential father. Hence, women's market participation has stalled far short of full market equality with men. Unless conditions change—such as less maternal value being placed on time with children, fewer women having sole responsibility for raising children, men helping more, or policies making it easier to combine both childrearing and market work—the trend toward greater gender similarity in market work may have reached a new "equilibrium" in the United States. There is considerably less gender specialization in the home and the market than there was in the 1950s, but mothers continue to concentrate more on family care whereas fathers continue to concentrate more on breadwinning. What implications does this have for reaching gender equality?

Two models of gender equality, or "nirvanas," have been proposed in the feminist economic literature.[46] The first model has three characteristics: men's and women's full-time labor force participation rates are equivalent; societal tax systems are not structured to encourage women to specialize in household labor; and housework and child care are performed efficiently through public-sector or private-sector provision. The second model has two characteristics: men increase their time in household labor and decrease their time in paid employment, and public policies encourage and reward shared paid and unpaid work between women and men.

Under both models, women's and men's time use will become more similar, but for different reasons. In the first model, women reallocate their time away from unpaid work to paid work, and their time use becomes more like men's. In contrast, in the second model men reallocate their time away from paid work to unpaid work and their time use becomes more like women's.

Convergence due to men's time use becoming more similar to women's time use is more likely to result in gender equality. Women and men do not want to purchase all household goods and services from the market, because "family work" such as cooking meals, doing chores around the house, and caring for children helps reinforce family relationships.[47] If men do not continue to increase their time in unpaid work, women will continue to do more than their fair share. And if women continue to be responsible for housework and child care, their paid work time will continue to be less than men's and they will continue to be at a financial disadvantage. Men will also continue to be emotionally deprived of the benefits women experience from their participation in caring for families, friends, and community.

But there are problems with this solution. First, husbands and fathers face long work weeks already. Certainly among married couples, while fathers are not doing half of the work in the home, they work many hours in the market, such that their total workloads look very similar to those of mothers.[48] Married fathers express even greater feelings of inadequate time with their children than do mothers in the United States, largely because work hours are so long.[49] How much ability men have to curtail those long work hours is not clear, but one suspects this curtailment is unlikely to happen in an economy where job tenure is uncertain and interesting and well-remunerated work often comes with the price of long hours. Fathers still feel strong pressure to provide adequately for their families, and couples manage work and family demands with one partner, usually the mother, scaling back market work hours, thereby placing greater pressure on the other partner to work long hours. Married couples also generally need to have at least one spouse in a full-time/year-round job because these jobs have higher wages and usually offer health insurance. Because husbands continue to earn more than wives, most couples make the rational choice that husbands will work full time and wives part-time. In the absence of constraints, both spouses might choose to work fewer paid work hours. But this choice is not available for most people. Even Robert Reich and Penny Hughes, arguably valuable employees whom employers should have wanted to retain, were not able to change their paid work situation enough so that they could better balance work and family.

Second, as a nation we have fairly high expectations for consumption, and scaling back work hours has implications for our ability to realize those expectations. Owning a home is highly valued. Having many cars is common in families for the commute to work and other activities. As more adults work outside the home, more market substitutes for work in the home are needed, desired, and afforded. For parents, an important aspect of rising expectations is greater emphasis on the need for children to attend and complete postsecondary education and for parents to finance that education. Public education is universally provided in the United States through secondary school but not thereafter. Even a college education at a public institution in the United States is an expensive proposition, so parental investment in their children's education promotes market work. Hence, men's and women's paid and unpaid work time has become more similar, but the social policies designed to facilitate and encourage a more equitable division of labor are lacking. The United States appears to have merged elements from both nirvanas, leaving American men and women and their families in a decidedly less-than-utopian state.

Government policies allowing for more successful integration of work and family lives are few and far between in this country, and the laws governing workplace schedules are woefully outdated and have not evolved with the changing workforce and economy. However, *Working Mothers* list of the "100 Best Companies

for Working Mothers" has spotlighted some of the most innovative corporate practices and programs that improve their workers' work and family lives. The list was introduced in 1986 and has spawned intense competition among CEOs to implement change in their workplaces so that their companies will make the list and become employers of choice for working mothers. These companies have made many changes. For example, they have added child-care programs and child-care referral services. But most of these companies are large, and they employ only about 2 percent of all employees.

It is doubtful that more progress will be made to close the gender gap in paid and unpaid work unless more widespread work-family policies are adopted. However, Americans have been very resistant to the high taxes that fund generous family-friendly policies. For public or private provision of such support to be successfully implemented in the United States, a case must be made to a wider audience that the lack of work and family policy is costly to employers or to governments, either in terms of lack of adequate nurturance of children; lack of necessary investment in the productivity of future workers; increased absenteeism, lower worker productivity and higher turnover of employees; or increased health costs of current workers that result from work and family stress.[50]

Making the case for greater government and private-sector involvement in the work and family arena is in its infancy in the United States. The challenge is to implement policies that fit the needs of workers at all socioeconomic levels and all life stages—for all those who need child-care or elder-care services, adequate wages and more and better work hours, reduction in work hours, or greater flexibility in meeting family demands.[51] Policies must address an employer's need to remain competitive in an increasingly global marketplace, and must build upon rather than erode the progress made toward gender equality in paid and unpaid work.[52]

It is possible that the increased educational attainment of Generation X women may portend a surge in full-time/year-round employment. Yet our results suggest that women and men may have reached their limits in terms of individual change. Without some adjustments on the part of employers and the government, gender differences in paid and unpaid work are likely to continue.

ACKNOWLEDGMENTS

The authors would like to thank John Haaga and Reynolds Farley and the anonymous reviewers for helpful comments on earlier drafts of the manuscript; Matthew Hayden for technical assistance with the figures and tables; Ellen Carnevale and Mary Kent for editorial suggestions; and the Population Reference Bureau and Russell Sage Foundation for supporting this report.

REFERENCES

If provided by the authors, additional text and data associated with this report are available at www.prb.org/AmericanPeople.

1. National Consumers League, "Dealing With Stress," accessed online at www.nclnet.org/stress/summary.htm, on June 3, 2004.
2. National Consumers League, "Dealing With Stress."
3. Susan Seitel, "Stress: Epidemic of the 21st Century," *Work and Family Trend Report* (Minnetonka, MN: Work and Family Connection, 2001), accessed online at www.work family.com/sub_services/tr/, on June 3, 2004.
4. Paula Rayman, "Life's Work: Generational Attitudes Toward Work and Life Integration," *Radcliffe Public Policy Center* (Cambridge, MA: President and Fellows of Harvard College, 2000), accessed online at www.radcliffe.edu/research/pubpol/lifeswork.pdf, on June 3, 2004.
5. Sara McLanahan and Lynne Casper, "Growing Diversity and Inequality in the American Family," in *State of the Union: America in the 1990s*, ed. Reynolds Farley (New York: Russell Sage Foundation, 1995); and Lynne M. Casper and Suzanne M. Bianchi, *Continuity and Change in the American Family* (Thousand Oaks, CA: Sage Publications, 2002).
6. Reynolds Farley, *The New American Reality: Who We Are, How We Got Here, Where We Are Going* (New York: Russell Sage Foundation, 1996); and Frank Levy, *The New Dollars and Dreams: American Incomes and Economic Change* (New York: Russell Sage Foundation, 1998).
7. Andrew J. Cherlin, *Marriage, Divorce, Remarriage* (Cambridge, MA: Harvard University Press, 1992).
8. Suzanne M. Bianchi and Lynne M. Casper, "American Families," *Population Bulletin* 55, no. 4 (2000).
9. McLanahan and Casper, "Growing Diversity and Inequality in the American Family"; Farley, *The New American Reality*; and Suzanne M. Bianchi, "Changing Economic Roles of Women and Men," in *State of the Union: America in the 1990s*, ed. Reynolds Farley (New York: Russell Sage Foundation, 1995).
10. Levy, *The New Dollars and Dreams*.
11. McLanahan and Casper, "Growing Diversity and Inequality in the American Family."
12. Casper and Bianchi, *Continuity and Change in the American Family*.
13. William G. Axinn and Arland Thornton, "The Transformation in the Meaning of Marriage," in *The Ties That Bind: Perspectives on Marriage and Cohabitation*, ed. Linda J. Waite (New York: Aldine de Gruyter, 2000); and Arland Thornton and Linda Young-DeMarco, "Four Decades of Trends in Attitudes Toward Family Issues in the United States: The 1960s Through the 1990s," *Journal of Marriage and the Family* 63, no. 4 (2001): 1009-37.
14. Claudia Goldin, *Understanding the Gender Gap: an Economic History of American Women* (New York: Oxford University Press, 1990).
15. Rachel Rosenfeld, "Women's Work Histories," *Population and Development Review* 22, Suppl. S (1996): 199-222.
16. Suzanne M. Bianchi and Daphne Spain, "Women, Work, and Family in America," *Population Bulletin* 51, no. 3 (1996).
17. F. Thomas Juster et al., "Time Use in Economic and Social Accounts, 1975-76," *Survey Research Center, Institute for Social Research, The University of Michigan, ICPSR 7580* (Ann Arbor, MI: Inter-university Consortium for Political and Social Research , 1979); John P. Robinson, "Americans' Use of Time, 1985," *Survey Research Center, University of Maryland College Park, ICPSR 9875* (Ann Arbor, MI: Inter-university Consortium for Political and Social Research, 1997); and Suzanne M. Bianchi, John P. Robinson, and Liana C. Sayer, "Family Interaction, Social Capital, and Trends in Time Use Study," *Survey Research Center, University of Maryland College Park* (Ann Arbor, MI: Inter-university Consortium for Political and Social Research, 2001).
18. Liana C. Sayer, "Gender, Time Use, and Inequality: Trends in Women's and Men's Paid Work, Unpaid Work, and Free Time" (paper delivered at the Annual Meetings of the Population Association of America, Atlanta, May 2002).
19. David Cotter, Joan Hermsen, and Reeve Vanneman, "Women's Work and Working Women: The Demand for Female Labor," *Gender & Society* 15, no. 3 (2001): 429-52.
20. Bianchi, "Changing Economic Roles of Women and Men."
21. Penny E. Becker and Phyllis Moen, "Scaling Back: Dual-Earner Couples' Work-Family Strategies," *Journal of Marriage and Family* 61, no. 4 (1999): 995-1007.
22. Gary S. Becker, *A Treatise on the Family* (Cambridge, MA: Harvard University Press, 1991).
23. Rae L. Blumberg and Marion T. Coleman, "A Theoretical Look at the Gender Balance of Power in American Couples," *Journal of Family Issues* 10, no. 2 (1989): 225-50; and Myra M. Ferree, "The Gender Division of Labor in Two-Earner Marriages," *Journal of Family Issues* 12, no. 2 (1991): 158-80.
24. Scott Coltrane, *Family Man: Fatherhood, Housework, and Gender Equity* (New York: Oxford University Press, 1996).
25. Scott J. South and Glenna Spitze, "Housework in Marital and Nonmarital Households," *American Sociological Review* 59, no. 3 (1994): 327-47.
26. Julie Brines, "Economic Dependency, Gender, and the Division of Labor at Home," *American Journal of Sociology* 100, no. 3 (1994): 652-88.
27. Scott Coltrane, "Research on Household Labor: Modeling and Measuring the Social Embeddedness of Routine Family Work," *Journal of Marriage and the Family* 62, no. 4 (2000): 1208-33.
28. Sanjiv Gupta, "The Effects of Transitions in Marital Status on Men's Performance of Housework," *Journal of Marriage and the Family* 61, no. 3 (1999): 700-11.
29. Becker and Moen, "Scaling Back: Dual-Earner Couples' Work-Family Strategies."
30. Bianchi and Casper, "American Families."
31. Bianchi and Casper, "American Families."
32. Amara Bachu, "Is Childlessness Among American Women on the Rise?" (paper delivered at the Annual Meetings of the Population Association of America, New York, March 1999).
33. Claudia Goldin, "Career and Family: College Women Look to the Past," in *Gender and Family Issues in the Workplace*, ed. Fran D. Blau and Ronald G. Ehrenberg (New York: Russell Sage Foundation, 1997).

34. Deborah S. Carr, "The Psychological Consequences of Work-family Trade-offs for Three Cohorts of Men and Women," *Social Psychology Quarterly* 65, no. 2 (2002): 103-24.

35. Casper and Bianchi, *Continuity and Change in the American Family.*

36. Mai Weismantle, "Reasons People Do Not Work: 1996," *Household Economic Studies* P70-76 (Washington, DC: U.S. Census Bureau, 2001).

37. Shelley Coverman and Joseph F. Sheley, "Change in Men's Housework and Child-Care Time, 1965-1975," *Journal of Marriage and the Family* 48, no. 2 (1986): 413-22; Cathleen D. Zick and W. K. Bryant, "A New Look at Parents' Time Spent in Child Care: Primary and Secondary Time Use," *Social Science Research* 25, no. 3 (1996): 260-80; Joseph H. Pleck, "Paternal Involvement: Levels, Sources, and Consequences," in *The Role of the Father in Child Development*, ed. Michael E. Lamb (New York: John Wiley & Sons, Inc., 1997); and John F. Sandberg and Sandra L. Hofferth, "Changes in Children's Time With Parents: United States, 1981-1997," *Demography* 38, no. 3 (2001): 423-36.

38. Shelley Coverman, "Explaining Husbands' Participation in Domestic Labor," *The Sociological Quarterly* 26, no. 1 (1985): 81-97; Coverman and Sheley, "Change in Men's Housework and Child-Care Time, 1965-1975"; William Marsiglio, "Paternal Engagement Activities With Minor Children," *Journal of Marriage and the Family* 53, no. 4 (1991): 973-86; and Zick and Bryant, "A New Look at Parents' Time Spent in Child Care."

39. Ronald Oaxaca, "Male-Female Wage Differentials in Urban Labor Markets," *International Economic Review* 14, no. 3 (1973): 693-709.

40. Myra M. Ferree, "Beyond Separate Spheres: Feminism and Family Research," *Journal of Marriage and the Family* 52, no. 4 (1990): 866-84; and Candace West and Don H. Zimmerman, "Doing Gender," *Gender & Society* 1, no. 2 (1987): 125-51.

41. Philip N. Cohen, "Replacing Housework in the Service Economy: Gender, Class, and Race-Ethnicity in Service Spending," *Gender & Society* 12, no. 2 (1998): 219-31.

42. John P. Robinson and Melissa A. Milkie, "Back to the Basics: Trends in and Role Determinants of Women's Attitudes Toward Housework," *Journal of Marriage and the Family* 60, no. 1 (1998): 205-18.

43. Kevin Heubusch, "Goodbye to the White Glove," *American Demographics* 19, no. 1 (January 1997): 39.

44. Liana C. Sayer, Suzanne M. Bianchi, and John P. Robinson, "Are Parents Investing Less in Children? Trends in Mothers' and Fathers' Time With Children," *American Journal of Sociology* (forthcoming).

45. Teresa Arendell, "The New Care Work of Middle Class Mothers: Managing Childrearing, Employment, and Time," in *Minding the Time in Family Experience: Emerging Perspectives and Issues*, ed. Kerry J. Daly (Oxford, England: Elsevier Science, 2001); and Sharon Hays, *The Cultural Contradictions of Motherhood* (New Haven, CT: Yale University Press, 1996).

46. Heather Joshi, "The Opportunity Costs of Childbearing: More Than Mothers' Business," *Journal of Population Economics* 11, no. 2 (1998): 161-83.

47. Marjorie L. Devault, *Feeding the Family: The Social Organization of Caring as Gendered Work* (Chicago: The University of Chicago Press, 1991).

48. Sayer, "Gender, Time Use, and Inequality"; and Suzanne M. Bianchi and Sara B. Raley, "Time Allocation in Working Families," in *Work, Family, Health, and Well-Being*, ed. Suzanne M. Bianchi, Lynne M. Casper, and Rosalind B. King (Mahwah, NJ: Erlbaum, forthcoming).

49. Melissa A. Milkie et al., "Feelings about Time with Children: The Influence of Employment, Family Structure, and Gender" (paper delivered at the Annual Meetings of the Population Association of America, Atlanta, May 2002).

50. Lynne M. Casper, Suzanne M. Bianchi, and Rosalind B. King, "Conclusion," in *Work, Family, Health, and Well-Being*, ed. Suzanne M. Bianchi, Lynne M. Casper, and Rosalind B. King (Mahwah, NJ: Lawrence Erlbaum Associates, forthcoming).

51. Casper, Bianchi, and King, "Conclusion."

52. Casper, Bianchi, and King, "Conclusion."

FOR FURTHER READING

Bianchi, Suzanne M. "Maternal Employment and Time with Children: Dramatic Change or Surprising Continuity?" *Demography* 37, no. 4 (2000): 401-14.

Bianchi, Suzanne M. "Changing Economic Roles of Men and Women." In *State of the Union: America in the 1990s*, vol. 1, ed. Reynolds Farley. New York: Russell Sage Foundation, 1995.

Bianchi, Suzanne M., Lynne M. Casper, and Rosalind B. King, eds. *Work, Family, Health and Well-Being*. Mahwah, N.J.: Lawrence Erlbaum Associates, forthcoming.

Bianchi, Suzanne M., Melissa A. Milkie, Liana C. Sayer, and John P. Robinson. "Is Anyone Doing the Housework? Trends in the Gender Division of Household Labor." *Social Forces* 79, no. 1 (2000): 191-228.

Browne, Irene. *Latinas and African American Women at Work: Race, Gender, and Economic Inequality*. New York: Russell Sage Foundation, 1999.

Casper, Lynne M., and Suzanne M. Bianchi. *Continuity and Change in the American Family*. Thousand Oaks, CA: Sage, 2002.

Cohen, Philip N. "Extended Households at Work: Living Arrangements and Inequality in Single Mothers' Employment." *Sociological Forum* 17, no. 3 (2002): 445-63.

Cohen, Philip N., and Suzanne M. Bianchi. "Marriage, Children, and Women's Employment: What Do We Know?" *Monthly Labor Review* 122, no. 12 (1999): 22-31.

Cotter, David, Joan Hermsen, and Reeve Vanneman. *Gender Inequality at Work*. New York: Russell Sage Foundation, 2004.

"Decade in Review: Understanding Families in the New Millennium." *Journal of Marriage and Family*, special issue (2000).

Goldin, Claudia. *Understanding the Gender Gap: An Economic History of American Women*. New York: Oxford University Press, 1990.

Jacobs, Jerry A., and Kathleen Gerson. *The Time Divide: Work, Family, and Gender Inequality*. Cambridge, MA: Harvard University Press, 2004.

Lichter, Daniel, and Rukamalie Jayakody. "Welfare Reform: How Do We Measure Success?" *Annual Review of Sociology* 28 (2002): 117-41.

McLanahan, Sara, and Lynne Casper. "Growing Diversity and Inequality in the American Family." In *State of the Union: America in the 1990s*, vol. 2, ed. Reynolds Farley. New York: Russell Sage Foundation, 1995.

Presser, Harriet B. *Working in a 24/7 Economy: Challenges for American Families*. New York: Russell Sage Foundation, 2003.

Sayer, Liana C., Suzanne M. Bianchi, and John P. Robinson. "Are Parents Investing Less in Children? Trends in Mothers' and Fathers' Time With Children." *American Journal of Sociology*, forthcoming.

Thornton, Arland, and Linda Young-DeMarco. "Four Decades of Trends in Attitudes Toward Family Issues in the United States: The 1960s Through the 1990s." *Journal of Marriage and the Family* 63, no. 4 (2001): 1009-37.

Waite, Linda J., ed. *The Ties That Bind: Perspectives on Marriage and Cohabitation*. New York: Aldine de Gruyter, 2000.

Williams, Joan. *Unbending Gender: Why Family and Work Conflict and What to Do About It*. New York: Oxford University Press, 2000.

SUGGESTED RESOURCES

U.S. Census Bureau website on families
www.census.gov/population/www/socdemo/hh-fam.html

The Families and Work Institute
www.familiesandwork.org

The Institute for Women's Policy Research
www.iwpr.org

The Urban Institute
www.urban.org

Gender Inequality at Work

By David A. Cotter, Joan M. Hermsen, and Reeve Vanneman

INTRODUCTION

A cigarette advertising slogan of the 1980s targeting women proclaimed: "You've come a long way, baby." By all accounts, this slogan is true. The transformation of men's and women's work roles stands out among the many technological, economic, social, and cultural changes in the last half of the 20th century. In 1950, only a small number of women (29 percent) worked outside the home; but in 2000, nearly three-quarters of women did. In 1950, women who were employed worked in a relative handful of nearly exclusively female occupations; but by 2000, women worked in nearly the entire spectrum of occupations. On average, a woman in 1950 earned 59 cents for every dollar earned by a man, while in 2000, she earned 73 cents. The scale of this change is indeed monumental, and its momentum has made it in retrospect seem almost inevitable.

Despite this progress, however, inequality remains between men and women. In 2000, men were still more likely than women to have access to paid employment, to be employed in better jobs, and to be better paid in those jobs. Additionally, across three main dimensions—work outside the home, kind of job, and pay—progress for women slowed and even reversed in the last decade of the century.

This report tracks changes in work-related gender inequality in the 1990s, placing these changes in the context of trends over the last 50 years in educational attainment, work experience, politics, and attitudes. The report also examines variations in inequality across race and ethnic groups, education levels, and age cohorts. The analysis contained in the report relies on data from the 1950 to 2000 censuses as well as from Current Population Surveys (CPS) from 1963 to 2002.

For the most part, the report focuses on the working-age population, people between the ages of 25 and 54. These people can be expected to have finished their education, but they are not likely to have begun to retire.

Three central conclusions emerge from our analysis of changes in gender inequality over time:

● Gender inequality in the labor market persists. While nearly nine of every 10 men are in the labor force, only three of four women are working. In addition, women and men continue to be highly concentrated in typically female and typically male jobs, respectively. Women continue to earn substantially less than men.

● The declines in gender inequality in the labor market that have been evident since at least 1950 have essentially stalled. The 1990s were a time of stability and possibly even retrenchment with regard to gender inequality. This decade may mark the end of an era of profound changes in women's labor market position. For each of the primary outcomes examined—labor force participation, occupational segregation, and earnings—the end of the 1990s closely resembled the beginning of the 1990s: a pattern of stability not seen in over 50 years.

● Notable variation exists across demographic groups in the pattern and degree of inequality experienced. For example, blacks and Hispanics lag behind whites in rates of labor force participation, the degree of occupational integration, and the level of earnings; and important differences in labor force participation and earnings have become more pronounced when comparing female high school dropouts with female college graduates.

Thus, our findings suggest that while both women and men have "come a long way," there is still a long way to go, and progress in the United States on gender equality seems to be slowing.

DAVID A. COTTER is an associate professor of sociology at Union College in Schenectady, New York, where he teaches a variety of courses on inequality. His research addresses occupational gender inequality and poverty.

JOAN M. HERMSEN is an associate professor of sociology at the University of Missouri, Columbia. Her research explores work-related gender inequality in the United States, including the wage gap, occupational segregation, and women's careers in information technology. She teaches courses on social inequality and research methods.

REEVE VANNEMAN is a professor of sociology at the University of Maryland, College Park. His current research investigates patterns of gender inequality across metropolitan areas in the United States and across districts in India. He teaches courses on stratification and multilevel methods.

LABOR FORCE PARTICIPATION

Women's increased participation in paid work is a central change in gender relations over the last 50 years. The question is no longer whether the average woman will work or not, but rather when during her life course she will work. Most women now work—women at all education levels, of each racial and ethnic group, and across successive family statuses.

Labor force participation is often seen as the prime indicator (and cause) of changes in women's status. As far back as Friedrich Engels' or Charlotte Perkins Gilman's writings on the subject in the late 1800s, social scientists and other observers have identified employment outside the home as the starting point for understanding women's position in society. Social theory often focuses on women's employment because employment determines their access to resources and their ability to make independent decisions.

By the year 2000, only a small margin separated men's and women's presence in the labor force. Nearly 74 percent of women ages 25 to 54 were in the paid labor force, either looking for work or actually working at least part-time. (See Box 1 for a discussion of employ-

---

Box 1
MEASURES OF EMPLOYMENT

Measuring employment can be simple: Either you have a job or you don't. However, social scientists use many different measures to draw distinctions about one's relationship to the labor market. Several of these measures are discussed below, and corresponding data are presented in the table.

In the Labor Force
The labor force participation rate accounts for individuals currently employed or seeking employment—the percentage of people who want or already have jobs. The advantage of this measure is that it indicates how widespread the desire for paid work is, an issue particularly important when considering how women's roles have changed over time. In 2000, nearly 74 percent of women and 86 percent of men were in the labor force. Of those in the labor force, some were unemployed and seeking work (between 4 percent and 5 percent of women and men in the labor force were classified as such).

Usual Hours and Number of Weeks Worked
Because the labor force participation rate is a gross measure of employment, it tells us little about how much those who are employed actually work. For this information, one would need to examine the distribution of hours and weeks worked. A measure of usual hours worked tells us whether someone typically works part-time or full time, which is an important consideration when evaluating women's work patterns because women are more likely than men to work part-time. An indicator based on the number of weeks worked in a year accounts for the potential instability of employment and the movement of people in and out of jobs. As with hours worked, women work fewer weeks per year than do men.

Full-Time/Year-Round Employment
Information on usual hours worked and weeks worked in the past year can be used to construct a measure of full-time (35+ hours/week)/year-round (50+ weeks/year) employment. Estimates of employment made using this measure are considerably lower than those for labor force participation because these estimates are based on stringent restrictions. Gender differences in employment, however, are substantially higher when considering full-time/year-round employment, because women are more likely than men to be out of the labor force,

Measures of Employment

Employment status	Women (%)	Men (%)
Out of labor force in 2000	26.5	14.4
Of whom:		
Did not work in 1999	69.3	51.9
Worked in 1999	30.7	48.1
In labor force in 2000	73.5	85.6
Of whom:		
Unemployed, 2000	4.5	4.2
Employed, 2000	95.5	95.8
Of whom:		
Did not work in 1999	2.4	1.5
Worked in 1999	97.6	98.5
Usual hours worked		
1–16	4.6	1.3
17–34	15.5	4.0
35–40	58.2	49.4
41–59	17.5	32.6
60+	4.3	12.6
Number of weeks worked in 1999		
1–24	5.7	3.1
25–49	21.3	14.8
50–52	73.0	82.1
Worked full-time (35+ hours/week)/ year-round (50+ weeks/year) in 1999	45.6	67.9

Note: Labor force participation calculated for men and women ages 25–54.
Source: Authors' calculations using Census 2000 5% Public Use Microdata Sample (PUMS).

unemployed, or working part-time or part-year. In 1999, nearly 46 percent of women and 68 percent of men were employed full-time/year-round.

Out of the Labor Force
Individuals who are not employed or actively seeking work are considered out of the labor force. In 2000, approximately 27 percent of women and 14 percent of men were out of the labor force. Some of these people had work-limiting disabilities, others chose not to work, and still others stopped seeking work when their earlier job searches failed.

ment measures.) Men's rates were only slightly higher, at 86 percent. Gender difference was somewhat larger for full-time/year-round employment. In 1999, 46 percent of women and 68 percent of men ages 25 to 54 were employed full-time/year-round.

These gender differences are small in historical perspective. Consistent with popular perception, women were much more likely to work outside the home by the end of the 20th century than at any time since 1950. As shown in Figure 1, women ages 25 to 54 have increased their labor force participation rate steadily, by between 8 percentage points and 14 percentage points for each decade from 1950 to 1990. In 1950, only 33 percent of women were in the paid labor force. By 1970, that figure had increased to 49 percent, and by 1990, to 74 percent. This upward trend has often been interpreted to signify women's increasing equality with men. The growth in labor force participation is also cited as an underlying cause for other changes in gender relations such as marital power, fertility patterns, and political representation.

Census 2000 shows no similar increase in women's labor force participation rate during the 1990s. The reported 2000 women's labor force participation rate of 74 percent is not notably different from the 1990 rate. Some of the stagnation in the 1990s is exaggerated by a slight change in wording of the Census 2000 employment question that depressed reports of labor force participation. But stagnation during the 1990s was also seen in the annual CPS, where the question's wording did not change. Like the census, the CPS recorded large increases in the past—from 48 percent in 1970 to 74 percent in 1990. The CPS rate in 2000 was 78 percent, slightly higher than the 1990 Census rate but still far below what would have been expected based on increases of previous decades.

The end of increasing labor force participation for women in the 1990s is surprising. It is too early to say if this lack of change is temporary; perhaps the strong 1990s' economy allowed a reemergence of the single-paycheck family. To understand this finding, it is important to recognize how the patterns of women's labor force participation, and particularly how the changes in the 1990s, have varied across groups of women.

Labor Force Participation by Family Status

The prime employment years of 25 to 54 are also the prime childrearing years. The concurrent demands of work and family have long shaped the ways in which women and men engage in the labor market. Nevertheless, the patterned ways in which families reconcile these demands have changed over the past five decades. The 1990s were no exception. Tracing the changes in labor force participation separately by family status confirms that the 1990s represent a break from the recent past.

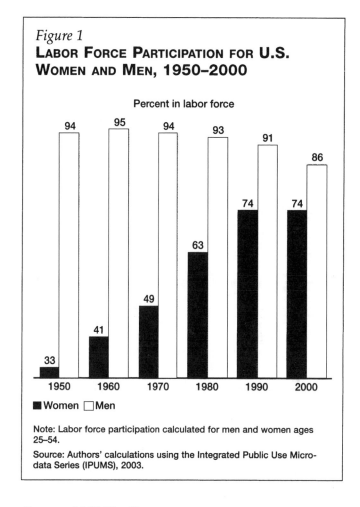

Figure 1

LABOR FORCE PARTICIPATION FOR U.S. WOMEN AND MEN, 1950–2000

Percent in labor force

Note: Labor force participation calculated for men and women ages 25–54.

Source: Authors' calculations using the Integrated Public Use Microdata Series (IPUMS), 2003.

Census 2000 Findings

Married mothers of young children are less likely to be in the labor force than are any other women or men of comparable age. Nevertheless, a majority of even these women were employed or looking for work in 2000. Sixty percent of married mothers with a child younger than 6 years old at home were in the labor force. This compares with between 72 percent and 82 percent of women with other family statuses (see Table 1, page 110). Once their children are in school, married mothers increase their labor force participation to levels approaching those of married women with no children at home. These mothers are less likely to work full-time/year-round than are married women with no children at home. Part-time or seasonal employment is common among all mothers, but even among mothers with young children at home, full-time/year-round employment is the most common option among those mothers in the labor force.

The presence of children at home makes less difference for never-married or formerly married mothers. Single women, whether mothers or not, are more likely to be in the labor force than married women. In fact, divorced and separated women with school-age children were more likely to be in the labor force than were women

Table 1
LABOR FORCE PARTICIPATION RATES FOR U.S. WOMEN AND MEN BY FAMILY STATUS, 2000

	Women			Men		
Marital status	Children under age 6 at home	Only children ages 6 to 17 at home	No unmarried children under 18 at home	Children under age 6 at home	Only children ages 6 to 17 at home	No unmarried children under 18 at home
Labor force participation (%)						
Currently married	60	74	76	92	92	84
Formerly married	77	82	77	88	88	80
Never married	72	75	80	85	84	80
Full-time/year-round employment (%)						
Currently married	31	41	51	77	78	69
Formerly married	45	56	54	69	72	59
Never married	39	47	54	62	61	55

Note: Data are for men and women ages 25–54 in a single-family household.

Source: Authors' calculations using Census 2000 5% Public Use Microdata Sample (PUMS).

without children. Never-married mothers also had high labor force participation rates in 2000, contrary to the stereotype of idle welfare mothers living off the dole.

Long-Term Trends

Single and married mothers' labor force participation diverged sharply in the 1990s. Married mothers' labor force participation held constant through the last half of the 1990s—reversing the long trend of these mothers for the fastest increases in labor force participation (see Figure 2). In contrast, single mothers' labor force participation increased significantly in the 1990s—also a change from their recent past pattern of little change in labor force participation since the late 1970s. Single mothers

have always worked more than their married counterparts, but the difference between them had been narrowing for some time. In the mid-1990s, the two groups went in opposite directions. Single mothers increased their rates of labor force participation to levels almost equal to single women without children. This increase rules out a ceiling effect as an explanation for the stagnation of married women's rates in the 1990s. If there is some upper bound on women's labor force participation, the increases for single mothers in the 1990s showed it has not yet been reached. Thus, the end of the growth in married mothers' labor force participation is the most unexpected gender turnaround of the 1990s.

Women with no children at home showed little change in entering the labor force during the 1990s. Women without children work more often than mothers do, but Figure 2 shows that those high levels held constant during the 1990s. Married women without children, like married mothers with children at home, had been increasing their labor force participation through much of the century, although at less dramatic rates. Those increases stalled in the 1990s, as did the employment rates of married mothers.

Single women with no children have the highest rates of labor force participation, but that has always been true, and those high rates have not changed much in the last quarter-century. Married women had been narrowing the gap with single women, but that ended in the 1990s.

Labor Force Participation by Age, Period, and Cohort

Age, Period, and Cohort Effects

When demographers examine social change, one of the first things they check is whether these changes come

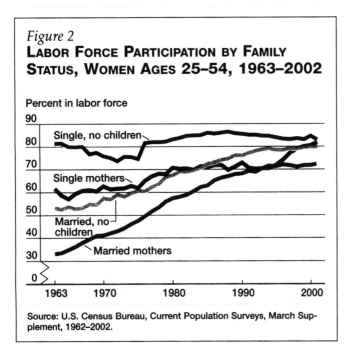

Figure 2
LABOR FORCE PARTICIPATION BY FAMILY STATUS, WOMEN AGES 25–54, 1963–2002

Source: U.S. Census Bureau, Current Population Surveys, March Supplement, 1962–2002.

from time-period effects common across the whole population or whether the changes result more from the distinctive characteristics of new cohorts replacing quite different older cohorts. To distinguish cohort effects from period effects requires analysis of age effects as well, since in any year what appear to be cohort differences may just be age effects.

● *Age effects* describe how individuals change over their lifetimes. Retirement is a typical example of an age effect. Social and legal prohibitions also prevent children from entering the labor force, another age effect. Age also has indirect effects on labor force participation by helping to pattern life course events such as marriage and childbearing. These age effects are strong enough so that we limit most of our analyses to the "prime years" between 25 and 54. We make an exception in this section in order to capture the full range of age variations.

● *Period effects* tell us about how historical changes in a society affect all individuals in that society. Specific events often lead to changes in gender inequality. The advent of the birth control pill in the early 1960s dramatically affected women's ability to control fertility, and therefore may have increased their participation in the labor force. The passage of equal employment legislation in the 1960s and 1970s is another example of a possible period effect on gender differences. Sometimes period effects are harder to date exactly but are nevertheless likely to have had broad impacts—for instance, when the women's movement of the 1970s raised fundamental issues about gender equality.

● *Cohort effects* identify generations of people who move together through history and who share common historical experiences that uniquely affect them. The baby-boom cohort is perhaps the most familiar contemporary example. Another cohort, The Depression Generation, came to political maturity during the Depression and New Deal and were forever marked by that experience. For gender issues, an important cohort is women who came of age after the advent of the pill and during the feminist revolution of that time; they are particularly important in understanding changes in gender relations. What makes cohort effects so interesting is that a whole society can change without any particular individuals changing what they think or do. For example, if recent cohorts accept more feminist positions than previous cohorts, eventually the society will adopt the positions of the recent cohort without any individual having changed her own behavior.

Of course, most social changes present some combination of all three of these effects, and disentangling the effects has become something of an art form because of the implicit and easily overlooked relationships between age, period, and cohort differences. If we know any two of these relationships, then the third is completely specified by the other two. Age can always be computed as census year minus birth year, and therefore age effects can always be expressed as the difference between cohort and period effects. Or period effects can always be expressed as the combination of cohort differences and aging. Any attempt to disentangle these three effects that does not acknowledge these identities will be misleading. Below are descriptions of the complex patterns of how labor force participation varies across time and cohorts (and thus across age).

Census 2000 Findings

The likelihood that a woman will be in the labor force varies substantially over her life. As we have seen, many women exit the labor force when they become mothers; therefore, labor force participation rates have traditionally been lower for women in their late 20s through early 40s than for younger or older women—a characteristic referred to as the "double maxima pattern." However, the 2000 age profiles of women's and men's labor force participation are strikingly similar. Women's labor force participation by age is comparable to men's (albeit at a lower level)—sharply rising from the teen years into early adulthood, remaining fairly stable in the prime years, falling sharply after the mid-50s, and then trailing off. In 2000, there was some evidence of a slight dip in labor force participation rates as women reached their mid-20s to mid-30s. However, women in their early 40s worked at the same rates as women in their early 20s.

Long-Term Trends

By age, women's labor force participation rates have not always so closely resembled men's. In the 1960s and 1970s, the labor force participation rates of women in their mid-20s to mid-30s were substantially lower than those of younger and older women, giving the trend line for women's labor force participation by age a roller-coaster appearance (see Figure 3, page 112). By 1980, the roller-coaster track began to flatten, reflecting lower fertility and fewer women leaving the labor force at marriage and childbirth. The dip also shifts to somewhat later ages at which women were marrying and having their first child. By 2000, the trend line hardly dips for women in their 20s and 30s. The pattern is also somewhat attenuated in 1950, but for different reasons than in 2000. In 1950, many fewer women returned to work after their children were in school or left home, so the labor force participation rates for women in their 50s never approached the peak of 20-year-old women.

Cohort Differences

The cross-sectional, point-in-time analysis presented above—while fairly clear—implies a problematic con-

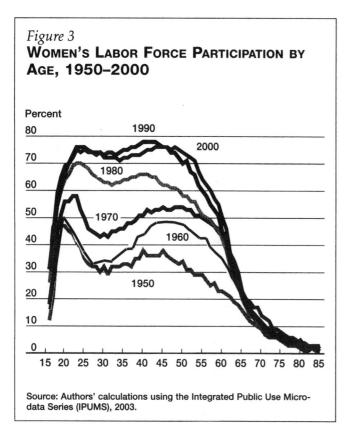

Figure 3

WOMEN'S LABOR FORCE PARTICIPATION BY AGE, 1950–2000

Source: Authors' calculations using the Integrated Public Use Microdata Series (IPUMS), 2003.

it ages across the life span (see Table 2). Reading across rows, one sees an age effect—what each generation of women actually experienced. For instance, for the cohort born between 1935 and 1944, labor force participation rose steadily until retirement age, when the rates declined sharply.

Reading down columns, one sees how cohorts differ from one another. For instance, the second column, at ages 25 to 34, shows how the late baby boomers, born between 1955 and 1964, differ from an earlier generation, born between 1925 and 1934. This comparison illustrates the cohort effect because it compares different birth cohorts at the same point in their life cycle. Enormous labor force increases occurred across young-adult cohorts. For example, 35 percent of those born between 1925 and 1934 were in the labor force at ages 25 to 34. This is much lower than the 74 percent of women born between 1955 and 1964 who were in the labor force at ages 25 to 34.

However, the increases from 32 percent in the earliest cohort to 73 percent in the latest cohort may not be the result of true cohort effects. These increases may be just a period effect common to all cohorts: Women born between 1915 and 1924 reached early adulthood around 1950, when few women were in the labor force at any age. And post-baby-boom women born between 1965 and 1974 reached early adulthood around 2000, when labor force participation rates were much higher. Unfortunately, this arrangement of a cohort table obscures the period effect of changes over time. To know rates for any census year, one has to read along the diagonal in Table 2—which is shaded to represent results from the 2000 Census.

If the cohort differences in column 2 of Table 2 represent lasting cohort effects, those differences should

clusion: The rates for women who are now 55 predict the future life course for women who are now 25. But perhaps the differences between current 25-year-olds and current 55-year-olds reflect permanent differences between generations that will not disappear with time.

Cohort analyses are often offered as a solution to this problem. By using multiple censuses, cohort analyses track the labor force patterns for each generation as

Table 2

WOMEN'S LABOR FORCE PARTICIPATION BY BIRTH COHORT, AGE, AND CENSUS YEAR, 1950–2000

Birth cohort	% in labor force by age							% in labor force by census year					
	16–24	25–34	35–44	45–54	55–64	65–74	75–84	1950	1960	1970	1980	1990	2000
1885–1894					24	13	5	24	13	5			
1895–1904				33	35	14	4	33	35	14	4		
1905–1914			35	47	42	12	4	35	47	42	12	4	
1915–1924		32	43	53	42	13	5	32	43	53	42	13	5
1925–1934	38	35	51	59	45	15		38	35	51	59	45	15
1935–1944	39	45	65	71	51				39	45	65	71	51
1945–1954	46	65	77	74						46	65	77	74
1955–1964	58	74	74								58	74	74
1965–1974	62	76										62	73
1975–1984	62												62

Note: Labor force participation calculated for women ages 16–84. Outlined cells are for the prime working ages 25–54. Shaded cells are from Census 2000.
Source: Authors' calculations using the Integrated Public Use Microdata Series (IPUMS), 2003.

remain even after the earlier cohorts enter the times of elevated labor force participation at the end of the 1990s. That persistence of effect doesn't happen. For instance, at ages 25 to 34, women born between 1935 and 1944 had participation rates that were 20 percentage points lower than those women in the very next cohort (45 versus 65). But by the time of later adulthood, at ages 45 to 54, the women born between 1935 and 1944 had almost caught up with the cohort that followed them (71 versus 74), suggesting that the early difference was more of a period effect than a lasting cohort effect. Baby-boom women had the advantage of entering the labor market at a time when labor force participation rates were increasing for all women. These time-period effects are more clearly seen on the right side of Table 2, which shows how each cohort progressed through each period rather than through each age range. Every birth cohort that had not yet reached retirement increased its labor force participation between 1960 and 1990. Even for the earlier cohorts, the retirement decline is weaker because these cohorts reached retirement ages just as labor force participation rates were growing.

These observations suggest that the best way to interpret the increases in women's labor force participation during the last half of the last century is as a period effect that changed labor supply for all cohorts. The age distributions from Figure 3 are probably the most parsimonious way to describe the changes: Each succeeding decade had higher rates of labor force participation, and these period effects were especially important for women ages 25 to 40.

Labor Force Participation by Race and Ethnicity

Race matters in the United States. It shapes our everyday experience and our life chances in as fundamental a way as gender does. In fact, some observers contend that race and gender interact to create unique patterns of gender inequality across racial and ethnic groups. Others note that many of the transformations in gender inequality have been so broad as to cross racial and ethnic lines. Thus, the story is simultaneously one of diversity and similarity.

Census 2000 Findings

Women's labor force participation rates varied widely across racial and ethnic groups. White women and Filipinas had the highest participation rates of any groups (see Table 3). Black women had a rate almost as high as white women's. Hispanic women tended to have lower rates, but there was substantial variability among Hispanics: Only 58 percent of Mexican American women were in the labor force, while 69 percent of Cuban American women were. There was even greater

Table 3

LABOR FORCE PARTICIPATION RATES FOR U.S. WOMEN AND MEN BY RACE AND ETHNICITY, 2000

Race/ethnicity	Women (%)	Men (%)	Ratio women/men
White (only)	75	89	0.85
African American	73	72	1.02
Hispanic (any)	61	77	0.79
Mexican	58	78	0.75
Puerto Rican	63	73	0.85
Central American	64	80	0.80
South American	66	82	0.81
Cuban	69	77	0.89
Dominican	61	71	0.86
Asian (any)	67	84	0.80
Chinese	70	86	0.82
South Asian	59	88	0.68
Filipina	77	84	0.92
Southeast Asian	65	78	0.84
Korean	61	80	0.77
Japanese	68	89	0.76
American Indian	69	78	0.88
Pacific Islander	71	80	0.88

Note: Labor force participation calculated for men and women ages 25–54.

Source: Authors' calculations using Census 2000 5% Public Use Microdata Sample (PUMS).

variability among Asian ethnic groups: Filipinas had the highest rates (77 percent), and South Asian women had the lowest (59 percent). American Indian and Pacific Islander women had rates slightly below white women's. Full-time/year-round employment rates were lower for each group, but the pattern across racial and ethnic groups (not shown) was similar. White, black, and Pacific Islander women were most likely to work full-time/year-round; American Indian and Hispanic women were least likely to do so.

Although women from most racial and ethnic groups were less likely to be in the labor force than white women, the same racial and ethnic groups may have had more gender equality in participation rates because of the low participation rates among men. The rate for Hispanic men (77 percent), for instance, was almost as far below the rate for white men (89 percent) as the rate for Hispanic women was below that for white women. The level of gender inequality in labor force participation was not very different when comparing Hispanics (79 percent) with non-Hispanic whites (85 percent).

Gender differences among African Americans were even more distinctive. While African American women were slightly less likely than white women to be in the labor force, African American men were far less likely than white men to be in the labor force. In fact, the African American women's labor force participation rate was slightly *higher* than the African American men's rate, one of the few instances when the usual gender inequality was reversed and favored women.

Gender inequality among Asian labor force participation rates varied widely across ethnic groups. The high participation rate of Filipina women was close to that of Filipino men, but the low rate of South Asian women contrasted with a high rate among South Asian men—one that approached the rate of white men.

The question of gender differences among racial and ethnic groups is complicated because two comparisons are possible. The above calculations use within-race comparisons, but such comparisons have the disadvantage that a racial and ethnic group may be more gender-equal than whites not because women in the group work more but because the men work less. An alternative between-race comparison keeps a constant comparison group, usually white men, because they are the most privileged group. Thus, inequality for black women is greater than for white women when using this between-race measure, but not when using the within-race comparison. Within-race comparisons appear throughout this report but do not mean that, when gender inequality within a racial or ethnic group is less than among whites, the women in that group work more than white women.

Long-Term Trends
The dramatic increases in labor force participation rates between 1950 and 1990 affected women of all racial and ethnic groups. For most of the period, black women and Asian women had the highest rates of participation, while American Indian women and Hispanic women reported the lowest rates. The participation rates of white women have equaled those of black women and Asian women only since 1990.

Similarly, the 1990s was a period of stagnation in labor force participation rates for women of all racial and ethnic groups. While the change in the wording of the race question in the 2000 Census exaggerates the declines (especially among African Americans and Hispanics), data from the Current Population Survey confirm the stagnation for all groups. Thus, both the increases from 1950 to 1990 and the unexpected plateau in the 1990s were shared across racial and ethnic groups.

Labor Force Participation by Education Level
Education is frequently seen as preparation for the labor force—as training for employment. As such, education is often thought of as an investment in human capital or skills to be brought to market. The more education one has invested in, the more skills one has obtained and the better job one can expect. The higher the income one

expects, the greater the incentive to be in the labor force. But education can also be thought of as a proxy for class, especially in terms of life chances. In either interpretation, education strongly conditions both the likelihood that an individual will be in the labor force and the type of work he or she does.

For married women, education has dual consequences: It increases their value in the labor market and thus raises the incentive to work. On the other hand, educated women tend to marry educated men, and these men have a higher incentive to work and have higher incomes. For women, this "unearned income"—income available whether women work or not—is a disincentive for employment. For most women, the incentive effects of higher education outweigh the disincentives.

Census 2000 Findings
In 2000, labor force participation rates increased at each higher education level for both men and women (see Table 4). Ninety-four percent of male and 82 percent of female college graduates were in the labor force. Similarly, 83 percent of male and 69 percent of female high school graduates were in the labor force. The rates dropped off sharply for high school dropouts, but the gender gap remained similar.

Long-Term Trends
Women of all education levels increased their labor force participation steadily from 1960 to 1990 (see Table 4). However, all groups saw a decline in participation from 1990 to 2000. There was also a decline among college women between 1950 and 1960. Only among high school dropouts was there a noticeable growth in labor force participation in the 1950s. Since the 1950s, however, labor force participation rates among high school dropouts, always the lowest, have grown more slowly than for other women, so the gap between high school dropouts and those with at least a high school diploma has grown since 1970. For women, education has become an increasingly important predictor of labor force participation.

Among men, labor force participation rates fell for all education groups from 1960 to 2000. Surprisingly little attention has been paid to the decline in men's labor force participation. Most research suggests some combination of men dropping out of the labor force due to declining wages, and a decline among married men whose wives' income allows the men to leave the labor force. This decline was particularly pronounced for high school dropouts. Until 1970, men's labor force participation rates differed little by education level. By 1980, high school dropouts had fallen behind high school graduates, and the pattern worsened through 2000. The percentage of men who have less than a high school degree has declined substantially over time, and some immigrant groups are disproportionately located among groups

Table 4

LABOR FORCE PARTICIPATION RATES FOR U.S. MEN AND WOMEN BY EDUCATION, 1950–2000

Education	1950	1960	1970	1980	1990	2000
High school dropout						
Women (%)	35	39	45	50	53	49
Men (%)	89	93	90	85	79	68
Ratio women/men	0.39	0.42	0.50	0.59	0.67	0.72
High school graduate						
Women (%)	41	41	50	63	72	69
Men (%)	94	97	96	94	91	83
Ratio women/men	0.43	0.42	0.52	0.67	0.79	0.84
Some college						
Women (%)	48	44	51	69	79	78
Men (%)	88	96	95	94	93	89
Ratio women/men	0.54	0.46	0.54	0.73	0.85	0.88
College graduate						
Women (%)	60	55	61	76	84	82
Men (%)	92	97	97	96	96	94
Ratio women/men	0.65	0.56	0.63	0.79	0.88	0.88

Note: Rates calculated for men and women ages 25–54.

Source: Authors' calculations using the Integrated Public Use Microdata Series (IPUMS), 2003.

with less than a high school degree. Overall, education is now as important a predictor of labor force participation for men as it is for women.

Gender differences in labor force participation rates are dominated by the larger changes among women, so gender inequality ratios are driven more by changes to women's labor force participation than to men's (see Table 4). A ratio of 1.0 indicates men and women have equal labor force participation rates, while a ratio below 1.0 indicates women are less likely to be in the labor force than similarly educated men. Since 1960, there has been an upward trend in all participation ratios, indicating growing similarity between women and men for all education groups. The gender revolution in labor force participation spread across levels of education just as it spread across racial divisions.

Sweeping Change

The data reviewed above present a picture of broad-based change. Most women today are in the labor force regardless of racial, age, education, marital, and parental status. This situation represents an enormous change from the 1950s, when most women were not active in the labor force. At the same time, the rate of increase in women's labor force participation may have slowed in the last decade, and even begun to reverse among married mothers. The next question is: Where are the women who have entered the labor force in the last 50 years?

TRENDS AND PATTERNS IN MEN'S AND WOMEN'S OCCUPATIONS

Women and men in the labor force do very different kinds of work. In general, the differences in women's and men's work persist, but are much reduced from a half-century ago. The integration of work marks another aspect of stunning change. Little more than 30 years ago, the idea of women becoming doctors, clergy, bartenders, or bus drivers in numbers equal to men would have seemed naive. But, as the data reveal, this equalization is precisely what has happened. However, as with labor force participation, there is still a considerable gap in the occupations that men and women hold. Many have remained decidedly male or female and, as with labor force participation, there is good evidence that integration has stopped in recent years.

Census 2000 Findings

Despite the fact that women make up nearly half of the labor force, men and women work in very distinct occupations. An occupation is a convenient way of categorizing the many different kinds of work that people do, grouping similar kinds of work performed in different settings. For instance, people who examine other people's physical and psychological condition and make recommendations about their treatment (doctors, psychiatrists, psychoanalysts, chiropractors, and nurses) are all "health diagnosing and treating practitioners." Similarly, people who sell things, such as art dealers, insurance agents, or gas station attendants, are all in sales and related occupations. Different coding systems categorize occupations into greater or lesser degrees of detail and make gross or fine distinctions among the types of work done.

The level of occupational detail is important for understanding gender differences, since the more detailed the coding system, the more segregated men's and women's work will appear. This can be illustrated by the difference between "teachers" at various levels. If all teachers are grouped, 74 percent of them are women. But if this group of teachers is disaggregated by grade level, 97 percent of preschool, 78 percent of elementary and middle school, 58 percent of secondary school, and 46 percent of college teachers are women. Thus, greater detail allows a more accurate estimate of how much segregation there is. In fact, some researchers have analyzed cross-classifications of industries and occupations or even organization-level data on job titles, and each analysis results in higher estimates of the "true" degree of gender segregation.[1]

The Census Bureau uses several occupational coding systems with varied degrees of detail. In 2000, there were

505 categories, but the microdata file collapses that number slightly to 475. The percentage of women in each of these occupations ranges from 98 percent for preschool teachers to 1 percent for heavy-vehicle mechanics.

Scholars examining gender segregation have commonly treated occupations in which more than 70 percent of the workers are of one sex as "sex-typed" occupations.[2] By this standard, more than half (52 percent) of all women work in occupations that are more than 70 percent female, and 57 percent of men work in occupations that are more than 70 percent male. Conversely, only 11 percent of women work in "male" occupations, while 7 percent of men work in "female" occupations. That leaves less than half of men (41 percent) and women (37 percent) working in "mixed" occupations (those between 31 percent and 69 percent female). Among the most heavily female occupations in 2000 were secretaries, cashiers, and elementary- and middle-school teachers; while the overwhelmingly male occupations were truck drivers, laborers and material movers, and janitors and building cleaners. The predominantly mixed occupations were retail sales workers, supervisors of retail sales workers, and miscellaneous managers.

A principal tool that scholars use to describe patterns of gender segregation is the dissimilarity index.[3] This measure can be interpreted as the percentage of women or men who would have to change occupations in order for each occupation to be evenly female—that is, to match the gender distribution in the labor force as a whole. Using this set of occupations, more than half (52.0 percent) of all women or men would have to change occupations in order for all occupations to match the 46.5 percent female rate found in the labor force as a whole.

Long-Term Trends

The Census Bureau has changed the occupational classification system almost every decade. The 2000 Census was no exception. These changes reflect, in part, changes in the type of work we do, but also changes in our understanding of that work.[4] These changes in classification cause problems for comparing changes in the kinds of work that women and men do. To have comparable occupations over these 50 years, it was necessary to recode all the occupations into a standard set of 179 occupations. This smaller set, however, limits the detail about the types of occupations, resulting in underestimates of the levels of segregation.

The rapid entry of women into the labor market in the 1960s, 1970s, and 1980s had consequences for the types of jobs they held. During these decades, women gained access to many occupations that had previously (whether formally or informally) been closed to them. But women's entry into occupations was uneven. Many occupations remain nearly as heavily male or female as they were in the 1950s. Some occupations have even *become* predomi-

Table 5

WOMEN'S SHARE OF SELECTED OCCUPATIONS, 1950–2000

Occupation	Percent of workers who are women			
	1950	1980	1990	2000
Male occupations				
Electricians	1	2	3	3
Firefighters	0	1	2	4
Airplane pilots	0	1	4	4
Truck drivers	1	3	6	6
Electrical engineers	1	5	10	9
Clergy	4	5	11	15
Police	2	5	13	16
Architects	2	9	16	21
Mixed occupations				
Physicians	6	15	23	30
Lawyers	4	15	26	33
Mail carriers	1	14	28	34
Managers	13	25	34	36
Real estate agents	16	50	53	52
Bartenders	8	47	55	57
Bus drivers	4	53	55	57
Accountants and bookkeepers	13	37	53	60
Female occupations				
Bill collectors	17	62	68	72
Medical and dental technicians	41	67	73	73
Teachers	73	67	74	75
Waiters and waitresses	83	88	82	76
Librarians	91	84	85	80
Nurses (professional)	97	91	91	92
Bank tellers	43	94	94	94
Secretaries and typists	94	99	98	97

Note: Labor force participation calculated for men and women ages 25–54.

Source: Authors' calculations using the Integrated Public Use Microdata Series (IPUMS), 2003.

nantly female since the 1950s (see Table 5). For example, while women have made some inroads into the skilled trades, women are only slightly more likely to be electricians or mechanics today than in 1950. Similarly, despite much popular attention to the phenomenon of the male nurse, a patient is nearly as likely today to have a female nurse as in 1950, children are equally likely to have a female teacher in 2000 as in 1950,[5] and the office secretary is just as likely to be a woman today as in 1950.

In other occupations, though, changes have been far more substantial. For instance, in 1950 it was extremely unlikely to find a woman driving a bus or mixing drinks in a bar—but by 2000, the probability was more than 50 percent. Much the same can be said about real estate agents, accountants, and bill collectors; each of those occupations had female majorities by 2000. Finally, some occupations that in 1950 were fairly evenly split between women and men have now become predomi-

Table 6

CHANGES IN GENDER SEGREGATION IN OCCUPATIONS, 1950–2000

Source of change	1950	1960	1970	1980	1990	2000
Occupational segregation	60.8	62.0	56.8	53.1	48.4	46.6
Actual change from previous decade	—	+1.2	−5.2	−3.7	−4.7	−1.8
Change from integration of occupations	—	+1.8	−3.3	−4.6	−3.4	+0.7
Change from shifts in the occupational structure	—	−1.0	−1.7	+1.6	−1.2	−2.1

— Not applicable.

Note: Includes men and women ages 25–54. The dissimilarity index is the percentage of men or women who would have to change occupations for each occupation to be evenly female—that is, to match the gender distribution in the general labor force.

Source: Authors' calculations using the Integrated Public Use Microdata Series (IPUMS), 2003.

nantly female. Both medical and dental technicians and bank tellers went from being just under half female in 1950 to being predominantly female by 2000.

Again, the dissimilarity index is useful for summarizing the changes throughout the occupational structure. Based on the smaller set of 179 occupations, the dissimilarity index was 46.6 for 2000 (see Table 6). This figure represents a total decline of 14.2 points in the index of dissimilarity between 1950 and 2000—just under one-third of a point each year for 50 years. At that rate, occupational segregation would disappear by the year 2150. The decline, however, has not been evenly paced over the period. Most of the change occurred from 1960 to 1990; both the 1990s (1.8 point decline) and 1950s (1.2 point increase) experienced much lower levels of change.

Declines in segregation come from two main sources. The most obvious type of change is the integration of previously segregated jobs—for example, women becoming doctors and men becoming nurses. Less obvious is the more rapid growth of already integrated occupations (the growth of the number of cooks) or the decline of segregated ones (declining numbers of miners since 1950 or of telephone operators and secretaries since 1970). Tools to decompose the changes in occupational segregation into these two components have been developed. Table 6 identifies what portion of each decade's changes represents changes in the gender composition of occupations and what percentage is just the consequence of differential occupational growth and decline. The declines in segregation seen in censuses from 1960 to 1990 resulted mostly from occupational integration, although in the 1960s and the 1980s, the more rapid growth of integrated occupations also contributed. All of the rather small decrease between 1990 and 2000 can be

attributed to the growth of integrated occupations. In fact, without changes in the occupational structure, the 2000 Census would have registered an increase in occupational segregation. This reversal is consistent with the labor force participation trends that also identified the 1990s as a break from the previous decades.

Another question frequently asked about integration is how much of the change stems from women entering occupations that had been male-dominated and how much from men entering occupations that had been female-dominated. That is, are women becoming carpenters and clergy, or are men becoming librarians and nurses? The specific occupational changes summarized in Table 5 suggest that most of the change came from women entering previously male occupations. More detailed calculations confirm this conclusion. If we look at the 13.6 point drop between 1960 and 1990, about 6.3 points of that drop are the result of women's changes (women's 1990 occupational distribution looking more like men's in 1960 than women's did in 1960). None of the drop is due to changes in men's occupations: Men's occupations in 1990 looked less like women's 1960 occupations than was the case 30 years earlier. A large portion of the declining segregation is due to the simultaneous changes in men's and women's occupations to look more like each other. So, however interesting the phenomena of male nurses and librarians may be, these phenomena do not account for much of the occupational integration. The changes in the middle portion of Table 5, occupations that shifted from male-dominated to integrated, drove the decline in occupational segregation.

Occupational Segregation by Age, Period, and Cohort

How much of the decline in occupational segregation between 1960 and 1990 was a period change common to all workers, and how much was the result of newer, more-integrated cohorts replacing earlier, more-segregated cohorts? As with labor force participation rates, the segregation trends can be disaggregated into age, period, and cohort trends (see Table 7, page 118). For segregation, the pattern is much clearer: Virtually all the change was a period change in which occupations for everybody in the labor force became more integrated, regardless of age or birth cohort. The rows in the table show the period change. Occupational segregation dropped for each cohort between 1960 and 1990. The three cohorts whose work lives extended through the entire period all dropped about 10 points in occupational segregation. The stagnation between 1990 and 2000 can also be observed for each cohort, with the possible exception of the recent 1965–to–1975 birth cohort (but in 1990, this cohort was between 16 and 24 years old, so levels of segregation may not represent the career jobs that many in this cohort would have begun after 1990).

Table 7

OCCUPATIONAL SEGREGATION BY BIRTH COHORT AND CENSUS YEAR, 1950–2000

Birth cohort	1950	1960	1970	1980	1990	2000
1875–1884	59.4					
1885–1894	60.5	61.6				
1895–1904	61.6	61.8	56.5			
1905–1914	61.2	62.3	58.0	56.0		
1915–1924	60.4	62.8	58.3	55.8	52.8	
1925–1934	59.3	61.8	58.2	55.4	51.9	50.6
1935–1944		61.0	56.1	54.5	50.2	49.7
1945–1954			56.0	51.6	48.6	48.4
1955–1964				54.6	47.9	47.7
1965–1974					49.4	46.0
1975–1984						42.9

Note: Includes men and women ages 16–84. Outlined cells are for prime working ages 25–54. The dissimilarity index is the percentage of men or women who would have to change occupations for each occupation to be evenly female—that is, to match the gender distribution in the general labor force.

Source: Authors' calculations using the Integrated Public Use Microdata Series (IPUMS), 2003.

Table 8

OCCUPATIONAL SEGREGATION BY GENDER AND BY RACE AND ETHNICITY, 2000

Race/ethnicity	Gender segregation (women vs. men)		Racial segregation (from whites of same gender)	
	Within race/ethnicity	Versus white men	Women	Men
White (only)	52.7	52.7	—	—
African American	47.7	57.4	21.7	26.5
Hispanic (any)	51.4	55.9	23.5	28.3
Mexican	52.1	57.5	28.3	34.7
Puerto Rican	47.0	53.9	17.1	23.2
Central American	47.7	58.1	37.9	37.3
South American	42.6	50.8	21.1	20.4
Cuban	44.7	48.5	10.5	13.6
Dominican	46.4	56.8	31.3	31.8
Asian (any)	39.6	51.7	23.4	30.2
Chinese	34.4	49.8	30.7	38.1
South Asian	36.6	52.0	28.7	41.8
Filipina	40.9	56.6	24.5	28.5
Southeast Asian	37.3	55.3	40.8	35.8
Korean	38.3	48.3	28.6	30.5
Japanese	39.5	48.9	15.5	22.9
American Indian	48.3	50.7	13.7	16.3
Pacific Islander	45.4	50.1	15.3	17.1

— Not applicable.

Note: Occupations for men and women ages 25–54. The dissimilarity index is the percentage of men or women who would have to change occupations for each occupation to be evenly female—that is, to match the gender distribution in the general labor force. Racial segregation is measured by a dissimilarity index defined as the percentage of same gender whites or other races (such as African American or Hispanic) that would have to change occupations for each occupation to be evenly white—that is, to match the racial distribution in the labor force for each gender group.

Source: Authors' calculations using Census 2000 5% Public Use Microdata Sample (PUMS).

There are much smaller differences among birth cohorts. Since 1970, the entering cohorts (born from 1935 to 1944) tend to have less occupational segregation than the cohorts that came before them (see the columns in the table). By 2000, the 1935–to–1944 cohort was entering retirement age and was about 4 points less integrated than the 1965–to–1974 cohort, whose members were beginning their adult careers. So the cohort differences over 30 years were less than half of the period changes that each cohort experienced between 1960 and 1990. Thus, the phenomenal changes in occupational segregation witnessed over the last 50 years have been experienced more within than between generations. The fact that everybody's occupation became more gender integrated accounted for most of the change.

There is also little evidence of age effects in these data. Most cohorts became more integrated as they passed through the life course, but that was because most cohorts in these censuses lived through the rapid changes from 1960 to 1990. Age differences within each census show small increases in occupational segregation with age, especially in the more recent censuses. Those age differences are the result of the small cohort differences that begin to emerge with the 1935–to–1944 cohort.

Occupational Segregation by Race and Ethnicity

Census 2000 Findings

As with labor force participation, occupational segregation varies by race and ethnicity as well as by gender. Not only are occupations racially segregated, but levels of gender segregation also may vary by race. Separate gender segregation indices can be calculated within each racial and ethnic group, and racial segregation indices can be calculated within each gender (see Table 8).

Two conclusions emerge from these calculations. First, women of color are generally far less segregated from white women (column 3) than from men of their own race or ethnicity (column 1). Asian women are an exception: Their racial segregation levels often approach the levels of gender segregation.

Second, levels of occupational gender segregation are quite similar across all racial and ethnic groups, except for Asians, who have substantially lower levels of gender segregation. Other groups also have lower gender segregation than whites, but the differences are small. Hispanics are about 1 percentage point below whites; African Americans and American Indians, 5 percentage points below. The lower levels of gender segregation among people of color are not the result of any privileged position of minority women. Rather, the lower segregation results because minority men are less privileged than white men. Segregation based on race and ethnicity is greater among men (column 4) than among women (column 3).

Long-Term Changes

Changes in occupational gender segregation over the last half-century roughly parallel the general gender story: limited change in the 1950s, followed by declines from the 1960s through the 1990s, when declines slowed or ended. Like labor force participation, the changes over the last 50 years cross racial and ethnic divisions fairly consistently. Indeed, changes over time within any one racial or ethnic group are greater than the differences across these same groups (with the exception of Asians). Even Asians have experienced the same changes as other groups since 1970, although at a lower level. African Americans have seen the largest drop: In the 1950s and 1960s, their gender segregation was greater than for whites or any other group. Only since 1970 have whites had more occupational gender segregation than other racial or ethnic groups.

Occupational Segregation by Education and Class

Education is the major determinant of the types of occupations people can enter. Does it also determine levels of gender segregation? Is gender segregation of occupations a working-class phenomenon? Many of the most male-dominated occupations are working-class occupations, especially skilled crafts (mechanics, electricians) and service work (firefighters, truck drivers). Similarly, many of the female-dominated occupations, while white collar, involve routine work that has many working-class characteristics (secretaries, bank tellers). On the other hand, some of the most dramatic changes in gender segregation are in the classic professional positions of doctors and lawyers. And the gender integration of managers has probably accounted for more of the overall integration of the labor force than has any other occupation. There are important exceptions, of course: Airplane pilots and nurses remain among the most gender-segregated occupations, while bartenders and bus drivers are now more gender-integrated than they were in the 1950s.

The class nature of gender segregation manifests itself in comparisons based on education and occupation. Comparing college-educated workers with workers who have no more than a high school diploma reveals the class division among workers. Separating working-class occupations from middle-class occupations also sheds light on the subject. The middle class includes professionals and managers (including nonretail sales), while the working class includes all other occupations. Both analyses tell similar stories: Gender segregation in occupation is stronger among the working class, and most of the change in such segregation has occurred for the middle class.

Census 2000 Findings

In an analysis of groups by level of education—high school dropouts, those with only a high school diploma, those who went beyond high school and attended a college without getting a bachelor's degree, and those who graduated from college (including those who continued for more advanced degrees)—only college graduates were in less gender-segregated occupations than any of the other three groups. This shift was not a gradual change with more education, but an abrupt division between college graduates and those with less education. This disparity is substantial: People who did not graduate from college are in occupations that are almost half again as segregated as the occupations of college graduates.

One reason why college-educated working women are less segregated from college-educated men in occupation is that these women hold middle-class jobs, and middle-class occupations are now far less segregated than working-class occupations. In the 2000 Census, the 316 working-class occupations produced a segregation coefficient of 62; for the 155 middle-class occupations, the coefficient was only 40 (a lower coefficient signifies less segregation).

Long-Term Trends

While the occupations of college-educated workers are now less gender-segregated than those of workers without college degrees, has this disparity always been the case? How much of the decline in occupational gender segregation from 1960 to 1990 was limited to the college-educated? Separate trends by education show that occupational segregation declined for everybody during the period, but it was most dramatic for the college-educated. The rapid decline of gender segregation among the college-educated was undoubtedly because primarily middle-class occupations were integrating. There was almost no decline in segregation for the working class. Middle-class occupations began being slightly more integrated in 1960; but by 1990, a major difference had emerged (see Figure 4, page 120).

Social class is obviously important for how integrated our jobs are. This difference is especially notable because gender segregation is almost constant across the other demographic characteristics we have examined. Race, ethnicity, age, and birth year do not seem to matter much for the degree of segregation. Not so for class: It is primarily the college-educated and those in middle-class occupations who have enjoyed the benefits of occupational integration that occurred between 1960 and 1990. On the other hand, education and class do not matter much for the rapid changes in women's labor force participation: Female high school graduates increased their labor force participation at about the same pace (although at a lower level) as female college graduates. But when female high school graduates got

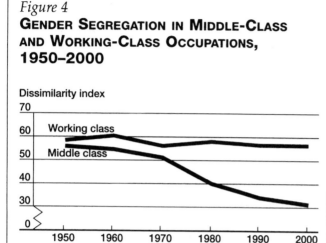

Figure 4

GENDER SEGREGATION IN MIDDLE-CLASS AND WORKING-CLASS OCCUPATIONS, 1950–2000

Note: Includes working people ages 25–54. Middle-class occupations include professional and managerial (including nonretail sales) occupations. All other occupations are considered working-class occupations. The dissimilarity index is the percentage of men or women who would have to change occupations in order for each occupation to be evenly female—that is, to match the gender distribution in the labor force as a whole.

Source: Authors' calculations using the Integrated Public Use Microdata Series (IPUMS), 2003.

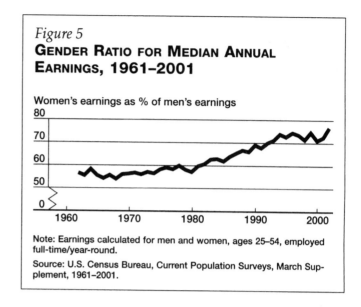

Figure 5

GENDER RATIO FOR MEDIAN ANNUAL EARNINGS, 1961–2001

Note: Earnings calculated for men and women, ages 25–54, employed full-time/year-round.

Source: U.S. Census Bureau, Current Population Surveys, March Supplement, 1961–2001.

to work in 2000, they found a much more segregated workplace than did their college-educated sisters.

Changing Work

The trends and patterns outlined in this section indicate a considerable integration of men's and women's work, but a substantial amount of segregation persists. Whether one looks at individual occupations, overall distributions, or summary statistics, it is clear that the barriers that kept women from certain occupations and trapped them in others have been lowered. But it is also clear that men and women continue to occupy separate spheres in the world of work. It also appears from this data that the pace of change has slowed. For almost all groups, there was less change in integration in the 1990s than in any decade since the 1950s. Again, it remains to be seen if this is a temporary slowing or the beginning of a reversal of the trends of the 1960s, 1970s, and 1980s.

EARNINGS

To some extent, changes in both labor force participation and occupational segregation over time are easily observable. We see more women working today and working in a wider variety of occupations than in the past. In fact, the sight of women in large numbers in previously male occupations, such as police officers and politicians, can sometimes mask the persistence of inequality. While perhaps the least directly visible of the

three dimensions of work-related gender inequality, differences in men's and women's pay may have garnered the most public attention. Each year, when the U.S. Bureau of Labor Statistics releases results from the March Current Population Survey, a spate of newspaper stories appear on the gender gap in earnings. These stories tell both good news (a narrowing gap) or bad (a widening gap). Cumulatively, as we will see, the last 50 years have brought good news—but the differences remain large, and the gap between men's and women's earnings widened again in the last half of the 1990s.

Women still earn less than men. The average woman age 25 to 54 who worked full-time/year-round in 1999 reported earnings of $28,100. That is only 73 percent of the $38,700 reported by the average man age 25 to 54. The ratio is somewhat better if hourly wages for all workers are estimated by adjusting annual earnings for the reported usual hours worked and the number of weeks worked last year. Women's average hourly wage of $12.44 is 79 percent of men's $15.72.

The gender gap in earnings declined during much of the last quarter of the 20th century. That advance appears to have ended in the mid-1990s. Census data from 1950 through 2000 show the ratio of women's to men's earnings to have hit bottom in 1969 and 1979 at 56 percent (the higher the ratio, the smaller the gender gap). In 1989, the ratio jumped to 66 percent, and it continued to improve to 71 percent in 1999. (Because the census collects data about last year's earnings, the 2000 Census yields estimates for 1999 earnings, the 1990 Census for 1989 earnings, etc.) More detailed annual data from the Current Population Survey (see Figure 5) suggest that the increase in the 1990s occurred entirely in the first half of that decade. Since the mid-1990s, there has been little improvement in the gender earnings ratio.

Changes in men's earnings are more closely correlated with changes in the gender ratio than are changes

Figure 6
MEDIAN ANNUAL EARNINGS FOR U.S. MEN AND WOMEN, 1961–2001

Median earnings (thousands)

Note: Earnings calculated for men and women, ages 25–54, employed full-time/year-round.

Source: U.S. Census Bureau, Current Population Surveys, March Supplement, 1961–2001.

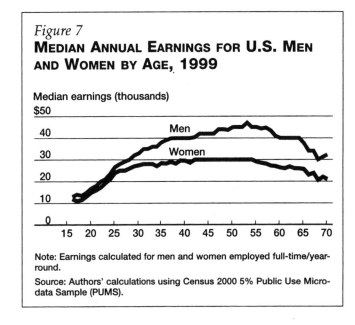

Figure 7
MEDIAN ANNUAL EARNINGS FOR U.S. MEN AND WOMEN BY AGE, 1999

Median earnings (thousands)

Note: Earnings calculated for men and women employed full-time/year-round.

Source: Authors' calculations using Census 2000 5% Public Use Micro-data Sample (PUMS).

in women's earnings (see Figure 6). Women's average earnings have increased steadily since the 1960s. Men's average earnings, on the other hand, increased in the 1960s through the early 1970s, but then plateaued and even declined somewhat until the mid-1990s. In the mid-1990s, men's earnings again began to increase after two decades of stagnation. Thus, over the last 40 years, when men's earnings have risen, the gender earnings gap has held constant or even grown. But when men's earnings have stagnated or declined, the gender earnings gap has closed. Times of progress in gender equality have come mainly when men's earnings have stagnated.

Earnings by Age, Period, and Cohort

It is not simple to determine how much of the change in the earnings ratio can be ascribed to period effects that all workers experienced and how much to cohort-replacement effects. Unlike occupational integration, which was clearly a period effect that happened among all workers with few age or cohort differences, changes in the earnings ratio reflect each of the possible patterns of age, cohort, and period effects—and none of these patterns are simple linear trends. We begin with the age patterns, which are especially strong for the earnings gap.

Census 2000 Findings

The gender difference in earnings is dramatically larger among older workers than among younger workers (see Figure 7). In 1999, the average 25-year-old woman earned 90 percent of what the average 25-year-old man earned. But 55-year-old women earned only 65 percent of what 55-year-old men earned. In what are

usually the post-retirement years, the gender difference diminishes somewhat.

However, the growing gender gap in 1999 between 16-year-olds and those in their late 50s does not mean that the gender gap increases over people's careers. When the same individuals are studied over time, the gender earnings gap between the average woman and the average man is quite stable across their work lives. Women earn less than men throughout their careers, but the disadvantage for the average woman doesn't change much after working many years. The age differences in Figure 7 occur for two other reasons: a cohort effect and an out-of-labor-force effect. First, the older workers in 1999 were born before the end of World War II; gender gaps for this generation have been higher than for any generation before or after. Second, women interrupt their careers for child care and family responsibilities more often than men do. This time out of the labor force puts older women at a disadvantage when they return to work. By age 55, the typical woman has accumulated fewer years of work experience than a man. If we compare men and women with the same years of work experience (something we cannot do with census data), the earnings difference between the average man and the average woman remains fairly constant over their work lives.

Although career earnings trajectories are quite similar for the average man and woman, these trajectories do diverge among higher earners. Men's chances of getting into the top fifth of earners increase faster than women's over time. Some women do reach that level later in their careers, but their rates of advancement into these top levels are slower than men's. As a result, the gender gap in earnings at the 80th percentile is higher than at the median, and that gap grows larger with more years in the labor force. The difference between career trajectories

Box 2

GLASS CEILINGS

In a 1986 *Wall Street Journal* article on women in the work force, Carol Hymowitz and Timothy Schellhardt coined the term "glass ceiling" to describe the experience of female executives who seemed unable to reach the highest levels of corporate success.

Since that time, a large number of reports have addressed the problem. The Federal Glass Ceiling Commission, founded in 1991, defined the glass ceiling as the "unseen, yet unbreachable barrier that keeps minorities and women from rising to the upper rungs of the corporate ladder, regardless of their qualifications or achievements."[1] Typical signs of a glass ceiling are the lack of women on corporate boards of directors, the relative absence of women as CEOs or presidents of large companies, and the scarcity of women at the top of government and education institutions. For instance, a report from the Catalyst organization showed that, in 2003, women held just 13.6 percent of the nearly 6,000 seats on Fortune 500 boards.[2]

Though useful, the idea of a glass ceiling has been increasingly used to describe so broad a variety of circumstances that it has become difficult to discern a difference between a glass ceiling and a generic form of gender inequality. In addition, scholars have generated a series of related metaphors, including "glass escalators" (to denote men's rapid upward mobility in female occupations); "sticky floors" (to point out the way that women and minorities often were relegated to the lowest rungs on corporate ladders); "glass walls" (to describe the way that women and minorities were relegated to certain departments like human resources or public relations); and even "concrete ceilings" (to emphasize the near total absence of women of color from positions in corporate governance).

We developed four criteria to distinguish glass ceilings from other forms of gender or racial inequality. A glass-ceiling inequality represents:

● A gender or racial difference not explained by other job-relevant characteristics of the employee;
● A gender or racial difference greater at higher levels of an outcome than at lower levels;
● A gender or racial inequality in the chances of advancement into higher levels, not merely the proportions currently at those higher levels; and
● A gender or racial inequality that increases over the course of a person's career.

Results of studies using these criteria to analyze individual work histories suggested that there are glass ceilings for women, and that for minority women, the glass ceiling falls quite low with respect to both earnings and advancement to managerial status.[3] At high earnings levels, defined in this research as chances of reaching white men's 75th percentile in earnings, the gap between white men's and white women's chances grows larger over time. By definition, 25 percent of white men are at this level at any given point in time, but only 10 percent are at it at the beginning of their careers, and 30 percent are at it at the end of their careers. For white women, fewer start at this high level of earnings, and the rate at which they attain high earnings is much slower than white men's, so the gap between white women and white men grows over the course of their careers. This gap grows only at the higher level of earnings, not at moderate or low levels. African American women see no increase in their chances of attaining high earnings, and their gap compared with white men grows substantially over their careers.

Both findings suggest a glass ceiling in earnings for women. In contrast, there is less evidence of such a glass ceiling for African American men. While African American men are less likely than white men to achieve each of the earnings benchmarks, the gap does not grow larger later in their careers, nor is it especially stronger at high earnings levels than at low earnings levels. In contrast, the research on advancement to managerial status shows that, relative to white men, chances for advancement among white women, black women, and black men gradually diminish, even among the youngest cohorts of college-educated workers.

References

1. Federal Glass Ceiling Commission, *Solid Investment: Making Full Use of the Nation's Human Capital* (Washington, DC: U.S. Department of Labor, 1995): 4.

2. Catalyst Inc., *2003 Catalyst Census of Women Board Directors*, accessed at http://catalystwomen.org/research/censuses.htm#2003wbd, on Sept. 7, 2004.

3. David A. Cotter et al., "The Glass Ceiling Effect," *Social Forces* 80, no. 2 (2001): 655–81; and David J. Maume, "Is the Glass Ceiling a Unique Form of Inequality? Evidence from a Random-Effects Model of Managerial Attainment," *Work and Occupations* 31, no. 2 (2004): 250–74.

at the average and among top earners suggests a "glass ceiling" for women: Women are at more of a disadvantage at the top of the earnings distribution than in the middle; and as their careers develop, their rate of advancement into the top category of earners falls behind men's (see Box 2).

Long-Term Trends

The earnings gap decreased between the mid-1970s and the mid-1990s partly because of changes that happened to all cohorts and, to a lesser extent, because of newer, more gender-equal cohorts replacing older, less-equal cohorts. Women fall further behind men through middle age and then catch up slightly nearing and after retirement ages (see Table 9). For instance, women born between 1935 and 1944 began their work lives earning 86 percent of what men earned, but that earning power fell to just 50 percent by the middle of the work lives of these women, and then rebounded to 65 percent when they were between 55 and 64. This age pattern is common to most cohorts, with some variations resulting primarily from period effects discussed below.

There are, at best, weak cohort differences. On the left side of Table 9, most columns show the lowest ratios in the middle cohorts. The two cohorts of 1925-to-1934 and 1935-to-1944 have particularly low gender ratios in their middle years, with both the cohorts that came before and after having more equal earnings ratios. But in their later years, these cohorts no longer look so unequal—primarily because that time frame is when the period effect of the 1980s catches up with them. Moreover, the low point in each column is not fixed on the same cohort but tends to move up diagonally with each decade of age, reflecting a period effect: the low point reached in the 1980 Census.

The stronger period effects are more evident in the right side. Most of the cohorts showed declining gender ratios from 1950 through 1980. In fact, the 1950 starting point looks surprisingly equal in this table. Only in 1990 had most of the ratios turned upward. Each of the cohorts between 1915 and 1944 became more equal during the 1980s. The two cohorts that followed (the baby boomers) did not experience the same equalizing trend—but for baby boomers, the 1980s were the early parts of their work lives, when gender earnings ratios typically decline rapidly. The 1980s' gender benefit for the boomers was that their early career declines were relatively modest.

Thus, the interesting result from these analyses is the strength of the period effect of the 1980s that brought rising equality to all cohorts in similar measure. Cohort differences are not especially consistent over the five decades, although the curved age effect is common to all groups.

Earnings by Race and Ethnicity

Gender gaps in earnings vary across racial and ethnic groups somewhat more than does occupational segregation. Again, gender inequality is somewhat stronger among whites. The earnings of white women were just 70 percent of white men. Women's earnings were several percentage points closer to men's earnings among African Americans (83 percent) and Hispanics (84 percent) (see Table 10, page 124). Although black and Hispanic women earned less than white women, black and Hispanic men were even further behind white men, so gender differences are smaller. The gender earnings ratios of Asian Americans, American Indians, and Pacific Islanders are also larger than that of whites, although there are substantial differences among Asian groups as there are for occupational segregation and labor force participation.

The gender inequality trends from 1950 to 2000 for earnings were shared across most racial and ethnic groups. The gender earnings gap widened during the 1950s and 1960s, peaked or leveled off in the 1970s, and decreased in the 1980s and 1990s. The one exception was African Americans: Their gender earnings gap decreased substantially during the 1960s and 1970s, a period of little change or increased gaps for other racial and ethnic groups. Average earnings for African American women increased especially fast in the 1960s and 1970s as many women shifted from domestic service to higher-paying jobs that were newly open to them. As a result, by 1980, earnings by gender for African Americans had shifted from the most unequal of all racial and ethnic groups to the most equal. Equality continued in the 1980s and at a slightly reduced rate in the 1990s for African Americans.

Table 9

RATIO OF WOMEN'S EARNINGS AS PERCENT OF MEN'S EARNINGS BY BIRTH COHORT, AGE, AND CENSUS YEAR, 1950–2000

Birth cohort	Birth cohort by age						Birth cohort by census year					
	16–24	25–34	35–44	45–54	55–64	65–74	1950	1960	1970	1980	1990	2000
1885–1894					61	58	61	58				
1895–1904				65	60	67	65	60	67			
1905–1914			65	58	60	63	65	58	60	63		
1915–1924		70	56	56	55	67	70	56	56	55	67	
1925–1934	90	64	53	50	59	71	90	64	53	50	59	71
1935–1944	86	60	50	58	65			86	60	50	58	65
1945–1954	78	65	63	67					78	65	63	67
1955–1964	80	76	73							80	76	73
1965–1974	90	81									90	81
1975–1984	88											88

Note: Median earnings calculated for men and women ages 16–84, working full-time/year-round. Shaded cells are from the 2000 Census. Outlined cells are for prime working ages 25–54.

Source: Authors' calculations using the Integrated Public Use Microdata Series (IPUMS), 2003.

Table 10
MEDIAN EARNINGS FOR U.S. WOMEN AND MEN BY RACE AND ETHNICITY, 1999

Race/ethnicity	Women	Men	Women's earnings as % of men's	
			Same race/ ethnicity	White men
White (only)	$28,000	$40,000	70	70
African American	$25,000	$30,000	83	63
Hispanic (any)	$21,000	$25,000	84	53
Mexican	$20,000	$23,900	84	50
Puerto Rican	$25,000	$30,000	83	63
Central American	$18,000	$22,500	80	45
South American	$24,000	$30,000	80	60
Cuban	$26,000	$31,000	84	65
Dominican	$20,000	$24,700	81	50
Asian (any)	$30,000	$40,000	75	75
Chinese	$34,000	$43,000	79	85
South Asian	$30,300	$35,000	87	76
Filipina	$32,300	$50,000	65	81
Southeast Asian	$23,100	$30,000	77	58
Korean	$35,000	$48,500	72	88
Japanese	$27,700	$38,000	73	69
American Indian	$24,000	$30,000	80	60
Pacific Islander	$25,000	$30,000	83	63

Note: Earnings calculated for men and women ages 25–54, employed full-time/year-round.

Source: Authors' calculations using Census 2000 5% Public Use Microdata Sample (PUMS).

Figure 8
MEDIAN ANNUAL EARNINGS OF U.S. WOMEN AND MEN BY EDUCATION, 1999

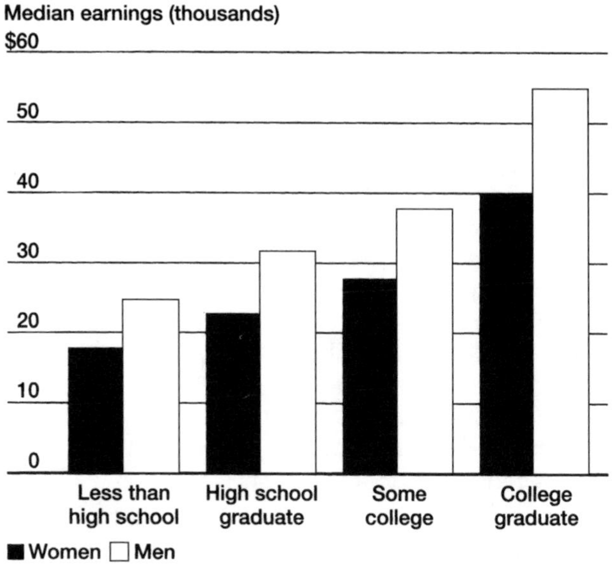

Note: Earnings calculated for men and women, ages 25–54, employed full-time/year-round.

Source: Authors' calculations using Census 2000 5% Public Use Microdata Sample (PUMS).

Earnings by Education

The gender earnings ratio is quite uniform across education levels. High school dropouts have almost as large a gender ratio (72 percent) as college graduates (73 percent). Although more education means higher earnings for both women and men, more education makes almost no difference for the size of the gender ratio across education groups (see Figure 8). Moreover, the increase in the gender ratio over the last 25 years is quite similar at each level of education.

Unlike occupational integration, which has been primarily a middle-class trend, gender earnings equality improved among all levels of education. And the trends within education levels have followed an inverted U-shaped pattern similar to those for racial and ethnic groups. The gender earnings gap among college graduates was its largest in 1960, while for high school dropouts, high school graduates, and those with some college, the gender gap reached its highest point in the 1970s. There is some evidence that gender differences by education have narrowed since 1970, with the largest declines happening in the 1980s. Since 1950, the gender earnings gap has been smaller among college graduates

than among high school graduates; that difference became negligible by 1999. Annual CPS data document the same convergence.

Earnings by Occupational Segregation

The segregation of women into female-dominated occupations has long been thought to be a principal cause of the gender earnings gap. Female-dominated occupations pay less, the argument goes, regardless of whether men or women work in those occupations. But because women more often work in these predominantly female occupations, they earn less on average. The association between occupation and earnings suggests two resolutions. If female occupations paid what male occupations paid, or if occupational segregation could be eliminated so that there were no predominantly female occupations, much of the gender earnings gap would be eliminated.

As in earlier decades, in 2000 women's occupations garnered lower earnings than men's. And regardless of occupation, men earned more than women. Median earnings for workers in men's occupations (30 percent female or less) averaged $38,240, while in mixed occupations (31 percent to 69 percent female) these earnings were slightly higher ($39,178). Across women's occupations (at least 70 percent female), the average was substantially lower ($27,219). But even within the same

124   THE AMERICAN PEOPLE

Table 11
WOMEN'S AND MEN'S MEDIAN ANNUAL EARNINGS IN SELECTED OCCUPATIONS, 1999

Earnings in 1999	Women	Men	Gender ratio (%)
Male occupations			
Electricians	$33,000	$39,100	84
Firefighters	$40,000	$47,000	85
Airplane pilots	$44,000	$59,000	75
Truck drivers	$23,000	$32,400	71
Electrical engineers	$54,000	$64,000	84
Clergy	$29,000	$32,000	91
Police	$40,000	$45,600	88
Architects	$40,100	$52,000	77
Mixed occupations			
Physicians	$86,000	$134,000	64
Lawyers	$65,000	$88,000	74
Mail carriers	$36,700	$40,000	92
Managers	$36,000	$51,000	71
Real estate agents	$35,000	$50,000	70
Bartenders	$16,000	$22,000	73
Bus drivers	$21,000	$32,000	66
Accountants and bookkeepers	$36,000	$51,000	71
Female occupations			
Bill collectors	$25,700	$30,000	86
Medical and dental technicians	$30,000	$35,000	86
Teachers	$33,000	$40,300	82
Waiters and waitresses	$15,200	$21,000	72
Librarians	$35,000	$38,000	92
Nurses (professional)	$42,000	$45,000	93
Bank tellers	$19,000	$22,000	86
Secretaries and typists	$26,000	$32,000	81

Note: Earnings calculated for men and women, ages 25–54, employed full-time/year-round.

Source: Authors' calculations using the Integrated Public Use Microdata Series (IPUMS), 2003.

Figure 9
MEDIAN ANNUAL EARNINGS BY PERCENT FEMALE IN OCCUPATION, 1999

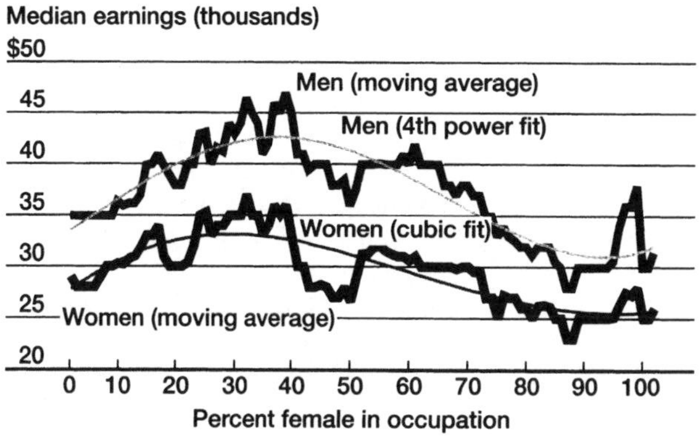

Note: The two lines indicating "4th power fit" and "cubic fit" represent attempts to fit a line that comes closest to all the points in the series. The relationship between earnings and occupational sex composition has often been assumed to be a straight line: the higher the percent female, the lower the earnings. However, as this figure shows, the pattern is not linear and is best described by the "wavy" lines created by fitting a more complex equation. The best-fitting curve for women included three coefficients, and for men, four. Earnings are highest among occupations predominantly (but not entirely) male, and lowest among those predominantly (but not entirely) female. Earnings calculated for men and women, ages 25–54, employed full-time/year-round.

Source: Authors' calculations using Census 2000 5% Public Use Microdata Sample (PUMS).

occupations, men earned more than women. An examination of the selected occupations presented in Table 11 shows that even where earnings were closest (nurses, librarians, mail carriers, and clergy), women earned less than men. For example, the average male nurse working full-time/year-round earned $45,000, while his female counterpart earned $42,000. But there are also occupations where the differences are quite large (physicians and bus drivers), and these examples span the spectrum of occupations both in terms of gender composition and social class. So, the typical male physician earned $134,000, while the typical female physician's earnings were $86,000. Among male bus drivers, the median earnings were $32,000, compared with women's $21,000.

In fact, the connection between occupational gender segregation and the earnings gap is more complex than usually thought. Figure 9 shows median annual earnings for occupations along the full range of occupational gender composition. Although female-dominant occupations generally pay less than male-dominant occupations, there are two important exceptions. First, the most male-dominated occupations pay less than those occupations that are partially integrated. Second, the most female-dominated occupations pay at least as well if not better than those occupations with more men. These exceptions at the two ends of the gender composition scale mean that the relationship between the gender segregation of occupations and their earnings cannot be summarized by a straight line. This nonlinearity is not well recognized in the extensive research literature on occupational gender segregation and earnings. Some of the nonlinearity can be explained by other factors such as education, but even after extensive statistical controls for the personal characteristics of workers, the nonlinear shape of the relationship remains, although somewhat attenuated (results not shown).

The nonlinearity is not a new phenomenon; each census since 1950 shows a similar curve. Over this last half-century, both the maximum and the minimum median incomes have moved slightly to the right, toward the female end of the gender composition scale, but the general shape of the curve has not changed substantially.

Box 3

SPATIAL VARIATION IN GENDER INEQUALITY

The places where we live are quite varied, and one of the ways in which those places vary is in their level of gender inequality. That variation can sometimes be as great or greater than the differences in gender inequality observed over time. For instance, women's labor force participation rates range from a low of 66 percent in Los Angeles to a high of 83 percent in Minneapolis-St. Paul, more than the total change in this ratio seen in the 1970s. The ratio of women's earnings to men's earnings ranges from a low of 64 percent in Detroit to a high of 77 percent in Sacramento, Calif., as much as the change from 1977 to 2000. These variations are, in fact, smaller than the total variations across places, in part because smaller metropolitan areas have greater variation (especially higher levels of gender inequality), although there are few substantial differences in gender inequality between metropolitan and nonmetropolitan areas.[1]

Attention to spatial variation is important because most Americans work in local rather than national labor markets. We tend to look for jobs within occupations in particular cities or regions. Thus, some of us may be working in places with labor markets in which men and women are more equal, or in labor markets with less equality. The underlying dynamics of these differences across places are not limited to gender inequality,

and their origins and interrelationships are the subject of recent research.[2] Some of the variation can be traced to compositional differences in the populations of these places—we would expect lower levels of labor force participation in areas with concentrations of people less likely to be in the labor force. For example, the larger Hispanic population in Los Angeles relative to Minneapolis may account for some of the difference in women's labor force participation. But part of the explanation may also involve differences in occupational or industrial compositions. For example, in Texas, Austin's high tech and government employment may be more "female friendly" than Houston's energy industry.

Some of the spatial variations may be cultural—norms about appropriate male and female roles may vary across different parts of the country. In any case, it is notable that conditions are far from uniform across the United States.

References

1. David A. Cotter et al., "Nonmetropolitan and Metropolitan Gender Inequality," *Rural Sociology* 61, no. 2 (1996): 272–88.

2. David A. Cotter, Joan M. Hermsen, and Reeve Vanneman, "Systems of Gender, Race, and Class Inequality: Multilevel Analyses," *Social Forces* 78, no. 2 (1999): 433–60; and Leslie McCall, *Complex Inequality: Gender, Class and Race in the New Economy* (New York: Routledge, 2001).

Gender Inequality Across 25 Largest Metropolitan Areas, 2000

Metropolitan area	Women's labor force participation (%)	Occupational segregation	Gender earnings ratio (%)
Minneapolis-St. Paul, MN-WI	83	0.44	71
Orlando, FL	79	0.46	68
Kansas City, MO-KS	79	0.46	70
Milwaukee-Racine, WI	79	0.48	68
Washington-Baltimore, DC-MD-VA-WV	78	0.42	74
Indianapolis, IN	78	0.46	69
Boston-Worcester-Lawrence, MA-NH-ME-CT	77	0.44	71
St. Louis, MO-IL	77	0.50	67
Seattle-Tacoma-Bremerton, WA	76	0.43	70
Cleveland-Akron, OH	76	0.49	66
Portland-Salem, OR-WA	76	0.46	72
Philadelphia-Wilmington-Atlantic City, PA-NJ	75	0.48	70
Atlanta, GA	75	0.46	70
Tampa-St. Petersburg-Clearwater, FL	75	0.47	72
San Francisco-Oakland-San Jose, CA	74	0.42	71
Miami-Fort Lauderdale, FL	74	0.47	71
Chicago-Gary-Kenosha, IL-IN-WI	73	0.47	67
Sacramento-Yolo, CA	73	0.45	77
Dallas-Fort Worth, TX	72	0.47	69
Detroit-Ann Arbor-Flint, MI	72	0.49	64
Phoenix-Mesa, AZ	71	0.47	71
San Diego, CA	71	0.45	72
New York-Northern New Jersey-Long Island	70	0.47	70
Houston-Galveston-Brazoria, TX	68	0.51	66
Los Angeles-Riverside-Orange Co., CA	66	0.45	75

Note: All statistics based on population ages 25–54. Earnings ratios calculated for people employed full-time/year-round.

Source: Authors' calculations using Census 2000 5% Public Use Microdata Sample (PUMS).

A substantial gender earnings gap remains even at similar levels of the gender composition of occupations (see Figure 9). Men earn more than women even within the same occupation. This disparity is true among all occupations—those that are predominately male, predominately female, and integrated. For example, as shown in Table 11, the average female electrician earned $33,000 in 1999, while the average male electrician earned $39,100. Similarly, the average female secretary earned $26,000, while her male counterpart earned $32,000. The gap persists even among integrated occupations where, for example, the typical female lawyer earned $65,000 and the typical male lawyer earned $88,000.

But the fact that most men hold jobs on the left (high earnings) side of Figure 9 while most women hold jobs on the right (low earnings) side must explain some of the overall gender earnings gap. How much is due to this gender segregation of occupations? The nonlinearity of the gender segregation/earnings relationship creates difficulties for answering this question. Most prior research has evaluated this question using a linear approximation to the occupation-earnings relationship. The nonlinear shape of the relationship renders any such estimate suspect. Instead, we can use women's average earnings within each detailed occupation to estimate what would be the mean earnings of women if women had the same occupational distribution as men. If women worked in the same set of occupations as men, their mean earnings would increase from $34,471 to $37,877; this would be 75 percent of men's mean earnings ($50,541) instead of the actual 68 percent. By these calculations, occupational segregation explains about 21 percent of the overall earnings gap. (A more realistic experiment of changing both men's and women's occupational distributions to match the overall occupational distribution reduces men's predicted earnings and raises women's predicted earnings to yield an expected earnings ratio of 74 percent—a gender gap about 18 percent smaller than the actual observed gap.) Thus, although most of the gender earnings gap occurs within occupations, about a fifth is directly attributable to gender segregation (see Box 3).

CAUSES AND CONSEQUENCES OF CHANGING INEQUALITY AT WORK

Thus far, we have outlined a series of changes over time following the general pattern of increasing equality between men and women, with particularly dramatic changes in the 1960s, 1970s, and 1980s and less dramatic ones in the 1950s and 1990s. Each of the three major facets of gender and work had a series of potential explanations. This section provides an overview of the general utility of these explanations in accounting for both change over time and persisting differences regarding inequality at work. We focus on several of the most commonly cited reasons for the changes: shifts in human capital and other attributes of women and men (such as education, experience, and family status); changes in the normative climate; and changes in the political and legal environment in which men and women work. All of these changes both affect and are affected by changes in women's work status. For instance, while increasing levels of approval for women's participation in the labor market may increase employment among women, it is also true that larger numbers of working women have led to greater approval of women's employment. Three criteria apply in assessing these explanations:

- The cause has to precede the effect. Increases in women's education should come before increases in women's earnings relative to men.
- There must be an empirical correlation. As women gain more education, their average levels of earnings should increase.
- The cause and effect should not both be the product of a third causal factor. For example, legislation leading to lower levels of discrimination by both schools and employers may have caused both more education for women and more equal pay between men and women.

Micro-Level Change
Several explanations relate to changes in women's and men's characteristics that may make these characteristics more attractive to employers, or may indicate a greater commitment to employment, or may show an increased need for women to be employed, and thus bring women the earnings associated with employment.

Education
Among the most frequently touted explanations for an individual's economic status is education. Our education substantially determines the kind of work we do and therefore the amount of pay and prestige we can expect. Thus, analysts seeking to explain changes in women's status often look first to education. Entering a particular occupation involves at least three hurdles, as illustrated by a doctor's career: training and certification (attending medical school); acceptance by employers and co-workers (working in a hospital or private practice); and acceptance by clients or consumers (treating patients). Any one of these hurdles can block a woman's entry into a particular field. The importance of access to certification is most obvious in the professions, but it is equally true in the trades—in fact, it is true wherever the supply of practitioners is limited by stringent train-

ing and licensing requirements.[6] The added benefit of certification is that relevant data are readily available. Acceptance by fellow workers and clients, on the other hand, is much more difficult to track. Being hired as a lawyer in a given firm does not guarantee equal treatment in pay, promotion, or partnership. Likewise, a woman on a carpentry crew may not be allowed to move from apprentice to journeyman, or given the same amount of overtime, or allowed to become a crew leader or site supervisor.

While the 2000 Census reveals generational patterns in gender differences in the completion of college or post-baccalaureate degrees, the gender differences across generations in completing a high school degree are quite similar. There is relatively little (if any) difference between men's and women's attainment of a high school degree. For men and women ages 45 and older, differences in the rates of high school completion are no more than 1 percentage point (favoring men). Among younger age groups, however, women hold a slight advantage: 86 percent of women ages 25 to 34 have completed high school, compared with 82 percent of their male peers. Among women ages 35 to 44, 87 percent have completed high school, while 83 percent of men ages 35 to 44 have done so. In short, since early in the 20th century, men and women have had nearly equal access to a high school education, with each subsequent generation becoming more likely to complete high school.

With regard to college, Figure 10 shows more substantial differences among older cohorts, with men being considerably more likely than women to receive a college education. This difference narrows with each subsequent cohort until women ages 35 to 44 and ages 25 to 34 begin to obtain college educations at higher rates than men. Much the same can be said about post-baccalaureate degrees: substantial differences among older cohorts that narrow (and even reverse) among the more recent cohorts. For example, among women ages 65 to 74 in 2000, only 5 percent had completed an advanced degree, while twice as many men in those ages had. Yet, nearly equal percentages of men and women ages 25 to 44 (7 percent to 9 percent) had completed an advanced degree.

While census data indicate who obtained a particular level of education, the data are much less able to specify the type or kind of education. Data from the National Center for Education Statistics (NCES) fill this gap. These data show much the same story as the census—a growing share of associate's, bachelor's, master's, doctoral, and professional degrees were granted to women between 1950 and 2000 (see Figure 11). Moreover, more than half of all degrees went to women after the late 1970s for associate's and in the early 1980s for bachelor's and master's degrees. Even in doctoral and professional degrees, women were approaching parity in 2000.

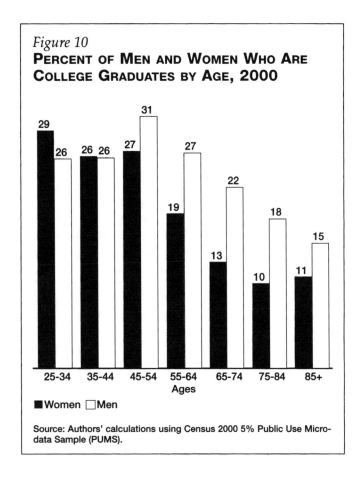

Figure 10

PERCENT OF MEN AND WOMEN WHO ARE COLLEGE GRADUATES BY AGE, 2000

■ Women □ Men

Source: Authors' calculations using Census 2000 5% Public Use Microdata Sample (PUMS).

So, on its face, the argument that access to or investment in education accounts for the substantial and persistent differences in employment, occupation, and earnings appear flawed. However, it may be that it is not just the difference in the amount of education but also in the type or kind of education that women and men have invested in that may make the difference. Trend data from NCES show college majors by gender. Women have made considerable inroads into many, if not all, fields of study. Of particular note are agriculture and natural resources, business and management, and law and legal studies. Some fields became substantially less female (library and archival sciences, probably because of Internet technologies), and some fields remained heavily female (education, languages, and health sciences). The index of dissimilarity calculated from these data shows a substantial decline—dropping from 47.3 percent to 27.8 percent of women or men having to switch majors in order for women and men to be evenly distributed across majors. (It is notable that these overall segregation measures are lower than what is observed for occupations. Much of this decline is due to the coarser classification scheme for field of degree. However, the much larger decline—19.5 points for majors, compared with 8.8 points for occupations—may well indicate more substantial change over the period.) Much of this

Figure 11
WOMEN'S SHARE OF DEGREES, 1950–2000

Percent

Bachelor's
Master's
Doctorates
Professional

| 1949– | 1959– | 1969– | 1979– | 1989– | 1999– |
| 1950 | 1960 | 1970 | 1980 | 1990 | 2000 |

Note: The data for women's share of bachelor's, master's, and doctorate degrees is for the academic year 1949–1950, and then for the years starting at 1959–1960. The data for women's share of professional degrees begins with the academic year 1960–1961.

Source: U.S. Dept. of Education, *Digest of Education Statistics* (2001): table 247.

change took place between 1971 and 1985, and a slowing of integration has been found in the subsequent period.[7]

Beyond the bachelor's degree, women's progress with regard to graduate, medical, dental, legal, and theological degrees is evident. In 1950, women made up just 10 percent of the recipients of doctoral and professional degrees. In each of the other fields, women represented less than 5 percent of the recipients. But rapid change took place in the 1970s and 1980s; by 2000, women were receiving more than 40 percent of all medical, dental, legal, and academic degrees. As with entry into occupations, however, the pace of change slowed in the 1990s, marking the smallest percentage-point gains for all fields since the 1960s. For these occupations, then, the first hurdle to access may have been passed: Women in large numbers have obtained the formal education credentials that should provide entrée into these types of work. Moreover, as cohorts of medical, dental, and law students move forward, their occupations will continue to become more balanced (unless women's dropout rates increase).

The trends reviewed above generally fit together—as women's educational attainment increased, their labor force participation increased, their access to occupations increased, and their earnings relative to men's increased. But closer examination reveals that this is only part of the story. Women's labor force participation shows similar increases within each level of education, so the growth of the share of the highest-educated who are most likely to work can account for some but not all of the increase in women's labor force participation. Similarly, gender earn-

ings gaps have narrowed mostly within levels of education, so women's increased educational attainment is not primarily responsible for the narrowing of the earnings gap. Moreover, women's levels of education have increased relative to men's throughout the last half-century, even before the earnings gap began to close in the 1970s and after it stopped closing in the mid-1990s.

Experience
Along with education, experience is one of the primary characteristics that make employees valuable to employers. In part, this is because much of the skill required to do a particular job is gained by having done that job. The experienced plumber (or surgeon) has encountered the same or similar situation, and knows how to respond. The novice, on the other hand, may have sufficient knowledge and information about how to handle the problem, but may take longer or do an inferior job. Thus, differences in experience are often responsible for differences in men's and women's pay, and contribute to differences in occupation and even labor force participation. Being in the labor force longer makes individuals less likely to drop out (and not dropping out, of course, increases their time in the labor force). Longer time in the labor force also opens access to occupations, particularly through promotion based on tenure and experience.

Scholars wishing to assess changes in experience must rely on longitudinal data, which follow individuals over time. Complicating matters, those who wish to assess changes in experience must use data that track different generations over time. While several such sources exist, few studies assess these changes. One suggests that, between 1979 and 1988, the gender difference in full-time experience dropped from 7.5 years to 4.6 years. This substantial decline was associated with approximately one-third of the decline in the gender gap in earnings.[8] Some evidence also ties changes in work experience to changes in labor force attachment. Unfortunately, more contemporary estimates of changes in experience and their effects are not yet available.

Second Incomes
One commonsense answer to the question of why women are more likely to be working today than in the past is that their earnings are more necessary to support a family. This possibility rings true for many women, and would appear at first glance to meet the tests outlined above. There are several ways in which changes in family life may have led to changes in women's work. First, the family itself has changed. More women today are raising children alone, there are more couples without children, and more women remain single longer. The expansion in the share of single women, who have always been more likely to work, could well lead to higher overall rates of labor force activity for women. Yet it is among married

mothers that the greatest changes in employment took place, so changes in family structure cannot account for all of the increase in women's employment. Moreover, single mothers' labor force participation, which had been high, stagnated from the late 1970s to the early 1990s and increased only in the late 1990s, while overall rates of women's labor force participation leveled off or declined.

A second source of this change, then, may have to do with men's earnings. A conventional account of this dynamic goes as follows: As husbands' and fathers' incomes stagnated and declined, wives and mothers were forced into the labor force. As those husbands' and fathers' earnings rebounded in the 1990s, wives and mothers pulled back from participating in the labor force. How much of the rise and plateauing of women's labor force participation is due to changes in incomes for husbands? An important determinant of labor force participation is the extent of other family income beyond a person's own earnings. The more family income a person has without being employed, the more she or he is permitted not to work and to enjoy leisure instead (or, especially for parents, to devote more time to unpaid work at home). In the 1990s, men's median earnings increased for the first time in decades; so for the first time in a long while, married mothers' opportunities to stay home increased. In an analysis not shown here, women's labor force participation rates still plateaued during the 1990s even after controls for other income, although the trend is attenuated. Thus, while changes in men's earnings may account for some of the changes in women's labor force participation, it is clear that most of the changes come from other sources.

Macro-Level Changes

The three issues addressed above relate to how changes in individuals' characteristics may have led to the increases in equality seen in the 1960s, 1970s, and 1980s, and why these same changes may have led to the stalling of these increases seen in the 1990s. Changes in social structural conditions are also thought to have contributed to improvements in equality.

Economic Structure

In many ways, the Industrial Revolution can be thought of as a source of contemporary forms of work-related gender inequality. When most of the population was engaged in agriculture, there was less differentiation in the type of work men and women did, and less distinction between those who were in or out of the labor force. Some scholars have suggested that, as the demand for traditional women's labor declined in industrial societies, so did women's status, but that as demand has increased with the emergence of service-sector employment, so has women's status.[9] In identifying a demand for female labor as central to explaining gender stratification, these theorists make three assumptions: there is a gender segregation of tasks in society that specifies some tasks as performed exclusively or generally by women; the importance of these female tasks varies over time and across societies in association with other factors such as technology; and this variation determines the relative autonomy or subordination of women across a wide range of political, economic, demographic, and ideological outcomes. Empirical assessments of this theory show some support for the effect of the demand for female labor, particularly on labor market outcomes and education, but less so on family, politics, or normative structures.[10] It is unclear at this point whether changes in occupational structure may have been related to diminished progress toward gender equality in the 1990s.

Technology

Along with inducing changes in the occupational structure, technological change may have had other effects on women's status. One way in which this may have happened is through the introduction of many labor-saving devices that may have reduced the amount of work and time required to maintain a home, thus freeing up women for employment outside the home. The research on such developments suggests that, while technology may have reduced some kinds of domestic work, it actually has increased other kinds.[11] Other technological developments, such as changes in reproductive technology, have had clearer effects. Women's increasing ability to control whether and when they have children has undoubtedly affected their presence in the labor force and likely their access to occupations and even their relative pay.[12] Control over fertility also may be the ultimate labor-saving device, as increasing numbers of children in the household have a strong negative effect on both labor force participation and pay for women who are employed.

Politics and Policy

Another set of potential explanations for changes in women's status in the world of employment is political. We offer a brief overview of three such explanations: women's access to political office; public policy oriented toward gender equality at work; and litigation that has challenged (or supported) workplace inequality. For convenience, we focus on the federal level, but many states and localities have similar policies aimed at lessening workplace inequality. At the beginning of the 1950s, many employers had explicit rules regarding appropriate jobs and pay for women. These rules included formal and informal restrictions on jobs; separate male and female sections in employment ads; differential pay scales for men and women in the same jobs within firms; pay scales set in accordance with the gender composition of jobs; and "marriage bars," which banned employment of married, let alone pregnant, women. (In fact, to avoid dismissal in the middle of the school year, the grandmother of one of this report's authors did not inform the school district where she taught that she'd gotten married.) Such rules were legal and binding into the 1960s; thereafter, informal rules served to limit women's pay and positions.

Officeholding

The political representation of women by women may have consequences for gender equality. Female elected officials may pursue with a more concerted effort than do their male peers legislation and public policies that address the unequal status of women in American society. This increased attention to women's issues may in turn contribute to normative changes in the larger society.

Although ideal for some issues, the census is a fairly poor source for information about women's presence and progress in the political arena. (The 2000 Census identified 15,406 people as legislators; 5,461, or 35 percent of them, are women. In the 1990 Census, 42 percent of the 12,716 legislators were women.) But even a casual observer knows that there are many more women in prominent political offices today than in the 1950s or 1960s. Before the 1980s, few women held political office, though many were involved in politics either as volunteers or as advisers to and supporters of their husbands' careers. Moreover, many of the women who held office prior to the 1970s did so by the so-called "widows model," assuming seats vacated by the death of husbands or (less frequently) fathers.[13] The late 1980s and 1990s marked women's entry into high-level elected office at both the state and national level. The proportion of female U.S. House members rose from 5 percent in 1987 to nearly 14 percent in 2003, while the Senate went from being 2 percent female to 13 percent (see Figure 12). In the states, women now hold 25 percent of elected executive offices, which include everything from governor and lieutenant governor (the most common office for women) to secretary of state, attorney general, education commissioner, and chief agricultural officer. Nonetheless, the 1990s did see a leveling off of women's officeholding at the state level. A possible consequence of this plateauing is that fewer women will hold office at the national level; holding a state-level political office is a pipeline to national office. Thus, while women's increased presence in politics marks progress, as does their increased access to many powerful and traditionally male occupations, this increase likely does not explain improvements in women's economic position because it occurred with economic progress rather than preceding it.

Public Policy

The first major national legislation affecting gender inequality in the workplace—the Equal Pay Act—came in

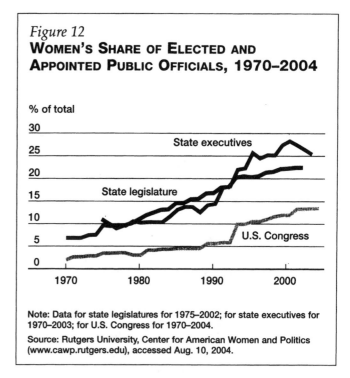

Figure 12
WOMEN'S SHARE OF ELECTED AND APPOINTED PUBLIC OFFICIALS, 1970–2004

% of total

Note: Data for state legislatures for 1975–2002; for state executives for 1970–2003; for U.S. Congress for 1970–2004.
Source: Rutgers University, Center for American Women and Politics (www.cawp.rutgers.edu), accessed Aug. 10, 2004.

1963. The act mandated equal pay for men and women doing the same work. Much in analyzing occupational gender inequality comes to depend on one's definition of "same." Is the term only applicable to people holding the same job titles, or also to those doing substantively similar or comparable work? Next, the Civil Rights Act of 1964, particularly Title VII, prohibited employment discrimination on the basis of race or sex. The 1972 Equal Pay Act Amendments extended the coverage of the Equal Pay Act to federal, state, and local agencies; education institutions; and employers with 15 or more employees (it had been 25 or more). In addition, the amendments expanded the Equal Employment Opportunity Commission's ability to file suit, and extended the time period in which discrimination complaints could be filed. In 1978, the Pregnancy Disability Act banned discrimination based on pregnancy or childbirth, essentially equating these physical states with any other disability that might cause a worker to be temporarily unable to work. The final piece of federal legislation, the Family and Medical Leave Act (introduced in Congress in 1985, passed in 1990, vetoed by President George H.W. Bush, and later signed by President Bill Clinton in 1996), allows an employee in a company of more than 50 workers to take up to 12 weeks of unpaid leave to care for a newborn or newly adopted child, or to care for a family member with a serious illness. Employers must allow such workers to return to their original or equivalent jobs.

Perhaps as telling in public policy efforts towards gender equality are the laws that never were. Notable among these is the Equal Rights Amendment, first introduced in 1923. It passed Congress in 1972, but was not ratified by the required number of states and thus expired in 1982. There have also been pieces of legislation that have failed. In an empirical analysis of Congressional sponsorship of bills, three categories of work, family, and gender legislation were identified: separate spheres, equal opportunity, and work-family balance.[14] Separate-spheres legislation allows pay differences, restricts access to occupations, and provides leave for mothers but not fathers. Of 13 such bills introduced between 1945 and 1990, only three were enacted: one each in the 1940s, 1950s, and 1980s. Equal opportunity bills, which would require equal treatment in access to and rewards for positions, were both more numerous than separate-spheres legislation over the entire period (63 bills) and more successful, with 29 laws enacted. Moreover, these laws were most common in the middle period, with three enacted in the 1940s, eight in the 1950s, six in the 1960s, 11 in the 1970s, and just one in the 1980s. The third type of bill, work-family balance, seeks to make both fathers and mothers more able to care for children and fulfill other family responsibilities, through mechanisms like flexible schedules and child care. All nine bills in this category, including the two that were enacted, were introduced in the 1980s.

These laws have been paired with a set of actions from the executive branch, notably President Lyndon Johnson's 1965 Executive Order 11246, which banned discrimination on the basis of race, color, sex, or religion on the part of government employers, contractors, subcontractors, or unions, and required them to " ... take affirmative action to ensure that applicants are employed and employees are treated during employment without regard to their race, color, religion, sex, or national origin."[15] That order has led to the set of policies and procedures known collectively as affirmative action, which applies to employees of federal contractors, employees of federal agencies, employees and contractors for many state and local governments, private employers under court-ordered remediation plans, and private employers who voluntarily adopt standards and guidelines for diversifying their workplaces. In total, one-third to one-half of the labor force is thought to work in organizations that practice some form of affirmative action.[16]

Enforcement and Litigation

A third "act" to this story is the executive enforcement and judicial interpretation of these laws. The guarantee of equality in the workplace is not effective if undermined by weak enforcement or application of the law.

At the federal level, the Equal Employment Opportunity Commission (EEOC) has primary responsibility for enforcing nondiscrimination laws. One of EEOC's major mechanisms is gathering complaints from workers and seeking to settle these complaints either through mediation or litigation. There were few such claims into the mid-1980s; but then there was a steep rise in complaints between 1985 and 1988, slower and uneven increases from the late 1980s to the early 1990s, a burst of filings from 1991 to 1995, and a leveling off thereafter. Approximately one-third of all claims to the EEOC since the mid-1980s have been gender-based claims.

Judicial interpretation of these and other laws greatly affects the process and progress of work-related gender inequality. An enormous body of case law has developed around these issues. Generally, employees who file suit against employers under any of the above-named legislation or regulations must be able to prove either disparate treatment or disparate impact based on one of the protected categories.[17] In disparate-treatment cases, the employee must prove by a preponderance of the evidence that he or she was paid less, promoted less, or not hired because of his/her sex (or race, religion, etc.). That is, the employee must prove that the employer intended to discriminate. With disparate-impact cases, the argument is that the apparently neutral policies or practices of an organization serve to disadvantage one of the protected groups. For instance, the physical strength test for firefighters gives men an advantage over women. If it can be shown that the standards or procedures for establishing qualifications (how strong a firefighter must be) are unrelated to the given job, then disparate impact has been shown. The trend in judicial interpretation has been in favor of disparate treatment rather than impact. Moreover, the pattern of case law shows a move toward a narrow interpretation of the laws.

Among the critical issues regarding the 1963 Equal Pay Act and subsequent legislation and litigation is the question of what constitutes "similar" work. This question frames the debates and litigation over "comparable worth"—that jobs similar not in content or function but in broader ways such as requisite skill and training, complexity, and conditions should have equal remuneration. Though showing some promise in the late 1970s and early 1980s, especially after the 1981 case of County of Washington v. Gunther, this legal strategy seems to have fallen out of favor with the courts after the early 1980s.[18]

Effect of Law, Policy, and Politics

Estimating the effects of these political changes on gender inequality is neither straightforward nor easy. However, some attempts to do so have suggested that, despite inadequate enforcement and narrowing interpretations, the legislative and executive actions detailed above have had a substantial and considerable effect on reducing discrimination against women, particularly on occupational segregation and pay differences.[19] At the same time, a number of studies find mixed effects of maternity leave policies on women's labor force participation and earnings.[20]

Norms and Attitudes

Other causes of macro-level changes are the broad cultural changes called "normative shifts," or the shared notions of what is appropriate behavior for women and men. While there is little doubt that these notions changed in the second half of the 20th century, were they primarily causes or consequences of changes in gender inequality? Public opinion did not shift toward women's equality until the 1970s. During the 1960s, when polls reported that Americans were increasingly willing to vote for a well-qualified Catholic, Jew, or African American for president, people's willingness to vote for a woman for president remained unchanged, at about half of the electorate. Public opinion seemed stuck. Only in the 1970s did attitudes begin to shift in a more egalitarian direction.[21]

Since the mid-1970s, the General Social Survey has asked a variety of questions tapping public attitudes toward gender roles. A broad scale created from responses to seven of these questions provides the most reliable indicator of the public's changing thoughts about women's political, household, and work roles.[22] Figure 13 shows the substantial shift in public opinion about gender roles from the late 1970s through the mid-1990s. But 1994 was the apogee of egalitarian thought about gender roles. After 1994, public opinion again plateaued.

Much of the egalitarian shift in public opinion from the late 1970s to the mid-1990s resulted from liberal recent cohorts replacing conservative older cohorts. This cohort-replacement effect continues even now to push public opinion toward more liberal gender roles. Thus, the overall slight conservative shift for the last decade masks a much stronger conservative shift within each cohort. Most individuals have become more conservative in the last 10 years; this trend has been offset somewhat because younger generations are far more liberal than their grandparents. But since the mid-1990s, young people have become more conservative, as has the rest of America.

The conservative trends in public opinion mirror the declining proportion of married mothers who work. It is unclear whether changing attitudes contributed to this decline or whether the changing attitudes merely reflect changes in the actual social structure induced by other causes. But the similarity in the timing is striking. In fact, the mid-1990s also marked the end of the trend toward gender equality in earnings, the stalling of the shift toward occupational integration in the 1990s, and the end of growth in the number of women in local and state elective office. The variety of changes that experienced a similar turning point suggests a broad cultural base to the changes of

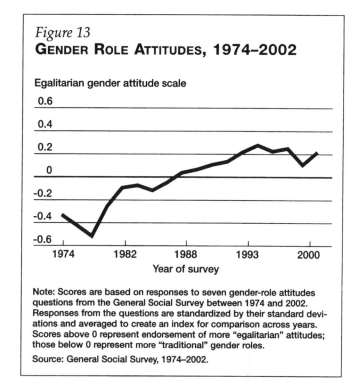

Figure 13
GENDER ROLE ATTITUDES, 1974–2002

Egalitarian gender attitude scale

Year of survey

Note: Scores are based on responses to seven gender-role attitudes questions from the General Social Survey between 1974 and 2002. Responses from the questions are standardized by their standard deviations and averaged to create an index for comparison across years. Scores above 0 represent endorsement of more "egalitarian" attitudes; those below 0 represent more "traditional" gender roles.

Source: General Social Survey, 1974–2002.

the last decade. The cultural explanation certainly seems more plausible than human capital or fertility explanations.

ASSESSING AND INTERPRETING CHANGE

The scope of change in the second half of the 20th century is nothing short of incredible. At midcentury, it was expected that women would spend much of their adult lives out of the labor force; that employers would specify whether they wished to hire a man (or perhaps a woman) for a particular job; and that women would be paid less than men, even for doing the same job. In the ensuing decades, all this changed. Today, most women work outside the home, even when their children are quite young, and employer discrimination in hiring and pay has been banned. Despite these changes, as we have shown, gender inequality persists. Women remain less likely than men to be active in the labor force, more than half of all women are in jobs that are predominantly female, and they still get paid less than men, even for the same kind of work.

General Patterns

In 2000, women were still somewhat less likely than men to be active in the labor force—74 percent of women and 86 percent of men ages 25 to 54 were in the labor force in 2000, with 46 percent of women and 68 percent of men working full-time/year-round. While men's labor force participation has declined since the 1950s, women exhibited rapid increases in labor force participation in each decade up to the 1990s, when women's rates then showed a stagnation or retrenchment in labor force participation. These trends are even more exaggerated for married women, and especially those with children, among whom both the increase in participation and its retrenchment in the 1990s are most pronounced. On the other hand, labor force participation of single mothers increased greatly in the late 1990s after having remained stable from the late 1970s to the mid-1990s. While women have made great strides in gaining entry into previously closed areas of employment, the occupations that men and women hold remain largely segregated. The typical man works in an occupation where just over one-third of his peers are women, and the typical woman works in an occupation that is 71 percent female. The overall level of segregation today—just under half of women or men would have to change occupations to eliminate segregation—is substantially less than what was observed in the 1950s, when a shift of nearly two-thirds would have been required. Finally, the difference in earnings for men and women remains large, with women earning only 73 cents for every dollar earned by their male counterparts. But this too marks progress: The figure was 59 cents in 1950. In part, this progress is because women's inflation-adjusted earnings have increased steadily since the 1950s, while men's increased through the early 1970s and then stagnated or fell until the mid-1990s. The narrowing of the gender pay gap was a combination of women's steady progress and men's uneven advances. Broadly, gender differences remain in engagement with paid work, the type of work done, and the pay received for that work. And after having narrowed since 1950, the pace of change appears to have slowed in the last decade.

Age, Period, and Cohort Effects

One of the consistent themes examined here is how these patterns and trends play out across age groups, and to what extent the changes we observed are attributable to episodic changes (period effects) or generational shifts (cohort effects). Patterns of labor force participation over the life course were shown to be differentiated by gender—men's remaining fairly constant through the prime years of 25 to 54, and women's dropping in the prime childbearing and childrearing years—but the degree of differentiation was shown to be declining across cohorts to the extent that it was nearly indiscernible by 1990 or 2000. Both men's and women's earnings increase with age—but because men's earnings rose faster, the gender gap grew across the life course. In addition, there were both cohort and period effects over time: Women born in later cohorts started

closer to men's earnings and experienced faster growth in earnings over time, losing less ground to their male counterparts than had women of earlier cohorts. Segregation declined fairly uniformly across cohorts, indicating that the changes that took place were largely period effects: Each cohort experienced about the same amount of change decade to decade, though newer cohorts entered the labor market somewhat less segregated than the ones before them. Thus, across these three dimensions, period effects have broad impact across cohorts, but the cohort changes in gender differences accentuate these shifts.

To a large degree, the story of persistent inequality despite substantial progress holds true for women regardless of race and ethnicity. All women today have rates of labor force participation, occupational distributions, and earnings that are closer to men of the same race and to those of white men than what was the case in 1950. But no group of women has attained parity with men on all of these measures. Gender differences in earnings and labor force participation comparing men and women of color appear smaller than the differences among whites, but this narrowing is mostly due to the lower levels of earnings or labor force participation of men in minority groups. Only Asians show within-race occupational segregation notably different from the pattern observed for whites.

Education has gone a long way toward determining how individuals fare in the labor market in the United States, and increasingly so for the past half-century. Education does little, however, to explain gender inequality. Education raises levels of earnings and labor force participation for both women and men. Thus, levels of gender inequality for these two dimensions were fairly similar across levels of education. The patterns of change over time were also similar across levels of education, leading to convergence on both of these dimensions. However, occupational gender segregation did vary by education, with college graduates having been notably less segregated than those with less education.

Explaining the 1990s

The forms, causes, and consequences of the shifts observed from the 1950s through the 1980s are by now fairly well known and well documented elsewhere. But what about the reversal of the 1990s: Is it real? Is it permanent or temporary? Is it a period or cohort effect? What caused the change? Is it significant?

Is it Real?

That the downturn crosses the three dimensions, is reflected in some changes beyond the world of work, and appears to mirror findings in some other sources all support the notion that the reversal is real. But, as noted above, between the 1990 and 2000 censuses, there were some changes in the wording of the question about employment, which may contribute to the lower estimates of labor force participation. Also, the changes are not uniform across all three dimensions, and have at least as much to do with men's earnings as with women's. Moreover, some indicators of gender inequality, such as education and political representation, show signs of continued progress toward equality. For the time being, a tentative answer is that the downturn is probably real.

Permanent or Temporary? Period or Cohort Effect?

These two questions are linked. This is not to say that generational changes are permanent and historical ones temporary (or vice versa). Nor would it be realistic to think of any such change as being truly permanent. But a relatively long-term shift is different from one that lasts less than a decade. A change in response to historical events felt by all generations is different from one experienced primarily by those who are young (or old) at a given point in time. For instance, if the stagnation in women's labor force participation in the 1990s was just a response to an abnormally good economy, which allowed some women to opt out of the labor force in favor of family (a temporary period effect), then a return to work during the more economically troubled times of the last few years would be expected. But if young mothers leaving the labor force represent instead a more profound cultural shift—say, a rejection by women of this generation of the "career-then-family" or "career-and-family" model created by baby-boom women— then the change is more a permanent cohort effect.[23] Additionally, though, even if it is simply a result of good times, this pattern of career interruption may have effects that reverberate through the lives of women of that generation in terms of pay, promotions, and access to occupations. There is no way to know whether these changes have ceased or whether observers will mark the 1990s as a turning point in gender equality.

What Caused the Change?

It is unlikely that a single factor that led to these changes could ever be identified. At the same time, this report offers some clues and tempting leads on suspects. Given that increases in both education and experience continued right through the 1990s, even at accelerated rates, it seems unlikely that human capital will account for much of the change in this period. The rebound in men's wages associated with the strong economy is a more promising, though still partial, explanation. Politics and policy also may hold some promise. Two of the major legislative efforts of the 1990s may have had profound impacts on women's employment. The first, the Family and Medical Leave Act, may have reduced women's employment by allowing families to have one worker (usually the wife or mother) leave the labor force for up to three months of unpaid leave. The other legislation, the Personal Opportunity and Work Reconciliation Act, put strict time limits on welfare receipt and mandated work requirements for single mothers. Both of these pieces of legislation may have affected women's choices about work.

What Would a Shift Mean?

This final question may be the most difficult of all, because it hinges somewhat on the answers to the above questions. What follows are a few scenarios—all of which assume that the changes are in fact real.

Real but relatively unimportant. While the shifts of the 1990s may be real, they are also fairly small. A close look at some of the other trend data shows periods that, at the time, may also have looked like reversals or retrenchment. Some of the appearance of reversal may simply have to do with timing. In a few years, the apparent stagnation might look like a simple blip. Still, the growing gap in labor force participation among married and single mothers may mean that children in these two types of families will have experienced childhood quite differently.

Temporary change driven by a good economy. This sort of change would have short-term effects on all women and little effect on men, but would have some potentially powerful and pervasive effects on women whose careers were in their formative stages in the 1990s. These women entered the labor force with strong expectations for career attainment; and then, in the mid-1990s, they opted out in favor of family. They may well be able to opt in and seamlessly return to their careers, but more likely they will earn less, have shorter career ladders, and have limited access to high-level positions. Such a situation is true for women born between World War I and World War II, who, in comparison to cohorts before and after them, experienced higher levels of gender inequality in pay over their entire working lives. These women pressed for the Equal Pay Act of 1963 and the Civil Rights Act of 1964, and they led the women's liberation movements of the 1960s and 1970s.

Permanent shifts due to cultural change. By many accounts, something changed in the culture in the 1960s and 1970s that made it possible for many, even most, women to have careers. Polls showed that increasing numbers of women and men approved of a married woman earning money if her husband was capable of supporting her. But some observers suggest that something may have changed again in the late 1980s and 1990s, a "backlash" against the upheaval in work and family life.[24] While it seems improbable that the gains of the last 50 years could be erased, it is possible.

The baby boomers were different. In explaining the differences in the 1990s from the differences in the three earlier decades, we might be tempted to say that the baby boomers were just different. Many of the mothers of the baby boomers briefly worked, often in nontraditional jobs, during World War II. Even though many of these women left the labor force for a time to raise children, their brief work experience undoubtedly had an impact on the employment hopes, desires, and expectations of baby-boom women. In addition, the new model for work and family (career then family, or career and family) significantly differentiates baby boomers from cohorts before and perhaps after them. The actions of the baby boomers led to massive changes in gender, work, and family (along with other institutions) that by now have quieted. Other generations may show patterns more similar to earlier ones or may simply replicate the patterns of the baby boomers.

The limits of change. A final possible scenario is that the 1990s represent neither a temporary resting place nor a turning point for change, but instead represent a new semistable balance. By the middle of the 1990s, all of the cumulative change of the 1960s, 1970s, and 1980s ended, and a new equilibrium was established. Women who chose to work did so; those who preferred to stay at home with children did so. Women who chose to enter mixed occupations did so—but some women also chose female occupations, and a few even chose male occupations. The notable emphasis on choice in the preceding sentences is important. It implies that these changes are a result of individual actions or of expressions of preferences rather than responses to constraints or to external conditions. Such "rhetoric of choice," although the dominant mode of thinking not just in social science but in society as well, has limitations and inadequacies.[25] A *New York Times Magazine* article in late 2003 relates the experiences of five women, all Princeton graduates, who chose to interrupt career for family.[26] Careful reading reveals not just choice—affirmation of childrearing as rewarding and fulfilling work—but also constraint. Each woman faced rising burdens and barriers in her career.

The scenarios we have outlined call for different responses. The next several years may tell whether the apparent retrenchment of the 1990s is real. Once that question is answered, perhaps a brighter light can then be cast about the causes of this reversal, and a more accurate set of responses to it can be prescribed.

REFERENCES

If provided by the authors, additional text and data associated with this report are available at www.prb.org/AmericanPeople.

1. Trond Petersen and Laurie A. Morgan, "Separate and Unequal: Occupation Establishment Sex Segregation and the Gender Wage Gap," *American Journal of Sociology* 101, no. 2 (1995): 329–65.
2. Jerry A. Jacobs, *Revolving Doors: Sex Segregation and Women's Careers* (Stanford, CA: Stanford University Press, 1989).
3. Otis Dudley Duncan and Beverly Duncan, "A Methodological Analysis of Segregation Indexes," *American Sociological Review* 20, no. 2 (1955): 210–17.
4. Attempts to describe Americans' occupations based on census data are complicated by the fact of change. The objectives of this report are to describe the contemporary differences between the jobs men and women have, and to compare men's and women's presence in occupations over time. Trying to compare the occupations listed for 1950 with those seen today is complicated. In light of changes in the types of work Americans do, the U.S. Census Bureau thoroughly revised its system of classifying occupations for the 2000 Census, the most substantial changes since the system was developed in the 1940s. Casual inspection of the new codes suggests that, between 1990 and 2000, some occupations seem to have disappeared (charwoman), whereas others have been created (computer software engineers). In truth, there are still charwomen (they cleaned the last hotel room you stayed in); and there were software engineers in 1990, but they had a different occupational classification. In some cases, these kinds of occupations were grouped with larger occupations, or were split among several more-detailed occupations.
5. This characterization may be a little misleading because this occupational classification lumps all teachers—from kindergarten through college—into the same occupation. From the 1950s through the 1990s, there have been increases in the proportion of women among college faculty, and some increases in male elementary/secondary school teachers.
6. Kim A. Weeden, "Why Do Some Occupations Pay More than Others? Social Closure and Earnings Inequality in the United States," *American Journal of Sociology* 108, no. 1 (2002): 55–102.
7. Jerry A. Jacobs, "Gender and Academic Specialties: Trends Among Recipients of College Degrees During the 1980s," *Sociology of Education* 68, no. 2 (1995): 81–98.
8. Francine D. Blau and Lawrence M. Kahn, "Swimming Upstream: Trends in the Gender Wage Differential in the 1980s," *Journal of Labor Economics* 15, no. 1 (1997): 1–42.
9. Rae Lesser Blumberg, "A General Theory of Gender Stratification," in *Sociological Theory*, ed. Randall Collins (San Francisco: Jossey-Bass, 1984); Janet Saltzman Chafetz, *Sex and Advantage: A Comparative, Macro-Structural Theory of Sex Stratification* (Totowa, NJ: Rowman and Allenheld, 1984); and Valerie K. Oppenheimer, *The Female Labor Force in the United States* (Berkeley: University of California Press, 1970).
10. Dawn Michelle Baunach and Sandra L. Barnes, "Competition, Race, and the Measurement of Female Labor Activity," *Sociological Inquiry* 73, no. 3 (2003): 413–40; and David A. Cotter et al., "The Demand for Female Labor," *American Journal of Sociology* 103, no. 6 (1998): 1673–712.

11. Ruth Cowan, *More Work For Mother: The Ironies Of Household Technology From The Open Hearth To The Microwave* (New York: Basic Books, 1983).

12. Claudia Goldin and Lawrence F. Katz, "The Power of the Pill: Oral Contraceptives and Women's Career and Marriage Decisions," *Journal of Political Economy* 110, no. 4 (2002): 730–70.

13. Brigid C. Harrison, *Women in American Politics: An Introduction* (Belmont, CA: Wadsworth, 2003).

14. Paul R. Burstein, Marie Bricher, and Rachel L. Einwohner, "Policy Alternatives and Political Change: Work, Family and Gender on the Congressional Agenda, 1945–1990," *American Sociological Review* 60, no. 1 (1995): 67–83.

15. Equal Employment Opportunity Commission, Executive Order No. 11246, accessed online at www.eeoc.gov/abouteeoc/35th/thelaw/eo-11246.html, on April 4, 2004.

16. Barbara F. Reskin, *The Realities of Affirmative Action in Employment* (Washington, DC: American Sociological Association, 1998).

17. Robert L. Nelson and William P. Bridges, *Legalizing Gender Inequality* (Cambridge, England: Cambridge University Press, 1999); and Paula England, *Comparable Worth: Theories and Evidence* (New York: Aldine de Gruyter, 1992).

18. Nelson and Bridges, *Legalizing Gender Inequality*; and England, *Comparable Worth*.

19. Barbara F. Reskin, "Employment Discrimination and Its Remedies," in *Sourcebook of Labor Markets: Evolving Structures and Processes*, ed. Ivar Berg and Arne L. Kalleberg (New York: Kluwer/Plenum, 2001).

20. Jacob Alex Klerman and Arleen Leibowitz, "Labor Supply Effects of State Maternity Legislation," in *Gender and Family Issues in the Workplace*, ed. Francine Blau and Ronald Ehernberg (New York: Russell Sage Foundation, 1997).

21. Myra Marx Ferree, "A Woman for President? Changing Responses: 1958–1972," *Public Opinion Quarterly* 38, no. 3 (1974): 390–99.

22. The number and content of the questions have varied over time, so an exactly equal measure cannot be constructed over time. Fortunately, the same seven gender role questions were asked in 1977 and between 1985 and 1998. Answers to these questions are correlated highly enough to suggest that the questions tap different aspects of a common attitude toward more traditional or more egalitarian gender roles. To extend the comparison to years when only some of these questions were asked, responses to the questions were first standardized according to the means and standard deviations of the surveys in which all seven questions were asked.

23. Claudia Goldin, "Career and Family: College Women Look to the Past," in *Gender and Family Issues in the Workplace*, ed. Francine Blau and Ronald Ehernberg (New York: Russell Sage Foundation, 1997).

24. Susan Faludi, *Backlash: The Undeclared War Against American Women* (New York: Doubleday, 1991).

25. Joan Williams, *Unbending Gender: Why Family and Work Conflict and What to do About It* (New York: Oxford University Press, 2002).

26. Lisa Belkin, "The Opt-Out Revolution," *New York Times Magazine*, Oct. 26, 2003.

FOR FURTHER READING

Amott, Theresa, and Julie Matthaei. *Race, Gender, and Work: A Multi-cultural Economic History of Women in the United States*. Boston: South End Press, 1996.

Bergmann, Barbara. *The Economic Emergence of Women*. 2d ed. New York: Palgrave, St. Martin's Press, 2002.

Bianchi, Suzanne, and Lynn M. Casper. *Continuity and Change in the American Family*. Thousand Oaks, CA: Sage Publications, 2002.

Blackwelder, Julia Kirk. *Now Hiring: The Feminization of Work in the United States, 1900–1995*. College Station, TX: Texas A&M University Press, 1997.

Blair-Loy, Mary. *Competing Devotions: Career and Family Among Women Executives*. Cambridge, MA: Harvard University Press, 2003.

Blau, Francine D., Marianne A. Ferber, and Anne E. Winkler. *The Economics of Women, Men, and Work*. 4th ed. New York: Prentice Hall, 2001.

Crittenden, Ann. *The Price of Motherhood: Why the Most Important Job in the World is Still the Least Valued*. New York: Owl Books, 2002.

England, Paula. *Comparable Worth: Theories and Evidence*. New York: Aldine de Gruyter, 1992.

Goldin, Claudia. *Understanding the Gender Gap: An Economic History of American Women*. New York: Oxford University Press, 1990.

Gornick, Janet, and Marcia K. Meyers. *Families That Work: Policies for Reconciling Parenthood and Employment*. New York: Russell Sage Foundation, 2003.

Jacobs, Jerry A. *Revolving Doors: Sex Segregation and Women's Careers*. Stanford, CA: Stanford University Press, 1989.

Jacobs, Jerry A., and Kathleen Gerson. *The Time Divide: Work, Family, and Gender Inequality*. Cambridge, MA: Harvard University Press, 2004.

Landry, Bart. *Black Working Wives: Pioneers of the American Family Revolution*. Berkeley: University of California Press, 2000.

Padavic, Irene, and Barbara F. Reskin. *Women and Men at Work*. Thousand Oaks, CA: Pine Forge Press, 2003.

Reskin, Barbara F. *The Realities of Affirmative Action in Employment*. Washington, DC: American Sociological Association, 1998.

Sayer, Liana C., Philip N. Cohen, and Lynne M. Casper. *Women, Men, and Work*. New York: Russell Sage Foundation, 2004.

Spain, Daphne, and Suzanne M. Bianchi. *Balancing Act: Motherhood, Marriage, and Employment Among American Women*. New York: Russell Sage Foundation, 1996.

Tomaskovic-Devey, Donald. *Gender and Racial Inequality at Work: The Sources and Consequences of Job Segregation*. Ithaca, NY: ILR Press, 1993.

Williams, Christine L. *Still a Man's World: Men Who Do "Women's Work."* Berkeley: University of California Press, 1995.

Cohorts and Socioeconomic Progress

By Dowell Myers

INTRODUCTION

How best can we measure socioeconomic progress across decades? Why do many of us worry that young adults are failing to match the progress of their parents, or that immigrants are failing to get ahead in America? Often, two different dimensions of progress are at play. On the one hand, people typically achieve progress in their socioeconomic status as they move through their careers. At the same time, society progresses as each generation exceeds the achievements of its predecessors. The picture is often confused by skewed averages, however, when a major shift occurs in the makeup of society because there are more young people, or more immigrants, or more minorities. How much progress are people really experiencing?

The measurement of progress is best addressed by analysis of cohorts—groups of people passing through time together—observed in this report in decades from 1960 to 2000. Defined by shared year of birth, or by year of entry to the United States, cohorts' progress is traced in two important ways: *over the lifetime*, as socioeconomic status changes with passing time; and *between cohorts*, as one cohort replaces another at each life stage.

Between 1960 and 2000, the socioeconomic status among the elderly (ages 65 to 74) increased much more rapidly than among young adults (ages 25 to 34). Where once the elderly had a poverty rate twice as high as the young, by 1990, the poverty rate among the elderly was lower than the rate among the young. The elderly's homeownership advantages over the young also increased, especially from 1980 to 2000, and the elderly's educational disadvantage relative to the young rapidly narrowed. The growing status of the elderly reflects lifelong advantages, because a status such as educational attainment or homeownership is highly persistent over time.

A cohort's status at ages 25 to 34 has great implications for the group's future well-being, because cohorts occupying that age group are launching into adult careers. For most of the 20th century, each cohort launched on higher and higher trajectories, but there was stagnation or decline on several indicators between 1980 and 1990. A crucial question to be answered from the 2000 Census is whether the decline observed at ages 25 to 34 across successive cohorts has continued or has reversed. Welcome evidence presented in this report reveals a resumption of progress, with strong increases in college completion and improvement in home-ownership rates.

Rapid growth in the foreign-born population has obscured the socioeconomic progress for younger cohorts, especially among Latinos. Although it appears from the overall numbers that high school completion rates fell among Latinos, that decline is an artifact of growing numbers of immigrant arrivals. Among U.S.-born Latinos, high school completion actually increased 4 percentage points for recent cohorts. Similarly, college completion rates among U.S.-born Latinos also increased by nearly 5 percentage points.

Among the immigrants, cohort dynamics also reveal substantial socioeconomic progress in the 1990s. At first glance, immigrant poverty appears to have worsened, but when we disaggregate immigrants by year of arrival and trace those cohorts across decades, we draw a different conclusion: On average, immigrants have experienced sharp declines in poverty the longer they have resided in the United States. For example, among Latinos who arrived in the United States in the 1980s, poverty declined from 33 percent in 1990 to 22 percent in 2000. Steeper declines are observed among Asian immigrants.

The age of immigrants combines with their length of residence in shaping their trajectories into homeownership. Very sharp improvements are found among immigrant cohorts under age 45, and those who arrive later in life also have less time to reach as high an ultimate level of homeownership. Cohorts that arrive at very young ages never experience the dislocation of immigration, and those children grow up to achieve the highest rates of homeownership, with trajectories that track even higher than their U.S.-born counterparts.

The changing composition of the population obscures the socioeconomic progress experienced by the average person. Examining trends for specific cohorts

DOWELL MYERS is professor of urban planning and demography in the School of Policy, Planning, and Development at the University of Southern California. He is the director of the Population Dynamics Research Group. His research has focused on the upward mobility of immigrants to the United States and California, as well as on cohort trajectories.

within racial and ethnic groups provides a much more promising picture of actual progress in America. The rhetoric used to describe change needs to account for the different time dimensions of change revealed by an analysis of cohorts.

TRENDS IN THE INDICATORS

Changes in the average social and economic status of the U.S. population are often seen as barometers of well-being. Popular indicators include the poverty rate, the percentage of adults who have college degrees, or the percentage of adults who are homeowners. Trends in these indicators imply a rise or fall in the nation's well-being; but how well do the overall trends reflect the average person's experience or the average experience of a specific ethnic or age group?

A person's fortune depends a lot on timing. Was the person born into a larger cohort with many peers competing for the same set of opportunities? And what was the state of the economy when the person was first looking for a full-time job? Not only is an employment search made easier when many companies are hiring, but the occupations people choose often depend on which new industries were emerging. And how low were mortgage rates at that time? Future housing purchases and employment can be greatly influenced by timing today. In subsequent years, a person can make up much of what was delayed in the present—but on average, a head start accelerates progress.

Not all groups track on the same course: While one group may be sharply elevating its status, another could be left behind. Key groups for social concern include the elderly, young adults, minority group members, and immigrants. Indeed, rapid change in the composition of the U.S. population is placing added weight on the success of rapidly growing groups such as Latinos and Asians, many of whom have immigrated to the United States in the last two decades.

Seeing Through Compositional Biases

Simple comparisons of status over time are often deceiving. Changes in the makeup of the population, called a "compositional shift," can often skew the overall trend. One of the most dramatic illustrations of such a shift occurred in the decade from 1960 to 1970, when the formation of the giant baby-boom generation caused the median age of the nation to decrease by 1.4 years, even though all the individuals alive in both 1960 and 1970 surely grew 10 years older. This movement in median age reflected the rapid growth in the number of children, not the average experience of growing younger.

Two major compositional shifts have been changing the nation recently. First, the rise and fall of fertility over the last century has created a peculiar national age structure that affects our measurement of socioeconomic status. The aging of the baby-boom generation is shifting the national age structure to weigh more heavily on older age groups that are typically more advantaged. This age shift could well elevate average status while obscuring declines for smaller groups. Indeed, the shift toward older, more advantaged age groups could well disguise a decline in average welfare among young adults in their 20s or 30s.

Second, the resumption of high levels of immigration, beginning in the 1970s but accelerating into the 1990s and mostly coming from Asia and Latin America, is affecting the average status attainments of Asians and Latinos. Because immigrants tend to have lower achievements when they first arrive in the United States, their large numbers have depressed the average status for the entire ethnic grouping, creating a false appearance of downward mobility.

In general, a few larger cohorts can outweigh many smaller ones, and recent immigrants who are young adults or elderly can shift the nation's average socioeconomic status up or down, much as the formation of the baby-boom generation caused the nation's median age to fall. Such compositional shifts are deceiving when it comes to describing actual progress. We need to see through these average trends and track the status changes of specific groups over time.

Need for a Lifetime Cohort Perspective

The "cohort" is a unit of analysis that helps us answer the above questions about socioeconomic change in the U.S. population. Historically, a cohort was a unit of troops in the ancient Roman army, a battalion of 600 men in a legion of 6,000. Marching through time together, the progress of the cohort represents the average progress for each of its members. The cohort concept was first popularized in demography in the 1940s by P.K. Whelpton,[1] not for the analysis of fighting men but for analysis of the fertility of women. As each cohort of young women came of age, the percentage of women having babies would grow from age 15 and peak in their 20s. Some cohorts would launch into motherhood more quickly than others, with consequences for the ultimate number of children born to that cohort.

Cohort analysis is widely applicable for representing the average experience of groups of people passing through their life course, for comparing this experience to that of previous generations, and for measuring overall changes in society. The cohort is ideal for measuring average experience because it is an aggregate unit whose members share the same age or length of experience.

A cohort perspective enables us to distinguish two important insights on trends in the well-being of a population: lifetime progress and generational progress.

Aggregate Experience

The progress of a cohort provides insight on aggregate experience, such as the increasing rates of home-ownership as the cohort ages from 35 to 45. As time passes, we are able to observe the net improvements or losses for a specific group of people.

Cohort Succession or Generational Progress

Over time, cohorts enter a given life stage in succession. The replacement of earlier cohorts by more-advantaged ones fosters socioeconomic progress. Alternatively, the entry of less-advantaged cohorts leads to less progress for society. For example, the most recent cohort to reach age 30 may have a homeownership rate that is 5 percentage points lower than the previous cohort that occupied that age group. Although this most recent cohort is only one age group, the young adult cohorts reveal the direction of generational progress. And, if the latest cohort has a lower status than its predecessor at every age throughout its life, this lower status will eventually depress the overall status of society.

Thus, the socioeconomic progress of the population should be measured on both dimensions—improvement over lifetime, and progress between generations. Both dimensions are needed to adequately describe people's well-being.

The key assumption that underlies both insights from cohorts is the notion of persistence of status or experience over the lifetime. People do not remake their lives every year; there is carryover from one year to the next. Cohorts' size, identity, experiences, and relative advantages persist across decades. Wartime experiences shared among young men mark their cohort for life. Similarly, early political or social experiences common to many in a cohort (such as the Great Depression or civil rights protests) may shape that cohort's outlook well into its elderly years. Early economic disadvantages also persist via their impacts on health and nutrition or via their prevention of educational or investment opportunities. Thus, the differences observed among the elderly are found to reflect differences at younger ages, and the differences observed today at young ages are assumed to indicate likely future differences. The powerful effects of persistence are examined throughout the examples contained in this report.

Growing Concerns of Loss of Progress

In recent years there has been a concern that the United States may be losing some of the socioeconomic gains of past generations. With the exception of the Great Depression in the 1930s, people who have entered adulthood in every decade since 1900 have rightly assumed they would be at least as successful as those who preceded them. Beginning in the 1970s or 1980s, however, a restructuring economy and rising cost of living have created doubt about the positive outlook for the current generation of young adults. Rising immigration has added to this negative perception because the number of poor people has increased. Many question how well these newcomers will assimilate and what their lifetime progress will be as they settle longer in the United States.

In fact, with regard to many indicators, the 1990 Census captured a portrait of faltering socioeconomic progress. Young adults from the baby-boom generation, blacks, Latinos, and new immigrants appeared to be falling below the trajectories of lifetime progress we have grown to expect. The results of the 2000 Census are thus crucial for confirming whether this trend has continued down as feared. Alternatively, the findings from the 2000 Census may indicate a revival of progress.

Measuring the potential downward shift in socioeconomic progress could proceed in one of two ways. Research could focus on the slowing rates of lifetime progress within cohorts. For example, has the latest cohort of young adults advanced more slowly into homeownership as they aged from 30 to 40, or have recent immigrants improved their status more slowly as they settled 10 years longer in the United States? Alternatively, research could focus on changes in the progress between generations, as the upward succession in homeownership attainment between cohorts of young adults in past decades gives way to downward succession in recent years. Both factors may be at work simultaneously, or one or the other may have turned for the better in the 2000 Census.

Questions Addressed in This Report

This report takes a long view of socioeconomic progress. Weaving together the findings from Census 2000 with previous data collected in 1960, 1970, 1980, and 1990, we are able to track lifetime achievements. We also can contrast the rates of progress in different decades. A high point appears to have been 1980, capping the post-World War II era of rising educational attainment and homeownership for young adults. A slower period of progress followed in the 1980s, and our major interest is to discover whether the 1990s continued this slippage or whether the American people may have regained the socioeconomic progress of an earlier era.

The progress of the American people is best addressed through the changes observed for two key population segments that reflect broader social forces and growing size or political significance.

First, we examine the status of the elderly over time. Have the elderly continued to rise above the disadvantaged status that plagued them earlier in the 20th century? Every decade, a new group of people advances to age 65; the rotating membership in this age group gives the group ample opportunity for socioeconomic change.

The reason for our special interest in the elderly (and why we address them first) is that changes in that age range reflect a legacy borne by cohorts entering with statuses carried from middle age or younger. As new cohorts enter their elderly years, how much have the successes enjoyed by cohorts who were middle-aged two decades earlier persisted in later decades? Even if cohorts' status has trended down as they cross age 65, it is still possible that the replacement of earlier cohorts by newer and more-advantaged ones has elevated the status recorded each decade for those ages 65 to 74.

Second, we examine adults ages 25 to 34, who are just launching their careers. The status of young adults is a major concern because deficits accrued at this age are likely to persist into middle age and beyond. Young people who have already graduated from college or who have already become homeowners have a head start and a superior economic position that will return benefits well into middle age and beyond. The key question is whether the young, who have recently entered adulthood, are continuing the decline discovered in the 1980s when a sizable gap in socioeconomic achievement opened up between young and old. Was this decline stopped by young adults in 2000, and did they resume the progress across generations long expected in the United States?

Answers to these questions can be pursued for the U.S. population as a whole, but there has been a significant national trend in recent decades toward growing racial and ethnic diversity. Change for the entire population might disguise opposite trends for different groups. Therefore, one must consider how each of the four major racial and ethnic groups has fared: non-Hispanic whites, blacks, Asians and Pacific Islanders, and Latinos. The emphasis is less on the differences between these groups and more on the equality of trends over time within these groups.

Analysis of socioeconomic progress for Latino and Asian residents of the United States is especially confounded by the arrival of new immigrants in both groups. In the U.S. population in 2000, 57 percent of all Latinos ages 25 and older were foreign-born, as were 86 percent of all Asians. Tracking the progress of these groups requires more explicit treatment of immigrants, their growing share of the population, and the experience of immigrant cohorts as they reside longer in the United States. It is important to separately examine the trajectories of the U.S.-born population and to trace the progress of earlier immigrant arrivals who have lived in the United States for some decades.

Indicators of Socioeconomic Status

Measuring the socioeconomic progress of all these groups requires selecting key indicators that tap different dimensions of socioeconomic status. In this report,

three measures are used: poverty rate, homeownership rate, and educational attainment.

The *poverty rate* of each group over time is frequently used to measure the percentage of people who live in households with incomes falling below the threshold deemed necessary to subsist at a low standard of living. The threshold is adjusted for household size and is computed roughly as three times the amount of a low-cost food budget. As such, the poverty rate is most useful for measuring what proportion of a group is deprived. In prior decades, the elderly were often afflicted by high rates of poverty. How have they managed to improve that status over time? Poverty has also been a particular public concern with regard to immigrants. Is there any evidence that immigrants have been able to escape from poverty?

The *homeownership rate* of each group measures the percentage of householders who are homeowners instead of renters. This indicator is also interpreted frequently as the proportion who have moved into a more-advantaged middle-class status. Homeownership is also distinguished by its quasicumulative nature, growing over the entire lifetime. It thus reflects the status of the elderly somewhat better than would income alone. How much does homeownership grow over the lifetime for different groups? Have young adults been able to attain homeownership as readily in the past decade as was true in the 1970s or 1980s? And how well have immigrants been able to achieve the American dream of homeownership?

The third indicator is *educational attainment*, examined here as both the proportion who have completed high school and the proportion who have completed four years of college. Educational status lays the basis for other socioeconomic achievements and is a rather fixed attribute for most adults. The educational attainment of young adults is especially crucial as they start their careers. Until 1990, each generation coming of age in the 20th century enjoyed markedly better preparation than earlier generations. In 1990, improvements leveled off and may have started downward. For this reason, it is crucial to learn how well the next cohort, which came of age in 2000, fared.

Method of Analysis

This report adopts cohort representation as its primary means of exposition. The cohort perspective is an important and uniquely demographic way of viewing society's changes, and is applicable to both the U.S.-born and foreign-born population. Defined by their common temporal identity (year of birth or year of arrival in the United States), cohorts have the analytical convenience of aggregation while retaining the temporal experience (lifetime and historical position) of individuals. In cohort analysis of social and economic data, the same individuals are not followed over time. Rather, separate surveys repeated at two or more points in time (such as the sequence of decennial censuses) sample the population members from the cohort groups at each point in time. Thus, the groups are followed over time to reflect the average experience of their members.

The underlying data are tabulations from the successive censuses of 1960 through 2000, with appropriate adjustments to data definitions and universes to maintain consistency across the decades. To draw meaningful longitudinal inferences from repeated censuses, the long-term trends must not be biased by short-term economic fluctuations. Over the course of the economic cycle, annual unemployment and poverty can rise and fall with considerable volatility. If the once-a-decade census observation happens to fall in a year when annual fluctuations are unfavorable, then the measurement of long-term trends could be biased upward or downward. By great fortune, all of the decennial censuses from 1960 through 2000 happened to fall at the same favorable point in the economic cycle (see Box 1), indicating that the measurement of long-term trends is not biased.

The findings in this report represent a highly descriptive picture of socioeconomic progress in Amer-ica, and much of what follows is presented graphically. Adopting a cohort perspective gives a better sense of the average person's experience over time, and that experience can be separated from the impact of large new cohorts entering adulthood or arriving in America. Overall, the trends of the 1990s suggest a more hopeful outlook for the coming decade than was earlier believed.

UNDERSTANDING SOCIAL CHANGE WITH COHORTS

America's population is comprised of a series of age groups. All these groups are at different life stages: Some are just entering the workforce and housing market, others are much further along, and still others are nearing or past retirement. With the passing of time, a series of new cohorts is formed by birth, and the existing cohorts pass through successive life stages as they grow older. All cohorts carry with them their distinctive life experiences as well as the legacy of past cohorts' advantages or disadvantages.

Box 1
ANNUAL FLUCTUATIONS AND LONG-TERM TRENDS

A little-recognized yet fortunate feature of the decennial census is its uncanny timing with regard to the national economic cycle of expansion and recession. During recessionary times, incomes fall, poverty and unemployment rise, and economic conditions appear very unfavorable. In contrast, during periods of expansion, job opportunities abound, incomes rise, and poverty falls.

The decennial census, the once-a-decade checkup on the nation's social and economic conditions, will be heavily influenced by its timing relative to an economic cycle. If the census one decade is conducted at the peak of an economic cycle, and the next decade at the trough, then the trends measured over the decade would be skewed downward. Conversely, comparing the results of a census taken near the trough of an economic cycle (when conditions are least favorable) and matching it later to a census near the peak would produce an inflated impression of improving well-being. To counteract these fluctuations, we need a method of factoring out the short-term fluctuations of the economic cycle so that we can better see the long-term trends.

Fortunately, every census since 1960 has fallen on a date that is roughly at the same point in the economic cycle. As shown in the accompanying figure, every census, by total happenstance, has been conducted shortly before the peak is reached of an economic cycle. In the figure, we have marked the years ending in "9" to show the data that were collected for the year preceding an April census. The figure depicts the annual fluctuations of poverty and unemployment rates, and each census has been conducted near the low point in those unfavorable indicators. The figure also shows the official date

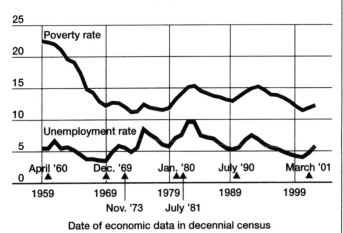

Timing of Census Relative to Business Cycle Peaks, Poverty, and Unemployment Rates

Date of economic data in decennial census

▲ NBER peak

Source: National Bureau of Economic Research, Inc.; and www.census.gov/hhes/poverty/histpov/recession.html, accessed Nov. 16, 2003.

of the peak of the economic expansion as determined by the National Bureau of Economic Research.

The decennial census is a good barometer of long-term trends. In measuring socioeconomic status from peak-to-peak of successive censuses, we gain insights that are relatively free of contamination by short-term fluctuations.

Adding to this mix, another series of cohorts is formed by the year of arrival of immigrants, who merge into the existing birth cohorts but have different histories because their time in the United States begins at later ages. Moreover, immigrants all share the life-shaping event of leaving their home and relocating to the United States. Their socioeconomic progress (particularly for foreign-born Asians and Latinos) must be tracked separately from their U.S.-born counterparts.

Progress Across Generations

A useful way to think about the social and economic formative experiences of the American people is to view the succession of cohorts as they enter young adulthood. Table 1 borrows from a characterization used by Reynolds Farley to describe the sequence of cohorts.[2] Each birth cohort is designated by its birth year, period of coming of age, and key events at those times. The table also shows the ages that each cohort occupies as it grows older across each successive census.

Throughout American history, the presumption has been that each generation enjoys a higher socioeconomic status than the last. This belief was supported by centuries of technological innovation and economic growth that led to a steadily rising standard of living. This steady progress was disrupted in the 1930s, however, by the calamitous and sustained Great Depression, which rocked the middle class into unprecedented high rates of unemployment and home foreclosures. The 1930s was the only time in our nation's history when home-ownership markedly declined, falling from 47 percent to 44 percent of households.

This setback was followed by an even higher rebound of consumer lifestyles. The crises of the Great Depression triggered President Franklin Roosevelt's New Deal, an agenda of innovative social and economic federal programs that are still in force. High-profile crises of the Great Depression included an epidemic of mortgage defaults, foreclosures, evictions of homeowners, and the failure and closure of the banks and lending institutions that owned the mortgages. Accordingly, remedying the home-mortgage problem was a priority of the New Deal. Federal insurance programs for home mortgages made homeownership more secure and protected banks at the same time. These insurance programs bolstered access to homeownership for greater numbers of householders at an earlier point in their life cycles. The key advantage was to enable someone to purchase a home with a down payment of only 10 percent or 20 percent instead of the prior convention of 50 percent or more of the purchase price. Federal support for a secondary-mortgage market also led to the restructuring of the mortgage industry, spreading payments over 30 years in much lower monthly amounts than those required by the then-commonplace 10-year mortgages. The result of this revolution was to stimulate great increases in homeownership after 1940, especially among younger adults who would have previously needed to save for many years to purchase a home.

Table 1

EIGHT BIRTH COHORTS, BORN 1906–1985

Year of birth	Cohort	Became young adults	Key events during young adult years	Ages in censuses of				
				1960	1970	1980	1990	2000
1976–1985	Generation Y	Mid-1990s–2000s	Era of digital dominance				5–14	15–24
1966–1975	Generation X	Mid-1980s–1990s	Era of economic polarization and HIV/AIDS			5–14	15–24	25–34
1956–1965	Late Baby Boom	Mid-1970s–1980s	Era of employment restructuring		5–14	15–24	25–34	35–44
1946–1955	Early Baby Boom	Mid-1960s–1970s	Era of civil rights and sexual revolutions	5–14	15–24	25–34	35–44	45–54
1936–1945	World War II	Mid-1950s–1960s	Post–World War II boom	15–24	25–34	35–44	45–54	55–64
1926–1935	Parents of the Baby Boom	Mid-1940s–1950s	Post–World War II boom	25–34	35–44	45–54	55–64	65–74
1916–1925	Parents of the Baby Boom	Mid-1930s–1940s	World War II	35–44	45–54	55–64	65–74	75–84
1906–1915	Grandparents of the Baby Boom	Mid-1920s–1930s	Great Depression	45–54	55–64	65–74	75–84	85–94

Adapted from: R. Farley, *The New American Reality* (1996): table 2-1.

Although the nation's economy began to recover markedly toward the end of the 1930s, the onset of World War II was the catalyst for industrial recovery; once the war ended, the country experienced a tremendous employment and consumer boom. Major new federal assistance programs were targeted directly at the youngest adults who were returning soldiers; the G.I. Bill promoted college education, and the Veterans Administration loan program for home mortgage assistance lowered down payments to as little as 5 percent of purchase price.

Imagine the difference in outlook between two cohorts closely spaced in time. One group graduated from high school and then was age 20 in 1930, preparing to begin careers when established workers were being laid off in great numbers and people were losing their homes. Family formation was surely a great uncertainty as well, and fertility did plunge to its lowest level recorded at that time in the United States (but in the 1980s, fertility declined even lower, to 2.03 children per woman). In contrast, young adults reaching age 20 in 1950 were too young to have fought in World War II and were sheltered from the worst impacts of the Great Depression. But, as young adults, they benefited from an expanding postwar economy and the programs established under the New Deal.[3]

The young adults who came of age in the late 1940s and 1950s—the "parents of the baby boom"—enjoyed so much success that they have also been called the "Good Times" cohort.[4] This group benefited from the federal programs instituted after World War II, and they had an added demographic advantage. Born in the low-fertility era of the late 1920s and Great Depression, this group had fewer members than previous or subsequent groups, and their small numbers led to less competition for schooling, housing, and jobs. They also enjoyed marvelous timing in a booming economy. As a result, their career trajectories were greatly accelerated. One study reported that the average adjusted income for these parents of the baby boom increased more than 100 percent in just 10 years as they passed from their 20s to their 30s.[5] As argued by Richard Easterlin, fertility soared far above that in recent preceding decades because new-found material comforts so greatly exceeded the modest expectations formed in Depression-era childhoods.[6] By the 2000 Census, these parents of the baby boom were now elderly, and many of their accumulated advantages elevated their status at that age far above what had been common for the elderly in 1960.

The cohort that immediately followed the 1926-to-1935 birth cohort (the World War II generation born from 1936 to 1945) entered adulthood in the late 1950s and also enjoyed the most favorable opportunities for socio-economic success. This group was too young to experience firsthand the Great Depression or World War II, but they continued to enjoy favorable conditions for entering the labor and housing markets, and they continued the

Table 2

RELATIVE SIZE OF BIRTH AND ARRIVAL COHORTS EXISTING IN 2000

Age	Cohort	Cohort members (millions)	Relative size (% of World War II cohort)
0–4	—	19.0	—
5–14	—	41.2	171
15–24	Generation Y	38.9	161
25–34	Generation X	39.6	164
35–44	Late Baby Boom	45.9	190
45–54	Early Baby Boom	37.6	155
55–64	World War II	24.2	100
65–74	Late Parents of Baby Boom	18.5	77
75–84	Early Parents of Baby Boom	12.3	—
85+	—	4.2	—
Total		262.4	

Arrival decade	Decade of arrival cohort	Cohort members (millions)	Relative size (% of 1970s arrivals)
1990–1999	1990s	13.2	281
1980–1989	1980s	8.5	181
1970–1979	1970s	4.7	100
pre–1970	Mid-century immigrants	4.8	102
Total foreign-born		31.1	

— Not applicable.

Source: Author's calculations using Census 2000, Summary File 3.

family lifestyles of the baby-boom era. Between 1940 and 1960, homeownership rates soared to levels nearly 50 percent better than in 1940, climbing only very slowly thereafter. With each new cohort of young adults prospering more than the last, expectations grew for continued progress across future cohorts as well.

For many reasons, the progress of subsequent cohorts began to falter. Those cohorts born after 1945 constituted the large baby-boom generation, and their sheer size created competition that began to slow their success in the job and housing markets. As of 2000, the early baby-boom cohort was 56 percent larger than the World War II cohort that preceded them, and the late baby-boom cohort was even larger—90 percent more numerous than the World War II cohort (see Table 2). The larger size of both baby-boom cohorts was to follow them at every step of their careers. Used to the smaller cohorts born in the 1930s and 1940s, institutions had to greatly expand their capacities to handle this new generation. The first impact was felt in elementary schools during the early 1950s, leading to much larger class sizes, double shifts for classrooms, and many temporary classrooms. Predictably, elementary school overcrowding progressed to high schools, then to colleges, and finally to increased unemployment rates for young people. The housing market was also affected, spurring new home construction and gentrification but also creating affordability problems because of rising prices due to excess demand among young cohorts.

The oil shock and recession of 1973 made socio-economic progress even more difficult for the large baby-boom cohorts. Employment opportunities moderated and, after 1975, housing prices began to escalate dramatically for the first time. Whereas home prices (adjusted for inflation) grew only 4 percent in the 1960s, they grew by 11 percent in the 1970s, by 8 percent in the 1980s, and then slowed to 3 percent growth in the 1990s.[7] The sheer numbers of would-be homebuyers in the baby-boom generation helped create this price inflation in the 1970s and 1980s. This price growth was a boon to the financial well-being of earlier cohorts, and the rising prices may have even stimulated more rapid investment in home purchases by the early baby boomers.[8] Nonetheless, this inflation created a growing challenge to young adults who were not yet homeowners, and the younger brothers and sisters constituting the late baby boom (born from 1955 to 1964) were caught at a disadvantage. Members of Generation X, born from 1966 to 1975, inherited a similar disadvantage. The latter group is only ages 25 to 34 as of the 2000 Census, so we can view their status just as they launch their adult careers. One advantage of Generation X, and especially of the subsequent Generation Y (born from 1976 to 1985), is that the members of these two cohorts are less numerous than the members of the baby-boom cohort; members of Generations X and Y face less competition with their peers for entry-level rungs in the housing and labor markets, but their eventual progress remains an open question.

Black, Latino, and Asian cohort members face the additional dimension of historical change. The crumbling of legal segregation and the rise of equal opportunity after the 1960s created new opportunities for those best able to take advantage. For example, only those who were young enough in the 1960s could take full advantage of new educational opportunities. Similarly, only adults under age 45 were likely to benefit fully from new job and housing opportunities. For middle-aged and older generations, these past restrictions remain indelibly imprinted.

The Renewed Story of Immigrant Assimilation

The resurgence of immigration after 1965 has created (or renewed) another prominent dimension of socio-economic progress. Following restrictive legislation in the mid-1920s, a 40-year pause ensued during which immigrant status faded from public awareness. Many theories of socioeconomic progress are rooted in the 1960s and 1970s before mass immigration was renewed in earnest. A contemporary evaluation, however, requires explicit attention to this factor.

Despite their relative invisibility in later years, the early 20th-century immigrants and their children (the second generation) were integrally woven into American social history. On the eve of World War II, fully 19 percent of the U.S. population was second generation,[9] and was heavily concentrated in age groups eligible for military service. Indeed, no group likely benefited more from the educational and housing programs following the war than the young-adult cohorts belonging to this second generation.

Just how substantial the progress across the generations was is shown in demographer Richard Alba's study of the Italian American population, highlighting the pivotal period from 1940 to 1960.[10] The educational leap was especially dramatic, and there was a strong convergence of the Italian immigrants with the U.S.-born stock of white Anglo-Saxon Protestants (WASPs). In 1980, the oldest cohorts of Italian Americans still carried the educational, occupational, and marriage profiles of the new immigrants of 1920. In contrast, the youngest cohorts—the third generation to live in America—had simultaneously reached college graduation rates and had entered occupations very similar to the WASPs. Not only had the previous ethnic distinctions been drastically reduced, but high rates of intermarriage were blurring the boundaries of Italian American identity: More than two-thirds of Italian Americans under age 30 had married spouses who had no Italian ancestry. Indeed, Alba declared Italians in America were entering the "twilight of ethnicity."

For the U.S. population, little more than 5 percent to 6 percent were foreign-born in 1960, 1970, or 1980. However, the share of foreign-born surged to 11 percent by 2000. These foreign-born shares were not distributed equally across cohorts. In fact, the nation's population was made up of two types of foreign-born: older adults who were part of the pre-1925 mass immigration, and children and adults newly arrived in the resurgent immigration boom of the 1980s and 1990s.

More than 18 percent of those ages 65 and older in 1960 were foreign-born, but members of that cohort are now deceased. Meanwhile, the sharply growing volume of new immigration since 1970 represents a rising share of all U.S. residents in the younger age groups. Among all U.S. residents ages 25 to 34, the foreign-born share climbed from 7 percent in 1980 to 18 percent in 2000. These foreign-born shares were dramatically higher in the case of Asians and Latinos, representing well over one-half of the young adults in these ethnic groups. Thus, the immigrant life history of Asians and Latinos is integral to their cohort history.

The cohort history described above may not apply well to individuals who immigrated later in life and did not experience U.S. events as children. Also important to consider is how the growing share of foreign-born may alter the trajectories of socioeconomic progress, especially for Asians and Latinos. In those cases, we must be careful to discern the effects of assimilation in addition to the life-course trajectories of the U.S.-born in these groups. The rapid escalation in the size of the foreign-born population strongly affects the overall trends observed in recent years. As shown in Table 2 (page 145), foreign-born residents who arrived in the United States in the 1980s are 81 percent more numerous than those who arrived in the 1970s, and those who arrived in the 1990s are 181 percent more numerous than those who arrived in the 1970s. Immigrants who have resided in the United States for less than 20 years account for two-thirds of all the foreign-born.

LIFE PROGRESS AND SOCIAL CHANGE

Trajectories Over the Lifetime

The slopes of trajectories represent aggregate life-course measures of progress because they illustrate change as a group ages. Over time, cohorts usually improve their socioeconomic status, which reaches a peak in late middle age before leveling, declining, or even continuing to rise.

Roughly parallel trajectories are observed for successive cohorts passing through the same age range in different decades. Upward succession across cohorts is indicated when more-recent cohorts track on higher trajectories; downward succession is indicated when successive cohorts track on lower trajectories than their predecessors.

These patterns of lifetime progress and cohort succession are illustrated in Figure 1 using three different indicators. Four selected cohorts are displayed, each of which launched their adult careers 20 years apart: Generation X (ages 25 to 34 in 2000); early baby boom (ages 25 to 34 in 1980); parents of baby boom (ages 25 to 34 in 1960); and grandparents of baby boom (ages 25 to 34 in 1940). Each cohort represents the same group of people as they age from 25 to 74. Only the trajectory of the baby-boom parents is observed over the entire age span because it was ages 25 to 34 in 1960 and ages 65 to 74 in 2000. The earlier cohort—baby-boom grandparents—began their adult careers in 1940 before our data begin, so that cohort is only observed from the time they were ages 45 to 54. And because the early baby-boom cohort and the Generation X cohort have entered adulthood more recently, they have not yet passed through most of the age ranges.

The proportion of each cohort at ages 25 to 34 that has completed four or more years of college forms a relatively flat trajectory over time because college completion is rarely attained after age 25. However, there appears to be a steady upward creep in college completion of 4 percentage points to 7 percentage points throughout the life course of each cohort. In the case of college completion,

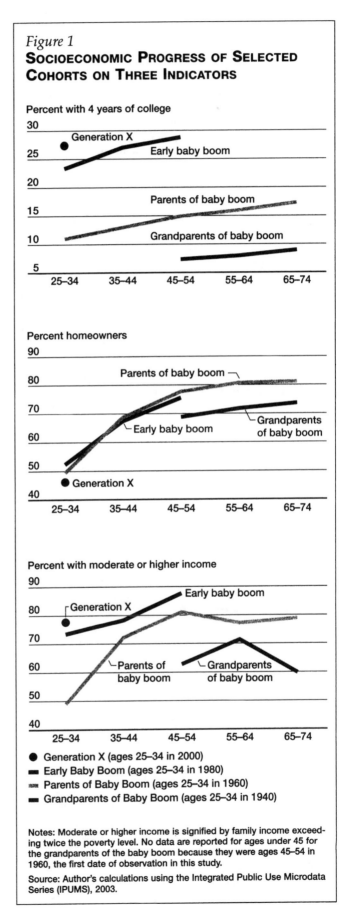

Figure 1

SOCIOECONOMIC PROGRESS OF SELECTED COHORTS ON THREE INDICATORS

● Generation X (ages 25–34 in 2000)
■ Early Baby Boom (ages 25–34 in 1980)
▨ Parents of Baby Boom (ages 25–34 in 1960)
■ Grandparents of Baby Boom (ages 25–34 in 1940)

Notes: Moderate or higher income is signified by family income exceeding twice the poverty level. No data are reported for ages under 45 for the grandparents of the baby boom because they were ages 45–54 in 1960, the first date of observation in this study.

Source: Author's calculations using the Integrated Public Use Microdata Series (IPUMS), 2003.

the greatest change is the upward succession observed between cohorts. Among the baby-boom grandparents, only 7 percent achieved this level of education by ages 45 to 54, compared with 15 percent for the baby-boom parents and 29 percent for the early baby boomers. Clearly, there has been dramatic intergenerational change.

The proportion of adults with moderate or higher family incomes has incomes more than twice the poverty threshold in the 2000 Census, or greater than $35,206 for a family of four. Among the baby-boom parents, the proportion with better incomes rose markedly during ages 45 to 54 before leveling and declining slightly in the elderly years. In the grandparents' generation, the proportion with better incomes was substantially lower than that of the baby-boom parents at ages 45 to 54 (observed in 1960), and their status rose moderately before falling by ages 65 to 74 in 2000. For the early baby-boom and Generation X cohorts, incomes are initially much higher, but the early baby-boom increase is more gradual during ages 45 to 54. Thus, on this indicator of socioeconomic status, we find evidence of both substantial lifetime improvement and intergenerational progress.

In this report, homeownership is regarded as the percentage of householders who own or are buying their currently occupied home. Nearly three times as many people achieve this status as those who completed four years of college (note the difference in the vertical scales in Figure 1). The major point about homeownership is how much it rises over one's life, approximately doubling between ages 25 to 34 and ages 65 to 74. Relatively less progress is made between generations, with the greatest improvement occurring between the baby-boom grandparents and baby-boom parents (rising from 68 percent to 78 percent at ages 45 to 54). Among the baby boomers, improvement over their parents has faltered, and homeownership among Generation X is also little different from that of the baby boomers.

Social Change Through a Succession of Cohorts

The above examples suggest how a cohort's social and economic status changes both as a cohort ages and as newer cohorts replace older ones. Given that the cohort trajectories for the most part are fairly parallel, the major dynamic of change is the succession of cohorts. Each decade, a new cohort enters adulthood and is launched on its trajectory from a (usually) higher starting point. From there, the cohort advances through the life course, progressively replacing the cohort that precedes it in each age group.

This insight on the importance of cohorts in social change was established in a seminal essay by Norman Ryder written near the peak of the baby-boom era. Others had written that generations came of age with distinctly different consciousness due to the economic,

political, and cultural climate during their teen and young adult years, and that such a generational identity persists for their lifetime. Ryder argued that the cohort was a more precisely defined temporal unit from which generations were constructed. His argument was that birth cohorts provide the fundamental mechanism by which social change is introduced into a population. The infusion of new cohorts and the flow of cohorts toward older ages, together with the deaths of older individuals, constitute a "massive process of personnel replacement, which may be called 'demographic metabolism.'"[11]

The great advantage of the cohort concept is that it provides what some regard as an ideal compromise between the benefits of aggregation and the longitudinal representation of individuals. According to Ryder, "[The cohort concept] is a device for providing a macroscopic link between the movement of the population and movements of individuals... The cohort is a macroanalytic entity like the population, but it has the same temporal location and pattern of development as the individuals that constitute it."[12] Thus, cohorts have the analytical convenience of aggregates while retaining the temporal properties of individuals. Age, duration, and other temporal properties advance for cohorts just as for individuals over time.

Persistent Traits of Cohorts

Cohort members absorb each year's history when they are the same age. The impact of the same event is different for individuals in different ages, so different birth cohorts experience a different shared history. The economic impact of the Great Depression was less severe for very young adults than it was for those in their 30s who had homes to lose, and it had the least impact on children, who could only vaguely perceive the trauma of what was lost. Yet, the young are more socially impressionable, and the lessons of frugality and lowered material aspirations learned in the Great Depression were absorbed more deeply by teens than by middle-aged adults.[13]

Later, during the social upheavals of the 1960s, the baby boomers were more influenced than their parents were by that decade's political and social currents. Not having established adult lifestyles meant that the baby boom was more impressionable; and not having families, possessions, and positions to protect left them free to experiment with new lifestyles and beliefs. Young men in that cohort were being drafted, and the events surrounding the Vietnam War clearly had a more lasting effect on them than on their parents or even on women of the same generation. More recently, Generation X has been more affected by the threat of AIDS than their parents or even older siblings, because the latter two groups were more likely by the advent of AIDS to be settled in stable sexual relationships and thus protected from risk. Those who are young and in flux are the ones who most urgently feel the need for changing practices and beliefs.

One of the unique cohort attributes most likely to persist over the decades is the relative size of the cohort—small for those born in the 1930s, large for those born in the 1950s and 1960s, and small again for those born in the 1970s. Relative size indicates the amount of competition among the peer group for focused age-specific activities such as schooling, entry-level jobs, and subsequent job promotions. Relative size also indicates the amount of political or economic clout the cohort might wield within the larger society.

A further persistent trait for cohorts is the legacy of socioeconomic achievement. Cohorts come of age with a given educational attainment, and retain that status for life. Occupational patterns entered into during young adulthood also persist, on average, throughout one's career, reflecting both training and new opportunities that became available at the time of career entry.[14] And, as shown later in this report, the socioeconomic status of the elderly reflects the momentum of accomplishments carried forward by cohorts from the time they were middle-aged. Without explicit attention to this carryover across decades, it becomes difficult to explain socioeconomic trends.

Pitfalls of Ignoring Cohorts

Cohorts are readily identifiable with census data that use familiar variables such as age. But age and cohort are not the same thing. To gain the longitudinal insights provided by cohorts, we must link the observations from a series of censuses, each of which provides a separate age cross-section of the population. Then we can trace cohorts as they grow older from decade to decade. Cohorts can be defined for any temporally identified variable based on the date when people entered a given status (for example, birth year, year of immigrant arrival in the United States, or year of occupancy in a residence). The method is well known to demographers.[15]

Despite this simplicity of construction, cohorts are often ignored in favor of age groups. The results of such analysis are often extremely misleading or shortsighted. A series of well-known fallacies of interpretation are highlighted in Box 2, page 150.

Another disadvantage of neglecting cohorts when analyzing age groups is that, even if the cross-sectional fallacies are avoided, the persistence factor is eliminated from consideration. It is very difficult to make any sense of changes in older age groups, for example, without examining the next-younger age group at a previous point in time. Today's 30-year-olds or 60-year-olds moved into the present age group by leaving a younger one. A cohort's persistent characteristics and differences can often be detected when that cohort's members were younger, and these characteristics help explain the nature of those who later occupy an older age group.

THE INCREASING GENERATIONAL WELL-BEING OF THE ELDERLY

The first group we shall examine for trends in socioeconomic status are the elderly. Because this is a very broad and open-ended age range, we will focus on those who have newly entered this status, the 65-to-74 age group. In the cohort perspective, each decade's elderly population represents the culmination of forces shaping adult fortunes over the last four decades or more. Those reaching ages 65 to 74 in 2000 came of age in the decade after World War II. Their careers were heavily shaped by postwar prosperity, unlike the elderly of 1980, who came of age in the Great Depression.

The elderly have long held a special position in the social policies of the United States. Respect for the elderly is a widespread value, if for no other reason than that this group includes one's own parents or grandparents. Unlike other class divisions, all voters also hope and fully expect to join this group one day, adding further emotional and political endorsement. When President Lyndon Johnson announced the War on Poverty in 1964, the elderly were a severely disadvantaged group.

A number of programs for the elderly were introduced or expanded in the 1960s. Especially important was the introduction of Medicare in 1965, complementing aid received through Social Security, a program set up in 1935. Initially, Social Security benefits were small, averaging only 26 percent of preretirement earnings in 1940; but this income "replacement rate" increased over the years, climbing from 31 percent in 1965 to 42 percent in 1975 before eventually peaking at 54 percent in 1980.[16]

Age Group Trends

Policies aimed at improving the welfare of the elderly are targeted to the age group, not to cohorts. Accordingly, we first should examine the age group trends, comparing people ages 65 to 74 to young adults ages 25 to 34 in the same year. Then, cohort trends that link age groups over time can be studied, particularly three indicators of social and economic welfare: the poverty rate, homeownership, and educational attainment.

Poverty Trends

A new poverty rate calculation was first proposed by the Social Security Administration in the early 1960s.[17] To define the poverty threshold, a low-priced, nutritionally adequate food plan was multiplied by 3 to represent the minimum annual income needed to elevate members of a family above the poverty line. This threshold has been updated in subsequent years in accordance with the Consumer Price Index. Despite weaknesses in the poverty definition—such as the same

Box 2
CROSS-SECTIONAL FALLACIES

At the single moment in time when a decennial census is taken in the United States, every cohort is captured at a different point in its life course: Some cohorts are young adults, others are middle-aged, and others are elderly. A common fallacy is that age differences at a single moment in time represent a path of *aging*—that today's 45-year-olds will become, 10 years later, like today's 55-year-olds. In reality, there are unique differences among cohorts, so cohorts should be followed over time by linking successive ages in successive censuses.

Asian Gardeners

One illuminating example of a fallacy is that of U.S.-born Asian American men's participation in the gardening occupation. Two contrasting views are shown in the accompanying figure. Gardening is a long-established occupational choice, and it is clear that older men have a much higher likelihood than younger men of pursuing this occupation. In the age cross-sectional view, it would appear that preference for the gardening occupation rises as these men get older.

The alternative view of cohorts shows the percentage choosing the gardening profession by supplementing the 1990 data with an earlier, 1980 cross-section and simply connecting the dots between 1980 and 1990. As these men grew older, there is little evidence of a preference for gardening. Instead, the older cohorts persist in their occupational choices (probably made 30 to 40 years ago), and young men will never join their fathers or grandfathers in gardening. Therefore, conclusions based on age groups at a single moment in time are clearly a naive, cross-sectional fallacy.

Will Baby Boomers Depress Housing Prices?

A second example of a cross-sectional fallacy drew enormous attention on Wall Street and among housing and real estate analysts. George Mankiw and David Weil's forecast called for a 47 percent plunge in house prices from 1990 to 2010, based on declines in population at young adult ages and the expectation that the large baby-boom generation would reduce its consumption as it grew older.[1] The econometrics behind the study embedded an age cross-section of house prices. At the time of the 1980 Census, people around age 40 occupied the highest price homes, and the value of homes was lower at older ages. Given the great number of boomers, Mankiw and Weil's model assumed the entire housing market would suffer from lowered demand and reduced prices as the boomers headed down the slope to lower-priced homes—a fallacy, as it turned out.

This cross-sectional fallacy of downward movement was created because earlier cohorts—now older—long ago purchased smaller, older, and lower-priced homes. The great majority of older homeowners remain in the very same homes for 10 and even 20 years or longer.[2] Thus, the baby boomers are not falling down the cross-sectional age slope to lower housing prices.

The Borjas-Chiswick Debate on Economic Assimilation

A final example of a cross-sectional fallacy is from the field of labor economics, applied to immigrant earnings. The 1970

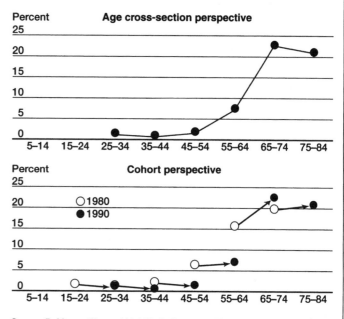

Percent of U.S.-Born Asian Men Employed as Gardeners, Viewed From the Age Cross-Section and Cohort Perspectives

Source: D. Myers, "Upward Mobility in Space and Time: Lessons From Immigration," in *America's Demographic Tapestry*, ed. J.W. Hughes and J.J. Seneca (New Brunswick, NJ: Rutgers University Press, 1999): figure 8.1.

Census was the first census in several decades to ask immigrants when they had entered the United States. With those data, Barry Chiswick was able to investigate the relationship between years since migration and earnings.[3] Chiswick followed the common practice of describing differences in earnings across categories of arrival dates as income growth. After the 1980 Census provided a second cross-section with earnings and arrival data, George Borjas was able to observe cohorts of immigrant arrivals at two points in time.[4] Immigrants who had been in the United States for at least 10 years as of 1980 did not see their earnings increase as much as the 1970 cross-section implied. Borjas showed that the longer-settled immigrants in 1970 and 1980 had been tracking on higher earnings trajectories all along, while more recent arrivals were tracking on lower trajectories. The cross-sectional relationship summed the effects of actual earnings growth over time for cohorts plus the positive gap between trajectories of high-tracking early arrivals and low-tracking recent arrivals.

References

1. N. George Mankiw and David N. Weil, "The Baby Boom, the Baby Bust, and the Housing Market," *Regional Science and Urban Economics* 19, no. 2 (1989): 235–58.

2. Dowell Myers and John Pitkin, "Evaluation of Price Indices by a Cohort Method," *Journal of Housing Research* 6, no. 3 (1995): 497–518.

3. Barry R. Chiswick, "The Effect of Americanization on the Earnings of Foreign-Born Men," *Journal of Political Economy* 86, no. 5 (1978): 897–921.

4. George Borjas, "Assimilation Changes in Cohort Quality, and the Earnings of Immigrants," *Journal of Labor Economics* 3, no. 4 (1985): 463–89.

threshold being used nationwide despite large differences in housing costs and other factors—the poverty calculation has become one of the most standardized social indicators in America.[18]

Applied to data from the 1960 Census, the new calculations found the elderly to be in deep financial distress: In 1960, fully 33 percent of those ages 65 to 74 had incomes falling below the poverty line. An even greater percentage of those ages 85 and older (44 percent) also fell below the poverty line. Here we will focus just on those ages 65 to 74 because they represent the new group of elderly each decade (having been ages 55 to 64 at the last census). Focusing on this one age group also helps avoid confounding effects of growing life expectancy that have increased the relative number of the old-old (ages 85 and older) over recent decades.

The improvement in poverty among the elderly has been dramatic since 1960, plunging from 33 percent to 7 percent in 2000 (see Figure 2). For comparison, we also show the poverty rate in the same year of young adults ages 25 to 34. The poverty rate of the young was half as great as that of the elderly in 1960, but after falling to a low in 1970, by 1990 the youth's rate had exceeded that of the elderly.

Homeownership Trends

Another indication of rising fortunes among the elderly is provided by homeownership, defined as the percentage of householders who own (with or without a mortgage) rather than rent their residence. The cohort membership of the household is given by characteristics of the householder (formerly known as "household head"). While poverty measures current economic distress, homeownership indicates a longer, lifetime economic well-being. Among young adults, home purchase reflects an anticipation of future earnings levels and family needs; among the elderly, homeownership reflects the persistence of decisions made decades before. Homeownership among the elderly climbed steadily over the last half-century, from 69 percent in 1960 to 81 percent in 2000, the highest rate for any age group (see Figure 2). For comparison, the homeownership rate of young adults ages 25 to 34 is roughly two-thirds that of the elderly, reaching a peak of 52 percent in 1980 before declining to 46 percent in 2000.

Educational Attainment Trends

Underlying these favorable trends for the elderly is a sharp improvement in their educational status. As recently as 1960, only 20 percent of the elderly had attained a high school degree or equivalent. That figure rose sharply to 70 percent in 2000 (see Figure 2). Education also increased for young adults in this time period, although not as dramatically. High school com-

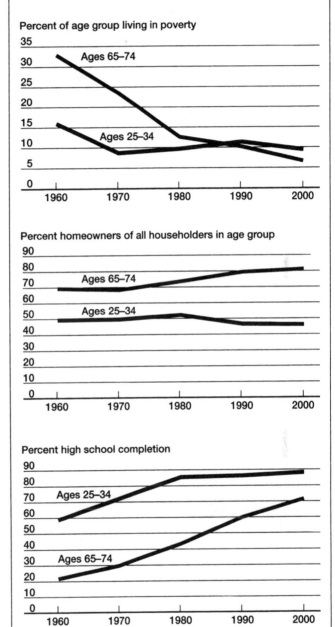

Figure 2

AGE GROUP COMPARISONS OF SOCIOECONOMIC PROGRESS OF THE ELDERLY AND YOUNG ADULTS, 1960–2000

Percent of age group living in poverty

Percent homeowners of all householders in age group

Percent high school completion

Source: Author's calculations using the Integrated Public Use Microdata Series (IPUMS), 2003.

pletion among adults ages 25 to 34 rose from 58 percent in 1960 to 84 percent in 1980, holding roughly constant until 2000. College completion in the general population also has increased for the elderly, but not as markedly as it did for high school completion. College completion rates rose from 4 percent in 1960 to 17 percent in 2000.

DISPLAYING SOCIAL DATA IN AN AGE-PERIOD-COHORT FRAMEWORK

		Percent of adults completing high school				
Age	Ⓐ Ⓑ	1960	1970	1980	1990	2000
25–34		58.1	72.2	84.2	84.1	83.8
35–44		51.7	62.2	76.8	85.6	84.9
45–54		37.8	54.5	66.1	78.1	85.8
55–64		26.7	40.4	56.9	67.6 Ⓒ	78.6
65–74		19.6	29.6	42.7	59.3 Ⓓ	69.2
75–84		17.7	25.0	33.5	46.7	62.9
85+		17.5	25.2	29.8	38.2	54.0

How to "slice" the data matrix for display:
A — Period trends from 1960–2000 are repeated for each age.
B — Age cross-section is repeated for each period.

In contrast, cohorts run down the diagonals, growing older each decade, and can be displayed alternatively as:
C — Period trajectories that show historical dates on the horizontal axis, or
D — Age trajectories that show ages on the horizontal axis.

Source: Author's calculations using the Public Use Microdata Sample (PUMS) from the 1960–2000 censuses.

Figure 3

HIGH SCHOOL COMPLETION TRAJECTORIES OF COHORTS ACROSS AGE AND DECADES

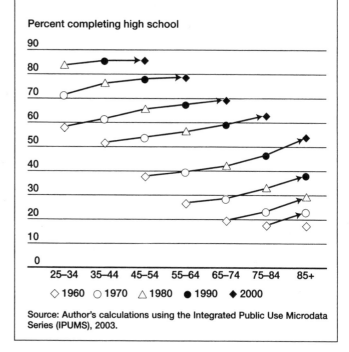

Source: Author's calculations using the Integrated Public Use Microdata Series (IPUMS), 2003.

Cohort Perspective on Rising Status Among the Elderly

The above indicators describe age group trends, measuring differences across successive cohorts ages 65 to 74 or ages 25 to 34. However, the socioeconomic status of the elderly does not solely, or even mainly, reflect the economic or policy conditions at the time of observation. For many outcomes, current status is a legacy of persistent effects inherited from middle age and before. To illuminate these lifetime conditions, a series of graphs presented here plot the cohort trajectories through time by displaying their movement across ages. Given age cross-sections from multiple periods, the conversion from age group to cohort data is illustrated in Box 3.

Educational Attainment Trends

The most dramatic example of cohort differences is educational attainment. Given that education is largely completed by age 25, cohorts retain a relatively constant educational status as they age (see Figure 3). With minor but notable exceptions, virtually all of the change in educational attainment is achieved between cohorts instead of within the lifetime of any one cohort. The increase in high school completion between successive cohorts is astounding, in some cases exceeding 10 percentage points in just one decade.

So great has the improvement been in educational attainment across successive cohorts that the percentage of people with a high school degree at ages 65 to 74 rises sharply as each successive cohort enters that age

over the five decades. Tracing the trajectories of younger cohorts, we can predict that the early baby-boom cohort (ages 45 to 54 in 2000) will likely enter their elderly years with a high school educational attainment of at least 88 percent, far above the 69 percent recorded for the elderly age group in 2000, and close to the level attained by the 25-to-34 age group in that year.

Certain aspects of these educational trajectories deserve explanation. First, despite our expectation, educational attainment is not absolutely constant for cohorts ages 25 and older. Curiously, the cohorts all appear to slowly inflate their educational attainments over time, creating trajectories that slope slightly upward by two or three percentage points per decade. This upward creep is prevalent for all cohorts in all decades, and is probably not a result of inconsistencies between censuses.[19] If there were an inconsistency, we would expect to see a bump or dip in the smooth cohort trajectories. The best explanation for the upward creep is that it reflects progressive respondent error, likely a form of resume padding and "selective amnesia," causing census respondents to forget that their final year of school was not actually completed. In any event, the effect is slight and consistent across groups, so it does not bias analysis.

The one exception to the constant slope of these educational trajectories is the accelerated upslope of high school completion for cohorts after ages 65 to 74. This is likely the result of mortality differences. If less economically advantaged cohort members do not have

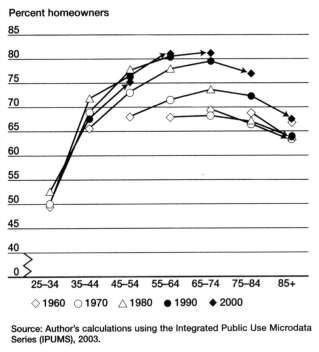

Figure 4

HOMEOWNERSHIP ATTAINMENT TRAJECTORIES OF COHORTS ACROSS AGE AND DECADES

Percent homeowners

◇ 1960   ○ 1970   △ 1980   ● 1990   ◆ 2000

Source: Author's calculations using the Integrated Public Use Microdata Series (IPUMS), 2003.

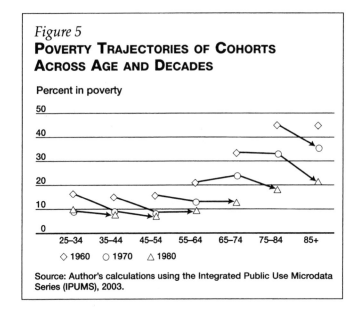

Figure 5

POVERTY TRAJECTORIES OF COHORTS ACROSS AGE AND DECADES

Percent in poverty

◇ 1960   ○ 1970   △ 1980

Source: Author's calculations using the Integrated Public Use Microdata Series (IPUMS), 2003.

high school degrees, and if they are prone to higher mortality due to poorer health care and other factors, then the educational attainment of those who survive at older ages will slant toward higher prevalence rates of high school completion.

Homeownership Trends

Homeownership is not constant over people's lifetimes, and the increase in homeownership from young to old can be dramatic. Less dramatic but still important is the increase in homeownership that occurs between successive cohorts. The increase observed at ages 65 to 74 amounts to 12 percentage points between 1960 and 2000 (see Figure 4). Today's elderly cohorts, who were ages 25 to 34 in 1950 or 1960, were ideally positioned to take advantage of new homeownership opportunities and economic prosperity in the post-World War II era. Government-sponsored mortgage programs stimulated home buying among the young because their much-lower requirements for down payments (5 percent to 10 percent instead of 40 percent to 50 percent) meant the young could buy without saving for many years. Rapid increases in average earnings for young men in the 1950s and 1960s further accelerated the pace of home buying. Smaller increases in home buying in the 1970s were spurred by the growing importance of women's earnings, not simply because of women's rising labor force participation but because new legislation required

lenders to count women's earnings as fully as men's in mortgage applications.

Now that the young from the early years after World War II are aging, they are bringing their accumulated high homeownership rates with them. For example, those entering ages 65 to 74 in 2000 had homeownership rates when they were ages 45 to 54 (some 20 years earlier) that are 9 percentage points higher than the 45-to-54 age homeownership rates of the cohort that entered ages 65 to 74 in 1980. Thus, this earlier difference in homeownership is carried forward, roughly matching the 8 percentage point difference recorded between the two cohorts at ages 65 to 74.

The pattern is more confused among more recent cohorts positioned in younger ages because these cohorts have lagged below the trajectories set by the earlier cohorts. Some of this decrease in homeownership may be due to delayed marriage or lengthened educational training periods, both of which discourage members of a cohort from launching homeownership at a very young age. In addition, rising interest rates from 1980 through the mid-1990s and rising house prices made homes less affordable. As a result, we find a polarization of housing status, with large increases in homeownership among the elderly and declines among the young.[20] The cohort ages 55 to 64 in 2000 will likely have a trajectory that exceeds all previous cohorts.

Poverty Trends

Poverty is much more closely tied to current economic conditions, and yet it also reflects prior cohort experience. The poverty rate at ages 65 to 74 is clearly linked to the level of poverty recorded 10 years earlier when the cohort was 10 years younger (see Figure 5). Poverty rates were unusually high for all age groups in 1960. The cohort trajectories from 1960 to 1970 show the sharpest improvement for young cohorts, indicating that the improvement in poverty was due to more than just Social Security or Medicare benefiting the elderly. Broad economic expansion and welfare support for families played a role in the improvements of the 1960s. Nonetheless, the poverty trajectories since 1970 reveal a substantially more-disadvantaged status for the elderly in earlier cohorts than those reaching ages 65 to 74 since 1980. Social policy reforms of the 1960s surely helped improve the status of the elderly; however, the entry into elderly status of the formerly middle-aged who possess higher education, higher homeownership, and a lower legacy of poverty also has boosted that group's current average status.

Summary

Analysis of trends for age groups shows that socio-economic status has improved markedly for the elderly since 1960, especially with regard to rising education levels and falling poverty. Young adults have enjoyed much less success, and, on some indicators, the elderly have now achieved a status superior to young adults. This reverses the pattern common in 1960.

Most of the improvements for the elderly appear to be the result of successes in middle age or before. Cohorts arriving at age 65 in recent years have a much higher socioeconomic status. In contrast, among the young, there has been a general downward shift since 1980. Thus, it is upward cohort succession among the elderly and downward cohort succession among the young that yields the divergent trends for age groups.

Looking ahead to the next two decades when the baby-boomers enter their elderly years, one could expect them to continue their current advantages of high educational attainment and low poverty. With regard to homeownership, the later baby-boom cohorts may not sustain the high homeownership rates of the elderly from the early baby-boom or World War II cohorts. Nonetheless, the socioeconomic status of the baby boomers will likely exceed that of any cohort who entered their elderly years before 1980.

CONTINUED LAGGING PROGRESS FOR YOUNG ADULTS?

The improving socioeconomic status of the elderly is one of the great successes in America over the last half-century. However, the sharp improvements among the elderly do not seem to have been equally enjoyed over this period by young adults. At one time, the elderly had poverty rates twice as high as the young, but, by 1990, their poverty rates had plunged below those of the young. Similarly, the elderly not only closed much of

their education deficit relative to the young, but they also widened their sizable advantage in homeownership.

Whatever the direction of change, trends among young adults have far greater implications for the future than do trends for the elderly. Whereas the elderly are nearing the end of their life and changes in their status reflect the culmination of 40 to 50 years of progress, young adults are just launching their careers and setting a course of 40 to 50 years of *future* progress. If the young-adult cohorts launch on trajectories that track lower than their successors, this downward cohort succession could likely characterize their careers as they age.

In fact, the cohorts of the baby-boom generation have fallen below the trajectory set by the baby-boom parents and World War II-born generations. This trend was especially clear at the time of the 1990 Census. An urgent question to be addressed with the 2000 Census data is whether this decline has continued for Generation X, those born from 1966 to 1975 and now emerging into young adulthood. If downward succession continues for Generation X, the risk is increased that the subsequent generation now in college—those born from 1976 to 1985—will also experience this downward succession.

Some of the apparent decline in socioeconomic achievement among the young may be due to the rapid racial and ethnic changes in the U.S. population that are most dramatic among children and young adults. If groups that are growing in prevalence have distinctly lower socioeconomic attainments, that may depress the average achievement level for the overall cohort. Not only should we be concerned about these minority groups, but the implication could be that the average non-Hispanic white is experiencing a more favorable path of progress than indicated by the population as a whole. Accordingly, it is important to separately track the cohort trajectories of non-Hispanic whites, blacks, Asians, and Latinos.

In the case of Asians and Latinos, an additional confounding factor is the arrival of new immigrants (see Box 4), so that the overall Asian or Latino cohorts may have their average status shifted up or down by the new arrivals. Adjustments are made for this factor in some analyses in the present section, while the next section focuses directly on socioeconomic progress of the immigrants.

Educational Attainment

Overall Changes Between Cohorts
As previously shown, educational attainment trajectories are fairly flat after age 25 because education is largely completed by that age. Accordingly, it is more efficient to focus on the young-adult launching points for educational trajectories, viewing these separately for non-Hispanic whites, blacks, Asians, and Latinos.

Between 1960 and 2000, cohorts in each racial and ethnic group have entered adulthood with ever-higher levels of high school completion and college education (see Figure 6, page 156). For each cohort, the figure displays the percentage that have completed high school and the smaller percentage that have completed both high school and four years of college.

As young adults in 1960, the later parents of the baby boom were less educated than young adult cohorts in more recent decades. The difference in high school completion among blacks is especially striking; those who came of age in 1980 were substantially better pre-

pared than those in 1960. A similar generational improvement is found among Latinos.

The sharpest gains in high school completion were achieved between cohorts entering adulthood in 1960 and 1980. Since that time, the gains have leveled off at about 90 percent completion for both U.S.-born and foreign-born whites and Asians, 80 percent completion for blacks, and 60 percent completion for Latinos (see Table 3, page 156). Despite the leveling, high school completion rates still increased by 2 percentage points to 4 percentage points among whites, blacks, and Asians. In contrast, among Latinos, high school completion fell by

---

Box 4
PROPORTION FOREIGN-BORN AMONG COHORTS

The growing presence of foreign-born residents complicates the analysis of socioeconomic progress. Given that immigrants tend to have lower status than U.S.-born residents, an influx of new immigrants can drive socioeconomic trends down. Most often, we are interested in the progress recorded across decades by U.S.-born residents. Separately, we should give explicit attention to the progress of immigrants after they arrive in the United States.

The nation's foreign-born population changed dramatically between 1960 and 2000, but this change affects some age groups much more than others. The great majority of immigrants are young when they arrive in the United States. Seventy percent of recent arrivals were under age 35 at the time of the 2000 Census; among Latinos, this figure reached 78 percent. As a consequence of this concentration of the young, the rising tide of recent immigration to the United States has most swelled the younger age groups. Given that roughly two-thirds of all the foreign-born have resided for less than 20 years in the United States, there has not been time for these immigrants to move into the older age cohorts.

We should not neglect, however, the large group of immigrants who have aged while in the United States. The accompanying table shows that, in 1960 and 1970, a fairly high percentage of elderly Americans were foreign-born. These large numbers reflect a previous era of young people's migration, one that came to a close with immigration restrictions after 1925. By 1990, the last vestiges of this earlier migration were visible in the 15 percent of adults ages 85 and older who were foreign-born.

The new immigration of the post-1965 era is slowly beginning to build a concentration among young adults, reaching about 18 percent of all Americans ages 25 to 34. Relatively low concentrations are found in any decade among young adults who are non-Hispanic whites or blacks.

Among Asians and Latinos, very high proportions of all age groups in all decades are foreign-born. Because of rising immigration, the proportion foreign-born among Asian adults in 2000 (83 percent) is almost twice as great as it was in 1960. An even greater increase has occurred among Latinos, although the proportion of foreign-born Latinos was only 58 percent in 2000.

Percent Foreign-Born by Race and Age, 1960–2000

Age	1960	1970	1980	1990	2000
Total population					
0–14	1.2	1.3	2.5	2.8	3.8
15–24	2.2	2.7	4.9	8.1	11.5
25–34	4.0	5.1	7.1	10.4	17.6
35–44	4.4	5.5	8.2	10.0	14.6
45–54	7.4	5.0	7.3	10.0	12.2
55–64	13.9	7.5	6.3	8.6	11.5
65–74	19.7	13.4	9.1	7.2	10.3
75–84	21.0	17.6	15.0	9.3	8.5
85+	19.7	17.7	18.6	15.1	9.3
Foreign-born Asians					
0–14	9.9	13.0	37.4	24.9	22.8
15–24	20.5	28.7	56.8	63.9	56.7
25–34	40.5	56.4	73.7	78.4	82.8
35–44	30.0	48.3	78.0	82.6	86.1
45–54	51.5	31.8	64.4	83.7	86.3
55–64	78.0	51.8	51.1	75.3	86.9
65–74	80.9	71.5	63.3	66.9	80.3
75–84	94.4	74.1	67.7	73.4	70.6
85+	84.6	71.0	73.2	79.3	70.2
Foreign-born Latinos					
0–14	3.5	7.9	10.4	11.5	11.8
15–24	12.7	17.9	28.7	38.0	40.3
25–34	15.8	27.2	38.2	49.5	58.1
35–44	21.9	29.4	42.6	49.0	58.1
45–54	36.5	28.6	39.5	49.7	54.8
55–64	51.4	37.7	39.5	45.0	53.8
65–74	53.6	48.8	49.1	44.5	49.7
75–84	57.7	48.2	56.7	53.7	48.2
85+	49.3	44.3	57.8	62.8	55.3

Source: Author's calculations using the Integrated Public Use Microdata Series (IPUMS), 2003.

The rapidly growing immigrant share of the U.S. population is most prominent among young adults, who can significantly affect the overall socioeconomic trends for Asians and Latinos, including both young and elderly adults.

nearly 2 percentage points (from 58 percent to 56 percent). This downward trend from an already low level of education is of considerable concern.

More dramatic changes are evident for college completion rates, with rapid gains followed by stagnation and then renewal. Although strong increases occurred from 1960 to 1980 with regard to the proportion of each cohort that completed four years or more of college, there were no further increases in college completion between 1980 and 1990 (see Figure 6). In fact, it appeared that the past trend of progress for each new cohort had stalled and might even reverse. Fortunately, between 1990 and 2000, the upward trend in college completion resumed. The upturn was greatest among Asians (+12 percentage points); followed by whites (+7 percentage points); blacks (+3 percentage points); and Latinos (+1 percentage point). This recent resurgence is so significant that it is explored later in this report.

Filtering Out the Effect of New Immigrants

How might the infusion of new immigrants be altering these trends in educational attainment? Among whites and blacks, no more than 9 percent of the young-adult cohorts in any decade are foreign-born, so there is little likelihood that this factor could substantially shift the aggregate educational attainment for those cohorts. However, among Asians, at least 40 percent of the young cohorts each decade are foreign-born, with the highest percentage (83 percent) reached in 2000 (see Box 4, page 155). Similarly, among Latinos, at least 16 percent of the young cohorts each decade are foreign-born, with the highest percentage (58 percent) reached in 2000. Accordingly, there is a good chance that immigrants will alter the trend observed across cohorts arriving in young adulthood.

In fact, the influx of immigrants has a pronounced effect on trends in Latino educational attainment. When

Table 3

EDUCATIONAL ATTAINMENT OF COHORTS LAUNCHED INTO ADULTHOOD BY DECADE, TOTAL U.S. POPULATION AND TOTAL U.S.-BORN POPULATION, AGES 25–34, BY RACE/ETHNICITY

Percent of cohort completing high school	1960	1970	1980	1990	2000
Total population	58.1	71.6	84.2	84.1	83.9
White	67.7	76.8	88.0	88.9	91.0
Black	42.5	52.9	74.4	77.1	81.0
Asian	73.6	84.6	86.5	85.7	89.6
Latino	25.5	44.6	57.4	58.0	56.3
U.S.-born only					
Total	58.7	72.1	85.5	86.4	88.3
White	67.9	77.2	88.2	88.9	91.1
Black	42.4	52.6	74.3	76.8	80.8
Asian	85.5	89.9	93.9	92.6	93.3
Latino	27.3	45.7	66.0	72.7	76.6

Percent of cohort completing 4 years of college	1960	1970	1980	1990	2000
Total population	11.0	15.9	23.3	22.7	27.5
White	14.7	18.1	25.8	25.5	32.5
Black	5.1	6.5	11.6	12.3	15.1
Asian	17.5	37.5	42.1	41.7	53.6
Latino	3.1	5.2	9.3	9.7	10.4
U.S.-born only					
Total	11.0	15.7	23.3	22.6	27.9
White	14.7	18.1	25.7	25.2	31.9
Black	5.0	6.2	11.3	11.5	14.3
Asian	21.7	27.3	40.4	40.5	52.5
Latino	3.0	4.3	9.8	11.4	16.1

Source: Author's calculations using the Integrated Public Use Microdata Series (IPUMS), 2003.

Figure 6

PERCENT HIGH SCHOOL COMPLETION AND PERCENT FOUR-YEAR COLLEGE COMPLETION AMONG NEW COHORTS LAUNCHED INTO ADULTHOOD EACH DECADE, AGES 25–34, BY RACE/ETHNICITY

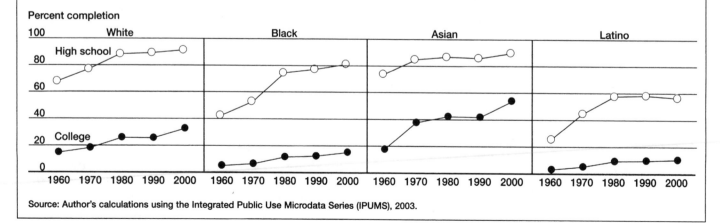

Source: Author's calculations using the Integrated Public Use Microdata Series (IPUMS), 2003.

the data for U.S.-born young adults are evaluated, Asians have high school completion rates for 1980 through 2000 that are only moderately elevated, about 93 percent (see Table 3). Among Latinos, however, the flat trend of 58 percent high school completion from 1980 to 2000 is replaced with steadily increasing educational attainment, growing from 66 percent to 77 percent. Between 1990 and 2000, U.S.-born Latinos increased their high school completion rate by 4 percentage points, more than any other group. But the growing numbers of foreign-born Latinos clearly have depressed the overall high school completion rate by that group. It is erroneous to refer to these lower-educated individuals as high school "dropouts." In fact, immigrants from Mexico and other Latin American countries often complete their schooling in the eighth grade and never enroll in U.S. schools.[21]

Once the effect of immigrants is removed, an even greater shift in status occurs with regard to four-year college completion. There is little change among U.S.-born Asians, because the large numbers of foreign-born have college completion rates much like the U.S.-born. In the case of Latinos, however, the college completion rate increases from a flat trend post-1980 to 16 percent in 2000. Once again, the apparent lack of educational progress across generations among Latinos is due to the growing numbers of foreign-born in Latino cohorts.

Progress Again From 1990 to 2000

Between 1980 and 1990, the upward trend of higher educational attainment across successive cohorts appeared to stall out. Fortunately, after 1990, the trend toward higher college completion resumed, especially among whites, Asians, and blacks. The upturn is also present for U.S.-born Latinos. This development is an extremely favorable omen for the socioeconomic achievements of Generation X (ages 25 to 34 in 2000).

The resumption of this upward trend is so noteworthy that it deserves closer scrutiny. Could the apparent turnaround simply be a reflection of a reporting error in the census time series of educational attainment, one that either exaggerated the attainments in 2000 or perhaps depressed the attainment observed in 1990? In fact, further investigation has shown this upturn to be credible.[22] The census questionnaire items on educational attainment were virtually identical in 1990 and 2000, and U.S. Census Bureau staff confirm this finding. The upturn is also observable in annual data from the Current Population Survey, which show that most of the upturn occurred after 1995.

A challenge to the veracity of the earlier trend between 1980 and 1990 may be of greater concern: If the 1990 attainment level had been erroneously depressed, it would contribute to a false impression of a resumed upward trend between 1990 and 2000. In fact, the Census Bureau changed its questionnaire items with regard to

educational attainment in 1990, switching from a focus on years of education to one of degrees completed. After appropriate adjustments to the education coding, however, careful testing shows that the trend from 1980 to 1990 can be integrated into a seamless series of measurements of educational attainment. The best evidence is that the cohort trajectories used in this report indicate no dips or jumps in either 1990 or 2000 (see Figure 3, page 152). The trajectories evidence a smooth and continuous record of educational attainment. The *only* change found in 2000 is for the youngest cohort entering adulthood. This group is the product of educational changes in the preceding decade, and the group reflects a true upturn in achievement. After a period of stagnation in educational progress, it is a welcome sign that young adults are again elevating their educational attainment.

Homeownership

As discussed previously, homeownership rates rise rapidly over one's life. Unlike educational status, homeownership tends to increase markedly into elderly years. However, the baby boom and more recent generations have gotten off to a slower start in the housing market. This could be due to both a later age at marriage and family formation and also to rising housing costs. For whatever reason, recent cohorts appear to have lower homeownership rates than their elders.

Here we look much more closely at the achievements of young adults by major racial and ethnic groups and education level. Because the trajectories overlap in early adult years, a cohort *period* trajectory format, and not a cohort *age* trajectory format, shows the different trajectories more clearly. This cohort period format highlights the decade when the cohort entered adulthood (at ages 25–34), showing the level entered and also the slopes of subsequent upward trajectories.

A summary of young adult homeownership rates for the U.S. population is given in Figure 7 (page 158). This figure displays trajectories of homeownership achievement beginning from the year the cohort was ages 25 to 34. (Homeownership is defined as the percentage of householders living in an owner-occupied home.) The early baby-boom cohort began adulthood with a 52 percent homeownership rate in 1980, slightly higher than preceding cohorts. The subsequent cohorts of the late baby boom and Generation X fell to substantially lower initial homeownership rates, lagging more than 5 percentage points behind the early baby boom.

Equally notable is the unusual shape of the homeownership trajectory for the early baby-boom cohort. Although the cohort started with higher initial homeownership in 1980, its trajectory was less steep in the subsequent decade than either the preceding or following cohorts. This indicates that the cohort made slower additional progress between 1980 and 1990 than did

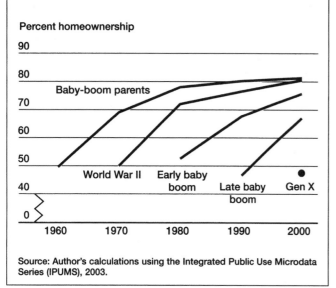

Figure 7

HOMEOWNERSHIP TRAJECTORIES OF COHORTS LAUNCHED INTO ADULTHOOD EACH DECADE, FROM AGES 25–34

Percent homeownership

Baby-boom parents

World War II Early baby boom Late baby boom Gen X

Source: Author's calculations using the Integrated Public Use Microdata Series (IPUMS), 2003.

other cohorts. However, in the 1990s, the early baby-boom cohort experienced a steeper rise than was true for earlier cohorts. Thus, the early baby boom got off to a fast start, slowed down relative to other cohorts in its first decade, and then sped up again in the next decade. The latter relative acceleration was echoed in the 1990s by the rapid increase in homeownership of the late baby-boom cohort.

Three factors could account for this pattern of variable progress across decades. The first factor is the rate at which the price of a house appreciates. During the 1990s, average house prices rose only 3 percent net of inflation—slowing down from the 8 percent increase of the 1980s—thus making homeownership far more affordable (even if the investment incentives may have dimmed). Also, in the late 1990s, interest rates fell to very favorable levels (although not to the historic lows still to come in the early 2000s). Finally, the Clinton administration, aided by the secondary mortgage market brokers Fannie Mae and Freddie Mac, instituted policies after 1995 to promote homeownership among racial and ethnic minorities by increasing counseling services and lowering mortgage-qualifying standards.[23] The result was that both the youngest and older households found it easier to own homes during the 1990s than in the 1980s.

Homeownership Trajectories by Race and Ethnicity

The above summary suggests a hopeful pattern of progress for the most recent cohorts, but it is not clear if that outlook is shared for all racial and ethnic groups or if it is present only among the best-educated members of

the cohorts. A parallel analysis of homeownership trajectories has been completed for each of the four major racial and ethnic groups, showing differences between higher- and lower-educated cohorts (see Figure 8). The left column of plots compares racial and ethnic groups without accounting for education. This pattern shows a slower entry into homeownership among the recent cohorts, followed by a steeper upward trajectory. Overall, non-Hispanic whites begin with higher homeownership rates and climb to higher ultimate levels than the other groups. Latinos start from slightly higher levels than do blacks, but both have lower launching points and flatter upward trajectories than Asians and Pacific Islanders. A positive note is that, among Latino and black cohorts, the late baby-boom cohort achieved steeper increases in homeownership between ages 25 to 34 and ages 35 to 44 (from 1990 to 2000) than earlier cohorts in their racial and ethnic group. This might reflect the workings of Clinton administration housing policies.

Differences by Education

These homeownership achievements differ markedly by educational attainment. Those with college educations are likely to have higher earnings and an easier time qualifying for mortgages. Nonetheless, college education holds students off the labor market longer than it does for less-educated peers, and that delay can produce lower initial homeownership at ages 25 to 34. People without a high school education may also benefit from working in manual trades that hone skills useful for do-it-yourself home construction and remodeling. Thus, many members of the lower-educated cohorts could own a home at an early age, but they are not likely to keep up in terms of household equity with their higher-educated peers in middle age.

Homeownership and race and ethnicity must be considered simultaneously, because racial and ethnic groups have very unequal educational profiles. Accordingly, there is a chance that what seems to be a racial or ethnic difference may be due to education, or vice versa. In this report, two education groups are contrasted: those with four years or more of college, and those with less than a high school degree.

Among non-Hispanic whites, higher-educated cohort members enjoy higher initial homeownership levels and steeper upward trajectories in the following decade than do their lower-educated peers. In both education classes, however, the rate of progress of the late baby boomers exceeds that of the early baby boomers. Also, in both education classes, the Generation X cohort has virtually the same level of initial homeownership as the late baby boomers. This is a welcome sign, as it curbs the decline in initial position that was observed between the early and late baby boomers. One hopes Generation X can also replicate or exceed the progress of its predecessor cohort as well.

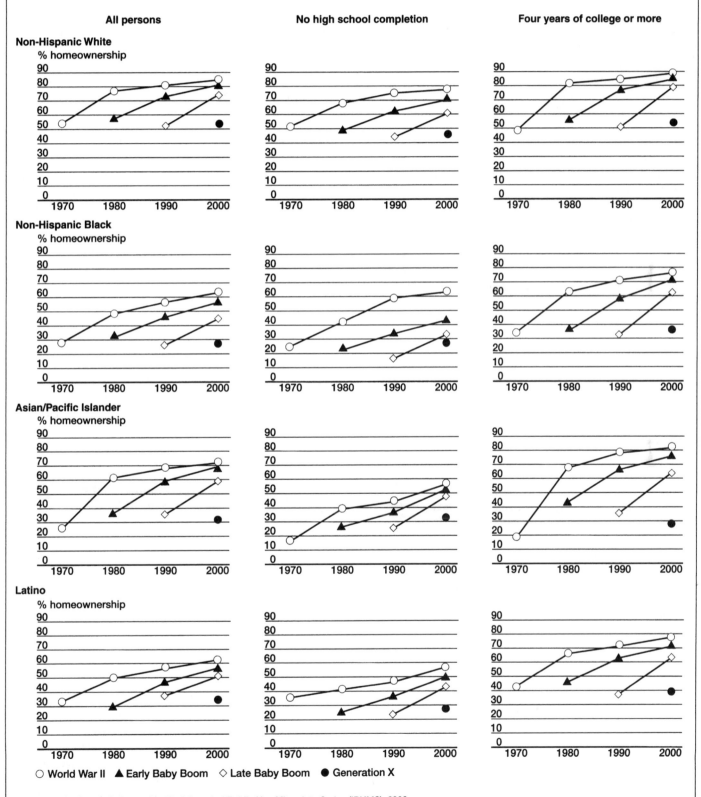

Figure 8

HOMEOWNERSHIP TRAJECTORIES OF COHORTS LAUNCHED INTO ADULTHOOD EACH DECADE, FROM AGES 25–34, BY RACE/ETHNICITY AND EDUCATIONAL ATTAINMENT

All persons   No high school completion   Four years of college or more

Non-Hispanic White
% homeownership

Non-Hispanic Black
% homeownership

Asian/Pacific Islander
% homeownership

Latino
% homeownership

○ World War II   ▲ Early Baby Boom   ◇ Late Baby Boom   ● Generation X

Source: Author's calculations using the Integrated Public Use Microdata Series (IPUMS), 2003.

A very similar pattern to that observed for non-Hispanic whites holds for blacks and Latinos. But there is one major exception: The homeownership trajectories for blacks and Latinos begin about 10 percentage points to 15 percentage points lower than the trajectory for non-Hispanic whites. In these groups, the late baby boomers achieved much greater progress in their first 10 years than the progress achieved by the early baby boomers. Among blacks who are college-educated, Generation X has a higher initial homeownership rate than the initial rate for the late baby boomers. Accordingly, among both blacks and Latinos, we find evidence for substantial gains in homeownership across recent cohorts.

In the case of Asian residents, there is an even larger gap in homeownership rates between the college-educated and other cohort members. The higher-educated begin with higher homeownership, and they demonstrate markedly steeper progress. What is alarming about Asian progress is that this group fails to demonstrate an improved position for Generation X; similarly, the late baby-boomer cohort does not show a steeper upward trajectory than what was observed for the early baby boomers. It is likely that this lagging progress reflects the greater weight of immigrant arrivals among Asians (an issue addressed later in this report).

Overall, the homeownership prospects of cohorts depend greatly on their educational status. Cohorts who are better-educated have better occupational and earnings prospects than less-educated cohorts, and better-educated cohorts may also have an easier time getting a mortgage.

Lagging No Longer

With few exceptions, the youngest generation of adults is no longer lagging behind its predecessors. Educational attainment has increased across successive cohorts, and homeownership has ceased its decline. Recent cohorts also show an even steeper upward trajectory into homeownership than the early baby boomers achieved.

It is too soon to say what the socioeconomic progress of Generation X or its followers will be. However, the initial starting position of this cohort is the most favorable we have witnessed since 1980. It is a hopeful outlook.

THE EFFECT OF IMMIGRATION ON MEASURED SOCIOECONOMIC PROGRESS

Analysis of the socioeconomic progress of Latinos and Asians is confounded by the large share of foreign-born residents of those two groups, and many of these residents are recent immigrants. Thus, an assessment of the changing population mix and the progress of the foreign-born population is integral to understanding socioeconomic progress for both those minority groups and for the total U.S. population. Indeed, in recent years, some of the deepest concerns about socioeconomic progress in America have been focused on the achievements and well-being of immigrants.[24] (In this report, the terms "foreign-born" and "immigrant" are used interchangeably to describe people born outside the United States or its outlying territories (such as Puerto Rico or Guam), and people whose parents are not U.S. citizens.)

Reversing the Longstanding Trend of Growing Immigrant Poverty

How immigration alters the perception of socioeconomic progress—and the underlying dynamics of this progress—is well illustrated by the incidence of poverty. Prior to the 2000 Census, despair about the fortunes of immigrants to the United States was fueled in particular by two key poverty indicators. For one, the poverty rate of recent arrivals (entering the United States in the decade preceding each census) had been rising for all immigrants since 1970, including Latinos and Asians. Recent immigrants had poverty rates of 15 percent, 23 percent, and 25 percent in 1970, 1980, and 1990, respectively. Latino newcomers had poverty rates of 21 percent, 28 percent, and 32 percent in 1970, 1980, and 1990, respectively. The poverty rates for Asian newcomers were 15 percent, 20 percent, and 22 percent in 1970, 1980, and 1990, respectively. Until 1990, poverty was clearly on the rise for newcomers to America.

A second basis for concern was that the total poverty rate of all foreign-born residents, particularly Latinos, had also steadily risen between 1970 and 1990. Among all the foreign-born, the total poverty rate rose from 14 percent in 1970 to 16 percent in 1980, and then to 17 percent by 1990. Among foreign-born Latinos, the rate increased from 21 percent in 1970 to 23 percent in 1980, and then to 25 percent in 1990. In contrast, the overall poverty rate of foreign-born Asians rose from 13 percent in 1970 to 16 percent in 1980 before leveling off at 16 percent in 1990. In sum, immigrants had experienced rising poverty rates, and the growing number of immigrants threatened economic progress for the nation.

One welcome finding from the 2000 Census is that the poverty rate of new arrivals and of all foreign-born residents in general has decreased since 1990. The poverty rate of new arrivals in the decade prior to 2000 decreased by nearly 2 percentage points, reversing a longstanding upward trend. This improvement for newcomers may be due to lower unemployment in the late 1990s versus the late 1980s. The higher status of newcomers in 2000 could also reflect the effects of stronger border enforcement, which has the effect of selecting migrants with greater economic resources.

A second finding from the 2000 Census is that the total poverty rate of all foreign-born also decreased for the first time in decades, albeit slightly. This overall improvement was a combined result of several forces. One reason the improvement was not greater is that Latinos' share of all immigrants increased from 38 percent to 44 percent, thus placing a greater weight on their higher poverty in forming the average for all immigrants.

Cohort Trajectories, Sizes of Arrival Cohorts, and Total Change

The explanation for the declining overall poverty rate of the foreign-born rests partially on the improving fortunes of newcomers; other explanations include the pace of upward mobility for previously arrived immigrants and the relative size of different arrival cohorts within the overall foreign-born population. Understanding an immigrant's progress out of poverty is an excellent application of the cohort framework, which emphasizes launching points and subsequent trajectory slopes of lifetime progress, combined with the effects of cohort succession as newer cohorts replace earlier ones. The emphasis here is somewhat novel because the literature on cohorts and socioeconomic progress has not traditionally focused on immigrant arrival cohorts. Data on year of arrival were absent from the census for most of the 20th century, and these data were not reintroduced until 1970; studies using the new data emphasized technical analyses in labor economics conducted apart from the broader cohort tradition.[25] In fact, data on immigrant year of arrival may be used to construct arrival cohorts in a fashion nearly as accurate as for birth cohorts.

Especially noteworthy in such an analysis of poverty rates and trajectories of improvement are the substantial downward slopes of immigrant cohorts' subsequent poverty trajectories as the cohorts reside longer in the United States. The example of poverty rates for Latino immigrant arrival cohorts illustrates this clearly (see Figure 9). Among Latinos who arrived in the 1980s, the poverty rate recorded in 1990 was 33 percent; the rate dropped to 22 percent by 2000. These downward poverty trajectories measure the pace of upward mobility within the lifetime of each immigrant arrival cohort. The declines among Asians are even steeper during their first full decade living in the United States. The longer immigrants settle in the United States, the better adapted they become economically. It takes time to "learn the ropes" and find employment in favorable occupations. By virtue of their migration, the cohort is economically dislocated, and the largest amount of status recovery occurs in the first decade of U.S. residence, with slower improvement thereafter.

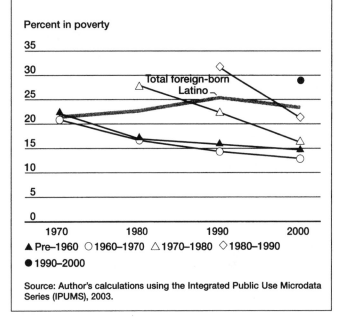

Figure 9
POVERTY TRAJECTORIES OF LATINO IMMIGRANTS BY DECADE OF ARRIVAL, COMPARED WITH THE OVERALL TREND IN FOREIGN-BORN LATINO POVERTY

Source: Author's calculations using the Integrated Public Use Microdata Series (IPUMS), 2003.

Despite these sharp reductions in poverty as immigrants settled for longer periods of time in the United States, the total poverty of the foreign-born continued to rise, at least until 1990. At the same time that the total poverty rate was rising, all the cohorts were experiencing downward trends in their poverty rates (see Figure 9).

A question to ask is: How much of the improvement between 1990 and 2000 in poverty for immigrants is due to the lower poverty of recent arrivals in 2000? Alternatively, we might ask: How much of the downturn is due to the improvement enjoyed by previously arrived immigrants, as signified by the downward sloping poverty trajectories from 1990 to 2000? Or: How much of the decline is due to changes in the mix of foreign-born with varying amounts of duration of residence in the United States (how many are newcomers versus settled immigrants)?

A separate analysis shows that the overall decline in foreign-born poverty between 1990 and 2000 results from offsetting factors. The poverty rates for all groups were affected by the continued growth in immigration, because immigrants who are in this country for less than 20 years generally have higher poverty rates than the average for all foreign-born. If this growth effect were the only factor, poverty rates would have climbed more than 3 percentage points for all foreign-born.

Fortunately, new arrivals in the 1990s had lower poverty rates than those arriving in the 1980s. Weighting these declines by the relative numbers of new arrivals versus settled immigrants, the lower poverty rates of new arrivals contributed to a reduction of anywhere from 0.5 percentage points to 2.0 percentage points in the groups' overall poverty rate. However, an even larger downward effect was wielded by the poverty reduction among previously arrived immigrants. The downward sloping trajectories shown previously are a considerable force. After weighting for the relative size of each cohort, the effect of poverty improvement among the settled immigrants is to reduce the groups' overall poverty rates by 3 percentage points to 4 percentage points.

In the data for the four racial and ethnic groups examined here, the effect of poverty reduction among the settled immigrants is the largest factor; when that factor is combined with a reduction in the initial poverty of new arrivals in the 1990s versus those who arrived in the 1980s, the two factors offset the pressure of mounting numbers of new immigrants. The pattern is remarkably similar for every group. The upward mobility of previously settled immigrants is a pervasive force in reducing poverty.

What is the Trend of Poverty for Immigrants?

Our analysis shows that the trajectory of immigrant poverty could be characterized by three different trends. Political commentators often seize on one or another of these trends to depict the prospects for the immigrant population:

- *Aggregate trend.* From 1970 to 1990, the overall poverty rate of the foreign-born rose 3 percentage points; but between 1990 and 2000, the poverty rate fell by 0.3 percentage points (2 percentage points for Latinos). Does that mean immigrants are doing better than before?
- *Poverty of new arrivals.* From 1970 to 1990, the poverty rate of recently arrived immigrants increased 9 percentage points, but that rate fell by 2 percentage points (3 percentage points for Latinos) between 1990 and 2000. Is poverty of new arrivals decreasing?
- *Poverty of settled immigrants.* From 1970 to 2000, the poverty rates of settled immigrants decreased by 10 percentage points or more, especially for immigrants with fewer than 20 years' residence in the United States. Does that mean immigrants are doing better over time?

During the 1990s, all the poverty measures pointed to improvement. However, before 1990, only the settled-immigrant trend led to poverty declines. If we wish to represent the average experience of settled immigrants, the cohort poverty trajectories provide the best measure. If we wish to represent the trend in immigrant newcomers' status, then the poverty rate shortly after arrival is the best measure. Finally, if our focus is on the overall status of the immigrant population, we need to recognize how this overall status is a composite of the other trends, each of which is weighted by the relative sizes of different cohorts in different stages of settlement.

IMMIGRANT AGE AND ARRIVAL COHORT TRAJECTORIES

The previous section addressed the socioeconomic progress of immigrant arrival cohorts irrespective of age. But age is often as important for immigrants as for U.S.-born residents. Not only does immigrants' socioeconomic status improve with age, as it does for U.S.-born residents, but immigrants' eventual socioeconomic status also depends on how old immigrants were when they arrived in the United States and how long they have lived here. In general, immigrants reach higher status levels the younger they are at arrival. For example, men and women in their 20s achieve greater economic success than those arriving in their 30s, and those arriving as children do best of all once they reach middle age. This illustrates again the power of cohort-defining events. The act of moving from a foreign country to the United States is a signal event in people's lives, the timing of which has substantial consequences.

How fully are immigrants able to move into the middle class? Answering this question is among the richest and most rewarding applications of the concept of cohorts to analysis of socioeconomic progress. Escape from poverty is only one criterion of socioeconomic advancement. Homeownership is widely regarded as a prime indicator of middle-class status. Homeownership also differs from poverty in that it is cumulative and slowly changing over the lifetime. Typically, the highest levels of homeownership are attained late in life, and the trajectories established as young adults lay the foundation for future higher or lower homeownership levels.

Homeownership and Immigrant Assimilation

Assimilation of immigrants is a process that results from the growing experience of immigrants in the U.S. society and economy. The process continues into the second and third generations of settlement, as the children and grandchildren of immigrants continue to adapt. Assimilation results in social incorporation, economic integration, and a lessening of ethnic differences. In a recent review, Richard Alba and Victor Nee define four key dimensions of assimilation: acculturation, socioeconomic achievement, residential integration, and social integration.[26] Of these four dimensions, socioeconomic achievement is of greatest concern in this report.

Homeownership occupies a pivotal position in the assimilation process. Often one of the principal economic objectives of immigrants, homeownership is a prime indicator of socioeconomic achievement. Because it is so commonly achieved, homeownership does not represent an elite status, as do certain higher-level occupations; instead, homeownership signifies entry into the middle class. Homeownership is also important because it represents a central element of family life. The home is the staging ground for a family's daily trips to work, to school, and to neighborhood socializing. Home purchase buys a stake in a particular community and school system, so homeowners acquire an economic interest in their communities that encourages political participation.[27] Homeownership fosters residential assimilation, bringing the family into contact with higher-status members of society, often from different ethnic backgrounds. The benefits of homeownership are transmitted across generations because children growing up in these homes have improved access to a middle-class lifestyle and the mainstream of society. Ultimately, this intergenerational transmission facilitates both acculturation and social integration.

Cohort Age Trajectories of Homeownership

The following analysis makes use of the "double cohort" design that tracks birth cohorts within immigrant arrival cohorts, albeit in a descriptive (not statistical) variation of the method.[28] Among immigrants, added factors are the length of time since immigration and the age at arrival. In this report, a unique graphic design shows trajectories across multiple dimensions as Latino immigrant cohorts pass through successive age groups in successive decades. To place these multiple immigrant trajectories in context, we have superimposed the homeownership trajectories for U.S.-born non-Hispanic whites and Latinos who were ages 25 to 34 in 1970.

The longest history of homeownership is that of immigrants who arrived in the 1960s. The homeownership status of these immigrants was recorded between 1970 and 2000 (see Figure 10). Among Latinos, trajectories rise sharply from low initial homeownership rates, especially for those younger than 45 at time of arrival (indicated by their age in 1970), given their length of residence in the United States.

People who immigrate later in life do not have time to reach the high homeownership rates of those who come at younger ages. For example, the 1960s arrivals who arrived at ages 25 to 34 reached 60 percent homeownership by ages 55 to 64. Those who arrived at ages 35 to 44, although starting with higher initial home-

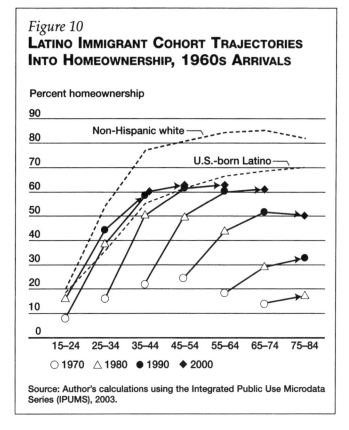

Figure 10

LATINO IMMIGRANT COHORT TRAJECTORIES INTO HOMEOWNERSHIP, 1960S ARRIVALS

Source: Author's calculations using the Integrated Public Use Microdata Series (IPUMS), 2003.

ownership than the younger group, only reached 58 percent homeownership by ages 55 to 64. And those who arrived at ages 45 to 54, while they had a still higher initial level than their younger peers, only reached 43 percent homeownership by ages 55 to 64.

The findings for Asians are very similar to those for Latinos, but there are a few major differences. First, Asian immigrants have homeownership rates substantially higher than those of Latinos.

Second, Asian immigrants ages 25 to 34 exhibit very steep upward homeownership trajectories in their first complete decade of U.S. residence. Among 1960s arrivals, that steep trajectory amounts to a 64 percentage point rise in homeownership (versus 34 percentage points for Latinos).

So high is initial homeownership among Asians, and so steep are their trajectories, that Asians rapidly surpass 70 percent homeownership, after which their trajectories abruptly flatten out or even turn downward.

The Trajectory of Immigrant Children

Although the success of immigrant children is not revealed until decades after arrival, evidence of this achievement can be found as arrivals from the 1960s approached middle age. The youngest immigrant children from that era are the equivalent of a U.S.-born second generation. Their mothers gave birth to them five years before immigrating instead of five years after.

Either way, these children would have entered U.S. schools from the first grade. Indeed, these immigrant children are often called the "1.5 generation," and they are pooled together with the second generation in many studies.

The new second generation (U.S.-born children of immigrants) commands attention because their fate signifies the ultimate success of the current wave of immigration.[29] However, the second generation is not specifically identified in the census, and alternative data sources that contain information on the second generation (the largest of which is the Current Population Survey) lack sufficient sample size to permit analysis of specific age groups within ethnic groups. Accordingly, this report assumes that the cohort trajectories showing the 1.5 generation with census data may be the best available proxy for the trajectories of the true second generation.

The youngest members of arrival cohorts ultimately rise to homeownership levels comparable with U.S.-born Latinos and Asians. This phenomenon is best observed in the case of 1960s arrivals. Those people ages 35 to 44 in 2000 would have been ages 5 to 14 in 1970 after their arrival. These immigrant children grow to have homeownership levels that are tracking equal to or above the trajectories shown for U.S.-born Latinos in Figure 10.

As these data on homeownership attainment make clear, the new second generation, or at least its 1.5-generation proxy, is faring very well among both Latinos and Asians. This offers a relatively more optimistic outlook than suggested by other, more pessimistic interpretations of prospects for the second generation. But a more detailed analysis is clearly needed, one that examines different nationality groups of Asians and Latinos and several different outcome variables of socio-economic progress or assimilation.

Summary

This analysis of homeownership trajectories of immigrants has exploited the full potential for cohort analysis of evidence contained in the decennial censuses. The repeated collection of census data in temporal categories allows for construction of cohorts that link these observations. This summary traces both the arrival cohorts and the birth cohorts within each arrival cohort.

Foreign-born residents pass through many of the same life-cycle dynamics as U.S.-born residents. One major difference is that immigrants' arrival is not marked by their birth but by migration after birth. Accordingly, we cannot assume that immigrant residents have lived through the social, political, and economic conditions prevailing in different decades. Those who arrived in the United States in the middle of their lives have skipped the early decades of experience shared by others in the same birth cohort.

Given the growing share of foreign-born residents among adult cohorts, especially among Asians and Latinos, it is important to expressly identify this group's socioeconomic progress. The dynamics revealed are among the most fascinating of any population group.

OUTLOOK FOR SOCIOECONOMIC PROGRESS

Cohort trends help us to better understand the American people's experience of socioeconomic progress. Using this perspective, we have learned about accumulated progress over lifetimes, the progress across generations, and the prospects for the future. We also have seen how the insights from cohorts differ from the misleading conclusions drawn from single historical snapshots or from simple trends over time.

Major Findings

The great strength of cohort analysis is the ability it gives researchers to trace persistent effects across decades as cohorts grow older. The educational advantages of more recent cohorts will surely last a lifetime, as will homeownership; but the latter also reveals evidence that past deficits can be somewhat compensated for by more rapid lifetime progress in subsequent years. However, the flip side of the advantage of cohort analysis is its blind spot for the status of future new cohorts. Since we have so little information on new cohorts (save for cohort size), we must be especially observant of trends. The launching points for life trajectories of cohorts just entering adulthood or just entering the United States are crucial to their future success.

Looking ahead to 2010 and 2020, when the World War II and early baby-boom cohorts will have entered their elderly years, what trends do we foresee in their status? These cohorts, now middle-aged, have substantial advantages over their predecessors. Comparing the cohorts when they were all ages 45 to 54, albeit in different decades (1980, 1990, and 2000), we see substantial gaps in high school completion. These gaps are being carried into cohorts' elderly years, so that the cohort scheduled to reach ages 65 to 74 in 2010 has high school completion rates 12 percentage points higher than does the elderly cohort of 2000. The still younger cohort (early baby-boom) has high school completion rates 20 points higher than does the elderly cohort of 2000. Similar gaps are also found for college completion rates, indicating that the future elderly population will have rising educational status.

The outlook for homeownership and poverty at ages 65 to 74 is much less certain. The gaps in homeownership trajectories observed at ages 45 to 54 are much smaller than for education. Indeed, the cohort that had advanced to ages 65 to 74 by 2000 actually had slightly higher homeownership rates than its successors at ages 45 to 54. If anything, this suggests that the future elderly population may have slightly lower home-ownership rates. The evidence for poverty is even less clear, in part because this status is more changeable over time. It appears, however, that the early baby-boom cohort (ages 45 to 54 in 2000) may be tracking on a lower poverty trajectory than either of its predecessors.

The question of immigrant upward mobility is important in its own right, and has drawn widespread concern recently. Immigrants' poverty levels are extremely sensitive to time dimensions. In every decade, the newest immigrants have the highest poverty, but poverty declines for each cohort of new arrivals the longer they reside in the United States. The rapid growth in the number of new arrivals means that each decade's foreign-born population includes a high pro-portion of people with a relatively high likelihood of liv-ing in poverty. This compositional effect creates the illusion that poverty is rising for the foreign-born and obscures the underlying lifetime trajectory of upward mobility for immigrant arrivals. Similar issues are raised for immigrant homeownership, although our findings on that topic add still more time dimensions: age at arrival and advancing age that accompanies longer duration in the United States.

Matching Rhetoric to Reality

No longer does it make sense to speak so simply about socioeconomic progress over time. There are multiple dimensions of time across which progress is measured, and the trends do not all run in the same direction. Our language and conceptualization of socio-economic progress are intertwined, because how we think about progress depends on the words we have available to describe it. Without a clear grasp of the alter-natives, politics can bias any interpretation, as one dimension or another is seized upon.

Based on the findings in this report, we should reflect upon the following:

● Does the average for a population reflect the aver-age person's experience over time? For example, is it really true that a declining median age for the popu-lation means that most people are getting younger? The average may fall, but cohorts still grow older.
● If educational attainment declines for older age groups, does that mean people lose their education

as they grow older? Obviously not. Rather than an age cross-section, we need to trace cohorts as they advance through age groups over time. That analy-sis shows that education is relatively fixed for each cohort after age 25. The age cross-section is reflect-ing differences between cohorts, not aging within a cohort.
● If educational attainment holds constant, does that mean there is no progress for cohorts? It may show there is no *lifetime* progress within cohorts' careers, but there can still be substantial *generational* progress among successive cohorts.
● If homeownership attainment is declining for the most recent cohorts, does that mean that young adults are experiencing lower homeownership rates? This case shows downward mobility across cohorts, even though each cohort is experiencing sharp upward mobility.
● What of immigrant poverty, which has been steadily rising since 1970? Does this trend mean that immigrants are losing ground and failing to assimi-late economically? Our evidence shows that immi-grants experience strong upward mobility as U.S. residents, but the growing number of new immi-grants skews the average poverty rate toward the higher poverty of newcomers. Again, the average figure does not represent the average experience.

Overall trends in averages are widely used to describe the experience of people, but the actual lan-guage chosen to interpret the trend usually emphasizes the experience of individuals. These trends, of course, would be more truthfully represented by the slopes of cohort trajectories (lifetime progress), or by the gaps between cohort trajectories (generational progress or cohort succession). The journalist, policy analyst, or advocate owes this clarification to his or her audience. And the audience has every right to question intent. Only through this clarification and questioning will we reach an accurate understanding of socioeconomic progress and its implications for American society.

Acknowledgments

The University of Southern California's Population Dynamics Research Group provided much needed support for the research underlying this report. In particular, Zhou Yu delivered exceptional research assistance. The author is grateful for helpful com-ments and direction from Reynolds Farley and John Haaga. Lessons from George Masnick were a key foundation.

REFERENCES

If provided by the author, additional text and data associated with this report are available at www.prb.org/AmericanPeople.

1. P.K. Whelpton, *Cohort Fertility: Native White Women in the United States* (Princeton, NJ: Princeton University Press, 1954).

2. Reynolds Farley, *The New American Reality: Who We Are, How We Got Here, Where We Are Going* (New York: Russell Sage Foundation, 1996): table 2-1.

3. Glen H. Elder, Jr., *Children of the Great Depression* (Chicago: University of Chicago Press, 1974).

4. Carl L. Harter, "The 'Good Times' Cohort of the 1930s: Sometimes Less Means More (and More Means Less)," *PRB Report* 3, no. 3 (1977): 1-4.

5. Frank Levy, *The New Dollars and Dreams: American Incomes and Economic Change* (New York: Russell Sage Foundation, 1998).

6. Richard A. Easterlin, *Population, Labor Force, and Long Swings in Economic Growth: The American Experience* (New York: Columbia University Press, 1968).

7. Calculations are based on house price indexes described in Dowell Myers and John Pitkin, "Evaluation of Price Indices by a Cohort Method," *Journal of Housing Research* 6, no. 3 (1995): 497-518. Subsequent extension to 2000 was completed with data supplied by the Office of Federal Economic and Housing Oversight. The house price index series is adjusted for general inflation in monetary value using the Consumer Price Index for all items. These data are for the nation as a whole; the patterns for individual metropolitan areas could be more variable.

8. In an apparent paradox of the affordability of homeownership, rising prices can escalate homeownership rates. Research of homeownership changes in the 1980s and 1990s has shown that homeownership by young adults is elevated in states where prices are rising most rapidly and depressed in states where prices are falling sharply. See Dowell Myers, "Advances in Homeownership Across the States and Generations: Continued Gains for the Elderly and Stagnation Among the Young," *Fannie Mae Foundation Census Notes* 8 (2001). The explanation for the paradox is that rising prices create an investment incentive as well as a fear that future increases will put homeownership out of reach.

9. Jeffrey Passel and Barry Edmonston, "Immigration and Race: Recent Trends in Immigration to the United States," in *Immigration and Ethnicity: The Integration of America's Newest Arrivals*, ed. Barry Edmonston and Jeffrey Passel (Washington, DC: Urban Institute Press, 1994).

10. Richard D. Alba, *Italian Americans: Into the Twilight of Ethnicity* (Englewood Cliffs, NJ: Prentice-Hall, 1985).

11. Norman Ryder, "The Cohort as a Concept in the Study of Social Change," *American Sociological Review* 30, no. 6 (1965): 843-61.

12. Norman Ryder, "Notes on the Concept of a Population," *American Journal of Sociology* 69, no. 5 (1964): 447-63.

13. Elder, *Children of the Great Depression*.

14. Dowell Myers and Cynthia J. Cranford, "Occupational Mobility of Immigrant and Native-Born Latina," *American Sociological Review* 63, no. 1 (1998): 68-93.

15. The method is well known to demographers. See William H. Frey, *Investigating Change in American Society: Exploring Social Trends with U.S. Census Data* (Belmont, CA: Wadsworth Publishing Company, 2004); Glenn Firebaugh, *Analyzing Repeated Surveys* (Thousand Oaks, CA: Sage Publications, 1997); and Norvall D. Glenn, *Cohort Analysis* (Thousand Oaks, CA: Sage Publications, 1997). Also see: www.rcf.usc.edu/~dowell/cohortgallery.htm.

16. Marilyn Moon and Janemarie Mulvey, *Entitlements and the Elderly: Protecting Promises, Recognizing Reality* (Washington, DC: The Urban Institute Press, 1996).

17. Mollie Orshansky, "Children of the Poor," *Social Security Bulletin* 26, no. 7 (1963): 3-13.

18. Judith Eleanor Innes, *Knowledge and Public Policy: The Search for Meaningful Indicators*, 2d ed. (New Brunswick, NJ: Transaction Publishers, 1990).

19. A major change was introduced in the 1990 census questionnaire with regard to questions on educational attainment. Whereas prior questionnaires asked about years of education, the questionnaires in 1990 (and in 2000) asked about degrees completed. This change created some inconsistency in responses over time. The principal problem involved those who had completed some post-high school training but were short of a college degree. Educational attainment remained consistent over time for those who attained a high school degree (or 12 years of schooling) or who had attained a college degree (or 16 years of schooling).

20. Dowell Myers and Jennifer Wolch, "Polarization of Housing Status," in *State of the Union: Volume 1, Economic Trends*, ed. Reynolds Farley (New York: Russell Sage Foundation, 1995).

21. Georges Vernez and Allan Abrahamse, *How Immigrants Fare in U.S. Education* (Santa Monica, CA: RAND, 1996).

22. Zhou Yu and Dowell Myers, *Research Memorandum: Verifying the Upturn in Educational Attainment at Age 25-34 in Census 2000* (Los Angeles: Population Dynamics Research Group, School of Policy, Planning, and Development, University of Southern California, Los Angeles, 2003).

23. Patrick A. Simmons, "A Coast-to-Coast Expansion: Geographic Patterns of U.S. Homeownership Gains During the 1990s," *Fannie Mae Foundation Census Notes* 5 (2001).

24. Philip Martin and Elizabeth Midgley, "Immigration: Shaping and Reshaping America," *Population Bulletin* 58, no. 2 (2003).

25. Barry R. Chiswick, "The Effect of Americanization on the Earnings of Foreign-Born Men," *Journal of Political Economy* 86, no. 5 (1978): 897-921; and George J. Borjas, "The Economics of Immigration," *Journal of Economic Literature* 32, no. 4 (1994): 1667-717.

26. Richard D. Alba and Victor Nee, *Remaking the American Mainstream: Assimilation and Contemporary Immigration* (Cambridge, MA: Harvard University Press, 2003).

27. William Rohe, Shannon Van Zandt, and George McCarthy, "Home Ownership and Access to Opportunity," *Housing Studies* 17, no. 1 (2002): 51-61.

28. Dowell Myers and Seong Woo Lee, "Immigrant Trajectories into Homeownership: A Temporal Analysis of Residential Assimilation," *International Migration Review* 32, no. 3 (1998): 593-625.

29. Reynolds Farley and Richard Alba, "The New Second Generation in the United States," *International Migration Review* 36, no. 3 (2002): 669-701.

PART III

FAMILIES, HOUSEHOLDS, AND CHILDREN

Marriage and Family in a Multiracial Society

By Daniel T. Lichter and Zhenchao Qian

BACKGROUND

Today's American family is hard to define. The so-called "traditional family"—working husband, his stay-at-home wife, and their children—represents only a small fraction of all American households. In "Leave It to Beaver," the popular late-1950s television show, the Cleaver family—Ward and June and their children Wally and Theodore ("the Beaver")—epitomized the American dream of economic success, a happy marriage, loving parents, respectful children, a nice house in the suburbs, and a big car in the garage. But the Cleaver family model represents only about 10 percent of all households today. The most popular television shows in recent years were about urban single people: "Seinfeld," "Friends," and "Sex and the City."

Television shows undoubtedly reflect America's changing family and demographic profile. Marriage rates have plummeted. Unmarried cohabitation has supplanted marriage as the first coresidential union for most young adults. Married couples have only one or two children, some couples have no children, and out-of-wedlock childbearing has become common. Many couples get divorced, yet many divorced people marry again and begin new families. Serial monogamy may have become the new norm. Many gays and lesbians seek legal changes that would allow same-sex marriages or civil unions that include the same rights and benefits enjoyed by heterosexual couples.

These general demographic trends are no longer news to most of us. In fact, we are often inured to them, mostly because we have experienced them firsthand. Preachers, politicians, and pundits worry that the decline in marriage and the breakdown of the traditional family are responsible for many societal ills: child poverty, racial inequality, delinquency, mental illness,

and moral decay. Some people look back nostalgically to the old ways. Others are more sanguine, viewing today's family patterns as a natural response to relentless cultural or economic pressures in our fast-paced society that make marriage less central in people's lives or more difficult to maintain.

History tells us that family change is inevitable and often adaptive, and therefore should not be a source for alarmist rhetoric. Family change may also be the price of personal freedom and the rise of individualism over communalism. It also reflects growing gender equality both in the home and in the workplace, as well as changing economic exigencies of modern American life, such as geographic mobility and job dislocation, work-family imbalances, and work-related stress. Sociologist Andrew Cherlin has argued that most Western societies have moved to "individualized marriage," placing much greater emphasis on personal choice and self-development rather than companionship.[1] He suggests that marriage is being deinstitutionalized, which simply means that the family values and norms that proscribe appropriate behavior regarding mate selection processes, gender relations, and marital interaction have weakened. The rules of courtship and marriage are less widely shared today.

Debates about cultural and family values require up-to-date information on America's changing marriage and family patterns, especially in light of rapid demographic and economic shifts over recent decades. More than ever before, these debates must also be informed by America's new racial and ethnic mix and its distinctive family forms. National statistics on marriage and living arrangements may misrepresent or even distort the family circumstances of many average Americans, especially racial minorities and recent immigrants from Latin America and Asia. Foreign nationals and other immi-

DANIEL T. LICHTER is the Robert F. Lazarus Professor in population studies and professor of sociology at The Ohio State University. Lichter is director of Ohio State University's new Initiative in Population Research. He has published widely on topics related to the family and welfare policy, including studies of marriage and family living arrangements, cohabitation and mate selection, child poverty, and welfare incentive effects on the family. Much of his recent work has focused on racial and ethnic variation in child poverty, and on marriage among welfare-dependent unwed mothers.

ZHENCHAO QIAN is associate professor of sociology and research associate of the Initiative in Population Research at The Ohio State University. Qian's research focuses on changing patterns of union formation and assortative mating. He has published work on changes in cohabitation and marriage, racial differences in intermarriage, racial identification of biracial children, and fertility and prospects of family planning in China. Currently, he is working on the impact of individual characteristics and marriage market compositions on mate selection.

grants living in the United States often remain separated in fundamental ways by race and ethnicity, national origin, social class, and geography. Family forms and relationships often differ widely from one group to another; but, as history shows, these forms and relationships also can converge quickly over time as social mobility and economic assimilation take root. Growing racial diversity makes it difficult to project the future of the family in the United States. One type of family (U.S.-born whites) is becoming less dominant, and the future characteristics of the family will increasingly be influenced by what minority families look like and do.

America can no longer be viewed in simple black and white terms; the fastest-growing segments of the U.S. population must not be ignored in the family debate or in family policy. The 2000 Census revealed that Hispanics were replacing non-Hispanic blacks as the largest minority in America. By 2002, the foreign-born population numbered 33 million, or more than 11 percent of the total population.[2] Hispanics accounted for 52 percent of this total. When we add U.S.-born children of foreign-born parents, these numbers increase even more dramatically. For example, recent estimates suggest that these second-generation children of immigrants represented 15 percent of the U.S. population under age 18.[3]

This report provides a comprehensive demographic portrait of recent changes in the contemporary American family, with special emphasis on racial and ethnic diversity. We will answer four questions:

● To what extent have marriage and families in America changed over the past few decades? As background, we first provide an overview of why marriage matters, along with a discussion of current key trends in the family and the demographic and economic processes that undergird these trends.
● To what extent has the "retreat from marriage" continued in the 1990s for different racial and ethnic groups? Guided by data from the decennial censuses, our analysis and discussion will focus on the timing of marriage—especially entry into marriage—and permanent singlehood.
● To what extent have new or different family forms become more prevalent in the United States? We document the proliferation of new family forms across racial and ethnic groups: cohabiting couples (with and without their own children); female-headed families with children; father-headed families; female provider/male homemaker families; and multigenerational families. We also illustrate the effects of family change on children's poverty and economic status.
● To what extent have racial and ethnic minorities crossed the "color line" by marrying people of different races? We examine patterns of marital assimilation; in other words, if the family-building

strategies of today's new immigrants and racial minorities mirror those of the U.S.-born population. Do immigrants wed U.S.-born Americans in small or large numbers? Do immigrants marry within or outside "color lines"? The answers tell us about social distance and race relations in America—whether racial lines are blurring or are remaining sharp and difficult to cross.

To fully understand today's families and tomorrow's future requires a fuller appreciation of the different cultural traditions rooted in the marriage patterns and family lives of America's racial and ethnic minorities. As in the past, America's next generation of adults promises to be very different from the current one, especially if intermarriage among groups accelerates. When today's children and youth grow into adulthood and start families of their own, their definitions of the ideal family are likely to differ from their grandparents' or even their parents'.

The 2000 Census provides an unusual opportunity to highlight family and household diversity in our increasingly multicultural and multiethnic society. Most surveys, even large ones, simply do not provide samples of sufficient size for some population groups (such as Koreans or Puerto Ricans) to give reliable family indicators for these groups. The usual, but often unsatisfactory, practice is to identify and analyze various panethnic groups, such as Asian Americans and Hispanics, that include smaller populations that may or may not share common cultural traits or economic circumstances. The Public Use Microdata Sample (PUMS) from the 1990 and 2000 U.S. censuses, because of its large sample sizes and national geographic coverage, provides an unprecedented opportunity to uncover major changes in the American family.

But, what is a family? The U.S. Census Bureau uses a very specific definition of households and families. A *household* contains all people living in a housing unit. Households are distinguished by whether they are family households (or families) or nonfamily households. A *family* includes household members who are related by blood, marriage, or adoption, and who share a common domicile. *Family households* include families in which a family member is the householder—the person who owns or rents the residence. These households can also include nonfamily members, such as a boarder or a friend. A *nonfamily household* includes the householders who live alone or who share a residence with individuals unrelated to the householder, such as two college friends sharing an apartment. Some nonfamily households sometimes substitute for traditional families and serve many of the same functions: Same-sex couples are one example. Close friends living together also sometimes regard themselves as a family, but this type of household does not satisfy the Census Bureau's strict definition.

Why Marriage and Family Matter

Attitude surveys indicate that the large majority of Americans expect to marry, and most will marry at some point in their lives.[4] Survey data indicate that, in 1997 and 1998, 72 percent of respondents reported that "having a good marriage and family life is 'extremely important.'"[5] At the same time, Americans are more tolerant today than in the past about alternative living arrangements. The stigma associated with single motherhood, unmarried cohabitation, and gay unions has lessened. Perhaps paradoxically, this increased tolerance has validated the significance of marriage as a freely chosen lifestyle decision rather than as a normative "requirement" or an expectation. Choosing to marry or not is a life-changing decision. Indeed, the symbolic significance and cultural meanings attached to marriage have perhaps never been more important to average Americans, or more hotly contested.

Disagreement about the significance of declines in marriage and traditional families is at the heart of the broader debate about the culture wars in America.[6] Many view the decline in marriage and the family as a cause of society's most pressing social problems. For example, delays in marriage, coupled with earlier and more frequent nonmarital sexual activity, have placed young women at much greater risk of out-of-wedlock childbearing than in the past. But, declines in marriage and marital fertility, not increases in nonmarital fertility, are most responsible for the post-1960s rise in the share of out-of-wedlock births.[7] Roughly one of every three births in the United States occurs outside of marriage, mostly to single women in their late teens and early 20s. Not so long ago, a pregnant teenage girl would have to leave her home and community, returning only after her baby was born and given up for adoption.

There also was a time when the woman married the man if she became pregnant with his child, but these marriages are no longer the cultural norm or viewed as necessary to legitimize the birth of the child. Demographer R. Kelly Raley has shown that, in the early 1990s, only about one of every 10 pregnant women ages 15 to 29 married before the birth of their babies.[8] The corresponding figure in the early 1970s was four of every 10.

High divorce rates have reinforced the rise in female-headed families. Nearly one-half of all marriages end in divorce.[9] More than 1 million marriages end in divorce each year.[10] About one-half of all divorces involve children, who usually live with their mothers despite recent increases in joint custody arrangements. The economic implications of these trends are obvious and serious. In 2002, about 40 percent of children living with single mothers fell below the poverty line.[11] The rise in female-headed families with children is associated with higher rates of family and child poverty and welfare dependency. And the growth in female-headed families with children—growth that occurred disproportionately among historically disadvantaged racial and ethnic minorities—has slowed progress toward racial economic equality.[12] Understanding family change is arguably key to better understanding racial inequality, but researchers disagree on the direction of this association and whether it is causal. One theory is that racial economic inequality is the cause for existing racial differences in marriage and family structure.

Other deleterious effects of family change are largely indirect, but nonetheless important. Children and adolescents raised in married-couple families have, on balance, clear emotional and cognitive advantages over children from single-parent families.[13] Youths who grow up in single-parent families are at greater risk for delinquency, school dropout, and teenage pregnancy and childbearing. Children who live with stepparents fare no better than children living alone with single parents. For adults, marriage appears to confer physical and emotional health advantages and promotes longevity; marriage provides social support and buffers the deleterious health effects of stress. Marriage also appears to make men more productive in the workplace.[14] This large body of empirical evidence is now difficult to ignore. Yet, the health and productivity effects of marriage may also simply reflect the self-selection of healthy and productive people.

Not surprisingly, the widely acknowledged statistical association between marriage and positive social and economic outcomes has given impetus to the marriage movement. We see this in men's groups such as the Promise Keepers; in nonprofit organizations like Smart Marriages; in rallies like the Million Man March; in the proliferation of faith-based initiatives that aim to strengthen traditional marriage; and in new legislative efforts to legally define marriage as only between a man and a women.[15] Indeed, we see increasing government involvement in family life. The 1996 welfare reform law, the Personal Responsibility and Work Opportunity Reconciliation Act, included among its goals the promotion of marriage as a context for childbearing and childrearing. The new law encourages the formation and support of two-parent families and promotes job preparation, work, and marriage. Many Americans believed that the old welfare system (administered through Aid to Families with Dependent Children) trapped families in poverty and reinforced an antifamily subculture that encouraged out-of-wedlock childbearing, single parenting, and welfare dependency. To date, however, welfare reform has apparently had only a modest, if any, effect on promoting marriage and two-parent families.[16] Goals of the reauthorized welfare bill, as currently proposed by the U.S. Congress, place less emphasis on marriage *per se* but more on "healthy marriages" that are emotionally satisfying and financially secure, and are beneficial for children.

Other official efforts to promote marriage have sought to remove its existing economic disincentives. These efforts include eliminating the marriage penalty in the tax code and in the Earned Income Tax Credit for low-income workers with children, and upping the earnings disregards of husbands (income counted against the welfare grant) in determining women's eligibility for welfare under Temporary Assistance for Needy Families (TANF). Some states have sought to reduce divorce rates by providing marriage preparation and enrichment courses that emphasize relationship skills and conflict management. But critics argue that such proposals are unlikely to gain widespread public approval or be successful because they ignore structural conditions (such as a bad economy) that predispose couples to greater conflict. Covenant marriages, such as the recent marriage legislation initiated in Louisiana, give couples greater opportunity to strengthen their commitment to marriage and make it more difficult to dissolve because of longer waiting periods for divorce. To date, however, few couples have chosen covenant marriages, and these marriages have not been shown to lower divorce rates.[17]

The politics of family changes have also been disconcerting to many social and political observers. Policy debates are often contentious, and appropriate policy courses often lack clear and widely shared goals. But marriage is likely to continue to occupy a distinctive place in the lives of most Americans. Most Americans seem to understand the positive economic, social, and psychological benefits of marriage; they also understand that children benefit from being raised in economically stable and loving married-couple families. Even poor single mothers do not have to be convinced of the value of marriage.[18]

Opponents of government programs that promote marriage fear government intrusion into their private lives, and they fear that official efforts to promote marriage will unfairly privilege marriage at the expense of other viable personal and family relationships, such as single-parent families, cohabiting couples, or same-sex couples. These observers worry that abused women will face new obstacles to ending bad marriages or will be forced out of economic necessity to stay in relationships that neither benefit them nor their children. They are also concerned about the reemergence of patriarchy and traditional views of marriage that historically undermined women's equality in the home and workplace. But these scenarios are unlikely. The American public gives little indication that they want to return to the days when the rules of courtship and marriage, gender relations, and appropriate marital roles were clearly defined. Those days are now viewed as overly restrictive, old-fashioned, and sexist.

FAMILIES IN AMERICA

The American family has experienced major changes over the past 25 years. But in *Continuity and Change in the American Family*, authors Lynne Casper and Suzanne Bianchi refer to a "quieting" of family change over the past several years.[19] Some trends, such as the rise in female-headed families, have slowed or even reversed for some groups. Some analysts claim that divergent trajectories of American family life are rooted in the unequal economic fortunes and access to opportunity of different segments of American society. Harvard professors David Ellwood and Christopher Jencks, for example, argue that income inequality has inevitably led to growing differences in marriage and family structure across population groups.[20] Ellwood and Jencks worry that current economic trends not only disadvantage those at the bottom of the income distribution but also reduce one's chances for marriage and for raising children with an economically and emotionally supportive spouse or partner.

More than ever before, merchants and marketers also have both the interest and the ability to target particular ethnic and economic segments of the American population, thus potentially crystallizing differences between groups rather than fostering cultural homogeneity or even assimilation. For example, the programs on Spanish-speaking television stations in most large cities reflect and reinforce distinct cultural values and appetites. The growing diversity and economic balkanization of American family life also is evident in less obvious ways. In 2000, labor force participation rates among mothers in white middle-class couples declined for the first time in decades.[21] Yet the growth of low-wage jobs and the new work requirements of recent welfare reform legislation pushed employment rates among single mothers to an all-time high.[22]

Recent Trends

The typical or average American family is difficult to characterize accurately. In this report, we discuss five trends that have reshaped American families and households over the past 20 years: the decline in traditional families; delayed marriage; the rise in single-parent families; more individuals living alone; and the surge in the number of cohabiting couples.

Decline in Traditional Families

One marker of the changing American family is the decline in the share of families and households headed by married couples. In 1970, 71 percent of all American households were headed by married couples. By 2000, the percentage had dropped to 53. More significant, married couples today are more likely than in the past to be dual earners and to have no children. The percentage of married-couple families with children has declined over the last three decades. In 1970, 25 million married-couple families included children. In 2000, the number remained largely unchanged but represented a much smaller percentage of all married-couple families or all family households.

These patterns reflect increases in childlessness, but the patterns also are the result of more effective control of unwanted fertility—especially at older reproductive ages—through modern contraception, voluntary surgical sterilization, and legal abortion. Increases in life expectancy also mean that growing shares of married couples have, literally and figuratively, survived the childrearing stage. Their children have grown up and moved away. Married couples may have half a lifetime to spend together without dependent minor children.

Delays in Marriage

Without question, the decline in the traditional American family has been shaped by the retreat from marriage. The marriage rate (marriages per 1,000 unmarried women) declined from 76 in 1970 to 54 in 1990, according to the National Center for Health Statistics. This means that only about 5 percent of unmarried women marry in a given year. On the other hand, from 1960 to 1980, the divorce rate increased from 9 to 23 divorces per 1,000 married women, and this rate has remained relatively constant and high. For women who married in the late 1970s, 39 percent divorced within 10 years, a figure much higher than for women who married in the late 1940s (14 percent).

Between 1970 and 1990, the remarriage rate among divorced women dropped from 123 to 76 per 1,000 divorced or widowed women. Despite this drop, more than one-half of those who had previously divorced were remarried in 1996.[23] About nine in 10 remarriages followed a divorce rather than the death of a spouse. Most remarriages took place within three years of divorce. For a large percentage of Americans, getting a divorce does not deter them from trying marriage again: Divorce rates are no lower for second marriages than for first marriages.[24]

America's retreat from marriage is revealed most easily in the changing marital status composition of the adult population. The percentage of American women who are married declined only modestly from 56 percent in 1970 to 52 percent in 2000, while the percentage of divorced women grew from 6 percent to 13 percent. Data on marital status by age are more dramatic. Young adults are much less likely today to be married. Among women ages 20 to 24, for example, the percentage of never-marrieds grew from 36 percent in 1970 to a stunning 73 percent in 2000. Among women ages 30 to 34, an even larger gap exists between 1970 and 2000—from nearly 11 percent never married to 39 percent never married. Americans today clearly are less likely to get married at younger ages.

As a result, the entry into marriage is less useful today as a key marker of adult status. In the past, marriage typically coincided with leaving home for the first time and the end of formal schooling. Marriage also began one's regular sexual activity and childbearing with the only intimate partner young adults would have in their lifetimes. Today, most young adults have had sex before marriage, often with several different partners. Most young adults will leave home long before they marry, and a significant percentage will experience pregnancy and childbirth before marriage. The end of formal schooling no longer segues directly into marriage, but typically begins a period of single living and personal independence.[25] More formal education, strong career aspirations, and greater financial independence mean that marriage is no longer the only or main defining role of young women today. Women of all ages have choices that their mothers were denied.

More Single-Parent Families

The usual progression of love, marriage, and babies is being reordered in American society. For a majority of adolescents and young adults today, sexual intimacy often comes before love. Children increasingly come before marriage; in 2002, one-third of all births were to unmarried women.[26] Many Americans believe that premarital sexual activity and out-of-wedlock childbearing are responsible for the rise in single-parent families, poverty, and welfare dependency. In truth, most single-parent families are not poor or welfare-dependent, and single-parent families are more often a consequence of divorce than of out-of-wedlock-childbearing. At the same time, single-parent families are heterogeneous and difficult to stereotype. Nontraditional families, including single-parent families with children, increased by over 50 percent between 1970 and 2000, and grew from 11 percent to 16 percent of all families. Declines in marriage and increases in divorce have played obvious roles.

The fact that single parents are less likely now than in the past to live with other family members also has increased family and child poverty rates.[27] Such changes have been fueled by declines in the stigma associated with raising children alone and with changing cultural values regarding economic and residential independence from parents. With increasing education and higher occupational status among women over this period, many single mothers are no longer economically dependent. They can now choose to live on their own if they prefer and can afford it. Indeed, the poverty rate for single mothers with children in 2003—32.5 percent—was the lowest level on record.[28] Despite this bit of good news, this figure is a high rate of poverty using almost any standard in the developed world.

In the 1979 movie "Kramer vs. Kramer," actor Dustin Hoffman played a newly divorced father struggling in his unexpected role as primary caretaker of his young son and fighting a battle to maintain custody. The 1970s had been a period of rapidly increasing divorce rates in America, and this box-office hit movie resonated with many single fathers. The movie helped increase public sensitivity to the estrangement of many single fathers from their children and to the situation of divorced men faced with the legal challenges of gaining physical custody of their children. More than 20 years after that movie, however, only about 17 percent of all children who live with a single parent live with their unmarried fathers.[29]

Rise in People Living Alone

Over the past three decades, the number of households containing only one person rose sharply, from 17 percent in 1970 to more than 25 percent of all households by 2000. These are important changes that reflect delays in marriage: The years between leaving school and marriage have increased rapidly over this period, thus increasing the chances that young adults live alone. Data from the U.S. Census Bureau's Current Population Survey indicate that, between 1970 and 2000, the median age at first marriage increased from 20.8 years to 25.1 years for women, and from 23.2 years to 26.8 years for men. Increases in persons living alone are not just limited to young adults. Today, single people of all ages are more likely than in the past to live alone rather than to live with family or friends.[30] This trend undoubtedly reflects increasing individualism; the desire for personal privacy; greater financial independence; and less pressure for nonmarried adults, especially women, to live with family or others.

The rise in single-person households also results from the aging of the population and the growing mortality differential between older men and women. Simply put, traditional families are less significant numerically because many families end through the death of a partner, and there are simply not enough older men for widows to marry. In 2000, the sex ratio for the population age 65 or older was 70, meaning that there were only 70 elderly men for every 100 elderly women.[31] At ages 85 and older, the sex ratio drops to 41. The demographic implications are clearly apparent in older men's and women's living arrangements. Men over age 75 are more likely than men at other ages to live with a spouse (67 percent), while women over age 75 are most likely to live alone. Unlike previous generations, today's growing population of widows are better able financially to live on their own rather than to live with other relatives or in a group home.

The Recent Surge in Cohabitation

The recent decline in marriage has been offset completely by increases in cohabitation—unmarried couples living together. Age at first marriage has increased significantly over the past decade or two, but studies suggest that age at first union (marriage or cohabitation) has

hardly changed over this period.[32] Couples have not stopped partnering in early adulthood: They simply are not marrying like they used to. The U.S. Census Bureau estimates that the number of opposite-sex cohabiting couples grew from 440,000 in 1960 to 3.8 million in 2000. Cohabitation now appears to be a normative step in the marriage process: Similar percentages of whites, blacks, and Hispanics experience cohabitation. Significantly, most cohabitors (about 75 percent) expect to marry their partners, but these partners do not necessarily discuss marriage plans before entering into a cohabiting union.[33]

Scholars have hotly debated the reasons for the upward climb in unmarried cohabitation. Some attribute this climb to America's changing sexual attitudes and behavior. The wide availability of the birth control pill in the 1960s helped separate sex from reproduction. Nonmarital sexual activity, especially for women, also became much less stigmatized. Another view is that the rise in divorce has made young couples more cautious about entering marriage. After witnessing and experiencing the effects of their own parents' divorce, these observers say, many couples fear the possibility of their own divorce. Cohabitation may give some couples greater confidence that they can get along with their partners; it gives them some idea about what to expect in marriage. But regardless of motivation, cohabitation is a short-lived arrangement. Most cohabiting couples end their relationships in a year or two. For many heterosexual couples, cohabitation is one step in the progression to marriage. This step also may soon be true for same-sex couples (see Box 1). For other heterosexual couples, cohabitation is an alternative to marriage, one that provides a marriage-like living arrangement without the legal ramifications associated with dissolution. Cohabitation can also be an adaptation to economic hardship or uncertainty—a kind of "poor person's" marriage.

The implications of cohabitation for American society and its families are difficult to forecast. Cohabitation is associated with delays in marriage and childbearing for many young couples, and thus is partly responsible for the recent delays in first marriage. Perhaps surprisingly, divorce rates are unusually high for cohabiting couples who later marry—around 30 percent to 40 percent higher than for couples who do not cohabit. Cohabitation may simply attract individuals who are less committed to marriage as an institution, which means they may also be at greater risk of later dissolution if things go wrong. Cohabitation itself may undermine the stability of subsequent marriage. In fact, the experience of cohabitation may not be representative of the kinds of interactions couples actually experience in marriage.[34] In this sense, cohabitation may not be a good testing ground for marriage. Cohabitation may provide little preparation for making difficult decisions about spending priorities, work, or childbearing and childrearing. A seemingly idyllic or carefree cohabiting experience may

SAME-SEX COUPLES

For the first time in the 1990 Census, and again in Census 2000, individuals could indicate whether they were "unmarried partners" of a householder or head of the household. These new data give researchers the opportunity to identify opposite-sex cohabiting couples and same-sex couples.

The results from the 2000 Census indicate that there were 594,000 same-sex cohabiting couples in the United States. This represents roughly 1 percent of all coupled households (married and unmarried), split almost evenly between gay and lesbian couples. San Francisco and Fort Lauderdale had the highest percentages of same-sex couples. Roughly one in four same-sex couples has children under age 18.

Our analyses of the 2000 Census data indicate that householders of same-sex couples had, on average, the highest levels of educational attainment of all householders. In 2000, 35 percent of same-sex couples had a college education or higher. In comparison, only 29 percent of married-couple householders were college-educated. The median household income of same-sex couple households was $60,000 in 1999, roughly the same as for married-couple households. The median incomes of same-sex and married-couple households were higher than for any other American household. These data show that, as a minority group, gay and lesbian couples are not economically marginalized.

The data reported here pertain to same-sex couples who share a common residence; the data are not the estimates of the overall gay and lesbian population in the United States. Yet these are important estimates from a policy standpoint. Cohabiting same-sex couples are probably most likely to choose same-sex marriages or civil unions if those marriages are legalized. In the heterosexual population, roughly 50 percent of cohabiting couples will marry. If a similar percentage of same-sex cohabiting couples married, roughly 300,000 weddings or civil ceremonies would take place. To put this number in perspective, there were roughly 2.3 million marriages in the United States in 2000.

References

Gary Gates and Jason Ost, *The Gay and Lesbian Atlas* (Washington, DC: Urban Institute Press, 2004); and Tavia Simmons and Martin O'Connell, "Married-Couple and Unmarried-Partner Households," *Census 2000 Special Reports*, CENSR-5 (Washington, DC: U.S. Census Bureau, February 2003).

thus set the stage for later disillusionment when tough decisions about children and money in marriage require a new level of negotiation and compromise to avoid conflict. Some cohabiting couples also may be poorly matched and therefore at greater risk of subsequent divorce. Many enter sexual and cohabiting relationships quickly and without much forethought about whether their partner is "Mr. or Ms. Right."[35] Intimate relationships, even quickly formed or unhealthy ones, often take on a momentum of their own as the relationship progresses inexorably toward marriage. This dynamic plays itself out later in higher divorce rates.

Explanations for Family Change

Many scholars ultimately attribute family changes to fundamental shifts in gender roles in American society. In his seminal 1991 book, *A Treatise on the Family*, Nobel Prize-winning economist Gary Becker identifies declining gender specialization in families as the cause of shifts away from marriage and rising divorce.[36] As the argument goes, men and women bring different comparative advantages to the marriage bargaining table. In the traditional breadwinner-homemaker marriage, men specialize in market work and women specialize in home production, including bearing and rearing children. Men and women "trade" their main assets in the marriage market; each is presumably better off by marrying than by remaining single. In the trade, men who make a good living presumably gain access through marriage to companionship, a sexual partner, someone to keep house, and children (who, in earlier periods of America history, were economic assets available to work on the farm or in the factory). As homemakers, women benefit from men's economic support and protection. This trade is especially the case when women face discrimination in the workplace and lack opportunities for economic self-sufficiency and upward mobility. The gains to marriage also increase if the trade is equitable—that is, when partners share similar characteristics such as physical attractiveness, socioeconomic background, race, and education.

Conversely, the blurring of traditional gender roles reduces the gains to marriage. Not surprisingly, observers often attribute recent declines in marriage to the rapid entry of women into the labor force and to the growth of women's earnings. The benefits of marriage presumably have declined with women's rapid entry into the labor force. Women have become less economically dependent on men, and these economic gains have removed a major incentive for women to marry. Working women are less likely to marry and more likely to divorce when faced with unhappy marriages.

The declining economic fortunes of young men—especially low-skilled minority men—and the rise in the welfare state have presumably reinforced declines in marriage. With greater economic independence, marriage-seeking women are more inclined to search longer for economically attractive male partners. Work subsidizes the marital search. For poorly educated men with low wages, their diminished ability to attract a wife is reflected in their rapidly declining marriage rates over the past several decades. The declines in real wages among low-educated workers as well as rising underemployment, especially in poor minority communities and neighborhoods, have presumably accelerated marriage declines among low-income and minority populations. Sociologist Valerie Oppenheimer has argued that men's changing circumstances—not women's work patterns—have steered America's marriage trends throughout history.[37]

At the same time, government-sponsored subsidies have arguably provided an alternative source of economic support and, therefore, a disincentive to—even a substitute for—marriage. According to critics of welfare, cash assistance has helped women leave their husbands, while also encouraging out-of-wedlock childbearing. The empirical evidence supporting this view, however, is weak.[38]

The benefits from marriage increase with the specialization along traditional gender roles. When mutually beneficial, marriage is the preferred state, and marriage rates are high. To many people, especially the romantically inclined, this coldly rational view of marriage undoubtedly seems anathema to their idealistic notions about the institution. They much prefer to believe that mate selection is largely beyond their control, governed by uncontrollable strong emotions.

Economic perspectives also provide a plausible explanation for racial differences in marriage and family structure. For example, black women's historically higher rates of labor force participation mean that they have always had greater economic independence than white women. Moreover, black men face higher rates of unemployment than do white men, and black men are also less likely to earn a family wage. The marriage imperative, therefore, is lower for black women and other disadvantaged minorities, and marriage rates are expected to be lower for these groups than for economically advantaged populations.

The empirical evidence on these questions, however, is much less compelling.[39] For one thing, delays in marriage have been broadly observed across almost all segments of the U.S. population. This trend has not simply been observed among high earning (and economically independent) women, low-earning or economically unattractive men, or welfare-dependent women. Indeed, highly educated women—those with the *greatest* earnings potential—are more likely than poor women to marry today. And declines in marriage rates have been especially pronounced among the most highly educated men.[40] This decline is seemingly contrary to most economic models of marriage.

Robert Moffitt, a welfare expert at Johns Hopkins University, suggests that the decline in marriage for low-income women reflects the declining earnings of low-educated, low-skilled men who are available for those women to marry.[41] For highly educated women, on the other hand, declines in marriage presumably reflect increases in economic independence associated with their own higher earnings. The important lesson is straightforward: Changes in marriage and family forms may have different causes for different segments of the American population. There is no single cause for declines in marriage, and there is no silver bullet or single prescription that will return America to the days when virtually everyone expected to marry, to stay married, and to have children cared for by a stay-at-home mom (see Box 2).

Widespread declines in marriage among most population groups and the upsurge in alternative living arrangements suggest another explanation for recent changes to family forms in the United States. Pervasive changes in cultural values and attitudes regarding marriage may have played a key role in family change. What causes these cultural values and attitudes to change? Some observers believe that marriage attitudes and values ultimately respond to changes in the economy and to urbanization. Technological changes have also played a large role. The introduction of modern contraception in the early 1960s changed the risks associated with sexual intercourse outside of marriage, including the risk of unintended pregnancy. The media, and television in particular, have also undoubtedly exposed Americans to alternative living arrangements and greater acceptability of sexual activity outside of marriage, while reducing the stigma associated with single parenthood, divorce, and homosexuality. But these media messages may also simply reflect preexisting public attitudes and behavior.

Race and the Family

Any discussion of racial variation in the family must begin with an acknowledgment of the long-standing debate about the strengths and weaknesses of the black family. Ever since the 1965 publication of Daniel Patrick Moynihan's *The Negro Family: The Case for National Action*, the discussion of racial and ethnic group variation in America's families has been culturally sensitive.[42] As Moynihan argued: "At the center of the tangle of pathology is the weakness of the family structure. Once or twice removed, it will be found to be the principal source of most of the aberrant, inadequate, or antisocial behavior that did not establish but now serves to perpetuate the cycle of poverty and deprivation." Critics charged that Moynihan unfairly blamed the victims.

We have learned a good deal more about changing marriage and family patterns among African Americans and other ethnic groups since Moynihan's prescient comments. The family life of blacks remains distinctive in many ways, as we shall report in the next section, and black family trends may be harbingers of change for all Americans.[43]

Nearly 70 percent of African American children are born outside of marriage. Most black children today grow up in female-headed families, which are often poor. If rates of marriage are our measure, traditional marriage occupies a much less central place in the lives of most American blacks than for other Americans. A

DOES EDUCATION HURT WOMEN'S CHANCES FOR MARRIAGE?

The conventional wisdom is that a highly educated young woman often has a difficult time finding a suitable mate for marriage. Presumably, the fear is that prospective husbands may be intimidated by women who are their educational equals or who earn more than they do. Indeed, the typical pattern is that women generally marry up in social status, including educational status. Sociologists call this "marital hypergamy." The implications are clear: As women's education increases, the potential demographic pool of similar or more highly educated men necessarily contracts. Highly educated women may therefore "price" themselves out of the marriage market and jeopardize their chances of marriage. Of course, this expectation also is consistent with standard economic arguments that women's specialization in roles other than homemaker makes them financially independent and therefore less dependent on men for support.

The truth is that the percentage of young women who are currently married does not vary greatly by education level (see figure). In fact, in 2000, unlike in earlier periods, college-educated women ages 25 to 34 were more likely than less-educated women to be married. This pattern is different from 1980, when college-educated women were slightly less likely than other education groups to be married. At the same time, the percentage of women who are married at ages 25 to 34 declined for each education group.

Young women who hope to marry do not need to worry that a good education will ruin their chances for love and marriage. If anything, a good education is now positively associated with getting married and staying married.

Percent of Currently Married Women Ages 25–34 by Education, 1980, 1990, and 2000

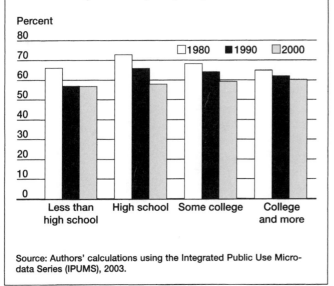

Source: Authors' calculations using the Integrated Public Use Microdata Series (IPUMS), 2003.

disproportionate share of young black mothers have a series of relationships with live-in partners and have children from multiple partners.[44] For black women who do marry, the large majority of their marriages do not last. The implications for intergenerational poverty, long-term welfare dependency, and children's developmental trajectories are real and profound.

These are the unvarnished facts. Their interpretation, however, has been the subject of much debate. Statistics on the black family beg the question about the root causes of these shifts. Are blacks themselves to blame for situations such as unwed childbearing, serial partners, and lack of education? Or are changes in the black family a product of racial oppression, economic inequality, and the lack of equal access to mainstream social and educational institutions? Is this trend a failure of our economic or political system? Or is the current state of the black family a cultural legacy of matrifocal family patterns extending back to slavery—when legal marriage was often denied to blacks, when the family unit centered on slave women and their children, and when black men were denied their traditional patriarchal roles as the family head and economic provider?

Census data alone cannot answer all these questions. The data can, however, provide a first glimpse of the changes in black marriage and family patterns from 1990 to 2000. A voluminous literature on African American family life also provides a social and political context for studying other minority and immigrant groups. Sociologist R. Salvador Oropesa, for example, has coined the term "paradox of Mexican American nuptiality," meaning that the currently high rates of marriage among both U.S.-born and immigrant Mexicans suggest a strong basis for cultural explanations of marriage.[45] Indeed, Mexican Americans, while often sharing the same impoverished circumstances as African Americans, exhibit much different patterns of marriage and family structure. Culture may trump economics. Whether foreign-born Mexicans will adopt the marriage and family patterns of the white majority as they blend into American society, or instead will maintain their cultural heritage of strong families, is far from certain. Mexican Americans are also much more likely than blacks to marry whites.

The typically stable families of most Asian Americans have been widely applauded as a source of great strength and upward social mobility. But in many ways, Asian Americans, as a panethnic group, are considerably more heterogeneous than Hispanics, who come from different Spanish-speaking countries but share certain cultural traits such as language and religion. Pan-Asian averages, on the other hand, may mask wide differences among different Asian-origin populations. Asians differ widely on language, religion, and economic resources. Chinese and Japanese have been in the United States in large numbers for more than 100 years, while other

Asian minorities have only recently arrived in the United States. Many are refugees, such as Cambodians and Vietnamese, who lack the same economic resources that often characterize Asian and other immigrants who entered the country long ago. The experiences of recent Asian immigrant groups have been different in uncertain ways from those of other Asian immigrant groups with large third-generation populations. Fortunately, the 2000 Census provides an unprecedented opportunity to chart the family and demographic experiences of diverse pan-Asian ethnic groups, and also to compare these groups with diverse groups of African Americans, Hispanics, and non-Hispanic whites.

RACIAL DIVERSITY: DELAYED MARRIAGE OR NO MARRIAGE?

Race is only one dimension of diversity. Indeed, America's new racial diversity does not necessarily connote a new diversity of attitudes, values, or behavior. The fact that most young people—of every race and creed—hope to marry, illustrates this point.

For Americans who would like to marry, previous research has shown that most of them will realize their aspirations for marriage, regardless of race. Typically, most groups do not forgo marriage, but simply delay it.[46] Less clear is whether the recent trend toward postponement of marriage is similar for most racial or ethnic groups, or whether some groups have had higher nonmarriage rates in the 1990s. Demographers usually measure the timing of marriage by showing how the percentage married differs by age group. Declines in the percentage of young adults, say at ages 20 to 24, who have married during their lives (including currently married, divorced, and widowed persons) suggest a pattern of marital delay. On the other hand, permanent singlehood is often represented by the percentage who have never married later in life. The likelihood of a first marriage declines with age and is very low among older Americans, so the percentage never married, at ages 50 to 54 for example, is therefore a good indicator of the level of singlehood in society.

Delayed Marriage

Young Americans today are not especially anxious to rush into marriage. In 1980, nearly one-half of women and one-third of men ages 20 to 24 were or had been married. Nearly 80 percent of women and 68 percent of men ages 25 to 29 had married (see Figure 1). By 2000, 63 percent of women and 52 percent of men had married. Women marry earlier than men. Generally, men catch up at later ages, perhaps as they become more secure financially. Clearly, young men and women in

their 20s are much less likely to tie the knot today; most wait to marry until they have finished school and established themselves in their jobs, usually by their late 20s.

We begin our discussion of racial diversity in marriage timing by examining broad racial and ethnic trends in delayed marriage. Not surprisingly, the overall U.S. trend directly reflects continuing delays in marriage among non-Hispanic whites. Only 38 percent of black women ages 25 to 29 had ever been married in 2000 (see Table 1). This is a large decline from 1980, when 63 percent of black women had married. African American women continued to have a sharper downward trend in marriage than women from other racial groups. The drop among Asian women ages 25 to 29 was also very rapid over this period, from 76 percent to 59 percent. Yet, in 2000, 81 percent of Asian women ages 30 to 34 had married. For black women, on the other hand, the percentage ever married was still very low by ages 30 to 34—56 percent, compared with the national figure of 79 percent.

Today, Hispanics wed much earlier than other racial and ethnic groups. But like other groups over the last 20 years, Hispanics are also significantly delaying marriage. In 2000, about 10 percent of Hispanic female teenagers had married, compared with 6 percent of all female teens. Moreover, 42 percent of Hispanic women had married by ages 20 to 24, a figure higher than any racial or ethnic group considered here. For these age ranges, there is little evidence of convergence with the marital patterns of white women, and it seems that age patterns of marital timing have diverged between Hispanic women and white women. By ages 30 to 34, however, the percentages of white women and Asian women who had married were similar to the rate for Hispanic women.

The potential impact on American society of rapid increases in the Asian American and Hispanic populations is magnified by the growing diversity of these groups in their countries of origin. The diverse experiences of these ethnic groups are clearly reflected in their marriage patterns. Of the various Asian American populations, Japanese, Korean, and Chinese women had the lowest percentages of 15-to-24-year-olds in 2000 who were currently married or had been married (see Table 2, page 180). However, the percentage of these groups who were ever married converges with other Asian ethnic groups by ages 45 to 54. In other words, Japanese, Koreans, and Chinese delayed marriage to a greater extent than other Asians. Japanese men are the exception to this marriage delay. The percentage of Japanese men who had gotten married by ages 45 to 54 was high (84 percent) but remained considerably lower than the rate for other groups.

In contrast, Asian Indians marry at much earlier ages than other Asian Americans. Among Asian Indians in 2000, about one-quarter of women ages 15 to 24 were married, as were 63 percent of men and 84 percent of women ages 25 to 34, and 97 percent of men and women

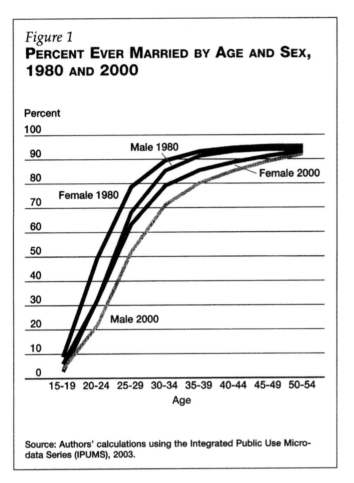

Figure 1

PERCENT EVER MARRIED BY AGE AND SEX, 1980 AND 2000

Percent

Male 1980

Female 2000

Female 1980

Male 2000

15-19 20-24 25-29 30-34 35-39 40-44 45-49 50-54

Age

Source: Authors' calculations using the Integrated Public Use Microdata Series (IPUMS), 2003.

cultural prescriptions regarding traditional mate selection practices favored by their parents and grandparents.

Regardless of country of origin, most Hispanics marry at earlier ages than Asians. The percentage married is particularly high for Mexicans ages 15 to 24. For this age group, 19 percent of men and 29 percent of women were already married in 2000. In contrast, Puerto Ricans had the lowest percentage ever married for every age group. These percentages are closer to those of African Americans than to other Hispanic groups, because Puerto Ricans and blacks share similar social and economic disadvantages.

Permanent Singlehood

A once common card game, "Old Maid," left little doubt about attitudes toward marriage and toward women who remained single. In this game, the "loser" is the one stuck with the card showing the old maid. There is no male version of "Old Maid." Instead, older single men are more likely to be stereotyped as immature or irresponsible, as swinging bachelors or playboys, or as gay.

The truth is that Americans remain single for many reasons, and stereotypes change slowly. Indeed, singlehood is often freely chosen today. Some people choose to be unmarried and celibate. Some people give higher priority to their careers than to marriage and children. Still others, such as gays and lesbians, are simply unlikely to enter into heterosexual marriages. Some people, despite their aspirations, are unable to find someone to marry. Still, the main point remains: Whether by choice or not, only a small percentage of men and women remain single throughout their lifetimes.

Yet, as Figure 2 (page 181) shows, the low incidence of singlehood may be changing, albeit slowly. For each panethnic group shown in Figure 2, the proportion never married by ages 50 to 54 increased between 1980 and 2000. For some smaller groups, change has been modest or nonexistent. For example, in 2000, only about

ages 45 to 54. This may reflect the prominent role that parents play in Asian Indian families, especially in arranging marriages for their children.[47] Asian Indians consist of mostly first- and second-generation Americans, who maintain strong cultural traditions and family unity. But the historical experiences of other immigrant populations suggest that this pattern of early marriage among Asian Indians is likely to shift as the children of today's second generation grow into adulthood and cast aside

Table 1

PERCENT OF WOMEN EVER MARRIED BY AGE AND RACE/ETHNICITY, 1980 AND 2000

Age group	White 1980	White 2000	Black 1980	Black 2000	Hispanic 1980	Hispanic 2000	Asian 1980	Asian 2000	American Indian 1980	American Indian 2000
Total	72	72	58	51	69	66	71	68	68	62
15–19	9	5	5	5	13	10	5	5	12	6
20–24	52	33	33	17	55	42	39	23	54	33
25–29	81	68	63	38	80	68	76	59	79	58
30–34	91	83	78	56	89	80	89	81	90	73
35–39	95	89	86	66	92	85	92	89	93	79
40–44	96	91	89	72	93	88	93	92	94	85
45–49	96	93	92	80	93	91	95	94	95	89
50–54	96	95	93	85	94	92	95	94	96	92

Source: Authors' calculations using the Integrated Public Use Microdata Series (IPUMS), 2003.

Table 2
PERCENT EVER MARRIED BY NATIONAL ORIGIN FOR U.S. ASIANS AND HISPANICS, BY AGE AND SEX, 2000

Age and sex	Asian						Hispanic			
	Chinese	Japanese	Filipino	Asian Indian	Korean	Southeast Asian	Mexican	Puerto Rican	Cuban	South and Central American
Men										
15–24	6	7	7	8	6	7	19	13	14	14
25–34	49	43	52	63	48	49	65	57	65	58
35–44	87	72	84	92	92	83	84	76	82	81
45–54	94	84	93	97	98	93	91	86	88	90
Women										
15–24	10	11	12	24	9	17	29	18	20	24
25–34	66	61	71	84	64	68	76	63	77	71
35–44	90	85	89	95	95	89	88	80	90	86
45–54	94	91	92	97	98	93	92	87	92	89

Source: Authors' calculations using the Integrated Public Use Microdata Series (IPUMS), 2003.

6 percent of whites and Asians and about 10 percent of Hispanics and American Indians remained unmarried by ages 50 to 54. For American blacks, the changes in singlehood have been more substantial. The percentage still single nearly doubled among black women, from 8 percent in 1980 to 15 percent in 2000. The percentage of single black men experienced a similar increase, from 9 percent in 1980 to 15 percent in 2000. Clearly, for African Americans, the retreat from marriage is both one of delayed marriage and growing singlehood.

What do these data forecast for today's young people? Our estimates of the percentage of people remaining single are based on the actual experiences of men and women born shortly after World War II (the 1945-to-1949 birth cohort). Significantly, the trajectory of recent trends implies much higher future levels of permanent singlehood; for black women in particular, nearly one-third of black women in their early 30s today will remain single during their lifetimes if current trends continue. Singlehood for these black women is well on its way to being an alternative to marriage. This is a very different situation from the past. There is little evidence to indicate that the decades-old declines in marriage among blacks ended in the 1990s. Trends in marriage and family life have not responded positively to improvements among blacks over recent decades in average education, occupational status, and earnings. The implication seems clear: Family change is not rooted simply in economics. Of course, averages hide the situation of lower-class disadvantaged blacks, whose marriage patterns may have diverged from middle-class blacks.[48]

The data in Figure 2 also reveal wide differences between the percentages of men and women who had married during their lives and those who were still married. These differences are driven mostly by patterns of divorce and subsequent remarriage. For whites, a much higher percentage of men than women are currently married. Older women are much more likely than older men to be currently divorced; this gender difference widened during the 1990s and reflects both the upward trend in divorce rates and declining remarriage rates during the young adult years of post-World War II women. Essentially, women are disadvantaged in the remarriage market. For one thing, the ratio of men to women decreases with age. Opportunities for marriage become more unfavorable for women and more favorable for men as they get older. The effects of demographic imbalances between the sexes are compounded by the seeming preferences of divorced men to remarry younger women. Most divorced women have custody of their children and therefore have fewer opportunities to remarry.[49] Prospective husbands may be unwilling to assume the burden of parenting another man's children, especially if the supply of childless single women is abundant.

The marriage patterns of black women are particularly affected by a unique set of disadvantages. Sex ratio imbalances are large in the black population (especially in inner-city neighborhoods), reflecting much higher death rates and prison incarceration rates among black men. In 2000, there were 89 black men ages 25 to 44 for every 100 black women of the same age.[50] By definition, demographic shortages of black men mean that 11 percent of America's black women of marriageable age will not have a black partner. This shortage is compounded if we also consider black men's marriageability. High unemployment and low earnings among the black male population provide a poor basis for getting and staying married. Not surprisingly, compared with other racial and ethnic groups, an unusually large share (roughly 40 percent) of older black women are currently divorced and not likely to remarry. The percentage divorced changed very little between 1980 and 2000. In 2000, less than 45 percent of black women were married, although 85 percent had been married at some point in their lives.

DIVERSE FAMILY AND HOUSEHOLD FORMS

Unmarried Americans of all ages have many lifestyle options. They can live alone or with other relatives, they can cohabit (without much stigma), or they can move in with friends or other nonrelatives. If divorced, they need not remarry. This means that families and households are different today than in the past, as mar-

riage has lost some of its cultural grip on contemporary American society. Sociologists Sara McLanahan and Lynne Casper documented shifts from 1980 to 2000 in the number of female-headed families, male-headed families with children, and cohabiting couples.[51] McLanahan and Casper provided a convincing case that declines in marriage and rising marital instability have profoundly affected American family life.

Trends in the 1990s

Our results for the 1990s show that the percentage of white married-couple households continued to decline, from 63 percent in 1990 to 58 percent in 2000 (see Table 3, page 182). Traditional families—a working husband, his nonworking wife, and their children—declined from 14 percent in 1990 to 11 percent in 2000. The tradi-

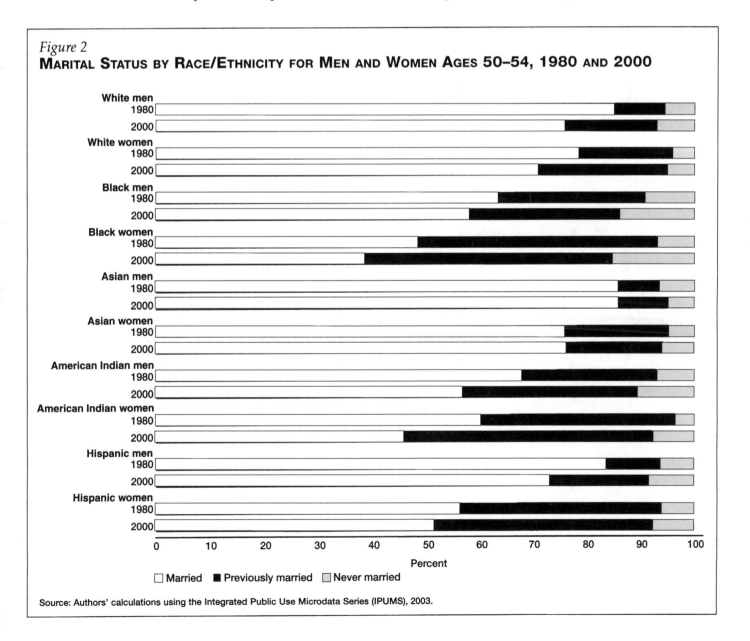

Figure 2
MARITAL STATUS BY RACE/ETHNICITY FOR MEN AND WOMEN AGES 50–54, 1980 AND 2000

□ Married ■ Previously married □ Never married

Source: Authors' calculations using the Integrated Public Use Microdata Series (IPUMS), 2003.

tional family represents only a small fraction of all households today.

Families represented by stay-at-home fathers are still relatively rare. As a percentage of all households, those households with homemaker fathers and working mothers increased slowly, from 1.2 percent to 1.9 percent between 1990 and 2000. There is little indication that husbands and wives now play interchangeable roles in the home and in the workplace, or even that couples are moving in this direction. In a large share of American families, women are still the caretakers of family members. They continue to do the lion's share of household chores and child care, even as they have entered the workforce in large numbers.[52]

Growth in less-traditional households predominated in the 1990s. The current interest in new family forms is rooted not only in recent demographic trends but also in new federal and state welfare policies implemented with passage of welfare reform in 1996. Early evidence in Minnesota, New Jersey, and other states suggests that time-limited welfare and the new emphasis on work and family may have resulted in declining nonmarital fertility rates, lower headship rates among teen mothers, and transitions to marriage rather than cohabitation among single mothers.[53] The implication is that, compared with the 1980s, recent rates of female headship may have stabilized or even declined among historically disadvantaged population groups, including blacks and Latinos. Results from the 2000 Census provide a mixed picture, at least for the 1990s. The share of unmarried female-headed households actually increased slightly during the 1990s, from 22 percent to 24 percent. But the share of households headed by previously married (mostly divorced) women with children declined slightly, from 9 percent to 8 percent; households headed by never-married women with children increased slightly, from 2 percent to 3 percent. Most female-headed households with children result from divorce rather than from out-of-wedlock childbearing. Together, female-headed families with children numbered nearly 8 million, or slightly less than 10 percent of all U.S. families in 2000.[54]

While some studies provide evidence that paternal involvement is associated with more positive behavior among children and adolescents, the evidence remains surprisingly weak or inconclusive. It is unclear whether fathers matter beyond providing a regular child support check.[55] Most judges still routinely award child custody to mothers rather than to fathers. Divorced fathers are increasingly seeking custody of their children, but few are awarded custody. Although unmarried male-headed households increased from 14 percent of all households in 1990 to 16 percent in 2000, comparatively few of them involved children. Most of these households were single men living alone. Families headed by unmarried men with children represented only a small fraction of all households and increased only slightly, from 1.6 percent in 1990 to 2.1 percent in 2000. Moreover, a significant share of single fathers do not live alone; they often have other adult caretakers in the home to help out (see Box 3).

In 2000, cohabiting couples headed 6 percent of all American households. It is common to assume that unmarried cohabitation is simply an extension of dating. Cohabitation provides an opportunity for young people to experiment with alternative lifestyles and new adult roles. But this rationale is not true for all cohabitors. Our estimates indicate that a surprisingly large share of cohabitors—43 percent—had coresidential minor children. Many of these families resemble typical married-couple families, with the children the biological offspring of both partners. And a 2004 study based on data from the 1999 *National Survey of America's Families* reported that 28 percent of children in cohabiting-couple households were born into them.[56] Although cohabitation has increased rapidly over the past decade or so, cohabiting-couple households still represent only a small fraction of all households. Only now is research helping us to better understand the developmental consequences of parental cohabitation—which is often a highly transitory arrangement—on children's cognitive and psychosocial development.[57]

Cross-sectional data from the 2000 Census misrepresent the demographic significance of cohabitation in American society. These data seriously underrepresent lifetime experiences of cohabitation; well over one-half of young persons are currently cohabiting or have cohabited in the past.[58] But most cohabiting unions do not last very

Table 3

PERCENT OF MAJOR FAMILY FORMS BY RACE/ETHNICITY, 1990 AND 2000

Family head	White		Black		Hispanic		Asian		American Indian	
	1990	2000	1990	2000	1990	2000	1990	2000	1990	2000
Unmarried man	14	17	15	17	12	13	11	12	16	19
Unmarried woman	18	20	42	42	21	21	13	14	27	28
Married couple	63	58	37	34	60	59	67	64	52	47
Other types	5	5	6	7	7	7	9	9	5	6

Source: Authors' calculations using the Integrated Public Use Microdata Series (IPUMS), 2003.

long. Recent evidence indicates that one-half or more of all first unions (cohabitations and marriages combined) are cohabitations. The majority of cohabiting unions end in marriage rather than disruption, although there is some new evidence that marriage rates are lower if co-residential children are biologically related to only one of the partners.[59] Poor women are less likely than nonpoor women in a cohabiting relationship to marry. Less than 25 percent of poor women marry within five years of entering a cohabiting union; the largest share separate.[60]

Racial and Ethnic Differences

The families and households of American blacks continue to be distinctive among the racial and ethnic groups considered in Table 3. Data from the 2000 Census show that married-couple families constituted the majority of households for all major racial and ethnic groups, except for African Americans. Only about one-third of all black households were headed by married couples. Instead, unmarried women headed two-fifths of black households. There is little evidence from the 1990s that the shift from married-couple households to households headed by single women has abated in the black community.

The percentage of traditional, one-earner married-couple families continued to decline in the 1990s. In 2000, such families accounted for only 10 percent of white households, 4 percent of black households, 8 percent of American Indian households, 14 percent of Asian American households, and 15 percent of Hispanic households (see Figure 3, page 184). The comparatively high percentage of traditional families among Hispanics, on the other hand, reinforces the commonplace perception that some Hispanic groups have retained their strong family values and social support. In fact, for all racial groups except Hispanics, dual-earner married-couple families with children outnumbered traditional families 2-to-1. Dual-earner Hispanic families were only about 6 percentage points more prevalent than traditional Hispanic families. For all groups, dual-earner married couples were the most common category, and for all groups except Hispanics, married-couple families without children exceeded the number of traditional families.

The number of female-headed households continued to climb in the 1990s for each racial and ethnic group. As shown in Figure 4 (page 184), a woman living alone represented the most common type of female-headed household among whites and Asians. For African American households, never-married and previously married single women with children outnumbered those living alone. The high percentage among African Americans undoubtedly reflects the high share of unmarried women—the result of past nonmarital fertility, divorce, low remarriage, and early widowhood (reflecting high mortality among black males). Black

---

Box 3

SINGLE FATHERS RAISING CHILDREN ALONE . . . OR NOT?

The media often ballyhoo the fact that more single fathers now have sole or joint custody of their children. The obvious implication is that these men—mostly divorced—are both the primary provider and, more significantly, the primary caretaker for their children. But this media attention gives the wrong impression about men's changing roles in families. In fact, a high percentage of single fathers are not raising children alone (see table). This table includes single fathers who are householders as well as those who are family members. Significantly, the rise in single-father families with children has occurred simultaneously with declining shares, between 1990 and 2000, of fathers raising their children alone.

This trend is especially true for disadvantaged minority fathers. In 2000, among black single fathers, only about 50 percent were living alone with their children. The other fathers were living with a cohabiting female partner or with their parent(s). Among Hispanic men, the percentage of single fathers living alone with their children was only about 40 percent. For white and Asian men, roughly two-thirds were living alone with their children, without any help from their mothers or their live-in girlfriends. Other data from Census 2000 also show that college-educated fathers are overrepresented among fathers living alone with their children. Fathers who are high school dropouts are much more likely to be living with other women who may be both economic providers and caretakers.

Living Arrangements of Single Fathers by Race and Ethnicity, 1990 and 2000

Race/ethnicity	Living with parents (%)		Cohabiting (%)		Living by themselves (%)	
	1990	2000	1990	2000	1990	2000
White	10	10	22	25	68	65
Black	24	24	24	26	52	50
American Indian	17	20	37	34	46	47
Asian	15	17	18	20	67	63
Hispanic	13	15	39	44	47	41

Source: Authors' calculations using the Integrated Public Use Microdata Series (IPUMS), 2003.

---

female-headed families contrast vividly with Hispanic female-headed families: A much smaller percentage of Hispanic women lived alone.

The percentage of households headed by cohabiting women with children is very low for each racial group (below 3 percent), but especially so among whites and Asians. This trend is true even for Hispanics, who have a long history of consensual or informal unions. However, racial differences in the percentage of households headed by previously married (mostly divorced) women with children are also large: 13 percent for African Americans, 10 percent for American Indians, 9

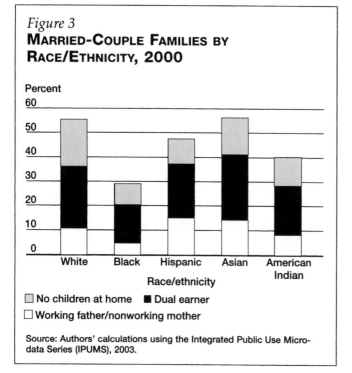

Figure 3

MARRIED-COUPLE FAMILIES BY RACE/ETHNICITY, 2000

Percent

Race/ethnicity

☐ No children at home   ■ Dual earner
☐ Working father/nonworking mother

Source: Authors' calculations using the Integrated Public Use Micro-data Series (IPUMS), 2003.

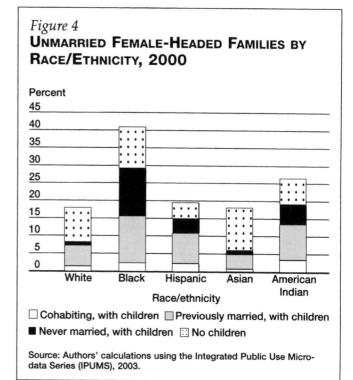

Figure 4

UNMARRIED FEMALE-HEADED FAMILIES BY RACE/ETHNICITY, 2000

Percent

Race/ethnicity

☐ Cohabiting, with children   ☐ Previously married, with children
■ Never married, with children   ⬚ No children

Source: Authors' calculations using the Integrated Public Use Micro-data Series (IPUMS), 2003.

percent for Hispanics, 6 percent for whites, and 4 percent for Asian Americans. These differences reflect, at least in part, significant racial differentials in divorce and remarriage. Specifically, African Americans have higher levels of divorce and lower rates of remarriage compared with other racial groups.

Large racial differences are probably most evident when it comes to households headed by never-married women with children. In 2000, never-married women with children headed 14 percent of African American households, a reflection of much higher rates of out-of-wedlock childbearing among black women (about 70 percent) than the national average (about 33 percent). The percentage of out-of-wedlock children was 5 percent among American Indians, 4 percent among Hispanics, and 1 percent among whites and Asians.

Households headed by men with children were on the rise in the 1990s (see Figure 5), but the increase was modest for each racial group. Unlike female-headed households, the overwhelming share of male households involved men living alone. In 2000, these shares ranged from a high of about 12 percent for white men to a low of 6 percent for Hispanic men. Only small shares of male-headed households included children: from 1 percent to 3 percent for each racial group. Cohabiting families with children that were headed by men represented around 1 percent to 2 percent—a range very similar to that of cohabiting families with children headed by single women.

Our analysis of the 1980, 1990, and 2000 censuses shows that multigenerational households vary substantially by race. Although multigenerational families have

increased steadily among whites since 1980, these families represent less than 2 percent of all households. But the percentages of these families are two to three times greater among blacks, American Indians, and Hispanics; and roughly 50 percent higher among Asians. Except for blacks, the percentage of multigenerational families among all these groups increased in the 1990s, and the percentage increased faster for American Indians, Hispanics, and Asians than it did for whites. Doubling up in multigenerational households is sometimes viewed as an adaptation to economic hardship. These data provide little indication of racial convergence in the prevalence of multigenerational households and, by implication, of economic well-being. Clearly, there is little indication that racial variation in multigenerational households has converged recently, and this variation also suggests that, in the 1990s, the multigenerational household has changed in ways that suggest less economic inequality and less need for household adaptation.

Asian and Hispanic Diversity

Substantial diversity within the Asian American and Hispanic populations is apparent in their family forms. In 2000, 20 percent of Asian Indian households are defined as traditional families (see Table 4). In fact, Asian Indians top all other ethnic groups in the percentage of households headed by married couples. This standing is balanced by extremely low percentages for Asian Indians of unmarried male- and female-headed households, indicating the importance of marriage and traditional family values for Asian Indian families.

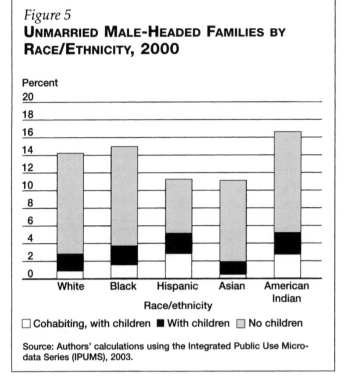

Figure 5

UNMARRIED MALE-HEADED FAMILIES BY RACE/ETHNICITY, 2000

Percent

□ Cohabiting, with children ■ With children □ No children

Source: Authors' calculations using the Integrated Public Use Microdata Series (IPUMS), 2003.

In contrast, only 8 percent of Filipino households are traditional families. Yet, among U.S. Asians, Filipinos have the highest percentage of households headed by working couples with children. Unlike some other Asian populations, Filipino families are unusually egalitarian, and traditional patrilineal principles are weak.[61] Filipinos have advantages in their occupational training

for U.S. labor markets (a high percentage of Filipinos are health-care providers); their job skills (especially English-speaking ability); and the cultural and economic effects brought by America's long military presence in the Philippines. Filipino women take more active economic roles in the family than do most women from other racial minorities, and this active role also helps explain the higher percentage of Filipino households headed by previously married women. Compared with women from other Asian ethnic groups, Filipino women tend to end unhappy marriages.

Single-person households are relatively more common among Japanese Americans, perhaps reflecting an older age structure. Less than two-fifths of Japanese households are single-person households (14 percent for women only and 18 percent for men only). Most Japanese Americans are U.S.-born (reflecting low recent immigration rates). Their incorporation into the social and economic fabric of American society is reflected in many ways, including their scattered residential patterns throughout many big city neighborhoods. Surprisingly, interracial marriage is very high for Japanese Americans (discussed below); their families have often been in the United States for decades and have adopted the ways of most U.S.-born white Americans, such as language and standards of consumption. Very low fertility among Japanese Americans also means, in the event of divorce, that fewer parents will have to raise children in single-parent families.

Among the various Hispanic groups in the United States, the traditional family household is most common among Mexicans (18 percent) and least common among

Table 4

PERCENT OF HOUSEHOLD FORMS BY NATIONAL ORIGIN FOR U.S. ASIANS AND HISPANICS, 2000

Ethnicity/ national origin	Married-couple			Female-headed				Male-headed			
	Working father/ nonworking mother	Dual-earner	No children	Cohabiting, with children	Previously married, with children	Never married, with children	Living alone	Cohabiting, with children	Unmarried, with children	Living alone	Other
Asian American											
Chinese	13	28	16	0	3	0	8	0	1	10	19
Japanese	13	18	17	0	4	0	14	0	1	18	14
Filipino	8	34	13	1	7	1	7	1	1	6	21
Asian Indian	20	26	20	0	2	0	5	0	1	11	16
Korean	17	22	14	0	5	0	11	0	1	9	20
Southeast Asian	15	27	11	1	6	2	4	1	2	6	24
Hispanic											
Mexican	18	23	10	2	8	3	3	3	2	6	22
Puerto Rican	9	18	10	4	12	9	8	3	2	9	18
Cuban	11	25	15	1	8	2	6	2	2	9	20
South and Central American	14	23	11	2	9	3	4	3	2	6	24

Source: Authors' calculations using the Integrated Public Use Microdata Series (IPUMS), 2003.

Puerto Ricans (9 percent). Family forms of Puerto Ricans mirror those of African Americans. In 2000, for example, 4 percent of Puerto Rican families in the United States were cohabiting households with children, 12 percent were previously married female-headed households with children, and 9 percent were never-married female-headed households with children. The high percentage of female-headed single families with children among Puerto Ricans in the United States reflects many factors, including the high levels of unemployment and low wages facing many Puerto Ricans in economically declining labor market areas in the Northeast. Such factors can reduce the marriage pool and the economic foundations of existing marriages.[62]

FAMILY CHANGE AND CHILDREN AT RISK

In *A Generation at Risk: Growing Up in an Era of Family Upheaval*, Paul Amato and Alan Booth chronicled the recent unprecedented transformation of America's children. Over the past four decades, children have been buffeted by the strong winds of family change—increased maternal employment, high divorce rates, growing rates of out-of-wedlock childbearing, and increased rates of cohabitation. The decisions parents make about family life profoundly affect their children—for good or ill.[63] A concern for the family's effect on children's well-being has prompted the U.S. government to become much more interested and active in family policy.

Indeed, children are a public good. All Americans have a clear stake in ensuring that today's children grow into healthy and productive citizens. Today's children will become tomorrow's parents, spouses, and employees. The government's interest in marriage is probably best reflected in the reauthorized welfare bill, which proposes to spend federal dollars to promote marriage and reduce divorce, mostly through counseling and marriage education. But expansions in the federal and state Earned Income Tax Credit (EITC), Medicaid, child tax credit, and childcare subsidies also have strengthened the economic foundations of America's families. In a 2004 study, economists Craig Gunderson and James Ziliak show that after-tax poverty was reduced in the 1990s more by EITC expansions ("making work pay") than by either welfare reform or the economic boom.[64] Such policies have helped address real concerns that rapid family change has placed a greater share of America's children at risk.

Children's Living Arrangements

To fully understand the changing family circumstances of children, we need to highlight the situation of chil-

dren rather than infer their circumstances from changes in households or families. Indeed, children's family living arrangements have changed significantly over the past few decades, but even though the pace of children's changing circumstances slowed during the 1990s, racial disparities regarding these changes remained large (see Box 4).

Figure 6 shows the percentage of children living in various household types. The typical national pattern was for children to live with a working married couple, although the share of children in this category declined to about 41 percent in 2000. In 2000, 21 percent of children lived in traditional families (working father and stay-at-home mother), down slightly from 24 percent in 1990. These new data provide the basis for another significant finding: Only a fraction of America's children are cared for by stay-at-home married mothers. Not long ago, Americans believed that this family form was the ideal child-care arrangement, especially for young children. Many people believed that mothers who chose otherwise selfishly put their own interests and ambitions above the interests of their family and children, and that working mothers risked harming their children's development. If actions speak louder than words, most Americans no longer believe this to be true.

In fact, most children are now raised by two working parents. And although the numbers for these categories remained small in 2000, children also are increasingly either living with their fathers, with never-married mothers, or with cohabiting couples or grandparents. For example, from 1990 to 2000, the percentage of children living with fathers increased from 1.7 percent to 2.3 percent, while the share of children living with never-married mothers increased from 3.8 percent to 5.0 percent. The number of children in cohabiting-couple households increased an astounding 50 percent during this same period, but still only grew from 2.8 percent to 4.1 percent of all children. Unfortunately, our understanding of the developmental consequences of these arrangements for children remains incomplete. We do know that, on average, children do better in married-couple families, but the majority of children in other kinds of family arrangements also grow up to be productive and well-adjusted citizens.[65] Growing up in single-parent families or in another nontraditional arrangement does not automatically bring unhappiness.

With the passage of welfare reform legislation in 1996, some scholars were concerned that single mothers would lose their welfare eligibility and that the children of those mothers would suffer. Another fear was that these mothers would be unable to adequately care for their children, and these mothers would turn this responsibility over to their own parents or other relatives. Indeed, from 1990 to 2000, the percentage of children living in families headed by their grandparents increased from 5 percent to 6 percent (see Figure 6).

ADULT CHILDREN LIVING AT HOME WITH THEIR PARENTS

Early adulthood is marked by a rapid succession of significant changes. It is a time to finish school, leave home for the first time, find a job, get married, and have children. More recently, with delays in marriage, many young adults have moved back into their parents' homes. Some young adults never left, because living with parents was both convenient and inexpensive. Some young adults found it difficult to maintain the economic lifestyle they had experienced while growing up. Others got divorced, had children outside of marriage, or were between jobs and needed a helping hand.

As shown in the figure, roughly 30 percent of young adults ages 18 to 29, regardless of race or ethnicity, lived with one or both of their parents in 1980, 1990, and 2000. The rate was lowest among Hispanics and whites, and highest among American Indians, blacks, and Asians. While the share of young adults increased during the 1980s, the percentage declined slightly for all racial and ethnic groups in the 1990s. This occurred at the same time that young adults were delaying marriage.

Percent of Young Adults Living With Parents by Race, 1980, 1990, and 2000

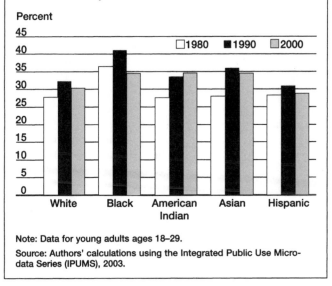

Note: Data for young adults ages 18–29.

Source: Authors' calculations using the Integrated Public Use Microdata Series (IPUMS), 2003.

These children are often at serious risk for poverty and developmental delays. Few people would blame the grandparents for these risks. Parents' physical or mental health problems, child abuse, substance abuse, and divorce are often factors in children going to live with grandparents. Some incorrigible adolescents may move in with their grandparents to provide relief to their parents. To be sure, many grandparents gladly assume responsibility for their grandchildren in a time of need. But the added responsibility of raising grandchildren can be psychologically and economically burdensome for grandparents.

Figure 6

CHILDREN'S LIVING ARRANGEMENTS, 1990 AND 2000

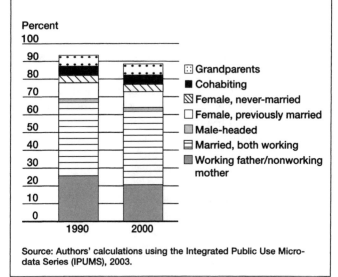

Source: Authors' calculations using the Integrated Public Use Microdata Series (IPUMS), 2003.

For children, the developmental risks associated with family changes are distributed unequally across America's racial and ethnic populations (see Table 5, page 188). Data from the 2000 Census show that Asian American children were most likely to live in traditional families (26 percent), followed by white children (24 percent) and Hispanic children (22 percent). Only 6 percent of African American children and 14 percent of American Indian children lived in traditional families. White children were most likely to live with two parents who are in the labor force (48 percent), followed by Asian American children (44 percent). Children living in cohabiting-couple families showed substantial racial diversity—9 percent of American Indian children lived with their cohabiting parent, while only 1 percent of Asian American children lived in such an arrangement.

Disparities by race in the number of children living alone with their fathers are minimal, but large disparities exist among children living with single mothers. In 2000, 20 percent of African American children lived with single mothers who were never married, and another 15 percent lived with single mothers who were previously married. White, American Indian, Asian American, and Hispanic children are much less likely to live with single mothers. Grandparents also apparently play a much larger parenting role among black and American Indian families than in other families. The high percentages of historically disadvantaged children living with single parents (and the comparatively large role of grandparents in their childrearing) are often interpreted as marks of families in crisis. A more benign interpretation is that disadvantaged families have developed more flexible family roles and patterns of kin support as an adaptive response to economic hardship. The incidence of children living with grandparents can be interpreted as a measure of family strength rather than family weakness.

Family Structure and Child Poverty

Children's economic welfare is inextricably tied to their family living arrangements. Indeed, the effects of single parenthood on various developmental outcomes are mediated in part by changes in income. One study showed that roughly one-half of the association between single parents and the various negative outcomes of their adolescent children was due to declines in income.[66]

Divorce is associated with increased poverty and declines in family income.[67] A divorced woman loses her husband's income, which typically represents the largest share of predivorce family income. Yet women often must be the sole financial support for their children. For single women, many were poor before they had children; childbearing only served to reinforce their cycle of poverty. For both single and divorced women, marriage or remarriage is often the best route to economic recovery.[68]

The good news from the 1990s is that the percentage of children living in poor families declined (see Figure 7). Perhaps surprisingly, the decline was most dramatic among children living in never-married female-headed families. More than 70 percent of children in these families lived below the poverty line in 1990, but less than 60 percent were poor in 2000. Some observers have attributed the improved economic circumstances of these children to the 1996 creation of a new welfare system emphasizing that welfare was temporary and that single mothers must find jobs. Other observers believe that job growth simply reflected the robust performance of the economy in the last half of the 1990s. More poor mothers were able to enter the labor force, if only at low-wage, low-skill jobs. Still, in

2000, close to three-fifths of children in never-married female-headed families remained poor.

However, welfare reform and a strong economy did little to reduce long-standing racial or ethnic differences in children's economic well-being. In 2000, racial and ethnic variation in child poverty in the United States was enormous. Official rates varied from a low of only 5 percent among Japanese American children to a high of 35 percent among Dominican children. Child poverty rates also exceeded 30 percent among non-Hispanic blacks, American Indians, and Puerto Ricans. These rates are high by almost any standard.

Child poverty may largely reflect variations in family structure that result from out-of-wedlock childbearing, divorce, and cohabitation. Poverty rates were lowest in 2000 for children living in families headed by married couples (4 percent), and highest among children living alone with never-married mothers (58 percent) and previously married mothers (34 percent). The official poverty rate for children living with a cohabiting parent and co-resident partner also was very high (38 percent). These high rates were also observed among all the racial and ethnic groups studied in this report.

Differences in children's living arrangements are not, by themselves, responsible for inequality across these racial and ethnic groups. Within each family type, historically disadvantaged children—blacks, Puerto Ricans, and American Indians—had substantially higher poverty rates than their white or Asian American counterparts. For example, the poverty rate for black children living in married-couple families was 14 percent, but only 5 percent for white children living in married-couple families. Similarly, the poverty rate for white children living in never-married female-headed families was very high (43 percent), but still substantially lower than the roughly 56 percent of black or American Indian children in those same family circumstances. The impli-

Table 5

CHILDREN'S LIVING ARRANGEMENT BY RACE, 2000

Family type/family head	White	Black	American Indian	Asian American	Hispanic
Couple families					
Husband working, wife not working (%)	24	6	14	26	22
Dual-earner couple (%)	48	22	29	44	28
Cohabiting couple (%)	3	6	9	1	6
Single-parent families					
Male (%)	2	2	3	1	2
Female, previously married (%)	9	15	12	4	9
Female, never married (%)	2	20	7	1	5
Grandparents (%)	4	13	12	4	7
Other types (%)	8	15	16	18	22

Source: Authors' calculations using the Integrated Public Use Microdata Series (IPUMS), 2003.

cation seems clear: Even if children of different racial and cultural backgrounds were distributed in the same proportions across low-risk and high-risk families, poverty rates would still be higher than the national average for blacks, American Indians, and other historically disadvantaged minority children in America. Family structure alone does not explain racial differences in child poverty.

Another common view about child poverty is that poverty rates are artificially inflated for children living in cohabiting-couple households. Our calculations indicate that if the incomes of both partners in cohabiting unions were combined and then compared against an adjusted poverty line (one that reflected the larger family size), poverty rates for these children hypothetically could be cut in half—from about 40 percent to 20 percent (compare the "official" and "adjusted" cohabiting-couples columns in Table 6, page 190). Poverty rates would be similarly affected for each racial or ethnic group considered here. For example, the poverty rate for black children in cohabiting-couple families would drop from the official rate of 44 percent to about 27 percent.

While the poverty-reducing effects of marriage are substantial for cohabiting children (assuming, perhaps unrealistically, that these children do not already receive income support from their parents' partners), the overall effect of marriage on child poverty rates is not large in absolute terms (compare the last two columns in Table 6). Even if all cohabiting couples actually got married, the effects on child poverty rates overall would be a drop of about 1 percentage point from 16 percent to 15 percent. Clearly, children in cohabiting unions still represent only a small share of all American children, and they are disproportionately more likely to be living with a disadvantaged parent and a similarly disadvantaged partner of that parent. The poverty rate of cohabiting couples, if they married, is still high by conventional standards.

Some scholars are concerned that this focus on poverty ignores other indicators of economic hardship. Many nonpoor children may be living in families or households that are only slightly above the poverty threshold. A singular focus on poverty may misrepresent overall changes in children's standard of living; it may also hide the growing gap between affluent and poor children.[69] Yet our analysis indicates that the 1990s ushered in a rise in median family/household income (in 1999 inflation-adjusted dollars) for virtually every type of American household, including families with children. The only exception to this upward trend was for cohabiting female householders with children and for male-headed families with children. Income inequality across types of households with and without children, however, remained substantial in 2000. For example, average family incomes ranged from a low of $15,000 among never-married females heading families with children to a high of $60,200 among dual-earner married couples with no children. The median income of dual-earning married couples with children was also more than $66,500. Clearly, recent changes in the family, especially the rise in female-headed families, suggest that America's children today take very different economic pathways to adulthood.

Family differences in economic well-being may be even larger if we account for differences in family size,

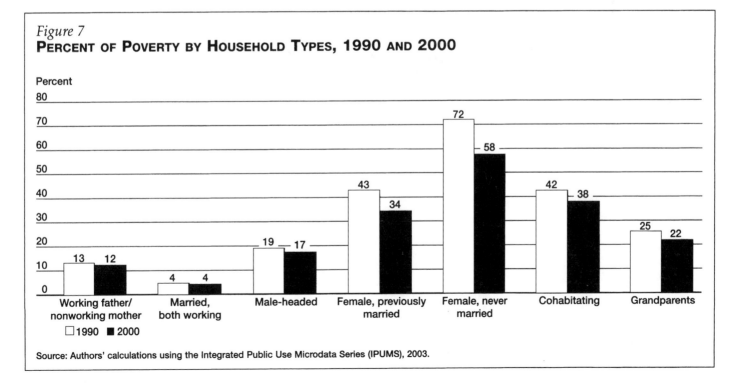

Figure 7
PERCENT OF POVERTY BY HOUSEHOLD TYPES, 1990 AND 2000

Percent

Household type	1990	2000
Working father/nonworking mother	13	12
Married, both working	4	4
Male-headed	19	17
Female, previously married	43	34
Female, never married	72	58
Cohabiting	42	38
Grandparents	25	22

□ 1990   ■ 2000

Source: Authors' calculations using the Integrated Public Use Microdata Series (IPUMS), 2003.

which differ substantially across household types. By definition, the household size is one for a male or female living alone. Traditional male-earner/female-homemaker families represent the nation's largest households (4.2 members in 2000). A big family with many children places obvious constraints on a woman's ability and inclination to work outside the home (and thus to contribute to family income). But it is also true that women in traditional families may desire more children than women who work outside the home. One way to measure economic well-being that takes family size into account is to divide a family's or household's income by the official poverty line for that family size. The poverty line, as defined by the federal government's Office of Management and Budget, increases with family size but also takes economies of scale into account. The poverty line is therefore set higher for larger families. By dividing family income by the poverty line, we can estimate adjusted family incomes that allow appropriate comparisons among families of different sizes.

Not surprisingly, this calculation finds that married couples without children are most advantaged; their average incomes were 4.1 times the poverty threshold. Never-married women with children had the lowest income-to-poverty ratio—1.4 times the poverty threshold. Declines in poverty do not mean that children living in female-headed families have attained a high standard of living.

Whether inequality across household types has increased during the 1990s can be determined by comparing the income-to-poverty ratios in 1990 and 2000. In most cases, observed changes were small. However, for never-married women with children, the income-to-poverty ratio increased by 26 percent. At the other extreme—married couples with no children—size-adjusted household income increased by only 3 percent. The implication is that historically disadvantaged groups, such as single women with children, have done better than other groups in the 1990s. As other studies have suggested, improvements in the standard of living among these never-married women with children may reflect the effects of their increased employment required by the 1996 welfare bill and the effects of the resurgent economy in the late 1990s. At the same time, the family incomes of these never-married women with children often remain very low by national standards, generally only slightly above poverty levels.

MATE SELECTION AND MARITAL MATCHING

To fully understand today's American families requires some understanding of how men and women sort themselves into marriages. Demographers call this matching process "assortative mating."[70] The conventional mate-selection pattern is for men and women to match on the same personal characteristics; indeed, this basic principle of mate selection has been

---

Table 6
POVERTY RATES BY RACE/NATIONAL ORIGIN AND FAMILY STRUCTURE, 2000

Race/ethnicity and national origin	Married couple	Single male	Single ever-married female	Single never-married female	Cohabiting couple (official)	Cohabiting couple (adjusted)	Total official	Total adjusted
All races/origins (percent)	9	17	32	54	40	20	16	15
Non-Hispanic white	5	12	25	43	37	14	9	8
Non-Hispanic black	14	27	39	57	44	27	33	31
American Indian	20	29	44	56	52	32	31	29
Chinese	11	18	22	26	31	19	12	12
Japanese	4	7	16	19	21	6	5	5
Filipino	4	10	12	14	28	10	5	5
Korean	11	9	24	40	29	8	12	12
Asian Indian	9	23	24	31	24	13	9	9
Southeast Asian	23	21	48	56	37	25	27	26
Mexican	22	23	45	57	43	31	28	27
Puerto Rican	16	26	46	64	46	27	33	31
Cuban	10	19	28	53	34	19	15	15
Dominican	22	30	52	64	41	25	35	34
Middle Eastern	3	4	12	35	34	10	5	5

Note: Adjusted rates include the income of the cohabiting partner in the family.

Source: Authors' calculations using the Integrated Public Use Microdata Series (IPUMS), 2003.

---

exploited with much success by the burgeoning dating-service industry. Young women marry young men, college-educated women marry college-educated men, black women marry black men, Catholics marry Catholics, and so on.

In the 1800s, satirist and novelist William Thackeray wrote, "It is just as easy to marry a rich man as a poor man." But this advice may not be true, especially for poor women. The empirical evidence indicates that it is difficult to cross status boundaries of any kind through marriage. For example, researchers Megan Sweeney and Maria Cancian suggest that patterns of assortative mating on income are more rigid.[71] There is less opportunity for low-income women to "marry up." High-earning men are increasingly choosing to marry high-earning women rather than less-educated homemakers. As a result, assortative mating by social class may exacerbate family income inequality in the United States and reinforce the existing social stratification system between rich and poor families. Marriage under these circumstances has a polarizing effect on American society. Out-group marriage, on the other hand, indicates the breakdown of social and economic boundaries. Recent increases in interfaith marriage, for example, provide evidence of secularization and the declining significance of religion in everyday life.

Racial intermarriage may similarly reveal the social significance of race in America's increasingly multicultural and multiracial society. Whether Americans are more likely to marry across racial and ethnic boundaries today than in the past reveals whether racial and ethnic boundaries have weakened over time or have become more rigid. Intermarriage provides a measure of the social distance between racial and ethnic groups and is a good indicator of the assimilation of minorities and immigrants into the majority society.[72] In fact, Milton Gordon, in his classic work *Assimilation in American Life*, argued that intermarriage is the final step in the assimilation process, occurring only after economic and residential assimilation.[73]

For much of America's history, romance and sex between men and women of different races was considered taboo. State antimiscegenation laws forbade people of different races from marrying. These laws were ruled unconstitutional and abolished nationwide in 1967 by the U.S. Supreme Court. Over the ensuing 35 years, interracial marriages have increased rapidly, especially between whites and blacks (who were the prime targets of state antimiscegenation laws). Census data show that the number of marriages between African Americans and whites increased nearly sixfold between 1970 and 2000, from 65,000 to 363,000 couples. Over the same period, marriages between whites and individuals of other racial groups increased from 233,000 to 1 million.

The rise in interracial marriage is a result of the narrowing of racial gaps in socioeconomic status and education; this narrowing has helped break down negative racial stereotypes in the United States. The integration of racially segregated universities, along with modest declines in neighborhood racial segregation, have brought together individuals of diverse backgrounds.[74] Propinquity obviously is a necessary but not sufficient condition for establishing interracial contact and for developing interracial friendships, relationships, romance, and marriage.

Attitudes about racially mixed marriages have also become more tolerant. In the 1960s, less than 10 percent of whites expressed approval of interracial marriages; in the 1990s, more than two-thirds approved of such marriages. White support for equal access of racial minorities to schools, housing, and jobs, however, was even more dramatic, at 96 percent, 86 percent, and 97 percent, respectively.[75] As Americans, we clearly support racial integration and equality in public accommodations and in other impersonal arenas, but we remain less tolerant of interracial intimacy and marriage. We also may increasingly accept intermarriage in principle, but we are less approving of such relationships among family members. Most of us do accept partners of another race in our own lives, but we still look twice at interracial couples. The statistical evidence reflects America's continuing aversion to interracial marriages. Marriages involving interracial couples only increased from less than 1 percent of all marriages in 1970 to almost 3 percent in 2000. Love is not blind when it comes to race.[76]

Racial Intermarriage Among U.S.-Born Americans

It is important to distinguish marriages involving U.S.-born Americans from marriages of immigrants who have not yet been fully incorporated into American society or who married before coming to America (see Tables 7 and 8, page 193). Racial endogamy, or within-group marriage, is the norm for U.S.-born whites and blacks. In 1990, 96 percent of U.S.-born white men were married to U.S.-born white women. This percentage dropped to 94 percent in 2000. Blacks, especially black women, are much less likely than other minorities to marry whites or other nonblacks. Black women also experienced much smaller declines in racial endogamy in the 1990s, from 95 percent in 1990 to 93 percent in 2000. For black men, endogamy declined from 91 percent in 1990 to 84 percent in 2000.

Intermarriage is one indicator of social distance between groups. For example, in New York City in 2000, more than two-thirds of African and West Indian black men marry endogamously.[77] The rest of these black men are married mostly to U.S.-born blacks. A similar percentage (about two-thirds) exists for West Indian women, but African women have slightly higher percentages of in-group marriage than U.S.-born black women. African and West Indians are only about one-half as likely as African Americans to marry whites. Clearly, racial endogamy prevails, but it also seems that nativity status and country of origin also create barriers to marriage within the black community.

Interracial marriage is especially common among U.S.-born American Indians. In 1990 and 2000, less than one-half of American Indians were married to spouses of the same race. During this time, Asian Americans also had high out-marriage rates to whites, but Asians were much different from American Indians in the extent of marriage to foreigners. In 2000, 23 percent of U.S.-born Asian men had foreign-born Asian spouses, and 45 percent of U.S.-born Asian men were married to U.S.-born women of different racial groups. Meanwhile, only 15 percent of U.S.-born Asian women were married to foreign-born Asian men, but 58 percent of U.S.-born Asian women married across racial boundaries (mostly to U.S.-born white men). If intermarriage is our measure, Asians are clearly assimilating rapidly into American society.

Asians are highly diverse with respect to national origin, religion, language, and history of immigration, and this diversity can affect their intermarriage patterns. For example, U.S.-born Chinese and Asian Indians had the highest endogamy rates in 2000 (48 percent and 44 percent, respectively); while Filipinos, Japanese, and Koreans had the lowest endogamy rates (29 percent, 31 percent, and 27 percent, respectively). Perhaps surprisingly, Asian Americans marry whites in higher percentages than they do members of another Asian ethnic group.[78] In recent years, however, interethnic marriage has been on the rise, especially between U.S.-born Japanese and Chinese who have lived in the U.S. for several generations. This rise in the Asian interethnic marriage rate may provide early evidence of a growing pan-Asian identity.

Compared with American Indians and Asians, endogamy among Hispanic Americans takes an intermediate position. In 2000, 51 percent of U.S.-born Hispanic men and 46 percent of U.S.-born Hispanic women were married to other U.S.-born Hispanics. Interestingly, the sex differences in endogamy were due mostly to differences in marriage to foreign-born Hispanics. In 2000, U.S.-born Hispanic women were more likely than U.S.-born Hispanic men to marry foreign-born Hispanics (22 percent for women, compared with 15 percent for men).

Our findings clearly indicate greater social distance between whites and blacks than between whites and other racial minorities. The growth of the black middle class has increased their presence in integrated neighborhoods, but African Americans still remain more residentially segregated than other racial minorities. Blacks also face more discrimination. Historically, black/white marriages were strongly discouraged and subject to legal penalties. In comparison, American Indian/white marriages were actually promoted for political and economic reasons.[79] Moreover, the racial background of Hispanics is a less significant barrier to intermarriage

than it is for blacks. At least one-half of Hispanics identify as being white and therefore find it much easier to marry non-Hispanic whites.[80] For Asian Americans, educational attainment is an important factor underlying intermarriage patterns. Asian Americans have the highest rates of college completion. And across all racial groups, college-educated people are more likely to marry interracially than those who have less education.

The 1990s saw a slowdown in the decline in racial endogamy for Asian Americans and Hispanics. In our view, the large influx of immigrants from Asia and Latin America enlarged the marriage pool for U.S.-born Asian Americans and Hispanics. But these small changes must be interpreted with care, because racial classifications changed with the 2000 Census. Some biracial individuals who in 1990 were identified as minorities are now identified as multiracial (they chose two or more races when answering the race question on the census). Multiracial individuals are less likely to marry others who also are multiracial than they are to marry individuals classified as belonging to a single race. In 2000, only 30 percent of multiracial men and 28 percent of multiracial women were married to spouses of multiple racial identifications.

Sex Differences in Interracial Marriage

More than 75 percent of black/white marriages in 2000 were between a black man and a white woman. Highly educated African American men are more likely than their female counterparts to marry into different racial groups (see Box 5, page 194). In fact, the black husbands of white women have much higher educational levels than the black husbands of black women.

Throughout the Western world, fair skin tone has long been perceived as a desirable feminine characteristic. In fact, until recently, black women rarely won the ultimate tests of beauty—the Miss Universe and Miss America beauty pageants. In 1977, Janelle Commissiong of Trinidad and Tobago became the first black winner in the 26-year history of the Miss Universe pageant. It was not until 1984 that a black woman was chosen as Miss America. The first black woman to win the Miss Florida title did so in 2003.

Beauty is socially constructed. With respect to race, sociologist Mark Hill has shown that fair skin color of African American women is associated strongly with attractiveness ratings.[81] The coupling of skin color with femininity and physical attractiveness may explain, at least in part, the larger share of black/white marriages involving black men rather than black women. For some, white women still seem to represent the highest standard of beauty.

Sex differences are also strong for Asian Americans regarding intermarriage. Among the U.S.-born population in 2000, three-fifths of Asian American/white couples were Asian women married to white men. The Asian culture's strong emphasis on the patrilineal line of

Table 7

RACE/ETHNICITY AND NATIVITY OF SPOUSES OF U.S.-BORN MEN AND WOMEN AGES 20–34, 1990 AND 2000

Race/ethncity and sex	1990 Spouse of same race (%) U.S.-born	Foreign-born	1990 Spouse of different race (%) U.S.-born	Foreign-born	2000 Spouse of same race (%) U.S.-born	Foreign-born	2000 Spouse of different race (%) U.S.-born	Foreign-born
U.S.-born men	93	2	4	1	90	2	7	1
White	96	2	2	1	94	1	3	1
Black	91	1	7	1	84	2	14	1
American Indian	42	z	57	1	43	z	56	1
Asian American	38	13	46	3	30	23	45	2
Hispanic	57	10	32	1	51	15	32	2
Multiracial	—	—	—	—	28	3	65	5
U.S.-born women	93	2	4	1	90	3	7	1
White	96	2	2	1	94	1	4	1
Black	95	2	3	z	93	2	5	1
American Indian	42	z	57	1	42	z	55	2
Asian American	35	8	53	4	24	15	58	3
Hispanic	52	16	31	1	46	22	30	2
Multiracial	—	—	—	—	25	3	66	6

z = Less than 0.5 percent.

— Not available.

Note: Percentages may not add to 100 due to rounding errors.

Source: Authors' calculations using the Integrated Public Use Microdata Series (IPUMS), 2003.

Table 8

RACE/ETHNICITY AND NATIVITY OF SPOUSES OF FOREIGN-BORN MEN AND WOMEN AGES 20–34, 1990 AND 2000

Race/ethncity and sex	1990 Spouse of same race (%) U.S.-born	Foreign-born	1990 Spouse of different race (%) U.S.-born	Foreign-born	2000 Spouse of same race (%) U.S.-born	Foreign-born	2000 Spouse of different race (%) U.S.-born	Foreign-born
Foreign-born men	47	41	2	11	59	27	4	10
White	16	78	2	3	22	70	3	5
Black	40	47	3	11	45	36	5	14
American Indian	14	12	16	59	22	14	8	56
Asian American	70	5	3	22	73	6	3	18
Hispanic	63	23	1	13	70	20	2	9
Multiracial	—	—	—	—	45	10	20	26
Foreign-born women	49	37	2	12	62	23	4	12
White	17	79	1	3	22	70	4	5
Black	46	43	3	8	51	37	3	9
American Indian	10	14	9	67	24	15	9	52
Asian American	54	6	3	37	61	6	3	30
Hispanic	72	15	1	12	77	13	3	7
Multiracial	—	—	—	—	47	7	18	28

— Not available.

Note: Percentages may not add to 100 due to rounding errors.

Source: Authors' calculations using the Integrated Public Use Microdata Series (IPUMS), 2003.

descent puts pressures on Asian American men to marry an Asian woman. As a result, endogamy for Asian men is strong regardless of whether the woman is a U.S.-born or a foreign-born Asian.

Interracial Cohabitation

Cohabitation is an increasingly popular living arrangement for interracial couples and perhaps even an alternative to marriage.[82] In 2000, 10 percent of cohabiting couples were in interracial relationships, while only 6 percent of married couples were interracial. A higher percentage of cohabiting than married couples include partners of different races. Cohabiting relationships, by most counts, are much less stable than marriages—levels of commitment are typically lower and rates of childbearing are lower for cohabiting couples than for married couples. Interracial couples may, in fact, choose to cohabit rather than marry because cohabiting relationships are less public and involve fewer formal interactions with families and friends. Sociologists Kara

Joyner and Grace Kao find that adolescents who have same-race partners are much more likely than adolescents with different-race partners to introduce their partners to their family.[83] Interracial couples express concerns about potential rejection when families become aware of such relationships.

Black/white cohabiting couples are especially common. In 2000, these couples accounted for almost 30 percent of interracial cohabiting relationships, but only 18 percent of interracial marriages. Black/white couples are more likely to opt for cohabitation than marriage, compared with other minority/white couples. The instability of black/white cohabitating couples may reflect a lack of family and community support for these relationships.

Intermarriage Patterns Among Immigrants

Marriages of immigrants to U.S.-born Americans of the same or different racial or ethnic background provide an

---

Box 5

MARRIAGE PROSPECTS OF BLACK COLLEGE-EDUCATED WOMEN

In *Too Many Women? The Sex Ratio Question*, Marcia Guttentag and Paul Secord argue that the shortage of men affects women's marriage patterns, forcing women to marry later or even to remain unmarried throughout their lives.[1] Indeed, in recent decades, age at marriage and the percentage never married have risen rapidly for women. Empirical evidence does not show a strong link between the sex ratio and changes in marriage patterns for white women.

For black women, however, sex ratios may play an important role in marriage patterns.[2] The availability of male partners is much lower at every age for black women than it is for white women. College-educated black women are no exception; they are much less likely to be married than similarly educated white women. Among women ages 25 to 44, almost three-fourths of white college-educated women were married, but only a little more than one-half of black college-educated women were married. Almost one-third of black college-educated women were never married, twice the percentage for white college-educated women.

Black college-educated women are less likely to marry because black college-educated women outnumber black college-educated men. In 2002, 29 percent of white men and 25

percent of white women had attended college. In contrast, the percentages were 16 percent and 17 percent, respectively, for black men and black women. This data indicate that the possibility of "like marrying like" cannot be fully achieved for black college-educated women. A high level of interracial marriage among black men further diminishes the marriage prospects of black college-educated women. Interracial marriage is especially common among highly educated black men.

College-educated black women are doubly squeezed in the marriage market. More than one-half of black college-educated women who were married were married to men who had less education than these black women had (see table). In contrast, only a little more than one-third of white college-educated women who were married were married to men with less education than they had.

References

1. Marcia Guttentag and Paul F. Secord, *Too Many Women? The Sex Ratio Question* (Thousand Oaks, CA: Sage Publications, 1983).
2. Zhenchao Qian and Samuel H. Preston, "Changes in American Marriage, 1972 to 1987: Availability and Forces of Attraction by Age and Education," *American Sociological Review* 58, no. 4 (1993): 482–95.

Marital Status and Assortative Mating Among College-Educated Women, 2000

College-educated women	Marital status (%)				Of those married, % married to men with			
	Currently married	Separated/ divorced	Widowed	Never married	Less than high school	High school	Some college	College+
White	74	8	z	17	1	11	23	65
Black	51	16	1	32	2	16	34	48

z = less than 0.5 percent

Note: Data for women ages 25–44.

Source: Authors' calculations using Census 2000 5% Public Use Microdata Sample (PUMS).

indicator of immigrants' incorporation into American society. Indeed, the extent of racial endogamy among the foreign-born helps us understand the trajectories in adaptation among different immigrant groups and their descendants.[84] For much of the 20th century, intermarriage among white ethnics of different European ancestries eroded cultural and homeland identities and ties. European immigrants (such as Italians or Poles) were, until recently, much less likely to marry descendants of early European settlers. Even then, clear status distinctions of white Europeans were reflected in mate selection patterns.[85]

Immigrants are often married when they arrive in the United States. In this report, we examined only the data for immigrants who arrived in the United States prior to age 20, when the overwhelming majority of them are unmarried. Immigrants' subsequent decisions about when and whom to marry are affected by marriage market conditions in the United States rather than in their home countries. Compared with adult immigrants, immigrants who arrived as children were exposed to the U.S. education system and were more likely to become immersed in American culture and institutions. As these children grow up, their intermarriage patterns, especially with whites or other U.S.-born Americans, arguably reflect their cultural adaptation in American society.

Not surprisingly, the foreign-born in the United States have much different patterns of racial endogamy than their U.S.-born counterparts. In 2000, about 70 percent of foreign-born white men and women were married to U.S.-born whites, reflecting little social distance between U.S.-born whites and immigrants. The story is much different for U.S.-born blacks and black immigrants. Only about one-third of black immigrants were married to U.S.-born blacks. Foreign-born blacks also have much higher rates of interracial marriage than their U.S.-born black counterparts. Perhaps surprisingly, incorporation into mainstream society through marriage is more evident among black immigrants than among U.S.-born blacks. For some black immigrants, marriage to U.S.-born blacks is regarded as downward mobility or as an indicator of downward assimilation.[86]

While U.S.-born Hispanics and Asians are more likely than blacks to marry across racial boundaries, foreign-born Hispanics and Asians are less likely than blacks to do so. One reason is that Hispanic and Asian immigrants are far more numerous than black immigrants, and the opportunities to find mates of the same race are relatively plenty for Hispanic and Asian immigrants. In 2000, nearly 75 percent of Asian immigrant men who came to the United States prior to age 20 married Asian immigrant women. A significantly lower percentage of Asian immigrant women (61 percent) married Asian immigrant men. This suggests that Asian immigrant women have more mate choices, a pattern also observed for their U.S.-born counterparts. Mean-

while, Hispanic immigrant women had a higher percentage of racial and nativity endogamy than Hispanic immigrant men—77 percent and 69 percent, respectively. The different intermarriage patterns of Hispanic and Asian immigrants may be explained in part by the higher educational levels among Asian than among Hispanic immigrants.

Racial boundaries may break down even more as racial minorities make socioeconomic progress and become fully incorporated into American society. Racial boundaries, however, are not likely to disappear quickly, as boundaries did among European white ethnics during much of the 20th century. Marriages between African Americans and whites are still comparatively rare, and there is little evidence over the past decade that this pattern is likely to change quickly over the foreseeable future. For U.S.-born Hispanics and Asians, interracial marriage with whites may even slow in the near future. The continuing influx of foreign-born Hispanics and Asians provides a ready marriage market, expanding the marriage pool for the U.S.-born population of these minorities. In the early 20th century, immigration from Europe was essentially cut off, thus encouraging marriage among different immigrant groups and fostering assimilation. In contrast, U.S.-born racial minorities are now exposed to a continuing influx of potential spouses with similar racial or ethnic backgrounds. Whether the current slowing of racial intermarriage will reverse itself if the U.S. Congress tightens America's borders to new immigrants is far from certain.

FORECASTING AMERICA'S FUTURE

What can we conclude about the state of marriage and family in the United States? What can we forecast about the future of all of America's families, including racial and ethnic minorities? Will differences in family life continue to be both a cause and a consequence of persistent differences in family and child poverty and well-being?

The optimistic view is that marriage and family are resilient institutions that will continue to evolve in function and form in response to changing social conditions. Indeed, globalization and technological progress have accelerated, to an unprecedented degree, the pace of cultural and economic change in the United States and around the world. The family has responded in kind. Stockbrokers often marvel that the stock market "knows" how to respond daily to changing economic conditions, fiscal and monetary policies, and national and world politics. Those who are optimistic about the state of the American family would probably say that the family also "knows" how to respond or adapt to changing conditions. These optimists believe that family change will play itself out in due course, but they recognize that the family has, from its beginnings, been highly fluid yet resilient.

On the other hand, pessimists are concerned that family changes over the past three decades—divorce, out-of-wedlock-childbearing, delayed marriage, and cohabitation—have so destroyed the social and moral fabric of American life that the nation may never fully recover. The pessimists believe that, from generation to generation, the stable nuclear family was a source of great national strength and unity. The nuclear family served its primary function well: bearing and raising generation after generation of productive and engaged citizens. If recent studies are our guide, America's new families—such as single-parent families or cohabiting couples—may be performing these primary functions less effectively than traditional families do. The current diversity in American family values and behavior, along with growing racial diversity, also portend a future of accelerated cultural change when today's children reach adulthood and assume adult roles, including starting (or not starting) families of their own.

Our examination of marriage and family change over the past decade has probably only reinforced whichever optimistic or pessimistic view our readers already held. Optimists will point to a slowdown or at least a leveling off of the rapid family change that took place in the 1970s and 1980s. They can point to the overwhelming share of people who want to marry and will marry. The fact that 70 percent of America's children live in married-couple families suggests that most children have two providers and caretakers. Divorce and remarriage mean that children today have more family members who care about them—stepparents and stepsiblings, additional sets of grandparents, and a larger kin network. Immigrants from Asia and Latin America, in many ways, have infused America with values and behaviors that largely support traditional family life.

Pessimists will emphasize that many of the trends of the 1970s and 1980s continued unabated in the 1990s. The percentage of families headed by unmarried single parents increased. Cohabitation supplanted marriage as the first-union experience for most young adults. Sexual activity, pregnancy, and childbirth outside of marriage, along with declines in marital fertility, elevated the percentage of children born outside of marriage to its highest level ever during the 1990s. The children and grandchildren of America's new immigrants are rapidly adopting the marriage and family patterns of the majority population. Marriage and family life for these children of immigrants may ultimately be the modern American life, much as it has been for most of America. Clearly, our results for the 1990s have provided something for both sides of the family debate and the broader debate about America's cultural decline.

Our portrait of America's future is necessarily an ambiguous one. This portrait, however, does highlight several important dimensions of contemporary American families likely to accelerate. For one, our analysis questions whether America's future will even include a typical American family. Growing racial and cultural diversity reinforces this conclusion. While each racial and ethnic group has somewhat different marriage and family profiles, African Americans in particular remain distinctive in many ways: a continuing matrifocal family structure, high rate of out-of-wedlock childbearing, and apparent family fluidity or instability. Our results provide little evidence that the retreat from marriage among African Americans has slowed much in the 1990s, or that it will slow or reverse in the near future. That so many black children today grow up in single-parent families will only add momentum to the continuing transformation of the black family from this generation to the next.

In the "old days," most Americans were born into two-parent families that stayed together. These families had extensive kin networks of social support. Marriage and family life were institutionalized—there was agreement about what it meant to be a husband and wife, mother and father, sister and brother, or grandfather and grandmother. Indeed, there was a set of commonly understood expectations about these roles; and most people lived up to these expectations. But with the proliferation of alternative family forms and their new and ambiguous roles, there aren't today many shared expectations. The family trajectories of young children take many different paths, with different implications for these children's success or failure. Remarriage and now cohabitation have been called "incomplete institutions" precisely because common understandings and behavioral expectations regarding these new forms have remained underdeveloped. Sociologist Andrew Cherlin believes that marriage itself is being deinstitutionalized, as many previously taken-for-granted aspects of marriage and family life disappear. The diverse portrait of American family life presented here provides little reason to dispute Cherlin's claim.[87]

Perhaps more than any other recent demographic or family change, cohabitation has fundamentally altered the family lifecourse. The upward trend in cohabitation is likely to accelerate. Data from the 2000 Census indicate that nearly 500,000 couples are currently cohabiting in America. But the rate of growth of cohabitation accelerated in the 1990s. Cohabitation has served to precede and delay most marriages today. Cohabitation is also especially high among divorced people, and this high cohabitation rate may be one reason why remarriage rates have declined significantly over the past quarter-century.

The once-common attitude that out-of-wedlock childbearing is a social problem that shapes the life course of young mothers can now be questioned if, as one recent study has shown, roughly 40 percent of all such births occur to cohabiting couples.[88] In these cases, both biological parents are raising these children. Moreover, our own analysis indicates that more than four of 10 cohabiting couples are raising children. Clearly, any attempt to understand modern marriage and family life must take cohabitation into account. Cohabitation has affected the measurement and meaning of virtually every conventional statistic related to marriage, fertility, and divorce. It seems that cohabitation is being institutionalized as a regular part of adult life at the same time that marriage is being deinstitutionalized. Moreover, cohabitation's growing popularity is evident across the panoply of racial and ethnic groups in America, with the exception of most Asian groups.

If rapid changes in the American family have one obvious downside, it is in regard to their negative implications for children's social and economic well-being and their futures. As our analysis demonstrates, children's economic well-being is inextricably linked to the decisions their parents make about marriage, divorce, cohabitation, and out-of-wedlock childbearing. The recent policy push for marriage promotion is a novel social experiment initiated by the federal government, but success is far from certain. To be sure, success may mean a better economic life and future for America's children. But another approach, preferred by most other Western industrialized societies, is to focus less on marriage and more on implementing policies or practices that eliminate the threat of particular parental choices (such as divorce) on children's well-being. In *Poor Kids in a Rich Country*, Lee Rainwater and Timothy Smeeding show that the United States has the highest poverty rate and most inequality among children of 14 other Western industrialized societies, including Sweden, the United Kingdom, and Canada.[89] Ensuring a family wage, adequate child care, better access to secondary and higher education, and sufficient government cash assistance all help make children's economic well-being independent of the good or bad decisions of their parents regarding marriage and family life. Great Britain's Prime Minister Tony Blair has a national goal to eliminate child poverty. In America, we now seem to have the political will and resources to promote marriage and support traditional two-parent families, but we lack the will to fully address the child poverty problem through government subsidies.

Poverty and low income will undoubtedly continue to shape the marital and family trajectories of racial and ethnic minorities, including immigrants. Patterns of racial intermarriage will also surely play a large role in shaping these trajectories. Over the past decade, large percentages of Hispanics and Asians have married U.S.-born whites, a sign that social distances between these groups and whites have narrowed in the 1990s. For most Asians and Hispanics, these numbers grew during the 1990s, as second- and third-generation immigrants

gained footing in the United States. The only exception to this trend was among Hispanics, but this relative lack of intermarriage may reflect the recent heavy immigration and growing ancestral and racial diversity of these new entrants to America. Whether this trend indicates Hispanics' growing social distance with U.S.-born whites is difficult to assess without additional study. Still, despite the slowdown of ethnic intermingling, nearly one-half of all Hispanics in America were married to non-Hispanics (mostly whites) in 2000. The implications of interracial marriage patterns will not become fully apparent until the mixed-race children of these couples choose to embrace or self-identify with one culture or the other, or these children choose to become part of a true melting pot.

The implications for assimilation and acculturation are broad, regardless of the answer. At the same time, race constitutes a major barrier for intermarriage between blacks and whites. For blacks, the pace of change has been slow, despite the increases in the economic status of average African Americans. Again, evidence for black exceptionalism remains strong.

Finally, our analysis suggests a growing balkanization of family life in America along economic and racial lines. While the income of single-parent families at the bottom of the income distribution increased during the 1990s, these families often represent the "other" America—the low-income and minority families and children under great stress to make ends meet in a rapidly restructuring and global economy. Job insecurity, little or no health care, inadequate child care, and poor public transportation conspire against struggling single-parent families living from paycheck to paycheck.

The gulf between this other America and U.S.-born, white, dual-career couples with good jobs, employer-paid health benefits and pensions, big houses in the suburbs, and first-rate public schools seems vast. To an unparalleled extent, fulfilling the American Dream depends on the luck of the draw, on the kind of family we are born into and grow up in. Nevertheless, the American public still holds strongly to the belief—and for some, the mistaken belief—in equal opportunity for all.

ACKNOWLEDGMENTS

The authors thank editors Reynolds Farley and John Haaga and several anonymous reviewers for their helpful comments, as well as the editorial staff of the Population Reference Bureau and the Russell Sage Foundation.

REFERENCES

If provided by the authors, additional text and data associated with this report are available at www.prb.org/AmericanPeople.

1. Andrew J. Cherlin, "The Deinstitutionalization of American Marriage," *Journal of Marriage and Family* 66, no. 4 (2004): 848-61.

2. Diane Schmidley, "The Foreign Born Population in the United States, March 2002," *Current Population Reports* P20-539 (2003): 1-2.

3. According to Child Trends, in 2001, 15 percent of all children has at least one foreign-born parent.

4. Matthew D. Bramlett and Willam D. Mosher, "First Marriage Dissolution, Divorce, and Remarriage, United States," *Advanced Data from Vital and Health Statistics* 323 (Hyattsville, MD: National Center for Health Statistics, 2001); and Maureen R. Waller, "High Hopes: Unwed Parents' Expectations About Marriage," *Children and Youth Services Review* 23, no. 6-7 (2001): 457-84.

5. Arland Thornton and Linda Young-DeMarco, "Four Decades of Trends in Attitudes Toward Family Issues in the United States: The 1960s Through the 1990s," *Journal of Marriage and Family* 63, no. 4 (2001): 1009-37.

6. Scott Coltrane, "Marketing the Marriage 'Solution': Misplaced Simplicity in the Politics of Fatherhood," *Sociological Perspectives* 44, no. 4 (2001): 387-418; Daniel T. Lichter, *Marriage as Public Policy* (Washington, DC: Progressive Policy Institute, 2001); Theodora Ooms, *Toward More Perfect Unions: Putting Marriage on the Public Agenda* (Washington, DC: Family Impact Seminar, 1998); and Isabel Sawhill, "Is Lack of Marriage the Real Problem?" *The American Prospect*, Spring Supplement (2002): 8-9.

7. Herbert L. Smith, S. Philip Morgan, and Tanya Koropeckyj-Cox, "A Decomposition of Trends in the Nonmarital Fertility Ratios of Blacks and Whites in the United States, 1960-1992," *Demography* 33, no. 2 (1996): 141-52.

8. R. Kelly Raley, "Increasing Fertility in Cohabiting Unions: Evidence of the Second Demographic Transition in the United States?" *Demography* 38, no. 1 (2001): 59-66.

9. Bramlett and Mosher, "First Marriage Dissolution, Divorce, and Remarriage"; and Robert Schoen and Nicola Standish, "The Retrenchment of Marriage: Results from Marital Status Life Tables for the United States, 1995," *Population and Development Review* 27, no. 3 (2001): 553-63.

10. The crude divorce rate in 2002 was 4.0 divorces per 1,000 population. With a U.S. population of roughly 290 million in 2004, we estimate that about 1.2 million marriages result each year in divorce.

11. See http://ferret.bls.census.gov/macro/032003/pov/new02_100_01.htm, accessed on May 1, 2004.

12. David J. Eggebeen and Daniel T. Lichter, "Race, Family Structure, and Changing Poverty Among American Children," *American Sociological Review* 56, no. 6 (1991): 801-17; and John Iceland, "Why Poverty Remains High: The Role of Income Growth, Economic Inequality, and Changes in Family Structure, 1949-1999," *Demography* 40, no. 3 (2003): 499-519.

13. Sara McLanahan and Gary Sandefur, *Growing Up With a Single Parent* (Cambridge, MA: Harvard University Press, 1994).

14. Jeffery S. Gray, "The Fall in Men's Return to Marriage: Declining Productivity Effects or Changing Selection," *Journal of Human Resources* 32, no. 3 (1997): 481-504.

15. In June 2000, the Coalition for Marriage, Family and Couples Education issued *The Marriage Movement: A Statement of Principles*. The document asked for a reconsideration of no-fault divorce laws; greater support of marriage over cohabitation and more communication to children about the value of abstinence and marriage; the promotion of *covenant* marriages, which make divorce more difficult; greater government effort to promote marriage as a goal of family policy; more government effort to collect complete statistics on marriage and divorce; reform of court-connected divorce education to facilitate reconciliation; the use of welfare funds to finance promarriage programs; and encouragement of marriage counseling to support troubled marriages.

16. Marianne P. Bitler et al., "The Impact of Welfare Reform on Marriage and Divorce," *Demography* 41, no. 2 (2004): 213-36; and John M. Fitzgerald and David C. Ribar, "Welfare Reform and Female Headship," *Demography* 41, no. 2 (2004): 189-212.

17. Laura Sanchez, Stephen L. Nock, and James D. Wright, "Setting the Clock Forward or Back? Covenant Marriage and the 'Divorce Revolution'," *Journal of Family Issues* 23, no. 1 (2002): 91-120; and Katherine B. Rosier and Scott L. Feld, "Covenant Marriage: A New Alternative for Traditional Families," *Journal of Comparative Family Studies* 31, no. 3 (2000): 385-94.

18. Daniel T. Lichter, Christie M. Batson, and J. Brian Brown, "Welfare Reform and Marriage Promotion: The Marital Expectations and Desires of Single and Cohabiting Mothers," *Social Service Review* 748, no. 1 (2004): 2-25.

19. Lynne M. Casper and Suzanne M. Bianchi, *Continuity and Change in the American Family* (Thousand Oaks, CA: Sage Publications, 2002).

20. David T. Ellwood and Christopher Jencks, "The Uneven Spread of Single-Parent Families: What Do We Know? Where Do We Look for Answers?" in *Social Inequality*, ed. Kathryn Neckerman (New York: Russell Sage Foundation, 2004).

21. David Cotter, Joan Hermsen, and Reeve Vanneman, *Gender Inequality at Work* (New York: Russell Sage Foundation, 2004).

22. Daniel T. Lichter and Rukamalie Jayakody, "Welfare Reform: How Do We Measure Success?" *Annual Review of Sociology* 28 (2002): 117-41.

23. Rose M. Kreider and Jason M. Fields, "Number, Timing, and Duration of Marriages and Divorces: 1996," *Current Population Reports* P70-80 (2002): 6.

24. Teresa Castro Martin and Larry L. Bumpass, "Recent Trends in Marital Disruption," *Demography* 26, no. 1 (1989): 37-51.

25. See www.cdc.gov/nchs/releases/95facts/fs_4312s.htm, accessed on May 2, 2004. Based on evidence from 1995, June was (and still is) the most popular month for marriage, with more than twice as many marriages (280,218) as January (117,310), the least popular month.

26. Joyce A. Martin et al., "Births: Final Data for 2002," *National Vital Statistics Reports* 52, no. 10 (2003): 8-9.

27. Maria Cancian and Deborah Reed, "Changes in Family Structure: Implications for Poverty and Related Policy," *Focus* 21, no. 2 (2000): 21-26.

28. Joseph Dalaker, "Poverty in the United States," *Current Population Reports* P60-214 (2001).

29. Jason Fields, "Children's Living Arrangements and Characteristics: March 2002," *Current Population Reports* P20-547 (2003): 4-5.

30. George Masnick and Mary Jo Bane, *The Nation's Families: 1960–1990* (Cambridge MA: The Joint Center for Urban Studies of MIT and Harvard University, 1980).

31. U.S. Census Bureau, "Age Groups and Sex: 2000," Census 2000 Summary File 1, accessed online at http://factfinder.census.gov/servlet/SAFFPeople?_sse=on, on Nov. 5, 2004.

32. Larry L. Bumpass, James A. Sweet, and Andrew Cherlin, "The Role of Cohabitation in Declining Rates of Marriage," *Journal of Marriage and Family* 53, no. 4 (1991): 913-27; and Larry Bumpass and James A. Sweet, "National Estimates of Cohabitation," *Demography* 26, no. 4 (1989): 615-25.

33. Susan L. Brown, "Moving From Cohabitation to Marriage: Effects on Relationship Quality," *Social Science Research* 33, no. 1 (2004): 1-19; and Sharon Sassler, "The Process of Entry in Cohabiting Unions," *Journal of Marriage and Family* 66, no. 2 (2004): 491-505.

34. Steven L. Nock, "A Comparison of Marriages and Cohabiting Relationships," *Journal of Family Issues* 16, no. 1 (1995): 53-76. Nock shows that the quality of cohabiting relationships is typically lower on a number of dimensions than for married couples. This finding contributes to his view that cohabitation remains an incomplete institution.

35. Sassler, "The Process of Entry in Cohabiting Unions."

36. Gary Becker, *A Treatise on the Family* (Cambridge: MA: Harvard University Press, 1991).

37. Valerie Kincade Oppenheimer, "A Theory of Marriage Timing," *American Journal of Sociology* 94, no. 3 (1988): 563-91.

38. Robert Moffitt, "The Effect of Welfare on Marriage and Fertility: What Do We Know and What Do We Need to Know?" in *Welfare, the Family, and Reproductive Behavior: Research Perspectives*, ed. Robert A. Moffitt (Washington, DC: National Academies Press, 1998): 50-97.

39. Ellwood and Jencks, "The Uneven Spread of Single-Parent Families."

40. Andrew J. Cherlin, "Toward a New Home Socioeconomics of Union Formation," in *Ties That Bind: Perspectives on Marriage and Cohabitation*, ed. Linda Waite et al. (New York: Aldine de Gruyter, 2000): 126-44.

41. Robert A. Moffitt, "Female Wages, Male Wages, and the Economic Model of Marriage: The Basic Evidence," in *Ties That Bind: Perspectives on Marriage and Cohabitation*, ed. Linda Waite et al. (New York: Aldine de Gruyter, 2000): 302-19.

42. Daniel Patrick Moynihan, *The Negro Family: The Case for National Action* (Washington, DC: U.S. Department of Labor, 1965)

43. The family situation of blacks in the 1960s is similar to the situation of whites today: Roughly one of every five children is born to an unmarried woman. Whites have followed similar family trajectories to blacks, but have lagged by a quarter-century.

44. Ronald B. Mincy, "Who Should Marry Whom? Multiple-Partner Fertility Among New Parents," *Center for Research on Child Well-Being Working Paper* 02-03FF (Princeton, NJ: Princeton University Press, 2002).

45. R.S. Oropesa, Daniel T. Lichter, and Robert A. Anderson, "Marriage Markets and the Paradox of Mexican-American Nuptiality," *Journal of Marriage and Family* 56, no. 4 (1994): 889-907.

46. Joshua R. Goldstein and Catherine T. Kenney, "Marriage Delayed or Marriage Foregone? New Cohort Forecasts of First Marriage for U.S. Women," *American Sociological Review* 66, no. 4 (2001): 506-19.

47. Jean Bacon, *Life Lines: Community, Family, and Assimilation Among Asian Indian Immigrants* (Oxford, England: Oxford University Press, 1996); and Johanna Lessinger, *From the Ganges to the Hudson: Indian Immigrants in New York City* (Boston: Allen and Bacon, 1995).

48. William Julius Wilson, *The Truly Disadvantaged* (Chicago: University of Chicago Press, 1988); and Daniel T. Lichter et al., "Race and the Retreat From Marriage: A Shortage of Marriageable Men?" *American Sociological Review* 57, no. 6 (1992): 781-99.

49. Megan M. Sweeney, "Remarriage of Women and Men After Divorce: The Role of Socioeconomic Prospects," *Journal of Family Issues* 18, no. 5 (1997): 479-502.

50. U.S. Census Bureau, Census 2000 Summary File 2, accessed online at http://factfinder.census.gov/servlet/SAFFPeople?_sse=on, on June 3, 2004. The comparable sex ratio for the nation's population ages 25-44 was 100.2 in 2000.

51. Sara McLanahan and Lynne M. Casper, "Growing Diversity and Inequality in the American Family," in *State of the Union*, Vol. 2, ed. Reynolds Farley (New York: Russell Sage Foundation, 1995): 1-46.

52. Scott Coltrane, "Research on Household Labor: Modeling and Measuring the Social Embeddedness of Routine Family Work," *Journal of Marriage and Family* 62, no. 4 (2000): 1208-33.

53. Bitler et al., "The Impact of Welfare Reform on Marriage and Divorce"; and Lisa A. Gennetian and Virginia Know, "Getting and Staying Married: The Effects of a Minnesota Welfare Reform Program on Marital Stability," *Population Research and Policy Review* 23 (forthcoming).

54. U.S. Census Bureau, "Family Type by Presence and Age of Own Children," Census 2000 Summary File 1 (Table P-34), accessed online at www.census.gov, on May 7, 2004.

55. Paul R. Amato and Fernando Rivera, "Paternal Involvement and Children's Behavior Problems," *Journal of Marriage and Family* 61, no. 3 (1999): 557-73.

56. Susan L. Brown, "Family Structure and Child Well-Being: The Significance of Parental Cohabitation," *Journal of Marriage and Family* 66, no. 2 (2004): 351-67.

57. Brown, "Family Structure and Child Well-Being"; and Wendy D. Manning and Kathleen A. Lamb, "Adolescent Well-Being in Cohabiting, Married, and Single-Parent Families," *Journal of Marriage and Family* 65, no. 4 (2003): 876-93.

58. Larry L. Bumpass and Hsien-Hen Lu, "Trends in Cohabitation and Implications for Children's Family Context in the United States," *Population Studies* 54, no. 1 (2000): 29-41.

59. Bumpass and Lu, "Trends in Cohabitation"; and Daniel T. Lichter and Deborah R. Graefe, "Finding a Mate? The Marital and Cohabitation Histories of Unwed Mothers," in *Out of Wedlock: Trends, Causes, and Consequences of Nonmarital Fertility*, ed. Lawrence L. Wu and Barbara Wolfe (New York: Russell Sage Foundation, 2001): 317-42.

60. Daniel T. Lichter, Zhenchao Qian, and Leanna Mellott, "Transitions of Disadvantaged Cohabiting Women Into Marriage," paper presented at the Population Association of America meeting, Boston, April 2004.

61. Pauline Agbayani-Siewart, "Filipino American Culture and Family Values," in *Contemporary Ethnic Families in the United*

States, ed. Nijole V. Benokraitis (Upper Saddle River, NJ: Prentice Hall, 2002): 36-42.

62. Nancy S. Landale, "Migration and the Latino Family: The Union Formation Behavior of Puerto Rican Women," *Demography* 31, no. 1 (1994): 133-58.

63. Paul R. Amato and Alan Booth, *A Generation at Risk: Growing Up in an Era of Family Upheaval* (Cambridge, MA: Harvard University Press, 1997); and Robert Haveman and Barbara Wolfe, "The Determinants of Children's Attainments: A Review of Methods and Findings," *Journal of Economic Literature* 33, no. 4 (1995): 1829-78.

64. Craig Gundersen and James Ziliak, "Poverty and Macroeconomic Performance: A View from the States in the Welfare Reform Era," *Demography* 41, no. 1 (2004): 61-86.

65. Rachel Dunifon and Lori Kowaleski-Jones, "Who's in the House? Race Differences in Cohabitation, Single Parenthood, and Child Development," *Child Development* 73, no. 4 (2002): 1249-64; Wendy D. Manning, "The Implications of Cohabitation for Children's Well-Being," in *Just Living Together: Implications of Cohabitation on Families, Children, and Social Policy,"* ed. Alan Booth and Ann C. Crouter (Mahwah, NJ: Lawrence Erlbaum, 2002): 121-52; and Wendy Manning and Daniel T. Lichter, "Parental Cohabitation and Children's Economic Well-Being," *Journal of Marriage and Family* 58, no. 4 (1996): 998-1010.

66. McLanahan and Sandefur, *Growing Up with a Single Parent*.

67. Pamela J. Smock, Wendy D. Manning, and Sanjiv Gupta, "The Effect of Marriage and Divorce on Women's Economic Well-Being," *American Sociological Review* 64, no. 6 (1999): 794-812.

68. Saul D. Hoffman and Greg J. Duncan, "What Are the Economic Consequences of Divorce?" *Demography* 25, no. 4 (1988): 641-45; Donna R. Morrison and Amy Ritualo, "Routes to Children's Economic Recovery After Divorce: Are Maternal Cohabitation and Remarriage Equivalent?" *American Sociological Review* 65, no. 4 (2000): 560-80.

69. Daniel T. Lichter and David J. Eggebeen, "Rich Kids, Poor Kids: Changing Income Inequality among American Children," *Social Forces* 71, no. 3 (1993): 761-80. The income of the poorest children declined absolutely in the 1980s, but the income of the richest children grew rapidly in that decade. This pattern of increasing income inequality occurred among black and white children in both married-couple and female-headed families.

70. Matthijs Kalmijn, "Intermarriage and Homogamy: Causes, Patterns, Trends," *Annual Review of Sociology* 24 (1998): 395-421.

71. Megan M. Sweeney and Maria Cancian, "The Changing Importance of White Women's Economic Prospects for Assortative Mating," *Journal of Marriage and Family* 66, no. 4 (2004): 1015-28.

72. Debra L. Blackwell and Daniel T. Lichter, "Mate Selection Among Married and Cohabiting Couples," *Journal of Family Issues* 21, no. 3 (2000): 275-302; and Zhenchao Qian, "Breaking the Racial Barriers: Variations in Interracial Marriage Between 1980 and 1990," *Demography* 34, no. 2 (1997): 263-76.

73. Milton M. Gordon, *Assimilation in American Life: The Role of Race, Religion, and National Origins* (New York: Oxford University Press, 1964).

74. In Census 2000, for the first time in census history, Americans were able to mark one or more racial categories. Most African American/white and Asian American/white couples identified their children as biracial (65 percent for children born to black/white couples and 55 percent for children born to Asian/white couples). However, while African American/white couples were twice as likely to identify their children as black rather than white only, Asian American/white couples were more than two times more likely to identify their children as white rather than Asian only. American Indian/white couples were least likely to identify their children as biracial. Also see: John R. Logan, Brian J. Stults, and Reynolds Farley, "Segregation of Minorities in the Metropolis: Two Decades of Change," *Demography* 41, no. 1 (2004): 1-22.

75. Howard Schuman et al., *Racial Attitudes in America: Trends and Interpretations* (Cambridge, MA: Harvard University Press, 1997).

76. In fact, if marriages between non-Hispanic whites and all other groups were completely random—that is, couples randomly "fell in love"—about 15 percent of non-Hispanic white women would be married to nonwhites. The observed figure is less than 5 percent.

77. Christie D. Batson, Zhenchao Qian, and Daniel T. Lichter, "Interracial Unions: Variations among Black Americans," paper presented at the Southwestern Social Science Association meeting, Corpus Christi, TX, March 2004.

78. Zhenchao Qian, Sampson Lee Blair, and Stacey Ruf, "Asian American Interracial and Interethnic Marriages: Differences by Education and Nativity," *International Migration Review* 35, no. 134 (2001): 557-86.

79. Gary D. Sandefur and McKinnell Trudy, "American Indian Intermarriage," *Social Science Research* 15, no. 4 (1986): 347-71.

80. Zhenchao Qian and Jose A. Cobas, "Latinos' Mate Selection: National Origin, Racial, and Nativity Differences," *Social Science Research* 33, no. 2 (2004): 225-47.

81. Mark E. Hill, "Skin Color and the Perception of Attractiveness Among African Americans: Does Gender Make a Difference?" *Social Psychology Quarterly* 65, no. 1 (2002): 77-91.

82. Blackwell and Lichter, "Mate Selection Among Married and Cohabiting Couples."

83. Kara Joyner and Grace Kao, "School Racial Composition and Adolescent Racial Homophily," *Social Science Quarterly* 81, no. 3 (2000): 810-25.

84. Although the evidence is limited largely to anecdotes, some immigrants may seek marriage to U.S.-born Americans as a strategy to remain in the United States or to ensure citizenship.

85. Deanna Pagnini and S. Philip Morgan, "Intermarriage and Social Distance Among U.S. Immigrants at the Turn of the Century," *American Journal of Sociology* 96, no. 2 (1990): 405-32; and Sharon Sassler and Zhenchao Qian, "Marital Timing and Marital Assimilation," *Historical Methods*, 36, no. 3 (2003): 131-49.

86. Mary C. Waters, *Black Identities: West Indian Immigrant Dreams and American Realities* (New York: Russell Sage Foundation, 1999).

87. Cherlin, "The Deinstitutionalization of American Marriage."

88. Bumpass and Lu, "Trends in Cohabitation."

89. Lee Rainwater and Timothy Smeeding, *Poor Kids in a Rich Country: America's Children in Comparative Perspective* (New York: Russell Sage Foundation, 2003).

Trends in the Well-Being of America's Children

By William P. O'Hare

INTRODUCTION

The old African greeting, "How are the children?," reflects the extent to which a society's health is often based on the condition of its children. The well-being of children reflects the functioning of institutions responsible for the care of children, such as families, communities, schools, and social welfare agencies.

It is important to assess the trends in the well-being of America's children because today's children represent the next generation of American adults. Childhood conditions and experiences are clearly linked to well-being in later life in terms of health, educational attainment, and employment.[1] Consequently, how today's children are being cared for has important implications for America's future.

An assessment of America's children is particularly timely because many of the social, economic, demographic, and policy changes that took place in the United States during the 1990s affected children and families. For example:

- Welfare reform, enacted in 1996, ushered in a new relationship between the government and poor families, particularly poor families with children.
- Increased immigration contributed to a U.S. population in which one-fifth of all children were immigrants or were children of foreign-born parents.
- The percentage of mothers in the labor force reached an all-time high, and labor force participation rates for never-married mothers skyrocketed during the late 1990s.
- The number of children in the United States grew by nearly 9 million during the 1990s—the largest increase since the 1950s and a jarring change from the decreases of the 1970s and 1980s.

A good understanding of how children and families are faring is particularly important for policymakers, and data from the decennial census provide a solid grounding for public policy. Empirical scientific evidence is the best foundation for informed debate and policy decisions. In the absence of good data, decisions are likely to be based on anecdotes, ideology, rumors, or other unscientific grounds.

The large size of the decennial census sample gives very reliable data for many groups and geographic areas not reported regularly through other data collection activities. This report uses data from the 2000 Census to provide a detailed picture of today's children and youth in the United States; it also compares these results from the 2000 Census with similar data from the 1990 Census. Also examined are some of the demographic trends during the 1990s related to the well-being of children, and the economic and social forces associated with these trends. Finally, this report addresses post-2000 changes in child well-being, including a look at data from the U.S. Census Bureau's American Community Survey (ACS), which in 2010 will replace the census long questionnaire. The ACS provides an up-to-date assessment of how children have fared since 2000.

CHILD WELL-BEING IN THE 1990S

Comparing data from the 2000 Census to data from the 1990 Census shows that children have become better off on some key measures of well-being, but worse off on other measures.

The child poverty rate is perhaps the most global and widely used indicator of child well-being, in part because poverty is closely linked to a number of undesirable outcomes in areas such as health, education, emotional welfare, and delinquency.[2] Data from the 2000 Census show that children continue to have a higher poverty rate than any other age group, even the elderly (those ages 65 and older). In 2000, the poverty rate for children was 16 percent, compared with 10 percent for the elderly (see Figure 1, page 202).

WILLIAM P. O'HARE has directed the KIDS COUNT program at the Annie E. Casey Foundation since 1993. He has worked in a variety of nonprofit organizations in the Washington, D.C., area for almost 30 years. The focus of his work has been making data from federal statistical systems more readily available to policymakers and the public. He is a former president of the Southern Demographic Association; served on the U.S. Census Bureau's advisory committee; and was a contributing editor to *American Demographics* magazine.

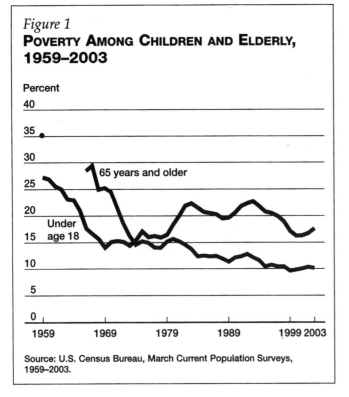

Figure 1

POVERTY AMONG CHILDREN AND ELDERLY, 1959–2003

Percent

65 years and older

Under age 18

1959   1969   1979   1989   1999 2003

Source: U.S. Census Bureau, March Current Population Surveys, 1959–2003.

The child poverty rate has been higher than the elderly poverty rate for the past three decades; but prior to 1973, the reverse was true. In 1959, the child poverty rate (27 percent) was well below the elderly poverty rate (35 percent). Samuel Preston's groundbreaking work showed that the improvement in the standard of living for older Americans is closely related to social policies such as Social Security and Medicare. Examining trends in the early 1980s, Preston concluded: "Conditions have deteriorated for children and improved dramatically for the elderly, and demographic change has been intimately involved in these developments."[3] The dramatic increase in Social Security and Medicare over the past 40 years—these two programs consumed about one-third of the federal budget in 2001—is testimony to the enormous political power of the elderly. Child advocates wonder why society doesn't make similar investments on behalf of children.

Comprehensive analysis of federal spending on children is rare because the federal budget is very complex, but one study found that the per capita expenditure on children in 1997 was $2,290, compared with around $14,000 for the elderly.[4] One major expenditure, coming largely from state and local budgets, is public education. The total outlay for preschool through grade 12 in public schools was $435 billion in 2001. However, even when government monies spent on public education are added to that total, public expenditures for the elderly are still greater than those for children.

The child poverty rate for related children (children who are related to the householder) fell from 20 percent

in 1990 to 16 percent in 2000. These figures reflect the official poverty rate, but this measure of poverty has several shortcomings (see Box 1). Despite its shortcomings, however, the poverty measure is useful because it identifies a set of families who have a very high probability of significant economic stress. Most Americans would agree that the prospect of trying to support oneself, a spouse, and two children on an income of less than $18,660 a year would be daunting anywhere in the country.

The decline of child poverty in the 1990s was also widespread. There was a decrease in child poverty between 1990 and 2000 in 39 states.[5] Only five states and the District of Columbia experienced an increase in child poverty rates between 1990 and 2000. It is clear that child poverty rates fell for blacks, Hispanics, Asians, and American Indians; however, because the 2000 Census allowed respondents to choose more than one race or ethnicity, we cannot make strict comparisons between the racial groups shown in the 1990 Census and those shown in the 2000 Census.

The decline in child poverty during the 1990s was accompanied by more children living in affluent households. Between 1990 and 2000, the number and share of children living in the most affluent households (yearly incomes greater than $100,000) increased. Census data show that 14 percent of children lived in affluent households in 2000, up from 10 percent in 1990. In terms of child outcomes, however, the movement from middle-income to upper-income households (reflected in the rise of children in affluent households) is not as important as the movement of families from low-income to middle-income status (reflected in the falling child poverty rate) because negative child outcomes are heavily concentrated in the low-income population.

The Big Picture

Fortunately, the examination of changes in the well-being of children during the 1990s has benefited from a flurry of measurement and reporting activity on child well-being during that decade (see Box 2, page 204). Much of this activity involved the creation and reporting of social indicators. Since social indicators reflect aggregate conditions of a society or population—such as the percentage of children who are in poverty—these indicators are very valuable in tracking whether a society or a certain population is moving in a desired direction.

Four widely respected reports, all showing trends in child well-being based on multiple indicators, indicate that child well-being improved during the last half of the 1990s.

The first report is a comprehensive index of child well-being developed by Kenneth Land and associates that tracks overall changes in child welfare since 1975.

This index, the Child Well-Being Index (CWI), shows that children's welfare clearly improved during the last half of the 1990s.[6] The CWI is based on 28 statistical indicators reflecting seven separate areas of well-being:

● Material well-being;
● Health;
● Safety and behavioral concerns;
● Educational attainment;
● Place in community;
● Social relationships; and
● Emotional and spiritual well-being.

The initial value of the index was set at 100, based on 1975 values. Subsequent index values above 100 reflect an improvement in child well-being relative to 1975, and values below 100 reflect a deterioration of child well-being relative to 1975.

Between 1975 and 1993, the index fell from 100.0 to 93.6, reflecting a general decline in the well-being of children. The value of the CWI was below 100 for all but two of the years between 1975 and 1993. But the index grew by 10 points between 1993 and 2000, indicating enormous improvement in child well-being during this relatively short period.

Second, the KIDS COUNT report, issued annually by the Annie E. Casey Foundation since 1990, tracks the well-being of children by state. The 2003 KIDS COUNT report shows improvement between 1990 and 2000 on eight of the 10 indicators that KIDS COUNT uses to track child well-being, and these improvements were widespread.[7] Forty-three states improved on six or more

---

Box 1
MEASURING POVERTY

While most of the data on poverty is provided by the U.S. Census Bureau, the U.S. Office of Management and Budget is the federal agency that determines the official definition of poverty.

The current definition of poverty was developed by Mollie Orshansky in the mid-1960s, in connection with President Lyndon Johnson's War on Poverty. Orshansky used a survey from 1955 that showed poor families spent about one-third of their income on food. Orshansky then multiplied the cost of the U.S. Department of Agriculture's economy food plan by three to derive the poverty line, and then adjusted the poverty line for families of various sizes.

The official poverty measure consists of a series of income thresholds based on family size and composition. The thresholds are adjusted every year to account for inflation. The 2003 poverty threshold was $14,824 for a family of one adult and two children, and $18,660 for a family of two adults and two children.[1]

However, a number of researchers have been critical of the official measure.[2] Some analysts think the current standard underestimates real poverty, while others think the measure overstates the number of needy families. In the last several years, the Census Bureau has published a set of experimental poverty measures that incorporate many of the changes called for in a study by the National Academies of Science, but the official definition of poverty has not yet changed.[3] Some data indicate that the poverty thresholds are unrealistically low. Polls show that the public would set the poverty thresholds about 25 percent higher than the current level.[4]

One problem with the current poverty measure is that it does not take taxes into consideration. The poverty measure assumes that all the income a family earns is available to cover expenses, but a portion of the income, even for families below the poverty line, must go to pay taxes. Another problem is that the poverty thresholds are the same across the country, ignoring the large geographic variation in the cost of living.

In addition, noncash government benefits like Medicaid, food stamps, and public housing are not including in calculat-

ing poverty. While excluding noncash benefits was not a big issue when the poverty definition was created in the 1960s, it is now: Noncash benefits account for about three-quarters of all government assistance distributed to low-income recipients. Excluding noncash benefits in the poverty calculation yields a poverty measure that does not reflect the impact of major antipoverty programs.

Finally, the poverty calculation also does not include such work costs as child care, transportation, and clothes. Increases in single-parent families and in the number of females in the labor force mean that more poor families must pay for child-care expenses. In low-income families, child-care costs often amount to 25 percent of monthly expenses.

Creating a new official poverty measure has been discussed for many years, but the outlook for change is not positive. No sitting president is likely to make a change in the poverty definition that would make it appear there are more poor people; and the political party out of power is unlikely to agree to changes that would make it appear there are fewer poor people. Despite these shortcomings in the poverty measure, it is still useful because it identifies a set of economically vulnerable families.

References

1. Carmen DeNavas-Walt, Bernadette D. Proctor, and Robert J. Mills, "Income, Poverty and Health Insurance Coverage in the United States: 2003," *Current Population Reports* P60-226 (2004): 39.

2. National Research Council, *Measuring Poverty: A New Approach* (Washington, DC: National Academies Press, 1995).

3. John Iceland, "Poverty Among Working Families: Findings From Experimental Poverty Measures, 1998," *Current Population Reports* P23-203 (2000); and Kathleen Short et al., "Experimental Poverty Measures: 1990 to 1997," *Current Population Reports* P60-205 (1999).

4. Steven Kull, *Fighting Poverty in America: A Study of American Public Attitudes* (Washington, DC: Center for Study of Public Attitudes, 1994); and William P. O'Hare et al., *Real Life Poverty in America: Where the American Public Would Set the Poverty Line* (Washington, DC: Center on Budget and Policy Priorities, 1999).

ADVANCEMENTS IN MEASURING AND REPORTING ON CHILD WELL-BEING

During the 1990s, many organizations and agencies created important annual reports and other data-gathering and dissemination vehicles, all of which broaden our understanding of child well-being.

The federal government now produces two annual reports on the well-being of children:

● In the mid-1990s, several federal statistical agencies formed the Federal Interagency Forum on Child and Family Statistics. Each year, the forum publishes *America's Children: Key National Indicators of Well-Being*. This report provides trend data for more than 25 key indicators of child well-being.

● In 1996, the U.S. Department of Health and Human Services began publishing *Trends in the Well-Being of America's Children and Youth*, which provides data on dozens of measures related to the well-being of children.

The 1990s also saw the creation of the Youth Risk Behavior Surveillance System from the Centers for Disease Control and Prevention (CDC). The CDC provides several annual measures of well-being for adolescents. Government statistical sources, such as the U.S. Census Bureau's *Current Population Survey* and the vital events reported by the National Center on Health Statistics, also provide annual data on trends.

More recently, the federal government's General Accountability Office and the National Academies of Science have begun working on a national well-being indicator system. While this system is broader than child statistics, the development of child indicators research and reporting during the 1990s undoubtedly helped stimulate support for this project.

Nongovernmental organizations such as the Annie E. Casey Foundation, Child Trends, the National Center on Child Poverty, and the Foundation for Child Development now produce regular, data-based reports on the well-being of America's children. *The Future of Children* series, initiated by the David and Lucile Packard Foundation in the early 1990s, provides the best scientific information on selected child topics. Also, the Children's Defense Fund has issued a data-rich *State of the Child Report* every year since the late 1980s.

Additionally, many state-level data books are now published every year. For example, in 2000, the Maryland Partner-

ship for Children, Youth, and Families started a yearly report to provide a comprehensive picture of the well-being of Maryland's children.[1] In 2001, the state of Maine began publishing *Maine Marks*, which provides statistical indicators for children, families, and communities in Maine.[2] The Alaska Department of Health and Social Services, along with the Alaska Department of Education and Early Development, publish *Building Blocks*.[3]

During the 1990s, infrastructure for developing the field of child indicators began to emerge. For example, in 1999, Child Trends started publishing a newsletter called *The Child Indicator*. And SINET (Social Indicators Network News) often includes information on indicators of child well-being. Also, the International Society for Quality of Life Studies has regular meetings focused on quality-of-life issues including child well-being.

Research conducted in 2000 found nearly 100 ongoing projects devoted to measuring and reporting the well-being of children and families; many more projects have emerged since then.[4]

Increased statistical reporting on children, particularly comprehensive reports, has stimulated government action. A recent report from the National Governors Association identified 16 states that have started Children's Cabinets,[5] and nearly all of those cabinets were started in the 1990s.

References

1. Maryland Partnership for Children, Youth, and Families, *Maryland's Results for Child Well-Being* (Baltimore: Maryland Partnership for Children, Youth, and Families, 2000).

2. Maine Children's Cabinet, *Maine Marks for Children, Families, and Communities: Leading by Results* (Portland, Maine: University of Southern Maine, Edmund S. Muskie School of Public Services, 2001).

3. Alaska Dept. of Health and Social Services and Dept. of Education and Early Development, *Building Blocks: Continuing the Progress of Smart Start—The Next Steps for Supporting Alaska's Young Children and Their Families* (Juneau, AK: Alaska Dept. of Health and Social Services and Dept. of Education and Early Development, 2001).

4. Child Trends, *Indicators of Child, Youth, and Family Well-Being: A Selected Inventory of Existing Projects* (Washington, DC: Child Trends, 2000).

5. National Governors Association, *A Governors Guide to Children's Cabinets* (Washington, DC: National Governors Association, 2004). To better coordinate efforts, a children's cabinet pulls together several state agencies with responsibilities for children.

indicators. While many of the improvements were not large or statistically significant, the overall trend is clear.

Most of the improvement during the 1990s occurred in the last half of the decade (see Table 1). Between 1990 and 1995, only five of the 10 KIDS COUNT indicators improved; but between 1995 and 2000, eight of the 10 indicators improved.

Third, the Federal Interagency Forum on Child and Family Statistics annual report, *America's Children*, shows that most of the 27 indicators used in that report to measure child well-being improved during the late 1990s.[8] The forum does not combine the data in its

report into an overall index, but a study that converted the data from the *America's Children* report into an overall index using the methodology developed by Land and Associates showed a 9 percent improvement in child well-being between 1995 and 2000.[9] Since most of the indicators used in the Land report come from the *America's Children* report, it is not surprising that the results are similar.

Fourth, another annual federal government report— *Trends in the Well-Being of American's Children and Youth*, a compendium of data on children and teenagers[10]— confirms the generally positive trend for children's well-

Table 1
CHANGES IN KEY INDICATORS OF CHILD WELL-BEING, 1990, 1995, AND 2000

Key indicator	1990	1995	2000
Low-birthweight babies (%)	7.0	7.3	7.6
Infant mortality rate (deaths per 1,000 live births)	9.2	7.6	6.9
Child death rate (deaths per 100,000 children ages 1–14)	31	28	22
Teen death rate by accident, homicide, and suicide (deaths per 100,000 teens ages 15–19)	71	65	51
Teen birth rate (births per 1,000 females ages 15–17)	37	36	27
Teens who are high school dropouts (ages 16–19) (%)	10	10	9
Teens not attending school and not working (ages 16–19) (%)	10	9	8
Children living in families where no parent works full-time/year-round (%)	30	30	24
Children living in poverty (%)	20	21	17
Children living in single-parent families (%)	24	27	28

Source: 2003 *KIDS COUNT Data Book*.

being. This report, while not as systematic as the three other reports cited above in assessing recent changes in the well-being of America's children, shows that several important indicators moved in a positive direction during the 1990s:

● In 2000, the child poverty rate reached its lowest point since the late 1970s.
● The teen birth rate fell steadily between 1991 and 2000.
● The steady, decades-long increase in the percentage of children living in single-parent families ended in the mid-1990s.
● The infant mortality rate decreased by 25 percent in the 1990s.

But not all trends were positive. For example, there was a large increase in obesity among children. The increase in the prevalence of obese children was so powerful that the health domain was the only domain in the Child Well-Being Index that moved in a negative direction during the late 1990s.

There are important geographic dimensions to trends in child well-being during the 1990s as well. Child well-being in California, Maryland, and New Jersey improved by 20 percent or more during the 1990s; Wisconsin and Nebraska experienced a decline in overall child well-being during the decade; and North Dakota and Kansas showed no change.[11]

There are large overlaps in the specific indicators used in these four reports, which is understandable because the reports are all trying to measure child well-being. While these reports are not independent in terms of the measures included, it is noteworthy that reports from the federal government, a major university, and a nonprofit organization all lead to the same conclusion.

Well-Being of Minority Children

A balanced reading of American history would show that most racial groups in the United States have experienced some degree of discrimination and unequal access to education, jobs, and housing. Consequently, it is not surprising that black, Latino, and American Indian children trail the non-Hispanic white population on most measures of well-being (see Table 2, page 206). Given these differences, it is important to disaggregate overall trends of well-being by looking separately at children in minority groups.

With respect to the well-being of minority children during the 1990s, there is a very important distinction to be made between *levels* and *trends*. The level of child well-being for a specific group reflects the relative status of a group of children at a given point in time, while trends reflect changes over time. During the 1990s, these two dimensions showed very different results when minority children were compared with white children.

The average well-being of African American, Hispanic, and American Indian children is lower than the well-being of non-Hispanic white children. Moreover, when decennial census data are examined, that pattern is seen on a host of indicators in nearly every state. The disadvantaged position of minority children today suggests that the long-standing gap between the majority white population and most minority groups is not likely to close soon without major new efforts.

The *America's Children* report for 2004 shows that, relative to white children, black and Hispanic children:[12]

● Have higher poverty rates;
● Have lower rates of secure parental employment;
● Have lower rates of health insurance;
● Have poorer health (as self-reported);
● Are more likely to be overweight;
● Are less likely to be immunized;

Table 2

SELECTED INDICATORS OF CHILD WELL-BEING BY RACE AND HISPANIC ORIGIN, VARIOUS YEARS

Key indicator	All children	White	Black	Asian*	American Indian*	Hispanic
Low birthweight babies, 2002 (%)	7.8	6.9	13.4	7.8	7.2	6.5
Infant mortality rate (deaths per 1,000 live births), 2001	6.8	5.7	13.5	4.7	9.7	5.4
Child death rate (deaths per 100,000 children ages 1–14), 2001	22	20	31	15	29	19
Teen death rate by accident, homicide, and suicide (deaths per 100,000 teens ages 15–19), 2001	50	48	63	28	92	47
Teen birth rate (births per 1,000 females ages 15–17), 2002	23	13	41	9	31	51
High school dropout rate (teens ages 16–19 not in school and not high school graduates), 2003 (%)	8	6	10	5	10	17
Teens not attending school and not working (ages 16–19), 2003 (%)	9	7	14	6	18	13
Children living in families where no parent works full-time/year-round, 2003 (%)	25	19	42	19	43	31
Children living in poverty, 2003 (%)	17	9	32	12	35	29
Children living in single-parent families, 2003 (%)	28	22	59	13	49	30

* The data for the following indicators for Asian and Pacific Islander children and American Indian and Alaska Native children include both those who selected Hispanic Origin and those who did not: low birthweight babies, infant mortality rate, child death rate, and teen birth rate.

Note: All data are reported for the most recent year available. Except where noted above, all data reported for white, black, Asian, and American Indian children are reported for non-Hispanic only.

Source: 2004 *KIDS COUNT Data Book* (www.aecf.org/kidscount/databook/indicators.htm, accessed Nov. 16, 2004).

● Have higher rates of adolescent mortality;
● Have higher teen birth rates;
● Are less likely to be read to as a child;
● Do less well on standardized tests;
● Are less likely to complete high school; and
● Are more likely to be out of school and out of work.

Every minority group, including Asians, has a higher child poverty rate than non-Hispanic whites. Blacks, Hispanics, and American Indians had child poverty rates two to three times those of non-Hispanic whites. Moreover, when compared with non-Hispanic white children, minorities are more likely to be deeper in poverty, to spend more of their childhood in poverty, and to live in neighborhoods with high poverty rates.[13]

The one major exception to this pattern is what is often called the "Hispanic paradox." Despite high levels of poverty and lower educational attainment among Hispanics, birth outcomes (infant mortality and low birthweight, for example) for Hispanics are as good as or better than those for non-Hispanic whites. There is little consensus among experts on the reasons for this paradox. But one theory is that young Hispanic women are less likely to smoke, drink alcohol, or use illegal drugs prior to or during pregnancy.

Among minority groups, Asians are relatively unique because they are more like non-Hispanic whites on most measures of child well-being—education and income among Asians are similar to education and income among non-Hispanic whites. It is worth noting, however, that there is a great deal of diversity in socio-economic status among Asian ethnic groups. For example, the child poverty rate among Japanese Americans (6 percent) and Asian Indians (12 percent) is relatively low, compared with the child poverty rate among Cambodians (38 percent) and Laotians (25 percent).

However, when it comes to assessing trends in child well-being during the last half of the 1990s, the situations for non-Hispanic whites and other racial and ethnic groups are reversed. On many measures, black and Hispanic children actually improved more than non-Hispanic white children during this period. During the last half of the 1990s, the Child Well-Being Index improved by 12 percent for black children, by 10 percent for Hispanic children, and by only 7 percent for white children.[14]

Other key measures show similar improvements for black, Hispanic, and American Indian children. For example, poverty among black children fell from 45 percent in 1990 to an all-time low of 30 percent in 2001, and Hispanic child poverty fell from 38 percent to 28 percent during the same period (also an all-time low).[15]

The poverty rate for American Indian children fell from 39 percent in 1990 to 32 percent in 2000. The poverty rate for non-Hispanic white children fell from 12 percent in 1990 to 10 percent in 2000.

The percentage of black and Hispanic children in poverty fell dramatically during the 1990s, but further analysis shows that the percent of black and Hispanic children living in near-poverty families (those families with household incomes between 100 percent and 200 percent of the poverty threshold) increased between the late 1980 and the late 1990s.[16]

Table 3
CHILDREN'S RECEIPT OF WELFARE BENEFITS BY POVERTY LEVEL, 2003

Welfare benefit	Percent of child beneficiaries living in families below 100% of poverty	Percent of child beneficiaries living in families between 100% and 200% of poverty	Total number of child beneficiaries (millions)
Food stamps	68	27	9.2
Free or reduced-price school lunches	45	40	17.6
State Children's Health Insurance Program or Medicaid	42	33	21.4
Subsidized housing	68	24	4.3
Cash public assistance or welfare	60	24	5.6
Child-care subsidy	45	30	1.8
Energy assistance	63	33	2.4

Note: Only children in the household and poverty universes are included.
Source: U.S. Census Bureau, March Current Population Survey, 2004.

Large numbers of black and Hispanic children moved out of the most dire circumstances during the 1990s, but many of these children remain in economically vulnerable families. This vulnerability is implicitly recognized in many government assistance programs, which set income eligibility thresholds well above the poverty line. Table 3 shows that a large share of recipients of government benefits—the majority of beneficiaries in some programs—have incomes above the poverty line.

Moreover, there is an intersection between geography and race. Among the five states that improved the most in child well-being during the 1990s (California, Maryland, New Jersey, Michigan, and Minnesota), 51 percent of the children in those states were racial or Hispanic minorities; among the five states that improved the least (Wisconsin, Nebraska, North Dakota, Kansas, and Montana), only 27 percent of children in those states were racial or Hispanic minorities.

In general, minority children were worse off than non-Hispanic white children in 2000, but on many measures of well-being, minority children improved more than non-Hispanic white children during the 1990s.

Child Well-Being and Public Perceptions

Despite all the positive trends for children during the 1990s, many people still have a gloomy view of the well-being of children.[17] The negative view of teenagers' well-being is particularly common, because a large share of the public is not aware of many of the most significant improvements during the 1990s in the welfare of children:

● The teen birth rate has decreased steadily since 1991.

● The percentage of teens committing violent crimes has decreased over the last five years.

A 2003 survey found that only 19 percent of the public thought that the number of children on welfare had decreased since federal welfare reform had been passed in 1996; in fact, that caseload was cut in half during this period.[18] The decline in the number of children on welfare is not necessarily a sign of improved child well-being, but the mismatch between public perceptions and data trends highlights the extent to which a large number of people are ill-informed about some major trends among children.

Some experts believe the mismatch between public perceptions and demographic reality is a reflection of the media's emphasis on bad news. A constant barrage of negative stories and images about children and youth distorts the public's view of this population. Also, news stories often focus on one person's experience and ignore broad trends or patterns. One example of this distortion is how the media focus on homicides among teenagers. Most big-city media outlets regularly reported on young homicide victims during the 1990s, leaving the impression that these homicides were increasing when, in fact, the teen homicide rate actually fell by almost 50 percent between 1990 and 2000.

Child advocates may have contributed to these misperceptions because some advocates constantly trumpet problems rather than highlighting improvements. Also, in some cases, positive trends of the late 1990s are a reversal of long-term negative trends, and long-term trends take more time to fade in people's minds.

Observers also feel that the public's failure to recognize many of the positive trends among children undermines support for government assistance programs. A broad segment of the public continues to feel that government programs just don't work, and that perception is reinforced by the incorrect but general perception that trends regarding children are getting worse.

IMPROVEMENTS DESPITE DEMOGRAPHIC COUNTERTRENDS

The improvements in child well-being that occurred in the 1990s are somewhat surprising in light of five major demographic trends that also occurred during that period:

- An increasing number of children;
- An increasing share of the child population from racial or Hispanic minority groups;
- An increasing number of immigrant children;
- An increasing concentration of children in states where child outcomes are below average; and
- An increasing number of children living in single-parent families.

One would expect any one of these demographic trends to depress child well-being. But the improvements in child well-being suggest that the forces behind these improvements were more powerful than the demographic trends outlined above.

More Children

The total number of children in the United States increased by almost 9 million during the 1990s. During the 20th century, the baby-boom decade of the 1950s was the only decade that saw a bigger numerical increase (see Table 4).

The increase in the number of children during the 1990s stands in stark contrast to the decreases of the 1970s. During the 1970s, the number of children fell by 8 percent, as the last of the baby boomers moved out of childhood. During the 1980s, the number of children also fell slightly.

The large increase in the number of children during the 1990s notwithstanding, the United States is much less of a child-centered society now than it has been. In 1900, 40 percent of the U.S. population was under age 18. Even as recently as 1960, near the height of the baby boom, 36 percent of the population was under age 18. However, just 40 years later, children's share of the U.S. population had dropped to 26 percent. The 1960 Census revealed that 51 percent of all households had at least one child, compared with slightly more than one-third of all households in 2000.[19]

The long-term decline in children as a percent of the population is the result of two major demographic trends. First, fertility rates fell over the last part of the 20th century. Second, increases in life expectancy led to

Table 4

CHILDREN IN THE U.S. POPULATION, 1900–2000

Year	Total U.S. population (millions)	U.S. population under age 18	
		Total (millions)	Percent
1900	76.1	30.7	40
1910	92.4	35.1	38
1920	106.5	39.6	37
1930	123.1	43.0	35
1940	132.1	40.4	31
1950	151.7	47.1	31
1960	180.7	64.5	36
1970	204.9	69.7	34
1980	226.5	63.8	28
1990	248.7	63.6	26
2000	281.4	72.3	26

Source: W.P. O'Hare, "The Child Population: First Data From the 2000 Census" (2001): table 1.

a larger adult population in 2000—more Americans now survive to older ages. The impact of these two trends has been mitigated to some extent during the 1990s because of increased immigration. Immigrants tend to be young adults who often bring children with them or have children soon after arriving. Very few older people migrate to new countries.

Geographic Dimensions of Child Population Change

Just as broad "national" data mask differences among racial and ethnic subgroups, these data also mask important differences among states and regions of the country. To illustrate this point, consider this: The most recent census data on income and poverty show that, of the 50 states, 42 had child poverty rates statistically significantly different from the national poverty rate.

The vast majority of children (83 percent) live in metropolitan areas, although most live in suburbs just outside the country's biggest cities. About 10 percent of all children live in "micropolitan areas"—smaller towns and surrounding areas outside metropolitan areas, with populations from 15,000 to 50,000. Less than 7 percent of all children live in the most rural and remote areas of the country outside metropolitan and micropolitan areas.

But the growth of the child population between 1990 and 2000 was not spread evenly across the country; most of the growth in the child population during the 1990s took place in metropolitan areas—a 16 percent increase during the 1990s, compared with a 4 percent increase in micropolitan areas; and no change in the number of children (5 million) living in the nation's most remote rural areas.

City and County Changes

Collectively, the number of children living in the 245 largest cities in the United States (those with 100,000 or more people) grew from 16 million in 1990 to 19 million in 2000. This 17 percent increase means that the child population in large cities grew more rapidly than did the child population in the rest of the country. Much of the population growth in large cities was from immigration.

There is an important regional overlay to the changes in cities and, to a lesser extent, counties. Cities in the Northeast and Midwest generally lost population or did not grow rapidly, while cities in the South and Southwest often experienced dramatic growth. This population loss and growth was due mainly to shifting economic opportunities and immigration.

One exception to this regional pattern is New York City. Not surprisingly, New York City, America's largest city, had the most children in 2000 (2 million), but it also had the biggest numerical increase between 1990 and 2000 of any large city (255,000). After New York City, the nine cities that added the most children in the 1990s were all in the South and West. Las Vegas was the largest of the fast-growing cities, adding 60,000 children (a 92 percent increase) during the 1990s.

Most of the cities with child population losses were located in the Northeast and Midwest. Baltimore lost the largest number of children between 1990 and 2000, followed by St. Louis and Cincinnati. The loss of good-paying jobs, especially manufacturing jobs, in these cities led to out-migration of families.

Children in Rural America

About one-fifth of all children in the United States live in rural areas. In some respects, they live in very different circumstances than their urban counterparts.

Overall, the number of children in nonmetropolitan counties grew by only 3 percent during the 1990s, and the number of children in many rural parts of the country actually declined during the 1990s, especially in a swath of counties from the Dakotas to West Texas. Moreover, in one-third of the rural counties that gained in overall population, the number of children fell during the 1990s, reflecting the sustained out-migration of young families with children and signaling big shifts in the age structure of these communities.

The out-migration of children from rural America is a reflection of more difficult conditions there. The child poverty rate in rural America fell during the late 1990s, but not as rapidly as it did in metropolitan areas.[20] In 1994, the child poverty rate for nonmetro children (23 percent) was only 1 percentage point above the poverty rate for children in metro areas; by 2000, this gap had grown to 5 percentage points (20 percent in rural areas, compared with 15 percent in metro areas). The 2000 Census also shows that, of the 50 counties with the highest child poverty rates, 48 were rural. It appears that the economic expansion of the 1990s benefited children living in central cities and suburbs more than rural children.

School Enrollment

The dramatic increase in the number of children also increased school enrollment. The number of school-age children (ages 5 to 17) increased from 45 million in 1990 to 53 million in 2000, and the number of 5-to-17-year-olds enrolled in school increased from 42 million in 1990 to 51 million in 2000. The number of children enrolled in elementary and secondary schools now matches the all-time high set when the youngest baby boomers were entering first grade in 1970.[21]

As a result of this surge in school enrollment, school construction costs doubled.[22] Funds for schools come mostly from state and local budgets. During the late 1990s, when state government budgets were flush because the economy was strong, construction funding was less of a problem, but state budgets have been squeezed since the economic downturn in 2000. The need for additional teachers sent administrators scrambling for new recruits, and too often administrators hired people who were not trained to teach.

Not only did the number of students increase during the 1990s, age-specific enrollment rates also increased over that decade. In 2000, 97 percent of 5-to-17-year-olds were enrolled in school, compared with only 93 percent in 1990.

One reason for the increased attendance rate in the 1990s is the enactment of more extensive provisions for students in need of special education. The Americans with Disabilities Act and the Individuals with Disabilities Education Act stimulated more programs and better outreach for children with disabilities. The number of disabled children served by special education programs increased from 4.4 million in 1991 to 5.7 million in 2000.[23]

On the other hand, in 2000, nearly 750,000 children between the ages of 6 and 16 were not enrolled in school. One explanation for these "missing" children is the increase in home-schooled children. There were an estimated 1 million children of all ages being home-schooled in 2003; the percentage of children being schooled at home has increased over the past 15 years.[24]

Finally, some of the pressure on the public school system caused by these record increases in the school-age population during the 1990s was reduced because more children are now going to private schools. In 2000, there were 6 million children enrolled in private schools, compared with around 5 million in 1990; the percentage of children in private school inched up from 10.2 percent in 1990 to 11.3 percent in 2000.

Americans are spending more time in school. More Americans are starting school younger and staying in school longer than they were a generation ago. The share of 3-to-5-year-olds enrolled in school increased from 42 percent in 1990 to 61 percent in 2000, and the high school dropout rate fell from 10 percent in 1990 to 8 percent in 2000. The share of young adults ages 18 to 24 who were enrolled in school also increased during the 1990s, from 55 percent in 1990 to 57 percent in 2000.

The Preschool Population

The preschool population (under age 5) is another important demographic group, and the increase in the number of preschoolers during the 1990s has implications for both child care and early education.

The number of preschoolers increased from 18 million in 1990 to 19 million in 2000. The nation's formal and informal child-care systems were already strained before this increase. Recent Census Bureau estimates indicate that, between 2000 and 2003, the number of children under age 5 increased by almost 600,000.[25]

The preschool population became the focus of attention during the 1990s because research showed that social stimulation experienced in the first few years of life plays a crucial role in later development. Researchers also tied early brain development, child care, and preschool activities to a child's readiness for school. As students entered kindergarten, scores on reading, math, and general knowledge were higher for those who participated in out-of-home care than for those who didn't participate in such care; and the scores were higher for those who participated in center-based care (more likely to be a preschool) than for those who were in home-based care.[26]

Recent studies show children from higher-income families are more likely than those from lower-income families to be proficient in reading and mathematics when they enter school because, in part, they are more likely to have attended preschool.[27] In this context, the federal government's Head Start program and other public programs that provide preschool experiences for needy children can play an important role in giving children from low-income families the same start in school as children from more affluent families.

The percentage of children ages 3 to 5 enrolled in preprimary education increased from 42 percent in 1990 to 61 percent in 2000. This increased number of preschoolers is partly a reflection of expanded prekindergarten programs offered by states. Forty states now fund prekindergarten programs for 4-year-olds. This increased emphasis on preschool education is reflected by the growing number of states (currently 21) that require prekindergarten teachers to have bachelor's degrees.[28]

Those who advocate more public support for preschool programs often point to a very favorable cost-benefit ratio for these programs. Quality preschool programs can reduce the need for remedial education or special education, increase high school graduation rates, increase employment and earnings, and reduce arrest rates later in life.[29]

More Minorities

Another major trend documented in the 2000 Census is the growing racial and ethnic diversity of the child population. Pinpointing the exact size of changes in racial groups is complicated because, in the 2000 Census—for the first time in any census—respondents could choose more than one race. Still, it is clear there was a significant change in the racial composition of the child population during the 1990s (see Table 5).

The share of non-Hispanic white children fell from 69 percent in 1990 to 61 percent in 2000; the number of non-Hispanic white children remained relatively stable (at about 44 million). But the number of minority children grew rapidly; during the 1990s, minority children accounted for about 98 percent of the growth in the child population of the United States.

Hispanic children accounted for about 5 million of the 9 million children added to the total U.S. population between 1990 and 2000. Racial minorities (Asians, blacks, and American Indians) accounted for most of the remaining increase. Only 200,000 of the 9 million children added to the population during the 1990s were non-Hispanic white children.

Racial diversity is also increasing more rapidly among children than it is among adults. Minority children accounted for 39 percent of the population under age 18 in 2000, compared with only 28 percent of the adult population. Minorities make up a larger share of the child population because immigrants tend to be younger and the recent immigration stream is heavily Hispanic and Asian. Racial diversity is also more advanced among children because some minority groups have higher birth rates than non-Hispanic whites.

Since minority children typically have poorer child outcomes than non-Hispanic white children, we would expect the growing minority youth population of the 1990s to have lower outcomes of child well-being. But those lower outcomes didn't materialize. Evidence from the 1990s indicates that the United States can accommodate growing numbers of minority children and still achieve improvements in child well-being.

More Children in Immigrant Families

During the 1990s, there was an upsurge in the number of children living in immigrant families (children born outside the United States or with at least one parent born outside the United States). While children born in the United States to immigrant parents are considered U.S. citizens and thus are not technically immigrants, these children would not be here if were not for immigration. The greater increase in racial and ethnic diversity among children than among adults is due mostly to immigration. Immigrants are typically young adults who are likely to immigrate with children or are likely

Table 5

PERCENT OF U.S. NON-HISPANIC WHITE, NON-HISPANIC RACIAL MINORITY, AND HISPANIC CHILDREN, 1980, 1990, AND 2000

Children	1980 (%)	1990 (%)	2000 (%)
White non-Hispanic	74	69	61
Non-Hispanic racial minority	17	19	22
Hispanic	9	12	17

Note: Children who marked white and another racial category in the 2000 Census are classified as minorities.

Source: Author's calculations using the Integrated Public Use Microdata Series (IPUMS), 2003.

Table 6

WELL-BEING OF CHILDREN BY IMMIGRANT STATUS, 2002

Immigrant status*	Immigrant children (%)	Nonimmigrant children (%)
Children under age 18		
Living in poverty	21	16
Living in single-parent families	22	33
Living in families where no parent works full-time/year-round	29	29
Living with a household head who is a high school dropout	35	11
Living in households without a telephone	3	4
Living in households without a vehicle	8	6
Children who have difficulty speaking English (ages 5–17)	22	1
Teens who are high school dropouts (ages 16–19)	15	6
Teens not attending school and not working (ages 16–19)	11	7

* An immigrant child is defined as not born in the United States, or at least one of the child's parents was not born in the United States.

Source: Author's calculations using the 2002 American Community Survey Public Use Microdata Sample (PUMS).

to have children soon after arriving. In 2000, there were 13.5 million immigrant children in the United States.

Unlike the 1950s, when the number of children grew because of an increased number of births to mostly U.S.-born white parents, much of the increase in the number of children in the 1990s was fueled by immigration. The number of immigrant children increased from 8.3 million in 1990 to 13.5 million in 2000, and this increase accounted for 60 percent of the total increase between 1990 and 2000 in the number of children in the United States.[30] By 2002, the number of immigrant children had risen to almost 16 million, or more than one of every five children in the United States.[31]

The surge of immigrants during the 1990s has important implications for some measures of child well-being. The child poverty rate for immigrant children in 2002 was 21 percent, compared with 16 percent for nonimmigrant children. In addition, a large share of children from immigrant families do not speak English as their primary language at home, and these children have cultural traditions unfamiliar to many educators and service providers. The number of 5-to-17-year-olds living in households where English was not the primarily language increased from 6 million in 1990 to 10 million in 2000. Census data show that among 18-to-24-year-olds, 10 percent of those who spoke only English had not finished high school, compared with 31 percent of 18-to-24-year-olds who were living in households where English was not the primary language.[32]

Table 6 shows several child outcome measures for children in immigrant families and for children in non-immigrant families. In general, immigrant children trail U.S.-born children, but on some indicators, children in immigrant families have better outcomes than nonimmigrants. For example, immigrant families are less likely than U.S.-born families to be headed by a single parent. In 2002, 22 percent of children in immigrant families were living in single-parent families, compared with 33 percent for nonimmigrant families. It is also important

to recognize that many immigrant children are not disadvantaged: Twenty-seven percent of immigrant children lived in households where at least one parent had a college degree, compared with 31 percent of nonimmigrant children.[33]

One of the unique challenges faced by many children in immigrant families is the large number—9 million—who are living in "mixed-status "families, in which the child is a U.S. citizen because he or she was born in the United States, but one or both of the parents are not citizens.[34] More than one of every 10 families with children in the United States is a mixed-status family. Children in these families are often eligible for the full range of benefits that all citizens enjoy, but their parents are often not eligible for some benefits depending on legal status and recency of immigration.

Concentration of Kids in States With Bad Outcomes

The child population is growing rapidly in many states where child outcomes are among the worst in the country. Of the five states that experienced the largest increases in the number of children during the 1990s (California, Texas, Florida, Georgia, and New York), all but California (ranked 21st) were in the bottom one-half of states based on a comprehensive measure of child well-being, according to the 2003 *KIDS COUNT Data*

Book.[35] These five states account for almost one-half of the growth in the number of children between 1990 and 2000.

Single-Parent Families and Poverty

The family is generally the most important social institution in determining a child's life chances. The dichotomy between married-couple and single-parent families, while relatively simplistic, provides a powerful set of categories for understanding child well-being. (According to the 2000 Census, 49 million children live in married-couple families and 19 million live in single-parent families.) While single-mother families constitute the vast majority of single-parent families (78 percent in 2000), the number of children living with single dads grew dramatically during the 1990s. And about 4 million children live with neither parent.

Much of the public interest in family structure is because children growing up in single-parent households typically do not have the same economic or human resources as those available to children growing up in two-parent families. Research shows that children in single-parent families have an increased risk for repeating grades, low academic marks, and low class standing; an increased likelihood of dropping out of high school; increased rates of early childbearing; and increased levels of depression, stress, anxiety, and aggression.[36] One recent study found that youths raised in fatherless families were much more likely to be incarcerated even after controlling for other factors such as poverty.[37]

When we talk about a particular family type, it is important to remember that we are talking about the average or typical child in a family, not all children. Many children growing up in single-parent families do fine, and many children growing up in married-couple families struggle. However, a growing body of research strongly suggests that children benefit when both parents, regardless of marital status, are active in those children's lives.[38]

Researchers typically point to three different reasons why child outcomes in married-couple families are generally better than those in single-parent families:

- Married-couples families have higher incomes than single-parent families.
- Children in married-couple families receive more time and attention from parents.
- Children in married-couple families experience childrearing skills of both the mother and father.

The economic disadvantage of growing up in a single-parent family is striking. Only 8 percent of children in married-couple households are living in poverty, compared with 37 percent of children in single-parent households. Single-parent families typically have only one adult earner; married-couple families often have two earners. Two-thirds of children living in married-couple households have more than one parent in the workforce.

Moreover, in single-mother families—the vast majority of single-parent families—the sole earner is a female, and women typically earn less than men. In 2003, for example, a man who worked full-time/year-round earned $40,332 annually, but a woman who worked full-time/year-round earned only $30,895 annually.[39]

Perhaps even more important to children's well-being than the income differential between married-couple and single-parent families is the difference in assets or net worth. The overall figures are distorted by the large number of relatively well-off widows, but, looking only at young families (where the householder is under age 35), the median net worth of female-headed families is only $1,500, compared with $17,350 for married-couple families.[40] Assets provide a safety net for married-couple families and resources for investments such as the purchase of a home or a college education for a child.

The economic disadvantage of single-mother families is exacerbated because a large share of single-mother families either do not receive any child support payments or receive modest payments. Only 41 percent of custodial mothers and 23 percent of custodial fathers reported receiving any child support in 2002.[41] The average amount of child support due single mothers was $5,138; among those single mothers who received child support, the average amount received was only $3,192. (Many custodial parents are not legally due any child support from the noncustodial parent.)

Measures that assess the time and attention received by children show that children under age 13 who live in two-parent families receive about twice as much daily time from parents as children under age 13 who live in single-parent families.[42] Moreover, children living in married-couple families are more likely than children in single-parent families to benefit from an extended family network of kinship ties of both mother and father.

Some researchers argue that men and women bring different parenting styles to childrearing, and children benefit from both styles. These researchers assert that women are more apt to focus on nurturing, while men are more focused on teaching. For example, in discussing the importance of fathers, David Blankenhorn notes that a father provides his children "with what might be termed paternal cultural transmission: a father's distinctive capacity to contribute to the identity, character, and competences of his children."[43]

The percentage of children living in single-parent families increased from 25 percent in 1990 to 27 percent in 2000, indicating that more kids were living in families with fewer resources. Nonetheless, overall child well-being improved.

Family Diversity

Recent changes in the American family have been the central topic of America's "culture wars." Some people feel that the changes in American families over the past few decades portend the passing of the traditional family; others celebrate the emergence of new family types.[44] It has been widely recognized that household and family relationships have become more complex and complicated during the second half of the 20th century. For example, increases in divorce and remarriage, births to unmarried mothers, and cohabitation have increased the number of children living in households of a different form than what is often described as a traditional family household, with two married adults and their biological offspring.

In 2003, 23 percent of children lived with their mother only; 5 percent lived with their father only; and 4 percent lived with neither parent (see Box 3). And because of divorce and remarriage, the percentage of children affected by the end of a marriage is actually higher than the single-parent figures suggest. Many children currently residing in married-couple families are actually living with stepparents. The Census Bureau recently reported that only 56 percent of all U.S. children are living with both biological parents.[45]

WHY DID CHILD WELL-BEING IMPROVE?

The improved well-being of children during the late 1990s is linked closely to increased resources (such as income) available to their parents.

Parental Employment

The decrease in child poverty during the 1990s is linked to changes in parental work effort. Table 7 (page 214). shows changes in the distribution of children by work status of their parent(s) between 1990 and 2000.

Box 3
NONTRADITIONAL LIVING ARRANGEMENTS

Although the vast majority of children in the United States live with at least one of their parents, there were 3 million children (4 percent of all children under age 18) living with neither parent in 2003. This rate is much higher for some groups: For black children, 8 percent live with neither parent. In addition to the two situations discussed here—living with grandparents and living in foster homes—there are about 300,000 children who live in group quarters such as boarding schools and juvenile justice facilities.

Grandparents
The 2000 Census was the first census to ask if grandparents have responsibility for a grandchild, and for how long they have had that responsibility. In 2000, 4.4 million children, or 6 percent of the child population in the United States, lived with a grandparent who was the head of the household. About 2.4 million grandparents have been responsible for the basic needs of their grandchildren for at least five years.[1]

Grandparents often take responsibility for the care of a grandchild when a parent has severe emotional or mental health problems, or has a drug addiction. Other times, grandparents step in when a child has been abused or neglected, and the grandparent does not want the child put in foster care.[2] An estimated 1.5 million children have a parent in prison. Grandparents will help out, but many are ill-equipped to provide for their grandchildren. In 2000, 19 percent of grandparent caregivers had incomes below the poverty line.[3]

Foster Care
Census data show almost 300,000 children in foster care in 2000, but administrative records indicate more than 540,000 children in foster care in 2001.[4] Because foster children move often, and often have a tenuous relationship with the house-holder, the likelihood of undercounting foster children in a census is high.

These 540,000 children growing up in foster care are particularly important to include in any assessment of child well-being because of their extremely high dropout rates, high incidence of teen pregnancy, difficulty in finding and keeping jobs, and likelihood of drug abuse and criminal behavior.

The foster-care population is very vulnerable, and data from several studies paint a troubling picture of children who age out of foster care. These children are more likely to have been held back a grade, suspended, or expelled from school. At age 17, on average, these foster youth read at the 7th grade level. More than one-half of the teens aging out of foster care report at least one arrest.[5] Only 50 percent of these kids have a high school degree, compared with about 85 percent of all young people. By age 17, one-fourth of foster children have endured a spell of homelessness; four of 10 have become parents; and one of four males has spent time in jail.

References

1. Tavia Simmons and Jane Lawler Dye, "Grandparents Living With Grandchildren: 2000," *Census 2000 Brief*, C2KBR-31 (2003).

2. Margaret Platt Jendrek, "Grandparents Who Parent Their Grandchildren: Circumstances and Decisions," *The Gerontologist* 34, no. 2 (1994): 206-16.

3. Generations United, *Grandparents and Other Relatives Raising Grandchildren: Grassroots Concerns and Solutions From Across the United States* (Washington, DC: Generations United, 2000); and Anne R. Pebley and Laura L. Rudkin, "Grandparents Caring for Grandchildren: What Do We Know?" *Journal of Family Issues* 20, no. 2 (1999): 218-42.

4. U.S. House of Representatives, Committee on House Ways and Means, *2004 Green Book: Background Material and Data on the Programs Within the Jurisdiction of the Committee on Ways and Means* (2004): table 11-7.

5. Martha Shirk and Gary Stangler, *On Their Own: What Happens to Kids When They Age Out of the Foster Care System* (Boulder, CO: Westview Press, 2004): 3; and Mark E. Courtney, Sherri Terao, and Noel Bost, *Midwest Evaluation of Adult Functioning of Former Foster Youth: Conditions of Youth Preparing to Leave State Care* (Chicago: University of Chicago Press, 2004).

Changes in the 1990s reflect the continuation of a long-term shift in work norms. The share of children living in a traditional breadwinner-father/homemaker-mother family fell from 16 percent in 1990 to 15 percent in 2000, while the share of children living in married-couple families in which both spouses work full-time/year-round increased from 17 percent in 1990 to 19 percent in 2000. There was also a slight increase in the share of children living in married-couple families in which the mother worked full-time/year-round and the father did not work, but the number of children living in this type of family is small—about 800,000.

The breadwinner-father/homemaker-mother family is more an idealized type than a bygone reality. Even in 1960, at the height of the baby boom, less than one-half (47 percent) of all families could be characterized as breadwinner/homemaker families.[46]

The biggest work status changes during the 1990s occurred in single-parent families. There was a large increase in the share of children living with a single parent who was working, and there was a significant decrease in the share of children living with a single parent who did not work at all. The share of children living with single parents who were working full-time/year-round increased from 9.1 percent to 12.9 percent from 1990 to 2000. On the other hand, the share of children in single-parent families where the parent did not work fell from 7.3 percent in 1990 to 5.7 percent in 2000.

Increased employment was particularly significant among never-married single mothers, a group that makes up a large share of the welfare population. Between 1995 and 2000, the percent of never-married single mothers who were employed increased from 49 percent to 66 percent.[47]

The reasons for this significant increase in parental employment during the 1990s are debatable. Some researchers point to the very robust economy of the late 1990s as the major reason for the increase in employment among parents, because employers needed workers and opportunities for low-income parents expanded greatly. Others conclude that the welfare reform legislation passed in 1996 was the main factor behind the increase in parental employment during the 1990s, particularly for single parents. By eliminating guaranteed long-term government support for poor families with children, these researchers argue, welfare reform motivated single parents to move into the labor force.

The Economic Expansion

There is widespread agreement that the improvements in child well-being during the late 1990s were linked to improvements in the employment situation of low-income families. And economic changes during the

Table 7
PERCENT OF CHILDREN BY FAMILY STRUCTURE AND PARENTAL EMPLOYMENT, 1990 AND 2000

Family/employment	1990 (%)	2000 (%)
Married-couple families	76.0	72.1
Both parents work full-time/ year-round	17.1	19.2
Father works full-time/year-round; mother works part-time/part-year	22.9	19.6
Father works full-time/year-round; mother doesn't work	16.3	14.9
Father works part-time/part-year; mother works full-time/year-round	3.4	3.3
Father works part-time/part-year; mother works part-time/part-year	7.3	6.4
Father works part-time/part-year; mother doesn't work	5.0	4.5
Single-parent families	24.0	27.9
Parent works full-time/year-round	9.1	12.9
Parent works part-time/part-year	7.6	9.4
Parent doesn't work	7.3	5.7
No resident parent works	9.5	7.6
All resident parents work	67.4	70.6

Note: Year-round means the person worked at least 50 weeks the previous year. Full time means the person worked at least 35 hours per week. Only children living with at least one parent are included in data.

Source: Author's calculations using the 1% Public Use Microdata Sample (PUMS) from the 1990 and 2000 censuses.

1990s have also had some positive influence on low-income neighborhoods. Neighborhood changes are important because research shows that the quality of the neighborhood where a child lives can have a significant impact on that child's life chances (see Box 4). But there is more to this story.

The economic expansion of the late 1990s was probably a *necessary* condition for the improvement of child well-being, but further analysis shows that the expansion was not a *sufficient* condition. Changes in child well-being during the periods of economic growth during the late 1970s and late 1980s illustrate that good economic times don't automatically translate into improved outcomes for children.

Indeed, falling unemployment rates during the late 1970s and late 1980s did little to improve the well-being of children. For example, the unemployment rate fell from 8.5 percent in 1975 to 5.8 percent in 1979, but the Child Well-Being Index was essentially unchanged during this period. Likewise, the unemployment rate fell from 9.7 percent in 1982 to 5.3 percent in 1989, but the index actually decreased slightly during this period. On the other hand, as the unemployment rate fell from 7.5 percent in 1992 to 4 percent in 2000, the index increased by about 9 points.[48]

One could argue that the economic expansion of the last half of the 1990s was longer and deeper than those of the late 1970s and late 1980s, but that situation alone does not explain why the experience of the late 1990s is so qualitatively different than the experience of the late 1970s and late 1980s with regard to the connection between economic expansion and changes in child well-being. If the robust economy of the late 1990s does not fully explain why child outcomes improved, what does?

Welfare Reform

One major event in the mid-1990s often linked to increased employment among single parents is the historic welfare reform legislation passed by Congress in 1996: the Personal Responsibility and Work Opportunity Reconciliation Act (PRWORA). This legislation ended Aid to Families with Dependent Children (AFDC) and enacted Temporary Assistance for Needy Families (TANF). PRWORA also ended entitlement to welfare payments; required that recipients work; limited the

time a family could remain on welfare; and gave states more control over how programs were structured by making the welfare program into a series of block grants. Under these block grant programs, states are given money and a great deal of flexibility to figure out how to best use the funds for a given purpose.

In terms of trends in child well-being, PRWORA was probably not as important as broader changes in how the government interacts with poor families. Many of the positive trends in child indicators started before the key provisions of PRWORA were implemented, and most of those provisions only applied to a small share of all American families. On the other hand, welfare reform did not have the disastrous impact some critics envisioned, such as contributing to a significant increase in child poverty.

Public policy changes during the 1990s signaled a major reorientation and change in emphasis of the relationship between government assistance programs and low-income families, and it is best to view PRWORA in this broader context. The emphasis during the 1990s was increasingly on supporting low-income workers.

Box 4

IMPROVING NEIGHBORHOODS

In addition to improving the economic conditions of individual families, the strong economy of the late 1990s also changed neighborhood environments for many children.[1] The neighborhood in which a child lives determines his or her choice of peers and playmates; the quality of schools; and the availability of amenities such as parks, playgrounds, and libraries. In addition, neighborhoods often determine the type of child-care services available, the level of personal safety, and the availability of jobs. The neighborhood has a major impact on the role models a child sees on a regular basis. Neighborhood norms can help launch a child toward college and a stable work life, or increase the likelihood that he or she will commit a crime or become a teenage parent.[2]

The number of children living in concentrated poverty neighborhoods (where the poverty rate was 40 percent or higher) fell by more than 25 percent between 1990 and 2000, or from 3.2 million to 2.3 million children (see table). It is not clear whether the number of high poverty tracts declined because poor families moved to less poor neighborhoods, or if a significant number of people in high poverty tracts moved out of poverty altogether. It is clear, however, that poor black and Hispanic children are more concentrated in high poverty neighborhoods than poor non-Hispanic white children.[3] About 20 percent of poor black children, and 14 percent of poor Hispanic children, lived in concentrated poverty neighborhoods in 2000, compared with about 2 percent of poor non-Hispanic white children.

The demolition of some public housing and the implementation of federal programs designed to disperse public housing residents also contributed to this deconcentration. But neighborhood change during the 1990s was not uniformly positive. For example, there was no change in the proportion

Children Living in High and Very High Poverty Neighborhoods, 1990 and 2000

Neighborhood poverty rate	Population under age 18 (millions)	
	1990	2000
Census-designated poverty area (20%+ in poverty)	14.6	14.7
Concentrated poverty (40%+ in poverty)	3.2	2.3

Source: U.S. Census Bureau, 1990 and 2000 censuses.

of children living in census-designated poverty areas—where the poverty rate was 20 percent or higher.

Additionally, a more comprehensive measure of neighborhood quality did not show similar neighborhood improvements over the 1990s.[4] The percent of children living in distressed neighborhoods—identified as those with high levels of poverty, female-headed families, unemployed working-age men, and high school dropouts—increased from 5.3 percent in 1990 to 6.1 percent in 2000.

References

1. Paul A. Jargowsky, *Stunning Progress, Hidden Problems: Dramatic Decline of Concentrated Poverty in the 1990s* (Washington, DC: The Brookings Institution, 2003).

2. Jeanne Brooks-Gunn et al., *Neighborhood Poverty: Context and Consequences for Children* (New York: Russell Sage Foundation, 1997).

3. U.S. Department of Health and Human Services, *Trends in the Well-Being of America's Children and Youth* (2003): figure PF 3.2.

4. William P. O'Hare and Mark Mather, *The Growing Number of Children in Severely Distressed Neighborhoods: Evidence From the 2000 Census* (Washington, DC: Population Reference Bureau, 2003).

The programmatic approach that emerged in the 1990s also recognizes that there are a significant number of working families in poverty or with incomes just above the poverty line who deserve assistance.

Total government spending on needy families did not change much during the last half of the 1990s, but there were significant shifts in where the funds were spent. Table 8 shows that overall government spending on benefits for low-income recipients rose only 4 percent between 1995 and 2000, in sharp contrast to the 48 percent increase seen in the first half of the 1990s. Between 1995 and 2000, there was actually an 11 percent decline in cash aid and a 21 percent decline in food benefits, reflecting the decreasing number of people in poverty or eligible for these programs. However, between 1995 and 2000, expenditures on education benefits increased by 12 percent; expenditures on jobs and job training increased by 20 percent; and expenditures for work support services increased by 62 percent.

Programs that aid working-poor families affect a large proportion of low-income children, because most parents in poor or low-income families are working and the share of poor children living in working-poor families is increasing. Between 1976 and 2001, the number of poor children living in families totally dependent on welfare fell from 3 million to just under 1 million, while the number of poor children living in families with income from earnings and none from public assistance increased from 4 million in 1976 to 7 million in 2001.[49]

Three of the most important programmatic trends during the 1990s that brought increased support for low-income working families were:

● Expansion of the Earned Income Tax Credit (EITC);
● A new health insurance program for low-income children (SCHIP); and
● Growth in government child-care subsidies.

Earned Income Tax Credit

The Earned Income Tax Credit (EITC) is a federal program that allows low-earning workers to enhance their income. EITC targets low-income families with children and with at least one working parent. EITC has enjoyed strong bipartisan support since it was first enacted in 1975 to blunt the effect of payroll taxes on low-income working families. The credit is generally available to families with incomes below 200 percent of the poverty line, or about $35,000 a year for a family of four. In 2003, the average EITC recipient received $1,784.

The importance of the EITC program can be seen by looking at federal government outlays, which show that the credit now provides twice as much cash income to low-income families as does the major cash welfare program, Temporary Assistance for Needy Families (TANF). In 2002, EITC outlays were $28 billion, compared with $13 billion for TANF. Some states also provide funds for state EITC programs, and all states contribute to TANF. As of mid-2004, 18 states have enacted a state EITC, and many others are considering one. State EITC programs give low-income working families with children an additional income boost because the families get a break on paying state taxes. But even with the state contributions, low-income families receive far more cash through EITC than through TANF.

Since EITC was expanded in 1993, the number of recipient families increased by 25 percent, while the average amount received per recipient family grew by more than 50 percent.[50] The EITC has lifted as many as 2.5 million children above the poverty line each year (but not officially, because EITC is part of the tax system and taxes are not included when measuring poverty). EITC has also increased the family income for millions of other families.[51] While changes in family income due to EITC may seem small, studies show that,

---

Table 8

GOVERNMENT EXPENDITURES ON BENEFITS FOR LOW-INCOME RECIPIENTS, 1990, 1995, AND 2000

	1990 (millions)	1995 (millions)	2000 (millions)	% change 1990–1995	% change 1995–2000
Total benefits*	$282,815	$418,484	$436,985	48	4
Medical	115,250	196,922	225,858	71	15
Cash aid	72,019	103,291	91,703	43	-11
Food	33,326	43,558	34,347	31	-21
Housing	23,926	35,764	34,906	49	-2
Education	19,102	18,146	20,385	-5	12
Jobs/training	5,631	6,132	7,347	9	20
Services**	11,267	12,775	20,724	13	62
Energy aid	2,294	1,896	1,715	-17	-9

* Total benefits are in constant 2000 dollars.

** Includes Title XX Social Services; child care for TANF recipients/ex-recipients; Child Care and Development Block Grant services; and TANF services.

Source: U.S. Census Bureau, *Statistical Abstract of the United States* (2003): table 539.

among low-income families, even small increases in income can lead to better child outcomes.[52]

State Children's Health Insurance Program

Data for 2003 show that about 11 percent of all children lack health insurance, and 19 percent of all poor children lack health insurance.[53] However, this measure includes only those children who lacked health insurance for the entire year. More than 37 percent of all children lacked health insurance for some period during 2002 and 2003.[54]

In response to growing concerns about lack of health care coverage in the 1990s—and spurred by President Bill Clinton's effort to enact comprehensive health insurance legislation—Congress passed the State Children's Health Insurance Program (SCHIP) in 1997 to help states provide health care coverage for children in low-income families. States can establish their own income cutoffs for eligibility, within certain boundaries. By 2001, almost 5 million children had been enrolled in the SCHIP program.[55]

SCHIP helped sever the link between welfare and health insurance for poor families by allowing low-income parents to obtain health care for their children while they continue to work. SCHIP eases the transition from welfare to work for these low-income parents, who typically find jobs that do not offer health insurance.

Child-Care Subsidies

The majority of children live in households in which all resident parents work (see Table 7, page 214).

A critical barrier for low-income parents trying to move into the workforce or wanting to expand the number of hours they work is the high cost and difficulty of finding appropriate child care; the odd and constantly changing work schedules faced by these low-wage workers make child care even harder to find. About two-fifths of employed Americans now work during nonstandard times.[56] Blue-collar and pink-collar jobs are the most likely jobs to require nonstandard work hours.

Data from the National Survey of American Families show that about one-half of all working families with children under age 13 pay at least some child care expenses, averaging $286 a month, or about 9 percent of earnings.[57] For low-income working parents, child-care costs consume an enormous portion of their budget. Census Bureau data show that, among low-income families with employed mothers (incomes less than $1,500 a month), child-care costs consume more than 25 percent of their income.[58]

As growing numbers of low-income parents, especially single mothers, moved into the workforce during the late 1990s (and many of these women moved from welfare to work), their need for child care grew dramatically. In the last half of the 1990s, federal and state child-care subsidies for low-income working families nearly tripled, in part because PRWORA allowed states to use TANF dollars for child care. In 2003, $2 billion in TANF money went into child care.

Federal and state government child-care funding increased from $3 billion in 1995 to almost $8 billion in 2001. States and localities, as well as some private-sector companies, also helped many low-income working families find affordable child care. Unlike the EITC and SCHIP programs, however, child-care assistance provided by the government involves several programs and includes direct subsidies as well as tax credits.

The Child Care Development Fund is the chief form of direct federal child-care assistance. Income limits for participation in this program are determined by states, but the income limit in most states is less than 200 percent of poverty. Child-care support is not an entitlement, and many eligible families do not receive child-care subsidies because support funds are limited. About one-half of states have waiting lists, and more than 500,000 children were on the waiting lists in 2003.[59] While there were still many eligible low-income workers who did not receive a child-care subsidy, the expansion of this support system undoubtedly helped low-income families.

Additional help for low-income parents is provided through the federal tax code. The Child and Dependent Care Credit is a tax credit which provides another $3 billion, but only about one-quarter of this benefit goes to low-income families for partial reimbursement of child-care costs.

EITC is part of the tax system, while child-care subsidies and public health insurance are noncash benefits. Therefore, these benefits are not considered as income in determining poverty status for families. Since official poverty status is based only on cash income, the expansion of EITC, child-care subsidies, and public health insurance is not reflected in the official poverty figures. However, analysts show that this expansion has significantly improved the standard of living for millions of Americans during the 1990s.[60]

Expanded Support

Expanded support for low-income working families during the 1990s helped struggling parents fulfill their work obligations and their responsibilities at home. While the mechanisms that translate higher incomes into better outcomes for children are not always clear, the connection between family economic status and outcomes for children is indisputable. On virtually every measure of child well-being, children from families with more resources do better than children living in families with fewer resources. Consequently, it is reasonable to expect that providing more resources for low-income working families will improve outcomes for children in those families.

Moreover, since negative outcomes for children are concentrated in the low-income population (see Table 9,

Table 9

CONCENTRATION OF NEGATIVE CHILD OUTCOMES IN LOW-INCOME FAMILIES, 2002

Negative child outcome	Percent in low-income families (less than 200% of poverty)
1. Children living in single-parent families	66
2. Children living in families where no parent works full-time/year-round	68
3. Children living with a household head who is a high school dropout	72
4. Children living in households without a telephone	84
5. Children living in households without a vehicle	84
6. Children who have difficulty speaking English (ages 5–17)	66
7. Teens who are high school dropouts (ages 16–19)	64
8. Teens not attending school and not working (ages 16–19)	64

Note: For outcomes 1–6, data are for related children only; also, persons under age 18 who are a householder, spouse, or unmarried partner are not included. For outcomes 7–8, all persons ages 16–19 are included.

Source: Author's calculations using the 2002 American Community Survey Public Use Microdata Sample (PUMS).

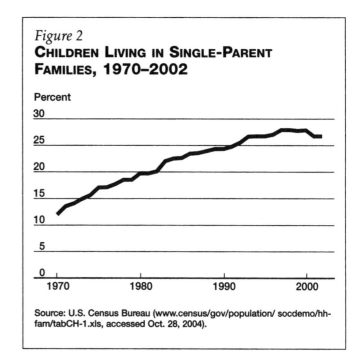

Figure 2

CHILDREN LIVING IN SINGLE-PARENT FAMILIES, 1970–2002

Source: U.S. Census Bureau (www.census.gov/population/ socdemo/hh-fam/tabCH-1.xls, accessed Oct. 28, 2004).

page 218), reducing the number of children living in low-income families will likely have a disproportionately positive effect on overall child well-being. For example, almost two-thirds of high school dropouts come from low-income families; more than 80 percent of children with no phone at home or no vehicle at home come from low-income families; and teens growing up in poverty are more likely to become pregnant than are teens from other income groups.

Given the expansion of programs to help low-income working families, it is not surprising that the well-being of children in low-income families improved during the 1990s. By some measures, the biggest improvements in child well-being during the 1990s were in low-income families. One major reason for the overall improvements in child well-being during the last half of the 1990s is better outcomes for children in low-income families.

Declining Share of Children in Single-Parent Families

For some groups, the share of children in single-parent families has shown a significant decline since the mid-1990s. For example, the percent of black children living in single-parent families fell from 58 percent in 1991 to 53 percent in 2002. Among Hispanics, the share of chil-

dren in single-parent families declined from 33 percent in 1995 to 29 percent in 2001. These beneficial trends in family structure occurred most often in low-income populations, suggesting that the trends are tied to expanded economic opportunity and support for low-income populations in the 1990s.[61]

In 2002, the share of children living in single-parent families was still below what it was in 1996, and this share is well below where it would have been if it had followed the trajectory of the early 1990s (see Figure 2). If the pace of change seen between 1990 and 1996 had continued for another six years, 31 percent of children would have been living in single-parent families in 2002, instead of the 27 percent observed in 2002.

Because the share of children in married-couple families stabilized during the mid-1990s, the impact of the booming economy and low-income family support programs of the late 1990s was not undermined by growing numbers of children in difficult family situations.

Sadly, Americans still fail to acknowledge the decrease in the number of children in single-parent families, a perception reflected in a poll taken in 2002. This poll found that 76 percent of adults believed that the percentage of children living in single-mother families had *increased* over the last five years.[62]

Decline in Teen Childbearing

Recent changes in the teen birth rate have resulted in fewer children living in single-parent families. Almost four of every five teen births (79 percent) are out-of-wedlock births. A recent report from the National Center for Health Statistics showed a 26 percent decline in the teen birth rate between 1991 and 2001.[63] One analysis indicates that this decline explains 26 percent of the reduction in child poverty in the 1990s.[64]

The increased risk for a child born to a teen mother can be illustrated by the following stark comparison. The poverty rate for children born to teenage mothers who never married and who did not graduate from high school is 78 percent. Conversely, the poverty rate for children born to women over age 20 who were married and did graduate from high school is 9 percent. Fortunately, relatively few children are born to teen mothers who have not completed high school and are not married.

The teen birth rate declined between 1991 and 2001 in every major racial and ethnic group and in every state, and teen pregnancy rates and teen abortion rates have been falling as well.[65] Teen birth rates have been falling for two simple reasons: Fewer teens are having sex, and more teens who do have sex are using contraception. The Youth Risk Behavior Surveillance System found that 46 percent of the nation's high school students reported having ever had sex in 2001, compared with 54 percent in 1991.[66]

POST-2000 TRENDS

Since the economy peaked in April 2000, there have been troubling signs that the momentum established in the late 1990s regarding improved child well-being may be dissipating. Most of the measures of child well-being available in 2004 reflect experiences through 2003 only, so it is likely that the current child well-being measures do not reflect the full impact of the prolonged post-2000 economic slump.

The Child Well-Being Index shows that the rate of improvement in overall child well-being slowed significantly between 2000 and 2002, but the rate still moved in a positive direction. The average gain of 1.6 points per year between 1995 and 2000 fell to an average gain of 0.8 points per year between 2000 and 2002.

In contrast to the large positive changes in child outcomes between 1995 and 2000, the evidence since 2000 for individual measures of child well-being is mixed. For example, the child poverty rate fell steadily between 1993 and 2000, but both the Current Population Survey (CPS) and the American Community Survey (ACS) show that child poverty rates increased between 2000 and 2003. The ACS data for state-level child poverty rates from 2000 to 2003 show that child poverty increased in 32 states, although the increase was statistically significant in only eight states plus the District of Columbia.

Despite the significant gains made in the late 1990s, the poverty rate for children was a little over 17 percent in 2003: More than one of every six children is growing up in poverty in the United States—a much higher child poverty rate than any other developed country and a sad situation for the wealthiest country in the world.

A Jobless Economic Recovery

Post-2000 economic performance has been dismal, as the 2001 recession gave way to a "jobless" recovery. The unemployment rate rose from 3.8 percent in April 2000 to 6.0 percent in April 2003; the rate then fell slightly to 5.6 percent in June 2004.[67] Real mean household income fell by 3 percent (or by $2,000) between 2000 and 2003.[68]

The recent economic slump has hit some of the most vulnerable families the hardest. Between 1995 and 2000, the percent of never-married single mothers who were employed increased by an incredible 17 percentage points (from 49 percent to 66 percent); but between 2000 and 2003, the figure fell by 4 percentage points, to 62 percent.[69]

One of the key stories of the post-2000 economy is that jobs with good benefits are being replaced by jobs without such benefits. Manufacturing and production jobs, for which median weekly earnings are $522, are being replaced by service jobs, for which median weekly earnings are $410. New jobs pay less and have fewer benefits. In 2002, only 46 percent of working parents in poverty had any paid leave (including sick leave), while 84 percent of parents above 200 percent of poverty had paid leave.[70]

Cutbacks in Government Support

There are also signs that the fiscal stress experienced by federal and state governments since 2000 has led to cutbacks in support programs. To appreciate trends in social support programs, it is important to understand the changing federal and state budget situations. The $200 billion annual federal budget surplus in 2000 has turned into a more than $400 billion deficit in 2004. And equally important, the post-2000 era has ushered in the largest fiscal crisis in decades for many states. To close the gap between revenues and expenditures, many states have cut spending. For example, child-care subsidies have been cut in 21 states since 2000.

Moreover, looking ahead 10 years, the situation will likely become much worse. If current trends continue, experts predict that the entire federal budget will be consumed by military spending, Social Security and Medicare, and interest on the national debt, leaving no funds for discretionary programs that support children and families.

While the EITC has enjoyed strong bipartisan support for many years, nagging questions about the level of erroneous payments have led the Bush administration to consider new EITC rules. Currently, families ask for the EITC benefits when they file their regular income tax forms. If audited by the IRS, an EITC recipient must provide documentation, as must anyone going through an IRS audit. However, proposed new "precertification" rules would require EITC families to provide much more documentation *before* they can receive the benefit.

Requiring more documentation will most likely lower participation rates among eligible families.[71]

Since 2000, there has been a steady erosion in the number of children who typically gain health insurance through an employed parent. The proportion of children covered by employer-based health insurance fell from 66 percent in 2000 to 61 percent in 2003.[72] The share of children in low-income families with employer-sponsored health insurance went from 39 percent in 1999 to 32 percent in 2002. Nonetheless, the share of all children with health insurance stayed relatively constant over this period because children covered by government health insurance increased dramatically. The expansion of public-sector insurance through SCHIP helps lessen the impact of private-sector health insurance cutbacks. But even SCHIP enrollment has inched downward; a lower enrollment in December 2003 than in June 2003 was the first decline in SCHIP enrollment since the program began in 1997.[73] Budget cuts adopted in 34 states will cause about 1.5 million low-income people to lose health insurance, and 21 states have new or higher copayments for public health insurance.[74]

After many years of steady decline, TANF caseloads are now increasing in many states. From September 2002 to September 2003, TANF caseloads increased in 30 states and the national caseload increased by 0.4 percent.[75] As the welfare caseload declined during the late 1990s, there was a debate about the relative contributions to this decline of the good economy and the new welfare law. Since the welfare rules have not changed since 1996, the post-2000 leveling off of TANF caseloads suggests that the good economic times of the late 1990s were a necessary condition for caseload declines. The slight uptick in TANF caseloads is also a sign of the difficulty that low-income workers have in getting and holding jobs, but the increase in caseloads is also a sign that those welfare recipients still on the rolls have the hardest time finding jobs.

TANF was up for reauthorization in 2002, but Congress thus far has not been able to come to agreement on some key welfare issues, such as increasing work requirements among TANF recipients.

WILL THE IMPROVEMENTS ERODE?

Examining the trends in the well-being of U.S. children in the 1990s helps dispel two common misperceptions: that children are enduring worsening conditions, and that government programs to help the needy either don't work or don't work well. The evidence presented in this report shows both perceptions to be incorrect. There were widespread improvements in the lives of children during the late 1990s (particularly for children in low-income working families), and much of the credit goes to the implementation and expansion of government programs.

Moreover, the overall improvements during the 1990s were led by improved outcomes for black and Hispanic children. This report shows that America can improve the lives of its children even while minority children are becoming a growing percentage of the U.S. population.

Although many post-2000 trends are troubling, overall child well-being continues to improve, but at a slower pace than in the late 1990s. Some government programs to help needy families and children are under pressure, largely because of budget constraints. The next few years will be critical in determining if the improvements in child well-being during the late 1990s begin to erode.

ACKNOWLEDGMENTS

The author would like to thank the three anonymous reviewers for the helpful comments on earlier drafts of the manuscript; Martye T. Scobee of the Urban Studies Institute at the University of Louisville and Jean D'Amico of the Population Reference Bureau for research assistance; Ellen Carnevale for her skillful editing; and the Population Reference Bureau and Russell Sage Foundation for supporting this report.

References

If provided by the author, additional text and data associated with this report are available at www.prb.org/AmericanPeople.

1. Mark D. Hayward and Bridget K. Gorman, "The Long Arm of Childhood: The Influence of Early-Life Social Conditions on Men's Mortality," *Demography* 41, no. 1 (2004): 87-107

2. Susan E. Mayer, *What Money Can't Buy: Family Income and Children's Life Chances* (Cambridge, MA: Harvard University Press, 1997): table 3.1; and Children's Defense Fund, *Wasting America's Future* (Washington, DC: Children's Defense Fund, 1994).

3. Samuel H. Preston, "Children and the Elderly: Divergent Paths for America's Dependents," *Demography* 21, no. 4 (1984): 436.

4. Rebecca L. Clark et al., "Federal Expenditures on Children: 1960-1997, Assessing the New Federalism," *Occasional Paper* 45 (Washington, DC: Urban Institute Press, 2001).

5. Federal Interagency Forum on Child and Family Statistics, *America's Children: Key National Indicators of Well-Being, 2004* (Washington, DC: U.S. Government Printing Office, 2004).

6. Kenneth Land, *The Child Well-Being Index (CWI) 1975-2002, with Projections for 2003: 2004 Report* (Durham, NC: Duke University Press, 2004).

7. William P. O'Hare, Nicole L. Bramstedt, and Vicky Lamb, "Assessing the KIDS COUNT Composite Index," *KIDS COUNT Working Paper* (Baltimore: Annie E. Casey Foundation, 2003).

8. Federal Interagency Forum on Child and Family Statistics, *America's Children, 2004.*

9. O'Hare, Bramstedt, and Lamb, "Assessing the KIDS COUNT Composite Index": 10.

10. U.S. Department of Health and Human Services, Office of the Assistant Secretary for Planning and Evaluation, *Trends in the Well-Being of America's Children & Youth: 2003* (Washington, DC: U.S. Government Printing Office, 2004).

11. William P. O'Hare and Vicky Lamb, "Ranking States Based on Improvements on Child Well-Being During the 1990s," *KIDS COUNT Working Paper* (Baltimore: Annie E. Casey Foundation, 2004).

12. Federal Interagency Forum on Child and Family Statistics, *America's Children, 2004.*

13. Karl Ashworth, Martha Hill, and Robert Walker, "Patterns of Childhood Poverty: New Challenges for Policy," *Journal of Policy Analysis and Management* 13, no. 4 (1994): 658-80.

14. Kenneth Land, "Figure 1: Race/Ethnic Group-Specific Child Well-Being Index, 1985-2001," *The Child Well-Being Index*, accessed online at www.soc.duke.edu/resources/child_wellbeing/section_g.html, on Nov. 30, 2004.

15. Bernadette D. Proctor and Joseph Dalaker, "Poverty in the United States: 2002," *Current Population Reports* P60-222 (2003): table A-2.

16. Hsien-Hen Lu et al., "Children Facing Economic Hardships in the United States: Differentials and Changes in the 1990s," *Demographic Research* 10, no. 11 (2004): 285-338.

17. Public Agenda, *Children These Days '99: What Americans Really Think About the Next Generation* (New York: Public Agenda, 1999).

18. Lina Guzman et al., "How Children Are Doing: The Mismatch Between Public Perception and Statistical Reality," *Child Trends Research Brief* 2003-12 (2003).

19. The 1960 data come from Steven Ruggles and Mathew Sobek, *Integrated Public Use Microdata Series: Version 2.0* (Minneapolis: Historical Census Projects, University of Minnesota, 1997, www.ipums.umn.edu/usa/cite.html). The 2000 data are from the U.S. Census Bureau, "Profile of General Demographic Characteristics for the United States, 2000," accessed online at www.census.gov/Press-Release/www/2001/cb01cn67.html, on Oct. 25, 2004.

20. William P. O'Hare and Kenneth M. Johnson, "Child Poverty in Rural America," *Population Reference Bureau Reports on America* 4, no. 1 (2004).

21. Amie Jamieson, Andrea Curry, and Gladys Martinez, "School Enrollment in the United States—Social and Economic Characteristics of Students: October 1999," *Current Population Reports* P20-533 (2001): 3-4.

22. Alex Frangos, "School Districts Spend to Ensure Good Acoustics," *The Wall Street Journal*, July 30, 2003.

23. U.S. Census Bureau, *Statistical Abstract of the United States: 2002* (Washington, DC: U.S. Government Printing Office, 2002): table 241.

24. Patricia M. Lines, "Homeschoolers: Estimating Numbers and Growth," accessed online at www.ed.gov/ofices/OERI/SAI/homeschool/homeschoolers.pdf, on Oct. 27, 2004; and U.S. Department of Education, National Center for Educational Statistics, "1.1 Million Homeschooled Students in the United States in 2003," *NCES Issue Brief* 2004-115 (2004).

25. U.S. Census Bureau, "Table 1: Annual Estimates of the Population by Sex and Five-Year Age Groups for the United States: April 1, 2000 to July 1, 2003" (released June 14, 2004), accessed at www.census.gov/popest/national/asrh/NC-EST2003/NC-EST2003-01.xls, on June 28, 2004.

26. National Research Council, *From Neurons to Neighborhoods: The Science of Early Childhood Development* (Washington, DC: National Academies Press, 2000); National Research Council, *Eager to Learn: Educating Our Preschoolers* (Washington, DC: National Academies Press, 2001); and Gary Ritter and Peter Moyi, "The Impact of Day Care on School Readiness: New Information From Early Childhood Longitudinal Study," accessed online at http://policy.uark.edu/ritter/researchpapers-childcare.html.

27. Richard J. Coley, *An Uneven Start: Indicators of Inequality in School Readiness* (Princeton, NJ: Education Testing Service, 2002).

28. Kathleen Vail, "Ready to Learn," *American School Board Journal* 190, no. 11 (2003): 14-17; and *Education Week*, "Quality Counts 2002: Building Blocks for Success" (Bethesda, MD: Editorial Projects in Education, 2002).

29. Lunn A. Karoly et al., *Investing in Our Children: What We Know and Don't Know About the Costs and Benefits of Early Childhood Intervention* (Santa Monica, CA: The Rand Institute, 1998); Arthur J. Reynolds et al., "Age 21 Cost Benefit Analysis of the Title 1 Chicago Child-Parent Center," *Dis-*

cussion Paper 1245-02 (Madison, WI: University of Wisconsin, Institute for Research on Poverty, 1998); Barbara Wolfe and Scott Scrivner, "Providing Universal Preschool for Four-Year-Olds", in *One Percent Solution: New Policies, Brighter Futures for America's Children*, ed. Isabel Sawhill (Washington, DC: The Brookings Institution, 2003); and Robert G. Lynch, *Exceptional Returns: Economic, Fiscal, and Social Benefits of Investment in Early Childhood Development* (Washington, DC: Economic Policy Institute, 2004).

30. Laura Beavers and Jean D'Amico, "Children in Immigrant Families: Evidence from the 2000 Census" (Washington, DC: Population Reference Bureau, forthcoming).

31. Beavers and D'Amico, "Children in Immigrant Families."

32. Steven Klein et al., "Language Minorities and Their Educational and Labor Market Indicators—Recent Trends," *NCES 2004-009* (Washington, DC: U.S. Department of Education, National Center for Education Statistics, 2004): v.

33. Beavers and D'Amico, "Children in Immigrant Families."

34. Randy Capps, "Immigrant Issues in Child and Family Policy," presentation at the annual Annie E. Casey Foundation KIDS COUNT Conference, 2004.

35. Annie E. Casey Foundation, 2003 *KIDS COUNT Data Book* (Baltimore: Annie E. Casey Foundation, 2003).

36. Gary Sandefur and Sara S. McLanahan, *Growing Up With a Single Parent: What Hurts, What Helps* (Cambridge, MA: Harvard University Press, 1994): 1-2.

37. Cynthia Harper and Sara S. McLanahan, "Father Absence and Youth Incarceration," paper delivered at the annual meeting of the American Sociological Association, 1998.

38. Sara McLanahan et al., *The Fragile Families and Child Well-Being Study*, March 2003, accessed online at http://crcw.princeton.edu/fragilefamilies/files/nationalreport.pdf, on Nov. 19, 2004.

39. Carmen DeNavas-Walt, Bernadette D. Proctor, and Robert Mills, "Income, Poverty and Health Insurance Coverage in the United States: 2003," *Current Population Reports* P60-226 (2004): table 1.

40. Shawna Orzechowsi and Peter Sepielli, "Net Worth and Asset Ownership of Households: 1998 and 2000," *Current Population Reports* P70-88 (2003): table J.

41. Timothy Grall, "Custodial Mothers and Fathers and Their Child Support: 2001," *Current Population Reports* P60-225 (2003): table A.

42. Child Trends, *Charting Parenthood: A Statistical Portrait of Fathers and Mothers in America* (Washington, DC: Child Trends, 2002): 26.

43. David Blankenhorn, *Fatherless America: Confronting Our Most Urgent Social Problem* (New York: Harper Collins, 1995): 25.

44. David Popenoe, "American Family in Decline, 1960-1990: A Review and Appraisal," *Journal of Marriage and Family* 55, no. 3 (1993): 527-55; Barbara White and Barbara Defoe, "Dan Quayle Was Right," *Atlantic Monthly* (April 1993); Blankenhorn, *Fatherless America*; and Karen Struening, *New Family Values: Liberty, Equality, Diversity* (Lanham, MD: Rowman and Littlefield, 2002). For a good description of some of the ways in which relationships are more complicated, see Lynne M. Casper and Suzanne M. Bianchi, *Continuity and Change in the American Family* (Thousand Oaks, CA: Sage Publications, 2003).

45. U.S. Census Bureau, "Living Arrangements of Children," accessed online at www.census.gov/population/www/socdemo/child/la-child.html, on Oct. 27, 2004.

46. Donald J. Hernandez, *America's Children: Resources From Family, Government and the Economy* (New York: Russell Sage Foundation, 1993): table 5.1.

47. Arloc Sherman, Shawn Fremstad, and Sharon Parrot, *Employment Rates for Single Mothers Fell Substantially During Recent Period of Labor Market Weakness* (Washington, DC: Center on Budget and Policy Priorities, 2004): table 1.

48. Land, *The Child Well-Being Index (CWI) 1975-2002.*

49. Analysis of the U.S. Census Bureau, March Current Population Surveys, 1976 and 2001.

50. Tax Policy Center, "EITC, Historical Recipients, 1975-2000," accessed online at www.taxpolicycenter.org/TaxFacts/lowincome/eitc_recipients.cfm, on Oct. 27, 2004.

51. Craig Gunderson and James P. Ziliak, "Poverty and Macroeconomic Performance Across Space, Race, and Family Structure," *Demography* 41, no. 1 (2004): 61-86.

52. Greg J. Duncan et al., "How Much Does Childhood Poverty Affect the Life Chances of Children?" *American Sociological Review* 63, no. 3 (1998): 406-23; and Virginia Knox, Cynthia Miller, and Lisa A. Gennetian, *Reforming Welfare and Rewarding Work: A Summary of the Final Report on the Minnesota Family Investment Program* (New York: Manpower Demonstration Research Corporation (MDRC), 2000).

53. DeNavas-Walt, Proctor, and Mills, "Income, Poverty and Health Insurance Coverage in the United States: 2003": table C-2.

54. Families USA, *One in Three: Non-Elderly Americans Without Health Insurance, 2002-2003* (Washington, DC: Families USA, 2004): 7.

55. U.S. Department of Health and Human Services, "SCHIP Quarterly Enrollment Report: FY 2001," accessed online at www.os.dhhs.gov/, on Nov. 5, 2004.

56. Harriet B. Presser, *Working in a 24/7 Economy: Challenges for American Families* (New York: Russell Sage Foundation, 2003).

57. Linda Giannarelli and James Barsimantov, "Child Care Expenses of American Families," *Assessing the New Federalism, Occasional Paper 40* (Washington, DC: Urban Institute Press, 2000): figure 1.

58. U.S. Census Bureau, "Who's Minding the Children? Child Care Arrangements: Spring 1999," Detailed Tables PPL-168 (2003): table 6.3.

59. Karen Schulman and Helen Blank, *Child Care Assistance Policies 2001-2004: Families Struggling to Move Forward, States Going Backward* (Washington, DC: National Women's Law Center, September 2004).

60. Kathryn Porter et al., *Strengths of the Safety Net: How the EITC, Social Security and Other Government Programs Affect Poverty* (Washington, DC: Center on Budget and Policy Priorities, 1998).

61. William P. O'Hare, "Recent Changes in the Percent of Children Living in Single-Mother Families," *KIDS COUNT Working Paper* (Baltimore: Annie E. Casey Foundation, 2003).

62. Lina Guzman et al., "Public Perceptions of Children's Well-Being," paper delivered at the annual meeting of the American Association of Public Opinion Researchers, May 2003.

63. Joyce A. Martin et al., "Births: Final Data for 2001," *National Vital Statistics Reports* 51, no. 2 (December 2002).

64. U.S. House of Representatives, Committee on Ways and Means, "Steep Decline in Teen Birth Rate Significantly Responsible for Reducing Child Poverty and Single-Parent Families," *Issue Brief*, April 23, 2004.

65. Federal Interagency Forum on Child and Family Statistics, *America's Children: Key National Indicators of Well-Being, 2003.*

66. U.S. Centers for Disease Control and Prevention, *Youth Risk Behavior Surveillance System, United States 2003,* accessed online at www.cdc.gov/HealthyYouth/yrbs/index.htm, on Nov. 17, 2004.

67. U.S. Bureau of Labor Statistics, accessed online at http://data.bls.gov/servlet/SurveyOutputServlet, on Nov. 5, 2004.

68. DeNavas-Walt, Proctor, and Mills, "Income, Poverty and Health Insurance Coverage in the United States: 2003": table A-1.

69. Sherman, Fremstad, and Parrot, *Employment Rates for Single Mothers.*

70. Katherin Ross Phillips, "Getting Time Off: Access to Leave Among Working Parents," *New Federalism: National Survey of America's Families* Series B, no. 57 (Washington, DC: Urban Institute Press, 2004): table 2.

71. Mary Williams Walsh, "I.R.S. to Ask Working Poor for Proof on Tax Credits," *New York Times*, April 25, 2003.

72. DeNavas-Walt, Proctor, and Mills, "Income, Poverty and Health Insurance Coverage in the United States: 2003": table C-2.

73. Vernon K. Smith, David M. Rousseau, and Molly O'Malley, *SCHIP Program Enrollment: December 2003 Update* (Washington, DC: The Kaiser Commission on Medicaid and the Uninsured, 2004).

74. Elizabeth McNichols, *States' Heavy Reliance on Spending Cuts and One-Time Measures to Close Their Budget Gaps Leaves Programs at Risk* (Washington, DC: Center on Budget and Policy Priorities, 2004).

75. Hedieh Rahmanou and Mark Greenberg, *Welfare Caseloads Increase in 27 States Between June and September 2003* (Washington, DC: Center for Law and Social Policy, 2004).

The Lives and Times of the Baby Boomers

By Mary Elizabeth Hughes and Angela M. O'Rand

INTRODUCTION

In the late 1940s, after several decades of declining births, the United States experienced a surprising and dramatic increase in fertility rates. Even more surprising, high birth rates continued until the mid-1960s, after which they dropped sharply. The large number of births in these years, combined with lower numbers immediately before and after, produced a birth cohort substantially larger than the preceding and subsequent cohorts—what we now know as the baby boom.

The first thing that comes to the minds of most Americans when the baby boom is mentioned is its sheer size. As the boomers moved through childhood, young adulthood, and into midlife, the education, labor, and housing markets were forced to adapt to larger numbers. More recently, attention has been directed to the potential impact of aging boomers on the economy, the health care system, and social programs for the elderly.

However, the baby boom is more than exceptionally large, it is *pivotal*. The boomers inherited, encountered, and redirected social change. Members were born into a nation already transformed by four long years of world war. As their lives unfolded, they experienced the profound changes that marked the decades between World War II and the 21st century, such as the Civil Rights Movement and the shift to a service economy. For the most part, the boomers did not initiate these changes. But since they encountered these shifting social contexts in young adulthood, their lives were disproportionately affected. The choices the boomers made about education, work, and family then reinforced some existing trends and set other trends in motion. The boomers are pivotal because they responded to historical change by living in new ways that set patterns for succeeding cohorts.

The lives of the boomers thus embody the post-World War II transformation of American society. At midlife, their experiences show some continuity with those of people born earlier in the 20th century. More noticeable, however, are the ways in which their lives differ from and have been less predictable than the lives of their counterparts in earlier cohorts. Consequently, boomer experiences are not just different from those of their predecessors; their experiences are different from each other's. Due in part to the heterogeneity of their lives, members of the baby boom are highly unequal in achievements and economic attainments.

This report is about the lives and times of the baby boomers. We use Census 2000 to describe them at midlife, linking their current circumstances to their life histories. Using other census sources, we compare them to members of cohorts born earlier in the 20th century. We conclude by looking ahead, offering a set of stylized expectations for the boomers' future.

LIVES IN HISTORY

If you ask three people to tell their life stories, you will hear three very different tales. Each story will have its own location, characters, and plot, reflecting the distinct circumstances and viewpoints of that person. But you will also hear the same topics and themes echoing through the stories. Each person will probably tell you where he or she grew up and talk about his or her family. They will all tell you about their educations, what they have done for a living, whether they married and had children, and how they have fared financially. If you listen closely, you will hear how these parts intertwined over time and how the whole played out against a backdrop of what was considered possible, appropriate, and important.

The emergence of common topics and themes in otherwise distinct biographies reflects these individuals' shared participation in society. Individual lives are unique, rich, and complex. However, as social beings, we are not simply idiosyncratic products of our own desires and imaginations. Our biographies are trajectories of socially defined roles enacted in contexts that present both opportunities and constraints.[1]

MARY ELIZABETH HUGHES is a late boomer who is currently an assistant professor of sociology at Duke University. She is a social demographer whose research interests focus on family processes such as marriage and coresidence, patterns of consumption, and individual health. She's been married to Fred Thomsen for 15 years and gave birth to Joel and Mark in the last six years. Joel is in first grade and Mark is an energetic 2-year-old.

ANGELA M. O'RAND is a War Baby born four months ahead of the baby boom. She is a professor of sociology at Duke University. Her research is concerned with patterns of stratification across the life course, with a special focus on socioeconomic outcomes such as earnings and pension wealth. She's been married to Mike O'Rand since 1967 and her 31-year-old son Chris is a lawyer in Miami. And, yes, she has a grandson, Dylan.

As they tell their stories, the three people will probably compare their lives and times to those of their parents and grandparents and perhaps of their children. They will reflect on how times have changed and how this has made their lives different from the lives of earlier or later generations. One person might note how World War II shaped his life because he served in the Army and subsequently went to school on the G.I. Bill. Another might observe that she would have liked to continue working after her children were born but that this simply wasn't done in her day.

Comparing lives and times is one of the ways we all make sense of social change. Social scientists usually make these comparisons using birth cohorts. A *birth cohort* is a group of people born in the same year or set of years. Members of a birth cohort move through life together, encountering at the same ages the same historical events and forces. The accumulated experience of a particular cohort thus reflects the intersection of lives and history.

Historical change alters the social context in which people make choices; so as history unfolds, lives change. At the same time, people's responses to historical change can redirect or even create change, so history reflects people's experiences. A particular cohort will be unique in some ways because cohort members experienced history differently than people born earlier or later. Events in early adulthood are usually considered especially important to the way a cohort develops. But cohort members can also be affected by events later in their lives (see Box 1).

Historical events, changes in social institutions such as the economy, and shifts in cultural ideas are what social scientists call *structural change*. People usually find themselves in the midst of these types of changes, which alter the context in which they have to live their lives. Comparing cohorts is one way of observing such structural changes. But by comparing cohorts, we can also observe how people react to structural change in their day-to-day lives. These *behavioral changes* are also a form

---

Box 1
AGE, PERIOD, OR COHORT?

Social scientists use the concepts of age, period, and cohort to analyze the relationship between individual lives and social change.

Age reflects biographical time and individual physiological and social development. A person's chronological age corresponds, at least loosely, with his or her social status and roles. For example, young people are often in school, while middle-aged people are in the labor force. However, many scholars argue that the links between chronological age and social age are weakening. For example, recent research shows that many middle-aged people return to school.[1]

Period refers to historical time. Historical time includes the major events or changes that define a particular slice of history, such as the Great Depression, the Vietnam War, technological innovations, public policy adjustments, and shifts in attitudes. Period conditions set the opportunities and constraints that individuals encounter as they age.

The term *cohort* refers to a group of people who experience a particular event at a specific time. The baby boom is a birth cohort, a group of people who are born in the same year or, in the case of the boomers, the same group of years. Members of a birth cohort grow up together, grow old together, and experience particular historical events at similar ages. Birth cohorts are often referred to as "generations." However, social scientists typically reserve the term *generation* to distinguish stages within a family lineage.[2]

Tradition argues that a cohort's experiences in childhood and young adulthood leave a permanent imprint on the behaviors, values, and beliefs of that cohort.[3] Thus, particular cohorts think and act in particular ways and any observed differences between cohorts are due to these cohort effects. Because this argument is intuitively appealing, it is widely embraced. In fact, it has entered popular consciousness and is the basis for many popular images of the baby boom.

However, the expectation of cohort effects rests on three assumptions:[4]

● Individuals are particularly impressionable early in the life course. Research on human development shows that this is the most solid of the three assumptions.
● These youthful impressions are lasting; individuals do not change their behavior and beliefs in response to shifts in political, economic, or social context. This assumption has less support; although some core personal characteristics are set early in life, people also adapt their behaviors and attitudes in response to period conditions.
● All cohort members experience the same early events and in the same ways. However, an enormous body of sociological research has shown that race/ethnicity, gender, and social class stratify life experiences.

These complexities suggest that superficial generalizations about the baby boom based on the idea of shared experience are unwise.

References

1. Cheryl Elman and Angela M. O'Rand, "The Race is to the Swift: Social Origins, Adult Education, and Economic Attainment," *American Journal of Sociology* 110, no. 1 (2004); 123-60.

2. Duane F. Alwin and Ryan J. McCammon, "Generations, Cohorts and Social Change," in *Handbook of the Life Course*, ed. Jeylan T. Mortimer and Michael J. Shanahan (New York: Kluwer, 2003): 23-49.

3. See, for example, Karl Mannheim, "The Problem of Generations," in *Studying Aging and Social Change: Conceptual and Methodological Issues*, ed. Melissa A. Hardy (Thousand Oaks, CA: Sage, 1997); and Norman B. Ryder, "The Cohort as a Concept in the Study of Social Change," *American Sociological Review* 30, no. 6 (1965): 843-61.

4. Alwin and McCammon, "Generations, Cohorts and Social Change."

of social change—changes in what people do, such as going on to college or marrying late. Large-scale changes in behavior create new ways of living and new ideas about how to live.

Since World War II, the United States has undergone profound social change. In this report we describe the role of the baby-boom cohorts in the transformation of American society. We show that the boomers both inherited changes from the past and directly experienced extensive structural change. As they adjusted and adapted to these changes, they created new ways of living. Reviewing the lives and times of the boomers helps to make sense of our new American society and our new American lives.

Six 20th-Century Cohorts

The baby boom was unexpected. On the eve of World War II, births were at an all-time low in the United States. In fact, some demographers were concerned that they were far too low and warned about population decline. No one would have predicted that 10 years later the United States would be in the midst of a baby boom, much less that the boom would continue unabated for nearly 20 years (see Box 2).

The baby boom began with a sharp increase in the number of births between 1945 and 1946, as couples "made up" for births postponed during the war (see Figure 1). Births continued to climb and reached a peak in 1957, when 4 million babies were born, compared

with just 2 million in 1937. The baby boom ended in 1964 just as dramatically as it began.

The demographic causes of the baby boom are well understood. From the end of World War II through the early 1960s, couples married earlier and started families more quickly than their counterparts in the 1920s and 1930s. During the 1950s, the average age at which men and women married and the fraction of people who never married dipped to historic lows. Once married, couples had a first child relatively quickly, pushing the

---

Figure 1
ANNUAL BIRTHS AND BIRTHS PER WOMAN, UNITED STATES, 1909–2000

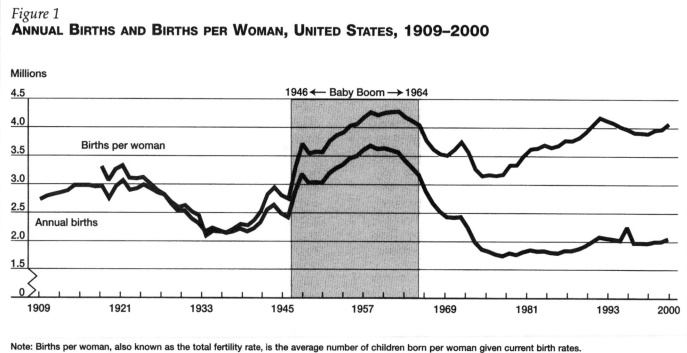

Note: Births per woman, also known as the total fertility rate, is the average number of children born per woman given current birth rates.

Sources: U.S. Center for Health Statistics, *Vital Statistics of the United States*, various volumes; *National Vital Statistics Reports* 51:12; and R. Heuser, *Fertility Rates by Color, United States*, 1917-1973 (1976).

Table 1

SIX 20TH-CENTURY AMERICAN COHORTS

Cohort	Birth years	Census year when ages 44–53*
Young Progressives	1906–1915	1960
Jazz Age Babies	1916–1925	1970
Depression Kids	1926–1935	1980
War Babies	1936–1945	1990
Early Boomers	1946–1955	2000
Late Boomers**	1956–1964	2010

* Age is as of year prior to the census. Because the census is taken on April 1, most people will not have had their birthday by census day.

** Most of the data presented in this report for late boomers are from the 2000 Census, when this cohort was ages 35–43.

average age at which women had their first birth lower as well. In contrast to the 1930s, nearly all couples went on to have a second child. These behavioral shifts were pervasive and visible across all races and social classes. In fact, most developed nations experienced similar, if shorter, postwar baby booms.[2]

Members of the baby boom were born over the course of 19 years; the last boomers were born as the earliest boomers were reaching adulthood. This means that even within the baby boom, individuals experienced history differently. For example, boomers are often associated with the Vietnam War protests of the late 1960s. However, only the boomers born earliest were involved in those protests; boomers born after the midpoint of the baby boom in 1955 were not in high school yet, and some were still in preschool. Similarly, people born in the first half of the baby boom entered a labor market with a shortage of workers in some expanding sectors; people born later in the boom entered a labor market crowded by their older brothers and sisters.

Because members of the baby boom did not experience history in the same ways, we divide the baby boom into two cohorts: the early boomers, born between 1946 and 1955; and late boomers, born between 1956 and 1964. The early boomers were ages 44 to 53 at the time of the 2000 Census, while the late boomers were ages 35 to 43.

To gain a longer-term historical and social perspective, we compare the early and late boomers to four 10-year birth cohorts from earlier in the 20th century. These cohorts are identified in Table 1, along with the census year in which they were ages 44 to 53.

Cohorts in History

Each of the six cohorts has lived through its own particular segment of U.S. history. The segments overlap because the earlier cohorts were still alive when the later ones were born. But each cohort experienced events and trends in a particular way. For example, during the Great Depression, the Young Progressives were young adults, the Jazz Age Babies were teenagers, and the Depression Kids were babies. Cohorts born later encountered the Depression only secondhand, through history books and the stories of their parents and grandparents.

The boomers' fate was to come of age in a time of great social transformation. Structural change accelerated in the United States after the Second World War, especially during and after the 1960s. As these forces combined with long-term secular changes already in place, society changed at a dizzying pace.

First, the United States underwent a series of economic shifts and shocks. The United States emerged from World War II as a dominant economic power with an expanding industrial base. In the 20 years after the war, the U.S. economy grew rapidly, incomes rose, and millions of Americans made their way into the middle class. Members of the baby boom were born during these prosperous times. However, a series of structural changes began around the time the early boomers entered the labor market. These forces transformed the United States into a largely service and information-based economy enmeshed in increasingly competitive globalized markets. This process extended over three decades, encompassing more than half of the boomers' working lives.

As the baby boomers entered the workplace, large-industry employers began seeking cheaper labor markets outside of the highly unionized North and Midwest. Unskilled and semiskilled workers in the inner cities were left behind, resulting in reduced wages and growing unemployment. These conditions sparked riots across large cities in the late 1960s and early 1970s. An even bigger jolt came with the 1973 oil crisis, which ushered in a new era of painful economic adjustment and readjustment.

Technological innovations in manufacturing, communications, health services, and other sectors created markets without boundaries. The international division of labor continuously moved domestic jobs offshore to cheaper labor markets. Rapidly expanding computer-supported communications networks facilitated this new division of labor and created a new area of job growth that required higher technical skills. High-end and low-end service jobs became the new dominant sectors of employment. Professional and technical jobs grew in research and development, health care delivery, and business services, while positions expanded in the seemingly ever-growing discount retail sector and in personal services such as day care and home care. The era culminated in the dot-com revolution, economic boom, and technology bubble of the mid-1990s.[3]

Second, the role of the government in the redistribution of resources, the provision of welfare support, and the extension of legal protections underwent equally dramatic shifts after World War II. While the boomers were growing up, public resources poured into building schools, highways, hospitals, and houses. Growing prosperity and the legacy of the New Deal appeared compatible. By the beginning of the 1960s, the discovery of larger-than-expected poverty led to enactment of policies for a wider sharing of this prosperity. Extensions of the 1935 Social Security Act such as early, reduced retirement benefits; Medicare; and Aid to Families with Dependent Children were followed in the early 1970s by cost-of-living adjustments and the Supplemental Security Income program for the elderly.

The Great Society of the Kennedy-Johnson era also sought to extend the protection of the law and the opportunities of democracy to African Americans. Black boomers were born under de jure Jim Crow segregation in the South and de facto Jim Crow segregation in the North. These restrictive policies and practices were challenged by the Civil Rights Movement in the 1950s and 1960s, resulting in laws aimed at redressing racial inequalities, including the Civil Rights Act and the Open

Housing Act.[4] Although America has yet to achieve full racial equality, these changes profoundly altered life for black and white Americans. The boomers were the first to reach adulthood in the post-civil rights era.

But ideology reversed in the 1970s. The jolt of the oil crisis and the growing threat of global competitiveness shifted policies in the direction of fewer regulations for industry and retrenchment of welfare programs. The remaining decades of the 20th century would bring increased privatization of former public services, growing retreat of employers from occupational benefits such as pensions and health insurance, and programs moving welfare recipients to work. As they reached adulthood, the boomers experienced weaker social safety nets as risk was increasingly borne by individuals.

Third, a major change in U.S. immigration policy opened the doors to millions of newcomers. Prior to 1965, immigration law in the United States kept people from some countries out entirely and subjected others to

---

Box 3
BOOMER BEGINNINGS: RACE, ETHNICITY, NATIVITY

The baby-boom cohorts are more racially and ethnically diverse than previous cohorts, and the late boomers are substantially more diverse than the early boomers. A full 30 percent of the late-boomer cohort is composed of minority groups.

The percentage of blacks increased very little across cohorts. Increases in the percentage of "others" have been proportionately, if not absolutely, large. This growth can be traced to two factors. The likelihood that people of American Indian heritage will identify themselves as such on the census has increased over time. American Indians are the largest component of the "other" category for every cohort prior to the boomers. The large increase in the "other" category among the boomer cohorts is because Census 2000 was the first census to allow people to identify themselves as members of more than one racial or ethnic group. Most of the growth across cohorts in the minority population is due to increases in the Hispanic and Asian groups. A great deal of this growth is due to immigration; high percentages of Asians and Hispanics in both boomer cohorts are foreign-born (57 percent and 86 percent, respectively, for both cohorts). In fact, the percentage of immigrants of all ethnicities is quite high in the boomer cohorts in 2000: 12 percent among early boomers and nearly 15 percent among late boomers.

The above statistics reflect increasing yearly immigration and the fact that immigrants are usually between the ages of 20 and 50. Thus in the past 30 years, the baby-boom cohorts have been in the prime "receiving years" for immigrants.

The figure makes plain that the boomer cohort is not the only cohort inflated by immigration. The impact on the boomers has been the most spectacular among the cohorts we observe because of the historical timing of migration increases and the age pattern of migration. In this respect, the boomers are again pivotal—the impact of immigration on future cohorts may be even more pronounced.

To varying degrees, immigrants have shared boomers' history. Half of early-boomer immigrants have been in the United

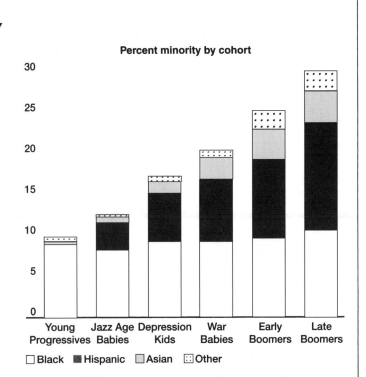

Percent minority by cohort

Source: Authors' calculations using the Integrated Public Use Microdata Series (IPUMS), 2003.

States over 20 years. When they were 10 years younger, about a quarter had been in the United States this long, about the same proportion among late boomers now.

Despite considerable progress in expanding opportunities to all subgroups of the population, race and ethnicity persist as major bases for inequality. Race and ethnicity also shape individual ideas about what is normal, appropriate, and important. Clearly, in the boomer cohorts, nativity is an additional basis for stratification.

IMAGES OF THE BABY BOOM

The image of the boomers that has emerged in recent media coverage is quite colorful and has several consistent themes. In drawing this conclusion, we conducted two random samples of articles published in major U.S. newspapers that contained references to the baby boom in the headline or lead paragraphs: articles published between June 1993 and June 2003; and articles published between December 2002 and June 2003.

Homogeneity. The most striking feature of recent commentary on baby boomers is the extent to which they are viewed as a homogeneous group. Nearly all commentary refers to them as an undifferentiated whole, lacking within-cohort differences.

Shared History. Members are assumed to share similar upbringings and a common set of cultural references. For example, boomers are often characterized as products of affluent, suburban childhoods; events such as the Vietnam War or Woodstock are considered pivotal in the lives of all boomers. Following from the assumption of shared experience is an image of boomers as a cohesive generation with a collective set of core values and beliefs.

Well Educated. Boomers are frequently referred to as the best-educated cohort in American history. This statement is then discussed as if it means that all boomers have college degrees. Hand in hand with this image is the perception that all members of the baby boom are professional and managerial workers.

Married with Children? In recent writing, boomers are most often portrayed as married with teenage or college-age children. Much attention is focused on the twin issues of empty nests and caring for aging parents. However, some commentary contradicts this family-centered image by focusing on the instability or even absence of boomer families.

Affluent. Boomers are widely perceived as financially comfortable and even wealthy. Marketers anticipate that aging boomers will drive up demand for high-end products such as vacation homes, luxury travel, and investment services.

Innovators. Boomers are viewed as the agents of the tremendous social and economic changes the United States has experienced in the last 40 years. Boomers are frequently described as pioneers: rewriting the rules, reinventing each life stage they pass through, and remaking society.

The Me Generation. One of the most pervasive characterizations of the boomers is that they are individualistic to the point of self-absorption. For example, baby boomers are viewed as self-indulgent consumers who have accumulated high levels of debt instead of prudently saving for retirement. Boomers are also described as obsessed with health and youth; they refuse to grow old gracefully, but will rely on products such as Botox, Viagra, and the latest herbal remedies to stave off biological aging.

quotas. In 1965, policies restricting immigration based on national origin were lifted and replaced with a system of preferences in which people with family already in the United States or with high-demand skills were given highest priority. These changes, combined with the pull of the U.S. economy and the push of demographic pressure in countries of origin, dramatically increased the flow of migrants from abroad.[5] Because immigrants tend to be young, these newcomers disproportionately swelled the ranks of the baby-boom cohorts relative to older cohorts (see Box 3, page 228). These "immigrant boomers" increased the size—and changed the face—of the boomer cohorts as they came of age.

Fourth, a revolution in cultural values changed the way Americans thought about "self." Individualism in some form has always been central to American culture. For example, self-reliance is a recurring theme in American history and literature. But the new individualism went beyond a materialistic self-reliance to a concern for autonomy, identity, and empowerment. Some scholars link these ideas to a broader shift in cultural values that became evident in all Western societies in the postwar period. This shift was away from a concern with the material conditions of day-to-day life and toward "post-materialist" concerns including self-expression and individual fulfillment. The result of these shifts was twofold: a decline in the power of traditional authority,

especially with regard to life choices; and an increase in the legitimacy of individual goals over family or communal goals.[6]

This cultural shift was particularly evident in the way Americans thought about gender roles and sexual activity. Beginning in the 1960s, ideas surrounding appropriate roles for men and women began to change, spurred on by women's movement into higher education and the labor force. Changes in the workplace were assisted by the inclusion of gender as a protected category in the Civil Rights Act of 1964. Originally inserted by conservative legislators in an attempt to defeat the bill, the law had a tremendous impact in legally redefining women's rights. At the same time, attitudes toward sexual relationships became much more liberal and once-taboo premarital sex became more accepted.[7]

Although the boomers are often credited with inventing these ideas, it seems more likely that the ideas were part of a broader cultural shift. But the boomers did appear to adopt the new ideas wholeheartedly as reflected by their behaviors.

Finally, the size of the baby boom was itself a potent force. Some scholars argue that the baby boom caused many postwar social changes through the pressures and adjustments required to accommodate such large cohorts.[8] We agree up to a point with this argument, but we propose that the pivotal role of the boomers in history is both continuous and discontinuous. The boomers inherited social change, they lived through social change, and in their day-to-day lives redirected social change. Their large size amplified what may otherwise have been small differences, magnified what may have become modest effects, and made both larger than life. This probably explains why the public seems fascinated with the boomers, who have become a cultural icon for Americans of all ages (see Box 4).

SCHOOL DAYS

Universal education has always been a distinctive (and some would say exceptional) characteristic of American society. In fact, the ideology of the American Dream is based in large measure on education accessible to all. In the common school movement of the 19th century, local economies of farmers and shopkeepers levied taxes to develop schools with the aim of ensuring literacy and local prosperity, which led to nearly universal access to primary school education. In the first half of the 20th century, the economy added factories and then large bureaucracies to farms and small businesses as its major sites of employment. Technical and verbal skills were required in factories and offices and increasingly on farms and in small businesses. Accordingly, secondary education was required and sought after.[9] By the eve of World War II, nearly universal access had been extended to secondary education.

Following World War II and beginning with the G.I. Bill of Rights, higher education became a mass institution, with unprecedented levels of government and private resources directed toward the development of a technically skilled workforce.[10] As the Cold War heated up with the launching of the Soviet

Union's Sputnik in the late 1950s and the U.S. mission to the moon in the 1960s, the ascendance of higher education on the national agenda and in the aspirations of the young accelerated. The boomers were thus born and brought up in a period when the demands for secondary and postsecondary education were the highest in history and were largely accommodated by a prosperous society. They inherited an educational system with nearly seamless opportunities to attain college diplomas and with improved chances for postsecondary attainment.

The Best-Educated Cohort
The legacy of the American educational system is visible in the educational attainment of the boomer cohorts, often called the best-educated cohorts in the history of the United States. High school completion is nearly universal among boomer men and women (see Table 2), significantly higher than among their Jazz Age and Depression Kid parents. However, high school attainment leveled off across the boomer cohorts and dropped slightly among late-boomer men. The increased prevalence of less-educated immigrant groups in this cohort offers only a partial explanation for this phenomenon, because high school graduation dropped even among U.S.-born whites.

The boomers also have higher levels of college participation and completion than their parental cohorts. Taken together, those with some college and those with college degrees account for over half of the boomer cohorts. Contrary to the most exaggerated baby-boomer mythology, college completion is far from prevalent. Just under one-third of early-boomer men and a little over one-fourth of early-boomer women have baccalaureate degrees; among late boomers, only about one in four have graduated from college.

Table 2
EDUCATIONAL ATTAINMENT BY GENDER AND COHORT

	Ages 44–53					Ages 35–43	
Highest level of education	Young Progressives 1960	Jazz Age Babies 1970	Depression Kids 1980	War Babies 1990	Early Boomers 2000	Early Boomers 1990	Late Boomers 2000
Women	100%	100%	100%	100%	100%	100%	100%
Less than high school	59	44	33	18	10	11	10
High school graduate	26	39	43	39	32	33	31
Some college	9	10	14	26	32	31	33
College degree or higher	6	7	11	18	27	25	26
Men	100%	100%	100%	100%	100%	100%	100%
Less than high school	63	47	33	18	11	12	13
High school graduate	21	30	33	31	29	28	33
Some college	8	11	14	25	29	30	28
College degree or higher	8	13	20	27	31	30	26

Source: Authors' calculations using the Integrated Public Use Microdata Series (IPUMS), 2003.

Notably, the percentage of early boomers with baccalaureate degrees increased by 2 percentage points between 1990 and 2000. Such an increase in a maturing cohort is unique, both historically and from a cross-national standpoint. It reflects at least two distinctive cohort phenomena: the immigration of more highly educated adults over the decade, and the return to school by adult boomers to gain baccalaureate credentials. In the 1990s, economic factors increased the college premium, and the perceived threat of job loss motivated many workers to return to school.[11] However, the pursuit of higher education in adulthood can be motivated by life style choices as well. People who have some college but did not graduate are the most likely to return to college as adults. Large portions of the boomer cohorts had some college earlier in their lives, suggesting substantial potential for increased educational attainment later. Nearly one-third of boomer women had some college, exceeding men's levels. Recent studies have shown that women are especially likely to return to college after dropping out.[12]

The long-term increase in the level of educational attainment has been driven in part by changes in the economy described earlier and in part by successively better-educated parents passing this advantage on to their children.[13] Thus, each cohort has tended to be better educated than the last. In the case of college attainment levels, the trends display a notable surge upward beginning with the War Babies. A large share of this earlier cohort actually grew up in boomer families, with younger siblings born after 1945. They shared the same parents, whose educational backgrounds were improvements over earlier generations and whose aspirations for their children affected these adjacent cohorts in the same ways as they grew up in the 1950s and 1960s.

The War Babies and boomers were both exposed to enriched and expanded school curricula over the 1950s and 1960s and into the 1970s. An increased emphasis on science, mathematics, and foreign languages was motivated in large measure by the Cold War and supported by the passage of legislation like the National Defense Education Act of 1958. These funds built science labs in high schools, often managed by teachers whose own educations were supported by the G.I. Bill. They also affected other curricula. At higher rates than earlier cohorts, War Babies and boomers read American literature as varied as Henry David Thoreau's "On the Duty of Civil Disobedience," J.D. Salinger's Catcher in the Rye, and British literature including Beowulf and the works of Lord Byron and Jane Austen. They had access in public schools to music lessons, drama classes, debate teams, and sports. But school expansion in this period also introduced curricular tracking, which channeled a minority of boomers into precollege tracks and others into general educational and vocational training tracks.[14]

Differential exposure to higher education would influence early diversity in political ideologies among the War Babies and early boomers. Images of the 1960s and 1970s often include scenes of rebellious youth, usually on college campuses, marching for free speech and civil rights and against the Vietnam War. These images distorted the actual diversity of their lives at that time. About one-third of the early boomers served in Vietnam.[15] Polls taken during the period disclosed highly divergent values and ideologies among them. Younger voters (including boomers) were significantly more likely to support right-wing candidates. Supporters of George Wallace during the 1968 presidential election were disproportionately young, from the South and rural regions, and less-educated and poor.[16] This schism would foreshadow a persistent theme in boomer politics.

Educational Advantage For Late-Boomer Women

Levels of education have risen for men and women alike. But a crossover in men and women's attainments emerged among late-boomer women. These women are more likely than men to have participated in college and as likely to have obtained a college degree or higher. Their average years of schooling are higher than men's. A gender gap appears at the bottom of the educational distribution as well—a higher percentage of men than women have not completed high school. Women appear more likely both to persist and to return to school in adulthood following interruptions related to work and family roles.[17]

These patterns have continued among cohorts younger than the boomers.[18] In this respect, the baby boomers—and particularly the late boomers—are pivotal. Their lives embody the redirection of long-term increases in gender equality toward educational advantages for women.

Racial Inequality in Diplomas

Access to quality education has never been equally distributed. Race, class, and gender have stratified opportunities for educational attainment throughout U.S. history. The common-school movement of the 19th century and the secondary school expansion of the early 20th century were not equally inclusive in all regions of the United States. Segregated and unequally funded school systems prevailed in the South and adjacent regions until the 1960s, when desegregation was actively implemented following Brown v. Board of Education and passage of the Civil Rights Act a decade later.

Segregation suppressed the educational attainment of nonwhite and lower-class students. Indeed, African Americans began migrating to Northern cities after World War I seeking better school and job opportunities.[19] Similarly, the most elite colleges remained segregated by gender until the boomers had already begun to enter them. Finally, immigrants entering the United States during the 20th century arrived with different levels of prior educational attainment and encountered differential opportunities for school participation and educational attainment.

The pattern of increasing educational attainment has therefore not been the same in all racial, ethnic, and nativity groups. Groups have improved their educational attainment at different rates, eliminating some disparities and reinforcing or creating others. Except for Hispanic immigrants, all groups have experienced a steep increase in the likelihood of completing a high school diploma. The proportion of high school graduates among black War Babies increased dramatically over previous cohorts, then rose more gradually among the boomers. These increases probably reflect the improvement of educational opportunities before and after World War II, first among black cohorts who migrated to Northern or Western cities, then among those growing up during the expansion of secondary and postsecondary education under integration policies.

Although racial and ethnic disparities in high school completion have narrowed, gaps remain. U.S.-born Asian and white advantages relative to blacks persist. The low levels of high school completion among immi-grant Hispanics no doubt reflects educational opportunities in their nations of origin and shows that the Hispanic immigration stream is dominated by people of lower education. This disadvantaged group represents a higher percentage of the boomer cohorts than previous cohorts.

Cohort rates of college completion diverge dramatically across race, ethnic, and nativity groups (see Figure 2). All groups have similarly low levels of college attainment in the Young Progressive cohort. Over the next four cohorts, the fraction of college-educated among U.S.-born and foreign-born Asians rises sharply, while the percentage of college-educated among foreign-born Hispanics does not increase at all. The percentage of white college graduates increased a great deal, but not as much as among Asians. Although the proportionate gains among U.S.-born Hispanics and blacks were larger than the gains among whites, in absolute terms their gains lagged far behind those of whites.

Thus, there is a negative side to cohort increases in educational attainment: Absolute race/ethnic/nativity differentials in college completion are wider in the boomer cohorts than in any previous cohort. Despite decades of efforts to extend the opportunity for higher education to all, differential attainment has persisted and is magnified in the boomer cohorts.

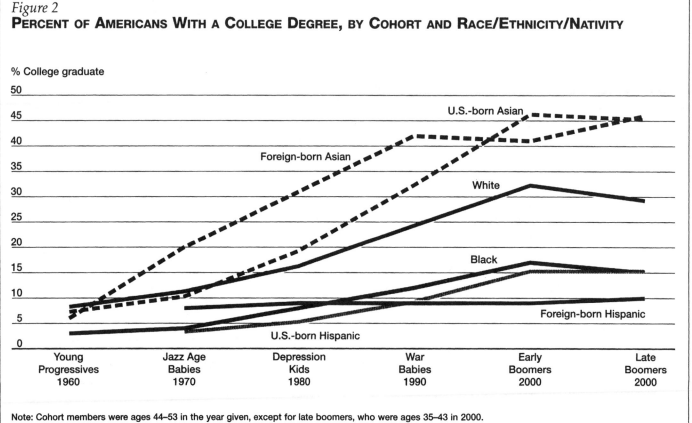

Figure 2

PERCENT OF AMERICANS WITH A COLLEGE DEGREE, BY COHORT AND RACE/ETHNICITY/NATIVITY

% College graduate

U.S.-born Asian

Foreign-born Asian

White

Black

Foreign-born Hispanic

U.S.-born Hispanic

| Young Progressives 1960 | Jazz Age Babies 1970 | Depression Kids 1980 | War Babies 1990 | Early Boomers 2000 | Late Boomers 2000 |

Note: Cohort members were ages 44–53 in the year given, except for late boomers, who were ages 35–43 in 2000.

Source: Authors' calculations using the Integrated Public Use Microdata Series (IPUMS), 2003.

BOOMERS AT WORK

The growth of the U.S. economy through history can be attributed in large measure to the growing size of the labor force and to the productivity of American workers. Generations of immigrants have come to the United States to find work and begin new lives. The 20th century began with the highest level of immigration in history, welcomed by industrialists like Henry Ford, John D. Rockefeller, and Andrew W. Mellon who were building manufacturing industries that initiated the elevation of the United States to a world power by the end of World War II. These male-dominated industries became ladders of upward social mobility in which employment security, wage growth, and job promotions were expected in exchange for employee loyalty. Worker compensation was based on a family wage system, predicated on the male breadwinner family. This occupational welfare system was reinforced by New Deal policies. The pattern was interrupted only briefly by World War II, when masses of young American men were mobilized for military service and women went to work in previously male-dominated industries. Following the war, the labor market returned to "normal"—until things began to change about the time the War Babies and baby boomers began to work.[20]

As the earliest boomers came of age, the U.S. economy began to shift more rapidly than before toward service and knowledge industries and away from traditional heavy manufacturing. These shifts were driven by technology and by global processes including competition and the reorganization of the international division of labor. As mentioned earlier, the oil crisis of the early 1970s was a watershed event after which manufacturing jobs in the United States steadily disappeared. The new jobs required intellectual ability, social skills, and postsecondary credentials, and they suited women as well as men. Also, in part as a result of affirmative action legislation in the 1960s, the ideology of meritocracy was spreading in the workplace, where bureaucratic institutions began rationalizing their procedures and policies in the direction of gender neutrality.[21]

Meanwhile, in addition to the disappearance of traditional manufacturing jobs in the major heavy industries, workplace institutions associated with these male-dominated jobs also declined. Union membership, which had almost never exceeded 30 percent of the labor force in the United States, began a steady decline. Many of the gains from labor-management accords that had bolstered job security, wages, and fringe benefits in male-dominated sectors disappeared with accelerating speed over the 1980s and 1990s. Worker power declined and employers increasingly shifted their allegiance toward stockholders and away from workers.[22]

Young Boomers Confront a Changing Economy

Young baby-boomer cohorts entered this changing workplace and increased the number of people employed in the 1970s by over 21 million and in the 1980s by more than 18 million.[23] A large share of this growth was due to boomer women's increased participation—and persistence—in the workforce. Indeed, as the War Baby and baby-boom cohorts matured, the lives of men and women began to look more similar in important respects. Both spent more years in school followed by more years working than earlier cohorts. Compulsory military service still applied to War Baby and early-boomer men but disappeared for the youngest boomers and later cohorts. Accordingly, boomer men and women began following generally similar paths into adulthood by moving from school to work.[24]

The behavior of these young adults changed the age pattern of women's participation in the labor force. During the first two decades following the war, middle-aged and older women accounted primarily for labor force increases. War Baby and early-boomer women—and later, late-boomer women with young children—accounted for the continued growth in employment rates. The common thread across cohorts was married women's dramatic increase in employment. But the pivotal change among War Babies and boomers was the pattern of spending more years continuously at work after entering the workplace earlier in their lives and while maintaining family roles over their lives.[25]

Some scholars have associated these changes with the birth control pill. The Food and Drug Administration approved the pill in 1960. Five years later, 40 percent of young married women were on the pill. In another five years, use of the pill spread rapidly among unmarried women.[26] The control of fertility not only reduced the necessity to marry in order to have sex, it also reduced the costs of investing in higher education and committing to work and family careers simultaneously. But the pill can only help in explaining women's labor supply. As noted earlier, the demand for women's work had also increased.

Women Working Much More, Men a Little Less

Work is central to the lives and identities of baby boomers. In midlife, nearly nine of 10 boomers work, representing the highest employment levels of all cohorts. Underlying these averages are two related but countervailing trends: the steady increase in women's employment at middle age and a less dramatic decline in men's employment in middle age. Boomer women's employment levels are higher than the average for all working-age women. While two-thirds of all working-

Table 3

PERCENT OF MEN AND WOMEN EMPLOYED PREVIOUS YEAR BY COHORT

Cohort	Year	Employed last year		
		All	Female	Male
At ages 44–53				
Young Progressives	1960	73	52	95
Jazz Age Babies	1970	76	58	95
Depression Kids	1980	76	62	91
War Babies	1990	83	75	91
Early Boomers	2000	84	79	89
At ages 35–43				
Early Boomers	1990	86	79	93
Late Boomers	2000	85	79	91

Source: Authors' calculations using the Integrated Public Use Microdata Series (IPUMS), 2003.

age women were employed in 1999, four of five boomer women were working (see Table 3). The biggest change for women occurred between the War Babies and the two preceding cohorts. Boomer employment rates are only slightly higher than War Babies' rates.

The 1990s produced a slight downward shift in employment of baby-boom men. Early-boomer employment rates are slightly lower than War Babies at the same age and reflect a drop of 4 percentage points between 1990 and 2000. And late boomers had slightly lower employment rates than early boomers at the same age.

These apparent declines among prime working-age men have been variously attributed to early retirement, disability, and job instability. Job instability is arguably the major contributor. The boomers, especially those born in the later years, have faced greater job instability over their work lives than their older siblings and their parents. Sectoral shifts, recessions, and corporate strategies to cut costs by trimming workforces through layoffs, contingent work, and outsourcing have confronted the late boomers nearly continuously since entering the labor market. Those without educational credentials were the most vulnerable to these shocks—so much so that some scholars suggest that the American dream of upward mobility may have been denied to a significant share of the baby boom.[27]

The growing instability of jobs and the decline of the so-called "employment relationship," which promised lifetime work with the same employer, may influence how boomers look toward retirement. Frequent job shifts and unemployment during the traditional peak earnings years (between ages 45 and 55) can retard pension saving. For those climbing the promotion and wage ladder with each job change, the pension consequences may be positive. But for those losing jobs and experiencing involuntary unemployment, retirement may be more problematic. In any case, boomer men and women are approaching retirement with different work histories and with different retirement saving opportunities than earlier cohorts. The budgetary risks that the boomers may present to the U.S. pension and health care systems are now matters of considerable concern, bordering on alarm (see Box 5, page 235).

Men's Jobs and Women's Jobs

The occupational distribution of workers across boomer cohorts has been influenced by at least three interdependent forces:

● Accelerating structural shifts away from blue-collar work toward high-end (professional/technical) and low-end (clerical and sales) white-collar work;
● Changing patterns of occupational segregation on the basis of gender and race/ethnicity; and
● Increasing demand for postsecondary credentials.

Table 4 (page 236) compares the occupational distribution of men and women across cohorts in their prime working years. The largest category of male workers continues to be blue collar (crafts, operatives, and related occupations), but the proportion of men working in these occupations declined by about 25 percent between the Young Progressives and the early boomers. Meanwhile, the share of men working in professional and technical occupations between these cohorts doubled.

The largest occupations among boomer women continue to be clerical and sales, although this reflects a decline from the high of 40 percent among Jazz Age Babies. The more dramatic change has been in women's participation in professional and technical occupations. Nearly one-third of early-boomer women are in this category and nearly the same proportion of both boomer groups falls into this category at ages 35 to 43. Women have also moved into managerial and administrative occupations; one in 10 boomer women is in this category.

In short, women's growing employment across cohorts has been channeled steadily into low-end (clerical and sales) and increasingly into high-end (professional and technical) white-collar work. Men typically remain concentrated in blue-collar jobs but have shifted to managerial and professional categories as well. Among boomers, men's and women's occupational segregation has persisted with respect to blue-collar and low-end white-collar work, but diminished with respect to professional, technical, and managerial work.

Indices of sex segregation calculated for comparable occupations across censuses suggest that sex segregation has declined within occupational categories.[28] Indices of sex segregation range from 0 to 1.0 and indicate how many of every 100 women would have to

Box 5
WILL RETIRING BOOMERS GO BUST OR BUST THE BUDGET?

When the oldest boomers reach age 59 1/2 (in 2005), some of them may begin withdrawing money from their retirement accounts; when they reach age 62 (in 2008) they are eligible for reduced Social Security benefits; and when they reach age 66 (in 2012) they may begin receiving full Social Security benefits. Is the federal budget ready for them to retire?

Average retirement ages steadily dropped below the age when workers are eligible for Social Security benefits, beginning with the Young Progressives and ending with the War Babies. The trend reflected two different sets of circumstances. First, workers covered by defined benefit pensions in major industrial and public sectors left the labor force voluntarily after many years in their jobs. Defined benefit pensions promise a calculable lifetime retirement annuity based on years of service and salary level at the end of the career. In addition, the manufacturing sectors contracted during the 1970s and 1980s; plant closings and downsizings encouraged employers to reduce their older workforces by offering retirement packages.[1]

A second set of workers retired early for different reasons. Some low-wage workers, usually without employer pension coverage, tended to retire at age 62 when they qualified for reduced Social Security benefits. The earnings replacement rates of Social Security provided incentives to leave often physically demanding jobs or poor working conditions. Many of these early retirees were in poor health or were disabled.[2]

By the mid-1990s, the median retirement age for men and women was age 62, but the labor force behaviors of older workers appeared to be changing. The three-decade long trend toward early retirement among men halted, while older women's labor force participation continued to increase.[3] Workers between ages 55 and 65 stayed in the labor force at higher rates than only a few years earlier. These workers included members of the War Baby cohort, whose educational and occupational histories have looked much like those of boomers.

Defined benefit pensions have declined as the major retirement benefit offered by employers, while defined contribution plans are spreading rapidly. Defined contribution plans are tax-sheltered retirement accounts accumulated as investments in portfolios of equity, bond, money market, and other speculative products. Workers are responsible for participation and contribution levels and bear the financial risks. Employers usually, but not always, also contribute to these accounts. The so-called 401(k) is the fastest growing type of defined contribution plan.

This innovation in the workplace has exposed workers directly to the bond and stock markets as investors. The stock market bubble between 1995 and 2002 first doubled stock prices and increased portfolios by nearly 60 percent during the boom phase of the bubble. This increased retirement by over 3 percent. However, in the bust that followed, which nearly wiped out the earlier gains, a comparable decline in retirement occurred.[4]

Recent evidence suggests that the late boomers are less likely to have retirement plan coverage than the older cohort at the same age. Early-boomer men's and women's coverage by a pension plan was 70 percent and 66 percent, respectively, in 1998; late-boomer men's and women's coverage was 66 per-

cent and 64 percent, respectively. Overall pension savings appeared to be low. In defined contribution plans, early-boomer men had median account balances of $26,000 in 1998, and early-boomer women had $22,000; late-boomer men had $22,000 and women $8,000.[5]

Three major changes in the Social Security system already signal delays in eligibility for full benefits to later ages for the baby boomers, increasingly less-generous benefits for boomers who retire early at age 62, and the elimination of mandatory retirement in 1986. For boomers born between 1946 and 1954, the age of eligibility for full Social Security benefits is 66; for those born later the eligibility age rises by two months for each year of birth until 1960, after which full retirement benefit eligibility begins at age 67. Retirement after eligibility ages brings higher benefits with each year of continued work. Meanwhile, reduced benefits at age 62 will decline for younger boomers.

The most recent change in the Social Security system is the elimination of the earnings test, which limited the amount retirees ages 65 to 69 could earn without benefit penalties.

Recent surveys of boomers suggest that they plan to work later and to continue to work after they retire. More advantaged members of the cohort with higher educations, better jobs, and high consumption levels may want to continue working; less advantaged members of the cohort with lower educations, bad jobs, and higher risks for poverty may have to continue working.

The issue of inequality is particularly poignant for disadvantaged minorities and women who are at higher risk of non-coverage by pensions because of their labor market locations. Women live longer than men, have longer experiences with disability, and greater requirements for long-term care. Widows and divorced or never-married women who find themselves alone in old age with limited retirement incomes are permanent concerns of retirement policymakers.

The proposed Social Security personal retirement account is a response to the fear that the baby boom's looming retirement presents a long-term financing problem and intergenerational burden. Concerns about the solvency of the Social Security Trust Fund have already led to major changes in the Social Security system to discourage early retirement.[6]

References

1. Melissa A. Hardy, Lawrence Hazelrigg, and Jill Quadagno, *Ending a Career in the Auto Industry* (New York: Plenum, 1996).

2. Robert Haveman et al., "Social Security, Age of Retirement, and Economic Well-Being: Intertemporal and Demographic Patterns Among Retired-Worker Beneficiaries," *Demography* 40, no. 2 (2003): 369-94.

3. Joseph F. Quinn, "Retirement Trends and Patterns in the 1990s: The End of an Era?" *Public Policy and Aging Report* 8, no. 2 (1997): 10-15.

4. Alan L. Gustman and Thomas L. Steinmeier, "Retirement and the Stock Market Bubble," *NBER Working Paper 9494* (Cambridge, MA: National Bureau of Economic Research, 2002).

5. Jules H. Lichtenstein and Ke Bin Wu, "Retirement Plan Coverage and Savings Trends of Baby Boomer Cohorts by Sex: Analysis of the 1989 and 1998 SCF," *Data Digest DD-93* (Washington, DC: Public Policy Institute, American Association of Retired Persons, 2003).

6. Steven A. Sass, "Reforming the U.S. Retirement Income System: The Growing Role of Work," *Global Brief No. 1* (Boston: Center for Retirement Research, Boston College).

Table 5
PERCENT OF U.S. MEN AND WOMEN IN HIGH-LEVEL PROFESSIONAL/TECHNICAL OCCUPATIONS, BY COHORT

Cohort	Year	Men	Women
Young Progressives	1960	8	4
Jazz Age Babies	1970	12	6
Depression Kids	1980	14	8
War Babies	1990	17	12
Early Boomers	2000	19	18
Late Boomers	2000	18	18

Note: Nurses and elementary and high school teachers were excluded. Cohort members were ages 44–53 in the year given, except for late boomers, who were ages 35–43 in 2000.

Source: Authors' calculations using the Integrated Public Use Microdata Series (IPUMS), 2003.

switch jobs from a predominantly female to a predominantly male occupation to produce a fully integrated labor force. The highest segregation index was 0.69 in 1910, implying that two-thirds of women would have to switch jobs. This level of segregation persisted until the boomers began to enter the workforce. Over the three decades following 1970, the figure fell from 0.68 in 1970 to about 0.53 in 2000.[29]

In addition, boomer women have broken paths into nontraditional professional/technical occupations; and they have been followed by younger cohorts with even higher entry levels who have encountered less resistance in more meritocratic workplaces.[30] Along these lines, when we compare cohort rates of employment in high-level professional and technical careers (excluding the traditional female professions of nursing and elementary and secondary teaching), the pattern of gender convergence is straightforward (see Table 5). Boomer men and women are equally represented in high-level professional and technical occupations at midlife; one of every five from both groups is located in an elite occupation.

These trends reveal the extraordinary occupational mobility of a significant minority of men and women in the boomer cohorts. Furthermore, they underscore the convergence of men's and women's commitments to careers because these occupations involve long-term investments in education and high time demands at work. For well-educated boomer women, these choices signaled a preference for a personally and economically satisfying career path as part of their lives, over and above family relationships.

Race, Ethnicity, and Occupational Achievement
While we have observed some gender convergence among boomers in education and upward occupational mobility, the pattern among race/ethnic and nativity groups has been divergence. Mobility into high-level professional, technical, and managerial positions increased significantly between the Jazz Age Babies and early boomers for all white and U.S.-born groups, but rates of mobility have been highly unequal across these groups (see Table 6, page 237). Beginning with the War Babies, U.S.-born Asians have been the most successful in achieving these positions; over half of U.S.-born Asian boomers were employed in these jobs in 1999. Non-Hispanic white boomers followed at 10 percentage points lower, and blacks and U.S.-born Hispanics were approximately 20 percentage points lower than U.S.-born Asians.

The divergence is even more dramatic when immigrant groups are compared. Foreign-born Hispanics have not experienced any occupational mobility across cohorts. But Asian immigrant groups, who have come to represent relatively large portions of the boomer cohorts, have fared generally as well as non-Hispanic whites.

These inequalities follow directly from differential educational achievement levels. Higher levels of educational attainment moved boomers upward in occupational hierarchies. These advantages cumulated over time and brought other rewards, including higher occupational achievement. The credential advantage is evi-

Table 6

PERCENT OF AMERICANS IN HIGH-LEVEL PROFESSIONAL, TECHNICAL, AND ADMINISTRATIVE OCCUPATIONS, BY RACE/ETHNICITY/NATIVITY AND COHORT

Cohort	Year	Non-Hispanic whites	Non-Hispanic blacks	U.S.-born Hispanics	Foreign-born Hispanics	U.S.-born Asians	Foreign-born Asians
Jazz Age Babies	1970	26	10	12	13	24	27
Depression Kids	1980	32	18	18	15	37	35
War Babies	1990	40	24	25	17	43	44
Early Boomers	2000	43	28	32	16	52	41
Late Boomers	2000	41	26	29	15	51	48

Note: Nurses and elementary and high school teachers were excluded. Cohort members were ages 44–53 in the year given, except for late boomers, who were ages 35–43 in 2000.

Source: Authors' calculations using the Integrated Public Use Microdata Series (IPUMS), 2003.

dent in the differential rates of occupational mobility that place men and women in the non-Hispanic white and U.S.-born Asian groups ahead of others. In turn, these occupational achievement levels influence earnings inequality among boomers.

Unequal Paychecks

The last few years of sustained wage growth in the postwar United States arrived in the late 1960s and early 1970s as the early boomers began entering the workforce. Between 1945 and 1973, wages grew between 2 percent and 3 percent per year. After 1973, the growth in wages in the restructuring economy slowed to between 0 percent and 1 percent and actually declined in some sectors. One consequence of these trends has been an increase in wage inequality that accelerated over the 1980s and 1990s.[31]

Wage growth over the work career ideally begins with early job shopping, quickly followed by stable employment. Among early boomers, even lower levels of education could be overcome as handicaps to wage mobility if young workers quickly moved to stable employment within the first decade of their work careers. Stability built experience that improved long-term wage rewards.[32] However, this ideal scenario became increasing elusive over the 1980s and 1990s. Employment instability, including job changes and periods of involuntary unemployment, became more and more pervasive among young workers by spreading from the manufacturing sector to mid-level white-collar sectors. Over time, wage penalties for these work patterns grew in tandem with an increased demand for college degrees.

The result at midlife for the boomers is the highest wage inequality of all cohorts (see Figure 3). Wage patterns (in constant dollars) across cohorts reveal a widening of the difference between mean and median wages for men and women, although the level of inequality has increased more dramatically among boomer men. The level of wages in a population can be measured in two different ways. The mean wage shows the arith-

metic average. The average is sensitive to values at the very high or very low ends. The median wage is the point at which half the group has higher wages and half has lower wages. The median is not sensitive to extreme values. Because of the differences in how the mean and median measure wages, comparing them shows the degree of wage inequality in the population.

The intercohort rise of mean wages relative to median wages indicates that when wage growth occurred it was at the top of the distribution. The intercohort trend in median wages indicates that men in these age groups generally experienced wage deterioration after 1980. Stagnation and then decline occurred for men at the bottom of the wage distribution and, for the boomers, wage decline at the bottom was accompanied by no gain at the top.[33] Early-boomer men at the bottom of the wage distribution in their 30s fell further by their 40s. Moreover, late-boomer men in their 30s looked worse than their older counterparts at the same ages.

Boomer women, on the other hand, show steady increases across the wage distribution, although higher wages moved up more between the War Baby and early-boomer cohorts. Late-boomer women are doing better than their counterparts at the same ages. These patterns probably reflect the educational advantages of boomer women, especially late-boomer women.

The Gender Wage Gap Narrows a Bit

In 2000, early-boomer women earned 63 cents for every dollar their male counterparts earned. In that year, the gender wage gap for workers of all ages was narrower, 73 cents. Ten years earlier, the early-boomer gender gap was 55 cents, indicating a relative improvement for women in this cohort over the 1990s (although it is important to remember that men's median wages declined by 2 percent). The late-boomer gender gap equals their older sisters' in the same year. Early-boomer women experienced improved wages relative to men over the 1990s, but their younger sisters came closer to men in their cohort earlier in their lives. Both trends reflect declines in men's wages as much as increases in women's for these cohorts.

Gender wage inequality occurs across the occupational distribution and even among boomers in the highest occupational categories. As we reported earlier, higher educational attainment moved more boomers into high-end service, professional, and managerial occupations. And men and women were equally represented in high-level careers by midlife. These men and women earned higher average wages than middle-aged workers generally, but they were still unequal among themselves (see Table 7). The gender wage gap among these privileged workers was higher; boomer professional women's median earnings were 58 percent of men's. The gap between the mean earnings of these groups was even larger at 52 percent, suggesting even higher inequality at the top of the distribution. The gender wage gap among well-educated workers is evident even in the most elite occupations that require extensive investments in educational preparation (meaning more than baccalaureate degrees) and extended work weeks and work years. For example, a recent longitudinal study following samples of late-boomer cohorts of male and female scientists from middle school to their early careers found that marriage and childbearing persistently depressed women's career advancement in the sciences.[34]

Table 7
MEN'S AND WOMEN'S MEAN AND MEDIAN WAGES IN HIGH-LEVEL PROFESSIONAL/TECHNICAL OCCUPATIONS, BY COHORT, IN 1989 DOLLARS

Cohort	Year	Men Mean	Men Median	Women Mean	Women Median
Young Progressives	1960	$35,362	$31,737	$18,177	$18,105
Jazz Age Babies	1970	47,006	42,545	21,760	20,510
Depression Kids	1980	46,255	41,306	20,078	18,705
War Babies	1990	51,610	42,000	24,333	22,000
Early Boomers	2000	52,225	39,760	27,120	22,720
Late Boomers	2000	47,247	36,920	26,512	21,513

Note: Nurses and elementary and high school teachers were excluded. Cohort members were ages 44–53 in the year given, except for late boomers, who were ages 35–43 in 2000.

Source: Authors' calculations using the Integrated Public Use Microdata Series (IPUMS), 2003.

The explanations for this effect reside both in the workplace (where family support policies have not been widespread over the childbearing and childrearing years of boomer women) and in the household (where the gender division of labor in housework and childcare has stubbornly persisted). Legislation in the 1990s to support

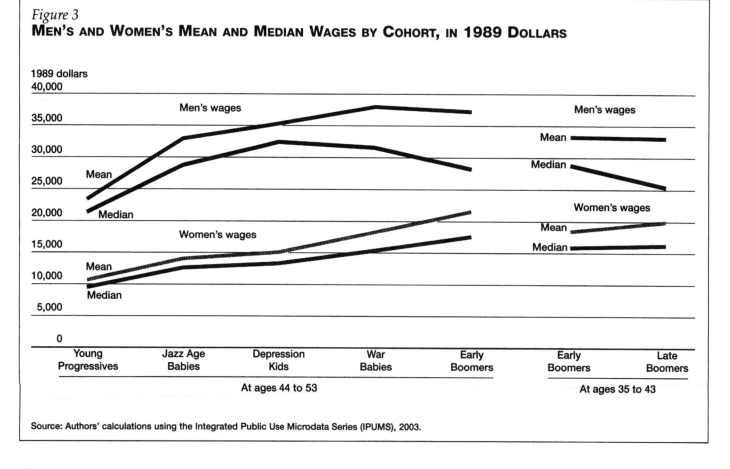

Figure 3
MEN'S AND WOMEN'S MEAN AND MEDIAN WAGES BY COHORT, IN 1989 DOLLARS

Source: Authors' calculations using the Integrated Public Use Microdata Series (IPUMS), 2003.

family leave policies represents a beginning effort to confront these problems, but the legislation arrived too late to benefit the majority of boomer women.[35]

FAMILY AFFAIRS

Americans are often surprised to learn that late marriage, permanent singlehood, small families, childlessness, and divorce have a long past in the United States. As in many Western nations, Americans have always waited to marry until they were economically self-sufficient, which meant that they often married in their mid- to late 20s and sometimes were not able to marry at all. Average family size declined in the United States throughout the 19th century, mirroring fertility declines in European nations. American divorce rates increased steadily between the Civil War and the outbreak of World War II. These family patterns, which reflect the long-term demographic history of the United States, were well established at the turn of the 20th century.[36]

The baby boom was the outcome of an extraordinary but temporary shift in these patterns. Between the end of World War II and the early 1960s, young adults married and had children at historically young ages. Few people remained single, and although divorce rates increased, they did so more slowly than they had in previous decades. The result, of course, was a large increase in the number of children born in those years. However, by the time the leading edge of early boomers reached adulthood in the mid-1960s, earlier family patterns were reemerging. Among late War Babies and the earliest boomers, marriage and childbearing shifted back to patterns more consistent with historical trends.

The bulk of the boomer cohorts inherited a modern family pattern with deep roots in the social and economic history of the United States. As the boomers came of age, they transformed this pattern. New experiences with education and work stemming from social change combined with new ideas about the importance of the individual to alter the context in which the boomers made decisions about family life. As they responded to new realities, the boomers adapted traditional family behaviors and created new family behaviors.

Marriage Delayed and Transformed

Because marriage is at the heart of the American family, changes in marriage were fundamental to the boomers' transformation of family life. New economic and cultural realities dramatically altered not just the context in which boomers decided about marriage but the institution of marriage itself. The result was that the boomers, especially late boomers, married later in life than earlier cohorts.

Table 8 shows the percentage of ever-married women by age in each of our cohorts (cohort patterns of

Table 8

PERCENT OF WOMEN EVER-MARRIED BY SELECTED AGES AND COHORT

Cohort	Age				
	20	25	30	35	40
Young Progressives	35	73	87	92	93
Jazz Age Babies	41	79	89	92	94
Depression Kids	51	84	91	94	95
War Babies	51	82	89	92	94
Early Boomers	45	75	84	88	91
Late Boomers	33	63	78	—	—

— Not applicable.

Source: Authors' estimates based on the Surveys of Income and Program Participation, 1986 and 1996.

family formation are generally symmetric for men and women, so to simplify the presentation we show results only for women). The age pattern of marriage among early boomers is not unprecedented. Members of this cohort married later than the previous three cohorts, but their age pattern closely resembles the pattern for the Young Progressives, the cohort that most closely matches historical patterns. However, the age pattern of marriage among late boomers is historically unusual. Late-boomer women and men are delaying marriage to a degree never recorded in the United States.

One cause of these marriage patterns was male boomers' experiences with education and work. Americans have always waited to marry until they were economically secure. This imperative applied especially to men, who were expected to provide most of a family's income. When economic conditions were inauspicious, marriage was postponed because establishing economic security was more difficult. As we have seen, boomer men entered the work world as educational credentials became more important to labor market success, lengthening the time required to attain economic security. At the same time, a restructuring and stagnant economy made attaining this security more difficult regardless of educational level. For boomer men with lower levels of education, such security was often simply out of reach. Some of the delay in marriage among boomers reflected the traditional response to the effects of an unfavorable economy on men's economic prospects.[37] This response was most marked among the late boomers, who had the more difficult time in the labor market.

But difficult economic conditions are only part of the story. The "silent revolution" in cultural values that began in the 1960s also affected marriage in the boomer cohorts. The weakening influence of traditional authority and increasing legitimacy of individual freedom profoundly altered Americans' ideas about gender, sexuality, and the family.[38]

New ideas about the appropriate roles for men and women were probably the most important catalysts for family change. Boomers grew up with a breadwinner-homemaker model of the family, in which men worked for pay and women cared for the home and children. This model, which had emerged with industrialization, depended on men's wages being high enough to support a family and the consequent exclusion of married women from market work. As structural economic change pulled women into the labor force, they were confronted by the formal and informal rules upholding this system. Bolstered by the new ideas emphasizing the power of the individual, women challenged these arrangements through the women's movement of the 1960s and 1980s. Although not all women actively participated in the movement, it had a tremendous impact on perceptions about what women—and men—could and should do and be.[39]

Boomer women encountered these ideas at the threshold of adulthood just as they were making decisions about education, work, and family. As they increasingly viewed work as a lifetime commitment central to their identities, boomer women took time to invest in education and establish work histories prior to marriage. Moreover, the economic foundations of marriage shifted so that women's earnings became a much more important part of family income. Thus, in contrast to previous cohorts, women's economic security appeared to be a prerequisite for marriage among late boomers.[40] Women's investments in education and work became necessary for marriage but further delayed marriage.

Women's growing economic roles posed a direct challenge to the breadwinner-homemaker family. This challenge was strengthened by the other half of the gender revolution, which concerned men's family roles.[41] A new model of masculinity encouraged boomer men to play a more active role in housework and childrearing. However, in contrast to women who moved overwhelmingly into paid work, men remained, on average only modestly engaged in the household.

Changes in attitudes toward sexuality were a second important catalyst for changes in marriage and family. Prior to the 1960s, sex was considered a matter for married people only; couples had sex only upon marriage or shortly before marriage. These attitudes were codified in a collection of laws prohibiting particular sex acts and the distribution (and even discussion) of contraception. The 1960s' cultural shift capped a century of changing attitudes, and many of these laws were abolished as norms became much more tolerant.[42] Sex before marriage became more accepted as sexual decisions became a matter of private and not public morality. These changes were helped along by important new advances in contraceptive technology, notably the pill and the IUD. These methods made control of reproduction much more effective and placed this more effective control in women's hands.

Boomer men and women quickly adopted these new norms. Greater freedom surrounding sexuality meant that one of the main drawbacks to delaying marriage, delaying regular and sanctioned sexual activity, was removed. In addition, women's increased control over their reproduction and sexuality amplified the effects of the gender revolution on the family.

Changing gender roles and shifting sexual norms altered the meaning of marriage. A third effect of changing values was to change the place of marriage in individual lives. For previous cohorts, marriage was a central goal and an important symbol of adulthood. For boomers, increased emphasis on self-fulfillment and personal growth meant that other kinds of goals, including interesting work, material satisfaction, and self-expression, became equally important. As marriage for marriage's sake became less important, marrying as soon as possible was no longer necessary. Paradoxically, the shift toward self-fulfillment also meant that people expected more out of their family relationships, especially from the conjugal relationship. Love and affection were certainly a part of marriage for prior cohorts. However, among boomers, an emotionally satisfying and sexually charged relationship became the main foundation of marriage. Finding such a soul mate is difficult, which probably contributed to delayed marriage among boomers.[43]

All of these economic and cultural forces increased the uncertainty surrounding courtship, and that uncertainty also contributed to delayed marriage among late boomers.[44] Changes in the meaning of marriage made the old rules of courtship obsolete. But the new rules were incomplete. For example, while women's new roles in the economy were quite clear, men's new roles in the household were not. Control over fertility changed women's bargaining position in complex ways. Some people embraced new ideas while others rejected them. Combined with a model of marriage based on egalitarian roles and emotional intensity, the lack of a map led to confusion and even distrust, as men and women struggled to make sense of these social changes in the context of their own lives.

The boomers, especially the late boomers, were thus the first participants in the retreat from marriage that characterizes the contemporary American family. Many people have wondered whether these lower marriage rates mean that late boomers are delaying marriage or forgoing marriage all together. A recent set of forecasts suggests that late-boomer women will marry at relatively high rates in their 30s and 40s. Thus, though they will not reach the nearly universal marriage of the Jazz Age Babies and Depression Kids, their levels of marriage will eventually be comparable to historical cohorts.[45] This forecast is consistent with survey data suggesting that boomers, as well as all Americans, value marriage and intend to marry.[46] What seems to have changed is how we think and decide about marriage, not the desire for marriage.

These marriage patterns appear to be here to stay. Marriage patterns in successive cohorts are similar to those among late boomers.[47] American marriage has changed dramatically, and the boomers, by reacting to economic and cultural change, played a pivotal role in effecting these changes.

New Challenges to Marriage and Family Life

Although boomers married at higher ages than preceding cohorts, the age at which they left home increased only slightly and only among the youngest boomers. This meant that the gap between major family roles—being a child and being a spouse or parent—widened. The boomers filled this gap with new forms of independent living, which transformed not only the family but also the entire transition to adulthood.

Historically, young unmarried people typically lived with their parents or in another household as boarders or lodgers. Young adults rarely established independent households, a transition associated only with marriage. Cohorts coming of age in the first half of the 20th century followed this pattern. When these young people left home prior to marriage, they usually did so to go to school, to serve in the military, or to find work. In each of these cases, they lived in some kind of institutional housing arrangement. Leaving home before marriage was much more common among men; women generally stayed at home until marriage.[48]

This long-term pattern changed with the boomers, although it first became visible among their older brothers and sisters, the War Babies. Unmarried boomer men and women left home in larger numbers. More important, they set up independent households, either immediately upon leaving or after they completed their educations. Some lived with roommates, others lived alone. Living alone in cities became a new, glamorous stage in the transition to adulthood, symbolized by television shows such as "Mary Tyler Moore" or "That Girl."

These new living arrangements can be traced directly to changing values about the individual and the family.[49] Apparently, both boomers and their parents desired greater autonomy, more privacy, and freedom from family roles. Boomers were much more likely to leave home simply to gain independence than to find work or go to school. Parents were willing to subsidize their children's autonomy—although they often welcomed them home again when things didn't work out.

Increases in nonfamily living prior to marriage were coupled with the rise of a new living arrangement: nonmarital cohabitation. In earlier cohorts, living with a partner outside the bonds of marriage was rare, con-

fined mostly to people of lower socioeconomic status who formed consensual unions. For most people, coresidence with a sexual partner was synonymous with marriage. Boomers were the first to depart from this pattern and live in sexual relationships outside of marriage in large numbers.

Cohabitation began among the earliest boomers and diffused rapidly. Among women born between 1945 and 1949 (the first four years of the early-boomer cohort), only 7 percent had cohabited prior to age 25. The corresponding figure for women born between 1960 and 1964, the last four years of the late-boomer cohort, was 37 percent.[50] High levels of cohabitation are one reason the late boomers show such low levels of marriage; the percentage of late-boomer women who have formed unions of any kind is much closer to the percent married among earlier cohorts.[51]

Changes in norms about sexual behavior were quite important in the spread of cohabitation. The stigma once attached to such unions was based on the sexual activity it indicated. Once this stigma was removed, or at least reduced, cohabitation became more acceptable. Some scholars have argued that cohabitation also served as a step in the courtship process. With marriage an increasingly risky proposition, boomer couples could use cohabitation to test out their compatibility prior to marriage.

These new living arrangements challenge the family because they are ways of living outside the boundaries of traditional family roles. But they also have taken on some of the characteristics of families. Both household formation and living with a sexual partner were once restricted to marriage. Thus the boundaries between family and nonfamily are blurring—or, as some would say, are being redefined.

Forming an independent household while unmarried is normative in the contemporary transition to adulthood.[52] Cohabiting with a partner is now so common that we forget how stigmatized it once was. Both of these behaviors originated largely in the boomer cohorts.

The Rise of Serial Monogamy

Boomers sought a different kind of marriage and married later than their counterparts in earlier cohorts. Once formed, their marriages were less stable than the marriages of members of earlier cohorts. The high incidence of divorce among boomers is reflected in Figure 4. At every age, a higher fraction of both early- and late-boomer women have been divorced than women in previous cohorts.

High levels of divorce among boomers are rooted in the same economic and cultural forces that changed the nature and timing of marriage and living arrangements. Women's economic emancipation and new ideas about self-fulfillment meant that couples were more willing to

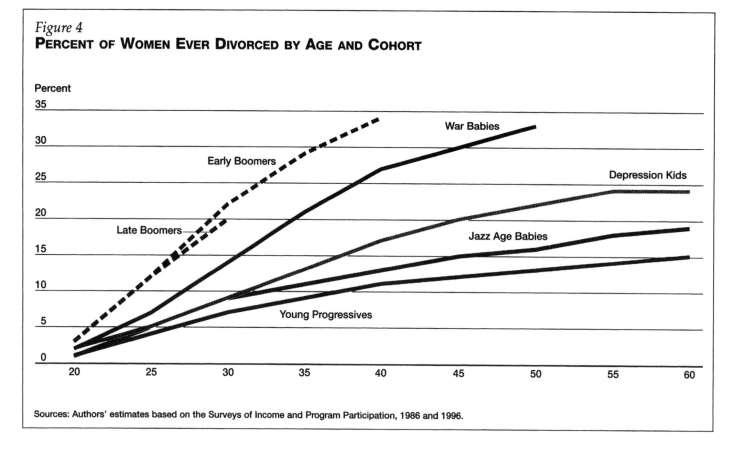

Figure 4

PERCENT OF WOMEN EVER DIVORCED BY AGE AND COHORT

Percent

War Babies

Early Boomers

Depression Kids

Late Boomers

Jazz Age Babies

Young Progressives

Sources: Authors' estimates based on the Surveys of Income and Program Participation, 1986 and 1996.

end a marriage that wasn't working well. To the extent that the basis of marriage shifted more toward an intense emotional tie, the always-subjective standard for marital success may have risen.

However, in contrast to patterns of marriage and living arrangements, the boomers were not in the vanguard of increases in divorce. The War Babies brought the sharpest increase in divorce rates over earlier cohorts. The War Babies were at risk for divorce in the late 1960s, just when the long-term secular increase spiked sharply upward.[53]

Thus, boomers watched as their older brothers and sisters experienced historically high rates of marital disruption. This likely reinforced an attachment to the labor market among boomer women, who could not be sure that their marriages would last. Overall, high levels of divorce increased uncertainty about marriage among boomers. The trend toward cohabitation may have strengthened, as it became a "trial run" for marriage. By the time the boomers had married, attitudes had shifted in the direction of greater tolerance of divorce leading them to divorce at even higher rates.

Some claim that increases in divorce signal abandonment of marriage among boomers. The best evidence against this is the relatively high level of remarriage. In fact, by age 30, 12 percent of late-boomer women have been married twice. Remarriage existed in earlier cohorts, but a much higher fraction of these

remarriages occurred following the death of a spouse rather than divorce.

The pattern of high levels of divorce combined with fairly common remarriage has been called "serial monogamy." Although this pattern did not emerge among the boomers, they reinforced it and by their large numbers made it more visible. Moreover, serial monogamy is the outgrowth of the same forces that shaped other aspects of boomer life.

The Variable Experience of Parenthood

Parenthood stands with marriage at the core of American family life. Accordingly, changes in childbearing and childrearing were also an important factor in the boomers' transformation of family life. The same historical and social forces that shaped boomer marriage patterns led to greater variation in the experience of parenthood.

Boomer women bore fewer children than women in earlier cohorts (see Table 9, page 243). Late-boomer women have not all reached age 45, which by convention is considered the end of the childbearing years. If many of these women have children, their completed fertility may rise a bit. But a surge above the level of the early boomers seems unlikely. Interestingly, the proportion of boomer women who remained childless is comparable to levels seen among the earliest cohorts

Table 9

FERTILITY INDICATORS FOR U.S. WOMEN BY COHORT

Fertility indicators	Young Progressives*	Jazz Age Babies	Depression Kids	War Babies	Early Boomers	Late Boomers
Average number of children	2.4	2.6	3.1	2.6	1.9	1.8
Childless (%)	19	16	11	12	17	22
With four or more children (%)	22	26	35	24	12	10
First birth at age 19 or younger (%)	—	—	23	29	25	22
First birth at age 30 or older (%)	—	—	8	8	15	18
First birth while unmarried (%)	—	—	12	15	18	24

— Not available.

* Ever-married women only.

Sources: Authors' estimates using the Integrated Public Use Microdata Series (IPUMS), 2003; and the Surveys of Income and Program Participation, 1986, 1996, and 2001.

(remember that the Jazz Age Babies and Depression Kids, the cohorts that produced the baby boom, had historically low rates of childlessness). In addition, the proportion of women with large families declined dramatically among boomers. In this respect at least, boomer women are less diverse than women in earlier cohorts: Among women who have children, most have one or two.[54]

This apparent homogeneity masks important change and variation. The way these fewer births are distributed over women's lifetimes and the circumstances under which children are born diversified greatly in the boomer cohorts. These trends are boomers' main contributions to fertility change.

First, there is much greater diversity among boomers in the age at which women become mothers for the first time. Boomer women have births early, on time, and late.[55] Although the percentage of women having their first birth as teenagers dropped in the boomer cohorts, nearly a quarter had their first child as a teen. At the same time, a much higher proportion waited until their 30s to begin childbearing. Among the late boomers, this figure may well increase since not all of them are past childbearing age.

Second, the fraction of births to unmarried women is higher in the boomer cohorts. Nonmarital childbearing increased beginning with the War Babies, but the increase was particularly sharp among the late boomers. Thus, for many boomer women, marriage and childbearing are not coincident. Many of these births are to women in cohabiting unions.[56] But since cohabiting unions are less stable, these women may well end up raising children on their own.

Of course, nonmarital childbearing is not the only source of single-parent families among boomers.[57] High divorce rates have many parents raising children more or less alone. Since women were more likely to receive custody of children in divorce settlements, many of these single parents are women. The chal-lenges of single parenthood, including relationships with the noncustodial or joint-custody parent, remain an important part of boomer parenthood. Remarriage, which brings a stepparent and often stepchildren, has added complexity.

Finally, boomer women were more likely to work during pregnancy and to return to work within a year after giving birth, so they were much more likely to combine the roles of mother to young children and paid worker. This new pattern paralleled an increase in "involved fathering" on the part of some late-boomer men. But as with sharing the housework, changes in fathering have been uneven and there is great variation in fathers' roles from family to family.[58]

Changes in childbearing reflect both long-term trends and the boomers' reconfiguration of the life course in response to structural change. The decline in numbers is a continuation of the transition to low fertility interrupted by the baby boom, although more efficient methods of contraception led to new lows in fertility among the boomers. Variations in the timing of parenthood are directly related to women's patterns of education, work, and marriage. On average, women's higher levels of education and increased commitment to the workforce delayed childbearing just as they delayed marriage. This trend was also aided by the new methods of contraception that gave women greater flexibility in the timing of births. The heterogeneity in the timing of childbirth in boomer women's lives reflected variation in the ways they fit childbearing around their education and work. Increases in nonmarital childbearing reflected longer periods spent unmarried and sexually active, increasing the likelihood of premarital births even with better methods of contraception. Most of the increase in nonmarital fertility among boomers can be traced to the higher number of women at risk of such a birth, not to increased rates of nonmarital fertility. Boomer women were much less likely to marry after a premarital conception than women in earlier cohorts.

Table 10

LIVING ARRANGEMENTS BY COHORT

| | Ages 44–53 | | | | | Ages 35–43 | | | | |
Living arrangements	Young Progressives 1960	Jazz Age Babies 1970	Depression Kids 1980	War Babies 1990	Early Boomers 2000	Jazz Age Babies 1960	Depression Kids 1970	War Babies 1980	Early Boomers 1990	Late Boomers 2000
With spouse*	69	72	71	66	61	75	76	72	65	59
With spouse and relatives*	13	10	8	8	7	10	7	6	5	6
Alone	5	5	7	9	11	3	3	6	8	9
With children only	3	4	5	5	5	2	4	6	6	6
With children and others	3	3	3	5	6	2	2	4	5	6
With relatives*	6	5	4	4	6	7	5	4	6	8
With nonrelatives	2	1	1	3	4	1	1	2	4	6

* May include children.

Source: Authors' calculations using the Integrated Public Use Microdata Series (IPUMS), 2003.

Many Kinds of Families

Boomers' family experiences have been quite different from the experiences of previous cohorts. In addition, on nearly every dimension the boomers' families are more heterogeneous than families in previous cohorts. Not only are boomers likely to live in family constellations that differ from those of the past, their families are also likely to differ from the families of at least some of their contemporaries.

Table 10 shows the proportion of people in each cohort who were living in different kinds of households in the cross-sectional snapshot of the census. Household structure summarizes patterns of marriage, divorce, cohabitation, and parenthood. For example, later age at marriage combined with the rising incidence of divorce leads to more people living alone. An increasing likelihood that the elderly will stay in their own homes reduces the fraction of multigenerational households. Since living arrangements change with age, we show data for most cohorts at two age ranges, from ages 35 to 43 and ages 44 to 53.

Two patterns appear. First, the diversity of living arrangements is higher in the baby-boom cohorts than in the cohorts preceding them. That is, the percentage in the most common arrangements, living with a spouse with or without children and other relatives, is less common, while the percentage in less common arrangements such as living alone is higher. The increased diversity is noticeable at both ages, suggesting that family diversity extends across the life course and that a smaller proportion of the boomers' lives will be spent in traditional households. Second, the fraction of people living in nonfamily households—alone or with nonrelatives—has risen dramatically in the boomer cohorts. The higher percentage of boomers living with nonrelatives primarily reflects the higher levels of cohabitation among boomers. Although these two patterns are strongest among boomers, and especially late boomers, they appear to have started with the War Baby cohort.

One of the implications of different and more heterogeneous families in the boomer cohorts is a greater variety of family roles and a greater range in family relationships. Change in roles has taken two forms: the redefinition of traditional roles and the creation of new roles. For example, boomer women redefined the role of mother to "working mother" by combining motherhood with work outside the home. Some observers suggest that the role of father is bifurcating into the "good" dads, who are fully involved with their children and are equal partners in maintaining the household, and the "bad" dads, who, as noncustodial parents, are absent from their children's lives.[59] Family change has also brought new roles. Most obviously, the cohabitating relationship has introduced the live-in partner. Divorce has brought ex-spouses and ex-in-laws, and remarriage brings stepchildren.

These new roles are not well defined, so there are no rules for appropriate behaviors and obligations. Consequently, individuals have to adapt in their own ways and they have often been confused by their own lives.[60]

So far, we have described boomer families as a whole. This broad-brush picture conceals great variation in family structure by race, ethnicity, and nativity. The general pattern of increasing diversity over time is true of all groups but Asian immigrants. However, within groups the level and pattern of change for each arrangement vary. For example, foreign-born and U.S.-born Hispanics show no decline in the likelihood of living as part of a married couple in a complex household. This is consistent with research suggesting the greater salience of extended family living in the Hispanic community. Hispanic and Asian immigrants show no increase in the likelihood of living alone. Blacks are especially likely to be living alone with children. These differences are due both to economic constraints and cultural conventions.

THE BOTTOM LINE

The prosperity the boomers experienced in childhood was the culmination of several decades of improvement in the American standard of living, interrupted only by the Great Depression. Income and wealth steadily increased over most of the 20th century, accompanied by a decline in overall inequality until sometime before 1980. Since then, the standard of living has arguably continued to improve, but a reversal in the earlier trend toward equality has occurred. A general pattern of dispersion in earnings, household income, and wealth has dominated the last two decades.[61]

Households are the basic units of economic activity in the United States and thereby serve as a gauge for the standard of living of families. Resource accumulation, consumption, and reproduction activities all occur in the context of the household, and household members produce significant goods and services as well. As such, households are more than addresses and social arrangements; they are complex economic relationships within which individual resources are pooled to manage both the expected and unexpected opportunities and difficulties of daily life.

The economic well-being of households has been a matter of increased concern among policymakers over the past four decades as the War Babies and baby boomers have aged. Changes in household arrangements have increased this preoccupation, since families have changed from the once predominant married male-breadwinner form to the current mixed complement of dual earner, single family-headed, and never-married single types. As a result, the incomes, poverty levels, and net worth of households are monitored to take account of the well-being of the nation.

At midlife, the boomers live with an even higher standard of living than their parents. But they also live with more inequality. The inequality is evident in their household incomes, home ownership patterns, and net worth. Their labor market histories contribute to this inequality, but so too do their family histories and current household arrangements.

The Polarization of Household Income

Household income closely monitors the general day-to-day well-being of individuals and families. It represents the capacity to meet the ordinary and extraordinary needs of household members. After World War II, average household income grew until 2000. But beginning in 1980, inequality in household income increased dramatically. Households in the top fifth of the income distribution have increased their share of aggregate income, while those in the bottom four-fifths have lost ground.[62]

Table 11

MEAN AND MEDIAN HOUSEHOLD INCOME BY COHORT, IN 1989 DOLLARS

Cohort	Year	Mean	Median
At ages 44–53			
Young Progressives	1960	$31,473	$27,264
Jazz Age Babies	1970	44,070	38,646
Depression Kids	1980	47,469	43,186
War Babies	1990	53,225	45,000
Early Boomers	2000	54,593	43,310
At ages 35–43			
Early Boomers	1990	48,147	41,200
Late Boomers	2000	49,340	39,544

Source: Authors' calculations using the Integrated Public Use Microdata Series (IPUMS), 2003.

These trends have held for the boomer cohorts. Median household income (in constant dollars) increased across successive cohorts, including both boomer cohorts (see Table 11). However, household income inequality was higher in the boomer cohorts relative to the War Babies, who up to that point had the highest level of inequality.

Increased income inequality is evident in the difference between cohort mean and median household incomes. As in the case of wages, the level of household income in a population can be measured two different ways. The mean income shows the arithmetic average. The average is sensitive to values at the very high or very low ends. The median income is the point at which half the group has higher income and half the group has lower income. The median is not sensitive to extreme values. Because of the differences in how the mean and median measure income, comparing them shows the degree of income inequality in the population. For example, increases in mean income combined with stability in median income indicate that incomes are increasing at the high end of the income distribution, but the middle point is remaining the same. Thus, a small proportion of high-income households have experienced income growth, but most did not, leading to higher levels of income inequality. This intercohort pattern mirrors the one observed earlier for earnings inequality, since earnings are the principal source for most preretirement households.

These trends in household income have been affected by the diversification of living arrangements and patterns of employment instability described earlier. Dual earner households and single family-headed households are not on level ground for household income attainment. In addition, involuntary job loss or wage decline—even in dual earner households—can depress household income.

Table 12

PERCENT OF AMERICANS IN POVERTY OR AFFLUENCE BY COHORT

Cohort	Year	Near poverty	Poverty	Affluence
At ages 44–53				
Young Progressives	1960	17	10	12
Jazz Age Babies	1970	9	6	25
Depression Kids	1980	8	6	33
War Babies	1990	8	5	40
Early Boomers	2000	9	5	38
At ages 35–43				
Early Boomers	1990	9	7	28
Late Boomers	2000	12	7	26

Note: Near poverty is 150 percent of the poverty threshold. Affluence is 500 percent of the poverty threshold.

Source: Authors' calculations using the Integrated Public Use Microdata Series (IPUMS), 2003.

Rising Affluence and Rising Poverty

The increase in household income inequality among boomers is visible also by examining changes at the extremes of the household income distribution (see Table 12). Poverty and affluence represent these extremes. The U.S. Census measures poverty by matching the total household money income from all sources before taxes to estimates of need based on family size and ages of family members (adjusted annually for inflation). If total household income falls below estimated need, the family is in poverty. Some scholars also examine families who are at or below 150 percent of the poverty threshold and are at high risk of falling into poverty. A common measure of affluence that permits comparisons across cohorts and over time is 500 percent of the poverty level, generally above the 80th percentile of the income distribution.

Poverty rates for people in midlife are generally lower than for the general population. The faces of poverty in the United States are primarily those of young children, the elderly, and disadvantaged ethnic groups. In 2000, the national poverty rate was 11 percent, higher than those for the War Babies and early boomers but lower than that of the late boomers.

The highest rate of poverty and the lowest rate of affluence were experienced at midlife by the Young Progressives: Nearly one in five was officially poor and one in four was near poverty. The discovery of this stark level of poverty across all age groups motivated the War on Poverty and related social programs such as Medicare and Medicaid. The effect was that, a decade later, poverty rates had fallen to half their 1960 levels. Poverty levels then remained relatively constant across cohorts.

However, between ages 35 and 44, the late boomers are significantly more at risk of poverty and near

poverty than the three previous cohorts. In fact, the late boomers have the highest levels of poverty of any cohort since the Young Progressives. One in 10 late boomers is in poverty at middle age, while two in 10 are in poverty or at risk of poverty.

Household incomes that reach affluent levels (500 percent above the poverty threshold) are most likely to occur in mature households, which have benefited from career wage growth. These levels increased across 20th-century cohorts, peaked with the War Babies, but fell somewhat among the early boomers. Affluence increased by 10 percentage points among the early boomers between 1990 and 2000. Meanwhile, late boomers had slightly lower affluence levels than early boomers at the same ages—coupled with higher poverty rates.

Ethnic Classes and Power Couples

Household income inequality in the boomer cohorts is crosscut by income inequality between subgroups of boomers. We see the persistence of income inequality by race, ethnicity, and nativity. These differences are so entrenched that in effect they create ethnic classes. In addition, however, a new basis for inequality has emerged among boomers: the combination of education and marital status.

Earlier we showed a divergence across cohorts in the likelihood of college completion by race/ethnicity and nativity. We saw persistent differences by race, ethnicity, and nativity in occupational mobility and wage growth. Household structure also varies among ethnic groups, with more single family heads among blacks and more married couples among U.S.-born Asians. These differences have produced enduring ethnic classes across cohorts. The cumulative effects of differences in education, occupation, and household structure have maintained the relative advantage in household income of non-Hispanic white and Asian groups compared with other groups. These intractable inequalities underlie some of the increased inequality in household income in the boomer cohorts.

Table 13 (page 247) reports household incomes of race, ethnic, and nativity groups as a percent of non-Hispanic white household incomes. The patterns of difference are diverse and dramatic. Blacks' household incomes have been about two-thirds of non-Hispanic whites since the War Babies, clearly showing little gain. On the other hand, U.S.-born Hispanics have gained relative to whites, especially in the boomer cohorts. U.S.-born Hispanic households have four-fifths the incomes of white households. Hispanic immigrants have lost ground across cohorts and are at the level of blacks. Asians have fared much better. U.S.-born Asians' household incomes exceed whites, while foreign-born Asians achieved parity with whites beginning with the Depression Kids.

Table 13

HOUSEHOLD INCOME OF SELECTED RACE AND NATIVITY GROUPS COMPARED WITH NON-HISPANIC WHITE INCOME, BY COHORT

| | | Household income as percent of non-Hispanic white household income | | | | |
Cohort	Year*	U.S-born Blacks	U.S-born Hispanics	Foreign-born Hispanics	U.S.-born Asians	Foreign-born Asians
Jazz Age Babies	1970	59	71	71	115	87
Depression Kids	1980	63	72	70	118	95
War Babies	1990	67	70	69	126	104
Early Boomers	2000	66	77	66	121	99
Late Boomers	2000	68	80	66	124	104

* Cohort members were ages 44–53 in the year given, except for late boomers, who were ages 35–43 in 2000.

Source: Authors' estimates using the Integrated Public Use Microdata Series (IPUMS), 2003.

The boomer cohorts came of age after the changes initiated by the Civil Rights Act. However, we see little evidence of the equalization intended by this legislation in household income with respect to race. Blacks in the boomer cohorts are no better off relative to whites than their parents and grandparents.

Ethnic classes in the baby-boom cohorts are not new. What is new is a pattern of income inequality by education and marital status. Households with multiple earners are at a significant advantage in household income. If both of these earners have college degrees, the advantage is of course increased. Table 14 reports percentage differences in income between marital groups by educational levels. With the exception of the Depression Kids, the divergence of household income by marital status and education is pronounced. These inequalities are bolstered by the high likelihood that married couples will have the same level of education.[63] Moreover, in the boomer cohorts, marriage is more likely and perhaps more stable among college-educated people.[64] Together these trends signal an important shift in the boomer cohorts: Marriage is becoming a class status as well as a family status.

A Home of One's Own

In the United States, owning one's home is a widely shared symbol of social and material success. Surveys show that the overwhelming majority of Americans desire to own their own homes. This remarkable consensus on the importance of property ownership reflects deep cultural values of individualism and self-sufficiency. Homeownership is key to financial well-being; home equity commonly accounts for the largest share of one's net worth.[65] Beyond financial advantages, ownership benefits the family and children by anchoring family lifestyle. Ownership has positive effects on the community through increased social integration and civic engagement.[66]

In keeping with the importance of homeownership to Americans, rates of ownership are higher in the United States than those in most other developed

Table 14

DIFFERENCES IN HOUSEHOLD INCOME BETWEEN HIGH SCHOOL AND COLLEGE GRADUATES, BY MARITAL STATUS AND COHORT

| | Ages 44–53 | | | | | Ages 35–43 | |
Education and marital status	Young Progressives 1960	Jazz Age Babies 1970	Depression Kids 1980	War Babies 1990	Early Boomers 2000	Early Boomers 1990	Late Boomers 2000
Married college graduates' income as a percentage of married high school graduates' income	149	149	141	159	168	153	167
Unmarried college graduates' income as a percentage of unmarried high school graduates' income	138	155	152	164	168	158	165
Married college graduates' income as a percentage of unmarried college graduates' income	165	164	171	176	179	157	158

Source: Authors' calculations using the Integrated Public Use Microdata Series (IPUMS), 2003.

Table 15

PERCENT OF AMERICANS WHO OWN THEIR HOMES, BY AGE GROUP AND COHORT

Cohort	Ages 35–43	Ages 44–53
Young Progressives	—	64
Jazz Age Babies	62	71
Depression Kids	68	77
War Babies	71	74
Early Boomers	64	71
Late Boomers	61	—

— Not available.

Source: Authors' calculations using the Integrated Public Use Microdata Series (IPUMS), 2003.

nations. In fact, homeownership is one of the post-World War II success stories in the United States. Home ownership rates increased dramatically between 1940 and 1960. These increases were due in part to the favorable economic situation. But they also reflected a policy environment supportive of ownership, including programs that subsidized the construction of suburban single-family homes, favorable tax treatment for homeowners, and institutions designed to facilitate mortgage lending.[67]

The Young Progressives, Jazz Age Babies, and Depression Kids capitalized on this environment. The prevalence of homeownership increased in each of these cohorts (see Table 15). However, this favorable trend ended with the War Babies, who were less likely to be owners than the Depression Kids were at the same age. Early and late boomers are even less likely to be homeowners.

Some of the decline in homeownership can be traced to the characteristics of the boomers. A higher percentage of them are minorities and immigrants. Despite increases in the overall likelihood of ownership, significant disparities reflect both economic inequality and outright discrimination in housing markets.[68] However, this downward trend is visible in all racial and ethnic groups, including non-Hispanic whites.

Shifts in family composition also account for some of the decline. Married couples are most likely to be homeowners. Delayed marriage, cohabitation, and divorce (where at least one former partner loses the house), mean that the boomer cohorts are more likely to be living in situations not associated with homeownership.

A final explanation for the boomer shortfall in ownership is that the same difficult economic circumstances that have increased income inequality have affected wealth accumulation. Since the mid-1970s, prospective homeowners have been caught between stagnant wages on one side and rising housing prices on the other. Increases in housing costs have come from both housing price inflation, which some scholars have argued is due

to the large baby-boom cohorts entering the housing market, and an increase in the overall quality of the housing stock.[69] Lower-income people have thus effectively been priced out of the ownership market.[70] The downward trend in ownership rates between the Depression Kids and late boomers is strongest among people with either high school or less than high school educations (29 percent and 17 percent, respectively). The decline is modest for college-educated people (2 percent). Education differentials in home ownership have therefore widened considerably. Among the Depression Kids, the high school graduate ownership rate was 2 percent lower than the college graduate rate. Among late boomers, the comparable figure is 17 percent.

The effects of new family patterns, stagnating wages, and housing price inflation have combined to increase inequality in home ownership in the boomer cohorts. The decline in homeownership signals a new era in which a significant proportion of the population is shut out of the American Dream.

Unequal Fortunes

Considerable research using sources other than census data has considered how much wealth baby boomers accumulated over their lifetimes. Some studies have found that, on average, the boomers have been wealthier at younger ages (ages 25 to 34 and 35 to 44) than their parents were at those ages. Early boomers have also been compared to current retirees and found to be relatively better off prior to retirement than the currently retired were. The conclusions from these studies are that the boomers are not—and probably will not be in old age—worse off than their parents.[71] Other studies have found that boomers are not saving enough for their retirements. These cohorts have accumulated more wealth over their lifetimes with high average levels of consumption. However, their savings behavior has not included as much traditional savings in bank accounts but more wealth accumulation in home equity and pension accounts—although these are unequally distributed in these cohorts. Moreover, their high levels of secured and unsecured debt raise some concerns about whether they are prepared for retirement.

The decennial census does not collect data that allow comparison of wealth across cohorts, and no other data source is available to compare all cohorts of interest in this study. But other surveys can provide a picture of the wealth of boomer cohorts. We used the Surveys of Income and Program Participation in 1986 and 1996 to review boomer wealth at midlife (see Table 16, page 249).

Table 16 summarizes the average levels of selected components of wealth and debt and the degree of wealth inequality among the boomer cohorts. At ages 31 to 40, the older cohort was more affluent (in constant dollars) than the younger cohort, having both higher

Table 16
WEALTH AND DEBT OF TWO BABY-BOOM COHORTS, 1986 AND 1996

| | Ages 31–40 | | | | | | Ages 41–50 | | |
| | Early Boomers | | | Late Boomers | | | Early Boomers | | |
Indicators of wealth	Mean	Median	Gini inequality index*	Mean	Median	Gini inequality index*	Mean	Median	Gini inequality index*
Total net worth, in 1989 dollars	$68,877	$34,269	0.66	$52,719	$15,799	0.78	$104,623	$43,195	0.74
Total wealth	72,532	37,703	0.63	59,911	20,634	0.74	109,406	47,396	0.70
Total debt	42,929	23,587	0.61	62,136	37,224	0.65	44,697	19,800	0.66
Selected sources of wealth									
Home equity	$34,048	$17,010	0.66	$25,594	$13,000	0.71	$41,546	$23,760	0.67
Stock equity**	3,109	0	0.96	3,626	0	0.97	26,960	0	0.95
Other savings	7,839	1,133	0.80	6,148	367	0.86	13,293	1,077	0.85

* Gini coefficients index the degree of inequalty in the distribution of wealth: 0 represents no inequality, while 1 represents maximum inequality. The Gini coefficients exclude people who do not have any of the asset in question.

** Excludes pension plan stock investments. Between 18 percent and 27 percent of cohort members owned stocks.

Source: Authors' calculations using the Surveys of Income and Program Participation, 1986 and 1996.

---

levels of wealth and lower levels of debt. The median net worth of early boomers in their 30s was almost twice that of late boomers. Early-boomers' assets exceed late-boomers' assets with the exception of average equity in stocks.

Late boomers display higher levels of inequality. The inequality is first evident in the difference between mean and median wealth levels, which show (as in the cases of earnings and household income presented earlier) that wealth is highly concentrated above the median in these cohorts, and especially among the younger one. Inequality is also measured by Gini co-efficients, which index the degree of inequality in the distribution of wealth: zero represents no inequality, while 1 represents maximum inequality. The late boomers are more unequal in wealth, net worth, and home equity.

Finally, when we compare the early boomers over 10 years between 1986 and 1996, we see that inequality has increased among them. Average wealth and net worth have increased for the boomers and debt has declined. But inequality in wealth and net worth have increased.

The Top Takes All

The highly skewed distribution of wealth in the United States is well established.[72] The most recent findings (2001) using the Survey of Consumer Finances' comprehensive estimates of wealth are that the top 1 percent of the population held one-third of total wealth; the next 9 percent in the highest decile held one-third; and the remaining 90 percent of the population held one-third.[73] Wealth distributions in boomer cohorts are less highly

skewed but nevertheless highly unequal. Based on our analyses using the Surveys of Income and Program Participation, the top 10 percent of early boomers hold 54 percent of total cohort wealth in 1996, and the top 10 percent of late boomers hold 59 percent of total cohort wealth. In both cohorts nearly all wealth (at or over 95 percent) is held by those above the medians of the respective wealth distributions.

In sum, the boomer cohorts have on average higher standards of living than earlier cohorts. However, these averages conceal high levels of economic inequality, levels higher than those in the cohorts immediately preceding them. These inequalities reflect the accumulation of education, work, and family histories. The late boomers exhibit more inequality because their journey through the last three decades has been somewhat more treacherous in the labor market and more heterogeneous in family life. The extent to which the economic highs and lows of the 1990s will have permanent effects on boomer wealth levels is yet to be determined. But we can be certain that heterogeneity and inequality will follow them.

WHAT'S AHEAD

We have called the baby-boom cohorts pivotal because, while their lives are rooted in the past, in most respects they point toward the future. The boomers inherited a society with a strong tradition of universal education and a modern industrial economy. Most grew up in traditional breadwinner families. As they grew up they encountered structural changes that transformed the economy, civil society, and culture.

Their choices negotiated between traditions from the past and the volatile present. As they responded to new circumstances, boomers redirected social change. More than any other cohort, they represent the transition from an old America to a new America.

As pivotal cohorts, the boomers show continuities with past cohorts, but also many discontinuities. On average, they received more education than prior cohorts; they were more likely to work in technical or service jobs; and they were more likely to marry late, divorce, and have few children. But these averages conceal great variation. In almost every respect, the boomer cohorts are more heterogeneous than prior cohorts and they are highly unequal in economic status.

Although the boomers are still in their prime working years, their later years are visible on the horizon. The prospect of the baby-boom cohorts entering later life has raised concerns among academics, policymakers, and the public. Most of this concern is based on the sheer size of the boomer cohorts. Just as the baby boom once crowded public schools, some observers caution that they will overwhelm public programs for the elderly, notably Social Security and Medicare. Others warn of a tremendous impact of aging boomers on the health care system, and fear that their long-term care will strain social and familial resources. Although the aging of the baby boom should lead to vibrant markets for products for the elderly, some marketers dread the boomers' exit from the high-income, high-spending midlife years. Other analysts predict declines in American productivity as retiring boomers shrink the labor force. Some commentators even worry that the withdrawal of the boomers from housing and equity markets will cause a meltdown in housing and stock prices.

The impact of the aging baby boom depends greatly on the current circumstances and future choices of the boomers themselves. As we have seen, the baby-boom cohorts enter old age with life histories that differ markedly from those of current elderly. Boomer men and women have worked longer and many plan to work later than earlier cohorts. Most boomers will confront the disabilities associated with aging later in their lives than earlier cohorts. And their diverse family histories and current living arrangements raise more uncertainties about the patterns of their lives in old age. The boomers have surprised us before. Will they surprise us again? Given these differences, projections based on size alone are not likely to be helpful. Indeed, the variability in the boomer cohorts that we have discovered promises that generalizations are likely to be misleading.

Based on our review of the boomers lives and times, what can we add to the debate about the impact of aging boomers? On the one hand, the boomers' status at midlife provides a rough map to their future because

the life course is sequentially dependent: Later events and statuses are conditional on earlier events and statuses. Consequently, their old age will reflect the accumulation of experiences. For example, their marital histories will shape their family relationships in later life. Similarly, their education and earnings histories will be an important determinant of their economic well-being. We also know where the boomers are continuous and where they are discontinuous with prior cohorts. To the extent that the boomers are continuous with past cohorts, differences between the boomers and current elderly will be a matter of degree. The experience of current elderly, and especially the experience of the War Babies, can provide useful clues about what to expect from the boomers.

On the other hand, reviewing the history of the baby boom has demonstrated the tremendous flexibility of individual biography. For example, the baby boom was itself a response to historical conditions. Their lives unfolded as responses to contemporaneous changes. At midlife, their most recent experiences have included the 1990s economic boom and bust, the War on Terror, and continuing technological change. How these experiences and experiences to come will bear upon their futures is not yet clear. Since we cannot predict historical change, conclusions about the future of the baby boom are not wise.

With this caveat, the following is a set of reasonable expectations for the aging of the baby boom.

The Extension of Midlife

Based on the patterns we observe in their lives to this point, we expect that the boomers will extend midlife well into what used to be considered old age. The organization of their lives has already deviated considerably from what was once considered normative. New roles and differences in the timing of roles have led to new life trajectories that will continue to develop and perhaps move in new directions as they grow old.

Longer Working Lives

A number of factors point to boomer men and women working later in their lives than previous cohorts. First, they have worked in less hazardous and less physically demanding occupations that have traditionally had later ages of retirement. Second, across all levels of education, their employment histories have been less stable due to labor market changes, which have slowed their progress in saving for retirement. Third, some boomers will continue to work because they are satisfied with their jobs, their incomes, and the lifestyles these afford. Others will continue to work from economic necessity. Finally, a number of structural changes will likely lead to longer work lives among the boomers. Chief among these changes will be disincentives to retire early.

Complex Family Lives

We have shown the enormous heterogeneity in the boomers' family lives. These family histories suggest that the boomers will extend midlife family roles and relationships beyond the middle years. For example, boomers who have had children later in life will find that some parental responsibilities, such as coresidence with children or paying for college, will extend to older ages than in previous cohorts. Longer lives among the boomers' parents may mean that older boomers will be caring for their very old parents.

Healthy and Active Lives

The image of old age often includes the disengagement of older people from lifelong interests and activities, implying that old age is a discreet, discontinuous stage. This image may never have been completely true, but among boomers it seems especially unlikely. The combination of better health and heterogeneous lives suggests that boomers will remain actively engaged in all dimensions of their lives and push back the boundaries of old age.

Golden Years or Tarnished Years?

Our analyses demonstrate the enormous inequalities in the baby-boom cohorts at midlife. These inequalities mean that while some boomers will have a comfortable old age, others will not. The boomers are generally better off than earlier cohorts, but the high dispersion of income and wealth among them will persist into retirement. Also, boomers are generally healthier than earlier cohorts, but health disparities among them will probably lead to diverging trajectories of disability in old age. These inequalities coincide with policy changes that may make things worse.

Persistent Inequality

Persistent economic inequalities combined with health disparities will mean that the least well off may face higher risks of unemployment and earlier and more protracted declines in health. Economic inequality among the boomers will coincide with policy changes that encourage them to remain at work later, further disadvantaging those who are least advantaged. Early retirement is common among lower-wage and disabled workers. However, the Social Security system has already altered the eligibility rules for the boomers in ways that will penalize earlier retirement and reward later retirement at higher levels than earlier cohorts. Recent increases in the federal deficit have fueled additional concerns over the financial burden of boomer retirees and raised the prospect of further adjustments that will again cut benefits for the boomers. The easiest way to cut benefits is to postpone them. These kinds of adjustments work to increase the relative disadvantage of boomers with lower incomes.

Less-advantaged boomer workers will encounter the same problems that current older workers encounter. Those who retire early become progressively worse off with time, but working later may also be problematic. Unemployment and underemployment are higher for less-skilled older workers; and jobs are low in pay and benefit coverage. Health insurance is becoming more scarce and expensive for older workers who hang on as long as they can until Medicare eligibility. The poorest among them are uninsured and turn to disability coverage under Social Security if possible.

The Devolution of Risk

Economic and health risks largely devolve on families and individuals and will do so even more in the boomer cohorts. Economic inequality and health disparities have coincided with changes in workplace provisions for pension saving and health insurance over the past two decades. Individuals and their families are increasingly responsible for retirement saving in risky financial markets and for the provision of health care, both through higher out-of-pocket costs and through the personal provision of care.

In this environment, some boomers will do fine, but others will be vulnerable to economic and health risks and to devastating consequences from lack of an adequate safety net. Risks will be highest for people with fewer resources and reserves. However, the importance of family members in sharing risk means that variations in family structure will affect the kinds of safety nets available. For example, much speculation has centered on the old-age prospects for "absent" fathers. Lacking strong bonds with children, many fear that these men will be left alone in old age. Similar issues arise for people who have never married or never had children. New family situations and configurations with ambiguous expectations or strained relations may weaken the family safety net.

Family histories will have an enduring impact well into old age. The oldest old (those 85 and over) are most in need of long-term care and most at risk for poverty. They will be especially vulnerable to variations in the family safety net. These issues will loom particularly large for women, who typically live much longer than men.

The Challenges of Diversity

More than any cohort before them, the boomers represent the diversification of American society. The boomers differ from each other in the kinds of education they received, the kinds of work they do, and the kinds of families they live in. These patterns are often crosscut by race, ethnicity, and nativity. They culminate in socioeconomic inequality. This diversity will continue to challenge the boomers.

Making Sense of Lives

The boomers have replaced the traditional life course with a varied set of trajectories. Not only are old rules obsolete, variability in lives means that they have not been replaced with new rules. The boomers lack standards for evaluating success and life satisfaction. Part of their project in midlife and old age will include the creation of these standards.

Potential Policy Mismatches

Social policy is typically based on assessments of the average experience in the population. Such an approach will be problematic with the boomer cohorts. Their diverse experiences will challenge policymakers to avoid enacting universal policies that create more problems than they solve. For example, health policies built on the assumption that family members are available to care for older people will not fit with the family circumstances of many boomers.

Different Life Worlds

Differences in life experiences create different life worlds. Life worlds in turn frame identities, values, and allegiances that are transmitted to younger generations. A multiplicity of life worlds can enrich society and promote tolerance and generosity. However, living in separate worlds can also lead to insulation and distance from others. These barriers can undermine social solidarity and lead to mistrust. They can also lead the boomer cohorts to underestimate their common interest to act collectively on their own behalf.

EPILOGUE

This report has centered on the experience of the baby boomers, but many of the issues raised as boomer issues are relevant to the entire American society. The best evidence suggests that succeeding cohorts are following patterns set by the boomers. Educational inequality has not abated and may even have increased. The workplace has become even more unpredictable for young workers entering the labor market. Younger cohorts have inherited the family complexity of the boomers. Diversity in the boomer cohort, while pronounced compared with earlier cohorts, is only a taste of what is to come. What is certain is that their past is our past and their future is our future.

ACKNOWLEDGMENTS

We are grateful for the constructive comments of David Brady, James Cook, Reynolds Farley, John Haaga, Phil Morgan, Martin O'Connell, and the three anonymous reviewers. Kara Bonneau, Melissa Buckmiller, Ben Dalton, Tracey LaPierre, Rob Marks, and Yong Yi Li provided research assistance.

REFERENCES

If provided by the authors, additional text and data associated with this report are available at www.prb.org/AmericanPeople.

1. Glen H. Elder, "The Life Course and Human Development," in *Handbook of Child Psychology, Volume 1: Theoretical Models of Human Development*, ed. Richard M. Lerner (New York: Wiley, 1998): 939-91.

2. S. Philip Morgan, "The Post-World War II Baby Boom," in *Encyclopedia of Population*, ed. Paul Demeny and McNicoll Geoffrey (New York: Macmillan Reference, 2003): 73-77.

3. Frank Levy, *The New Dollars and Dreams* (New York: Russell Sage Foundation, 1998).

4. Reynolds Farley, *The New American Reality: Who We Are, How We Got Here, Where We Are Going* (New York: Russell Sage Foundation, 1996).

5. Philip Martin and Elizabeth Midgley, "Immigration: Shaping and Reshaping America," *Population Bulletin* 58, no. 2 (2003): 1-44.

6. R.N. Bellah, et al., *Habits of the Heart: Individualism and Commitment in American Life* (Berkeley: University of California Press, 1985); Ronald Inglehart, *Cultural Shift in Advanced Industrial Society* (Princeton, NJ: Princeton University Press, 1990); and Ron Lesthaeghe, "The Second Demographic Transition in Western Countries: An Interpretation," in *Gender and Family Change in Industrialized Countries*, ed. Karen Oppenheim Mason and An-Magritt Jensen (Oxford: Clarendon Press, 1995): 17-62.

7. Farley, *The New American Reality*; and Arland Thornton and Linda Young-DeMarco, "Four Decades of Trends in Attitudes Toward Family Issues in the United States: The 1960s Through the 1990s," *Journal of Marriage and the Family* 63, no. 4 (2001): 1009-37.

8. Richard A. Easterlin, *Birth and Fortune: The Impact of Numbers on Personal Welfare* (New York: Basic Books, 1980); and Diane J. Macunovich, *Birth Quake: The Baby Boom and Its Aftershocks* (Chicago: University of Chicago Press, 2002).

9. Pamela Barnhouse Walters, "Educational Access and the State: Historical Continuities and Discontinuities in Racial Inequality in American Education," *Sociology of Education* (Extra Issue, 2001): 35-49.

10. Pamela Barnhouse Walters, "The Limits of Growth: School Expansion and School Reform in Historical Perspective," in *Handbook of the Sociology of Education*, ed. Maureen T. Hallinan (New York: Kluwer Academic/Plenum, 2000): 241-59.

11. Cheryl Elman and Angela M. O'Rand, "Perceived Labor Market Insecurity and the Educational Participation of Workers at Midlife," *Social Science Research* 31, no. 1 (2002): 49-76.

12. Jerry A. Jacobs and Rosalind B. King, "Age and College Completion: A Life History Analysis of Women Aged 15-44," *Sociology of Education* 75, no. 3 (2002): 211-30.

13. Robert D. Mare, "Changes in Educational Attainment and School Enrollment," in *State of The Union: America in the 1990s. Volume One: Economic Trends*, ed. Reynolds Farley (New York: Russell Sage Foundation, 1995): 155-214.

14. Philip Cusick, *The Egalitarian Ideal and the American High School* (New York: Longman, 1983).

15. Annette Bernhardt et al., *Divergent Paths: Economic Mobility in the New American Labor Market* (New York: Russell Sage Foundation, 2001).

16. Seymour Martin Lipset and Earl Raab, *The Politics of Unreason: Right-Wing Extremism in America* (New York: Harper & Row, 1970).

17. Jacobs and King, "Age and College Completion."

18. Adam Gamoran, "American Schooling and Educational Inequality: A Forecast for the 21st Century," *Sociology of Education* (Extra Issue, 2001), 135-53.

19. Stanley Lieberson, *A Piece of the Pie: Blacks and White Immigrants Since 1880* (Berkeley: University of California Press, 1980).

20. Sanford M. Jacoby, *Employing Bureaucracy: Managers, Unions and the Transformation of Work in American Industry*, 1900-1945 (New York: Columbia University Press, 1985); and Sanford M. Jacoby, *Modern Manors: Welfare Capitalism Since the New Deal* (Princeton NJ: Princeton University Press, 1997).

21. Robert Max Jackson, *Destined for Equality: The Inevitable Rise of Women's Status* (Cambridge, MA: Harvard University Press, 1998).

22. Levy, *The New Dollars and Dreams*.

23. U.S. Department of Labor, Bureau of Labor Statistics, *Handbook of U.S. Labor Statistics* (Washington, DC: Government Printing Office, 2003); and Robert F. Szafran, "Age-Adjusted Labor Force Participation Rates, 1960-2045," *Monthly Labor Review* 125, no. 9 (2002): 25-39.

24. Suzanne Bianchi, "Changing Economic Roles of Women and Men," in *State of the Union: America in the 1990s*, ed. Reynolds Farley (New York: Russell Sage Foundation, 1995): 107-54.

25. Francine Blau, "Trends in the Economic Well-Being of American Women 1970-1995," *Journal of Economic Literature* 36 (1998): 112-65.

26. Claudia Goldin and Lawrence F. Katz, "Career and Marriage in the Age of the Pill," *The American Economic Review* 90, no. 2 (2000): 461-65.

27. Bernhardt et al., *Divergent Paths: Economic Mobility in the New American Labor Market*.

28. Jerry A. Jacobs, "Evolving Patterns of Sex Segregation," in *Sourcebook of Labor Markets: Evolving Structures and Processes*, ed. Ivar Berg and Arne L. Kalleberg (New York: Kluwer/Plenum, 2001): 535-50.

29. Paula England, "Toward Gender Equality: Progress and Bottlenecks," in *The Declining Significance of Gender?* ed. Francine Blau, Mary Brinton, and David Grusky (Ithaca, NY: Cornell University, 2003).

30. Sandra E. Black and Chinhui Juhn, "The Rise of Female Professionals: Are Women Responding to Skill Demand?" *The American Economic Review* 90, no. 2 (2000): 450-55.

31. Levy, *The New Dollars and Dreams*; and Sheldon H. Danziger and Peter Gottschalk, *America Unequal* (New York: Russell Sage Foundation, 1995).

32. Bernhardt et al., *Divergent Paths: Economic Mobility in the New American Labor Market*.

33. Finis Welch, "Effect of Cohort Size on Earnings: The Baby Boom Babies' Financial Bust," *Journal of Political Economy* 85, no. 5 (1979): s65-97.

34. Yu Xie and Kimberlee A. Shauman, *Women in Science: Career Processes and Outcomes* (Cambridge, MA: Harvard University Press, 2003).

35. England, "Toward Gender Equality: Progress and Bottlenecks."

36. Catherine A. Fitch and Steven Ruggles, "Historical Trends in Marriage Formation: The United States 1850-1990," in *The Ties That Bind: Perspectives on Marriage and Cohabitation*, ed. Linda J. Waite et al. (New York: Aldine de Gruyter, 2000): 59-88; Michael R. Haines, "Long-Term Marriage Patterns in the United States from Colonial Times to the Present," *The History of the Family* 1, no. 1 (1996): 15-39; Ansley J. Coale and Susan Cotts Watkins, *The Decline of Fertility in Europe* (Princeton, NJ: Princeton University Press, 1980); Andrew J. Cherlin, *Marriage, Divorce, Remarriage* (Cambridge, MA: Harvard University Press, 1992); and Samuel H. Preston and John McDonald, "The Incidence of Divorce within Cohorts of American Marriages Contracted Since the Civil War," *Demography* 16, no. 1 (1979): 1-26.

37. Valerie Kincade Oppenheimer, "Women's Rising Employment and the Future of the Family in Industrial Societies," *Population and Development Review* 20, no. 2 (June 1994): 293-342; Valerie Kincade Oppenheimer, Matthijs Kalmijn, and Nelson Lim, "Men's Career Development and Marriage Timing During a Period of Rising Inequality," *Demography* 34, no. 3 (1997): 311-30; and William Julius Wilson, *The Truly Disadvantaged* (Chicago: University of Chicago Press, 1987).

38. Thornton and Young-DeMarco, "Four Decades of Trends in Attitudes Toward Family Issues in the United States: The 1960s Through the 1990s."

39. Blau, "Trends in the Economic Well-Being of American Women 1970-1995"; Janet Saltzman Chafetz, "Chicken or Egg? A Theory of the Relationship Between Feminist Movements and Family Change," in *Gender and Family Change in Industrialized Countries*, ed. Karen Oppenheim Mason and An-Magritt Jensen (Oxford: Clarendon Press, 1995): 63-81; and Cherlin, *Marriage, Divorce, Remarriage*.

40. Megan M. Sweeney, "Two Decades of Family Change: The Shifting Economic Foundations of Marriage," *American Sociological Review* 67, no. 1 (2002): 132-47; and Lynn White and Stacy J. Rogers, "Economic Circumstances and Family Outcomes: A Review of the 1990s," *Journal of Marriage and the Family* 62, no. 4 (2000): 1035-51.

41. Steven L. Nock, *Marriage in Men's Lives* (New York: Oxford University Press, 1998); and Frances K. Goldscheider and

Linda J. Waite, *New Families, No Families?* (Berkeley: University of California Press, 1991).

42. Farley, *The New American Reality.*

43. Lesthaeghe, "The Second Demographic Transition in Western Countries: An Interpretation."

44. Andrew J. Cherlin, "Toward a New Home Socioeconomics of Union Formation," in *The Ties That Bind: Perspectives on Marriage and Cohabitation*, ed. Linda J. Waite et al. (New York: Aldine de Gruyter, 2000): 126-44; and Valerie K. Oppenheimer, "A Theory of Marriage Timing: Assortative Mating Under Varying Degrees of Uncertainty," *American Journal of Sociology* 94, no. 3 (November 1988): 563-91.

45. Joshua R. Goldstein and Catherine T. Kenney, "Marriage Delayed or Marriage Forgone? New Cohort Forecasts of First Marriage for U.S. Women," *American Sociological Review* 66, no. 4 (2001): 506-19.

46. Thornton and Young-DeMarco, "Four Decades of Trends in Attitudes Toward Family Issues in the United States: The 1960s Through the 1990s."

47. R. Kelly Raley, "Recent Trends and Differentials in Marriage and Cohabitation: The United States," in *The Ties That Bind: Perspectives on Marriage and Cohabitation*, ed. Linda J. Waite et al. (New York: Aldine de Gruyter, 2000): 19-39.

48. Frances Goldscheider and Calvin Goldscheider, "Leaving and Returning Home in 20th Century America," *Population Bulletin* 48, no. 4 (1994).

49. Frances K. Goldscheider and Calvin Goldscheider, *Leaving Home Before Marriage: Ethnicity, Familism, and Generational Relationships* (Madison, WI: University of Wisconsin Press, 1993).

50. Larry L. Bumpass and James A. Sweet, "National Estimates of Cohabitation," *Demography* 26, no. 4 (1989): 615-25.

51. Raley, "Recent Trends and Differentials in Marriage and Cohabitation: The United States."

52. Goldscheider and Goldscheider, *Leaving Home Before Marriage.*

53. See also Cherlin, *Marriage, Divorce, Remarriage*: figure 1-6.

54. Martin O'Connell, "Childbearing," in *Continuity and Change in the American Family*, ed. Lynne M. Casper and Suzanne M. Bianchi (Thousand Oaks, CA: Sage Publications, 2002): 67-94.

55. S. Phillip Morgan, "Characteristic Features of Modern American Fertility," in *Fertility in the United States: New Patterns, New Theories*, ed. John B. Casterline, Ronald D. Lee, and Karen A. Foote (New York: Population Council, 1996): 19-67.

56. R. Kelly Raley, "Increasing Fertility in Cohabiting Unions: Evidence for the Second Demographic Transition in the United States?" *Demography* 38, no. 1 (2001): 59-66.

57. Irwin Garfinkel and Sara S. McLanahan, *Single Mothers and Their Children: A New American Dilemma* (Washington, DC: Urban Institute Press, 1986); and Marilyn Coleman, Lawrence Ganong, and Mark Fine, "Reinvestigating Remarriage: Another Decade of Progress," *Journal of Marriage and the Family* 62, no. 4 (2000): 1288-307.

58. Andrew J. Cherlin, "On the Flexibility of Fatherhood," in *Men in Families*, ed. Alan Booth and Ann C. Crouter (Mahwah, NJ: Lawrence Erlbaum Publishers, 1998): 41-52; and Martin O'Connell, "Childbearing."

59. Frank F. Furstenberg, "Good Dads/Bad Dads: The Two Faces of Fatherhood," in *The Changing American Family and Public Policy*, ed. Andrew J. Cherlin (Washington, DC: Urban Institute Press, 1988): 193-218.

60. Phyllis Moen, "Recasting Careers: Changing Reference Groups, Risks, and Realities," *Generations* 22, no. 1 (1998): 40-45.

61. Seymour Spilerman, "Wealth and Stratification Process," *Annual Review of Sociology* 26 (2000): 497-524.

62. Arthur F. Jones Jr. and Daniel H. Weinberg, "The Changing Shape of the Nation's Income Distribution," *Current Population Reports* P60-204 (Washington, DC: U.S. Census Bureau, 2000).

63. Blau, "Trends in the Economic Well-Being of American Women 1970-1995."

64. Goldstein and Kenney, "Marriage Delayed or Marriage Forgone?"

65. Shawna Sepielli and Peter Orzechowski, "Net Worth and Asset Ownership in Households: 1998 and 2000," *Current Population Reports* P70-88 (Washington, DC: U.S. Census Bureau, 2003): 70-75.

66. Denise DiPasquale and Edward L. Glaeser, "Incentives and Social Capital: Are Homeowners Better Citizens?" *Journal of Urban Economics* 45, no. 2 (1999): 354-84.

67. Albert Chevan, "The Growth of Home Ownership: 1940-1980," *Demography* 26, no. 2 (1989): 249-66; and Peter D. Linneman and Isaac F. Megbolugbe, "Housing Affordability: Myth or Reality?" *Urban Studies* 29, no. 3/4 (1992): 369-92.

68. John Yinger, *Closed Doors, Opportunities Lost* (New York: Russell Sage Foundation, 1995).

69. N. Gregory Mankiw and David N. Weil, "The Baby Boom, the Baby Bust, and the Housing Market," *Working Paper 2794* (Cambridge, MA: National Bureau of Economic Research, 1988).

70. Joseph Gyourko, "The Changing Strength of Socioeconomic Factors Affecting Home Ownership in the United States," *Scottish Journal of Political Economy* 45, no. 4 (1998): 466-90; and Mary Elizabeth Hughes, "What's Happening to the American Dream? Changes in the Transition to Home Ownership 1968-97," unpublished paper, Duke University.

71. Lisa A. Keister and Natalia Deeb-Sossa, "Are Baby Boomers Richer Than Their Parents? Intergenerational Patterns of Wealth Ownership in the United States," *Journal of Marriage and the Family* 63, no. 2 (2001): 569-579; U.S. General Accounting Office, *Retirement Income: Intergenerational Comparisons of Wealth and Future Income*, GAO-03-429 (Washington, DC: Government Printing Office, 2003).

72. Lisa A. Keister and Stephanie Moller, "Wealth Inequality in the United States," *Annual Review of Sociology* 26 (2000): 63-81; and Arthur B. Kennickell, "A Rolling Tide: Changes in the Distribution of Wealth in the U.S., 1989-2001," *Federal Reserve Board, Survey of Consumer Finances*, accessed at www.federalreserve.gov/pubs/oss/oss2/scfindex.html>, on Aug. 31, 2003.

73. Kennickell, "A Rolling Tide."

For Further Reading

Alwin, Duane, and Ryan McCammon. "Generations, Cohorts, and Social Change." In *Handbook of the Life Course*, ed. Jeylan T. Mortimer and Michael J. Shanahan. New York: Klewer, 2003.

Bernhardt, Annette, et al. *Divergent Paths: Economic Mobility in the New American Labor Market*. New York: Russell Sage, 2001.

Casper, Lynne M., and Suzanne M. Bianchi. *Continuity and Change in the American Family*. Thousand Oaks, CA: Sage Publications, 2002.

Easterlin, Richard A. *Birth and Fortune: The Impact of Numbers on Personal Welfare*. New York: Basic Books, 1980.

Elder, Glen H. "The Life Course and Human Development." In *Handbook of Child Psychology, Volume 1: Theoretical Models of Human Development*, ed. Richard M. Lerner. New York: Wiley, 1998.

Farley, Reynolds. *The New American Reality: Who We Are, How We Got Here, Where We Are Going*. New York: Russell Sage Foundation, 1996.

Goldin, Claudia, and Lawrence F. Katz. "Career and Marriage in the Age of the Pill." *The American Economic Review* 90 (2000).

Inglehart, Ronald. *Cultural Shift in Advanced Industrial Society*. Princeton NJ: Princeton University Press, 1990.

Keister, Lisa A., and Natalia Deeb-Sossa. "Are Baby Boomers Richer Than Their Parents? Intergenerational Patterns of Wealth Ownership in the United States." *Journal of Marriage and the Family* 63, no. 2 (2001).

Levy, Frank. *The New Dollars and Dreams*. New York: Russell Sage Foundation, 1998.

Macunovich, Diane J. *Birth Quake: The Baby Boom and Its Aftershocks*. Chicago: University of Chicago Press, 2002.

Mannheim, Karl. "The Problem of Generations." In *Studying Aging and Social Change: Conceptual and Methodological Issues*, ed. Melissa A. Hardy. Thousand Oaks, CA: Sage Publications, 1997.

Martin, Philip, and Elizabeth Midgley. "Immigration: Shaping and Reshaping America." *Population Bulletin* 58, no. 2 (2003).

Pampel, Fred, and H. Elizabeth Peters. "The Easterlin Effect." *Annual Review of Sociology* 21 (1995).

Uhlenberg, Peter, and Sonia Miner. "The Life Course and Aging: A Cohort Perspective." In *Handbook of Aging and the Social Sciences*, ed. Robert H. Binstock and Linda K. George. San Diego: Academic Press, 1996.

PART IV

IMMIGRATION AND AMERICA'S RACIAL GROUPS

Immigration and a Changing America

By Mary M. Kritz and Douglas T. Gurak

INTRODUCTION

Immigration has deep roots in American history and continues to be a dynamic force in reshaping America. People from many nations helped America settle and expand its frontiers, build its industrial complex and service economy, and become the leading economic and military power in the world.

The United States is now in the midst of its fourth immigration wave. In the 1990s, the foreign-born population increased by 57 percent and reached 31 million in 2000. If this population lived in a single country, it would be larger than the population of Canada; larger than the combined populations of Austria, Denmark, Finland, Norway, and Sweden; and the 33rd-largest country in the world. No other country has a foreign-born population of this size, although some do have larger shares of their populations who are foreign-born. Because of immigration, the United States has a relatively high population growth rate and will see its 2000 population of 281 million rise to over 400 million by 2050 if immigration continues at its current pace.[1]

America's current immigration wave, called the Globalization Wave in this report, started in the 1960s. At that time, immigrants had a diminishing profile in the U.S. population, but they have since become an important social and economic group in America. The portrait of immigration that emerges in this report is one of change. Since 1960, foreign-born numbers have tripled; major shifts have also occurred in the geographic origins and characteristics of the foreign-born population. Given these trends, the U.S. Census Bureau projects that the size of the overall U.S. population will increase rapidly in the years ahead, as will its race and ethnic diversity.[2] While today's immigrants come to America with the same hopes and dreams that earlier immigrants had, growing numbers are not traditional settlers, but rather come to America to study or work for a few years and then return home or move to another country. This means that while many foreigners residing in America today form part of the large foreign-born population recorded in the 2000 Census, they are not immigrants in the historic sense (see Box 1, page 260).

In addition to the unexpected surge in immigrant numbers recorded by the 2000 Census, other factors since then have renewed interest in immigration. The terrorist attacks on the World Trade Center and the Pentagon on Sept. 11, 2001, prompted a federal review of immigration policy and management and led to the passage of the USA Patriot Act. That legislation gave law enforcement officials the authority to track, detain, and deport foreigners suspected of terrorist connections or intent. Critics of the Patriot Act charge that it threatens the civil liberties of both Americans and foreigners and undermines the values on which America was built. Congress set up the Department of Homeland Security (DHS) in 2003 in order to reduce the likelihood of immigration abuse and to improve the management and coordination of domestic security (see Box 2, page 261).

Concern about terrorism sparked these government initiatives, while continued immigration of unauthorized labor migrants from Mexico and elsewhere sparked other initiatives. In early 2004, President George W. Bush asked Congress for the authority to set up a temporary worker program that would allow the estimated 8 million to 10 million unauthorized migrants in the United States from Mexico and other countries to work here legally for up to six years. That proposal was quickly criticized by some in Congress and the public for not granting unauthorized migrants permanent immigration status and by others as being too generous to a population that has broken U.S. laws.

Questions about immigration are increasingly being raised not only by Congress but also by the media and

MARY M. KRITZ holds appointments as senior research associate, Population and Development Program, Department of Development Sociology, Cornell University; and as secretary general and treasurer of the International Union for the Scientific Study of Population (IUSSP). Her research focuses on U.S. immigration determinants and consequences. With funding from the National Institute of Child Health and Human Development (NICHD), she is studying changing settlement patterns of immigrants and the growth of foreign-born populations in nonmetropolitan areas during the 1990s.

DOUGLAS T. GURAK is a professor in Cornell University's Department of Development Sociology and an associate of its Population and Development Program. His research focuses on immigrant integration processes in the United States. Current work includes a study of linkages between the composition and magnitude of recent immigration and the internal migratory responses of U.S.-born and foreign-born Americans, supported by NICHD. Another project focuses on the dynamics behind the significant expansion of foreign-born populations in rural, nontraditional settlement areas of New York and Wisconsin.

Box 1
WHO IS AN IMMIGRANT?

Legally, foreigners living in the United States can be classified into four categories depending upon their mode of admission:

● Permanent residents who have been admitted for long-term residence;
● Nonimmigrant residents who have been issued visas (subject to renewal) that admit them to perform specific activities for a fixed period of time;
● Asylees and refugees admitted for humanitarian reasons; and
● Illegal or unauthorized migrants who either enter surreptitiously or overstay a temporary visitor visa.

Under U.S. immigration law, only permanent residents would be considered immigrants, but all foreigners present for more than one year would satisfy the United Nations definition of an immigrant.

Americans tend to equate foreigners with immigrants. The fact that the 14th Amendment set forth the birthright principle of citizenship reinforces the idea that foreigners already in the United States have the right to stay and that physical presence is a sufficient basis for claiming access to American rights.

In the 1900s, Congress increasingly drew legal distinctions between different categories of foreigners and between citizens and immigrants. Whereas permanent immigrants now have most of the same rights as citizens (except the right to vote), the rights of unauthorized migrants remain unclear. In the 1982 case of Plyer v. Doe, the U.S. Supreme Court ruled that children of unauthorized migrants have the same rights to a public education as children of legal aliens or citizens. In 1996, Congress passed the Illegal Immigration Reform and Immigrant Responsibility Act and the Personal Responsibility and Work Opportunity Reconciliation Act, both of which restricted unauthorized migrants' access to public assistance.

Increasing numbers of foreigners living in the United States are nonimmigrant residents, a group that mainly includes managers, professionals, technical personnel, and other highly skilled people admitted to the United States on a temporary basis to work for the institutions that recruit or sponsor them. Immediate family members of those immigrants are admitted with the same status.

While the *Yearbook of Immigration Statistics* provides data on the number of permanent residents and refugees arriving in a given year, the *Yearbook* has poor data on nonimmigrant residents, and no data on unauthorized migrants. Since the census does not ask about a foreigner's legal status, we do not know the distribution of the 31 million foreign-born counted in the 2000 Census across the above-mentioned four legal status categories.[1] Moreover, the United States gathers no data on the number of foreigners and Americans who move outside the country, although both outflows are thought to be substantial; and the return migration of Americans living abroad is also growing.

The decennial census has the richest data on foreigners in America, but anyone who uses this data has to decide how people should be classified. Should naturalized citizens be classified as Americans or immigrants? Should foreigners who have lived in America for decades be classified as immigrants? Should a person born abroad of an American parent be considered an American or an immigrant? And comparisons across time may be biased because foreigners present at the time of one census may have left the country by the next census.

In this report, the term "foreign-born" refers to the total population of foreigners counted in the U.S. census regardless of legal status or citizenship. The term "recent immigrant," in contrast, refers to foreigners who arrived in the 10-year period preceding the census. Both the foreign-born and recent-immigrant categories may include some naturalized Americans, since foreigners admitted for permanent residency can apply for naturalization within five years of their arrival in the United States.

Reference

1. Daniel B. Levine, Kenneth Hill, and Robert Warren, eds., *Immigration Statistics: A Story of Neglect* (Washington, DC: National Academies Press, 1985); and Barry Edmonston, ed., *Statistics on U.S. Immigration: An Assessment of Data Needs for Future Research* (Washington, DC: National Academies Press, 1996).

the public, but immigration has always been a polarizing issue, particularly during previous historic periods of high immigration. In order to inform these discussions, this report focuses on three issues: the historical context that set the stage for contemporary immigration to America; the policy, economic, and social forces that shape immigration today; and the demographic, sociocultural, and economic diversity of America's foreign-born population and changes in that population since 1960. The report draws heavily on data from the 2000 Census as well as on data from earlier censuses. While census data provide rich information on the origins and characteristics of the foreign-born population, the data are silent about immigrants' reasons for coming to America or about their values, beliefs, and dreams. Since the United States is a country where the latter group is believed to be as important as one's background and characteristics in shaping one's life, the rest of the immigration story will be written by immigrants and Americans themselves in the years ahead.

IMMIGRATION TO AMERICA: HISTORICAL BACKGROUND

For four centuries America has received immigrants from other continents. However, the number of immigrants, their national origins, the causes of immigration, and the policy context guiding immigration have changed greatly over time. In order to highlight differences between the current wave and earlier immigration waves, this report reviews U.S. immigration history.[3] To frame this discussion, we use Philip Martin and Elizabeth Midgley's classification of American immigration:[4]

- Colonization.
- Frontier Expansion.
- Industrialization.
- Post-1965 Wave (Globalization).

Colonization Wave: 1600–1820

This period lasted almost 200 years and established the roots of the population and culture that characterize America, but it in fact brought the smallest number of foreigners to America's shores (see Table 1, page 262). While England needed immigrants in the 1600s to settle its North American colonies, it was difficult to recruit large numbers of people willing to make the difficult and long journey across the North Atlantic to settle in territories perceived as wilderness. England had a population of only 4.1 million in 1600 and needed people at home to advance its economic and political interests. But since England also wanted to establish control over its distant North American colonies, it pursued a wide range of recruitment practices to get people to move to the colonies, including offers of free land in America, indentured servitude, free transport, and forced deportation of convicted criminals and other social outcasts. Fernand Braudel claimed that "men, women and children were kidnapped into emigration in Bristol; or heavy criminal sentences were passed to increase the number of 'volunteers' for the New World who could save themselves from the gallow or from the galleys."[5]

By 1700, the American colonies had a European-origin population of about a quarter-million; and this population, composed largely of people born in the colonies, was growing rapidly through natural increase—reaching 2 million by 1775. While England continued to treat the colonies as dumping grounds for its paupers and criminals, the colonists had started to object. In 1722, Pennsylvania responded to England's settlement there of several thousand religiously persecuted Palatines from Germany by passing a law requiring shipowners to pay a fee for every undesirable person landed. Pennsylvania was also the first state to set a head tax on immigrants in order to discourage immigration of the poor and destitute. Public antipathies toward particular origin groups began to rise and became an important political issue in the 1700s. The Irish were the first group singled out as "undesirables" and unlikely to assimilate—because they were Catholics. Most of the colonies passed legislation in the late 1700s that restricted the entry of Catholics.

By the mid-1700s, England realized that its practice of deporting undesirables had become a major source of conflict within the colonies. Although England then started to change its emigration policies, requiring for the first time that heavy taxes be levied on all people from England and Ireland seeking to emigrate to North America, it was too late. In 1776, the colonies issued their Declaration of Independence, citing England's emigration practices as one of their grievances.[6]

In the 1700s, England spearheaded another unfortunate episode in American history: the forced importation of slaves from Africa. Slavery was one way for

Table 1
FOUR U.S. IMMIGRATION WAVES, 1607–2000

Period	Number of immigrants arriving	Top national origins of immigrants	Underlying economic forces	Policy highlights
1607–1820	600,000 Europeans	England, Scotland, Ireland, Netherlands, France, Germany, Sweden	Colonization	England placed no restrictions on emigration.
	300,000 Africans	West Africa	Plantation economy	1808: slavery importation abolished.
1820–1870	7.4 million	Ireland, United Kingdom, France, Germany, Mexico	Frontier expansion	Few policy restrictions.
				1876: Supreme Court affirms federal authority over immigration.
				1875 Act prohibited immigration of criminals and prostitutes.
1880–1925	25 million	1860–1890—Germany, United Kingdom, Ireland, Canada, Scandinavia	Industrialization and urbanization	Federal numeric restriction of immigration begins.
		1890–1920—Austria/Hungary, Italy, Russia, Germany, Ireland, Canada		1882: Chinese Exclusion Act.
				1921 and 1924: National Origins Quota acts.
1965–present	26.4 million	Mexico, China, Soviet Union, India, Philippines, Vietnam, Dominican Republic, Korea, El Salvador, Canada	Global interdependence	1965: Immigration Act abolished national origin quotas.
				1986: IRCA amnesty; increasing federal regulation.

Source: Immigration and Naturalization Service, *2001 Statistical Yearbook of the Immigration and Naturalization Service* (2003).

southern tobacco and cotton plantation owners to obtain a secure supply of workers. In the 1600s, England had encouraged indentured workers from Western Europe in order to meet the growing need for labor in the colonies. But supply did not keep up with demand. After working for a few years to pay off their passage, the freemen usually opted for land ownership rather than wage labor. The colonists also were unsuccessful at enslaving indigenous Indians, because Indians knew the terrain and often escaped and went back to their tribes.[7]

The colonists then turned to Africans, who were thought to be an ideal labor population because they could be identified by color, were already accustomed to working in a tropical climate since their homeland had a climate similar to that of the southern United States, and were generally viewed at that time as racially inferior.[8] Although the first Africans had arrived in Jamestown in 1619 as indentured servants, their status changed to that of slaves in the late 1600s as the need for labor grew. The slave trade took off in the 1700s and continued until 1808, when the young U.S. federation passed a law prohibiting slave importation. By then an estimated 300,000 Africans had been forcibly uprooted and taken to Britain's colonies in the Americas. Many more died en route. Vernon Briggs claims that slave importation did

not end in 1808 but continued until President Abraham Lincoln issued the Emancipation Proclamation in 1863.[9] If so, this suggests that the first illegal immigration to the United States occurred from 1808 to 1863 because shipowners and their financial backers ignored U.S. law and continued to import slaves.

Frontier Expansion Wave: 1820–1870

The beginning of the second immigration wave is usually set at 1820, perhaps because government data on immigration began to be compiled from that date onward. But 1820 is an arbitrary date, and the roots of the second immigration wave were established during the presidency of Thomas Jefferson (1801 to 1808), following passage by Congress of two pieces of legislation favorable to immigrants. The first action was the repeal of the 1798 Naturalization Act, which required a 14-year residency period before foreigners could apply for naturalization; the second was a decision not to renew the 1798 Alien and Sedition Acts, which facilitated the deportation of foreigners deemed dangerous. While Jefferson was not a proponent of immigration, he had ambitions for America—namely, that it should stretch from the Atlantic to the Pacific—that eventually would require immigrants. To achieve that vision, Jefferson made the Louisiana Purchase in 1803 and then sponsored the Lewis and Clark expedition in 1804. He was unsuccessful in his bid to acquire Florida from Spain; the treaty with Spain that deeded Florida to the United States was not signed until 1819.

The ensuing westward expansion needed settlers. Immigrants from northwestern Europe were encouraged to migrate by offers of free land in the West. Although the West was already sparsely populated by Indians, many of whom had resettled there after being pushed out of the eastern colonies and told that lands west of the Mississippi were theirs, the westward movement of Europeans did not slow. Throughout American history, neither Britain nor the United States felt it important to honor pledges to the indigenous Indian populations. Nor did Britain or the United States ever make a serious effort to incorporate Indians into the growing American population.

By 1820, frontier expansion was well underway, setting off increased immigration of Europeans to a new peak of more than 400,000 people annually in the 1850s. Further settlement was stimulated by the acquisition of additional land in 1848, after President James Polk forced Mexico to cede the Southwest Territories following the Mexican War. Gold was discovered shortly thereafter in California's Sacramento Valley and fueled the rush of both Americans and immigrants to this new territory. In just one year, 1849, California's population increased from 20,000 to 100,000.

California's settlement not only attracted migrants from Europe and the eastern United States but also lured the first Chinese immigrants to America. Gold initially attracted the Chinese, but as labor shortages developed in the West, they were recruited for low-wage jobs. In order to attract Chinese workers, the United States signed the Burlingame Treaty with China, which guaranteed Chinese immigrants the same rights as other foreigners.[10] Western entrepreneurs then started to recruit Chinese men to work in the mining industry and to help build the transcontinental railroads. By 1870, a quarter of California's population was of Chinese origin.[11] The growth of the Chinese population in California was not welcomed either by those U.S.-born citizens concerned that the Chinese would dilute the country's racial stock, or by labor organizers concerned that Chinese workers would be willing to work for lower wages than U.S.-born workers and thus would drive down wages. In response to this growing opposition, Congress passed the Chinese Exclusion Act in 1882 and banned immigration of new Chinese workers for 10 years. That law allowed some Chinese to continue to come to the United States, including wives and children of citizens and returning residents; foreign students; visitors and government diplomats; and family members, servants, and employees of dipomats.[12] The Chinese Exclusion Act was renewed decennially until 1945.

For immigrants from northwestern Europe, there was an open-door policy in the 1800s. Most immigrants from that region came from Ireland, England, Germany, France, Sweden, and Norway. According to Philip Martin and Elizabeth Midgley, large numbers of Frontier Wave immigrants were Catholics, which led to the emergence of Catholicism as the largest U.S. religious denomination in the 1860s.[13] The Catholic immigrants, mainly Irish and German, were feared by Protestant Americans because of Catholics' tendency to develop parochial schools along with their own churches. Germans were also the first large non-English-speaking immigrant group and were widely viewed as separatists because they developed social clubs, newspapers, and schools. As the number of new immigrants increased, opposition to immigration grew. The Native American Movement emerged in 1835 in New York, Massachusetts, and Pennsylvania and demanded restrictions on immigration. The "Know-Nothings" organized in secret societies in the 1850s and sought to get anti-immigration politicians elected who would ensure that Americans ruled America.[14] Though ultimately unsuccessful, the "Know Nothings" influenced the political discourse of their day and illustrated the strong anti-immigrant attitudes often generated during periods of large-scale immigration.

During the Frontier Wave, states continued to take the lead in the recruitment and processing of immigrants, but authority over immigration began to shift toward the federal government. Although Congress took no steps to restrict immigration during the Frontier Wave, it did pass a law in 1819 that sought to reduce crowding and improve conditions on ships that transported immigrants to America. The law responded to reports that sailing vessels were riddled with disease, were poorly provisioned with water and food, and caused many deaths of passengers during the crossing.[15] The 1800s were an important period for sorting out whether the federal government or states could regulate immigration. Before affirming in 1876 that Congress rather than states had authority over immigration, the U.S. Supreme Court addressed several questions: Did state regulation of immigration interfere with international commerce? Could states extract a head tax from shipowners who transported immigrants to America? Could states require shipowners to provide a written report on the characteristics and origins of their passengers? Although the Supreme Court vacillated in its decisions as to which government body had authority over immigration, it eventually sided with Congress (see Box 3, page 264).

Industrialization Wave: 1880–1925

After a drop in European immigration during the Civil War years, America's third immigration wave took off in the 1880s and reached historic levels before being

SUPREME COURT CASES ON ALIENAGE AND COMMERCE IN THE 1800S

Before America's independence from England in 1776, immigration had been controlled by Britain and by each American colony. After independence, the newly created states continued to regulate immigration, and many states enacted passenger laws in order to control the type of immigrants who would come. One set of laws focused on how to prevent ship captains from bringing in paupers, criminals, and other foreigners deemed undesirable. New York, Massachusetts, and other states required shipowners to submit a written report of passengers' names, places of birth, ages, occupations, and last place of residence. In order to minimize the costs to cities and states, some states imposed a head tax on immigrants.

In the 1800s, these state regulations began to be challenged in the courts on the grounds that they interfered with international commerce. In 1824, the U.S. Supreme Court upheld the authority of Congress over international commerce in the case of Gibbons v. Ogden. In 1827, in Brown v. Maryland, the Supreme Court declared unconstitutional a Maryland law that imposed fees and restrictions on interstate and international commerce.

It still remained unclear whether transporting foreigners to America was the equivalent of international commerce. The Supreme Court had acknowledged in its 1824 and 1827 decisions that states had the right to police and secure the welfare of their citizens. In the 1837 case of New York v. Miln, the Supreme Court upheld a New York State law that required ship captains to submit a list of passengers within one day of docking, held that immigrants were not equivalent to international commerce, and said that the New York statute was a police-power matter rather than one of international commerce. But in an 1849 ruling on several Passenger Cases, the Supreme Court took a different direction and decided that a head tax on immigrants did interfere with international commerce.

Following that decision, New York and other states attempted to get around the head tax prohibition by requiring shipowners to pay a temporary bond on foreigners and collect fees from all arriving passengers, including Americans. The New York State law was challenged in 1875 in the case of Henderson v. Mayor of the City of New York, and in 1876 the Supreme Court ruled that, while New York had the right to request that a shipowner submit a list of foreign passengers, the collection of a bond or fee was equivalent to a head tax on immigrants, which had been ruled unconstitutional in the 1849 Passenger Cases.[1] The Supreme Court also opined that Congress was the appropriate authority in the United States to develop a system of laws to regulate immigration.

Reference

1. Craig T. Friend, "An Omen of Change: State Power to Regulate Commerce," in *Historic U.S. Court Cases: An Encyclopedia*, 2d ed., ed. John W. Johnson (New York: Routledge, 2001): 365–67; and The Dillingham Commission, *Abstracts of Reports of the Immigration Commission*, Vol. 2 (Washington, DC: Government Printing Office, 1911).

checked by the National Origins Quota acts of 1921 and 1924. Immigration during this wave was fueled by the growing demand for workers in urban areas, the building of a transcontinental rail system, and improvements in the North Atlantic voyage. Steamship travel had become common by the 1880s, reducing the Atlantic crossing to less than a week compared with the seven to 10 weeks that the crossing used to take. By 1873, 97 percent of immigrants were arriving by steamship rather than sailing vessel.[16] The Industrialization Wave also brought a shift in the national origins of immigrants, from northwestern Europe to southern and eastern Europe. Since immigrants from the new origin areas were widely viewed by Americans as racially and ethnically inferior to earlier immigrants, a strong anti-immigrant movement emerged in the early 1900s that culminated in the passage of restrictive immigration acts in 1917, 1921, and 1924. Opposition to immigration came from several sectors, including followers of the eugenics movement, labor unions, and social service agencies.

Despite the importance of urban industrial growth as the major stimulant underlying immigration in this period, not all immigrants in this wave settled in urban areas. Although Frederick Jackson Turner claimed that the frontier had closed by 1890, in actuality, "in the forty years after 1890 the government gave away almost four times as much land as it had given away before that year."[17] The continued availability of free land in rural areas meant that the immigrants who continued to come from Germany, the United Kingdom, and Scandinavia flowed westward to take advantage of land opportunities there rather than settling in the rapidly growing industrial cities in the Northeast.

Nevertheless, the demand for cheap labor to support rapidly expanding urban industries meant that new sources of immigrants had to be found elsewhere. Southern and eastern Europe were sources for those new workers. To attract migrants from those regions, labor recruiters and state governments stimulated outmigration by developing flyers, posters, and other material to spread information about job opportunities in America. By 1900, migration flows to the United States from Italy, Poland, Austria-Hungary, Greece, Russia, Bulgaria, and Rumania were well established.[18] Although the new immigrants were similar to northwestern European immigrants in that they also were mainly rural peasants or farmers fleeing poverty and seeking economic opportunity in a new land, the recruitment networks that brought them to America differed. While migration from northwestern Europe was encouraged by existing social networks between earlier settlers and people in their homelands, migration from eastern and southern European was stimulated by U.S. labor recruiters who worked for companies or state governments. Cultural differences in language and dress between the new immigrants and Americans made the immigrants highly visible targets in urban areas for xenophobes, who believed they would never assimilate.

In response to the growing public debate over the appropriate number and characteristics of immigrants, President Theodore Roosevelt set up the Dillingham Commission in 1909. When the commission released its 41-volume report three years later, its principal conclusion—that a slower pace of immigration would make it easier for America to assimilate the newcomers—quickly became lost in the rhetoric. Charges of "racism" and "anti-immigrant" were made against the commission, and most of its findings were eventually dismissed. Nonetheless, one of its recommendations—that a concerted effort should be made to ensure that the newcomers did assimilate—was heeded by a wide range of agencies seeking to promote social justice in America.[19] Social service agencies reached out to immigrants in the early 1900s in order to help them and their children adjust to America. In adult education classes, immigrants were taught English and sufficient history and government to enable them to pass the test required to become naturalized citizens. Other "proassimilation" agencies reached out to ethnic churches, newspapers, and clubs. Efforts were also made to educate the public about the contributions and special needs of immigrants. Social service groups promoted legislation to protect the rights of foreigners and ensure that immigration laws were fairly administered.

During the Industrialization Wave, about 25 million immigrants arrived before the southern and eastern European flows were effectively shut down following passage of the 1917, 1921, and 1924 Immigration acts. The 1917 law banned immigration from Asia and required that immigrants over age 16 be given a literacy test in their own language. To change the source of immigration back to northwestern Europe, the 1921 law limited the total number of foreign-born from a given country to 3 percent of the total number of foreign-born already in the United States from that country in 1910. That restriction applied to Eastern Hemisphere immigrants (who were then mainly Europeans) and implied an annual numeric ceiling on immigration of about 358,000.[20] In response to continued anti-immigration lobbying, in 1924 Congress passed the National Origins Quota Act, limiting the total number of immigrants from a given country to 2 percent of the 1890 foreign-born population from that country. This percentage implied an annual quota of about 164,000 immigrants from the Eastern Hemisphere, most of whom would be from northwestern Europe.

Immigration became a routine part of governance. Almost yearly in the late 1800s and early 1900s, Congress passed legislation or the Supreme Court ruled on some aspect of immigration.[21] Immigrant processing at U.S. seaports became the responsibility of the federal government following passage of the Immigration Act of 1891. That act also authorized the creation of a federal immigration facility, Ellis Island, where foreigners could be inter-viewed and receive medical exams to determine whether they should be admitted to America. However, after numeric restrictions on immigration began in the 1920s, a new method had to be found to screen prospective immigrants before they made the long journey to America. The consular visa system was the method developed. Under that system, which continues today, prospective immigrants are screened at U.S. overseas consulates to determine whether they are eligible to immigrate and, if so, with what type of visa. After overseas processing started in 1924, Ellis Island was no longer needed for that purpose, and its buildings were abandoned.

Globalization Wave: 1965–Present

U.S. immigration slowed to a trickle from 1925 to 1950. The Great Depression and World War II, along with immigration restrictions in the 1920s, combined to create this pause in immigration. With trans-Atlantic migration on hold, a shortage of U.S.-born agricultural workers developed during World War II. Western agricultural employers lobbied Congress for a temporary worker program with Mexico. Earlier, from 1912 to 1922, a temporary worker program with Mexico had operated, and employers wanted a new program to admit workers during harvests and other seasons when labor demands were high. These employers were successful in their efforts—Mexico and the United States signed the Mexican Labor Program Agreement in 1942. Commonly known as the *bracero* program, the agreement was renewed several times until 1964. A similar program for Caribbean seasonal workers was set up in the 1940s. The British West Indies temporary worker program was approved by Congress in 1943 and allowed nationals from Jamaica, the Bahamas, St. Lucia, and other parts of the West Indies to be admitted as seasonal agricultural workers throughout Florida and the East Coast.

Although immigration picked up during the 1950s, the numbers coming to the United States were still modest—265,000 permanent immigrants were admitted in 1960—and most analysts thought that the era of large-scale immigration had ended. That view seemed reasonable given that other countries of permanent immigration —Canada, Australia, and New Zealand—had seen their immigration flows slow to a trickle after passing similar restrictions on immigration. It was widely believed in the United States and elsewhere that the passport and consular visa system, along with policy restrictions on immigration, were effective tools for managing immigration. Moreover, there was no strong demand for increased U.S. immigration in the period after World War II. The American frontier was definitely closed and labor needs in industry and urban areas were being met by south-to-north migration of U.S.-born blacks, internal migration of white Americans from rural to urban areas, and increased labor force participation of women.

Changes in the global economy play a major role in America's fourth immigration wave, the Globalization Wave, so named because of the growing interdependence among countries.

The international economic and political forces transforming this era are complex.[22] International flows of capital, raw materials, goods, information, and people have increased dramatically since World War II and have led to increased interdependence among countries. International migration of highly skilled people has become an important dynamic between countries and an integral part of international exchange. Many institutions are part of the growing global apparatus that facilitates international migration of highly skilled people, including governmental and multilateral agencies, multinational corporations and private companies, universities, churches, development agencies, and a wide array of other nonprofit social and humanitarian agencies.

Just as growing numbers of Americans have gone abroad in recent decades to work for the U.S. government, corporations, nongovernmental organizations (NGOs), and other institutions, so too are growing numbers of foreigners coming to the United States to do similar work for their government and other institutions. These migrants are usually highly skilled managers, professionals, and technical personnel. From a legal standpoint, they require institutional sponsorship and are admitted to the United States as nonimmigrant residents for varying periods of time. Their visas are readily renewed and they often become permanent immigrants after being in the United States for several years. The fact that this category of migrant virtually did not exist in previous immigration periods indicates that forces propelling migration now differ from past forces.

The number of unauthorized labor migrants has grown in the Globalization Wave, increasing not only in the United States but also in the European Union and other relatively prosperous countries in Asia (Japan, Korea, Malaysia, and Thailand); Africa (South Africa, Senegal, and Egypt); and South America (Argentina and Brazil). Differential relative prosperity and geographic proximity underlie unauthorized migration flows, and easier and cheaper international communication and travel facilitate these flows. In addition, social networks between earlier migrants and their relatives and friends back home encourage more workers to migrate and take advantage of low-wage opportunities in economically prosperous countries. Rapid population growth in Africa, Asia, and Latin America in recent decades contributes to labor migration because of the burgeoning numbers of young people and rapidly growing labor forces that stagnant economies cannot absorb. As such, if economic opportunities appear better in neighboring countries, migrants are likely to vote with their feet and move to those countries.

Refugees have been ubiquitous throughout history, but as national borders have been sealed, growing numbers can no longer find refuge in neighboring countries. Since World War II, a system of international and nongovernmental organizations has been developed to meet the needs of refugees and facilitate their resettlement. The United Nations High Commissioner for Refugees (UNHCR) leads these global efforts, along with an array of bilateral and nongovernmental organizations. In 2002, UNHCR estimated the world's refugee population at 10.4 million. If asylum seekers, returned refugees, stateless persons, internally displaced migrants, and other quasi-refugees who receive some protection and assistance from the UNHCR are included, that number doubles.[23] While the United States, Canada, Australia, and a few other industrialized countries admit some refugees annually for permanent resettlement, most refugees subsist in camps in neighboring countries and live on assistance from the UNHCR until they can return home. In 2002, for instance, an estimated 2 million Afghan refugees were displaced to neighboring Pakistan and Iran, and 750,000 civilians displaced within Afghanistan returned home.

Current U.S. Immigration Policy

These changing global forces set the context for contemporary U.S. immigration policy. In 1965, Congress passed the Immigration and Nationality Act, which is generally credited with starting America's fourth immigration wave. Passed during the Civil Rights Movement of the 1960s, the act abolished the use of race and origin criteria for selecting immigrants, and it opened up immigration to nationals of all countries. Nonetheless, numeric controls remained: 120,000 migrants annually from the Western Hemisphere and 170,000 from the Eastern Hemisphere.

After eliminating national origin as the criteria for selecting immigrants, another basis was needed for allocating the limited number of permanent immigrant visas. Family reunification became the new mechanism. Under the 1965 plan, Congress decided that 74 percent of visas should be allocated to foreigners with a familial relationship to a U.S. citizen or permanent resident; 10 percent to professionals, scientists, and artists; 10 percent to skilled and unskilled workers in short supply in the United States; and 6 percent to refugees. While country quotas of 20,000 were set for Eastern Hemisphere countries, immediate relatives of U.S. citizens (spouses, minor children, and parents of citizens over age 21) were exempted from both the country and hemisphere quotas. Family reunification remains the centerpiece of U.S. immigration policy, although the distribution of visas in different preference categories has changed (see Table 2).

Since 1965, the federal government has passed legislation almost annually to address the main problem that regulation of international travelers and migrants now poses—namely, how to control unauthorized labor

Table 2

FOREIGNERS ENTERING THE UNITED STATES FOR PERMANENT OR TEMPORARY RESIDENCE, 2002

Category	Number
I. Permanent immigrants	**[1,063,732]**
Family-sponsored	673,029
Immediate relatives of U.S. citizens (no limit)	485,960
Spouses	294,798
Children (including orphans)	97,099
Parents	94,063
Other family-sponsored	187,069
Spouses of permanent residents	84,860
Siblings of U.S. citizens	57,570
Adult sons and daughters of U.S. citizens	44,639
Employment-based	174,968
Refugee and asylees	126,084
Diversity immigrants	42,829
Other immigrants	46,822
II. Nonimmigrant residents*	**[800,000]**
H-1B skilled workers	104,000
Foreign students*	344,000
Foreign government officials and families*	47,000
Businessmen/women (company transfers) and families*	150,000
NAFTA workers and families*	30,000
Other temporary workers and families*	141,000
III. Unauthorized migrants or illegal migrants*	**[550,000]**

* Estimates.

Note: The three categories in this table are not mutually exclusive across time and are not net additions to the U.S. population in 2002 because emigration is not considered here. Half of foreign students and their families were assumed to be newly arriving rather than returning foreigners. A third of people arriving in the other nonimmigrant categories were considered to be newly arriving. Only H-1B workers who are considered new or initial workers are included in the total shown. The annual estimate of unauthorized migrants was assumed to be the same as the Department of Homeland Security estimated that it was in the 1990s: 550,000 annually.

Source: Department of Homeland Security, *2002 Yearbook of Immigration Statistics* (2003): tables 4 and 25; page 216.

become an immediate relative of a U.S. citizen. In 2002, 72 percent of visas in the family-sponsored category were granted to exempt family members. Most of these people had already lived in the United States an average of three to four years before adjusting their status.[24]

A review of immigration policy efforts in recent decades indicates much back and forth. The difficulties Congress has in formulating and managing immigration policy stem from an inherent tension between policy measures intended to control unauthorized labor migration and other measures intended to facilitate immigration of immediate family members, nonimmigrant residents, and refugees whose admission is widely accepted by the American public because of underlying social, economic, and humanitarian interests. However, rather than taking a comprehensive look at the forces driving immigration trends, Congress tends to focus on specific problems and passes legislation that has unintended consequences.

The 1986 Immigration Reform and Control Act (IRCA) is an example of legislation that was passed to halt unauthorized immigration, but that might have contributed to its increase. To find the votes, both pro- and anti-immigration legislators had to compromise. To appease proimmigration forces, IRCA allowed unauthorized migrants who were continuously in the United States after Jan. 1, 1982, to apply for permanent immigration status. To address the concerns of those seeking to deter unauthorized migration, the bill increased funding for border control and imposed sanctions on employers who "knowingly" hired unauthorized aliens, but only after legislators had removed provisions that would have made these steps enforceable. Nearly 2.7 million foreigners received permanent immigrant status under IRCA. The bulk of those whose status was legalized were Mexicans, but significant numbers were Salvadorans, Guatemalans, and Canadians. Many IRCA status adjusters were from distant countries (such as Poland, Italy, and the Philippines) that also send large numbers of legal migrants to the United States.[25] Studies suggest that a substantial number of applications may have been fraudulent.[26]

IRCA was unsuccessful in reducing unauthorized immigration because neither employer sanctions nor increased border deterrence worked as expected. Employer sanctions failed to work because, in the absence of a secure national identity system, employers inspect documents such as driver's licenses and social security cards that are easily forged and hard to verify. A verification system initially included in the bill was dropped in order to secure the votes needed to pass IRCA. While significant investments were made following IRCA to expand the personnel, resources, and technology needed to police borders, the fact is that the United States has about 6,000 miles of land borders with Canada and Mexico and close to 5,000 miles of coastline

migration while maintaining ready access for highly skilled foreigners, refugees, and others whose admission is considered to be in the national interest. Achieving this balance is not easy because immigration policy continues to be based on the premise that the United States is screening foreigners overseas to determine their eligibility for a permanent immigration visa. However, most foreigners who receive permanent immigration visas today are nonimmigrant residents and unauthorized migrants already living here who are converting their legal status to that of permanent immigrant. In 2002, 64 percent of all permanent immigrant visas were granted to foreigners already living in the United States as nonimmigrant residents or as unauthorized migrants who had petitioned for an adjustment of their legal status. The most common basis for the petition was that these foreigners had not including Hawaii, Alaska, or Puerto Rico.[27] Dramatic efforts such as the construction of concrete walls in densely populated areas along the Mexican border appear to only alter entry patterns.

The Department of Homeland Security estimates that 7 million unauthorized migrants lived in the United States in 2000,[28] a higher number than was present in the early 1980s before IRCA was passed. Some immigration experts estimate that the current number of unauthorized migrants is even higher—8.5 million or more.[29]

Congress has passed dozens of other bills in recent decades to facilitate the immigration of nonimmigrant residents, refugees, and their family members. Since passage of the Displaced Persons Act of 1949, which granted refugee status to European Jewish survivors from World War II, similar laws have been passed to admit other refugee groups of special interest to the United States. Following the Soviet Union's repression of the 1956 uprising in Budapest, Hungarian refugees were granted asylum in the United States. The Cuban revolution in the late 1950s led to the first admission of a large refugee group to the United States. To reduce the fiscal impact of Cuban refugee resettlement on states and communities, Congress authorized a refugee assistance program in the 1960s, a practice subsequently continued for other refugee populations, including the Vietnamese, Cambodians, and Laotians.

In the 1990s, as civil conflicts developed in many parts of Africa, the United States responded by offering to resettle refugees from Somalia, Ethiopia, Liberia, the Sudan, and Sierra Leone. In Africa and elsewhere, the United States extended resettlement largely to refugees from countries in which it had a special interest. Refugees from Rwanda, Burundi, the former Zaire, Angola, and other parts of Africa in which the United States has little foreign policy interest have not been admitted for resettlement. Although the United States passed the 1980 Refugee Act to bring its refugee admission policy into conformity with the United Nations Protocol on Refugees, most refugee admissions continue to be selective and linked to U.S. national interests.

Other legislation opened up immigration to other groups. The 1979 Panama Canal Act granted permanent resident status to Panamanians and other foreigners who had worked in the Panama Canal Zone when it was controlled by the United States. A 1991 act granted special immigrant status to aliens who had served honorably in the Armed Forces of the United States for 12 years. Several nursing relief acts have been passed by Congress to admit nurses willing to work in areas with nursing shortages or to allow nurses previously admitted on temporary visas to adjust to permanent resident status. Following the collapse of the Soviet Union, Congress passed the Soviet Scientists Immigration Act to admit highly skilled scientists who had worked in nuclear physics, germ warfare, or other war- or security-related

professions. The Nicaraguan Adjustment and Central American Relief Act of 1997 allowed Nicaraguans, Guatemalans, Salvadorans, and nationals of former Soviet bloc countries to remain in the United States.[30]

Most Americans would probably agree that the legislation described above has been responsive to the national interest and the humanitarian needs of specific groups of foreigners. The main point suggested by the increasing amount of targeted legislation passed by Congress in recent years is that foreigners increasingly need to be admitted to the United States for reasons that go beyond immigration policy. Moreover, group-specific legislation has received more support in the Globalization Wave because immigration responds to different forces today. Increasingly, U.S. political interests abroad play a role in determining which immigrants should come to the United States and the conditions under which immigrants should be admitted.

THE NEW IMMIGRANTS: RAPIDLY GROWING AND DIVERSE

The United Nations estimates that 175 million people were living outside their country of birth in 2002, double the number in 1975.[31] If this estimate is correct, almost one in five international migrants now lives in the United States. While the absolute size of the foreign-born population is at its highest level in U.S. history, foreigners make up a smaller share of the population today than they did in 1910, when foreigners constituted 15 percent of the population, compared with 11 percent in 2000 (see Figure 1). The Census Bureau estimated that the foreign-born population rose to 11.5 percent of the population in 2002,[32] and it is likely that its share of the total population will exceed the 1910 figure by the 2010 Census. The magnitude of the growth in the size of the foreign-born population becomes apparent when one considers that there were almost as many foreign-born Mexicans in the United States in 2000 (9.2 million) as the total number of foreigners from all countries in 1960 (9.7 million). While the Mexican-born population increased by 116 percent from 1990 to 2000, the foreign-born populations from six other countries increased at a higher rate: Brazil (158 percent); Pakistan (141 percent); Nigeria (161 percent); Honduras (143 percent); India (132 percent); and the former Soviet Union (121 percent).

As the size of the foreign-born population rose in the 1980s and 1990s, so too has the number of countries that send migrants to the United States. While most foreigners come from a relatively small number of countries, America now receives migrants from virtually every country in the world. Historically, international migration to the United States and other countries was more limited in size and geographic scope and consisted of flows that

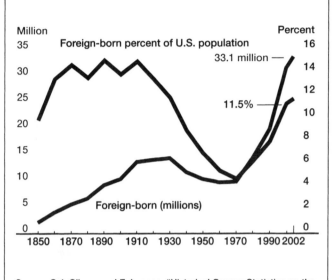

Figure 1
TRENDS IN THE ABSOLUTE AND RELATIVE SIZE OF THE FOREIGN-BORN POPULATION, 1850–2002

Source: C.J. Gibson and E. Lennon, "Historical Census Statistics on the Foreign-Born Population of the United States: 1850–1990," *Population Division Working Paper* No. 2 (1999); U.S. Census Bureau, 2002 March Current Population Survey; and authors' estimates using Census 2000 1% Public Use Microdata Sample (PUMS).

evolved from special ties between the sending and receiving countries.[33] While those elements remain important, the U.S. flow has been transformed from a relatively confined migration system as late as 1960 into a global migration system in 2000. The expansion of the U.S. migration system occurred because of several forces: the liberalization of U.S. immigration policy, the opening up of the U.S. migration system to nonimmigrant residents, and the increasing inflows of unauthorized migrants.[34]

The diversity of the U.S. flow is reflected in the numbers. In 2000, there were 24 immigrant groups in the United States with populations greater than 250,000; 20 had populations of 100,000 to 250,000, and 43 had populations of 25,000 to 100,000 (see Table 3). These 87 countries accounted for 97.5 percent of the foreign-born population in 2000. The remaining 2.5 percent came from more than 110 other countries. To underscore the point that nationals of all countries can migrate to America, Congress set up the diversity visa program in 1990 to give access to foreigners from countries underrepresented in immigration flows. Since then, the number of countries considered underrepresented has expanded. In 2002, the program allocated 55,000 visas through an annual lottery to which nationals of all but the top 15 senders of immigrants to the United States could apply. Immediate family members (spouse, unmarried children under 18, and parents) may accompany those who

Table 3
SIZE OF FOREIGN-BORN POPULATION BY COUNTRY OF ORIGIN, 2000

Population size category	Number of sending countries	Country of origin
9 million or more	1	Mexico
1 million to 2 million	3	China, Philippines, India
750,000 to 999,999	6	Vietnam, former Soviet Union, Cuba, Korea, Canada, El Salvador
500,000 to 749,999	5	Germany, Dominican Republic, United Kingdom, Jamaica, Colombia
250,000 to 499,999	9	Poland, Italy, Guatemala, Haiti, Japan, Iran, Peru, Ecuador, Honduras
100,000 to 249,999	20	Nicaragua, Pakistan, Brazil, Guyana, Laos, Trinidad and Tobago, Portugal, Thailand, Greece, Ireland, France, Romania, Cambodia, Nigeria, Argentina, Israel, Panama, Bangladesh, Egypt, Venezuela
50,000 to 99,999	22	Lebanon, Yugoslavia, Netherlands, Hungary, Iraq, Bosnia, Czechoslovakia, Chile, Spain, Indonesia, Turkey, Ethiopia, Costa Rica, Ghana, Bolivia, South Africa, Australia, Austria, Malaysia, Sweden, Barbados, Syria
25,000 to 49,999	21	Jordan, Afghanistan, Kenya, Croatia, Switzerland, Morocco, Liberia, Belgium, Bulgaria, Somalia, Burma, Belize, Denmark, Norway, Grenada, Albania, Azores, Fiji, Uruguay, Sri Lanka, Bahamas
Number of groups with a population of 25,000 or more	87	

Average population size of 87 groups: 347,266
Average population size of groups, excluding Mexicans: 244,776

Note: The 87 groups with a population of at least 25,000 in 2000 made up 97.5 percent of the foreign-born population. Origin groups are ranked from largest to smallest within size categories.

Source: Authors' calculations using Census 2000 1% Public Use Microdata Sample (PUMS).

receive a diversity visa but are not included in the annual quota. Applications have grown annually; 6.2 million applicants qualified for the 2003 lottery.

The diversity visa program and other policy measures opened up African immigration in the 1990s. Historically, relatively few immigrants to the United States have come from sub-Saharan Africa. But in the 1990s, migration from that region grew by 174 percent because of three policy forces: the diversity visa program; the U.S. decision to admit increased numbers of refugees from African war zones; and increased opportunities for graduate study in the United States. Most sub-Saharan Africans in America are from Nigeria, followed by Ethiopia, Ghana, South Africa, Liberia, Kenya, and Somalia. The number of African foreign students in the United States is still modest compared with those who come to study from Latin America or Asia, but their numbers are growing. To increase Africa's core of professionals and scientists, a number of institutions—including universities, private foundations, and bilateral and multilateral funding agencies—set up fellowship programs in the 1980s to recruit Africans for graduate study abroad.

Graduate study in the United States often results in permanent immigration because students find salaries and working conditions more attractive in the United States than in their homelands. Others stay because political or economic crises at home make it difficult for them to return. Whatever the cause, when highly educated nationals do not return home following their graduate studies, their origin countries lose the talent of some of their brightest young people. Often referred to as the "brain drain," investments made by students' sending countries in the education of these emigrants can be considered lost. However, sending countries may gain from remittances or by the professional and business ties that highly skilled emigrants often develop with their homelands. All types of migrants remit money to their homelands and thus contribute indirectly to economic improvements there.

U.S. immigration from all regions and most countries increased in the 1990s, but Mexican immigration soared: 34 percent of all recent immigrants in the 1990s came from Mexico, compared with 25 percent in the 1980s (see Figure 2). Recent immigrants are defined in this report as foreigners who arrived in the 10-year period prior to a U.S. census. According to demographer Francisco Alba, Mexican emigration to the United States is economically motivated by U.S. wages that are 10 times higher than Mexican wages, and by the inability of the Mexican economy to absorb the large and growing cohorts of Mexican workers that resulted from Mexico's high birth rates from the early 1970s to mid-1990s (see Box 4).[35]

Increased numbers of migrants to the United States in the 1990s also came from Europe and Canada. This rebound was unexpected and came after four

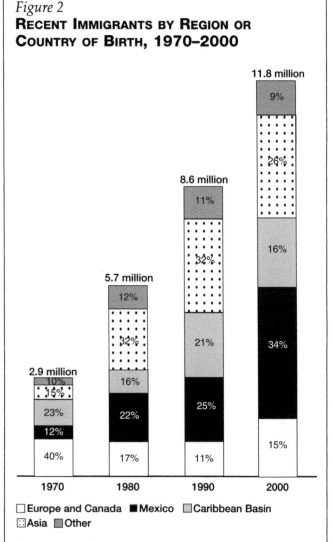

Figure 2

RECENT IMMIGRANTS BY REGION OR COUNTRY OF BIRTH, 1970–2000

☐ Europe and Canada ■ Mexico ☐ Caribbean Basin
▨ Asia ▨ Other

Note: Recent immigrants are those who arrived in the decade preceding the census year given. Caribbean Basin includes all countries, except Mexico, that border the Caribbean Ocean, plus Guyana, Suriname, French Guiana, and El Salvador. Percents may not add to 100 due to rounding.

Source: Authors' calculations using the 1% Public Use Microdata Sample (PUMS) from the 1970–2000 censuses.

decades of decline. In the 1990s, the size of the European/Canadian foreign-born population in the United States increased by 765,000, to 5.1 million. Almost 1.8 million recent immigrants from that region arrived in the 1990s, 84 percent more than came during the 1980s. These immigrants are mainly business executives, engineers, scientists, researchers, professors, diplomats, and graduate students who come to the United States as nonimmigrant residents. Some are relatively well-to-do retirees who spend part of the year in Florida, California, and other warm regions.

The absolute number of immigrants received from all regions increased in the 1990s, but the relative share from the Caribbean Basin, Asia, Africa, and South

MEXICAN IMMIGRATION: A SPECIAL CASE

The circumstances shaping Mexican immigration are unique, and stem from Mexico's sharing of a long and relatively porous land border with the United States, Mexican settlement in the U.S. Southwest that predates today's borders, a history of labor recruitment and migration to the United States, continued sharp economic disparities between the two countries, and strong social and economic ties between Mexicans living on both sides of the border.

While Mexican migration to the United States used to be a low-profile issue for both countries, that is no longer the case. Immigration from Mexico to the United States has grown as the Mexican economy worsened in the 1990s, and is now a "rite of passage" for a growing number of Mexicans.[1] An estimated 10 percent of all Mexicans now live in the United States, but they make a major contribution to Mexico's economy. In 2002, Mexico received $9.8 billion in remittances, almost equivalent to the income the country received from tourism and 80 percent of the value of foreign direct investment.[2] With an average annual income of less than $20,000, a Mexican working in the United States sends almost 10 percent of those earnings to relatives in Mexico each year.

Mexico has taken steps in recent years to enhance its ties to Mexicans living abroad and to retain the loyalty of those nationals, even amending its constitution to permit dual citizenship. In 2002, Mexican consulates started to issue matricula consular identification cards in order to improve Mexicans' access to services in the United States. These cards are used in the United States by local governments, banks, motor vehicle bureaus, and other agencies to verify the identity and residence of Mexicans. Other Mexican initiatives have focused on how to extend voting rights in Mexican elections to Mexicans living in the United States; currently Mexicans can vote in Mexican elections only by casting their votes in Mexico. Some political

groups in Mexico are lobbying for the United States to become Mexico's sixth electoral district and thus have full representation in the Mexican Congress; other groups want to extend political participation rights not only to U.S. foreign-born Mexicans but also to Mexicans born in the United States of Mexican parents.[3]

An agreement between Mexico and the United States on unauthorized migration was close to being reached before the terrorist attacks of 9/11 in the United States. Under the terms of that bilateral agreement, the United States would have regularized the status of unauthorized migrants already in the United States and set up a temporary worker program to allow Mexicans to continue to migrate in a legal, safe, and orderly manner. But these discussions were put on hold after 9/11, and remain so today.

In 2002, the Mexico-United States Border Partnership Action Plan was signed to improve the infrastructure and flow of people and goods across the border. In 2004, President George W. Bush renewed calls for a temporary worker program that would bring unauthorized migration into the open and enhance border security. While he viewed President Bush's call as a good first step, President Vicente Fox of Mexico stated that unauthorized migrants already in the United States should be legalized and that future policy initiatives should grow out of bilateral discussions rather than unilateral U.S. actions.

References

1. The Mexico-U.S. Binational Migration Study issued its final report in 1997. A number of studies were commissioned under this project and can be accessed online at www.utexas.edu/lbj/uscir.

2. Manuel Orozco and Michelle LaPointe, "Migration, Remittances, and the Rural Sector in Latin America," *Cooperation South* (New York: United Nations Development Program, 2003): 78–92.

3. Ken Bensinger, "Mexican Lawmaker Sees Voting in U.S.," *Washington Times*, July 10, 2003.

America decreased. While the Caribbean foreign-born made up 21 percent of recent immigrants in 1990, they constituted only 16 percent in 2000, despite an absolute increase (see Figure 2) from 1.8 million to 1.9 million in the 1990s. The same pattern held for Asian immigration: The percentage of recent immigrants from Asia in the 1990s decreased from 32 percent to 26 percent, but the absolute number of recent immigrants from Asia increased from 2.8 million to 3.1 million. These anomalous patterns occurred because of the 1990s' surge in immigration.

The Top Sending Countries

The focus on foreign-born regional groupings can obfuscate the fact that, while the U.S. migration system is global in scope, the bulk of its migrants continue to come from a small number of countries—one-third come from Mexico alone, and an additional one-third come from 10 other countries with close historical ties to

the United States. Table 4 (page 272) lists the top 10 countries of origin for recent immigrants from 1970 to 2000.[36] Until 1970, most recent immigrants still came from Europe or Canada, but Cuba and Mexico had emerged by then as the number one and number two top senders of migrants. Cuban refugee migration developed momentum quickly in the 1960s and benefited from America's willingness both to admit Cubans and provide them with generous resettlement benefits. After 1970, Cuba's rank as a sending country fell, though Cubans still constituted the 11th-largest recent immigrant group in 2000. By 2000, the top 10 sending countries included four geographically proximate ones (Canada, Dominican Republic, El Salvador, and Mexico); three Asian countries whose flows grew out of labor migration to the United States during the Industrialization Wave (China, India, and the Philippines); two Asian countries with which the United States has had close military ties (Korea and Vietnam); and one former political foe (the former Soviet Union).

Table 4

TOP-RANKED ORIGIN COUNTRIES OF RECENT IMMIGRANTS, 1970–2000

Cumulative % of recent immigrants	2000				
	Rank	Origin	1990 rank	1980 rank	1970 rank
34	1	Mexico	1	1	2
39	2	China	2	3	8
43	3	Former Soviet Union	15	12	29
48	4	India	7	7	17
51	5	Philippines	3	2	7
55	6	Vietnam	5	5	70
57	7	Dominican Republic	9	15	15
59	8	Korea	4	4	19
62	9	El Salvador	6	19	56
64	10	Canada	18	9	3
64		Cumulative percent and	60	54	58
7,513		number of immigrants (thousands)	4,859	3,044	1,675

Note: Recent immigrants are those who arrived within 10 years of the census year given. The cumulative percent and number for the top 10 groups refer to the top 10 groups at the time of each census.

Source: Authors' calculations using the 1% Public Use Microdata Samples (PUMS) from the 1970–2000 censuses.

Migration flows from Mexico, the Dominican Republic, and El Salvador evolved from a long history of political and economic contact with the United States. These migrations share several characteristics: They are from countries geographically proximate to the United States, they contain large numbers of unauthorized migrants, and they have resulted in the transfer of a relatively large share of the sending countries' populations to the United States. In 2000, an estimated 12 percent of Salvadorans, 9 percent of Mexicans, and 8 percent of Dominicans lived in the United States. The magnitude of this population transfer stands out particularly for Mexico because of its large population size of more than 100 million. By 2000, the Mexican foreign-born population in the United States had reached 9.2 million and constituted 30 percent of the total foreign-born U.S. population, dwarfing all other senders.

Canada, another neighboring country, rejoined the list as the 10th-largest sender in the 1990s after dropping from third in 1970 to 18th in 1990. This migration has different roots than flows from other countries. Canada is the largest U.S. trading partner and has a comparable level of development to that of the United States. Canadian immigration probably picked up in the 1990s because provisions in the North American Free Trade Agreement (NAFTA), signed in 1993 by Canada, Mexico, and the United States, specified that highly skilled people could migrate from one NAFTA country to another to work as businessmen/women, executives, scientists,

engineers, university teachers, or other professionals. Legally, Canadians admitted under NAFTA would be nonimmigrant residents. According to U.S. immigration statistics, Canada was the number one sender of nonimmigrant residents to the United States in 2002.

The inflows from China, India, and the Philippines can be traced to labor migrations to the United States that started in the 1800s or early 1900s.[37] Immigration from China got underway in the mid-1850s. In spite of restrictions on Asian immigration in the 1900s, the Chinese-born population in the United States had grown to 140,000 by 1950. After 1965, the family reunification provisions of the 1965 Immigration Act allowed members of the settled Chinese population to sponsor family members as permanent immigrants. Chinese immigration got another boost after Congress passed the Chinese Student Protection Act in 1992 in response to the Tiananmen Square prodemocracy demonstrations. Chinese graduate students were thus allowed to remain indefinitely in the United States. In addition, many other highly educated Chinese scientists and professionals have been admitted in recent decades under the skilled employment provisions authorized in U.S. immigration policy.

Filipino migration has its roots in both earlier labor migration and U.S. military actions in the Philippines. After Spain ceded the Philippines to the United States following the Spanish-American War in 1898, Filipinos were considered U.S. nationals (but not citizens) and thus were exempt from restrictions on Asian immigration.[38] Since U.S. employers in the West and Hawaii still wanted low-wage workers from abroad, they turned to the recruitment of Filipinos after the 1924 Oriental Exclusion Act was passed. Labor migration from the Philippines continued for about 10 years before being halted by the Depression and World War II. However, close links between the United States and the Philippines during and after World War II reestablished Filipino migration to the United States. While Indian immigration also had its roots in early-1900 labor migrations, it too was halted by the Oriental Exclusion Act. Indian laborers initially were recruited to help build railroads in Washington State, but they subsequently began relocating to California to replace aging Chinese agricultural workers there.[39]

The Korean War stimulated Korean migration to the United States. American involvement in that war provided an opportunity for American soldiers to marry Korean women and bring them home as war brides; other Koreans were granted permanent immigrant status because of their service on behalf of the U.S. war effort. While Korea had sent almost no migrants to the United States before the Korean War, by 1970 it was the 19th-ranked sender, and by 1980 it was the fourth-largest sender. This surge in Korean immigration stemmed directly from the U.S. military intervention and then was facilitated by family reunification provisions of U.S. immigration policy. Although still the eighth-ranked sender of recent immigrants to the United States in 2000, the volume of Korean immigration dropped by half in the 1990s from levels in the 1980s.

Korea is the first of the large Globalization Wave senders that has shifted from being a relatively poor country when its emigration flows to the United States started to being a relatively prosperous one today that imports immigrants from neighboring Asian countries. If Korean immigration continues to decline in the years ahead, that trend would suggest that economic development may indeed deter emigration and lead to declining emigration from other sending countries if they too are successful in their development efforts.[40] The strengthening of democracy in Korea in recent decades may have contributed to decreased desires to emigrate. Vietnamese immigration also had roots in a U.S. military action but differs from the Korean flow in that the Vietnamese were officially classified as a refugee group and thus granted resettlement assistance in the United States. While Vietnam's sending rank dropped from fifth in 1990 to sixth in 2000, it continued to send about the same number of migrants to America in the 1990s as it did in the 1980s.

As opportunities for nonimmigrant residents to America picked up in the Globalization Wave, immigrants from India, China, and the Philippines quickly stepped in to fill the applications submitted by U.S. companies for skilled nonimmigrant professionals from abroad. India became a large sender of highly skilled nonimmigrant residents in the 1990s, just as it previously was the largest sender of medical doctors and other health professionals in the 1980s. And many Filipino nurses, laboratory technicians, and other health personnel have migrated to the United States in recent decades on nonimmigrant visas.

THE DEMOGRAPHY OF IMMIGRANTS

Demographics reveal a great deal about a population's economic and social conditions because schooling, family formation, employment, health, and other life-cycle events are highly correlated with age and sex. Foreign-born populations have selective age and sex characteristics that change over time depending upon rates of return migration and new immigration. Recent immigrants tend to be heavily concentrated in the 20-to-30 age group, and are considerably more likely than the U.S.-born to be in the prime working ages of 15 to 40 (see Figure 3). In 2000, both the total foreign-born and recent immigrant populations had fewer children ages 10 and younger than the U.S.-born population,

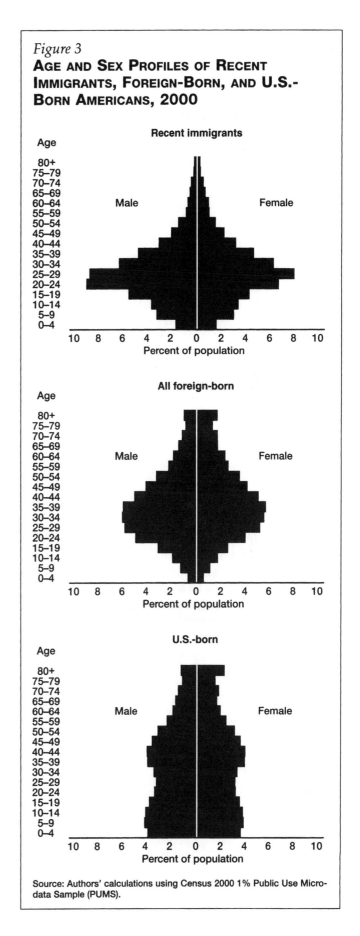

Figure 3

AGE AND SEX PROFILES OF RECENT IMMIGRANTS, FOREIGN-BORN, AND U.S.-BORN AMERICANS, 2000

Source: Authors' calculations using Census 2000 1% Public Use Micro-data Sample (PUMS).

because children born to immigrants are considered U.S. citizens and thus are classified as U.S.-born. Although the average ages of the foreign-born and U.S.-born populations have converged since 1960, the median age for the former is slightly older—37 years versus 35 years, respectively. In 1960, however, the foreign-born population was 22 years older than the U.S.-born. That disparity occurred because large numbers of elderly immigrants from the Industrialization Wave were present in the 1960 foreign-born population. By 2000, most of those elderly foreign-born had died, so both the foreign-born and U.S.-born had comparable percentages of their populations ages 60 and older (15 percent).

These averages mask considerable demographic diversity across foreign-born groups stemming from differential timing and causes of immigration. Labor migrants, for instance, come to the United States seeking low-wage work, are disproportionately young, and come largely from Mexico and the Caribbean Basin. As long as new labor migrants arrive, the mean age of foreign-born groups with large numbers of labor migrants remains relatively young. In contrast, foreign-born populations that include large numbers of refugees have a relatively young age structure in the decade when their immigration started, but these populations age in subsequent decades because they tend not to be replenished. The initial youthful pattern occurs because the underlying political causes of refugee flows tend to uproot entire families, including children. Cubans, Vietnamese, Cambodians, and Laotians are examples of aging foreign-born populations in the United States.

Sex Ratios of Immigrant Groups

Immigration used to be viewed as a staged process that began with a male family member migrating to America to find work. After securing a job and establishing himself, the man would then send for his wife and children or propose marriage to a woman from his homeland. Under this framework, which corresponded to cultural norms about appropriate gender roles, men were considered to be the breadwinners and women were seen mainly as wives and mothers. This pattern continues to exist for some immigrant groups, but women have emerged as principal actors in many migration flows.[41]

In 2000, women constituted almost half of the foreign-born population. In order to identify how origin groups vary in their sex composition, sex ratios were calculated for the 44 largest immigrant groups. Figure 4 shows the ratios for the groups that had the 10 highest and 10 lowest sex ratios. (Sex ratios measure the number of males in a population relative to the number of females.) Ratios greater than 100 indicate there are more men than women in the population and ratios under 100 indicate fewer men than women.

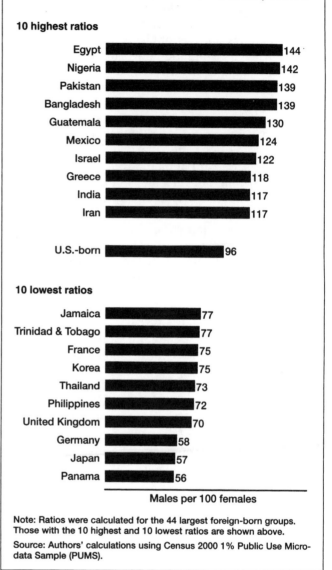

Figure 4
SEX RATIOS OF SELECTED FOREIGN-BORN POPULATIONS BY COUNTRY OF ORIGIN, 2000

10 highest ratios

Country	Males per 100 females
Egypt	144
Nigeria	142
Pakistan	139
Bangladesh	139
Guatemala	130
Mexico	124
Israel	122
Greece	118
India	117
Iran	117
U.S.-born	96

10 lowest ratios

Country	Males per 100 females
Jamaica	77
Trinidad & Tobago	77
France	75
Korea	75
Thailand	73
Philippines	72
United Kingdom	70
Germany	58
Japan	57
Panama	56

Males per 100 females

Note: Ratios were calculated for the 44 largest foreign-born groups. Those with the 10 highest and 10 lowest ratios are shown above.

Source: Authors' calculations using Census 2000 1% Public Use Microdata Sample (PUMS).

Differentials in sex ratios stem from immigration timing and causes. Men usually predominate in origin groups that have relatively large numbers of recent or labor migrants. Older established groups, in contrast, include more women and thus have lower sex ratios. The latter pattern characterizes the foreign-born populations from Japan, Germany, the United Kingdom, France, and Ireland. All those countries sent large numbers of immigrants to America during the Industrialization Wave. Panamanians also have a low sex ratio (56) that stems from special conditions of this migration flow. Many Panamanian women have immigrated as brides of American men who worked in the Panama Canal Zone; 58 percent of Panamanian women over the age of 19 and with spouse present were married to U.S.-born men in 2000. The percent married to U.S.-born men is considerably lower for other Caribbean Basin Hispanic-origin groups, ranging from 9 percent to 21 percent for Salvadoran, Mexican, Guatemalan, Dominican, Cuban, Nicaraguan, and Colombian women. Other migration flows with low sex ratios, such as those from the Philippines, Thailand, Trinidad and Tobago, and Jamaica, developed because women from those countries tend to migrate independently rather than as family members.

Foreign-born groups with high sex ratios in 2000 tended to be made up of large numbers of recent or labor migrants. For instance, the four origin groups with the highest sex ratios—Egyptians, Nigerians, Pakistanis, and Bangladeshis—only began to immigrate to the United States in large numbers in the 1990s and are relatively small in number. Because women from these origins have limited autonomy in their homelands, men were the pioneers. Gender inequality at origin could also explain why India and Iran are among the countries with relatively high sex ratios. Most Central American groups that include large numbers of labor migrants had high sex ratios. Guatemalans had a sex ratio of 130, Mexicans had a sex ratio of 124, and Salvadorans had a sex ratio of 108. Those ratios would be even higher were it not for the growing numbers of labor migrants from those origins who have now settled in the United States and brought their family members.

WHERE DO IMMIGRANTS LIVE?

The foreign-born live in every U.S. state and metropolitan area, but those from any given country tend to be highly concentrated in a few areas. Social networks channel immigrants from different origins toward geographic areas where others from their homelands are settled, and these networks discourage immigrants from moving elsewhere once they are settled.[42] During the Industrialization Wave, immigrants from northwestern Europe settled mainly in rural areas and small towns in the upper Midwest and New England, while southern and eastern Europeans concentrated in large urban areas and cities in the Northeast. The remnants of that settlement system were still in place in 1960 and visible on a map that shows the foreign-born share in each U.S. county in 1960 (see Figure 5, page 276). In 1960, many rural counties in states in the Upper Midwest—Michigan, Wisconsin, North Dakota, Montana, Washington, and Wyoming—had populations that were 5 percent to 10 percent foreign-born, and most counties in those states had foreign-born populations greater than 2.5 percent. Similarly, in 1960 most counties in New York and New England had foreign-born populations greater than 5 percent.

At the same time, the 1960 map indicates that a new type of immigration and settlement pattern was emerging in the West and Southwest. In California, northern Nevada, and southern parts of Arizona, New Mexico, and Texas, several counties were already 5 percent to 15 percent foreign-born in 1960. Six counties along the Mexican border that spread from South Texas (Hidalgo, Webb, Maverick, and Zavala) to Arizona (Santa Cruz) and to Southern California (Imperial) were more than 15 percent foreign-born. The foreign-born who lived in California were mainly Industrialization Wave immigrants who had migrated west after World War II, but growing numbers were Mexican, Central American, Asian, and South American foreign-born whose numbers had started to increase in the West. Elsewhere in the United States, only 15 percent of the foreign-born were from Mexico, Central America, Asia, or South America in 1960. Many of the counties in the West with more than 10 percent foreign-born populations in 1960 were rural, consistent with the *bracero* program's channeling of Mexican migrants into agricultural work.

In the rest of the country in 1960, foreign-born concentrations were largely limited to the New York metropolitan area and a scattering of other East Coast metro areas, including the city of Miami. Foreign-born populations were also growing elsewhere in Florida, including the counties north of Miami up to West Palm Beach, and on the Florida Gulf Coast around Tampa and Sarasota. Some of Florida's foreign-born were Cuban refugees who had started arriving there in the late 1950s, but most were Industrialization Wave immigrants from the Northeast who began retiring to Florida along with other Americans in the 1950s. As roads improved and car and air travel expanded in the post-World War II period, retirement and seasonal migration for the South took off. Air conditioning became affordable for homeowners in the 1950s, making it realistic for Northerners to consider living in Florida's hot and humid climate year-round.

By 2000, most Industrialization Wave foreign-born had died and the rural counties in the Upper Midwest, New York, and New England were among those with the smallest percentage foreign-born in the country (see Figure 6, page 276). In contrast, the settlement system that was getting established in the West and South in 1960 had greatly increased in size and spread into neighboring counties and states. Whereas in 1960, 70 percent of America's foreign-born lived in the Northeast and Upper Midwest, by 2000 two-thirds of them lived in states in the West and South. Historically, New York State was the gateway for new immigrants, but California had become America's new gateway by 1980. While New York was home to 24 percent of the foreign-born in 1960, by 2000 only 12 percent lived there. This drop occurred both because New York

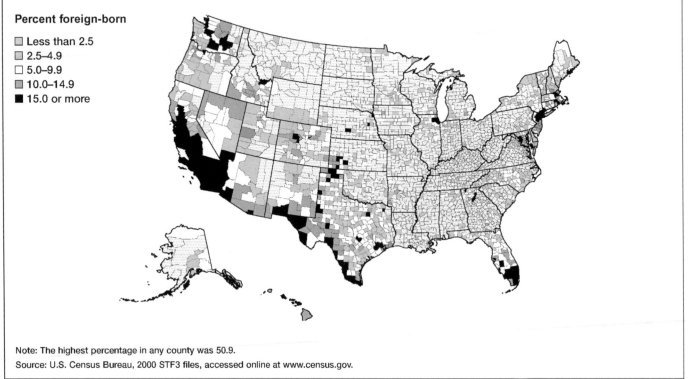

Figure 5
FOREIGN-BORN COMPOSITION OF U.S. COUNTIES, 1960

Percent foreign-born

☐ Less than 2.5
☐ 2.5–4.9
☐ 5.0–9.9
☐ 10.0–14.9
■ 15.0 or more

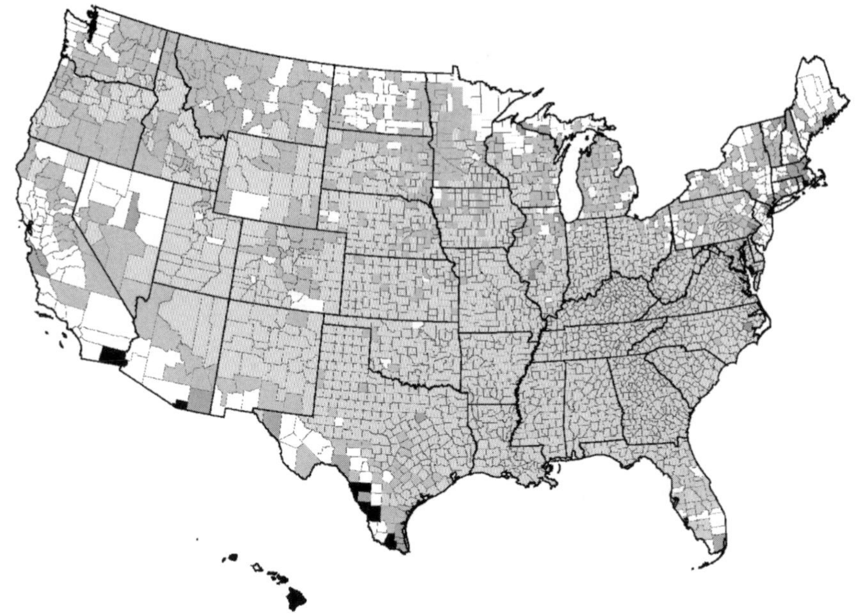

Note: The highest percentage in any county was 25. Data for Alaska were unavailable.

Source: U.S. Census Bureau, *City and County Data Book* (1962).

Figure 6
FOREIGN-BORN COMPOSITION OF U.S. COUNTIES, 2000

Percent foreign-born

☐ Less than 2.5
☐ 2.5–4.9
☐ 5.0–9.9
☐ 10.0–14.9
■ 15.0 or more

Note: The highest percentage in any county was 50.9.

Source: U.S. Census Bureau, 2000 STF3 files, accessed online at www.census.gov.

Box 5

IMMIGRATION AND REGIONAL POPULATION CHANGE

The growth rates of the foreign-born population in different regions of the United States in the 1990s ranged from a low of 38 percent in the Northeast to 91 percent in the South. These trends are the result of two processes: net internal migration of foreign-born, and net immigration and settlement by foreigners arriving from abroad.

The Midwest and Northeast lost the largest share of their 1995 foreign-born populations (see table). If the foreign-born migrated from one region of the country to another from 1995 to 2000, they were most likely to move to the South—43 percent moved to that region, but only 14 percent moved to the Northeast. The West, particularly the Mountain states, attracted 24 percent of internal foreign-born migrants.

This regional distribution of the foreign-born was also shaped by where recent immigrants who arrived from abroad decided to settle. Most of them settled in the South and West. Though the Midwest ranked third as a destination of foreign-born migrating internally, it was in distant last place as a destination for immigrants arriving from abroad, attracting just 14 percent of them. The Northeast, in contrast, attracted 21 percent of the recent immigrants, which compensated for the net loss of foreign-born through internal migration. All regions experienced net foreign-born increases from 1995 to 2000, with the largest net increase occurring in the South.

Population Change for U.S. Regions, 1995–2000

U.S. region	% 1995 foreign-born who left region	% 1995 foreign-born migrants from other regions who migrated to region	% foreign-born from abroad who immigrated from 1995–2000 and settled in region	Net foreign-born change 1995–2000 (thousands)
Northeast	6	14	21	1,003
South	5	43	33	2,102
Midwest	9	19	14	802
West	4	24	32	1,741

Source: Authors' calculations using Census 2000 5% Public Use Microdata Sample (PUMS).

attracted fewer immigrants than California in recent decades and because it experienced high out-migration of foreign-born. Nonetheless, the foreign-born population in the New York metropolitan area grew by 31 percent in the 1990s, compared with 19 percent in the Los Angeles metro area, suggesting that New York remains a major gateway.

The biggest change in immigrant settlement trends from 1960 to 2000 was the phenomenal growth in the size of the foreign-born population in the South. For decades the South has had higher rates of economic growth than other regions and has been a magnet for U.S.-born workers. As length of U.S. residence has increased among Globalization Wave immigrants, they too have learned of America's changing South and its economic opportunities. The opportunity to live in a climate more similar to that found in many immigrants' homelands may have been an added attraction. Whatever the reasons, foreign-born growth rates were higher in the South than in other regions in the 1990s (91 percent compared with 58 percent for the country as a whole). Moreover, from 1995 to 2000, the South attracted more internal foreign-born migrants and received more immigrants entering from abroad than any other region (see Box 5).

Mexicans accounted for the bulk of this growth in the South, increasing by 170 percent in the 1990s. If Texas and Florida are excluded from the calculation,

Mexicans grew by over 1,000 percent in the rest of the region. While the non-Mexican foreign-born also increased at above average rates in the South, their rate of increase (69 percent) was far lower than that of Mexicans. Groups that more than doubled the size of their populations in the South in the 1990s included Dominicans, former Soviet Union nationals, Salvadorans, Indians, and Vietnamese. The dispersal of the foreign-born to the South and other parts of the country that previously had few foreigners has implications for education, health care, and other services. It is too soon to evaluate whether the foreign-born migrating to nontraditional areas will be disadvantaged or advantaged relative to the foreign-born who settle elsewhere.

Beyond the large foreign-born concentrations in the West and in Florida, in 2000 only five other concentrations in the country spanned multiple counties. This group included the Northeast corridor that runs from Washington, D.C., to Boston; the Charlotte-Raleigh-Greensboro region of North Carolina; the city of Atlanta and its surrounding metropolitan counties; the Chicago-Milwaukee metropolitan region, including Rock and Dane counties in Wisconsin; and the city of Detroit and its metropolitan region. Other regional growth poles appeared to be getting underway in northwestern Arkansas and coastal Georgia and South Carolina, but were far smaller in scale.

Metro Concentration and Change From 1990–2000

The foreign-born are more likely than the U.S.-born to live in metropolitan areas. Just as America's Industrialization Wave immigrants from Europe concentrated in large urban areas, Globalization Wave immigrants also have shown a preference for such areas regardless of the region in which they settle. Large cities have experience working with people of diverse cultural backgrounds and traditionally have facilitated immigrant integration. They offer migrants a wide range of job opportunities and bilingual education, provide health care and other social services, and have good transportation systems. In the past, once immigrants acculturated, they often moved out of their urban ethnic communities.[43] Many question whether today's immigrants will do the same. Richard Alba and colleagues observed that recent immigrants were less likely to settle in central cities and were starting to locate in suburbs.[44]

Although the foreign-born remained more concentrated in metropolitan areas than U.S.-born in 2000, between 1990 and 2000 they became less concentrated in America's largest areas. The three largest metropolitan areas—Los Angeles, New York, and Chicago—dropped from 30 percent to 25 percent in their share of the total foreign-born. In contrast, smaller-size metropolitan areas, namely those with populations under 5 million, either experienced a relative increase in their share of the foreign-born or had no change. Metropolitan areas that experienced the largest percentage gains in foreign-born populations during the 1990s had populations under 1 million. Areas in the population category of 2.5 million to 4 million also experienced above-average increases in their foreign-born populations. There was a slight drop in the proportion of the foreign-born residing in nonmetropolitan areas in the 1990s, but the numbers of foreign-born in those areas actually increased by 31 percent in the 1990s, reaching 1.7 million in 2000. That anomaly occurred because of the strong overall growth of the foreign-born population in the 1990s.

Individual metropolitan areas differed greatly in the growth rates of their foreign-born populations in the 1990s. Whereas the foreign-born grew very rapidly in several metropolitan areas, Cleveland actually had a smaller foreign-born population in 2000 than it did in 1990. Since Cleveland's unemployment rates and other economic indicators were comparable to or even better than those of other metropolitan areas in the Northeast with increased immigration, the likely explanation for the foreign-born decline in Cleveland is the high mortality of Industrialization Wave immigrants and the length of time it takes for new immigrants to open up economic niches in new areas. Research by William Frey and colleagues indicates that cities such as Cleve-

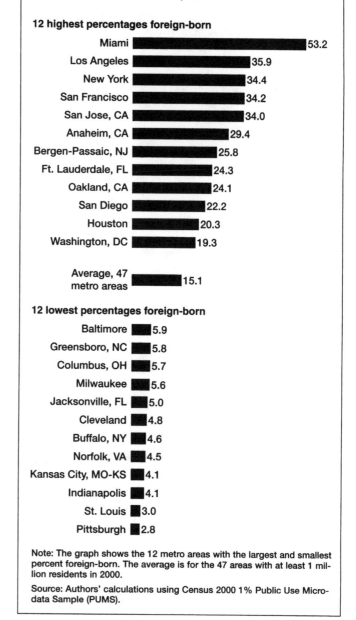

Figure 7

FOREIGN-BORN SHARE OF SELECTED U.S. METROPOLITAN AREAS, 2000

12 highest percentages foreign-born

Metro Area	Percent
Miami	53.2
Los Angeles	35.9
New York	34.4
San Francisco	34.2
San Jose, CA	34.0
Anaheim, CA	29.4
Bergen-Passaic, NJ	25.8
Ft. Lauderdale, FL	24.3
Oakland, CA	24.1
San Diego	22.2
Houston	20.3
Washington, DC	19.3
Average, 47 metro areas	15.1

12 lowest percentages foreign-born

Metro Area	Percent
Baltimore	5.9
Greensboro, NC	5.8
Columbus, OH	5.7
Milwaukee	5.6
Jacksonville, FL	5.0
Cleveland	4.8
Buffalo, NY	4.6
Norfolk, VA	4.5
Kansas City, MO-KS	4.1
Indianapolis	4.1
St. Louis	3.0
Pittsburgh	2.8

Note: The graph shows the 12 metro areas with the largest and smallest percent foreign-born. The average is for the 47 areas with at least 1 million residents in 2000.

Source: Authors' calculations using Census 2000 1% Public Use Microdata Sample (PUMS).

land have had stagnant populations in recent decades and have not attracted U.S.-born either.[45]

For metropolitan areas with populations greater than 1 million in 2000, 19 had foreign-born populations greater than the metropolitan average of 15 percent. Figure 7 shows that Miami had the highest foreign-born share (53 percent) and Pittsburgh the lowest (3 percent). About a third of the populations of Los Angeles, New York, San Francisco, and San Jose were foreign-born in 2000, as were 20 percent to 30 percent of the populations of several large metropolitan areas in California, Texas, Florida, and New Jersey. Washington, D.C.,

Chicago, Boston, and Nassau County, New York also had relatively large foreign-born populations. However, metropolitan size was not a direct correlate of immigrant settlement. Philadelphia and Detroit, America's fourth- and sixth-largest metropolitan areas in 2000, had foreign-born populations less than 8 percent and experienced little or no growth in their foreign-born populations in the 1990s. Two other relatively large metropolitan areas, St. Louis and Pittsburgh, had small shares of foreign-born populations (3 percent) that experienced little growth in the 1990s. In contrast, while Atlanta and Minneapolis had smaller-than-average shares of foreign-born populations in 1990, their foreign-born populations more than doubled by 2000.

Diversity Across Metropolitan Areas

Immigrant groups tend to settle in different metropolitan areas and differ in the extent to which they concentrate. The settlement system that an immigrant group develops is usually related to the forces that bring immigrants to America, to migrants' economic niche strategies, and to migrants' social networks. For instance, immigrants who come to the United States for graduate study locate initially in college communities and often settle in that type of place after they graduate. Mexicans, in contrast, are more likely than other groups to be located in rural areas because, both historically and today, many Mexicans are employed in agriculture. First-wave refugees often disperse initially because their settlement is sponsored by churches and other social agencies that locate them in communities throughout the country. Then, as refugees adjust, they often decide

to move toward communities where other refugees from their homeland are located. Today's concentration of Cubans in Miami resulted from secondary migration of Cubans from other parts of the United States to Miami in the decades after they arrived.

Although media attention often focuses on first-wave immigration and settlement in gateway cities and states, there is considerable internal migration among the foreign-born. This internal migration contributed to the shifting regional and metropolitan distribution of the foreign-born in the 1990s. The foreign-born are as prone to migrate within the United States as the U.S.-born. This contradicts a common perception that immigrants remain in their first destination cities. Since economic considerations underlie many immigrants' initial decision to immigrate, the foreign-born are highly sensitive to changing economic conditions in settlement areas and often migrate internally if economic conditions deteriorate in their areas of settlement. The declining attractiveness of California and Los Angeles to the foreign-born in the 1990s probably stemmed from deteriorating economic conditions there. The relatively young age of immigrants also predisposes them toward internal migration.

The largest foreign-born groups differed considerably in their propensity to concentrate in 2000 (see Table 5). While Canadians, Germans, and Indians were highly dispersed, 55 percent of Dominicans lived in New York and 56 percent of Cubans lived in Miami. Indeed, 72 percent of Dominicans lived in only five metropolitan areas, as did 68 percent of Cubans. Salvadorans were the only other group which had more than half its population concentrated in five metropolitan areas.

Table 5

METROPOLITAN AREAS OF CONCENTRATION OF THE LARGEST FOREIGN-BORN GROUPS, 2000

National origin of group	Group size (thousands)	% in top metro area	% in top 5 metro areas	Top 5 metro areas
Mexican	9,161	16	35	Los Angeles; Chicago; Houston; Orange Co., CA; Dallas
Chinese	1,493	17	47	New York; Los Angeles; San Francisco; San Jose, CA; Oakland, CA
Filipino	1,395	15	36	Los Angeles; San Diego; San Francisco; Oakland, CA; Chicago
Indian	1,018	8	29	Chicago; New York; San Jose, CA; Washington, DC; Middlesex-Somerset-Hunterdon, NJ
Vietnamese	986	12	33	Orange Co., CA; Los Angeles; Houston; Washington, DC; San Diego
Former Soviet Union	891	23	46	New York; Los Angeles; Chicago; Philadelphia; Boston
Cuban	878	56	68	Miami; Ft. Lauderdale, FL; New York; Jersey City, NJ; Tampa, FL
Korean	857	17	39	Los Angeles; New York; Washington, DC; Orange Co., CA; Chicago
Canadian	844	4	16	Los Angeles; Detroit; Ft. Lauderdale, FL; Seattle; Tampa, FL
Salvadoran	825	31	59	Los Angeles; Washington, DC; Houston; Nassau Co., NY; New York
Germans	712	4	16	Chicago; New York; Los Angeles; Philadelphia; Washington, DC
Dominican	711	55	72	New York; Bergen-Passaic, NJ; Jersey City, NJ; Miami; Boston

Note: Origin groups are ordered by group size. The metropolitan areas listed in the "Top 5 metro areas" column are ordered from highest to lowest percentage concentrated in each area. The data are for the total foreign-born in each group, including those who live in nonmetropolitan areas.

Source: Authors' calculations using Census 2000 1% Public Use Microdata Sample (PUMS).

At the other extreme, less than 40 percent of Filipinos, Koreans, Mexicans, Vietnamese, Indians, and Canadians were concentrated in five settlement areas. The largest foreign-born groups were less concentrated in 2000 than they were in 1990 or 1980, consistent with the idea that the new migrants are starting to disperse.

The tendency for the foreign-born from various origins to settle in different areas is illustrated in Table 5. For nine of the 12 largest foreign-born groups, Los Angeles was one of their top five settlement areas. New York was in the top five for eight groups; Chicago for six; Washington, D.C., for five; and Orange County (Calif.) and Houston for three groups each. Otherwise, the top five metropolitan areas where each group was concentrated differed considerably. Indeed, six metropolitan areas that attracted at least one group did not attract any of the other groups in large numbers. This set of areas and the group located in them included Dallas (Mexicans); Middlesex-Somerset-Hunterdon counties in New Jersey (Indians); Detroit (Canadians); Seattle (Canadians); Nassau County, N.Y. (Salvadorans); and Bergen-Passaic, N.J. (Dominicans).

Viewed from the standpoint of the metropolitan area, immigrant group diversity also varies. A comparison of the foreign-born populations of the two largest metropolitan areas, Los Angeles and New York, illustrates this point. Los Angeles received 44 percent of its foreign-born population from just one country, Mexico, while an additional 38 percent came from 10 other countries. In New York, in contrast, Dominicans were the largest foreign-born group but made up only 13 percent of New York's foreign-born population. The next 10 countries that sent the largest number of migrants to New York accounted for an additional 46 percent of New York's foreign-born. Putting these figures together indicates that, while 82 percent of Los Angeles' foreign-born population came from 11 countries in 2000, only 59 percent of New York's foreign-born population came from that number of origins. This means that New York's population is considerably more diverse than that of Los Angeles.

These numbers indicate that very different compositional dynamics can get established in metropolitan areas depending upon the size and diversity of the areas' foreign-born population. Beyond Los Angeles and New York, other metropolitan areas also differ in the extent to which they are developing relatively homogeneous versus diverse immigrant populations. Some western metropolitan areas among the top 10 settlement areas for Mexicans in 2000, for instance, had relatively large foreign-born settlements but almost no foreign-born other than Mexicans. McAllen-Edinberg, Texas, had a total population of 573,826 people in 2000, with 30 percent foreign-born. However, 161,819 (94 percent) of those foreign-born were from Mexico. Similar situations occured in El Paso, Phoenix, and Dallas, where Mexicans made up 90 percent, 67 percent, and 59 percent, respectively, of the foreign-born populations in 2000. Those metropolitan areas, in contrast, that are building diverse populations of immigrants from many lands include Boston, Chicago, New York, San Francisco, and Washington, D.C.

ADJUSTING TO AMERICA

Since education is a good predictor of people's earnings, unemployment, welfare use, and most other social and economic outcomes, the education levels of the foreign-born have implications for the nation's human capital and economic productivity. George Borjas found that, while the education levels of both the foreign-born and U.S.-born rose from 1960 to 1998, the education gap between those two groups increased in that period.[46] Figure 8 shows the trend observed by Borjas and also indicates that educational attainment rose faster among recent immigrants in the 1990s than it did for the U.S.-born. If recent Mexican immigrants are excluded from the comparison, by 2000 there was no gap in educational attainment between the U.S.-born and recent immigrants (line not shown in Figure 8). Both had a mean educational attainment just over 13 percent. Even with Mexicans included, the education profile of recent immigrants improved in the 1990s. This change was unexpected, since immigration greatly increased during the decade and most immigrants continued to come from regions of the developing world that have lower educational levels than the United States.

Reynolds Farley points to the bifurcation of the foreign-born population into two educational attainment groups: a highly educated segment with college degrees or some higher education, and a poorly educated segment with less than high school education.[47] This distinctive educational profile among the foreign-born is consistent with the two main types of migrants now coming to the United States—large numbers of unauthorized labor migrants from Mexico, Central America, and elsewhere in the Caribbean Basin who are poorly educated and fill low-wage jobs; and large numbers of highly skilled nonimmigrant residents coming from other origins who usually have college, graduate, professional, or technical degrees.

The pattern of educational bifurcation within the foreign-born population is heavily influenced by the characteristics of the Mexican foreign-born population. That group has considerably lower levels of educational attainment than Americans or the other foreign-born. Figure 9 gives the ratio of the percentage of recent immigrants, Mexicans versus non-Mexicans, who had college degrees relative to U.S.-born who had degrees in four census periods. Ratios above 1.0 indicate that recent immigrants had more college education than those born in the United States, and ratios below 1.0 indicate that recent immigrants had less college educa-

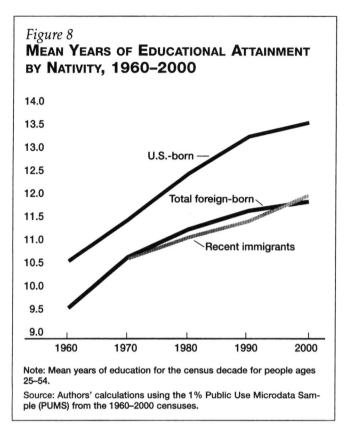

Figure 8
MEAN YEARS OF EDUCATIONAL ATTAINMENT BY NATIVITY, 1960–2000

U.S.-born

Total foreign-born

Recent immigrants

Note: Mean years of education for the census decade for people ages 25–54.

Source: Authors' calculations using the 1% Public Use Microdata Sample (PUMS) from the 1960–2000 censuses.

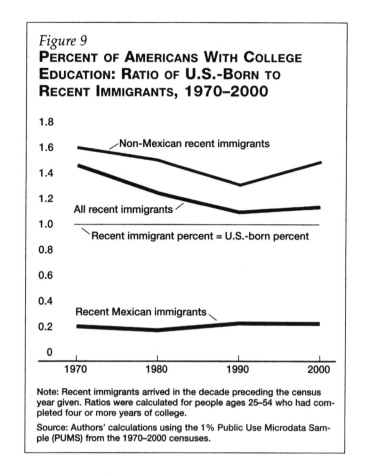

Figure 9
PERCENT OF AMERICANS WITH COLLEGE EDUCATION: RATIO OF U.S.-BORN TO RECENT IMMIGRANTS, 1970–2000

Non-Mexican recent immigrants

All recent immigrants

Recent immigrant percent = U.S.-born percent

Recent Mexican immigrants

Note: Recent immigrants arrived in the decade preceding the census year given. Ratios were calculated for people ages 25–54 who had completed four or more years of college.

Source: Authors' calculations using the 1% Public Use Microdata Sample (PUMS) from the 1970–2000 censuses.

tion. Figure 9 shows that in each period, recent immigrants were more likely than the U.S.-born to have college degrees or higher levels of education. The recent immigrant advantage was greatest in 1970. Those who arrived during the 1960s were 1.4 times more likely than the U.S.-born to have a college education. But that advantage decreased in the 1970s and 1980s, and then stabilized and started to climb again in the 1990s. The recent immigrant advantage over the U.S.-born in levels of college attainment would have been higher in 2000 if recent Mexican immigrants had the same levels of college attainment as other recent immigrants. Recent Mexican immigrants have been far less likely than other recent immigrants to have a college education and, as their share of the total foreign-born population has increased, so too has their effect on the overall educational profile of the U.S. foreign-born population.

In spite of the low educational attainment of immigrants from Mexico and several other origins, it is impressive that the overall educational attainment of the foreign-born kept up with and even made a slight gain relative to the U.S.-born in the 1990s. Given that labor migrants from Mexico and other Caribbean countries are heavily concentrated in the low education category, this slight improvement in the educational profile of the foreign-born in the 1990s resulted mainly from a dramatic improvement in the profile of immigrants from other origins. This situation can be evaluated as a glass half-full or half-empty. It appears that immigration can-

not be directly equated with a society experiencing increasingly lower levels of educational attainment. Nevertheless, educational attainment levels in the United States are lower now than they would have been given no immigration in the past 40 years. Furthermore, the distinct educational profile of recent immigrants, consisting of many very poorly educated and many very highly educated people, differs dramatically from that of the U.S.-born population.

Educational Diversity

Foreign-born groups differ considerably in their levels of educational attainment. In general, groups that include large numbers of unauthorized labor migrants or refugees have lower educational attainment. The precipitating cause of a refugee flow can shape skill composition. The foreign-born populations from Vietnam, Cambodia, and Laos, for instance, have low educational attainment levels, while the foreign-born from Cuba and the former Soviet Union (two other origin countries that include large numbers of refugees) have relatively high levels of educational attainment because Cold War politics influenced who emigrated. The Refugee Relief Act of 1953 encouraged skilled Soviet Union nationals to defect and granted refugee status to those who did. Technicians and professionals working in Soviet industries considered to be of security interest were encouraged to flee because such emigration was seen by Congress as a good way to disrupt Communism from the inside out.[48] After the Soviet Union started to disintegrate in the late 1980s, the United States granted permanent resident status to many scientists from the independent states of the former Soviet Union and the Baltic states.

For immigrant men in the 44 largest origin groups in 2000, the lowest levels of educational attainment occurred among Guatemalans, Salvadorans, Hondurans, and Mexicans. Less than 50 percent of foreign-born men ages 25 and older in those groups had completed high school, compared with 87 percent of the total U.S.-born and 68 percent of the total foreign-born. The figures were comparable for women from those origins except for Hondurans, a group in which women were more likely than men to be high school graduates. At the upper end of the education ladder, adult men from several origins had a very high probability of holding a college degree. Among the 44 largest origin groups, there were seven groups in which 60 percent or more of the men ages 25 to 54 were college graduates in 2000, including Indians (77 percent); Nigerians (70 percent); Egyptians (66 percent); Iranians (64 percent); Japanese (62 percent); French (61 percent); and Chinese (60 percent).

Although American women were slightly more likely than American men in 2000 to have a college degree—26 percent and 23 percent, respectively—the reverse pattern occurred among the foreign-born. Twenty-one percent of foreign-born women had a college degree, compared with 26 percent of the men. Indian women were the best educated—69 percent of them had four or more years of college. About 50 percent of foreign-born women from Egypt, France, the former Soviet Union, China, and the Philippines had college degrees. At the other end of the continuum, only 4 percent of Mexican women, 5 percent of Salvadoran women, and 10 percent of Dominican women had college degrees, and the modal education category for women in those groups was less than high school education.

Gender Gaps in Education and Group Diversity

Educational attainment not only varies greatly among migrants from different origins but also between foreign-born men and women from the same origin. Many of today's migrants come from societies in which men and women have differential access to formal education and work. Gender inequalities in migrant homelands can underlie gender inequalities among these groups. Although the social profiles of foreign-born groups in the United States should not be expected to be identical to those of homeland populations, it is common to find some comparability between these two groups.

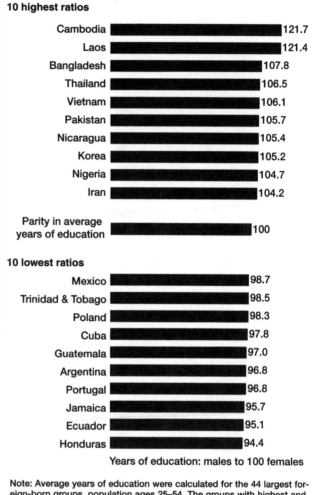

Figure 10

GENDER INEQUALITY IN EDUCATIONAL ATTAINMENT FOR SELECTED COUNTRIES OF ORIGIN, FOREIGN-BORN AGES 25–54, 2000

10 highest ratios

Cambodia	121.7
Laos	121.4
Bangladesh	107.8
Thailand	106.5
Vietnam	106.1
Pakistan	105.7
Nicaragua	105.4
Korea	105.2
Nigeria	104.7
Iran	104.2
Parity in average years of education	100

10 lowest ratios

Mexico	98.7
Trinidad & Tobago	98.5
Poland	98.3
Cuba	97.8
Guatemala	97.0
Argentina	96.8
Portugal	96.8
Jamaica	95.7
Ecuador	95.1
Honduras	94.4

Years of education: males to 100 females

Note: Average years of education were calculated for the 44 largest foreign-born groups, population ages 25–54. The groups with highest and lowest ratios are shown.

Source: Authors' calculations using Census 2000 1% Public Use Microdata Sample (PUMS).

Education sex ratios for the 44 largest foreign-born groups show gender differences across groups (see Figure 10). A ratio of 100 indicates that men and women have the same mean level of education; ratios above 100 indicate that men have more education than women, and those below 100 indicate that men have less education than women. Education sex ratios range from a low of 94 for Hondurans to a high of 122 for Cambodians and 121 for Laotians. All 10 of the groups with the lowest sex ratios had ratios below 100. However, considering that the education sex ratio for the U.S.-born was 99 and the ratio for the foreign-born was 98, not too much should be made of the female advantage for groups that have ratios close to parity.

At the other end of the continuum, high gender inequalities in education are concentrated among three types of foreign-born groups: ones that include large numbers of refugees or immigrants admitted as a result of group-targeted legislation (Cambodians, Laotians, Vietnamese, and Nicaraguans); ones that originate from countries where gender inequalities are high (Bangladeshis, Pakistanis, Nigerians, and Iranians); and ones that include large numbers of recent nonimmigrant residents and aging women from earlier immigration flows (Koreans, Germans, Japanese, and British). These groupings are not mutually exclusive in that two of the refugee populations, Laotians and Cambodians, come from societies in which gender inequities are also relatively high. The gender differences for the German, Japanese, and British foreign-born, in contrast, greatly exceed those common in their homelands and are being produced by the combination of increased recent immigration of men admitted as nonimmigrant residents and the continued presence of small numbers of foreign-born women from the Industrialization Wave cohorts. Whereas the recent cohorts of German, Japanese, and British men are relatively highly educated, the earlier cohorts of these groups are composed largely of older women who have relatively low education profiles.

English-Language Attainment

As the immigrant population has grown, so too have the number and percentage of people who live in America and speak a language other than English. The American ethnic pattern, according to Nathan Glazer, tolerates foreign-language maintenance within the home and community, but the public sphere requires communication in a single language, namely English.[49] For immigrants to get ahead economically, to become part of American society, and to participate in the American political process, it is important to know English. To facilitate immigrant adjustment and English-language acquisition, bilingual programs have been set up in public schools. Social agencies regularly provide information in multiple languages to ensure that immigrants have access to health and other services in America.

According to Richard Alba and Victor Nee: "All the evidence about the European and early Asian groups reveals a powerful linguistic gravitational pull that has produced conversion to English monolingualism on a wide scale within three generations; only a small minority of any group has escaped its grip."[50] Alba and Nee recognize, however, that because the United States is still in the midst of the Globalization Wave, the evidence is not yet in on whether today's immigrant groups will take a different course in their linguistic achievement and assimilation trajectories. Those concerned that the new immigrant groups will not assimilate linguistically worry that, as long as immigration continues at high

levels, origin cultural elements including language will be replenished; these analysts argue further that language retention is facilitated in this era by modern technologies. Immigrants often tend to maintain close ties with families and friends in their homelands and to participate in social and political life there rather than focusing on how to build a new life in America. Ties between immigrants and their homelands can be maintained at essentially no cost by e-mail; and for those desiring a more personal mode of communication, telephone services are also convenient and inexpensive.

Others are optimistic that today's immigrants will learn English. Such optimism is based on the historical evidence showing that Industrialization Wave immigrants had overwhelmingly adopted English as their mother tongue by the second and third generations, and that Globalization Wave immigrants are doing so today. Data from the 2000 Census showed a level of 67 percent English-language fluency among children 18 and younger who were born in the United States to parents who migrated from a Spanish-speaking country. That percentage rises if the children of recent immigrants are not included in the statistic. Since English is increasingly the international language of commerce and trade and is being taught as a second language in schools worldwide, it would be highly unlikely for English to diminish in importance in the United States as it continues to gain as the leading international language.

The major concern over language focuses on Spanish-language retention, since Spanish is the most common language other than English spoken in U.S. homes. Spanish retention is facilitated by growing concentrations of Spanish speakers in large urban areas and throughout the Southwest, and by the growth of Spanish-language media. In 2000, there were 28 million Spanish speakers in the United States, and 11 percent of the total population ages 5 and older spoke Spanish at home, as did 44 percent of the foreign-born. The geographic concentration of Spanish-speaking foreign-born adds to concern that Spanish will replace English in those regions in the years ahead. Some evidence supports this concern. For instance, in the metropolitan areas of El Paso and McAllen-Edinburg-Pharr-Mission, located on the Mexico/U.S. border in southern Texas, 72 percent and 82 percent, respectively, of the total population spoke Spanish at home in 2000. The foreign-born in those areas were almost all from Mexico and constituted one-third of the population. Since the number of people who spoke Spanish at home was more than double the size of the foreign-born population, these statistics indicate that language retention in the Texas border region remains high among U.S.-born Mexican Americans. However, speaking Spanish does not necessarily imply neglecting English, since 48 percent of the population in El Paso and 54 percent of the population in McAllen spoke English only or very well.

Miami is another metropolitan area with a large concentration of Spanish speakers from one origin, and where more than half of the population spoke Spanish at home in 2000. Over a half million Cubans live in Miami, as do growing numbers of Dominicans, Salvadorans, Puerto Ricans, Colombians, and Spanish speakers from other countries. While foreign-born Spanish speakers made up 44 percent of metropolitan Miami's total population in 2000, Spanish was spoken at home by 62 percent of the population. That pattern is similar to the one noted for El Paso and McAllen and indicates that in Miami also there is some language retention that stretches into the second and possibly third generations.

The patterns observed for Miami, El Paso, and McAllen probably stem from a convergence of very high levels of homogeneity of foreign-born from a single origin as well as extremely close and active links with an origin society. In both the McAllen and El Paso metropolitan areas, Mexicans constitute at least 95 percent of the foreign-born populations. In Miami, 81 percent of the foreign-born population is of Hispanic origin, with 59 percent coming from Cuba. The McAllen and El Paso regions are major border areas with very high and continuous contact and population exchange with Mexico. Historically, these regions' links with Mexico have rivaled in importance their links with the remainder of Texas. Miami is not literally a border area, but it has evolved as a major multidimensional gateway with very active links to Latin American countries. It appears that the combination of a large and homogenous foreign-born population and very active links with the origin society strongly encourages the use of Spanish or any language in the home.

Correlates of English-Language Skills

Immigrants' English-language skills vary greatly by country of origin, education, age, and length of U.S. residence. Some immigrants come from English-speaking regions such as the United Kingdom, Canada, or the British West Indies, and thus have a language advantage. Other immigrants come from countries in which English is the official language used in the public sphere and university education, but where it is not the mother tongue. This group includes India, Pakistan, and countries in English-speaking Africa. Spanish is the mother tongue spoken by the largest number of immigrants in the United States. The top 10 foreign languages other than Spanish spoken in the United States (ordered by number of speakers) include Chinese, Tagalog, Vietnamese, French, Korean, Russian, German, Arabic, and Portuguese.

The English-language skills of the foreign-born population correlate positively with education and negatively with age. If recent immigrants in the 1990s had a college degree, 59 percent of them spoke English only or very well, compared with 31 percent of those with less than four years of high school. Among recent immigrants from origins where English is not the mother tongue, sub-Saharan Africans with a college education were the most likely to speak English only or very well (85 percent), followed by: South Asians (76 percent); other Southeast Asians excluding Indochinese refugees (70 percent); West Asians and North Africans (68 percent); and Europeans (52 percent). Recent immigrants from some origins were unlikely to speak English only or very well even if they had a college education, including Mexicans (30 percent); East Asians (36 percent); and Indochina refugees (37 percent).

Immigrants between the ages of 5 and 24 were most likely to speak English only or very well. Children of immigrants should speak English better than their parents or grandparents because they are in an age group likely to be enrolled in school. Seventy-nine percent of all 5-to-24-year-olds, both U.S.- and foreign-born, were enrolled in school in 2000. Nonetheless, the younger cohorts from some foreign-born origins have relatively low percentages who speak English only or very well or who are enrolled in school. Among Mexicans ages 5 to 24, only 35 percent spoke English only or very well, and 45 percent were enrolled in school. Rates for the rest of the foreign-born were considerably higher. Sixty-six percent of children ages 5 to 24 spoke English only or very well and 72 percent were enrolled in school. The foreign-born elderly have the poorest English-language skills. Recent immigrants ages 55 or older were the least likely to speak English only or very well in 2000. While some of today's elderly foreign-born came to the United States when they were in their productive ages, worked, paid in to Social Security, and then retired, increasing numbers immigrate at the end of their productive life cycle in order to live with or be near their children who are settled in America.[51]

Immigrants' language abilities improve as length of U.S. residence increases. In 2000, the foreign-born who had been in the United States for less than 11 years were slightly less likely than those who had been in the country for a comparable length of time in 1980 to speak English only or very well. Moreover, in 1980, among the foreign-born who had immigrated 11 to 20 years before that year, 26 percent were likely to speak English only or very well, compared with 13 percent of those present for 11 to 20 years in 2000. These trends suggest that the Globalization Wave migrants are not learning English as quickly as those who arrived 20 years earlier. However, linguistic isolation, which the Census Bureau defines as living in a household in which no one age 14 or older speaks English only or very well, showed no change from 1980 to 2000. For the recent foreign-born cohorts in both 1980 and 2000, 42 percent of the foreign-born were linguistically isolated.

Naturalization and Citizenship

While serving as head of the U.S. Commission on Immigration Reform in the 1990s, Barbara Jordan argued that the civil incorporation of newcomers in America is an essential part of immigration policy. She noted: "The United States is the most successful multiethnic nation in history. It has united immigrants and their descendants from all over the world around a commitment to democratic ideals and constitutional principles."[52] The premise underlying American immigration from its outset has been that people from diverse lands can "become American." That phrase used to be equated with learning English and becoming a naturalized citizen. Critics of this view argue that it is an idealized version of American history and that many U.S.-born people were not accepted as citizens or allowed to participate in the polity. Even after the Supreme Court ruled in 1898 that Chinese and other foreigners born on American soil were protected under the 14th Amendment, groups such as American Indians, blacks, and women continued to be denied full citizenship rights.

There are several reasons why foreigners living in the United States as permanent immigrants should consider naturalization. Political participation in federal, state, and local elections is limited to citizens, although a few municipalities in Maryland recently started to allow foreigners to vote in local elections.[53] Since most foreigners who work in the United States pay taxes and Social Security, it is important for them to become citizens and have the right to vote for the politicians who make decisions about how that money is spent. Moreover, while naturalized citizens are not eligible to become president of the United States, they can run for other political offices. The highly visible election of Austrian-born Arnold Schwarzenegger as governor of California in 2003 symbolized the political possibilities open to immigrants should they choose to enter politics. American citizenship also entitles foreigners to a U.S. passport and its associated travel rights. Furthermore, naturalized citizens have the right under U.S. immigration law to bring to the United States immediate family members, including spouses, children, and elderly parents, without any delay in their admission.

Comparisons between naturalization rates among new immigrants and those among earlier immigrants are complicated because of differentials in naturalization rates across foreign-born groups, the changing composition of U.S. immigration, and the close link between naturalization and length of U.S. residency. To become a naturalized citizen, a foreigner must have been a permanent resident for five years (three years if married to an American citizen) and must pass two tests, one that examines English-language ability and one that evaluates knowledge of American history and political processes. Figure 11 shows how two foreign-born cohorts that

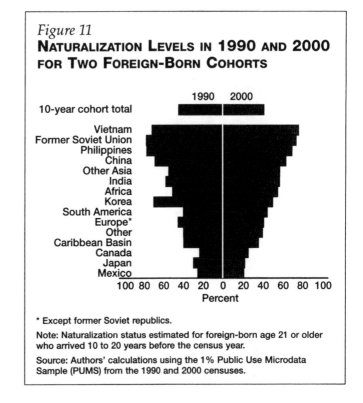

Figure 11

NATURALIZATION LEVELS IN 1990 AND 2000 FOR TWO FOREIGN-BORN COHORTS

* Except former Soviet republics.

Note: Naturalization status estimated for foreign-born age 21 or older who arrived 10 to 20 years before the census year.

Source: Authors' calculations using the 1% Public Use Microdata Sample (PUMS) from the 1990 and 2000 censuses.

arrived at different times compare in their naturalization rates. The first group arrived in the 1970s, and their naturalization rates are assessed 10 to 20 years later based on 1990 Census data; the second group arrived in the 1980s, and their naturalization rates are also assessed 10 to 20 years later based on 2000 Census data.

Overall, 45 percent of the 1970 cohort had naturalized by 1990, but levels for this naturalization vary considerably across origin groups. Canada, Japan, and Mexico had the lowest naturalization levels, from 23 percent to 29 percent. Rates were also relatively low among Caribbean Basin immigrants. That finding is consistent with the idea that immigrants from neighboring countries often view themselves as sojourners who regularly return home and plan to do so permanently at some point in the future. While Japanese settlers did come during the Industrialization Wave, now the Japanese foreign-born are mainly nonimmigrant residents who work for Japanese companies in the United States or who come to study. The foreign-born from China, Korea, the Philippines, Vietnam, and the former Soviet Union, on the other hand, are mainly settlers and had naturalization levels above 69 percent in 1990.

The second cohort examined in Figure 11 had, by 2000, the same amount of time to become citizens as the 1970 cohort; and its experience proved to be quite similar, though there was a weak suggestion of a trend away from naturalization. For instance, the overall level of naturalization among the 1980 cohort (41 percent) was slightly lower than that for the 1970 cohort (45 percent). Nevertheless, five groups (Vietnamese, Other Asians,

Africans, South Americans, and Canadians) had slightly higher levels of naturalization in 2000 than they did in 1990, and two other groups (Indians and the heterogeneous "Other" category) remained the same. Koreans were the only group that experienced a large drop in naturalization levels, from 70 percent naturalized in 1990 to 50 percent in 2000. This change, along with the drop in Korean recent immigration in the 1990s noted earlier, suggests that the dynamics of that flow changed in recent years. The declines in levels of naturalization that occurred for other groups, including Mexicans and Chinese, were quite small.

The comparison of the naturalization experiences of these two immigration cohorts suggests that the forces influencing the propensity to become a citizen have remained relatively stable in the midst of the tremendous growth of the foreign-born population and an array of other social, political, and economic changes in the legal statuses of the foreign-born. It is possible, however, that the view from the perspective of the foreign-born is more complex than this apparent stability would suggest. Increased numbers of nonimmigrant residents from Europe, Japan, and other origins are arriving in response to globalization. These foreign-born people would not be likely to have, initially at any rate, any intention to settle and become citizens. On the other hand, other foreign-born groups may be accelerating their movement toward becoming citizens in response to changes in the legal and political climate in the United States. Michael Fix, Jeffrey Passel, and Kenneth Sucher showed that, following the passage of legislation in the mid-1990s that restricted immigrants' access to public assistance, naturalization rates started to increase in the latter half of the 1990s, although they had been declining before then.[54]

WHAT WORK DO IMMIGRANTS DO IN AMERICA?

Debates about the effects of immigration on America invariably focus on the economic impacts of immigrants on the wages and employment of American workers and on the economy in general. Do immigrant workers take jobs that American workers will not do, or do they displace U.S.-born workers? Do they compete with American workers for low-wage jobs? How does immigration affect the employment of minority workers? Do immigrants fuel economic growth in the communities where they settle? The underlying economic issues are complex, and answers depend upon the level of analysis (federal, state, or local); whether analysts look at the short-term versus long-term impact of immigration; the costs and benefits considered; and the human capital characteristics of immigrants.[55] By look-

ing at the characteristics of immigrants, it is possible to obtain some sense of the range of possible effects. As such, the analysis that follows focuses on providing an overview of the trends and characteristics of the foreign-born in the American labor force and the diversity of the economic contributions of immigrants.

Labor Force Participation

Data from the 2000 Census indicate that, of the 8.7 million new immigrants ages 18 to 59 who arrived in the United States in the 1990s, 5.6 million were in the labor force in 2000. Between 1990 and 2000, the total U.S. labor force increased by 14.4 million. Thus, recent immigrants accounted for 41 percent of labor force growth in the 1990s, compared with only 11 percent in the 1960s. Moreover, the percentage of the total labor force that is foreign-born reached 12 percent in 2000, compared with 6 percent in 1960. The foreign-born, however, are not evenly distributed across the country and thus constitute a much greater share of the labor force in some metropolitan areas. At the high end, in 2000, over half of metropolitan Miami's population and 63 percent of its labor force were foreign-born. The large Cuban enclave in Miami stands out as a thriving foreign-born community that offers a wide range of employment opportunities to Cubans, other immigrants, and Americans. Immigrants also have a big impact on the economies of Los Angeles and New York. About one-third of the populations in those metropolitan areas and just over 40 percent of their labor forces were foreign-born in 2000. Other California cities had heavily foreign-born labor forces as well. One-quarter of California's population was foreign-born, as was 30 percent of its labor force. No other state exceeded those levels.

In several large metropolitan areas, immigration had very little impact on the labor force. Though larger metropolitan areas tended to have higher foreign-born labor force compositions, there were many exceptions. Chicago, the nation's third-largest metropolitan area, had a labor force 20 percent foreign-born; but in the fourth- and sixth-largest metropolitan areas, Philadelphia and Detroit, only 8 percent and 9 percent, respectively, of the labor force was foreign-born. In Washington, D.C., the fifth-largest area, 22 percent of the labor force was foreign-born. In general, the foreign-born constituted a smaller share of the labor force in moderate to small metropolitan areas. For instance, the 17 metropolitan areas that had populations from 400,000 to 500,000 in 2000 had foreign-born labor force compositions of 7 percent, on average.

Employment rates for U.S.- and foreign-born men have been comparable since 1960. About 90 percent of men, regardless of nativity, worked in the year prior to the 2000 Census (see Figure 12). The employment rates for foreign-born and U.S.-born women were also comparable in 1960, but then began to widen in subsequent

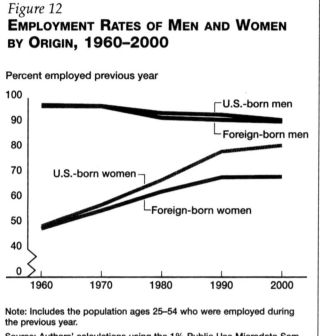

Figure 12
EMPLOYMENT RATES OF MEN AND WOMEN BY ORIGIN, 1960–2000

Percent employed previous year

Note: Includes the population ages 25–54 who were employed during the previous year.

Source: Authors' calculations using the 1% Public Use Microdata Sample (PUMS) from the 1960–2000 censuses.

decades as immigration increased. Women's employment rates increased dramatically from 1960 to 1990, rising from 48 percent in 1960 to 79 percent for U.S.-born women and from 48 percent to 68 percent for foreign-born women. While the employment of U.S.-born women continued to rise slowly during the 1990s and reached 81 percent by 2000, the rate of foreign-born women remained constant. By 2000, there was a 13 percentage point difference between U.S.-born and foreign-born women in employment rates.

America's foreign-born groups vary greatly in their employment rates. Among the 44 largest foreign-born groups, men ages 25 to 54 from France and the United Kingdom had the highest levels of employment in 2000 (95 percent and 94 percent, respectively). Indian and Canadian men also had above-average employment rates at 93 percent; and Irish, German, Polish, and Argentine men were at 92 percent. Lower levels of employment, in contrast, occurred among men from origin countries that sent large numbers of unauthorized labor migrants to America. That group included Dominican men (83 percent) and Haitian men (85 percent). Mexican men had an employment rate of 88 percent in 2000, close to the foreign-born average. Rates for men from origins that included large numbers of refugees were also relatively low—79 percent for Cambodian men and 82 percent for Laotian men. The highest levels of employment among foreign-born women were achieved by Jamaicans (85 percent); Filipinas (84 percent); Nigerians (79 percent); Trinidadians (79 percent); Haitians (77 percent); Romanians (77 percent); and

Panamanians (77 percent). The lowest rates of employment occurred for women from Pakistan (46 percent); Bangladesh (52 percent); Mexico (56 percent); Japan (56 percent); and Israel (60 percent).

Gender Inequality in Employment

The origin societies of recent immigrants differ considerably in their norms concerning appropriate economic activities for women outside the household. Many question whether those new immigrants who come from societies that have restrictive approaches toward women and where levels of gender inequality are high will change their values and practices over time as they become familiar with U.S. gender norms. The group differentials in women's employment rates just noted, for instance, could stem from gender norms in migrants' origin societies. That would definitely be the case for foreign-born women from Pakistan and Bangladesh, since Islam dominates in both countries. Throughout the Middle East and West Asia, the world region where Islam dominates, restrictive gender systems prevail. Most of these societies frown upon women's participation in the labor force and public sphere, and girls are segregated from boys in schools. These practices correlate with high levels of gender inequality in schooling, labor force participation, and marriage practices.

The relatively low rate of employment among Israelis in the United States probably stems from the Muslim component of that flow. The Israeli foreign-born population includes both Jews and Palestinian Arabs. Since data on people's religion are not gathered in the census, those two segments of the Israeli flow cannot be readily differentiated with census data. One study estimated that 31 percent of Israeli migrants were of Palestinian origin in 1990.[56] In the 1990s, immigration of Palestinian Arabs to the United States increased, as did immigration to the United States from Muslim countries in general.

Further light can be shed on gender differences across groups by examining employment sex ratios, which were calculated for adults ages 25 to 54 by dividing the percentage of men employed in the year before the census by the percentage of women employed. Ratios above 100 indicate that more men than women work, while those below 100 indicate that more women than men work. The employment sex ratio of 193 for Pakistanis in 2000 means that 193 Pakistani men were employed for every 100 employed Pakistani women (see Figure 13, page 288). Bangladesh has a ratio of 170, and a few other Asian and Middle Eastern groups also have relatively high employment sex ratios, including Indians, Japanese, and Israelis. While Laos is not a Muslim society, it does retain traditional attitudes toward gender.

In 2000, the employment sex ratio for U.S.-born was 112, compared with 132 for the foreign-born. For all 44 of the largest foreign-born groups, men were more

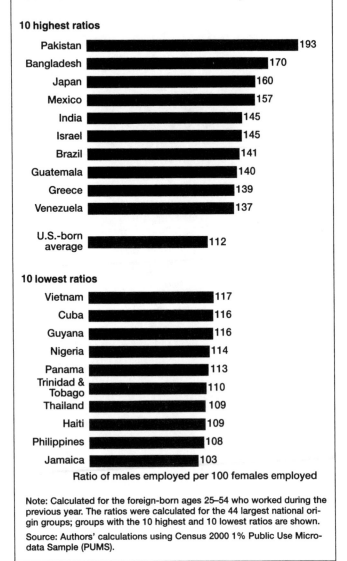

Figure 13

GENDER INEQUALITY IN EMPLOYMENT FOR SELECTED COUNTRIES OF ORIGIN, 2000

10 highest ratios

Pakistan	193
Bangladesh	170
Japan	160
Mexico	157
India	145
Israel	145
Brazil	141
Guatemala	140
Greece	139
Venezuela	137
U.S.-born average	112

10 lowest ratios

Vietnam	117
Cuba	116
Guyana	116
Nigeria	114
Panama	113
Trinidad & Tobago	110
Thailand	109
Haiti	109
Philippines	108
Jamaica	103

Ratio of males employed per 100 females employed

Note: Calculated for the foreign-born ages 25–54 who worked during the previous year. The ratios were calculated for the 44 largest national origin groups; groups with the 10 highest and 10 lowest ratios are shown.

Source: Authors' calculations using Census 2000 1% Public Use Microdata Sample (PUMS).

United States could be a legacy of a West African cultural pattern. Some anthropologists and African scholars have made that observation.[57] The foreign-born from Nigeria, Africa's largest country and one where many of America's slaves originated, also had a relatively low employment sex ratio in 2000, a finding that supports the cultural-pattern argument. Many of the slaves imported to Jamaica and other Caribbean islands came from Africa's Guinea coast, particularly the Bight of Benin and the Bight of Biafra, where Nigerians live.[58]

Filipinos also have relatively high levels of gender equality in employment. That pattern is consistent with Filipinos origin culture, which strongly encourages schooling for girls and women's work for pay outside the home. Moreover, the Filipino migration stream has been highly selective of females who migrate to fill technical and professional jobs in the health care industry. Fully 30 percent of employed Filipino women in the United States worked in medical services in 2000; an additional 17 percent worked in sales and 13 percent in education and professional services.

Gender inequality in employment can stem from the composition and dynamics of migration flows. Mexicans, for instance, have a high level of gender inequality even though they come from a country where the labor force participation of women is relatively high. Gender equality, however, is characteristic of urban Mexico and not typical of the rural areas and small towns where most unauthorized migrants originate. While many Mexican women in rural and urban parts of Mexico work as market traders, that activity is strictly regulated in the United States and thus not one that Mexican women can readily pursue after coming to the United States. Other factors stemming from Mexicans' rural origins are associated with reduced employment, including low levels of education and English-language ability and relatively high fertility rates. For all groups of women, both U.S.- and foreign-born, childbearing and childrearing dampen labor force participation.[59] Mexican men are more likely than other groups of foreign-born men to work in agriculture in rural and nonmetropolitan areas, a situation that also could depress Mexican women's employment rates because, in general, there are fewer jobs for women in rural areas.

Migration flows composed of large numbers of nonimmigrant residents tend to have relatively high employment sex ratios because accompanying spouses can only work if they too obtain institutional sponsorship. That pattern probably accounts for the relatively high employment sex ratios among the French, Japanese, and other foreign-born groups who mostly come to the United States as nonimmigrant residents. In 2002, for instance, very few French were admitted as permanent immigrants (4,596), but about 111,000 entered as nonimmigrant residents. While one cannot tell from official data on nonimmigrant entries whether these French

likely to have worked in the year before the 2000 Census than women. There were some groups that had lower levels of gender inequality in employment than U.S.-born, including Jamaicans (the lowest sex ratio of 103), Haitians, and Trinidadians. The ratios for Cuba, Panama, and Guyana exceeded that of the U.S.-born by an insignificant degree. Nicaragua also had a relatively low sex ratio. While these Caribbean Basin countries had different colonial experiences and their populations speak different languages today, they share a common historical experience and cultural heritage rooted in their West African slave origins. One can speculate about whether the relatively high levels of women's autonomy and work outside the home that characterize people of African origins in the Caribbean and the people were entering for the first time, or were residing in the United States already, traveled abroad, and then returned, a conservative estimate is that perhaps one-quarter to one-third of them would be foreigners coming for the first time. A similar situation occurs for Japan. Whereas in 2002, only 9,150 Japanese arrived as permanent residents, 87,000 arrived as nonimmigrant residents. Japanese companies have invested heavily in the U.S. automotive, hotel, and finance industries and regularly send Japanese managerial and technical personnel here to manage these investments. Since men outnumber women among corporate executives in France, Japan, and most countries of the world, accompanying spouses of nonimmigrant residents would likely be female and thus restricted from entering the labor force. In order to work, accompanying spouses would have to find employers willing to hire them as skilled workers and to go through the complicated official process to obtain labor certifications for them.

Occupational Shifts and Group Diversity

What jobs do the foreign-born fill in America and how has their economic activity changed in recent decades? Since the foreign-born population has highly diverse skills, there are many types of jobs that they do in America. It is difficult to provide more than a crude snapshot of the wide range of jobs and economic contributions that immigrants make in America.[60] Nonetheless, it is important to try to glean insights about their economic activities in order to understand how they survive after they arrive. The economy that recent immigrants entered in the 1990s has experienced broad structural changes in recent decades. For instance, between 1970 and 2000, the skill requirements of jobs shifted upward and manufacturing and agricultural jobs declined. In 1970, 25 percent of workers were managers or professionals, but 37 percent were in 2000. At the other end of the distribution, the percent employed as operators or laborers declined from 22 percent in 1970 to 15 percent in 2000.

This upward shift was not experienced by recent immigrants to the same extent as it was by the U.S.-born. While U.S.-born men increased their percentages employed as managers and professionals from 31 percent to 38 percent from 1970 to 2000, the percent of recent immigrant men employed as managers and professionals remained constant at 31 percent. Furthermore, although U.S.-born men were shifting out of the operator/laborer category (from 25 percent to 20 percent), the recent immigrant share in this category increased from 26 percent to 29 percent. These trends disguise another shift in the operator/laborer category: a decline in high-paying union jobs and an increase in low-wage jobs with limited benefits. Despite the divergence in the occupational distributions of U.S.-born and recent immi-

grant men from 1970 to 2000, the latter group worked in a wide range of occupations at both points in time.

The occupational distributions of U.S.-born and foreign-born women also diverged across these three decades, but in a different manner. Unlike men, recent immigrant women significantly increased their share working as managers and professionals, from 18 percent in 1970 to 29 percent in 2000. That gain, however, was outpaced by U.S.-born women, who increased their share working as managers and professionals from 21 percent in 1970 to 40 percent in 2000. In the same period, both U.S.-born and foreign-born women experienced big declines in their percentages working as operators/laborers, from 17 percent to 7 percent for U.S.-born and from 34 percent to 18 percent for recent immigrants. In the service sector, trends by nativity moved in different directions for women. While recent immigrant women's employment in service jobs increased from 20 percent to 28 percent between 1970 and 2000, U.S.-born women's share declined from 20 percent to 15 percent.

The type of work that people do in the U.S. labor force is closely related to their human capital, particularly their education and English-language skills. Indeed, when the population is differentiated by nativity and education, it becomes apparent that, for men, education is more important for occupational position than nativity or length of residence. Figure 14 (page 290) shows that the occupational distributions of recent immigrants, all foreign-born, and U.S.-born men with a college or advanced degree were almost identical in 2000, with about 75 percent of well-educated men in each group employed as managers and professionals. Moreover, virtually no men with a college education worked in farming, forestry, and fishing; and only about 10 percent worked in service occupations. College-educated men employed in other occupations, in contrast, do differ slightly in their employment patterns by nativity. For instance, recent immigrant men with a college education were more than twice as likely as U.S.-born men to hold jobs as machine operators, factory workers, and laborers; and U.S.-born men with college educations were more likely than the foreign-born to hold clerical and sales jobs. Despite these minor differences, the bottom line is that college-educated men have similar occupational distributions regardless of nativity.

The occupational distributions by nativity of men with fewer than four years of college show greater differences. One-third of foreign-born men with less than a college education worked as machine operators, factory workers, and laborers; followed by 22 percent in craft and repair jobs, 15 percent in service jobs, and 14 percent in managerial or professional occupations. Though the distribution of jobs for U.S.-born men with less than college education was similar, they were more likely than immigrant men to hold craft and repair jobs or managerial and professional jobs. Both recent immigrant and foreign-born men with less than college education were more likely than U.S.-born men to work in farming, forestry, and fishing. Research on the movement of unauthorized migrants into agriculture and rural industries in the upper Midwest and South suggest this movement is a growing trend.[61]

The patterns for women by nativity are comparable to those for men. Women who are college-educated have similar occupational distributions regardless of nativity, while those without a college degree diverge in their patterns (see Figure 14). In 2000, the vast majority of all college-educated women worked as managers and professionals—76 percent of U.S.-born women, 69 percent of all foreign-born women, and 65 percent of recent immigrants. If women had less than a college education, however, foreign-born and recent immigrant women tended to work in blue-collar jobs, while U.S.-born women worked in white-collar jobs (managers and professionals or sales and clerical). U.S.-born women were twice as likely as foreign-born women to be sales and clerical workers, but only half as likely to do service work or to work as operators, fabricators, and laborers.

Moreover, recent immigrant women were slightly more likely than all foreign-born women to be machine operators, factory workers, and laborers, or to be engaged in agricultural and rural jobs.

Understanding the diversity of occupational experiences of foreign-born men and women in America can be enhanced by looking at the situation of specific origin groups. Figure 15 shows the occupational distribution of Mexican, Vietnamese, and Indian men; and Figure 16 gives the same information for Mexican, Jamaican, and Filipino women. Mexican men and women were examined because they are the largest foreign-born group and include large numbers of unauthorized labor migrants who work for low wages. Indian men were examined because they were the fourth-largest foreign-born group in 2000 and represent the skilled immigrant sector. Vietnamese men are also a large foreign-born group—the fifth largest—and shed light on a group with roots in refugee migration. Filipino women were selected because of the prevalence of well-educated and employed women in that flow. More Jamaican women migrate than men and thus shed light on a predominantly black immigration flow.

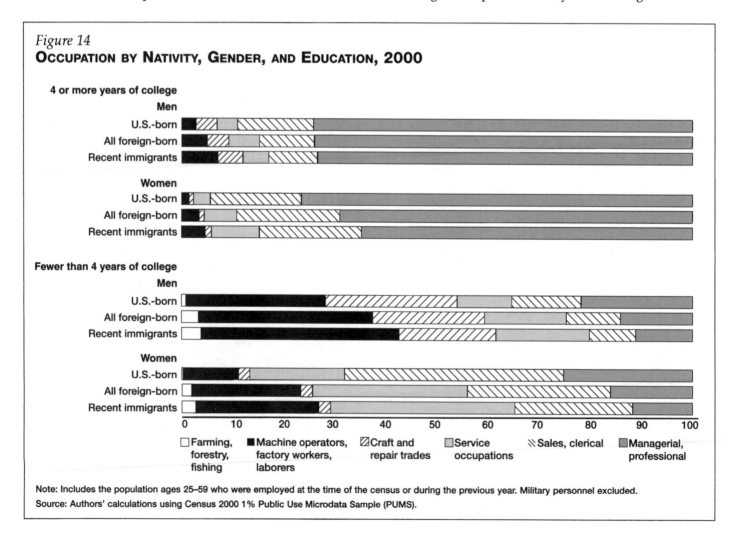

Figure 14
OCCUPATION BY NATIVITY, GENDER, AND EDUCATION, 2000

Note: Includes the population ages 25–59 who were employed at the time of the census or during the previous year. Military personnel excluded.

Source: Authors' calculations using Census 2000 1% Public Use Microdata Sample (PUMS).

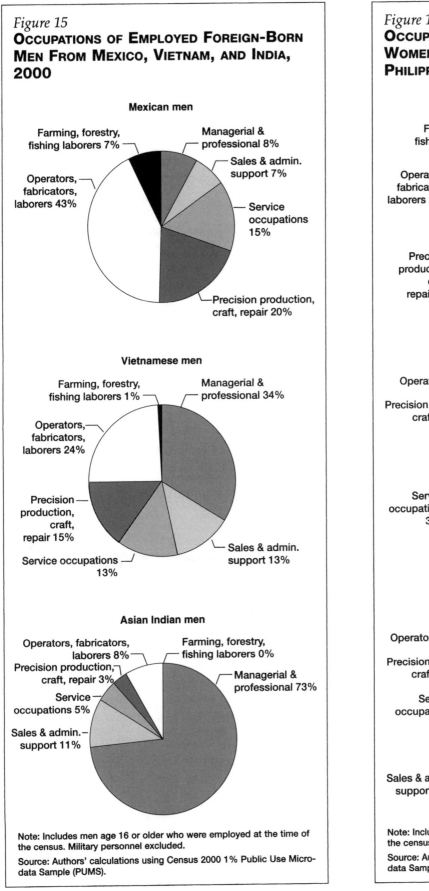

Figure 15

OCCUPATIONS OF EMPLOYED FOREIGN-BORN MEN FROM MEXICO, VIETNAM, AND INDIA, 2000

Mexican men

Farming, forestry, fishing laborers 7%
Managerial & professional 8%
Sales & admin. support 7%
Service occupations 15%
Precision production, craft, repair 20%
Operators, fabricators, laborers 43%

Vietnamese men

Farming, forestry, fishing laborers 1%
Managerial & professional 34%
Operators, fabricators, laborers 24%
Precision production, craft, repair 15%
Service occupations 13%
Sales & admin. support 13%

Asian Indian men

Operators, fabricators, laborers 8%
Farming, forestry, fishing laborers 0%
Precision production, craft, repair 3%
Managerial & professional 73%
Service occupations 5%
Sales & admin. support 11%

Note: Includes men age 16 or older who were employed at the time of the census. Military personnel excluded.

Source: Authors' calculations using Census 2000 1% Public Use Microdata Sample (PUMS).

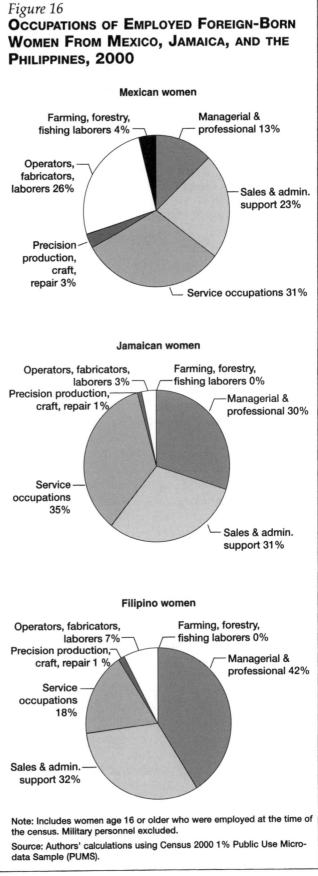

Figure 16

OCCUPATIONS OF EMPLOYED FOREIGN-BORN WOMEN FROM MEXICO, JAMAICA, AND THE PHILIPPINES, 2000

Mexican women

Farming, forestry, fishing laborers 4%
Managerial & professional 13%
Operators, fabricators, laborers 26%
Sales & admin. support 23%
Precision production, craft, repair 3%
Service occupations 31%

Jamaican women

Operators, fabricators, laborers 3%
Farming, forestry, fishing laborers 0%
Precision production, craft, repair 1%
Managerial & professional 30%
Service occupations 35%
Sales & admin. support 31%

Filipino women

Operators, fabricators, laborers 7%
Farming, forestry, fishing laborers 0%
Precision production, craft, repair 1%
Managerial & professional 42%
Service occupations 18%
Sales & admin. support 32%

Note: Includes women age 16 or older who were employed at the time of the census. Military personnel excluded.

Source: Authors' calculations using Census 2000 1% Public Use Microdata Sample (PUMS).

In 2000, most Mexican men (43 percent) worked as operators, fabricators, and laborers, compared with 24 percent of Vietnamese men and 8 percent of Indian men. In contrast, three-quarters of Indian men and one-third of Vietnamese men worked as managers and professionals, but only 8 percent of Mexicans. Other data indicate that 5 percent of Indian men and 5 percent of Indian women were employed in 2000 as medical doctors, compared with 0.5 percent of U.S.-born men and women. An additional 11 percent of Indian men worked in sales and administrative support occupations. While Vietnamese men had a more diverse occupational profile than Indian or Mexican men, the latter were primarily concentrated in low-wage occupations. An employment pattern unique to Mexicans is their tendency to work in farming, forestry, and fishing; 7 percent of them did so in 2000. That figure represented a decline, however, from the 32 percent of Mexican men who had those jobs in 1960.

Other 2000 Census data on rural industries indicate that 14 percent of all workers in those industries were Mexican men. Rural industries include a broader array of jobs than the occupational category of farming, forestry, and fishing laborers used to calculate the data in Figures 15 and 16. Included in the industry measure would be all workers engaged in farming, fishing, and forestry (not just laborers); workers engaged in meat packing, dairy processing, and vegetable/fruit packing; as well as those who handle farming, fishing, and forestry products. Since U.S.-born workers have been moving out of employment in rural industries, these statistics suggest that Mexican men have stepped in to fill an important niche in America's rural economy. The dispersal of Mexicans to different parts of the country in the 1990s could be linked to their niche in rural industries.

For the three groups of foreign-born women examined, the occupational distributions differ, but not as much as those of the men. The highest concentration among the women occurs for Filipino female managers and professionals (42 percent), but one-third of Jamaican women also worked as managers and professionals, as did 13 percent of Mexican women. Indeed, more Mexican women worked as managers or professionals than Mexican men, although that ratio is not the case for most foreign-born groups. The share of women in the three groups employed in service occupations is also comparable, ranging from one-third of Jamaican and Mexican women to just under one-fifth of Filipino women. In addition, the three groups have a comparable share employed in sales and administrative support work. The sharpest differential between the three groups of foreign-born women occurred in the operator, fabricator, and laborer category. While one-quarter of Mexican women worked in those occupations, only 7 percent of Filipino women and 3 percent of Jamaican women were in them. An additional 4 percent of Mexican women worked as farm laborers.

The type of work performed by the foreign-born in the United States is often dependent upon where they live. Eighteen percent of Filipino women, for instance, worked in service occupations in the country as a whole, but 37 percent of them worked in those occupations if they lived in Hawaii. But most Filipino women lived in California (48 percent), compared with only 8 percent in Hawaii. The differences that occur between the occupational distribution of Filipino women in Hawaii and California stem from the social networks that channel migrants from the same origin country into different states and metropolitan areas to settle. This occurs because people tend to form social relationships with people similar to themselves.

Some jobs in America are increasingly defined as "immigrant" jobs. Table 6 identifies the 10 occupations most likely to be held by recent immigrant men and women in 2000. Although recent immigrants constituted only 5.0 percent of employed men and 3.4 percent of employed women in 2000, they had concentrations three to four times larger in the occupations listed in Table 6. While most of the overrepresented occupations were unskilled ones, there were two highly skilled occupations in which recent immigrant men were overrepresented: biological scientists and other natural scientists. Recent immigrant women were also overrepresented among biological scientists and other natural scientists, as well as among chemists and statisticians and actuaries.

Most of the occupations in which recent immigrants were overrepresented, however, were unskilled and low-wage occupations. For recent immigrant men, that group of occupations included taxi drivers and chauffeurs, parking attendants and auto service workers, laundry workers, plasterers, tailors, and waiters. Recent immigrant women, in contrast, were most overrepresented among employed women working as produce graders and packers, farm laborers, private household workers, meat cutters, tailors, and laundry workers. While these national statistics would allow for the inference that recent immigrants were doing jobs in 2000 that American workers preferred not to do, they also indicate that, with the exception of taxi driving and produce grading and packing, most unskilled jobs in 2000 were still being done by U.S.-born workers. The overrepresentation of recent immigrant men and women in highly skilled occupations would seem to be more a failing of America's education system to train sufficient workers for those jobs rather than an inherent distaste for high-paying jobs.

Self-Employment

Immigrants are often described as entrepreneurs and more likely than U.S.-born workers to set up a business. The growth of ethnic communities in America's largest cities, and their accompanying ethnic restaurants and shops, reinforces this impression. Moreover, there has been a growth of chain firms in the food and hospitality industry that have ethnic themes, such as Chi-Chi's, Taco Bell, and Taco Maker. A simple Internet search identifies a wide range of entrepreneurial activities in which the foreign-born are engaged in the United States. While immigrants themselves have to take the initiative to set up small businesses, U.S. immigration policy encourages foreigners to invest in America. In 1990, Congress set up a new immigration category that authorizes up to 10,000 permanent residency visas annually to foreigners who commit to investing $1 million in a new commercial enterprise or at least $500,000 in a new enterprise in a targeted area of high unemployment.

Despite the widespread image of self-employed immigrants, when we look at the total foreign-born, there is very little difference between foreign-born and U.S.-born self-employed workers. Among people ages 25 to 59 who were employed at the time of the 2000 Census, 11 percent of the foreign-born and 10 percent of the U.S.-born declared themselves self-employed. Self-employment by nativity has converged since 1960, when 12 percent of the foreign-born and 9 percent of the U.S.-born were self-employed. When differentiated by sex, the picture changes. In 2000, U.S.-born men were slightly more likely than foreign-born men to be self-employed (12 percent versus 11 percent, respectively); and foreign-born women were more likely than U.S.-born women to be self-employed (9 percent versus 7 percent, respectively).

Self-employment rates vary greatly across foreign-born groups. In 2000, self-employment ranged from a low of 5 percent for Haitians to a high of 26 percent among Greeks (see Figure 17, page 294). Filipinos had the second-lowest rate of self-employment (6 percent), which is consistent with their heavy concentration in the health industry as professionals and technical workers. Laotians, an Asian group with refugee origins, also had a relatively low rate of self-employment. With these exceptions, the lowest rates of self-employment were concentrated among foreign-born groups from Mexico and the Caribbean Basin that include large numbers of unauthorized labor migrants.

Cubans had a self-employment rate slightly above the national average. The strong presence of Cubans in the Miami metropolitan area and the size of their economic enclave there undoubtedly opened up opportunities for entrepreneurship available to few other foreign-born groups. Nonetheless, given that the Mexican foreign-born population is almost 10 times larger than the Cuban population, it would be difficult to argue that size alone is a sufficient factor for entrepreneurship. A more likely explanation would build on the composition of Cuban refugees in the 1960s. The Cuban revolution disproportionately uprooted members of the upper-middle and middle classes. As such, entrepreneurs, managers, professionals, and other skilled Cubans predominated among the first generation of Cuban refugees. The high levels of human and real capital among these Cuban refugees, in turn, enabled them to build new businesses in Miami that turned that city within a couple of decades into the surrogate capital of Latin America.[62]

High rates of self-employment are largely concentrated among foreign-born groups from Europe, the Middle East, and Asia. Among the 10 countries shown in Figure 17 with the highest rates of self-employment

---

Table 6
OCCUPATIONS IN WHICH RECENT IMMIGRANTS ARE OVERREPRESENTED, 2000

Employed men			Employed women		
Occupation	% recent immigrants	Total number employed (1,000)	Occupation	% recent immigrants	Total number employed (1,000)
Biological scientists	19	79	Produce graders & packers	24	14
Taxi drivers, chauffeurs	19	130	Other natural scientists	19	65
Farm laborers	18	314	Biological scientists	19	65
Parking attendants, auto service workers	17	64	Farm laborers	16	97
Laundry and dry-cleaning workers	16	79	Private household workers	14	673
Other natural scientists	16	140	Meat cutters, except slaughter-house workers	13	44
Plasterers	15	32	Chemists	13	28
Tailors	15	19	Tailors	12	51
Service workers (not private households)	14	449	Statisticians and actuaries	12	14
Waiters	14	181	Laundry and dry-cleaning workers	11	121
All employed	5	49,544	All employed	3	43,445

Note: Data refer to employed men and women ages 25–54 and show recent immigrants as a percent of total employment in each occupation by sex. Recent immigrants are those arriving since 1990. Rankings are limited to occupations that employed at least 10,000 men or women.

Source: Authors' calculations using Census 2000 1% Public Use Microdata Sample (PUMS).

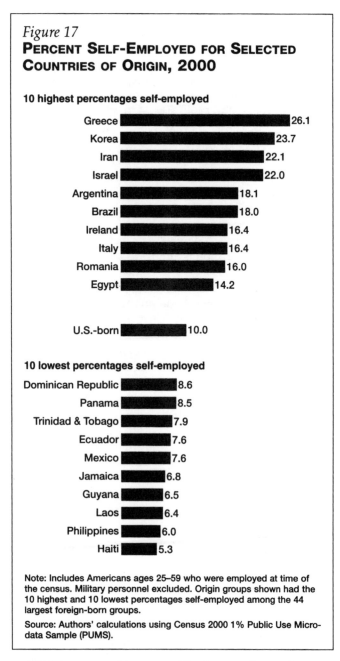

in 2000, four were European. The largest share of European self-employed operated businesses in the construction sector. This pattern of self-employment in construction holds for both sexes.

The popular image of the immigrant entrepreneur is of a man and his wife and perhaps their children operating a small family-based restaurant or grocery store in an ethnic neighborhood. There is some basis for that image for some origin groups, such as Greeks and Italians in the restaurant business. While Chinese and Japanese do not have exceptionally high rates of self-employment, if they are self-employed they are likely to be restaurant owners (26 percent and 22 percent, respectively). The food industry attracts large numbers of foreign-born—14 percent of the foreign-born worked in

that industry in 2000, compared with 7 percent of U.S.-born. Koreans stand out as a group that has both relatively high levels of self-employment (24 percent) and a high concentration in the food industry.[63]

Foreign-born groups from the Middle East also have high rates of self-employment—more than 14 percent of the foreign-born from Israel, Iran, and Egypt. Other Middle Eastern groups with high rates of self-employment include Syrians (30 percent) and Jordanians (20 percent), but those groups are not shown in Figure 17 because they are not among the 44 largest groups.

Economic Status

The economic status of foreign-born households in the United States can be expected to vary significantly given the diversity across origin groups. Diversity in economic status across origins can be assessed by comparing groups in terms of the extent to which their family incomes fall below or exceed the poverty line. The percentage of U.S.-born and foreign-born families with incomes more than five times the poverty line in 1990 and 2000 are represented by bars to the right of the vertical line in Figure 18, while those with incomes below the poverty line are shown to the left of the vertical line. Poverty is measured using 1990 threshold levels and is adjusted for inflation for 2000. Data are shown for the 10 largest foreign-born groups in 1990 and 2000, and for all other foreign-born aggregated by their region of origin. The "Other" category includes foreign-born from the South Pacific, stateless persons, and unclassified others.

Between 1990 and 2000, the poverty status of the U.S.-born remained unchanged. In both periods, 27 percent to 29 percent of the U.S.-born had incomes more than five times above the poverty line, and 10 percent were below. Poverty levels among the foreign-born also remained constant during the two periods at about 17 percent. Mexicans were more likely than any other foreign-born group to be in poverty in both decades, but their share in poverty (26 percent) did not increase in the 1990s even though the Mexican foreign-born grew by 43 percent. Only the foreign-born from the former Soviet Union experienced a sharp increase in poverty in the 1990s, rising from 16 percent to 21 percent. That increase probably occurred because that recent immigrant flow from the former Soviet Union included large numbers of refugees and children who would have been eligible for refugee assistance. However, that group is also relatively well educated, and thus their poverty disadvantage should diminish in the years ahead. A small increase in poverty occurred for the African and South American regional groupings. On the other hand, while Other Asians, Vietnamese, and the heterogeneous "Other" category experienced decreasing poverty levels in the 1990s, the poverty status of most groups remained unchanged.

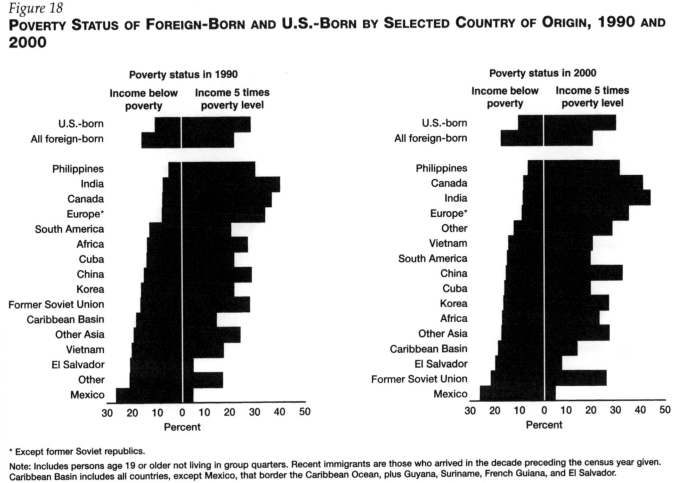

Figure 18

POVERTY STATUS OF FOREIGN-BORN AND U.S.-BORN BY SELECTED COUNTRY OF ORIGIN, 1990 AND 2000

Poverty status in 1990

Income below poverty   Income 5 times poverty level

U.S.-born
All foreign-born

Philippines
India
Canada
Europe*
South America
Africa
Cuba
China
Korea
Former Soviet Union
Caribbean Basin
Other Asia
Vietnam
El Salvador
Other
Mexico

30   20   10   0   10   20   30   40   50
Percent

Poverty status in 2000

Income below poverty   Income 5 times poverty level

U.S.-born
All foreign-born

Philippines
Canada
India
Europe*
Other
Vietnam
South America
China
Cuba
Korea
Africa
Other Asia
Caribbean Basin
El Salvador
Former Soviet Union
Mexico

30   20   10   0   10   20   30   40   50
Percent

* Except former Soviet republics.

Note: Includes persons age 19 or older not living in group quarters. Recent immigrants are those who arrived in the decade preceding the census year given. Caribbean Basin includes all countries, except Mexico, that border the Caribbean Ocean, plus Guyana, Suriname, French Guiana, and El Salvador.

Source: Authors' calculations using the 1% Public Use Microdata Sample (PUMS) from the 1990 and 2000 censuses.

At the other extreme, many foreign-born groups had percentages of households with incomes more than five times the poverty level. In both 1990 and 2000, four groups—Europe, India, Canada, and the Philippines—had higher percentages than did the U.S.-born. In 2000, almost 20 percent of all foreign-born had household incomes of this magnitude. If Mexicans are excluded from the calculation, the percentage of foreign-born with incomes more than five times the poverty level rises to 26 percent, fairly close to the 29 percent of U.S.-born. Between 1990 and 2000, the percent of U.S.-born households with this level of income increased by just under 2 percentage points and reached 29 percent. Eight of the 16 foreign-born categories also had increases of 2 points or greater. Three groups—the former Soviet Union, Africa, and Cuba—experienced declines of at least 2 points; while five—Mexico, Caribbean, South America, Europe, and the Philippines—experienced little change in the proportion of households with relatively high income.

While jobs are a core reason why many foreigners come to America, many foreign-born were out of the labor force at the time of the 2000 Census. This raises questions about the survival strategy of unemployed adults. Do they live with relatives who support them? Do they live off retirement income or investments? Table 7 (page 296) provides data on income sources and activities of nonworking men and women ages 21 to 65 by nativity status in 2000. If U.S.-born men were not working, they were likely to be receiving Social Security or other retirement income (47 percent) or to be in a household that had other members working (49 percent). Nonworking foreign-born men, in contrast, usually lived in households that had other members working (65 percent). Only 17 percent of foreign-born men received Social Security and 10 percent received some other form of public assistance or Supplemental Security Income (SSI), compared with 16 percent of U.S.-born men. In addition, 15 percent of nonworking foreign-born men were in school, compared with 7 percent of U.S.-born men. The relatively high levels of school attendance among foreign-born men are consistent with the presence of large numbers of nonimmigrant resident

Table 7

ECONOMIC ACTIVITIES AND SOURCES OF SUPPORT FOR PERSONS NOT EMPLOYED IN THE YEAR BEFORE THE CENSUS, BY NATIVITY AND GENDER, 2000

	Men		Women	
	U.S.-born	Foreign-born	U.S.-born	Foreign-born
Looking for work (%)	7	9	4	5
Receiving any investment income (%)	17	7	10	4
Receiving public assistance or SSI (%)	16	10	13	9
Receiving Social Security or other retirement income (%)	47	17	23	9
Attending school (%)	7	15	6	9
With other household members working (%)	49	65	65	80
With other household members receiving public assistance or SSI (%)	8	9	5	5
With other household members receiving investment income (%)	12	10	22	16
With other household members receiving Social Security or other retirement income (%)	15	8	14	7
Median age (years)	48	40	46	41

Note: Statistics are based on population ages 21–65 and not residing in group quarters. School and unemployment status are at the time of the census rather than the prior year. SSI refers to Supplementary Security Income.

Source: Authors' calculations using Census 2000 1% Public Use Microdata Sample (PUMS).

students in the United States. Only a small percentage of foreign-born and U.S.-born men who were not employed at the time of the census said they were looking for work—9 percent and 7 percent, respectively.

Among nonworking adult women, both U.S.-born and foreign-born women were about 15 percentage points more likely than their male counterparts to live in a household where another member worked. Whereas U.S.-born women were only half as likely as U.S.-born men to be receiving Social Security or other retirement income, they were more than twice as likely as foreign-born women to have income from that source. Nevertheless, regardless of nativity, nonworking women were less likely than men to be receiving Social Security income or investment income or attending school. Moreover, nonworking U.S.-born and foreign-born women were more likely than their male counterparts to be in a household where another household member received investment income, but just as likely as men to live in a household where another member received Social Security or other retirement income. Only a small share of women not in the labor force said they were looking for work.

FUTURE DIRECTIONS

Immigration has been and continues to be a significant force in building and changing America. But the forces that drive immigration today differ greatly from those that shaped earlier waves. While immigration used to be driven by America's need to populate its empty lands and obtain workers for its growing industries, immigration is now increasingly driven by forces that extend beyond America's borders and stem from growing interdependencies between countries. The forces shaping migration today are complex, as are the processes by which the growing foreign-born population is altering America's social landscape. This complexity is reflected in the growing diversity of immigrants' origins; in the presence of large numbers of highly educated migrants alongside equally large numbers of poorly educated migrants; and in the widening range of social, economic, and political scenarios emerging as the foreign-born settle and disperse throughout the United States.

A theme sounded throughout this report is that some immigration to the United States, possibly even a growing volume of immigration, will continue because international migration is now an integral element of international commerce, politics, and society. The number of foreigners who come to the United States to live or work (in particular, as nonimmigrant residents) is likely to continue to grow in number, as will the number of foreigners who seek admission because they have become an immediate relative of a U.S. citizen. Increases in the latter will occur because immigration law allows U.S.-born Americans and naturalized citizens to bring in their immediate family members. It is unlikely that this policy will change, nor should it change. Thus, as interactions between Americans expand both in the United States and abroad, marriages ensue and help build immigration momentum.[64] While permanent immigrants and unauthorized migrants also want the right to bring in their immediate family members, their right to do so is likely to remain restricted.

Other foreigners will need to be admitted to America in the years ahead for humanitarian reasons. In a world awash in civil and ethnic conflicts, international military actions, and nation-building, and if U.S. involvement in these international affairs continues, there will likely be more and more refugees, and some will have to be resettled in America. Given the leadership role and engagement of the United States in political conflicts throughout the world, it will be necessary to open our doors to foreigners whose lives have become endangered because of their political support for or military service to the United States.

If U.S. immigration is to be altered or reduced, more control must be exerted over unauthorized migration. A hot debate exists among immigration experts, however, regarding whether it is possible or even desirable to control unauthorized migration. Critics of regulation often argue that unauthorized migration from Mexico cannot be controlled because of the history and geography that binds Mexico to the United States. NAFTA and other integration efforts between North America, Mexico, and other countries in the Caribbean and Latin America are likely to strengthen and to generate increased demand for migration among countries in the region. Douglas Massey argues that the United States should recognize the special relationship between Mexico and the United States and set up a temporary worker program to admit Mexicans to work in the United States.[65] According to his argument, it is better to bring that movement into the open in order to reduce its negative effects on migrants and the economy. He also argues that increased efforts to deter unauthorized migrants in dense urban areas at the Mexican border are ineffective and only shift flows to remote rural areas where the risks to migrants are greatly increased. Other proponents of this view point to the social networks between unauthorized migrants and their homelands that recruit new migrants, and they argue that increased government efforts to control these flows will drive migrants further underground and increase their exploitation.[66]

Experts who believe that unauthorized migration should be controlled make three points. First, for a democracy built on law and order, it is inconsistent to ignore either the implications that large numbers of unauthorized migrants have for the economy and society or the potentially discriminatory effects of unauthorized status on the migrants themselves. A correlate of this argument is that prospective immigrants from other origins are encouraged to join the flow of unauthorized migration to America, since deportation is unlikely if they successfully make it past America's borders.

Second, opponents point to the economic effects of maintaining a large pool of unauthorized workers willing to work for low wages on the wage rates and employment levels of U.S.-born unskilled workers in general and U.S.-born minorities in particular. Nonetheless, while economic theory suggests that negative labor market effects should occur, empirical studies of the impact of immi-

grant workers have produced inconsistent findings. One reason may be that U.S.-born workers adjust by migrating out of metropolitan labor markets that receive large numbers of unauthorized migrant workers.[67]

Third, those who advocate immigration control argue that unauthorized migration could be controlled through serious policy reforms. The lack of political will to do something about unauthorized migration, in turn, these analysts argue, is reinforced by lobbying efforts from a diverse group of well-organized political constituencies. One group that has lobbied effectively for benign neglect consists of agricultural and other employers who benefit from the presence of foreign workers. While some employers argue forcefully that American workers are unavailable for the low-wage jobs that foreigners are willing to fill, other employers argue that highly skilled migrants are needed to keep America's science and technology industries competitive. Strong lobbying against stricter immigration control also comes from a range of political and advocacy groups who believe that foreigners already here should be permitted to stay if they are gainfully employed and not disturbing the peace. Some groups think in terms of how immigration might affect political alignments over the long run.[68] Politicians hesitate to act because of concern over how immigration policy reform will affect the next election. Together, these forces have led to a strong political alignment against change in immigration policy that crosscuts traditional liberal and conservative ideologies and party lines.

Immigration experts of all persuasions agree that border deterrence has been ineffective as a means of controlling unauthorized immigration. Therefore, if unauthorized migration is to be slowed, the options that remain would be to try to reduce unauthorized immigration through improved internal enforcement. The development of secure national identity cards and a system to allow employers to verify work eligibility are essential elements of improved enforcement. While momentum is building in the United States for some form of temporary worker program, skeptics point to the experience of Europe in the 1960s and 1970s. As Western Europe recovered from World War II, countries in that region set up temporary worker programs to meet labor demands. However, when their economies slowed in the early 1970s, the countries that had those programs found that temporary workers had become permanent and that large-scale deportation of foreign workers was inconsistent with their liberal democracies. Thus, the temporary workers stayed in Europe and Europe's immigration stock has continued to grow through family reunification.

Future policy directions will play an important and perhaps even decisive role in determining the directions that immigration to America will take. Although immigration policy is difficult to formulate, legislate, and successfully implement, it is nonetheless clear that immigration to the United States throughout its history has been extensively shaped by a series of federal policies, and continues to be shaped during the Globalization Wave by a growing and often contradictory set of policies. Given the controversy that surrounds immigration policy discussions, now may be the time to set up another bipartisan commission to look at U.S. immigration trends and policies. The last comprehensive review of U.S. immigration policy was undertaken by the bipartisan U.S. Commission on Immigration Reform a decade ago. That commission came down strongly on the side of continued legal immigration, noting the contributions that immigrants have made to American society and the opportunities that immigration presents for the nation. While another commission would have to build on the policy changes made by Congress since then and address increased concerns over national security, the critical questions to be addressed today are the same ones asked by the 1990 commission:

- How do we ensure that immigration is based on and supports broad national economic, social, and humanitarian interests rather than the interest of those who would abuse our laws?
- How do we gain effective control over our borders while still encouraging international trade, investment, and tourism?
- How do we maintain a civic culture based on shared values while accommodating the large and diverse population admitted through immigration policy?[69]

These questions remain unanswered. The last commission did lay out a number of measures that would regain control over immigration, and those recommendations should be looked at again as the United States decides what direction its immigration should take. At the same time, it has to be recognized that the world has greatly changed since 9/11. More people now recognize that the government needs to do a better job of monitoring who enters and exits the country and for what purposes. While this recognition is linked to security concerns rather than to specific concerns over the desired size and composition of immigration, measures taken for national security reasons have implications for immigration policy and thus become an important part of the picture.

As long as concern continues over national security at home, technologies, staffing, and policies for managing the entry and exit of foreigners are likely to become more sophisticated, even though the exact form of evolving controls remains to be determined. Should biometric data be used to manage immigration? Should there be secure identity cards for Americans and foreigners in America? Does America's tolerant attitude toward unauthorized migration compromise efforts to enhance security? Will measures taken to increase control of America's borders reduce American's civil liberties?

As momentum and pressure for immigration continue to grow, it has become increasingly important to address these issues in order to reach consensus on the future direction of immigration to America.

ACKNOWLEDGMENTS

We are particularly grateful to Kai Schafft for producing the county maps for this report; and to him and Lew Lama, Pilar Parra, Max Pfeffer, and the anonymous reviewers engaged by the Population Reference Bureau and Russell Sage Foundation, who gave us valuable feedback and suggestions on drafts of this report.

REFERENCES

If provided by the authors, additional text and data associated with this report are available at www.prb.org/AmericanPeople.

1. U.S. Census Bureau, "U.S. Interim Projections by Age, Sex, Race, and Hispanic Origin, 2004," accessed online at www.census.gov/ipc/www/usinterimproj/, on Aug. 27, 2004.
2. U.S. Census Bureau, "U.S. Interim Projections": table 1a.
3. Vernon M. Briggs, Jr., *Immigration Policy and the American Labor Force* (Baltimore: Johns Hopkins University Press, 1984); and David M. Reimers, *Still the Golden Door: The Third World Comes to America* (New York: Columbia University Press, 1985).
4. Philip Martin and Elizabeth Midgely, "Immigration: Shaping and Reshaping America," *Population Bulletin* 58, no. 2 (2003): 11–14.
5. Fernand Braudel, *The Perspective of the World: Civilization and Capitalism 15th-18th Century*, Vol. 3 (New York: Harper and Row, 1979): 396.
6. Mary M. Kritz, "The British and Spanish Migration Systems in the Colonial Era: A Policy Framework," in *The Peopling of the Americas, Conference Proceedings*, ed. International Union for the Scientific Study of Population (1992): 263–81.
7. Richard N. Current, T. Harry Williams, and Frank Freidel, *American History: A Survey* (New York: Alfred A. Knopf, 1967): 30.
8. Philip D. Curtin, "The Atlantic Slave Trade, 1600–1800," in *History of West Africa*, Vol. 1, ed. J.F. Ade Ajayi and Michael Crowder (Harlow Essex, England: Longman House, 1981): 313–15.

9. Briggs, *Immigration Policy:* 17.

10. Briggs, *Immigration Policy:* 26.

11. Richard D. Alba and Victor Nee, *Remaking the American Mainstream: Assimilation and Contemporary Immigration* (Cambridge, MA: Harvard University Press, 2003): 200.

12. Maurice R. Davie, *World Immigration* (New York: Macmillan Co., 1936): 308–9.

13. Martin and Midgley, "Immigration: Shaping and Reshaping America": 15.

14. Davie, *World Immigration:* 88–89.

15. Davie, *World Immigration:* 92–96.

16. Davie, *World Immigration:* 97.

17. Current, Williams, and Freidel, *American History:* 516.

18. Davie, *World Immigration:* 107–83.

19. Davie, *World Immigration:* 510–18.

20. Briggs, *Immigration Policy:* 43.

21. A listing of federal immigration and naturalization policy from 1790 to the present can be accessed online at http://uscis.gov/graphics/shared/aboutus/statistics/legishist/index.htm.

22. Immanuel Wallerstein, *The Modern World System II: Mercantilism and the Consolidation of the European World-Economy, 1600–1750* (New York: Academic Press, 1980); Saskia Sassen, *The Mobility of Labor and Capital: A Study in International Investment and Labour Flow* (Cambridge, England: Cambridge University Press, 1988); and Douglas S. Massey et al., *Worlds in Motion: Understanding International Migration at the End of the Millennium* (Oxford, England: Oxford University Press, 1998).

23. United Nations High Commissioner for Refugees (UNHCR), *Refugees by Numbers 2003* (Geneva: UNHCR, 2003): 4.

24. U.S. Department of Homeland Security, *Yearbook of Immigration Statistics* (Washington, D.C.: U.S. Government Printing Office, 2003): 6–7.

25. Martin and Midgley, "Immigration: Shaping and Reshaping America": 17.

26. Pia M. Orrenius and Madeline Zavodny, "Do Amnesty Programs Reduce Undocumented Immigration?" *Demography* 40, no. 3 (2003): 439.

27. Information on the U.S. Border Patrol can be accessed online at www.cbp.gov.

28. U.S. Department of Homeland Security, *Yearbook of Immigration Statistics:* 213.

29. Michael E. Fix and Jeffrey S. Passel, "U.S. Immigration at the Beginning of the 21st Century," testimony before the U.S. House of Representatives Committee on the Judiciary, Subcommittee on Immigration and Claims (Aug. 2, 2001), accessed online at www.urban.org/url.cfm?ID=900417, on Aug. 28, 2004.

30. U.S. Department of Homeland Security, *Yearbook of Immigration Statistics:* 56.

31. United Nations Population Division, *International Migration 2002* (New York: United Nations, 2003).

32. Jennifer Cheeseman Day, "Population Projections of the United States by Age, Sex, Race and Hispanic Origin: 1995 to 2050," *Current Population Reports*, P25–1130 (Washington, DC: U.S. Government Printing Office, 1996).

33. Hania Zlotnik, "Empirical Identification of International Migration Systems," *International Migration Systems: A Global Approach*, ed. Mary M. Kritz, Lin Lean Lim, and Hania Zlotnik (Oxford, England: Oxford University Press, 1998).

34. Kritz, Lim, and Zlotnik, *International Migration Systems*.

35. Francisco Alba, "Mexico: A Crucial Crossroads," *Migration Information Source* (Washington, DC: Migration Policy Institute, July 2002), accessed online at www.migrationinformation.org/feature/display.cfm?ID=211, on Aug. 28, 2004.

36. This report draws heavily on Public Use Microdata Samples (PUMS) from the 1960 to 2000 censuses. All of the 1% sample files were obtained from the Integrated Public Use Microdata Series (IPUMS) website based at the University of Minnesota (Steven Ruggles and Matthew Sobek et al., "Integrated Public Use Microdata Series: Version 3.0." Minneapolis: Historical Census Projects, University of Minnesota, 2003, www.ipums.org. The 5% PUMS files for 1980, 1990, and 2000 were also utilized. The 1980 and 1990 5% files were obtained from the data archive of the Cornell Institute for Social and Economic Research (CISER). For the 1960 and 2000 censuses, only one version of a 1% PUMS file exists. For 1990, we used the 1% Metro file. For 1980, we used the 1% Metro (B Sample). For 1970 it was necessary to utilize four 1% files, including both the Form 1 and Form 2 versions of the State and Metro samples. Most population estimates in this report are simply the weighted estimates from the 1% files. While these estimates are very close to those obtainable from larger databases such as aggregate reports and "American FactFinder" (www.census.gov), some insignificant deviations do occur.

37. For excellent summaries of immigration from selected Asian countries (Philippines, China, Vietnam, India, and Korea) and other countries in the Americas (Mexico, the Dominican Republic, Cuba, Jamaica, and El Salvador), see Alba and Nee, *Remaking the American Mainstream:* 167–214.

38. Alba and Nee, *Remaking the American Mainstream:* 205.

39. Alba and Nee, *Remaking the American Mainstream:* 208–9.

40. J. Edward Taylor and Douglas S. Massey, *International Migration: Prospects and Policies* (Oxford, England: IUSSP/OUP Series on International Studies in Demography, Oxford University Press, 2004).

41. UN Department for Economic and Social Information and Policy Analysis, *International Migration Policies and the Status of Female Migrants* (New York: UN Population Division, 1995); and Monica Boyd and Elizabeth Grieco, "Women and Migration: Incorporating Gender into International Migration Theory," *Migration Policy Institute Working Paper* (Washington, DC: Migration Policy Institute, 2003), accessed online at www.migrationinformation.org/Feature/display.cfm?ID=106, on Aug. 28, 2004.

42. Douglas T. Gurak and Mary M. Kritz, "The Interstate Migration of U.S. Immigrants: Individual and Contextual Determinants," *Social Forces* 78, no. 3 (2000): 1017–39.

43. Mary M. Kritz and June Marie Nogle, "Nativity Concentration and Internal Migration among the Foreign-Born," *Demography* 31, no. 3 (1994): 509–24; and Gurak and Kritz, "Interstate Migration."

44. Alba and Nee, *Remaking the American Mainstream:* 111–13.

45. William H. Frey and Kao-Lee Liaw, "The Impact of Recent Immigration on Population Redistribution Within the United States," in *The Immigration Debate*, ed. James P. Smith and Barry Edmonston (Washington, DC: Urban Institute Press, 1998): 388–448.

46. George J. Borjas, *Heaven's Door: Immigration Policy and the American Economy* (Princeton, NJ: Princeton University Press, 2001): ch. 2.

47. Reynolds Farley, *The New American Reality: Who We Are, How We Got Here, Where We Are Going* (New York: Russell Sage Foundation, 1996): 175–76.

48. Aristide R. Zolberg, Astri Suhrke, and Sergio Aguayo, *Escape From Violence: Conflict and the Refugee Crisis in the Developing World* (New York: Oxford University Press, 1989): 26–27.

49. Nathan Glazer, *Affirmative Discrimination*, as cited in Richard D. Alba and Victor Nee, *Remaking the American Mainstream: Assimilation and Contemporary Immigration* (Cambridge, MA: Harvard University Press, 2003): 143.

50. Alba and Nee, *Remaking the American Mainstream*: 72.

51. Mary M. Kritz, Douglas T. Gurak, and Likwang Chen, "Elderly Immigrants: Their Composition and Living Arrangements," *Journal of Sociology and Social Welfare* 27, no. 1 (2000), special issue on "The Changing American Mosaic": 85–114.

52. Barbara Jordan, as quoted in *Embracing America: A Look at Which Immigrants Become Citizens*, Leon Bouvier (Washington, DC: Center for Immigration Studies, *Center Paper* 11, 1996): 6, accessed online at www.cis.org/articles/embamer/embracing.html, on Aug. 28, 2004.

53. Robert F. Worth, "Push Is on to Give Legal Immigrants Vote in New York," *New York Times*, April 8, 2004.

54. Michael E. Fix, Jeffrey S. Passel, and Kenneth Sucher, "Trends in Naturalization," *The Urban Institute Series on Immigrant Families and Workers: Facts and Perspectives*, Policy Brief 3 (Sept. 17, 2003), accessed online at www.urban.org/urlprint.cfm?ID=8580, on Aug. 27, 2004.

55. George J. Borjas, "The Labor Demand Curve Is Downward Sloping: Reexamining the Impact of Immigration on the Labor Market," *The Quarterly Journal of Economics* (November 2003): 1335–74; David Card, "Immigrant Inflows, Native Outflows, and the Local Labor Market Impacts of Higher Immigration," *Journal of Labor Economics* 19, no. 1 (2001): 22–64; and James P. Smith and Barry Edmonston, eds. *The New Americans: Economic, Demographic, and Fiscal Effects of Immigration* (Washington, DC: National Research Council, 1997).

56. Yinon Cohen and Yitchak Haberfeld, "The Number of Israeli Immigrants in the U.S. in 1990," *Discussion Paper* 92 (Tel Aviv: Golda Meir Institute for Social and Labour Research, Tel Aviv University, May 1997): table 7.

57. Niara Sudarkasa, "Where Women Work: A Study of Yoruba Women in the Market Place and in the Home," *Anthropological Papers* 53 (Ann Arbor, MI: Museum of Anthropology, University of Michigan, 1973); Henrietta L. Moore, *Feminism and Anthropology* (Minneapolis: University of Minnesota Press, 1988); and Niara Sudarkasa, "The 'Status of Women' in Indigenous African Societies," in *Women in Africa and the African Diaspora*, ed. Rosalyn Terborg-Penn, Sharon Harley, and Andrea Benton Rushing (Washington, DC: Howard University Press, 1987).

58. Ajayi and Crowder, *History of West Africa*: 322–25.

59. Joan R. Kahn and Leslie A. Whittington, "The Labor Supply of Latinas in the United States: Comparing Labor Force Participation, Wages, and Hours Worked With Anglo and Black Women," *Population Research and Policy Review* 15, no. 1 (1996): 45–73.

60. In order to be able to compare occupations across censuses, we use the IPUMS occupational recode categories, which are based on the coding scheme used in the 1950 census. The description of these codes can be accessed online at www.ipums.org.

61. Philip Martin, "Immigration and the Changing Face of Rural America," accessed online at www.farmfoundation.org/martin/martin.htm, on Aug. 28, 2004.

62. Alejandro Portes and Robert Bach, *Latin Journey: Cuban and Mexican Immigrants in the United States* (Berkeley: University of California Press, 1985).

63. Ivan H. Light and Edna Bonacich, *Immigrant Entrepreneurs: Koreans in Los Angeles, 1965–1982* (Berkeley: University of California Press, 1988).

64. Guillermina Jasso and Mark R. Rosenzweig, *The New Chosen People: Immigrants in the United States* (New York: National Committee for Research on the 1980 Census, Russell Sage Foundation, 1990).

65. Douglas S. Massey, Jorge Durand, and Nolan J. Malone, *Beyond Smoke and Mirrors: Mexican Immigration in an Era of Economic Integration* (New York: Russell Sage Foundation, 2002).

66. Alejandro Portes and Rubén G. Rumbaut, *Immigrant America: A Portrait* (Berkeley: University of California Press, 1990): 232–39.

67. Smith and Edmonston, eds. *The New Americans*: 225–28.

68. Dudley L. Poston, Jr., Steven A. Camarota, and Amanda K. Baumie, "Remaking the Political Landscape: The Impact of Illegal and Legal Immigration on Congressional Apportionment," *Center for Immigration Studies Backgrounder* (October 2003); and James G. Gimpel, "Latinos and the 2002 Election: Republicans Do Well When Latinos Stay Home," *Center for Immigration Studies Backgrounder* (January 2003).

69. U.S. Commission on Immigration Reform, *U.S. Immigration Policy: Restoring Credibility*, 1994 Report to Congress, accessed online at www.utexas.edu/lbj/uscir/, on Aug. 28, 2004.

FOR FURTHER READING

Alba, Richard D., and Victor Nee. *Remaking the American Mainstream: Assimilation and Contemporary Immigration.* Cambridge, MA: Harvard University Press, 2003.

Bean, Frank D., and Gillian Stevens. *America's Newcomers and the Dynamics of Diversity.* New York: Russell Sage Foundation, 2003.

Borjas, George J. *Heaven's Door: Immigration Policy and the American Economy.* Princeton, NJ: Princeton University Press, 2001.

Briggs, Vernon M., Jr. *Mass Immigration and the National Interest: Policy Directions for the New Century.* 3d ed. Armonk, NY: M.E. Sharpe, 2003.

Castles, Stephen, and Mark J. Miller. *The Age of Migration: International Population Movements in the Modern World.* 3d ed. New York: The Guilford Press, 2003.

Farley, Reynolds. *The New American Reality: Who We Are, How We Got Here, Where We Are Going.* New York: Russell Sage Foundation, 1996.

Hirschman, Charles, Philip Kasinitz, and Josh DeWind, eds. *The Handbook of International Migration: The American Experience.* New York: Russell Sage Foundation, 1999.

Huntington, Samuel P. *The Challenges to America's National Identity.* New York: Simon and Schuster, 2004.

Jasso, Guillermina, and Mark R. Rosenzweig. *The New Chosen People: Immigrants in the United States.* New York: Russell Sage Foundation, 1990.

Martin, Philip, and Elizabeth Midgley. "Immigration: Shaping and Reshaping America." *Population Bulletin* 58, no. 2 (2003).

Portes, Alejandro, and Rubén G. Rumbaut. *Immigrant America: A Portrait.* Berkeley: University of California Press, 1990.

Smith, James, and Barry Edmonston, eds. *The New Americans: Economic, Demographic, and Fiscal Effects of Immigration.* Washington, DC: National Research Council, 1997.

Taylor, J. Edward, and Douglas S. Massey, eds. *International Migration: Prospects and Policies.* New York: IUSSP Series on International Studies in Population, Oxford University Press, 2004.

Waldinger, Roger, ed. *Strangers at the Gate: New Immigrants in Urban America.* Berkeley: University of California Press, 2001.

Zolberg, Aristide R., Astri Suhrke, and Sergio Aguayo. *Escape From Violence: Conflict and the Refugee Crisis in the Developing World.* New York: Oxford University Press, 1989.

Immigration and Fading Color Lines in America

By Frank D. Bean, Jennifer Lee, Jeanne Batalova, and Mark Leach

INTRODUCTION

In 1965, after 40 years of relatively low immigration, Congress passed the Hart-Celler Act, eliminating national origin quotas and reopening the nation's doors to increased flows of immigrants. One of the most dramatic and ongoing consequences of this legislation has been the diversification of the racial and ethnic landscape of the United States, a shift that has occurred for two primary reasons. First, immigrants coming to the United States over the past three to four decades, unlike those who arrived in the early years of the 20th century, have been mainly non-Europeans. During the 1980s and 1990s, for example, more than four of five came from Asia, Latin America, or the Caribbean, with only about one in seven originating in Europe or Canada. Second, the absolute number of newcomers settling in the country has been sizable. For example, 34 million foreign-born people lived in the United States in 2002 (after adjusting for the census undercount), with the size of the U.S.-born second generation numbering around 32 million, so that immigrants and their children together totaled almost 66 million people, or about 23 percent of the U.S. population.[1] Demographers expect the numbers of foreign-born who are non-European to remain high. As a result, according to National Research Council projections, Latinos and Asians could triple their shares of the U.S. population by the year 2050, growing to about 25 percent and 8 percent of total population, respectively.

These new immigrants have changed a largely biracial black-white nation with a very large white majority into a society composed of several racial and ethnic groups. Some observers find the arrival of contemporary immigrants a cause for concern, seemingly because of worries that the nonwhite population has been growing so rapidly. In a country where the black-white color line has historically constituted a sharp and impenetrable divide, those who assume that such fault lines are part of the natural order of things may worry about the growth of the nonwhite population, particularly if they perceive nonwhite newcomers as more similar to the black population than the white population. If matters of race (and most specifically black-white relations) have constituted the most intractable domestic difficulty the country has faced in its history, some may presume that an influx of mostly nonwhites will cause such problems to persist long into the future.

But immigrant newcomers from Latin America and Asia are neither black nor white. Their arrival and presence calls into question the relevance of the traditional U.S. black-white model, which reflects the legacy of slavery including its contemporary forms of discrimination and resultant socioeconomic disadvantages.[2] Because most of today's immigrants are nonwhite, they could be helping to break down the old black-white color line, challenging the very meaning of race in the United States and moving the nation beyond the traditional bipolar demarcation that has plagued the country. This fault line was famously forecast a century ago by the prominent African American social theorist W.E.B. DuBois when he noted that the "problem of the 20th century is the problem of the color-line."[3] Writing in 1903, itself a time of substantial immigration, DuBois could hardly have anticipated that America's racial and ethnic makeup would, as a result of immigration, so drastically shift by the late 20th century.

If the arrival of unprecedented numbers of Asians and Latinos is rendering a black-white portrait of America anachronistic, what is emerging to take its place? Is the old line disappearing altogether? Are new

FRANK D. BEAN is professor of sociology and co-director of the Center for Research on Immigration, Population and Public Policy at the University of California, Irvine. His areas of research and writing include Mexican migration to the United States, international migration, the economic sociology of U.S. immigration, family and fertility, the sociology and demography of racial and ethnic groups, and population policy.

JENNIFER LEE is associate professor of sociology at the University of California, Irvine. Her research interests include race/ethnicity, immigration, the new second generation, and multiracial identification.

JEANNE BATALOVA is a Ph.D. candidate in the Department of Sociology at the University of California, Irvine. Her research interests include skilled and professional migration, impacts of immigration on social structures and labor markets, and immigrant incorporation and mobility. Her dissertation focuses on the labor market implications of highly skilled migration in the United States.

MARK LEACH is a graduate student of sociology at University of California, Irvine. His research interests include immigrant incorporation, new settlement patterns of Mexican migrants in the United States, and historical Chinese immigration during the so-called Exclusion Era. Prior to his graduate studies, he was a business consultant.

lines emerging? If so, where are they being drawn? Or are shifts toward relatively easy boundary crossings occurring for some groups but not others? These questions are fraught with theoretical and social significance. Their answers are critical for social scientists and policymakers seeking to understand today's demographic scene and the changing nature of America's color lines.

This report seeks to ascertain whether today's immigrants are helping to blur racial and ethnic boundaries generally in the United States, whether immigrants are causing new color lines to emerge, or whether some of America's newcomers (but not others) are simply more easily able to traverse old color lines without eradicating them.[4] How are immigration and the experiences of immigrants in the United States changing both the racial and ethnic composition of the United States and ideas about race and ethnicity in America? The answers draw on current theories, recent research findings, and new data from the 2000 Census. We examined the volume and racial or ethnic composition of recent immigration and key aspects of immigrant economic and sociocultural incorporation, and focused on immigrant-group job quality and mobility, annual earnings, intermarriage, and multiracial identification.

Our analysis of recent immigration trends and patterns points to shifts in America's color lines.

THEMES OF CHANGING DIVERSITY

The central issue—the implications of immigration for changing racial and ethnic diversity in the United States—can be parsed into four closely related themes:

- How the concept of race has been historically measured in the U.S. Census. Several factors have influenced its change over time, including immigration patterns and trends.
- How immigration has affected both the nation's population growth and its racial and ethnic composition over the past 30 years or so. Furthermore, how have these patterns and trends varied in different parts of the country?
- Whether, given that most of today's immigrants are nonwhite, it is harder for them to become part of mainstream America than it was for earlier European immigrants. Some observers think this may be the case because nonwhite racial or ethnic groups in this country typically exhibit lower levels of education and earnings than whites. If the lower education and income levels occur because immigrants generally start out at the bottom of the socioeconomic ladder and are working their way up, one would expect to find considerable job mobility

among recent immigrants to the United States. If the lower education and income levels are due to racial or ethnic discrimination, one would expect to find considerably less mobility.
- Whether immigration is leading to changing ideas about race and color in America. Is it possible that immigration and immigrant incorporation may be modifying the very notions of how we view race and ethnicity, moving them from the relatively immutable categories of the past to much more dynamic and fluid notions today? The changes in racial identification that have moved many ethnic groups from nonwhite to white, or almost white, vividly illustrate that race is a cultural (rather than biological) category, one that has expanded over time to include new immigrant groups.

If racial and ethnic boundaries have stretched in the past and are continuing to do so now, questions emerge about the degree to which racial and ethnic divides are now fading, persisting in relatively unchanged form, or changing for some of today's immigrants but not others. While it is difficult to predict where new racial or ethnic boundaries are being drawn, demographic trends in intermarriage and reports of multiracial identities can provide a sense of the directions in the changes that the color lines appear to have taken up to this point in time.

Evolving Notions of Race

Such concepts as "nonwhite" and "race" have a complex and changing nature. For example, determining exactly who is a member of the nonwhite population is difficult, not only because the concept of race is problematic (and its measurement ambiguous and always changing), but also because nonwhites are hardly a monolithic group. Moreover, race must be recognized as a social and cultural rather than a biological category. To this end, contemporary social science research has documented the processes by which ethnic and racial boundaries have changed throughout this nation's history. For instance, previous immigrant groups—such as Irish, Italians, and Eastern European Jews—came to be viewed as white, often by deliberately distinguishing themselves from blacks. Historians such as Noel Ignatiev and Matthew Freye Jacobson describe how European ethnics (initially viewed as nonwhite) went to extreme measures to distance themselves from black Americans in order to achieve whiteness.[5]

Irish, Italians, and Eastern European Jews are not the only groups to have changed their status from nonwhite to white. Asian national origin groups also changed their racial status from nonwhite to almost white. James Loewen, for example, documents how Chinese Americans in the Mississippi Delta made conscious efforts to change their lowly status by achieving economic mobility, emulating the cultural practices of whites, intentionally distancing themselves from blacks, and rejecting both Chinese who married blacks and their Chinese-black multiracial children.[6] Paul Spickard notes a similar process of change among Japanese Americans, who were once with blacks at the bottom of the racial group ladder at the beginning of the 20th century but whose status had improved dramatically three-quarters of a century later.[7]

Many social scientists have noted that the very fact that Irish, Italians, and Jews were not subject to the same type of systematic legal discrimination as African Americans illustrates that they were on a different plane to begin with, a standing that facilitated their eventual racial treatment as whites. Moreover, the disappearance of national origin differences among European ethnics and the discontinuation of tendencies to view such differences not only in racial terms but in rigid black-white terms contributed to the development of the idea that, for many European immigrants, race could be modified rather than being fixed forever. But this was likely because such people were viewed as nonwhite rather than black. In the early 20th century's rigidly compartmentalized black-white world, governed by the "one-drop rule" of ancestry (which emphasized pure whiteness versus everything else), not being white did not mean actually being black, but it was perhaps often like being black. Thus, it is not surprising that certain national origin groups were sometimes treated as nonwhite. However, because in fact they were not black (in the sense of being the descendants of African origin who had been slaves), their status was eventually allowed to change, thus hastening the evolution and acceptance of the idea that at least some racial categories—maybe all except black—could be modified. That racial and ethnic boundaries have changed in the past (and will likely continue to stretch) illustrates that race is a dynamic rather than a fixed concept.

Something akin to a tripartite racial classification system has emerged in the United States, at least in a *de facto* sense. There are people who consistently report being white. There are people who consistently report being black. And there also are people who are not black but who do not appear to place themselves in the white category, at least not at the moment. Many of the recent Hispanic and Asian immigrants seem to be in this nonwhite category. A mixed-race class is also emerging, one that is formed by people crossing these tripartite group boundaries. The formation of this group indicates that it is much easier to cross the nonwhite to white line than it is to move out of the black class. It also implies that a new diversity in America is eroding color lines, although less for blacks than for others, and that the matter of race in America may be more dynamic than ever.

MEASURING RACE IN THE CENSUS

In order to assess how immigration has affected the racial and ethnic composition of the U.S. population over the past 35 years, one must understand how race and ethnicity have been measured by the census. The U.S. Constitution mandates an enumeration of the country's population every 10 years for the purpose of congressional apportionment. Since its inception in 1790, the census has been used to determine a national system of taxation, the number of U.S. representatives from each state, and the boundaries of congressional districts. Along with gender and age, the census has always counted the U.S. population by race, although in 1790, "color"—and not "race"—was the primary term of classification.

However, even before the first census was completed, Congress had to decide who should be counted, and in particular whether slaves should be counted as the equivalent of free people for the purposes of taxation. While Northerners contended that slaves should be the equivalent of free persons, Southerners argued that they should be counted as only a fraction of free persons. In 1783, Congress decided on a compromise, approving a motion to count states' slave populations at a ratio of three-fifths of their free populations.[8] Slavery was based on the system of racial hierarchy and oppression, and the counting of slaves as three-fifths of free people significantly marked the legitimization and institutionalization of the black-white color line in government policy and practice. Throughout the nation's history, color or race has been a central organizing principle of political, social, legal, and economic life, and census practices have often mirrored this emphasis.

Today, the Office of Management and Budget (OMB) largely determines which racial and ethnic categories the federal government uses in its statistical systems. In 1977, OMB standardized racial and ethnic categories to allow for consistent reporting and recording of federal data.[9] This classification scheme provides a basis for assessing compliance with civil rights directives and legislation on the part of both the public and private sectors, including the U.S. government. Thus, the main purpose of classifying the U.S. population by race and ethnicity does not stem from an interest in categorizing the population along these lines, but rather from one seeking to conform to the Constitution and to monitor and enforce civil rights laws.

Classification

The task of discerning how immigration has changed the nation's racial and ethnic landscape over time is complicated because the racial categories themselves have not remained constant. Although the U.S. government has collected data on race for more than two centuries, the way that race has been measured and even the racial categories themselves have undergone considerable change over time. Categories have been added, dropped, and altered throughout the history of the U.S. Census, so much so that only three racial categories—white, Chinese, and Japanese—consistently appeared on the census enumeration forms in the 20th century.[10] The category involving blacks in the United States has changed considerably. For example, in an attempt to accurately measure the black mixtures in the population, the census added the category mulatto in 1850 and the categories quadroon and octoroon in 1890. However, quadroon and octoroon were removed in 1900 because of inconsistencies in accurately measuring these populations. By 1918, the nation's mulatto population had grown so rapidly that the Census Bureau estimated that at least three-fourths of all blacks in the United States were ancestrally mixed; thus, the Census Bureau concluded that the mulatto category provided clearer data on the population with mixed blood than on the black population.[11] By 1930, however, the Census Bureau had dropped attempts to measure the mulatto population, eliminating the category altogether, partly because mulattos were so numerous and partly because they were not necessarily physically distinguishable from either the black or white populations. Furthermore, the laws of much of the country, with the census following suit, had come to follow the one-drop rule for assigning race.

Even the black category did not remain consistent in the censuses of the 20th century. For example, in 1900 and 1910, the Census used the category black, but in 1920 Negro replaced black and was used in the next four censuses. In 1970, Negro or black appeared as an option, and in the year 2000, the census listed black, African American, or Negro as a racial category. Other racial categories have similarly changed throughout the history of the census. For instance, in 1930 (and in this year alone) Mexican was listed as a possible response to the color or race question. However, the category was dropped from subsequent censuses because the Mexican government and Mexican Americans (at least the elite) strongly objected to the label—they did not consider themselves a separate racial group. Rather, Mexican Americans saw themselves as white and therefore did not want a distinct color or race category.

Census categories also expanded to reflect the arrival of new groups to the nation's shores, such as Asian origin groups that migrated after the mid-19th century. For example, in 1870, the census introduced Chinese as a color category and in 1890 added Japanese as an option. The migration of Filipinos, Hindus, and Koreans led to the addition of these categories in the 1920 Census. These categories remained distinct until 1977, when OMB merged the disparate Asian origin categories under the umbrella category of Asian/Pacific Islander, racializing the Asian national origin groups. In the late 1950s and early 1960s, racial categories came under scrutiny once again, and changes in the measurement of race (prompted in part by the Civil Rights Movement) eventually led to one of the most significant shifts in the political context and purpose of racial categorization. Debate spread that Americans should be able to mark their own race to identify themselves and their children rather than leaving this task to census enumerators. Before self-enumeration, a census taker would designate an individual's race upon visual inspection. Self-enumeration gave individuals control over their own racial identification. Taking into consideration public sentiment and cost, the 1970 Census replaced enumerator identification with self-enumeration, and for the first time the census was taken by mail.

At that time, special interest groups asserted that the racial categories should accurately reflect America's demographic diversity; these groups lobbied for new categories, the disaggregation of the white category, and the substitution of the term "ethnic" for the term "race." One unintended consequence of self-enumeration was the unexpected increase in the number of American Indians who had previously been identified by census enumerators as white. The American Indian population grew from 827,000 in 1970 to almost 2 million in 1990—growth far in excess of natural increase. The population increase reflected changes in identification among those who were previously identified as another race (largely white) and also reflected a greater willingness of respondents to claim the American Indian part of their mixed heritage.[12]

Hispanic Origin

With the introduction of self-enumeration in 1970, the census allowed Americans to choose from one of many color or race categories. Responding to criticism in the 1960s from the U.S. Interagency Committee on Mexican-American Affairs, and because of the growth of the Hispanic population due to the influx of immigrants from Latin America (primarily Mexico), the Census Bureau also added a question about Hispanic origin. However, because the short form of the 1970 Census was already in production, the Hispanic origin question was added only to the long form and administered to only about one in five households. This change signaled that Hispanics were to be recognized as a distinct group.[13] The 1970 Census asked whether a person's origin or descent was Mexican, Puerto Rican, Cuban, Central or South American, Other Spanish, or none of the above. By not listing Hispanic origin under the color or race question, the U.S. Census distinguished Hispanic origin or descent from color or race, effectively treating Hispanic as a set of national origins rather than as a race. In other words, one could mark a specific Hispanic origin and choose among the census race categories, meaning that Hispanics could be of any race. For the first time, this type of group identity was not racialized in its measurement. Whether intentional or not, because the Census Bureau did not treat Hispanic as a race, the racial boundaries have not been as rigid for Hispanics as they have been for blacks in the United States.

On the 1980 Census, the Hispanic origin question was included on the short form (which goes to all households), a change that coincided with a 60 percent increase in the Hispanic population during the decade. This substantial growth reflected not only improved coverage in the 1980 Census but also the significant expansion of this population resulting from new waves of immigration.[14] In 1980, the census substituted a question about a person's ancestry for the more costly and complicated questions about parental birthplace that had been used previously. This allowed for rough identification of the members (or partial members) of earlier arriving immigrant groups. Only the racial and Hispanic origin groups, however, enjoyed official statistical representation. Gaining such representation had two benefits: a category on the census that increased the count of the group, and opportunities for racial or ethnic minorities to qualify for federal programs for disadvantaged minorities.

As various ethnic groups sought statistical representation during this period, it was clear that America's demography was rapidly changing with the arrival of immigrants, especially those from Latin American and Asian countries. The growth in the Asian population prompted the census to add the categories Vietnamese, Asian Indian, Guamanian, Samoan, Eskimo, and Aleut to the 1980 Census. In 1990, the U.S. Census Bureau modified the racial categories so that the Asian/Pacific Islander category included those whose ethnic origins were Chinese, Filipino, Hawaiian, Korean, Vietnamese, Japanese, Asian Indian, Samoan, and Guamanian. But it was not the growth of the Asian population that led the Census Bureau to add the long list of Asian origins as races. Race questions proposed by the Census Bureau in the 1980s consistently had one check box for all Asians and a space for the individual to write his or her specific Asian race or ancestry. Rep. Robert Matsui, D-Calif., insisted that the 1990 Census address Asian origins, and President Reagan accepted his recommendations.

In addition to the race options, Americans also had the option of marking "other race" and printing the race of their choice. As in the 1970 and 1980 censuses, the Hispanic origin question came after the race question in the questionnaire. And, like the previous decennial censuses, the 1990 Census directed Americans to "fill ONE circle for the race that the person considers himself/herself to be," again with the explicit instruction to choose only one race. In both the 1980 and 1990 censuses, the fastest-growing category was "other race," chosen by almost 10 million Americans in the 1990 Census, 97 percent of whom were Hispanic. Furthermore, 40 percent of Hispanics chose this category, compared with only 1 percent of the non-Hispanic population,[15] but Census Bureau coding rules were partly responsible for this. A person who checked "other race" and wrote Irish or German (for example) was recoded into the white category. A person who wrote any phrase that denoted a Spanish origin remained in the Other race category. But also, Hispanics are more likely than any other group to choose this option, because Hispanics tend to see themselves as more than one race, with an interracial legacy that dates back to the mixing of Spaniards and the indigenous peoples of South and Central America. This long-standing and widespread history of racial mixing has created hybrid or *mestizo* backgrounds among many Hispanics, especially Mexicans, and that involves mixtures of earlier racial groups. Other Americans who marked the Other race option in 1990—a quarter of a million people—often reported multiracial designations, such as black/white, Eurasian, or Amerasian.[16]

One or More Races

During the early 1990s, new advocacy groups with different agendas arose. These groups criticized OMB for not accurately measuring the diversity in the country brought about by increases in immigration, interracial marriage, and growth in the multiracial population. They pressed OMB to reconsider the race and ethnic categories in the 2000 Census; in response, OMB set out to assess the adequacy of the existing categories, created principles to govern any revisions in categories, and solicited recommendations for changes. In 1994, OMB established a federal interagency committee that, over the next three years, conducted seven congressional subcommittee hearings, three national tests, and numerous focus groups and workshops to assess the needs of those who use federal data on race and ethnicity. The committee also heard the oral testimonies of 94 witnesses and reviewed nearly 800 letters.

Most prominent among OMB's critics were such groups as the Association for Multi-Ethnic Americans (AMEA) and Project RACE (Reclassify All Children Equally), which pressed the OMB to adopt a multiracial category. Susan Graham from Project RACE and Carlos Fernandez from AMEA argued that, in the interest of accuracy and fairness, OMB should add a multiracial category to the racial options and noted that the absence of this category undermined the accuracy of other racial data. Moreover, Graham and Fernandez asserted that it is an affront to force multiracial people or their children to choose only one race; they argued that forced monoracial identification was not only inaccurate because it denied the existence of interracial marriages but was also discriminatory. They proposed that multiracial should be a sixth category and that the five existing categories could be listed underneath, so that Americans could first check "multiracial" and then all that apply from the existing five racial categories.

Not everyone, however, was in favor of adding a multiracial category or allowing Americans to mark more than one race on government forms. For example, civil rights groups (including the National Coalition for an Accurate Count of Asians and Pacific Islanders, the National Council of La Raza, the Mexican American Legal Defense Fund, the Urban League, the National Council of American Indians, and the NAACP) opposed adding a multiracial category. These groups feared that those who would otherwise be counted as Asian, Hispanic, black, or American Indian would now choose to identify as multiracial, thus diminishing the count of specific minorities in the census. They thought that the shift could adversely affect enforcement of the Voting Rights Act, blur the categories of antidiscrimination and affirmative action programs, and potentially undermine the size and effectiveness of state and federal programs aimed at helping minorities. In addition, social scientists, OMB and Census Bureau officials, and representatives from other federal agencies cautioned against adopting a multiracial designation on the grounds that statistical categories should be discrete, few in number, capable of generating consistent responses, and comparable with past categories. Final hearings took place in July 1997, at which time the interagency committee recommended to the OMB that the census allow Americans to select multiple responses from the race categories, but recommended against adding multiracial as a sixth category. While representatives from AMEA accepted this recommendation, those from Project RACE were dissatisfied.

In October 1997, OMB announced its decision that all people would have the option to identify with one or more races starting with the 2000 Census and extending to all federal data systems by the year 2003. Hence, the racial options on the 2000 Census included white, black, Asian, Native Hawaiian or Other Pacific Islander, American Indian and Alaska Native, and Other, and allowed people to mark more than one category. While Latino or Hispanic was not a racial category on the 2000 Census, OMB mandated two distinct questions regarding a person's racial or ethnic background: one about race and a second about whether a person was Spanish/Hispanic/ Latino (see Figure 1). Since someone who self-designated as Spanish/Hispanic/Latino could be of any race, the census asked both questions in order to identify the Hispanic population in the United States. While OMB also reviewed a proposal that would group Hispanics into one race, it eventually decided against making Hispanics a separate race since this would result in fewer people being classified in the Hispanic category and in fewer whites being classified as white.[17] (Hereafter, the terms Hispanic and Latino are used interchangeably.)

OMB's decision to allow Americans to mark one or more races is a landmark change in the way the U.S. Census Bureau collects data on race, reflecting the growth of intermarriages and multiracial births. Popula-

Figure 1
QUESTIONS ON RACE AND HISPANIC ORIGIN, CENSUS 2000

→ NOTE: Please answer BOTH Questions 5 and 6.

5. Is this person Spanish/Hispanic/Latino? Mark ☒ the "No" box if not Spanish/Hispanic/Latino.
☐ No, not Spanish/Hispanic/Latino   ☐ Yes, Puerto Rican
☐ Yes, Mexican, Mexican Am., Chicano   ☐ Yes, Cuban
☐ Yes, other Spanish/Hispanic/Latino – *Print group.*

6. What is this person's race? Mark ☒ one or more races to indicate what this person considers himself/herself to be.
☐ White
☐ Black, African Am., or Negro
☐ American Indian or Alaska Native – *Print name of enrolled or principal tribe.* ▼

☐ Asian Indian   ☐ Japanese   ☐ Native Hawaiian
☐ Chinese   ☐ Korean   ☐ Guamanian or Chamorro
☐ Filipino   ☐ Vietnamese   ☐ Samoan
☐ Other Asian – *Print race.* ▼   ☐ Other Pacific Islander – *Print race.* ▼

☐ Some other race – *Print race.* ▼

Source: U.S. Census Bureau, Census 2000 questionnaire.

tion projections suggest that the multiple-race segment of the population will increase by 2 to 3 percentage points each decade for the next century. Based on these assumptions, by the year 2100, 95 percent of the American Indian population, 70 percent of the Hispanic population, 43 percent of the Asian population, 37 percent of the black population, and 35 percent of the white population could be of multiple-race origin.[18]

The option to mark more than one race gave official status and recognition to people who see their backgrounds as having involved racial mixing—an acknowledgment that speaks volumes about how far the country has come since the days of the one-drop rule. In essence, by allowing Americans to mark more than one race, OMB has rejected the premise of mutual exclusivity in racial categorization in the United States, has signified that race is no longer conceived as rigidly as in the past, and has perhaps indicated that the old racial divides may be fading.

CODING RACE AND ETHNICITY

Because the 2000 Census allowed people to record themselves in more than one racial category, we found it necessary to recode race and ethnicity in the 2000 data in order to study trends and patterns in immigration and race and ethnicity over the past few decades. This new categorization combines information on race and ethnicity, forcing mutual exclusivity among racial and ethnic categories and allowing comparative analyses of trends over time. This recoding has a hierarchy of rules that assign each individual to one of five groups:

- White.
- Black.
- Asian/Pacific Islander.
- Latino.
- AINLOR (American Indian or Non-Latino Other Race).

First, for all four censuses starting with 1970, people who indicated they were Latino were counted in the Latino group. Because of the multiple-race option in the 2000 Census, different criteria were used for the 2000 data than for data from the previous three censuses. In the 1970, 1980, and 1990 data, non-Latinos were categorized into one of the other four race groups according to the race category they selected, as described above. Due to the relatively small number of cases in the 1 percent sample, American Indians and Alaska Natives were grouped into the "Other" category. For 2000 Census data, non-Latinos who indicated multiple races were grouped into the largest racial minority with which they identified. Using this methodology, people reporting themselves as black, regardless of any other racial identification, were classified as black. If black was not indicated but Asian was, the person was classified as Asian. Someone who checked American Indian or "some other race" was classified as AINLOR. Finally, someone who checked only white was categorized as white.

We studied Hispanics as a separate group, even though the census does not treat them as a distinct racial or ethnic category. This approach was used for two reasons. First, many Latinos see themselves as a separate category, as indicated by the fact that so many chose "other race" in the census. Second, they have been legally treated as a separate group and often as a racial or ethnic minority group that qualifies for and benefits from federal programs designed to assist disadvantaged minorities, such as affirmative action programs. Latinos have also been protected by civil rights legislation and the Voting Rights Act, both of which are aimed at helping racial or ethnic minorities. That is, not only do Latinos see themselves as a separate category (although not necessarily a separate racial category), they are also treated as a separate category by the U.S. government.

Charting Population Changes

The considerable change that has occurred over the past 30 years in the ways the U.S. government measures race and ethnicity in its official surveys and censuses makes it a challenge to assess shifts over time in the racial and ethnic composition of the U.S. popula-

tion. But by applying certain rules to the ways that have been used to measure race or ethnicity, it becomes possible to chart changes in the relative sizes of racial or ethnic groups in the country. The most striking result is that in 2000 there were almost as many Latinos in the country as blacks (around 35 million each), even after counting as black all people listing black and one or more other races. Latinos constituted 13 percent of the population in 2000, as did blacks, reflecting the continuing substantial immigration from Latin America during the 1990s. Since shortly after the 2000 Census, the size of the Latino population has surpassed that of the black population. In 2000 almost all people reporting some other race were Latinos (more than 97 percent). Among the other notably sized racial or ethnic groups in the country in 2000 were Asians (12 million) and people in the residual race category (5 million, which includes those identified as AINLOR). As these results make clear, the United States can no longer be described in racial and ethnic terms as consisting almost entirely of black and white people.

However, this does not mean that America's white population is insignificant; more than 75 percent of the population still gave a white identification in 2000. Excluding those whites who also reported they were Latino (about 6 percent of the population), 69 percent reported themselves as non-Latino whites—just a little more than two of every three people. This ratio is down from three in four in 1990, from four in five in 1980, and from five in six in 1970 (see Table 1, page 309). The 14 percentage point decline in the non-Latino white population in the United States since 1970 means that there would have been about 40 million more whites in the country in 2000 if whites had been as relatively numerous in 2000 as they were in 1970. While the percentage of whites declined, Asians and Latinos increased. The former increased their share of the population by 4 percentage points, and the latter by 8. Non-Latino blacks and others increased their shares by a modest 1.6 and 1.2 percentage points, respectively. Thus, the major gains in share of the U.S. population since 1970 have taken place among Asians and Latinos, the groups that made up most of the shift in the composition of immigrants coming to the country since 1965, when the National Origin Quota Act was abolished.

Immigration's Contribution

Examining the racial and ethnic composition of immigrants over the past 30 years reveals the contribution of immigration to changes in the racial/ethnic composition of the U.S. population over this period. In 1970, the foreign-born population of the country was still predominantly non-Latino white, among both men and women (see Table 2, page 309). No other major racial or ethnic group, except the Latinos, constituted substantial

Table 1

Table 1
POPULATION BY FIVE MAJOR CENSUS RACIAL/ETHNIC CATEGORIES, UNITED STATES, 1970–2000

Race/Ethnicity[a]	1970 Number (millions)	1970 Percent	1980 Number (millions)	1980 Percent	1990 Number (millions)	1990 Percent	2000 Number (millions)	2000 Percent
Total	203.3	100	226.5	100	248.0	100	281.4	100
White	169.7	83	180.3	80	188.1	76	194.4	69
Black	22.1	11	26.2	12	29.1	12	35.3	13
Asian/Pacific Islander	1.5	1	3.6	2	7.0	3	11.9	4
Latino	9.1	4	14.7	6	21.7	9	35.2	13
AINLOR[b]	0.9	0	1.7	1	2.1	1	4.6	2

a Numbers are derived from Census questions on race and ethnicity. All people who identified themselves ethnically as "Hispanic" are classified Latino. All others are classified by race. Thus, Latinos are included only in the Latino group and may be of any race.

In the 2000 Census, non-Latinos reporting multiple races were classifed as belonging to the largest of the racial groups with which they identified.

b American Indian, Alaska Native, and non-Latino Other racial groups.

Source: Authors' calculations based on the Integrated Public Use Microdata Series (IPUMS), 2003.

Table 2
FOREIGN-BORN POPULATION BY GENDER AND FIVE MAJOR RACIAL/ETHNIC CATEGORIES, UNITED STATES, 1970 AND 2000

Race/ethnicity[a]	1970 Female Number (millions)	1970 Female Percent	1970 Male Number (millions)	1970 Male Percent	2000 Female Number (millions)	2000 Female Percent	2000 Male Number (millions)	2000 Male Percent
Total	5.3	100.0	4.5	100.0	15.6	100.0	15.4	100.0
White	3.9	73.8	3.2	72.0	3.7	23.5	3.2	20.5
Black	0.1	2.3	0.1	2.3	1.1	7.1	1.0	6.4
Asian/Pacific Islander	0.3	5.1	0.3	5.8	3.9	25.1	3.5	22.7
Latino	1.0	18.1	0.9	19.1	6.6	42.5	7.5	48.6
AINLOR[b]	—	0.6	—	0.8	0.3	1.7	0.3	1.8

a Foreign-born excludes U.S. citizens born in outlying territories and persons born abroad to U.S. citizens.

b American Indian, Alaska Native, and non-Latino Other racial groups.

— Less than 500,000.

Source: Authors' calculations based on the Integrated Public Use Microdata Series (IPUMS), 2003.

shares of the foreign-born population at that time; even then, however, the percentages of Asians who were foreign-born started to foreshadow the changes that were just beginning. Over the next 30 years, these changes would exert their cumulative impact ever more forcefully. In 1970, for example, 6 percent of foreign-born males and 5 percent of foreign-born females were Asian, percentages that were three to seven times the percentage of Asians in the total population, hinting at the dramatic growth in the Asian population yet to come. The percentages of foreign-born males and females who were Latinos were 19 percent and 18 percent, respectively, about three to four times the concentration of Latinos in the total population, again suggesting the growth to come.

In 1970, just a few years after implementation of the 1965 reforms opening U.S. doors to non-European immigration, these percentages were similar for males and females. In fact, except among whites, the percentage of foreign-born males within the various racial and ethnic groups tended to slightly exceed that for females. By 2000, however, the percent female exceeded the percent male in three of the four largest racial and ethnic groups. Only among Latinos were there fewer females than males (43 percent and 49 percent, respectively). This gap reflects the fact that so much Latino immigration involves low-skilled and often single unauthorized Mexican migrants coming to the United States to work. In other words, the labor migration of Latinos is more selective of men than the kinds of migration occurring from other countries, which tend to be more selective of women. Whatever such national origin differences, the much higher fractions of foreign-born among Asians and Mexicans in 2000 than in 1970 shows the cumulative importance of immigration for the growth of these two populations in the country.

New Diversity States

The growth in the nonwhite population over the past 30 years has been not only dramatic but also diverse in terms of both race and ethnicity and geographic location. The increase in the nonwhite population has tended to involve several racial or ethnic groups, with each increase largely fueled by immigration, and it has disproportionately occurred only in some places. The major recent racial and ethnic composition shift in the country is at once highly conspicuous (especially in those places where it is taking place most rapidly, thus sometimes exacerbating fears about a growing nonwhite population) and nonmonolithic (which, if better understood, would probably lessen anxieties about racial or ethnic relations and conflict). The most nonwhite state in the country is Hawaii, whose population is 77 percent nonwhite; and the least is Maine, whose nonwhite population is 3 percent.

But this nonwhiteness departs from the black-white pattern that once traditionally characterized the country. If the data from the states with the 20 largest nonwhite populations are broken down into the four major nonwhite components of black, Latino, Asian, and Other (see Table 3), three patterns emerge. First, the old black-white bipolar pattern is still somewhat in evidence, but only in Southern states such as Georgia, Louisiana, Maryland, and Mississippi—states referred to as black-white states. By 2000, several places were showing a new bipolar pattern of mostly whites and Latinos, such as Arizona, Nevada, and New Mexico—states referred to as Latino-white states. These states add a different dimension to the county's old bipolar racial division. Second, several states have populations containing at least three major racial or ethnic groups, each with relatively sizable percentages of the state's total population (defined here as consisting of 10 percent or more of the overall state population): California, Florida, Illinois, New Jersey, New Mexico, New York, and Texas. These states are designated new diversity states. Under a criterion of three groups, each with at least 7 percent of a state's population, five more states (and the District of Columbia) would also qualify: Connecticut, Hawaii, Nevada, Oklahoma, and Washington (see Figure 2, page 311). Third, the states with the most racially and ethnically diverse populations are also among the country's most populous and highest income places. Thus, increasing racial and ethnic diversity in the United States appears to characterize large and relatively prosperous states.

Similar patterns of bipolar concentration and diversity are also evident in metropolitan areas containing the largest nonwhite populations in the country (see Table 4, page 311). Of the 20 largest such metro areas, 60 percent (12) are places where at least three racial or ethnic groups are represented in their populations. Located in new diversity states, these urban locales are the centers of the country's new racial and ethnic diversity: Anaheim (Calif.), Fresno (Calif.), Houston, Jersey City

Table 3

PERCENT OF POPULATION IN SELECTED NONWHITE CATEGORIES IN U.S. STATES WITH AT LEAST 20 PERCENT NONWHITE RESIDENTS, 2000

State	Total Nonwhite	Black	Asian/Pacific Islander	Latino	AINLOR*
Black-white states					
Mississippi	39	36	1	2	1
Maryland	38	29	5	4	1
Georgia	37	29	2	5	1
Louisiana	37	33	1	2	1
South Carolina	34	30	1	2	1
Virginia	30	20	4	5	1
North Carolina	30	22	2	5	2
Alabama	30	26	1	2	1
Delaware	27	20	2	5	1
Arkansas	22	16	1	3	2
Michigan	22	15	2	3	2
Tennessee	21	17	1	2	1
White-Latino or white-AINLOR states					
Arizona	36	4	2	25	6
Alaska	33	4	6	5	19
Colorado	26	4	3	17	2
Diversity states					
Hawaii	77	3	66	7	1
District of Columbia	72	60	3	8	1
New Mexico	55	2	1	42	10
California	54	7	12	32	2
Texas	48	12	3	32	1
New York	38	16	6	15	1
Florida	35	15	2	17	1
Nevada	34	7	6	19	2
New Jersey	34	13	6	13	1
Illinois	32	15	4	12	1
Oklahoma	25	8	2	5	11
Connecticut	23	9	3	9	1
Washington	21	4	7	8	3

Note: Includes states with populations that are at least 20 percent nonwhite or Hispanic. In Diversity states, at least three ethnic groups (including whites) each accounted for 7 percent to 10 percent of the total population. Black-white states are nondiversity states in which blacks account for at least two-thirds of the nonwhites. Latino-white or white-AINLOR states are nondiversity states in which Latinos or AINLOR account for two-thirds of nonwhites.

* American Indian, Alaska Native, and non-Latino Other racial groups.

Source: Authors' calculations based on the Integrated Public Use Microdata Series (IPUMS), 2003.

(N.J.), Los Angeles, Miami, New York, Oakland (Calif.), Riverside-San Bernardino (Calif.), San Francisco, San Jose (Calif.), and Stockton (Calif.). Only eight of the top 20 nonwhite metro areas are bipolar places: five are Latino-white (El Paso, McAllen, and San Antonio, all in Texas; Bakersfield, Calif.; and Albuquerque, N.M.); two are black-white (Memphis, Tenn., and New Orleans), and one is Asian-white (Honolulu). Clearly, diversity is the emerging touchstone of the new racial and ethnic structure in the United States. California leads the coun-

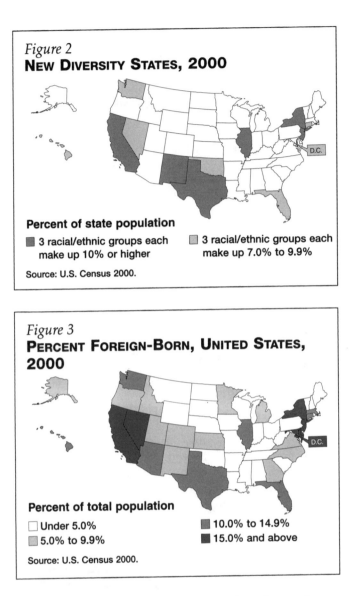

Figure 2
NEW DIVERSITY STATES, 2000

Percent of state population

■ 3 racial/ethnic groups each make up 10% or higher

□ 3 racial/ethnic groups each make up 7.0% to 9.9%

Source: U.S. Census 2000.

Figure 3
PERCENT FOREIGN-BORN, UNITED STATES, 2000

Percent of total population

□ Under 5.0%

■ 5.0% to 9.9%

■ 10.0% to 14.9%

■ 15.0% and above

Source: U.S. Census 2000.

Table 4

PERCENT IN VARIOUS RACIAL/ETHNIC CATEGORIES IN THE 20 U.S. METROPOLITAN AREAS WITH GREATEST PERCENT NONWHITE, 2000

Metropolitan areas, state(s)[a]	Total Non-White	Black	Asian/ Pacific Islander	Latino	AINLOR[b]
Black-white					
Memphis, TN/AR/MS	67.4	61.8	1.1	3.9	0.6
New Orleans, LA	55.0	45.9	3.0	5.1	1.1
Latino-white					
McAllen-Edinburg-Pharr-Mission, TX	88.7	0.2	1.0	87.4	0.1
El Paso, TX	83.7	2.7	1.3	79.3	0.5
Bakersfield, CA	50.9	6.3	3.3	38.8	2.6
Albuquerque, NM	49.8	2.8	2.2	40.5	4.3
Asian/Pacific Islander-white					
Honolulu, HI	78.3	2.8	68.6	6.2	0.8
Diversity metros					
Miami-Hialeah, FL	80.7	19.8	1.2	59.1	0.6
Jersey City, NJ	63.9	12.2	9.6	39.9	2.2
Los Angeles-Long Beach, CA	68.9	10.0	13.0	44.3	1.6
New York-Northeastern NJ	63.5	25.2	10.0	26.5	1.8
Fresno, CA	60.1	5.7	9.8	42.3	2.3
San Jose, CA	56.8	3.0	27.3	25.1	1.4
Riverside-San Bernadino, CA	54.5	9.5	5.1	38.1	1.8
San Francisco, CA	53.9	6.0	27.8	18.4	1.9
Houston-Brazoria, TX	53.8	17.6	5.5	29.6	1.0
Stockton, CA	52.9	6.4	14.3	29.9	2.3
Oakland, CA	52.7	12.9	19.1	18.9	1.7
Anaheim, CA	49.6	1.9	15.3	30.8	1.6
San Antonio, TX	64.4	7.2	2.3	53.8	1.1
Non-metro areas	20.3	9.3	1.8	7.2	2.0

[a] Metropolitan Statistical Areas.

[b] American Indian, Alaska Native, and non-Latino Other racial groups.

Note: Diversity metro areas have three or more racial/ethnic groups that each account for at 7 percent of the population.

Source: Authors' calculations based on the Integrated Public Use Microdata Series (IPUMS), 2003.

try in having the most metro areas with such populations, with eight of the 12 most diverse metropolitan areas.

While there is clearly an association between diversity and overall population size, there is also an association between diversity and high immigration. The most diverse states have relatively large foreign-born populations (see Figure 3).[19] Among the top 20 states with large foreign-born populations, six also have at least three racial or ethnic groups making up at least 10 percent of the population. Similarly, among the top 20 metro areas in terms of foreign-born population, 10 are high-diversity places. Thus, immigration is contributing substantially both to population growth and to the emergence of racial and ethnic diversity in this country.

Asian and Latino Growth

Immigration clearly accounts for much of the unusually rapid growth of the Asian and Latino populations in the United States and is the most important reason for these groups' increased shares of the population in 2000. There are two sources of population growth: immigration and the balance of births and deaths, or net natural increase. If one group has more births or fewer deaths than another group, its rate of population increase will be higher.

How much has immigration contributed to population growth among the major racial and ethnic groups in the country? Immigrants contribute to U.S. population growth in two ways. First, they contribute simply by coming to the United States. This is part of net immigration and constituted about 40 percent of overall U.S.

Table 5

NET IMMIGRATION AS PERCENT OF RACE/ETHNIC GROUP POPULATION GROWTH BY DECADE, UNITED STATES, 1970–2000

Racial/ethnic group	1970-1980		1980-1990		1990-2000	
	Foreign-born	Foreign-born plus their U.S.-born children[a]	Foreign-born	Foreign-born plus their U.S.-born children[a]	Foreign-born	Foreign-born plus their U.S.-born children[a]
White	13	24	18	34	35	55
Black	11	15	21	31	14	23
Asian & Pacific Islander	74	89	78	99	65	89
Latino	40	61	56	83	48	76
AINLOR[b]	10	14	10	17	11	16

[a] This includes net gain of foreign-born persons plus any children born in the U.S. during the decade to foreign-born persons.

[b] American Indian, Alaska Native, and non-Latino Other racial groups.

Source: Authors' calculations based on the Integrated Public Use Microdata Series (IPUMS), 2003.

Figure 4

IMMIGRATION AS PERCENT OF POPULATION GROWTH BY DECADE, UNITED STATES, 1970–2000

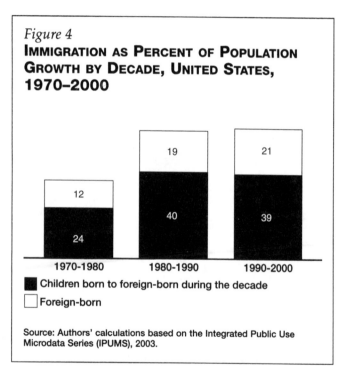

■ Children born to foreign-born during the decade

□ Foreign-born

Source: Authors' calculations based on the Integrated Public Use Microdata Series (IPUMS), 2003.

population growth during the 1980s and 1990s (see Table 5). Second, they have children after they come here. In a strict sense, the number of births immigrants have during the decade of their arrival is attributable to fertility and is a part of natural increase during that decade. This part of natural increase, however, would not have occurred without the immigration taking place, so it is reasonable to view this component as deriving from immigration, even if it represents part of the natural increase component.

The average percent increase in the populations of the major racial and ethnic groups in the country attributable to immigration per se and to the fertility of

immigrants during the decade for each of the three decades since 1970 are shown in Figure 4. Immigration per se constituted a fairly small fraction of population growth in the cases of the white, black, and other groups in each of the three decades since 1970 (although immigration made up a third of population growth among whites during the 1990s, a decade that saw a resurgence of white immigration from Eastern Europe and Russia in the wake of the collapse of the Soviet Union in 1989). By contrast, the percent of population growth due to immigration among Asians and Latinos was much higher. In the case of the former group, immigration accounted for most of the population growth, ranging from about 74 percent in the 1970s to 78 percent in the 1980s to 65 percent during the 1990s. The fertility of Asian immigrants during the decade accounted for only a slight bit more, so that immigration-related growth accounted for almost all the population growth of Asian Americans over the 30-year period.

The case of Latinos represents a striking contrast to that of Asians. Immigration constituted anywhere from about 40 percent to more than half of this group's total population growth during these decades. In addition, births to Latino immigrants during the decade added about half again as much to their immigration-related total. Thus, during the 1970s immigration and births accounted for three-fifths of Latino population growth in the country, a figure that grew to more than 80 percent during the 1980s and almost the same level during the 1990s. Two points are important to underscore here. One is that the Asian and Latino populations have both grown for largely immigration-related reasons over the past 30 years. The second is that among Latinos a much larger part of this growth results from births to immigrants after they arrive in the country than is the case among Asians.

Immigrant Economic Incorporation

Americans have always been ambivalent about immigration, concerned that immigrants might erode national identity and cohesion but responding positively to the economic benefits and inexpensive labor immigrants provide. Much of the contemporary anxiety about immigration may stem from the fact that the new immigrant groups are largely nonwhite. The new immigrants, however, are far from uniform in national origin and in racial or ethnic identification. They are rapidly increasing the racial and ethnic diversity of the United States, which may be more of an asset than a liability for many aspects of the country's well-being. One way to gauge the plausibility of this argument is to examine immigrant economic incorporation and, more specifically, the work and job mobility experiences of immigrants. This information helps discern whether the immigrants are best considered as newcomers to the society who have yet to complete their upward paths of movement into the economic mainstream, or whether they are best considered as discriminated-against members of racial or ethnic minorities who remain stuck in dead-end work situations long after they arrive here. Considerable upward job mobility among the new immigrants would suggest that the former view is more accurate, implying that fears about too much and the wrong kinds of immigration have often been exaggerated. Little job mobility and persistent disadvantage would suggest that the latter view is more accurate, implying that immigration is contributing to a growing underclass and the perpetuation of the problem of racial and ethnic inequality in the United States.

Whatever the country's historical ambivalence about immigration, the latter half of the 1990s in the United States witnessed a widening recognition that immigrants were playing an important and increasingly prominent role in the U.S. economy. Eleven percent of the country's total population was foreign-born in 2000, and 14 percent of the total was between the ages of 18 and 64, the prime employment years.[20] Among people in that age group actually working, the foreign-born percentage was even higher. Furthermore, the percentage of children in the population who were either immigrants or the children of immigrants was over 20 percent, indicating that the nation's future workforce will be even more dependent on immigration than today.[21]

Whether newcomers to the United States can experience upward mobility depends on important economic trends that affect the structure of opportunities for advancement. Over the past three decades, the role of immigrants in the nation's workforce has grown while employment structures have changed. The country has experienced a relative decline in manufacturing employment (especially high-wage union jobs), a relative increase in service-industry employment, declining or stagnant real earnings at the middle and the bottom of the income distribution, growing numbers of working-age males (especially young African Americans) who are dropping out of the labor force, and narrowing gaps in pay between men and women with similar levels of education.[22] These trends suggest that opportunities to improve one's economic position may not be as numerous as they once were and that growth in the number of middle-class jobs may not have kept pace with population growth.

The characteristics of the new immigrants mirror this possibility. For example, the new immigrants have tended to have either high levels of education (college degrees) or low levels (less than high school). In 2000, 24 percent of adult immigrants had at least a college degree, a figure about the same as that for the U.S.-born population. At the same time, 38 percent of all adult immigrants had not completed high school, compared with only 16 percent of U.S.-born adults. Immigrant adults were less likely to have a middle level of education (a high school diploma but not a college degree) than were U.S.-born adults (see Figure 5). This "hollowed-out" educational distribution reflects the pattern of change in the labor market in recent years, one that involved substantial growth in the numbers of high- and low-end jobs, with much lower increases in the number of middle-range jobs.

The substantial growth in low-education immigrants is puzzling. This migration has continued even as pay levels for workers without college degrees have stagnated and the employment opportunities for disadvantaged U.S.-born racial or ethnic minorities, especially blacks, have stalled. Because of the relative disappearance of factory jobs in cities (where many blacks live) and the movement of many middle-class black professionals to the suburbs, blacks in the central parts of American cities have become even more disadvantaged than they were previously.[23] Given this, and given that many new immigrants settle in the central parts of cities, how does one explain the growth in low-education immigrants? Why should larger numbers of less-skilled Mexican migrants come to the United States when the need for less-skilled labor appears to be declining? Part of the answer is the relative lack of jobs in Mexico, a deficiency still severe enough to make even the worst jobs and limited employment prospects in the United States attractive to many migrants. Moreover, social networks among low-educated immigrants foster further migration and confer recruitment and hiring advantages to immigrants (over comparable African American workers at the low end of the wage scale).[24]

The chances for low-education migrants to experience upward mobility in the United States are affected

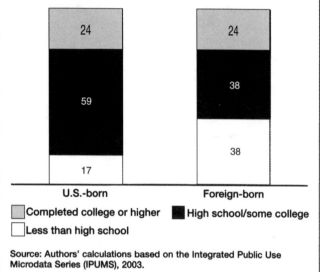

Figure 5

EDUCATIONAL ATTAINMENT FOR U.S.-BORN AND FOREIGN-BORN AMERICANS AGE 24 OR OLDER, 2000

	Completed college or higher	High school/some college	Less than high school
U.S.-born	24	59	17
Foreign-born	24	38	38

Source: Authors' calculations based on the Integrated Public Use Microdata Series (IPUMS), 2003.

by the role that race and ethnicity plays in the U.S. labor market. Does the new immigration, in particular its low-education component, represent something negative or something positive for the wage and job prospects of other low-skilled workers, including low-skilled U.S.-born minorities, earlier-arriving immigrants, and the recently arrived immigrants themselves? Over two decades, social science research on the labor market impacts of immigration has found that U.S.-born workers are not appreciably negatively affected overall, although this research has also shown that increased immigration of low-education workers does somewhat limit employment options for other low-education workers, especially previously arrived low-education immigrants.[25] Does this mean that the prospects for moving up the job ladder into the economic mainstream are diminishing for today's immigrants? Are opportunities for low-education immigrants also lessening because economic restructuring is losing middle-level jobs, leaving fewer pathways to upward mobility? To what degree is this worrisome possibility exacerbated by the fact that so many new immigrants are nonwhite and thus presumably subject to racial or ethnic discrimination?

In recent decades, the structure of job opportunities in the United States appears to have increasingly taken an hourglass or U-shaped form.[26] That is, there are relatively more jobs at the top and bottom of the job hierarchy than in the middle. The decline in the manufacturing sector of the economy (which shifted from employing 33 percent of private-sector workers in 1970 to 17 percent in 2000) may have resulted in fewer jobs that provide middle-class lifestyles, especially for people without college

educations. To the extent that the overall structure of the economy is becoming more U-shaped, opportunities for upward mobility in the United States may have been declining, particularly for those without higher education. Discrimination in hiring, pay, and promotion on the basis of such characteristics as race and ethnicity, nativity, and gender are harder to overcome under conditions of declining opportunities, especially for people at the bottom of the social hierarchy. Their chances for betterment depend on the number and kind of midrange employment opportunities as well as on the nature and strength of barriers to achievement. Research indicating that racial and ethnic groups, especially minority women, are concentrated at the bottom of the job distribution heightens concerns that emerging hourglass structures of employment may limit job mobility for new immigrants.

This is the context in which we assess the prospects for new immigrants. They are not only newcomers in American society but also members of racial or ethnic groups whose prospects for mobility may be impeded by treatment as racialized minorities (people whose race or ethnicity constitutes a basis for substantial discrimination). Evidence of upward mobility among low-end immigrants would suggest that immigrant status may not constrain opportunity to the degree that perspectives focusing on the discriminatory effects of race and ethnicity alone, without taking nativity into account, would imply. It is thus crucial to examine jobs for the foreign-born and U.S.-born separately, and to ascertain differences between men and women, given that immigrant women may start out in very low-level jobs.

We define job quality in terms of the relative earnings of jobs involving combinations of occupation and industry in 1980, 1990, and 2000, and we divide the resulting occupation-industry categories into segments based on pay. The occupation-industry combinations are arrayed into quintiles, from high to low, based on thresholds.[27] Because sizable numbers of people are in jobs at the various pay thresholds, the percentages in each segment do not exactly equal 20 percent (people on the threshold were placed in the higher fifth). These quintiles describe jobs as "good," "somewhat good," "middle," "somewhat bad," and "bad."

Changing Job Quality

Ascertaining whether racial and ethnic discrimination worsens the chances of upward mobility for today's low-skilled immigrants requires disentangling the effects of race and ethnicity in America from the effect of immigration. This, in turn, requires considering the extent to which theories about immigrants joining the economic mainstream emphasize that immigrants see themselves and are viewed by others as racialized minorities in America. Existing theories offer essentially optimistic (in the case of assimilation perspectives) or pessimistic (in

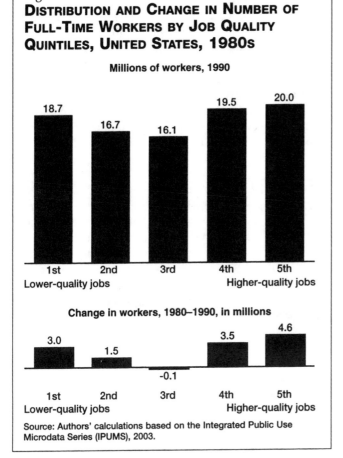

Figure 6

DISTRIBUTION AND CHANGE IN NUMBER OF FULL-TIME WORKERS BY JOB QUALITY QUINTILES, UNITED STATES, 1980S

Millions of workers, 1990

1st Lower-quality jobs	2nd	3rd	4th	5th Higher-quality jobs
18.7	16.7	16.1	19.5	20.0

Change in workers, 1980–1990, in millions

1st Lower-quality jobs	2nd	3rd	4th	5th Higher-quality jobs
3.0	1.5	-0.1	3.5	4.6

Source: Authors' calculations based on the Integrated Public Use Microdata Series (IPUMS), 2003.

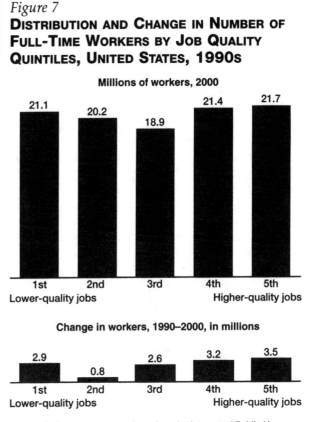

Figure 7

DISTRIBUTION AND CHANGE IN NUMBER OF FULL-TIME WORKERS BY JOB QUALITY QUINTILES, UNITED STATES, 1990S

Millions of workers, 2000

1st Lower-quality jobs	2nd	3rd	4th	5th Higher-quality jobs
21.1	20.2	18.9	21.4	21.7

Change in workers, 1990–2000, in millions

1st Lower-quality jobs	2nd	3rd	4th	5th Higher-quality jobs
2.9	0.8	2.6	3.2	3.5

Source: Authors' calculations based on the Integrated Public Use Microdata Series (IPUMS), 2003.

the case of ethnic disadvantage perspectives) pictures of the process, or a mixture of the two (in the case of segmented assimilation views). Which view best applies to a given immigrant group depends substantially, if not always explicitly, on whether the group was treated as a racialized disadvantaged minority group. Ethnic disadvantage perspectives tend to see immigrant groups as nonwhite minorities subject to discrimination. Assimilation perspectives tend to view them less in racial and ethnic terms than in nativity terms. Nonetheless, upward economic mobility depends on the extent to which the new immigrant groups become disadvantaged racialized minority groups in the United States.

Our analysis of job growth from 1980 to 2000 examines shifting patterns of employment by job quality in the United States during the 1980s and 1990s, focusing on results examined simultaneously by nativity, race or ethnicity, and gender, as well as on changes over time in job quality among immigrants. To a certain extent, the basic pattern of employment in the United States reveals a U-shaped structural form in 1990 and 2000. Some hollowing-out of the number of people holding midlevel jobs characterized the job quality distribution of the United States at the end of the 1980s. In 1990 about 20 million full-time workers were employed nationally in

high-quality jobs and 18 million in the lowest-quality jobs, with only about 16 million in the middle. The change during the decade definitely reduced the middle of the distribution (see Figure 6), indicating that processes of economic restructuring and technological change were at work during the course of the 1980s. A similar structure emerges in 2000 (see Figure 7). The structural shift during the economic boom of the 1990s did not eliminate (and possibly reinforced) an hourglass job pattern, resulting in disproportionate growth in both good and bad jobs. In other words, the numbers of people holding such jobs rose to a greater degree than did the numbers of people holding midlevel jobs.

The chances for immigrant upward mobility depend on the economy generating increases in higher-quality jobs as well as on the degree of immigrant upward mobility experienced over time. Assessing racial or ethnic group involvement in the growth of the five job quality categories during the 1990s requires separating the findings for men and women, because immigrant employment varies by gender and varies by group. Men and women from different racial or ethnic groups are concentrated disproportionately at lower and higher points in the U.S. job structure. As shown in Figure 8, Latino women appear to contribute more to the pattern of low-end job growth than Latino men do, and Asian men contribute disproportionately to growth at the high end. Together, these patterns are consistent with the fact that low-end job growth disproportionately involves the members of society with the lowest education and least experience (racial or ethnic minorities and immigrants, especially women).

It is important to determine the extent to which immigrants constitute a disproportionate share of this growth because immigrants may be more likely to start at low-end jobs because they are inexperienced newcomers, not because they are seen as members of racialized minority groups. To the degree that this is the case, their labor market outcomes might disproportionately improve as they gain more job experience. Figure 8 also indicates the degree to which immigrants have been involved in employment growth by job quality quintile in the United States. Variation in immigrant employment change across job quintiles indicates growth at both the high and low ends of the distribution. Thus, immigrants do appear involved in the emergence and maintenance of a U-shaped job pattern, representing from one-third to one-half of the growth in the extreme tails of the job quality distribution among males. But immigrants are not responsible for the U-shaped pattern, because the same tendency characterizes changes in job quality for U.S.-born workers.

Immigrant males also contribute substantially to growth in the middle part of the distribution, accounting for about half of the middle-quintile job increases. In fact, distinct differences among men and women characterize job quality dynamics when immigrants are compared to U.S.-born workers. Foreign-born males account for appreciable fractions of employment growth in the high and middle parts of the distribution (about one-third and two-fifths, respectively), but foreign-born females account for a large fraction (about one-third) of the growth only in the lower part of the distribution. The U-shaped distribution of job quality growth thus involves distinctive gender and nativity patterns, with both immigrant men and women accounting for the largest single nativity-gender component of low-end growth and immigrant men almost the largest component of high-end growth. In addition, immigrant men account for almost half the growth in the middle.

Immigrant Job Mobility

These results illustrate why it is important to consider the possibility that newcomer dynamics as well as racialized minority group dynamics may play an important role in affecting immigrants in the labor market. Specifically, the extent to which immigrants experience mobility in the labor market is germane to inferring whether the incorporation experiences of Latinos and Asians reflect those of other newcomers to American society more than those of members of racialized minority groups who undergo considerable labor market discrimination (such as African Americans). If immigrants are similar to African Americans in experiencing prejudice and discrimination in the labor market, then as long as such discrimination continues, little upward mobility among low-education immigrants is likely. On the other hand, if immigrants are more like newcomers who need experience and familiarity in the labor market, then immigrants can expect better prospects for job mobility. This

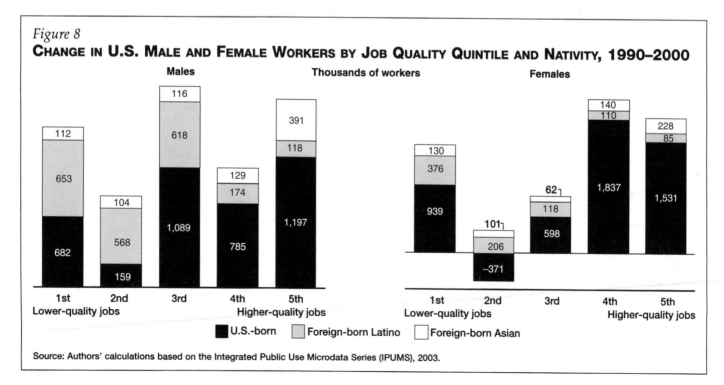

Figure 8

CHANGE IN U.S. MALE AND FEMALE WORKERS BY JOB QUALITY QUINTILE AND NATIVITY, 1990–2000

Source: Authors' calculations based on the Integrated Public Use Microdata Series (IPUMS), 2003.

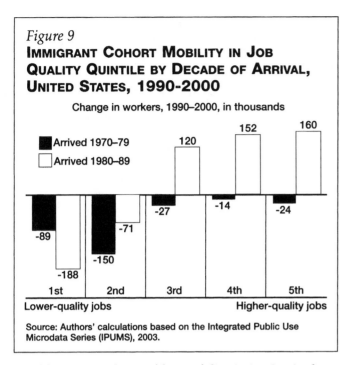

Figure 9

IMMIGRANT COHORT MOBILITY IN JOB QUALITY QUINTILE BY DECADE OF ARRIVAL, UNITED STATES, 1990-2000

Change in workers, 1990–2000, in thousands

■ Arrived 1970–79
□ Arrived 1980–89

	1st	2nd	3rd	4th	5th
Arrived 1980–89			120	152	160
Arrived 1970–79	−89	−71	−27	−14	−24
	−188	−150			

Lower-quality jobs   Higher-quality jobs

Source: Authors' calculations based on the Integrated Public Use Microdata Series (IPUMS), 2003.

would not mean that problems of discrimination in the labor market against Latinos and Asians are nonexistent, only that they are sufficiently different in kind and degree from those experienced by African Americans that their newcomer status might matter more than their racial or ethnic status.

Of course many U.S.-born and immigrant workers earn more as they mature and gain job experience. But for immigrants, years of working experience can be separated into total working experience, which often begins in the home country, and the years of working experience gained after entering the U.S. labor market. Upon arrival, many immigrants lack language and U.S.-specific job skills that improve over time and are rewarded with better jobs and earnings. Research on earnings is extremely nuanced, but it generally supports the assertion that the new immigrants earn less than U.S.-born workers who have equal years of work experience. But even after two decades of U.S.-specific experience, immigrants generally fail to catch up to the earnings levels of similarly skilled U.S.-born workers. Lacking longitudinal data, a fully adequate test of the earnings incorporation process is not possible, and one cannot adequately distinguish between mobility due to total working experience and that due to U.S.-specific experience.

Immigrant job quality mobility can be approximated by tracking cohorts over time. We grouped immigrants according to the decade they report arriving in the United States, and we examined two recent arrival cohorts (the 1970-1979 cohort and the 1980-1989 cohort). To the degree that job quality mobility occurs, immigrants in these arrival cohorts should shift into higher-quality jobs during the 1990s, a period marked by an economic boom.

First, the percentage was calculated of each arrival cohort's members who were employed in each of the five job quality categories. Then the percentage distribution in 1990 was subtracted from the percentage distribution in 2000, resulting in the percentage-point change across the time period (see Figure 9). This change was then converted to absolute numbers of workers in order to show the numbers of people involved in the change. The number of workers in the 1980s cohort in the highest job quality category increased by over 150,000 people during the 1990s. At the same time, the number in the 1970s cohort in the highest job quality category decreased slightly, reflecting the influence of attrition (retirement, emigration, and mortality). But the overall pattern of change is one of upward mobility, with the 1980s cohort showing the strongest employment losses in lower-quality jobs and the strongest gains in higher-quality jobs. But even the arrivals of the 1970s experienced substantial mobility out of lower-end jobs during the decade of the 1990s.

These findings indicate that the overall pattern of job quality change among immigrants mirrors that of the country as a whole, with some tendency toward a hollowing-out of the middle of the job distribution occurring in recent decades. However, considerable upward job mobility among immigrants has also been taking place during this time, indicating that the nonwhite racial or ethnic status of immigrants does not appear to represent an ironclad impediment to economic incorporation. This conclusion is buttressed by the fact that many Asian males start their job experience in the United States in the top part of the job distribution, not in the lower. Hence, the worry that recent immigrants are likely to constitute a drag on the American economy because they start out at the bottom of the job ladder and are likely to remain there without much prospect for improvement seems unwarranted. In fact, substantial mobility occurs even in the immigrant generation. What happens to the members of the immigrant group after the immigrant generation is also relevant to the question of the degree to which the members of immigrant groups are handicapped by their racial or ethnic status. In the United States, Asians do not appear to be particularly handicapped in the labor market, leaving Latinos as the group to whom such questions pertain most compellingly.[28] How are U.S.- and foreign-born Latinos, the groups most represented at the bottom of the job distribution, distributed across major industry categories, compared with majority U.S.-born whites? If U.S.-born Latinos tend to resemble U.S.-born whites more than they resemble foreign-born Latinos, improvement among immigrants in the United States would seem to be taking place across generations as well as in the first generation.

Figure 10 shows the distributions of male and female Latinos by nativity across major industry categories in the United States in 2000, along with that of

U.S.-born whites. In five of the 12 male categories, the differences among the three groups are not large, indicating that neither immigrant nor U.S.-born Latinos tend to be over- or underrepresented in that part of the economy. (The groups might hold different occupations within the sector, but this discussion focuses on industry differences.) In six categories, however, nativity differences emerge, with U.S-born Latinos being much closer to U.S.-born whites than to Latino immigrants in public administration, professional services, transport/communication/ utilities, nondurable goods manufacturing, construction, and agriculture/mining/forestry/fishing. The first three categories generally involve higher fractions of better-paying jobs; the latter three generally involve lower-paying jobs and substantial concentrations of the foreign-born. Only two industry categories show an ethnic difference: retail trade, in which the concentration of Latinos exceeds that of whites irrespective of nativity; and durable goods manufacturing, in which the concentration of whites exceeds that of Latinos irrespective of nativity. The concentrations of females in these industries reveal a similar tendency for nativity differences to predominate over ethnic differences, with the U.S.-born far more represented than the foreign-born in relatively higher-paying sectors.

These results suggest that failing to consider nativity when examining labor market outcomes of Latino immigrants often gives a misleading picture of the

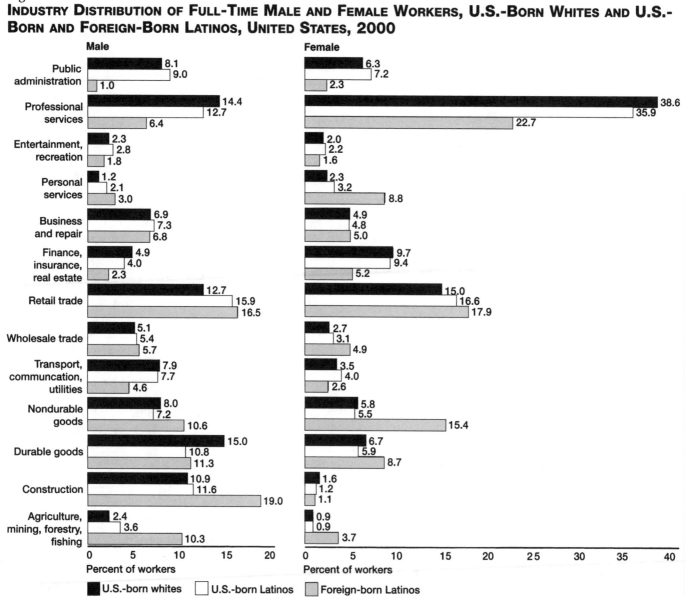

Figure 10

INDUSTRY DISTRIBUTION OF FULL-TIME MALE AND FEMALE WORKERS, U.S.-BORN WHITES AND U.S.-BORN AND FOREIGN-BORN LATINOS, UNITED STATES, 2000

Source: Authors' calculations based on the Integrated Public Use Microdata Series (IPMS), 2003.

degree of their economic accomplishment, thus generating confusion about whether the evidence offers more support to the assimilation or the ethnic disadvantage perspective. This is particularly problematic in the case of the Mexican origin population, whose members start out in the United States at lower employment levels than any other Latino immigrant group.

Observers of the rise in the importance of the Mexican origin population have often been uncertain how to characterize their experiences and their incorporation in the United States. Even though Mexican immigrants are diverse in terms of their migration status and modes of entry into the United States, they are often judged according to the prior experiences of either European immigrants or African Americans. An assimilation perspective views Mexican origin people primarily as an immigrant group whose members have mostly come to the United States only recently and whose incorporation may mirror that of earlier groups. In this view, natural incorporation processes need only run their course, usually over three or four generations. The alternative perspective tends to see them as members of a disadvantaged minority group whose progress toward full economic parity with other U.S. groups is retarded by discrimination. In this view, substantial progress is not likely to occur without policies that both help eradicate discrimination and compensate for its past effects.

Analysts influenced by these two ways of looking at the Mexican origin experience tend to organize economic statistics differently in seeking to shed light on the group's economic incorporation. Because the ethnic disadvantage viewpoint sees all members of the group as subject to discrimination, its adherents tend to marshal data on income and jobs and other indicators based on the entire national origin group, regardless of nativity status. Observers who treat Mexican origin

people as members of an immigrant group, by contrast, tend to distinguish the foreign-born from the U.S.-born on the grounds that the experience of those of Mexican origin vary so much by nativity that data on this group must be disaggregated. For example, rather than arguing that discrimination shapes immigrants' experiences in the labor market, these observers hold that such outcomes as immigrant wages and employment are influenced more by English-language proficiency, human capital variables, and U.S. work experience. From this perspective, the examination of labor market outcomes or other variables that include data on both foreign-born and U.S.-born people is likely to yield misleading assessments of the economic achievements of many members of immigrant groups, especially Mexican origin people.

Each viewpoint has some evidence to support its ideas. On the one hand, research suggests that people of Mexican origin often face job discrimination, though not as much as African Americans. Nonetheless, it is also evident that not disaggregating data by nativity generates an incomplete picture of the accomplishments of those of Mexican origin. For example, the annual earnings among U.S.-born white males exceeded those of Mexican-origin males by almost 30 percent in 2000, irrespective of education level. Earnings of white females exceeded comparably educated Mexican origin females by about 13 percent to 18 percent. These are substantial differences, and such earnings gaps stated in terms of ethnic group differentials give considerable weight to the argument that race or ethnicity plays a prominent role in earnings patterns. However, when U.S.-born Latinos and whites are compared, these differences shrink considerably (by about a fourth in the case of males and by almost a third in the case of females), although the gap is not eliminated (see Table 6).

Table 6

MEDIAN ANNUAL EARNINGS OF FULL-TIME WORKERS BY RACE/ETHNICITY, NATIVITY, GENDER, AND EDUCATION, UNITED STATES, 2000

Racial/ethnic group	Males Less than high school	Males High school	Males Any college	Females Less than high school	Females High school	Females Any college
Non-Latino white						
U.S.-born	$28,000	$34,000	$48,000	$18,000	$23,000	$33,000
Mexican origin						
Total	20,000	25,000	35,000	15,000	20,000	28,000
U.S.-born	22,000	27,000	38,000	16,000	22,000	29,000
Foreign-born	20,000	23,000	30,000	14,000	18,000	25,000
Percent difference						
White–all Latinos	28.6	26.5	27.1	18.3	13.0	15.2
White–U.S.-born Latinos	21.4	20.6	20.8	11.1	4.3	11.8

Source: Authors' calculations based on the Integrated Public Use Microdata Series (IPUMS), 2003.

These patterns illustrate that substantial earnings increases occur when immigrants are compared with subsequent generations. In fact, recent research on generational differences shows that these gaps close even more substantially when later-generation Mexican origin people are compared to non-Latino whites.[29] Results that group all Mexican origin people together miss these patterns. Gaps in education and earnings between immigrant and U.S.-born members of the same group clearly have more to do with origin-country differences in economic development than with discrimination. Bias resulting from the aggregation of nativity data is likely to be especially severe in times of high immigration, as in the 1990s, when immigration, particularly from Mexico, rose because of the legalization programs associated with the 1986 Immigration Reform and Control Act and because of an economic crisis in Mexico.[30]

Some scholars argue that several new immigrant groups risk the kinds of outcomes that disadvantaged blacks have often experienced. Efforts to sort out the degree of economic progress among immigrant groups must break down racial or ethnic groups by nativity or (preferably) generational status. While this may seem like a banal observation, it bears repeating, as Rebecca Raijman and Marta Tienda have also emphasized, because it continues to be overlooked.[31] Understanding what is happening among new immigrant groups requires recognizing that even as incorporation may be occurring in regard to economic factors, it may be moving in opposite directions in regard to some sociocultural factors (immigrants may be moving up the economic ladder even as they identify more strongly with many of the symbols of their ethnicity, such as food or celebration of holidays). Thus, neither perspective may fully characterize the experiences of many new immigrant groups, who not only have distinctive historical backgrounds but experience different modes of reception after they arrive in the United States.[32]

SOCIOCULTURAL
INCORPORATION

While studying trends in job mobility and earnings provides a window into the economic incorporation processes among today's immigrants, other important indicators of immigrant incorporation involve sociocultural patterns—namely intermarriage and multiracial reporting. Trends in intermarriage are significant because social scientists view racial or ethnic intermarriage as a measure of decreasing social distance, declining racial or ethnic prejudice, and changing racial or ethnic group boundaries.

Perhaps the most apparent trend is that over the past four decades—a time coinciding with the rise of the new immigration—intermarriage has increased substantially. For example, more than 30 percent of Asian or Latino individuals had a spouse of another race or ethnicity by the late 1990s, with the vast majority married to a white partner.[33] Similarly, more than 50 percent of third-generation Asian or Latino marriages during the 1990s (defined as those with at least one spouse being a member of the racial or ethnic group in question) included a white spouse.[34] Such rises in intermarriage have in turn led to a sizable and growing multiracial population. Currently, one in 40 people self-identifies as multiracial, and this figure is twice as high among those under the age of 18.[35] Population projections suggest that the multiple origin population will increase by 2 to 3 percentage points each decade for the next century; by the year 2050 as many as one in five Americans could claim a multiracial background.[36]

America's Newcomers

The process of sociocultural incorporation of new immigrant groups in the United States leads to various theories about the nature and degree of assimilation processes. The first is the classic "straight-line" model of assimilation, with its many variants. This model predicts that newcomers will both affect and be affected by the fabric of American life so that after several generations, the immigrant minorities and the majority become ever more indistinguishable from one another. Born of the predominantly European origin migration taking place at the beginning of the 20th century, the straight-line model emerged from how European immigrants established a foothold and gained economic mobility in the United States.

Milton Gordon canonized the view that there is one unidirectional pathway to successfully assimilating into the nation's economic and social structure and that acculturation not only preceded but was necessary for structural incorporation.[37] In the assimilation process, immigrants lose their ethnic distinctiveness; become ever more indistinguishable from the host society; intermarry with members of the host society; and eventually adopt an American identity, thereby marking the final stages of assimilation.

Gordon's model has two shortcomings: its imperfections in depicting the experiences of European migrants and its inability to explain the experience of either African Americans or today's immigrants. For example, white European groups continue to manifest aspects of ethnic distinctiveness despite their substantial structural incorporation—a phenomenon that cannot be accounted for with the straight-line assimilation model. Researchers have demonstrated, however, that much of the ethnic revival of this period was symbolic, giving rise to the concept of "symbolic ethnicity" for white ethnics.[38] The failure of the classic straight-line assimilation model to account for the experience of blacks in the United States is more fundamental. In the latter two decades of the 20th century, while black customs, practices, and ideals had come to mirror those of the larger population to a considerable degree—indicating their high level of acculturation—complete economic incorporation was still missing. The prevailing view at this time was that the removal of legal barriers would quickly lead to substantial structural incorporation among African Americans. By the 1980s, however, it was plain that the elimination of such barriers had resulted in only partial economic improvements for blacks.[39] Furthermore, despite the high level of acculturation among African Americans, the rate of intermarriage between blacks and whites remained and continues to remain low.

The straight-line model also fails to accurately characterize the incorporation pathways of America's newest immigrants, such as Asians, Latinos, and West Indians. Today, social scientists conceive of many different paths of incorporation for America's newcomers, a perspective first articulated in Alejandro Portes and Min Zhou's seminal article on segmented assimilation.[40] They posited three possible pathways of immigrant incorporation: straight-line assimilation into the white middle class (for example, light-skinned Cubans in Miami); assimilation into the minority underclass in inner-city poverty and culture (for example, Haitians in Miami); and selective assimilation, in which immigrants remain immersed in their ethnic community and preserve the immigrant community's values and solidarity (for example, Punjabi Sikh Indians in Northern California). Many of today's new Asian and Latino immigrants adopt a path of selective acculturation or accommodation without assimilation.[41] Social scientists have also documented that acculturation is no longer the surest path to successful economic incorporation, as the straight-line model suggests. For example, immigrants and their children who adopt a path of selective assimilation (assimilating along some dimensions but not others) use the resources within the immigrant ethnic community and maintain a strong sense of ethnic identity to shield themselves from the spiral of downward mobility in the face of economic disadvantage. In fact, among West Indians in New York and Vietnamese in Louisiana, casting off one's immigrant identity can lead to downward mobility—a concept that directly challenges the dominant sociological paradigm of straight-line assimilation.[42] Thus, if cultural accommodation facilitated structural incorporation in the past, it does not seem apparent or necessary for many of today's newcomers, illustrating the frequent decoupling of the traditional linkages thought to exist between acculturation and economic mobility.[43] In the path of selective assimilation, ethnicity acts as a resource to upward mobility and appears less constraining than previously presumed, becoming more useful, flexible, and non-bounding than emphasized by the straight-line model.

Intermarriage

At the beginning of the 20th century, intermarriage between white ethnics was rare and nearly caste-like, especially between "old" white ethnics and newer arrivals from Eastern and southern Europe.[44] Today, white ethnics intermarry at such high rates that only one-fifth of whites have a spouse with an identical ethnic background, reflecting the virtual disappearance of boundaries among white ethnic groups.[45] By contrast, marriage across racial groups, while on the rise, is still relatively uncommon between some groups, and all groups continue to intermarry at rates lower than would be predicted at random. For example, more than 90 percent of white and black marriages were endogamous in 1990, while about 70 percent of Asian and Hispanic and 25 percent of American Indian marriages were. Moreover, even though these percentages had increased by 2000, they remained relatively low.[46]

In one sense, it not surprising that interracial marriage is not as common as white interethnic marriage, given that it was illegal in 16 states as recently as 1967 when the U.S. Supreme Court (in Loving v. Commonwealth of Virginia) overturned the last remaining antimiscegenation laws. The ruling, along with the civil rights revolution, contributed to the rise in interracial marriage, which increased tenfold within a 30-year period (from 150,000 in 1960 to 1.6 million in 1990), far beyond what would be predicted by population growth alone.[47] Today, about 13 percent of American marriages involve people of different races, a considerable increase over the 35 years.[48] While the rise in interracial marriage might initially appear to indicate that racial boundaries are eroding, closer examination of recent findings indicates that not all racial or ethnic groups are equal partners in this growth. For instance, among the 30 percent or so of married U.S.-born Asians and Latinos who have a spouse of a different racial background, most spouses are white (see Table 7). Among young (25 to 34 years of age) U.S.-born Asians and Latinos, the intermarriage figures are even higher; nearly two-thirds of married Asians and two-fifths of Latinos outmarry, again mostly with whites.[49] By contrast, less than one-tenth of young blacks marry someone of a different racial background.[50]

While the rate of black-white intermarriage more than doubled in the 1970s and 1980s, on the whole the intermarriage rates for whites and blacks remain relatively low.[51] Even by 2000, of all marriages involving at least one white person, only 7 percent were exogamous; the comparable figure for blacks was 13 percent. The comparatively higher rates of intermarriage among U.S.-born Asians and Latinos indicate that as these groups incorporate into the United States, not only do they

Table 7

PERCENT OF MARRIED COUPLES WITH SPOUSE OF DIFFERENT RACE/ETHNICITY, BY RACE/ETHNICITY, 1990 AND 2000

Race/ethnicity	1990	2000
Total	4.4	6.4
White	4.7	7.0
Black	8.4	12.6
Asian	31.5	30.9
Latino	32.5	29.3
AINLOR[a]	74.8	70.7

[a] American Indian, Alaska Native, and non-Latino Other racial groups.

Source: Authors' calculations based on the Integrated Public Use Microdata Series (IPUMS), 2003.

become receptive to intermarriage, but whites also perceive them as suitable marriage partners.

Three distinct trends are emerging in interracial marriage in the United States. First, intermarriage for all racial groups has increased dramatically over the last 35 years and will probably continue to rise. Second, intermarriage is not uncommon in the cases of newer immigrant groups such as Asians and Latinos (particularly among the young U.S.-born populations). Third, compared to Asians, Latinos, and American Indians, intermarriage is still relatively uncommon among blacks.

The differential rates of intermarriage among nonwhite racial groups suggest that racial and ethnic boundaries are more prominent for some groups than for others. The significantly higher rates of intermarriage for Asians and Latinos indicate that racial or ethnic boundaries are more fluid and flexible, and racial or ethnic prejudice less salient. By contrast, the lower rates of intermarriage among blacks suggest that racial boundaries are more prominent and that the black-white divide is more salient than either the Asian-white or Latino-white divides. Thus, while boundaries are fading, boundary crossing among racial groups is not unconditional, and race is not declining in significance at the same pace for all groups.

Multiracial Population

The rise in interracial marriage has resulted in the growth of the multiracial population in the United States. This population became highly visible when the 2000 Census, for the first time in history, allowed Americans to select one or more races to indicate their racial identification. Brought about by a small but highly influential multiracial movement, this landmark change in the way the United States measures racial identification reflects the view that race is no longer conceived as a bounded category.[52] In 2000, 7 million people, or 2 percent of Americans, identified themselves as multiracial—about one of every 40 people. While these figures may not appear

large, a recent National Academy of Sciences study noted that the multiracial population could rise to 21 percent by the year 2050 when—because of rising patterns in intermarriage—as many as 35 percent of Asians and 45 percent of Hispanics might claim a multiracial background.[53] The growth of the multiracial population provides a new reflection on the nation's changing racial boundaries.

Because the multiracial population will clearly continue to grow, the phenomenon has begun to receive systematic attention in social science research. For example, several studies have examined the question of how interracial couples identify their multiracial children, revealing that about 50 percent of American Indian-white and Asian-white intermarried couples report a white racial identity for their children.[54] Other studies have examined the ways in which multiracial individuals self-identify, but often based on small samples that generate conflicting findings.[55] For example, Nelly Salgado de Snyder and colleagues found that 70 percent of multiracial children in California with one Mexican origin parent identified as Mexican, a rate much higher than Cookie White Stephan and Walter G. Stephan found for multiracial Hispanic college students in New Mexico, where only 44 percent adopted a Hispanic identity.[56]

Previous research indicates that several important variables affect the choice of racial identification among children of interracial unions, such as generational status, bilingualism, and proximity to a nonwhite community. For example, in their studies of biracial children with one Asian parent, Rogelio Saenz and colleagues and Yu Xie and Kimberly Goyette found that nativity and generational status matter.[57] First-generation biracial Asian children are more likely to be identified as Asian than are subsequent generations. However, the third generation is more likely to be identified as Asian than their second-generation counterparts. While this finding appears to contradict the classic assimilation model—which predicts fading ethnic identification with each successive generation—Xie and Goyette argue that choosing to identify one's child as Asian does not necessarily signify a stronger sense of racial identification. Rather, they posit that the racial identification of multiracial Asian children is to a large extent optional, likening it to the ethnic options available for whites. Providing further support for this claim, David Harris and Jeremiah Joseph Sim found in their study of multiracial youth that when asked to choose a single race, Asian-white youth are equally likely to identify as Asian or white, demonstrating that the racial identification of Asian-white multiracial individuals is largely a matter of choice.[58]

A second consistent finding is that speaking a language other than English at home significantly increases the likelihood that biracial children will adopt a nonwhite identity, supporting the thesis that language maintenance is critical in ethnic identity formation.[59] A third finding is that neighborhood context matters, and exposure to the minority parent's culture increases the likelihood that biracial children will adopt a nonwhite identity. For example, living among a large co-ethnic community or residing in a Public Use Microdata Area that is greater than 20 percent Asian positively affects the degree to which interracially married Asians and whites identify their multiracial children as Asian.[60] Furthermore, Stephan and Stephan posit that the higher rates of multiracial identification of the Japanese in Hawaii (73 percent) compared to the Hispanics in New Mexico (44 percent) reflect the greater multicultural milieu in Hawaii, including a variety of locally available labels for the multiracial or multiethnic population.[61] Karl Eschbach also discovers vast regional differences in the choice of an American Indian identity for American Indian-white multiracial individuals—ranging from 33 percent to 73 percent.[62]

Patterns of Multiracial Identification

About one in 40 Americans reported a multiracial background in the 2000 Census. Of these, 93 percent reported exactly two races, 6 percent reported three races, and only 1 percent reported four or more races. While most individuals who report a multiracial identification list exactly two races, the selection of these races is not evenly distributed across all racial groups. As Table 8 illustrates, groups with a high percentage of multiracial people as a percentage of the total group include Native Hawaiian or Other Pacific Islander, American Indian and Alaska Native, Other, and Asian. In both 1990 and 2000, slightly more than 97 percent of those who checked Other were Latinos.[63]

Also shown in Table 8, the groups with the lowest proportion claiming a multiracial background in 2000 were whites and blacks. However, because whites account for over three-fourths of the total U.S. population, most individuals who report a multiracial identity also claim a white background. More specifically, while 5 million whites report a multiracial background, this accounts for only 3 percent of the total white population. Like whites, the proportion of blacks who claim a multiracial background is also small, accounting for only 5 percent of the total black population. These figures stand in sharp contrast to those among American Indian/Alaska Native and Native Hawaiian/Other Pacific Islander, who show the highest percentage of multiracial reporting as a proportion of their populations. Asians and Latinos fall in between (14 percent and 17 percent, respectively), with significantly higher rates of multiracial reporting than blacks or whites, but lower rates than American Indian/Alaska Native and Native Hawaiian/Other Pacific Islander.

Expressed as a percentage of the total black, Asian, and Latino populations, the rates of black-white, Asian-white, and Latino-white multiracial combinations are 2

Table 8

AMERICANS IDENTIFYING WITH ONE OR MORE RACES, 2000

| Race | Millions indentifying with race | | | |
	Total[a]	This race alone[b]	This race and other race(s)[c]	Percent multiracial
White	216.9	211.5	5.5	2.5
Black	36.4	34.7	1.8	4.9
Asian	11.9	10.2	1.7	14.3
Other	18.5	15.4	3.2	17.3
American Indian, Alaska Native	4.1	2.5	1.6	39.0
Native Hawaiian, other Pacific Islander	0.9	0.4	0.5	55.6

[a] Racial/ethnic group totals do not sum to the total U.S. population because multiracial persons are counted in more than one group.

[b] Totals do not sum to the total U.S. population because multiracial persons are excluded.

[c] Multiracial persons are counted in each racial group with which they identified.

Source: U.S. Census 2000.

percent, 7 percent, and 5 percent, respectively (see Table 9). Compared with the black-white combination among blacks, the Asian-white multiracial combination is about three and a half times more likely to occur among Asians, and the Latino-white combination is more than two and a half times more likely to occur among Latinos. Mirroring trends in intermarriage, three conclusions can be drawn from the patterns of multiracial identification.

First, the multiracial population seems likely to continue to grow in the foreseeable future as a result of increasing intermarriage. Second, multiracial identification is not uncommon among the members of new immigrant groups, such as Asians and Latinos (particularly for those under the age of 18). Third, at only 5 percent, multiracial identification remains relatively uncommon among blacks.

Why blacks are far less likely to report a multiracial background is particularly noteworthy, considering that the U.S. Census Bureau estimates that at least three-quarters of the black population in the United States is ancestrally multiracial.[64] In other words, although at least 75 percent of black Americans have some mixed ancestry (mostly white) and thus could claim multiracial identities on that basis, less than 5 percent choose to do so. The tendency of black Americans to be less likely to report multiracial identifications undoubtedly owes to the legacy of slavery, including lasting discrimination, the formerly *de jure* and now *de facto* invocation of the one-drop rule that emerged to protect slavery and legitimize Jim Crow segregation, and the force of black pride,

Table 9

PERCENT OF AMERICANS IDENTIFYING WITH TWO RACES BY RACE, UNITED STATES, 2000

| Race/ethnicity | Additional racial identity | | | | |
	White	Black	Asian	American Indian	Other
Whites[a]	—	0.3	0.4	0.5	1.1
Blacks[a]	1.9	—	0.3	0.6	1.1
Asians[a]	7.0	0.8	—	1.5	2.2
American Indian[a]	25.5	4.6	4.1	—	2.4
Other race[b]	11.9	2.2	1.3	0.5	—
Latinos[c]	4.9	0.8	0.4	0.5	5.1

[a] Non-Latino.

[b] May be Latino or non-Latino reporting the other racial category alone or in combination with the white, black, Asian, or American Indian categories.

[c] Latino respondents reporting a dual racial identity involving the column race and any one other race.

Source: U.S. Census 2000.

which may prefer not to dilute black identification by invoking other identifications. For no other racial or ethnic group in the United States and in no other country does this rule so influence a group's identity choices.

While the historical legacy of the one-drop rule still strongly affects identity options among black Americans, F. James Davis posits that blacks are aware that their racial ancestry is mixed.[65] He also notes that while the rule served to protect a rigid racial hierarchy, blacks may be reluctant to insist on changing it. In fact, he argues that many blacks have taken the rule for granted, but more important, they may also feel they have a stake in maintaining it because it provides a strong basis for ethnic unity, pride, and political power. Ironically, then, although the rule is arbitrary, socially constructed, and fundamental for implementing certain practices of racial oppression, abandoning it could weaken black identity and political strength as well as possibly undermine the credibility of some of the strongest black community leaders.

However, recent studies reveal that not all multiracial blacks feel compelled to adhere to the one-drop rule, and that younger black-white multiracial people, in particular, feel less constrained to adopt an exclusively black monoracial identity. For example, Kathleen Odell Korgen's study of 40 black-white adults reveals that only one-third of her sample under the age of 30 exclusively identified as black.[66] Moreover, David Harris and Jeremia Joseph Sim's study of multiracial youth shows that 17 percent of black-white adolescents chose white as the single race that best describes them.[67] While younger blacks are less likely to report an exclusively black monoracial identity than are older black

cohorts, blacks overall are still far less likely to report multiracial backgrounds than are Asians or Latinos.

The absence of a one-drop rule for labeling among multiracial Asians, Latinos, and American Indians has left them more room for exercising discretion in selecting racial or ethnic identities. Higher rates of multiracial reporting among Latinos and Asians, both as a proportion of the total Latino and Asian populations and when compared with blacks, indicate that racial boundaries are less constraining for these groups than for blacks.

In addition, because a significant proportion of Latinos and Asians in the United States are either immigrants or the children of immigrants, their understanding of race, racial boundaries, and the black-white color divide is shaped by a different set of circumstances than those of African Americans. Most important, experiences of Latinos and Asians in the United States are not rooted in the same historical legacy of slavery, with its systematic and persistent patterns of legal and institutional discrimination and inequality from which the tenacious black-white divide was born and cemented. Unlike African Americans, who were forcibly brought to this country as slaves, the migration experiences of today's Latino and Asian newcomers are quite distinct from those of African Americans. The subjugation of black Americans in this country makes the black-white racial gap qualitatively and quantitatively different from the Latino-white or Asian-white racial divides. Thus, while boundary crossing may be more common for all groups, it appears that the legacy of institutional racism in the country more forcefully constrains identity options for blacks than for other nonwhite groups.

In fact, some research indicates that racial boundaries among Latinos, Asians, and American Indians are beginning to assume the fluidity and mutability of ethnicity. For example, in their longitudinal study of high school students, Karl Eschbach and C. Gomez note that only 68 percent of the more than 6,500 students interviewed between 1980 and 1982 consistently identified as Hispanic.[68] They suggest that the change in racial and ethnic identification points to a process of transformation from ascribed to optional ethnicity. Similarly, Karl Eschbach, Khalil Supple, and C. Matthew Snipp note that the American Indian population grew from 827,000 in 1970 to almost 2 million in 1990, positing that the change in racial identification from white to American Indian signifies the flexibility of racial boundaries for this group.[69] Furthermore, the racial identification for Asians has changed over time from almost black to almost white, pointing to the mutability of boundaries for at least some Asian ethnic groups. Thus, recent findings suggest that at least for some Asians, Latinos, and American Indians, race is adopting the optional and symbolic character of white ethnicity.

Shifting Geographic Boundaries

Another way of assessing America's changing racial and ethnic boundaries is to unearth where these boundaries are shifting most rapidly. Patterns of multiracial identification reveal that areas with high immigrant populations evince larger multiracial populations. The foreign-born population and the multiracial population are clustered in several cities and states. In fact, 64 percent of those who report a multiracial identification reside in just 10 states—California, Florida, Hawaii, Illinois, Michigan, New Jersey, New York, Ohio, Texas, and Washington—all of which have relatively high immigrant populations.[70] In essence, high-diversity states (as reflected in the percent of the population other than non-Hispanic whites and blacks) boast much larger multiracial populations than less racially diverse states. On the opposite end of the diversity spectrum are states like Maine and West Virginia, which have low racial minority populations and thereby exhibit very low levels of multiracial reporting. States like Alabama, Louisiana, Mississippi, and South Carolina, however, have relatively large black populations but nevertheless evince low levels of multiracial reporting. In these Southern states, the strong traditional dividing line between blacks and whites appears to constrain multiracial identification, leading people to identify monoracially as either white or black rather than adopting a multiracial identity.[71]

These patterns suggest that multiracial reporting is more likely in areas with greater levels of racial and ethnic diversity, which in turn have largely been brought about by the post-1965 wave of immigrants, particularly Latinos and Asians. This theory is consistent with much prior work in sociology. Racial and ethnic diversity implies both the presence of many racial and ethnic groups and the relative absence of statistical predominance on the part of any single group. Thus, the more a single racial or ethnic group dominates the population of some social, political, economic, or geographic group or area, the less the diversity; conversely, the greater the number of groups and the more equally they are distributed within an area, the greater the diversity. As used here for racial and ethnic groups, diversity is equivalent to the idea of heterogeneity as it is often more broadly invoked in sociology. All else equal, greater diversity should lead to increased multiracial reporting, because increased diversity (or heterogeneity) tends to promote more frequent intergroup associations and greater tolerance, results often found and noted in the sociological literature.[72]

In fact, it is precisely the lack of racial and ethnic tolerance in the Deep South that has tended to constrain the reporting of multiracial mixing. In general, increased tolerance and flexibility should generate increased multiracial reporting. Immigration increases the likelihood of multiracial identification because the greater diversity it fosters loosens racial or ethnic boundaries and allows more flexibility in the identity options for multiracial people. The geography of multiracial reporting indicates that the rate varies widely across the country, with the highest levels in areas that exhibit the greatest racial and ethnic diversity brought about by the arrival of immigrants to these areas. Thus, while national patterns in interracial marriage and multiracial identification indicate a loosening of racial boundaries, particularly for Latinos and Asians, these shifts appear to be taking place more rapidly in certain parts of the country and among certain groups.

Linking Diversity to Multiracial Identification

What kinds of research results might be further evidence of a connection between growing diversity and the breakdown of racial or ethnic color lines? Multiracial identifications are more likely among Asians and Latinos than among either black African-origin immigrants or U.S.-born blacks, as a consequence of both higher rates of intermarriage among the former groups and greater tendency for them to see themselves in multiracial terms. Places with more immigration may also have larger relative sizes of racial or ethnic minority groups (at least in the cases of Latinos and Asians) and increased diversity, with the latter loosening racial or ethnic boundaries and increasing the likelihood of multiracial self-identification.

But a minority group that is growing in size may also increase perceptions of threat in the majority group.[73] Under conditions of continuing immigration, a constant influx of new members of a given racial or ethnic group into a concentrated area will not only add to the group's relative size but it may also reinforce the group's distinctive behavioral and cultural patterns. This may heighten the group's distinctive sense of ethnicity, foster ethnic insularity, and tighten racial or ethnic boundaries. It may also make it less likely that the members of such groups will either come from multiracial backgrounds (due to declines in intermarriage) or come to perceive themselves in multiracial terms. In short, while larger relative group size may foster multiracial identification through one pathway, it may diminish intermarriage and multiracial identification through others.

Metropolitan-level data on multiracial identification can be used to assess the effects of relative group size and diversity on multiracial reporting. For example, Table 10 presents basic data for metropolitan areas on multiracial identification and racial and ethnic composition.

Many of the metropolitan areas with the highest percentages of multiracial residents are located in the Pacific West, and rank high on the diversity score. Many of those with low multiracial percentages are in the South and Midwest. Some of these also rank high on the diversity score, but they tend to be areas where blacks are the dominant minority group and where there are few Asians. In a multivariate analysis of a complete data set for metropolitan areas (not shown here), we confirmed that the effects of racial and ethnic diversity on multiraciality is more positive for metropolitan areas with a sizable proportion of Asians than for areas with relatively large black populations. This supports the idea that increasing racial and ethnic diversity loosens these traditional group boundaries in the United States, apparently more so for Asians and Latinos than for blacks.[74]

BLENDING AND FADING

Increases in intermarriage and the growth of the multiracial population reflect a blending of races and the fading of color lines. Because interracial marriage and multiracial identification indicate reduced social distance and racial prejudice, these patterns offer an optimistic portrait of weakening racial boundaries. For example, interracial marriage was illegal in 16 states as recently as 1967, but today about 13 percent of American marriages involve people of different races. At the end of the 19th century, rates of intermarriage among Asians in this country were close to zero, but today

---

Table 10
HIGHEST AND LOWEST PERCENT MULTIRACIAL U.S. METROPOLITAN AREAS, 2000

Metropolitan areas, state(s)	Multiracial persons (thousands)	Percent of metro population multiracial	Percent of metro population nonwhite	Diversity score*
Most multiracial				
Honolulu, HI	96.8	16.7	78	0.48
Stockton, CA	34.6	6.1	53	0.66
Jersey City, NJ	35.7	5.9	64	0.69
Oakland, CA	134.3	5.6	53	0.69
San Francisco, CA	81.2	5.5	54	0.67
Tacoma, WA	38.8	5.5	25	0.42
Vallejo-Fairfield-Napa, CA	28.4	5.5	47	0.65
Modesto, CA	23.7	5.4	43	0.57
Sacramento, CA	88.9	5.4	36	0.55
San Jose, CA	90.6	5.4	57	0.68
Los Angeles-Long Beach, CA	490.6	5.2	69	0.68
New York-Northeastern NJ	441.1	5.1	64	0.72
Riverside-San Bernadino, CA	136.2	5.1	55	0.64
San Diego, CA	143.1	5.0	46	0.61
Tulsa, OK	34.6	5.0	25	0.42
Least multiracial				
Sarasota, FL	8.2	1.4	15	0.27
Melbourne-Titusville-Cocoa-Palm Bay, FL	6.4	1.4	15	0.27
Canton, OH	5.4	1.3	9	0.17
Richmond-Petersburg, VA	7.5	1.3	39	0.51
Cincinnati OH/KY/IN	10.6	1.3	29	0.42
Pittsburgh-Beaver Valley, PA	18.1	1.2	14	0.25
Charlotte-Gastonia-Rock Hill, SC	8.6	1.2	38	0.53
Buffalo-Niagara Falls, NY	14.4	1.2	17	0.30
Harrisburg-Lebanon-Carlisle, PA	7.6	1.2	14	0.25
Greensboro-Winston Salem-High Point, NC	14.9	1.2	28	0.44
Dayton-Springfield, OH	6.2	1.1	23	0.37
Scranton-Wilkes-Barre, PA	6.6	1.1	5	0.10
Baton Rouge, LA	6.2	1.0	36	0.49
Birmingham, AL	5.3	1.0	45	0.53
Memphis, TN/AR/MS	4.9	0.9	67	0.51
Jackson, MS	2.7	0.6	47	0.52
Non-metro areas	2,367,456	1.9	20	0.35

* Diversity score is defined as one minus the sum of squared proportions of the population in each racial or ethnic group. A score of zero would mean that all residents belong to just one group; a score of 0.75 would mean equal proportions of the population in each of four groups.

Source: Authors' calculations based on the Integrated Public Use Microdata Series (IPUMS), 2003.

---

more than a quarter of all U.S.-born Asians and Latinos marry someone of a different racial background, mostly whites. These figures are even higher among younger Asians and Latinos and are likely to increase in future generations.

The rise in intermarriage has led to a visible and growing multiracial population that could easily account for one-fifth of the nation's population by the year 2050. Nowhere are these changes more apparent than in the West, where 40 percent of the multiracially identified population resides, most prominently in California—the state that leads the country with the highest level of multiracial reporting and the only state with a multiracial population exceeding 1 million. Multiracial individuals account for 5 percent of California's population, or one in 21 Californians, compared with one in every 40 for the country as a whole. Among Californians under the age of 18, one in every 14 (7 percent) reports a multiracial identification. At first glance, these statistics appear to indicate that boundary crossing is becoming more common and that racial divides are fading for all groups. But intermarriage and multiracial identification are fairly high among Asians and Latinos (especially among the younger cohort), and are far less common among blacks.

Before assessing the implications of these patterns for America's color lines, it is crucial to know how one interprets the findings on intermarriage and multiracial identification for Latinos and Asians. For instance, given the perspective that Latinos and Asians are racialized minorities, and thus fall closer to blacks than whites along some scale of social disadvantage, then the high levels of interracial marriage and multiracial identification among these groups suggest that boundaries are not only fading for these groups but also for all non-whites, including blacks. Such a conclusion would support the sanguine view that the long-standing black-white divide is breaking down and that racial prejudice and boundaries are fading for all groups. However, this interpretation risks attributing signs of integration to blacks that are in fact more the province of Latinos and Asians, thus inviting overly optimistic conclusions about the breadth of boundary dissolution.

If, on the other hand, Latinos and Asians are better represented as new immigrants whose disadvantage stems from not having had sufficient time to join the economic and social mainstreams, then their high levels of intermarriage and multiracial reporting signal that their experiences may be different from those of blacks altogether. Such a conclusion would support a more pessimistic view that the experiences and situations of Latinos and Asians do not imply similar improvements and results among blacks. That is, what may at first suggest a dissolution of color lines for all racial and ethnic groups may simply constitute less rigid boundaries among new immigrant groups transitioning toward incorporation. This distinction is critical, and helps to differentiate whether color lines are shifting for all racial and ethnic minorities or whether they are mainly accommodating new nonblack immigrant groups.

Our analysis affirms that racial boundaries are not eroding at the same pace for all groups. The nature of these divergent patterns indicates that the color line is less rigid for Latinos and Asians. Although the color line may be shifting for blacks, this change is occurring more slowly, placing Asians and Latinos closer than blacks to whites and demonstrating the tenacity of the black-white divide. In essence, while boundary crossing may be rising, and the color line fading, a shift has yet to occur toward a pattern of unconditional boundary crossing or a declining significance of race for all groups.

It appears that Latinos and Asians may be accepted as almost white or even white, and consequently may participate in a new color line that is still somewhat exclusionary of blacks, especially if they do not have college degrees. If much of America's racial history has revolved around who was white and who was not, it is important to strive to ensure that the next phase in this story does not revolve around who is black and who is not. While rising rates of intermarriage and patterns of multiracial identification clearly indicate that immigration is breaking down barriers, the fact that boundary dissolution is neither uniform nor unconditional indicates little basis for complacency about the degree to which prospects are good for all racial and ethnic groups in America.

REFERENCES

If provided by the authors, additional text and data associated with this report are available at www.prb.org/AmericanPeople.

1. Michael Fix, Jeffrey Passel, and Kenneth Sucher, *Trends in Naturalization* (Washington, DC: Urban Institute, 2003); and U.S. Census Bureau, *Current Population Survey: Monthly Demographic File, March* (Washington, DC: U.S. Census Bureau, 2002).

2. Lawrence Bobo, "The Color Line, the Dilemma, and the Dream: Race Relations in America at the Close of the Twentieth Century," in *Civil Rights and Social Wrongs*, ed. John Higham (University Park: Pennsylvania State University Press, 1997); Kenneth Clark, *Dark Ghetto: Dilemmas of Social Power* (New York: Harper and Row, 1965); St. Clair Drake and Horace R. Cayton, *Black Metropolis: A Study of Negro Life in a Northern City* (Chicago: University of Chicago Press, [1945] 1993); Reynolds Farley and Richard Allen, *The Color Line and the Quality of Life in America* (New York: Russell Sage Foundation, 1987); Gunnar Myrdal, *An American Dilemma: The Negro Problem and Modern Democracy* (New York: Harper, 1944); Orlando Patterson, *The Ordeal of Integration* (Washington, DC: Civitas, 1998); Orlando Patterson, *Rituals of Blood* (Washington, DC: Civitas, 1998); Neil J. Smelser, William Julius Wilson, and Faith Mitchell, *America Becoming: Racial Patterns and Their Consequences* (Washington, DC: National Academies Press, 2001); and William Julius Wilson, *The Truly Disadvantaged: The Inner City, the Underclass, and Public Policy* (Chicago: University of Chicago, 1987).

3. DuBois, *The Souls of Black Folk* (Boston: Bedford Books, 1997 [1903]).

4. Alba, "Immigration and the American Realities of Assimilation and Multiculturalism"; Frank D. Bean and Gillian Stevens, *America's Newcomers and the Dynamics of Diversity* (New York: Russell Sage Foundation, 2003); Herbert J. Gans, "The Possibility of a New Racial Hierarchy in the Twenty-first Century United States," in *The Cultural Territories of Race*, ed. Michele Lamont (Chicago and New York: University of Chicago Press and Russell Sage Foundation, 1999); Todd Gitlin, *The Twilight of Common Dreams* (New York: Metropolitan, 1995); David A. Hollinger, "Amalgamation and Hypodescent: The Question of Ethnoracial Mixture in the History of the United States," *American Historical Review* 108, no. 5 (2003): 1363-90; David A. Hollinger, *Postethnic America: Beyond Multiculturalism* (New York: Basic Books, 1995); Jennifer Lee and Frank D. Bean, "Beyond Black and White: Remaking Race in America," *Contexts* 2, no. 3 (2003): 26-33; Clara E. Rodríguez, *Changing Race: Latinos, the Census, and the History of Ethnicity in the United States* (New York: New York University Press, 2000); Roger Sanjek, "Intermarriage and the Future of the Races," in *Race*, ed. Steven Gregory and Roger Sanjek (New Brunswick, NJ: Rutgers University Press, 1994); John Skrentny, *Color Lines: Affirmative Action, Immigration, and Civil Rights Options for America* (Chicago: University of Chicago Press, 2001); and Mary C. Waters, *Black Identities: West Indian Immigrant Dreams and American Realities* (New York; Cambridge, MA: Russell Sage Foundation; Harvard University Press, 1999).

5. Alba, "Immigration and the American Realities of Assimilation and Multiculturalism"; Karen Brodkin, *How Jews Became White Folks, and What That Says About Race in America* (New Brunswick, NJ: Rutgers University Press, 1998); Nancy Foner, *From Ellis Island to JFK: New York's Two Great Waves of Immigration* (New Haven and New York: Yale University Press and Russell Sage Foundation, 2000); Gary Gerstle, "Liberty, Coercion, and the Making of Americans," in *The Handbook of International Migration*, ed. Charles Hirschman, Josh DeWind, and Philip Kasinitz (New York: Russell Sage Foundation, 1999); Noel Ignatiev, *How the Irish Became White* (New York: Routledge, 1995); Matthew Freye Jacobson, *Whiteness of a Different Color: European Immigrants and the Alchemy of Race* (Cambridge, MA: Harvard University Press, 1998); Joel Perlmann and Roger Waldinger, "Second Generation Decline? Children of Immigrants, Past and Present—A Reconsideration," *International Migration Review* 31, no. 4 (1997): 893-922; and David Roediger, *The Wages of Whiteness* (New York: Verso, 1991).

6. James Loewen, *The Mississippi Chinese: Between Black and White* (Cambridge, MA: Harvard University Press, 1971).

7. Paul R. Spickard, *Mixed Blood: Intermarriage and Ethnic Identity In Twentieth-Century America* (Madison: University of Wisconsin Press, 1989).

8. Margo J. Anderson, "Counting by Race: The Antebellum Legacy," in *The New Race Question: How the Census Counts Multiracial Individuals*, ed. Joel Perlmann and Mary C. Waters (New York: Russell Sage Foundation, 2002); and Kim Williams, *Boxed in: The United States Multiracial Movement*, unpublished dissertation, Cornell University, 2001.

9. Margo J. Anderson and Stephen E. Fienberg, *Who Counts? The Politics of Census-Taking in Contemporary America* (New York: Russell Sage Foundation, 1999).

10. Reynolds Farley, "Racial Identities in 2000: The Response to the Multiple-Race Response Option," in *The New Race Question: How the Census Counts Multiracial Individuals*, ed. Joel Perlmann and Mary C. Waters (New York: Russell Sage Foundation, 2002).

11. F. James Davis, *Who is Black? One Nation's Definition* (University Park: The Pennsylvania State University Press, 1991).

12. Karl Eschbach, Khalil Supple, and C. Matthew Snipp, "Changes in Racial Identification and the Educational Attainment of American Indians, 1970-1990," *Demography* 35, no. 1 (1998): 35-43

13. Harvey M. Choldin, "Statistics and Politics: The 'Hispanic Issue' in the 1980 Census," *Demography* 23, no. 3 (1986): 403-18; and Peter Skerry, "Multiracialism and the Administrative State," in *The New Race Question: How the Census Counts Multiracial Individuals*, ed. Joel Perlmann and Mary C. Waters (New York: Russell Sage Foundation, 2002).

14. Frank D. Bean and Marta Tienda, *The Hispanic Population of the United States* (New York: Russell Sage Foundation, 1987).

15. Anderson and Fienberg, *Who Counts? The Politics of Census-Taking in Contemporary America*.

16. Barry Edmonston, Joshua Goldstein, and Juanita Tamayo Lott, eds., *Spotlight on Heterogeneity: The Federal Standards for Racial and Ethnic Classification, Summary of a Workshop* (Washington, DC: National Academies Press, 1996).

17. Rodríguez, *Changing Race: Latinos, the Census, and the History of Ethnicity in the United States.*

18. Barry Edmonston, Sharon M. Lee, and Jeffrey S. Passel, "Recent Trends in Intermarriage and Immigration and their Effects on the Future Racial Composition of the U.S. Population," in *The New Race Question: How the Census Counts Multiracial Individuals*, ed. Joel Perlmann and Mary C. Waters (New York: Russell Sage Foundation, 2002).

19. For a discussion of this measure of diversity, see Bean and Stevens, *America's Newcomers and the Dynamics of Diversity.*

20. U.S. Census Bureau, "Foreign-Born Population of the United States," *Current Population Survey, March 2000, Revised Detailed Tables*, accessed online at www.census.gov/population/www/socdemo/foreign/ppl-160.html, in February 2002.

21. Donald J. Hernandez, *Children of Immigrants: Health, Adjustment, and Public Assistance* (Washington, DC: National Research Council, 1999).

22. Frank D. Bean and Stephanie Bell-Rose, eds., *Immigration and Opportunity: Race, Ethnicity and Employment in the United States* (New York: Russell Sage Foundation, 1999); Bean and Stevens, *America's Newcomers and the Dynamics of Diversity.*

23. Wilson, *The Truly Disadvantaged: The Inner City, the Underclass, and Public Policy*; William Julius Wilson, *When Work Disappears: The World of the New Urban Poor* (New York: Alfred A. Knopf, 1996).

24. Douglas S. Massey et al., *Return to Aztlan: The Social Process of International Migration from Western Mexico* (Berkeley: University of California Press, 1987); Roger Waldinger, ed., *Strangers at the Gates: New Immigrants in Urban America* (Berkeley: University of California Press, 2001); and Roger Waldinger and Michael I. Lichter, *How the Other Half Works: Immigration and the Social Organization of Labor* (Berkeley: University of California Press, 2003).

25. Frank D. Bean, Mark A. Fossett, and Jennifer Van Hook, "Immigration, Spatial and Economic Change, and African American Employment," in *Immigration and Opportunity: Race, Ethnicity and Employment in the United States*, ed. Frank D. Bean and Stephanie Bell-Rose (New York: Russell Sage Foundation, 1999); and Rachel M. Friedberg and Jennifer Hunt, "Immigration and the Receiving Economy," in *The Handbook of International Migration: The American Experience*, ed. Charles Hirschman, Josh DeWind, and Philip Kasinitz (New York: Russell Sage Foundation, 1999).

26. Daniel Bell, *The Coming of Post-Industrial Society* (New York: Basic Books, 1973); Michael J. Piore and Charles Sabel, *The Second Industrial Divide* (New York: Basic Books, 1984); Erick Olin Wright and Rachel Dwyer, "The Patterns of Job Expansions in the United States: A Comparison of the 1960s and 1990s," accessed online at www.ssc.wisc.edu/~wright/JobsAJS.pdf, on March 20, 2004.

27. Frank D. Bean and Lindsay Lowell, *Unauthorized Mexican Migration to the United States: IRCA, NAFTA and Their Migration Implications* (Washington, DC: Migration Policy Institute and the Carnegie Endowment for International Peace, 2003).

28. Bean and Stevens, *America's Newcomers and the Dynamics of Diversity.*

29. Bean and Stevens, *America's Newcomers and the Dynamics of Diversity*; and James P. Smith, "Assimilation Across the Latino Generations," *American Economic Review* 93, no. 2 (2003): 315-19.

30. Frank D. Bean et al., "Immigration and the Social Contract," *Social Science Quarterly* 78, no. 2 (1997): 249-68; and Douglas Massey, Jorge Durand, and Nolan J. Malone, *Beyond Smoke and Mirrors: Mexican Immigration in an Era of Economic Integration* (New York: Russell Sage Foundation, 2002).

31. Rebecca Raijman and Marta Tienda, "Immigrants' Socioeconomic Progress Post-1965: Forging Mobility or Survival?" in *The Handbook of International Migration*, ed. Charles Hirschman, Josh DeWind, and Philip Kasinitz (New York, NY: Russell Sage Foundation, 1999).

32. Alejandro Portes and Rubén G. Rumbaut, *Legacies. The Story of the Immigrant Second Generation* (Berkeley and New York: University of California Press and Russell Sage Foundation, 2001); and Alejandro Portes and Min Zhou, "The New Second Generation: Segmented Assimilation and Its Variants," *The Annals of the American Academy of Political and Social Science* 530 (November 1993): 74-96.

33. Bean and Stevens, *America's Newcomers and the Dynamics of Diversity:* 195.

34. Tamar Jacoby, "An End to Counting by Race?" *Commentary* 111, no. 6 (2001): 37-40; Waters, *Black Identities: West Indian Immigrant Dreams and American Realities.*

35. Frank D. Bean and Jennifer Lee, "America's Changing Color Lines: Immigration, Racial/Ethnic Diversity, and Multiracial Identification," paper delivered at the Center for Comparative Studies in Race and Ethnicity, Stanford University, April 2002; and Elizabeth M. Grieco and Rachel C. Cassidy, *Overview of Race and Hispanic Origin* (Washington, DC: Government Printing Office, 2001).

36. Edmonston, Lee, and Passel, "Recent Trends in Intermarriage and Immigration and their Effects on the Future Racial Composition of the U.S. Population"; Reynolds Farley, *Identifying with Multiple Races: A Social Movement That Succeeded but Failed?* (Ann Arbor: Population Studies Center, University of Michigan, 2001); James P. Smith and Barry Edmonston, *The New Americans: Economic, Demographic, and Fiscal Effects of Immigration* (Washington, DC: National Academies Press, 1997).

37. Milton M. Gordon, *Assimilation in American Life: the Role of Race, Religion, and National Origins* (New York: Oxford University Press, 1964).

38. Alba, *Ethnic Identity: The Transformation of White America*; Herbert J. Gans, "Symbolic Ethnicity: The Future of Ethnic Groups and Cultures in America," *Ethnic and Racial Studies* 2, no. 1 (1979): 1-20; and Mary C. Waters, *Ethnic Options: Choosing Identities in America* (Berkeley: University of California Press, 1990).

39. Bean and Bell-Rose, eds., *Immigration and Opportunity: Race, Ethnicity and Employment in the United States*; Nathan Glazer, *We Are All Multiculturalists Now* (Cambridge, MA: Harvard University Press, 1997); Neil Smelser, William Julius Wilson, and Faith Mitchell, *America Becoming: Racial Patterns and Their Consequences* (Washington, DC: National Academies Press, 2001); and Wilson, *The Truly Disadvantaged: The Inner City, the Underclass, and Public Policy.*

40. Portes and Zhou, "The New Second Generation: Segmented Assimilation and Its Variants."

41. Margaret A. Gibson, *Accommodation without Assimilation: Sikh Immigrants in an American High School* (Ithaca, NY: Cornell University Press, 1988); Portes and Rumbaut, *Legacies: The Story of the Immigrant Second Generation*; Min Zhou

and Carl L. Bankston, *Growing Up American: How Vietnamese Children Adapt to Life in the United States* (New York: Russell Sage Foundation, 1998).

42. Waters, *Black Identities: West Indian Immigrant Dreams and American Realities*; Zhou and Bankston, *Growing Up American: How Vietnamese Children Adapt to Life in the United States.*

43. Kathryn M. Neckerman, Prudence Carter, and Jennifer Lee, "Segmented Assimilation and Minority Cultures of Mobility," *Ethnic and Racial Studies* 22, no. 6 (1999): 945-65; Portes and Zhou, "The New Second Generation: Segmented Assimilation and Its Variants."

44. Deanna L. Pagnini and S. Philip Morgan, "Intermarriage and Social Distance among U.S. Immigrants at the Turn of the Century," *American Journal of Sociology* 96, no. 2 (1990): 405-32.

45. Alba, *Ethnic Identity: The Transformation of White America*; Stanley Lieberson and Mary C. Waters, "The Ethnic Responses of Whites: What Causes Their Instability, Their Simplification, and Inconsistency?" *Social Forces* 72, no. 2 (1993): 421-50; Stanley Lieberson and Mary C. Waters, *From Many Strands: Ethnic and Racial Groups in Contemporary America* (New York: Russell Sage Foundation, 1988); and Waters, *Ethnic Options: Choosing Identities in America.*

46. Rachel F. Moran, *Interracial Intimacy: The Regulation of Race and Romance* (Chicago: University of Chicago Press, 2001).

47. Jacoby, "An End to Counting by Race?"; Mary C. Waters, "Multiple Ethnicities and Identity in the United States," in *We Are A People*, ed. Paul Spikard and W. Jeffrey Burroughs (Philadelphia: Temple University Press, 2000).

48. Bean and Stevens, *America's Newcomers and the Dynamics of Diversity*; and Lee and Bean, "Beyond Black and White: Remaking Race in America."

49. Zhenchao Qian, "Breaking the Racial Barriers: Variations in Interracial Marriage between 1980 and 1990," *Demography* 34, no. 2 (1997): 263-76.

50. Joel Perlmann, "Reflecting the Changing Face of America: Multiracials, Racial Classification, and American Intermarriage," in *Interracialism: Black-White Intermarriage in American History, Literature, and Law*, ed. Werner Sollars (New York: Oxford University Press, 2000).

51. Matthijs Kalmijn, "Trends in Black-White Intermarriage," *Social Forces* 72, no. 1 (1993): 119-46.

52. Kimberly DaCosta, *Remaking the Color Line: Social Bases and Implications of the Multiracial Movement*, unpublished dissertation, University of California-Berkeley, 2000; Farley, *Identifying with Multiple Races: A Social Movement That Succeeded but Failed*; Charles Hirschman, Richard Alba, and Reynolds Farley, "The Meaning and Measurement of Race in the U.S. Census: Glimpses into the Future," *Demography* 37, no. 3 (2000): 381-93; Lee and Bean, "America's Changing Color Lines: Immigration, Race/Ethnicity, and Multiracial Identification"; Lee and Bean, "Beyond Black and White: Remaking Race in America."; Mary C. Waters, "Immigration, Intermarriage, and the Challenges of Measuring Racial/Ethnic Identities," *American Journal of Public Health* 90, no. 11 (2000): 1735-37; and Williams, *Boxed In: The United States Multiracial Movement.*

53. Smith and Edmonston, *The New Americans: Economic, Demographic, and Fiscal Effects of Immigration.*

54. Eschbach, "The Enduring and Vanishing American Indian"; Nampeo R. McKenney and Claudette E. Bennett, "Issues Regarding Data on Race and Ethnicity: The Census Bureau Experience," *Public Health Reports* 109, no. 1 (1994): 16-25; Rogelio Saenz et al., "Persistence and Change in Asian Identity Among Children of Intermarried Couples," *Sociological Perspectives* 38, no. 2 (1995): 175-94; Waters, "Multiple Ethnicities and Identity in the United States."; Yu Xie and Kimberly Goyette, "The Racial Identification of Biracial Children with One Asian Parent: Evidence from the 1990 Census," *Social Forces* 76, no. 2 (1997): 547-70.

55. Heather M. Dalmage, *Tripping on the Color Line: Black-White Multiracial Families in a Racially Divided World* (New Brunswick, NJ: Rutgers University Press, 2000); David Harris and Jeremiah Joseph Sim, "Who is Multiracial? Assessing the Complexity of Lived Race," *American Sociological Review* 67, no. 4 (2002): 614-27; Timothy P. Johnson et al., "Dimensions of Self-Identification Among Multiracial and Multiethnic Respondents in Survey Interviews," *Evaluation Review* 21, no. 6 (1997): 671-87; Kathleen Odell Korgen, *From Black to Biracial: Transforming Racial Identity Among Americans* (Westport, CT: Praeger, 1998); Maria P. Root, *The Multiracial Experience: Racial Borders as the New Frontier* (Thousand Oaks, CA: Sage Publications, 1996); Maria P. Root, *Racially Mixed People in America* (Newbury Park, CA: Sage Publications, 1992); Nelly Salgado de Snyder, Cynthia M. Lopez, and Amado M. Padilla, "Ethnic Identity and Cultural Awareness Among the Offspring of Mexican Interethnic Marriages," *Journal of Early Adolescence* 2, no. 3 (1982): 277-82; Paul Spickard, *Mixed Blood: Intermarriage and Ethnic Identity In Twentieth-Century America*; Cookie White Stephan and Walter G. Stephan, "After Intermarriage: Ethnic Identity Among Mixed-Heritage Japanese-Americans and Hispanics," *Journal of Marriage and the Family* 51, no. 2 (1989): 507-19; Barbara Tizard and Ann Phoenix, *Black, White or Mixed Race? Race and Racism in the Lives of Young People of Mixed Parentage* (New York: Routledge, 1993); and Naomi Zack, *Race and Mixed Race* (Philadelphia: Temple University Press, 1993).

56. Salgado de Snyder, Lopez, and Padilla, "Ethnic Identity and Cultural Awareness Among the Offspring of Mexican Interethnic Marriages"; and Stephan and Stephan, "After Intermarriage: Ethnic Identity Among Mixed-Heritage Japanese-Americans and Hispanics."

57. Saenz et al., "Persistence and Change in Asian Identity Among Children of Intermarried Couples"; Xie and Goyette, "The Racial Identification of Biracial Children with One Asian Parent: Evidence from the 1990 Census."

58. Harris and Sim, "Who is Multiracial? Assessing the Complexity of Lived Race."

59. Portes and Rumbaut, *Legacies: The Story of the Immigrant Second Generation*; Rogelio Saenz et al., "Persistence and Change in Asian Identity Among Children of Intermarried Couples"; and Zhou and Bankston, *Growing Up American: How Vietnamese Children Adapt to Life in the United States.*

60. Saenz et al., "Persistence and Change in Asian Identity Among Children of Intermarried Couples"; Xie and Goyette, "The Racial Identification of Biracial Children with One Asian Parent: Evidence from the 1990 Census."

61. Stephan and Stephan, "After Intermarriage: Ethnic Identity Among Mixed-Heritage Japanese-Americans and Hispanics."

62. Eschbach, "The Enduring and Vanishing American Indian: American Indian Population Growth and Intermarriage in 1990."

63. Anderson and Fienberg, *Who Counts? The Politics of Census-Taking in Contemporary America.*

64. Davis, *Who is Black? One Nation's Definition;* Jon Michael Spencer, *The New Colored People: The Mixed-Race Movement in America* (New York: New York University Press, 1997).

65. Davis, *Who is Black? One Nation's Definition.*

66. Korgen, *From Black to Biracial: Transforming Racial Identity Among Americans.*

67. Harris and Sim, "Who is Multiracial? Assessing the Complexity of Lived Race."

68. Karl Eschbach and Christina Gomez, "Choosing Hispanic Identity: Ethnic Identity Switching among Respondents to High School and Beyond," *Social Science Quarterly* 79, no. 1 (1998): 74-90.

69. Eschbach, Supple, and Snipp, "Changes in Racial Identification and the Educational Attainment of American Indians, 1970-1990."

70. Bean and Stevens, *America's Newcomers and the Dynamics of Diversity.*

71. Bean and Stevens, *America's Newcomers and the Dynamics of Diversity;* Farley, *Identifying with Multiple Races: A Social Movement That Succeeded but Failed;* and Harris and Sim, "Who is Multiracial? Assessing the Complexity of Lived Race."

72. Gordon W. Allport, *The Nature of Prejudice* (Reading, MA: Addison-Wesley, 1954); Hubert M. Blalock, *Toward a Theory of Minority-Group Relations* (New York: John Wiley & Sons, 1967); Peter M. Blau, *Inequality and Heterogeneity* (New York: The Free Press, 1977); Garth Massey, Randy Hodson, and Dusko Sekulic, "Ethnic Enclaves and Intolerance: The Case of Yugoslavia," *Social Forces* 78, no. 2 (1999): 669-93.

73. Hubert M. Blalock, *Toward a Theory of Minority-Group Relations* (New York: John Wiley & Sons, 1967); Herbert Blumer, "Race Prejudice as a Sense of Group Position," *Pacific Sociological Review* 1, no. 1 (1958): 3-7; Mark A. Fossett and K. Jill Kiecolt, "The Relative Size of Minority Populations and White Racial Attitudes," *Social Science Quarterly* 70, no. 4 (1989): 820-35; and Howard Schuman, Charlotte Steeh, and Lawrence Bobo, *Racial Attitudes in America: Trends and Interpretations* (Cambridge, MA: Harvard University Press, 1985).

74. This measure of multiracial reporting excludes those Latinos who responded to the U.S. Census question on race that they possess both white and other racial backgrounds. Some scholars have suggested that such people should not be included as multiracial because their response may reflect confusion about the meaning of race question. Alternatively, among many Latinos, the categories white and other reflect white and *mestizo* backgrounds, meaning that these indicate actual multiracial backgrounds.

FOR FURTHER READING

Alba, Richard, and Victor Nee. *Remaking the American Mainstream.* Cambridge, MA: Harvard University Press, 2003.

Anderson, Margo J., and Stephen E. Fienberg. *Who Counts? The Politics of Census-Taking in Contemporary America.* New York: Russell Sage Foundation, 1999.

Bean, Frank D., and Gillian Stevens. *America's Newcomers and the Dynamics of Diversity.* New York: Russell Sage Foundation, 2003.

Bean, Frank D., and Stephanie Bell-Rose, eds. *Immigration and Opportunity: Race, Ethnicity and Employment in the United States.* New York: Russell Sage Foundation, 1999.

Hollinger, David A. "Amalgamation and Hypodescent: The Question of Ethnoracial Mixture in the History of the United States," *American Historical Review* 108, no. 5 (2003): 1363-90.

Lee, Jennifer, and Frank D. Bean. "American's Changing Color Lines: Immigration, Race/Ethnicity, and Multiracial Identification," *Annual Review of Sociology* 30 (2004): 221-42.

Nobles, Melissa. *Shades of Citizenship: Race and the Census in Modern Politics.* Palo Alto, CA: Stanford University Press, 2000.

Perlmann, Joel, and Mary C. Waters, eds. *The New Race Question: How the Census Counts Multiracial Individuals.* New York: Russell Sage Foundation, 2002.

Rodriguez, Clara E. *Changing Race: Latinos, the Census, and the History of Ethnicity in the United States.* New York: New York University Press, 2000.

Smelser, Neil, William Julius Wilson, and Faith Mitchell. *America Becoming: Racial Patterns and Their Consequences.* Washington, DC: National Academies Press, 2001.

Waters, Mary C. *Black Identities: West Indian Immigrant Dreams and American Realities.* New York; Cambridge, MA: Russell Sage Foundation; Harvard University Press, 1999.

Who Chooses to Choose Two?

By Sonya M. Tafoya, Hans Johnson, and Laura E. Hill

Prior to Census 2000, most Americans were accustomed to selecting a single racial response on state and federal forms. But with an ever more racially diverse population and an increasing rate of intermarriage, the U.S. Census Bureau created a new format for the race question on the 2000 Census: Respondents could now mark one or more races. This change was welcomed by some as an overdue acknowledgement of their multiracial identity and criticized by others who feared its consequences.

In the 1990 Census, even though the instructions indicated that only one box should be checked, almost half a million people filled in more than one race box. After the 1990 Census, estimates of the U.S. multiracial population ranged as high as 6.6 percent, so that many scholars anticipated that at least 4 percent to 6 percent of the American population would be counted as multiracial in 2000. In the end, Census 2000 counted only about 7 million multiracial people, about 2.4 percent of the population. Clearly, not all who could have claimed a multiracial identity chose to. Yet, despite their relatively small share of the total population, multiracial Americans generated a great deal of interest. Given the significance of race in America, understanding this new population is relevant not only because it builds on our historical understanding, but also because it provides insight into the future significance of race in America.

The multiracial Americans counted in Census 2000 are not aptly described with any one summary of their characteristics. To understand this group we must understand the specific multiracial combinations encompassed by this broad category. In this report we describe the diverse demographic, geographic, social, and economic profiles of multiracial Americans. We draw on what is well known about the social and economic status of the single-race groups and present data to show the extent to which multiracial Americans occupy a status in between that of their component single-race groups.

For some people, responses to questions of race and ethnic identity are not static. Their response to a particular inquiry about racial identity may vary with the context in which it is asked—at home or school, in the presence of others, or without observers.[1] Furthermore, racial identity can develop and change as a person matures. An individual's racial/ethnic identity can be influenced by age, family member's racial identity, friends, community composition, or even society at large.[2] Many multiracial Americans are so identified by their parents. Almost half of multiracial Americans are children. However, not all mixed-race couples choose to identify their children as multiracial. Within the family context, the racial identity of parents influences their children's racial identity. And even though intermarriage has increased substantially, the fact that some parents do not identify their children as multiracial suggests that for many of today's adults, single-race categories may be more salient.

Although the new enumeration of multiracial Americans has certainly complicated the traditional working definition of race in America, 98 percent of all Americans continue to identify themselves as only one race.[3]

HISTORY AND POLITICS OF CENSUS RACE CATEGORIES

For the first time in U.S. census history, the 2000 Census allowed residents to check more than one racial category. This change in the reporting of race is only the latest in a long history of census changes in collecting and reporting racial data. In fact, the Census Bureau has never used the same race categories for more than three consecutive censuses.

Table 1 (page 333) shows that in the very first census, in 1790, enumerators were asked to distinguish among free

SONYA M. TAFOYA is a research associate with the Pew Hispanic Center, in Washington D.C. Her current research focuses on the intersection between Latin American immigration and racial and ethnic identity. Prior to joining the Pew Hispanic Center, she was a research associate at the Public Policy Institute of California. She has a master's degree in biology from the University of California, Davis.

HANS JOHNSON is a research fellow with the Public Policy Institute of California. His research interests include international and domestic migration, population estimates and projections, and determinants and consequences of population growth. Prior to joining PPIC, he was senior demographer at the California Research Bureau, where he conducted research for the state legislature and governor's office on population issues. He has a Ph.D. in demography from the University of California, Berkeley.

LAURA E. HILL is a research fellow at the Public Policy Institute of California, where she researches immigrants, international migration, race/ethnicity, and youth. Before joining PPIC as a research fellow, she was a research associate at the SPHERE Institute and a National Institute of Aging postdoctoral fellow. She has a Ph.D. in demography and a master's in economics from the University of California, Berkeley.

Table 1
CENSUS RACIAL CATEGORIES, 1790–2000

Year	Race values
1790-1810	Free Whites, All Other Free Persons, Slaves
1820	Free Whites, Free Colored Persons, Slaves, All Other Persons (except Indians not taxed)
1830-1840	Free Whites, Free Colored Persons, Slaves
1850	White, Black, Mulatto
1860	White, Black, Mulatto, Indian
1870-1880	White, Black, Mulatto, Chinese, Indian
1890	White, Black, Mulatto, Quadroon, Octoroon, Chinese, Japanese, Indian
1900	White, Black, Chinese, Japanese, Indian
1910	White, Black, Mulatto, Chinese, Japanese, Indian, Other
1920	White, Black, Mulatto, Chinese, Japanese, Filipino, Hindu, Korean, Indian, Other
1930	White, Negro, Indian, Chinese, Japanese, Filipino, Hindu, Korean, Mexican, Other
1940	White, Negro, Indian, Chinese, Japanese, Filipino, Hindu, Korean, Other
1950	White, Negro, American Indian, Japanese, Chinese, Filipino, Other race
1960	White, Negro, American Indian, Japanese, Chinese, Filipino, Hawaiian, Part Hawaiian, Aleut, Eskimo, Other
1970	White, Negro or Black, American Indian, Japanese, Chinese, Filipino, Hawaiian, Korean, Aleut, Eskimo, Other
1980	White, Black or Negro, Japanese, Chinese, Filipino, Korean, Vietnamese, American Indian, Asian Indian, Hawaiian, Guamanian, Samoan, Eskimo, Aleut, Other
1990	White, Black or Negro, American Indian, Eskimo, Aleut, Chinese, Filipino, Hawaiian, Korean, Vietnamese, Japanese, Asian Indian, Samoan, Guamanian, Other Asian or Pacific Islander, Other race
2000	White; Black, African American, or Negro; American Indian or Alaska Native; Asian Indian; Chinese; Filipino; Japanese; Korean; Vietnamese; Other Asian; Native Hawaiian; Guamanian or Chamorro; Samoan; Other Pacific Islander; Some other race

appeared and disappeared. For example, "free colored person" appeared as a race in 1820, but was subsumed by black and mulatto in 1850. In 1890, variations of mulatto appeared, but by 1930, Negro was added as a category and black, mulatto, and similar categories were omitted. In 1930 "Mexican" was added as a race category, but by 1940 census enumerators were given instructions to consider Mexicans white unless they were "definitely Indian or some other race other than White." By 1970, Hispanics could indicate their ethnicity on a separate question, but still had to indicate a race from the choices of white, black, Indian, Asian, or some other race. Since 1970, the dual questions of race and ethnicity have been a consistent feature on the census questionnaire.

The appearance of the multiracial option in 2000 can best be understood in reference to recent changes that occurred during and after the civil rights era.[4] The Civil Rights acts of 1964 and 1968, the Voting Rights Act of 1965, and many programs associated with Lyndon Johnson's Great Society program were aimed squarely at ending racial discrimination and disenfranchisement. Because racial and ethnic data was paramount for monitoring legislative compliance and allocating grants-in-aid, civil rights activists embraced racial and ethnic categorization, and looked to the census as a tool for redressing inequalities. Official recognition of racial groups by the Census Bureau in this new context both conferred political and economic advantages for racial and ethnic minority groups and raised the stakes on accurate and scientifically defensible racial statistics.

In this new context, the Census Bureau was drawn into contentious legal debates that continue to this day.[5] The debates span the issues of respondent confidentiality, differential undercount of racial minorities, reapportionment of Congress, and the working definition of race itself. In response to the 1980 and 1990 census categories, many lobbying groups began to challenge the categorization system petitioning for inclusion within a group (Native Hawaiians in the American Indian group), exclusion from a group (Arab Americans as separate from whites), establishment of new groups (multiracial advocates), and even the deletion of the race and ethnic questions altogether. In an attempt to resolve many of the problems associated with the 1980 and 1990 censuses, the Office of Management and Budget (OMB) called for a comprehensive review of the racial and ethnic classification system that had guided the Census Bureau since 1977.

The results of this intensive review have been codified in a 1997 OMB document entitled "Revisions to the Standards for the Classification of Federal Data on Race and Ethnicity," which outlines the following minimum race categories:

● American Indian or Alaska Native.
● Asian.

whites, other free persons, and slaves. And since 1850, enumerators were provided with instructions for properly assigning race. For example, in 1860 enumerators were instructed to "insert the letter 'B' in all cases where the person is black without admixture" and "if a mulatto, or of mixed blood, write 'M'." Over the 200-plus years of census taking, various racial categories have

- Black or African American.
- Native Hawaiian or Other Pacific Islander.
- White.

The Census Bureau is the most visible agency that employs these categories, although all federal data collection efforts must comply with OMB guidelines. Unlike other federal agencies, however, the Census Bureau also employs the residual category "some other race" to capture respondents who would not otherwise respond to the minimum standard categories. Under its exemption, the Census Bureau included the "some other race" category on the 1980, 1990, and 2000 censuses. In 1990, the Census Bureau tallied more than 250,000 respondents who used the Other race category to express their multiracial heritage. These respondents either wrote in several race categories, or used terms such as "Eurasian." Because Census 2000 allowed respondents to check one or more races, the "some other race" category is no longer the preferred category for multiracial respondents, but rather is more commonly used by those of Hispanic origin.

As in the past, the OMB and consequently the Census Bureau view Hispanic origin as an ethnic identity rather than a race. Collection of data on Americans of Hispanic ethnicity is required to fulfill the obligations of Public Law 94-311, passed in 1976 to remedy discrimination suffered by those of Hispanic origin. The result of this distinction is a data collection method that consists of two related questions: an Hispanic ethnicity question and a race question. Hispanics may identify with any racial group or combination of groups.

Given that race and ethnic data are used to monitor civil rights, and that much of the legislation predates the 2000 Census with its proliferation of multiracial categories, the OMB has issued a set of rules for the purposes of civil rights monitoring and enforcement:

- Responses in the five single-race categories are not allocated.
- Responses that combine one minority race and white are allocated to the minority race.
- Responses that include two or more minority races are allocated as follows: If the enforcement action is in response to a complaint, allocate to the race that the complainant alleges the discrimination was based on. If the enforcement action requires assessing disparate impact or discriminatory patterns, analyze the patterns based on alternative allocations to each of the minority groups.

Although the OMB outlines five minimum race categories, there were actually 15 boxes on the census form (see Figure 1). For example, Asians are subdivided into Asian Indians, Chinese, Filipinos, Japanese, Koreans, Vietnamese, and Other Asians. While there is no indication on the census form that someone who selects both

Figure 1

QUESTIONS ON RACE AND HISPANIC ORIGIN, CENSUS 2000

→ NOTE: Please answer BOTH Questions 5 and 6.

5. Is this person Spanish/Hispanic/Latino? Mark ☒ the "No" box if not Spanish/Hispanic/Latino.
   ☐ No, not Spanish/Hispanic/Latino   ☐ Yes, Puerto Rican
   ☐ Yes, Mexican, Mexican Am., Chicano   ☐ Yes, Cuban
   ☐ Yes, other Spanish/Hispanic/Latino — *Print group.*

6. What is this person's race? Mark ☒ one or more races to indicate what this person considers himself/herself to be.
   ☐ White
   ☐ Black, African Am., or Negro
   ☐ American Indian or Alaska Native — *Print name of enrolled or principal tribe.*

   ☐ Asian Indian   ☐ Japanese   ☐ Native Hawaiian
   ☐ Chinese   ☐ Korean   ☐ Guamanian or Chamorro
   ☐ Filipino   ☐ Vietnamese   ☐ Samoan
   ☐ Other Asian — *Print race.*   ☐ Other Pacific Islander — *Print race.*

   ☐ Some other race — *Print race.*

Source: U.S. Census Bureau, Census 2000 questionnaire.

Filipino and Japanese will not be tabulated as multiracial, such respondents are officially tabulated as monoracial Asian. If someone checked the boxes indicating Native Hawaiian, Guamanian or Chamorro, Samoan, and Other Pacific Islander, they would not be counted as belonging to four race groups, but rather would be tallied as monoracial Native Hawaiian or Other Pacific Islander.

For official use, only combinations of the broad race categories count in multiracial tabulations. Based on the five broad groups plus the additional "some other race" residual group, there are six possible monoracial choices and therefore 15 unique biracial combinations, 20 unique three-race combinations, 15 four-race combinations, six five-race combinations, and one final combination of six races. All combined, there are 63 possible unique racial identities. If we consider Hispanic ethnicity and assign respondents to two categories, Hispanic or non-Hispanic, we have 126 unique race-ethnic categories (63 race categories multiplied by two ethnicity categories).

Finally, the questionnaire does not specify how write-in responses will be treated. For example, if a respondent writes an ethnic identity in the space below "some other race" (SOR), that response is often recoded into a specific race group (see Box 1, page 335). The rule employed by the Census Bureau is that if at least 90 percent of an ethnic group typically identifies with a single-race group, the write-in ethnic response will be recoded as a standard race category. Thus, a write-in response of "Jamaican" would be coded as black or African Ameri-

Box 1

ABBREVIATIONS AND USAGE

In this report, the following terms and symbols are used:

White = white
Black = black or African American
Asian = Asian
AIAN = American Indian and Alaska Native
NHOPI = Native Hawaiian and Other Pacific Islander
SOR = Some Other Race

Multiracial = Person belonging to more than one of the above six groups.
Biracial = Person belonging to two of the above six groups

Hispanic or Latino are used interchangeably.

A "+" sign denotes individuals identified as more than one race. For example, a person who marked the box for white and the box for Asian is referred to in this report as Asian+white.

A "/" denotes the racial identification of married couples. For example, a couple in which one partner is black and the other partner is Asian is described as a black/Asian couple. If one partner is multiracial, Asian+black, and the other partner is white, the couple is described as Asian+black/white.

Table 2

TOTAL POPULATION BY NUMBER OF RACES REPORTED IN CENSUS 2000

Number of Races	Total	% of total	% of total two+ races
Total Population	281,421,906	100.0	(X)
One race	274,595,678	97.6	(X)
Two+ races	6,826,228	2.4	100.0
Two races	6,368,075	2.3	93.3
Three races	410,285	0.1	6.0
Four races	38,408	<0.1	0.6
Five races	8,637	<0.1	0.1
Six races	823	<0.1	<0.1

Source: U.S. Census Bureau, Census 2000 Redistricting Data Summary File: table PL1.

made up about 12 percent of the population; Asians represented nearly 4 percent; and the remaining 3 percent identified as American Indian or Alaska Native (AIAN), Native Hawaiian or Pacific Islander (NHOPI), or SOR. Given that the nation has nearly six times as many non-Hispanic whites as it does Hispanics or blacks, it should not be surprising that most (about four-fifths) biracial responses included white as one of the racial choices.[6] This preponderance of biracial Americans who identify as white and another race is a direct result of the relative population sizes of the single-race groups.

Of the 15 possible biracial combinations, only two—SOR+white and AIAN+white—have population counts over 1 million (see Table 3). The racial combination most frequently selected is that of SOR+white (2.2 million respondents, or 35 percent of all biracial responses). The inclusion of the SOR category among the single-race categories allows the Census Bureau to enumerate those who do not identify with the standard racial categories. The majority of those who selected SOR alone were Latino.[7] Thus, in trying to understand the SOR+white biracial group, one confronts several issues. First, two-thirds of these respondents also identified as ethnically Latino. And in a separate census question that elicits ancestry, the non-Latino third of this group reported an array of different ancestries including Greek, Italian, Irish, Russian, Ukrainian, Albanian, Egyptian, Iranian, and Arab. For these respondents, their identity may reflect mixed parentage, an understanding of race at odds with census categories, or an ancestry that is nominally white but an experience in the society at large as only marginally white.

The second most frequent racial combination was AIAN+white (1 million respondents). Unlike the SOR+white respondents, this group was almost entirely non-Hispanic (90 percent). The high rates of out-marriage among AIAN and the difficulties in determining legitimate American Indian identity have been well documented.[8] In this case, the addition of a biracial group of AIAN+whites compounds the level of difficulty in classifying American Indians.

can because 90 percent of Jamaicans typically identify as black. On the other hand, a write-in response of "Mexican" would be coded as SOR, since fewer than 90 percent of Mexicans identify as white. This rule explains the preponderance of Hispanics in the SOR category, a topic addressed later in this report.

WHO ARE MULTIRACIAL AMERICANS?

Who are the 6.8 million Americans who were counted as more than one race in Census 2000? Overwhelmingly they are Americans who identified as members of two racial groups (see Table 2). The most common combinations are:

- SOR+white, non-Hispanic (SOR+white).
- SOR+white, Hispanic (SOR+white, Hispanic).
- AIAN+white, non-Hispanic (AIAN+white).
- Asian+white, non-Hispanic (Asian+white).
- Black+white, non-Hispanic (black+white).

It is important to place these findings in the context of the American population as a whole. According to the 2000 Census, the share of the nation's population that identified as non-Hispanic white was 69 percent, Hispanics (of any race) and non-Hispanic blacks each

The two next-largest groups—Asian+white and black+white—each have counts greater than half a million but less than 1 million. These two combinations are made up primarily of non-Hispanics. Ninety-three percent of all Asian+white respondents were non-Hispanic as were 89 percent of black+white respondents. These two groups account for about one-quarter of the biracial population. These groups are much more likely to arise from intermarriage of the standard single-race categories than SOR+white Hispanics.

There are six groups whose populations are between 100,000 and 500,000, and together they account for nearly 20 percent of the entire biracial population: SOR+black, Asian+SOR, AIAN+black, NHOPI+Asian, NHOPI+white, and Asian+black. The first two combinations have the largest share of Latinos: the SOR+black group is nearly 40 percent Latino, and the Asian+SOR group is one-quarter Latino. The vast majority of the respondents in the remaining combinations are non-Latinos (more than 89 percent).

The last few biracial combination groups make up less than 5 percent of the entire biracial population, with fewer than 100,000 people in each category. The two biracial categories that include SOR, AIAN+SOR and NHOPI+SOR, each have a large share of Latinos, 77 percent and 68 percent respectively.

Even though fewer than 500,000 Americans (or less than 0.2 percent of the population) were enumerated as members of three or more racial groups, some triracial groups merit attention. Whereas national figures show that 93.3 percent of multiracial respondents are biracial, in the state of Hawaii 68 percent of multiracial people are biracial, and 28 percent are triracial. In fact, slightly more residents of Hawaii answered that they were

NHOPI+Asian+white (55,189) than answered that they were biracial Asian+white (55,028). Of the nearly 90,000 NHOPI+Asian+white respondents counted nationally, 62 percent resided in Hawaii. The only other triracial group that numbered over 50,000 was the AIAN+black+white group. Nationally they numbered 112,207. About 17 percent of this group resided in California, 9 percent in New York, and 10 percent in Ohio and Michigan combined. Less than 1 percent of multiracial Americans identified as of four or more races.

In the remainder of this report, we focus on the five most common biracial combinations.

Demographic Characteristics

To understand multiracial Americans, we need to examine their demographic characteristics, which vary by the particular racial combination. Multiracial and monoracial Americans have similar sex ratios. Forty-nine percent of the monoracial population is male, while 50 percent of the multiracial population is male. There are no appreciable differences for any of the major biracial combinations.

The foreign-born are somewhat more likely to identify as more than one race than are the U.S.-born (6 percent versus 2 percent). However, this appears to be due largely to the popularity of the SOR+white combination among both non-Hispanics and Hispanics (see Table 4, page 337). For all other biracial combinations, the percent foreign-born is much lower than we might expect based on the percent foreign-born found among each single-race group.

Early analysis of the multiracial population has shown that multiracial individuals, as a group, are

Table 3
BIRACIAL POPULATION BY HISPANIC ETHNICITY, 2000

	Biracial Total	Biracial Percent	Non-Hispanic, biracial Total	Non-Hispanic, biracial Percent	Hispanic, biracial Total	Hispanic, biracial Percent	Hispanic share of total biracial population
Population of two races	6,368,075	100.0	4,257,110	100.0	2,110,965	100.0	33.1
SOR+white	2,206,251	34.6	731,719	17.2	1,474,532	69.9	66.8
AIAN+white	1,082,683	17.0	969,238	22.8	113,445	5.4	10.4
Asian+white	868,395	13.6	811,240	19.1	57,155	2.7	6.5
Black+white	784,764	12.3	697,077	16.4	87,687	4.2	11.1
SOR+black	417,249	6.6	255,966	6.0	161,283	7.6	38.6
SOR+Asian	249,108	3.9	185,754	4.4	63,354	3.0	25.4
AIAN+black	182,494	2.9	168,022	3.9	14,472	0.7	7.9
NHOPI+Asian	138,802	2.2	129,130	3.0	9,672	0.5	6.9
NHOPI+white	112,964	1.8	100,702	2.4	12,262	0.6	10.8
Asian+black	106,782	1.7	99,513	2.3	7,269	0.3	6.8
AIAN+SOR	93,842	1.5	21,477	0.5	72,365	3.4	77.1
AIAN+Asian	52,429	0.8	43,052	1.0	9,377	0.4	17.8
NHOPI+SOR	35,108	0.6	11,288	0.3	23,820	1.1	67.8
NHOPI+black	29,876	0.5	27,479	0.6	2,397	0.1	8.0
NHOPI+AIAN	7,328	0.1	5,453	0.1	1,875	0.1	26.0

Source: Authors' tabulations of Census 2000 Redistricting Data Summary File.

Table 4
PERCENT FOREIGN-BORN FOR BIRACIAL AND MONORACIAL GROUPS, 2000

Group	Percent foreign-born
Non-Hispanic	
White	4
Black+white	2
Black	5
AIAN+white	1
AIAN	1
Asian+white	19
Asian	69
SOR+white	42
SOR	31
Hispanic	
White	39
SOR+white	37
SOR	44

Source: Authors' calculations using Census 2000 1% Public Use Micro-data Sample (PUMS).

Figure 2
MEDIAN AGE OF BIRACIAL AND MONORACIAL GROUPS, 2000

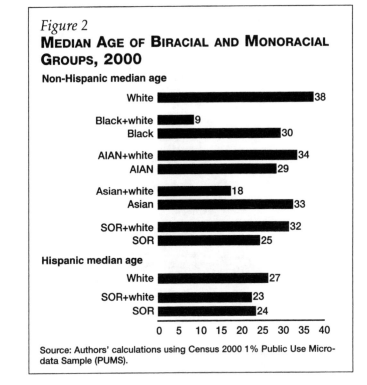

Source: Authors' calculations using Census 2000 1% Public Use Micro-data Sample (PUMS).

younger than their monoracial counterparts. Of the 6.8 million Americans who reported more than one race, 42 percent were under the age of 18 compared to only 25 percent for monoracial Americans.[9] Figure 2 shows the median age for the most common biracial groups as well as their corresponding monoracial groups.

The most striking age difference is the relative youth of black+white Americans as compared with either monoracial blacks or monoracial whites, suggesting that multiracial identities among this group are being taken up primarily by the very young, perhaps chosen by their parents. Asian+white biracial individuals are also quite young relative to both white and Asian monoracial groups. Both AIAN+white and SOR+white median ages are in between those of each monoracial groups. Hispanics as a group are relatively young, and because SOR+white Hispanics are the largest multiracial group (1.5 million), they contribute strongly to the overall age structure of the broader multiracial population. Age differences by gender within each biracial category are few and small, but females appear to be the same age or a year or two older on average than their male multiracial counterparts. These differences are examined more closely in age and sex profiles for the biracial groups whose median age differs dramatically from their component monoracial groups (see Figure 3).

Black+white individuals are significantly younger than either single-race whites or blacks, and much younger than the other multiracial groups. Asian+white individuals are also significantly younger than Asians or whites. For AIAN+white and SOR+white groups, age

and sex profiles appear to be an average of the component monoracial group age profiles.

Reasons for the relative youth of the multiracial population are explored later in this report. However, two merit note here. First, to the extent that interracial couples are more common recently, the biracial offspring of these couples will be relatively young. Second, younger individuals might feel less constrained by racial boundaries that have historically forced people to choose a single racial identity. For example, multiracial black/white marriages have increased over time, making the pool of potential black+white individuals larger now than ever before. In addition, younger black+white individuals may be more likely to identify as such than older cohorts, who are more likely to choose only one race.

The relative youth of the multiracial population raises an important caveat about census data collection. Since data are collected by household, generally one person in each home provides information on all household members. Thus, while 42 percent of the multiracial population may be under the age of 18, the probability that these youths actually filled out the census form themselves is exceedingly low. Census follow-up studies have shown that less than 4 percent of those who fill out the census are 18 or younger. It is a parent, and likely a mother, who completes the census form for minors in the household.[10]

The multiracial population is not evenly distributed across the nation. The greatest share (40 percent) of multiracial Americans lives in the West. Another 27 percent live in the South, 18 percent in the Northeast, and the remaining 15 percent in the Midwest.[11]

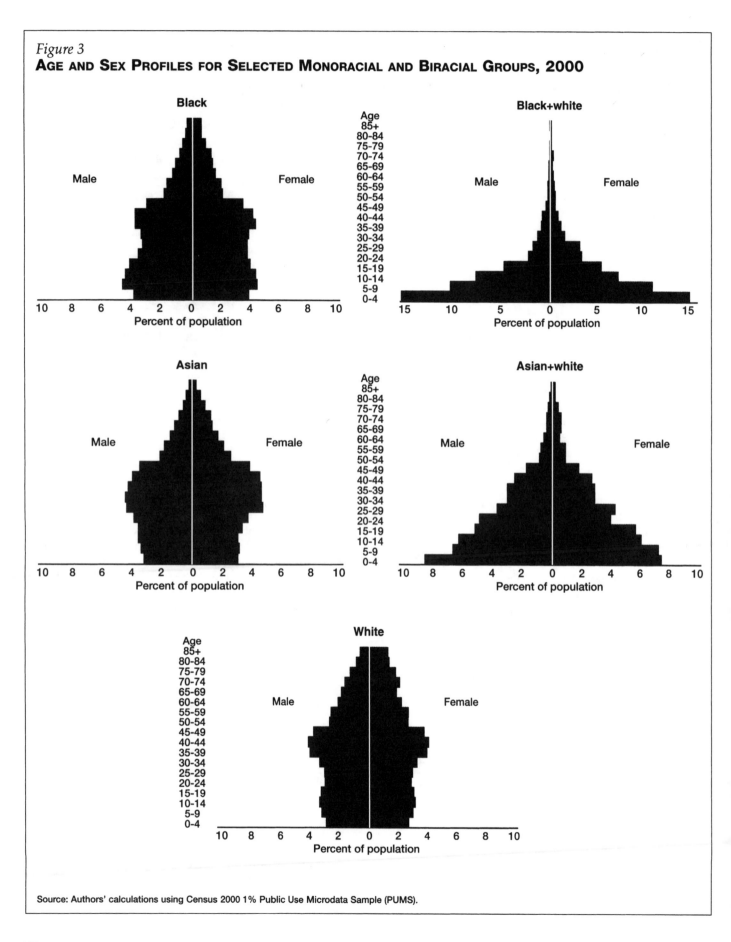

Figure 3

AGE AND SEX PROFILES FOR SELECTED MONORACIAL AND BIRACIAL GROUPS, 2000

Source: Authors' calculations using Census 2000 1% Public Use Microdata Sample (PUMS).

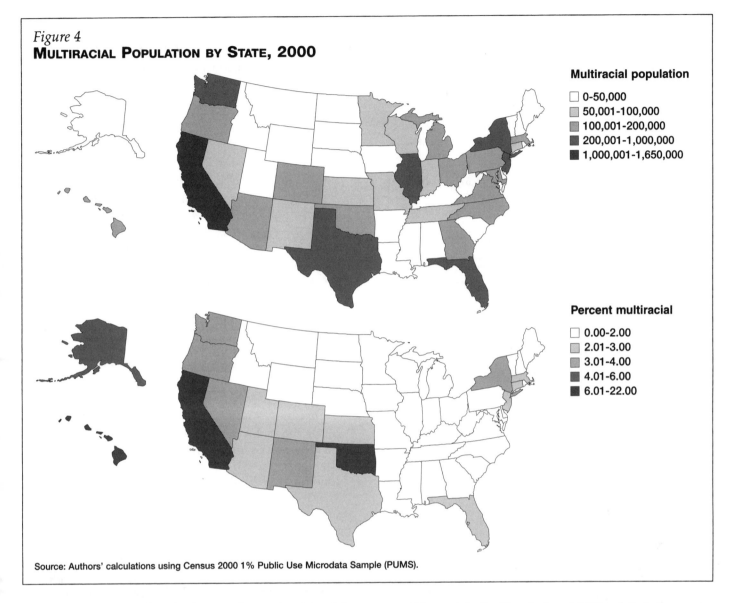

Figure 4
MULTIRACIAL POPULATION BY STATE, 2000

Multiracial population
- 0-50,000
- 50,001-100,000
- 100,001-200,000
- 200,001-1,000,000
- 1,000,001-1,650,000

Percent multiracial
- 0.00-2.00
- 2.01-3.00
- 3.01-4.00
- 4.01-6.00
- 6.01-22.00

Source: Authors' calculations using Census 2000 1% Public Use Microdata Sample (PUMS).

Although Hawaii has the largest share of multiracial persons (21 percent), the more populous states have the largest numbers of multiracial persons (see Figure 4). The three most populous states, California, Texas, and New York, each have more than a half-million multiracial residents. California is the only state with over 1 million multiracial residents. Hawaii, Illinois, New Jersey, and Washington all have greater than 200,000 multiracial residents.

Because one-third of all biracial Americans are also Hispanic, the geographic distribution of Hispanics has an influence on the overall distribution of biracial Americans. Over one-third (37 percent) of biracial Americans in the West are also Latinos. This differs most notably from the Midwest, where only 19 percent of biracial Americans are also Latino.

Historically, answers to the race question have been complicated for Latinos, and an examination of their multiracial combinations at the regional level sheds light on this complexity. The choice of SOR+white is the most common biracial response, and is particularly common in the West (see Table 5). The second most-common biracial combination for Latinos is the SOR+black combination. It is most common in the Northeast, where Puerto Rican and Dominican national origin groups compose a large share of the regional Latino population (53 percent). Puerto Ricans and Dominicans are more likely than other national origin groups to identify as racially black.[12]

Evidence from California suggests that people who identify as multiracial are less likely to live in ethnic and immigrant enclaves than in other kinds of neighborhoods.[13] Because many immigrants arrive in the United States already married, or speak a language other than English, marriage with a co-ethnic is a more common occurrence for the foreign-born than the U.S.-born. In metropolitan areas of the nation, multiracial Americans are the least segregated of any minority group.

Table 5

MOST COMMON BIRACIAL COMBINATIONS FOR U.S. HISPANICS, BY REGION, 2000

Hispanic combination	Percent distribution				
	Northeast	Midwest	South	West	Total
SOR+white	16	10	28	46	1,493,986
SOR+black	40	9	26	25	161,643
AIAN+white	9	13	21	57	110,721
AIAN+SOR	13	8	25	54	83,125
Asian+SOR	13	5	21	61	80,937
Black+white	41	14	22	24	80,348
Asian+white	13	6	19	61	49,917
Other 2-race combination	21	8	21	50	82,168

Source: Authors' calculations using Census 2000 1% Public Use Microdata Sample (PUMS).

Socioeconomic Characteristics

If biracial Americans were simply a combination of their monoracial counterparts, we would expect their socioeconomic characteristics to fall between those measured for their monoracial counterparts. For most measures and groups, this is the case.

The level of educational attainment for most biracial American adults is intermediate when compared with their component monoracial groups (see Figure 5). While this is generally true at all levels of education, Figure 5 shows only the percent in each group with a bachelor's or higher degree.

For example, the largest non-Hispanic biracial combination is AIAN+white, and in comparison to whites alone and AIAN alone, the biracial group is intermediate. The percentage of these populations with a bachelor's or higher degree is 31 percent for whites, 18 percent for AIAN+whites, and 13 percent for AIAN. The same pattern prevails when comparing white, black+white, and black groups. Whites show the highest educational attainment, black+white biracials are intermediate, and the black group has the lowest educational attainment. In the comparison of whites with Asian+whites and Asians, the biracial groups are again intermediate; however, the monoracial Asian group has the highest level of educational attainment, while whites have the lowest educational attainment of the three groups.

The final two sets of bars in Figure 5 show comparisons of whites with SOR+white and monoracial SORs. The first comparison shows that non-Hispanic SOR+whites do not exhibit a clear pattern relative to either monoracial group. But among Hispanics, those who identify as white have the highest educational attainment, those who identify as SOR have the lowest educational attainment, and those who identify as Hispanic SOR+white are intermediate in their educational attainment.

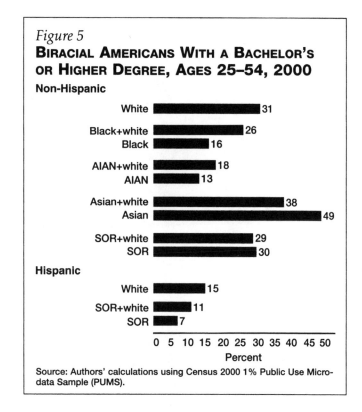

Figure 5

BIRACIAL AMERICANS WITH A BACHELOR'S OR HIGHER DEGREE, AGES 25–54, 2000

Non-Hispanic

White 31
Black+white 26
Black 16
AIAN+white 18
AIAN 13
Asian+white 38
Asian 49
SOR+white 29
SOR 30

Hispanic

White 15
SOR+white 11
SOR 7

Source: Authors' calculations using Census 2000 1% Public Use Microdata Sample (PUMS).

In comparisons of hourly wages, we restrict our analysis to males only since their labor force histories are generally continuous, while those of women are often punctuated by interruptions in labor force participation due to childbearing. The general absence of labor force interruptions among males makes the modeling and interpretation of results more straightforward.

In this analysis, we limit the sample to U.S.-born men, ages 25 to 54, who were neither in the military nor enrolled in school and worked full-time 40 or more weeks in the prior year. Because the age structure and educational attainment levels vary considerably among each race/ethnic group and combinations of groups, hourly wages are estimated after controlling for age, educational attainment, and region of the country.

Once age, educational attainment, and region were controlled for, black+white biracial men's wages were not significantly different from black-alone men's wages, but were significantly lower than white-alone men's wages (see Figure 6, page 341). Likewise, Aisan+white men's wages and Hispanic SOR+white men's wages were not significantly different from their monoracial men's component groups. AIAN+white biracial men's wages were significantly less than white men's wages, but not significantly different from American Indian men's wages. For biracial men who identified as non-Hispanic SOR+white, wages were significantly higher than those of non-Hispanic men who identified as SOR, but significantly lower than those who identified as white alone. These differences reflect many factors, including but not limited to employment discrimination. For example, a biracial man

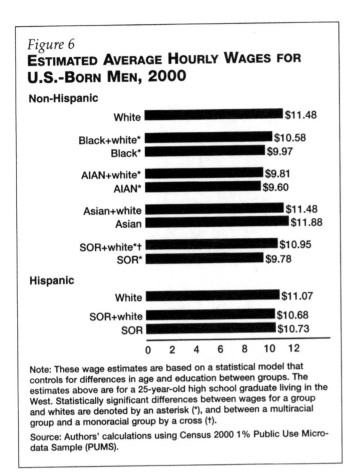

Figure 6
ESTIMATED AVERAGE HOURLY WAGES FOR U.S.-BORN MEN, 2000

Non-Hispanic

White	$11.48
Black+white*	$10.58
Black*	$9.97
AIAN+white*	$9.81
AIAN*	$9.60
Asian+white	$11.48
Asian	$11.88
SOR+white*†	$10.95
SOR*	$9.78

Hispanic

White	$11.07
SOR+white	$10.68
SOR	$10.73

Note: These wage estimates are based on a statistical model that controls for differences in age and education between groups. The estimates above are for a 25-year-old high school graduate living in the West. Statistically significant differences between wages for a group and whites are denoted by an asterisk (*), and between a multiracial group and a monoracial group by a cross (†).

Source: Authors' calculations using Census 2000 1% Public Use Microdata Sample (PUMS).

who appears "very white" might be seen as white by employers, and thereby benefit. Other sources of wage differentials between the groups could arise from school quality or major, work history, and local labor market effects.

Political Attitudes and Participation

While several groups advocated for recognition in the 2000 census, without a doubt multiracial groups were the most successful. Does this recognition reflect an engaged and highly political population? Because the census does not include questions about political participation or beliefs, a telephone survey of 2,000 randomly selected California adults sheds light on the political views and activities of the multiracial population.[14] In addition to being asked to identify themselves as belonging to one of the standard race categories, the survey respondents were also asked to indicate if they had ever identified as mixed race. Of the 2,000 surveyed adults, approximately 14 percent indicated that they had "ever identified" as multiracial. For these individuals, we know not only if they have ever identified as multiracial, but also with which race they primarily identify when forced to choose just one.

Using the survey results to compare multiracial adults to monoracial adults, there are few differences in political attitudes and participation. Those small differences that do stand out tend to suggest that the multiracial population is slightly more likely to be registered as Democrats and Independents, less likely to be registered Republicans, more likely to not be registered at all, and less likely to say that they "always" or "nearly always" vote than are adults who have never identified as multiracial. These small differences do not suggest that the multiracial population is dramatically different in any way than the monoracial population.

At the national level, the Kaiser Family Foundation conducted a similar study in which 1,709 adults were surveyed.[15] In this survey, the results were similar to those in California. They found that biracial adults (here defined to be those with parents of different races, 169 adults in total) were slightly more likely to be Democrats, less likely to be Republicans, and less likely to be registered to vote.

Returning to the California survey, we examine the association between multiracial identity and two indicators of political participation. We examine party affiliation and self-reported voter participation, holding age, education level, and nativity constant. The multiracial population is not uniform in their political views or their political participation. While mixed-race individuals are slightly less likely to be registered Republicans, the greatest variation occurs between the different monoracial groups. For example, blacks who have "ever" identified as multiracial are more similar to monoracial blacks than to other multiracial groups.

When asked how often they vote, most respondents answered "always" or "nearly always." Relative to their monoracial counterparts, multiracial respondents were slightly less likely to answer "always" or "nearly always." However, these differences were not statistically significant. In general, rather than being a politically engaged force, multiple-race individuals in this survey were not more likely to vote or unified in their party affiliation. While the respondents in this survey were slightly more likely to be liberal leaning overall, these differences were hardly universal.

MULTIRACIAL IDENTITY FORMATION

The formation of a multiracial identity takes place within the broader historical context of race and ethnic ideas in the United States. The significance of race in society has changed over time and racial boundaries have become more blurred. These changes occur not only as the population composition changes, but also as political, social, and cultural attitudes evolve. For example, some changes occur as new immigrants arrive with different concepts of race and ethnicity. Increased intermarriage also leads to changes in the racial composition of the population. Political uses of racial data and purposes for collection of data have also changed across time, from primarily serving as a means of exclusion to more recently serving as a means of inclusion. Within this larger context, families and broader social networks influence racial and ethnic identity formation.

Not only have racial boundaries and categories changed throughout history, but there is also considerable evidence that racial and ethnic identity can change over an individual's life course and in different contexts. Indeed, the Census Bureau's own validation study found that just six months later, some 40 percent of the multiracial population of Census Day 2000 was identified as monoracial using the very same question. In contrast, 99 percent of the monoracial population identified with only one race when asked again in September.[16] Why do these identities change for some individuals over such a short time period?

Previous research on racial and ethnic identity suggests a role for age, particular multiracial combination, family, school, neighborhood, peers, and general societal views about particular races or ethnicities. Some combinations of multiracial/ethnic identity are more consistently reported among individuals with multiple racial/ethnic backgrounds: white+Asian and white+black multiracial individuals were the most likely to be identified the same way in both the Census and the Census Quality Survey,[17] and in school and home surveys of adolescent youth.[18]

Research on ethnic identification, as distinct from racial identification, has a long tradition and informs the question of racial identity. Ancestry identification for whites changes with age: Older people are more likely to choose a single ethnic identity than are younger people, although those still living with their parents are more likely to maintain multiple ethnic identities into their late twenties.[19]

Research on adolescents' self-identification may prove to be the most informative in helping predict who might maintain a multiracial/multiethnic identity into adulthood. Harris and Sim find that the adolescent multiracial population is somewhat fluid.[20] Youth who self-identify as more than one race at school do not always identify as being more than one race at home where an interviewer poses the question, possibly in front of other family members. Their estimates of the multiracial population of adolescent youth range from 4 percent to 11 percent, depending on the context of the interview.

In families with multiple ethnic or racial backgrounds, the father's racial or ethnic identity may be a more important predictor of the child's identity than the mother's. This suggests that surname is important, not only in terms of self-identification, but also in the way in which one is perceived by society at large.[21] However,

consistency of multiracial reporting is higher among multiracial adolescents who do not live with both biological parents.[22] It is possible that each parent views his or her child's identity differently.

An analysis of matched birth and death certificates for children who died prior to reaching 1 year of age found dramatic inconsistencies in racial identification. Inconsistencies among white (1 percent) and black infants (4 percent) were small in comparison with the over 40 percent of infants of other races who were classified with a different race at death than at birth.[23] In theory, immediate family members should have reported the race of the infant on both the birth and death certificate; however, the family members may be different in each case or unrelated individuals may have made the racial classification.

Among groups with large immigrant populations, language usage is clearly important in forming identity. Adolescent children of immigrants from Latin America are more likely to self-identify as Hispanic (as opposed to American or hyphenated Americans) if they have poor English skills[24] or speak Spanish.[25] Among children with one Asian and one non-Asian parent, those who use a language other than English are more likely to identify as Asian than those who do not.[26]

Community context also plays a role in determining the racial and ethnic identification of youth. Studies have shown that youth who consistently identify as Hispanic are more likely attend school with greater numbers of Hispanics, live in urban areas, and live in areas with other Hispanics.[27] Similarly, youth with one Asian parent are more likely to identify as Asian if they live in neighborhoods with high concentrations of other Asians.[28] However, the importance of neighborhood may depend on the immigrant generation.[29] Consistently identified multiracial adolescents are more likely to live in racially diverse neighborhoods, neighborhoods with a higher concentration of Hispanics, and neighborhoods with more nonpoor residents.[30] These findings do not apply universally to all multiracial combinations. Consistently self-identified black+white adolescents are more likely to live in predominantly white neighborhoods than those black+white youths who do not consistently identify as multiracial.[31] This suggests the importance of neighborhood and English-language ability in ethnic or racial identity over the life course.

The context for multiracial identification is changing with the new census choices.[32] Many people with multiracial backgrounds may have seen their new race options for the first time in April 2000 when they filled out the census form. In 2010, many more may avail themselves of the option to choose more than one race. Furthermore, discussions of the prevalence of multiracial/ethnic populations in the 2000 Census are likely to cause others who have not previously chosen a multiracial/ethnic identity to consider doing so if they are already aware of their ancestry, and may even spark interest in learning about one's diverse ancestry. Similarly, the popularity of particular ancestries and racial identities may wax and wane over time. Many scholars have noted the increasing popularity of American Indian identification since 1960.[33] Among whites, English and Irish ethnic identifications are considerably more popular than others, such as German and Polish, among those who could claim any or all of those combinations,[34] and the population of Americans who claim Irish ancestry far exceeds those who could do so based on ancestry.[35] And particular national origin groups within the Asian category are more likely to identify as simply Asian. For example, Chinese and Japanese are more likely to also say they are Asian than those who identify ethnically as Filipino, Indian, or Korean.[36]

This report has taken the Census 2000 results at face value; however, racial identity can be fluid, and consistency varies by race category. After each recent decennial census, the Census Bureau conducts follow-up surveys to both evaluate the data quality in the current census, and to inform planning for the upcoming census. One such study, the Census Quality Survey (CQS), conducted one year after the 2000 Census, reveals much about which categories are most fluid.

Census data show that 99 percent of non-Latinos who reported one race in the census also reported one race in the CQS. For non-Latino monoracial white, black, and Asian respondents, there was an extremely high degree of consistency in racial reporting. Non-Latino white, black, and Asian Americans accounted for 85 percent of the nation's population in 2000. It is the combination of this measure of consistency as well as the sheer size of this segment that leads us to conclude that, for most Americans, standard racial categories are alive and well in the United States.

On the other hand, among non-Latinos who reported two or more races in Census 2000, only 40 percent responded by offering the same response in the CQS. Rather, 60 percent selected only one race in the CQS follow-up. The single race most often selected was white. This choice is not surprising since 75 percent of non-Latino biracial Americans identify as at least partly white.

Census 2000 showed that 48 percent of Latinos identified as white alone, 42 percent as SOR alone, and 6 percent as more than one race. With certainty one can say that white, SOR, and SOR+white are the preferred racial responses for Latinos; however, individual's responses shift considerably among these choices. Of Latinos who reported only one race in Census 2000, 94 percent also reported one race in the CQS. But the single-race choices changed for many monoracial Latinos between the two surveys. For example, among Census 2000's white Latinos, 49 percent also said they were white in the CQS, but 45 percent gave the response SOR in the CQS. Of those Latinos who said they were SOR in Census 2000, 27 percent said they were white in the

CQS. Of those who selected more than one race, 70 percent selected white and SOR in Census 2000. However, of those who reported more than one race, only 22 percent also reported two or more races in the CQS. More than 29 percent selected SOR alone, and even more (43 percent) selected white alone.

Multiracial Unions and Births

Interracial unions have the potential to dramatically increase the numbers and proportion of the multiple race/ethnic population. Over time, intermarriage rates have been increasing and births to parents of different races have been increasing.

The level of out-marriage varies tremendously by race or ethnic group. American Indians, Hispanics, and Asians have the highest out-marriage rates, while blacks and whites have the lowest.[37] Within mixed-race pairings, outmarriage varies by gender as well. For example, black men are much more likely to be married to nonblacks than are black women.[38] The opposite is true for Asians; women are much more likely to marry non-Asians than are men.[39] Among the race/ethnic groups with large immigrant populations (Asians and Hispanics), out-marriage is inversely related to the number of people in the group—Hispanics and Asians in states with small populations of those groups are most likely to marry outside their group.[40] These patterns are also affected by immigrant generation. Out-marriage increases by immigrant generation for Asians and Hispanics, but declines by generation among whites and blacks (see Table 6).[41]

We consider another measure of mixed-race couples by using birth records from California. California has a relatively long history of collecting data on parents' race and ethnicity on birth records.[42] That data allow us to examine 20-year trends in multiracial births—children born to parents of different races—in one of the most diverse states in the country. From 1980 to 2000, California experienced a dramatic change in its population. In 1980, two-thirds of the state's population was non-Hispanic white, and by 2000 no racial or ethnic group represented a majority of the state's population. Over roughly the same period, the number and percentage of multiracial births in California grew tremendously. By 2001, one in every 14 births in California was to parents of different racial groups (see Figure 7).

During this time period, the percentage of multiracial births to foreign-born mothers has stayed relatively low, hovering around 4 percent or 5 percent. Foreign-born mothers are generally less likely to have a spouse or partner of a different race than U.S.-born mothers, because many women arrive in the United States already married, and even those who arrive single are less likely to marry out of their race or ethnic group due to cultural and language differences. On the

Table 6

ESTIMATED INTERMARRIAGE RATES BY POPULATION GROUP AND GENERATION, 2000–2100

| Group | All | Percent intermarried by generation | | |
		First	Second	Third+
AIAN	40	20	30	50
Asian	20	13	34	54
Black	10	14	12	10
Hispanic	30	8	32	57
White	8	10	9	8

Source: B. Edmonston et al., "Recent Trends in Intermarriage and Immigration and Their Effects on the Future Racial Composition of the U.S. Population," in *The New Race Question: How the Census Counts Multiracial Individuals* (2002).

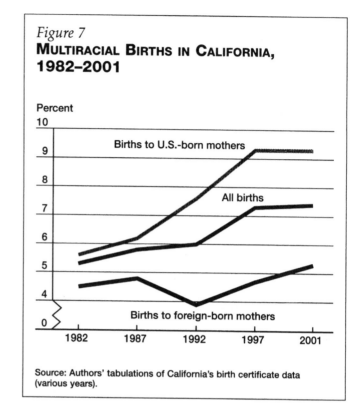

Figure 7

MULTIRACIAL BIRTHS IN CALIFORNIA, 1982–2001

Source: Authors' tabulations of California's birth certificate data (various years).

other hand, over the last 20 years multiracial births to U.S.-born women have risen from one in 18 to one in 11.

Group size is also an important determinant of multiracial births. Groups with relatively few members are much more likely to have spouses or partners of a different race, since by chance alone their social networks are more likely to include people of another race. In contrast, those belonging to majority groups can easily form large social networks among members of their own group. American Indians for example, represent less than 1 percent of California's population and are especially likely to have multiracial children. Seventy-six percent of AIAN mothers gave birth to multiracial children in 2001 (see Figure 8); only 6 percent of non-Hispanic white mothers gave birth to multiracial children.

Group size is not the only determinant. Although populations of Asians and African Americans are of similar sizes in California, Asian mothers are much more likely to have a child with a spouse or partner of another race than are African American mothers. However, as shown in Figure 8, the percentage of multiracial births to black mothers has more than doubled since 1982. This pattern is consistent with patterns in intermarriage and clearly is not exclusively a function of group size. Despite these differences, multiracial births are becoming more common for parents of all races and ethnic groups in the state.

Models of Multiracial Identity

To examine the determinants of multiracial identity in the 2000 Census, we developed statistical models (regression models) to identify the demographic and socioeconomic characteristics most strongly associated with multiracial identity. We report findings from two sets of models. In the first set, we restrict our analyses to the person in each household who responded to the census (the "householder" in census terminology), and developed separate models for each multiracial group in addition to a model for all groups together. Restricting the analysis to the person in each household who responded to the census allows us to examine how individuals self-identify, rather than how respondents identify the race of other members of the household. In the

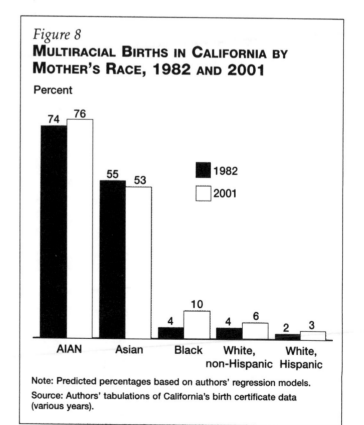

Figure 8

MULTIRACIAL BIRTHS IN CALIFORNIA BY MOTHER'S RACE, 1982 AND 2001

Note: Predicted percentages based on authors' regression models.
Source: Authors' tabulations of California's birth certificate data (various years).

second set, we examine how parents of different races identify the race of their children, again running separate models for each multiracial group. In this set of models, we consider how and why some multiracial couples identify their children as multiracial and why some do not. Both sets of models allow us to develop a deeper understanding not only of who chooses to choose two, but also how racial identity is formed and established.

Multiracial Identity Among Householders

Even after controlling for differences in age, region of the United States, education, nativity, and gender, we find that black householders are less likely to identify as multiracial than any other group of respondents to the 2000 Census (see Table 7). That blacks would be less likely to identify as more than one race is not unexpected, especially among older segments of the population. Prior to the 1960s Civil Rights Movement, legislation sought to harden the boundary between white and black America. For example, census enumerators for the 1930 Census were instructed to classify any person of white and Negro blood as Negro, no matter how small the percentage of Negro blood. This practice became known as "the one-drop rule." Antimiscegenation laws and Jim Crow statutes were widespread and meant to separate blacks from whites.

Although the civil rights era in the United States marked a turning point in American race relations, recent studies still show that blacks are the most segregated racial group in the United States.[43] Even among those identifying with more than one race, multiracial black+whites are more segregated than other multiracial combinations. Intermarriage rates between blacks and other groups are substantially lower than among Asians, American Indians, and Latinos.

Age is also a strong predictor of multiracial identity. Multiracial respondents to the 2000 Census tend to be younger than their monoracial counterparts. This is especially the case for multiracial blacks, but it is also true for multiracial Asians and multiracial SOR+white respondents as well. Twenty-year-old black householders are nine times more likely to report a multiracial identity than 60-year-old blacks, and 20-year-old Asian householders are almost twice as likely to identify as multiracial as 60-year-old Asians. This age pattern is undoubtedly a reflection of increasing rates of intermarriage over time. Younger individuals are more likely to have been born to parents of different races than older individuals. In addition, younger adults developed their own racial identities in very different social, political, and cultural settings than older adults, and might feel less restricted by traditional monoracial categories.

Multiracial identification also varies across regions of the United States. These regional patterns illustrate the importance of group size and social networks in

Table 7	
HOUSEHOLDERS IDENTIFYING AS MULTIRACIAL, 2000	
Householder	**Percent**
Black	0.4
American Indian	35.1
Asian	3.1
SOR, non-Hispanic	73.3
SOR, Hispanic	8.8

Note: Predicted percentages based on authors' regression models.
Source: Authors' calculations using Census 2000 1% Public Use Microdata Sample (PUMS).

multiracial identity. Racial groups that are concentrated geographically and have large populations are less likely to have social contacts and networks that include people of other races. Blacks in the South are especially unlikely to report more than one race, whereas blacks in the West are the most likely to do so (six times the rate in the South). Blacks are a greater share of the population of the South than in any other region, and are least represented in the West. Thus, blacks in the West are more likely to have social networks and parents of different races than blacks in the South. In contrast, Asians and American Indians in the West are least likely to report a multiracial identity. Relatively high concentrations of American Indians and Asians in the West result in relatively low proportions of those groups identifying as multiracial. In the West, Asian populations are concentrated in Hawaii and a few large metropolitan areas. For similar reasons, American Indians in nonmetropolitan areas—places that include reservations—are less likely to identify as multiracial.

Immigrants to the United States are less likely to identify as multiracial than U.S.-born residents. For the same reasons that intermarriage is less common among immigrants relative to the native born, so too is multiracial identity. Many immigrants come to the United States from countries with less racial diversity than the United States (many Asian countries, for example) or with racial typologies that are different from those in the United States and do not lend themselves to multiracial identity in the United States. One exception to this pattern is among non-Hispanic foreign-born individuals of other races, who are more likely to report a multiracial identity than their single-race counterparts.

Household living arrangements are another indication of the social networks and contacts that could have implications for the determination of racial identity. Among blacks, American Indians, and other-race Latinos, single mothers are less likely to identify as multiracial than women who are married. Interactions with a spouse of a different race could change an individual's own conception of race, leading her to be more likely to identify as of more than one. Of course, it is also possible that single mothers are less likely to have parents of different races, or that multiracial women are more likely to be married, or both.

Multiracial Identity of Children of Mixed-Race Couples

Racial identity in the United States is first established within the context of families. In the census, parents report the racial identity of their children. To what extent do parents of different races identify their children as multiracial? Do patterns of multiracial reporting depend on the specific race of each parent? In the most common intermarriage case where one parent is white and one is nonwhite, does reporting depend on whether it is the mother or the father who is nonwhite?

One of the most striking results of the 2000 Census is that most interracial couples do not report their children as multiracial. Overall, we estimated that less than half (44 percent) of children living with parents of different races are identified as multiracial. The proportions are especially low for two of the largest biracial groups, with only 13 percent of American Indian/white couples and only 3 percent of Latino SOR/white couples identifying their children as biracial (see Table 8).

The likelihood of reporting a child as multiracial depends very much on the specific racial combination of the parents. Children of Asian/white and black/white interracial couples are far more likely to report their child as multiracial than American Indian/white, non-Latino SOR/white, and Latino SOR/white parents. However, even among Asian/white and black/white couples, only about half report their children as multiracial. Among black/white couples, most who do not report their children as multiracial report them as black. Among Asian/white and Latino SOR/white couples, most who do not report their children as multiracial report them as white. American Indian/white couples are about evenly divided between reporting their children as only American Indian or only white. Just as the levels of multiracial reporting vary between the racial combinations of the parents, we believe that the reasons for multiracial reporting are particular to each combination of multiracial parents.

The very low levels of multiracial reporting among American Indian/white couples may be due to the nature of the American Indian population in the United States. That population includes a large number of people of mixed ancestry with varying degrees of strength in an AIAN identity.[44] Those who strongly identify as American Indian are likely to report their children as monoracial American Indian, even if one parent is white. Most American Indian tribes allow as members individuals who have only one "full-blooded" grandparent.[45] Thus, an AIAN parent who has strong ancestral connections to a tribe is likely to report his or her

child as American Indian regardless of spouse ethnicity. Those who do not strongly identify as AIAN, an apparently large and perhaps growing share of the AIAN population in the United States, and who have a child with a white spouse, report the child as white.

The low levels of multiracial reporting among Latino mixed-race SOR/white couples can be attributed to the prominence of Latino identity rather than racial identity. For many Latinos, the racial categories on the census are not meaningful. Large proportions of Latinos respond that they are SOR, and even slightly larger proportions respond that they are white. A large majority of Latinos would prefer to have "Hispanic, Latino, or of Spanish origin" added to the list of racial categories used in the census.[46] For many Latinos, the choice between SOR and white is somewhat arbitrary. Choosing both identities for their children would be superfluous, since the Latino identity is most salient.

Couples most likely to identify their children as multiracial are those in which both parents are multiracial: 83 percent of such couples report their children to be more than one race. Although such couples are a small share of all married couples, their children represent a substantial share of all multiracial children. Indeed, 25 percent of multiracial children in the United States have parents that both identify as multiracial. In contrast, only 1 percent of all children in married-couple households have two multiracial parents (see Figure 9, page 347). Even having only one multiracial parent leads to a relatively high probability of a child being identified as multiracial. Altogether, over half of multiracial children have at least one multiracial parent.

Multiracial reporting of children is extremely uncommon among parents of the same race. Overall, only 0.3 percent of parents of the same single race identify their child as multiracial. Because the vast majority (93 percent) of children in married-couple households have two parents of the same race, even this low rate of multiracial reporting among such couples' children results in a substantial number of multiracial children (120,000 children, or 8 percent of all multiracial chil-

---

Table 8

CHILDREN IDENTIFIED AS MULTIRACIAL, BY PARENT'S RACE, 2000

Parent's race	Percent
Black/white parents	49
AIAN/white parents	13
Asian/white parents	52
SOR, Hispanic/white parents	3
Both parents multiracial	83

Note: Predicted percentages based on authors' regression models.

Source: Authors' calculations using Census 2000 1% Public Use Microdata Sample (PUMS).

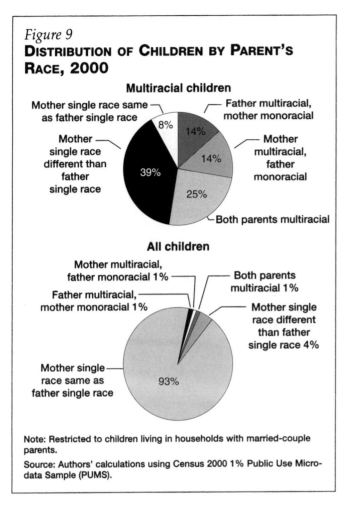

Figure 9

DISTRIBUTION OF CHILDREN BY PARENT'S RACE, 2000

Multiracial children

- Mother single race same as father single race — 8%
- Father multiracial, mother monoracial — 14%
- Mother single race different than father single race — 39%
- Mother multiracial, father monoracial — 14%
- Both parents multiracial — 25%

All children

- Mother multiracial, father monoracial 1%
- Both parents multiracial 1%
- Father multiracial, mother monoracial 1%
- Mother single race different than father single race 4%
- Mother single race same as father single race — 93%

Note: Restricted to children living in households with married-couple parents.

Source: Authors' calculations using Census 2000 1% Public Use Microdata Sample (PUMS).

Table 9

PERCENT OF CHILDREN IDENTIFIED AS BIRACIAL, BY PARENT'S RACE, 2000

Children	Parent's race		
	Black/ white	AIAN/ white	Asian/ white
Overall	49	13	52
Age 1	57	11	54
Age 17	42	12	50
South U.S.	46	10	40
West U.S.	52	20	61
Mother black	41	na	na
Father black	52	na	na
Mother AIAN	na	15	na
Father AIAN	na	11	na
Mother Asian	na	na	53
Father Asian	na	na	51
Both parents college grads	54	13	58
Both parents less than h.s.	35	12	49

na = Not applicable

Source: Authors' calculations using Census 2000 1% Public Use Microdata Sample (PUMS).

dren). Couples in which both partners are non-Hispanic SOR are the most likely to report their children as multiracial, but even among those couples only 1.5 percent of their children are identified as multiracial.

Gender also matters in the assignment of racial identity to children of mixed-race couples. Multiracial identity is more commonly selected for children of a mixed-race black/white couple if it is the father who is black rather than the mother. Black men are more likely to be married to whites than are black women.[47] If these marriage patterns continue, the population of black+white children may grow more rapidly than if there were no gender imbalance in rates of black out-marriage. The opposite pattern prevails among American Indians; multiracial identity is chosen more often if the mother in a mixed-race marriage is AIAN than if the father is AIAN.

When a multiracial identity is not chosen for the child, the father's race is more commonly selected. That is, if the father is black and the mother is white and only one race is chosen for the child, the choice is more often black than white. If the father is white and the mother is black, the choice is more often white when only one race is selected for the child. Similar results are found for Asian/white couples.

Mixed-race couples with young children are more likely to identify that child as multiracial than mixed-race couples with older children. This age pattern is especially pronounced for children with one black parent and one white parent (see Table 9). For those children, well over half of 1-year-olds are identified as multiracial black+white, whereas only 42 percent of 17-year-olds are so identified. The pattern is also found among Asian and white parents, though it is much less pronounced.

There are several reasons for this age pattern. First, parents with older children had those children many years ago when the only categories available on most forms and surveys were monoracial categories. Those parents are less likely to adopt the multiracial format for reporting their children's racial identity precisely because they have become accustomed to reporting their children as monoracial. Second, older children might be more likely to have a say in the reporting of their racial identity by their parents. Those older children might have had experiences that have led them to strongly identify with only one racial identity. Those experiences could include facing discrimination directed at a mono-racial group, identifying with a set of monoracial peers, or education that has raised an individual's ethnic or cultural awareness. Third, the finding could be measurement error, as older children are less likely to be the biological child of both parents in the household.[48]

Regionally, mixed-race parents in the West are most likely to identify their child as multiracial, while those in the South are least likely to do so. Probabilities in the

Northeast and Midwest are generally midway between the low levels in the South and the high levels in the West. These differences persist even when we control for regional differences in age, parent's education, and whether or not the family lives in a metropolitan area. The pattern is particularly strong for children of an Asian/white couple and an American Indian/white couple but is also evident for black/white couples.

Why are interracial couples in the West more likely to report multiracial identity for their children and those in the South less likely to do so? Social attitudes undoubtedly play a role. Interracial couples in the West tend to live in the most socially liberal states of the West (California, Hawaii, and Washington) where social norms and histories are less pronounced than in the South. In addition, the West has lower levels of segregation of both monoracial and multiracial residents than other regions.

Finally, college-educated mixed-race couples are more likely to identify their children as multiracial than less-educated parents. More-educated parents might be more savvy with respect to census forms than other parents, and are probably more likely to have followed debates and discussions about changing racial and ethnic understandings and categories.

Because the census reports the relationship of a child to the householder and not to the householder's spouse, we cannot determine if a child is biologically related to the householder's spouse. In our sample of married parents of different races, children may be the stepchildren or adopted children of the householder's spouse, but are reported to be the biological children of the household head. Since we cannot exclude the nonbiological children of the householder's spouse, our estimates of the share of married parents of different races who identify their children as multiracial may be biased.

However, it is unlikely that the bias is large. In order to estimate the size of this bias, we assume that the same share of children are step and adopted for the spouse of the householder as for the householder (8 percent of all children of the householder).[49] A liberal estimate of the bias assumes that all multiracial children are the biological children of both parents, which would increase the overall estimate of mixed-race couples that identify their children as multiracial from 44 percent to 48 percent.

RATES AND BRIDGES: CHALLENGES FOR DATA USERS

Beyond the social and political dimensions of multiracial identity discussed above, changes to the federal system of race classification have major implications for social scientists and demographers who use these data. The following are two examples of challenges faced by data users.

Using Census Data to Estimate Base Populations

Many social scientists and health researchers use census data to provide denominators in the calculation of race-specific rates—including birth rates, death rates, rates of morbidity, crime rates, and arrest rates. However, combining data from one set of data with census data can be problematic, especially for multiracial individuals for whom the reporting of racial identity may not be consistent.

For example, measures of fertility for multiracial women vary depending on the data set(s) used. Administrative data from California birth records suggest that AIAN+white women have substantially higher fertility than whites. These rates are derived from a single data source, and therefore do not involve inconsistent measures of race between numerators and denominators. Measures of fertility are very different, however, when we combine birth records with census data to estimate total fertility rates in California. These results suggest that AIAN+white women in California have astonishingly low levels of fertility, with a total fertility rate of 1.0 (lower than the total fertility rate for women in any country in the world).

Of course, both results cannot be correct. It is probable that many women who identified as AIAN+white on the 2000 Census were not identified that way when they gave birth in California. Thus, combining administrative data on births with census data on populations understates fertility rates for this group.

Special care must also be taken in working with the SOR category. The census found substantially more SOR+whites than did the Census Supplementary Survey (C2SS), a survey conducted at the same time as the census. Though the content was identical in the two questionnaires, the formatting was different. In the C2SS, it was much more difficult to locate the SOR category, as it was not offset as in the census questionnaire. Overall, the C2SS places the SOR population at 10.6 million, compared to 15.2 million in the census. The number of multiracial SOR+whites among Latinos (1,468,000) was more than half again as large in the census as the C2SS (962,000), and the number of non-Latino SOR+whites was more than four times as large in the census (841,000) as in the C2SS (200,000).

Bridging Issues and Civil Rights Monitoring

Because racial categorizations between the 1990 and 2000 censuses are not consistent (with the addition of the ability to choose more than one race in 2000), analyzing changes in racial populations from one census to the next is difficult. The same problem exists in other data sets, such as the Current Population Survey, which has modified its racial and ethnic categories to allow more than one race beginning in 2003. The severity of the problem depends on how many people choose to identify as more than one race and the extent to which those people are different from monoracial respondents. For non-Latino whites, the problem is not so severe. The proportion of multiracial whites among all whites is small: less than 2 percent; and the characteristics of those multiracial whites are not so different from monoracial whites. For American Indians, the problem is severe. The most important and basic temporal measure of any population—changes in its size—is in serious doubt. The 2000 Census counted 2.1 million non-Latinos who identified only as American Indian, and 3.4 million who identified either as American Indian alone or as American Indian and another race. The higher count suggests that the American Indian population almost doubled from 1990 to 2000, while the lower count suggests the increase was only 15 percent. Characteristics of the American Indian population in the U.S., including measures of economic well-being, depend on whether we choose to include multiracial American Indians, who tend to be better educated and have higher wages than monoracial American Indians.

Demographers have devised several alternative methods of bridging categories across censuses. These methods range from counting multiracial people as fractions of persons for each race checked—for example, a black+white individual would add one-half to the black population and one-half to the white population—to counting multiracial people as whole individuals for each race checked (essentially doublecounting for biracial people).

THE FUTURE OF RACE IN AMERICA

There are two extreme views of the future of racial categorization in the United States. In one view, racial categories would no longer exist—the Census Bureau and other government agencies would cease to collect and disseminate data on the basis of race. Proponents of this view argue that racial categorization has no scientific basis and only serves to promote divisive identity politics. In California, this view was put to the voters in October 2003 (see Box 2). In the other extreme view, there will be an ever-expanding list of groups seeking and gaining inclusion in the federal statistical system.[50]

The 2000 Census, the first ever to allow respondents to choose more than one race, could be seen as a step

---

Box 2

CALIFORNIA'S RACIAL CLASSIFICATION INITIATIVE

California, home to the largest number of multiracial Americans and the third-highest percentage of multiracial Americans, recently voted on an initiative that would have prevented the state from classifying individuals on the basis of race and ethnicity. This was the first time citizens in any state had been asked to vote on the collection of racial and ethnic data.

The initiative, known as Proposition 54 ("Classification by Race, Ethnicity, Color, or National Origin") appeared on the Oct. 7, 2003, ballot. It would have prevented the state from using such categories for the purposes of public education, public contracting, public employment, and other government operations. The only exemptions would have been those data collection efforts needed to comply with federal law; for certain law enforcement activities; for medical research; and for the California Department of Fair Employment and Housing to collect certain race-related information through 2014.

The initiative's proponents argued that the initiative signaled America's "first step toward a color-blind society." Opponents argued that demographic information "helps us make smart choices."

California voters rejected the initiative by 64 percent to 36 percent. Support for the initiative varied substantially among California's racial and ethnic groups. According to a Los Angeles Times exit poll, 38 percent of non-Hispanic whites, 13 percent of blacks, 25 percent of Latinos, and 28 percent of Asians voted in favor of the initiative.

---

toward this second view. But relatively few Americans responded as multiracial. In fact, the number who responded as multiracial was much lower than the potential number who could do so. One accounting prior to the 2000 Census suggested that between 3.1 and 6.6 percent of the U.S. population was likely to respond as multiracial, yet only 2.4 percent of the population did so.[51] Not even a majority of mixed-race couples identified their children as multiracial, and the single largest multiracial group in America is Latino SOR+white. If we exclude that group, only 1.6 percent of Americans identified as multiracial.

Race still matters in America. In particular, the divide between blacks and whites, while narrowing, is still large. With respect to wages, for example, blacks still earn significantly less than whites even after controlling for age, education, and occupation.[52] Nonetheless, racial disparities have been reduced. The collection of racial data by government agencies has allowed us to measure this improvement. Indeed, the U.S. Supreme Court has affirmed the salience of these categories, and census results show that the vast majority of Americans identify with a single race. And the government has issued guidelines for civil rights monitoring that largely rely on monoracial categories.

The large and growing Latino population is just as likely as the multiracial population to pose a challenge to the current racial paradigm. Many Latinos do not identify with the traditional monoracial categories and place themselves in the category that the Census Bureau uses to collect residual racial responses. Indeed, a Current Population Survey of racial identities found that a large majority of Latinos would prefer that Hispanic or Latino be listed as a racial category.[53]

Racial categories will change. Since the first decennial census in 1790, no more than three consecutive censuses have used the same racial categories. The multiracial population is of great interest not only because it is a newly recognized racial identity but also because of what it tells us about race in America.

REFERENCES

If provided by the authors, additional text and data associated with this report are available at www.prb.org/AmericanPeople.

1. David R. Harris, "Does it Matter How We Measure? Racial Classification and The Characteristics of Multiracial Youth," in *The New Race Question: How the Census Counts Multiracial Individuals*, ed. Joel Perlmann and Mary C. Waters (New York: Russell Sage Foundation, 2002).
2. Mary C. Waters, *Ethnic Options: Choosing Identities in America* (Berkeley: University of California Press, 1990).
3. Michael Bentley et al., "Census Quality Survey to Evaluate Responses to the Census 2000 Question on Race: An Introduction to the Data" (Washington, DC: U.S. Census Bureau, Census 2000 Evaluation B.3, April 3, 2003).
4. Kim M. Williams, "Boxed In: The United States Multiracial Movement" (unpublished dissertation, Cornell University, 2001).
5. Hugh D. Graham, "The Origins of Official Minority Designation," in *The New Race Question: How the Census Counts Multiracial Individuals*, ed. Joel Perlmann and Mary C. Waters (New York: Russell Sage Foundation, 2002).
6. Nicholas A. Jones and Amy S. Smith, "The Two or More Races Population," *Census 2000 Brief* (Washington, DC: U.S. Census Bureau, 2001).
7. Elizabeth M. Grieco and Rachel C. Cassidy, "Overview of Race and Hispanic Origin 2000," *Census 2000 Brief* (Washington, DC: U.S. Census Bureau, March 2001); and Sonya M. Tafoya, "Latinos and Racial Identification in California," *California Counts: Population Trends and Profiles* 4, no. 4 (2003).
8. Matthew Snipp, "Some Observations about Racial Boundaries and the Experiences of American Indians," *Ethnic and Racial Studies* 20, no. 4 (1997): 667-89; and Matthew Snipp, "American Indians: Clues to the Future of Other Racial Groups," in *The New Race Question: How the Census Counts Multiracial Individuals*, ed. Joel Perlmann and Mary C. Waters (New York: Russell Sage Foundation, 2002).
9. Jones and Smith, "The Two or More Races Population."
10. Elizabeth Sweet, *1990 REX Memorandum Series # PP-9* (Washington, DC: U.S. Census Bureau, Decennial Statistical Studies Division, 1994); and Elizabeth Sweet, *1990 REX Memorandum Series # PP-11* (Washington, DC: U.S. Census Bureau, Decennial Statistical Studies Division, 1994).
11. Jones and Smith, "The Two or More Races Population."
12. Authors' calculation of Census 2000 1 Percent Public Use Microdata Sample (PUMS). Costa Ricans and Panamanians also tend to have a higher share of respondents who identify racially as black; however, these groups together constitute less than one-half of 1 percent of the Latino population in the United States.
13. Tafoya, "Latinos and Racial Identification in California."
14. Public Policy Institute of California, *Californians and Their Government* (San Francisco: Public Policy Institute of California, August 2000).
15. The Washington Post/Kaiser Family Foundation/Harvard University, *Race and Ethnicity in 2001: Attitudes, Perceptions, and Experiences* (Menlo Park, CA: The Henry J. Kaiser Family Foundation, 2001).
16. Bentley et al., "Census Quality Survey to Evaluate Responses to the Census 2000 Question on Race."
17. Bentley et al., "Census Quality Survey to Evaluate Responses to the Census 2000 Question on Race."
18. David R. Harris and Jeremiah J. Sim, "Who is Multiracial? Assessing the Complexity of Lived Race," *American Sociological Review* 67, no. 4 (2002): 614-27.
19. Waters, *Ethnic Options: Choosing Identities in America*.
20. Harris and Sim, "Who is Multiracial? Assessing the Complexity of Lived Race."
21. Waters, *Ethnic Options: Choosing Identities in America*; Rogelio Saenz, Sean-Shong Hwang, and Robert Anderson, "Persistence and Change in Asian Identity Among Children of Intermarried Couples," *Sociological Perspectives* 38 (1995): 175-94; and Yu Xie and Kimberly Goyette, "The Racial Identification of Biracial Children with One Asian Parent: Evidence from the 1990 Census," *Social Forces* 76, no. 2 (1997): 547-70.
22. David R. Harris, "Does it Matter How We Measure? Racial Classification and The Characteristics of Multiracial Youth," in *The New Race Question: How the Census Counts Multiracial Individuals*, ed. Joel Perlmann and Mary C. Waters (New York: Russell Sage Foundation, 2002).
23. Robert A. Hahn, Joseph Mulinare, and Steven M. Teutsch, "Inconsistencies in Coding of Race and Ethnicity Between Birth and Death in U.S. Infants: A New Look at Infant Mortality, 1983 through 1985," *Journal of the American Medical Association* 267, no. 2 (1992): 259-63.
24. Alejando Portes and Dag MacLeod, "What Shall I Call Myself? Hispanic Identity Formation in the Second Generation," *Ethnic and Racial Studies* 19, no. 3 (1996).
25. Karl Eschbach and Christina Gómez, "Choosing Hispanic Identity: Ethnic Identity Switching among Respondents to High School and Beyond," *Social Science Quarterly* 79, no. 1 (1998).

26. Saenz, Hwang, and Anderson, "Persistence and Change in Asian Identity Among Children of Intermarried Couples"; and Xie and Goyette, "The Racial Identification of Biracial Children with One Asian Parent."

27. Eschbach and Gómez, "Choosing Hispanic Identity."

28. Saenz, Hwang, and Anderson, "Persistence and Change in Asian Identity Among Children of Intermarried Couples"; and Xie and Goyette, "The Racial Identification of Biracial Children with One Asian Parent."

29. Xie and Goyette, "The Racial Identification of Biracial Children with One Asian Parent."

30. Harris, "Does it Matter How We Measure?"

31. Harris, "Does it Matter How We Measure?"

32. Joshua Goldstein and Ann Morning, "The Multiple-Race Population of the United States: Issues and Estimates," *Proceedings of the National Academy of Sciences* 97, no. 11 (2000): 6230-35.

33. Jeffrey Passel, "The Growing American Indian Population, 1960-1990: Beyond Demography," *Population Research and Policy Review* 16, no. 1-2 (1998): 11-31; Snipp, "Some Observations about Racial Boundaries and the Experiences of American Indians"; and Karl Eschbach, "The Enduring and Vanishing American Indian: American Indian Population Growth and Intermarriage in 1990," *Ethnic and Racial Studies* 18, no. 1 (1995): 89-108.

34. Waters, *Ethnic Options: Choosing Identities in America.*

35. Michael Hout and Joshua Goldstein, "How 4.5 Million Irish Became 40 Million Irish-Americans: Demographic and Subjective Aspects of Ethnic Composition of White America," *American Sociological Review* 59, no. 1 (1994).

36. Xie and Goyette, "The Racial Identification of Biracial Children with One Asian Parent."

37. Zhenchao Qian, "Who Intermarries? Education, Nativity, Region and Interracial Marriage, 1980 to 1990," *Journal of Comparative Family Studies* 30, no. 4 (1999): 579-97.

38. Tim B. Heaton and Stan L. Albrect, "The Changing Pattern of Interracial Marriage," *Social Biology* 43, no. 3-4 (1996); and Qian, "Who Intermarries?"

39. Qian, "Who Intermarries?"

40. Matthijs Kalmijn, "Intermarriage and Homogamy: Causes, Patterns, and Trends," *Annual Review of Sociology* 24 (1998): 395-421; and Roberto Suro, "Mixed Doubles," *American Demographics* 21, no. 11 (1999): 56-62.

41. Sharon M. Lee and Marilyn Fernandez, "Trends in Asian American Racial/Ethnic Intermarriage: A Comparison of 1980 and 1990 Census Data," *Sociological Perspectives* 41, no. 2 (1998): 323-42; Zai Liang and Naomi Ito, "Intermarriage of Asian Americans in the New York City Region: Contemporary Patterns and Future Prospects," *International Migration Review* 33, no. 4 (1999); and Qian, "Who Intermarries?"

42. Sonya M. Tafoya, "Check One or More ... Mixed Race and Ethnicity in California," *California Counts: Population Trends and Profiles* 1, no. 2 (2000).

43. William Frey and Dowell Myers, "Neighborhood Segregation in Single-Race and Multirace America: A Census 2000 Study of Cities and Metropolitan Areas," *Fannie Mae Foundation Working Paper* (Washington, DC: Fannie Mae Foundation, 2002).

44. Snipp, "American Indians: Clues to the Future of Other Racial Groups."

45. Russell Thornton, "Tribal Membership Requirements and the Demography of Old and New Native Americans," in *Changing Numbers, Changing Needs*, ed. Gary D. Sandefur, Ronald R. Rindfuss, and Barney Cohen (Washington, DC: National Academies Press, 1996).

46. Clyde R. Tucker et al., "Testing Methods of Collecting Racial and Ethnic Information: Results of the Current Population Survey Supplement on Race and Ethnicity," *Statistical Notes*, no. 40 (1996).

47. Heaton and Albrect, "The Changing Pattern of Interracial Marriage."

48. Rose M. Kreider, "Adopted Children and Stepchildren: 2000," *Census 2000 Special Reports* (Washington, DC: U.S. Census Bureau, 2003).

49. Kreider, "Adopted Children and Stepchildren: 2000."

50. Kenneth Prewitt, "Race in the 2000 Census: A Turning Point," in *The New Race Question: How the Census Counts Multiracial Individuals*, ed. Joel Perlmann and Mary C. Waters (New York: Russell Sage Foundation, 2002).

51. Goldstein and Morning, "The Multiple-Race Population of the United States: Issues and Estimates."

52. Deborah Reed and Jennifer Cheng, *Racial and Ethnic Wage Gaps in the California Labor Market* (San Francisco: Public Policy Institute of California, 2003).

53. Tucker et al., "Testing Methods of Collecting Racial and Ethnic Information."

Latinos and the Changing Face of America

By Rogelio Saenz

LATINOS ARE US

Over the last 100 years, few racial or ethnic groups have had as great an impact on the demography of the United States as Latinos. In 1900, there were only slightly more than 500,000 Latinos.[1] Today, the national Latino population numbers more than 35 million and represents one of the most dynamic and diverse racial/ethnic groups in the United States.

The most dramatic impact of the Latino population on the demography of the nation has taken place over the last few decades. The number of Latinos in the United States more than doubled between 1980 and 2000, accounting for 40 percent of the growth in the country's population during that period. And in 2003 the U.S. Census Bureau designated Latinos as the nation's largest minority group, an amazing event given that in 1980 the Latino population was only slightly more than half the size of the African American population.

The rapid growth of the Latino population has been due to various demographic factors. First, the Latino population is significantly younger than the general population, signifying that a relatively large proportion of Latinas (females within the Latino population) are in or approaching the childbearing ages. Second, the Latino population has higher levels of fertility compared with other groups. Third, more immigrants arriving in the United States originate from Latin America than from any other region. Given these trends, Latinos will undoubtedly continue to have an impact on the composition of the U.S. population. Indeed, population projections suggest that the Latino population could increase its share of the overall U.S. population from 13 percent in 2000 to 33 percent in 2100.[2]

The Latino population has had an impact not only on the demography of the U.S. population, but also on other aspects of U.S. society. This can be seen, for example, in the increasing popularity of Latin American food and music and in the prevalence of Spanish-language signage, advertisements, and media. In addition, the business community has discovered the economic clout of the Latino population. It has been estimated that the disposable income of the Latino population will surge nearly fourfold to $1,014 billion in 2008 from $222 billion in 1990.[3] The increase in buying power of the Latino population over this 18-year period is expected to be greater than that of the white, African American, American Indian, and Asian populations. Politicians increasingly recognize the political muscle of the Latino population, especially with the group's concentration in the most populous states in the nation. The growing presence of the Latino population has already caused a rethinking of racial and ethnic relations in the United States, a country that has commonly examined race and ethnicity from the perspective of blacks and whites.

Despite the growing interest in Latinos, there is relatively limited knowledge of this population. The emergence of panethnic (broad, inclusive) terms such as "Latinos" and "Hispanics" has fostered a view of this population as a monolithic group, despite the diverse nature of the groups making up the Latino population.[4] These groups exhibit different histories, demographic characteristics, and patterns of social and economic integration. The U.S. Latino population includes segments that can trace their roots in the United States over numerous generations and others that have recently arrived. Alejandro Portes and Cynthia Truelove describe this great diversity within the Latino population:

> "Under the same label, we find individuals whose ancestors lived in the country at least since the time of independence and others who arrived last year; we find substantial numbers of professionals and entrepreneurs, along with humble farm laborers and unskilled factory workers; there are whites, blacks, mulattoes, and mestizos; there are full-fledged citizens and unauthorized aliens; and finally, among the immigrants, there are those who came in search of employment and a better economic future and those who arrived escaping death squads and political persecution at home."[5]

Their great diversity presents challenges in understanding the rate and extent of Latino groups' integra-

ROGELIO SAENZ is professor and head of the department of sociology at Texas A&M University. He received his doctorate in sociology from Iowa State University in 1986. Saenz is the author of numerous journal articles, book chapters, and technical reports on the demography of Latinos, immigration, social inequality, and race and ethnicity. He is a past president of the Southwestern Sociological Association and a past vice president of the Rural Sociological Society. Saenz is the recipient of the American Association of Higher Education Hispanic Caucus 2003 Outstanding Latino Faculty Award in Research and Teaching in Higher Education and is a former American Sociological Association Minority Fellow.

tion into mainstream U.S. society. Educators, policy-makers, businesspeople, and others in the United States require knowledge about the Latino population and the groups within it to more effectively understand and serve the particular needs of Latino populations. This is particularly true now that the Latino population has expanded geographically beyond its traditional hub areas into places that have historically had few Latinos.

This report examines the contemporary demographic and socioeconomic characteristics of the diverse groups that form the Latino population, as well as the changes that these groups experienced over the last decade (1990-2000). It reviews the factors that have contributed to the growth of the Latino population in the United States, discusses how U.S. Latinos are faring, and outlines the challenges to improving the social and economic conditions of Latinos in the coming decades.

COMING TO AMERICA

For the last several centuries, Latinos have made their way to the United States, a movement that continues today. Yet the timing of their movement and the reasons for it differ, as do their experiences here.

War and Political Turmoil

For some Latino groups, the initial entrance into the United States was associated with the outcome of war. For example, the U.S. victory over Mexico in the Mexican-American War, ending with the signing of the Treaty of Guadalupe Hidalgo in 1848, resulted in Mexico ceding approximately half of its territory to the United States; most of the relatively small number of Mexicans living in this territory—estimates range between 75,000 and 86,000[6]—became U.S. citizens in the process. Similarly, the U.S. victory in the Spanish-American War resulted in the United States gaining control of Puerto Rico in 1898; the passage of the Jones Act in 1917 eventually granted U.S. citizenship to Puerto Ricans, who continue to enjoy the ease of moving back and forth between the island and the U.S. mainland.[7]

Short of war, other political developments have boosted Latin American immigration to the United States. For example, in response to a period of political turmoil and revolution in Mexico, approximately 678,000 Mexicans immigrated to the United States legally between 1911 and 1930. Similarly, the rise to power of Fidel Castro in Cuba in 1959 was immediately followed by the first major flow of Cuban immigrants to the United States.

Nearly 209,000 Cubans immigrated to the United States legally between 1961 and 1970.[8] The U.S. govern-

---

Box 1
THE FREE FLOW OF GOODS AND PEOPLE

The last couple of decades have seen important developments related to Latino immigration. These changes have enlarged the economic, social, familial, and political worlds of Latino immigrants.

For example, Latino immigrants continue to maintain ties with their home countries and communities. Many regularly send money to family members remaining behind. Roberto Suro estimates that some 6 million Latin American immigrants in the United States sent nearly $30 billion in remittances to Latin American and Caribbean countries in 2003.[18] These funds are extremely important for the families and home communities of immigrants.

In addition, many Latin American immigrants are transnational migrants that move back and forth between the United States and their home countries for varying lengths of time. Many are part of transnational families, with some immediate family members living in the United States and others in the country of origin. The number of transnational migrants is not known; transnational migrants who were in the United States on April 1, 2000, and who were enumerated are part of the census data reported here; those who were back in their home countries at that time are not included in this analysis.

The increase of women as immigrants has even resulted in rising levels of transnational motherhood, with immigrant women working in the United States while their children remain behind in the home community under the care of relatives or friends.[19] Such living arrangements give rise to mixed-status families, in which some family members are U.S.-born citizens; others, U.S. naturalized citizens; and still others, undocumented immigrants.[20] These arrangements lead to variations within the family in access and entitlement to societal resources, services, rights, and benefits. Mixed-status families illustrate the blurring of boundaries between the nation's U.S.- and foreign-born populations.

During the 1990s, more Latin American countries recognized dual nationality, allowing people to hold nationality in more than one country. While only El Salvador, Panama, Peru, and Uruguay recognized dual nationality prior to 1990, an additional six countries—Brazil, Colombia, Costa Rica, the Dominican Republic, Ecuador, and Mexico—did so during the 1990s.[21] The recognition of dual nationality has important implications for sustaining transnational migration, as well as for the incorporation of immigrants in the United States.

---

ment, with its opposition to communism and Fidel Castro, embraced Cuban exiles, many of them drawn from the middle and upper classes of Cuba, and seeking refuge in the United States.[9]

Political instability and large-scale violence in the Dominican Republic from the mid-1960s to the mid-1970s led to major flows of Dominicans to the United States. From 1961 to 1970, nearly 209,000 Dominicans came to this country legally.[10]

The late 1970s and early 1980s saw major political turmoil and civil wars in Central American countries including El Salvador, Guatemala, and Nicaragua, complete with U.S. intervention.[11] Nearly 603,000 Central Americans immigrated to the United States legally between 1971 and 1990.[12]

The Refugee Act of 1980, which allowed for the admission and incorporation of political refugees on humanitarian grounds, provided entry to 125,000 Cuban refugees. Known as *Marielitos* due to the location from which they departed Cuba (Mariel Bay), they sought sanctuary from repression and fled when Castro temporarily lifted restrictions against leaving the island. Compared with their compatriots who had arrived in the United States earlier, *Marielitos* were more likely to be black and of lower- and working-class origins;[13] their reception in the United States was colder than that extended to earlier Cuban refugees.[14]

Economic Factors

Economic and demographic forces have also played a significant role in the movement of Latin Americans to the United States. Operation Bootstrap, which was initiated in 1947 to industrialize Puerto Rico by opening it up to U.S. investors, uprooted many Puerto Ricans from rural areas, some of whom moved to urban areas of the island and others to the U.S. mainland. Latin American countries experienced major population growth beginning in the 1950s and 1960s, making it difficult for them to provide adequate employment opportunities for their people. The high unemployment rates and low wages resulting from population pressures and from regional economic difficulties spurred immigration from Latin America to more favorable economic conditions in the United States.

U.S. Immigration Policy

While the proximity of Latin Americans to the United States has played a role in increased immigration flows, U.S. policies also have helped Latin American immigrants enter the country. When the United States established immigration quotas to stem the tide of immigration from southern and Eastern Europe and from Asia, Mexicans and other Latin Americans were exempted from quotas and from related entry requirements.[15] Moreover, World War II brought labor shortages that caused the United States to establish the Bracero Program, allowing Mexicans to work in the United States as contract laborers. The program was so popular among U.S. employers, especially those in agriculture, that it was extended until 1964. Approximately 4.8 million Mexicans worked as part of this program between 1942 and 1964.[16]

The liberal Hart-Cellar Act of 1965, which abolished the national quotas system that restricted immigration

from southern and Eastern Europe and lifted the ban on immigration from Asia, also provided for family reunification; naturalized citizens, many of them Latinos, were allowed to petition to have their close relatives immigrate to the United States.

The bulk of immigration from Mexico and other Latin American countries has occurred since the 1960s. During that period, a total of nearly 11 million people from Latin American countries, including 5 million from Mexico alone, entered the United States legally. In each decade since 1960, Latin Americans have accounted for between 45 percent and 47 percent of all legal immigrants to this country. Yet these numbers do not accurately reflect the much larger volume of immigration from Latin America because they do not include undocumented immigrants.

The Immigration Reform and Control Act (IRCA) of 1986 contained an amnesty provision that allowed undocumented immigrants who had been living in the United States continuously since 1982 (for at least 90 days working in agriculture since 1985 in the case of seasonal workers) to become permanent residents and eventually naturalized citizens. Roughly 3 million people—about three-fourths of them Mexican—gained legal status through IRCA.[17]

The various groups that make up the Latino population in the United States differ significantly in the forces that have brought them to the United States, the timing of their entrance, and the length of their stay. For some Latino groups, such as Mexicans, a significant share of the population has had family living in the United States for several generations, while another noticeable portion has arrived just in the last few years. Indeed, U.S.-born Latinos who are third generation or higher—especially Mexicans—are often overlooked in current discussions and debates regarding Latinos. For other Latino groups, the overwhelming majority of members of their populations were born outside the United States. The various Latino groups have distinct experiences in the United States and differ in socioeconomic status.

DEMOGRAPHIC PROFILE

Gathering information on how Latinos are faring in the United States first requires some understanding of the term "Latino." The emergence of groups described as Hispanics and Latinos has taken place over the course of the last quarter-century in the United States.

From Many to One—to Many

People throughout Latin America generally identify themselves on the basis of their nationality—for example, Cubans, Mexicans, Puerto Ricans, or Salvadorans—rather than as Hispanics or Latinos. Accordingly, prior to the late 1970s, Latinos living in the United States commonly viewed themselves by their (ancestors') national origin. For instance, people of Mexican origin tended to view themselves as Mexican or Mexican American.[22]

On May 12, 1977, the Office of Management and Budget (OMB) issued OMB Directive 15, which declared that, for data collection on the U.S. population, there would be two ethnic categories: the panethnic label of "Hispanic," and non-Hispanic.[23] This decision occurred several years after President Nixon, responding to pressures from the U.S. Interagency Committee on Mexican American Affairs, requested that the 1970 census include an item to count Hispanics.[24] The request came too late for the Hispanic item to be included in the 1970 Census short-form questionnaire, but was included in the 5 percent sample long-form questionnaire.

The Hispanic label, according to OMB Directive 15, referred to people of Mexican, Puerto Rican, Cuban, Central or South American, or other Spanish culture or origin.[25] Despite much debate over the federal government using this term to identify such diverse groups, the term became increasingly popular. Much of this popularity was stimulated by the dissemination in the media of statistics for the Hispanic population after the 1980 Census. In addition, Hispanic politicians, leaders, and political organizations increasingly used the panethnic term and forged coalitions across national origin groups.[26] Hispanic leaders trumpeted the 1980s as the "decade of the Hispanic."[27]

Nonetheless, by the mid-1980s many people who had never accepted the Hispanic term began to mount efforts to replace it. These individuals asserted that the U.S. federal government had imposed the label on the ethnic group and that the label emphasized the Spanish element of the panethnic group while neglecting its indigenous roots.[28] Opponents of the Hispanic identity put forth the term "Latino," a label that they saw as more inclusive of the experience of Latin American groups in the United States.[29] The newer term has gained popularity among ethnic leaders and the media. This does not mean, however, that the Latino identity has completely replaced the Hispanic identity. Indeed, there is a significant segment of the ethnic community that continues to prefer the Hispanic label.[30] In sum, the Latino label emerged in reaction to the Hispanic term, and both panethnic terms have their roots in the United States. Latin American immigrants coming to the United States soon realize that these labels are used to describe them.

Indeed, collection of demographic data on people of Latin American descent depends on their identifying themselves in the census using these labels. For this analysis, data on Latinos come from the responses of people who answered that they were "of Spanish/Hispanic origin" in the 1990 Census and "Spanish/Hispanic/Latino" in the 2000 Census.

Changes occurred between the 1990 and 2000 censuses in the manner in which people were asked about their ethnic origin. The 1990 and 2000 questionnaires allowed only Mexicans, Puerto Ricans, and Cubans to indicate their specific Latino group directly. Latinos not belonging to these three groups had to indicate that they belonged to the residual category of "Other Spanish/ Hispanic" (1990 Census) or "Other Spanish/Hispanic/ Latino" (2000 Census). They were also asked to print their specific group. However, the 1990 Census questionnaire presented a set of examples of specific groups—for example, Argentinean, Colombian, Dominican, Nicaraguan, Salvadoran, Spaniard, and so on— which helped prompt respondents to indicate their specific Latino group. These examples were dropped from the 2000 Census questionnaire. The outcome of this change appears to be that people were less likely to print their national-origin group in 2000 than in 1990.[31] Therefore, it is likely that individuals who classified themselves as Dominican, Central American, or South American in 1990 ended up in the residual Other Latino group in 2000. The Other Latino group as used in this analysis is a catchall category that includes Spaniards, individuals who view themselves in distinct terms that are unavailable on the census questionnaire (for example, Californios, Hispanos, or Tejanos), and people who failed to provide their specific national-origin group. Hence, caution is in order in interpreting the patterns associated with this group.

For much of the analysis presented below, the focus is on seven Latino groups: Mexicans, Puerto Ricans, Cubans, Dominicans, Central Americans, South Americans, and Other Latinos. Non-Latino whites and non-Latino African Americans are the primary groups used for comparison in the analysis. (In the 2000 Census, people could select more than one race. For the analysis that follows, based on the 2000 Census, non-Latino whites include those who selected only the white racial category, and non-Latino African Americans include those who chose only the black or African American racial category.)

Population Change and Distribution

During the 1990s, the Latino population marked its dominance as the ethnic group most responsible for population growth in the United States. The Latino population expanded from 22.4 million in 1990 to 35.3 million in 2000, a growth rate of 58 percent (see Table 1). The growth rate of the Latino population was nearly 4.5 times greater than that of the total U.S. population and more than six times that of the non-Latino population in the country. By 2000 Latinos accounted for one in eight people in the United States, compared with one in 11 people in 1990.

Among Latinos, it was Mexicans and members of the Other Latino group that experienced the fastest growth rates between 1990 and 2000, with Puerto Ricans and Cubans increasing at a moderate pace. Mexicans continue to represent the largest segment of the Latino population; 60 percent of Latinos are Mexican. Nevertheless, each of the three major Latino groups—Mexicans, Puerto Ricans, and Cubans—saw its relative share of the Latino population slip during the decade, while people in the Other Latino group expanded its share from 23 percent of the total Latino population in 1990 to 28 percent in 2000.

The five major national origin groups making up the Other Latino group in 2000 included Dominicans, Salvadorans, Colombians, Guatemalans, and Ecuadorians. It is likely that the population estimates for these groups are artificially low due to people from these groups being more likely in 2000 than in 1990 to label themselves as Other Latino instead of providing information on their specific national origin.

Regional Clustering

The Latino population is clustered in specific parts of the country. Because of the unique geographic distribution patterns of Mexicans, the largest Latino group, five regions, rather than the Census Bureau's four regions, are used in this analysis. Five states where Mexicans are concentrated—Arizona, California, Colorado, New Mexico, and Texas—are grouped in this analysis to form the Southwest region. As such, the South as defined here excludes Texas, while the West excludes Arizona, California, Colorado, and New Mexico (see Figure 1).

Comparison of the regional distributions of the overall U.S. population and the overall Latino population

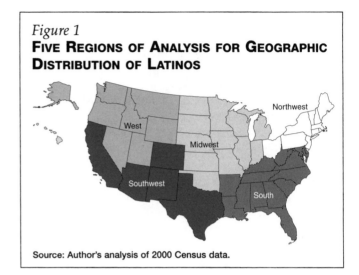

Figure 1

FIVE REGIONS OF ANALYSIS FOR GEOGRAPHIC DISTRIBUTION OF LATINOS

Source: Author's analysis of 2000 Census data.

shows that Latinos are disproportionately concentrated in the Southwest (see Table 2, page 357). While nearly 25 percent of people in the United States made their home in the Southwest in 2000, close to 60 percent of Latinos were located in this region. Latinos make up nearly a third of residents of the Southwest. This geographic preference for the Southwest is particularly true for Mexicans. In contrast, Puerto Ricans are primarily clustered in the Northeast; Cubans are principally concentrated in the South; and the Other Latino population is located predominately in the Southwest and Northeast.

Despite the continued concentration of Latinos in certain parts of the country, their regional distribution shifted between 1990 and 2000. For example, Mexicans were less likely to live in the Southwest in 2000 than

Table 1

GROWTH OF LATINO POPULATION BY ETHNIC GROUP AND OF NON-LATINO POPULATION BY RACE, 1990–2000

Group	1990	2000	Change 1990-2000	% change 1990-2000	% of U.S. population 1990	% of U.S. population 2000	% of U.S. population growth 1990-2000
Total U.S. population	248,709,873	281,421,906	32,712,033	13.2	100.0	100.0	100.0
Latino	22,354,059	35,305,818	12,951,759	57.9	9.0	12.5	39.6
Mexican	13,495,938	20,640,711	7,144,773	52.9	5.4	7.3	21.8
Puerto Rican	2,727,754	3,406,178	678,424	24.9	1.1	1.2	2.1
Cuban	1,043,932	1,241,685	197,753	18.9	0.4	0.4	0.6
Other Latino	5,086,435	10,017,244	4,930,809	96.9	2.0	3.6	15.1
Non-Latino*	226,355,814	246,116,088	19,760,274	8.7	91.0	87.5	60.4
White	188,128,296	194,552,774	6,424,478	3.4	75.6	69.1	19.6
African American	29,216,293	33,947,837	4,731,544	16.2	11.7	12.1	14.5
American Indian and Alaska Native	1,793,773	2,068,883	275,110	15.3	0.7	0.7	0.8
Asian and Pacific Islander	6,968,359	10,476,678	3,508,319	50.3	2.8	3.7	10.7
Other race	249,093	467,770	218,677	87.8	0.1	0.2	0.7

* Non-Latino groups are single-race groups.

Sources: Author's estimates using Census 1990 Summary Tape File 1 (STF1) and Census 2000 Summary File 1 (SF1).

they were a decade earlier, and they were more likely to be found in the South, where their number more than tripled between 1990 and 2000.

Similarly, Puerto Ricans, Cubans, and Other Latinos increasingly shifted from the Northeast to the South. The percentage of Puerto Ricans living in the South increased 1.5 times between 1990 and 2000. The Northeast actually experienced a drop of 8 percent in the number of Cubans during this period. By 2000, 72 percent of Cubans were located in the South. Finally, Other Latinos shifted from the Northeast and increasingly to the Southwest and South.

All regions were significantly affected by the growth in their Latino populations. The Latino population more than doubled in the West and South, while it almost doubled in the Midwest. Its growth was more modest in the Southwest and the Northeast. The Latino population expanded at a significantly faster pace than the overall population in all the regions, accounting for a disproportionate share of the overall population change in each: 62 percent of the people added in the Southwest; 54 percent in the Northeast; 30 percent in the Midwest; 24 percent in the West; and 23 percent in the South.

The shift in the regional distribution of Latinos is consistent with changes in regional employment patterns. Indeed, the South (excluding Texas) and West (excluding Arizona, California, Colorado, and New Mexico) experienced the greatest employment growth

between 1990 and 2000—16 percent and 26 percent, respectively. In contrast, the Northeast and California (the largest state in the Southwest) experienced much slower employment growth from 1990 to 2000—2 percent and 5 percent, respectively. The shift of Latinos from the Northeast and Southwest reflects movement in response to job opportunities.

Destination States

The Latino population is concentrated in particular states. The 10 states with the largest Latino populations in 2000 were home to slightly more than 80 percent of U.S. Latinos (see Figure 2). These states represent traditional hub areas for Latinos, with all but one (Washington) being among the top-10 most populous Latino states in 1990 as well. California and Texas alone accounted for one of every two Latinos in the United States.

The growth in the Latino population between 1990 and 2000 was also concentrated in specific states. The 10 states that experienced the largest absolute growth in the Latino population during this period—the same as those shown in Figure 2 but with Georgia and North Carolina substituting for Washington and New Mexico—accounted for three-fourths of the nearly 13 million Latinos added to the U.S. population between 1990 and 2000. Most of the 10 states are traditional enclave areas for Latinos. Indeed, three states accounted for slightly more than half of this growth—California, Texas, and

Table 2

LATINO AND TOTAL POPULATION BY REGION, 1990 AND 2000

Group	Northeast 1990	Northeast 2000	Midwest 1990	Midwest 2000	South 1990	South 2000	West 1990	West 2000	Southwest 1990	Southwest 2000
Population (millions)										
Total population	50.8	53.6	59.7	64.4	68.5	79.4	14.6	18.1	55.2	66.0
Latino	3.8	5.3	1.7	3.1	2.4	4.9	0.7	1.6	13.7	20.4
Mexican	0.2	0.5	1.2	2.2	0.5	1.5	0.5	1.1	11.2	15.4
Puerto Rican	1.9	2.1	0.3	0.3	0.4	0.7	0.5	0.7	0.2	0.3
Cuban	0.2	0.2	0.4	0.5	0.7	0.9	0.1	0.2	1.0	0.1
Other Latino	1.5	2.5	0.3	0.6	0.9	1.9	0.3	0.4	2.2	4.7
% distribution										
Total population	20.4	19.0	24.0	22.9	27.5	28.2	5.9	6.4	22.2	23.4
Latino	16.8	14.9	7.7	8.8	10.9	13.9	3.2	4.5	61.4	57.9
Mexican	1.3	2.3	8.5	10.7	3.4	7.2	3.5	5.4	83.3	74.5
Puerto Rican	68.6	60.9	9.4	9.6	13.3	20.3	1.7	2.1	6.9	7.2
Cuban	17.6	13.6	3.5	3.6	68.7	72.1	1.1	1.8	9.1	8.8
Other Latino	30.0	25.3	5.5	5.5	17.6	18.5	3.7	3.7	43.2	47.0
% of regional population										
Latino	7.4	9.8	2.9	4.9	3.5	6.2	5.0	8.7	24.8	31.0
Mexican	0.3	0.9	1.9	3.4	0.7	1.9	3.3	6.1	20.3	23.3
Puerto Rican	3.7	3.9	0.4	0.5	0.5	0.9	0.3	0.4	0.3	0.4
Cuban	0.4	0.3	0.1	0.1	1.0	1.1	0.1	0.1	0.2	0.2
Other Latino	3.0	4.7	0.5	0.9	1.3	2.3	1.3	2.1	4.0	7.1

Sources: Author's estimates using Census 1990 Summary Tape File 1 (STF1) and Census 2000 Summary File 1 (SF1).

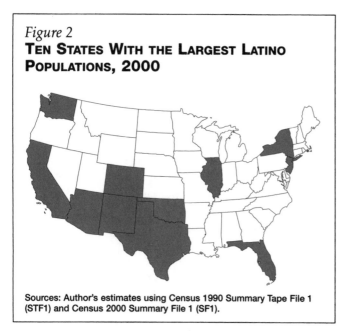

Figure 2

TEN STATES WITH THE LARGEST LATINO POPULATIONS, 2000

Sources: Author's estimates using Census 1990 Summary Tape File 1 (STF1) and Census 2000 Summary File 1 (SF1).

Figure 3

TEN STATES WITH THE FASTEST GROWTH IN LATINO POPULATION, 1990–2000

Sources: Author's estimates using Census 1990 Summary Tape File 1 (STF1) and Census 2000 Summary File 1 (SF1).

Florida. However, Georgia and North Carolina represent new destinations for Latinos, who have been drawn by jobs in construction, services, agriculture, and meat and poultry processing.

The Latino population has grown quite rapidly in states that have traditionally had relatively few Latinos (see Figure 3). Among the 10 states with the most rapid growth in the Latino population, the percentage increases ranged from a low of 155 percent in Nebraska to 394 percent in North Carolina. This growth has primarily been associated with the restructuring of the meat-processing industry and the expansion of low-wage jobs in the South and the Midwest,[32] primarily in nonmetropolitan areas.[33] Nevada stands apart from the other nine states. Drawn by a dynamic economy dominated by service jobs and the gaming industry, Nevada's Latino population tripled between 1990 and 2000.

International migrants (people who lived abroad in 1995) and interstate migrants (people who lived in different U.S. states in 1995 and 2000) contributed to this state-by-state growth in the Latino population. Seventy-one percent of the 3 million Latinos who came to the United States from abroad between 1995 and 2000 headed to eight states that have traditionally attracted Latino immigrants: California, Texas, Florida, New York, Illinois, New Jersey, Arizona, and Georgia. These "gateway" states are places where Latino immigrants can tap into social networks that help them adjust to life in the United States.

As the name gateway implies, however, these states are both a destination and a point of departure. In the interstate migration of Latinos between 1995 and 2000, five gateway states experienced net losses of Latinos. That is, they lost more Latinos to other states than they gained from these states. This group included California, New York, Illinois, New Jersey, and Texas. The

remaining three gateway states—Florida, Arizona, and Georgia—each experienced net gains of interstate Latino migrants between 1995 and 2000. Five other states had net gains of Latino interstate migrants exceeding 20,000 during the five-year period: Nevada, North Carolina, Colorado, Indiana, and Minnesota.

The Latino population and the national-origin groups within it grew significantly from 1990 to 2000. Although Latinos continue to be concentrated in particular parts of the country, there was a shift in their regional distribution, with the South, in particular, experiencing an increase in its share of the Latino population. It is clear that Latinos continue to move to different parts of the country, largely in response to job opportunities.

Age Structure

The relatively fast pace at which the Latino population grew during the 1990s is due in part to its age structure (see Figure 4, page 359). Latinos (whose median age is 25) are younger than African Americans (median age 30) and much younger than whites (median age 38) in the United States. The age and sex profiles reveal a few important features related to the Latino population: The long bars at the youngest ages reflect a high fertility rate; the long bars at the prime working ages (20 to 44) indicate the presence of foreign-born people who have moved to the United States in search of employment; and the longer bars associated with males in the primary working-age groups hint at the greater relative presence of males than females among Latin American, especially Mexican, immigrants to the United States.

Approximately 30 percent of Latinos were younger than age 15 in 2000, compared with 26 percent of African Americans and 19 percent of whites. In contrast, older people (ages 65 and older) accounted for only one in 20 Latinos compared with one in 12 African Americans and one in nearly seven whites. The Latino population is also more heavily male (with a sex ratio of 111 males per 100 females) than the African American (90) and white (96) populations.

Among Latino groups, Mexicans and Other Latinos, in particular, have the youngest populations (see Figure 5) . The median age of members of these two groups is 24, with about 33 percent being younger than age 15. In contrast, Cubans, with a median age of 40, represent the oldest Latino group. Approximately 20 percent of the Cuban population is age 65 or older, while people younger than 15 make up slightly less than 15 percent of the group's population. The Central American and South American populations are heavily dominated by people in the prime working ages, with relatively low percentages of children under the age of 15 (approximately 20 percent) and older people (3 percent to 5 percent). This reflects the relatively recent arrival of Central Americans and South Americans in the United States compared with other Latino groups.

While there is significant variation in the age and sex profiles of the Latino groups, the groups are similar in one important respect: The U.S.-born population is significantly younger than the foreign-born population. The median age of U.S.-born Latinos ranges from 9 among Central Americans to 19 among Other Latinos. In contrast, the median age of Latinos born outside of the United States varies from 31 among Mexicans to 50 among Cubans. These distinctions are associated in part with differences in the immigration histories of the different groups. One of the main reasons for the relationship between place of birth and median age is that the U.S.-born children of foreign-born Latinos are part of the native population, resulting in the relatively low presence of young children among the foreign-born population.

Citizenship

As noted, Latino groups vary tremendously with respect to their immigration histories and timing of arrival in the United States. These differences affect the share of each population that is foreign-born—segments whose socioeconomic progress may not keep track with that of their U.S.-born counterparts—and the rate at which members of each group have become U.S. citizens.

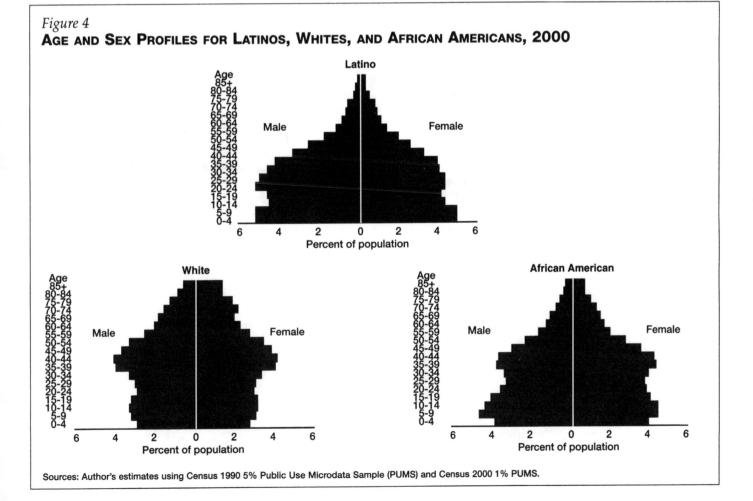

Figure 4

AGE AND SEX PROFILES FOR LATINOS, WHITES, AND AFRICAN AMERICANS, 2000

Sources: Author's estimates using Census 1990 5% Public Use Microdata Sample (PUMS) and Census 2000 1% PUMS.

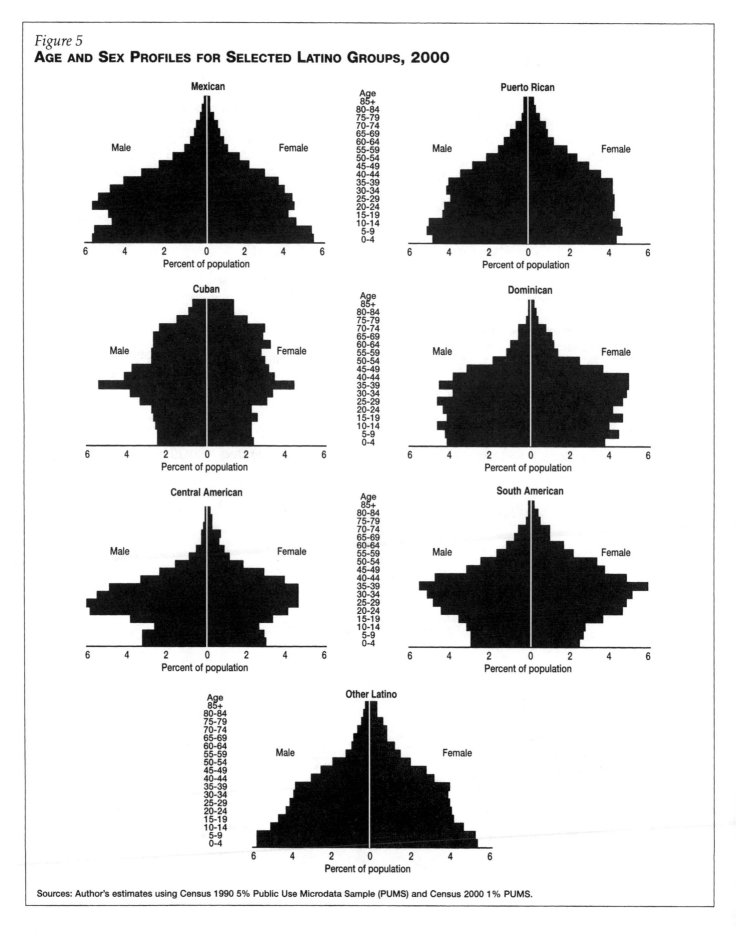

Figure 5

AGE AND SEX PROFILES FOR SELECTED LATINO GROUPS, 2000

Sources: Author's estimates using Census 1990 5% Public Use Microdata Sample (PUMS) and Census 2000 1% PUMS.

Table 3
SHARE OF AND CITIZENSHIP STATUS AMONG FOREIGN-BORN LATINOS BY ETHNIC GROUP, 1990 AND 2000

Group	% foreign-born 1990	% foreign-born 2000	% naturalized citizens 1990	% naturalized citizens 2000
White	3.3	3.5	60.3	54.8
African American	4.1	5.5	33.5	44.6
Latino	35.7	40.1	26.2	27.7
Mexican	33.1	41.3	22.4	22.1
Puerto Rican	1.3	1.4	38.4	38.8
Cuban	71.3	68.9	50.4	60.6
Dominican	70.0	69.1	26.4	35.0
Central American	79.0	76.1	18.4	26.5
South American	75.1	76.6	28.3	36.4
Other Latino	21.1	27.7	37.6	32.7

Sources: Author's estimates using Census 1990 5% Public Use Microdata Sample (PUMS) and Census 2000 1% PUMS.

Because Puerto Ricans born in Puerto Rico are automatically U.S. citizens, only slightly more than 1 percent of Puerto Ricans were foreign-born in 2000 (individuals who have Puerto Rican parents but were themselves born outside of the U.S. mainland and Puerto Rico). Nonetheless, 40 percent of Puerto Ricans were born outside of the U.S. mainland. In addition, Other Latinos and Mexicans had moderate portions of their members born outside of the United States (28 percent and 41 percent, respectively), as a result of a long presence in the United States and continued immigration (see Table 3).

In contrast, the groups that have most recently immigrated to the United States—Central Americans and South Americans—had approximately three-fourths of their members born outside of the United States; Cubans and Dominicans had percentages of foreign-born nearly as high.

Comparison of the percentages of people who were foreign-born in 1990 and 2000 indicates that the foreign-born group increased its share of the overall Latino population, rising from 36 percent in 1990 to 40 percent in 2000. The relative increase of the foreign-born was most prominent among Mexicans and Other Latinos, while the relative presence of this segment of the population declined slightly among Cubans and Central Americans.

Less than a third of foreign-born Latinos were naturalized citizens in 2000 (see Table 3). Cubans have the highest naturalization rate due to the relatively long presence of Cuban immigrants in the United States and their status as political refugees. The naturalization rates of whites (55 percent) and African Americans (45 percent) surpass those of the other Latino groups. Although the naturalization rate of the overall Latino population remained fairly stable in 1990 and 2000, the naturalization rates of Cubans, Dominicans, Central Americans,

and South Americans rose noticeably during this period. Mexicans and Central Americans have the lowest naturalization rates of any of the groups, likely reflecting the increasing presence of foreign-born individuals within these groups between 1990 and 2000.

Marriage, Family, and Living Arrangements
The Latino population is commonly depicted as a family-centric group, with stable marriages and living arrangements that include members of the extended family. It is commonly believed that such features of family and household life decline with length of residence in the United States.

Prevalence of Marriage
Latinos are commonly thought to have high rates of marriage. In fact, in 2000, Latino men and women ages 25 to 44 were slightly less likely than whites but more likely than African Americans to be married (see Table 4). Latinas (females within the Latino population) and white females were more likely than their male counterparts to be married, while the opposite was true among African Americans. Mexicans were the most likely and Puerto Ricans the least likely of the Latino groups to be married.

In the 25-to-44-year-old group, foreign-born people were more likely to be married than their U.S.-born counterparts in 2000. The high rate of marriage among foreign-born Mexican females—75 percent—is likely due to the imbalanced sex ratio (more males than females) among foreign-born Mexicans in the United States. Foreign-born Latinas also tended to have higher marriage rates than males, the exceptions being women from Puerto Rico and the Dominican Republic.

These marriage patterns have implications for other aspects of family life and living arrangements, as well as for the socioeconomic standing of the different Latino groups.

Female-Headed Families
Slightly more than one-fifth of Latino families had spouseless females as householders in 2000 (see Table 5, page 363). By way of comparison, Latino families were almost twice as likely as white families to be headed by single females, but half as likely as African American families to have such family household arrangements.

In 2000, the highest rates of female headship occurred among Dominicans and Puerto Ricans, groups with low rates of marriage. In contrast, single females headed less than 20 percent of Cuban and South American families. The U.S.-born had a higher prevalence of female-headed families than did the foreign-born for all Latino groups except Dominicans and South Americans, with Mexicans registering the greatest difference by place of birth.

Table 4

MARRIAGE RATES OF LATINO MEN AND WOMEN BY ETHNIC GROUP AND NATIVITY, 1990 AND 2000

| | Percent of people ages 25-44 who are currently married | | | |
| | Male | | Female | |
Group	1990	2000	1990	2000
White	66.0	62.3	70.1	67.3
African American	44.4	46.2	38.4	37.7
Latino	62.2	61.7	63.2	64.0
Mexican	65.2	64.6	67.4	68.3
U.S.-born	59.7	55.6	62.7	59.1
Foreign-born	70.5	69.3	73.4	74.6
Puerto Rican	53.7	51.6	48.9	48.6
Mainland-born	51.2	49.5	49.2	47.7
Non-mainland-born	55.6	54.2	48.7	49.6
Cuban	58.5	58.8	63.9	67.3
U.S.-born	50.5	54.3	55.6	62.0
Foreign-born	60.4	60.4	66.0	69.5
Dominican	58.6	57.5	51.5	52.6
U.S.-born	44.7	43.6	50.7	50.2
Foreign-born	59.8	59.4	51.5	52.9
Central American	59.7	56.5	60.0	61.9
U.S.-born	49.8	48.3	55.2	53.1
Foreign-born	60.4	57.1	60.3	62.6
South American	62.9	59.7	65.4	67.3
U.S.-born	50.3	44.9	52.7	60.5
Foreign-born	64.0	62.0	66.5	68.4
Other Latino	55.9	59.5	61.0	59.5
U.S.-born	54.4	55.0	59.0	54.3
Foreign-born	59.7	65.2	66.3	66.7

Sources: Author's estimates using Census 1990 5% Public Use Microdata Sample (PUMS) and Census 2000 1% PUMS.

Living Arrangements of Children

Marriage and female headship patterns are related to the extent to which children live in married-couple families. Slightly more than 60 percent of Latino children under age 18 were living in such families in 2000, a percentage that is somewhat lower than that of whites but significantly higher than that of African Americans.

South American, Cuban, and Mexican youngsters were most likely to be part of married-couple families. In contrast, Puerto Rican and Dominican children were the least likely to be part of such families. There are not great differences between U.S.- and foreign-born groups regarding the portion of children living in married-couple families, with the largest differences occurring in the Central American and Other Latino populations. The lack of differences on the basis of nativity reflects the blurring of nativity, especially among children. Children of a given family may be in different nativity categories, with some being born in the United States and others being foreign-born.

Overall, children were slightly less likely to be living in married-couple families in 2000 than a decade earlier across the Latino groups and the white and African American populations.

Extended-Family Households

For many families with limited economic resources, extended households represent a survival strategy to maximize resources. Roughly 12 percent of Latinos were members of extended family households in 2000, a level that is comparable to that of African Americans. In contrast, Latinos were nearly four times more likely than whites to be living in an extended family household arrangement.

Latino groups with high rates of immigration and limited economic resources were the most likely to be part of extended-family households. More than 12 percent of Central Americans, Dominicans, and Mexicans were living in the households of relatives in 2000, with Puerto Ricans being the least likely group to be in such living arrangements. With the exception of Puerto Ricans, foreign-born people had a higher prevalence of residing in extended family households than U.S.-born individuals. Foreign-born Mexicans, in particular, were the most likely to be living with relatives. In contrast, U.S.-born South Americans and U.S.-born Cubans had the lowest tendency to be part of extended-family households.

Between 1990 and 2000, the extended family rates of Latinos increased slightly. In contrast, those of whites and African Americans remained fairly stable.

Marriage, family, and living arrangement patterns differentiated the various Latino groups in 2000. Mexicans, South Americans, and to a certain extent Cubans tended to have relatively high rates of marriage, low rates of female headship, and high rates of children living in married-couple households; Puerto Ricans and Dominicans tended to exhibit contrasting patterns. In general, foreign-born groups tended to have high rates of marriage and lower female headship rates. And immigrant groups with limited resources tended to rely most heavily on extended-family households for economic survival.

Acculturation and Assimilation

Latino groups differ significantly on a variety of factors that are commonly associated with acculturation and assimilation. These factors include length of residence in the United States, level of education, and structural factors such as the size of the ethnic group and the volume of immigration from the home country. Acculturation and assimilation are measured in a variety of ways, including language patterns, racial identification, and interracial marriage.

Language Patterns

Sociologists have observed that ethnic groups do not completely shed their cultures, but may develop new ones that incorporate segments of their own ethnic culture and parts of the mainstream culture. Latino groups vary enormously in the extent to which they retain their ethnic cultures and absorb that of the United States. Two items from the census—language spoken at home and fluency in English among those that speak a language other than English—are used to assess the language patterns of Latinos and place them in language categories:

- Monolingual English (person speaks English at home);
- Monolingual Spanish (person speaks a language other than English at home and speaks English "not well" or "not at all"); and
- Bilingual (person speaks a language other than English at home and speaks English "well" or "very well").

Bilingualism was the most common language form among Latinos (see Table 6). In contrast, whites and African Americans were almost exclusively monolingual English speakers.

Similarly, bilingualism was the most prevalent language form among the different Latino groups in 2000, ranging from 48 percent of Mexicans to 71 percent of Puerto Ricans. The one exception was foreign-born Mexicans, most of whom were monolingual Spanish speakers.

The degree to which Latinos are fluent in English can be gauged by aggregating bilingual and monolingual English language forms. The majority of U.S.-born Latinos were fluent in English in 2000, with the range extending from a low of 94 percent among Central Americans to a high of 99 percent among Cubans. Among the foreign-born, the variation in English fluency is greater. More than 70 percent of non-mainland-born Puerto Ricans, foreign-born South Americans, and foreign-born Cubans were fluent in English. In contrast, only 48 percent of foreign-born Mexicans were fluent in English.

Table 5

LATINO FAMILY AND HOUSEHOLD CHARACTERISTICS BY ETHNIC GROUP AND NATIVITY, 1990 AND 2000

Group	% of families with female householders		% of children under age 18 living with two parents		% of people living in extended-family households	
	1990	2000	1990	2000	1990	2000
White	11.8	12.5	80.5	77.2	3.0	3.1
African American	43.1	44.6	37.1	34.5	10.3	10.0
Latino	21.5	21.6	64.2	62.3	10.1	11.7
Mexican	18.1	17.5	67.9	65.8	10.5	12.8
U.S.-born	21.4	23.1	68.1	65.8	7.9	9.4
Foreign-born	14.2	13.7	66.4	66	15.8	17.5
Puerto Rican	36.4	37.0	45.3	43.7	7.8	8.1
Mainland-born	35.4	38.8	45.5	43.9	8.5	8.2
Non-mainland-born	36.9	35.7	44.5	42.9	7.0	8.0
Cuban	16.2	15.9	70.4	67.3	9.1	9.8
U.S.-born	19.9	17.9	70.5	66.6	7.7	7.2
Foreign-born	15.8	15.5	70.0	70.7	9.7	11.0
Dominican	41.3	39.5	44.9	43.8	12.1	13.6
U.S.-born	31.4	38.6	44.5	44.4	9.9	9.8
Foreign-born	41.9	39.6	45.9	42.3	13.0	15.3
Central American	22.9	21.7	61.3	58.4	15.0	14.3
U.S.-born	19.5	24.2	64.7	60.1	9.0	10.4
Foreign-born	23.1	21.6	57.2	53.8	16.5	15.5
South American	18.3	19.3	71.7	69.9	9.8	11.1
U.S.-born	16.6	16.7	73.3	70.2	5.9	6.5
Foreign-born	18.4	19.5	68.4	69.3	11.1	12.4
Other Latino	20.6	25.3	64.4	61.1	7.4	9.7
U.S.-born	21.7	27.8	64.3	60.7	6.1	8.0
Foreign-born	17.2	21.6	65.3	65.9	12.2	14.4

Sources: Author's estimates using Census 1990 5% Public Use Microdata Sample (PUMS) and Census 2000 1% PUMS.

Comparison of the distribution of language patterns between 1990 and 2000 shows some changes. For Latinos as a whole, the percentage of monolingual Spanish speakers rose by nearly 5 percentage points over the decade, while the percentage who were bilingual or were monolingual English speakers slipped by the same level. This combination of changes is likely due to the increasing relative presence of the foreign-born in the Latino population in 2000 compared with a decade earlier.

Nonetheless, across Latino groups there were some differences. For example, the increasing prevalence of the monolingual Spanish pattern between 1990 and 2000 was driven primarily by foreign-born Mexicans, foreign-born Cubans, and foreign-born Other Latinos. Several U.S.-born groups experienced rising percentages of bilingual speakers—Cubans, Dominicans, Central Americans, South Americans, and Other Latinos. Finally, Puerto Ricans, Mexicans, and foreign-born

Dominicans experienced slight gains in the percentage of individuals in their populations that spoke only English.

The census data on language usage is quite limited, however, and does not capture the dynamic nature of language. People may speak English at home but still be fluent in Spanish. In addition, people may vary their language use depending on social context. Furthermore, many Latinos engage in code switching (the simultaneous use of two languages when speaking), a form of speech commonly referred to as "Spanglish." Moreover, many Latino entertainers—for example, singers, actors, and comedians—have made a transition to the English language or have combined Spanish and English. Finally, the Spanish language has become more prevalent in the United States and continues to be by far the most popular foreign language taught in colleges and universities throughout the United States.[34]

Table 6
LANGUAGE PATTERNS OF LATINOS BY ETHNIC GROUP AND NATIVITY, 1990 AND 2000

Percent of people ages 25-44

Group	1990 Monolingual Spanish	Bilingual	Monolingual English	2000 Monolingual Spanish	Bilingual	Monolingual English
White	0.5	4.3	95.2	0.6	5.3	94.1
African American	0.7	5.2	94.1	0.8	6.2	93.0
Latino	23.7	56.6	19.7	28.6	53.2	18.2
Mexican	25.1	54.2	20.7	33.5	48.2	18.4
U.S.-born	3.5	60.5	36.0	3.2	56.9	40.0
Foreign-born	48.8	47.2	4.0	51.7	43.0	5.3
Puerto Rican	12.6	71.9	15.5	8.9	70.7	20.4
Mainland-born	2.9	69.6	27.5	2.6	67.7	29.7
Non-mainland-born	20.0	73.6	6.4	17.0	74.5	8.5
Cuban	16.2	71.7	12.2	20.9	66.7	12.5
U.S.-born	2.5	60.7	36.9	0.9	68.1	31.0
Foreign-born	19.5	74.4	6.2	28.7	66.1	5.2
Dominican	43.2	51.6	5.2	36.2	58.2	5.7
U.S.-born	20.8	57.8	21.4	2.1	85.3	12.7
Foreign-born	45.0	51.1	3.9	40.8	54.5	4.7
Central American	42.9	50.5	6.6	39.3	54.9	5.8
U.S.-born	9.1	47.9	43.0	6.7	59.7	33.6
Foreign-born	45.2	50.7	4.1	41.7	54.5	3.7
South American	26.0	65.7	8.3	24.7	67.4	7.8
U.S.-born	6.2	51.1	42.7	3.3	66.0	30.7
Foreign-born	27.8	67.1	5.2	28.0	67.7	4.3
Other Latino	8.4	45.4	46.2	18.4	53.0	28.6
U.S.-born	2.6	37.8	59.6	2.5	52.5	44.9
Foreign-born	23.2	65.3	11.6	39.7	53.6	6.7

Note: The entries for the "monolingual Spanish" column for whites and African Americans refer to any language other than English—rather than only Spanish—spoken at home. It is assumed that, among Latinos, those speaking a language other than English at home speak Spanish.

Sources: Author's estimates using Census 1990 5% Public Use Microdata Sample (PUMS) and Census 2000 1% PUMS.

The language patterns of Latinos are likely related to other forms of acculturation and assimilation, as well as to Latinos' access to the mainstream labor market.

Racial Identification

The large majority of Latinos in the United States are offspring of the racial mixing of the various groups that met in Latin America beginning in the late 15th century. In particular, many Latinos are products of the intermixing of a combination of Africans, Indians, and Spaniards. Although race has commonly been associated with physical characteristics of people, our understanding of race has been enhanced by the view that race is socially constructed.[35] That is, racial classifications are the product of human beliefs and ideas regarding group differences.

The concept of race is particularly interesting in the case of U.S. Latinos. The Census Bureau does not treat Latinos/Hispanics as a racial group but as an ethnic group. Therefore, Latinos are free to place themselves in the varying racial categories that the Census Bureau provides. Most Latinos label themselves as "white" or "other" in the census. While it is tempting to place these terms on different poles on a continuum, white being associated with ethnic assimilation and other with ethnic retention, this is difficult to justify because people may choose between these terms for many different reasons—for example, assimilation, rejection of the white racial classification, lack of understanding of the concepts, ancestry, and the like.[36]

Moreover, it is also likely that U.S.- and foreign-born individuals have different notions about race. For example, many foreign-born Latinos in the United States were not members of minority groups in their home countries. In addition, Latin American societies typically view race as a continuum with a significant amount of fluidity—Brazil, for instance, has more than 140 racial categories[37]—while those in the United States view race in a more restricted and static fashion.[38] Furthermore, upward mobility in Latin America allows dark-skinned individuals to become "white," although it is clear that blacks and indigenous people in Latin America remain at the bottom of the stratification system. Finally, a change in the ordering of the race and Hispanic/Latino items took place in the census questionnaire in 2000. In an apparently unsuccessful attempt to get more Latinos to choose a race besides "other," the race item was placed after the Hispanic/Latino item in 2000, while the opposite order was used in 1990. The change in the ordering of these items could affect comparisons in the racial identities of Latinos between 1990 and 2000.

As a group, Latinos were split between the white and other racial classifications in 2000 (see Table 7). In addition, about 6 percent considered themselves multiracial, while a very small portion classified themselves as black.

Among Latino groups, however, there is considerable variation, with four general patterns emerging. The first pattern describes the situation of Cubans, who showed a heavy preference (85 percent) for the white racial category in 2000. Only 7 percent of Cubans selected the other racial category, with an even smaller percentage seeing themselves as multiracial or black.

The second pattern is associated with South Americans, a group that also showed a clear preference (60 percent) for the white racial classification in 2000, although 30 percent preferred the other racial category.

The third pattern is associated with Mexicans, Puerto Ricans, and Other Latinos. These groups favored the white racial identification by a slight margin over the other racial category in 2000. The diverse nature of the Puerto Rican population is apparent even within this pattern, in that about 8 percent viewed themselves as multiracial and 6 percent classified themselves as black. A significant portion (9 percent) of Other Latinos also classified themselves as multiracial.

The fourth pattern describes Dominicans and Central Americans. For these groups, the other racial term was the preferred racial category in 2000. Nonetheless, Dominicans and Central Americans differed significantly in some respects. For instance, Dominicans were much more likely to prefer the other racial category than were Central Americans, while Central Americans were much more likely to see themselves as white than were Dominicans (40 percent compared with 23 percent, respectively). Among all Latino groups, Dominicans were the most likely to see themselves as black.

Comparison of U.S.- and foreign-born people on the basis of their preferences for racial categories also shows some noteworthy patterns. First, there were significant variations in the racial classification of these groups in the case of Mexicans and Other Latinos in 2000. In each of these cases, U.S.-born individuals were more likely to prefer the white racial category, with their foreign-born counterparts being more likely to choose the other racial classification. Second, Puerto Ricans born outside of the U.S. mainland were more likely to prefer the white racial term compared with those born on the mainland. The same pattern exists among Cubans; indeed, approximately 88 percent of foreign-born Cubans saw themselves as white. Third, foreign-born Dominicans and Central Americans were more likely to prefer the other category and somewhat less likely than their U.S.-born counterparts to select the white racial category.

Because the ways in which racial classification data were collected in 1990 and 2000 are not comparable, it is difficult to make direct comparisons between years. Nonetheless, some general patterns are evident in how Latinos classified themselves. On the whole, the percentages of Latinos classifying themselves as white, black, and other declined somewhat between 1990 and 2000. It is likely that these declines, at least in part, are associated with the multiracial option that was available to respondents in 2000.

In addition, major shifts took place in how Dominicans classified themselves racially. Overall, the share of Dominicans viewing themselves as black dropped by close to 19 percentage points between 1990 and 2000. In contrast, the percentage of Dominicans reporting themselves racially as other increased by about 15 percentage points over the decade, and in 2000 close to 9 percent of Dominicans classified themselves as multiracial. While some of the change may be due to the distinct ways in which racial information was collected in 1990 and 2000, the differences are large enough to suggest that a more interesting set of social dynamics may be responsible for the observed changes. One such dynamic may involve a conscious decision to distance themselves from blacks.[39] This may be a strategy adopted by more upwardly mobile individuals. However, this is only speculation that requires further study.

Finally, a similar pattern exists in the case of Other Latinos. The percentage of these individuals viewing themselves as white dropped by 16 percentage points between 1990 and 2000, while the percentage selecting

the other racial category rose by 15 percentage points. Furthermore, approximately 9 percent of Other Latinos reported themselves as multiracial in 2000. It should be noted, however, that some of this change among Other Latinos might reflect the inclusion of Dominicans, Central Americans, and South Americans in 2000 in this residual category.

Census data provide only hints about how Latinos view themselves racially. In reality, the construction of race is much more complex and dynamic. For instance, Latinos may shift their racial identification in varying contexts and circumstances. In addition, the salience of race as an identifier is likely to vary significantly among groups of Latinos.

Intermarriage

The choice of a spouse represents one of the most intimate decisions that people make. Sociologists have viewed the crossing of racial and ethnic lines in the selection of a spouse as the primary indicator of assimilation.[40] Individuals who have been in the United States for a longer period of time are more likely to be married outside their racial/ethnic groups. The percentage of

Table 7

RACIAL SELF-CLASSIFICATION OF LATINOS BY ETHNIC GROUP AND NATIVITY, 1990 AND 2000

Ethnic group	% white 1990	% white 2000	% black 1990	% black 2000	% other race 1990	% other race 2000	% multiracial 2000
Latino	52.2	47.8	2.9	1.8	43.2	42.6	6.4
Mexican	50.4	47.3	0.9	0.7	47.4	45.4	5.2
U.S.-born	53.5	49.8	1.1	0.9	43.8	41.5	6.1
Foreign-born	44.1	43.7	0.6	0.4	54.8	51.0	3.9
Puerto Rican	45.8	47.0	5.9	5.8	47.2	38.4	7.8
Mainland-born	45.6	45.3	6.8	6.8	45.8	36.9	9.7
Non-mainland-born	46.0	49.6	4.7	4.3	48.7	40.5	4.9
Cuban	83.6	84.5	3.8	3.6	12.2	7.2	4.3
U.S.-born	81.8	77.6	5.9	5.7	11.6	8.6	7.3
Foreign-born	84.3	87.6	3.0	2.7	12.5	6.5	2.9
Dominican	28.2	22.5	27.3	8.8	43.2	58.6	8.7
U.S.-born	31.2	25.0	25.1	10.4	42.3	54.1	9.5
Foreign-born	26.9	21.3	28.3	8.1	43.6	60.6	8.4
Central American	44.2	40.4	5.3	3.0	49.3	47.8	7.8
U.S.-born	49.0	40.7	7.6	3.8	41.7	43.6	10.6
Foreign-born	43.0	40.3	4.7	2.7	51.3	49.1	6.9
South American	64.6	59.4	1.5	0.8	32.9	30.2	8.6
U.S.-born	68.2	59.8	1.7	1.2	28.6	27.2	10.8
Foreign-born	63.5	59.3	1.4	0.7	34.3	31.2	7.9
Other Latino	61.1	44.9	4.8	2.1	26.6	41.5	9.4
U.S.-born	63.9	46.9	3.9	2.1	26.6	39.2	9.6
Foreign-born	50.5	39.6	8.3	2.0	26.4	47.5	8.8

Note: The white, black, and "other" racial categories for 2000 are based on individuals who chose a single race.

Sources: Author's estimates using Census 1990 5% Public Use Microdata Sample (PUMS) and Census 2000 1% PUMS.

married Latinos having a non-Latino spouse is used to measure intermarriage. Due to data restrictions associated with the three aggregate Latino groups (Central Americans, South Americans, and Other Latinos), the Latina/o boundary is set broadly, resulting in marriage among members of different Latino groups being treated as "in-marriage" rather than "intermarriage."

Overall, less than 20 percent of married Latinas/os were married to a non-Latina/o in 2000, with females being more likely to be in such marriages than males (see Table 8, right-most columns). However, there is much variation across Latino groups on the prevalence of intermarriage. In general, Puerto Ricans, Central Americans, South Americans, and Other Latinos were the most likely to have a non-Latina/o spouse in 2000. In contrast, Mexicans, Cubans, and Dominicans were the least likely to go outside of the Latino group in selecting a spouse.

U.S.-born individuals are more likely to be intermarried than the foreign-born. The greatest tendency for marriage outside of the Latino group existed among three U.S.-born groups in 2000: Central Americans, South Americans, and Cubans. In contrast, foreign-born Mexicans were the least likely to be wed to non-Latinos, followed by foreign-born Dominicans and Cubans.

Comparison of the intermarriage rates of Latinos between 1990 and 2000 shows a declining tendency to marry outside of the Latino group. This may be due to the relatively larger presence of foreign-born people in the Latino population in 2000 compared with a decade earlier, many of whom are married to people from the same ethnic group. Indeed, background analysis (not shown) reveals that in-married Latinas/os were more likely to consist of foreign-born individuals in 2000 than in 1990, the percentage increasing from 56 percent to 66 percent among Latino men and from 54 percent to 64 percent among Latinas.

This trend held regardless of place of birth. For example, 19 percent of U.S.-born Latino men were married to a foreign-born Latina in 2000 (compared with 15 percent in 1990), while 23 percent of U.S.-born Latina

Table 8

MARRIAGE CHARACTERISTICS OF LATINO MEN AND WOMEN BY ETHNIC GROUP AND NATIVITY, 1990 AND 2000

Ethnic group	% of currently married Latinas/os with a co-ethnic spouse*				% of currently married Latinas/os with a non-Latina/o spouse			
	Male		Female		Male		Female	
	1990	2000	1990	2000	1990	2000	1990	2000
Latino	81.5	84.4	79.9	81.5	18.5	15.7	20.2	18.5
Mexican	81.5	81.7	80.7	80.3	16.0	13.3	16.9	15.1
U.S.-born	72.4	68.0	72.1	65.1	25.4	27.8	25.7	30.4
Foreign-born	91.2	89.7	91.1	90.6	5.7	4.9	6.1	4.9
Puerto Rican	66.0	59.7	67.6	60.7	22.4	25.2	21.5	25.1
Mainland-born	48.5	44.5	51.0	47.3	40.3	40.1	37.3	37.6
Non-mainland-born	74.0	69.4	76.3	70.5	14.3	15.8	13.1	15.9
Cuban	72.7	68.5	76.6	72.8	14.9	16.7	15.3	16.9
U.S.-born	30.1	33.1	37.0	35.3	53.9	49.6	48.1	47.5
Foreign-born	77.1	74.2	81.5	80.1	10.8	11.5	11.2	10.9
Dominican	76.8	70.0	73.0	67.9	7.3	5.3	8.4	12.1
U.S.-born	43.8	42.7	52.6	37.1	28.8	22.7	23.1	21.6
Foreign-born	79.2	72.1	74.9	71.1	5.7	4.0	7.1	11.1
Central American	72.9	62.9	63.1	56.7	11.5	10.3	18.6	17.7
U.S.-born	29.8	28.2	21.3	16.5	55.1	50.1	59.8	60.2
Foreign-born	75.4	65.1	65.6	59.2	8.9	7.9	16.1	15.0
South American	65.2	62.6	60.1	54.6	19.6	17.2	26.2	29.1
U.S.-born	25.0	34.4	23.2	25.3	59.5	45.8	58.4	57.9
Foreign-born	67.8	65.1	62.5	57.7	17.0	14.7	24.1	26.0
Other Latino	50.5	61.9	47.2	55.7	40.9	22.3	43.3	26.1
U.S.-born	46.3	57.8	44.5	52.4	47.4	31.7	47.2	35.1
Foreign-born	62.0	67.4	54.4	60.0	23.1	9.8	33.1	14.2

* Co-ethnic spouse refers to cases where the husband and wife belong to the same specific Latino group (i.e., Mexican, Puerto Rican).

Sources: Author's estimates using Census 1990 5% Public Use Microdata Sample (PUMS) and Census 2000 1% PUMS.

women were married to a foreign-born Latino man in 2000 (compared with 19 percent in 1990).

These trends are even more magnified for Mexicans, the largest Latino group. While foreign-born people made up about half of all in-married Mexican spouses in 1990, 10 years later they accounted for nearly 70 percent of all in-married Mexican spouses. Moreover, 23 percent of U.S.-born Mexican men were married to foreign-born Latinas in 2000 (versus 17 percent in 1990), while 28 percent of U.S.-born Mexican women were married to foreign-born Latino men in 2000 (versus 22 percent in 1990).

The most pronounced declines in intermarriage rates between 1990 and 2000 occurred among Other Latinos and three groups of U.S.-born males: Dominicans, Central Americans, and South Americans. At least a portion of the declines among these groups may be associated with the greater presence of Dominicans, Central Americans, and South Americans in the residual Other Latino group in 2000.

A few groups, most notably U.S.-born Mexicans, experienced slight increases in their propensity to marry non-Latinos between 1990 and 2000.

The observed intermarriage patterns are undoubtedly related to structural factors such as the size of the group (especially true in the case of Mexicans) and sex ratios (number of males per 100 females) within Latino groups.[41] Overall, it is clear that Latino groups vary significantly on the indicators of acculturation and assimilation examined in this report. Place of birth is strongly related to language use, racial identification, and intermarriage.

In a broad sense, certain groups (for example, Cubans and South Americans) have experienced greater acculturation and assimilation. In contrast, Mexicans have generally experienced less acculturation and assimilation, a pattern that is likely to be associated with the large presence of recent immigrants in the population. The acculturation and assimilation patterns observed here influence the socioeconomic standing of Latino groups.

Socioeconomic Status

Research has consistently shown that, as a group, Latinos tend to occupy the lower rungs on the socioeconomic ladder of the United States. Historically, Latinos have had relatively low levels of education, high levels of unemployment, low levels of income, and high poverty rates. Nevertheless, significant variation exists within Latino groups. The standing of these Latino groups depends largely on factors such as the stock of human capital that people possess (for example, education, skills, training, and experience); characteristics of the labor markets where Latinos live; access to higher education; and, for immigrants, the resources that they bring with them to the United States. In general, U.S.-born Latinos and immigrants who have been in the

country longer tend to fare better socioeconomically than the foreign-born and recently arrived immigrants.

Educational Attainment
Education represents the primary form of human capital in which workers can invest to maximize their economic returns in the labor market.

High School and College Completion
Overall, only a slight majority of Latinos ages 25 and older were high school graduates in 2000, and only about 11 percent were college graduates (see Table 9, page 369). The educational attainment levels of Latinos are below those of African Americans and far below those of whites. The high school completion rates of African Americans (72 percent) and whites (86 percent) were higher than that of Latinos in 2000. In addition, African Americans were 1.4 times and whites were 2.6 times more likely to hold a college diploma than were Latinos.

Still, Latino groups varied significantly in their educational attainment levels in 2000. For example, Mexicans and Central Americans were the least likely to be high school or college graduates in 2000. In contrast, South Americans had the highest rates of high school and college completion, with a noticeable share of Cubans also having such educational credentials. Only South Americans had a higher rate of high school completion than African Americans, while South Americans and Cubans were the only Latino groups more likely than African Americans to have finished college.

The educational attainment levels of U.S.-born Latinos surpassed those of the foreign-born in 2000. The high school and college completion rates of U.S.-born South Americans and Cubans tied or surpassed those of whites, while the college completion rate of U.S.-born Central Americans was also higher than that of whites.

Regardless of place of birth, however, Mexicans stand apart from other Latino groups in education. Mexicans rank at the bottom in the percentage holding a high school diploma and a college degree. For instance, Mexicans were the only U.S.-born group to have a high school completion rate less than 70 percent in 2000. U.S.-born Mexicans also had the lowest percentage of college graduates among all U.S.-born Latino groups and also were less likely to hold a college diploma than were foreign-born South Americans and Cubans. Foreign-born Mexicans were least likely to complete high school and college. The educational standing of U.S.-born Other Latinos was similar to that of U.S.-born Mexicans.

Comparison of the educational attainment levels in 1990 and 2000 reveals that Latinos as a whole made only slight improvements compared with whites and African Americans. For example, the Latino high school completion rate increased by a mere 3 percentage points, compared with 9 percentage points for African

Americans and 6 percentage points for whites. Similarly, the Latino college completion rate increased only slightly compared with that of whites and African Americans.

With few exceptions, however, almost all of the Latino groups experienced improvements in the percentages of group members completing a high school or college degree between 1990 and 2000. The greatest improvements in high school completion over the decade were recorded by U.S.-born Dominicans and non-mainland-born Puerto Ricans, both of whom increased their high school completion rates to a greater degree than did African Americans. In addition, U.S.-born Cubans and both U.S.- and foreign-born South Americans showed the greatest absolute improvement in college completion rates, with each of these groups showing greater gains than whites.

Dropout Rate

The educational patterns of late teens and young adults provide indications of the educational levels of Latinos in the near future. Nearly one-third of Latinos ages 16 to 24 were high school dropouts in 2000, a significantly higher share than for whites and African Americans. Indeed, Latino youth were approximately four times more likely than their white peers and nearly two times more likely than their African American counterparts to be high school dropouts in 2000.

Variations among the Latino groups on the basis of high school dropout rates mirror the educational attainment patterns described earlier. In particular, Central American and Mexican youth had the most elevated dropout rates in 2000, while Cubans and South Americans had the lowest rates.

Furthermore, foreign-born Latinos ages 16 to 24 were at least twice as likely as their U.S.-born counterparts to be high school dropouts, the one exception being Puerto Ricans, whose rate was similar to that of the mainland-born. Foreign-born Mexicans had the highest dropout rates in 2000, with the majority not having a high school diploma; nearly half of foreign-born Central Americans were in the same situation. It is likely that some of these young people are not really

Table 9
EDUCATIONAL STATUS OF LATINOS BY ETHNIC GROUP AND NATIVITY, 1990 AND 2000

Group	% of people ages 25 and older High school graduates		College graduates		% of 16-to-24-year-olds High school dropouts	
	1990	2000	1990	2000	1990	2000
White	79.1	85.5	22.0	27.0	10.3	8.7
African American	63.3	72.4	11.5	14.3	17.7	16.8
Latino	50.0	52.5	9.1	10.5	30.5	31.5
Mexican	44.5	45.8	6.3	7.6	34.3	35.9
U.S.-born	61.0	68.6	8.6	12.4	21.1	19.5
Foreign-born	24.8	30.0	3.5	4.3	53.0	55.4
Puerto Rican	53.5	63.2	9.5	12.2	26.0	23.6
Mainland-born	72.2	76.0	13.0	14.3	23.4	21.4
Non-mainland-born	44.8	54.3	7.9	10.7	31.4	29.2
Cuban	56.7	63.1	16.5	21.1	14.3	13.6
U.S.-born	81.0	85.2	26.3	35.9	9.8	9.2
Foreign-born	53.7	59.1	15.3	18.4	20.4	22.6
Dominican	43.1	51.6	7.8	10.3	26.3	19.6
U.S.-born	63.0	77.6	14.9	19.4	15.4	12.2
Foreign-born	41.7	49.1	7.3	9.5	31.8	23.7
Central American	45.5	45.8	8.8	9.5	35.7	38.7
U.S.-born	80.7	79.8	25.4	30.1	11.4	11.3
Foreign-born	43.3	43.6	7.8	8.2	40.1	45.6
South American	70.6	77.0	19.2	25.1	12.4	12.8
U.S.-born	85.7	87.7	34.7	40.6	6.2	6.2
Foreign-born	69.5	75.9	18.1	23.4	16.1	15.7
Other Latino	65.9	60.7	14.8	11.9	18.7	24.0
U.S.-born	69.2	70.7	13.6	12.9	16.9	18.8
Foreign-born	57.4	46.6	18.1	10.5	25.3	37.7

Sources: Author's estimates using Census 1990 5% Public Use Microdata Sample (PUMS) and Census 2000 1% PUMS.

"dropouts" because they never "dropped in" to schools in the United States. That is, they came to this country to work and never did enroll in school. In contrast, South American youth had the lowest dropout rate among foreign-born groups.

Finally, while the dropout rate of white and African American youth declined slightly between 1990 and 2000, the rate of Latino youth increased slightly. Although the dropout rates of most Latino groups remained fairly stable during the decade, the rates of foreign-born Dominican youth fell substantially, while those of foreign-born Other Latinos and foreign-born Central Americans increased noticeably. Again, interpreting the changes among these groups requires caution due to the greater presence of Dominicans, Central Americans, and South Americans in the residual Other Latino group in 2000.

As a group, Latinos do not fare well in educational attainment. However, low standing in education is particularly apparent in the case of Mexicans, with South Americans and Cubans faring much more favorably.

Work

The low educational levels of Latinos, especially Mexicans, determine the types of jobs that they hold.

Employment and Unemployment

Nearly 70 percent of Latino males 16 and older were in the labor force in 2000, a rate that was somewhat lower than that of white males, but significantly higher than that of African American males (see Table 10). However, Latina females had a substantially lower rate of labor force participation in 2000 than did African American and white females.

Central Americans and South Americans had the highest rates of labor force participation within the Latino population in each sex category, with nearly 75 percent of males and slightly below 60 percent of females being in the labor force. The rates of males from these groups surpass the labor force participation rate of white males, while those of females approximate those of white and African American females.

Table 10

LABOR FORCE CHARACTERISTICS OF LATINO MEN AND WOMEN BY ETHNIC GROUP AND NATIVITY, 1990 AND 2000

Group	% of people ages 16 and older in the labor force Males 1990	Males 2000	Females 1990	Females 2000	% of workers with earnings who are self-employed 1990	2000
White	75.1	72.5	56.4	57.8	10.2	10.7
African American	66.6	60.5	59.6	59.6	3.6	4.4
Latino	78.8	69.3	56.0	53.1	6.1	6.8
Mexican	80.3	71.3	55.3	51.9	5.5	6.2
U.S.-born	76.0	68.3	59.0	59.7	5.3	5.2
Foreign-born	85.1	73.4	50.2	44.8	5.8	7.1
Puerto Rican	71.3	63.4	50.7	55.0	3.9	4.5
Mainland-born	73.3	68.1	59.8	63.7	3.3	4.3
Non-mainland-born	69.9	58.9	44.8	47.2	4.4	4.8
Cuban	75.2	61.7	55.8	49.3	11.3	11.7
U.S.-born	73.1	68.2	67.6	66.1	6.0	7.3
Foreign-born	75.7	59.9	53.4	45.0	12.5	13.1
Dominican	75.0	65.6	53.4	53.9	6.1	7.8
U.S.-born	62.6	62.3	58.0	61.8	3.2	4.2
Foreign-born	77.0	66.2	52.8	52.6	6.5	8.5
Central American	84.8	74.7	64.1	57.2	6.2	7.9
U.S.-born	74.4	69.4	66.8	66.2	4.3	4.8
Foreign-born	85.7	75.2	63.9	56.3	6.3	8.2
South American	84.2	74.3	63.1	59.2	9.3	9.8
U.S.-born	71.5	75.0	68.4	68.8	5.2	5.0
Foreign-born	86.1	74.1	62.3	57.8	9.9	10.6
Other Latino	73.4	63.8	58.2	53.2	7.5	7.4
U.S.-born	72.6	64.7	58.3	57.3	7.1	6.2
Foreign-born	75.5	62.5	58.1	46.6	8.5	9.3

Sources: Author's estimates using Census 1990 5% Public Use Microdata Sample (PUMS) and Census 2000 1% PUMS.

In contrast, Cuban, Puerto Rican, and Other Latino men had the lowest rates of participation in the labor force, while Cuban and Mexican females were the least likely be part of the labor force. The relatively low labor force participation rates of Cubans are due to the group's relatively older age structure: Close to one-fourth of the Cuban working-age population 16 and older was age 65 or older in 2000.

There are clear distinctions in the labor force participation rates of females on the basis of nativity. In each of the seven Latino groups, U.S.-born females were significantly more likely than their foreign-born counterparts to be part of the labor force in 2000, with the nativity gap being the greatest among Cubans, Puerto Ricans, and Mexicans. Five groups of U.S.-born Latinas had participation levels that surpassed 60 percent: South Americans, Central Americans, Cubans, mainland-born Puerto Ricans, and Dominicans. Among foreign-born females, South Americans and Central Americans had the highest levels of labor force involvement, with Mexicans and Cubans being the least likely to be part of the labor force. The low levels of participation in the labor force among foreign-born women, especially Mexicans, Other Latinas, and non-mainland-born Puerto Ricans, have important implications for the sustenance of families as well as for gender role changes. The difference in labor force rates between the sexes is greatest among foreign-born Mexicans.

In the case of males, nativity was not as important a distinguishing factor of labor force participation in 2000 as it was in 1990. In 1990, with only one exception (Puerto Ricans), foreign-born males had higher rates of labor force activity than U.S.-born Latino males. This changed in 2000, with the foreign-born labor force participation rates being higher than those of the U.S.-born in only three cases—Mexicans, Dominicans, and Central Americans. Four groups of males had labor force participation rates above 70 percent: foreign-born Central Americans, foreign-born and U.S.-born South Americans, and foreign-born Mexicans. In contrast, four other groups had rates lower than 63 percent: non-mainland-born Puerto Ricans, foreign-born Cubans, U.S.-born Dominicans, and foreign-born Other Latinos. Again, the low rate of Cubans reflects their older age structure. However, the low labor force participation rates of non-mainland-born Puerto Ricans and foreign-born Other Latinos among males and females places members of these groups in a vulnerable economic position. The labor force participation rates of U.S.-born Dominican males and females are quite similar, a pattern that parallels African Americans.

Comparison of labor force participation rates between 1990 and 2000 shows fairly consistent declines. The rates of Latino males dropped from 79 percent in 1990 to 69 percent in 2000, with the labor force participation rate of African American males also falling by 6 percentage points. While white males also experienced a

decline in labor force participation, it was fairly modest. The labor force declines were greatest for foreign-born men in the following order: Cubans, Other Latinos, South Americans, Mexicans, non-mainland-born Puerto Ricans, Dominicans, and Central Americans.

Among U.S.-born males, Other Latinos and Mexicans experienced the steepest declines in labor force activity rates. U.S.-born South American males were the only group of males that experienced an increase in their labor force activity rates. The changes were more moderate among females.

The labor force participation rates of Latinas dropped only slightly, from 56 percent in 1990 to 53 percent in 2000, although the rate of white females increased slightly and that of African American females remained unchanged. The greatest declines in female labor force participation rates took place among three foreign-born groups: Other Latinas, Cubans, and Central Americans. However, there were some groups of women that actually experienced increases in their labor force participation rates—Puerto Ricans, U.S.-born Dominicans, U.S.-born Mexicans, and U.S.-born South Americans.

It is not clear what factors are associated with the significant drops in the labor force participation rates of Latino males, especially among the foreign-born. A series of background analyses failed to reveal any adequate explanation. One possibility that could have had some effect on the slippage of the labor force participation rates is a change that occurred in the census item asking people about their labor force activities. In 1990, the census asked (about all members of each household), "Did this person work at any time LAST WEEK?" In 2000, the form asked, "LAST WEEK, did this person do ANY work for either pay or profit?" It is possible that the addition of "for either pay or profit" may have caused some confusion or resulted in people responding differently than they would have if these words had not been part of the question.

Another potential reason could be that Latino workers, especially foreign-born males, dropped out of the labor force because of difficulties in obtaining employment. That is, they may have become discouraged workers who were not actively seeking employment at the time of the 2000 Census. There are some hints that this could have taken place.

For example, during the same 10-year period when the Latino male labor force participation rate dropped significantly, the unemployment rate of Latino males dropped from 10 percent in 1990 to 8 percent in 2000. The drop was less than a percentage point for Latina workers, whose rate was around 11 percent. Moreover, among four groups of Latino males—Mexicans, Puerto Ricans, Dominicans, and Central Americans—the foreign-born experienced greater declines in their unemployment rates between 1990 and 2000 than did the U.S.-born. Each of these groups of foreign-born males had relatively high unemployment rates in 1990—foreign-born Dominicans, non-mainland-born Puerto Ricans, foreign-born Mexicans, and foreign-born Central Americans.

Yet another possibility for the significant decline in the labor force participation rate of Latinos is associated with the reduction in the undercount between the 1990 and 2000 censuses. If people who were not counted in 1990 were not well off socioeconomically, their enumeration in 2000 could possibly skew socioeconomic comparisons including labor force participation rates. Nonetheless, these potential explanations are tentative; they have not been subjected to empirical examination.

Type of Job

Despite changes in the levels of labor force involvement between 1990 and 2000, Latino workers continue to be clustered in particular types of jobs. Sixty-eight percent of Latino male workers worked in three occupational categories in 2000: production, transportation, and material moving; construction, extraction, and maintenance; and service. White and African American males were also clustered in certain occupations, albeit somewhat different ones: 70 percent of white men were employed in three occupations (managerial, professional, and related; production, transportation, and material moving; and sales and office); 67 percent of African American men were employed in three occupations (production, transportation, and material moving; service; and sales and office). Women were even more concentrated in a narrow set of occupations. For example, 81 percent of Latina workers worked in three occupations in 2000: sales and office; service; and managerial, professional, and related. White and African American women were even more concentrated in these same three occupations.

However, there are significant differences across Latino groups in the type of jobs that people perform. Among males, South Americans and Cubans have similar occupational profiles. U.S.- and foreign-born males from these groups, which have the highest levels of education, are the most likely to hold jobs in management, professional, and related occupations. Approximately one-third of U.S.-born South Americans, U.S.-born Cubans, and whites work in this category of occupations.

On the other hand, Mexican and Other Latino males, as well as foreign-born Central Americans, were the most likely to be working in blue-collar occupations: production, transportation, and material moving; and construction, extraction, and maintenance. African Americans, foreign-born Central Americans, foreign-born Mexicans, and foreign-born Dominicans, along with mainland-born Puerto Ricans, were the most likely to be employed in service occupations.

Among women, U.S.-born Cubans, South Americans, and Central Americans, as well as whites, were the most likely to hold management, professional, and related occupations. In addition, U.S.-born Latinas in all groups had the highest levels of work in sales and office occupations. In contrast, five groups of foreign-born Latinas (Central Americans, Other Latinas, Mexicans, Dominicans, and South Americans) were the most likely to be working in service occupations. A significant percentage of foreign-born Mexican, Dominican, Other Latina, and Central American women worked in production, transportation, and material-moving occupations.

The types of jobs that people hold are related to their place of birth, human capital resources, and gender. Certain occupations that offer low wages and limited benefits tend to be filled quite heavily by immigrant workers. Census data indicate that Latino immigrants are disproportionately involved in building, constructing, transporting, serving, cleaning, and taking care of the day-to-day needs of the U.S. public.

Self-Employment

When opportunities are limited in the general labor market, some workers may opt for self-employment.[42] Overall, about 7 percent of Latino paid workers worked for themselves in 2000, a rate that is lower than that of whites (11 percent) but somewhat higher than that of African Americans (around 4 percent).

Among Latinos, foreign-born groups with greater economic resources are more likely to pursue self-employment. Foreign-born Cubans and South Americans were the most likely to be working for themselves. In contrast, U.S.-born Dominicans, Central Americans, South Americans, and Mexicans, as well as mainland-born Puerto Ricans, were the least likely to be self-employed.

Overall, between 1990 and 2000, most Latino groups as well as whites and African Americans experienced relatively small increases in the percentages of their members who were self-employed.

The labor market patterns of Latinos show one commonality: declining labor force participation rates, especially among foreign-born males. This may reflect rising discouragement among workers, who then drop out of the labor force. Nonetheless, Cubans and South Americans had the most favorable labor market experiences across the different indicators examined. These groups were also the most likely to be self-employed. In contrast, foreign-born Mexicans, Central Americans, Dominicans, and Other Latinos were clustered in low-paying jobs with limited benefits that rely heavily on immigrant workers.

Income and Earnings

The educational and labor force experiences of Latinos are important in determining their earnings and household incomes. Being an immigrant is another determinant, tending to reduce earnings and income. Given the differences among Latino groups in schooling, work, and nativity, their economic positions are apt to vary as well.

Median Hourly Wage

On average, Latino workers earned a median hourly wage of $10 in 1999, with the median hourly pay of whites and African Americans being noticeably higher (see Table 11). Latino workers earned 69 cents and 83 cents for each dollar that whites and African Americans earned in hourly wages, respectively.

The Latino groups differed noticeably, however, in their median hourly wages. Cubans, Puerto Ricans, and South Americans had the highest hourly wages in 1999, while Central Americans, Mexicans, and Dominicans had the lowest. In general, U.S.-born individuals earned higher wages than their foreign-born counterparts. Nonetheless, some foreign-born groups are included among the five groups with the highest median hourly

wages: U.S.-born Cubans, U.S.-born South Americans, mainland-born Puerto Ricans, foreign-born Cubans, and non-mainland-born Puerto Ricans. Moreover, the median earnings of foreign-born South Americans surpassed those of three U.S.-born groups: Other Latinos, Dominicans, and Mexicans.

Four foreign-born groups had median hourly pay below $10 in 1999: Mexicans, Central Americans, Dominicans, and Other Latinos. Mexicans again ranked at the bottom of each nativity group on the basis of their median hourly wage. This ranking reflects the group's low level of education and its concentration in low-paying jobs, especially in the case of foreign-born Mexicans.

The median hourly wage of Latino workers remained unchanged between 1989 and 1999, while the median hourly wage of whites rose by 9 percent, and that of African Americans increased by more than 8 percent. Thus, Latino workers lost economic ground compared with both white and African American workers

Table 11

ECONOMIC CHARACTERISTICS OF LATINOS BY ETHNIC GROUP AND NATIVITY, 1989 AND 1999

Group	Median hourly wages ($) of workers employed for at least 1,040 hours in		Median household income ($)		% of people in poverty	
	1989*	1999	1989*	1999	1989	1999
White	13.24	14.42	40,986	45,100	8.9	8.0
African American	11.09	12.02	25,635	29,200	29.1	24.6
Latino	9.98	10.00	31,149	33,800	25.0	22.4
Mexican	9.36	9.62	30,876	33,600	26.0	23.4
U.S.-born	10.63	11.06	32,554	36,100	24.2	21.6
Foreign-born	8.11	8.55	28,553	31,900	29.5	26.0
Puerto Rican	11.83	11.98	27,255	30,300	31.3	25.0
Mainland-born	12.12	12.02	32,447	35,000	31.5	24.9
Non-mainland-born	11.51	11.54	24,775	27,400	31.2	25.2
Cuban	11.68	12.12	36,083	36,900	14.3	14.6
U.S.-born	12.17	13.58	42,180	48,300	13.7	12.6
Foreign-born	11.58	11.72	35,042	34,600	14.6	15.4
Dominican	9.46	9.62	25,957	29,000	32.4	25.7
U.S.-born	10.04	11.13	31,149	35,000	37.9	28.8
Foreign-born	9.36	9.62	25,459	28,350	30.1	24.3
Central American	8.56	9.13	31,994	35,000	23.8	19.8
U.S.-born	11.63	11.43	40,705	40,000	20.1	21.9
Foreign-born	8.32	8.99	31,186	35,000	24.8	19.2
South American	11.23	11.54	39,195	40,320	14.2	15.3
U.S.-born	11.72	12.61	41,547	39,800	13.4	13.4
Foreign-born	11.23	11.30	38,936	40,710	14.5	15.9
Other Latino	11.23	10.49	33,095	33,100	19.8	21.0
U.S.-born	11.38	11.15	32,447	33,500	19.8	20.6
Foreign-born	10.92	9.62	36,335	33,000	19.7	21.9

*The 1989 median hourly wages and median household incomes have been adjusted to 1999 dollars using the Bureau of Labor Statistics' experimental Consumer Price Index (CPI-U-RS). The index for the 1947-2002 period is available at www.census.gov/hhes/income/income02/cpiurs.html.

Sources: Author's estimates using Census 1990 5% Public Use Microdata Sample (PUMS) and Census 2000 1% PUMS.

between 1989 and 1999. However, this is likely due to the larger presence of foreign-born people in the Latino population in 2000 compared with the earlier decade.

Indeed, in analyses by nativity, most Latino groups experienced increases in their median hourly wages between 1989 and 1999. Two U.S.-born groups, Cubans and Dominicans, recorded the greatest gains in earnings over the decade, surpassing even the level of wage increases of whites and African Americans. Among the four Latino groups that experienced declines in their earnings, foreign-born Other Latinos had the steepest fall in their wages. Again, caution should be used in interpreting this finding given the greater presence of Dominicans, Central Americans, and South Americans in the residual Other Latino group in 2000.

Median Income

The patterns related to household income are somewhat different from those based on the hourly wage. Latino households had a median income of $33,800 in 1999, compared with a median household income of $45,100 for whites and $29,200 for African Americans. Hence, the typical Latino household had about 75 cents for every one dollar that a white household possessed in 1999 and $1.16 for every one dollar held by an African American household. Yet Latinos lagged significantly behind both whites and African Americans when the focus was on median hourly wages. What could explain the different results? Put simply, the median hourly wage reflects the earnings of individual workers, while the median household income is based on the income of all household members. Latino households were more likely to contain three or more workers than were white and African American households. In 1999, 23 percent of Latino households had at least three workers, compared with 15 percent of white and 14 percent of African American households.

There are significant variations in the median household incomes of Latino groups. South Americans, Cubans, and Central Americans had the highest median household incomes in 1999, at $35,000 or higher. On the other hand, Dominicans and Puerto Ricans—the groups with the highest percentages of female-headed households—had the lowest median household incomes.

With only one exception (South Americans), households with U.S.-born householders had higher median incomes than those with foreign-born householders. Households headed by U.S.-born Cubans had a median income of $48,300 in 1999, a level that surpassed the median income of white households. Three other groups—foreign- and U.S.-born South Americans and U.S.-born Central Americans—had median incomes that were approximately $40,000. On the other side of the continuum, non-mainland-born Puerto Ricans, foreign-born Dominicans, and foreign-born Mexicans had the lowest median household incomes, with the median household incomes of the first two of these groups being lower than that of African Americans.

Between 1989 and 1999, the median income of Latino households rose by 8.5 percent. Nevertheless, the median incomes of African American and white households increased at a faster pace during the same period.

Most Latino groups saw increases in their median household incomes between 1989 and 1999. Households headed by U.S.-born Cubans experienced the sharpest rise, with their median income going up by more than 14 percent during the decade, outpacing the gains of white and African American households. Six other Latino groups had changes in their median household incomes that were greater than 10 percent: U.S.-born Dominicans, foreign-born Central Americans, foreign-born Mexicans, foreign-born Dominicans, U.S.-born Mexicans, and non-mainland-born Puerto Ricans. The median incomes of each of these groups increased at a slightly faster rate between 1989 and 1999 than did that of white households.

Poverty

Slightly more than 20 percent of Latinos were living in poverty in 1999, compared with 8 percent of whites and 25 percent of African Americans.

There is some variability in the poverty rate across Latino groups. The highest poverty rates in 1999 occurred among Dominicans, Puerto Ricans, and foreign-born Mexicans—all with rates around 25 percent. The former two groups have relatively high rates of female-headed households, and the latter has a low average level of education. In contrast, less than 17 percent of South Americans and Cubans were impoverished. However, there does not appear to be an association between nativity and poverty rates. This is likely due to the young age structure of the U.S.-born population, which includes the U.S.-born children of foreign-born individuals.

The poverty rate of the overall Latino population declined by 3 percentage points between 1989 and 1999, compared with a drop of 1 percentage point among whites and 5 percentage points among African Americans (see Table 11, page 373). With few exceptions, most Latino groups experienced reductions in their poverty rates between 1989 and 1999 as well. The most impressive absolute declines in poverty rates during the decade took place among Dominicans (regardless of nativity), mainland-born Puerto Ricans, and foreign-born Central Americans. Each group experienced greater reductions in its poverty rate than did African Americans. Still, caution is in order in interpreting these changes because it is likely that some Dominicans and Central Americans were part of the residual Other Latino group in 2000.

Certain groups are especially likely to be in poverty. In particular, the risk of poverty is significantly higher

Table 12

POVERTY RATES FOR LATINO HOUSEHOLD AND FAMILY TYPES BY ETHNIC GROUP, 1999

Ethnic group	Poverty rate of households with own children (%)		Poverty rate of children in household (%)	
	Married-couple	Female-headed	Married-couple	Female-headed
Latino	17.1	46.6	19.8	49.5
Mexican	19.6	46.8	22.3	50.0
Puerto Rican	11.1	49.0	13.1	52.0
Cuban	7.9	32.3	10.4	37.6
Dominican	14.5	51.0	17.3	54.7
Central American	13.7	44.7	15.5	45.3
South American	10.9	36.4	12.1	41.2
Other Latino	14.8	46.7	15.9	47.5

Source: Author's estimates using Census 2000 1% Public Use Microdata Sample (PUMS).

for female-headed families with children. Overall, about 47 percent of Latino families with children headed by females were in poverty in 1999, a rate that was nearly three times higher than that of Latino married-couple families (see Table 12). This pattern exists across the seven Latino groups, the gaps being especially great in the case of Puerto Rican and Cuban family households. The highest poverty rates among female-headed families occurred among Dominicans, Puerto Ricans, Mexicans, and Other Latinos. This household form was most prevalent among Puerto Ricans and Dominicans.

Overall, one of two Latino children living in female-headed families were poor in 1999, compared with one of five Latino children who were part of married-couple families. Female-headed households are likely to have special needs—including the need for economic resources, child care, flexible work schedules, and health insurance. The poverty rates of Mexican married-couple families with children are also relatively high, with more than 20 percent of such families being poor.

The results of this analysis show some segments of the Latino population are doing well along many dimensions, in some instances having social and economic patterns that mirror those of the white population. South Americans and Cubans, in particular, consistently surpass their Latino counterparts socioeconomically. On the other hand, Mexicans, Dominicans, Puerto Ricans, and Other Latinos tend to fare worse on a variety of socioeconomic indicators. Across the different Latino groups, female-headed families with children are especially at risk for being in poverty.

The foregoing analysis did not consider the extent to which social and economic patterns vary by the length of time that immigrants have lived in the United States, or the degree to which the observed differences between U.S.- and foreign-born groups are associated with differ-

ences in age structure. These matters are taken up next, focusing on Mexicans, the largest Latino population.

THE SPECIAL CASE OF MEXICANS

For this analysis, Mexicans are divided into five categories: U.S.-born; immigrated before 1970; immigrated during the 1970s; immigrated in the 1980s; and immigrated in the 1990s. The focus is on several indicators: English fluency, U.S. citizenship status, high school completion, labor force participation, occupation, median hourly wage, and poverty.

One word of caution is that these data are cross-sectional, based on one point in time; thus, the data provide merely a snapshot of the social and economic standing of these groups at the time of the 2000 Census. It is impossible to know the social and economic characteristics of foreign-born Mexicans who had previously been in the United States but were not in the country at the time of the 2000 Census. To the extent that individuals who returned to Mexico fare poorly on social and economic characteristics, this analysis could potentially be overestimating the influence of length of time in the United States on the social and economic indicators of interest.

Overall, foreign-born Mexicans ages 25 to 44 who had been in the United States for a longer period fared better on a variety of social and economic dimensions than those who had been in the country for a shorter period of time (see Table 13). In some cases, those who immigrated before 1970 did as well or better than U.S.-born Mexicans. Mexicans who had been in the United States for a longer time were more likely to be fluent in English, to be U.S. citizens, to have higher wages, and to have lower poverty rates. They were also more likely to hold management, professional, and related occupations and less likely to be working in the other five occupations than were Mexican immigrants who had been in the country for a shorter period. In addition, Mexican women who had been in the United States longer were more likely to be in the labor force. However, length of residence was more modestly related to educational attainment and to men's labor force participation.

These findings augment the results presented earlier based on comparisons between U.S.- and foreign-born Mexicans. The cross-sectional results do not support accusations commonly leveled against Mexican immigrants that they fail to learn English, shun U.S. citizenship, and remain trapped at the bottom of the socioeconomic ladder. Nonetheless, longitudinal data are necessary to more fully examine the veracity of such claims.

LATINOS AND THE FUTURE U.S. POPULATION

Over the last several decades, the racial and ethnic composition of the U.S. population has changed markedly. Minorities are increasing their presence in the United States and will continue to do so for the foreseeable future. The Latino population is driving these transformations. While today one of every eight residents of the United States is Latino, it is projected that Latinos could account for one of every five residents by 2035, one of every four by 2055, and one of every three by 2100. Latinos are already having a significant impact on the various societal institutions and on all segments of society in the United States. Although Latinos represented hardly a blip on the national radar screen only a few decades ago, demographic processes have made Latinos critical to the future social and economic direction of the United States.

Ongoing immigration has significantly affected the Latino experience in the United States. The continued flows of Latino immigrants ensure that the Spanish language and diverse Latino cultures will endure in the United States. The combination of established and newcomer Latinos in the United States further enhances the diversity that exists across and within Latino groups. The growth of the Latino population has led to a blurring of many boundaries. Transnational migration has blurred international and identity boundaries. Immigration has blurred the boundaries associated with nativity, even within families. The increasing use of Spanish through its dominance in foreign-language instruction in colleges and universities, its entrance into mainstream popular culture, and the bilingual context in which many Latinos operate have also blurred language boundaries.

The experiences of the various Latino groups in the United States have been quite different, and even the blurring of place and linguistic boundaries has not eliminated one important distinction. Mexicans and Puerto Ricans are the two groups that were initially incorporated into the United States through warfare. They have been viewed as "colonized groups."[43] Throughout their long history in the United States, Mexicans and Puerto Ricans have occupied a low position in the nation's social and economic hierarchy. As the analysis presented above has shown, even U.S.-born Mexicans and mainland-born Puerto Ricans occupy a low socioeconomic position among the various groups that constitute the Latino population. In contrast, other Latino groups have come to the United States as voluntary immigrants, either escaping political persecution or in search of economic opportunity. By and large, these groups have tended to fare better socially and economically, the exception being Dominicans and foreign-born Central Americans.

There are looming questions related to the future of Latinos in the United States. Will their experience in the United States be similar to that of European and Asian immigrants, or to that of African Americans? It is fairly clear that some segments of the Latino population are experiencing upward mobility, suggesting that they are

---

Table 13

SELECTED SOCIAL AND ECONOMIC CHARACTERISTICS OF MEXICANS AGES 25 TO 44, BY NATIVITY AND PERIOD OF U.S. ENTRY, 2000

Characteristic	U.S.-born	% of foreign-born by period of U.S. entry			
		< 1970	1970-1979	1980-1989	1990-2000
Percent speaking English well/very well	96.9	90.8	71.7	51.8	32.4
Percent U.S. citizens	100.0	67.9	47.1	25.6	6.5
Percent high school graduates	75.4	62.0	38.8	30.9	30.9
Percent in labor force					
Males	79.4	82.3	77.7	75.9	78.3
Females	71.6	68.8	59.4	49.2	42.6
Percent of workers by occupation					
Management, professional, and related	24.8	24.2	11.9	7.5	6.4
Service	16.3	17.3	18.4	23.3	27.3
Sales and office	28.8	25.3	18.7	11.6	10.1
Farming, fishing, and forestry	1.2	3.3	4.9	6.9	7.4
Construction, extraction, and maintenance	12.1	10.9	16.5	18.7	20.5
Production, transport, and material moving	16.7	19.1	29.7	32.1	28.3
Median hourly wage (1,040+ hours in 1999)	$12.02	$13.02	$10.94	$9.23	$7.69
Percent in poverty	13.4	14.4	17.2	23.7	29.5

Source: Author's estimates using Census 2000 1% Public Use Microdata Sample (PUMS).

following the path of European and some groups of Asian immigrants. In particular, Cubans and South Americans lead the various social and economic hierarchies within the Latino population. With some exceptions, members of these groups have arrived in the United States with human capital and socioeconomic resources that have helped them achieve upward mobility. Moreover, especially in the case of Cubans, the development of ethnic business enclaves has provided opportunities for upward mobility for co-ethnics who lack English abilities to compete in the larger labor market.[44] In addition, Central Americans show evidence of some degree of upward mobility, suggesting that with the passage of time they could follow the social and economic paths of Cubans and South Americans and more generally of European immigrants.

It is less clear what path the remaining four groups (Mexicans, Puerto Ricans, Dominicans, and Other Latinos) will follow. This set includes groups viewed as colonized minority groups (Mexicans and Puerto Ricans) as well as groups that have a relatively high proportion of members who are black (Puerto Ricans and Dominicans). Because of its diverse nature and because of the potential methodological problems in identifying the group, it is difficult to draw any substantive conclusions or inferences about the Other Latino population. Furthermore, Latinos with darker skins and indigenous features fare worse in the United States, as they do in the Latin American countries from which they originate, thus adding complexity to the determination of the social and economic future of the diverse Latino groups.[45]

The case of the Mexican-origin population stands out. On many crucial socioeconomic indictors, Mexicans are ranked at the bottom among U.S.-born and foreign-born groups. Foreign-born Cubans and South Americans consistently fared better socioeconomically than did U.S.-born Mexicans. Particularly disturbing is that Mexicans represent the largest segment of the Latino population—nearly 60 percent—and that this is the group that has been in the United States the longest.

The extremely low educational attainment of Mexicans does not bode well. This trend is consistent with the research of Alejandro Portes and Ruben Rumbaut, who observe that Mexican youth are consistently at the bottom on educational achievement and aspirations as well as on self-esteem.[46] They observe that third- and higher-generation Mexican Americans are especially disadvantaged in these respects. They conclude:

"This comparison offers no grounds for expecting that academic performance [of the third- and higher-generation Mexican Americans] will improve and dropout rates will decline over time."[47]

Given the ongoing population changes, the importance of lifting the educational attainment levels of Mexicans cannot be exaggerated. The challenge is made more difficult given that Mexican families and households have limited resources. David Lopez and Richard Stanton-Salazar point out that Mexicans "lack many of the resources that have allowed other recent groups of newcomers to thrive."[48] Although Mexicans face the biggest challenges, Puerto Ricans and Dominicans also have hardships, with high poverty rates and low median household incomes.

Measures to improve the social and economic standing of Mexican and other Latino groups need to be considered in the context of projected U.S. population changes. The major growth in the Latino population will occur among the school-age and working-age populations. The white population will continue to age and decline over the next several decades as baby boomers retire. The nation will increasingly have to rely on Latinos to provide the resources necessary to sustain an aging population.[49] It is imperative that Latino youth be prepared to participate effectively in an increasingly technological and global labor force. This is a massive task given the low socioeconomic resources and educational attainment levels of major segments of the Latino population.

To improve the educational standing of Mexicans and all Latinos, teachers, parents, and policymakers need to keep children in school. Many measures would help do this:

● Partnerships between local schools and universities that introduce high school students to future academic possibilities and ease the transition to college;
● Mentoring and internship programs that allow youth to learn from professionals in their fields of interest;
● Programs that integrate older immigrant children into academic life at the middle school and high school levels;
● Programs that integrate Latino parents into local schools; and
● Legislation that removes financial and legal barriers preventing noncitizen children who have been residing in the United States for a certain period of time from pursuing higher education.

The improvement of the social and economic conditions of Latinos will also require the elimination of discrimination and racism, which have historically hindered the progress of Latinos.

The Latino population needs to be seen as a valuable resource for this country. U.S. institutions will increasingly be affected by and dependent on Latinos in the coming decades. For example, the business community will increasingly rely on Latinos as entrepreneurs, employees, investors, and consumers. The bilingual and bicultural nature of the Latino population also makes Latinos a valuable resource as the U.S. business community expands its consumer markets and business operations into Latin America. The higher education system will increasingly find Latinos among the ranks of potential students and educators. Political institutions will find that Latinos will play an increasingly powerful role in the outcome of elections, both as voters and as political candidates. Additionally, the health care system will increasingly see Latinos as health care recipients and providers. Religious institutions will find that their potential adherents and leaders will increasingly be Latinos. These trends are well underway in the largest states and at the national level; the rising dispersion of Latinos into parts of the country that traditionally have not had Latino populations suggests that all parts of the country will feel the impact of Latino growth.

ACKNOWLEDGMENTS

The author acknowledges the helpful comments of Judith Linneman, Edward Murguia, and Isao Takei; the technical assistance of Isabel Ayala, Brandi Ballard, and Daniel Saenz, and the editorial assistance of Ellen Carnevale and Allison Tarmann. The author also appreciates the helpful comments and suggestions of the series editors, Reynolds Farley and John Haaga, and the advisory panel.

REFERENCES

If provided by the author, additional text and data associated with this report are available at www.prb.org/AmericanPeople.

1. Brian Gratton and Myron P. Gutmann, "Hispanics in the United States, 1850-1990: Estimates of Population Size and National Origin," *Historical Methods* 33, no. 3 (2000): 137-53.
2. U.S. Census Bureau, "Projections of the Resident Population by Race, Hispanic Origin, and Nativity: Middle Series, 1999 to 2100," accessed online at www.census.gov/population/www/projections/natsum-T5.html, on Feb. 10, 2004.
3. Jeffrey M. Humphrey, *The Multicultural Economy 2003: America's Minority Buying Power* (Athens, GA: Selig Center for Economic Growth, Terry College of Business, University of Georgia, 2003).
4. Benigno E. Aguirre and Rogelio Saenz, "A Future Assessment of Latinismo," *Latino Studies Journal* 2, no. 3 (1991): 19-32.
5. Alejandro Portes and Cynthia G. Truelove, "Making Sense of Diversity: Recent Research on Hispanic Minorities in the United States," *Annual Review of Sociology* 13 (1987): 360.
6. Gratton and Gutmann, "Hispanics in the United States, 1850-1990"; Oscar J. Martinez, "On the Size of the Chicano Population: New Estimates, 1850-1900," *Aztlan* 6, no. 1 (1975): 43-67; and Carey McWilliams, *North from Mexico: The Spanish-Speaking People of the United States* (New York: Greenwood Press, 1968).
7. Hector A. Carrasquillo and Virginia Sanchez-Korrol, "Migration, Community, and Culture: The United States-Puerto Rican Experience," in *Origins and Destinies: Immigration, Race, and Ethnicity in America*, ed. Silvia Pedraza and Ruben G. Rumbaut (Belmont, CA: Wadsworth, 1996).
8. U.S. Immigration and Naturalization Service (INS), *2001 Statistical Yearbook of the Immigration and Naturalization Service* (Washington, DC: U.S. Government Printing Office, 2003).
9. Silvia Pedraza, "Cuba's Refugees: Manifold Migrations," in *Origins and Destinies: Immigration, Race, and Ethnicity in America*, ed. Silvia Pedraza and Ruben G. Rumbaut (Belmont, CA: Wadsworth, 1996).
10. INS, *2001 Statistical Yearbook*.
11. Leo R. Chavez, "Borders and Bridges: Undocumented Immigrants from Mexico and Central America," in *Origins and Destinies: Immigration, Race, and Ethnicity in America*, ed. Silvia Pedraza and Ruben G. Rumbaut (Belmont, CA: Wadsworth, 1996); Juan Gonzalez, *Harvest of Empire: A History of Latinos in America* (New York: Penguin Books, 2001); and Nestor P. Rodriguez and Jacqueline Hagan, "Central Americans in the United States," in *The Minority Report: An Introduction to Racial, Ethnic, and Gender Relations*, ed. Anthony Gary Dworkin and Rosalind J. Dworkin (Fort Worth, TX: Harcourt Brace College Publishers, 1999).
12. INS, *2001 Statistical Yearbook*.
13. Pedraza, "Cuba's Refugees: Manifold Migrations."
14. Benigno E. Aguirre, Rogelio Saenz, and Brian Sinclair-James, "Marielitos Ten Years Later: The Scarface Legacy," *Social Science Quarterly* 78, no. 2 (1997): 487-507.
15. Richard A. Easterlin et al., *Immigration* (Cambridge, MA: Belknap Press of Harvard University Press, 1980); and Rogelio Saenz, Maria Cristina Morales, and Maria Isabel Ayala, "United States: Immigration to the Melting Pot of the Americas," in *Migration and Immigration: A Global View*, ed. Maura I. Toro-Morn and Marixsa Alicea (Westport, CT: Greenwood Press, 2004).
16. Manuel G. Gonzales, *Mexicanos: A History of Mexicans in the United States* (Bloomington: Indiana University Press, 1999).
17. Leo R. Chavez, "Borders and Bridges"; and Karen A. Woodrow and Jeffrey S. Passel, "Post-IRCA Undocumented Immigration to the United States: An Assessment Based on the June 1988 CPS," in *Undocumented Migration to the United States: IRCA and the Experience of the 1980s*, ed. Frank D. Bean, Barry Edmonston, and Jeffrey S. Passel (Washington, DC: The Urban Institute Press, 1990).
18. Roberto Suro, *Remittance Senders and Receivers: Tracking the Transnational Channels* (Washington, DC: Pew Hispanic Center, 2003).

19. Pierrette Hondagneu-Sotelo and Ernestine Avila, "'I'm Here, But I'm There': The Meanings of Latina Transnational Motherhood," *Gender & Society* 11, no. 5 (1997): 548-71.

20. Michael Fix and Wendy Zimmermann, "All Under One Roof: Mixed-Status Families in an Era of Reform," *International Migration Review* 35, no. 2 (2001): 397-419.

21. Michael Jones-Correa, "Under Two Flags: Dual Nationality in Latin America and Its Consequences for Naturalization in the United States," *International Migration Review* 35, no. 4 (2001): 997-1029.

22. Rogelio Saenz and Benigno E. Aguirre, "The Dynamics of Mexican Ethnic Identity," *Ethnic Groups* 9, no. 1 (1991): 17-32.

23. C. Matthew Snipp, "Racial Measurement in the American Census: Past Practices and Implications for the Future," *Annual Review of Sociology* 29 (2003): 563-88.

24. Harvey M. Choldin, "Statistics and Politics: The 'Hispanic Issue' in the 1980 Census," *Demography* 23, no. 3 (1986): 403-18.

25. Office of Management and Budget, *Directive No. 15, Race and Ethnic Standards for Federal Statistics and Administration Reporting* (Washington, DC: Office of Management and Budget, 1977).

26. Ignacio Garcia, "Backwards From Aztlan: Politics in the Age of Hispanics," in *Chicanas and Chicanos in Contemporary Society*, ed. Roberto M. De Anda (Boston: Allyn and Bacon, 1995).

27. Gonzales, *Mexicanos: A History of Mexicans in the United States*: 232.

28. Marta Cruz-Janzen, "Ethnic Identity and Racial Formations: Race and Racism American-Style and *a lo Latino*," in *Transnational Latina/o Communities: Politics, Processes, and Cultures*, ed. Carlos G. Velez-Ibanez and Anna Sampaio (Lanham, MD: Rowman and Littlefield, 2002); and Garcia, "Backwards From Aztlan."

29. Cruz-Janzen, "Ethnic Identity and Racial Formations."

30. Geoffrey Fox, *Hispanic Nation: Culture, Politics, and the Construction of Identity* (Secaucus, NJ: A Birch Lane Press Book, 1996).

31. Roberto Suro, *Counting the 'Other' Hispanics: How Many Colombians, Dominicans, Ecuadorians, Guatemalans and Salvadorans Are There in the United States?* (Washington, DC: Pew Hispanic Center, 2002).

32. Lourdes Gouveia and Rogelio Saenz, "Global Forces and Latino Population Growth in the Midwest: A Regional and Subregional Analysis," *Great Plains Research* 10, no. 2 (2000): 305-28; Ruben Hernandez-Leon and Victor Zuniga, "'Making Carpet by the Mile': The Emergence of a Mexican Immigrant Community in an Industrial Region of the U.S. Historic South," *Social Science Quarterly* 81, no. 1 (2000): 49-66; and Donald D. Stull, Michael J. Broadway, and David Griffith, eds., *Any Way You Cut It: Meat Processing and Small-Town America* (Lawrence, KS: University Press of Kansas, 1995).

33. Rogelio Saenz and Cruz Torres, "Latinos in Rural America," in *Challenges to Rural America in the Twenty-First Century*, ed. David L. Brown and Louis E. Swanson (University Park, PA: Pennsylvania State University Press, 2003).

34. Modern Language Association, "MLA's Fall 2002 Survey Shows Increase in Foreign Language Enrollments," *MLA Newsletter* 36, no. 1: 5.

35. Clara E. Rodriguez, *Changing Race: Latinos, the Census, and the History of Ethnicity in the United States* (New York: New York University Press, 2000).

36. Rodriguez, *Changing Race.*

37. Rodriguez, *Changing Race.*

38. Cruz-Janzen, "Ethnic Identity and Racial Formations"; and Rodriguez, *Changing Race.*

39. Mary C. Waters, *Black Identities: West Indian Immigrant Dreams and American Reality* (Cambridge, MA: Harvard University Press, 2001).

40. Milton M. Gordon, *Assimilation in American Life: The Role of Race, Religion, and National Origin* (New York: Oxford University Press, 1964).

41. Peter M. Blau, Terry C. Blum, and Joseph E. Schwartz, "Heterogeneity and Intermarriage," *American Sociological Review* 47, no. 1 (1982): 45-62.

42. Alejandro Portes and Leif Jensen, "The Enclave and the Entrants: Patterns of Ethnic Enterprise in Miami and After Mariel," *American Sociological Review* 54, no. 6 (1989): 929-49; and Jimy W. Sanders and Victor Nee, "Immigration Self-Employment: The Family as Social Capital and the Value of Human Capital," *American Sociological Review* 61, no. 2 (1996): 231-49.

43. Robert Blauner, *Racial Oppression in America* (New York: Harper and Row, 1972).

44. Portes and Jensen, "The Enclave and the Entrants."

45. Walter Allen, Edward Telles, and Margaret Hunter, "Skin Color, Income and Education: A Comparison of African Americans and Mexican Americans," *National Journal of Sociology* 12, no. 1 (2000): 129-80; Rodolfo Espino and Michael M. Franz, "Latino Phenotypic Discrimination Revisited: The Impact of Skin Color on Occupational Status," *Social Science Quarterly* 83, no. 2 (2002): 612-23; Christina Gomez, "The Continual Significance of Skin Color: An Explanatory Study of Latinos in the Northeast," *Hispanic Journal of Behavioral Sciences* 22, no. 1 (2000): 94-103; Edward Murguia and Rogelio Saenz, "An Analysis of the Latin Americanization of Race in the United States: A Reconnaissance of Color Stratification Among Mexicans," *Race & Society* 5, no. 1 (2002); Edward Murguia and Edward E. Telles, "Phenotype and Schooling Among Mexican Americans," *Sociology of Education* 69, no. 4 (1996): 276-89; Edward E. Telles and Edward Murguia, "Phenotypic Discrimination and Income Differences Among Mexican Americans," *Social Science Quarterly* 71, no. 4 (1990): 682-96; and Eric Uhlmann et al., "Subgroup Prejudice Based on Skin Color Among Hispanics in the United States and Latin America," *Social Cognition* 20, no. 3 (2002): 198-226.

46. Alejandro Portes and Ruben G. Rumbaut, *Legacies: The Story of the Immigrant Second Generation* (Berkeley and New York: University of California Press and Russell Sage Foundation, 2001).

47. Portes and Rumbaut, *Legacies: The Story of the Immigrant Second Generation.*

48. David E. Lopez and Richard Stanton-Salazar, "Mexican Americans: A Second Generation at Risk," in *Ethnicities: Children of Immigrants in America*, ed. Ruben G. Rumbaut and Alejandro Portes (Berkeley, CA: University of California Press, 2001): 57.

49. David E. Hayes-Bautista, Werner O. Schink, and Jorge Chapa, *The Burden of Support: Young Latinos in an Aging Society* (Palo Alto, CA: Stanford University Press, 1988); and Steve H. Murdock et al., *The New Texas Challenge: Population Change and the Future of Texas* (College Station, TX: Texas A&M University Press, 2003).

African Americans and the Color Line

By Michael A. Stoll

CONTINUING DEBATE

Almost 100 years ago, W. E. B. Dubois, the world-renowned scholar and political activist, declared that in America, "The problem of the twentieth century is the problem of the color-line."[1] With 350 years or so of legalized slavery abolished just 40 years before, recent efforts at Reconstruction firmly defeated, and Jim Crow-style racial segregation taking hold in the South, where most blacks lived, few students of race relations at the time would have disputed DuBois' claim. Indeed, many would have agreed then that race was the most important, if not the sole, factor determining the life chances of African Americans in the United States.[2]

But much has changed in America's political economy in the 100 years since DuBois' prophetic declaration. Blacks' migration out of the South to the North, coupled with steady economic growth after the Great Depression and postwar periods, began to change the socioeconomic profile of African Americans. This change, in conjunction with the enduring struggle of the civil rights movement, which helped end de jure segregation and codify blacks' rights in the civic sphere in the 1960s, brought new hope that African Americans' dreams and aspirations for a better life could actually be realized.

Events in the late 1960s and early 1970s bolstered these aspirations. As a result of Great Society program efforts, strong federal enforcement of antidiscrimination laws, and expanding affirmative action programs, blacks made their greatest social and economic gains in the 20th century on a host of dimensions—both absolutely and especially relative to whites.[3]

The persistence of gains made during the 1980s introduced a new debate about the future prospects of African Americans. Some argued that, as a result of declining negative attitudes and behaviors toward African Americans, race was no longer the sole or even the most important determinant of African Americans' opportunities in the social and economic sphere. As evidence, many pointed to steady, absolute black progress on social and economic indicators and to the growth of a solid black middle class.[4] The implication of this argument is profound in the modern era, suggesting a declining need for government intervention to improve the lives of African Americans since social and economic mechanisms appear to be ensuring this progress.

Others, however, held that race was still an important influence in the life chances of blacks in the United States. They argued that persistent discrimination, coupled with a reduced federal role, continued to limit the potential economic and social gains of African Americans. As evidence they showed that, when viewed in relation to gains among whites, African Americans' progress on a host of dimensions either stalled or reversed during the 1980s, implying a continuing need for a government role in providing a level societal playing field and in securing continued black economic and social progress.[5]

This report advances the continuing discussion of African Americans' economic and social progress in America. Using the latest results from Census 2000 and other current data sources, it examines whether African Americans continued to make gains during the 1990s, especially relative to whites. Some would argue that a focus on black-white comparisons in this age of rapidly growing diversity is too narrow. The swift growth of other minority populations, in particular of Hispanics, in the last 20 years or so perhaps justifies a more dynamic comparison among racial and ethnic groups. Yet it is arguable that the racial division between blacks and whites shapes the unfolding racial and ethnic relations in the United States precisely because of the historically significant role of slavery, legalized segregation, and black-white conflict. In response to these concerns, this report focuses on comparisons between blacks and whites but does examine—where appropriate and where space permits—other groups that are growing rapidly, such as Hispanics and Asian Americans.

The African American experience since the beginning of slavery in the 16th century has been shaped by the fight to gain equal rights—the right to freedom, the right to own property, and the right to attend school. In the modern era, these fights have included movements to secure the right to vote, to enjoy public accommodations, and to choose where to live.

But since the 1960s, especially in the 1970s and 1980s, after civil rights were achieved at least on paper,

MICHAEL A. STOLL is an associate professor of policy studies in the School of Public Policy and Social Research, and associate director of the Center for the Study of Urban Poverty, at the University of California, Los Angeles. He is the author of numerous publications on race, poverty, and labor markets, especially as these pertain to welfare reform, transportation, and mass incarceration in the United States. He received his Ph.D. in urban studies and planning from the Massachusetts Institute of Technology and recently served as a visiting scholar at the Russell Sage Foundation in New York City.

African Americans' struggles for equality have increasingly moved to the economic sphere. This report focuses on blacks' relative gains during the 1990s in employment, earnings, family income, poverty reduction, and wealth. Except where noted, the analysis compares the non-Hispanic black population to the non-Hispanic white population. Also examined is the incarceration rate of African Americans.

POPULATION CHANGE AND GROWTH

The African American population in the United States grew over the 1990s in absolute terms but not as a percentage of the total population (see Figure 1). The black share of total population held steady in each decade from 1980 to 2000, while the shares of those with Asian and especially Hispanic ancestries grew. Indeed, the Hispanic share of total population nearly doubled. In contrast, the share of the total white population dropped by nearly 10 percentage points. The overall U.S. population grew from about 227 million in 1980 to about 281 million in 2000.

The rate of growth of racial and ethnic minorities in the U.S. population during the 1990s exceeded that of the country over this period (13 percent). The black population increased by 16 percent, or from about 30 million to 36 million, while the Hispanic population increased a phenomenal 58 percent, from 22.4 million to 35.3 million. With this rate of growth, the Hispanic population surpassed the black population in the United States as the nation's largest ethnic minority group in the early 2000s; this was true even if black Hispanics were counted as black. (The 2000 Census was the first to allow respondents to describe themselves as being of more than one race. The total shown here for blacks includes those who reported black only, as well as those who reported black and one or more other race. "Hispanic," as discussed in Box 1, is an ethnic, rather than a racial, designation.) On the other hand, the white population grew by only 6 percent, from about 199 million to 211 million.

Recent evidence on racial differences in age structure and in fertility rates suggests that the growth of the black, Hispanic, and Asian populations will continue to outpace that of whites, at least in the very near future. The age composition of populations strongly influences their future growth rates. On average, younger populations grow faster than older ones because most births occur among younger females. Census 2000 data show that the median age of the black population is significantly younger than that of whites. In fact, in 2000 black men were about nine years younger than white men, on average, while black

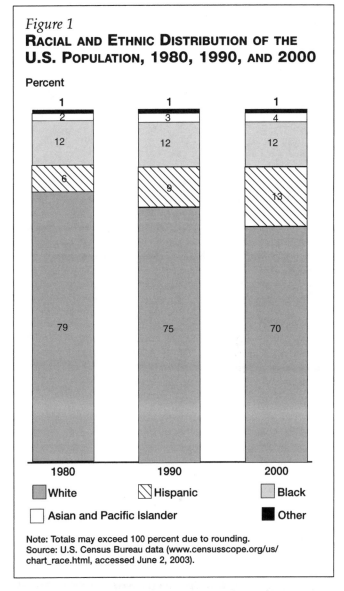

Figure 1
RACIAL AND ETHNIC DISTRIBUTION OF THE U.S. POPULATION, 1980, 1990, AND 2000

Percent

	White	Hispanic	Black

| | Asian and Pacific Islander | Other |

Note: Totals may exceed 100 percent due to rounding.
Source: U.S. Census Bureau data (www.censusscope.org/us/chart_race.html, accessed June 2, 2003).

women were nearly seven years younger than white women, on average. The Asian and Hispanic populations were younger still than whites.

The fertility rate of blacks is also higher than that of whites. Data from the National Center for Health Statistics indicate that in 1999 there were 70 births per 1,000 black women and about 65 births per 1,000 white women.[6] Thus, the older age of the white population and the lower fertility rate of white women suggest slower population growth of this group relative to blacks in the near future. This prediction is tempered, however, by the higher mortality rates of blacks, especially of black men, reflected in their lower life expectancy. In 2000, the average life expectancy of black men was 68 compared with 75 for white men, and 75 for black women compared with 80 for white women. Although the life expectancy for both blacks and whites has improved over the last 20 years, the racial gap has yet to close; and, at least for men, the racial gap widened over this period.[7]

Box 1

'MULTIRACIAL' BLACKS IN 2000

Census 2000 for the first time permitted respondents to describe themselves using more than one racial category. In previous censuses, respondents were allowed to mark only one box for race—white, black, Asian, American Indian and Alaska Native, or Other. Given the opportunity to mark more than one racial category, about 1.4 million non-Hispanic blacks reported more than one race in 2000. This represents about 4 percent of the total non-Hispanic black population of 35 million. However, non-Hispanic blacks under the age of 18 were much more likely to report more than one race (7 percent) than those over 18 (3 percent).[1]

Although the reasons for the difference between older and younger individuals in reporting more than one racial background are not yet well understood, they are likely to include an increasing number of children from interracial marriages, and greater openness and awareness of the diversity of racial backgrounds among younger generations.[2]

What other racial backgrounds were blacks likely to identify in the 2000 Census? Among non-Hispanic blacks who reported more than one race, a near majority (49 percent) indicated they were "black and white," 18 percent "black and some other race," 12 percent "black and American Indian," and 7 percent "black and Asian." These data are consistent with interracial marriage rates of blacks; most of those who marry outside their race marry whites.[3]

The 1990 and 2000 censuses allowed respondents to identify whether they were of Hispanic ancestry in addition to providing their racial background. Thus, in the census, Hispanic is not considered a racial group. However, as noted, individuals who are of Hispanic origin can report their racial background. Thus, race and ethnicity are considered two distinct concepts by the federal system. That is, Hispanics may be of any race, and blacks can be Hispanic or non-Hispanic. In Census 2000, about 1 million blacks reported being of Hispanic ancestry, the majority from the Dominican Republic and Puerto Rico.

References

1. Calculations based on data from Jesse McKinnon, "The Black Population: 2000," *Census 2000 Brief* C2KBR/01-5, accessed online at www.census.gov/prod/2001pubs/c2kbr01-5.pdf, on March 18, 2004.

2. David R. Harris, "Does It Matter How We Measure? Racial Classifications and the Characteristics of Multiracial Youth," in *The New Race Question,* ed. Joel Perlmann and Mary C. Waters (New York: Russell Sage Foundation, 2002).

3. David R. Harris and Hiromi Ono, "Cohabitation, Marriage, and Markets: A New Look at Intimate Interracial Relationships," *Discussion Paper* (Ann Arbor, MI: Institute for Social Research, University of Michigan, 2003).

Box 2

THE GROWING DIVERSITY OF THE BLACK POPULATION IN THE UNITED STATES

The diversity of the black population in the United States grew rapidly over the 1990s. A report on black diversity shows that the number with origins in the Caribbean (from places such as Jamaica, Haiti, and Guyana) increased by over 60 percent. The number of black Americans with recent roots in sub-Saharan Africa (from places like Nigeria and Ghana) more than doubled during the 1990s.[1] Blacks in the United States with recent Caribbean roots number over 1.5 million; blacks from Africa numbered over half a million in 2000. Combined, these groups represented only about 6 percent of the total black population in 2000, but they accounted for nearly 25 percent of the growth of the black population between 1990 and 2000.[1]

In some major metropolitan regions, these "new" black groups represent about 20 percent or more of the total black population. For example, Afro-Caribbeans are heavily concentrated on the East Coast. Six out of 10 live in the New York, Miami, and Fort Lauderdale, Fla., metropolitan regions. Moreover, more than half of blacks in Miami are Haitian.

Haitians are also well represented but outnumbered by Jamaicans in New York and Fort Lauderdale.

America's African population, on the other hand, is much more geographically dispersed. The largest numbers are in Washington, D.C., and New York. In both places West Africans predominate, with the largest groups from Ghana and Nigeria. Ethiopians and Somalis are the other main groups.

The social and economic profile of Afro-Caribbeans and Africans is somewhat better than that of African Americans, in part because migrants from these places tend to be well educated and relatively well-off. Still, like African Americans, Afro-Caribbeans and Africans are highly segregated from whites.

Reference

1. See John. R. Logan and Glenn Deane, *Black Diversity in Metropolitan America* (Albany, NY: Lewis Mumford Center for Comparative Urban and Regional Research, State University of New York at Albany, 2003) for a more detailed discussion of these trends.

Thus, the American population over the 1990s became increasingly diverse. During this time, the white share of the U.S. population declined by almost 10 percentage points. To put this change in perspective, in the recent past it took nearly 40 years for the white share of the U.S. population to decline by 10 percentage points, from 90 percent to 80 percent between 1940 and 1980. Certainly, the growth in the African American population has contributed to these changes, and blacks' younger age and higher fertility rates relative to whites suggest blacks' numbers will continue to grow absolutely in the United States. But to what extent the African American share of the total population will continue to grow rests crucially on the population growth rates of Hispanics and Asians, which have been phenomenal in recent years.

Diversity within the African American population also will grow in the next decade. Interracial marriage rates and births will continue to increase as they did over the 1990s, thus increasing the number and percentage of multiracial blacks in the United States. And the continuing and perhaps increasing flow of black immigrants from the Caribbean, Africa, and elsewhere will increasingly change the profile of the African American population in the United States (see Box 2, page 382).

These trends raise a number of important questions about the future of race relations and politics in the United States. These include whether multiracial blacks will adopt racial identities that are neither black nor white, or whether the historically significant "one-drop rule," in which those with at least one drop of African blood are considered black, will continue to dominate any alternative definition or concept of race that may emerge with mixed-race status. The continued growth of immigrant black populations in the United States raises the question of whether their socioeconomic progress will diverge from that of the U.S.-born black population, or whether the machinery of race in America will ensure convergence of outcomes.

Whether we will have answers to these questions will depend on continued consensus on the merits of collecting information about race. In California, for example, attempts were made as part of the Racial Privacy Initiative to keep private information about individuals' racial background during public data collection efforts.

RISING EDUCATIONAL ATTAINMENT

The African American fight for equal schooling has a long history. Even during the period of slavery, personal accounts tell of slaves learning to read and write (many times with the help of benevolent slave-owning families) despite the dreadful consequences of being found out. In the post-slavery era, education has also been an important pathway pursued to combat discrimination and poverty in the United States. Indeed, besides the black church, many of the first black institutions built in the post-slavery period were schools and institutions of higher learning, such as the Tuskegee Institute, some with assistance from white philanthropists (such as Cheyney University of Pennsylvania, which was built before slavery ended) and from state and federal governments (such as North Carolina Central University). And in the recent past, it was the fight over the integration of segregated schools in the landmark court case of Brown v. Board of Education in 1954 (in which African Americans and their major civic organizations played a prominent legal and political role) that helped fuel the civil rights movement in America.

Education has also played a key role in social mobility in the United States. For many marginalized and immigrant groups, education has been one of the few institutions available for social advancement. But over the past few decades, the importance of education in society appears to have accelerated, especially in the labor market. With the rise of, and rapid changes in, technology in the workplace and the continuing specialization of work, jobs require ever-more skills and credentials. Many of these skills are learned in places of higher education, such as colleges and universities. Perhaps in part for these reasons, rates of college attainment have grown rapidly over the past 20 to 30 years for most racial and ethnic groups.

For all these reasons, it is critically important to examine how the educational attainment of blacks changed over the 1990s, especially the degree to which blacks made advances in college attainment, because of its growing importance in economic mobility. Before doing this, it is important to point out that, since the 1960s, blacks have made tremendous gains relative to whites in educational attainment in primary and secondary education. Blacks have significantly closed the racial gap in high school completion since the 1960s.[8]

Black men have made steady progress in educational attainment (see Figure 2). The share of black men who earned a college degree or more rose by 3 percentage points from 1980 to 2000, while the share who did not earn a high school degree fell dramatically.[9] Also, the percentage of black men who attained at least some college education rose rather dramatically over this period, although the increase was more pronounced in the 1980s than in the 1990s.

The gains made by black men relative to whites in the 1980s in the attainment of a college degree or more stalled in the 1990s. In 1980, the black/white ratio in the attainment of a college degree or more was 0.41. This fraction rose to 0.44 in 1990, suggesting that black men attained this educational level at a faster rate than whites during the 1980s, thus narrowing the racial gap in this measure. However, during the 1990s, and although black men's college attainment improved, the black/white ratio in this measure remained at 0.44, indicating that black men made no gains relative to white men in college attainment.

The story among women is somewhat different. Like black men, black women have made steady progress in educational attainment since the 1980s. The percentage of black women who did not earn a high school degree fell by over 15 percentage points from 1980 to 1990, while the percentage of black women who earned a college degree or more rose by 6 percentage points during this period. The rise in college attendance by black women and men is attributed to a number of factors, including the improvement in primary and secondary schools that blacks attend, affirmative action in college, and increasing academic preparedness.[10] Black women also made dramatic gains in the attainment of some college education, although again the increase was more dramatic in the 1980s than in the 1990s.

Unlike black men, black women made no gains relative to white women in the 1980s or 1990s in the attainment of a college degree or more. In fact, they lost ground over this period, as the black/white ratio in attaining at least a college education dropped from 0.66 in 1980 to 0.62 in 2000. Recent research has yet to address the reasons for these declines in racial equality in educational attainment, especially in the attainment of a college degree during the 1990s. However, a variety of factors—including the somewhat lower high school graduation rates and academic preparedness of blacks as compared with whites—account for the racial gap in college attendance over the 1980s. The socioeconomic status of families, particularly parents' educational attainment, also influences college attendance, and blacks have both lower socioeconomic levels and parents with lower levels of educational attainment than do their white counterparts. Rising college costs are also likely to be identified as a major explanation of the racial gap in educational attainment, with blacks less able to afford college than whites.[11]

Thus, over the 1990s, black men and women made absolute gains in educational attainment. The dramatic decline in the percentage of high school dropouts observed for blacks over the 1970s and 1980s continued through the 1990s, and so did the attainment of a college degree or more. To the extent that blacks attend schools that are inferior to those of whites, improvements documented here could overstate the extent to which blacks are reaching educational parity with whites. Standardized test scores, however, show that blacks have narrowed the gap with whites (despite claims of test bias), although this narrowing was more significant in the 1980s than 1990s.[12] Moreover, research by psychologist Claude Steele shows that blacks' test scores are likely

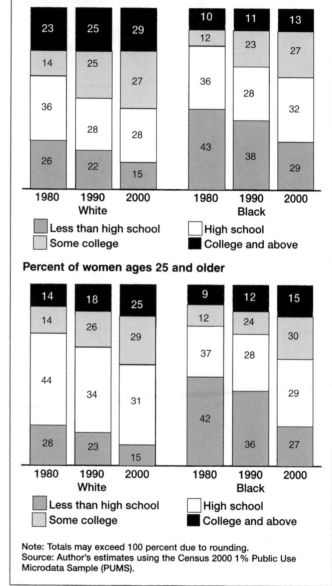

Figure 2
DISTRIBUTION OF U.S. POPULATION BY HIGHEST EDUCATIONAL ATTAINMENT AND BY RACE, 1980, 1990, AND 2000

Note: Totals may exceed 100 percent due to rounding.
Source: Author's estimates using the Census 2000 1% Public Use Microdata Sample (PUMS).

biased downward because of poorer performance on tests than what blacks' ability suggests.[13]

Despite these causes for optimism, other trends raise concern about racial equality in educational attainment. Blacks either lost or made no ground relative to whites in the attainment of a college degree or more. This concern is magnified in light of the recent Supreme Court ruling (in the case against the University of Michigan Law School) on the uses and limits of affirmative action in higher education. The limits on affirmative action imposed by the Supreme Court will affect highly com-

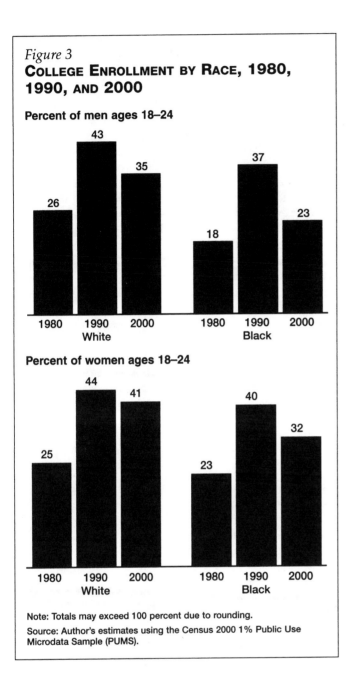

Figure 3

COLLEGE ENROLLMENT BY RACE, 1980, 1990, AND 2000

Percent of men ages 18–24

White: 1980 = 26, 1990 = 43, 2000 = 35
Black: 1980 = 18, 1990 = 37, 2000 = 23

Percent of women ages 18–24

White: 1980 = 25, 1990 = 44, 2000 = 41
Black: 1980 = 23, 1990 = 40, 2000 = 32

Note: Totals may exceed 100 percent due to rounding.

Source: Author's estimates using the Census 2000 1% Public Use Microdata Sample (PUMS).

College enrollment rates of 18-to-24-year-olds with at least a high school degree give an even clearer picture of changes in college attendance (see Figure 3). On first inspection, the rates for 1990 and 2000 appear to contradict the finding that college attainment rose over the 1990s for all groups. The apparent inconsistency, however, is largely explained by the fact that the college enrollment data reflect choices at one point in time, whereas the college attainment figures reflect events and choices made over the decade.

So, for example, in 2000, wages and salaries were relatively high because the economy was booming and the labor market was tight. During periods such as these, one should expect college enrollment rates to decline as people choose to enter the labor market rather than go to school because current earnings opportunities appear strong. College attendance rates rose over the 1990s, as previously stated, despite declines in college enrollment in 2000.

College enrollment among all groups jumped sharply and nearly equally between 1980 and 1990, changing the black-white difference in these measures only slightly. However, between 1990 and 2000, the decline in college enrollment for blacks was much sharper than for whites. As a result, the racial difference in college enrollment for both men and women jumped steeply over the 1990s.

Whether to view the increase in the racial difference in college-going among the young as a social concern depends on the factors that drove the decline. It is plausible that young black men and women who were eligible for college entered the labor market at greater rates than whites because of increased employment opportunities. It is well known that young blacks face more difficulties in the labor market than others as a result of discrimination and other barriers, and thus their employment opportunities improve greatly during tight labor markets. To the extent that such young black men and women attain employment, remain employed long enough to gain significant human capital and skills, or return to college if employment prospects weaken, the dramatic drop in their college enrollment perhaps should be not viewed with concern. But to the extent that human capital formation does not take place, those with employment difficulties do not to return to college, or this pattern becomes a long-term trend, there may be cause for concern.

Still, the enrollment rates confirm the trend of black women entering college at greater rates than black men. Even in 2000, when college enrollments dropped for both, the share of young black women enrolled in college was nearly 10 percentage points higher than the share of black men. No doubt these trends have deep implications, especially in the marriage market. Again, to the extent that women tend to marry those with equal or higher levels of education, the imbalance in college attainment between black men and women will reduce

petitive and very prestigious institutions the most. Since attending these institutions confers numerous benefits and privileges, such as higher earnings and greater access to elites, increasing barriers to African Americans' admission to these schools will surely harm African Americans' social and economic mobility.

Another concern is that black women have surpassed black men in the level of college attainment. This reordering first occurred in the 1980s, but rose more dramatically in the 1990s. Over the 1980s and 1990s, college attainment rose by 31 percent for black women but by only 19 percent for black men. To the extent that women in the United States tend to marry men with higher educational attainment levels, this trend is likely to contribute to the decline in marriage among blacks.

the pool of marriageable black men. More research is needed to fully understand these changes and their educational and social consequences.

UNEVEN EMPLOYMENT CHANGES

Blacks' fight for justice in the contemporary period includes the right to employment. The right to jobs is key because most families rely on employment as their main source of income and economic stability. Before industrialization in the United States, most blacks lived in the South, where agricultural work was readily available, albeit at extremely low pay. With the movement of blacks from Southern to Northern cities in response to industrialization, blacks, especially black men, began to experience significant employment problems that have persisted to this day (see Box 3).

The 1990s saw the biggest economic expansion in the United States in the last 30 years, significantly and positively influencing most Americans' economic outcomes. But because African Americans have typically fared relatively poorly on a host of economic dimensions in the United States, whether blacks' labor-market outcomes and general economic standing improved during the economic boom is an open question.

Two measures aid in answering that question. One is the unemployment rate, the standard measure used by the federal government to report the extent to which individuals are employed. It is calculated as the percentage of the labor force that is unemployed. The other measure is the employment-to-population ratio, also known as the employment rate, the fraction of the population under study that is employed. The unemployment rate is based on the labor force, which is composed of individuals who are employed and those who are unemployed—that is, those who have been actively searching for work within the past six months but not working. The employment rate takes into account people who are in and people who are out of the labor force; in other words, it includes potential workers—those who are not in the labor force but are willing to work. These individuals, usually referred to as discouraged workers, have abandoned the search for work and dropped out of the labor force as a result of not receiving suitable job offers. Blacks make up a larger share of

---

Box 3

THE CHARACTERISTICS OF JOBLESS MEN

Census 2000 allows a close-up look at the characteristics of men, especially African American men, who experienced long periods of unemployment. This inquiry is particularly relevant given the low employment rates of African American men. The inability of many black men to secure employment, even during the economic boom of the 1990s, raises the question of who these men are.

The table provides some data from Census 2000 on the characteristics of men (ages 18 to 64) who never worked in the previous year, 1999. First, according to the census, a much larger percentage of black than white men never worked in 1999, a finding consistent with the data on employment-to-population ratios. Indeed, the share of black men who never worked (28 percent) is over twice that of white men (12 percent). Of those who never worked in 1999, black men are younger and more likely to have dropped out of high school. Moreover, these black men are also less likely ever to have been married than white men who did not work in 1999.

Not working could be related to physical conditions that limit work, or to incarceration, which prevents individuals from realizing an opportunity to work. Census 2000 provides data on both of these statuses. The disability data indicate that white men who never worked in 1999 were more likely than their black counterparts to report that they had employment (from a work-related injury), physical, or mental disabilities. On the other hand, the data indicate that black men who never worked in 1999 are nearly three times more likely than their white counterparts to be incarcerated.

Men Ages 18–64 Who Never Worked in 1999 by Race

	White	Black
Never worked in 1999 (%)	12	28
Characteristics		
Average age	40	35
No high school degree (%)	41	53
Enrolled in school (%)	28	26
Never married (%)	45	57
Disabilities (%)		
Employment	24	19
Physical	17	14
Mental	26	19
Currently incarcerated (%)	6	16
Looking for work (%)	9	17

Source: Author's calculations using the Census 2000 5% Public Use Microdata Sample (PUMS).

Thus, the data suggest that black men are much more likely to be jobless than their white counterparts and that the factors associated with this joblessness may be different for these groups. White men seem to be limited from work more by disabilities, while the factors associated with a lack of work for black men appear to be more connected to nonphysical disadvantages. These conclusions are supported by the table: Black men who never worked in 1999 are nearly two times more likely than their white counterparts to be looking for work.

Figure 4
EMPLOYMENT BY RACE AND SEX, 1980–2000

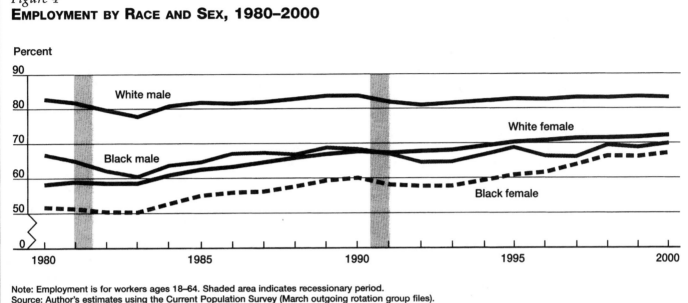

Note: Employment is for workers ages 18–64. Shaded area indicates recessionary period.
Source: Author's estimates using the Current Population Survey (March outgoing rotation group files).

Box 4
DOES RACE STILL MATTER IN THE LABOR MARKET?

A number of recent studies document that racial discrimination continues to be a significant barrier to employment, especially for black men. Reynolds Farley, Harry Holzer, Sheldon Danziger, and Ted Mouw have all shown that black men in the Detroit area were less likely to get jobs, especially blue-collar jobs in manufacturing, than were similar white men. A recent audit study in Milwaukee by sociologist Devah Pager found similar results. Most strikingly, in this study, white men who admitted being incarcerated for cocaine possession with intent to distribute were more likely to be recruited for low-skill jobs than identical black men who had never been incarcerated. Finally, a recent study by economists Marianne Bertrand and Sendhil Mullainathan showed that employers were less likely to interview applicants with black-sounding names like Lakisha than those with white-sounding names like Emily.

Increasingly, the racial discrimination against black men in the labor market occurs on the basis of perceived criminality. In a recent study in Atlanta, Boston, Detroit, and Los Angeles, Harry Holzer, Steven Raphael, and Michael Stoll found that black men were significantly less likely to be hired for jobs that did not require a college degree because employers perceived the men as being criminally prone, although most were not. Employers are averse to hiring ex-offenders for a variety of reasons and use social markers like

race to infer criminality. Hiring on this basis discriminates against black men who have never been incarcerated.

Discrimination against blacks also occurs at other stages in the employment process. Economists Marta Elvira and Christopher Zatzick found that blacks were less likely to be promoted and more likely to be laid off at firms than similar whites, even after a variety of important factors were controlled for, including firm and job characteristics. However, monitoring personnel decisions and actively enforcing affirmative action policies reduce this discrimination, as has been shown elsewhere.[1]

Reference

1. For all these studies, see Reynolds Farley, Sheldon Danziger, and Harry J. Holzer, *Detroit Divided* (New York: Russell Sage Foundation, 2001); Ted Mouw, "Job Relocation and the Racial Gap in Unemployment in Detroit and Chicago, 1980 to 1990," *American Sociological Review* 65, no. 5 (2000): 730-53; Devah Pager, "The Mark of a Criminal Record," *American Journal of Sociology* 108, no. 5 (2003): 937-75; Marianne Bertrand and Sendhil Mullainathan, "Are Emily and Greg More Employable than Lakisha and Jamal? A Field Experiment on Labor Market Discrimination," *Working Paper* #W9873 (Cambridge, MA: National Bureau of Economic Research, 2003); Harry Holzer, Steven Raphael, and Michael A. Stoll, "Perceived Criminality, Criminal Background Checks, and the Racial Hiring Practices of Employers," *Discussion Paper* 1254-02 (Madison, WI: Institute for Research on Poverty, University of Wisconsin, 2002); and Marta M. Elvira and Christopher D. Zatzick, "Who's Displaced First? The Role of Race in Layoff Decisions," *Industrial Relations* 41, no. 2 (2002): 329-61.

discouraged workers than whites. Thus, for many blacks, the employment rate is a more comprehensive measure of employment.

An analysis of employment rates by race and sex from 1980 to 2000 reveals two clear patterns (see Figure 4). First, there is a large and persistent racial gap in employment for both men and women, consistent with that observed since the 1960s. These gaps range from 10 percentage points to 20 percentage points among men, and from 5 percentage points to 10 percentage points among women.

Second, the employment rate for blacks is much more sensitive to business-cycle fluctuations than that of whites, consistent with the practice of "last hired, first fired." That is, for a variety of reasons, blacks are last to be hired during an upswing in the economy and are first to be let go during a downswing. While the employment rate for white men was virtually unchanged from 1980 to 2000, that of white women increased steadily (consistent with trends in their employment), despite fluctuations in the economy. Black women's employment rate also rose absolutely over this period, from about 50 percent to 66 percent, but was slightly more affected by changes in the economy than that of white women. After dropping dramatically in the early 1980s, the rate for black men rose only modestly: The boom of the late 1990s raised their employment rate only to prerecession 1989 levels.

Despite these gains, the black-white employment gap was only slightly smaller in 2000 than at the beginning of the 1980s or the 1990s. By 2000, black women reduced the employment gap with white women to 5 percentage points (down from a high of about 10 percentage points in the recessionary early 1990s), with much of this reduction occurring during the economic boom of the late 1990s. But the racial gap in employment among men improved only slightly during this period and remained virtually the same in 2000 (at 12 percentage points) as it had been in 1995, before the boom began.

Thus, African Americans' employment rate did rise over the 1990s, but the increase was much more pronounced for black women than for black men. Even so, the inclusion of all adult men in this figure masks the employment problems of young black men over this period. Research by economists Harry Holzer and Paul Offner has shown that the employment rate of young black men actually declined over the 1990s, despite the boom.[14] Given that black women's employment rate rose at a slightly faster rate than that of white women, the racial gap in employment among women actually narrowed by the end of the decade. Black men, however, gained virtually no ground relative to their white counterparts in employment over this period, leaving the racial gap in employment for men in 2000 almost as big as it was at the beginning of the decade (see Box 4).

MODEST EARNINGS GAINS

Equal pay for equal work has been a central concern for African Americans. Yet African Americans' lower educational attainment relative to whites—despite significant black progress on this dimension over the past century—limits the extent to which blacks are able to command similar wages. So, too, could discrimination and other factors.

The rising employment rates over the 1990s surely must have affected workers' earnings and the racial divide therein. This is because employers must offer higher wages to attract job candidates as it becomes more and more difficult for them to find workers, let alone qualified ones. During the economic boom of the late 1990s, as labor markets became tighter than they had been in almost 30 years, earnings paid to workers rose. An important question is whether the earnings of African Americans rose over the 1990s, and whether they did so enough to narrow the historic racial gap in earnings.

Black men and women have enjoyed substantial gains in earnings relative to whites since the early 1900s. But the magnitude of these gains and their persistence over time depend on the measure used. Research that focuses on hourly wages has shown that black workers have made substantial progress in catching up with whites, while research using annual earnings indicates that this progress has been less significant.

Why? These conclusions are driven partly by how the different earnings measures are defined. Weekly or annual earnings measures factor in both the wages that individuals earn per hour and the amount of time they spend working. Thus, these measures can fluctuate in response to changes in compensation rate or to changes in the number of hours spent working.

On the other hand, hourly earnings can change only with changes in compensation. Of course, changes in compensation can reflect either changes in the human capital or skills that individuals bring to the job, or changes in how tight labor markets are. Individuals may therefore receive vastly different weekly or annual earnings depending on how many hours of work they put in during the relevant time frame, even though they may receive the same hourly wage rate.

These differences in earnings measures have important implications. Blacks are much more likely to suffer a bout of unemployment and to experience a longer period of unemployment once unemployed than whites; they are therefore likely to work less time during a particular period than whites. This fact makes the hourly wage rate a more conservative measure of racial inequality in earnings.

Blacks' wages, like overall wages in the United States, stagnated in the mid-1970s. The wages of black men, especially those of young black men, actually fell from 1975 through the late 1980s. These trends led to a stalling of black-white wage convergence since the 1970s and, on some dimensions, relative losses through the 1980s.

Hourly earnings for most race and sex groups declined from the late 1980s to about 1994 (see Figure 5). White women saw their hourly earnings remain relatively constant during this period, and black women's earnings began to rise earlier, around 1991. Hourly earnings then began to rise for all groups in 1996, just as the economic boom began to take hold. Indeed, wages of black men rose fairly rapidly, from about $10.50 per hour in 1996 to nearly $12 per hour in 1999, nearly a 15 percent gain. Black women also experienced steady wage gains and saw them start to rise earlier than those of black men. Black women's wage gains began at the end of the early 1990s recession in 1994 and increased by nearly $2 to $10 per hour by 2000.

Despite these wage gains made by black men and women over the 1990s, in 2000 the racial gap in earnings still remained. For women, the racial gap remained fairly constant from the early to the mid-1990s at about $2 per hour, but declined somewhat to nearly $1.75 per hour by 2000. So, over the 1990s some progress was made in reducing racial earnings inequality for women. However, the racial gap in earnings for men remained as large in 2000 (at nearly $4 per hour) as it was in 1988, despite the significant wage gains made by black men in the late 1990s.

In fact, the gap was likely much bigger. As noted earlier, the hourly wage rate is a conservative measure of racial wage inequality because it does not take into account earnings that accrue from additional hours worked. And blacks work fewer hours per year than whites in large part because blacks experience more bouts of joblessness that last a significantly longer time than those of whites. Thus, other earnings measures such as annual earnings are likely to provide a gloomier picture of racial inequality than that shown here.

But the degree of racial inequality in hourly earnings shown above is underestimated for other reasons as well. This is because the hourly earnings are only measured for those in the labor force who were employed. A significant share of black men (nearly 5 percent) who were incarcerated during this time (see section on incarceration) and a large and growing fraction of black men who were not in the labor force (but not incarcerated) were missing from these data. Had these men been included in the data presented here, they would likely have driven black men's median hourly earnings downward. This is because the characteristics of those who are incarcerated and not in the labor force—such as being young, disproportionately high school dropouts, and so on—suggest that these men would likely earn wages closer to the bottom of blacks' wage distribution if they became employed. This factor would significantly increase the racial gap in earnings between back men and white men.[15]

Similarly, among women, there is a racial difference in the composition of those not in the labor force that

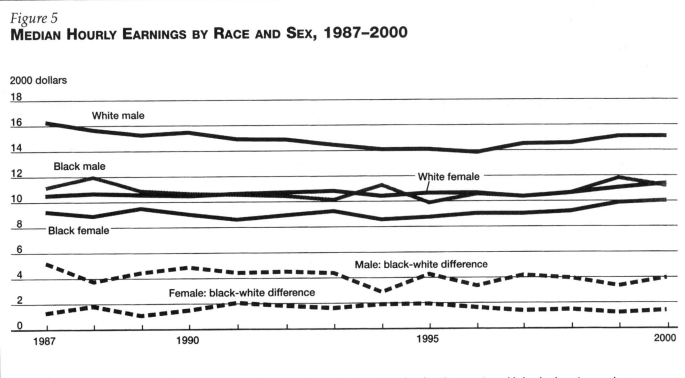

Figure 5
MEDIAN HOURLY EARNINGS BY RACE AND SEX, 1987–2000

Note: Earnings are for workers ages 18 to 64 who were not in school. The median is shown rather than the mean to avoid skewing by extreme values.
Source: Author's estimates using the Current Population Survey.

leads to an underestimation of the racial differences in hourly earnings. Among white women, those out of the labor force are disproportionately married women in high-income households (relative to black women).[16] Relative to white women, black women who are out of the labor force are disproportionately poor women with children (and this was truer before the passage of the Personal Responsibility and Work Opportunity Reconciliation Act of 1996, or PRWORA, which put time limits on welfare receipt). Because such black women would likely earn significantly lower wages than such white women if both entered the labor force, the true racial gap in earnings is wider than that shown here. These same factors also apply to the interpretation of employment-to-population figures shown earlier for men and women; the racial difference in employment between whites and blacks is likely understated because of the high incarceration and labor force dropout rates of black men and the racial differences in the composition of women not in the labor force.

Many explanations of the racial gap in employment and earnings have been offered. These can be most conveniently organized into supply- and demand-side explanations. Supply-side explanations refer to the characteristics, behaviors, and choices of the individuals themselves, while demand-side explanations include the characteristics, behaviors, and choices of employers.

The most prominent supply-side explanations include skills and education, cultural or urban underclass behavior, crime, and—in the case of women—government dependency. The skills and education argument holds that blacks have accumulated less education, fewer skills, and less productive social networks than whites. This, combined with observations that skill requirements for jobs are quickly rising in the modern economy, suggests a persistent racial gap in employment and earnings. However, though education and skills explain a large chunk of these differences as should be expected, even when education and skills are taken into account, blacks are still relatively less likely to be employed and are likely to earn lower wages than whites.[17]

The urban underclass hypothesis argues that blacks, especially those who are poor, are more likely than others to exhibit qualities that are unattractive to employers. These "soft skills" include low motivation and aspirations and "ghetto" styles of dress, presentation, and language. These kinds of behaviors are argued to be products of living in neighborhoods that are characterized by extreme poverty and racial concentration, and that are typically isolated from mainstream society. Blacks are more likely than others to grow up and live in such neighborhoods, and thus these behaviors are learned and reinforced through contact with neighborhood peers.

These same neighborhood effects are argued to extend to criminality and welfare dependence among blacks, especially young blacks. Poor neighborhoods that also have high concentrations of criminal activity such as petty drug dealing serve as employment alternatives to the formal labor market, especially for young black men. The landmark study of sociologist William Julius Wilson documents that poor, jobless neighborhoods also have high concentrations of welfare use, so much so that such use is seen as the norm and thus influences young women's decisions to choose welfare over work, at least until welfare reform in 1996.[18]

On the demand side, prominent explanations of blacks' employment problems include racial discrimination, spatial mismatch (discussed below), aggregate demand, and job-competition hypotheses, among others. The racial discrimination argument holds that employers discriminate against blacks in hiring and/or in wages either through statistical discrimination or racial animus. Statistical discrimination refers to employers' use of real or perceived information about groups when making hiring or recruiting decisions. If, for example, employers view blacks as a group as less desirable workers—as untrustworthy, unmotivated, or prone to crime—employers may be reluctant to hire any individual black that applies, even if the black individual is the most qualified. This is particularly true if employers cannot access full information about individuals. Or employers may use recruitment methods that bias the applicant pool toward nonblacks; examples of these include advertising for workers in community newspapers based in white neighborhoods, or recruiting through white employees.

The final demand-side explanations are closely linked. The aggregate demand hypothesis states that blacks' employability and earnings are much more sensitive to the strength of the overall economy than that of other groups, as presented above. This is because blacks, in the eyes of employers, may be a least-preferred group of workers on average. If this is true, then blacks are likely to be hired at greater rates only when there is a tightening in the labor market, which occurs when the economy is in a boom cycle and there are fewer workers available for employment. Similarly, the job-competition hypothesis holds that other demographic groups, in particular women and immigrants, compete with blacks for employment and are preferred by employers. In this scenario, blacks are pushed lower down the hiring ladder as a consequence of these labor substitutes and employer preferences.[19]

In sum, the economic expansion during the late 1990s had different effects on different groups. The expansion drew both black and white women into the labor force, increased their employment, and—at least in the late 1990s—increased employment faster for black women than for white women. It also led to increases in both groups' real earnings, with earning gains coming slightly faster for black women than for white women at the end of the decade. For men, especially black men, however, such unambiguous improvements were not realized. This same economic expansion did not significantly increase the employment of white or black men. This is particularly troubling for black men since so many of them were out of the labor force over the 1980s and 1990s. The expansion did raise the wages of employed black men, though not enough to close the racial gap in wages.

RISING FAMILY INCOME

The following examination of African Americans' employment and earnings trends suggests that blacks' family income should have risen modestly over the 1990s. This is because wages and salaries make up roughly three-fourths of total family income and, as just seen, these rose steadily over the 1990s. Family income is an important part of understanding racial inequality because it is the most common measure of the nation's standard of living.[20] It reflects all income resources available to the family—wages and salaries, interest and dividends, government transfer payments, alimony and child support, and disability payments.

Historically, median family income levels have followed trends in the national economy. After World War II, when the economy expanded rapidly for nearly 20 years, family income grew steadily as well. From 1947 to about 1959, median income grew by about 40 percent and then grew about another 40 percent between 1959 and 1969. However, after 1973 when the oil-shock-

induced recession took hold, year-to-year increases in family income came to a halt. Family income stagnated between 1973 and 1979, rising only somewhat during the economic recovery of the early 1980s.

Black family incomes, relative to those of whites, remained virtually unchanged from 1949 to the mid-1960s. However, because of the civil rights movement, antidiscrimination laws, affirmative action programs, and a tight labor market, blacks made real gains relative to whites in family income from the late 1960s to the mid-1970s. From this point, with the national recession firmly rooted, black family income gains relative to whites stalled and on many accounts reversed through the mid-1980s.[21]

Two clear patterns emerge in median family income during the 1990s. First, the median family income of whites and blacks over this period followed trends in the general economy (see Figure 6). Median family income for whites and blacks rose modestly during the economic expansion of the late 1980s and declined somewhat during the early 1990s recession. However, blacks and whites made strong gains in family income during the late 1990s economic expansion. Both whites' and blacks' family income was at its highest level at the end of the expansion in 2000. From 1994 to 2000, whites' family income grew from nearly $45,000 to $53,000, a gain of $8,000, or about 17 percent. Blacks' family income grew over this period at an even stronger rate, 24 percent, from nearly $25,000 to $31,000, a gain of about $6,000.

Second, relative to whites, blacks' family income levels still remained relatively low from 1980 to 2000.

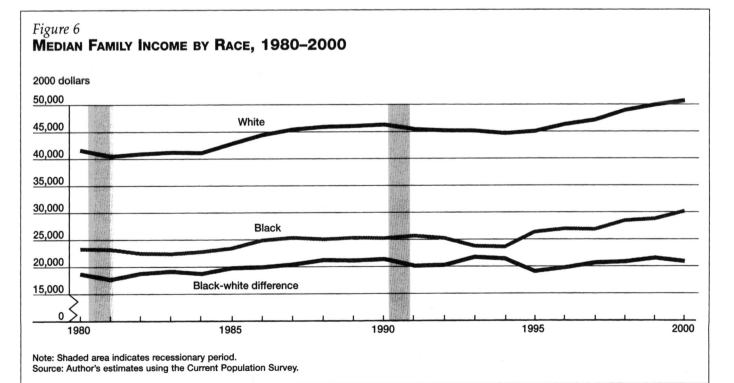

Figure 6
MEDIAN FAMILY INCOME BY RACE, 1980–2000

Note: Shaded area indicates recessionary period.
Source: Author's estimates using the Current Population Survey.

Over this period, the median family income of blacks never surpassed $35,000. To put this number in perspective, median family income in the United States in 2000 was about $52,000, or about $17,000 higher than the median figure for blacks. Alternatively put, blacks' median family income level of $31,000 in 2000 was about the median family income level in the United States in 1965 (using constant 2000 dollars).[22] Moreover, the racial gap in family income hovered consistently around $20,000 over this period.

The black/white family income ratio increased from 0.54 in 1990 to 0.58 in 2000. This suggests that blacks made up some ground relative to whites in family income during the last economic expansion. However, an examination of the absolute difference in income between blacks and whites, which indicates the true resource difference between the races, shows that these relative gains disappear. The racial difference in family income remained at virtually the same level at the end of the expansion in 2000 as it was at the beginning of the decade (about $21,500), despite strong gains by blacks in family income over this period. In fact, the racial gap in family income widened somewhat during the peak period of the economic expansion, from 1995 to 2000.

Of course, the difference in annual earnings between blacks and whites is a major explanation of the racial gap in family income. But so too is the racial difference in family structure. Blacks are less likely to be married and more likely to have families headed by females than are whites. Thus, black families have fewer members contributing to family income than do white families, and this difference contributes to part of the racial gap in earnings. This factor has become more important in recent years as the share of wives' earnings in family income has risen. In 1970, about 27 percent of family income came from wives' earnings; by 2000 this percentage had risen to nearly 34 percent.[23] To the extent that black families are disproportionately headed by females, these factors are likely to influence the racial gap in family income.

Alternatively, the absolute growth in the racial gap in family income in the late 1990s could be related to differences in growth in family income for different household types—two-parent and female-headed families (see Figure 7). The greatest influence on the growth of the racial gap in family income in the late 1990s came from racial differences in family income among married (two-parent) families. The racial gap in family income for this group fluctuated between $10,000 and $12,000 between 1985 and 1992, before rising to nearly $14,000 in 2000. Interestingly, while this racial gap declined somewhat during the economic expansion in the late 1980s, it rose rather dramatically during the economic boom of the late 1990s for reasons that are not well understood.

The racial gap in family income among female-headed families declined somewhat during the late 1990s. This gap remained fairly constant at about $8,000 between 1980 and 1994. Thereafter, the racial gap declined precipitously from about $8,000 in 1994 to just under $6,000 in 2000.

A possible explanation for the rise in the racial gap in family income for two-parent households is the role that income from financial assets plays in overall family income. Family income comes from many sources—wages and salaries, government transfer payments, other business income, and income from investments—

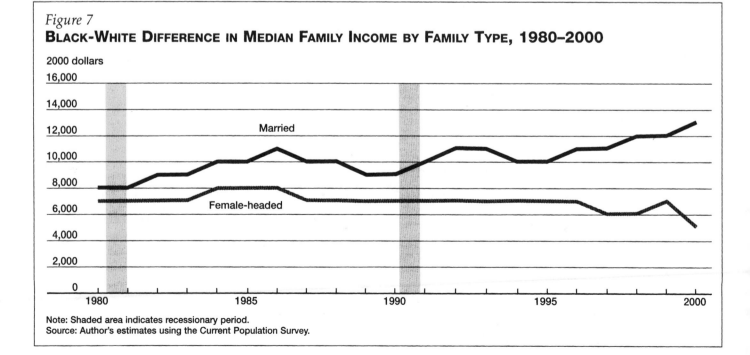

Figure 7
BLACK-WHITE DIFFERENCE IN MEDIAN FAMILY INCOME BY FAMILY TYPE, 1980–2000

Note: Shaded area indicates recessionary period.
Source: Author's estimates using the Current Population Survey.

although wages and salaries make up the lion's share. The economic boom of the 1990s was characterized by a run-up of stock market prices. Thus, some that were heavily invested in the stock market during this period realized significant income gains as a result of either rising dividend payments or capital gains income from the selling of shares of rising stocks. Whites are more heavily invested in the stock market than are blacks, as are two-parent or married families relative to other types of families. Therefore, racial differences in income-generating assets are also a plausible explanation of the rise in the racial gap in family income observed between two-parent households in the late 1990s.

What factors explain the decline in the racial gap in family income among female-headed families during the late 1990s? One plausible hypothesis is the role of welfare reform legislation. PRWORA effectively ended the federal guarantee of cash assistance to poor and needy families and imposed stringent work requirements and time limits on welfare recipients. Black mothers are disproportionately on welfare compared with their white counterparts. But since the mid-1990s, welfare caseloads declined dramatically, and employment rates among current and former recipients, as well as single female heads of household more broadly, rose substantially. Indeed, the number of adults on welfare in the United States declined by a record 30 percent between August 1996 and September 1998, to the lowest level in 30 years. The research of economists Rebecca Blank and Robert Schoeni indicates that about 50 percent of this decline was due to economic factors such as the tight labor market at the time, and

nearly 40 percent was due to policy changes in the rules governing welfare receipt.[24] Furthermore, during the late 1990s, the gains accruing to welfare recipients from employment generally seemed to outweigh the costs, and thus incentives for them to gain employment seemed strong.[25]

Analyzing the percentage of family income derived from public assistance between 1980 and 2000 reveals interesting trends (see Figure 8). First, as expected, black female-headed families had the highest percentage of family income coming from welfare in any year. In the early 1980s, 35 percent to 37 percent of income among black female-headed households derived from public assistance, while the percentage among equivalent whites hovered around 15 percent.

Second, the percentage of family income derived from public assistance began to decline slightly before welfare reform legislation, especially among all black families and among white and black female-headed families. However, the decline in these percentages, especially among black female-headed families, accelerated after 1996 probably because of welfare reform legislation and a strong economy. Welfare reform put pressure on mothers to enter the labor force if they received public assistance monies or to avoid using public assistance if they were already in the labor force. Economic conditions at the time enabled single mothers to secure employment that paid wages superior to income received from welfare. From 1994 to 2000, the share of income from public assistance declined by 20 percentage points for black female-headed families. The decline for

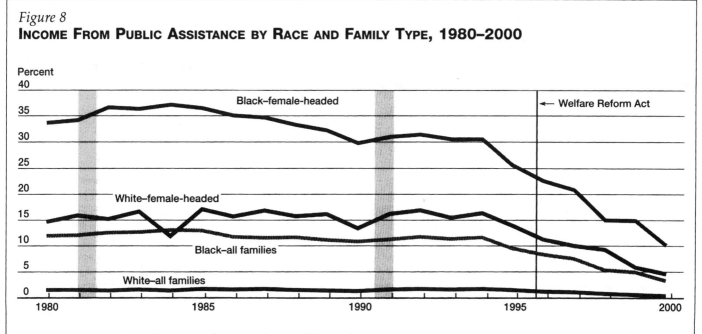

Figure 8
INCOME FROM PUBLIC ASSISTANCE BY RACE AND FAMILY TYPE, 1980–2000

Note: Assistance includes Aid to Families with Dependent Children (AFDC) and Temporary Assistance for Needy Families (TANF). Shaded area indicates recessionary period.
Source: Author's estimates using the Current Population Survey.

white female-headed families was about 11 percentage points. This occurred despite the fact that black welfare recipients were shown to have a much harder time entering employment (or exiting the welfare roles) than white welfare recipients after welfare reform.[26]

Third, as a result of these trends, the black-white difference in the percentage of income that female-headed families derived from public assistance was significantly reduced over this period. This difference declined by 10 percentage points, from nearly 15 percentage points in 1994 to 5 percentage points in 2000. Thus, the data suggest that to the extent that welfare leavers over the 1990s gained employment with wages higher than welfare payments, the racial gap in family income among this group was likely to decline. This is because black single mothers received a much greater share of income from public assistance than did their white counterparts, but the decline in this percentage over the 1990s was much greater for blacks than for whites.

FALLING POVERTY

The rise in blacks' employment, earnings, and family income over the 1990s suggests that their poverty rates should have declined as well during this period of economic robustness. The federal poverty rate,

developed 40 years ago (see Box 5), can be used for this analysis.

However, it should be noted that this official approach to measuring poverty has been widely criticized. Some argue that the rate fails to reflect changes in consumption and spending since the early 1960s, as ideas of material needs in the nation have changed rapidly. Some also argue that the current approach to measuring poverty fails to include noncash contributions or resources that clearly increase the buying power of the poor, such as food stamps; welfare income; and, more important, income from the Earned Income Tax Credit. Finally, some also argue that the official measure neglects important differences in the cost of living. Living costs vary wildly from one metropolitan area to the next, between urban and rural areas, and even across regions.

Despite these concerns, the federal poverty rate is an absolute measure that provides a uniform and consistent way to measure deprivation in the United States and how it changes over time.

The poverty rate, like family income, has historically fluctuated with the overall state of the economy. With the persistent economic growth that followed World War II and federal antipoverty efforts begun in the 1960s, the poverty rate fell from about 22 percent in 1959 to about 11 percent in 1973. However, unlike family income, the poverty rate has not improved significantly since 1973. As a result of the recession of the late

---

Box 5
HOW IS THE FEDERAL POVERTY LINE DETERMINED?

The federal poverty standards are set by determining a baseline income needed for individuals or families to enjoy a reasonable living standard. For the most part, the income baseline varies by the size of the family, with higher baselines for larger families. For example, in 2000, a single person was considered poor if his or her income fell below $9,214, while a mother with two children was considered poor if her annual income was less than $14,269. People or families with incomes below these thresholds are considered poor. The poverty rate is the percentage of the population that falls below the poverty threshold.

The poverty threshold does not vary geographically but is updated annually for inflation using the Consumer Price Index. The official poverty definition counts money income before taxes and does not include capital gains or noncash benefits (such as public housing, Medicaid, and food stamps). Poverty is not defined for people in military barracks or institutional group quarters, or for unrelated individuals under age 15 (such as foster children). These individuals are excluded from the poverty universe.

The federal poverty standards were determined in 1964 with the assistance of economist Mollie Orshansky, who worked for the Social Security Administration. Orshansky began with the price of the Department of Agriculture's Econo-

my Food Plan, which was, according to the department, the cheapest plan that still provided adequate nutrition. Since the average family in the 1960s spent one-third of its income on food (the other two-thirds on rent, utilities, clothing, transportation, and other household expenditures), Orshansky multiplied that price by three and called it a poverty threshold.

Orshansky's purpose was not to introduce a new general measure of poverty in the United States. Instead, her intent was to develop a measure to assess the relative risks of low economic status (or, more broadly, differentials in opportunity) among different demographic groups of families with children. However, her work coincided with the announcement by the Johnson administration of a War on Poverty in January 1964. The Office of Economic Opportunity was being set up to address poverty and adopted Orshansky's poverty thresholds as a working definition of poverty for statistical, planning, and budget purposes in May 1965. In 1969, the Bureau of the Budget designated the somewhat-revised poverty thresholds as the federal government's official statistical definition of poverty.[1]

Reference
1. Patricia Ruggles, *Drawing the Line: Alternative Poverty Measures and Their Implications for Public Policy* (Washington, DC: Urban Institute Press, 1990).

1970s and early 1980s, the national poverty rate increased from 12 percent in 1978 to nearly 15 percent in 1983, before declining to 12.5 percent in 1989 with the economic expansion. However, by the end of the economic boom of the 1990s, the poverty rate had declined only to its 1973 level of 11 percent.[27]

The poverty rate of African Americans has historically been at least two to three times higher than that of whites, and it surpassed the rate for any other racial or ethnic group until the early 1990s, when Hispanic and black poverty rates began to converge. Moreover, blacks' poverty rate has been particularly sensitive to changes in economic conditions. In response to the early 1980s recession, blacks' poverty rate increased from about 30 percent in 1978 to 36 percent in 1983.[28] Did blacks' poverty rate decline over the 1990s, during the strongest economic expansion in 30 years? If so, did it decline enough to reduce the historic racial gap in poverty?

A close analysis of poverty rates by race and family type between 1980 and 2000 reveals that blacks' poverty rate declined absolutely and relative to that of whites during the economic boom of the 1990s, for all families (see Figure 9). Among all black families, the poverty rate declined from a 20-year high of about 40 percent in 1982 and 1993 to 25 percent in 2000. During this period, the poverty rate for white families remained fairly constant, at about 10 percent.

Among female-headed families, the black poverty rate also dropped dramatically over this period, but especially over the late 1990s during the economic boom. From 1990 to 2000, the poverty rate among black female-headed families dropped by 20 percentage points, reaching a 20-year low of 40 percent. While the poverty rate for white female-headed families declined

over this period too, it did so less dramatically. During the 1990s, this poverty rate declined by about 10 percentage points, reaching a 20-year low in 2000 at 25 percent, the same poverty rate for all black families.

The racial difference in the poverty rate declined during this period for both all families and those headed by females. The racial gap in poverty among all families declined by about 10 percentage points (or 37 percent) over the 1990s, while the gap among female-headed families dropped by about 8 percentage points (or 35 percent) over this period. Though not as impressive, the black/white poverty ratio for all families declined from 3.6 in 1990 to 3.2 in 2000, a drop of about 11 percent; the ratio for female-headed families declined from 1.7 in 1990 to 1.6 in 2000, a drop of 6 percent.

Second, as expected, the poverty rate of blacks (either all families or those headed by females) is much more sensitive to economic fluctuations that that of their white counterparts. This is partly due to the fact that blacks' labor-market outcomes are much more sensitive to economic conditions for reasons discussed previously. Still, these facts remain interesting when viewed in relation to whites' poverty rate over time. Indeed, despite peaks in the economy in 1989 and 2000, whites' poverty rate for all families remained relatively unchanged at about 10 percent over this 20-year period. To a lesser extent, the same pattern was true for the poverty rate of white families headed by females, but that poverty rate declined rather sharply with the economic boom of the late 1990s, from about 32 percent between 1980 and 1992 to nearly 25 percent in 2000. Among all black families and those headed by females, poverty rates declined significantly during the economic boom of the 1990s.

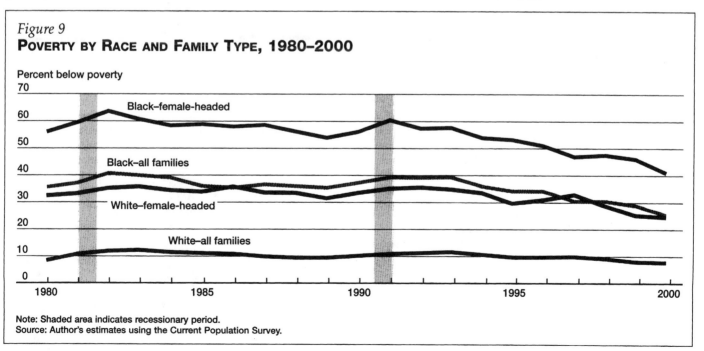

Figure 9
POVERTY BY RACE AND FAMILY TYPE, 1980–2000

Note: Shaded area indicates recessionary period.
Source: Author's estimates using the Current Population Survey.

Clearly, these trends indicate substantial progress in lowering blacks' economic deprivation over the 1990s. The data suggest that strong economic growth plays an important role in reducing poverty among those for whom poverty has been high and persistent. One caveat in interpreting these data is that the poverty rates especially for blacks are likely to be downwardly biased, painting a rosier picture of black progress in overcoming poverty than what actually occurred. This is because, as noted earlier, the poverty rate calculation does not include the incarcerated who, if included, would likely be counted as poor. Their inclusion would drive up the black poverty rate, especially that of all families, since a disproportionate number of the incarcerated are men.

What is alarming is that, despite the strongest growth in the economy in 30 years, black poverty remained high at an absolute level. In 2000, at the height of the economic boom, nearly a quarter of black families were poor and nearly 40 percent of black female-headed families were poor. Since the economic boom of the 1990s was a rare event, extreme black poverty is likely to remain a permanent feature of American social life in the absence of any other intervention.

Still, the absolute decline of the black poverty rate in the United States over the 1990s likely had positive spillover effects. Beyond falling poverty rates, the United States experienced significant declines in the number and fraction of people who lived in high-poverty neighborhoods over the 1990s. High-poverty neighborhoods are defined as those where more than 40 percent of the residents are living in poverty. The research of Paul Jargowsky showed that, over the 1970s and 1980s, the number of people living in high-poverty neighborhoods doubled. This was especially true for blacks, who had a higher share of their population living in high-poverty neighborhoods than any other racial or ethnic group by 1990. The chance that a poor black child lived in a high-poverty area increased from 25 percent in 1980 to 33 percent in 1990.[29]

Some have argued that the poor may benefit from having poor neighbors because they may develop and share coping strategies and draw on and produce neighborhood networks that help them manage in impoverished conditions. However, research by sociologists Greg Duncan, Jeanne Brooks-Gunn, and others clearly demonstrates that the cost of poor people living side by side and isolated from others exceeds any possible benefits that might derive from these living arrangements. There is now a reasonable degree of certainty that the concentration of poor families and children in high-poverty neighborhoods compounds or even causes the problems faced by the poor. Consistent with this interpretation, crime, dropping out of high school, and joblessness, among other problems, are disproportionately experienced in these neighborhoods because of a lack of resources, institutions, or role models; social isolation and discrimination; or all of the above.[30]

Consistent with the falling poverty rate in the United States over the 1990s, the number of people living in high-poverty neighborhoods declined significantly. In his recent work, Paul Jargowsky estimates the decline at 2.5 million between 1990 and 2000 (from about 10.3 million to 7.9 million). Moreover, the number of neighborhoods in the United States that are characterized by high poverty declined from 3,417 to 2,510.[31]

While the falling poverty rate certainly contributed to these declines, the falling black poverty rate contributed disproportionately since blacks are overrepresented in these neighborhoods. Jargowsky's recent research also documents that the share of the poor living in high-poverty neighborhoods also declined over the 1990s and that this decline was strongest for African Americans. Whether the decline in high-poverty neighborhoods was caused by residents in these areas gaining more income or by the migration of the poor out of these areas is an open question. The decline in such neighborhoods is definitely good news. But whether the decline will continue when the poverty rate begins to rise again, especially for African Americans, remains uncertain.

LIMITED GAINS IN WEALTH ACCUMULATION

Most researchers interested in assessing the degree of racial economic inequality in American society have focused on measures of income, earnings, and poverty. Recently, however, researchers have broadened their focus to include wealth. Wealth is arguably an important measure of economic well-being, and of racial differences in economic well-being in particular. To the extent that racial differences in wealth are much greater than differences in measures such as income, the extent of racial inequality between blacks and whites is likely to have been underestimated and policy efforts directed at closing the gap are likely to have been insufficient.

Unlike income, which measures flows of money over a set period of time, wealth is a stock of owned assets. Income does allow individuals and families to purchase goods and services, thereby helping determine a standard of living. But wealth signifies the command of financial resources that individuals or families have accumulated over a lifetime, along with those assets that have been inherited across generations. In the long run, individuals and families accumulate wealth to finance education, purchase a house, start a small business, or finance retirement. In the short run, wealth, particularly those liquid financial assets such as checking and savings accounts, can help families cope with financial emergencies related to unemployment or illness, something that income alone cannot do. Wealth, when combined with income, can also widen opportunities to secure a better life for individuals, families, and their children. This is because the accumulation of wealth opens opportunities to enhance income through investment. Thus, wealth is arguably a more encompassing measure of economic well-being.

Wealth distribution in the United States is very unequal. The wealthiest 1 percent of all households control about 38 percent of national wealth, with the bottom 80 percent of households holding about 17 percent. This inequality in wealth is even greater for stock ownership. The top 1 percent of stockholders hold almost 50 percent of all stock value, with the bottom 80 percent owning about 4 percent. This is because most individuals in the United States do not have a meaningful stake in the stock market. In 1998, 48 percent of households in the United States owned stock, while about 36 percent held stock worth $5,000 or more.[32]

Recent studies of wealth and assets by sociologists Melvin Oliver and Harold Shapiro and others have documented large racial differences. Moreover, almost all studies show that the racial differences in wealth are much larger than those for typical earnings or income measures. This is true even in those studies that match blacks and whites on the basis of educational attainment. For example, in the late 1980s, Oliver and Shapiro showed that the median net worth for a white person with a college degree was about $75,000, while it was roughly $17,500 for a black person with a college degree—a difference of nearly $60,000. This racial gap in wealth is even bigger for the population as a whole. During this period, the racial gap in net worth was estimated to be about $82,000.[33]

There are a number of explanations for the racial gap in wealth. Some, like Oliver and Shapiro, argue that it is heavily influenced by public policy. The enslavement of African Americans, the barring of blacks from certain occupations, the erection of racial housing covenants through local ordinances, and federal policy on homesteading and homeownership—which in many instances excluded blacks—have all reduced blacks' accumulation of wealth. So, too, has private market discrimination against blacks in labor, credit, and capital markets. This discrimination has lowered blacks' earnings and ownership rates of assets such as houses and businesses below what would be expected given their economic or human capital profile. This setback has disadvantaged blacks cumulatively by reducing intergenerational transfers of wealth, which serve to build wealth within families and racial groups.[34]

Others have examined racial differences in personal and family characteristics and other factors to explain the racial gap in earnings. Economists Francine Blau and John Graham have shown that racial differences in income, family structure, residential location, and education explain a small portion of the racial gap in wealth. So, too, do racial differences in the composition of wealth and in the rates of return on assets. For example, whites are much more likely than blacks to have their wealth held in stocks, which historically have had higher rates of return than typical savings accounts. Blacks, on the other hand, are much more likely than whites to have their wealth held in savings accounts. Even so, racial differences in the composition of wealth and the components' rates of return explain a small portion of the racial gap in wealth. In fact, according to Blau and Graham, when all of the above factors are taken into account, about three-quarters of the racial gap in wealth remains unexplained.[35]

Did the economic boom of the 1990s, which saw stock prices rise to historic levels, widen or narrow the racial gap in wealth? Either effect would seem plausible. Blacks are less invested in the stock market than whites, so it would be reasonable to expect that the racial gap widened. On the other hand, over the 1990s black homeownership rates rose significantly for a variety of reasons: rising income, lower mortgage rates, greater enforcement of the Community Reinvestment Act, and federal policy directed at increasing minority homeownership rates. For example, in 1990 about 40 percent of blacks owned their own homes, compared with 69 percent of whites. By 2000, about 47 percent of blacks owned homes compared with 74 percent of whites. Put another way, from 1990 to 2000, the black/white homeownership ratio increased from 0.58 to 0.64.[36] Given rising black homeownership rates both absolutely and relative to whites, and given that for most Americans the largest share of wealth is held in home equity, it is reasonable to expect that the racial gap in wealth could have narrowed over the 1990s.

Median net worth increased for both blacks and whites over the 1990s (see Figure 10). But it increased more for whites than for blacks, so that the racial difference in net worth was much bigger in 1999 than 1989. Indeed, blacks' net worth increased very modestly over the 1990s (by $1,000 on average), while that for whites increased by $19,000 on average. Thus, over this period the racial gap in net worth increased by about $18,000, or by 32 percent. An examination of the change in the black/white ratio of net worth leads to the same general conclusion. From 1989 to 1999, the black/white net worth ratio decreased from 0.096 to 0.085.

What are the factors that influenced the rise in the racial gap in wealth over the 1990s? Data on the composition of total wealth by race provide some insight into this question (see Figure 11). The composition of blacks' and whites' wealth is very different. Whites' wealth is disproportionately held in financial assets. For example, in 1989, before the run-up in stock prices in the late 1990s, 10 percent of whites' wealth was held

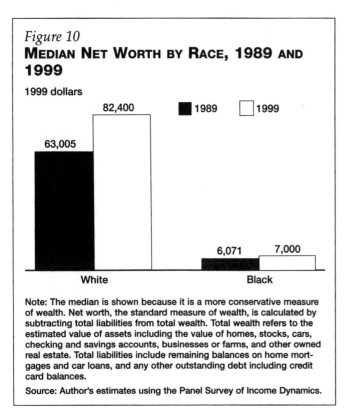

Figure 10

MEDIAN NET WORTH BY RACE, 1989 AND 1999

1999 dollars

1989 ■   1999 □

White: 63,005 (1989), 82,400 (1999)
Black: 6,071 (1989), 7,000 (1999)

Note: The median is shown because it is a more conservative measure of wealth. Net worth, the standard measure of wealth, is calculated by subtracting total liabilities from total wealth. Total wealth refers to the estimated value of assets including the value of homes, stocks, cars, checking and savings accounts, businesses or farms, and other owned real estate. Total liabilities include remaining balances on home mortgages and car loans, and any other outstanding debt including credit card balances.

Source: Author's estimates using the Panel Survey of Income Dynamics.

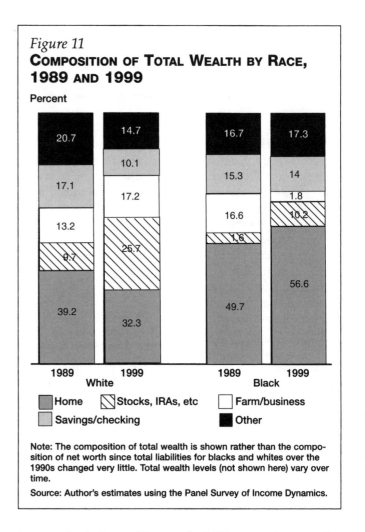

Figure 11

COMPOSITION OF TOTAL WEALTH BY RACE, 1989 AND 1999

Percent

White 1989: Other 20.7, Savings/checking 17.1, Farm/business 13.2, Stocks/IRAs 9.7, Home 39.2
White 1999: Other 14.7, Savings/checking 10.1, Farm/business 17.2, Stocks/IRAs 25.7, Home 32.3
Black 1989: Other 16.7, Savings/checking 15.3, Farm/business 16.6, Stocks/IRAs 1.6, Home 49.7
Black 1999: Other 17.3, Savings/checking 14, Farm/business 1.8, Stocks/IRAs 10.2, Home 56.6

■ Home   ▨ Stocks, IRAs, etc   □ Farm/business
▨ Savings/checking   ■ Other

Note: The composition of total wealth is shown rather than the composition of net worth since total liabilities for blacks and whites over the 1990s changed very little. Total wealth levels (not shown here) vary over time.

Source: Author's estimates using the Panel Survey of Income Dynamics.

in stocks and other related assets, while the comparable figure for blacks was 2 percent.

On the other hand, blacks' wealth is disproportionately held in the value of their homes. In 1989, 50 percent of blacks' wealth was held in home value, while the comparable percentage for whites was 40 percent. Among blacks, this percentage increased to 57 percent in 1999. An alternative way to examine the extent to which blacks' wealth is disproportionately held in home value is to measure the percentage of net worth that is made up of home equity (home value minus mortgage balance). The data (not shown) reveal that in 1989, 43 percent of blacks' net worth was composed of home equity, while the comparable figure for whites was 32 percent. This gap actually increased during the 1990s. By 1999, 46 percent of blacks' net worth was composed of home equity, while the comparable figure for whites dropped to 24 percent.

Blacks also have a relatively large share of wealth in savings and checking accounts. The higher unemployment rates, longer unemployment spells, and greater income uncertainty faced by blacks relative to others in the labor market may increase their demand for liquid assets. However, rates of return on these types of assets are much lower than those on stock or bond markets and thus may further disadvantage blacks in long-run wealth accumulation.

The factors that influenced the rise in total wealth over the 1990s were different for whites and blacks. The data for whites suggest that the major source of the

increase in their wealth over the 1990s came from stocks and other related assets. In 1989, about 10 percent of whites' total wealth was in the form of stocks and other financial assets; by 1999, this percentage had increased to 26 percent. Surely, the rise in the value of stocks during the economic boom of the 1990s had much to do with this change. Interestingly, although home prices rose fairly strongly during the 1990s and although nearly 75 percent of whites owned their own homes, home value as a percentage of whites' wealth declined over this period. This suggests that the increase in wealth generated by the rapid increase in stock value over the 1990s exceeded any increase in home equity that whites saw contribute to their overall wealth.

In contrast, the data suggest that the moderate rise in blacks' wealth over the 1990s was fueled by home value. In 1989, about 50 percent of blacks' wealth came from their homes' value, and by 1999 this percentage had increased to 57 percent. Blacks' increasing homeownership rates over this period, coupled with rising home prices, contributed to this increase. The data also suggest that had blacks' been more invested in the stock market in the 1990s, their total wealth would have increased substantially more than it did over this period.

Thus, the analysis of racial inequality in wealth over the 1990s suggests two things. One is that the pattern of racial inequality over the next decade is likely to look different than the pattern seen during the 1990s. The prime contributor to the rise in racial inequality in wealth over the 1990s appears to be racial differences in participation in the stock market. But the popping of the stock market bubble in 2000 must have decreased total wealth, especially for those heavily invested in the stock market. Thus, the drop of stock market prices in 2000 and the closing of the racial gap in homeownership rates suggest that the racial gap in wealth is likely to be lower over the coming decade.

The other thing that is clear from the data is that racial inequality in wealth grew over this period, despite blacks' increased homeownership rates. The racial wealth gap will persist, and given the long-run importance of stocks and other related financial assets to the formation of wealth in the United States, the continued racial difference in the participation in the stock market is likely to perpetuate racial inequality in wealth.

GROWING STABILITY IN FAMILY STRUCTURE

Changing economic conditions clearly influence economic outcomes of individuals, but they can also influence social decisions, such as those pertaining to marriage and childbearing. Yet the effect of economic conditions on these decisions is sometimes ambiguous. For example, better economic opportunities such as those that came about in the 1990s may influence some people's decisions to marry and have children because greater economic security enhances one's ability to provide. For others, especially women, better economic conditions may mean that leaving a marriage or remaining single becomes more viable. What effect did the period of sustained economic opportunity in the 1990s have on African Americans' family structure?

Before proceeding, it is important to consider that notions of family as a principal unit of social organization are virtually universal, but the specific definition or form of families, and the extent to which such family types are socially acceptable, vary widely across countries and cultures and time. After a prolonged period in the United States in which the nuclear family was the main form of family structure, family and living arrangements have undergone serious changes. For example, from 1960 to 1980, the marriage rates for white men and women fell from 70 percent and 67 percent, respectively, to 65 percent and 60 percent. The decline among African Americans was even more dra-

matic, falling from about 60 percent for black men and women in 1960 to 49 percent and 45 percent, respectively, in 1980.[37] Did this trend continue during the economic boom of the 1990s, and was the decline still more pronounced for blacks than for whites?

The marriage rates for both blacks and whites declined over the 1980s, but declined only for whites over the 1990s. Between 1980 and 1990, the proportion married declined for whites by 5 percentage points or by about 7 percent, and for blacks, by about 7 percentage points or 15 percent. Given the faster rate of decline of black than white marriages over the 1980s, the racial difference in this rate grew by 3 percentage points, or by 13 percent.

The decline in the percentage of individuals married continued over the 1990s, but only for whites (see Figure 12). The rate declined for whites by about 2 percentage points, or by about 3 percent. The percentage of blacks who were married remained virtually the same in 2000 as in 1990 at about 40 percent. As a result, the black-white difference in the percentage married dropped slightly over the 1990s by slightly more than 2 percentage points to near 1980 levels. Thus, in 2000, the percentage of whites who were married reached an historic low, while the percentage of blacks who were married stabilized after nearly five decades of decline.

Since the findings for blacks concerning marriage represent a major departure from historic trends, it is helpful to look at data for those ages 20 to 34 to examine this question in more detail. This age range corresponds more closely with the period of entry into marriage (or first marriage) and thus may shed more light on the extent to which the stabilization in the percentage married for blacks occurred.

The data for this age group confirm the trends observed for those ages 20 to 64. The only major difference in these trends is that the percentage married for both blacks and whites at all three points in time is lower than that for the age group 20 to 64, as should be expected since older individuals are more likely to be married than younger ones. Moreover, in 2000, the racial difference in the percentage married for younger individuals is smaller than that for those ages 20 to 64.

These changes have implications for the living arrangements of children and how such arrangements differ by race (see Figure 13).[38] In contrast to the pattern in the 1980s, the percentage of black children living in female-headed families stabilized over the 1990s, at 51 percent, while the comparable fraction for white children grew by about 3 percentage points, or 17 percent, thus closing slightly the racial gap in female-headed families. For both black and white children, the percentage that lived with married families declined during the 1990s, as it also did during the 1980s, but did so more for whites than for blacks. Indeed, the decline was 6 percentage points (or 7 percent) for whites and 2 percentage points (or 5 percent) for blacks. Finally, for both white and black children, the percentage who lived in other family types, such as with grandparents and in male-headed families, increased over the 1990s as well.

While the rise in the percentage of children in female-headed families could occur through divorce, separations, or deaths of spouses, much of it is being driven by births to unmarried women. Much of the racial difference in the percentage of children living in female-headed families is driven by earlier racial differences in the rate of childbirth between white and black women. In the 1940s, 1950s, and 1960s, the unmarried fertility rate for blacks remained nearly 10 times that for whites. However, since the 1960s, the rate for blacks in most age cohorts has declined, while that for whites has increased. Indeed, by 1995, the unmarried fertility rate for blacks had dropped to 2.6 times that for whites.[39]

The changing patterns of family formation, especially the decline of marriage, suggest that there are changes in macro forces influencing all racial groups' marriage decisions, but especially those of whites over the 1990s. These likely include shifting norms, attitudes, and values regarding marriage and the growing economic independence of women.[40] In addition, there appear to be specific factors associated with the large racial gap in marriage rates between whites and blacks.

A number of well-substantiated hypotheses about racial differences in family formation and marriage have been documented. Some have shown that the peculiar nature of the African American slave experience created and fostered critical differences in family formation between African Americans and whites that have persisted through time. Historian Brenda Steven-

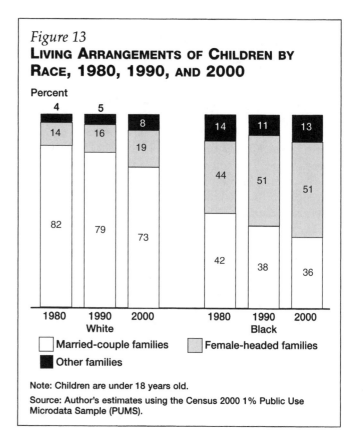

Figure 13
LIVING ARRANGEMENTS OF CHILDREN BY RACE, 1980, 1990, AND 2000

Note: Children are under 18 years old.
Source: Author's estimates using the Census 2000 1% Public Use Microdata Sample (PUMS).

son argues that the brutal effects of slavery on the family forced African Americans to adopt and be open to a variety of forms including extended roles of more distant family members.[41] Others, such as anthropologist Carol Stack, have extended this line of reasoning in the contemporary period by arguing that some poor and working-class African American women share a

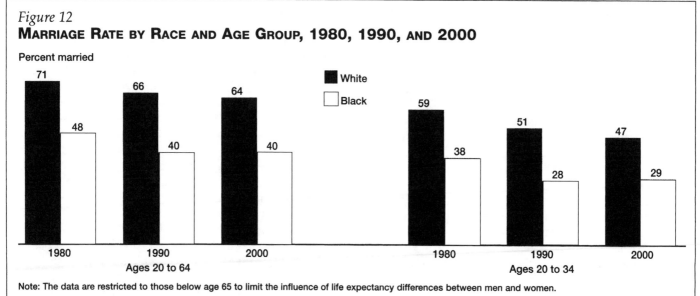

Figure 12
MARRIAGE RATE BY RACE AND AGE GROUP, 1980, 1990, AND 2000

Note: The data are restricted to those below age 65 to limit the influence of life expectancy differences between men and women.
Source: Author's estimates using the Census 2000 5% Public Use Microdata Sample (PUMS).

notion of community-based independence that emphasizes kin-based support networks and long-term partnerships with men, but not necessarily marriage.[42]

Even more contemporaneously, interracial marriage and dating are likely to be associated with lower African American marriage rates, especially those of black women. The growing tendency of black men, relative to black women, to date and marry those of other races may be a factor in the lower marriage rate of black women. For example, the rate at which black men marry white women (the most frequent black male interracial marriage) jumped from about 1.5 percent in 1990 to over 4 percent by 1999. During this period, the interracial marriage rate between black women and white men (the most frequent black female interracial marriage) increased from about 0.8 to 1.8 percent.[43]

Moreover, interracial cohabitation may be influencing these trends as well. Interracial cohabitation rates are rising, and are much higher among black men than among black women. For example, in 1990, about 4.5 percent of black women were cohabiting with white men (the most frequent black female interracial cohabitation type), while 15 percent of black men were cohabiting with white women (the most frequent black male interracial cohabitation type).[44] Given the continuing liberalization of racial attitudes in this recent period, it is expected that such unions are likely to have increased over the 1990s. Surprisingly, although interracial marriage and cohabitation increased during the 1990s, the percentage married did not decline for all blacks or for those in their marriage-entry years (ages 20 to 34).

There is great debate about the relative importance of these factors in explaining the lower marriage rates of blacks, but the one factor that has received the most attention is the black male marriageability hypothesis. Some, such as sociologist William Julius Wilson, have argued that blacks are less likely to marry because of the increasing economic marginality of black men. As noted earlier, the decline in the economic fortunes of black men, especially those who are less-educated, sharpened since the 1970s as a result of several factors, including the loss of manufacturing jobs on which black men were disproportionately reliant. These changes have hurt black men's attractiveness as potential spouses, especially since the 1960s, and affected black men's views of themselves as breadwinners. That is, an increasing number of black males are less willing to marry and become husbands because they perceive that they cannot meet the socially defined responsibilities of husbands.[45] The apparent stabilization of black men's economic fortunes (at least of those who were employed) as a result of the 1990 boom should have positively influenced black marriages during this period.

The data provide some support for this hypothesis. As the percentage married for blacks remained steady over the 1990s while declining for whites, the economic stability of black men is perhaps an important factor in marriage for blacks and may act to buffer against any national cultural trends influencing lower marriage rates in the United States.

Alternatively, sociologist Robert Sampson and others have argued that demographic factors are associated with lower marriage rates among blacks. This argument holds that there are simply not enough black men as potential mates for black women, especially in the prime marriage years of 20 to 34. Thus, a sex-ratio imbalance between young black women and men has developed and is growing as a result of factors including high mortality rates of black men, especially young black men.[46] Sampson and others see the sex-ratio imbalance as playing a large role in lower black marriage rates, particularly since a vast majority of black marriages are of the same race. In the 1990s, the growing incarceration rate of black men is likely to have further influenced sex-ratio imbalances among young blacks. This factor may help account for the racial difference in marriage rates, but is not consistent with the marriage rate of blacks over time, especially over the 1990s, as the data previously shown suggest.

CHANGING RESIDENTIAL LOCATION PATTERNS

The slave economy served to concentrate blacks in the South, where the largest share of blacks still reside today (about 55 percent). When slavery ended, blacks in the South still faced the oppression of Jim Crow and limited economic opportunities. From 1910 to 1920, the nation's black population shifted away from underdeveloped rural areas in the South to industrial centers in the cities, particularly in the North and Midwest. The same type of migration but on a massive scale occurred before, during, and shortly after World War I: Between 500,000 and a million African American men, women, and children left the South, settling in New York, Chicago, Detroit, and other parts of the North and Midwest. Chicago's black population increased from 44,000 to 110,000 during this period. This mass movement has been called the Great Black Migration.[47]

Although the distribution of blacks became less skewed toward the South as a result of migration, racial housing covenants and residential housing discrimination ensured that blacks remained concentrated and residentially segregated in mostly big Northern and Midwestern cities. Within these cities, they lived in the worst neighborhoods, which again limited their economic and social opportunities.

How much have black geographic and residential distributions changed over the years, especially during the 1990s? New York, California, and Texas, the top three states according to the size of their black populations in 2000, have had the largest black populations for the past 30 years. The top 10 states with the largest black populations (see Table 1) house about 58 percent of the total black population, while they represent 48 percent of the total U.S. population. The ranking of these states, however, is likely to change. The states that gained the most blacks during the 1990s included a disproportionate share of Southern states such as Florida, Georgia, Texas, and Maryland; California, for the first time in 30 years, was not among the top five states with the largest black gains.[48]

In all but one of the cities with the largest black populations (see Table 1), blacks made up over 20 percent of the overall population (the exception was Los Angeles). Big urban areas in the North still topped the list, as they have for the past 30 years. But Southern urban areas enjoyed the largest growth in black population over the 1990s, especially Atlanta, Houston, and Washington, D.C., and thus they are likely to overtake some of those in the North in the coming decades as cities with the largest black populations.[49]

The return of blacks to the South that occurred during the 1980s continued and perhaps accelerated in the 1990s. As alluded to earlier, the South experienced net out-migration of blacks for every decade from 1880 to 1970. But for the first time in 100 years, blacks began returning to the South in much greater numbers than they were leaving during the 1970s and 1980s.

As for the pattern during the 1990s, the Southern share of the black population increased yet again over the decade, suggesting continued return migration. The South's black population increased by 3.6 million, about two times the number the South gained in the 1980s (1.7 million). The Southern share of the population also increased for whites, though to a lesser extent. Of

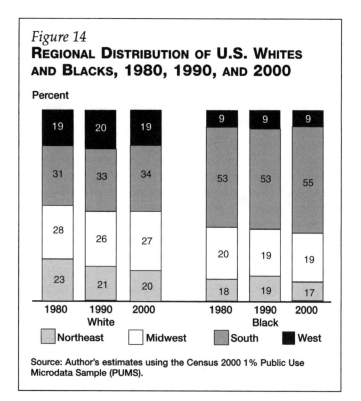

Figure 14
REGIONAL DISTRIBUTION OF U.S. WHITES AND BLACKS, 1980, 1990, AND 2000

Source: Author's estimates using the Census 2000 1% Public Use Microdata Sample (PUMS).

course, there are other factors besides interregional migration that are likely to be driving these changes, such as regional birth or death rate differences by race or by immigration, among others.

Still, the magnitude of the change in the share of blacks living in the South appears to be strongly influenced by black out-migration from all other regions (see Figure 14). The share of blacks living in the Northeast and Midwest, and to a lesser extent in the West, declined from 1990 to 2000. In fact, the 1990s was the first decade in which each of these regions (besides the South) registered a net out-migration of blacks.

Table 1
TOP 10 PLACES IN UNITED STATES WITH LARGEST BLACK POPULATIONS, 2000

State		Count	Share of U.S. black population (%)	City		Count	Share of city population (%)
1.	New York	3,234,165	9	1.	New York	2,274,049	28
2.	California	2,513,041	7	2.	Chicago	1,084,221	37
3.	Texas	2,493,057	7	3.	Detroit	787,687	83
4.	Florida	2,471,730	7	4.	Philadelphia	672,162	44
5.	Georgia	2,393,425	7	5.	Houston	505,101	26
6.	Illinois	1,937,671	5	6.	Los Angeles	444,635	12
7.	North Carolina	1,776,283	5	7.	Baltimore	424,449	65
8.	Maryland	1,525,036	4	8.	Memphis	402,367	62
9.	Michigan	1,474,613	4	9.	Washington, D.C.	350,455	61
10.	Louisiana	1,468,317	4	10.	New Orleans	329,171	67
	U.S. Total	36,419,434					

Source: Jesse McKinnon, "The Black Population," *Census 2000 Brief* C2KBR/01-5 (www.census.gov/prod/2001pubs/c2kbr01-5.pdf, accessed March 18, 2004).

Table 2
INTERREGIONAL MIGRATION BY RACE, 1995–2000

Region of residence in 1995 (movers)	Region of residence in 2000			
	Northeast	Midwest	South	West
White				
Northeast	85%	2%	9%	3%
Midwest	1%	88%	7%	4%
South	2%	4%	91%	3%
West	2%	4%	15%	79%
Black				
Northeast	84%	1%	13%	1%
Midwest	1%	90%	7%	2%
South	1%	2%	96%	1%
West	1%	2%	38%	59%
Black/white ratio				
Northeast	0.99	0.56	1.40	0.39
Midwest	0.59	1.02	1.12	0.40
South	0.51	0.51	1.06	0.41
West	0.76	0.65	2.44	0.74

Note: The table reads that, of whites who moved from the Northeast in 1995 (i.e., in the first row), 85 percent moved within the Northeast, 2 percent moved to the Midwest, 9 percent moved to the South, and 3 percent moved to the West.

Source: Author's calculations using the Census 2000 5% Public Use Microdata Sample (PUMS).

As for whether the propensity to move to the South is greater for blacks than for whites, analysis of Census 2000 data on interregional migration by race (see Table 2) indicates a few clear patterns. First, most people who moved between 1995 and 2000 moved within their region of residence. For example, for white and black movers living in the Northeast at the end of the decade, 85 percent and 84 percent of them, respectively, had moved there since 1995 from other locations within the Northeast. The second strong pattern is that black movers were much more likely than white movers to move to the South, confirming expectations. For example, for black movers who lived in the Northeast in 1995, about 13 percent of them moved to the South by the end of the decade, while the comparable figure for whites was about 9 percent.

The ratio of black to white percentages in these figures (the bottom panel of data in the table) confirms blacks' greater propensity to move south. Ratios above 1 indicate that blacks were much more likely than whites to move to a particular region, while scores below 1 indicate the reverse. The shaded area of the table indicates that blacks were more likely than whites to move to the South irrespective of their region of residence in 1995, something that was especially true for movers out of the West and to a lesser extent the Northeast.

Although researchers have yet to examine the factors underlying blacks' interregional migration patterns in the 1990s, some have studied these for the 1970s and 1980s. The factors that emerged from that research are likely to go a long way in explaining the continued trend of black return migration to the South in the 1990s.

There are two major explanations of blacks' return to the South: the traditional push-pull framework and historical social networks. Demographer Larry Long argues that the recent black return to the South is a result of a push out of the Northeast and Midwest and a pull to the South. He reasons that the black dream of the North as a place of "milk and honey" never materialized and that the changing South represented new opportunities for blacks. In Long's view, deteriorating social and economic conditions for blacks in the North, caused by deindustrialization and persistent discrimination, were the push factors; improvements in the general economic and social environment of the South—increasing school integration, improved race relations, and the rise of Sunbelt cities as centers for capital investment and economic opportunities—were the pull factors.[50]

The ethnographic work of anthropologist Carol Stack argues that historically significant social and familial ties play a key role in blacks' decisions to return to the South. Stack maintains that black Northerners, even those born outside the South, kept strong ties to home communities in the South, and passed these on from one generation to the next. These kinship and familial ties have been shown to be strong predictors of migration decisions by blacks.[51]

Underlying these regional trends are changing residential patterns by blacks within metropolitan areas. It is well known that, as a result of historical migration patterns, housing discrimination and affordability, and to some extent, preferences to live near other blacks, African Americans' residential locations have long been concentrated in central cities. Although the percentage of blacks living in central cities has been one of the highest of any racial or ethnic group over the past three decades, this percentage declined among blacks for every decade since the 1970s. This trend continued during the 1990s. The 2000 Census shows that for large metropolitan areas with populations of 500,000 or more, 61 percent of African Americans lived in the central city, down from 66 percent in 1990. The similar percentage of whites living in the central city was 34 percent in 1990 and 29 percent in 2000.[52]

Black suburbanization increased over the 1990s. Blacks moved in greater numbers to the suburbs for greater homeownership and economic opportunities, among other factors. The increase in black suburbanization over the 1990s may have been spurred in part by the economic boom of the 1990s, which led the black unemployment rate to drop to a record low. With more blacks working, housing demand among black households grew, and black homeownership (discussed earlier) increased over this period. Given that single-family homes are disproportionately found in the suburbs, these trends suggest greater black representation in suburban communities over the 1990s.

Still, most of the suburbs into which blacks are moving are inner-ring suburbs (usually in close proximity to central cities). Some argue that economic conditions in these inner rings do not differ dramatically from those in the central cities.[53] Hence, for many, it is an open question as to whether blacks experienced greater economic opportunities as a result of the increased residential mobility over the 1990s.

PERSISTENT RESIDENTIAL SEGREGATION

The increased residential mobility of blacks over this period is likely to have affected residential segregation patterns in the United States. Social scientists measure the degree of residential segregation between groups using indices of dissimilarity. The dissimilarity indices shown in Figure 15 are based on data for the 316 Primary Metropolitan Statistical Areas in the United States and are weighted by the total black population in each of these metropolitan areas. The dissimilarity index ranges from 0 to 100, with higher values indicating greater residential segregation between racial groups. Hence, the index value between blacks and whites for all metropolitan areas in the United States describes the extent to which the neighborhoods that blacks tend to reside in are different from the neighborhoods whites live in.

The actual numerical value of the dissimilarity index has a convenient interpretation. Specifically, the index can be interpreted as the percentage of either population that would have to be relocated to different neighborhoods to completely eliminate any geographic imbalance. For example, the 1990 index value describing the imbalance between the residential distribution of blacks and whites is 64. This indicates that in 1990, about 64 percent of blacks would have had to relocate within the metropolitan area to be spatially distributed in proportion to the residential distribution of whites.

Over the 1990s racial segregation between blacks and other groups declined modestly. However, these declines were more dramatic between blacks and Hispanics and between blacks and Asians than between blacks and whites. The index of dissimilarity between blacks and whites declined by 4 percentage points, or 6 percent, from 1990 to 2000. The equivalent decline between blacks and Hispanics was 6 percentage points, or 11 percent; and between blacks and Asians, 6 percent-

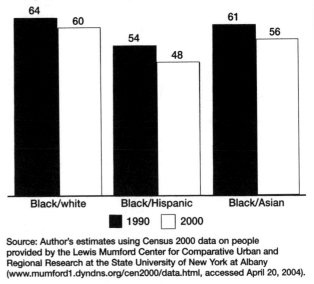

Figure 15

METRO NEIGHBORHOOD SEGREGATION BETWEEN BLACKS AND OTHER GROUPS, 1990 AND 2000

Average black dissimilarity indices

Black/white 1990: 64, 2000: 60
Black/Hispanic 1990: 54, 2000: 48
Black/Asian 1990: 61, 2000: 56

■ 1990 □ 2000

Source: Author's estimates using Census 2000 data on people provided by the Lewis Mumford Center for Comparative Urban and Regional Research at the State University of New York at Albany (www.mumford1.dyndns.org/cen2000/data.html, accessed April 20, 2004).

age points, or 8 percent. Thus, by the end of the decade, segregation between blacks and whites still remained higher than that between blacks and other racial and ethnic groups.

The decline in black segregation over the 1990s seems to be linked to demographic changes in metropolitan areas. Additional analysis of the 2000 Census reveals that the biggest declines in black segregation occurred in metropolitan areas that were growing quickly and in places where the percentage of blacks in the population was rising rapidly. This suggests either that metropolitan areas where blacks are migrating are areas where black segregation is lower than the average, or that black movers within metropolitan areas are moving to increasingly nonblack neighborhoods. Bigger declines still in the indices of segregation occurred in places where blacks made up a small proportion of the population in 1990. However, segregation of blacks changed very little in the largest metropolitan areas, where segregation historically has been the highest, and in metropolitan areas where the black population is the largest.[54] The latter trends cause concern since these areas house a disproportionate share of the nation's population and of the U.S. black population.

The degree of racial segregation is influenced by a number of factors. Among these, suburban housing discrimination plays a key role. This kind of discrimination can take many forms, one of which is discrimination against blacks in obtaining home mortgages. Indeed, numerous studies have documented that blacks are less likely than whites to be approved for home mortgages, even after racial differences in income, debt, creditworthiness, residential location, and other relevant personal characteristics are taken into account.[55] Since single-family homes are disproportionately located in the suburbs, discrimination against blacks in mortgage approvals will likely contribute to racial segregation.

Housing discrimination can also take the form of discrimination by real estate agents and landlords. Suburban landlords discriminate against blacks in rental housing, while many real estate agents steer blacks away from certain neighborhoods that are disproportionately white. But other factors also perpetuate segregation. The limited availability of low-income housing in suburban areas limits the extent to which many blacks can move there. Growth controls, the setting of high impact fees on developers by cities and municipalities, as well as other development regulations (such as limits on multiunit housing) are chief reasons for the lack of affordable housing in suburban areas. Of course, suburban whites' fear of blacks could also contribute to these housing development barriers.

Blacks' racial preferences to live near those of their own race play a smaller role in perpetuating segregation. Housing segregation by income plays an even smaller role, as the black middle class is just as likely to be segregated from whites as the black poor.[56]

RACIAL SEGREGATION AND ECONOMIC OPPORTUNITY

The modest decline in the segregation of blacks observed in the United States over the 1990s is likely to have affected blacks' proximity to employment opportunities.[57] During the latter half of the 20th century, employment opportunities have grown more distant from predominantly black residential areas. As a result of innovations in transportation, such as the development of highways and of cargo trucks in the mid-20th century, and of cheaper land prices on the suburban fringe, firms, and therefore employment, have decentralized toward suburbs and exurbs, where a disproportionate share of whites also located. However, for a variety of reasons discussed above, black residential locations have remained fairly centralized and concentrated in older urban neighborhoods of the nation's central cities.

Many social scientists argue that this "spatial mismatch" between black residential locations and employment opportunities is in part responsible for the stubbornly inferior labor-market outcomes experienced by African Americans. Given the difficulties of reverse commutes in many metropolitan areas and the fact that traveling long distances imposes high money and time

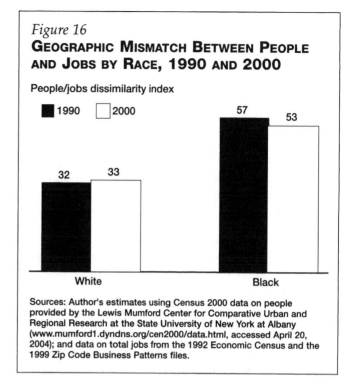

Figure 16

GEOGRAPHIC MISMATCH BETWEEN PEOPLE AND JOBS BY RACE, 1990 AND 2000

Sources: Author's estimates using Census 2000 data on people provided by the Lewis Mumford Center for Comparative Urban and Regional Research at the State University of New York at Albany (www.mumford1.dyndns.org/cen2000/data.html, accessed April 20, 2004); and data on total jobs from the 1992 Economic Census and the 1999 Zip Code Business Patterns files.

costs on commuters, such spatial mismatch may render impossible many jobs for which black workers are suited. Thus, an important question is whether the modest decline in the segregation of blacks observed over the 1990s is associated with improvements in blacks' spatial proximity to economic opportunity.

There is a clear racial difference in the degree of mismatch between people and jobs (see Figure 16). In both 1990 and 2000, all of the dissimilarity index values for blacks indicate that more than 50 percent of blacks would have had to relocate to even out the distribution of blacks relative to jobs (the lowest value was 53 percent for total employment in the year 2000). The comparable figures for whites are 25 percentage points lower. Thus, in both 1990 and 2000, there are large racial differences in the imbalance between people and jobs, and African Americans are far more physically isolated from jobs than whites. And though not shown here, the data also indicate that blacks residing in metropolitan areas in the Northeast and the Midwest are the most physically isolated from employment opportunities, whereas blacks residing in the South are the least isolated.

However, blacks' geographic separation from jobs declined during the 1990s. Figure 16 confirms this, as the total employment mismatch index for blacks declined by more than 3 points. Over this period, there are very small changes in the average mismatch values for whites. These changes narrow the black-white difference in geographic mismatch by approximately 13 percent.

The modest improvements in blacks' proximity to employment opportunities occurred in nearly every U.S.

metropolitan area. Such declines were smallest in the Northeast, where segregation is high and economic growth sluggish. The mismatch between blacks and jobs is also most severe in areas where a relatively large percentage of the population is black and where the black population is large in absolute terms. In addition, the absolute declines in the mismatch indices are largest for metropolitan areas with small black populations (in both relative and absolute terms).[58]

Several factors could explain the modest declines in blacks' geographic separation from economic opportunities during the 1990s. One of these is the possibility that job development began to occur in minority neighborhoods as a result of the economic boom. The boom brought with it tremendous economic and employment growth, slowing and in some cases reversing the hemorrhaging of jobs from central cities that characterized the previous four decades. With talk of the revival of central cities, many middle- and upper-income households began to repopulate older urban neighborhoods, bringing with them consumer dollars and businesses that cater to such demand. With this revival came talk of the "competitive advantage of the inner city." Poor, distressed, and predominantly minority urban neighborhoods were increasingly seen as strategic areas of capital investment because of their underserved retail markets and proximity to central business districts.[59] In fact, in some instances, the development and repopulation of these neighborhoods proceeded to the point where many observers increasingly turned their attention to the potential negative consequences of urban gentrification.[60]

This reasoning, it turns out, has little explanatory power. All of the declines that occurred during the 1990s in blacks' segregation from jobs were driven by the residential mobility of blacks within metropolitan areas.[61] That is, most of the reduction in blacks' geographic separation from jobs occurred because blacks moved closer to where jobs are located within metropolitan areas—in or near suburban areas. In fact, changes in the location of jobs during the 1990s actually precipitated higher levels of black isolation from employment. Had black residential mobility out of mostly disadvantaged black communities not occurred to the extent that it did over the 1990s, blacks' geographic isolation from jobs would have worsened significantly during the economic boom. This is because little job growth occurred in inner-city minority communities during the boom of the late 1990s, despite the fact that job development occurred to a significant extent in other areas of central cities.[62]

Despite improvements in these measures for blacks, the geographic imbalances between blacks and jobs are magnified by racial differences in how individuals travel to work. The different ways in which individuals travel to work, in addition to their residential locations,

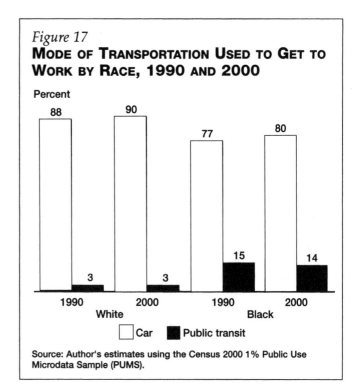

Figure 17

MODE OF TRANSPORTATION USED TO GET TO WORK BY RACE, 1990 AND 2000

Source: Author's estimates using the Census 2000 1% Public Use Microdata Sample (PUMS).

strongly influence employment opportunities. Cars, for example, provide the greatest flexibility during travel and allow individuals to search for and maintain more distant jobs, thus improving employment opportunities, especially for those that are physically isolated from jobs, such as African Americans. But blacks are significantly less likely than whites to drive to work. In both 1990 and 2000, blacks were less likely than whites to travel to work by car (see Figure 17). In 1990, 88 percent of whites traveled to work by car, whereas only 77 percent of blacks did, resulting in a difference of about 11 percentage points, or 13 percent. The work of Steve Raphael and Michael Stoll indicates that differences between the races in car access are greater for the less-educated. For example, in the mid-1990s, the car ownership rates among those with a high school degree or less were 74 percent, 47 percent, and 48 percent for whites, blacks, and Hispanics, respectively.[63]

Many factors help explain these racial differences in car ownership: differences in income and earnings between whites and blacks, differences in insurance premiums that these groups face, and discrimination against blacks in the car loan market. Indeed, in black and other poor minority neighborhoods, auto insurance premiums are much higher than elsewhere because of redlining by insurance companies and higher theft and traffic accident rates in these areas.[64] Also, blacks are charged significantly higher interest rates for private car loans than are similar creditworthy whites and therefore pay significantly more interest over the course of a car loan. This problem led to a recent lawsuit against and subsequent settlement by GMAC, a wholly owned subsidiary of General Motors that was found to engage in these discriminatory practices.

By 2000, the percentage of whites and blacks traveling to work by car increased, consistent with the long-run trends in these measures. This increase could also have been triggered by the economic boom of the 1990s, in which employment rates and earnings for many groups increased, giving more individuals the ability to purchase a car. Still, the rate of increase in car travel to work was similar for both whites and blacks, leaving the racial difference in this measure virtually unchanged by 2000.

Because lack of car access diminishes employment prospects and limits the ability to search for a job, it harms African Americans in the labor market. As a consequence of the relative lack of car access, blacks are much more likely than others to travel by public transportation. In 1990, about 15 percent of blacks traveled to work by public transit, while only 3 percent of whites did. These percentages changed very little for either group over the 1990s, maintaining the racial difference in mode of travel by 2000.

Economists Edward Glaeser, Matt Kahn, and Jordan Rappaport intimate that the poor, including a disproportionate share of blacks, live in cities because they cannot afford cars and precisely because public transit is reasonably available there.[65] Accordingly, blacks disproportionately use public transit to get to work. But even if this were true, in most metropolitan areas, traveling to work by public transit increases travel burden in a number of ways and therefore diminishes labor-market opportunities. Because commuting by public transit takes considerably longer than commuting by car, individuals using public transit are less likely to search for or maintain a distant job. In boom economies like that experienced over the 1990s, this may be less of a problem as central-city employment opportunities become more numerous. But during recessions, distant suburban employment becomes more important because central-city employment dries up fastest during hard times.

Moreover, reverse commutes from central cities to suburbs, where there is greater employment opportunity, are difficult because of transit service unavailability, particularly for rail. And relative to other workers, blacks and other minority workers are increasingly working nonstandard work schedules, such as the graveyard shift, when public transit is even less available. Finally, suburban firms are more physically distant from public transit stops than are central-city firms, making many suburban employment opportunities that much less accessible. Indeed, in the mid-1990s, nearly half of all jobs in suburban areas where employment growth has been strong were inaccessible by public transportation (defined as being more than a quarter of a mile away from the nearest public transit stop), while the comparable figure for jobs in the central city was about 20 percent.[66]

RAPID GROWTH IN INCARCERATION

Blacks' pursuit of equal rights, particularly in the nation's criminal justice system, has been long-standing. The criminal victimization of blacks by whites that went unpunished (such as lynching), the imprisonment of blacks for crimes that they did not commit, and the differential treatment and sentencing of blacks have led to sustained fights by African Americans for equal treatment under criminal law and for changes in unjust laws. Changes within the criminal justice system since the 1960s in due process and equal rights have led to a substantial reduction in racial inequalities in the administration of justice.

Despite this, blacks have been overrepresented in the criminal justice system as a result of past and present socioeconomic disadvantages, differential policing and enforcement by race, and other factors. Many social scientists have documented a fairly strong relationship between economic opportunities and crime, suggesting that groups such as African Americans that are disproportionately poor, have limited educational attainment and limited skills, and lack good jobs have higher crime and incarceration rates. This, combined with research showing that racial disparities in arrests and sentencing remain, whether or not the defendant committed the crime, suggests that blacks' incarceration rate should be higher than that of whites, something that has historically been true.[67]

For much of the postwar period, the nation's incarceration rate remained fairly stable, and the fraction of the prison population made up of blacks remained fairly constant as well. Throughout the 1980s and until the mid-1990s, rates of incarceration in the United States rose dramatically, particularly for blacks, despite the fact that rates of most major types of crime, such as violent and property crime, dropped dramatically during this period. The reasons for the decline in crime during the 1990s are not fully understood but include a strong economy, changes in sentencing and policing policies, a decline in the share of young people in the population, and the imprisonment of more offenders.[68]

Over the 1990s, the number of those incarcerated in the United States nearly doubled, from about 600,000 to 1.2 million. The rise in incarceration in the United States has been disproportionately fueled by prison and jail admissions of blacks, in particular black men (see Figure 18). The share of black men under correctional supervision is higher than that for other racial or gender groups.

Moreover, the percentage of black men under supervision grew rapidly over the late 1980s and early 1990s, while the same was not true for others, suggesting that the black male fraction of the prison population also

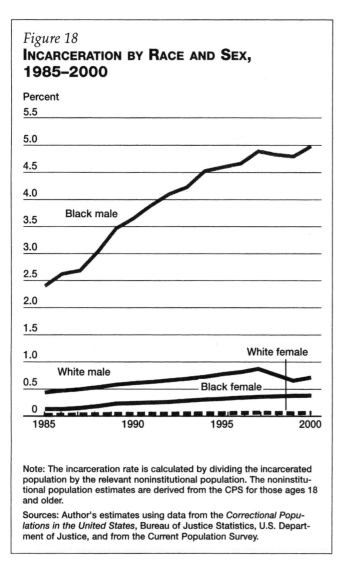

Figure 18

INCARCERATION BY RACE AND SEX, 1985–2000

Percent

Black male

White female

White male

Black female

Note: The incarceration rate is calculated by dividing the incarcerated population by the relevant noninstitutional population. The noninstitutional population estimates are derived from the CPS for those ages 18 and older.

Sources: Author's estimates using data from the *Correctional Populations in the United States*, Bureau of Justice Statistics, U.S. Department of Justice, and from the Current Population Survey.

rose over this period. In 1985, between 2 percent and 3 percent of black men were incarcerated, but by 2000 this number had swelled to 5 percent, thus driving the black-white male difference in incarceration to 4 percentage points, up from 2 percentage points in 1985. With black men in the United States numbering 16 million in 2000, the data suggest that about 800,000 black men were incarcerated at any given point in time in the late 1990s. But those imprisoned were disproportionately young, so the percentage of young black men who were imprisoned was even higher. There were roughly 5 million young black men ages 16 to 34 in the population in 2000. Of these, perhaps 600,000 to 700,000 were incarcerated, representing about 14 percent of this population. Furthermore, when the flows of young black men in and out of prison are taken into account, the Bureau of Justice Statistics estimates that during the 1980s and 1990s nearly 17 percent of African American men had been incarcerated at least once.[69]

Is the rapid rise in black male incarceration over the 1980s and 1990s accounted for by a rise in blacks'

propensity to commit crimes relative to whites? The data indicate that this is not the case. Indeed, tabulations from the U.S. Department of Justice's Uniform FBI Crime Reports indicate that from 1976 to 1999 the percentage of crime committed by African Americans was fairly stable. In fact, over this period, African Americans committed between 43 percent and 47 percent of violent crime (down to 40 percent in 1999) and between 33 percent and 37 percent of overall crime (down to 29 percent in 1999).[70] Thus, the rise in black incarceration over this period was not accounted for by any increase in black criminality. Moreover, if anything, the strong economy should have helped lower black incarceration rates, as well as others, all else being equal, because of the relationship between economic opportunities and crime.

Alternatively, some indicate that the spread of mandatory sentencing laws across states and the increasing use of plea bargaining in the 1980s and 1990s may have increased incarceration, but these factors account more for the rise in overall incarceration than for the disproportionate rise in black incarceration.

What has fueled black male incarceration most over this period is the rise in drug-related arrests and convictions and the differential sentences imposed on those in possession of crack versus powder cocaine. Although violent and property crime declined over the 1990s, drug-related crime rose rapidly, and by the end of the decade became slightly more prevalent than violent crime. This increase is due partly to stricter drug laws and enforcement in the war on drugs, which became prevalent during the Reagan, first Bush, and Clinton administrations. In particular, the harsher penalties on those in possession of crack cocaine, which is disproportionately possessed by blacks, versus powder cocaine, which is disproportionately held by whites, has contributed mightily to the recent run-up in black male incarceration. In 2000, for example, the median cocaine possession sentence (for 25 grams or less) was about 14 months for powder cocaine versus 65 months for crack cocaine.[71] This sentencing differential for apparently equal substances has led to the question of whether blacks are receiving equal treatment under the law.

In any case, the rising contribution of drug offenders to the prison population has disproportionately involved black men. It is estimated that over the 1990s black men accounted for 35 percent of arrests, 55 percent of convictions, and 74 percent of prison sentences for drug-related crimes such as possession. These events have occurred despite the fact that blacks are estimated to represent about 13 percent of monthly drug users in the United States. Moreover, the rise in the number of drug offenders over the late 1980s and early 1990s accounted for 42 percent of the total growth among black inmates but only 26 percent of the growth among white inmates.[72]

The problem of incarceration does not end with the imprisonment of these mostly young black men. Given that the median time served for imprisoned offenders at the end of the 1990s was about two to three years, this suggests that a large share of the 800,000 incarcerated black males are reentering society now. Most of these ex-offenders return to poor, mostly black communities in America's biggest urban centers, where job opportunities are already limited. Even if those who were incarcerated had skills that employers valued, the stigma of ex-offender status would likely dampen any potential labor-market opportunities. Harry Holzer, Steve Raphael, and Michael Stoll show that employers are averse to hiring ex-offenders, for reasons that include fear of negligent hiring lawsuits.[73] Still, many ex-offenders have other disadvantages including personal deficits that may have limited their labor-market opportunities in the first place and may have influenced their incarceration. To the extent that policy supports are not in place to help ex-offenders rejoin society, further stress will be put on these already vulnerable urban and minority communities over the coming decade.

THE COLOR LINE'S UNCERTAIN FUTURE

The evidence provided in this report points to an uncertain future of continuing black progress and declining racial inequality in America, based on uneven progress in the 1990s (see Box 6). African Americans made real, continued progress during the 1990s. By 2000, African Americans' poverty and unemployment rates were reduced to the lowest levels in 30 years, and black family income rose strongly over the 1990s. These factors, in conjunction with historically low interest rates, contributed to rising African American home-ownership rates, some of the highest ever recorded. The sustained period of economic growth over the 1990s contributed to these positive developments, as perhaps did a reduction in private market discrimination and declining negative attitudes toward African Americans.

Black progress was also evident on social measures. The dramatic decline in the percentage of black high school dropouts over the 1970s and 1980s continued through the 1990s, while blacks' college completion rates continued to rise. By 2000, blacks' attainment of a college or advanced degree was higher than ever before. And the percentage of blacks who were married and the percentage of black children living in female-headed families stabilized over the 1990s, after falling and rising, respectively, over the previous two decades. To the extent that important outcomes for children, such as educational attainment, tend to be poorer in female-

headed families than other family types, stabilization of these trends suggests positive developments.

Despite these signs of unambiguous progress, African Americans' advancement on many other measures inched along, stalled, or reversed. Residential segregation between blacks and whites declined modestly over the 1990s, not as significantly as that between blacks and other racial minorities. This decline occurred despite the fact that black suburbanization and migration to the South where segregation levels are lower increased during this period. This suggests that the increasing residential mobility of blacks is leading to only slight increases in residential integration. Moreover, blacks' proximity to areas with greater economic opportunity increased only modestly during this period, despite the increasing residential mobility. Finally, notwithstanding a robust economy and stock market in the 1990s and increasing homeownership rates that provided greater opportunities to build home equity, African Americans' wealth grew very little over the 1990s.

Box 6
THE UNEVENNESS OF BLACK PROGRESS DURING THE 1990S

Blacks made important gains during the 1990s. Many of these occurred through high-profile government appointments: David Satcher became the 16th Surgeon General of the United States, while Colin Powell and Condoleezza Rice were appointed as the U.S. Secretary of State and the National Security Adviser, respectively. Other gains came in the private sector. Oprah Winfrey and Robert Johnson of Black Entertainment Television became black billionaires, while Franklin Raines, Ken Chenault, and Lloyd Ward became the first black CEOs of Fortune 500 companies (Fannie Mae, American Express, and Maytag, respectively). These events, and others like them, were visible signs that blacks were "making it" in mainstream America.

Yet other events during this period suggested that blacks still had a long way to go to achieve equality in America. The police beating of Rodney King (and beatings of others like him that were less publicized), the modern lynching of Donald Byrd in Texas (Byrd was a disabled man who was tied to the back of a truck and dragged to his death), the discrimination against black Secret Service agents at a prominent restaurant chain, and the largest racial discrimination class-action suit on behalf of black employees at Coca-Cola were reminders that racial discrimination and perceptions of blacks as second-class citizens had not been erased. Moreover, the diverging opinions of blacks and whites of O.J. Simpson's guilt and the contentious hearings surrounding the Clarence Thomas appointment to the Supreme Court provided evidence that race still mattered and was a powerful force in America.

Other important indicators offer cause for greater concern, especially among black men. Black men's employment and wages improved very little during the 1990s. Indeed, their employment rate was only slightly higher at the height of the late 1990s economic boom than at the peak of the late 1980s economic expansion. And among young black men, the employment rate fell in absolute terms during this period of economic robustness. By 2000 the percentage of black men in prison had doubled since the 1980s; among young black men, nearly 14 percent were incarcerated in 2000.

While understanding whether blacks made absolute gains is important for assessing the degree of racial progress in America, understanding whether the racial divide is closing is equally important. Many have argued that groups view their well-being in relation to how dominant groups are faring.[74] Indeed, DuBois' prophetic declaration about the color line in America suggests a comparative framework for understanding racial progress.

But when viewed in this light, the degree of racial progress observed over the 1990s was limited. For most of the social and economic outcomes examined here, African Americans either made up very little ground or lost ground relative to whites. This pattern was true for most measures in education, the labor market, wealth, family structure, and incarceration. One of the few exceptions to this trend was poverty, in which the racial difference declined by nearly half during the 1990s.

Taken as a whole, the events that occurred over the 1990s are likely to provide evidence to both optimists and pessimists regarding racial progress in America. Optimists will point to the continued absolute gains that blacks made over the 1990s in education, poverty reduction, and family income. These gains can be interpreted to mean that private mechanisms are sufficient to ensure black progress in this modern era and that government involvement in these affairs is no longer warranted. Pessimists will highlight the lack of relative gains made by blacks during this period of economic robustness in education, wealth, and employment. These findings will serve as evidence of a continuing need for government involvement—if not for social justice, especially in light of the history of the "Negro question" in America, then for policy purposes and civil rights.

The debate is likely to continue for at least the next decade. Economic and political conditions are likely to be, by and large, unfavorable to significantly more African American progress. Persistent racial discrimination against African Americans in labor, housing, and credit markets is unlikely to disappear in the next decade or so. And the economic downturn that began in early 2000 is likely to have erased many of the labor-market gains made by African Americans over the 1990s, perhaps even resulting in losses when compared with whites. And there is little evidence that in the next decade the strength of the American economy will return to its late 1990s level, which was impressive by historic standards.

The persistence of criminal justice policies that clearly have racially disparate effects, the continuing shrinking role of the federal government, the increasing stress on state and local governments to meet unfunded federal mandates, and the lack of enforcement of antidiscrimination laws in key sectors of the economy and society will surely harm African Americans. These factors, combined with the narrowing of coverage of affirmative action policies, will reduce blacks' opportunities to move into the middle class. Though controversial and limited in the extent to which they affect the black population, affirmative action programs in higher education, the labor market, and contracting, among others, remain one of the few viable policy options shown to spur black progress as well as narrow racial gaps in important outcomes. But continued softening of public support for these programs suggests that they will remain tenuous at best as policy solutions to address discrimination and social justice issues in the foreseeable future.

Finally, growing diversity in America and within the African American population may limit the degree of African American progress in the near future as well. The rapid growth of other racial and ethnic minority populations is likely to create greater competition for government resources, policies, and attention to address race- and ethnic-specific problems, thus limiting the extent to which the public listens and remains concerned about the unique challenges affecting black social and economic progress. And the growing diversity within the black population, spurred by the growing immigration and higher birth rates of blacks from Africa and the Caribbean and by the growing black "biracial" population, raises the question of whether African Americans' political unity, which has helped overcome numerous injustices and indignities, will remain intact. All the evidence suggests that the problem of the color line will be an important question that will continue to be raised, studied, and debated.

ACKNOWLEDGMENTS

The author would like to thank Yan Lee and Sarah Ramsey for their invaluable research assistance, and Ren Farley, John Haaga, and the advisory panel for their very helpful comments and suggestions.

REFERENCES

If provided by the author, additional text and data associated with this report are available at www.prb.org/AmericanPeople.

1. W.E.B. DuBois, *The Souls of Black Folk: Essays and Sketches* (Cambridge: University Press John Wilson and Son, 1903).

2. In this report, the terms "African American" and "black" are used interchangeably and refer to non-Hispanics. However, the term "African American" refers to people of African descent who were born and raised in the United States. On the other hand, "black" could describe those of African descent, including immigrants from places such as the Caribbean and Africa. Since recent black immigrants represent only 6 percent of the total black population, this report does not distinguish among these groups. However, the author acknowledges that this approach masks differences among these groups (for more on the two groups, see Box 2).

3. Gerald D. Jaynes and Robin W. Williams, Jr., *A Common Destiny: Blacks and American Society* (Washington, DC: National Academies Press, 1989).

4. Abigail Thernstrom and Stephan Thernstrom, *America in Black and White: One Nation, Indivisible* (New York: Simon & Schuster, 1997).

5. Lawrence D. Bobo, "The Color Line, the Dilemma, and the Dream," in *Civil Rights and Social Wrongs: Black-White Relations Since World War II*, ed. John Higham (University Park, PA: Pennsylvania State University Press, 1997): 31-55; Melvin L. Oliver and Thomas M. Shapiro, *Black Wealth/White Wealth: A New Perspective on Racial Inequality* (New York: Routledge, 1995); and Andrew Hacker, *Two Nations: Black and White, Separate, Hostile, Unequal* (New York: Charles Scribner, 1992).

6. National Center for Health Statistics, *Vital Statistics of the United States*, accessed online at www.cdc.gov/nchs/products/pubs/pubd/vsus/vsus.htm, on March 26, 2004.

7. National Center for Health Statistics, "United States Life Tables," accessed online at www.cdc.gov/nchs/datawh.htm, on March 22, 2004.

8. Jaynes and Williams, *A Common Destiny*.

9. The category "college and above" includes those that completed a bachelor's, master's, doctorate, or other professional degree.

10. Kurt J. Bauman, "Schools, Markets and Family in the History of African American Schooling," *American Journal of Education* 106, no. 4 (1998): 500-31.

11. Thomas J. Kane, "College Entry by Blacks Since 1970—The Role of College Costs, Family Background, and Returns to Education," *Journal of Political Economy* 102, no. 5 (1994): 878-911.

12. Christopher Jencks and Meredith Phillips, eds., *The Black-White Test Score Gap* (Washington, DC: Brookings Institution Press, 1998).

13. This situation is termed "stereotype threat" and refers to the hypothesis that blacks perform worse on standardized tests than their abilities suggest they are capable of because certain testing, like performance testing, taps into blacks' insecurities about confirming the stereotype that they are not intelligent. This mental frame triggers psychological anxieties during testing, lowering cognitive efficiencies and therefore performance, especially of academically inclined black students. See Claude M. Steele and Joshua Aronson, "Stereotype Threat and the Test Performance of Academically Successful African Americans," in *The Black-White Test Score Gap*, ed. Christopher Jencks and Meredith Phillips (Washington, DC: The Brookings Institution, 1998): 401-30.

14. Harry J. Holzer and Paul Offner, "Trends in Employment Outcomes of Young Black Men, 1979-2000," *JCPR Working Paper #245* (Evanston and Chicago, IL: Joint Center for Poverty Research, Northwestern University/University of Chicago, 2001).

15. For more on this argument, see Bruce Western and Becky Pettit, "Incarceration and Racial Inequality in Men's Employment," *Industrial and Labor Relations Review* 54, no. 1 (2000): 3-16. They demonstrate that incarceration of young black men understates black-white inequality in young adult labor markets by as much as 45 percent. See also Amitabh Chandra, "Labor Market Dropouts and the Racial Wage Gap: 1940-1990," *American Economic Review* 90, no. 2 (May 2000): 333-38, for a similar discussion on the effect of labor market dropouts.

16. Derek Neal, "The Measured Black-White Wage Gap Among Women Is Too Small," *Journal of Political Economy* 112, no. 1 (February 2004): S1-S28.

17. William M. Rodgers and William E. Spriggs, "What Does the AFQT Really Measure: Race, Wages, Schooling and the AFQT Score?" *Review of Black Political Economy* 24, no. 4 (1996): 13-46.

18. For these arguments, see Linda Datcher-Loury and Glenn Loury, "The Effects of Attitudes and Aspirations on the Labor Supply of Young Men," in *The Black Youth Employment Crisis*, ed. Richard Freeman and Harry J. Holzer (Chicago: University of Chicago Press, 1986): 377-402; and William J. Wilson, *The Truly Disadvantaged: The Inner City, The Underclass, and Public Policy* (Chicago: University of Chicago Press, 1987).

19. For evidence on these, see Marc Bendick Jr., Charles Jackson, and Victor Reinoso, "Measuring Employment Discrimination through Controlled Experiments," *Review of Black Political Economy* 23, no. 1 (1994): 25-48; Holzer and Offner, "Trends in Employment Outcomes"; and Kristin Butcher, "An Investigation of the Effect of Immigration on the Labor-Market Outcomes of African Americans, Help or Hindrance?" in *The Economic Implications of Immigration for African Americans*, ed. Daniel S. Hamermesh and Frank D. Bean (New York: Russell Sage Foundation, 1998): 149-82.

20. In this analysis, a family refers to a group of two or more persons residing together who are related by blood, marriage, or adoption. The count of families is for "primary" families only—that is, the householder and all other persons related to and residing with the householder. Not included are unrelated subfamilies. Families are classified either as married-couple families or families maintained by women or men without spouses.

21. Lawrence Mishel, Jared Bernstein, and John Schmitt, *The State of Working America, 2002/2003* (Ithaca, NY: Cornell University Press, 2003): figure 1A, 36.

22. Mishel, Bernstein, and Schmitt, *The State of Working America*: table 1.1, 37.

23. Mishel, Bernstein, and Schmitt, *The State of Working America:* table 1.1, 37.

24. Rebecca M. Blank and Robert Schoeni, "What Has Welfare Reform Accomplished? Impacts on Welfare Participation, Employment, Income, Poverty, and Family Structure," *Working Paper #7627* (Cambridge, MA: National Bureau of Economic Research, 2000).

25. Sheldon Danziger, Colleen M. Heflin, and Mary E. Corcoran, "Does It Pay to Move From Welfare to Work?" *Journal of Policy Analysis and Management* 21, no. 4 (2002): 671-92.

26. Harry J. Holzer and Michael A. Stoll, "Employer Demand for Welfare Recipients by Race," *Journal of Labor Economics* 21, no. 1 (2003): 210-41; and Cheryl Miller and Kenya C. Cox, "Has Welfare Reform Been Successful for All Groups? Examining Racial Variations in Caseload Declines," *Working Paper* (Baltimore: University of Maryland, Baltimore County, 2003).

27. Mishel, Bernstein, and Schmitt, *The State of Working America:* figure 5A, 313.

28. Mishel, Bernstein, and Schmitt, *The State of Working America:* figure 5A, 315.

29. Paul A. Jargowsky, *Poverty and Place: Ghettos, Barrios, and the American City* (New York: Russell Sage Foundation, 1997).

30. Jeanne Brooks-Gunn, Greg J. Duncan, and J. Lawrence Aber, *Neighborhood Poverty: Policy Implications in Studying Neighborhoods* (New York: Russell Sage Foundation, 1999).

31. Paul A. Jargowsky, "Stunning Progress, Hidden Problems: The Dramatic Decline of Concentrated Poverty in the 1990s," *Living Cities Census Series* (Washington, DC: The Brookings Institution, 2003).

32. Mishel, Bernstein, and Schmitt, *The State of Working America:* table 4.1, 269 and table 4.9, 287.

33. Melvin L. Oliver and Thomas M. Shapiro, *Black Wealth/White Wealth: A New Perspective on Racial Inequality* (New York: Routledge, 1995): table 5.1, 94.

34. Oliver and Shapiro, *Black Wealth/White Wealth.*

35. Francine D. Blau and John W. Graham, "Black-White Differences in Wealth and Asset Composition," *The Quarterly Journal of Economics* 105, no. 2 (1990): 321-39.

36. U.S. Census Bureau, "Housing Vacancies and Homeownership: Annual Statistics 2001," accessed online at www.census.gov/hhes/www/housing/hvs/annual01/ann01ind.html, on March 22, 2004.

37. U.S. Census Bureau, "Marital Status and Living Arrangements: March 1998 (Update)," *Current Population Reports* P20-514 (1999).

38. The "other families" category includes children who are living with the father only, other relatives (such as grandparents), or other nonrelatives.

39. M. Belinda Tucker, "Considerations in the Development of Family Policy for African Americans," in *New Directions: African Americans in a Diversifying Nation,* ed. James S. Jackson (Washington, DC: National Policy Association, 2000).

40. See Alice S. Rossi, "Parenthood in Transition: From Lineage to Child to Self-Orientation," in *Parenting Across the Life Span: Biosocial Dimensions,* ed. Jane B. Lancaster et al. (Hawthorne, NY: Aldine Publishing Co., 1987): 31-81; and Suzanne Bianchi, "Changing Economic Roles of Women and Men," in *The Changing American Family: Sociological and Demographic Perspectives,* ed. Reynolds Farley (Boulder, CO: Westview Press, 1995).

41. See Brenda E. Stevenson, "Black Family Structure in Colonial and Antebellum Virginia: Amending the Revisionist Perspective," in *The Decline in Marriage Among African Americans: Causes, Consequences and Policy Implications,* ed. M. Belinda Tucker and Claudia Mitchell-Kernan (New York: Russell Sage Foundation, 1995); S. Philip Morgan et al., "Racial Differences in Household and Family Structure at the Turn of the Century," *American Journal of Sociology* 98, no. 4 (1993): 799-828; and Antonio McDaniel, "Historical Racial Differences in Living Arrangements of Children," *Journal of Family History* 19, no. 1 (1994): 57-76.

42. Linda M. Blum and Theresa Deussen, "Negotiating Independent Motherhood: Working-Class African American Women Talk about Marriage and Motherhood," *Gender and Society* 10, no. 2 (1996): 199-211; and Carol Stack, *All Our Kin: Strategies for Survival in a Black Community* (New York: Harper & Row, 1975).

43. U.S. Census Bureau, "Interracial Married Couples: 1960 to Present," accessed online at www.census.gov/population/socdemo/ms-la/tabms-3.txt, on March 24, 2004.

44. David R. Harris and Hiromi Ono, "Cohabitation, Marriage, and Markets: A New Look at Intimate Interracial Relationships," *Discussion Paper* (Ann Arbor, MI: Institute for Social Research, University of Michigan, 2003).

45. Wilson, *The Truly Disadvantaged.*

46. Marcia Guttentag and Paul F. Secord, *Too Many Women: The Sex Ratio Question* (Beverly Hills, CA: Sage Publications, 1983); and Robert Sampson, "Unemployment and Imbalanced Sex Ratios: Race-Specific Consequences for Family Structure and Crime," in *The Decline in Marriage Among African Americans: Causes, Consequences and Policy Implications,* ed. M. Belinda Tucker and Claudia Mitchell-Kernan (New York: Russell Sage Foundation, 1995): 229-54.

47. See Daniel M. Johnson and Rex Campbell, *Black Migration in America: A Social Demographic History* (Durham, NC: Duke University Press, 1981).

48. William H. Frey, "Census 2000 Shows Large Black Return to the South, Reinforcing the Region's 'White-Black' Demographic Profile," *Population Studies Center Research Report* 01-473 (Ann Arbor, MI: University of Michigan, May 2001).

49. Frey, "Census 2000 Shows Large Black Return to the South."

50. Larry H. Long, *Migration and Residential Mobility in the United States* (New York: Russell Sage Foundation, 1988); and James H. Johnson Jr. and Stanley D. Brunn, "Spatial and Behavioral Aspects of Counterstream Migration of Blacks to the South," in *The American Metropolitan Systems: Present and Future,* ed. Stanley D. Brunn and James O. Wheeler (New York: Wiley & Sons, 1980).

51. Carol B. Stack and John Cromartie, "Reinterpretation of Black Return and Nonreturn Migration to the South, 1975-1980," *Geographical Review* 79, no. 3 (1989): 297-310.

52. William H. Frey, "Melting Pot Suburbs: A Census 2000 Study of Suburban Diversity," *Census 2000 Report* (Washington, DC: The Brookings Institution, June 2001); and U.S. Census Bureau, *1990 Census of the Population.* Vol. 1 (Washington, DC: U.S. Department of Commerce, 1993).

53. See George G. Galster, "Black Suburbanization: Has It Changed the Relative Location of the Races?" *Urban Affairs Quarterly* 26, no. 4 (1991): 621-62.

54. Edward L. Glaeser and Jacob L. Vigdor, "Racial Segregation in the 2000 Census: Promising News," *Survey Series Report* (Washington, DC: The Brookings Institution, April 2001).

55. See John Yinger, "Cash in Your Face: The Cost of Racial and Ethnic Discrimination in Housing," *Journal of Urban Economics* 42, no. 3 (1997): 339-65.

56. Douglas S. Massey and Nancy A. Denton, *American Apartheid: Segregation and the Making of the Underclass* (Cambridge, MA: Harvard University Press, 1993); Jan Ondrich, Alex Stricker, and John Yinger, "Do Landlords Discriminate? The Incidence and Causes of Racial Discrimination in Rental Housing Markets," *Journal of Housing Economics* 8, no. 3 (1999): 185-204; Jan Ondrich, Stephen Ross, and John Yinger, "Geography of Housing Discrimination," *Journal of Housing Research* 12, no. 2 (2001): 217-38; and John Goering and Ron Wienk, eds., *Mortgage Lending, Racial Discrimination, and Federal Policy* (Washington, DC: Urban Institute Press, 1996).

57. Steven Raphael and Michael A. Stoll, "Modest Progress: The Narrowing Spatial Mismatch between Blacks and Jobs in the 1990s," *Living Cities Census Series* (Washington, DC: The Brookings Institution, December 2002).

58. Raphael and Stoll, "Modest Progress."

59. Michael E. Porter, "The Competitive Advantage of the Inner City," *Harvard Business Review* (May/June 1995): 55-71.

60. Jacob L. Vigdor, "Does Gentrification Harm the Poor?" *Brookings-Wharton Papers on Urban Affairs* 3 (2002): 133-82.

61. Raphael and Stoll, "Modest Progress."

62. Kenneth T. Rosen, Grace J. Kim, and Avanti A. Patel, "Shopping the City: Real Estate Finance and Urban Retail Development," *Discussion Paper* (Washington, DC: Center on Urban and Metropolitan Policy, The Brookings Institution, July 2003).

63. Steven Raphael and Michael A. Stoll, "Can Boosting Minority Car Ownership Rates Narrow Interracial Employment Gaps?" *Brookings-Wharton Papers on Urban Affairs* 2 (2001): 99-137.

64. Paul Ong and Hyun-Gun Sung, "Exploratory Study of Spatial Variation in Car Insurance Premiums, Traffic Volume and Vehicle Accidents," *Working Paper* (Los Angeles: Lewis Center for Regional Studies, University of California at Los Angeles, 2003).

65. Edward L. Glaeser, Matthew E. Kahn, and Jordan Rappaport, "Why Do the Poor Live in Cities?" *Discussion Paper* #1891 (Cambridge, MA: Harvard Institute of Economic Research, 2000).

66. Martin Wachs and Brian D. Taylor, "Can Transportation Strategies Help Meet the Welfare Challenge?" *Journal of the American Planning Association* 64, no. 1 (1998): 15-20; Thomas M. Beers, "Flexible Schedules and Shift Work: Replacing the '9-to-5' Workday?" *Monthly Labor Review* 123, no. 6 (June 2000): 33-40; Harry J. Holzer and Keith R. Ihlanfeldt, "Spatial Factors and the Employment of Blacks at the Firm Level," *New England Economic Review* (May/June 1996): 65-86; and Michael A. Stoll, Harry J. Holzer, and Keith R. Ihlanfeldt, "Within Cities and Suburbs: Racial Residential Concentration and the Distribution of Employment Opportunities Across Sub-Metropolitan Areas," *Journal of Policy Analysis and Management* 19, no. 2 (2000): 207-32.

67. Jaynes and Williams, *A Common Destiny*; Jeff Grogger, "Market Wages and Youth Crime," *Journal of Labor Economics* 16, no. 4 (1998): 756-91; and Shawn D. Bushway and Anne M. Piehl, "Judging Judicial Discretion: Legal Factors and Racial Discrimination in Sentencing," *Law and Society Review* 35, no. 4 (2001): 733-64.

68. Elliott Currie, *Crime and Punishment in America* (New York: Henry Holt and Co., 1998).

69. U.S. Department of Justice, *Sourcebook of Criminal Justice Statistics* (Washington, DC: Bureau of Justice Statistics, 2000).

70. Federal Bureau of Investigation, *Uniform Crime Reports*, accessed online at www.fbi.gov/ucr/ucr.htm, on March 26, 2004.

71. Darnell F. Hawkins and Cedric Herring, "Race, Crime, and Punishment: Old Controversies and New Challenges," in *New Directions: African Americans in a Diversifying Nation*, ed. James S. Jackson (Washington, DC: National Policy Association, 2000); Harry J. Holzer, Steven Raphael, and Michael A. Stoll, "How Do Crime and Incarceration Affect the Employment Prospects of Less-Educated Young Black Men?" in *Extending Opportunities to Young, Less-Skilled Men*, ed. Ronald Mincy (forthcoming); Jeremy Travis, Amy Solomon, and Michelle Waul, *From Prison to Home: The Dimensions and Consequences of Prisoner Reentry* (Washington, DC: Urban Institute Press, 2001); and U.S. Sentencing Commission, *Report to Congress: Cocaine and Federal Sentencing Policy* (Washington, DC: U.S. Sentencing Commission, 2002).

72. Marc Mauer and Tracy Huling, *Young Black Men and the Criminal Justice System: A Growing National Problem* (Washington, DC: The Sentencing Project, 1996).

73. Harry J. Holzer et al., "Will Employers Hire Ex-Offenders? Employer Preferences, Background Checks and Their Determinants," in *Imprisoning America: The Social Effects of Mass Incarceration*, ed. Mary Pattillo, David Weiman, and Bruce Western (New York: Russell Sage Foundation, forthcoming); and Harry J. Holzer, Steven Raphael, and Michael A. Stoll, "Employment Barriers Facing Ex-Offenders" (paper prepared for Urban Institute Reentry Roundtable, New York University Law School, May 19-20, 2003).

74. For more on relative deprivation theory, see Edward Muller, "The Psychology of Political Protest and Violence," in *Handbook of Political Conflict: Theory and Research*, ed. Ted Robert Gurr (New York: Free Press, 1980).

FOR FURTHER READING

Hacker, Andrew. *Two Nations: Black and White, Separate, Hostile, Unequal.* New York: Charles Scribner, 1992.

Jackson, James S., ed. *New Directions: African Americans in a Diversifying Nation.* Washington, DC: National Policy Association, 2000.

Jaynes, Gerald D., and Robin W. Williams. *A Common Destiny: Blacks and American Society.* Washington, DC: National Academies Press, 1989.

Jencks, Christopher, and Meredith Phillips, eds. *The Black-White Test Score Gap.* Washington, DC: Brookings Institution Press, 1998.

Massey, Douglas S., and Nancy A. Denton. *American Apartheid: Segregation and the Making of the Underclass.* Cambridge, MA: Harvard University Press, 1993.

Mishel, Lawrence, Jared Bernstein, and John Schmitt. *The State of Working America 2002/2003.* Ithaca, NY: Cornell University Press, 2003.

Oliver, Melvin L., and Thomas M. Shapiro. *Black Wealth/White Wealth: A New Perspective on Racial Inequality.* New York: Routledge, 1995.

Smelser, Neil J., William Julius Wilson, and Faith Mitchell, eds. *America Becoming: Racial Trends and Their Consequences.* Washington, DC: National Academies Press, 2001.

Thernstrom, Abigail, and Stephan Thernstrom. *America in Black and White: One Nation, Indivisible.* New York: Simon & Schuster, 1997.

Tucker, M. Belinda and Claudia Mitchell-Kernan, eds. *The Decline in Marriage Among African Americans: Causes, Consequences and Policy Implications.* New York: Russell Sage Foundation, 1995.

Wilson, William J. *The Truly Disadvantaged: The Inner City, the Underclass, and Public Policy.* Chicago: University of Chicago Press, 1987.

SUGGESTED RESOURCES

Lewis Mumford Center for Comparative Urban and Regional Research, Census 2000, State University of New York at Albany:
www.albany.edu/mumford/census/index.html

Center on Metropolitan and Urban Policy, Census 2000 Series, The Brookings Institution:
www.brookings.org/urban

U.S. Census Bureau:
www.census.gov

U.S. Department of Labor, Bureau of Labor Statistics:
www.bls.gov

A Demographic Portrait of Asian Americans

By Yu Xie and Kimberly A. Goyette

Asian Americans are a diverse group who either are descendants of immigrants from some part of Asia or are themselves such immigrants. They come from East Asia (China, Japan, and Korea); Southeast Asia (Cambodia, Indonesia, Laos, Malaysia, the Philippines, Thailand, and Vietnam); and South Asia (Bangladesh, India, Myanmar, Nepal, and Pakistan). Cultural heritage, economic conditions, political systems, religious practices, and languages are quite different across these countries and, in some cases, have changed over time. As a result, ethnic differences among Asian Americans are so large that they call into question the use of a single, overarching category to group them.

The broad category of Asian Americans is used for several reasons. Besides the practical need to collapse racial categories in statistical tabulations, there are also many ways in which Asian Americans are distinct from other major racial groups in the United States. First, Asian Americans are physically and culturally distinguishable from whites and other minorities. Second, except for those of Japanese descent, most Asian Americans arrived in the United States recently, as beneficiaries of the 1965 Immigration and Nationality Act (Chinese, Koreans, Filipinos, and Asian Indians) or as refugees (Vietnamese, Laotians, and Cambodians). Finally, again with the exception of Japanese Americans, most Asian Americans speak their native languages at home and maintain their distinct ethnic cultures and values, signaling that they either face difficulties fully assimilating into the American mainstream or purposefully resist full assimilation. As this report will show, Asian Americans have socioeconomic experiences and demographic profiles that are overall distinct from those of whites and blacks.

With available census data and supplemental material, this report documents racial differences in demographic and socioeconomic characteristics between Asian and non-Asian Americans, as well as ethnic differences in these characteristics among Asian Americans. The report begins with an historical review of the immigration history of the major Asian groups. It then examines the educational achievements of Asian Americans relative to whites and blacks and across Asian ethnicities over the past 40 years; the labor force outcomes of Asian Americans relative to whites and blacks and variations across Asian ethnicities over time; Asian Americans' family characteristics and marriage patterns; and spatial distribution and residential patterns in the United States.

HISTORY OF ASIAN AMERICANS

Although Asian ethnic groups in the United States have had diverse immigration and settlement experiences, these experiences can be divided into two broad historical periods demarcated by the landmark 1965 Immigration and Nationality Act (also known as the Hart-Celler Act). The first, prior to 1965, is characterized by a U.S. economy hungry for low-wage labor and by severe racial conflicts. In this period, Asian Americans faced competition, racial violence, and discrimination. The second period, after 1965, reflects a relatively more tolerant racial environment following the Civil Rights Movement and a growing need in the U.S. economy for an educated, skilled labor force. Since 1965, Asian Americans have been perceived more positively, in the words of some, as a "model minority."[1] A brief review of the immigration histories of the most populous Asian ethnic groups in the United States follows, highlighting some of the similarities and differences in immigration experiences by Asian American ethnicity.

Chinese

Chinese were among the first Asians to settle in the United States.[2] Some Chinese were present in Hawaii as early as 1835, but thousands of Chinese arrived both in Hawaii and on the mainland during the 1840s and 1850s. The 1860 U.S. Census documented almost 35,000 Chinese on the mainland (see Box 1, page 416). These Chi-

YU XIE holds several faculty appointments at the University of Michigan. He is Otis Dudley Duncan Professor of Sociology and Statistics and Research Professor in the Survey Research Center and the Population Studies Center, Institute for Social Research (ISR), where he directs the Quantitative Methodology Program (QMP). He is also a faculty associate at the Center for Chinese Studies. Xie's areas of interest are social stratification, demography, statistical methods, and the sociology of science.

KIMBERLY A. GOYETTE is an assistant professor of sociology at Temple University. Her research interests include education, Asian Americans, and stratification. Kim has recently explored the influence of social class on graduate school attendance and major choice. She is beginning a project on how families choose schools through their choice of residences.

nese immigrants came to the United States for various reasons. Some sought shelter from wars and rebellions in the mid-1800s. Others sought better economic opportunities. Tremendous social and political turmoil in China during this period led the Imperial Qing Dynasty to levy high taxes, and in trying to pay them, peasants often lost their land. Frequent floods destroyed crops, and the population lived under the threat of starvation.

Early Chinese immigrants were primarily peasants, with little or no formal schooling. Large waves of them came to the United States as manual workers when the rapid development of the West demanded cheap labor. Immigrants were also drawn by the promise of the discovery of gold in California. Most Chinese immigrants to the United States in the 19th century were men. They envisioned making money in the United States and then returning to China at some future date. Married women remained home to care for their children and for their husbands' parents. At the turn of the century, only 5 percent of all Chinese on the mainland, and 14 percent in Hawaii, were female.

Chinese immigrants initially settled in rural areas but soon gravitated toward urban centers: San Francisco, and later New York and Boston. By 1900, 45 percent of Chinese in California lived in the city of San Francisco. Chinese in urban areas were predominantly employed in service-sector jobs—working in laundries, for example—and lived in their ethnic communities. Because Chinese in these communities were isolated from mainstream American society, many children of Chinese immigrants grew up speaking only Chinese and interacting with few whites. Some supplemented their American public school experiences by attending Chinese schools at the end of the day or on weekends.

Chinese immigrants found work outside their enclaves in agriculture, in construction, in mining, and as shopkeepers. Chinese laborers represented 90 percent of the workforce responsible for the construction of the Central Pacific Railroad. Chinese workers were often brought into factories after white workers went on strike over labor disputes. Because of this practice, Chinese in the United States were perceived as a threat to white workers and were often a target of hatred and racial violence. In the late 1870s, federal courts ruled that Chinese immigrants should be barred from naturalization as "aliens ineligible for citizenship." Later, Chinese immigration was legally restricted by the Chinese Exclusion Act of 1882. Immigration of all Asians except Filipinos, who were residents of a U.S. territory at that time, was prohibited by the National Origins Act of 1924, which barred the immigration of all "aliens ineligible for citizenship." From a high of over 107,000 in 1890, the Chinese population in the United States dwindled over the following decades. Chinese immigration practically stalled until 1965, when immigration law changed significantly.

Box 1

ASIAN AMERICANS IN THE U.S. CENSUS

The U.S. census has counted Asian Americans in different ways since the 1850s. Early Chinese in the United States were first documented through questions on nativity. Later, as more Chinese immigrated and sentiment against them among U.S.-born laborers grew, U.S. state and federal courts struggled with their racial classification and the classification of other immigrants from Asia. In 1870, Chinese were classified as a "race" on the census form, followed by Japanese in 1890. The practice of enumerating Asian ethnicities as separate racial groups has continued to this day, with new major groups (such as Filipino, Korean, Asian Indian, and Vietnamese) added to the list as their populations grew in the United States. In the 1990 Census, there was a short-lived attempt to group different ethnicities of Asian Americans along with Hawaiians and Pacific Islanders under a heading "Asians and Pacific Islanders."

In this report, Asians include East Asians, Southeast Asians, and South Asians, but not individuals with ancestry from West Asia, who are identified racially as "white" or "Other." The 2000 Census was the first one that allowed racial identification with more than one race. The race question from the 2000 Census is shown below.

→ NOTE: Please answer BOTH Questions 5 and 6.

5. Is this person Spanish/Hispanic/Latino? *Mark ☒ the "No" box if not Spanish/Hispanic/Latino.*
   ☐ No, not Spanish/Hispanic/Latino   ☐ Yes, Puerto Rican
   ☐ Yes, Mexican, Mexican Am., Chicano   ☐ Yes, Cuban
   ☐ Yes, other Spanish/Hispanic/Latino – *Print group.*

6. What is this person's race? *Mark ☒ one or more races to indicate what this person considers himself/herself to be.*
   ☐ White
   ☐ Black, African Am., or Negro
   ☐ American Indian or Alaska Native – *Print name of enrolled or principal tribe.* ▱

   ☐ Asian Indian   ☐ Japanese   ☐ Native Hawaiian
   ☐ Chinese   ☐ Korean   ☐ Guamanian or Chamorro
   ☐ Filipino   ☐ Vietnamese   ☐ Samoan
   ☐ Other Asian – *Print race.* ▱   ☐ Other Pacific Islander – *Print race.* ▱

   ☐ Some other race – *Print race.* ▱

Note: For further reading on how the race question is asked in the Census, see M.J. Anderson and S.E. Fienberg, *Who Counts? The Politics of Census-Taking in Contemporary America* (1999); and N. Mezey, "Erasure and Recognition: The Census, Race and the National Imagination," *Northwestern Law Review* 97, no. 4 (2003): 1701-68.

Although small numbers of Chinese people were allowed to immigrate following the repeal of the Chinese Exclusion Act in 1943, immigration of Chinese and other Asians to the United States did not really flourish until the passage of the Immigration and Nationality Act in 1965. This act repealed all previous quotas and immigration restrictions, and established preferences for immigrants who wished to reunite with family members or who had skills valued in the U.S. labor market. Following the passage of this landmark legislation, Chinese immigrating to the United States tended to be highly educated, to have professional and technical occupations, and to arrive with their families. Many came from Hong Kong and Taiwan, places where they had taken refuge after the 1949 military defeat of the Nationalists in China. Some of these new immigrants settled in urban ethnic enclaves like Chinatowns, while others, especially those with professional occupations, established themselves in suburban communities. Before 1900, Chinese made up the largest Asian group in the United States, though eventually the Japanese overtook them. Since 1970, Chinese have again been the most populous Asian ethnic group in the United States (see Table 1). Currently, there are more than 2.6 million Americans of Chinese descent in the United States.

Japanese

Japanese first started immigrating to the United States in the 19th century. Like Chinese, they came as agricultural workers. Unlike Chinese, a large proportion of Japanese immigrants became plantation workers in Hawaii. In the 1920s, 43 percent of the Hawaiian population was Japanese. On the mainland, many Japanese who were initially employed as agricultural workers soon became self-employed merchants and farmers. By 1925, 46 percent of Japanese immigrants were involved in agriculture. In cities like San Francisco, they established small enclaves where they could support and socialize with each other, eat familiar food, and speak their native language. After Japanese men had established themselves with farms or businesses, they sent for their wives, and the wives worked with their husbands in businesses and on farms. Japanese, more than other early Asian immigrants, came to the United States to settle and raise families.

Given their intention to settle, Japanese emphasized to their children the importance of learning to be American to avoid discrimination. Japanese sent their children to American public schools and encouraged their children to become fluent in English. They saved money for their children to go to college, believing education would help them overcome discrimination.

Their efforts did not protect them from massive government-sponsored discrimination, however. Because white workers saw the Japanese, as they had the Chinese, as a source of unfair competition, immigration of Japanese was restricted by the Gentlemen's Agreement of 1907-1908. Japanese immigration was later completely prohibited in 1924. Further, during World War II, over 100,000 Japanese from California and other states in the Pacific Northwest were placed in internment camps by the U.S. government. Whole families were herded into camps under suspicions that they had colluded or would collude with Japan to attack the mainland United States. Many Japanese families lost their land while residing in these camps. Some Japanese Americans fought in the U.S. Army to show their loyalty to the United States.

Because many Japanese had settled in the United States with their families, their numbers increased through natural population growth. They were the most populous Asian American group from 1910 to 1960 (see Figure 1, page 418). Because Japan's economy was well developed by 1965, relatively few Japanese entered the United States after the major overhaul of immigration laws in 1965. And because of this, many Japanese ethnic enclaves have not been sustained. Greater proportions of Japanese speak English well, and Japanese tend to be more structurally assimilated—that is, to have attainment in education and occupation that is equal to that of whites—than other ethnic groups such as Chinese and Koreans. Currently, fewer than 1 million people are estimated to be Japanese Americans.

Filipinos

Few Filipinos lived in the United States before the turn of the 20th century. Most of the early Filipino immigrants arrived as American nationals after 1898, the year that the United States acquired the Philippines at the conclusion of the Spanish-American War. Filipinos immigrated to the United States in search of employment on plantations in Hawaii and other agricultural work on the mainland. Filipinos also worked in fisheries in the Pacific Northwest and as domestic and other service workers. Many Filipino workers organized labor unions during the early 20th century, but their efforts to win wage increases were met with hostility not only from their employers but also from white workers who feared competition. More likely to intermarry than Chinese and Japanese, Filipino immigrant men also provoked racial hatred and violence by marrying white women. Because a large portion of the Filipino population worked as plantation or migrant agricultural workers, they did not establish ethnic communities in urban centers. As a result of their geographical dispersion and their propensity to intermarry, Filipinos soon

became more structurally assimilated in the United States than Chinese and Japanese.

Filipinos were the only Asian ethnic group not prohibited from immigrating by the 1924 National Origins Act, because they came from an American territory. However, when the Philippines was established as a commonwealth of the United States in 1934, severe restrictions were placed on Filipino immigration. The Filipino population in the United States dropped from about 108,000 to 98,000 in the following decade.

After changes to immigration laws were enacted in 1965, many Filipinos came to the United States fleeing the repressive Marcos regime and seeking better economic opportunities. For example, Filipino doctors, nurses, and pharmacists were better compensated for their skills in the United States than in the Philippines. From 1980 on, Filipinos constituted the second most populous Asian American group in the United States. Currently, Filipino Americans number slightly over 2 million.

Koreans

Most early Korean immigrants, both men and women, began their journey to the U.S. mainland working on plantations in Hawaii. Plantation owners in Hawaii capitalized on ethnic enmity, using Korean plantation workers to break strikes by Japanese workers. About 40 percent of Korean immigrants were Christians. They built many churches and formed Christian associations in Hawaii. By 1907, almost 1,000 had left Hawaii for the U.S. mainland.

Other Koreans came to the mainland after Japan annexed Korea in 1910. The 1910 Census counted around 4,500 Koreans. Korean Americans maintained a strong loyalty to Korea and an intense desire to liberate their country from Japanese rule. Korean Christian churches often served to maintain this nationalism, as did Korean language schools, in which second-generation Koreans not only spoke Korean but also learned about the culture and politics of the homeland.

Many Koreans immigrating to the U.S. mainland worked in mines and fisheries; others formed gangs of migrant farm workers. Some Koreans also became business owners, running laundries and hotels that served whites. Because they were so few in number, they did not establish ethnic enclaves, though they maintained a distinct sense of Korean identity. Along with Japanese, Koreans were prohibited from immigration by the 1924 National Origins Act.

The majority of the present Korean population in the United States is the result of an immigration wave that began after 1965. Since then, in major metropolitan centers such as New York and Los Angeles, Korean ethnic enclaves have sprung up. Most post-1965 emigrants were middle class and well educated. In the 1960s and 1970s, educational attainment increased in Korea, but

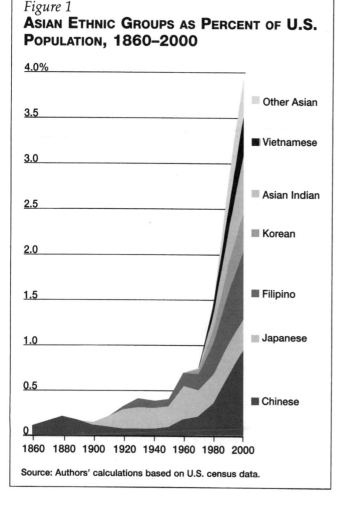

Figure 1
ASIAN ETHNIC GROUPS AS PERCENT OF U.S. POPULATION, 1860–2000

Source: Authors' calculations based on U.S. census data.

there was no corresponding increase in skilled jobs in densely populated cities such as Seoul. Skilled professionals, such as doctors and pharmacists, immigrated to many places, including the United States. Some Koreans arrived with capital and established grocery stores and other small businesses. As a result, Koreans have the highest rate of self-employment among all Asian ethnic groups in the United States. Today there are over 1 million Korean Americans.

Asian Indians

The first Asian Indian immigrants to the United States were recruited to work on plantations in Hawaii. Others came to Washington and California to find agricultural work, and Asian Indian workers were often used as strike breakers in both construction and mining industries. Many early Asian Indian immigrants were from the Punjab, and about 80 percent were of the farming caste. By 1920, about 6,400 Asian Indians were in the United States. The majority of South Asian immigrants to the United States during the late 19th and early 20th centuries were single Sikh men, who kept the Sikh tradition of wearing long hair wrapped in a turban. Unlike Chinese and Japanese immigrants, Asian Indians did not concentrate geographically.

Asian Indians in the United States were first classified in court decisions of 1910 and 1913 as Caucasians. These decisions permitted Asian Indians to become naturalized and intermarry with U.S.-born whites. These decisions, however, were reversed in 1923, when Asian Indians were legally classified as nonwhite because their ancestry could not be traced to northern or Western Europe. Asian Indian immigrants, reclassified as nonwhite, were prevented from becoming citizens and barred from further immigration, as were other Asians, in 1924. Antimiscegenation laws prevented Asian Indians from marrying Caucasian women. However, many Asian Indian men married newly immigrated Mexican women.

Because the initial Asian Indian immigration was small and Asian Indians were not allowed to bring families to the United States, few Asian Indians lived in the United States prior to 1965. Since then, many highly educated professionals from India have immigrated to the United States in search of skilled employment. Most had been exposed to Western culture and education in India and had little trouble finding professions in which their education and skills were needed. Today 1.8 million Asian Indians live in the United States.

Vietnamese

Very few Vietnamese immigrated to the United States prior to 1970. However, U.S. involvement in the Vietnam War resulted in substantial Vietnamese immigration in the 1970s. In 1972, after the United States withdrew all its forces from Vietnam, many Vietnamese left the country. And during the months preceding the collapse of the South Vietnamese government in 1975, over 100,000 people were evacuated or airlifted out of the country. Many Vietnamese who left had prospered under the South Vietnamese government. Others left because they had aided the United States in some way, and the U.S. military made provisions for them. Refugees leaving Vietnam before 1975 were generally better off economically than the overall population of Vietnam.

The communists captured Saigon in 1975 and placed segments of the Vietnamese population in reeducation camps. Fearing political persecution, some Vietnamese left Vietnam as political refugees. Those who left after 1975 tended to be poorer than the earlier wave, often leaving without capital or possessions. Many were Chinese-Vietnamese who were ethnically Chinese but had lived in Vietnam for generations. This group was concentrated in the South and was particularly persecuted by the Vietnamese communists, who were suspicious of their class as merchants. Many escaped by boat, crossing the Mekong River into Thailand or crowding onto boats to cross the South China Sea. These "boat people" were desperate and faced extortion by those helping them escape. Once boat people were spotted on the sea or had made it safely to ports, they were sent to refugee camps in the Philippines, Malaysia, and Thailand, where many spent years waiting to be admitted to the United States. Children in refugee camps were schooled in the English language and Western etiquette but lost years of learning math, science, and other subjects.

Vietnamese who came as political refugees were originally sponsored by Midwestern churches and other charitable organizations in the United States. These groups provided refugees with shelter and food and helped them obtain temporary government assistance. Many immigrants got job training, and their children enrolled in public schools. After several years in the United States, Vietnamese began to know family members and friends settling in other parts of the United States and initiated a wave of secondary migration, concentrating in communities such as Orange County, Calif.; Houston; and even New Orleans. Vietnamese Americans now number over 1 million.

Other Asians

There are other Asian ethnic groups in the United States. They include Southeast Asians from Thailand, Indonesia, Malaysia, Laos, and Cambodia. Cambodians and Laotians are similar to Vietnamese in that they immigrated to the United States primarily as refugees from the Vietnam War. Other Asians came from South Asian countries such as Nepal, Pakistan, and Sri Lanka. They are similar to Asian Indians in that they were primarily immigrants seeking better economic opportunities. Like the groups discussed above, other Asians represent a diversity of languages, cultures, national heritages, and immigration and settlement experiences.

Demographic Characteristics

After the passage of the 1965 Immigration and Nationality Act, Asia quickly became the second-largest source of immigrants to the United States, and, as a result, the Asian American population has grown rapidly. For example, Asian Americans represented 1.4 percent of the population in 1980 and almost 4 percent in 2000 (see Table 1, page 417). With the exception of Japanese Americans, all Asian ethnic groups have more than doubled in population since 1980. By comparison, the total U.S. population increased by only 24 percent in this period.

The option to choose more than one race first available in the 2000 Census makes it difficult to compare Asian populations over time and, for 2000, across Asian ethnic groups (see Box 1, page 416). To compare the 2000 totals with earlier censuses in Table 1, we used a 50 percent rule to reallocate multiracial and multiethnic Asians to their appropriate groups (see Box 2). These numbers differ slightly from the 2000 Census figures released by the U.S. Census Bureau, shown in columns 1 and 3 of Table 2. In the 2000 Census, 10,019,405 individuals reported being of one Asian ethnicity (column 3), and 11,898,828 chose an Asian ethnicity either alone *or* in combination with some other category (column 1). Overall, 84 percent reported a single ethnic group among all who reported an Asian ethnicity. This percentage, which roughly gauges the

extent to which an Asian group does not have mixed ancestry, varied from 92 percent among Vietnamese to 69 percent among Japanese. Throughout this report, we focus mostly on those who chose a single ethnic group when comparing Asian ethnic groups.

Most of the increase in the Asian American population is due to immigration rather than to natural growth, a circumstance reflected in the proportions of foreign-born among Asians in the United States (see Table 2). Although these proportions vary greatly by ethnicity, with Japanese at the low end (41 percent) and Koreans at the high end (79 percent), overall 64 percent of Asians in the United States were born abroad.

Foreign birth and speaking a language other than English at home are crude measures of assimilation into American society. While the highest foreign-born fraction is found among Koreans, the highest percentage of non-English speaking at home is among Vietnamese (at 93 percent). Other than multiracial Asians, the Japanese have the lowest rates of foreign birth and of non-English speaking at home—both below 50 percent. The multiethnic and multiracial Asians are similar to the Japanese in having low rates of both being foreign-born and non-English speaking at home.

Despite a long history of disproportionately male immigration, the sex ratio among Asian Americans overall is either balanced or in favor of women. The only ethnic group with an underrepresentation of women is Asian Indians, at 47 percent female. The age composition varies greatly by ethnicity. The Japanese American population shows signs of aging, with 20 percent at age 65 or older and 12 percent below age 18. Among all the other groups, children constitute a much larger percentage (from 21 percent to 45 percent), and the elderly a much smaller percentage (from 4 percent to 10 percent). The relative youth

---

Box 2

THE ONE-DROP RULE VS. THE 50 PERCENT RULE

The 2000 U.S. Census allowed for the first time the enumeration of people with multiple racial/ethnic affiliations. For comparison with historical data and for simplicity, it is sometimes necessary to reclassify multiracial people in the 2000 Census into single-race categories in statistical tabulations.

There are two possible simple rules for such an objective: the "one-drop rule" and the 50 percent rule. The one-drop rule defines race in reference to the white majority. It specifies that anyone with any minority ancestry is considered nonwhite. The 50 percent rule evenly assigns biracial people to the two racial groups to which they partially belong for statistical purposes. These two rules serve as ideal types, as more rules can be devised to allocate multiracial people based on fourth or eighth fractions according to the mixture of their parents' and grandparents' races.

In much of U.S. history and culture, a common rule for categorizing multiracial blacks has been the one-drop rule,

although it is unclear how rigidly it has been practiced. For multiracial Asians, who are a relatively recent phenomenon, it appears that the 50 percent rule is a close approximation. Prior research has found children of parents who had one Asian and one white parent (the majority of multiracial Asians) were almost equally likely to be identified as Asian or white when forced to choose a single race.

For this report, the 50 percent rule was applied when it was necessary to reclassify multiracial Asians in the 2000 Census into single-race categories. For example, the size of the 2000 Asian American population was estimated at 11,070,913 (3.9 percent of total) if the racial classification system had not been changed (see Table 1, page 417). In most of the analyses presented in the report, rich information pertaining to multiracials in the 2000 Census was preserved by separating multiethnic and multiracial Asians.

Table 2
POPULATION SIZE AND KEY DEMOGRAPHIC CHARACTERISTICS BY ASIAN AMERICAN ETHNICITY, 2000

Race/ethnicity	Asian alone or in combination	% single ethnic group	Single-ethnic classification	% foreign-born	% speaking non-English language at home	% female	% children (ages 0–17)	% elderly (ages 65+)
All Asians	11,898,828	84	10,019,405	64	73	52	27	7
Chinese	2,879,636	84	2,432,585	72	86	52	21	10
Japanese	1,148,932	69	796,700	41	47	57	12	20
Filipino	2,364,815	78	1,850,314	70	71	55	22	9
Korean	1,228,427	88	1,076,872	79	82	56	24	6
Asian Indian	1,899,599	88	1,678,765	76	81	47	25	4
Vietnamese	1,223,736	92	1,122,528	77	93	50	27	5
Other Asian	1,449,087	73	1,061,641	68	87	50	35	3
Multiethnic Asian	223,593	—	223,593	50	61	51	33	4
Multiracial Asian	1,655,830	—	1,655,830	30	35	50	45	4

Note: Percentages for All Asians were based on the total in the "Asian alone or in combination" column; percentages for Asian ethnic groups were based on the "Single-ethnic classification" column.

— Not applicable.

Sources: Authors' calculations using Census 2000 5% Public Use Microdata Sample (PUMS); and J.S. Barnes and C.E. Bennett, *The Asian Population: 2000* (2002).

of the other Asian groups is due to immigration, as immigrants tend to be young people who either bring children to America or rear children soon after immigration.

From Discrimination to Model Minority

For the convenience of statistical reporting, Asian Americans are often treated as a single race and compared with other major racial groups such as whites and blacks. That is the practice adopted here. Yet cultural heritage and immigration paths vary greatly by country of origin among Asian Americans. Owing to this diversity, most Asian Americans would not accept the proposition that they belong to a single Asian race. When given a choice, they often would rather identify themselves as part of an Asian ethnic group (such as Chinese, Japanese, or Vietnamese) than as simply Asian American. However, because Asian groups are all numerically small and lacking in political strength, some Asian Americans feel the need to develop a panethnic Asian American identity.

In this context, three distinctions are drawn between race and ethnicity. First, it is commonly accepted that race refers to distinctions drawn from physical appearance, whereas ethnicity refers to distinctions based on cultural markers such as national origin, language, religion, and food. Second, race has serious social consequences for individuals' life chances, whereas ethnicity is for the most part considered optional in contemporary America. Third, individuals' freedom of racial identification is limited, in the sense that racial identification requires external consent from others, whereas ethnic identity can be internal.

Therefore, regardless of their own views concerning whether or not they belong to a single race, Asian Americans face categorization into a single race in America, as they are often defined in contrast to the other racial groups—whites, blacks, and American Indians. This categorization of Asian Americans as a racial minority has differed historically, geographically, and legally. In Hawaii, Asians often adopted the identity of Hawaiian, speaking a dialect of English called pidgin, which mixed elements of English, Portuguese, Native Hawaiian, and Asian languages. In Mississippi, early Chinese immigrants were subject to the same segregation as blacks, though later they would achieve "honorary" white status as they became economically successful. Despite these regional differences, U.S. Supreme Court cases such as People v. Hall (1854) and Saito v. United States (1893) ruled that Asians were either classified as "a lesser caste similar to Indians" (in the case of Chinese) or Mongolian (in the case of the Japanese), but not Caucasian or white. These two court cases, among others, reaffirmed that Asian immigrants could not obtain citizenship, because citizenship was only possible for "free whites" or for those born on U.S. soil. Asian Indians, first considered Caucasian according to two separate court cases in 1910 and 1913, were denied citizenship in 1923 (United States v. Bhagat Singh Thind) because they were not of northern or Western European descent.[3] The restriction on naturalization was lifted for Chinese immigrants in 1943 and for other Asian immigrants in 1952.

How Asian Americans were defined racially affected whether or not they could be citizens of the United States, own land, and hold certain jobs. Because the courts defined Asians as nonwhite, most Asian immigrants in the 19th and early 20th centuries were prevented from becoming citizens of the United States.

However, children of Asian immigrants who were born on U.S. soil were citizens. In 1913, alien land law acts prevented Asian immigrants from owning land or leasing land for more than three years. Taxes were levied on "foreign" miners' earnings in California in 1850. Race also determined where Asians lived and whom they could marry. Chinese people attempting to settle in Tacoma, Wash., were prevented from doing so by white residents of the town. Koreans were prohibited from settling in Riverside County, Calif. Antimiscegenation laws forbidding marriage specifically between whites and Mongolians were enacted in some states as early as 1880.

In different places and at various points in U.S. history, Asian Americans have also been subjected to prejudice, hatred, and racial violence. An 1870 poem, entitled "The Heathen Chinee," reflected a negative sentiment toward Chinese at that time. The poem was reprinted and republished across the country, and "its sensational popularity made Bret Harte [its author] the most celebrated literary man in America in 1870." It begins with:

> "Which I wish to remark,
> And my language is plain,
> That for ways that are dark
> And for tricks that are vain,
> The heathen Chinee is peculiar,
> Which the same I would rise to explain."[4]

Mob violence against Asian Americans was first documented in 1871, when European Americans entered neighborhoods in Los Angeles' Chinatown and shot and hanged 21 Chinese people. Settlements of Asians were burned, and Asian residents were forced out of towns. Fear of and prejudice toward Asian immigrants eventually led to the prohibition of all Asian immigration to the United States, a process that was enacted in stages. Chinese immigration was first limited in 1882 with the Chinese Exclusion Act; Japanese immigration was restricted in 1907-1908; and then in 1924 all Asian immigration was prohibited. Changes were not made to these discriminatory immigration laws until 1943 (see Box 3).

The generally negative image of Asian immigrants in America between the 1860s and 1920s is far from the "model minority" label widely used to characterize Asian Americans in recent decades.[5] Since the 1960s, Asian Americans' success in education and their high concentration in professional occupations have been widely publicized by the popular press. Asian Americans' values have been declared compatible with the Protestant work ethic of the United States.[6]

Demographic changes in the population of Asian immigrants are in part responsible for the shift in the public's image of them from negative to positive. When the prohibition of Asian immigrants was repealed in 1965, immigration priority was given to family members of immigrants and workers with needed skills. Therefore, Asian immigrants to the United States after the 1960s were more likely to be highly skilled workers than those who immigrated during the 19th century, and many had been exposed to the English language and Western culture.

Political refugees formed another major component of immigration to the United States during the 1970s and 1980s. During the 1970s, Vietnamese, Cambodian, Lao, and Hmong refugees who aided the United States in military operations were helped to escape from their countries. Other refugees left Vietnam after 1975, when the communist forces gained control over the South. Citizens of the United States were sympathetic to the plight of these noncommunist refugees, having waged war on behalf of these people against what they perceived to be a communist threat. Many aid organizations and churches organized the immigration and settlement of these groups.

Another popular explanation for the portrayal of Asian Americans as a model minority is that immigrant Asian Americans invest heavily in their children's education. Cultural explanations for this investment stress the compatibility of Confucian cultural values with the Protestant work ethic. Other research adds that anticipation of discrimination and marginalization in the labor force leads Asian Americans to choose education as a viable means to achieve upward mobility.

Despite the overall educational and economic successes of Asian Americans, heterogeneity among them is high. Just as the image of the model minority is an uninformed characterization of Asian Americans, the attribution of all observed disadvantages of Asian Americans to racial discrimination is too simplistic. Complex by nature, social phenomena routinely defy simple explanations and require nuanced analyses. The experience of Asian Americans is no exception. The remainder of this report focuses on the empirical question of how Asian Americans have fared in terms of measurable indicators of socioeconomic status relative to whites and blacks in this country.

EDUCATIONAL ATTAINMENT

One important empirical finding that distinguishes Asian Americans is that they have indeed attained socioeconomic status that is overall comparable with, and in some instances superior to, that of whites. In studying the relatively high socioeconomic status of Asian Americans, scholars have invariably pointed out that Asian Americans have successfully attained high levels of education.[7] Hence, a fruitful examination of the socioeconomic conditions of Asian Americans requires knowledge of their educational experiences.

New Entrants to the Labor Force

Asian educational attainment was higher than that of both blacks and whites as early as 1960, with 70 percent of Asians completing a high school education, compared with 61 percent of whites and 33 percent of blacks (see Table 3, page 424). However, the gap in high school completion narrowed over time. In 1990, whites showed slightly higher rates of high school completion than Asians, due to the influx of new refugees from Southeast Asia. In 2000, Asians overall had a slightly higher rate of achieving high school degrees.

The gap between Asians and whites in college completion is far more dramatic. In 1960, 19 percent of Asian Americans had completed college, compared with 12 percent of whites. This gap increased throughout subsequent decades. In 2000, 53 percent of Asians had completed a college degree, compared with 30 percent of whites.

A substantial portion of the widening gap between Asians and whites in college completion was driven by foreign-born Asian Americans, particularly those who immigrated after 1965. The impact of changes in immigration laws, which established preferences for skilled workers, is seen in the dramatic differences in college completion among foreign-born Asian Americans from 1960 to 1970. In 1960, 19 percent of both foreign- and U.S.-born Asian Americans had attained a college degree. In 1970, this percentage jumped to 46 percent for the foreign-born. Although some foreign-born Asian Americans were educated in the United States, the immigration of highly educated Asians is largely responsible for this jump. By comparison, the college completion rate among U.S.-born Asian Americans in 1970 was 26 percent, while whites' college completion rate was at 16 percent.

Variation in Asian Americans' educational attainment is evident not only by nativity but also by ethnicity. In 1960, Japanese had the highest level of high school attainment, but Chinese had the highest level of college attainment. In later decades, Chinese, Koreans, and Asian Indians are among the most educationally successful, with college completion rates of 67 percent, 59 percent, and 76 percent in 2000, respectively. Vietnamese are among the least successful, with rates of high school and college completion below whites, and rates of high school completion below blacks.

The comparison by nativity does not follow the same pattern over time. Among Filipinos, for example, the foreign-born seem to have had an advantage in education even before 1965. Foreign-born Japanese had a lower college completion rate than the U.S.-born in 1960, but this reversed in 1970 and reversed again in later years. Koreans show a different pattern still. While in earlier decades foreign-born Koreans had more education than their U.S.-born counterparts, in 2000, 58 percent of foreign-born Koreans had completed college, compared with 70 per-

cent of U.S.-born Koreans. It should be noted that, while some foreign-born Asians came as immigrant children who received all or most of their education in the United States, most foreign-born Asian Americans completed their education before immigrating to the United States.[8]

Elementary and Secondary

Asian American children were not always educationally advantaged. Data from the 1910 Census, for example, reveal that Chinese and Japanese children ages 7 to 17 were less likely to be enrolled in school than were whites (77 percent for Chinese and 73 percent for Japanese versus 88 percent for whites). In part, this disadvantage was due to segregation laws that prevented Chinese and Japanese children from attending schools with majority whites. In California in the late 1800s, the effect of such laws was to restrict Chinese and Japanese children to segregated schools for "Orientals." In states with smaller Asian populations, like Mississippi, Asian children were required to attend segregated schools

Table 3

PERCENT COMPLETING HIGH SCHOOL AND ATTAINING COLLEGE DEGREES BY ASIAN ETHNICITY AND RACE, AMERICANS AGES 25–34, 1960–2000

Race/ethnicity	High school or higher					College degree or higher				
	1960	1970	1980	1990	2000	1960	1970	1980	1990	2000
All Asians	70	84	87	85	90	19	37	42	43	53
U.S.-born	79	87	95	94	94	19	26	44	43	50
Foreign-born	58	82	84	83	89	19	46	42	44	54
Chinese	62	82	88	85	92	26	44	50	53	67
U.S.-born	80	90	97	97	96	28	32	58	63	73
Foreign-born	48	79	85	83	91	25	48	48	51	65
Japanese	77	90	96	98	97	16	32	45	49	57
U.S.-born	83	93	98	98	96	18	30	48	47	57
Foreign-born	63	84	93	97	98	11	37	40	52	57
Filipino	58	82	88	90	95	18	37	42	37	43
U.S.-born	53	76	87	89	97	11	10	15	23	43
Foreign-born	63	85	89	91	94	25	47	47	42	43
Korean	—	69	83	90	97	—	40	31	42	59
U.S.-born	—	40	91	97	98	—	6	33	57	70
Foreign-born	—	77	83	90	97	—	51	31	42	58
Asian Indian	—	—	90	90	94	—	—	60	60	76
U.S.-born	—	—	81	94	92	—	—	40	67	74
Foreign-born	—	—	90	89	94	—	—	61	60	76
Vietnamese	—	—	69	67	72	—	—	14	22	27
U.S.-born	—	—	—	42	52	—	—	—	8	23
Foreign-born	—	—	69	67	73	—	—	14	22	27
Whites	61	74	87	87	88	12	16	25	25	30
Blacks	33	52	75	77	81	4	6	12	12	15

— Data not available.

Source: Authors' calculations using the 1% Public Use Microdata Sample (PUMS) from the 1960–2000 censuses.

with blacks. Asians, like other minorities, fought vehemently for integration and educational opportunity. And, as early as 1930, Chinese and Japanese enrollment in elementary and secondary schools surpassed that of whites, although segregation laws were not removed officially in many states until the 1950s.

In today's elementary and secondary schools, the academic performance of Asian American students is generally high. According to the National Center for Education Statistics (NCES), in 1999, only 7 percent of Asians in grades K through 12 had ever repeated a grade, compared with 9 percent of whites. Additional results drawn from the 1988-1994 National Education Longitudinal Study (NELS), administered by NCES to a nationally representative sample of eighth-graders in 1988, show that Asian Americans scored significantly higher on a standardized math test than whites; differences in verbal scores were statistically insignificant between whites and Asians.

These results are confirmed by scores on the Scholastic Aptitude Test (SAT) in the academic year 2000-2001. On the verbal SAT, Asian American students taking the test scored slightly lower than their white peers (501 versus 528) but higher than blacks and Hispanics (at 430 and 460, respectively). On the math SAT during that same year, Asians scored higher than all the other groups, with an average score of 566 compared with whites at an average of 531.

Asian American high school students also attain higher grade point averages than do their white counterparts. Asian American eighth- and 10th-graders in NELS reported grade point averages of 3.2 and 3.0 on a four-point scale, compared with 2.9 and 2.7 for whites.[9] Furthermore, Asian American students take more advanced math and science courses than do students of other race and ethnic groups. In 1998, NCES reported that 74 percent of Asian high school graduates had taken advanced science and that 56 percent of them had taken advanced math. The comparable percentages for whites were 64 percent and 45 percent.

Asian American teenagers seem to have fewer behavioral problems in schools as well. From the 1999 National Household Survey, the NCES reports that the percentages of students in grades 7 to 12 who had ever been expelled or suspended from school were 13 percent for Asians, 15 percent for whites, 20 percent for Hispanics, and 35 percent for blacks. Asian American students are also unlikely to drop out of high school. According to data from the October 2000 Current Population Survey, 4 percent of Asian American 16-to-24-year-olds were considered high school dropouts, while the corresponding percentages were 7 percent among whites, 13 percent among blacks, and 28 percent among Hispanics. The high school completion rates among 18-to-24-year-olds in 2000 were 95 percent among Asians and 92 percent among whites. Similarly, 92 percent of Asians in the eighth-grade in 1988

Table 4

HIGH SCHOOL COMPLETION AND COLLEGE ENROLLMENT OF ASIAN ETHNIC GROUPS, WHITES, AND BLACKS WITHIN SIX YEARS OF EIGHTH GRADE, 1994

Race/ethnicity	Eighth graders in 1988	
	High school graduation by 1994 (%)	Enrollment in postsecondary institution by 1994 (%)
All Asians	92*	80*
Chinese	97*	87*
Japanese	95	80
Filipino	96*	76
Korean	93*	79*
South Asian	99*	87*
Southeast Asian	88	86*
Whites	85	68
Blacks	73*	57*

* Percentages for Asians and blacks were significantly different from percentages for whites.

Source: Authors' calculations based on the National Education Longitudinal Study of 1988.

received their high school diploma within six years, compared with 85 percent of whites (see Table 4).

Asian Americans' academic achievement in elementary and secondary schools is related to attitudes and behaviors of both Asian American children and their parents. Asian American parents expect their children to achieve higher levels of education than do parents of other racial groups. For example, data from NELS show that over a third of the mothers and fathers of Asian 10th-graders expect their children to achieve some graduate education, compared with less than a fifth of white parents. Further, Asian American children themselves expect to achieve more education than their white, black, and Hispanic peers. Over 20 percent of Asian 10th-graders in this same study reported the expectation of achieving a doctorate, compared with 14 percent or less among blacks, Hispanics, and whites.[10] It has been suggested that Asian American parents perceive effort rather than ability as the key to children's educational attainment, while white parents believe more in innate ability.[11] To achieve the goals that parents set for them and that they set for themselves, Asian American children also expend more effort on academic matters, doing on average close to one hour more of homework per week than whites.[12]

Postsecondary

Academic success in high school prepares Asian Americans well for entering postsecondary institutions. The NELS data show that Asian Americans of all ethnic groups, except Filipinos, apply for admission to two- and four-year colleges at much higher rates than do whites.[13] Furthermore, detailed analysis of the data reveals that Asian Americans tend to apply to more colleges than do whites, and that these colleges are more likely to be the top-tier schools (as measured by the average SAT scores of entering classes). Whites are more likely to apply to smaller, less expensive, and less selective schools.

The NELS data also indicate that Asian Americans have rates of acceptance to their first-choice schools that are comparable to those of whites overall. This is significant in light of the fact that, in recent decades, the admission policies concerning Asian American applicants at highly selective schools like Harvard, Princeton, Brown, and Stanford have been closely scrutinized. At issue is whether or not academically qualified Asian applicants are disadvantaged in admission processes that prioritize nonacademic factors such as extracurricular activities and athletic abilities. Despite perceived difficulties, the desire of Asian American applicants, or more precisely their parents, to enroll in these elite universities remains very high. Analysis of the NELS data reveals that Asian Americans do gain admission to and later attend the top tier universities in this country in large numbers.

Asian Americans are much more likely to enroll in a postsecondary institution than are whites and other minority groups (see Table 4, page 425). Among those who were eighth-graders in 1988 and who later received their high school diplomas, 80 percent of Asian Americans, compared with 68 percent of whites, had enrolled in either a two-year or four-year postsecondary school by 1994. The enrollment rates vary by Asian ethnicity, ranging from 76 percent among Filipinos to between 86 percent and 87 percent among South Asians, Chinese, and Southeast Asians.

Some Asian American ethnic groups are more likely to attend two-year colleges than are whites. For example, Filipinos in the 1988 eighth-grade cohort of NELS were almost twice as likely to be enrolled in two-year colleges as whites. Japanese and Southeast Asians also report higher rates of enrollment in two-year institutions than do whites. Two-year schools may be perceived as less-expensive paths to four-year degrees, with many students who cannot immediately afford tuition at four-year schools receiving their first two years of education at community colleges. These students may later transfer to four-year institutions to complete coursework for a bachelor's degree.

Much media attention has focused on Asian Americans' overrepresentation in America's elite colleges. The NCES found that Asians were over two times more likely than whites to attend "Tier 1" national universities (top 50 national universities according to *U.S. News & World Report).*[14] Analysis of the NELS data shows that the proportion attending such universities among Asian students is very high, ranging from 18 percent and 22 percent among Japanese and South Asians to 42 percent

and 44 percent among Korean and Chinese students. This can be compared with whites' rate of about 9 percent. However, Asian Americans are not more likely than whites to attend first-tier liberal arts colleges.

Asian American college students differ from white students in choice of majors. Asians are more likely than whites to major in science, math, and engineering, and less likely than whites to choose fields in the humanities and education. Data from the 1993-1994 Baccalaureate and Beyond study indicate that 20 percent of Asian American graduates were granted bachelor's degrees in science or math, compared with 13 percent of whites. By comparison, 9 percent of Asians received degrees in the humanities, compared with 14 percent of whites.

For 1999-2000, the NCES reports that Asian Americans received about 5 percent of all the associate's degrees and 6.5 percent of all the bachelor's degrees conferred in the United States.

Postgraduate

Data from the Educational Testing Service show that Asian Americans' scores on the Graduate Record Examination during the 1980s were close to those of whites, with higher quantitative scores and slightly lower verbal scores. For example, Asian Americans in 1984-1985 scored 479 on verbal, 603 on quantitative, and 533 on the analytic portions of the test, compared with 513, 537, and 550 for whites. Similar Asian-white patterns have been observed in scores for the business, law, and medical school entrance exams.[15]

Asian Americans appear to be about as likely to enroll in master's and doctoral graduate degree programs as whites. However, analysis of data from the Baccalaureate and Beyond study reveals that Asian Americans are more likely than whites to enroll in graduate professional programs even when family background, test performance, and other undergraduate characteristics are taken into account. Among those in professional schools, Asians are more likely to be in medical school, while whites are more likely to be in law school. Similar to the situation for undergraduate majors, Asian Americans in doctoral programs are more likely than whites to be found in science and engineering programs and less likely to be in the liberal arts.

According to the NCES, Asian Americans received 5 percent of the master's degrees, 11 percent of the professional degrees, and about 5 percent of the doctoral degrees conferred between 1999 and 2000.

Explanations

What accounts for Asian Americans' overall high educational achievement? There are five potential explanations.

Socioeconomic background. The socioeconomic explanation highlights the role of family socioeconomic resources in Asian American children's educational success. Many Asian ethnic groups arrive in the United States with high levels of education. Others arrive with financial capital to enable them to set up small businesses. Asian parents may make good use of these socioeconomic resources to facilitate their children's educational achievement. However, it is important to recognize the diverse backgrounds of Asian Americans. Vietnamese and other Southeast Asians immigrated with little human or financial capital, and variation in income within groups like Chinese and Koreans is also very high. Poverty rates among Chinese, Koreans, and Vietnamese are higher than they are among whites. Thus, the socioeconomic explanation is simply not applicable to all Asian Americans.

Ability. The second popular explanation for high Asian American academic achievement focuses on their ability. On various standardized tests, Asian Americans show a greater proficiency in math and only slightly lower verbal aptitude than do whites. Popular attention to racial differences in tested proficiency has led to much speculation about the sources of these differences. While some contend that the differences are biological in nature, others attribute differences in measured proficiency to parents' socioeconomic resources, neighborhood and community environments, immigration selectivity, and perhaps culture.

Community and identity. Another explanation for Asian American educational success considers the community-level support, encouragement, and information that is available to students. Because Asian Americans hold high educational expectations, they serve as examples for each other, encourage and support each other's achievement, and serve as sources of information about colleges and application procedures. For example, Asian American adults who have attended college act as role models for Asian American high school students. Asian Americans may also benefit from peer groups composed predominantly of other Asian Americans. Students in close-knit ethnic communities, like the New Orleans Vietnamese community, benefit from the supervision and support of community members. Children who maintain their ethnic distinctiveness through their native language and ethnic self-identification link themselves to this community. They are then accountable to the community and closely supervised by its members. Children not only learn norms that contribute to their success from this community, but also benefit from the connectedness of its members.[16]

Attitudes, values, and beliefs concerning education. Attitudes, values, and beliefs held by Asian Americans that differ from those of whites may have their origins in Asian cultures or in the self-selection of immigrants. Researchers suggest that one legacy of Confucianism in many Asian countries (notably China, Korea, Japan, and Vietnam) is the notion that human beings are perfectible if they work hard to improve themselves. Given this cul-

tural heritage, some Asian Americans may be more likely than whites to believe that hard work in school will be rewarded. It is also argued that Asian Americans may presume greater returns to education, both material and symbolic, than do whites and other minorities, based on beliefs originating in Asian home countries. In traditional Confucian societies, individuals of low social origin are encouraged to achieve upward mobility through intensive study. In particular, sought-after civil service jobs are tied to the successful completion of examinations. Because of this culture, Asian American parents and their children may be more likely to view education as a prominent, if not the sole, means to greater occupational prestige, social standing, and income. In addition, Asian Americans may be more likely to hold particular values, attitudes, and beliefs because they are voluntary immigrants to the United States. Voluntary immigrants are self-selected in having high motivations to achieve, evidenced by the fact that they chose to immigrate. Therefore, values encouraging success and hard work may be a product of the self-selected immigration process itself rather than of any particular ethnic or cultural heritage.

Blocked opportunities. The blocked opportunities perspective is closely related to the last two explanations. It suggests that Asian Americans use education as a means to overcome obstacles to social mobility.[17] As recent immigrants, Asian Americans lack social networks to help them obtain good jobs in the mainstream economy, although they may have ethnic networks that are conducive to educational attainment. For example, Asian Americans may lack access to social networks that will help them obtain well-paid manufacturing jobs after graduating from high school because few Asian Americans work in such occupations. They also lack population bases for political careers. Thus, Asian parents stress education as a means for their children to overcome their disadvantages in achieving social mobility. In an economy where the demand for knowledge-based skill is high and meritocracy is held as a norm (even if not fully implemented in practice), this strategy for social mobility is quite appealing, especially when accompanied by the Confucian cultural norm that human imperfections can be improved by persistent learning and practice. Asian Americans' strong belief in the connection between hard work and success underlies their heavy investment in education as a means to achieve the social mobility that might otherwise elude them.

The five explanations overlap. Together, they provide plausible explanations of the educational achievement of Asian Americans. Many Asian American youths have highly educated parents and/or high family incomes. Overall, Asian Americans perform better on standardized math tests than do whites. Asian American students may also have highly educated role models and motivated peers, and reside in interconnected ethnic communities. Some Asian Americans, either because they are selective immigrants or because of their cultural backgrounds, may believe hard work is rewarded with success and may perceive high returns to education. Further, these values—coupled with limited opportunities for Asian Americans' social mobility through means other than education—may lead Asian American families to stress education as a means to high social standing and economic success in the United States.

LABOR FORCE OUTCOMES

Socioeconomic status is multidimensional, with education and labor force outcomes as two of its main components. Thus, racial inequality or ethnic inequality usually refers to racial or ethnic differences in education and labor force outcomes. The last section examined education and found that Asian Americans overall have surpassed whites in key outcomes, despite substantial differences across ethnic groups among Asian Americans. This section focuses on labor force outcomes.

Labor force outcomes are quite different from educational outcomes in some respects. First, labor force outcomes have direct economic consequences for individuals and their families, whereas the consequences of educational outcomes are indirect, mostly mediated by their effects on labor force outcomes. Second, labor force outcomes are not only affected by individuals' own efforts and family resources but also by relationships with others—employers, supervisors, and co-workers. Third, except for slots in prestigious universities, the educational achievement of Asian Americans does not necessarily pose a threat to whites and other minorities. Some workers, however, feel that, as more positions are taken by Asians in the labor market, fewer are available for non-Asians.

Because labor force outcomes are more likely than educational outcomes to be influenced by racial resentment or discrimination, they are more direct indicators of Asian Americans' social status in American society. This section analyzes three dimensions of labor force outcomes—labor supply, earnings, and occupation— and draws comparisons by race and ethnicity as well as by gender. A focus on gender is necessary because work has been traditionally segregated by gender in American society.

Labor Supply

The labor force participation rate refers to the proportion of the adult population who are either employed or actively looking for work. Labor force participation excludes people who are not employed and not seeking employment. If nonparticipation in the labor force reflects not only an individual's own choice but also market forces (such as little hope of finding meaningful

Table 5

LABOR FORCE PARTICIPATION BY RACE AND ASIAN ETHNICITY, AMERICANS AGES 21–64, 1960-2000

Race/ethnicity	% in labor force				
	1960	1970	1980	1990	2000
All Asians					
Men	92	89	87	86	80
Women	48	56	65	68	65
Chinese					
Men	89	85	86	86	81
Women	45	53	67	69	66
Japanese					
Men	94	93	88	88	84
Women	51	57	65	64	65
Filipino					
Men	90	90	92	91	80
Women	39	61	75	80	73
Korean					
Men	—	77	87	83	78
Women	—	36	61	61	59
Asian Indian					
Men	—	—	92	91	85
Women	—	—	57	64	59
Vietnamese					
Men	—	—	74	81	74
Women	—	—	53	63	61
Whites					
Men	93	91	89	88	84
Women	39	48	59	70	71
Blacks					
Men	86	83	79	76	68
Women	51	57	64	70	69

— Data not available.

Source: Authors' calculations using the 1% Public Use Microdata Sample (PUMS) from the 1960–2000 censuses.

employment), labor force participation confounds labor supply with demand.

Here, labor force participation is treated as labor supply. To interpret number of hours worked as labor supply, it is assumed that workers can increase the number of hours worked at will. That is, part-time workers can work full time if they wish, even if this change requires them to change employment. No results concerning employment are shown, for two reasons. First, employment (or unemployment) measures demand more than supply. Second, preliminary analysis indicates very small, unsystematic racial differences in employment rates between Asians and non-Asians and across Asian ethnic groups.

An interesting pattern that emerges from examining labor force participation rates is that gender differences vary by race (see Table 5). In the earlier decades, gender differences were much larger for whites than for blacks: A lower fraction of black men than white men, and a higher fraction of black women than white women, participated in the labor force. Black women's higher rates of labor force participation are a reflection of greater economic need—in part because of black men's lower labor force participation rates, and in part because of black women's lower marriage rates. For Asian Americans, both men and women have had relatively high labor force participation rates.

In particular, Japanese and Chinese women had high rates of labor force participation during the period. In 1960, for example, the rates were 51 percent for Japanese women and 45 percent for Chinese women, compared with 39 percent for white women and 51 percent for black women. However, unlike blacks, relatively few Chinese and Japanese women remained unmarried. It appears that these working Asian women contributed significantly to family income, in part because not many Asian husbands had high incomes.

A clear trend from 1960 onward is the steady increase in women's labor force participation. Although all the racial/ethnic groups experienced the increase, it was sharpest among whites, for whom labor force participation increased rapidly from 39 percent in 1960 to 71 percent in 2000. For Asian women, the rate increased from 48 percent to 68 percent in 1990 and held at 65 percent in 2000—a trend that was very similar to that of black women. By 1990, the rate for white women was slightly higher than blacks' and had surpassed Asians'. Asian men's labor force participation rates declined gradually over the decades, as they did for whites and blacks.

There is also substantial ethnic variation in labor force participation between 1960 and 2000. Among Asian American men, Vietnamese had the lowest participation rates (74 percent to 81 percent between 1980 and 2000). Among Asian American women, both Vietnamese and Koreans had low participation rates (between 36 percent and 63 percent between 1970 and 2000). Because Vietnamese Americans were mostly refugees, they were disadvantaged in the labor market by a lack of both human and financial capital. Korean women's low levels of labor force participation in part reflect a cultural norm that women should stop working outside the home after marriage and childbirth. While this cultural norm is shared to some degree by all the groups (as revealed in the data), its influence on labor force participation is more pronounced among Korean Americans. Low levels of labor force participation among Korean women may also reflect the underreporting of their participation in family-owned businesses.

In terms of average hours worked per week, Asian men worked slightly less than white men and Asian women worked slightly more than white women (by one to two hours per week overall). The real divergence between Asians and whites is seen in gender differ-

ences. While women overall worked fewer hours per week than men, the gender disparity is wider for whites than for Asians—a difference that emerged after 1970, as the gender gap substantially narrowed for Asians but remained at a similar level for whites. In 1980, for example, Asian men worked an average of 43 hours and Asian women worked 38, a gender difference of about five hours. In contrast, white men worked 44 hours and white women worked 36 hours, an eight-hour difference. The gender differences in hours worked were even smaller among blacks: four hours in 1990 and 2000.[18]

The extent to which the gender gap in hours worked is smaller for Asians than for whites varies by ethnicity. The smallest gender gap is found among Vietnamese: two hours in 1980 and 1990, and three hours in 2000. After 1960, the gender gap in hours worked was also very small for Filipinos: two hours in 1970, 1990, and 2000. Vietnamese and Filipinos on average had lower socioeconomic status than the other major Asian ethnic groups. As with blacks, the narrowing gender gap in hours worked among Vietnamese and Filipinos is attributable both to a lower number of hours worked by men and to a higher number of hours worked by women, who needed to compensate for men's lower labor supply and earnings.

Earnings

In contrast to education and labor supply, earnings directly reflect the demand for a worker's skill and productivity in the labor market. If there is discrimination against Asian Americans because of their race or country of origin, it is more likely to be reflected in earnings than in any other indicator.

An analysis comparing U.S.-born Asians' earnings to whites' earnings, separately by gender, appears in Table 6 (page 430). Because education attained abroad may not be as highly valued in the American labor market as education acquired in the United States, immigrants who completed their education prior to immigration may suffer an earnings disadvantage.[19]

The entries in Table 6 are the Asian/white earnings ratios, observed and adjusted. An observed earnings ratio is the ratio of Asians' average earnings to whites' average earnings. An adjusted earnings ratio accounts for education and experience and indicates whether Asian Americans suffer an earnings disadvantage after adjustment for schooling and years of work experience. Asians are said by some to achieve economic parity with whites through "overeducation"; this is called the net disadvantage thesis.[20] Since Asian Americans are advantaged relative to whites in education but not in work experience, the difference between observed earnings ratios and adjusted earnings ratios is attributable to Asians' higher educational attainment.

A value of 1.00 in Table 6 means earnings equity. A ratio value less than 1.00 indicates Asians' disadvantage.

Likewise, a number greater than 1.00 indicates Asians' advantage. For example, in 1959 all Asian men earned 98 percent as much as white men on average, but the racial difference is not statistically significant (in other words, it could be due to chance). However, after adjusting for human capital, Asians earned 94 percent as much as comparable whites in 1959, and this racial difference is statistically significant (not likely to be due to chance). Thus, the apparent equality of observed earnings is the result of Asians' higher levels of educational attainment.

Several findings emerge from the earnings results. First, Asian Americans compared more favorably with whites in observed earnings than in adjusted earnings. Asians' advantage over whites in observed earnings is particularly large in 1989 and 1999, in part reflecting the increased return to higher education in the U.S. labor market during this period. Second, there is a significant and steady trend over the decades in Asians' favor. Without adjustment, Asian men earned about as much as white men between 1959 and 1979, but earned 9 percent more in 1989 and 14 percent more in 1999. After

adjustment, Asian men experienced an earnings disadvantage of 6 percent in 1959 and 5 percent in 1979, but a 4 percent advantage in 1999. Similar increases in the Asian/white ratio for the six major ethnicities are also apparent. Third, Asian women have fared well relative to white women. Throughout the period and for all the groups considered, Asian women's earnings were not significantly lower than white women's. In fact, Asian women's observed earnings and adjusted earnings began to surpass those of white women in 1969, and the Asian advantage continued to grow. By 1999, Asian women earned 32 percent more than white women before adjustment and 17 percent more after adjustment.

Finally, substantial variation occurred across Asian ethnic groups. Of the three major Asian groups that were observed throughout the four-decade period, Filipinos did not do as well as Chinese and Japanese. In 1959, Filipino men earned 79 percent as much as whites before adjustment and 87 percent as much as white men after adjustment. The gap between Filipino men and white men gradually closed by 1999. However, in no

Table 6

RATIO OF ASIAN AMERICANS' EARNINGS TO WHITES' EARNINGS: OBSERVED AND ADJUSTED FOR EDUCATION AND EXPERIENCE, 1959–1999

| Race/ | 1959 | | 1969 | | 1979 | | 1989 | | 1999 | |
ethnicity	Observed	Adjusted*	Observed	Adjusted*	Observed	Adjusted*	Observed	Adjusted*	Observed	Adjusted*
All U.S.-born Asians										
Men	0.98	0.94**	1.04**	0.98	1.01	0.95**	1.09**	1.02	1.14**	1.04**
Women	1.04	1.02	1.13**	1.08**	1.17**	1.09**	1.28**	1.16**	1.32**	1.17**
Chinese										
Men	0.99	0.94	1.01	0.90**	1.03	0.95	1.29**	1.11**	1.35**	1.12**
Women	1.10	1.07	1.18**	1.09	1.31**	1.18**	1.44**	1.24**	1.65**	1.35**
Japanese										
Men	1.00	0.95**	1.08**	1.02	1.08**	0.99	1.13**	1.01	1.19**	1.00
Women	1.04	1.02	1.15**	1.11**	1.17**	1.09**	1.31**	1.17**	1.37**	1.15**
Filipino										
Men	0.79**	0.87**	0.80**	0.89**	0.80**	0.86**	0.87**	0.95**	0.93**	1.00
Women	0.86	0.88	0.94	0.95	0.99	0.98	1.07**	1.07**	1.09**	1.09**
Korean										
Men	—	—	0.97	1.00	0.85	0.86	1.04	1.11	1.15**	1.13**
Women	—	—	0.92	0.91	1.25	1.18	1.28**	1.20**	1.24**	1.20**
Asian Indian										
Men	—	—	—	—	0.74**	0.67**	1.03	0.94	1.10	1.09
Women	—	—	—	—	1.02	0.97	1.33**	1.15	1.34**	1.20**
Vietnamese										
Men	—	—	—	—	0.94	0.97	0.65**	0.77	0.87	1.08
Women	—	—	—	—	1.02	1.12	1.11	1.24	0.83	0.97

*Ratios adjusted for differences in education and experience.

**U.S.-born Asians' earnings were significantly different from those of whites.

— Data not available.

Note: Analysis was restricted to full-time/year-round workers with positive earnings who were ages 21–64.

Source: Authors' calculations using the 1% Public Use Microdata Sample (PUMS) from the 1960–2000 censuses.

year were the earnings of Filipino men higher than those of white men, either observed or adjusted. The Filipina-white gap for women was not statistically significant between 1959 and 1979, after which the gap turned to Filipinas' favor. In fact, in 1999 Filipinas earned 9 percent more than white women, in both observed and adjusted earnings. While Vietnamese overall had relatively low earnings, the only statistically significant disparity between Vietnamese and whites was for observed earnings in 1989. Asian Indians actually had low earnings relative to whites as recently as in 1979, when Indian men earned 74 percent as much as white men before adjustment and 67 percent as much after adjustment. After 1989, Asian Indian men reached parity with white men in both observed and adjusted earnings. Asian Indian women had about one-third higher observed earnings than white women in 1989, and about one-fifth higher adjusted earnings in 1999.

These results suggest that the net disadvantage thesis may be a valid characterization of the experiences of Asian American men prior to 1989. However, it does not appear to hold for either Asian American women in general, or for Asian American men since 1989. Due to both their higher educational attainment and higher earnings within levels of education, Asian American women have had an advantage over white women since 1969. Relative earnings of Asian American men also improved dramatically, to the point of surpassing white men, even after adjusting for education and experience. If there is evidence that Asian American men's lower adjusted earnings relative to white men's earnings reflected racial discrimination from 1959 to 1979, this ceased to be true after 1989.

Occupation

Occupation has been of central interest to those who study inequality for several reasons. First, one's occupation is usually known to friends, relatives, and acquaintances, and it is often considered a shorthand description of social status. In contrast, earnings are customarily private and are seldom used by others to describe a person's social status. Second, occupation is a relatively stable attribute that does not change much over the life cycle or the business cycle. In some ways, occupation can be thought of as a proxy measure of one's permanent income. Third, occupations are concrete social positions that are filled by actual workers. Forces such as technological innovation or economic development change the occupational structure and generate new positions, which in turn provide opportunities for social mobility. Sociologists have long been interested in who benefits and who loses as a result of such structural changes.

Occupation is significant for another reason that is especially germane to the discussion of inequality among Asian Americans. Some occupations may provide channels of mobility that are less subject to poten-

tial discrimination.[21] First, the extent to which objective criteria can be used for performance assessment varies, or is perceived to vary, from occupation to occupation. For example, universalism is a core normative principle in science, where extraneous factors—such as race, gender, nationality, and religion—should not play a role in the evaluation of performance. Similarly, in occupations such as engineering and computer programming, delivery of products and services can be more directly observed and assessed than in other occupations such as the military, teaching, and clerical work.

Furthermore, there is a direct correspondence between educational credentials and entry into certain occupations. For example, it usually takes a doctoral degree in science to be a scientist, and a medical degree to be a physician. Attaining such credentials is a long and arduous process, and no matter how privileged a person is—either because of family background or race—he/she cannot become a scientist or a physician without the requisite educational credentials. However, regardless of one's social origin (including race), job opportunities in these fields are widely available once one attains the educational credentials. This close link between education and entry into many prestigious occupations makes it reasonable for Asian Americans to use educational attainment as an effective channel of mobility to overcome either real or perceived barriers to some high-status occupations.

Given that Asian Americans have achieved high educational and academic credentials, they may rationally seek to work in occupations in which they can demonstrate their skills and in which objective criteria are used to evaluate performance. One 30-year-old Korean American summed up Asians' motivation in this way:

"I don't think that Asians prefer the sciences. Sometimes it is the only avenue open to them. In the sciences, empirical results matter more than in the esoteric discussion of humanities. So that at least as an engineer, you know how to put machines in, and you can be a useful bolt and nut. And I think the job opportunities for us lie in this field."[22]

Asians, then, may be concentrated in certain occupations on the basis of their desire to maximize socioeconomic outcomes. However, racial concentration in certain occupations can also occur through other social mechanisms. An historical example illustrates how this can happen. In San Francisco in the late 19th century, a small group of Chinese people began working in the laundry service occupation in response to discrimination and labor competition from whites. Their success demonstrated that they could operate laundries, not necessarily that they were best suited to running laundries relative to other kinds of work. Somehow, through social networks and role modeling, many other Chinese

Table 7

PERCENT ASIAN BY OCCUPATION AND INDEX OF DISSIMILARITY, 1960-2000

Occupation	1960	1970	1980	1990	2000
Life scientists	3.6	4.2	4.4	6.7	14.7
Physical scientists	0.7	2.6	4.8	7.0	15.3
Social scientists	0.3	1.3	2.0	2.4	4.3
Mathematicians	0.6	2.7	2.4	5.6	11.1
Engineers	0.9	1.6	4.5	6.7	9.9
Architects	1.5	2.5	5.1	6.3	6.9
Physicians, dentists, and related practitioners	1.4	3.7	7.9	9.0	13.6
Nurses, dietitians, therapists	0.7	1.4	3.5	4.2	6.2
Elementary and preschool teachers	0.4	0.6	1.1	1.3	1.9
Secondary and vocational teachers	0.5	0.6	1.1	1.7	2.8
Postsecondary teachers	1.7	1.7	3.6	7.0	8.7
Health technicians	0.6	1.7	3.8	4.4	5.4
All other technicians	0.7	1.2	2.6	4.2	4.3
Computer specialists	—	1.2	4.2	7.0	13.2
Writers, artists, and media workers	0.4	1.0	1.9	2.6	4.1
Lawyers and judges	0.3	0.3	0.7	1.3	2.7
Librarians, archivists, curators	0.5	1.8	2.0	3.2	3.5
Social and recreation workers	0.9	0.9	1.3	1.7	2.3
Religious workers	0.2	0.4	1.2	2.9	4.0
Accountants and financial analysts	0.8	1.1	2.9	4.3	6.1
Administrators and public officers	0.5	0.6	1.1	1.8	2.4
Managers and proprietors	0.6	0.7	1.6	2.6	4.1
Sales workers, retail	0.4	0.7	1.4	3.3	4.8
Sales workers, other	0.5	0.5	1.3	2.6	3.8
Clerical workers	0.5	0.8	1.8	2.9	3.8
Bookkeepers	0.5	0.8	1.7	2.9	3.8
Secretaries	0.6	0.7	1.2	1.7	2.3
Mechanical workers	0.5	0.5	1.2	1.8	2.5
Carpenters	0.5	0.6	0.7	1.0	1.3
Electricians	0.3	0.6	1.1	1.5	1.5
Construction workers	0.3	0.4	0.6	1.0	1.0
Craftsmen	0.3	0.4	1.3	3.0	4.7
Textile machine operators	1.1	1.4	3.5	6.7	10.1
Metalworking and transportation operators	0.3	0.3	0.7	1.2	2.3
Other operators	0.3	0.5	1.3	2.5	4.0
Laborers, except farm	0.4	0.7	1.2	1.7	2.1
Farmers and farm laborers	1.1	0.8	1.0	1.2	1.5
Cleaning and food service workers	1.1	1.4	2.7	3.9	4.7
Health service workers	0.2	0.6	1.5	2.3	3.3
Personal service workers and barbers	0.5	0.8	1.6	2.8	5.1
Protective service workers	0.1	0.4	0.6	1.1	1.8
Total	0.5	0.8	1.7	2.8	4.1
Index of dissimilarity	18.6	17.7	19.7	17.8	18.1

— Data not available.

Note: Analysis was restricted to all workers ages 21–64. The index of dissimilarity measures the percent of Asians who would need to change occupations for Asians and non-Asians to have identical occupational distributions.

Sources: Authors' calculations using the 1% Public Use Microdata Sample (PUMS) from the 1960-2000 censuses; and Census 2000 5% PUMS.

followed suit and started their own laundry businesses, thus creating a concentration of Chinese in the laundry service through the 1920s.[23]

The clustering of Asian workers in certain occupations is presented in Table 7. Values in each row should be compared with the corresponding entries in the second row from the bottom, the total percentage of Asian workers in the civilian labor force within each census year. A number greater than the total percentage reveals an overrepresentation of Asians in a particular occupation. Likewise, a number smaller than the total percentage reveals an underrepresentation of Asians. The last row of the table presents the index of dissimilarity, measuring the occupational segregation of Asians from non-Asians.

The table supports the notion that Asians may consciously pursue certain occupations, such as life scientists, architects, physicians, and dentists, to maximize their chances for upward social mobility, since these are high-status occupations requiring high educational attainment. Asians' presence in some other occupations, like farmers and textile operators, reflects the labor niches that early Asian immigrants occupied.

As described earlier, the Asian population grew rapidly after 1965. This growth is reflected in the steady increase in the percentage of Asians in the labor force, from 0.5 percent in 1960 to 4.1 percent in 2000—an eightfold increase in four decades. However, the increase in Asian representation was much steeper in some occupational areas than in others. Foremost among these areas were scientific and engineering occupations. For example, the percentage of Asians in physical science jobs jumped from an unremarkable 0.7 percent in 1960 to an astonishingly high 15.3 percent in 2000. The percentage of Asians among computer specialists, an occupation that did not exist in the 1960 census occupation classification, increased from 1.2 percent in 1970 to 13.2 percent in 2000. Also, Asians' representation increased markedly in all other professional jobs except for elementary and preschool teachers, secondary and vocational teachers, lawyers and judges, and social and recreation workers. For example, the percentage of Asians among physicians, dentists, and related occupations increased rapidly from 1.4 percent in 1960 to 13.6 percent in 2000. Third, and surprisingly, Asians rapidly increased their share in some skilled manual jobs, such as textile operators, craftsmen, and other operators (respectively to 10.1 percent, 4.7 percent, and 4.0 percent in 2000). Finally, Asian representation increased among personal service workers and barbers, both in absolute terms (from 0.5 percent in 1960 to 5.1 percent in 2000) and in relation to the increase in the representation of Asian Americans in the labor force (from 0.5 percent in 1960 to 4.1 percent in 2000). Asian Americans' representation among cleaning and food service workers, at 1.1 percent in 1960, increased in absolute terms (to 4.7 percent in 2000) but not in relative terms.

Asians' presence remained small and the group as a whole was underrepresented in such occupations as librarians, clerical workers, and teachers (except teachers in higher education). Although these are all white-collar jobs, they are relatively low-status and low-paying occupations with flat career trajectories, and they tend to be filled predominantly by women. Somehow, Asians have avoided these occupations,[24] a fact that might help explain why Asian women earn more than white women. However, Asian Americans were underrepresented in 2000 in two high-status occupations: lawyers and judges (2.7 percent), and administrators and public officers (2.4 percent). Asians' presence is also hardly felt in certain skilled manual occupations: carpenters, electricians, and construction workers. One reason for Asians' absence is historical, as competition between whites and minority workers in skilled trades has been fierce, and Asians were discriminated against in dominant trade unions of the 19th and early 20th centuries, such as the American Federation of Labor. Another related reason is a lack of social networks and role models, as few Asians worked in these occupations. Finally, it is interesting to observe that Asians' representation in farming stayed low, although many Asians (especially Japanese) historically were engaged in these occupations. Many Japanese Americans may have left farming after losing land while interned in camps during Word War II, but other Asians, especially new Asian immigrants, may now view the lifestyle associated with farming as undesirable and prefer to work and live in urban settings.

It is important to consider the source of changes in Asians' representation across the census years. There is a great inertia in labor force composition in the sense that the structure of the labor force does not change much within a 10-year window. Aside from job mobility, two demographic factors account for the changes in Asian representation observed earlier—aging and immigration. Older workers (55 and older) in an earlier census left the labor force, and a new cohort of young workers (who were ages 11 to 20 in the previous census) entered the labor force. However, this source of change contributes only a small part to the changes. Most of the changes in occupational patterns are due to the influx of new immigrants and their children into the labor force.

The preceding discussion highlighted occupations in which Asians are either overrepresented or underrepresented. It is important to keep in mind that the overall differences in the distributions of Asians and non-Asians across occupations are small. This is shown in the last row of Table 7, which presents the index of dissimilarity measuring the racial occupational segregation. According to this index, which varies between 18 percent (in 1970, 1990, and 2000) and 20 percent (in 1980), levels of racial segregation are low. The index indicates that only 18 percent to 20 percent of all Asians (or non-

Asians) would need to change occupations in order for Asians and non-Asians to have identical distributions across the occupational classifications.

The Role of Education

Education is at the core of Asian Americans' social mobility. Their high educational achievement has facilitated their entry into many occupations that require college and advanced degrees. Asian Americans' large presence in science, engineering, and medicine evolved gradually from 1960 to 2000. While part of this transformation is attributable to the influx of new immigrants and their children, who increased the overall share of Asian Americans in the labor force, the main explanation is that a large portion (indeed most by 2000) of Asian Americans, either U.S.-born or foreign-born, attained postsecondary education. High educational credentials facilitated Asian Americans' entry into professional jobs in the labor market.

Asian Americans' high educational attainment is also a major reason for their relatively high earnings. Among U.S.-born workers, Asian American men reached parity in earnings with white men in 1959 and 1979 through higher educational attainment. Within levels of education, however, Asian American men suffered an earnings disadvantage of 5 percent. Education accounted for about a 5 percent difference in observed earnings between Asian Americans and whites before 1989. The difference attributable to education increased to 10 percent in 1999. By then, Asian American men earned more than white men not only in observed earnings (by 14 percent) but also in adjusted earnings (by 4 percent).

Among women, Asian Americans consistently outperformed whites in earnings throughout the period, in both observed and adjusted earnings. In recent decades, education seems to play a particularly large role in the higher earnings of Asian American women. In 1999, Asian American women's observed earnings were 32 percent greater than those of white women. This premium goes down to 17 percent for adjusted earnings, suggesting that education accounts for almost half of the observed advantage enjoyed by Asian American women. Again, Asian Americans' higher earnings, either observed or adjusted, did not happen instantly. In fact, Asian American men experienced a net disadvantage in 1959 and 1979.

Finally, there are substantial ethnic differences across Asian groups. In both education and earnings, Filipinos and Vietnamese lagged behind the other major Asian groups. Indeed, the Vietnamese (even U.S.-born Vietnamese) are the only Asian group that had a lower rate of college education than whites. However, socioeconomic conditions for Filipinos and Vietnamese have significantly improved over time, and both groups had earnings roughly comparable to whites in 1999.

MARRIAGE AND FAMILY

Asian Americans have effectively used education as a vehicle for social mobility. However, educational attainment normally occurs early in the life course, when an individual is still dependent on parents for both financial and emotional support. Because parents' emotional encouragement and financial support facilitate educational attainment, the high levels of education found among Asian American youth reflect the large investment of Asian American parents. Seen in this light, achieving social mobility through education is a family strategy. Thus, knowledge of Asian Americans' situations and experiences in the United States would be incomplete without understanding the Asian American family.

This section looks at family characteristics and marriage patterns of Asian Americans relative to those of whites and blacks. For simplicity, only the results from the 2000 Census are presented.[25] Tremendous change has occurred in American families in recent decades, such as increases in age of marriage (that is, the postponement of marriage), decreases in marriage, and increases in divorce and premarital cohabitation rates. These trends have affected all racial groups, and analysis of 2000 Census data provides sharp comparisons between Asians and non-Asians, and across different Asian ethnicities.

Another important trend has been the steady increase in women's labor force participation. Some scholars hypothesize that women's growing involvement in the labor force has contributed both to their postponement of marriage and to their disinclination toward marriage, as it has provided financial stability for women outside of marriage. This hypothesis may also explain why marriage rates are lower among blacks than among whites. Historically, black women have been more active than white women in the U.S. labor force; sizable fractions of black men have lacked steady employment, which made them less appealing as marriage partners.

The labor force participation rates of Asian women were historically higher than whites' and close to blacks' prior to 1990. Asian women also tended to work long hours and to earn more than their white or black counterparts. Thus, all available evidence indicates that Asian American women have been active in economic pursuits, although there is ethnic variation, with Korean women less economically active than other groups. However, this greater economic independence among Asian women has not caused them to avoid marriage. In fact, marriage rates are relatively high and divorce rates relatively low among Asian Americans.

Family Characteristics

Asian Americans are more likely to live in married-couple or husband-wife families than are whites or blacks (see Table 8). As defined here, a husband-wife family is not the same as a nuclear family—which includes solely a married couple and their own children—but it encompasses a nuclear family. For instance, an elderly woman who lives with her daughter and her son-in-law is considered to live in a husband-wife family, as is a child who lives with his or her grandparents. Individuals who live by themselves or in families headed by unmarried adults are not considered to live in a husband-wife family. The husband-wife family is used here as a measure of the stability and support—both emotional and material—of family life that are commonly associated with marriage.

For all people regardless of age, the share living in husband-wife families is 73 percent among Asian Americans, compared with 67 percent among whites and 40 percent among blacks. For children, the percentage is 84 percent among Asians, compared with 78 percent among whites and 40 percent among blacks. There is some cross-ethnic variation among Asian Americans. Most notable is that only 65 percent of all Japanese, the most assimilated Asian group, live in husband-wife families. However, the percentage of Japanese children living in husband-wife families is very high, at 88 percent. The only Asian American group with a significantly lower percentage of children living in husband- wife families is multiracial Asians, whose rate is similar to whites' on this measure. The overall picture that emerges from these numbers is that an overwhelming majority of Asians, especially Asian children, live in families headed by married couples and thus benefit from this living arrangement.

A family household is considered multigenerational if family members living in the same household are related to each other by blood and belong to three or more generations. An example of a multigenerational family consists of children, parents, and grandparents. Marital status is not specified; parents and grandparents in such a multigenerational family can be single, married, divorced, or widowed.

For elderly parents to live with adult married children is a cultural tradition in many Asian societies.[26] While this practice is less prevalent among Asian Americans than among Asians in Asia, it is still evident (see Table 8). Among all Asians, the percentage is 15 percent; among Asian children, the percentage is 17 percent. These numbers are much higher than those among whites (5 percent and 7 percent, respectively) and very similar to those among blacks (14 percent and 18 percent, respectively). However, the seeming similarity between Asians and blacks in percentages living in multigenerational families is misleading. Recall that Asian children live predominantly in husband-wife families. For them, having grandparents living in the same household usually means additional resources. For black children, grandparents often substitute for parents as primary caretakers. Additional analysis of Census 2000 data revealed that two-thirds of black children who live in multigenerational families do not live with two biological parents, whereas

Table 8

FAMILY CHARACTERISTICS BY RACE AND ASIAN ETHNIC GROUP, 2000

Race/ethnicity and age	% in husband-wife families	% in multigeneration families	Mean family size	1999 mean family income ($1,000)	1999 median family income ($1,000)	% in poverty, 1999
All persons						
All Asians	73	15	4.2	$77	$61	13
Chinese	73	15	3.9	82	63	13
Japanese	65	5	3.2	91	74	9
Filipino	73	22	4.4	81	70	6
Korean	74	10	3.7	71	53	15
Asian Indian	80	14	4.0	94	70	10
Vietnamese	72	16	4.7	65	52	15
Other Asian	74	19	5.3	56	44	23
Multiethnic Asian	72	13	4.3	78	64	12
Multiracial Asian	66	11	4.1	71	55	13
Whites	67	5	3.5	70	55	9
Blacks	40	14	3.9	45	35	24
Children (ages 0–17)						
All Asians	84	17	4.8	74	57	14
Chinese	88	19	4.5	82	63	13
Japanese	88	7	4.1	98	80	6
Filipino	82	27	5.0	77	67	6
Korean	88	11	4.2	73	56	12
Asian Indian	92	18	4.6	91	66	10
Vietnamese	81	17	5.1	59	45	20
Other Asian	82	21	6.1	49	38	30
Multiethnic Asian	84	15	4.7	80	65	11
Multiracial Asian	77	13	4.4	72	56	11
Whites	78	7	4.4	68	52	11
Blacks	40	18	4.4	39	29	32

Note: Mean family size, mean family income, and median family income were computed for individuals in each group.

Source: Authors' calculations using the Census 2000 1% (for whites and blacks) and 5% (for Asian groups) Public Use Microdata Sample (PUMS).

this type of family arrangement applies to only a small fraction (about 18 percent) of Asian American children.

Multigenerational living arrangements vary by Asian ethnicity. The prevalence of living in multigenerational families among Japanese is low, both for all people and for children. The rate is very high among Filipinos (22 percent for all people and 27 percent for children), Other Asians (19 percent for all people and 21 percent for children), and Vietnamese (16 percent for all people and 17 percent for children). One reason that a high proportion of Asian Americans live in multigenerational families is cultural, as noted earlier. Another reason is economic, since pooling resources across multiple generations saves money and reduces economic risk. A third reason is related to immigration. Recent immigrants may initially reside with other family members before establishing independent households of their own.

Except for Japanese, Asian Americans live in larger families than do whites and blacks (see Table 8). Note that family size is affected by many factors: the marital status of the household head, the number of children (that is, fertility), and the presence or absence of elderly

adults. However, fertility among Asian Americans is relatively low.[27] Thus, the larger family size on average among Asian Americans than among whites and blacks is not due to Asian Americans having more children per family but due to their higher rate of stable marriages and higher rate of elderly people living with married adult children. Thus, it is not surprising that there is a correspondence across Asian ethnicities between the percentage living in multigenerational families and family size, with Filipinos, Vietnamese, and Other Asians at the high end and Japanese at the low end on both measures.

Asian Americans overall have much higher family incomes than do blacks (see Table 8). And except for Vietnamese and Other Asians, Asian Americans have higher mean family incomes than whites. Since Asian Americans have larger families on average than whites, measuring family income per person reduces, or may even reverse, this advantage over whites.

The 1999 mean family income was $77,000 for all Asians, for example, compared with $70,000 for whites. Per capita mean family income was around $18,000 for all Asians, lower than the $20,000 for whites. There is also large ethnic variation in family income across Asian ethnicities. At the high end, Japanese had the highest median family income ($74,000) and the second-highest mean family income ($91,000); Asian Indians had the highest mean family income ($94,000) and the second-highest median family income ($70,000). At the low end, Vietnamese and Other Asians had mean and median family income at levels substantially lower than those of whites.

Family living arrangements have direct consequences for economic well-being. This is true because the family is usually the basic unit at which both income and consumption are shared. Everything else being equal, it is economically more efficient to live in a larger family due to economies of scale. Like family income, poverty status is a family attribute (although it is computed in Table 8 at the individual level). A person is considered to live in poverty if the combined gross cash income of his/her family falls below the official threshold income determined necessary for subsistence, which adjusts for family size and composition.

Contrary to the model minority image, a larger proportion of Asian Americans than whites live in poverty. Overall, 13 percent of Asians lived in poverty in 2000, compared with 9 percent among whites. Among children, the figures are 14 percent among Asians and 11 percent among whites. However, these poverty rates are much lower than those among blacks (at 24 percent for all people and 32 percent for children). The ethnic variation is also large. The poverty rate is low among the Japanese and Filipinos (in fact, lower among these groups than among whites) and high among Chinese, Koreans, Vietnamese, and Other Asians. The poverty rate is high among Vietnamese because they came to the United States as refugees. However, the average economic conditions for Chinese and Koreans are good—either comparable or superior to those of whites. These results suggest that there is a polarization in the economic conditions of Chinese and Korean Americans: Whereas a large portion of these groups has realized the American dream by achieving middle-class status, another large portion has been left behind and economically deprived. This economic diversity of Asian Americans within the same ethnic group is often overlooked.

Prevalence and Timing of Marriage

Examining Asian Americans' marriage patterns is not an easy task because census data provide information about current marital status only, not marital history. In particular, for respondents who said they were currently married, it is not known for how long they were married or whether they had previously married and divorced. For those who were divorced, neither the timing of the divorce nor the marital history preceding the divorce is known. The following analysis relies on a crude measure of divorce, calculated as the difference

between ever married and currently married, ignoring remarriage and widowhood.

Proportionately more Asian Americans are currently married than are whites and blacks (see Table 9). Among men ages 35 to 44, 78 percent of Asian Americans are currently married, compared with 69 percent of whites and 52 percent of blacks. Among women ages 35 to 44, 80 percent of Asian Americans are currently married, compared with 71 percent of whites and 42 percent of blacks. There is some evidence that, relative to whites, Asians' higher rates of current marriage are attributable to Asians' lower likelihood of divorce.

The rates of ever being married are comparable between Asian Americans and whites (85 percent for men and 90 percent for women). The difference between ever married and currently married for people ages 35 to 44, a crude measure of divorce, is 7 percentage points among Asian men and about 10 percentage points among Asian women. In contrast, the difference stands at 15 percentage points for white men and 18 percentage points for white women. Blacks' rates of being currently married are low for two reasons, both because a lower proportion ever marries (71 percent for men and 69 percent for women) and because a higher percentage of those who were previously married is no longer married (19 percent among men and 27 percent among women).

There are notable ethnic variations in the percentages currently married and ever married. The Japanese have relatively low marriage rates, and Koreans and Asian Indians have the highest marriage rates. Furthermore, multiracial Asians have marriage rates that closely resemble those of whites. In particular, the difference in the two marriage rates, ever married minus currently married, is slightly higher among multiracial Asian women (19 percentage points) than among white women (18 percentage points). This result suggests that multiracial Asians have assimilated to the degree that their marriage patterns resemble more closely those of whites than those of monoracial Asians.

The proportion of first marriages occurring in ages 45 to 54 is twice as high among Asian American men (8 percentage points) as it is among Asian American women (4 percentage points). A similar gender difference exists between white men (7 percentage points) and white women (4 percentage points). Overall, the data show that among Asian Americans and whites a very small proportion of people get married for the first time past age 44, because an overwhelming majority of them has already been married before that age. However, the proportion is much higher among blacks (around 12 percent).

Change across age groups in the proportion currently married is a net result of divorce, remarriage, or new marriage. The difference is a positive 7 percentage points for Asian American men but a negative 2 percentage points among Asian American women. This gender difference probably reflects the fact that a higher proportion of divorced men than divorced women get remarried, presumably to younger women. This gender asymmetry is also true for whites and blacks. In any

Table 9

PERCENT CURRENTLY MARRIED AND EVER-MARRIED AND MEDIAN AGE OF MARRIAGE, BY RACE/ETHNICITY AND GENDER, 2000

Race/ethnicity	% currently married (ages 35–44)	% ever married (ages 35–44)	% currently married (ages 45–54)	% ever married (ages 45–54)	Median age at marriage among all ever-married
All Asians					
Men	78	85	85	93	28
Women	80	90	78	94	25
Chinese					
Men	82	87	87	94	29
Women	82	90	81	94	27
Japanese					
Men	64	72	72	84	30
Women	74	85	75	91	27
Filipino					
Men	76	84	83	92	28
Women	77	89	76	92	25
Korean					
Men	85	91	90	98	30
Women	84	94	81	98	27
Asian Indian					
Men	88	92	92	97	27
Women	90	95	87	97	23
Vietnamese					
Men	75	80	84	93	30
Women	76	87	76	93	26
Other Asian					
Men	79	86	86	95	28
Women	81	92	76	94	24
Multiethnic Asian					
Men	76	82	83	93	—
Women	75	88	78	94	—
Multiracial Asian					
Men	67	80	74	90	28
Women	68	87	65	91	25
Whites					
Men	69	84	74	91	26
Women	71	89	70	93	24
Blacks					
Men	52	71	55	82	27
Women	42	69	43	82	28

— Insufficient data.

Source: Authors' calculations using the Census 2000 1% (for whites and blacks) and 5% (for Asian groups) Public Use Microdata Sample (PUMS).

event, in ages 45 to 54, 85 percent of Asian American men and 78 percent of Asian American women are still married, compared with 74 percent of white men and 70 percent of white women. Thus, the data show that Asian Americans, with the exception of Japanese and multi-racial Asians, are still more likely to be married than are whites in this later age range.

The median age of marriage is estimated to be 28 among Asian men and 25 among Asian women. Comparing these numbers to those of whites (26 for white men and 24 for white women) leads to two conclusions: First, Asian Americans marry at later ages than do whites. Second, the age gap between men and women in the median age of marriage is also slightly wider for Asian Americans (three years) than for whites (two years). The late age of marriage for Asian Americans may reflect a traditional expectation that a person (especially a man) needs to be economically established before marriage. The patterns of late marriage and a high gender gap in the age of marriage are true across all Asian American groups. For example, among Japanese Americans, the most assimilated Asian group, the median age of marriage is estimated to be 30 for men and 27 for women. Interestingly, black women have a high median age of marriage, 28.

Data from Census 2000 shed some light on Asian Americans' marriage patterns. Compared with whites and blacks, Asian Americans have relatively high rates of marriage and low rates of divorce, but a high median age of marriage. All of these results seem to suggest that Asian Americans are still influenced by a culture that emphasizes the importance of the family and family responsibility.

Intermarriage

Early Asian immigrants were predominantly male manual workers. There were very few Asian women in America who could be their marriage partners. To make the situation worse, Asian workers were not allowed to bring their wives to the United States. In fear of Asian men marrying U.S.-born white women, many states instituted antimiscegenation laws to prohibit marriages between Asians and whites. This situation lasted until the end of World War II, when U.S. servicemen who fought and were stationed overseas in Asia began to bring home war brides from Asia. This started a new era in which Asian women are accepted, and sometimes even preferred, as wives by white and black men.

Large-scale immigration from Asia did not occur until the landmark 1965 Immigration and Nationality Act. The beginning of this new wave of immigration coincided with the Civil Rights Movement, which resulted in the abolition of antimiscegenation laws in 1967. Intermarriage between Asian Americans and other racial groups began to increase. Whereas American culture has applied a one-drop rule when racially identifying children from white-black parentage, it does not have a similar norm concerning the race of children from white-Asian parentage (see Box 2, page 420). This may be because these interracial offspring are a relatively recent phenomenon, born after the Civil Rights Movement of the 1960s. Further, Asian-white relationships are not complicated by a history of intricate relationships between whites and blacks dating back to slavery. Our earlier study using data from the 1990 Census found that about half of biracial Asian children are identified as Asian, suggesting that how to racially identify this group is fluid and maybe even optional.[28] Out of nearly 12 million Asian Americans in 2000, 1.9 million were reported as mixed Asian—1.7 million being multiracial Asians (those with an Asian race plus a non-Asian race), and 223,593 being multiethnic Asians (those with more than one Asian ethnicity). These mixed Asians are mostly children of interracial or interethnic marriages, as only a small proportion of Asian Americans are born outside of marriage.

Although most Asian Americans still tend to marry other Asian Americans, intermarriage between Asians and non-Asians has become a significant phenomenon in American society today. Twelve percent of all married Asian American men have a non-Asian wife (see Table 10). The percentage of married Asian American women with a non-Asian husband is much higher, at 23 percent.

Interpretation of intermarriage rates is not always straightforward, because their magnitudes are subject to the influences of relative group sizes, also called exposure or "opportunity structure." Suppose that marriage occurs at random so that there is no assortative mating by race or ethnicity. Under this unrealistic ideal situation, the smaller a group, the smaller the probability of marrying a member of the group. Conversely, the larger the size of a group, the higher the probability of marrying someone from that group. Thus, there is a natural tendency for a person in a small group to marry someone outside the group due to the scarcity of supply. Similarly, there is a natural tendency for a person in a large group to marry someone else within the group. As a result, intermarriage rates for non-Asians are not shown in Table 10, since they are not comparable.

One of the most interesting observations from Table 10 is that Asian American women outmarry at higher rates than Asian American men. Among all Asian Americans, the outmarriage rate for women is about twice the rate for men (23 percent versus 12 percent). For Filipinos, the difference is almost threefold (33 percent versus 13 percent). Among Koreans, the contrast is even greater (27 percent versus 4 percent). Of course, part of the gender difference is attributable to the fact that some military men met and married their wives during their service in Asia. However, the gender difference is so large and so consistent across all ethnic groups that it goes beyond this factor alone. Even when the analysis is restricted to U.S.-born Asian Americans, a gender difference emerges:

Table 10
INTERMARRIAGE RATES AMONG ASIAN AMERICANS BY ETHNIC GROUP AND GENDER, 2000

Race/ethnicity	Spouse's race/ethnicity		
	Non-Asian (%)	Same Asian ethnicity (%)	Other Asian (%)
All Asians			
Men	12	—	—
Women	23	—	—
Chinese			
Men	6	90	5
Women	13	83	4
Japanese			
Men	20	69	11
Women	41	51	8
Filipino			
Men	13	83	4
Women	33	63	4
Korean			
Men	4	93	3
Women	27	69	4
Asian Indian			
Men	8	90	3
Women	5	92	3
Vietnamese			
Men	3	92	4
Women	10	86	4
Other Asian			
Men	9	—	—
Women	18	—	—
Multiethnic Asian			
Men	13	—	—
Women	26	—	—
Multiracial Asian			
Men	44	—	—
Women	54	—	—

— Data not applicable or not available.

Note: "Other Asian" for spouse's race/ethnicity includes multiethnic and multiracial Asians.

Source: Authors' calculations using Census 2000 5% Public Use Microdata Sample (PUMS).

Whereas 38 percent of married U.S.-born Asian American men are married to non-Asians, 49 percent of married U.S.-born Asian American women are married to non-Asians. While it is difficult to pin down precisely the social processes that underlie this gender difference, the social barrier for intermarriage is lower for Asian American women than for Asian American men.

Intermarriage is far more common among U.S.-born Asian Americans than among immigrant Asian Americans. Part of the reason, of course, is that a large portion of immigrants were already married before they came to

America. This pattern is also reasonable because U.S.-born Asian Americans are more assimilated than new immigrants and have had far more opportunities to get to know non-Asians. The high percentages of intermarriage suggests that second and higher generations of Asian Americans are now well integrated into American society, as a significant proportion of them meet the ultimate criterion of assimilation— "amalgamation," or racial mixing.[29] However, because high rates of intermarriage among U.S.-born Asian Americans are accompanied by high rates of continuing immigration of Asians, it seems unlikely that Asian Americans as a group will be completely assimilated into the mainstream in the near future.

The ethnic differences in intermarriage rates among Asian Americans also reflect their varying degrees of assimilation. Japanese Americans, the most assimilated group, have high outmarriage rates of 20 percent for men and 41 percent for women. Multiracial Asian Americans, who are structurally assimilated because of their mixed parentage, have even higher rates of marrying non-Asians, at 44 percent for men and 54 percent for women. In contrast, Vietnamese Americans have low rates of outmarriage, at 3 percent for men and 10 percent for women. Although Asian Indian Americans have high socioeconomic status, they immigrated to the United States only recently and have maintained their cultural distinction. They also have low rates of outmarriage (8 percent for men and 5 percent for women). Asian Indians are the only major Asian group in which women do not outmarry more often than men.

When an Asian American is married to another Asian American, the husband and the wife are not necessarily of the same ethnicity. If Asians do not marry within their own ethnic group, they are much more likely than members of the general population to marry other Asians than to marry non-Asians. For example, this is clear in the marriage patterns of Japanese men. Of those who do not marry Japanese women, 11 percent marry other Asians (such as Chinese and Koreans), while 20 percent marry non-Asians. This ratio of other Asian (11) to non-Asian (20), 0.56, is far above the ratio of 0.04 for the total population.

Continuity and Change

Asian Americans exhibit continuity and change in terms of their family behaviors. They still maintain certain practices that have had a long tradition in their countries of origin, such as high rates of (ever) marriage, low rates of divorce (especially when children are present), a relatively large gender gap in age of marriage, and multigenerational living arrangements. Furthermore, they tend to marry within their own ethnic groups. When they fail to do so, Asian Americans still prefer to marry members of other Asian ethnic groups rather than non-Asians.

They exhibit change in their assimilation into American society. With respect to divorce, for example, Asian Americans have a nontrivial divorce rate, albeit low relative to the rates of whites and blacks. In childbearing, Asian Americans have low fertility, although recent Asian immigrants have an age distribution with a larger proportion in young, childbearing ages and thus have relatively high birth rates. In residence, most Asians do not live in multigenerational families. The clearest manifestation of assimilation is seen in the variation among Asian Americans by ethnicity and nativity. The Japanese, the most assimilated group, exhibit marriage and family behaviors that closely resemble those of whites. In addition, U.S.-born Asian Americans have much higher intermarriage rates than foreign-born Asian Americans. It seems that more-assimilated Asians are less familial and less traditional in their family behaviors than are less-assimilated Asians.

Asian Americans exhibit a high degree of family orientation. One consequence is that Asian American children overwhelmingly live in two-parent families, sometimes with grandparents, and have fewer siblings. Such family living arrangements undoubtedly benefit Asian children's academic achievement. Asian parents also hold high educational expectations for their children and are willing to invest family resources in them. For these reasons, the family is the driving force behind the social mobility of Asian American youth.

RESIDENCE

America is a race-conscious society. Race relations take on particular prominence when individuals interact with each other across racial boundaries in the workplace and in schools, neighborhoods, parks, gyms, and at religious gatherings. Despite the rapid development of computer technology and telecommunication, the vast majority of such social settings are spatially situated and constrained. People who live closer to each other are more likely to interact with each other in such social settings than people who live farther apart. In other words, if Asian Americans live close to other Asian Americans, they tend to interact with other Asian Americans in social settings. Conversely, if Asian Americans are surrounded by members of another race (say whites), they are compelled by this configuration to have more interracial interactions.

Put into more concrete terms, residential patterns are an important dimension of race relations, influencing how likely one is to be exposed to people of different races and thus potentially to interact with those of different races. The fact that Asians tend to marry within their own ethnicity and/or among Asians may in part reflect the fact that Asians may be exposed more to other Asians (and particularly those of the same ethnicity) than to non-Asians in residence, schools, interest groups, and/or even work settings.

This section examines the residential patterns of Asian Americans—the geographic distribution of Asians across states and metropolitan areas, and what are the residential segregation patterns between Asians and non-Asians within metropolitan areas. The analyses are based on data from the 2000 Census.

Geographic Distribution

First it is important to distinguish between absolute distribution and relative distribution. Absolute distribution refers to the uneven allocation of Asian Americans to different geographic units (such as states and metropolitan areas); relative distribution refers to the differentials between the spatial allocation of Asians versus that of non-Asians. Spatial distribution is measured in relative terms because certain geographic units are larger or denser and thus draw more people, both Asian and non-Asian. The absolute distribution of Asian Americans indicates where they tend to live, whereas the relative distribution shows where Asian Americans are overrepresented relative to other racial groups in the U.S. population.

Again, analysis of the geographic distribution of Asian Americans using 2000 Census data is complicated by the fact that almost 14 percent of all Asians are multiracial. Whether or not to include them changes results significantly. The U.S. Census Bureau reports the percentage of Asian Americans by state, county, and place.[30] However, the figures given by the bureau are not ideal because they do not include multiracial Asians. To have a single-number estimate of the 2000 Asian population that is also comparable to historical figures, one simply imputes one-half of multiracial Asians to be Asian and the other half to be non-Asian. This raises the percentage of Asian Americans from 3.6 percent to 3.9 percent for the whole United States. Thus, a percentage greater than 3.9 indicates overrepresentation of Asian Americans in an area. Conversely, a percentage smaller than 3.9 indicates underrepresentation. By this criterion, Asian Americans are overrepresented in only 10 states (see Figure 2): Hawaii (50 percent); California (12 percent); Washington, New Jersey, and New York (all 6 percent); Nevada and Alaska (both 5 percent); and Maryland, Virginia, and Massachusetts (all 4 percent).

To see how concentrated Asian Americans are geographically, one may also look at their absolute distribution. Forty-one percent of all Asian Americans live in just two states—California and Hawaii. California alone accounts for 3.9 million, or 36 percent of all Asian Americans in the United States. This is a very high degree of Asian concentration. Only 12 percent of the U.S. population lives in California, and 13 percent lives in California and Hawaii combined. If New Jersey,

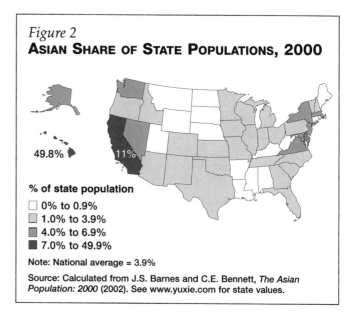

Figure 2
ASIAN SHARE OF STATE POPULATIONS, 2000

49.8%

11%

% of state population

☐ 0% to 0.9%
☐ 1.0% to 3.9%
☐ 4.0% to 6.9%
■ 7.0% to 49.9%

Note: National average = 3.9%

Source: Calculated from J.S. Barnes and C.E. Bennett, *The Asian Population: 2000* (2002). See www.yuxie.com for state values.

Washington, and New York are added to the list of states with the highest percentages of Asian Americans, they account for 59 percent of Asian Americans but only 24 percent of the total population. There are several reasons for Asian Americans' unique geographic distribution. One is historical, as Asian immigrants first came to California and Hawaii as laborers. Another is distance, as Hawaii and the West Coast are closer to Asia than is the rest of the country. However, there is also a cultural element to this distribution: Once Asians settled and established their own communities, they began to attract other, especially newly arriving, Asian immigrants. Now, well-entrenched old Chinatowns can be found in almost all the largest cities in the United States, and vibrant new Asian (Chinese, Korean, and sometimes Vietnamese) communities are found in middle-class suburbs in metropolitan areas such as Los Angeles, San Francisco, and New York.

Besides their affinity with Hawaii and the West Coast for historical and geographic reasons, Asian Americans now also tend to be concentrated in major metropolitan centers. This is in sharp contrast to the early waves of Asian immigrants, especially Japanese immigrants, a large portion of whom worked on farms. In fact, Asian Americans' presence in farming can still be seen in 1960 occupational data, which showed that their likelihood to be in occupations of "farmers and farm laborers" was twice as high as the average. Asian Americans' concentration in farming declined gradually. By 1980, they were no longer overrepresented in farming occupations. Asian immigrants of the latest waves do not work on farms.

Asian Americans are now concentrated in two types of occupations: high-status professional and technical occupations, and low-skilled service and manual jobs. Given their positions in the occupational structure, it is not surprising that Asian Americans tend to live in major metropolitan areas, which offer such job opportunities. Census tabulations show that Asian Americans with a single ethnicity made up 4.5 percent of all urban residents, compared with a mere 0.5 percent of all rural residents. Between metropolitan and nonmetropolitan areas, there is a similar gap; the share of Asian Americans was 4.3 percent among all residents in metropolitan areas and 0.8 percent among all residents in nonmetropolitan areas. Not surprisingly, the lowest presence of Asian Americans is found among rural residents in nonmetropolitan areas, at 0.3 percent.

Asian Americans' distributions, both absolute and relative, in the top 10 cities with the largest Asian American population are shown in Table 11. Since the definition of a city varies from place to place, it is not clear how to compare the absolute numbers across cities. However, the numbers reported in Table 11 give a sense of how concentrated Asian Americans are in major cities. New York, the largest city in the United States, also has the largest Asian population at 829,912. The percentage of Asian Americans in New York is 10.4 percent, a level more than twice the national average. Surprisingly, the percentage of Asian Americans in Los Angeles is similar to the share in New York, at 10.5 percent, and in absolute numbers, a large number of Asian Americans live in Los Angeles (388,349). Asian Americans are not well-represented in all large cities. Absent from Table 11, for example, are Dallas, San Antonio, Phoenix, and Detroit. The percentages of Asian Americans in these large cities all fall below the 3.9 percent national average.

Combining the 10 cities, the percentage of Asian Americans is on average 12.2 percent, three times the national level. Describing Asian Americans' concentration in another way, 23 percent of all Asian Americans live in these 10 cities, whereas only 7 percent of all the U.S. population lives in these same cities. Thus, the concentration of Asian Americans is on average three times as high in these cities as the national average.

Residential Segregation

Because residential proximity greatly influences the chances of interracial interaction, the analysis now turns to the residential patterns of Asian Americans within cities. Blacks' residential segregation from whites has long been thought to be both an indicator and a cause of racial discrimination in American society, and a major reason for their socioeconomic disadvantage. Earlier Chinese and Japanese immigrants to the United States also suffered severe racial discrimination and were restricted to living in ethnic ghettos.

For two reasons, contemporary Asian Americans are much less segregated from whites than either Asian Americans were in the past or blacks are today. First, Asian Americans have achieved relatively high socioeconomic status that on balance either equals or sur-

Table 11

TEN U.S. CITIES WITH THE LARGEST ASIAN POPULATIONS, 2000

City	Population	Asians	% Asian
Total U.S. population	281,421,906	11,070,913	3.9
Total in 10 cities	20,586,265	2,521,098	12.2
% of U.S. total	7.3	22.8	—
New York, NY	8,008,278	829,912	10.4
Los Angeles, CA	3,694,820	388,349	10.5
San Jose, CA	894,943	248,973	27.8
San Francisco, CA	776,733	246,521	31.7
Honolulu, HI	371,657	229,637	61.8
San Diego, CA	1,223,400	178,191	14.6
Chicago, IL	2,896,016	133,246	4.6
Houston, TX	1,953,631	108,917	5.6
Seattle, WA	563,374	79,280	14.1
Fremont, CA	203,413	78,072	38.4

— Not applicable.

Source: Calculated from J.S. Barnes and C.E. Bennett, *The Asian Population: 2000* (2002).

passes that of whites, especially in education. Second, the Asian American population is small in size, and individual Asian ethnic groups are particularly small. Given their small numbers in most places, when Asian Americans move into a white community, they do not pose the threat of soon dominating the community in the way that blacks are sometimes perceived to do. As a result, even though some whites may still prefer to live in neighborhoods without Asian Americans, they are now unlikely to act strongly on their racial preferences for neighbors. Attitude surveys indeed show that whites are not as hostile to the prospect of having Asian neighbors as they are to the prospect of having black neighbors.[31]

Except in a few isolated places, the barriers discouraging Asian Americans from living in white neighborhoods are relatively low, compared with those separating blacks and whites. However, even in the absence of such racial barriers, not all Asian Americans wish to live in integrated neighborhoods. Most Asian Americans are recent immigrants and maintain a strong identification with their home culture, speaking their native languages at home and relying heavily on ethnic communities for a successful transition to American life. Ethnic communities offer many practical resources to immigrants, including ethnic-specific goods and services, cultural events, information in native languages, and entrepreneurial opportunities.

Indeed, there are two related theoretical debates in sociology regarding the advantages to immigrants of living in ethnic communities.[32] The first debate is concerned with the potential economic benefits of working in an ethnic niche—an ethnic enclave economy. Some scholars argue that an enclave economy provides a protective work environment to new immigrant workers where they can derive economic benefits that would not be available in the mainstream economy. These benefits could include pay that reflects their skills, education, and experience; social mobility to supervisory positions; and opportunities to be entrepreneurs. However, other scholars contend that an enclave economy primarily benefits business owners of enclave firms rather than their co-ethnic workers, for whom working in the mainstream economy would facilitate assimilation and thus upward mobility.

The second debate is around segmented assimilation theory, which is concerned with the long-term (particularly educational) benefits for immigrant children of maintaining a strong ethnic identity and social networks among co-ethnics and thus not being fully assimilated into the American mainstream. The basis for this argument is that America is now extremely diverse and segmented, with an underclass residing in central cities where a large portion of new immigrant families first settle upon arrival. Thus, it is argued that there exist divergent assimilation paths for new immigrants. One path is full and direct assimilation into mainstream American society; another possible path of full assimilation, to which new residents of central cities are especially vulnerable, is downward assimilation into the urban underclass. To avoid this, according to the theory, it is better for immigrants to maintain their own culture while acquiring skills for the labor market. This middle path of assimilation is called "selective acculturation."

So far, empirical evidence pertaining to the enclave economy debate and the segmented assimilation debate leaves them unresolved. However, even without the hypothesized benefits, many Asians may still wish to live close together to share a common culture or for the convenience of seeing relatives and friends. Thus, one would expect to see clustering patterns of residence among Asian Americans.

A commonly used segregation index (the index of dissimilarity) is reported in Table 12 for the 10 cities with the largest Asian population. The index measures residential segregation between two population groups, in this case, Asians and whites.[33] Measurement of segregation is at the level of census tracts. The index between Asians and whites varies from a low of 29 percent in Fremont, Calif., to a high of 50 percent in San Diego. A dissimilarity index of 29 percent means that either 29 percent of Asian Americans or 29 percent of whites in the city would need to move to different census tracts for the two groups to reach equal distributions across all census tracts. The second column presents the dissimilarity index between Asian Americans and blacks, and the last column gives the dissimilarity index between whites and blacks for comparison. The segregation between Asian Americans and whites and the segregation between Asian Americans and blacks are still substantial. In Los Angeles, for example, the dissimilarity index is 47 percent between Asian Americans and whites and 69

Table 12
RESIDENTIAL SEGREGATION INDICES IN THE 10 U.S. CITIES WITH THE LARGEST ASIAN POPULATIONS, 2000

City	Asian and white	Asian and black	White and black
New York, NY	42	63	63
Los Angeles, CA	47	69	73
San Jose, CA	48	31	41
San Francisco, CA	41	58	59
Honolulu, HI	36	58	47
San Diego, CA	50	50	62
Chicago, IL	48	87	86
Houston, TX	45	68	72
Seattle, WA	48	34	60
Fremont, CA	29	26	24

Note: The segregation index measures the percentage of a racial group that would have to move to a different census tract to reach equal distribution across all census tracts.

Source: www.psc.isr.umich.edu/residentialsegregation, accessed June 21, 2004.

percent between Asian Americans and blacks, although the index between whites and blacks is even higher, at 73 percent. These numbers mean that residential segregation is very high between whites and blacks and between Asian Americans and blacks in Los Angeles. By comparison, residential segregation is moderately high between whites and Asians.

With the exception of Fremont and San Jose, the level of residential segregation between Asian Americans and whites is much lower than that between whites and blacks. Fremont is unusual also for having very low segregation levels between any two of the three groups (29 percent or lower). For six of the 10 cities—New York, Los Angeles, San Francisco, Honolulu, Chicago, and Houston—the segregation between Asians and whites is much lower than that between Asians and blacks. However, for the remaining cities, the segregation between Asians and blacks is either comparable to that between Asians and whites (San Diego and Fremont) or even smaller (San Jose and Seattle).

The results in Table 12 are crude in the sense that they do not present segregation indices separately by Asian ethnicity. This tends to understate levels of segregation for Asian Americans, if there is a tendency, as is the case, for residential clustering within an ethnic group. Japanese and Filipino Americans are less segregated from whites than are other Asian American groups (such as Chinese and Vietnamese).[34] Still, one can draw an overall observation that Asian Americans live in somewhat concentrated communities that are separate from whites and blacks on the whole. However, Asian Americans' residential segregation is less pronounced than residential segregation for blacks. The difference is also qualitative, in that at least in contemporary America, Asian Americans do not face the same kind of racial discrimination and prejudice that blacks do in the housing market. To the extent that Asian Americans' residential patterns show signs of concentration, they appear to reflect Asians' own preferences to live near other Asian Americans rather than external constraints limiting their residential choices.

However, culturally based preferences to live with co-ethnics indicate a lack of assimilation into the American mainstream and thus should weaken over time as immigrants become more assimilated. In the literature on immigrants, residence in desirable neighborhoods (such as those in suburbs with a high average family income and a high percentage of non-Hispanic whites) has long been viewed as spatial assimilation or residential assimilation.[35] Given the well-known relationship between assimilation and generation, second- and third-generation Asian Americans (such as most Japanese Americans) are likely to be less segregated residentially from whites than first-generation Asian Americans. One consequence of less segregation is a structural increase in Asian Americans' opportunities for interacting with non-Asians in daily life, thus promoting intermarriage with non-Asians. This partly explains why the Japanese, who are the most assimilated group of Asian Americans, also have the highest rates of outmarriage. In fact, all U.S.-born Asian Americans have high rates of outmarriage.

Geographic Concentration

For a variety of reasons, Asian Americans tend to live near other Asian Americans. This statement is true at two geographic levels. At the national level, Asian Americans tend to be concentrated in a few states (such as California and Hawaii) and a few metropolitan areas (such as New York and Los Angeles). At the city level, Asians tend to be concentrated in certain neighborhoods or communities, not fully assimilated into white or black neighborhoods. However, in most cities Asian Americans are more residentially integrated with whites than with blacks, and Asian Americans and whites are more integrated than are blacks and whites.

While these empirical findings are clear, theoretical interpretations of them are less so. Do Asian Americans live near other Asian Americans due to their desire to maintain their culture or out of the need to cope with the potential risks of racial discrimination? That is, are the unique residential patterns of Asian Americans really the result of their own choices or of a structural constraint imposed on them? These theoretically interesting questions cannot be answered with census data. But at least when compared with such barriers for blacks, Asians' barriers to living in white neighborhoods are relatively low. Thus, the level of segregation

between Asians and whites is relatively low. If blacks suffer dire socioeconomic consequences because of residential segregation from whites, Asians do not face similar disadvantages.

CONCLUSION

Although Asian Americans were first recorded in the U.S. census as early as 1860, their social significance in American society was not widely recognized until the post-1965 waves of immigrants fundamentally changed the demographic composition of the U.S. population. Because post-1965 immigrants are primarily from Asia and Latin America, traditional race relations in America constructed around whites and blacks have been further complicated by the presence of sizable and rapidly growing populations of Asians and Hispanics. Should Asian Americans be treated as a single race in the racial landscape of America? While this question was contemplated well before 1965, it is becoming more and more pressing due to the rapid growth of the Asian American population.

The answer to this question is mixed, depending on one's definition of race.[36] There are four simple bases for deriving a definition of race: psychological, physiological, social, and external. The psychological definition equates race to the self-identification of group membership based on one's ancestral origin. The physiological definition equates race to shared physical appearance. The social definition connects race to a common set of social consequences (such as confronting racial discrimination and residential segregation). The external definition links race to a common perception of a nominal group by people outside the group. Asian Americans are clearly not a race according to the psychological definition, as most of them prefer to be identified as members of their ethnic groups—such as Chinese and Koreans—rather than as Asians. Whether they are a race according to the physiological and social definitions is unclear. There is large variation in physical appearance, especially between South Asians (such as Asian Indians) and East Asians (such as Chinese). Further, social outcomes are similar for some Asian groups (Chinese and Koreans) but quite different for others (Japanese versus Vietnamese). It seems to us that the most plausible definition for Asian Americans is external, as non-Asians may perceive Asian Americans as a homogeneous group and treat them as a race. Indeed, the popular model minority label implicitly treats Asian Americans as a race, with minority meaning a racial minority.

Demographers explore the question of whether Asian Americans exhibit distinct demographic characteristics that differentiate them from whites and other minority groups. Thus, whether Asian Americans should be treated as a race is a question that can be addressed, in part, with demographic data. Based on the results presented in this report, the answer is a cautionary yes. It is yes because some distinct demographic characteristics among Asian Americans set them apart from whites and other minority groups:

● The residential patterns of Asian Americans are distinct. They live in different parts of the country, concentrated in Hawaii, California, and a few large metropolitan areas. Within cities, they also tend to be concentrated in communities that attract other Asian Americans.
● Asian Americans are familial in orientation. They have a high marriage rate and a low divorce rate, and they maintain traditional practices such as living in multigenerational family households.
● Asian Americans have high levels of educational attainment.
● Asian Americans have dramatically improved their labor force outcomes, such as earnings and occupation, since the 1950s.

However, substantial variations across Asian ethnic groups and by nativity have been seen in almost all the demographic dimensions examined in this report. These differences make the characterization of Asian Americans with a simple label like model minority problematic. For example, the earnings of Filipinos and Vietnamese lag behind those of other Asian Americans. The prevalence of multigenerational living arrangements also varies greatly by ethnicity, with the Japanese being less likely to be in multigenerational families than whites. Further, as the education results indicate, ethnic differences are more pronounced among foreign-born Asian Americans than among U.S.-born Asian Americans.[37] Assimilation may exert a homogenizing force, making Asian Americans of different ethnicities appear similar. However, it is also plausible that similarities among Asian Americans of different ethnicities arise because of the common difficulties they face. For example, Asian American families may make exceptional investments in their children's education as a conscious strategy to compensate for disadvantages they believe they face as a racial minority group, such as racial discrimination and a lack of mainstream social capital.

With further assimilation and continuing success in socioeconomic spheres, Asian Americans may more and more constitute part of the American mainstream rather than a racial minority. The finding that intermarriage rates are high among U.S.-born Asian Americans supports this prediction. However, given the constant flow of new immigrants from Asia, it is a demographic impossibility that all Asian Americans will be fully assimilated at any time in the near future. Indeed, a large portion of Asian Americans are, and for the foreseeable future will be, new immigrants. Because of this, it is highly likely

that Asian Americans will exhibit certain distinct demographic characteristics (such as residential segregation from non-Asians). At least part of this is attributable to the fact that many Asians are new immigrants.

With today's data, it is difficult to separate race effects from immigration effects, because most Asian Americans are immigrants. With time, however, there should be a steady increase in the share of U.S.-born second- and higher-generation Asian Americans. One possible scenario in the near future is that racial differences between Asians and whites become blurred, but differences between foreign-born Asian Americans and U.S.-born Asian Americans become more pronounced by comparison. Another possible scenario is that the continuous growth of the Asian American population and its gradual assimilation into the American mainstream will heighten the awareness of their racial distinction among second- and higher-generation Asian Americans. Whether or not Asian Americans are considered a single race in the future, one thing is certain: The ever-changing Asian American population and the diversity of Asian Americans' experiences by ethnicity and nativity present constant challenges to the logic of racial categorizations and to the understanding of race relations in the United States.

ACKNOWLEDGMENTS

The authors are grateful to Reynolds Farley, Emily Greenman, Arthur Sakamoto, Min Zhou, and anonymous reviewers for comments and suggestions; to Bill Frey, Emily Greenman, and John Logan for sharing their unpublished research results; to Justin Wu and Emily Greenman for research assistance; to Albert Anderson for programming assistance; and to Stacey Althouse, N.E. Barr, Sherry Briske, Debbie Fitch, Yan Fu, Judy Mullin, Lisa Neidert, and Rhonda Moats for research support. Computations for this report were performed at the Population Studies Center at the University of Michigan, which receives its core funding from NICHD. Additional information and explanations of our research for this report are available at www.yuxie.com.

Throughout the project, our spouses, Helen Yijun Gu and Michael Lim, gave us unreserved support. Our children, Raissa Xie, Kevin Xie, and Jasper Lim-Goyette, while too young to understand the report, also encouraged us to complete the report in subtle ways. The report is not about their experiences but about the experiences of many others who are like them. It is to them that we dedicate this report.

REFERENCES

If provided by the authors, additional text and data associated with this report are available at www.prb.org/AmericanPeople.

1. For a discussion of the origins of the term "model minority," see Sucheng Chan, *Asian Americans: An Interpretive History* (Boston: Twayne Publishers, 1991). Chan argues that this term was used politically to divide Asian Americans from other minority groups.

2. Most of the information in this section was drawn from Ronald Takaki, *Strangers from a Different Shore: A History of Asian Americans* (Boston: Little, Brown, and Company, 1989).

3. Tomás Almaguer, *Racial Fault Lines: The Historical Origins of White Supremacy in California* (Berkeley: University of California Press, 1994).

4. Bret Harte, "Plain Language from Truthful James," *The Overland Monthly Magazine* (September 1870), accessed online at http://etext.lib.virginia.edu/railton/roughingit/map/chiharte.html, on June 10, 2004.

5. Won Moo Hurh and Kwang Chung Kim, "The 'Success' Image of Asian Americans: Its Validity, and Its Practical and Theoretical Implications," *Racial and Ethnic Studies* 12, no. 4 (1989): 512-38; and Grace Kao, "Asian-Americans as Model Minorities? A Look at Their Academic Performance," *American Journal of Education* 103, no. 2 (1995): 121-59.

6. Despite this generally positive portrayal of Asian Americans, discrimination and hatred against Asian Americans have persisted. In 1982, for example, Vincent Chin, a Chinese American mistaken as Japanese, was beaten to death by unemployed autoworkers near Detroit.

7. See, for example, Charles Hirschman and Morrison G. Wong, "Socioeconomic Gains of Asian Americans, Blacks, and Hispanics: 1960-1976," *American Journal of Sociology* 90, no. 3 (1984): 584-607; and Yu Xie and Kimberly Goyette, "Social Mobility and the Educational Choices of Asian Americans," *Social Science Research* 32, no. 3 (2003): 467-98.

8. See Zhen Zeng and Yu Xie, "Asian Americans' Earnings Disadvantage Reexamined: The Role of Place of Education," *American Journal of Sociology* 109, no. 5 (2004): 1075-108.

9. Grace Kao, Marta Tienda, and Barbara Schneider, "Racial and Ethnic Variation in Academic Performance," in *Research in Sociology of Education and Socialization*, Vol. 11, ed. Aaron M. Pallas (Greenwich, CT: JAI Press, 1996).

10. See Kimberly Goyette and Yu Xie, "Educational Expectations of Asian American Youths: Determinants and Ethnic Differences," *Sociology of Education* 72, no. 1 (1999): 22-36; and Simon Cheng and Brian Starks, "Racial Differences in the Effects of Significant Others on Students' Educational Expectations," *Sociology of Education* 75, no. 4 (2002): 306-27.

11. Chuansheng Chen and Harold Stevenson, "Motivation and Mathematics Achievement: A Comparative Study of Asian-American, Caucasian-American, and East Asian High School Students," *Child Development* 66, no. 4 (1995): 1215-34.

12. Kao, Tienda, and Schneider, "Racial and Ethnic Variation in Academic Performance."

13. Much of the material in this section based on NELS was extracted from Kimberly Goyette, *The College Attendance of Asian Americans* (doctoral dissertation, University of Michigan, Ann Arbor, 1999).

14. National Center for Education Statistics, "Who Goes to America's Highly Ranked 'National' Universities?" *NCES 98-095* (Washington, DC: U.S. Department of Education, 1998).

15. Jayjia Hsia, *Asian Americans in Higher Education and at Work* (Hillsdale, NJ: Lawrence Erlbaum Associates, 1988).

16. Min Zhou and Carl L. Bankston III, *Growing Up American: How Vietnamese Children Adapt to Life in the United States* (New York: Russell Sage Foundation, 1998).

17. Kao, Tienda, and Schneider, "Racial and Ethnic Variation in Academic Performance"; Stanley Sue and Sumie Okazaki, "Asian-American Educational Achievements: A Phenomenon in Search of an Explanation," in *The Asian American Educational Experience: A Source Report for Teachers and Students*, ed. Don T. Nakanishi and Tina Yamano Nishida (New York: Routledge, 1995); and Xie and Goyette, "Social Mobility and the Educational Choices of Asian Americans."

18. For detailed information on hours worked, see www.yuxie.com.

19. Zeng and Xie, "Asian Americans' Earnings Disadvantage Reexamined."

20. Joe R. Feagin and Clairece B. Feagin, *Racial and Ethnic Relations* (Englewood Cliffs, NJ: Prentice-Hall, 1993).

21. For a fuller account of the argument, see Xie and Goyette, "Social Mobility and the Educational Choices of Asian Americans."

22. Joann Faung Jean Lee, *Asian American Experiences in the United States* (Jefferson, NC: McFarland and Company, 1991).

23. Takaki, *Strangers from a Different Shore: A History of Asian Americans.*

24. Indeed, in preliminary analyses of the 2000 Census data, Emily Greenman has found that Asian American women are more likely to be in certain professional (and traditionally male-dominated) fields than white women, particularly in science and engineering.

25. In order to compute reliable estimates across Asian ethnicities, we used the Census 2000 5% Public Use Microdata Sample (PUMS) for the analysis of Asian Americans. We then combined the results with those pertaining to whites and blacks from the 1% PUMS.

26. Albert Hermalin, ed., *The Well-Being of the Elderly in Asia: A Four-Country Comparative Study* (Ann Arbor, MI: University of Michigan Press, 2002).

27. Amara Bachu and Martin O'Connell, "Fertility of American Women: June 2000," *Current Population Reports* P20-543RV (Washington, D.C.: U.S. Census Bureau, 2001).

28. Yu Xie and Kimberly A. Goyette, "The Racial Identification of Biracial Children with One Asian Parent: Evidence from the 1990 Census," *Social Forces* 76, no. 2 (1997): 547-70.

29. Robert E. Park, *Race and Culture* (Glencoe, IL: Free Press, 1950).

30. See http://quickfacts.census.gov and www.census.gov/population/www/cen2000/phc-t6.html.

31. Lawrence Bobo and Camille L. Zubrinsky, "Attitudes on Residential Integration: Perceived Status Differences, Mere In-Group Preference, or Racial Prejudice?" *Social Forces* 74, no. 3 (1996): 883-909.

32. Alejandro Portes and Robert L. Bach, *Latin Journey: Cuban and Mexican Immigrants in the United States* (Berkeley: University

of California Press, 1985); and Alejandro Portes and Rubèn G. Rumbaut, *Legacies: The Story of the Immigrant Second Generation* (New York: Russell Sage Foundation, 2001). For counterarguments, see Richard Alba and Victor Nee, *Remaking the American Mainstream: Assimilation and Contemporary Immigration*. (Cambridge, MA: Harvard University Press, 2003).

33. Population Studies Center, University of Michigan, Racial Residential Segregation Measurement Project, accessed online at www.psc.isr.umich.edu/residentialsegregation, on June 10, 2004.

34. This statement is based on unpublished tabulations provided by John Logan, Lewis Mumford Center, State University of New York-Albany.

35. Richard D. Alba et al., "Immigrant Groups in the Suburbs: A Reexamination of Suburbanization and Spatial Assimilation," *American Sociological Review* 64, no. 3 (1999): 446-60.

36. The authors benefited from informal discussions with David Harris on this topic.

37. For similar results on earnings, see Zeng and Xie, "Asian Americans' Earnings Disadvantage Reexamined."

FOR FURTHER READING

Barnes, Jessica S., and Claudette E. Bennett. "The Asian Population: 2000." *Census 2000 Brief* C2KBR01-16 (February 2002). Accessed online at www.census.gov/prod/2002pubs/c2kbr01-16.pdf, on June 11, 2004.

Barringer, Herbert R., Robert W. Gardner, and Michael J. Levin. *Asians and Pacific Islanders in the United States.* New York: Russell Sage Foundation, 1993.

Goyette, Kimberly. *The College Attendance of Asian Americans.* Doctoral dissertation. University of Michigan, Ann Arbor, 1999.

Hirschman, Charles, and Morrison G. Wong. "Socioeconomic Gains of Asian Americans, Blacks, and Hispanics: 1960-1976." *American Journal of Sociology* 90, no. 3 (1984): 584-607.

Hsia, Jayjia. *Asian Americans in Higher Education and at Work.* Hillsdale, NJ: Lawrence Erlbaum Associates, 1988.

Kao, Grace. "Asian-Americans as Model Minorities? A Look at Their Academic Performance." *American Journal of Education* 103, no. 2 (1995): 121-59.

Kitano, Harry H.L., and Roger Daniels. *Asian Americans: Emerging Minorities.* Englewood Cliffs, NJ: Prentice-Hall, 1988.

Lee, Joanne Faung Jean. *Asian American Experiences in the United States.* Jefferson, NC: McFarland and Company, 1991.

Lee, Sharon M. "Asian Americans: Diverse and Growing." *Population Bulletin* 53, no. 2 (1998).

Takaki, Ronald. *Strangers from a Different Shore: A History of Asian Americans.* New York: Penguin Reports, 1989.

Xie, Yu, and Kimberly Goyette. "The Racial Identification of Biracial Children with One Asian Parent: Evidence from the 1990 Census." *Social Forces* 76, no. 2 (1997): 547-70.

Xie, Yu, and Kimberly Goyette. "Social Mobility and the Educational Choices of Asian Americans." *Social Science Research* 32, no. 3 (2003): 467-98.

Zeng, Zhen, and Yu Xie. "Asian Americans' Earnings Disadvantage Reexamined: The Role of Place of Education." *American Journal of Sociology* 109, no. 5 (2004): 1057-108.

Zhou, Min. "Are Asian Americans Becoming 'White?'" *Contexts* 3, no. 1 (2003): 25-27.

Zhou, Min, and James V. Gatewood. "Introduction: Revisiting Contemporary Asian America." In *Contemporary Asian America: A Multidisciplinary Reader,* ed. Min Zhou and James V. Gatewood. New York: New York University Press, 2000.

INDEX

Boldface numbers refer to figures or tables.

baby boom (*cont.*)
government, 227–28; historical view, 224–30; homeownership, 146; images of, 229; immigrants, 228–29; income, 245–49; midlife extension, 250–52; poverty, 245–49; retirement, 235; socioeconomic status, 140, 147–48; wealth accumulation, 248–49; work, 227, 233–38. *See also* cohorts

Batalova, Jeanne, ix, 302
Bean, Frank D., ix, 302
Becker, Gary, 175
behavioral change: cohorts, 225; work-family time, 99–101
Bertrand, Marianne, 387
Bianchi, Suzanne, 86, 172
biracial classification. *See* multiracial classification, Census 2000
birth cohorts, defined, 225. *See also* cohorts
blacks and African Americans, 380–414; about, ix, 380–81, 409–11; age, 358–59; baby boomers, 228, 236–67; census classification, ix, 14–15, 18–19, 21, 25, 28, 29, 41, 305–12, 333–41; children, 187–90, 202, 205–7, 210, 218, 399–401; civil rights laws, 18–19; cohabitation, 174; defined, 411*n*2; diversity, 310–11, 325, 382, 383; economic opportunity, 405–7; educational attainment, xi, 155–57, 232, 383–86, 397; family status, 176–77, 183–84, 186, 391–94, 399–401; gender inequality and work, 82, 113–14, 123, **124**, 383–84, **387**, 388, 389; historical view, 380–81, 383; homeownership, 158–60, **159**; incarceration, 407–9; income inequality, 246–47, 388–94, 396; intermarriage, 191, 192, 197, 200*n*74, 321–22, 401; marriage, 176–77, 179–84, 186, 399–401; multigenerational households, 184; multiracial identity, 323–26, 345, 365–66, 382; nonmarital childbearing, 176; occupational segregation, 118–19; population change, 381–83; poverty, 57–59, 68, 93, 160–61, 188–90, 202, 205, 394–96; residential segregation, 388–407; segregation, x, 118–19, 388–407; single-parent families, 93, 176–77, 183, **185**, 218, 392–93, 399–400; single-personhood, 179–80, **181, 182**; socioeconomic status, 146, 160–61, 388–99, 409; wealth accumulation, 396–99; work, 236–37, 316, 319, 386–88, 410, 428–29. *See also* multiracial classification, Census 2000

Blair, Tony, 72, 197
Blank, Rebecca, 393
Blankenhorn, David, 212
Blau, Francine, 397
BLS (Bureau of Labor Statistics), 52, 120
Booth, Alan, 186
Borjas, George, 150

Bracero Program, 265, 354
Braudel, Fernand, 261
Briggs, Vernon, 262
Brooks-Gunn, Jeanne, 396
Brown, Ron, 21
Brown v. Board of Education (1954), 383
Bryant, Barbara, 20
Bureau of Census. *See* Census and Census Bureau
Bureau of Labor Statistics (BLS), 52, 120
Burtless, Gary, 52
Bush, George H.W., 21, 408
Bush, George W., 35, 39, 259
Byrd, James Jr., 409

C2SS (Census Supplementary Survey), 348
California racial classification, 349
Canadian immigration, 265–72, 295, 302
careers. *See* gender inequality and work
Caribbean immigrants, **262**, 265–70, 275, 277, 279, 285, 287, 302
car ownership and race, 406–7
Casper, Lynne M., x, 76, 172, 181
Castro, Fidel, 353
Caucasians. *See specific topics*
CDC (Centers for Disease Control), 204
census and Census Bureau, 3–46; about, viii, 3; accuracy of, 7–16, 32–37; adjustment of, 19–20, 33–34; age and work, 111, **112**; Asian Americans, ix, 21, 25, 28, 41, 305–12, 333–41, 415, 420, 440; baby boom, defined, 226; budget for, 17–18, 27, 37; Census 2000, 26–32; challenges, 16–24; children, 201–2, 203, 208; Chinese immigrants, 415–16; cohabitation, 174; Constitutional requirements, vii, 3, 4–5, 10; count and subsequent decisions, 32–37; decisions on census figures, 32–37; democratic principles supported by, 3, 4–5, 37–43; economic cycles, 143; educational attainment, 157; elderly socioeconomic status, 151; family and household definitions, 51, 170; function of, vii–viii, 24; gender, age and work, 112–13; government guidance, 3–4, 28–30; historical view, vii–viii, 3, 4–6, 8, 13, 42; historic race categories, 332–33; language spoken at home, 363; mail-back rates, 16–17, 30–32; measurement of immigrant race, 304–7; misuse of, 4; multigenerational households, 184; multiracial, 322–23; occupational classification, 115–16, 136*n*4; outlook, 37–43; phases of, 6; population distribution, 277, 289–90; poverty, 51, 52, 54, 63, 202, 203; privacy and confidentiality, 38–40; recent immigrants, 268; same-sex couples, 175; scientific and technical approaches, 7, 28, 33–34; scrutiny of, 21–23; single-personhood, 174; traditional methods, 25–26,

28–30; 2010 census, 36–37; unpaid work and gender, 82, 86–87. *See also* Current Population Survey (CPS)
Census Quality Survey (CQS), 343
Census Supplementary Survey (C2SS), 348
Census 2000: accuracy, 7–16, 32–37; age and work, 111, **112**; attitude and demographic changes, 16–17; budget for, 27; challenges, 16–24; children, 201–2; coding race and ethnicity, 307–12, 334–35; cohabitation, 182–83, 196; cohort income, 148; design, 25–27; dual-system estimation, 14–15, 19–21; educational attainment, 114, 128; English language fluency, 283–84; family status, 109–10, 170; gender inequality and work, 109; immigration, 160–61, 259, 268–69; Latinos as largest minority, 170, 352; marriage, 182–83, 196; vs. 1990 census "failure," 17–18, 25, 30–31; occupational patterns, 115–16, 118–19; oversight and scrutiny, 21–24; partisanship and reapportionment, viii, 9–11, 18–21, 25, 33–36; political process, 25, 34–36; population count (enumeration), vii–viii, 7–16, 32–37; poverty, 57–59, 160–61; public cooperation, 27, 30–32; race and work, 113–14; sampling, vii, 26–27, 36–37; scientific recommendations, 33–34; socioeconomic status, 141; Supreme Court ruling, 6, 25–26, 32–33, 35; undercount, 12–15, 17, 25, 37; underrepresentation, 18–19, 41; work, 109–10; write-in ethnic response, 334–35. *See also specific topics*
Centers for Disease Control (CDC), 204
Central American immigrants, 266–70, 282, 294, 302, 354–61
Chenault, Ken, 409
Cherlin, Andrew, 78, 169, 196
Child and Dependent Care Tax Credit, 217
Child Care Development Fund, 217
children and child well-being, 201–23; about, ix, 201, 220; adult children living with parents, xi, 187; American Indians, 187–90, 202, 205–7, 210; Asian Americans, 424–26; baby boom parents, 242–44; behavior, and paternal involvement, 182; blacks, 399–401; census numbers of, 201, 208–12; childcare responsibilities, 76–80, 82–84, 317; cohabitation, 182, 186, 188, 213; demographic countertrends, 208–13; developmental concerns, 186, 187–88; economic impact, 214–15, 219; educational attainment, 202, 209–10, 424–26; EITC, 216–17, 219; English fluency, 284; family status, 62–63, 79–80, 88–89, 109–10, 171, 186–90, 196, 212–13; geographic dimensions, 205, 207, 208–9; government support, 202, 215–20; immigrants,